ROTHMANS RUGBY UNION YEARBOOK 1993-94

Editor: Stephen Jones
Statistician: John Griffiths

ROTHMANS

HEADLINE

First published in 1993
by HEADLINE BOOK PUBLISHING LTD

Cover photographs.Front: England's Jeremy Guscott is tackled by Didier Camberabero
(left) and Philippe Sella of France in the 1993 International Championship match
at Twickenham, which England narrowly won, 16-15. *Back:* South Africa's
James Small passes to team-mate Wahl Bartmann in the historic Test against the
All Blacks at Ellis Park which marked South Africa's return to international rugby.
The All Blacks won 27-24.

All photographs by Colorsport

10 9 8 7 6 5 4 3 2 1

ISBN 0-7472-7891-1

Photoset by Cylinder Typesetting Limited, London

Printed and bound in Great Britain by
Richard Clay Ltd, Bungay, Suffolk

HEADLINE BOOK PUBLISHING LTD
Headline House
79 Great Titchfield Street
London W1P 7FN

CONTENTS

EDITORIAL PREFACE

There are several improvements in this edition of the Yearbook. The recasting of the Clubs Section is completed by the re-inclusion of the section devoted to Irish club rugby; a full section on the Provincial Cup in England appears for the first time, together with the results of the Southern Hemisphere's Super-10 tournament, which ended in May 1993, and the Rugby World Cup Sevens, held at Murrayfield in April 1993. Coverage of French and South African rugby is expanded with more domestic detail.

Sincere thanks are due to everyone who contributes to this Yearbook, in Britain, Ireland and around the world; and welcome in particular to Chris Rhys, one of sport's great recorders, who is now in charge of the tours section. We are also grateful once again to Colorsport, who have provided all the photographs for the Yearbook. Thanks also to all the readers who have written in with suggestions for amendments.

Finally, yet another vote of thanks is due to Caroline North, who has been house editor of the Yearbook for 11 years. Her contribution cannot be over-praised, nor can her attention to detail and professionalism in overseeing all aspects of the production of the book with such dedication for so long.

Stephen Jones *Editor*
John Griffiths *Statistician*

PLEASE NOTE: The main statistical sections of the Yearbook are complete up to 1 May 1993. Full coverage of the British Lions tours to New Zealand and of all other major international tours taking place in the Northern Hemisphere summer of 1993 will be contained in the next issue, out in September 1994.

ENGLAND'S GLORY FADING IN THE COMPLICATED RULE OF LAW

REVIEW OF THE 1992-93 SEASON
The Editor

If the demands on leading players, and the tendency of many administrators to regard players as a combination of horse-meat and meal-ticket, were not already excessive, then they became so in season 1992-93. The amount of top-level rugby played in the British Isles can hardly nowadays be crammed into the season proper, and with more League matches imposed on English, Welsh and Irish clubs the months from September to May are now becoming a pressure-cooker without relief valve.

On the international scene, it often seemed last season that every team played every other, in every month. At the start of August 1992, New Zealand went to South Africa on tour (they had already undergone an onerous three-Test tour of Australia). The Test whirl carried on for a full 12 months because by early July 1993, the Kiwis had won their three-Test series against the touring British Lions (full details in the next edition of the Yearbook) and the Springboks, political considerations permitting, were to make a tour of Australia lasting well into August 1993. If any millionaire rugby globetrotter wished to watch top Test and tour rugby every week of the year then he could most certainly have done so in the season under review.

It is vital that the two groups in charge of the world game, the International Rugby Board and Rugby World Cup, together with all the national unions, now start to cut back these commitments. If the demands for increasing professionalism in rugby grow even higher – which they will – it is a travesty, not to mention a libel, to blame the players.

The drive towards professionalism is powered by the governing bodies of the game in a ferociously commercial world. There is no one else to blame. The whole situation was illustrated in microcosm at the Rugby World Cup Sevens, held at Murrayfield in April 1993. The event was a great success in many ways, the final day providing a brilliant machine-gun burst of top rugby, with world rugby history and sociology encapsulated every 14 minutes as South Africa played New Zealand, Western Samoa played Fiji, Fiji played Tonga, Australia played England, then New Zealand, and so on. Yet the gruelling three-day format (completely unnecessary) made it the survival of the fittest. Many teams were simply carrying injured players and were therefore not given the chance to compete properly. The extra day of action, of course, brought in more gate receipts, more television money, more sponsorship. So in paying tribute to an extraordinary England victory in the event, led with a dazzling flourish by the electric Andrew

Harriman, it is also appropriate to dole out black marks to the organisers, Rugby World Cup. They played the players to the bone, yet again.

Indeed, it has often been said in our annual review that rugby does not have the leadership it deserves from administrators. This was certainly true of season 1992-93. The difference is in execution, not in philosophy. Previously, the problem lay in the inertia of the IRB, their failure to grasp their role as global guardians and global marketing men of rugby. It is not their motivation that is now in question. It is their direction and modes of operation.

The RWC organisation, to the outsider impossibly labyrinthine and still too secretive and suspicious, is in some danger of becoming a monster. Some individual unions clearly regard RWC as a body outside any IRB control which, to some extent, it is. The body needs to be brought back under control and back into the public eye so that rugby's followers can be sure that they are getting the best possible deal from one of the jewels in the crown of the game. Even a smidgin of genuine public relations expertise would be welcome.

The IRB could certainly do with the latter, and while no one could deny the increasing internationalism of the Board, a welcome development, there are still areas in which the IRB are too staid and secretive and downright poor. The process by which they pass new law is flawed. Their laborious channels of communication do not trawl up, in any satisfactory way, the views of the leading players, coaches and referees. If they fail those three sections of the game then who, exactly, are they serving?

The widespread and justified criticism of the appalling new ruck/maul law, which gives possession at subsequent scrums to the teams not in possession at the start of indeterminate rucks and mauls, has changed the face of rugby, and profoundly not for the better. The lack of meaningful consultation with significant parties outside the IRB was damaging enough. The IRB needs to co-opt, or at least consult on a frequent and formal basis, the managements of the national teams, more and more players and referees. And referees, incidentally, are still coming over as the sheepish seen-but-not-heard body in the game.

Referees must demand, and they must be given, a higher profile; to stick in their oar for the laws, to defend themselves against the storm of criticism; to address themselves to the vast differences in interpretation which now exist from country to country, even town to town. And to own up to the fact that in the clammy hands of the IRB the game at the top level is becoming almost impossible to referee.

As ever, there was some momentous action when the game finally burst from the committee rooms on to the pitch. The Northern Hemisphere season was low-octane because of the shambles, the counter-productive frenzy, caused by the new laws. Yet the gladiatorial side of the game just about survived – England were thrown to the lions, beaten in the Five Nations Championship by Welsh and Irish sides who had lain too long under the yoke of a team which, in 1993, could not find a final gallop, and in which only a few players, notably Jeremy Guscott and Ben Clarke, approached the top of their game. It was France, quietly and with discipline, who won the title; they were unlucky to lose at Twickenham, won their three other games with some ease and therefore took some of the pressure from Pierre Berbizier, who always seems to be just one small step ahead of the hyenas of French rugby's legendary factions.

Scotland managed to arrest their slide somewhat in the international series, although they were well beaten in the Calcutta Cup when Stuart Barnes, finally recalled to England's colours, sparked off some attacking play the like of which English followers had not seen for some time. Ireland's passionate victory over England gave their morale the required boost, and if it serves to nudge along their team preparations into the modern era, then it will be doubly welcome. The Welsh victory flattered to deceive when the team lost its way later, lacking in key positions, and when, pathetically, the Welsh Rugby Union crashed in flames around the inertia of some of the committee, the jealousy of the clubs and a personality clash between the secretary and treasurer.

We also found that the long-awaited return to international rugby of South Africa, which saw the Springboks in Europe and both New Zealand and Australia in South Africa, was by no means the end of a sad story. It was simply the latest instalment of a difficult problem which continues to rumble on the field and off it.

Australia won both Tests on a gruelling tour of Ireland and Wales, finding that their status of world champions draws ferocity from any team they meet, and in this case from Llanelli, Swansea and Munster, who all beat the tourists. Yet the character of the team took them to resounding victories in the two Tests.

On the representative front, the Irish Inter-Provincial event was improved by the arrival of an Anglos XV; the Scottish Inter-District Championship may be devalued in the same proportion by the disappearance of such a team. The English County Championship now consists of Cornwall and Cornwall alone: the myth that Lancashire and Yorkshire are hotbeds of the county game was exploded when the teams played out a dismal final in front of a ground one-quarter full.

On the club front, although Bath and Llanelli were unquestionably the best teams of the year anywhere in the country when at their best, there must be honourable mentions for Young Munster, for the revived Cardiff and for the proud men of Dunvant, who completed their astonishing rise by entering the top division in Wales for next season. No less praiseworthy, in some senses, were the achievements of Penarth and West Hartlepool. Penarth, whipping-boys for most of their existence, pulled confidently clear of the relegation zone in Division 2 in Wales; West Hartlepool, a splendid club in the north-east, chose as their season in the top flight a year when four teams were relegated. Down they went, but with honour. They could easily have survived had narrow defeats fallen the other way and they will surely come again.

Young Munster, that wonderfully passionate Irish club, ruled the Irish roost as did Melrose, a well-organised and committed outfit, in Scotland. Still in Scotland, it was good to see that everyone realised the debt that the World Sevens owed to the Cathay Pacific-Hong Kong Bank event in Hong Kong, still the best gathering of the world game.

Irishmen signal the end of England's dominance of the Five Nations Championship as the whistle blows on their astonishing victory at Lansdowne Road and the team – and the country – prepares to celebrate.

ROTHMANS FIVE PLAYERS OF THE YEAR

The basis for selection for the Rothmans Five Players of the Year was the European season 1992-93. Those who thought there might be a lull after the World Cup were in for a rude shock – there was the incident-packed Wallaby tour of Ireland and Wales, a riveting Five Nations Championship and endless debate as to who would captain the Lions. The choices of our panel of contributors reflect the importance of these events.

The Five Players are **Gavin Hastings,** the Scottish full-back and captain of the British Lions, whose invigorating leadership was to help his country to second place in the Championship; **Laurent Cabannes,** the flanker, whose electrifying running underpinned France's title-winning campaign; **Phil Kearns,** the hooker, who stepped in when Australian captain Michael Lynagh was injured and held the injury-racked squad together in difficult circumstances; **Jean-Baptiste Lafond,** the full-back, who had the unenviable task of replacing the great Serge Blanco yet ceded nothing by comparison; **Waisale Serevi,** the Fijian fly-half, who has long been the magician in Hong Kong, conjuring tries from nowhere.

NB: No player can be nominated more than once. Career details given are correct up to 30 April 1993.

Previous nominations
1989-90: **Will Carling, Patrice Lagisquet, Steve McDowell, David Sole, Paul Ackford**
1990-91: **Dean Richards, Gary Armstrong, Wade Dooley, Serge Blanco, Rory Underwood**
1991-92: **Peter Winterbottom, Jonathan Webb, David Campese, Simon Poidevin, Marc Cecillon**

GAVIN HASTINGS

Ian McGeechan knew just the man he wanted to replace the imperious David Sole. 'He had to be able to draw the best from what would be an inexperienced side,' said McGeechan. 'He had to have presence. If you ever had an anonymous captain, you'd pretty soon end up with an anonymous team.'

Step forward Gavin Hastings. He took on the full mantle of responsibility for the Scotland team, which began the Championship with four new caps and few prospects. They finished a very creditable second, and Hastings was also to successfully lead the British Lions in New Zealand. Not bad for a first season in charge.

He has never been a shrinking violet, be it standing broad-shouldered under the high ball or giving his trenchant views on the game. He may

not have the most astute tactical brain, nor even beat the tartan drum with the passionate intensity of some of his immediate predecessors, but he does have charisma, that indefinable quality which inspires others to great feats. If there was one moment which captured the man perfectly it was during the third-place play-off in the World Cup. He had just fumbled a high kick. Furious, he took a pass a few moments later. In front of him stood All Black prop Richard Loe. But not for long. Loe took the full force of Hastings' dipped shoulder. Props aren't supposed to be smashed aside by backs.

One of four brothers who all played rugby for George Watson's College, Hastings always looked set for the highest honours in the game. A Cambridge Blue, he made his debut with brother Scott in 1986 against France, one of six new caps. If he was nervous it didn't show: Gavin kicked a world record-equalling six penalty goals to give Scotland victory by 18-17. He finished the season with a record haul of 52 points.

The statisticians have been busy with their pens ever since. He is the record points-scorer for his country with 424 points. His 27 points against Romania in the World Cup of 1987 is a record and he is within two caps of equalling Andy Irvine's record total of 47 for a Scottish full-back.

But the man is more than a mere cipher in a ledger. He symbolises vibrancy and courage; he exudes confidence and has always been a great ambassador for the game. At times his touch can desert him. These occasions are far outnumbered by the times when he plays the opposition on his own. The match against Wales had his mark all over it: the wind was swirling, Big Gavin stood firm and Wales collapsed at his feet.

Gavin Hastings *Born Edinburgh, 3 January 1962; full-back; plays for Watsonians; 45 caps since first cap against France in 1986.*

LAURENT CABANNES

But for the skill of a French surgeon Laurent Cabannes might have been lost to the game. Four years ago he was involved in a car crash which nearly cost him his life. Not many come back at all from being catapulted through a windscreen at 80mph, let alone to make such a remarkable impact on the rugby field.

Cabannes suffered a crushed chest, and all the nerve-endings in his right shoulder were severed. Six months later his right arm still flopped uselessly at his side. 'I was walking a tightrope between two worlds – the world of normal people and the world of the handicapped,' he said. Twelve screws and a four-inch metal plate did the trick and so Cabannes started out on the tortuous road to recovery. Within a year he had helped Racing Club to the 1990 French Championship, their first such success in 31 years, by scoring the decisive extra-time try in that gripping, turbulent final against Agen. A few months later he came on as a replacement for Abdel Benazzi in the Second Test against New

Zealand to win his first cap. Small wonder that his team-mates refer to him as *'le miracule'*.

As he swerved athletically outside the South African cover defence last autumn to launch yet another sweeping French attack, you had to wonder what he might have been if it had not been for that accident. For, at the time, he considers that he was playing some of the best rugby of his life. He made his first-class debut as a 17-year-old with Pau and first played for France B against Wales at Pontypridd in 1986.

Cabannes might have thought he was doing well but one influential figure did not – Jacques Fouroux. The little Napoleon was not too taken with flankers who ran round people: he preferred men who smashed through the opposition. Bulk was all the rage. And so the 14-stone lightweight Cabannes went about his business unrecognised; selling champagne for a living, and playing in the champagne style with his pink-bow-tied mates at Racing.

The Fouroux days came to end, as ever in French rugby, somewhat bloodily. In came Daniel Dubroca as coach, and with him Cabannes. He has been a virtual ever-present since, playing throughout the World Cup and the last two Championships. Again this year we have seen his ceaseless support of the ball-carrier; his wonderfully perceptive eye for an opening; his electric pace; his invaluable work at the tail of the line-out: all duties carried out, both on and off the field, with an easy, generous spirit. *Le miracule.*

Laurent Cabannes *Born Reims, France, 6 February 1964; flanker; plays for Racing Club de France; 23 caps for France since first cap against New Zealand (as a replacement) in 1990.*

PHIL KEARNS

Phil Kearns was always going to captain Australia one day. The problem was that he didn't particularly want it to be the day that he was actually given the job. It was a dirty day in Dublin, Ireland were threatening to blow up their usual storm and the last thing Kearns wanted to see was skipper Michael Lynagh leave the field, and the tour, with a shoulder injury at half-time. With Farr-Jones retired, Lynagh under the surgeon's knife, and defeated already by Munster, were the world champions about to fall apart? Not a chance. Kearns bore the responsibility magnificently. As Australian coach Bob Dwyer remarked at the end of the tour: 'It's necessary for a really strong side to show that, no matter what obstacles are thrown in their path, they can overcome them'.

That Dwyer was able to pay such a compliment to his team was due in no small part to Kearns' self-effacing leadership off the field and his defiant play on it. Injury was to be the motif of the tour, with men falling by the wayside every week. Kearns himself struggled through Wales with a series of niggling injuries, but never once asked for sympathy.

He got on with the job, and that is the sort of attitude an Aussie admires.

Kearns has gained many admirers since he was plucked from the obscurity of Randwick second team to play against the All Blacks in 1989. He has not missed a Test since. Aged only 26, he already has 28 caps to his credit and is over halfway towards eclipsing Colin Deans' world record for a hooker of 52 caps. Many thought that Dwyer, who had seen Kearns come through at his own club, Randwick, was merely indulging in favouritism when he thrust the young hooker into the heat of battle against the mighty All Blacks. Dwyer, though, has x-ray vision when it comes to spotting talent. He wanted to dismantle the pack which had just lost the series to the Lions, and Kearns was going to be at the core of the new generation.

Kearns had already captained New South Wales and Australia at Under-21 level. Dwyer saw also that Kearns' energetic driving play in the loose, allied to his technical mastery of the hooker's duties, would perfectly fit the tenor of the new Wallaby side, whose total football was to so enrich the 1991 World Cup. By then we already knew that Kearns was a player of substance. What we found out last season was more important still – Kearns is also a man of substance.

Phil Kearns *Born Sydney, Australia, 27 July 1967; hooker; plays for Randwick; 28 caps since first cap against New Zealand in 1989.*

JEAN-BAPTISTE LAFOND

Not many can step into the shoes of the great Serge Blanco and not suffer by comparison. Lafond was the backbone of France's Championship-winning side: dependable in defence, unwavering under the high ball and ever eager to add a cutting edge in attack.

Lafond had plenty of time to study the great man's virtues at close quarters, having made his own international debut in 1983 at Clermont-Ferrand. In fact he was chosen for that game, against Australia, as a full-back. Blanco in those days could only get in as a wing. Great things were expected of Lafond. 'I had never seen so much raw, natural talent,' wrote that doyen of French journalists Denis Lalanne.

Sadly, he was not to see too much of it. After dropping a goal Lafond was late-tackled by Wallaby second-row forward Steve Williams. He suffered a broken collarbone and shattered knee ligaments. Lafond, however, was never content to sit on the sidelines. He flared brightly on many occasions only for injury or a temporary loss of form to cause him to fall back down to earth. Until 1991, though, Lafond had scarcely done justice to his early rave notices. He had won only 16 caps by that point.

The arrival of Jean Trillo as the national backs coach helped him to focus his game and build his self-confidence. He finished the World Cup as joint top try-scorer with David Campese, both men scoring six

tries. At the start of the 1993 Championship 30 of his 33 caps had been won as a winger. With the departure of Blanco, he moved to his preferred position, full-back. He feels that his game has matured and that he is no longer as impulsive as he once was, preferring to stand back and size up the options before letting rip. Business commitments have caused another switch this season, from glitzy Racing to Bègles-Bordeaux. Lafond, a wine merchant, has over a million bottles of vintage Bordeaux in his cellars near Saint-Emilion.

Lafond has long been a supporter of the Barbarians, turning out for them once again last season against Leicester. Lafond is also a fervent anglophile, relishing in particular the camaraderie of the sport over here. His grandfather, André Lafond, won one cap on the wing for France against England in 1922. He would have been more than proud of his grandson's all-round contribution to France's victorious season. But for the Twickenham crossbar, which rebounded Lafond's late dropped goal attempt, some of that red stuff might have been uncorked in celebration of a Grand Slam.

Jean-Baptiste Lafond *Born Neuilly-sur-Seine, France, 29 December 1961; wing or full-back; plays for Bègles-Bordeaux; 36 caps since first cap against Australia in 1983.*

WAISALE SEREVI

Off the field he has a simple manner. He is shy, quiet and unobtrusive. In a suit and tie, he cuts a small, almost forlorn figure, indistinguishable from the rest. Placid, predictable and utterly conformist. Why on earth should anyone pay him any attention?

Strip away that suit and tie, toss him a rugby shirt and, if you want to be really sophisticated, a pair of boots, and you'll soon see why. Audacious, confrontational and ruthlessly self-assured, it's as if he learned his trade playing with the gods. No wonder Clem Thomas was moved to describe Waisale Serevi as 'the greatest living footballer'.

The arena Serevi has claimed as his own is the stadium in Hong Kong. There, he has defied the laws of the game. Not those tucked into the referee's back pocket, but the ones that state that if you have a man trapped in a corner with no way out, then he is finished. Time and again many a stony-faced All Black or concrete-shouldered Samoan has closed in on Serevi to inflict the inevitable. Time and again he has failed. Even the best of them have not managed to pin down the little 24-year-old Fijian fly-half.

This year it was Tim Horan's turn to eat dirt. Fiji were playing Australia in the semi-final of the Hong Kong Sevens. Serevi had already scored two tries when Horan moved in for what looked like a certain kill. Two goose-steps later Horan was on the floor, Serevi in the clear and the crowd in ecstasy.

Serevi has his detractors, who sneer that he only shines at the shortened game. Often those who disparage him also knock the sevens game itself, usually from their ringside seats about 500 miles away. If they actually bothered to come and watch, they too might be converted. For Serevi, and for Fiji, sevens *is* rugby. Fiji have made their name, and, whisper it gently, part of their living, from playing sevens. Of course they are capable of adapting to the fuller code, as they have shown so often, particularly when playing at home. For the moment their priorities are elsewhere. Perhaps they are wrong, and there is some evidence that their preoccupation with sevens success has provoked nasty elements of gamesmanship in them.

Serevi's audacious skills were not enough to resist the Samoan charge in Hong Kong. Nor were they sufficient a prompt to his rather listless team-mates in the inaugural World Sevens. No matter. A flickering of his talent of Murrayfield was richer in quality than the combined output of most teams.

Waisale Serevi *Born Suva, Fiji, 20 May 1969; fly-half or scrum-half; plays for Nabua; 11 caps since first cap against Scotland in 1989.*

TOURS 1992

NEW ZEALAND TO SOUTH AFRICA 1992

It was always likely that the South Africans would mark the end of their isolation with a tour by the team they rate above all others. Once the African National Congress were satisfied (only for the moment, as it turned out) that South African rugby was proceeding along multi-racial lines, it was only a matter of time before the All Blacks arrived.

Yet if South Africa had been starved of top-class rugby then the same could not be said of New Zealand. They departed for South Africa the day after the Third Test of a sapping series in Australia, and it was as well for their morale that they had won the last Test. They had lost the first two, and arriving in South Africa on the back of a whitewash would have been another problem to add to that of sheer tiredness. The absence of the injured flanker, Mike Brewer, was another drawback.

The countries had last met in New Zealand in 1981, and the one Test on the 1992 tour was the first official match for South Africa against another country since England toured in 1984. As it turned out, New Zealand came through well. They disposed of Orange Free State and Natal in high-scoring and loose matches; they had a few problems before overcoming the Junior Springboks, but none at all in seeing off the Central Unions.

The Test was a charged affair, in which South Africa lifted their morale with a storming comeback, but one that was always going to fall short. The massive Ellis Park Stadium was packed and a bitter controversy began when 'Die Stem', the national anthem, which is seen by non-whites as a symbol of white oppression, was played officially before the match, in defiance of the wishes of the ANC. The furore was still raging months later when the Springboks came to England.

In the touring party, there were massive contributions from Frank Bunce in the centre and Ian Jones, the lock. Jamie Joseph looked a marvellous prospect at blindside flanker and Grant Fox, restored to the team, played as if refreshed by the new challenge of rebuilding a side which had broken up after the World Cup.

THE TOURING PARTY

Manager N Gray **Coach** L W Mains **Assistant Coach** E W Kirton

Captain S B T Fitzpatrick

FULL-BACKS

J K R Timu (Otago)
M J A Cooper (Waikato)

THREEQUARTERS

J J Kirwan (Auckland)
V L Tuigamala (Auckland)
E J Rush (North Harbour)

T J Wright (Auckland)
F Bunce (North Harbour)
W K Little (North Harbour)
E Clarke (Auckland)
M C G Ellis (Otago)

HALF-BACKS

G J Fox (Auckland)
S J Bachop (Otago)

A D Strachan (Auckland)
J P Preston (Canterbury)

FORWARDS

O M Brown (Auckland)
R W Loe (Waikato)
S C McDowell (Auckland)
S B T Fitzpatrick (Auckland)
G W Dowd (North Harbour)
G H Purvis (Waikato)
I D Jones (North Auckland)

R M Brooke (Auckland)
M S Cooksley (Counties)
B P Larsen (North Harbour)
A T Earl (Canterbury)
D J Seymour (Canterbury)
J W Joseph (Otago)
M N Jones (Auckland)
A R Pene (Otago)
Z V Brooke (Auckland)

TOUR RECORD
All matches   Played 5   Won 5   Points for 167   Against 79
International matches   Played 1   Won 1   Points for 27   Against 24

SCORING DETAILS

All matches
For: 20T   14C   13PG   167 Pts
Against: 6T   5C   13PG   79 Pts

International matches
For: 3T   3C   2PG   27 Pts
Against: 3T   3C   1PG   24 Pts

MATCH DETAILS

1992	OPPONENTS	VENUE	RESULT
1 August	Natal	Durban	W 43-25
5 August	Orange Free State	Bloemfontein	W 33-14
8 August	Junior Springboks	Pretoria	W 25-10
10 August	Central Unions	Witbank	W 39-6
15 August	SOUTH AFRICA	Johannesburg	W 27-24

Scorers: 45 – Fox (9C 9PG); 27 – Cooper (1T 5C 4PG); 20 – Kirwan (4T); 10 – Rush, Timu, Wright (2T each); 5 – Loe, Strachan, Earl, I D Jones, Bunce, Little, Bachop, Seymour, Z V Brooke (1T each)

MATCH 1   1 August, King's Park, Durban

Natal 25 (1G 6PG)   **New Zealand XV 43** (4G 5PG)
Natal: H Reece-Edwards; J F van der Westhuizen, P G Muller, R Muir, A C Watson; H W Honiball, R J du Preez; G Harding, J Allan, L J J Müller, S Atherton, R J Visagie, W J Bartmann (*capt*), G Teichmann, A D Blakeway
Scorers *Try:* penalty try   *Conversion:* Reece-Edwards   *Penalty Goals:* Reece-Edwards (6)
New Zealand XV: Timu; Kirwan, Bunce, Clarke, Tuigamala; Fox, Strachan; Loe, Fitzpatrick (*capt*), Brown, I D Jones, Cooksley, Joseph, Z V Brooke, M Jones
Scorers *Tries:* Kirwan (2), Loe, Strachan   *Conversions:* Fox (4)   *Penalty Goals:* Fox (5)
Referee F Burger (Western Province)

MATCH 2   5 August, Bloemfontein

Orange Free State 14 (3PG 1T)   **New Zealand XV 33** (2G 3PG 2T)
Orange Free State: E von Gericke; H J Truter, J B Venter, H L Muller, C Badenhorst; J H de Beer, H Martens; J J Styger, A D Bester, P C Bester, R Opperman, D S van Zyl, J van Tonder, P G Human (*capt*), R J Kruger *Replacements* B Ludik for de Beer (40 mins); J Jonker for Venter (55 mins)
Scorers *Try:* Muller   *Penalty Goals:* de Beer (2), von Gericke
New Zealand XV: Cooper; Rush, Little, Bunce, Tuigamala; Bachop, Preston; McDowell, Dowd, Purvis, I D Jones (*capt*), Larsen, Earl, Pene, Seymour
Replacement Ellis for Tuigamala (36 mins)
Scorers *Tries:* Earl, I D Jones, Bunce, Rush   *Conversions:* Cooper (2)
Penalty Goals: Cooper (3)
Referee P Lombard (Northern Orange Free State)

MATCH 3   8 August, Loftus Versfeld, Pretoria

Junior Springboks 10 (1G 1PG)   **New Zealand XV 25** (2G 2PG 1T)
Junior Springboks: G Grobler (Northern Transvaal); J Olivier (Northern Transvaal),
H Fuls (Transvaal), B G Fourie (Transvaal), C Badenhorst (Orange Free State);
J H de Beer (Orange Free State), J van der Westhuizen (Northern Transvaal); J J Styger
(Orange Free State), H Roberts (Transvaal), P C Bester (Orange Free State), J J Wiese
(Transvaal), H Hattingh (Northern Transvaal), R J Kruger (Orange Free State),
C P Strauss (Western Province) (*capt*), P B Rossouw (Western Transvaal)
Replacements F C Smit (Western Province) for Wiese (21 mins); J T J van Rensburg
(Transvaal) for Badenhorst (48 mins)
Scorers *Try:* Badenhorst   *Conversion:* Grobler   *Penalty Goal:* de Beer
New Zealand XV: Timu; Kirwan, Little, Bunce, Clarke; Fox, Strachan; Loe,
Fitzpatrick (*capt*), Brown, I D Jones, R M Brooke, Joseph, Z V Brooke, M N Jones
Replacements Earl for Joseph (24 mins); Pene for M N Jones (74 mins)
Scorers *Tries:* Kirwan, Little, Timu   *Conversions:* Fox (2)   *Penalty Goals:* Fox (2)
Referee A Adams (Northern Transvaal)

MATCH 4   10 August, Witbank

Central Unions 6 (2PG)   **New Zealand XV 39** (3G 1PG 3T)
Central Unions: L Gilomee; G Jacobs, W van Aswegen, H le Roux, S van Vuuren;
E Herbert, K Coetzer; C du Plessis, T van der Walt, T Loubser, L Botha,
C van der Merwe, H Hattingh, A van Wyk (*capt*), S Wessels *Replacement* M McMahon
for Herbert (62 mins)
New Zealand XV: Cooper; Rush, Clarke, Ellis, Wright; Bachop, Preston; McDowell
(*capt*), Dowd, Purvis, Larsen, Cooksley, Earl, Pene, Seymour *Replacement* Z V Brooke
for Seymour (53 mins)
Scorers *Tries:* Wright (2), Bachop, Cooper, Seymour, Rush   *Conversions:* Cooper (3)
Penalty Goal: Cooper
Referee S Neethling (Boland)

MATCH 5   15 August, Ellis Park, Johannesburg   Test Match

SOUTH AFRICA 24 (3G 1PG)   NEW ZEALAND 27 (3G 2PG)

The game was not nearly as close as the final score suggests, although this momentous and thrilling occasion was certainly shaken out of its former course when South Africa fought back from 21-10 down in the last ten minutes. A mistake by referee Sandy MacNeill helped the Springboks' comeback. MacNeill missed a clear knock-up by Robert du Preez, the South African scrum-half. Later in that same move, Piet Müller in the centre raced over to score.

Late in injury time and with Müller, co-centre Danie Gerber and full-back Theo van Rensburg cutting swathes through the midfield, Gerber went storming over. Botha converted this, as well as the previous two tries, and in view of earlier events, South Africa were happy to settle for 24 points. The New Zealand tries came from John Kirwan, John Timu and Zinzan Brooke. The first two came after concerted driving up the midfield while Brooke's try was a simple affair – he took a quick tap to himself and raced through as most South Africans, on the pitch and in the stadium, looked on in amazement.

SOUTH AFRICA: J T J van Rensburg (Transvaal); J Small (Transvaal), D M Gerber (Western Province), P G Müller (Natal), P Hendriks (Transvaal); H E Botha

(Northern Transvaal) (*capt*), R J du Preez (Natal); P H Rodgers (Transvaal), U L Schmidt (Northern Transvaal), L J J Müller (Natal), A Geldenhuys (Eastern Province), A W Malan (Northern Transvaal), W J Bartmann (Natal), J C Breedt (Transvaal), I Macdonald (Transvaal) *Replacements* J J Styger (Orange Free State) for Rodgers (50 mins); H Fuls (Transvaal) for Small (80 mins)
Scorers *Tries:* Gerber (2), Müller   *Conversions:* Botha (3)   *Penalty Goal:* Botha
NEW ZEALAND: Timu; Kirwan, Bunce, Little, Tuigamala; Fox, Strachan; Loe, Fitzpatrick (*capt*), Brown, I D Jones, R M Brooke, Joseph, Z V Brooke, M N Jones *Replacements* Preston for Strachan (15 mins); Cooper for Tuigamala (80 mins)
Scorers *Tries:* Z V Brooke, Kirwan, Timu   *Conversions:* Fox (3)
Penalty Goals: Fox (2)
Referee A R MacNeill (Australia)

AUSTRALIA TO SOUTH AFRICA 1992

This tour, like New Zealand's, was hastily inserted into the schedule after the African National Congress finally gave the green light for South Africa's rugby return. That permission was given as a result of the amalgamation of the South African Rugby Board and the South African Rugby Union. The latter body represented black players and had consistently held out against amalgamation even when other non-white organisations joined.

The tour was a triumph for the world champions, and for Nick Farr-Jones and Bob Dwyer, captain and coach. They were in trouble in none of their matches, and won a splendid victory in the Test match at Newlands, Cape Town, despite the foul weather and the new laws, which they hated.

They also scored in another way. The Australians arrived at the tail-end of the New Zealand tour and were present at Ellis Park for the Test between the Springboks and the All Blacks where, against ANC demands, the South African national anthem was played. The resulting furore, in which the ANC accused South African rugby of hidebound conservatism, and worse, almost led to the cancellation of the Australian Test. But it was the diplomacy and statesmanship of the Australian party and the ARU president, Joe French, that saved the day.

THE TOURING PARTY

Manager J J Breen   **Coaches** R S F Dwyer, R I Templeton   **Captain** N C Farr-Jones

FULL-BACKS	HALF-BACKS
M C Roebuck (New South Wales)	M P Lynagh (Queensland)
T P Kelaher (New South Wales)	P Kahl (Queensland)
THREEQUARTERS	N C Farr-Jones (New South Wales)
	P J Slattery (Queensland)
D I Campese (New South Wales)	**FORWARDS**
P V Carozza (Queensland)	
D K Junee (New South Wales)	T A Lawton (Queensland)
R C Tombs (New South Wales)	P N Kearns (New South Wales)
T J Horan (Queensland)	A Blades (New South Wales)
J S Little (Queensland)	M Ryan (Queensland)
A G Herbert (Queensland)	E J A McKenzie (New South Wales)

A J Daly (New South Wales)
G Morgan (Queensland)
J A Eales (Queensland)
W W Waugh (Queensland)
R J McCall (Queensland)

T Coker (Queensland)
D J Wilson (Queensland)
V Ofahengaue (New South Wales)
B T Gavin (New South Wales)
S J N Scott-Young (Queensland)

TOUR RECORD

All matches Played 4 Won 4 Points for 130 Against 41
International matches Played 1 Won 1 Points for 26 Against 3

SCORING DETAILS

All matches
For: 15T 5C 15PG 130 Pts
Against: 4T – 7PG 41 Pts

International matches
For: 3T 1C 3PG 26 Pts
Against: – – 1PG 3 Pts

MATCH DETAILS

1992	OPPONENTS	VENUE	RESULT
11 August	Western Transvaal	Potchefstroom	W 46-13
14 August	Northern Transvaal	Pretoria	W 24-17
18 August	Eastern Province	Port Elizabeth	W 34-8
22 August	SOUTH AFRICA	Cape Town	W 26-3

Scorers: 22 – Kelaher (2C 6PG); 17 – Lynagh (1C 5PG); 16 – Roebuck (2C 4PG), 15 – Campese (3T); 10 – Gavin, Carozza (2T each); 5 – Waugh, Blades, Wilson, Morgan, Slattery, Junee, Kahl, Herbert (1T each)

MATCH 1   11 August, Openpark, Potchefstroom

Western Transvaal 13 (1PG 2T)   **Australia XV 46** (2G 4PG 4T)
Western Transvaal: W J van der Merwe; A Homan, N Engelbrecht, D P Swart,
G Bryant; G P Bouwer, E K Hare (*capt*); R Lotriet, J L D Putter, H Tromp, D P Berry,
L Swart, S Loots, T Stewart, B P Rossouw *Replacement* M Hurter for Tromp (69 mins)
Scorers *Tries:* Stewart, Hare   *Penalty Goal:* Bouwer
Australia XV: Roebuck; Campese, Herbert, Tombs, Junee; Kahl, Slattery (*capt*);
Ryan, Lawton, Blades, Waugh, Morgan, Ofahengaue, Gavin, Wilson
Scorers *Tries:* Gavin (2), Waugh, Blades, Wilson, Morgan   *Conversions:* Roebuck (2)
Penalty Goals: Roebuck (4)
Referee F Burger (Western Province)

MATCH 2   14 August, Loftus Versfeld, Pretoria

Northern Transvaal 17 (4PG 1T)   **Australia XV 24** (1G 4PG 1T)
Northern Transvaal: G Grobler; D E Oosthuizen, R van de Venter, F A Meiring,
J Olivier; L Smith, J van de Westhuizen; W G Hills, J A Truscott, D F du Plessis,
J J Strydom, P J W Schutte, P I L Pretorius, A Richter (*capt*), M J Fourie
Scorers *Try:* Schutte   *Penalty Goals:* Smith (3), Grobler
Australia XV: Kelaher; Campese, Horan, Little, Carozza; Lynagh, Farr-Jones (*capt*);
Daly, Kearns, McKenzie, McCall, Eales, Coker, Scott-Young, Wilson
Replacement Herbert for Lynagh (40 mins)
Scorers *Tries:* Campese (2)   *Conversion:* Kelaher   *Penalty Goals:* Lynagh (2), Kelaher (2)
Referee I Rogers (Natal)

MATCH 3   18 August, Boet Erasmus, Port Elizabeth

Eastern Province 8 (1PG 1T)   **Australia XV 34** (1G 4PG 3T)
Eastern Province: A F Fourie; C Noble, R Potgieter, M J du Plessis *(capt)*, J du Plessis;
G Miller, J Calitz; F S Erasmus, J Kirsten, W Meyer, D Joubert, N Meyer,
J J Oosthuizen, A Barnard, H Weber *Replacements* V Roodt for Kirsten (77 mins); M Catt
for Miller (79 mins)
Scorer *Try:* Miller   *Penalty Goal:* Miller
Australia XV: Kelaher; Junee, Herbert, Tombs, Carozza; Kahl, Slattery *(capt)*; Ryan,
Lawton, Blades, Waugh, Morgan, Ofahengaue, Scott-Young, Coker
Replacements Campese for Junee (12 mins); McCall for Coker (60 mins)
Scorers *Tries:* Slattery, Junee, Kahl, Herbert   *Conversion:* Kelaher
Penalty Goals: Kelaher (4)
Referee I Anderson (Transvaal)

MATCH 4   22 August, Newlands, Cape Town

SOUTH AFRICA 3 (1PG)   AUSTRALIA 26 (1G 3PG 2T)

Australia played one of the great halves of rugby in the World Cup
semi-final in Dublin in 1991. In the first half of that match against New
Zealand, they played with such style and authority that New Zealand
were shut out completely. The second-half effort of this momentous
Test, played on a filthy Cape Town day, ranked with that performance.
In the mud and against the highly-committed Springboks, Australia's
forward control and tactical mastery was a wonder.

They emphasised their superiority in almost every department with
two tries in the last six minutes. One of these came from David
Campese, lurking inevitably on the right wing – his 50th in international rugby. The other came from Paul Carozza, who slid over for a
momentum try down the left. The approach work for both was done by
Tim Horan, the centre, who had a titanic match, often grappling like a
forward but moving beautifully when the ball came back. His was one
of the great all-round individual efforts.

South Africa were bogged down in the conditions and in the past.
Their pack, and especially Bartmann in the back row, were too slack in
their play and gave away too many penalties. Botha, at fly-half, often
lost his footing on the treacherous surface and there was nothing to
praise from the Springbok threequarters, so dangerous a week earlier
against New Zealand on a dry pitch in Johannesburg.

SOUTH AFRICA: J T J van Rensburg (Tranvaal); J T Small (Transvaal), D M Gerber
(Western Province), P G Müller (Natal), P Hendriks (Transvaal); H E Botha
(Northern Transvaal) *(capt)*, R J du Preez (Natal); J J Styger (Orange Free State),
U L Schmidt (Northern Transvaal), L J J Müller (Natal), A Geldenhuys
(Eastern Province), A W Malan (Northern Transvaal), W J Bartmann (Natal),
J C Breedt (Transvaal), I Macdonald (Transvaal) *Replacement* H Hattingh (Northern
Transvaal) for Geldenhuys (64 mins)
Scorer *Penalty Goal:* Botha
AUSTRALIA: Roebuck; Campese, Little, Horan, Carozza; Lynagh, Farr-Jones *(capt)*;
Daly, Kearns, McKenzie, McCall, Eales, Ofahengaue, Gavin, Wilson
Scorers *Tries:* Carozza (2), Campese   *Conversion:* Lynagh   *Penalty Goals:* Lynagh (3)
Referee D J Bishop (New Zealand)

SOUTH AFRICA TO FRANCE AND ENGLAND 1992

This visit was by no means a glorious re-entry into international touring for the Springboks. There were shortcomings in the team and management structure, a structure largely cobbled together for the sake of political expediency. There were conflicting reports concerning the true unity of the party. Certainly, the team did not relish the drawbacks of touring France. The problems of language and culture can prove difficult to overcome, especially for a team which is essentially inward-looking. The Springboks were heavily criticised by their own Union following the tour for aspects of their off-field behaviour.

There were even reminders of the bad old days, the demo-plagued days. As the tour reached England, voices were raised in South Africa that the SARFU's efforts to take rugby into the townships and to the non-white population in general were decidedly weak. There were even a few days when, with the African National Congress threatening to withdraw consent for the tour, it appeared that the South Africans would return home without playing the England Test. The ANC, to their credit, allowed the tour to proceed but not before a few small groups of superannuated demonstrators had dusted down the banners.

South Africa did win a Test – they beat an abject French side in Lyons. But they were defeated comfortably in the Second Test in Paris, and also by England at Twickenham. They proved that they could raise the pace of their game and achieve a little continuity when they beat England B at Bristol in a superb match. Otherwise, pace and continuity were not hallmarks. In some of the French provincial matches there were signs of a surprising lack of pride and application.

Naas Botha, the captain, was hardly a dazzling springboard for attack but he bravely worked to keep the party moving forward and to present a friendly public face. He announced his retirement from Test rugby after the Twickenham defeat. The Springboks fielded a meaty pack yet ultimately, they were lacking. They were lacking at lock, they lacked consistency, they lacked ball-players and ball-winners.

Richter and Strauss were prominent in the back row, especially in the later stages of the tour; Wright forced the taller but limited du Preez out of the Test team at scrum-half and there was the odd sharp thrust from Gerber and Müller in the centre. Overall, it seemed as if this was a team from a bygone era, not one to bring South Africa back into the modern game. That probably went for their coaches and administrators, too.

THE TOURING PARTY

Manager G F Malan   **Assistant** J Abrahams   **SARFU Representative** J T Claasen
Coach J T Williams   **Assistant Coach** I Kirkpatrick   **Captain** H E Botha

FULL-BACKS

H **Reece-Edwards** (Natal)   **J T J van Rensburg** (Transvaal)

THREEQUARTERS

H Fuls (Transvaal)
D M Gerber (Western Province)
P Hendriks (Transvaal)
F Knoetze (Western Province)
P G Müller (Natal)
J Olivier (Northern Transvaal)
D E Oosthuizen (Northern Transvaal)
J Small (Transvaal)

HALF-BACKS

R J du Preez (Natal)
G D Wright (Transvaal)
H E Botha (Northern Transvaal)
H P Le Roux (Transvaal)

FORWARDS

K S Andrews (Western Province)

W G Hills (Northern Transvaal)
P H Rodgers (Transvaal)
J J Styger (Orange Free State)
H Roberts (Transvaal)
J A Truscott (Northern Transvaal)
S Atherton (Natal)
A Geldenhuys (Eastern Province)
H Hattingh (Northern Transvaal)
A W Malan (Northern Transvaal)
W J Bartmann (Natal)
I MacDonald (Transvaal)
P I L Pretorius (Northern Transvaal)
P B Rossouw (Western Province)
A Richter (Northern Transvaal)
C P Strauss (Western Province)
*F C Smit (Western Province)
*P J W Schutte (Northern Transvaal)

*Replacement during tour

TOUR RECORD

All matches   Played 13   Won 8   Lost 5   Points for 297   Against 236
International matches   Played 3   Won 1   Lost 2   Points for 52   Against 77

SCORING DETAILS

All matches
For: 30T 21C 28PG 7DG   297 Pts
Against: 16T 9C 42PG 4DG   236 Pts

International matches
For: 4T 4C 5PG 3DG   52 Pts
Against: 8T 5C 9PG   –   77 Pts

MATCH DETAILS

1992	OPPONENTS	VENUE	RESULT
3 October	French Selection	Bordeaux	L 17-24
7 October	Aquitaine XV	Pau	W 29-22
10 October	Midi-Pyrenées XV	Toulouse	W 18-15
13 October	Provence-Côte d'Azur XV	Marseilles	W 41-12
17 October	FRANCE	Lyons	W 20-15
20 October	Languedoc XV	Béziers	W 36-15
24 October	FRANCE	Paris	L 16-29
28 October	French Universities	Tours	L 13-18
31 October	French Barbarians	Lille	L 20-25
4 November	Midland Division	Leicester	W 32-9
7 November	England B	Bristol	W 20-16
10 November	Northern Division	Leeds	W 19-3
14 November	ENGLAND	Twickenham	L 16-33

Appearances: 10 – Hattingh (inc 1 as replacement), Richter (inc 1 as replacement); 8 – Wright, Botha, Andrews, Hills, Styger, Strauss, Olivier, van Rensburg (inc 1 as replacement), Müller (inc 1 as replacement); 7 – Gerber, Small, Malan, Fuls (inc 1 as replacement), Rodgers (inc 1 as replacement); 6 – Reece-Edwards, Knoetze, Oosthuizen, MacDonald, Le Roux (inc 1 as replacement), Roberts (inc 1 as replacement), Atherton (inc 1 as replacement), Pretorius (inc 1 as replacement); 5 – Hendriks, Bartmann, du Preez; 4 – Truscott, Geldenhuys, Smit (inc 1 as replacement); 2 – Rossouw, Schutte
Scorers: 74 – Botha (10C 11PG 7DG); 48 – van Rensburg (1T 5C 11PG); 30 – Reece-Edwards (6C 6PG); 20 – Olivier, Gerber (4T each); 15 – Hattingh, Small (3T each); 10 – Müller, Hendriks, Knoetze (2T each); 5 – Bartmann, MacDonald, Rossouw, Le Roux, du Preez, Oosthuizen, Richter, Roberts, Strauss (1T each)

MATCH 1   3 October, Bordeaux

French Selection 24 (1G 4PG 1T)   **South African XV 17** (3PG 1DG 1T)
French Selection: O Campan (Agen); D Berty (Stade Toulousain), F Mesnel

(Racing Club de France), T Lacroix (Dax), P Hontas (Biarritz); C Reigt (Lourdes), J Cazalbou (Stade Toulousain) (*capt*); L Benezech (Racing Club de France), F Landreau (Grenoble), S Graou (Auch), D Sanoko (Biarritz), H Chaffardon (Grenoble), X Blond (Racing Club de France), J Alibert (Bègles), L Loppy (Toulon) *Replacements* C Martos (Racing Club de France) for Graou (65 mins); M Courtiols (Bègles-Bordeaux) for Blond (40 mins); D Mandic (Grenoble) for Alibert (75 mins)
Scorers *Tries:* Hontas, Berty   *Conversion:* Lacroix   *Penalty Goals:* Lacroix (4)
South African XV: Reece-Edwards; Oosthuizen, Knoetze, Müller, Hendriks; Botha (*capt*), du Preez; Rodgers, Truscott, Andrews, Geldenhuys, Hattingh, Pretorius, Strauss, MacDonald *Replacements* Le Roux for Oosthuizen (59 mins); van Rensburg for Hendriks (47 mins)
Scorers *Try:* Hattingh   *Penalty Goals:* Botha (3)   *Dropped Goal:* Botha
Referee E F Morrison (England)

MATCH 2   7 October, Pau

Aquitaine XV 22 (1G 5PG)   **South African XV 29** (1G 4PG 2T)
Aquitaine XV: J-B Lafond (Bègles-Bordeaux) (*capt*); P Lacroix (Dax), F Ribreau (Lourdes), F Preux (Pau), P Bernat-Salles (Pau); F Pouyau (Bayonne), G Accocebery (Tyrosse); G Lascubé (Biarritz), L Verge (Bègles-Bordeaux), E Michaud (Bègles-Bordeaux), F Grec (Lourdes), O Roumat (Dax), A van Heerden (Tarbes), A Benazzi (Agen), P Benetton (Agen) *Replacements* L Salinas (Lourdes) for Lacroix (10 mins); A Agueb (Tarbes) for Grec (41 mins); M Del Maso (Agen) for Lascubé (56 mins); T Mentieres (Pau) for Michaud (72 mins)
Scorers *Try:* Salinas   *Conversion:* Pouyau   *Penalty Goals:* Pouyau (5)
South African XV: van Rensburg; Small, Fuls, Gerber, Olivier; Le Roux, Wright; Styger, Roberts, Hills, Malan, Hattingh, Richter, Strauss, Bartmann (*capt*)
Replacement Rodgers for Hills (56 mins)
Scorers *Tries:* Bartmann, Olivier, Small   *Conversion:* van Rensburg
Penalty Goals: van Rensburg (4)
Referee M Darroucq (Armagnac-Bigorre)

MATCH 3   10 October, Toulouse

Midi-Pyrenées XV 15 (5PG)   **South African XV 18** (1G 1PG 1DG 1T)
Midi-Pyrenées XV: H Mola (Stade Toulousain); P Garrigues (Graulhet), M Marfaing (Stade Toulousain), H Couffignal (Colomiers), D Dal Pos (Colomiers); B Bellot (Graulhet), F Galthié (Colomiers) (*capt*); F Ancelin (Colomiers), R Tremoulet (Graulhet), C Califano (Stade Toulousain), H Miorin (Stade Toulousain), F Pelous (Graulhet), A Carminati (Castres), N Hallinger (Colomiers), T Maset (Stade Toulousain) *Replacements* G Pages (Colomiers) for Pelous (44 mins); J-P Jusson (Valence-d'Agen) for Ancelin (56 mins); F Rui (Castres) for Bellot (70 mins)
Scorer *Penalty Goals:* Bellot (5)
South African XV: van Rensburg; Small, Fuls, Gerber, Olivier; Botha (*capt*), Wright; Styger, Roberts, Hills, Malan, Hattingh, Bartmann, Strauss, Richter *Replacements* Atherton for Malan (30 mins); Müller for Fuls (70 mins)
Scorers *Tries:* Olivier, Gerber   *Conversion:* van Rensburg   *Penalty Goal:* van Rensburg
Dropped Goal: Botha
Referee P Robin (Perigord-Agenais)

MATCH 4   13 October, Marseilles

Provence-Côte d'Azur XV 12 (3PG 1DG)   **South African XV 41** (5G 2PG)
Provence-Côte d'Azur XV: E Berdeu (Nice); P Tesseire (Toulon), E Artiguste (Nice), J-C Repon (Toulon), D Jaubert (Toulon); Y Delaigue (Toulon), J-E Piazza (Chateaurenard) (*capt*); C Barriere (Nîmes), E Desalmartini (Toulon), M Perie (Toulon), G Orsoni (Toulon), T Devergie (Nîmes), L Loppy (Toulon), E Melville (Toulon),

G Costello (Nîmes) *Replacements* J-M Monie (Chateaurenard) for Jaubert (41 mins); M Pujolle (Nice) for Melville (63 mins); M De Rougemont (Toulon) for Barriere (63 mins)
Scorers *Penalty Goals:* Tesseire (3) *Dropped Goal:* Berdeu
South African XV: Reece-Edwards; Olivier, Knoetze, Müller, Oosthuizen; Le Roux, du Preez; Andrews, Truscott, Rodgers, Geldenhuys, Atherton, Pretorius, MacDonald, Rossouw *Replacement* Richter for MacDonald (71 mins)
Scorers *Tries:* MacDonald, Rossouw, Olivier, Müller, le Roux
Conversions: Reece-Edwards (5) *Penalty Goals:* Reece-Edwards (2)
Referee M Thomas (Drome-Ardeche)

MATCH 5   17 October, Stade Gerlaud, Lyons   1st Test

FRANCE 15 (1G 1PG 1T)   SOUTH AFRICA 20 (2G 1PG 1DG)

France made a massive contribution to this surprising South African victory. Their selection for the match was odd, their tactics – running the ball on a soft pitch – were strange and their execution was miserably poor. Viars missed kick after kick and it was only at the end that the team awoke. They scored two tries in the last 25 minutes and could have pulled the match round at the end.

Yet South Africa's tackling was courageous and unfailing and they deserved to hold on for a victory which at least guaranteed that their tour would not be a complete disaster. Their scrummaging was solid and their upper-body strength generally tied up the ball in the mauls and close-quarter exchanges. They were well served by Botha's coolness and by the foraging back row of Bartmann, Richter and Strauss. The back row certainly cashed in on untidy French line-out work and on some poor play behind the French scrum.

Penaud tended to let the game run away from him at fly-half and the highly rated Deylaud did not live up to his promise in the centre. Hueber at scrum-half had a difficult ride.

FRANCE: J-L Sadourny (Colomiers); P Saint-André (Montferrand), F Mesnel (Racing Club de France), C Deylaud (Stade Toulousain), S Viars (Brive); A Penaud (Brive), A Hueber (Toulon); L Armary (Lourdes), J-M Gonzales (Bayonne), P Gallart (Béziers), J-M Cadieu (Stade Toulousain), O Roumat (Dax), J-F Tordo (Nice), M Cecillon (Bourgoin) *(capt)*, L Cabannes (Racing Club de France)
Replacements A Benazzi (Agen) for Cadieu (50 mins); P Benetton (Agen) for Tordo (62 mins)
Scorers *Tries:* Penaud (2) *Conversion:* Viars *Penalty Goal:* Viars
SOUTH AFRICA: Reece-Edwards; Small, Gerber, Müller, Olivier; Botha *(capt)*, Wright; Styger, Hills, Rodgers, Geldenhuys, Malan, Bartmann, Strauss, Richter
Scorers *Tries:* Gerber, Small *Conversions:* Botha (2) *Penalty Goal:* Botha
Dropped Goal: Botha
Referee B Kinsey (Australia)

MATCH 6   20 October, Béziers

Languedoc XV 15 (1G 1PG 1T)   **South African XV 36** (2G 4PG 2T)
Languedoc XV: P Bonhoure (Béziers); P Fabre (Montpellier), S Rouch (Narbonne), P Bondouy (Narbonne), J-P Bullich (Narbonne); D Camberabero (Béziers), P Cances (Montpellier); J-J Pineda (Narbonne), D Bes (Montpellier), C Musset (Montpellier), F Dejean (Narbonne) *(capt)*, J-F Gourragne (Béziers), P Chamayou (Béziers),

G Bourguignon (Narbonne), S Dispagne (Narbonne) *Replacements* J-P Alarcon (Béziers) for Dispagne (49 mins); J-V Bertrand (Narbonne) for Bonhoure (69 mins)
Scorers *Tries:* Chamayou, Fabre   *Conversion:* Camberabero
Penalty Goal: Camberabero
South African XV: van Rensburg; Oosthuizen, Fuls, Knoetze, Hendriks; Le Roux, du Preez *(capt)*; Styger, Roberts, Andrews, Atherton, Hattingh, Pretorius, MacDonald, Rossouw
Scorers *Tries:* du Preez, Hendriks, Hattingh, van Rensburg
Conversions: van Rensburg (2)   *Penalty Goals:* van Rensburg (4)
Referee F A Howard (England)

MATCH 7   24 October, Parc des Princes   2nd Test

FRANCE 29 (2G 5PG)   SOUTH AFRICA 16 (1G 2PG 1DG)

This was emphatically a better effort by the French. It took some of the pressure from the team and from the shoulders of Pierre Berbizier, the coach. There were many aspects in which the French improved, especially in the matter of points-scoring. Lacroix, the talented centre, missed his first two kicks but then banished the unhappy memories of the troubles of Viars the previous week by kicking six from the next six.

Even better, the French finally gained a return from the line-out. Benazzi had a fine game and his presence alone took some of the weight from the shoulders of Roumat. After many matches as the only target, Roumat revelled in the fact that France had someone else to throw to.

The flankers, Benetton and Cabannes, played explosively and even though it took the French a good deal of the match to impose themselves, they eventually ran out easy winners. Roumat scored the first French try on the end of a forward drive and Penaud side-stepped a path to the line later on. Gerber scored for South Africa, but on the day the visiting team looked slow; they lacked continuity and ideas, lacked a line-out and a general. After losing to the French Barbarians at the end of the month they departed France for England with some relief, but they did not appear to be a team which could win at Twickenham.

FRANCE: J-L Sadourny (Colomiers); J-B Lafond (Bègles-Bordeaux), F Mesnel (Racing Club de France), T Lacroix (Dax), P Saint-André (Montferrand); A Penaud (Brive), A Hueber (Toulon); L Armary (Lourdes), J-M Gonzales (Bayonne), P Gallart (Béziers), A Benazzi (Agen), O Roumat (Dax), P Benetton (Agen), M Cecillon (Bourgoin) *(capt)*, L Cabannes (Racing Club de France) *Replacement* S Viars (Brive) for Lafond (55 mins)
Scorers *Tries:* Roumat, Penaud   *Conversions:* Lacroix (2)   *Penalty Goals:* Lacroix (5)
SOUTH AFRICA: Reece-Edwards; Small, Gerber, Müller, Oliver; Botha *(capt)*, Wright; Styger, Hills, Rodgers, Malan, Geldenhuys, Bartmann, Strauss, Richter
Replacement Hattingh for Geldenhuys (49 mins)
Scorers *Try:* Gerber   *Conversion:* Botha   *Penalty Goals:* Botha (2)
Dropped Goal: Botha
Referee B Kinsey (Australia)

MATCH 8   28 October, Tours

French Universities 18 (5PG 1DG)   **South African XV 13** (1G 2PG)
French Universities: O Campan (Agen); E Fachan (Tarbes), B Daguerre (Bayonne),

Adri Geldenhuys, the Springbok lock, wins possession in the Second Test against France, in Paris. France levelled the series with a comprehensive victory.

P Fauthoux (Racing Club de France), P Lacroix (Dax); L Mazas (Colomiers), G Accocebery (Tyrosse) (*capt*); F Bernabeu (Perpignan), S Morizot (Perpignan), P Voisin (Racing Club de France) F Pellous (Graulhet), Y Lemeur (Racing Club de France), D Lacroix (Stade Toulousain), O Marin (Stade Toulousain), S Chonchy (Bègles-Bordeaux) *Replacements* C Savy (Grenoble) for Campan (67 mins); E Jamin (Stade Toulousain) for Morizot (76 mins)
Scorer *Penalty Goals:* Mazas (5)   *Dropped Goal:* Mazas
South African XV: van Rensburg; Hendriks, Fuls, Knoetze, Oosthuizen; Le Roux, du Preez (*capt*); Hills, Truscott, Andrews, Atherton, Hattingh, MacDonald, Richter, Pretorius *Replacement* Roberts for Truscott (45 mins)

Scorers *Try:* Hendriks   *Conversion:* van Rensburg
Penalty Goals: van Rensburg (2)
Referee P Galligot (Limousin)

MATCH 9   31 October, Stade du Nord, Lille

French Barbarians 25 (1G 5PG 1DG)   **South African XV 20** (2G 1PG 1DG)
French Barbarians: S Blanco (Biarritz) (*capt*); P Saint-André (Montferrand), P Sella
(Agen), D Charvet (Racing Club de France), P Lagisquet (Biarritz); D Camberabero
(Béziers), R N Jones (Swansea); G Lascubé (Biarritz), L Dal Maso (Agen), P Ondarts
(Biarritz), A Benazzi (Agen), J Condom (Biarritz), E Champ (Toulon), L Rodriguez
(Dax), L Loppy (Toulon)
Scorers *Try:* Lagisquet   *Conversion:* Camberabero   *Penalty Goals:* Camberabero (5)
Dropped Goal: Camberabero
South African XV: Reece-Edwards; Small, Müller, Fuls, Olivier; Botha (*capt*),
Wright; Styger, Roberts, Andrews, Atherton, Malan, Richter, Strauss, Smit
Scorers *Tries:* Small, Müller   *Conversions:* Botha (2)   *Penalty Goal:* Botha
Dropped Goal: Botha
Referee N Lasaga (FFR)

MATCH 10   4 November, Welford Road, Leicester

Midland Division 9 (2PG 1DG)   **South African XV 32** (3G 2PG 1T)
Midland Division: J Liley (Leicester); S Hackney (Leicester), S Potter (Leicester),
I Bates (Leicester), H Thorneycroft (Northampton); J Steele (Northampton),
A Kardooni (Leicester); M Linnett (Moseley), C J Olver (Northampton), G S Pearce
(Northampton), M Johnson (Leicester), M Bayfield (Northampton), P Shillingford
(Moseley), D Richards (Leicester) (*capt*), R Tebbutt (Leicester)
Scorers *Penalty Goals:* Liley (2)   *Dropped Goal:* Steele
South African XV: van Rensburg; Oosthuizen, Gerber, Knoetze, Hendriks;
Botha (*capt*), Wright; Rodgers, Hills, Andrews, Hattingh, Schutte, Bartmann, Richter,
MacDonald *Replacements* Smit for Schutte (19 mins); Pretorius for Bartmann (32 mins)
Scorers *Tries:* Knoetze (2), Oosthuizen, Gerber   *Conversions:* Botha (3)
Penalty Goals: Botha (2)
Referee J M Fleming (Scotland)

MATCH 11   7 November, Memorial Ground, Bristol

England B 16 (2PG 2T)   **South African XV 20** (1G 1DG 2T)
England B: I Hunter (Northampton); N J Heslop (Orrell), P R de Glanville (Bath),
D P Hopley (Cambridge U & Wasps), T Underwood (Leicester); S Barnes (Bath) (*capt*),
S M Bates (Wasps); M Hynes (Orrell), B C Moore (Harlequins), J A Probyn (Wasps),
N C Redman (Bath), A Blackmore (Bristol), T A K Rodber (Northampton), B B Clarke
(Bath), N Back (Leicester) *Replacements* A Buzza (Wasps) for Heslop (64 mins); J Steele
(Northampton) for Hunter (76 mins)
Scorers *Tries:* Hunter, Underwood   *Penalty Goals:* Barnes (2)
South African XV: van Rensburg; Small, Gerber, Müller, Olivier; Botha (*capt*),
Wright; Styger, Hills, Andrews, Hattingh, Malan, Strauss, Richter, Smit
Replacement Fuls for Müller (70 mins)
Scorers *Tries:* Hattingh, Olivier, Richter   *Conversion:* Botha   *Dropped Goal:* Botha
Referee J Dume (Bordeaux)

MATCH 12   10 November, Elland Road, Leeds

Northern Division 3 (1PG)   **South African XV 19** (1G 4PG)
Northern Division: J Mallinder (Sale); N J Heslop (Orrell), B Barley (Wakefield),
K G Simms (Liverpool St Helens) (*capt*), S Bromley (Rugby); G Ainscough (Orrell),
D Scully (Wakefield); P Lancaster (West Hartlepool), S Mitchell (West Hartlepool),

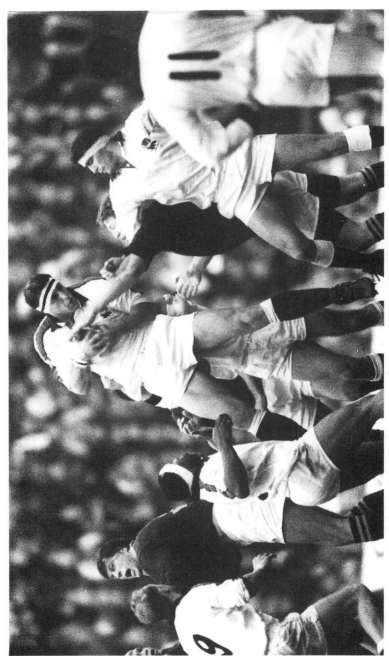

Wade Dooley (in possession) and Ben Clarke of England hold off Frederik Smit and the rest of the Springbok pack in a line-out in the Test match at Twickenham.

M Whitcombe (Sale), K Westgarth (West Hartlepool), S Bainbridge (Newcastle Gosforth), M Greenwood (Wasps), A Macfarlane (Sale), M Pepper (Nottingham)
Scorer *Penalty Goal:* Ainscough
South African XV: Reece-Edwards; Hendriks, Fuls, Knoetze, Oosthuizen; Le Roux, du Preez; Rodgers, Roberts, Truscott, Pretorius, Hattingh, Schutte, MacDonald, Atherton
Scorers *Try:* Roberts   *Conversion:* Reece-Edwards   *Penalty Goals:* Reece-Edwards (4)
Referee A J Spreadbury (Somerset)

MATCH 13   14 November, Twickenham

ENGLAND 33 (2G 3PG 2T)   SOUTH AFRICA 16 (1G 2PG 1DG)

South Africa had improved markedly in their short time in England and when they led 16-8 at one stage there was certainly a chance of a shock victory: whether that would have done long-term good for their game, or whether it would have masked inadequacies, is open to debate.

However, England reasserted themselves. They had struggled early on in the scrums and line-outs and for some time their demeanour was appropriate for a dismal, dank and wet day at Twickenham. They did score a splendid try in the first half when Rory Underwood fed brother Tony and the younger Underwood celebrated his first cap by streaking over in the corner to score. Yet a charging try by Strauss and some beautiful kicking by Botha set up that 16-8 lead.

England dominated the second half. Bayfield had a marvellous game in the line-out and Winterbottom was in storming form around the pitch, in all areas of the game. Guscott scored simply by running unopposed on to a superb chip ahead by Andrew, the perfect counter to the tactic of the South African backs of coming up just ahead of the offside line. Morris poached a try around the fringes of the scrum and Carling scored when a steepling kick by Andrew eluded the defence.

ENGLAND: J M Webb (Bath); T Underwood (Leicester), W D C Carling (Harlequins) (*capt*), J C Guscott (Bath), R Underwood (Leicester & RAF); C R Andrew (Wasps), C D Morris (Orrell); J Leonard (Saracens), B C Moore (Harlequins), V E Ubogu (Bath), M C Bayfield (Northampton), W A Dooley (Preston Grasshoppers), MC Teague (Gloucester), B B Clarke (Bath), P J Winterbottom (Harlequins)
Replacement P R de Glanville (Bath) for T Underwood (58 mins)
Scorers *Tries:* Carling, Guscott, Morris, T Underwood   *Conversions:* Webb (2)
Penalty Goals: Webb (3)
SOUTH AFRICA: van Rensburg; Small, Gerber, Müller, Olivier; Botha (*capt*), Wright; Styger, Hills, Andrews, Hattingh, Malan, Strauss, Richter, Smit
Scorers *Try:* Strauss   *Conversion:* Botha   *Penalty Goals:* Botha (2)
Dropped Goal: Botha
Referee S R Hilditch (Ireland)

AUSTRALIA TO IRELAND AND WALES 1992

The popular statement about this Australian visit was that it was a tour too far – that the world champions had been under so much sustained pressure as they took their mantle around the globe that they needed not another tour, but a rest. There was some truth in this, and certainly there were some tired players, both in body and in mind. The Australians also had problems against the Welsh clubs and against Munster. They learned, as the All Blacks learned long ago, that some teams have wonderful traditions against touring sides and will lift themselves far above normal form. Not the least of the problems was that by the end, both World Cup half-backs, Nick Farr-Jones and Michael Lynagh, were missing. Farr-Jones had retired and Lynagh suffered a shoulder injury against Ireland at Lansdowne Road. The rest of the tour proved, not surprisingly, that their replacements were not of the same class and influence and also that some of the back-up forwards were not as formidable as they looked.

And yet, having said all that, the Australians still won the two Tests convincingly, still disposed of the Barbarians in the tour finale and still departed for home as the unchallenged best in the world.

In many ways it was quiet tour. David Campese was often shackled by injury and heavy marking, although he had a major hand in the Tests. Tim Horan and Jason Little, the team anchors in the midfield, played powerfully even though their usual continuity was absent. Phil Kearns led well in the absence of Lynagh, the tour captain. In the back row, Willie Ofahengaue had an outstanding tour, especially in the tackle, where he upset the frenzied Welsh attacks at Cardiff.

For the home teams, there was glory for Munster, although only after a rough match; for Llanelli, with a typically passionate victory at Stradey; and most of all for Swansea, who took on and beat almost the best Australia could field on the day, and beat them very well indeed.

THE TOURING PARTY

Manager J J Breen   **Coach** R S F Dwyer
Assistant coach R I Templeton   **Captain** M P Lynagh

FULL-BACKS

M C Roebuck (Eastwood & NSW)
T P Kelaher (Randwick & NSW)

THREEQUARTERS

D I Campese (Randwick & NSW)
D K Junee (Randwick & NSW)
P V Carozza (Wests & Queensland)
D Smith (Souths & Queensland)
A G Herbert (GPS & Queensland)
T J Horan (Souths & Queensland)
J S Little (Souths & Queensland)
R C Tombs (Norths & NSW)

HALF-BACKS

M P Lynagh (University & Queensland)
P Kahl (Easts & Queensland)

P J Slattery (University & Queensland)
A Ekert (Gordon & NSW)
*T M Wallace (Gordon & NSW)
*L F Walker (Randwick & NSW)

FORWARDS

D J Crowley (Souths & Queensland)
A J Daly (Easts & NSW)
C P Lillicrap (University & Queensland)
E J A McKenzie (Randwick & NSW)
P N Kearns (Randwick & NSW)
D V Nucifora (University & Queensland)
J A Eales (Brothers & Queensland)
R J McCall (Brothers & Queensland)
G Morgan (Souths & Queensland)

W W **Waugh** (Randwick & NSW)
M **Brial** (Easts & NSW)
T **Coker** (Souths & Queensland)
V **Ofahengaue** (Manly & NSW)
D J **Wilson** (Easts & Queensland)
B T **Gavin** (Easts & NSW)

S J A **Scott-Young** (Souths & Queensland)
*M **Ryan** (Brothers & Queensland)
*A **Blades** (Gordon & NSW)
*D P A **Dix** (Cambridge U & NSW)
*S P **Poidevin** (Randwick & NSW)

Replacement during tour

TOUR RECORD
All matches Played 13 Won 10 Lost 3 Points for 312 Against 161
International matches Played 2 Won 2 Points for 65 Against 23

SCORING DETAILS
All matches
For: 32T 19C 38PG –   312 Pts
Against: 12T   4C 26PG 5DG 161 Pts

International matches
For: 8T 5C 5PG 65 Pts
Against: 1T   –   6PG 23 Pts

MATCH DETAILS

1992	OPPONENTS	VENUE	RESULT
17 October	Leinster	Dublin	W 38-11
21 October	Munster	Cork	L 19-22
24 October	Ulster	Belfast	W 35-11
27 October	Connacht	Galway	W 14-6
31 October	IRELAND	Dublin	W 42-17
4 November	Swansea	Swansea	L 6-21
7 November	Wales B	Cardiff	W 24-11
11 November	Neath	Neath	W 16-8
14 November	Llanelli	Llanelli	L 9-13
17 November	Monmouthshire	Ebbw Vale	W 19-9
21 November	WALES	Cardiff	W 23-6
24 November	Welsh Students	Bridgend	W 37-6
28 November	Barbarians	Twickenham	W 30-20

Appearances: 9 – McCall (inc 1 as replacement); Crowley (inc 2 as replacement); 8 – Roebuck, Little, Slattery, Kearns, McKenzie (inc 1 as replacement), Gavin, Smith, Coker (inc 2 as replacement); 7 – Kelaher (inc 1 as replacement), Horan, Ofahengaue, Wilson, Junee, Scott-Young; 6 – Campese (inc 1 as replacement), Carozza, Eales, Kahl; 5 – Tombs, Ekert, Nucifora, Morgan, Waugh, Ryan; 4 – Brial, Blades, Walker; 3 – Lynagh, Wallace; 2 – Herbert, Lillicrap; 1 – Dix, Daly Poidevin
Scorers: 100 – Roebuck (17C 22PG); 67 – Kelaher (3T 2C 16PG); 20 – Campese (4T); 15 – Little, Ryan, Smith (3T each); 10 – Lynagh, Wilson, Gavin, McKenzie, Horan (2T each), 5 – Eales, Morgan, McCall, Nucifora, Crowley, Kearns (1T each)

MATCH 1 17 October, Lansdowne Road, Dublin

Leinster 11 (2PG 1T) **Australia XV 38** (2G 3PG 3T)
Leinster: C Clarke (Terenure); D O'Brien (Clontarf), V J G Cunningham (St Mary's Coll), M P Ridge (Blackrock Coll), N Woods (Blackrock Coll); A McGowan (Blackrock Coll), L F P Aherne (Lansdowne); H Hurley (Old Wesley), J N Murphy (Greystones), D Dowling (St Mary's Coll), B J Rigney (Greystones), J O'Callaghan (Wanderers), K T Leahy (Wanderers), P J Lawlor (Bective Rangers), R Love (Old Wesley)
Replacement S Byrne (Blackrock Coll) for Murphy (43 mins)
Scorers *Try:* Woods *Penalty Goals:* McGowan (2)
Australia XV: Roebuck; Carozza, Little, Horan, Campese; Lynagh (*capt*); Slattery; Daly, Kearns, McKenzie, McCall, Eales, Ofahengaue, Gavin, Wilson
Replacement Crowley for Daly (23 mins)
Scorers *Tries:* Campese (2), Lynagh (2), Wilson *Conversions:* Roebuck (2)
Penalty Goals: Roebuck (3)
Referee W D Bevan (Wales)

33

MATCH 2   21 October, Cork

Munster 22 (1G 4PG 1DG)   **Australia XV 19** (1G 4PG)
Munster: C Haly (Cork Const); R M Wallace (Garryowen), P P A Danaher (Garryowen), B Walsh (Cork Const), J D Clarke (Dolphin); D Larkin (Garryowen), D Tobin (Young Munster); P D McCarthy (Cork Const), T J Kingston (Dolphin) *(capt)*, P Clohessy (Young Munster), M Galwey (Shannon), R Costello (Garryowen), G Clohessy (Young Munster), B Cronin (Garryowen), G Earls (Young Munster) *Replacements* J Galvin (Shannon) for Larkin (21 mins); E O'Sullivan (Old Crescent) for Costello (65 mins)
Scorers *Try:* penalty try   *Conversion:* Haly   *Penalty Goals:* Haly (4)
Dropped Goal: Galvin
Australia XV: Kelaher; Smith, Tombs, Herbert, Junee; Kahl, Ekert; Lillicrap, Nucifora *(capt)*, Crowley, Morgan, Waugh, Scott-Young, Coker, Brial
Replacement McKenzie for Crowley (33 mins)
Scorer *Try:* Kelaher   *Conversion:* Kelaher   *Penalty Goals:* Kelaher (4)
Referee M Desclaux (France)

MATCH 3   24 October, Ravenhill, Belfast

Ulster 11 (1PG 1DG 1T)   **Australia XV 35** (5G)
Ulster: C R Wilkinson (Malone); R Carey (Dungannon), M McCall (Bangor), M Field (Malone), K D Crossan (Instonians); P Russell (Instonians), A Blair (Dungannon); D Elliott (Instonians), S J Smith (Ballymena), A Miller (Ballymena), P Johns (Dungannon), D Tweed (Ballymena), S McKinty (Bangor), B F Robinson (London Irish), G F Hamilton (Ballymena) *(capt)* *Replacement* G Bell (Instonians) for Miller (45 mins)
Scorers *Try:* Robinson   *Penalty Goal:* Russell   *Dropped Goal:* McCall
Australia XV: Roebuck; Carozza, Little, Horan, Campese; Lynagh *(capt)*, Slattery; Lillicrap, Kearns, McKenzie, McCall, Eales, Ofahengaue, Gavin, Wilson
Replacement Crowley for Lillicrap (41 mins)
Scorers *Tries:* Eales, Gavin (2), McKenzie, Little   *Conversions:* Roebuck (5)
Referee R J Megson (Scotland)

MATCH 4   27 October, Sports Ground, Galway

Connacht 6 (2PG)   **Australia XV 14** (3PG 1T)
Connacht: A White (St Mary's Coll); C Leahy (Wanderers), S Tormey (Galwegians), M Cosgrave (Wanderers) *(capt)*, G Curley (Athlone); E Elwood (Lansdowne), K Lawless (Clontarf); T P J Clancy (Lansdowne), W Mulcahy (Skerries), D Henshaw (Athlone), T Coughlin (St Mary's Coll), S Jameson (St Mary's Coll), E Walshe (Dolphin), N P Mannion (Lansdowne), M P FitzGibbon (Shannon) *Replacement* P Brady (Wanderers) for Mannion (42 mins)
Scorer *Penalty Goals:* White (2)
Australia XV: Kelaher; Smith, Herbert, Tombs, Junee; Kahl, Ekert; Crowley, Nucifora, Ryan, Morgan, Waugh, Scott-Young, Coker *(capt)*, Wilson
Replacement Campese for Herbert (35 mins)
Scorers *Try:* Ryan   *Penalty Goals:* Kelaher (3)
Referee G Simmonds (Wales)

MATCH 5   31 October, Lansdowne Road, Dublin

IRELAND 17 (4PG 1T)   AUSTRALIA 42 (4G 3PG 1T)

It says everything about the relative strengths of these two teams that Australia could give their worst performance for at least two years and yet still threaten to score 50 points. Australia made too many mistakes and were profligate with their finishing – otherwise, it could have been desperate for Ireland. As it was, Ciaran Fitzgerald, their coach, resigned a few days after the match.

Australia reasserted themselves in the second half after Ireland had come back to the relative respectability of 17-28 with a try by Wallace, who burst past Campese, and a penalty by Russell.

Australia decided that enough was enough and Gavin and Ofahengaue began to drive on the narrow front. Kelaher (deputising for Lynagh, who departed at half-time) and Horan scored late tries to rub it in.

For Ireland, at least Geoghegan looked to have an appetite for the contest on the wing and Ireland's makeshift back row gave everything. The front row was solid but there was very little technical merit behind the scrum, no continuity and, perhaps worst of all, very little of the traditional Dublin passion. Campese, McKenzie and Little were the try-scorers in the first half. The Little try was the best, involving Campese with a typical burst then deft handling by the Australian forwards as they supported the move.

IRELAND: J E Staples (London Irish); S P Geoghegan (London Irish), P P A Danaher (Garryowen) (*capt*), V J G Cunningham (St Mary's Coll), R M Wallace (Garryowen); P Russell (Instonians), L F P Aherne (Lansdowne); N J Popplewell (Greystones), J N Murphy (Greystones), P McCarthy (Cork Const), M J Galwey (Shannon), P S Johns (Dungannon), B F Robinson (London Irish), P J Lawlor (Bective Rangers), G F Hamilton (NIFC)
Scorers *Try:* Wallace   *Penalty Goals:* Russell (4)
AUSTRALIA: Roebuck; Campese, Little, Horan, Carozza; Lynagh (*capt*), Slattery; Crowley, Kearns, McKenzie, McCall, Eales, Ofahengaue, Gavin, Wilson
Replacement Kelaher for Lynagh (40 mins)
Scorers *Tries:* Campese, McKenzie, Little, Kelaher, Horan   *Conversions:* Roebuck (4)
Penalty Goals: Roebuck (3)
Referee E F Morrison (England)

MATCH 6   4 November, Swansea

Swansea 21 (1G 2PG 1DG 1T)   **Australia XV 6** (2PG)
Swansea: A Clement; M H Titley, K Hopkins, I S Gibbs, Simon Davies; A Williams, R N Jones; C Clark, G R Jenkins, K Colclough, R D Moriarty, P Arnold, A D Reynolds, Stuart Davies (*capt*), R E Webster
Scorers *Tries:* Gibbs, Jenkins   *Conversion:* Williams   *Penalty Goals:* Williams (2)
Dropped Goal: Williams
Australia XV: Kelaher; Smith, Little, Horan, Carozza; Kahl, Slattery; Ryan, Kearns (*capt*), Blades, Waugh, Eales, Coker, Gavin, Scott-Young
Scorer *Penalty Goals:* Kelaher (2)

MATCH 7   7 November, Cardiff Arms Park

Wales B 11 (2PG 1T)   **Australia XV 24** (1G 4PG 1T)
Wales B: M A Rayer (Cardiff); I W Jones (Llanelli), M R Hall (Cardiff), N Davies (Llanelli), W T Proctor (Llanelli); C J Stephens (Llanelli), R H StJ B Moon (Llanelli) (*capt*); R Evans (Llanelli), D C Fox (Llanelli), H Williams-Jones (South Wales Police), S Roy (Cardiff), J D M Wakeford (South Wales Police), M A Perego (Llanelli), S Legge (South Wales Police), M S Morris (Neath) *Replacements* N Boobyer (Llanelli) for Jones (14 mins); N Meek (Pontypool) for Fox (19 mins)
Scorers *Try:* Davies   *Penalty Goals:* Stephens (2)
Australia XV: Roebuck; Smith, Tombs, Walker, Junee; Wallace, Ekert; Crowley, Kearns (*capt*), McKenzie, McCall, Morgan, Ofahengaue, Gavin, Wilson

Scorers *Tries:* Smith, Morgan   *Conversion:* Roebuck   *Penalty Goals:* Roebuck (4)
Referee B E Stirling (Ireland)

MATCH 8   11 November, Neath

Neath 8 (1PG 1T)   **Australia XV 16** (1G 3PG)
Neath: P H Thorburn; S Bowling, L Isaac, J Bird, J Reynolds; M McCarthy, R Jones;
B R Williams, K H Phillips, J D Davies, Glyn Llewellyn, Gareth Llewellyn (*capt*),
S Williams, A Kembery, M S Morris
Scorers *Try:* B R Williams   *Penalty Goal:* Thorburn
Australia XV: Kelaher; Smith, Little, Walker, Junee; Wallace, Slattery (*capt*); Ryan,
Nucifora, Blades, Eales, McCall, Coker, Scott-Young, Brial
Scorers *Try:* Little   *Conversion:* Kelaher   *Penalty Goals:* Kelaher (3)
Referee A Cuq (France)

MATCH 9   14 November, Stradey Park, Llanelli

Llanelli 13 (1G 2DG)   **Australia XV 9** (3PG)
Llanelli: H Williams; I C Evans, N Davies, S Davies, W T Proctor; C J Stephens,
R H StJ B Moon (*capt*); R Evans, A Lamerton, L Delaney, P T Davies, A H Copsey,
M A Perego, E W Lewis, L Jones *Replacement* D Joseph for Delaney (42 mins)
Scorers *Try:* Evans   *Conversion:* Stephens   *Dropped Goals:* Stephens (2)
Australia XV: Roebuck; Smith, Kelaher, Little, Junee; Horan, Slattery; Crowley,
Kearns (*capt*), McKenzie, McCall, Eales, Ofahengaue, Gavin, Wilson
Replacement Coker for Eales (10 mins)
Scorer *Penalty Goals:* Roebuck (3)
Referee F A Howard (England)

MATCH 10   17 November, Eugene Cross Park, Ebbw Vale

Monmouthshire 9 (3PG)   **Australia XV 19** (1G 4PG)
Monmouthshire: D Rees (Newbridge); J Westwood (Newport), K Orrell (Newport),
I Lewis (Bath), S White (Pontypool); P Turner (Sale) (*capt*), D Llewellyn (Newport);
A Dibble (Pontypool), A Peacock (Newport), L Mustoe (Pontypool), A Rees (Cardiff),
M Voyle (Newport), P Crane (Newbridge), R Goodey (Pontypool), G M George
(Newport) *Replacement* P Withers (Cross Keys) for Turner (73 mins)
Scorer *Penalty Goals:* Westwood (3)
Australia XV: Roebuck; Junee, Tombs, Walker, Smith; Kahl, Ekert; Ryan, Nucifora,
Blades, Waugh, Morgan, Brial, Scott-Young, Coker (*capt*) *Replacement* McCall for
Morgan (73 mins)
Scorers *Try:* Smith   *Conversion:* Roebuck   *Penalty Goals:* Roebuck (4)
Referee B Smith (Ireland)

MATCH 11   21 November, National Ground, Cardiff Arms Park

WALES 6 (2PG)   AUSTRALIA 23 (1G 2PG 2T)

There seemed just a chance for the emerging Welsh team because
Australia were without the injured line-out man, Eales, and there was
also the opportunity to put the pressure on Kahl, who had been
unconvincing on tour as the replacement for the injured Lynagh.

Wales played well. Copsey and Llewellyn and their colleagues fought
a draw in the line-out battle whereas the last time the teams had met, in
the World Cup, Australia had won every line-out in the match bar
three. There was welcome passion and organisation in Welsh ranks.

Yet it was by no means enough. Australia scored three tries and their
own line was threatened rarely. This was chiefly because Australia's

tackling was thunderous – Horan and Little in the centre and especially the explosive Ofahengaue on the flank hammered the life from any and every Welsh move, cutting down Wales around the fringes and in midfield. Wales lacked the ideas and penetration to cope and they subsided to a convincing defeat. Their scoring was confined to two penalties by Stephens, who was inconsistent at fly-half. The match was sealed with a try by Campese. He raced on to the ball after a mis-kick by Little in the centre. Campese scooped up the ball, sprinted down the right wing and made the line. The Cardiff crowd rose to him as he walked back. It was a touching tribute.

David Wilson was driven over for the first Australian try and Rod McCall stretched out for another through a forest of legs. The Wilson try had the hint of fortune: the ball rebounded to Australia from the Welsh post after Roebuck had made a hash of a kick at goal.

WALES: M A Rayer (Cardiff); I C Evans (Llanelli) (*capt*), M R Hall (Cardiff), I S Gibbs (Swansea), W T Proctor (Llanelli); C J Stephens (Llanelli), R N Jones (Swansea); M Griffiths (Cardiff), G R Jenkins (Swansea), H Williams-Jones (South Wales Police), G O Llewellyn (Neath), A H Copsey (Llanelli), E W Lewis (Llanelli), S Davies (Swansea), R E Webster (Swansea) *Replacement* A D Reynolds (Swansea) for Lewis (74 mins)
Scorer *Penalty Goals:* Stephens (2)
AUSTRALIA: Roebuck; Campese, Little, Horan, Carozza; Kahl, Slattery; Crowley, Kearns (*capt*), McKenzie, McCall, Morgan, Ofahengaue, Gavin, Wilson
Replacement Coker for Wilson (56 mins)
Scorers *Tries:* Wilson, McCall, Campese   *Conversion:* Roebuck
Penalty Goals: Roebuck (2)
Referee A J Spreadbury (England)

MATCH 12   24 November, Bridgend

Welsh Students 6 (2PG)   **Australia XV 37** (4PG 5T)
Welsh Students: L Evans (Welsh National S Medicine); C Thomas (Cardiff Inst HE), N Boobyer (Bridgend TC), S Hill (Welsh National S Medicine), O Robbins (South Bank Poly); M McCarthy (West London Inst), P John (Cardiff Inst HE); M Davis (Cheltenham & Gloucester Coll), J Humphreys (Poly of Wales), C Evans (Cardiff Inst HE), L Harvey (Cardiff Inst HE), S Roy (Bristol U), P Pook (Tyneside Poly), O Williams (Cardiff Inst HE), A Carter (Cardiff Inst HE) *Replacement* A Peacock for Humphreys (70 mins)
Scorer *Penalty Goals:* L Evans (2)
Australia XV: Kelaher; Smith, Tombs, Walker, Junee; Wallace, Ekert; Blades, Nucifora, Ryan, Waugh, Dix, Poidevin, Scott-Young, Brial
Scorers *Tries:* Ryan (2), Kelaher, Smith, Nucifora   *Penalty Goals:* Kelaher (4)
Referee D Leslie (Scotland)

MATCH 13   28 November, Twickenham

Barbarians 20 (1G 1PG 2T)   **Australia XV 30** (3G 3PG)
Barbarians: M A Rayer (Cardiff); I Hunter (Northampton), W D C Carling (Harlequins) (*capt*), I S Gibbs (Swansea), T Underwood (Leicester); S Barnes (Bath), R N Jones (Swansea); N J Popplewell (Greystones), N Meek (Pontypool), J A Probyn (Wasps), I D Jones (North Harbour), N Hadley (UBC OB, Vancouver), M G Skinner (Blackheath), B B Clarke (Bath), I R Smith (Gloucester)
Scorers *Tries:* Hunter, I D Jones, Probyn   *Conversion:* Rayer   *Penalty Goal:* Barnes

Australia XV: Roebuck; Campese, Little, Horan, Carozza; Kahl, Slattery; Crowley, Kearns (*capt*), McKenzie, McCall, Coker, Ofahengaue, Gavin, Scott-Young
Scorers *Tries:* Horan, Crowley, Kearns   *Conversions:* Roebuck (3)
Penalty Goals: Roebuck (3)
Referee J M Fleming (Scotland)

SCOTLAND TO AUSTRALIA 1992

Scotland's tour to Australia was expected to be the most demanding the country had undertaken, and so it proved – and not just because it was in the home of the world champions. The scene was set in the first game, when a Northern Territory Invitation XV won by 17-16 in Darwin, and the tour was half over before the Scots had their first victory.

Only two wins, both against country XVs, offset two draws and four defeats, including two by Australia. Yet the 15-15 draw with Queensland at Ballymore was a creditable result for the second match of the tour. A draw followed in the next game, when the Scots pulled back from 4-24 with four tries in 14 minutes to share the Hobart game with the Emerging Wallabies, an inappropriate title when the home team included experienced campaigners such as Anthony Herbert, David Knox, David Nucifora and Peter FitzSimons. David Sole, Scotland's captain and loose head, playing as a replacement wing forward, did much to urge the tourists to their comeback.

Injuries, as well as the demands of travelling in Australia, afflicted the tourists. More than one replacement was called on for the first time since the 1981 tour to New Zealand. Stuart Reid, the Boroughmuir breakaway forward, went home after he had played in only two games. A toe injury in the Darwin match kept John Robertson, the Heriot's flanker, out of action between the first and fifth matches, and both Sole and Gavin Hastings missed the Sydney game against New South Wales. The handicap of losing two such experienced players was too much, and the Scots succumbed by 35-15.

Creditably, Scotland led at half-time in the Sydney Test, the first international for the Wallabies since they won the World Cup seven months earlier. By then, however, the tourists were handicapped by the loss of Kenny Milne, and lapses in concentration by the Scots let Australia away. Milne dropped out early in that Test because of a damaged leg muscle, and the hooker was not alone in missing the second international. Hastings withdrew the night before. The Scots were never in the game.

Five new caps were called on for the two Tests. Carl Hogg and Peter Wright were chosen for their debuts in the first Test, and within ten minutes Ian Corcoran joined them as stand-in for the injured Milne. Martin Scott was capped as hooker in the Second Test, only five days after his arrival on tour as Milne's replacement, and Kenny Logan became Stirling's County's first home-bred cap when he deputised for Gavin Hastings.

THE TOURING PARTY
Captain D M B Sole   **Manager** C Ritchie
Coach J R Dixon   **Assistant Coach** D I Johnston

FULL-BACKS
P W Dods (Gala)
A G Hastings (Watsonians)

THREEQUARTERS
D C Bain (Melrose)
S Hastings (Watsonians)
S R P Lineen (Boroughmuir)
K M Logan (Stirling County)
A G Shiel (Melrose)
A G Stanger (Hawick)
D A Stark (Ayr)
I Tukalo (Selkirk)

HALF-BACKS
C M Chalmers (Melrose)
D B Millard (London Scottish)
A D Nicol (Dundee HSFP)
G P J Townsend (Gala)

FORWARDS
I Corcoran (Gala)
D F Cronin (London Scottish)
N G B Edwards (Harlequins)
C A Gray (Nottingham)
C D Hogg (Melrose)
P M Jones (Gloucester)
*A E D Macdonald (Heriot's FP)
D J McIvor (Edinburgh Academicals)
K S Milne (Heriot's FP)
S J Reid (Boroughmuir)
J Robertson (Heriot's FP)
L R Smith (Gloucester)
D M B Sole (Edinburgh Academicals)
*M W Scott (Dunfermline)
R I Wainwright (Edinburgh Academicals)
A G J Watt (Glasgow High/Kelvinside)
G W Weir (Melrose)
P H Wright (Boroughmuir)
Replacement during tour

TOUR RECORD
All matches   Played 8   Won 2   Drawn 2   Lost 4   Points for 150   Against 177
International matches   Played 2   Lost 2   Points for 25   Against 64

SCORING DETAILS
All matches
For: 20T   11C   12PG   4DG   150 Pts
Against: 22T   10C   22PG   1DG   177 Pts

International matches
For: 3T   2C   3PG   25 Pts
Against: 9T   2C   8PG   64 Pts

MATCH DETAILS

1992	OPPONENTS	VENUE	RESULT
28 May	Northern Territory Invitation XV	Darwin	L 16-17
31 May	Queensland	Brisbane	D 15-15
3 June	Emerging Wallabies	Hobart	D 24-24
6 June	New South Wales	Sydney	L 15-35
9 June	NSW Country Origin	Tamworth	W 26-10
13 June	AUSTRALIA	Sydney	L 12-27
17 June	Queensland Country Origin	Toowoomba	W 29-12
21 June	AUSTRALIA	Brisbane	L 13-37

Appearances: 7 – Logan (inc 2 as replacement); 6 – Hogg (inc 1 as replacement), Stanger (inc 1 as replacement); 5 – Cronin, Jones, Wright (inc 1 as replacement); 4 – Bain, Chalmers, Corcoran (inc 1 as replacement), Dods, Gray, S Hastings, Lineen, McIvor, Millard, Milne (inc 1 as replacement), Nicol, Shiel, Smith, Sole (inc 1 as replacement), Stark, Townsend, Tukalo, Wainwright, Watt, Weir; 3 – Edwards, Robertson; 2 – A G Hastings, Macdonald, Reid, Scott
Scorers: 29 – Dods (7C 5PG); 23 – Chalmers (1C 5PG 2DG); 14 – Townsend (2T 2DG); 12 – A G Hastings (3C 2PG), Stark (3T); 8 – Lineen, Millard (2T each); 4 – Cronin, Gray, Hogg, Milne, Reid, Robertson, Shiel, Sole, Stanger, Wainwright, Watt (1T each)

MATCH 1   28 May, Rugby Park, Darwin

Northern Territory Invitation XV 17 (3PG 2T)   **Scotland XV 16** (1G 1PG 1DG 1T)
Northern Territory Invitation XV: M Pitts-Brown; A Watson, M Coghlan,

A G Herbert, A Doidge; C Leach (*capt*), A Ekert; J Evans, C Snowden, A Blades,
M Unwin, G Morgan, M Brial, C Hodson, B Earley
Scorers *Tries:* Pitts-Brown, Coghlan   *Penalty Goals:* Ekert (3)
Scotland XV: Dods (*capt*); Stanger, Bain, Shiel, Logan; Townsend, Millard; Jones,
Corcoran, Watt, Gray, Cronin, McIvor, Robertson, Reid
Scorers *Tries:* Robertson, Reid   *Conversion:* Dods   *Penalty Goal:* Dods
Dropped Goal: Townsend
Referee B Leask (Queensland)

MATCH 2   31 May, Ballymore, Brisbane

Queensland 15 (1G 2PG 1DG)   **Scotland XV 15** (2G 1PG)
Queensland: M Pini; D Smith, J S Little, T J Horan, P V Carozza; P Kahl,
P J Slattery (*capt*); C P Lillicrap, T A Lawton, D Crowley, R J McCall, J A Eales,
D J Wilson, T Coker, S J Scott-Young
Scorers *Try:* Horan   *Conversion:* Kahl   *Penalty Goals:* Kahl (2)
Dropped Goal: Kahl
Scotland XV: A G Hastings; Stark, S Hastings, Lineen, Tukalo; Chalmers, Nicol;
Sole (*capt*), Milne, Wright, Edwards, Weir, Hogg, Smith, Wainwright
Replacement Logan for A G Hastings (43 mins)
Scorers *Tries:* Stark, Lineen   *Conversions:* A G Hastings (2)   *Penalty Goal:* Chalmers
Referee P Marshall (New South Wales)

MATCH 3   3 June, Bellerive Oval, Hobart

Emerging Wallabies 24 (2G 4PG)   **Scotland XV 24** (2G 3T)
Emerging Wallabies (*New South Wales unless stated*): M Burke; B Fielke
(Queensland), A G Herbert (Queensland), R Constable (Queensland), A Murdoch;
D J Knox, A Ekert; A Blades, D V Nucifora (Queensland) (*capt*), M Ryan (Queensland),
P FitzSimons, G Morgan (Queensland), M Miller, I Tabua (Queensland), M Brial
Scorers *Tries:* Herbert, Fielke   *Conversions:* Knox (2)   *Penalty Goals:* Knox (4)
Scotland XV: Dods (*capt*); Stark, Bain, Shiel, Logan; Townsend, Millard; Jones,
Corcoran, Watt, Cronin, Gray, McIvor, Hogg, Reid *Replacements* Sole for Watt
(50 mins); Milne for Reid (70 mins)
Scorers *Tries:* Hogg, Cronin, Shiel, Stark, Milne   *Conversions:* Dods (2)
Referee B Kinsey (New South Wales)

MATCH 4   6 June, Waratah Rugby Park, Sydney

New South Wales 35 (4G 1PG 2T)   **Scotland XV 15** (3PG 2DG)
New South Wales: M C Roebuck; D K Junee, R C Tombs, L F Walker, P Jorgensen;
J Allen, N C Farr-Jones (*capt*); A J Daly, P N Kearns, E J A McKenzie, T Kava,
W W Waugh, V Ofahengaue, B T Gavin, M Brial *Replacement* A Ekert for Farr-Jones
(79 mins)
Scorers *Tries:* Jorgensen (2), Gavin, Kava, Ofahengaue, Roebuck
Conversions: Roebuck (4)   *Penalty Goal:* Roebuck
Scotland XV: Logan; Stanger, S Hastings, Lineen, Tukalo; Chalmers, Nicol; Jones,
Milne, Wright, Edwards, Weir, McIvor, Wainwright, Smith (*capt*)
Scorer *Penalty Goals:* Chalmers (3)   *Dropped Goals:* Chalmers (2)
Referee B Fienberg (Queensland)

MATCH 5   9 June, Scully Park, Tamworth

New South Wales Country Origin XV 10 (1G 1T)   **Scotland XV 26** (2G 1PG 1DG 2T)
New South Wales Country Origin XV: S Munday; D Earp, G Thompson, P O'Brien,
M Crawford; J Lancaster, A Ekert; C Coulthart, P Palmer, K Whiteman, J Nowlan,
S Jones, S Whyte, S Talbot, S Heanly *Replacements* N Cobcroft for Whyte (70 mins);
M Delavere for Ekert (78 mins)

Scorers *Tries:* Heanly, Ekert   *Conversion:* Munday
Scotland XV: Dods (*capt*); Stanger, Bain, Shiel, Stark; Townsend, Millard; Jones, Corcoran, Watt, Gray, Cronin, Robertson, Macdonald, Hogg *Replacement* Logan for Bain (56 mins)
Scorers *Tries:* Watt, Millard, Townsend, Gray   *Conversions:* Dods (2)
Penalty Goal: Dods   *Dropped Goal:* Townsend
Referee F van der Westhuizen (New South Wales)

MATCH 6   13 June, Sydney Football Stadium   1st Test

AUSTRALIA 27 (1G 3PG 3T)   SCOTLAND 12 (1G 2PG)

Scotland led 9-7 near the start, and the game was there for the taking if they had kept cool heads. Instead, they played 20 minutes of slack rugby that was out of character with their game for the other hour, but it was enough to let Australia off the hook. The World Cup-holders needed no invitation to take charge. Michael Lynagh and David Campese relentlessly added to their world records.

Scotland earned their interval lead through secure, steady rugby in face of severe pressure up front. The Scottish scrummage was rarely secure, and Doddie Weir was subdued by John Eales on the touchline. Rob Wainwright, however, kept the Scots in contention in the line-out tail, once producing ball for a try. He also scored himself from Craig Chalmers' garryowen. Gavin Hastings converted to put the Scots two points clear.

Immediately after the interval, however, a loose kick by Gavin Hastings was gratefully accepted by Campese, who willingly ran back at the Scots. Lynagh hacked on for Carozza to score. Lynagh added two penalty goals, and the Wallabies led 17-9 after 52 minutes.

Gavin Hastings pulled the margin back with his second penalty goal, but Lynagh struck again and Tony Daly added a blindside try.

By then the game had gone from the Scots, but to their credit they responded to David Sole's unstinting example in pulling together a semblance of the game that had earned them the interval lead. Campese still had the last word, drifting in from the far wing to score off a goal-line ruck.

AUSTRALIA: M C Roebuck (Eastwood & NSW); D I Campese (Randwick & NSW), R C Tombs (Norths & NSW), T J Horan (Souths & Queensland), P V Carozza (Wests & Queensland); M P Lynagh (Queensland U & Queensland), N C Farr-Jones (Sydney U & NSW) (*capt*); A J Daly (Easts & NSW), P N Kearns (Randwick & NSW), E J A McKenzie (Randwick & NSW), R J McCall (Brothers & Queensland), J A Eales (Brothers & Queensland), V Ofahengaue (NSW), B T Gavin (Easts & NSW), D J Wilson (Easts & Queensland) *Replacement* P Jorgensen (Randwick & NSW) for Carozza (65 mins)
Scorers *Tries:* Campese (2), Carozza, Lynagh   *Conversion:* Lynagh
Penalty Goals: Lynagh (3)
SCOTLAND: A G Hastings; Stanger, S Hastings, Lineen, Tukalo; Chalmers, Nicol; Sole (*capt*), Milne, Wright, Edwards, Weir, Hogg, Wainwright, Smith
Replacement Corcoran for Milne (10 mins)
Scorers *Try:* Wainwright   *Conversion:* A G Hastings   *Penalty Goals:* A G Hastings (2)
Referee L L McLachlan (New Zealand)

MATCH 7   17 June, Gold Park, Toowoomba

Queensland Country Origin 12 (4PG)   **Scotland XV 29** (2G 3PG 2T)
Queensland Country Origin: P Sprecher; B Lea, M Hood, R Constable, W Burrows; P Weir, B Johnstone; D J Crowley, M Foley, G Oxenford, S Thorn, G Morgan, F Perrin, S J Scott-Young, B Curran (*capt*) *Replacement* A King for Weir (40 mins)
Scorer *Penalty Goals:* Sprecher (4)
Scotland XV: Dods (*capt*); Logan, Bain, Shiel, Stark; Townsend, Millard; Jones, Scott, Watt, Gray, Cronin, McIvor, Macdonald, Robertson *Replacements* Wright for Jones (34 mins); Stanger for Stark (62 mins); Hogg for Cronin (80 mins)
Scorers *Tries:* Stark, Millard, Townsend, Stanger   *Conversions:* Dods (2)
Penalty Goals: Dods (3)
Referee A Cole (Queensland)

MATCH 8   21 June, Ballymore, Brisbane   2nd Test

AUSTRALIA 37 (1G 5PG 4T)   SCOTLAND 13 (1G 1PG 1T)

Australia achieved a record sequence by winning the Second Test with a try count of 5-2. It was the Wallabies' eighth successive international win, the first time they have had such an extensive run. It was not the send-off the Scots would have wished for David Sole, who was an example to all, and Sean Lineen in their farewell to international rugby. Each of the departing pair, however, scored a try to mark his retirement.

Scotland did themselves no favours by conceding too many penalties – 21 against Australia's 15 – though Sole, as a parting gesture, severely criticised Colin Hawke, the New Zealand referee. Doddie Weir's line-out game was one of Hawke's targets, and the upshot was that John Eales again dominated on the touchline.

In the first half Michael Lynagh kicked four goals from five penalty attempts, Paul Carozza had a try off linkage by David Campese and David Wilson, and Australia led 16-3 at the interval. It was a relief to Scotland that the margin was not greater. Australia stretched to 27-3 after 51 minutes with two tries by Tim Horan sandwiching another Lynagh penalty goal. Campese's hoisted kick to the Scottish goal-line made the centre's first try, and a surge by Willie Ofahengaue, Nick Farr-Jones, Wilson and Tombs sucked the Scots in for Horan's second.

In the last 20 minutes, however, the Scots matched the Wallabies with two tries from each side. Percussion hammering on the Australian line eventually opened the way for Lineen to score. Carozza immediately replied after Campese had looped Marty Roebuck, and Eales then scored from an exchange of passes with Farr-Jones. The persistent Sole finished off after Cronin, Smith and Andy Nicol had assaulted the goal-line.

AUSTRALIA: M C Roebuck (Eastwood & NSW); D I Campese (Randwick & NSW), R C Tombs (Norths & NSW), T J Horan (Souths & Queensland), P V Carozza (Wests & Queensland); M P Lynagh (Queensland U & Queensland), N C Farr-Jones (Sydney U & NSW) (*capt*); A J Daly (Easts & NSW), P N Kearns (Randwick & NSW), E J A McKenzie (Randwick & NSW), R J McCall (Brothers & Queensland), J A Eales (Brothers & Queensland), V Ofahengaue (Manly & NSW), B T Gavin (Easts & NSW),

D J Wilson (Easts & Queensland) *Replacement* P Jorgensen (Randwick & NSW) for Campese (79 mins)
Scorers *Tries:* Carozza (2), Horan (2), Eales   *Conversion:* Lynagh
Penalty Goals: Lynagh (5)
SCOTLAND: Logan; Stanger, S Hastings, Lineen, Tukalo; Chalmers, Nicol; Sole *(capt)*, Scott, Wright, Cronin, Weir, Hogg, Wainwright, Smith
Scorers *Tries:* Lineen, Sole   *Conversion:* Chalmers   *Penalty Goal:* Chalmers
Referee C J Hawke (New Zealand)

IRELAND TO NEW ZEALAND 1992

The prospects for this trip were desperately poor and it all turned out even worse than the expectations. That is the only possible conclusion for the ill-fated Irish. By the end, the tour and the immediate prospects of a revival in Irish rugby fortunes were in disarray. Ireland travelled without three key back-row forwards – Phil Matthews, Phil Lawlor and Gordon Hamilton – and their chances in the line-out were all but wiped out when Neil Francis, their leading lock, also withdrew from consideration.

Ireland did give a brave and clever performance in the First Test in Dunedin and could even have won: they were 12-0 up in 12 minutes. However, the All Blacks played miserably badly in their match. A week later, they were restored and delivered an 11-try thrashing.

There was complete humiliation in the provincial matches: Auckland scored more than 60 and even Manawatu, far from a major force in New Zealand rugby, incredibly ran up 58 against the Irish second string in the midweek match between the two Tests.

It was doubly disappointing for coach Ciaran Fitzgerald, who might have hoped to have been able to set the record straight after his conspicuously unsuccessful tour as Lions captain in New Zealand in 1983. It was even worse for poor Phil Danaher, the captain. His knee gave out after 15 minutes of the first match, and he was not able to play again until the First Test, when he had to be replaced in the first half, his tour over.

All successes were relative, yet the marvellous efforts in adversity of Robinson and especially the storming Popplewell in the pack, and of Cunningham in the centre, at least gave Ireland a little to write home about. The only relief apart from that was the final whistle of a melancholy tour.

THE TOURING PARTY
Manager N A A Murphy   **Coach** C F Fitzgerald   **Assistant Coach** G Murphy
Captain P P A Danaher

FULL-BACKS

  K J Murphy (Cork Constitution)
  J E Staples (London Irish)

THREEQUARTERS

  R W Carey (Dungannon)
  D J Clarke (Dolphin)

J N Furlong (UC, Galway)
R M Wallace (Garryowen)
V J G Cunningham (St Mary's Coll)
P P A Danaher (Garryowen)
M C McCall (Bangor)
M P Ridge (Blackrock Coll)
*D O'Brien (Clontarf)

HALF-BACKS

D R McAleese (Ballymena)
P Russell (Instonians)
L F P Aherne (Lansdowne)
M T Bradley (Cork Constitution)

FORWARDS

T P J Clancy (London Irish)
G F Halpin (London Irish)
P McCarthy (Cork Constitution)
N J Popplewell (Greystones)
T J Kingston (Dolphin)

S J Smith (Ballymena)
R Costello (Garryowen)
J Etheridge (Northampton)
M J Galwey (Shannon)
B J Rigney (Greystones)
M P Fitzgibbon (Shannon)
P S Johns (Dungannon)
K T Leahy (Wanderers)
W D McBride (Malone)
N P S Mannion (Lansdowne)
B F Robinson (Ballymena)
*P Kenny (Wanderers)
* Replacement during tour

TOUR RECORD

All matches   Played 8   Won 3   Lost 5   Points for 153   Against 287
International matches   Played 2   Lost 2   Points for 27   Against 83

SCORING DETAILS

All matches
For: 21T 15C 12PG 1DG   153 Pts
Against: 50T 30C   8PG 1DG   287 Pts

International matches
For: 4T   4C 1PG   27 Pts
Against: 15T 10C 1PG   83 Pts

MATCH DETAILS

1992	OPPONENTS	VENUE	RESULT
13 May	South Canterbury	Timaru	W 21-16
16 May	Canterbury	Christchurch	L 13-38
20 May	Bay of Plenty	Rotorua	W 39-23
23 May	Auckland	Auckland	L 7-62
26 May	Poverty Bay-East Coast	Gisborne	W 22-7
30 May	NEW ZEALAND	Dunedin	L 21-24
2 June	Manawatu	Palmerston North	L 24-58
6 June	NEW ZEALAND	Wellington	L 6-59

Appearances: 7 – Murphy (inc 3 as replacement), Cunningham; 6 – Galwey (inc 1 as replacement), Robinson (inc 1 as replacement); 5 – Furlong, Johns, Bradley, Aherne (inc 2 as replacement), Popplewell, Smith, Staples, McAleese (inc 2 as replacement), McCall (inc 1 as replacement), Fitzgibbon; 4 – Russell, Clancy, Etheridge, Mannion, Clarke (inc 1 as replacement), Rigney (inc 1 as replacement), Halpin (inc 1 as replacement), Carey, McCarthy; 3 – Ridge, Kingston, Leahy, Costello, Kenny (inc 1 as replacement); 2 – Wallace, Danaher, O'Brien; 1 – McBride
Scorers: 38 – Russell (10C 5PG 1DG); 26 – McAleese (4C 6PG); 10 – Murphy (2T 1C); 8 – Wallace, Mannion, Furlong, Galwey, Cunningham, Aherne (2T each); 4 – Bradley, Popplewell, Carey, Rigney, Ridge, Staples, Clarke (1T each); 3 – McCall (1PG)

MATCH 1   13 May, Fraser Park, Timaru

South Canterbury 16 (3PG 1DG 1T)   Ireland XV 21 (3G 1PG)
South Canterbury: D Hunter; S J Todd, B J Laney, S B Tarrant (*capt*), C J Dorgan; B J Fairbrother, B A Matthews; G F Coughlan, S R Richards, R Morgan, J M Gregan, G F Stanley, J Mawhinney, K Wills, J P Simpson *Replacements* T G Miller for Hunter (22 mins); C Gard for Todd (47 mins)
Scorers *Try:* Matthews   *Penalty Goals:* Fairbrother (3)   *Dropped Goal:* Fairbrother
Ireland XV: Murphy; Wallace, Danaher (*capt*), Cunningham, Furlong; Russell, Bradley; Popplewell, Smith, Clancy, Galwey, Etheridge, Robinson, Mannion, McBride
Replacement Aherne for Bradley (74 mins)
Scorers *Tries:* Bradley, Wallace, Popplewell   *Conversions:* Russell (3)
Penalty Goal: Russell
Referee L L McLachlan (Otago)

MATCH 2   16 May, Lancaster Park, Christchurch

Canterbury 38 (3G 5T)   **Ireland XV 13** (1G 1PG 1T)
Canterbury: A F McCormick; P Bale, D Kerr, W K Maunsell, S K Seinafo; G P Coffey,
G T M Bachop; G Halford, M R Sexton, S J Loe, C A Philpott, M R McAtamney,
A T Earl, R H Penney, D J Seymour *Replacement* H Murray for Sexton (65 mins)
Scorers *Tries:* Kerr (2), Seinafo, Bachop, Bale, Seymour, McCormick, penalty try
Conversions: Coffey (3)
Ireland XV: Staples; Wallace, Ridge, Cunningham, Clarke; McAleese, Aherne (*capt*);
Popplewell, Smith, Halpin, Costello, Rigney, Robinson, Mannion, Fitzgibbon
Replacements Murphy for Wallace (69 mins); Galwey for Fitzgibbon (75 mins)
Scorers *Tries:* Wallace, Mannion   *Conversion:* McAleese   *Penalty Goal:* McAleese
Referee D J Bishop (Southland)

MATCH 3   20 May, International Stadium, Rotorua

Bay of Plenty 23 (2G 1PG 2T)   **Ireland XV 39** (4G 4PG 1DG)
Bay of Plenty: T R Jennings; P G Woods, C Yorston, J R Spanhake, G Rutene; E Cossey,
M D Haig; W Morehu, R George (*capt*), A McLean, J J Lillas, M Tinnock,
C Te Kowhai, R D Peacock, M R Jones *Replacement* C W Maika for Peacock (21 mins)
Scorers *Tries:* George, Jennings, Haig, Jones   *Conversions:* Cossey (2)
Penalty Goal: Cossey
Ireland XV: Murphy; Carey, Cunningham, McCall, Furlong; Russell, Bradley; Clancy,
Kingston, McCarthy, Etheridge, Johns, Leahy, Fitzgibbon, Galwey *Replacement* McAleese
for Fitzgibbon (68 mins)
Scorers *Tries:* Galwey (2), Carey, Murphy   *Conversions:* Russell (3), McAleese
Penalty Goals: Russell (3), McAleese   *Dropped Goal:* Russell
Referee C J Hawke (South Canterbury)

MATCH 4   23 May, Eden Park, Auckland

Auckland 62 (9G 2T)   **Ireland XV 7** (1PG 1T)
Auckland: S P Howarth; J J Kirwan, W Sotutu, E Clarke, V L Tuigamala; G J Fox,
J A Hewett; S C McDowell, S B T Fitzpatrick (*capt*), O M Brown, R M Brooke,
G J Whetton, Z V Brooke, P Lam, M P Carter
Scorers *Tries:* Howarth (3), Kirwan (2), Fox, Fitzpatrick, R M Brooke, Carter, Clarke,
Brown   *Conversions:* Fox (9)
Ireland XV: Staples; O'Brien, Clarke, Cunningham, Furlong; McCall, Bradley (*capt*);
Popplewell, Kingston, McCarthy, Johns, Etheridge, Galwey, Robinson, Fitzgibbon
Replacements Murphy for O'Brien (40 mins); McAleese for Clarke (44 mins); Halpin
for McCarthy (50 mins); Aherne for Furlong (62 mins)
Scorers *Try:* Furlong   *Penalty Goal:* McCall
Referee K H Lawrence (Bay of Plenty)

MATCH 5   26 May, Rugby Park, Gisborne

Poverty Bay-East Coast 7 (1PG 1T)   **Ireland XV 22** (2G 2PG 1T)
Poverty Bay-East Coast: E J Robinson; R S Tamatea, J R Kururangi, S D Fitzsimons,
R Riwaka; E J Manuel, N B Henare, D F B Mataira (*capt*), B J Davies, M Kingi,
G Williams, A Macky, M E Waitoa, S Pokai, J Martin *Replacements* F H J Walker for
Kururangi (21 mins); E B Poi for Pokai (41 mins); A Rangihuna for Manuel (54 mins)
Scorers *Try:* Martin   *Penalty Goal:* Manuel
Ireland XV: Murphy; Carey, Cunningham, Ridge, Staples; McAleese, Aherne; Clancy,
Smith, Halpin, Rigney, Costello, Kenny, Mannion, Leahy (*capt*)
Scorers *Tries:* Rigney, Ridge, Mannion   *Conversions:* McAleese (2)
Penalty Goals: McAleese (2)
Referee R Hill (Wellington)

MATCH 6   30 May, Dunedin   1st Test

NEW ZEALAND 24 (4G)   IRELAND 21 (3G 1PG)

It was a bizarre afternoon. Ireland had been battered throughout their tour but they found the All Blacks in unbelievably listless and fallible mood. Ireland led 12-0 after 12 minutes and their lead could have been even bigger. An attempt at an interception by Carey, which could have led to six points, did not quite go to hand and a drop-goal miss from close range by Russell was another golden chance missed.

Both Popplewell and Robinson played superbly for the Irish, who showed some penetration and pace. They even tried gamely to shrug off the injuries to Danaher – who stayed on for some time to rally the troops, eventually departing just before half-time – and to Leahy, who had to leave the field with a broken bone in his ankle.

For New Zealand, the half-back partnership of Little and Strachan was laboured in the extreme and the familiar collective drive of the pack was missing. The strength at close quarters of Bunce, who forced his way over for two tries, was a crucial factor in New Zealand's shaky but successful comeback.

NEW ZEALAND: G J L Cooper (Otago); J J Kirwan (Auckland), F Bunce (North Harbour), E Clarke (Auckland), V L Tuigamala (Auckland); W K Little (North Harbour), A D Strachan (Auckland); S C McDowell (Auckland), S B T Fitzpatrick (Auckland) *(capt)*, R W Loe (Waikato), I D Jones (North Auckland), B P Larsen (North Harbour), J W Joseph (Otago), A R Pene (Otago), P W Henderson (Southland) *Replacement* G W Dowd (North Harbour) for Loe (57 mins)
Scorers *Tries:* Bunce (2), Henderson, Clarke   *Conversions:* Cooper (4)
IRELAND: Staples; Carey, Danaher *(capt)*, Cunningham, Furlong; Russell, Bradley; Popplewell, Smith, McCarthy, Galwey, Johns, Fitzgibbon, Robinson, Leahy
Replacements McCall for Danaher (35 mins); Rigney for Leahy (40 mins)
Scorers *Tries:* Cunningham (2), Staples   *Conversions:* Russell (3)
Penalty Goal: Russell
Referee A R MacNeill (Australia)

MATCH 7   2 June, Showgrounds, Palmerston North

Manawatu 58 (6G 2PG 4T)   **Ireland XV 24** (1G 2PG 3T)
Manawatu: S C Doyle; J M Smith, G N Konia, P J Crosswell, P J Alston; L Stensness, P G Lloyd; R McLean, P J Doyle, G J Nesdale, K M F Otai, D A C Coleman, S N Cruden *(capt)*, K J Williams, S Hall
Scorers *Tries:* S C Doyle (3), Stensness (2), Smith, Cruden, McLean, Otai, Hall
Conversions: Smith (6)   *Penalty Goals:* Smith (2)
Ireland XV: Murphy; Clarke, McCall, Ridge, O'Brien; McAleese, Aherne; Clancy, Kingston *(capt)*, Halpin, Etheridge, Costello, Mannion, Johns, Kenny
Replacement Robinson for Etheridge (47 mins)
Scorers *Tries:* Aherne (2), Clarke, Murphy   *Conversion:* Murphy
Penalty Goals: McAleese (2)
Referee G Wahlstrom (Auckland)

MATCH 8   6 June, Athletic Park, Wellington   2nd Test

NEW ZEALAND 59 (6G 1PG 5T)   IRELAND 6 (1G)

This was a record defeat for Ireland in a Test, a desperate way to end the tour. The All Blacks, although still fallible, were well restored after the horrors of their performance in the First Test.

The second half was a shattering experience for the touring team. They conceded 44 points, including eight tries, after half-time and Matthew Cooper, the Waikato full-back making his first appearance in a Test, scored 23 points from two tries, six conversions and a penalty goal. This must have come as mixed news for Greg Cooper, the Otago full-back and Matthew's brother, who had been discarded after the First Test in favour of Matthew.

It was bad enough for Ireland but it could have been worse. Little was again pressed into service for New Zealand at fly-half and did not look at all comfortable. He duly reverted to centre for the tour of South Africa, with Grant Fox refreshed and restored in the pivotal role.

NEW ZEALAND: M J A Cooper (Waikato); J J Kirwan (Auckland), F Bunce (North Harbour), E Clarke (Auckland), J K R Timu (Otago); W K Little (North Harbour), A D Strachan (Auckland); S C McDowell (Auckland), S B T Fitzpatrick (Auckland) (*capt*), O M Brown (Auckland), I D Jones (North Auckland), R M Brooke (Auckland), M R Brewer (Otago), A R Pene (Otago), M N Jones (Auckland)
Scorers *Tries:* Bunce (2), Pene (2), Cooper (2), I D Jones, Clarke, Timu, Kirwan, Strachan   *Conversions:* Cooper (6)   *Penalty Goal:* Cooper
IRELAND: Staples; Carey, McCall, Cunningham, Furlong; Russell, Bradley (*capt*); Popplewell, Smith, McCarthy, Rigney, Johns, Galwey, Robinson, Fitzgibbon
Replacements Kenny for Fitzgibbon (18 mins); Murphy for Staples (38 mins); Clarke for Russell (45 mins)
Scorers *Try:* Furlong   *Conversion:* Russell
Referee A R MacNeill (Australia)

NEW ZEALAND TO AUSTRALIA 1992

This was a landmark tour in many ways. It contained the first Test series to be played under the new laws, with the ruck/maul experimental law attracting interest. It offered new All Black coach Laurie Mains an ideal opportunity to gather his new-look team around him to test the re-emergence of New Zealand rugby after the wholesale changes following the World Cup.

The final analysis must be that by All Black standards it was a disappointing tour. They lost the Test series and the Bledisloe Cup, and faced a whitewash until they rallied in the last Test in Sydney. They also suffered the humiliation of losing their midweek match against Sydney by 17-40. It was a remarkable result and indicated that All Black reserve strength was not nearly as well-marshalled as usual.

There were also controversial incidents throughout the tour, which reached a head in the Second Test at Ballymore. Paul Carozza, the Australian wing, had his nose broken after he dived to score, by what appeared to be a dangerous late lunge by Richard Loe, the All Black prop, who was later to be suspended from the game for gouging in New Zealand domestic rugby. Loe was allowed to escape by the New Zealand tour management, which was a black mark for the whole party. The All Blacks were distinctly unfortunate to lose the First Test in Sydney. Yet to be fair to the Australians, this was the fourth match under for new laws for the New Zealanders, and only the first for the Wallabies, who effectively had to change laws in mid-season. Although the series was already lost, the desperate need for victory in the Third Test could not be overstated. It was vital for morale, and to send off the party leaving for South Africa and another harsh tour soon afterward. There were some major successes among the tourists. John Timu played splendidly at full-back, adding a cutting edge to the attack. Timu had begun the tour at breakneck pace with four tries in the opener in Perth against Western Australia. Sean Fitzpatrick was a powerful force as hooker and captain, scoring two tries himself in the crushing of the highly rated New South Wales team. Jamie Joseph came through as a likely blindside flanker and Ian Jones was an anchor man in the line-out.

THE TOURING PARTY

Manager N Gray **Coach** L W Mains **Assistant Coach** E W Kirton
Captain S B T Fitzpatrick

FULL-BACKS

M J A Cooper (Waikato)
T J Wright (Auckland)

THREEQUARTERS

J J Kirwan (Auckland)
J K R Timu (Otago)
V L Tuigamala (Auckland)
F E Bunce (North Harbour)
M C G Ellis (Otago)
E Clarke (Auckland)
W K Little (North Harbour)
*E J Rush (North Harbour)

HALF-BACKS

S J Bachop (Otago)
G J Fox (Auckland)
J P Preston (Canterbury)
A D Strachan (Auckland)
*G T M Bachop (Canterbury)

FORWARDS

O M Brown (Auckland)
R W Loe (Waikato)
S C McDowell (Auckland)
G H Purvis (Waikato)
G W Dowd (North Harbour)
S B T Fitzpatrick (Auckland)
R M Brooke (Auckland)
M S B Cooksley (Counties)
I D Jones (North Auckland)
B P Larsen (North Harbour)
M R Brewer (Otago)
P W Henderson (Southland)
M N Jones (Auckland)
J W Joseph (Otago)
K J Schuler (North Harbour)
Z V Brooke (Auckland)
A R B Pene (Otago)
*D J Seymour (Canterbury)
*A T Earl (Canterbury)
*P R Lam (Auckland)
*G L Taylor (North Auckland)

Replacement during tour

TOUR RECORD

All matches Played 11 Won 8 Lost 3 Points for 400 Against 173
International matches Played 3 Won 1 Lost 2 Points for 58 Against 58

SCORING DETAILS

All matches

For: 55T 31C 20PG 1DG 400 Pts
Against: 16T   9C 22PG 3DG 173 Pts

International matches

For: 6T 5C 5PG 1DG 58 Pts
Against: 6T 2C 8PG   –   58 Pts

MATCH DETAILS

1992	OPPONENTS	VENUE	RESULT
21 June	Western Australia	Perth	W 80-0
24 June	South Australian XV	Adelaide	W 48-18
28 June	New South Wales	Sydney	W 41-9
1 July	Australian Capital Territory	Canberra	W 45-13
4 July	AUSTRALIA	Sydney	L 15-16
8 July	Victorian XV	Melbourne	W 53-3
12 July	Queensland	Brisbane	W 26-19
15 July	Queensland B	Cairns	W 32-13
19 July	AUSTRALIA	Brisbane	L 17-19
22 July	Sydney	Penrith	L 17-40
25 July	AUSTRALIA	Sydney	W 26-23

Appearances: 7 – Timu, Tuigamala (inc 1 as replacement), Strachan (inc 1 as replacement); 6 – Bunce, R Brooke, Joseph (inc 1 as replacement), Loe, Fitzpatrick, Brown, Kirwan, Little, Fox, I Jones, Z Brooke; 5 – Cooper, Clarke, S Bachop, Cooksley, Wright, Ellis, Purvis, Dowd, McDowell, M Jones, Larsen, Schuler (inc 1 as replacement), Pene (inc 1 as replacement); 4 – Preston, Rush; 3 – Brewer, Earl (inc 1 as replacement); 2 – Henderson; 1 – G Bachop, Lam, Seymour, Taylor (as replacement)
Scorers: 73 – Fox (14C 14PG 1DG); 44 – Cooper (3T 10C 3PG); 30 – Wright (4T 2C 2PG); 25 – Timu (5T); 20 – Tuigamala, Bunce, Clarke, Ellis (4T each); 18 – Preston (1T 5C 1PG); 15 – Little, Rush, Schuler (3T each); 10 – S Bachop, Joseph, Loe, Kirwan, Fitzpatrick (2T each); 5 – Cooksley, Brewer, Larsen, Strachan, G Bachop, Z Brooke, M Jones (1T each)

MATCH 1　21 June, WACA Ground, Perth

Western Australia 0　New Zealand XV 80 (6G 1PG 7T)
Western Australia: Robin Smith; D Hone, B Kini, S Bunce, T Waqanivavalagi; S McRoberts, M Ryburn; S Porter, A Box *(capt)*, B Ruddell, R Minty, J Wellborn, C Kovacs, T Tamanivalu, Ricky Smith *Replacement* D Woodham for Waqanivavalagi
New Zealand XV: Cooper; Tuigamala, Bunce, Clarke, Timu; S Bachop, Preston; Brown, Fitzpatrick *(capt)*, Loe, Cooksley, R Brooke, Joseph, Pene, Henderson
Replacement Strachan for Preston
Scorers *Tries:* Timu (4), Loe (2), Preston, Tuigamala, Joseph, Clarke, Bunce, Cooksley, Bachop *Conversions:* Cooper (4), Preston (2) *Penalty Goal:* Preston
Referee B Kinsey

MATCH 2　24 June, Hindmarsh Stadium, Adelaide

South Australian XV 18 (5PG 1DG)　New Zealand XV 48 (4G 5PG 1T)
South Australian XV: T P Kelaher; J Paitai, P Robinson, R Sadler, R Tuhou; P Kahl, M Berry; A Blades, D V Nucifora, O Porter, M Firth, P FitzSimons, H Dijksman *(capt)*, I Tabua, D Hargreaves
Scorer *Penalty Goals:* Kahl (5) *Dropped Goal:* Kahl
New Zealand XV: Wright; Kirwan, Ellis, Little, Tuigamala; Fox, Strachan; Purvis, Dowd, McDowell, I Jones, Larsen, M Jones, Z Brooke, Brewer *(capt)*
Scorers *Tries:* Wright (2), Little, Brewer, Larsen *Conversions:* Fox (4) *Penalty Goals:* Fox (5)
Referee M Keogh

MATCH 3　28 June, Waratah Rugby Stadium, Sydney

New South Wales 9 (3PG)　New Zealand XV 41 (4G 1PG 2T)
New South Wales: M C Roebuck; D K Junee, R C Tombs, L F Walker, P Jorgensen; J Allen, N C Farr-Jones *(capt)*; A J Daly, M Bell, E J A McKenzie, T P Kava, W W Waugh, W Ofahengaue, M Brial, S P Poidevin *Replacements* T P Kelaher for Roebuck; A Ekert for Junee; A Blades for Brial; T Dempsey for Ofahengaue; K O'Kane for Daly
Scorers *Penalty Goals:* Kelaher (2), Roebuck
New Zealand XV: Cooper; Kirwan, Bunce, Little, Timu; Fox, Strachan; Brown, Fitzpatrick *(capt)*, Loe, I Jones, R Brooke, Joseph, Pene, Henderson
Replacements Schuler for Henderson; Tuigamala for Bunce

49

Scorers *Tries:* Fitzpatrick (2), Strachan, Tuigamala, Bunce, Kirwan
Conversions: Fox (4)   *Penalty Goal:* Fox
Referee B Leask

MATCH 4   1 July, Manuka Oval, Canberra

Australian Capital Territory 13 (1G 2PG)   **New Zealand XV 45** (2G 2PG 5T)
Australian Capital Territory: R Kafer; D McLachlan, G Quinn, M O'Connor, V Crowe;
R Hayes, P Brown; R Lawton, J Taylor (*capt*), G Didier, G Chessell, C Sweeney, J Ross,
M McInness, G Emmery *Replacement* M Toma for Chessell
Scorers *Try:* Taylor   *Conversion:* O'Connor   *Penalty Goals:* O'Connor (2)
New Zealand XV: Timu; Rush, Ellis, Clarke, Wright; S Bachop, G Bachop; Purvis,
Dowd, McDowell, Larsen, Cooksley, Brewer (*capt*), Z Brooke, Schuler
Scorers *Tries:* Clarke (2), Wright, G Bachop, Ellis, Rush, Schuler   *Conversions:* Wright (2)
Penalty Goals: Wright (2)
Referee P Marshall

MATCH 5   4 July, Sydney Football Stadium   1st Test

AUSTRALIA 16 (2PG 2T)   **NEW ZEALAND 15** (1G 1PG 1T)
AUSTRALIA: T P Kelaher (NSW); D I Campese (NSW), J S Little (Queensland),
T J Horan (Queensland), P V Carozza (Queensland); M P Lynagh (Queensland),
N C Farr-Jones (NSW) (*capt*); A J Daly (NSW), P N Kearns (NSW), E J A McKenzie
(NSW), R J McCall (Queensland), J A Eales (Queensland), T Coker (Queensland),
S J N Scott-Young (Queensland), D J Wilson (Queensland) *Replacement* G Morgan
(Queensland) for Scott-Young (77 mins)
Scorers *Tries:* Campese, Horan   *Penalty Goals:* Lynagh (2)
NEW ZEALAND: Timu; Kirwan, Bunce, Little, Tuigamala; Fox, Strachan; Loe,
Fitzpatrick (*capt*), Brown, I Jones, R Brooke, Brewer, Pene, M Jones
Replacement Joseph for Brewer (64 mins)
Scorers *Tries:* Tuigamala, Bunce   *Conversion:* Fox   *Penalty Goal:* Fox
Referee J M Fleming (Scotland)

MATCH 6   8 July, Olympic Park, Melbourne

Victoria XV 3 (1PG)   **New Zealand XV 53** (4G 5T)
Victoria XV: D Ephriams; J Myers, A G Herbert, R Saunders, R Collier; T M Wallace,
S Waaka; N Raikuna, D V Nucifora, A Heath, T Curtis, S Pengelly, A Coombes,
B P Nasser, D Williams (*capt*) *Replacements* T Potae for Williams; C Sweeney for Pengelly
Scorer *Penalty Goal:* Wallace
New Zealand XV: Cooper; Rush, Ellis, Clarke, Wright; S Bachop, Preston; Purvis,
Dowd, McDowell, Cooksley, Larsen, Joseph, Z Brooke (*capt*), M Jones
Scorers *Tries:* Ellis (2), Cooper, Wright, Rush, Clarke, S Bachop, Z Brooke, M Jones
Conversions: Preston (3), Cooper
Referee F van der Westhuizen

MATCH 7   12 July, Ballymore Oval, Brisbane

Queensland 19 (2G 1T)   **New Zealand XV 26** (1G 3PG 2T)
Queensland: M Pini; D Smith, J S Little, T J Horan, P V Carozza; P Kahl, P J Slattery
(*capt*); D J Crowley, T A Lawton, C P Lillicrap, R J McCall, G Morgan, T Coker,
J A Eales, D J Wilson *Replacement* A G Herbert for Smith
Scorers *Tries:* Morgan (2), Smith   *Conversions:* Kahl (2)
New Zealand XV: Timu; Kirwan, Bunce, Little, Tuigamala; Fox, Strachan; Brown,
Fitzpatrick (*capt*), McDowell, R Brooke, I Jones, Joseph, Z Brooke, Schuler
Scorers *Tries:* Tuigamala, Little, Bunce   *Conversion:* Fox   *Penalty Goals:* Fox (3)
Referee W Erikson

Queensland B 13 (1G 2PG)   **New Zealand XV 32** (3G 2PG 1T)

Queensland B: G Holt; M Anderson, A G Herbert, D Maguire, B Fielke; T Mandrusiak, B Johnstone; P Volavola, D V Nucifora, A Skeggs, G Morgan, B Curran, F Perrin (*capt*), B P Nasser, I Tabua *Replacement* P Murdoch for Tabua
Scorers *Try:* penalty try   *Conversion:* Mandrusiak   *Penalty Goals:* Mandrusiak (2)
New Zealand XV: Cooper; Rush, Ellis, Clarke, Wright; S Bachop, Preston; Purvis, Dowd, Loe (*capt*), Cooksley, Larsen, Schuler, Pene, M Jones
Scorers *Tries:* Schuler (2), Cooper, Ellis   *Conversions:* Cooper (3)
Penalty Goals: Cooper (2)
Referee A Cole

MATCH 9   **19 July, Ballymore, Brisbane**   **2nd Test**

AUSTRALIA 19 (3PG 2T)   **NEW ZEALAND 17** (2G 1PG)
AUSTRALIA: M C Roebuck (NSW); D I Campese (NSW), J S Little (Queensland), T J Horan (Queensland), P V Carozza (Queensland); M P Lynagh (Queensland), N C Farr-Jones (NSW) (*capt*); A J Daly (NSW), P N Kearns (NSW), E J A McKenzie (NSW), R J McCall (Queensland), J A Eales (Queensland), T Coker (Queensland), S J N Scott-Young (Queensland), D J Wilson (Queensland)
Scorers *Tries:* Carozza (2)   *Penalty Goals:* Lynagh (3)
NEW ZEALAND: Timu; Kirwan, Bunce, Little, Tuigamala; Fox, Strachan; Brown, Fitzpatrick (*capt*), Loe, I Jones, R Brooke, Earl, Z Brooke, Schuler *Replacement* Pene for Schuler (8 mins)
Scorers *Tries:* Timu, Kirwan   *Conversions:* Fox (2)   *Penalty Goal:* Fox
Referee P Robin (France)

MATCH 10   **22 July, Penrith Stadium, Sydney**

Sydney 40 (3G 1PG 2DG 2T)   **New Zealand XV 17** (2G 1PG)
Sydney: T P Kelaher; D K Junee, R C Tombs, L F Walker, P Jorgensen; T M Wallace, A Ekert; M N Hartill, M Bell, A Blades, T P Kava (*capt*), W W Waugh, M Brial, B T Gavin, S P Poidevin *Replacements* T Dempsey for Poidevin; S Payne for Ekert
Scorers *Tries:* Junee (3), Ekert, Brial   *Conversions:* Wallace (3)   *Penalty Goal:* Wallace
Dropped Goals: Wallace (2)
New Zealand XV: Wright; Rush, Ellis, Cooper, Clarke; S Bachop, Preston; Purvis, Dowd, McDowell (*capt*), Cooksley, Larsen, Earl, Lam, Seymour *Replacement* Taylor for Lam
Scorers *Tries:* Rush, Cooper   *Conversions:* Cooper (2)   *Penalty Goal:* Cooper
Referee A R MacNeill

MATCH 11   **25 July, Sydney Football Stadium**   **3rd Test**

AUSTRALIA 23 (2G 3PG)   **NEW ZEALAND 26** (2G 3PG 1DG)
AUSTRALIA: M C Roebuck (NSW); D I Campese (NSW), J S Little (Queensland), T J Horan (Queensland), P V Carozza (Queensland); M P Lynagh (Queensland), N C Farr-Jones (NSW) (*capt*); A J Daly (NSW), P N Kearns (NSW), E J A McKenzie (NSW), R J McCall (Queensland), J A Eales (Queensland), T Coker (Queensland), S J N Scott-Young (Queensland), D J Wilson (Queensland) *Replacements* G Morgan (Queensland) for Eales (36 mins); A G Herbert for Scott-Young (42 mins)
Scorers *Tries:* Farr-Jones, Herbert   *Conversions:* Lynagh (2)
Penalty Goals: Lynagh (3)
NEW ZEALAND: Timu; Kirwan, Bunce, Little, Tuigamala; Fox, Strachan; Brown, Fitzpatrick (*capt*), Loe, I Jones, R Brooke, Joseph, Z Brooke, M Jones *Replacement* Earl for R Brooke (23 mins)
Scorers *Tries:* Little, Joseph   *Conversions:* Fox (2)   *Penalty Goals:* Fox (3)
Dropped Goal: Fox
Referee P Robin (France)

FRANCE TO ARGENTINA 1992

Even though the traditional measure of success on a tour is victory in the Test series, and even though in Argentina France easily won both Tests against the Pumas, this was not a tour to remember with any great affection. It was born in controversy when the unorthodox approach of Pierre Berbizier, the French coach, caused bother again: he left some major players at home, including Philippe Sella, stating that he was resting them. Sella declared that he needed no rest, and it seems a strange thing to leave your key back at home just when you are trying to establish a settled team for matches ahead. In any case, the French team in the two Test matches of this tour soon broke up: few players retained their places for subsequent French internationals at home. The tour captain, Marc Cecillon, did keep his place, but the captaincy was taken from him for the start of the 1993 Five Nations Championship.

France were harried a little in the non-Test matches, notably in Tucumán, where they lost to the ever-fierce home team, and in Mendoza, where they surprisingly lost to a Cuyo Selection. They were also trailing by two points against a Rosario Selection when the match was abandoned at half-time due to a floodlight failure.

Some of the promising young French backs disappointed on the trip, although Sadourny at full-back and Hueber at scrum-half played extremely well. The riches of French flank forward play were amply demonstrated in the performances of Benetton, Cabannes and Tordo, although the line-out weakness was never satisfactorily solved in the absence of the pair regarded by many as the leading French locks, Roumat and Benazzi.

Generally, the Tests were a success story. However, the comparative lack of power and invention in the Pumas' ranks should be taken into account. The basis of the young Argentinian team has now been together for some years, but their coaches were left looking anxiously for signs of development.

THE TOURING PARTY

Manager G Lesbats   **Assistant Managers** R Paparemborde, R Astre
Coach P Berbizier   **Captain** M Cecillon

FULL-BACKS

S **Ougier** (Stade Toulousain)
J-L **Sadourny** (Colomiers)

THREEQUARTERS

P **Bernat-Salles** (Pau)
P **Saint-André** (Montferrand)
M **Marfaing** (Stade Toulousain)
C **Coeurveille** (Agen)
C **Deylaud** (Stade Toulousain)
S **Viars** (Brive)

HALF-BACKS

C **Reigt** (Lourdes)
A **Penaud** (Brive)
A **Hueber** (Toulon)
F **Galthié** (Colomiers)

FORWARDS

J-M **Gonzales** (Bayonne)
L **Armary** (Lourdes)
J-P **Genet** (Racing Club de France)
F **Landreau** (Angoulême)
P **Gallart** (Béziers)

S Graou (Auch)
T Devergie (Nîmes)
C Deslandes (Racing Club de France)
J-M Cadieu (Stade Toulousain)
H Miorin (Stade Toulousain)

J-F Tordo (Nice)
X Blond (Racing Club de France)
M Cecillon (Bourgoin)
L Cabannes (Racing Club de France)
P Benetton (Agen)

TOUR RECORD

All matches Played 8   Won 5   Lost 3*   Points for 241   Against 136
International matches Played 2   Won 2   Points for 60   Against 21

SCORING DETAILS

All matches*
For: 25T   16C   23PG   5DG   241 Pts
Against: 6T   5C   30PG   2DG   136 Pts

International matches
For: 5T   4C   7PG   2DG   60 Pts
Against: –   –   5PG   2DG   21 Pts

MATCH DETAILS

1992	OPPONENTS	VENUE	RESULT
16 June	Cordoba XV	Cordoba	W 62-20
20 June	Buenos Aires XV	Buenos Aires	W 28-12
23 June	Tucumán	Tucumán	L 23-25
27 June	Invitation XV	San Juan	W 32-18
30 June	Cuyo XV	Mendoza	L 30-32
4 July	ARGENTINA	Buenos Aires	W 27-12
7 July	Rosario XV*	Rosario	L 6-8
11 July	ARGENTINA	Buenos Aires	W 33-9

* *Includes match against Rosario, abandoned at half-time due to floodlight failure*

Appearances: 7 – Cecillon, Gallart (inc 2 as replacement), Coeurveille (inc 3 as replacement), Gonzales (inc 2 as replacement), Viars; 6 – Deylaud, Penaud, Cabannes, Tordo (inc 2 as replacement); 5 – Marfaing, Saint-André, Benetton (inc 2 as replacement), Cadieu (inc 1 as replacement), Deslandes, Armary, Sadourny (inc 1 as replacement), Graou (inc 2 as replacement), Hueber; 4 – Ougier, Bernat-Salles, Reigt (inc 1 as replacement), Devergie (inc 1 as replacement), Blond (inc 1 as replacement), Miorin, Landreau (inc 1 as replacement); 3 – Galthié, Genet
Scorers: 112 – Viars (5T 9C 23PG); 30 – Saint-André (6T); 17 – Ougier (1T 6C); 15 – Bernat-Salles (3T); 13 – Penaud (2T 1DG); 10 – Marfaing, Benetton (2T each); 9 – Reigt (3DG); 8 – Hueber (1T 1DG), 7 – Deylaud (1T 1C); 5 – Gonzales, Sadourny (2T each)

MATCH 1   16 June, Cordoba

Cordoba XV 20 (2G 2PG)   **French XV 62** (6G 4T)
Cordoba *Tries:* Giaimo, Merlo   *Conversions:* Alvarez, Herrera
Penalty Goals: Alvarez (2)
French XV *Tries:* Saint-André (3), Benetton (2), Marfaing, Penaud, Ougier,
Bernat-Salles, Gonzales   *Conversions:* Ougier (6)
Referee R Blecqwedel (Tucumán)

MATCH 2   20 June, Velez Sarsfield Stadium, Buenos Aires

Buenos Aires XV 12 (4PG)   **French XV 28** (2G 2PG 1DG 1T)
Buenos Aires XV *Penalty Goals:* F J Mendez (4)
French XV *Tries:* Sadourny, Marfaing, Bernat-Salles   *Conversions:* Viars (2)
Penalty Goals: Viars (2)   *Dropped Goal:* Reigt
Referee J L Rolandi (Buenos Aires)

MATCH 3   23 June, Tucumán

Tucumán XV 25 (1G 6PG)   **French XV 23** (2G 3PG)
Tucumán *Try:* Bunader   *Conversion:* S Meson   *Penalty Goals:* S Meson (6)

French XV *Tries:* Penaud, Saint-André *Conversions:* Viars (2) *Penalty Goals:* Viars (3)
Referee M Peyrone (Rosario)

MATCH 4   27 June, San Juan

Invitation XV 18 (6PG) **French XV 32** (1G 5PG 2T)
Invitation XV *Penalty Goals:* Crexell (6)
French XV *Tries:* Viars (2), Saint-André *Conversion:* Viars *Penalty Goals:* Viars (5)
Referee E Sklar (Buenos Aires)

MATCH 5   30 June, Mendoza

Cuyo XV 32 (2G 6PG) **French XV 30** (1G 4PG 2DG 1T)
Cuyo XV *Tries:* Cassone, Nazzari *Conversions:* Cremaschi (2)
Penalty Goals: Cremaschi (6)
French XV *Tries:* Bernat-Salles, Viars *Conversion:* Viars *Penalty Goals:* Viars (4)
Dropped Goals: Reigt (2)
Referee J M Pavio (Buenos Aires)

MATCH 6   4 July, Velez Sarsfield Stadium, Buenos Aires   1st Test

ARGENTINA 12 (3PG 1DG) **FRANCE 27** (1G 4PG 1DG 1T)
ARGENTINA: L Criscuolo (Alumni); G M Jorge (Pucara), S E Meson (Tucumán),
H M Garcia Simon (Pueyrredon), D Cuesta Silva (San Isidro Club); L Arbizu (Belgrano),
G Camardon (Alumni); D M Cash (San Isidro Club), M A Bosch (Olivos), F E Mendez
(Mendoza), P L Sporleder (Curupayti), G A Llanes (La Plata), P Garreton (Tucumán U)
(capt), M Carreras (Olivos), R N Perez (Duendes)
Scorers *Penalty Goals:* Meson (3) *Dropped Goal:* Arbizu
FRANCE: Ougier; Saint-André, Marfaing, Deylaud, Viars; Penaud, Hueber; Armary,
Gonzales, Gallart, Deslandes, Cadieu, Benetton, Tordo, Cecillon *(capt)*
Replacements Sadourny for Ougier (42 mins); Coeurveille for Deylaud (78 mins)
Scorers *Tries:* Deylaud, Viars *Conversion:* Deylaud *Penalty Goals:* Viars (4)
Dropped Goal: Penaud
Referee F Burger (South Africa)

MATCH 7   7 July, Rosario

Rosario XV 8 (1PG 1T) **French XV 6** (2PG)
Abandoned at half-time due to floodlight failure
Rosario XV *Try:* Carmona *Penalty Goal:* Crexell
French XV *Penalty Goals:* Viars (2)
Referee S Pordeauch (Cordoba)

MATCH 8   11 July, Velez Sarsfield Stadium, Buenos Aires   2nd Test

ARGENTINA 9 (2PG 1DG) **FRANCE 33** (3G 3PG 1DG)
ARGENTINA: L Criscuolo (Alumni); M J Teran (Tucumán), S E Meson (Tucumán),
D Cuesta Silva (San Isidro Club), G M Jorge (Pucara); L Arbizu (Belgrano), G Camardon
(Alumni); D M Cash (San Isidro Club), M A Bosch (Olivos), F E Mendez (Mendoza),
P L Sporleder (Curupayti), G A Llanes (La Plata), P Garreton (Tucumán U) *(capt)*,
J M Santamarina (Tucumán), R N Perez (Duendes) *Replacement* R de la Arena
(Club Universitea Buenos Aires) for Teran (41 mins)
Scorers *Penalty Goals:* Meson (2) *Dropped Goal:* Arbizu
FRANCE: Sadourny; Saint-André, Coeurveille, Deylaud, Viars; Penaud, Hueber;
Armary, Gonzales, Gallart, Deslandes, Cadieu, Cabannes, Cecillon *(capt)*, Tordo
Replacements Benetton for Cadieu (59 mins); Devergie for Tordo (75 mins)
Scorers *Tries:* Hueber, Viars, Saint-André *Conversions:* Viars (3)
Penalty Goals: Viars (3) *Dropped Goal:* Hueber
Referee F Burger (South Africa)

ARGENTINA TO SPAIN, ROMANIA & FRANCE 1992

Argentinian rugby desperately needed this tour and the success it brought. Their Test record coming into the tour was very poor, but to succeed in the three Tests on the tour, against Spain, Romania and France, was an outstanding effort and the win over the French at Nantes was a result to be compared with any in their history.

The Pumas' problem before the tour was obvious. Their young team had been together for some years and the youthful forwards, especially, had not been expected to dominate other more experienced packs in the early stages of development. But results had not improved as the team gained that experience. One more disastrous tour and the Pumas may have concluded that they were on the wrong track all along. 'We had lost many games but all the time, our players were winning caps and experience,' said Luís Gradin, the Pumas coach, after the win over France. 'We proved we are now experienced enough to win.'

There was just one defeat on tour, when Argentina went down 13-21 to a powerful Côte Basque-Landes Selection at Bayonne. There were some encouraging successes amongst individuals – Santiago Meson, the medical student from Tucumán, had an exceptional tour; Martin Teran built on the reputation he had earned in the World Cup on the wing and the front five came of age, built as ever round the rock-like Frederico Mendez at prop.

The Test win at Nantes was well-deserved, even though the French scored three tries to nil through Galthié, Gonzales and Sella. The Puma hero was Meson, who kicked seven penalties. The French forwards frequently infringed in the loose. Lisandro Arbizu dropped a goal to complete the tourists' scoring. Argentina seemed to have scored a perfectly good try under the posts through Teran. However, the score was controversially ruled out by Ray Megson, the Scottish referee.

Perhaps the best achievement of all was for Argentina to put this behind them and to claw their way back from 3-15 down. It was a tribute to a new spirit, and the Pumas celebrated rapturously.

THE TOURING PARTY

Manager F Alvarez   **Coach** L Gradin   **Assistant Coach** L Imhoff
Captain L Arbizu

FULL-BACK
R de la Arena (CUBA)

THREEQUARTERS
G M Jorge (Pucara)
M E Roby (Mendoza)
M J Teran (Tucumán)
S Salvat (Alumni)

D Cuesta Silva (San Isidro Club)
L P Cremaschi (Los Tordos)
L Arbizu (Belgrano)
S Meson (Tucumán)

HALF-BACKS
F J Mendez (Los Tilos)

R Bullrich (Newman)
G Camardon (Alumni)
R Crexell (Rosario)

FORWARDS

E Garbarino (Belgrano)
R Le Fort (Tucumán)
E Noriega (Hindu)
F E Mendez (Mendoza)
J H Jalil (Tucumán Gymnasia)

M Corral (San Isidro Club)
P L Sporleder (Curupayti)
R N Perez (Duendes)
G A Llanes (La Plata)
J Santamarina (Tucumán)
F J Irarrazabal (Newman)
G Garcia Orsetti (Duendes)
N Ferrari (Alumni)
F Buabse (Los Tarcos)

TOUR RECORD

All matches Played 8 Won 7 Lost 1 Points for 259 Against 138
International matches Played 3 Won 3 Points for 88 Against 72

SCORING DETAILS

All matches					International matches				
For:	32T 24C 15PG 2DG			259 Pts	For:	9T 8C 8PG 1DG			88 Pts
Against:	18T 9C 9PG 1DG			138 Pts	Against:	9T 6C 5PG –			72 Pts

MATCH DETAILS

1992	OPPONENTS	VENUE	RESULT
20 Oct	Madrid XV	Madrid	W 94-10
24 Oct	SPAIN	Madrid	W 43-34
27 Oct	Romania B	Brasov	W 33-13
31 Oct	ROMANIA	Bucharest	W 21-18
4 Nov	Côte Basque-Landes	Bayonne	L 13-21
7 Nov	Roussillon	Perpignan	W 13-10
10 Nov	Limousin-Auvergne	Brive	W 18-12
14 Nov	FRANCE	Nantes	W 24-20

MATCH 1   20 October, Madrid

Madrid XV 10 (1G 1PG)   Argentina XV 94 (9G 2PG 5T)
Madrid XV *Try:* Serres   *Conversion:* Nunez   *Penalty Goal:* Nunez
Argentina XV *Tries:* Garcia Orsetti (3), Jorge (3), de la Arena (3), Roby (2), Teran, Cremaschi, Le Fort   *Conversions:* Crexell (9)   *Penalty Goals:* Crexell (2)

MATCH 2   24 October, Madrid

SPAIN 34 (4G 2PG)   ARGENTINA 43 (5G 1PG 1T)
SPAIN *Tries:* Puertas, Altuna, Sanchez, de la Calle   *Conversions:* Sanchez (4)
Penalty Goals: Sanchez (2)
ARGENTINA *Tries:* Cuesta Silva (2), F-J Mendez (4)   *Conversions:* Meson (5)
Penalty Goal: Meson
Referee M Darroque (France)

MATCH 3   27 October, Isai

Romania B 13 (1PG 2T)   Argentina XV 33 (4G 1T)
Romania B *Tries:* Colceriu, Negreci   *Penalty Goal:* Petre
Argentina XV *Tries:* de la Arena, Roby, Bullrich, Garcia Orsetti, Meson
Conversions: Meson (4)

MATCH 4   31 October, National Stadium, Bucharest

ROMANIA 18 (1G 2PG 1T)   ARGENTINA 21 (3G)
ROMANIA *Tries:* Dumitras (2)   *Conversion:* Nichitean   *Penalty Goals:* Nichitean (2)

ARGENTINA *Tries:* Camardon, Le Fort, penalty try   *Conversions:* Meson (3)
Referee M K McCartney (Scotland)

MATCH 5   4 November, Stade Saint-Leon, Bayonne

Côte Basque-Landes 21 (2PG 3T)   **Argentina XV 13** (1G 2PG)
Côte Basque-Landes *Tries:* Gouloumet, Beraz, Hontas   *Penalty Goals:* Arrieta (2)
Argentina XV *Try:* Roby   *Conversion:* Meson   *Penalty Goals:* Meson (2)

MATCH 6   7 November, Stade Aime-Giral, Perpignan

Roussillon 10 (1G 1DG)   **Argentina XV 13** (1G 1PG 1DG)
Roussillon *Try:* Arbo   *Conversion:* Tresene   *Dropped Goal:* Appy
Argentina XV *Try:* Perez   *Conversion:* Meson   *Penalty Goal:* Meson
Dropped Goal: Arbizu

MATCH 7   10 November, Brive

Limousin-Auvergne 12 (1G 1T)   **Argentina XV 18** (1G 2PG 1T)
Limousin-Auvergne *Tries:* Faugeron, Lhermet   *Conversion:* Nicol
Argentina XV *Tries:* Camardon, Arbizu   *Conversion:* Meson   *Penalty Goals:* Meson (2)

MATCH 8   14 November, Stade Beaujoire, Nantes

FRANCE 20 (1G 1PG 2T)   **ARGENTINA 24** (7PG 1DG)
FRANCE: S Viars (Brive); P Bernat-Salles (Pau), P Sella (Agen), A Penaud (Brive),
P Hontas (Biarritz); L Mazas (Colomiers), F Galthié (Colomiers); L Armary (Lourdes),
J-M Gonzales (Bayonne), P Gallart (Béziers), C Mougeot (Bègles-Bordeaux), O Roumat
(Dax), P Benetton (Agen), A Benazzi (Agen), J-F Tordo (Nice) (*capt*)
Replacement S Graou (Auch) for Gallart (41 mins)
Scorers *Tries:* Galthié, Gonzales, Sella   *Conversion:* Viars   *Penalty Goal:* Viars
ARGENTINA: Meson; Teran, Cuesta-Silva, Salvat, Jorge; Arbizu (*capt*), Camardon;
F E Mendez, Le Fort, Noriega, Sporleder, Llanes, Garcia Orsetti, Santamarina, Perez
Scorers *Penalty Goals:* Meson (7)   *Dropped Goal:* Arbizu
Referee: R J Megson (Scotland

ENGLAND B TO NEW ZEALAND 1992

Ultimately, this was a disappointing tour. It will have helped in the
development of players and in spotting those ready to slot into the
England side in the near future, but if the B player is judged on his
capacity to help his team to victory in tight corners in major matches
then the tour was not a success.

Both of the 'tests' against the New Zealand B team were lost,
although it must be said that fortune smiled on the home teams. Yet in
truth England were up against a third-string side – New Zealand had a
party of 30 in Australia for their full tour at the same time.

England found New Zealand rugby in traditional form – the forward
play was well organised and there was far too much stamping on the
prostrate player. Yet the fixture list was unbalanced: England played
only low grade provincial opposition, meeting none of the real giants of
the New Zealand domestic game, and they were therefore not well
prepared for the two international matches.

There were many individual successes in the party, which was well
led by Stuart Barnes at fly-half. Tony Underwood was a dangerous
wing, and Victor Ubogu came through strongly despite having his ear

almost severed in a raking incident in the first 'test'. Phil de Glanville showed real all-round expertise in the centre. In the end, however, the results in the major matches were not good enough to make England feel too sanguine about their immediate international future.

THE TOURING PARTY

Manager G Smith **Coach** J Rowell **Assistant Coach** M A C Slemen
Captain S Barnes

FULL-BACKS

J **Steele** (Northampton)
I **Hunter** (Northampton)

THREEQUARTERS

G C **Childs** (Wasps)
P R **de Glanville** (Bath)
A T **Harriman** (Harlequins)
D P **Hopley** (Wasps)
H S **Thorneycroft** (Northampton)
G J **Thompson** (Harlequins)
T **Underwood** (Leicester)
S **Hackney** (Leicester)

HALF-BACKS

S **Barnes** (Bath)
N J **Matthews** (Gloucester)
D A **Scully** (Wakefield)
A **Kardooni** (Leicester)

FORWARDS

N A **Back** (Leicester)
G P S **Baldwin** (Northampton)
M C **Bayfield** (Northampton)
J P S **Cassell** (Saracens)
B B **Clarke** (Bath)
R G R **Dawe** (Bath)
K A **Dunn** (Gloucester)
M **Greenwood** (Nottingham)
M **Haag** (Bath)
M P **Hynes** (Orrell)
D **Sims** (Gloucester)
V E **Ubogu** (Bath)
A R **Mullins** (Harlequins)
D **Ryan** (Wasps)
D **Baldwin** (Sale)
S **Ojomoh** (Bath)
M P **Russell** (Harlequins)

TOUR RECORD

All matches Played 8 Won 6 Lost 2 Points for 273 Against 127
International matches Played 2 Lost 2 Points for 36 Against 50

SCORING DETAILS

All matches

For:	45T	27C	12PG	1DG		273 Pts
Against:	10T	6C	22PG	3DG		127 Pts

International matches

For:	6T	3C	2PG	–		36 Pts
Against:	4T	2C	7PG	3DG		50 Pts

MATCH DETAILS

1992	OPPONENTS	VENUE	RESULT
10 June	North Otago	Oamaru	W 68-4
13 June	Southland	Invercargill	W 31-16
17 June	NZ Universities	Wellington	W 32-15
20 June	Wairarapa-Bush	Masterton	W 40-6
24 June	Wanganui	Wanganui	W 35-9
28 June	New Zealand XV	Hamilton	L 18-24
1 July	North Auckland	Whangarei	W 31-27
5 July	New Zealand XV	Pukekohe	L 18-26

Appearances: 6 – Kardooni (inc 1 as replacement), Hynes, Barnes, Mullins (inc 1 as replacement); 5 – Thompson (inc 1 as replacement), Bayfield, Ojomoh (inc 1 as replacement), Hopley, Underwood, Dawe (inc 1 as replacement), Back, Clarke; 4 – Steele, Childs (inc 1 as replacement), Dunn, Haag, Russell, Hunter, Harriman, de Glanville, Sims, Hackney; 3 – Thorneycroft, Ubogu, Cassell, Scully, G P S Baldwin (inc 1 as replacement), D Baldwin, Greenwood; 2 – Matthews
Scorers: 74 – Barnes (2T 15C 11PG 1DG); 25 – Steele (11C 1PG); 24 – Underwood, Harriman (6T each); 12 – Bayfield, Hackney, Thorneycroft, Ojomoh, de Glanville, Back (3T each); 10 – Hunter (2T 1C); 8 – Ubogu, Thompson (2T each); 4 – Dunn, Childs, Kardooni, Hopley, Russell, Cassell, pen try (1T each)

MATCH 1   10 June, Centennial Park, Oamaru

North Otago 4 (1T)   **England B XV 68** (6G 8T)
North Otago: A Lemon; R MacColl, J Taeiloa, G Hiscoke, S M Matthews; C Hore,
B Stevens; P Rowland, S Curle (*capt*), J Wilson, A Jones, C A Ross, S Talanoa,
A Matthews, P Mason
Scorer *Try:* Lemon
England B XV: Steele; Hackney, Childs, Thompson, Thorneycroft; Matthews,
Kardooni; Hynes, Dunn, Ubogu, Bayfield, Haag, Russell (*capt*), Ojomoh, Cassell
Scorers *Tries:* Thorneycroft (3), Hackney (3), Thompson (2), Ubogu (2), Dunn,
Bayfield, Ojomoh, Childs   *Conversions:* Steele (6)
Referee D J Bishop (Southland)

MATCH 2   13 June, Homestead Rugby Stadium, Invercargill

Southland 16 (4PG 1T)   **England B XV 31** (3G 3PG 1T)
Southland: E S Todd; S Forrest, A G James, G J Beardsley, G W Anderson;
S D Culhane, B D Murrell; R J Palmer, P Edwards, C C Corbett, W A Miller,
B J Morton, D B Henderson (*capt*), R T Smith, P W Henderson *Replacement* S Hayes for
Corbett (64 mins)
Scorers *Try:* Beardsley   *Penalty Goals:* Culhane (3), Beardsley
England B XV: Hunter; Harriman, de Glanville, Hopley, Underwood; Barnes (*capt*),
Scully; G P S Baldwin, Dawe, Mullins, D Baldwin, Sims, Greenwood, Clarke, Back
Replacement Kardooni for Scully (40 mins)
Scorers *Tries:* Underwood (2), Harriman, de Glanville   *Conversions:* Barnes (3)
Penalty Goals: Barnes (3)
Referee M L Fitzgibbon (Canterbury)

MATCH 3   17 June, Athletic Park, Wellington

New Zealand Universities 15 (1G 3PG)   **England B XV 32** (3G 2PG 2T)
New Zealand Universities: H Wong (Wellington); P Surridge (Auckland), J Leslie
(Otago), S Cottrell (Wellington) (*capt*), P Alston (Massey); S Kerr (Otago), J A Hewett
(Auckland); M Mika (Otago), N Mantell (Auckland), M Otai (Massey), B Timmons
(Otago), M Bradley (Wellington), D Tuaivi'i (Wellington), M Steffert (Waikato),
E Fuller *Replacement* D Love (Massey) for Hewett (78 mins)
Scorers *Try:* Surridge   *Conversion:* Kerr   *Penalty Goals:* Kerr (3)
England B XV: Hunter; Hackney, de Glanville, Hopley, Underwood; Barnes (*capt*),
Kardooni; Hynes, Dunn, Ubogu, Bayfield, Sims, Greenwood, Clarke, Back
Replacements Dawe for Dunn (46 mins); Ojomoh for Sims (50 mins)
Scorers *Tries:* Bayfield, de Glanville, Underwood, Back, pen try   *Conversions:* Barnes (3)
Penalty Goals: Barnes (2)
Referee P J O'Brien (North Otago)

MATCH 4   20 June, Memorial Park, Masterton

Wairarapa-Bush 6 (2PG)   **England B XV 40** (5G 2PG 1T)
Wairarapa-Bush: C Pepperell; M Foster, D Boyle, M J Berry (*capt*), J H Shirkey;
G R Gray, B J Lett; C F W Berry, N O'Neale, B E Styles, V M Boyce, J A Hutchins,
D Bassett, D Guildford, B D Bowie
Scorers *Penalty Goals:* Pepperell, Berry
England B XV: Steele; Harriman, Thompson, Hopley, Underwood; Barnes (*capt*),
Kardooni; Hynes, Dawe, Mullins, D Baldwin, Bayfield, Russell, Clarke, Cassell
Replacements G P S Baldwin for Hynes (34 mins); Childs for Hopley (37 mins)
Scorers *Tries:* Underwood (2), Bayfield, Barnes, Kardooni, Harriman
Conversions: Barnes (4), Steele   *Penalty Goals:* Barnes (2)
Referee G H Lempriere (Manawatu)

MATCH 5   24 June, Spriggens Park, Wanganui

Wanganui 9 (3PG)   **England B XV 35** (4G 1PG 2T)
Wanganui: L K Harding; R S Byam, C W Osborne, G Brennan, S Selby; K H Chase,
T W Scott; N N Ward, T J Cundy (*capt*), A M Bull, R Wallace, B J Scott, B W Hansen,
N B Bell, P Sullivan *Replacement* J Hamlin for Chase (77 mins)
Scorer *Penalty Goals:* Harding (3)
England B XV: Steele; Harriman, Childs, Thompson, Thorneycroft; Matthews, Scully;
Hynes, Dunn, Mullins (*capt*), Haag, Sims, Russell, Ojomoh, Back
Scorers *Tries:* Harriman (4), Back (2)   *Conversions:* Steele (4)   *Penalty Goal:* Steele
Referee M Thompson (Auckland)

MATCH 6   28 June, Rugby Park, Hamilton

New Zealand XV 24 (2G 2PG 2DG)   **England B 18** (1G 3T)
New Zealand XV: G J L Cooper (Otago); E J Rush (North Harbour), M S L Pierce
(North Harbour), M J Berry (Wairarapa-Bush), T D L Tagaloa (North Harbour);
L Stensness (Manawatu), S J Crabb (Waikato); M R Allen (Taranaki), W D Gatland
(Waikato) (*capt*), P H Coffin (King Country), S B Gordon (Waikato), C D Tregaskis
(Wellington), G L Taylor (North Auckland), R S Turner (North Harbour), D J Seymour
(Canterbury)
Scorers *Tries:* Crabb, Tagaloa   *Conversions:* Cooper (2)   *Penalty Goals:* Cooper (2)
Dropped Goals: Cooper (2)
England B: Hunter; Hackney, de Glanville, Hopley, Underwood; Barnes (*capt*),
Kardooni; G Baldwin, Dawe, Ubogu, D Baldwin, Bayfield, Greenwood, Clarke, Back
Replacement Mullins for Ubogu (4 mins)
Scorers *Tries:* Hunter (2), Hopley, Underwood   *Conversion:* Hunter
Referee L L McLachlan (Otago)

MATCH 7   1 July, Whangarei

North Auckland 27 (3G 3PG)   **England B XV 31** (3G 2PG 1DG 1T)
North Auckland: W B Johnston; N R Berryman, M Younger, M B Seymour (*capt*),
Q C Cherrington; R L J le Bas, P Thomas; C K Barrell, D J Jurlina, J Barrell, R Thomas,
G A Crawford, A Campbell, R C Hilton-Jones, M W Hilton-Jones
Scorers *Tries:* Berryman (3)   *Conversions:* Johnston (3)   *Penalty Goals:* Johnston (3)
England B XV: Steele; Harriman, Thompson, Childs, Thorneycroft; Barnes (*capt*),
Scully; Hynes, Dunn, Mullins, Haag, Sims, Russell, Ojomoh, Cassell
Scorers *Tries:* Russell, Cassell, Ojomoh, Barnes   *Conversions:* Barnes (3)
Penalty Goals: Barnes (2)   *Dropped Goal:* Barnes
Referee A G Riley (Waikato)

MATCH 8   5 July, Pukekohe

New Zealand XV 26 (5PG 1DG 2T)   **England B 18** (2G 2PG)
New Zealand XV: M J Berry (Wairarapa-Bush); A F McCormick (Canterbury),
M S L Pierce (North Harbour), L Stensness (Manawatu), T D L Tagaloa
(North Harbour); S J Mannix (Wellington), S J Crabb (Waikato); M R Allen (Taranaki),
W D Gatland (Waikato) (*capt*), G L Walsh (North Harbour), S B Gordon (Waikato),
C D Tregaskis (Wellington), G L Taylor (North Auckland), R S Turner
(North Harbour), D J Seymour (Canterbury)
Scorers *Tries:* Stensness, Turner   *Penalty Goals:* Mannix (5)   *Dropped Goal:* Stensness
England B: Hunter; Hackney, de Glanville, Hopley, Underwood; Barnes (*capt*),
Kardooni; Hynes, Dawe, Mullins, Haag, Bayfield, Ojomoh, Clarke, Back
Replacement Thompson for de Glanville (52 mins)
Scorers *Tries:* Ojomoh, de Glanville   *Conversions:* Barnes (2)   *Penalty Goals:* Barnes (2)
Referee C J Hawke (New Zealand)

FRANCE'S STEALTHY TITLE
AS ENGLAND DOMINANCE ENDS

THE INTERNATIONAL CHAMPIONSHIP 1993
Mick Cleary *The Observer*

We had a Championship but did we have a trophy? The news that silverware was to be awarded to the winners was delivered to us only in mid-season, as if it were a piece of classified information which some dastardly subversive had leaked. With it came paragraph 3.4, stating that for the first time ever points difference could settle the Championship.

It was all badly handled. On the surface, points difference did not matter, since France won and England lost their final matches. But did it influence things in a more subtle way? Would England have played with greater vigour in Dublin if they hadn't already trailed France by eight points going into that last game? Some of those English players certainly performed like men who had already given up the ghost.

There's little point bemoaning the committee's public relations inadequacies. The Five Nations has never needed any publicity. Once again there was drama at nearly every turn. Low on quality the games might have been, but for various reasons they were high on excitement. And this despite one of the monsters of the age: the new ruck/maul law. The worst fears of coaches such as Bob Dwyer – 'it's a nightmare', Alex Wyllie – 'the whole thing is a madness', and Dick Best – 'do they want us to play Rugby League?' seemed to be borne out by the dearth of tries scored. There were only 20 in total, the lowest aggregate per game for many years. Worse than that was the sight of rows of midfield muggers waiting to kill the ball, or the ball-carrier, and in so doing kill the game.

The referees varied in the degree of sympathy they showed to players. Some whistled far too quickly. If the referees had applied the old law more assiduously, and kept players on their feet, then there might never have been any lobbying for change. As it is the poor blighters have so much to do they are missing the greatest curse of all – off-side. It was also disturbing to see Fred Howard removed from England's panel. The game needs strong, sensitive officials like Howard and the sooner he is back in action, the better.

This was the first Championship of the five-point try. It seemed to make no tangible difference to any side's attacking inclination and all we could reflect on was that England would have drawn in Cardiff under the old values.

That defeat was seen as an aberration. England did everything but score and when the floodgates opened against Scotland, triggered by the appearance of Barnes in an England shirt, many assumed that the pre-tournament favourites were back in the groove. Dublin proved otherwise. Some of the old warriors, Dooley in particular, looked to be past their magnificent best. England's complement of 16 Lions for the summer tour was unduly favourable. Dooley, Winterbottom and Webb announced their retirements and the latter two retired. Probyn became England's most-capped prop and Carling the most successful international captain.

The Championship went to France. They had the perfect build-up: revolution in the air, Berbizier sacked, Berbizier reinstated, glorious victory over South Africa in the second Test, inglorious defeat by Argentina in Nantes a few weeks later. Total confusion – they couldn't have asked for anything better. It was not to be victory in the grand manner for France, however. Their chief virtue was defensive. England crossed their line only through a lucky rebound. Only a lick of paint on the Twickenham crossbar kept out Lafond's dropped goal, which would have meant a Grand Slam for France. The full-back retired at the season's end.

In Scotland they were mourning the retirement of Ian McGeechan. Again he showed his master touch in blooding Andy Reed and Ian Morrison. Gavin Hastings' first stint as captain ended with him leading the Lions. Chalmers' injury against England, a double break of the right forearm, was a grievous blow.

Ireland looked as if they were going to continue down the long dark chute. Defeats number ten and 11 in succession were chalked up before they edged home in Cardiff. And so to Dublin. What a match. Galwey's try was acclaimed by cheers which must have been heard on the other side of the Irish Sea. The big Kerry man's battling display earned him a Lions place. The new star, fly-half Eric Elwood, just missed out.

For Wales, the long slog back uphill continues. Victory over England was sweet but significant for only two weeks. The thrashing in Murrayfield gave a truer indication of what lies in store for Alan Davies and Bob Norster. Olympic hurdler Nigel Walker won his first cap, as did Rupert Moon. Robert Jones was dropped and still every Welshman scanned the horizon for the saviour in the No 10 shirt to appear.

FINAL TABLE

	P	W	D	L	F	A	Pts
France	4	3	0	1	73	35	6
Scotland	4	2	0	2	50	40	4
England	4	2	0	2	54	54	4
Ireland	4	2	0	2	45	53	4
Wales	4	1	0	3	34	74	2

16 January, Murrayfield   *(Sponsored by The Royal Bank of Scotland)*
SCOTLAND 15 (1G 1PG 1T)   **IRELAND 3** (1PG)
This was a satisfying victory for what was in large part an experimental Scottish team. Stark came in on the wing, Watt added his massive bulk to the loose-head prop position and Bath's Andy Reed, for many seasons a reserve player at the club, completed a meteoric rise for his first cap. He had played before huge crowds before, of course – as a lock for Cornwall in two County finals at Twickenham.

The new men proved to be a success and Scotland won comfortably. The only reservation must be that the opposition was so disjointed and limited. Ireland were afflicted by injury, especially to key forwards. They were still reeling from heavy defeats in New Zealand in the previous summer and also against Australia at Lansdowne Road. Their preparation was poor and they fielded too many players not used to the pace and atmosphere at the very top of the game. Although Popplewell had an outstanding match in the Irish front row, the team as a whole were under-powered.

As Noel Murphy, the manager, pointed out later, one of the key features was the hard core of experience that Scotland could muster, what with the Hastings brothers and the half-backs, Armstrong and Chalmers. Armstrong especially had a fine game for his country.

Scotland scored two excellent tries and the searing pace of Stark was evident in both. Milne, Turnbull and Reed handled well after a Scotland tap-kick and Stark went over down the left. It was an encouraging try, although Ireland's defence was extremely deficient.

Stark made a telling intrusion into a Scottish back movement later in the first half. He cleverly handed on an overhead pass to Stanger, bursting up from the opposite wing, and Stanger ran on to score. Gavin Hastings kicked a conversion and a penalty and although Scotland did not score in the second half, they did not need to. The only score after the interval was a penalty by Malone, the inexperienced young Oxford University student who made a steady debut.

SCOTLAND: A G Hastings (Watsonians) *(capt)*; A G Stanger (Hawick), S Hastings (Watsonians), A G Shiel (Melrose), D A Stark (Boroughmuir); C M Chalmers (Melrose), G Armstrong (Jedforest); A Watt (Glasgow High/Kelvinside), K S Milne (Heriot's FP), A P Burnell (London Scottish), A Reed (Bath), D F Cronin (London Scottish), D J Turnbull (Hawick), G W Weir (Melrose), I R Morrison (London Scottish)
Scorers *Tries:* Stark, Stanger   *Conversion:* A G Hastings   *Penalty Goal:* A G Hastings
IRELAND: C R Wilkinson (Malone); S P Geoghegan (London Irish), V J G Cunningham (St Mary's Coll), P P A Danaher (Garryowen), R M Wallace (Garryowen); N G Malone (Oxford U), M T Bradley (Cork Const) *(capt)*; N J Popplewell (Greystones), S J Smith (Ballymena), P D McCarthy (Cork Const), P S Johns (Dungannon), R A Costello (Garryowen), P J Lawlor (Bective Rangers), N P Mannion (Lansdowne), W D McBride (Malone)
Scorer *Penalty Goal:* Malone
Referee E F Morrison (England)

16 January, Twickenham *(Sponsored by Save & Prosper)*
ENGLAND 16 (1G 3PG)   **FRANCE 15** (1G 1PG 1T)
It may be a perverse summary to say that while France could have won and won comfortably, still England deserved this heart-stopping victory. There was certainly very little in it and the French deserve credit for their approach and endeavour. They could easily have snatched victory at the end.

Indeed, England's Five Nations campaign could have been scuppered almost before it began. Jean-Baptiste Lafond, the French full-back, who had a superb match in defence, dropped at goal with the score at 16-15 and the ball cannoned back from the cross-bar. It was as close as that.

France could rue the bounce of the ball. In the first half, as England struggled, Jon Webb was given a kick at goal. He mis-hit the ball slightly and it hit the post. But instead of bouncing to safety, as Lafond's effort was fated to do, it hopped up obligingly into the hands of the onrushing Ian Hunter. England's strapping wing scored easily and the conversion made it a seven-point disaster for the French.

France had issued a ringing statement of intent in the first half. They led 12-6 at one stage, were winning all the ball – especially from Roumat and Benazzi in the line-out – and scored two tries. The first came when Webb dropped an innocuous kick ahead from Lacroix in the French centre. There was an excuse in the fact that there was wicked, swirling wind. Saint-André came up and pounced for the try. Webb did kick two penalties for England but Saint-André came again soon afterwards. Camberabero lofted a garryowen and while England defenders on or about their own line remained earthbound, Saint-André jumped for the ball, caught it and scored.

England reasserted themselves with the fortunate Hunter try and as the match wore on, they made a major comeback in the line-out. In this phase, and also in other areas, there was a fine contribution from Johnson, the Leicester lock called in with scarcely more than 24 hours' notice after the withdrawal of the formidable Dooley.

ENGLAND: J M Webb (Bath); I Hunter (Northampton), W D C Carling (Harlequins) *(capt)*, J C Guscott (Bath), R Underwood (Leicester & RAF); C R Andrew (Wasps), C D Morris (Orrell); J Leonard (Saracens), B C Moore (Harlequins), J A Probyn (Wasps), M C Bayfield (Northampton), M Johnson (Leicester), M C Teague (Gloucester), B B Clarke (Bath), P J Winterbottom (Harlequins)
Scorers *Try:* Hunter   *Conversion:* Webb   *Penalty Goals:* Webb (3)
FRANCE: J-B Lafond (Bègles); P Saint-André (Montferrand), P Sella (Agen), T Lacroix (Dax), P Hontas (Biarritz); D Camberabero (Béziers), A Hueber (Lourdes); L Armary (Lourdes), J-F Tordo (Nice), L Seigne (Merignac), A Benazzi (Agen), O Roumat (Dax), P Benetton (Agen), M Cecillon (Bourgoin), L Cabannes (Racing Club de France) *Replacements* F Mesnel (Racing Club de France) for Sella; S Ougier (Toulouse) for Lacroix
Scorers *Tries:* Saint-André (2)   *Conversion:* Camberabero   *Penalty Goal:* Camberabero
Referee J M Fleming (Scotland)

Philippe Saint-André has scored his second try of the afternoon against the English at Twickenham. Abdel Benazzi begs to be the first to congratulate him.

7 February, Cardiff Arms Park (*The British Gas Challenge*)
WALES 10 (1G 1PG)   ENGLAND 9 (2PG 1DG)

There was just one try, and no score at all in the second half, but this was one of the most marvellous occasions even Cardiff Arms Park had seen. Before the match, Geoff Cooke, the England manager, had stated that Wales could not talk about a revival until they had started winning games. They won, and the revival was a possibility.

England failed to score a try and Alan Davies, the Welsh coach, called the Welsh tackling 'majestic'. The defensive wall set up by the Welsh back row and the midfield, where Scott Gibbs had an astonishing match, were the basis of the Welsh win. Having said that, England came perilously close to scoring tries, notably when Dewi Morris was twice hauled down just short. On the first occasion, he appeared to have stretched out and touched down legally but the referee disallowed the score. In the second half, after a dazzling, weaving run which took him past six defenders, Morris was cut down only by a desperate tackle from Mike Rayer, the Welsh full-back.

Yet any other result would have been unfair on the fighting Welsh. Apart from their virtues in defence, they were quicker on to the loose ball, they gained a half-share of the line-out possession against the vaunted England giants and they finished stronger. Gareth Llewellyn was outstanding in the second row. He took a stream of two-handed catches and was a dominant figure around the field.

The Welsh try came near half-time. England were leading 9-3 with two penalty goals by Jon Webb and a high dropped goal from the left foot of Guscott to set against a long penalty from Jenkins for Wales. Emyr Lewis appeared to strike a kick ahead a little too far and it seemed as though Rory Underwood had enough time to reach the ball first, even though Ieuan Evans, the Welsh captain, came sprinting up. Yet Underwood, for some reason, dawdled helplessly. Evans hacked the ball on, outpaced Webb and scored. Jenkins converted and Wales took a lead which they were never to surrender, despite all the English possession and scoring chances in the second half.

WALES: M A Rayer (Cardiff); I C Evans (Llanelli) (*capt*), M R Hall (Cardiff), I S Gibbs (Swansea), W T Proctor (Llanelli); N R Jenkins (Pontypridd), R N Jones (Swansea); R L Evans (Llanelli), N Meek (Pontypool), H Williams-Jones (South Wales Police), G O Llewellyn (Neath), A H Copsey (Llanelli), E W Lewis (Llanelli), S Davies (Swansea), R E Webster (Swansea)
Scorers *Try:* I Evans *Conversion:* Jenkins *Penalty Goal:* Jenkins
ENGLAND: J M Webb (Bath); I Hunter (Northampton), W D C Carling (Harlequins) (*capt*), J Guscott (Bath), R Underwood (Leicester & RAF); C R Andrew (Wasps), C D Morris (Orrell); J Leonard (Saracens), B C Moore (Harlequins), J A Probyn (Wasps), M C Bayfield (Northampton), M Johnson (Leicester), M C Teague (Gloucester), B B Clarke (Bath), P J Winterbottom (Harlequins)
Replacement P R de Glanville (Bath) for Hunter
Scorers *Penalty Goals:* Webb (2) *Dropped Goal:* Guscott
Referee J Dume (France)

7 February, Parc des Princes
FRANCE 11 (2PG 1T)   SCOTLAND 3 (1PG)

There was much publicity given to Scotland's territorial domination of much of the match and to their failure to take try-scoring chances, but in the end, France had that extra edge of incisiveness and they came through. Perhaps the luck which had deserted them at Twickenham had returned in some measure; in any event, by the end they were in control of the brave Scots. Scotland have still never won in France since the French moved their Test venue to Parc des Princes from Stade Colombes in the 1970s.

Scotland did carve out some try-scoring chances and Gary Armstrong was an electric influence at scrum-half. Craig Chalmers, his partner, strongly favoured the high kick ahead as the option in attack and Jean-Baptiste Lafond dealt expertly with most of his attempts. Gavin Hastings hampered the cause of his own team a little with his off-form goal-kicking, just when points on the board could have sustained Scotland's momentum. Scotland's threequarter line had precious little impact in attack, a major factor in their defeat.

The French try came from a shortened line-out on the right. Hueber, the outstanding French scrum-half, set Cabannes away. The French flanker handed on to Sella, who carved through the middle and found support from the impressive Benazzi. Eventually, the ball was spun to the right and although there was little space in which to move, some accurate passing sent Lacroix over for the try. The try arrived after 63 minutes. Camberabero had kicked two penalty goals against one from Gavin Hastings but the try settled the French and paved the way for their near-domination of the closing stages. They could have scored at least one more try in a series of impressive attacks.

Nevertheless, it was in many ways a promising day for Scotland. Their line-out men were given high praise by Pierre Berbizier, the French coach, and their impressive togetherness belied the fact that the Scotland team was in its infancy, and had been largely thrown together only short weeks before. The giant Reed at lock, playing in only his second Test match, was a real handful for the French.

FRANCE: J-B Lafond (Bègles); P Saint-André (Montferrand), P Sella (Agen), T Lacroix (Dax), P Hontas (Biarritz); D Camberabero (Béziers), A Hueber (Lourdes); L Armary (Lourdes), J-F Tordo (Nice), L Seigne (Merignac), A Benazzi (Agen), O Roumat (Dax), P Benetton (Agen), M Cecillon (Bourgoin) (*capt*), L Cabannes (Racing Club de France)
Scorers *Try:* Lacroix   *Penalty Goals:* Camberabero (2)
SCOTLAND: A G Hastings (Watsonians) (*capt*); A G Stanger (Hawick), S Hastings (Watsonians), A G Shiel (Melrose), D A Stark (Boroughmuir); C M Chalmers (Melrose), G Armstrong (Jedforest); P Wright (Boroughmuir), K S Milne (Heriot's FP), A P Burnell (London Scottish), A Reed (Bath), D F Cronin (London Scottish), D J Turnbull (Hawick), G W Weir (Melrose), I R Morrison (London Scottish)
Scorer *Penalty Goal:* A G Hastings
Referee W D Bevan (Wales)

20 February, Lansdowne Road
IRELAND 6 (2PG)   FRANCE 21 (1G 2PG 1DG 1T)

Some myths about Irish rugby were dismantled before this match, others confirmed during it. It has been said that the state of Irish rugby might be desperate, but it is never serious. That patronising cliché was shown to be nonsense in the build-up when Simon Geoghegan was disciplined behind closed doors for daring to speak out about the frustrations of playing in a losing side. Acrimony, dissent, disillusion – it was serious, all right.

Yet the portents of disaster were unreliable. True, the 11th loss in succession was recorded but there was merit in defeat. All the traditional Irish hallmarks were back in place: aggression, tenacity and a sense of purpose long since absent in the men in green. The old warriors, O'Hara and Galwey, exemplified the new mood, well supported by one of the two new caps, tight-head prop Clohessy. Another slight adjustment to old prejudices had to be made in that the storm did not blow out after 60 minutes. If international matches were played for just an hour, Ireland would probably be world champions. Here they sustained their efforts until the final ten minutes. It was only then that France managed to undeservedly embellish the scoreboard with two tries.

Malone's two penalties by the half-hour were just reward for Ireland's solid start. Camberabero edged France level by half-time with a dropped goal and a penalty, and added another penalty goal shortly after the restart. Ireland badly needed some imagination behind to complement the industry up front. It was singularly lacking. And so the depressing scenario of no victories in the Championship since 1990 took tangible shape with late tries from France. Saint-André surged past Wallace to gather Hueber's deft chip-kick in the 73rd minute. Then Sella, who played in the last French side to be beaten at Lansdowne Road in 1983, rounded off matters on the stroke of full-time, capitalising on the thundering midfield drives by the impressive second-row duo of Roumat and Benazzi.

IRELAND: C P Clarke (Terenure Coll); S P Geoghegan (London Irish), V J G Cunningham (St Mary's Coll), P P A Danaher (Garryowen), R M Wallace (Garryowen); N G Malone (London Irish), M T Bradley (Cork Const) *(capt)*; N J Popplewell (Greystones), T J Kingston (Dolphin), P M Clohessy (Young Munster), P S Johns (Dungannon), N P J Francis (Blackrock Coll), P T O'Hara (Cork Const), M J Galwey (Shannon), W D McBride (Malone) *Replacement* B T Glennon (Lansdowne) for Danaher
Scorer *Penalty Goals:* Malone (2)
FRANCE: J-B Lafond (Bègles); P Saint-André (Montferrand), P Sella (Agen), T Lacroix (Dax), P Hontas (Biarritz); D Camberabero (Béziers), A Hueber (Toulon); L Armary (Lourdes), J-F Tordo (Nice) *(capt)*, L Seigne (Merignac), A Benazzi (Agen), O Roumat (Dax), P Benetton (Agen), M Cecillon (Bourgoin), L Cabannes (Racing Club de France)
Scorers *Tries:* Saint-André, Sella   *Conversion:* Camberabero
Penalty Goals: Camberabero (2)   *Dropped Goal:* Camberabero
Referee D Leslie (Scotland)

20 February, Murrayfield   *(Sponsored by The Royal Bank of Scotland)*
SCOTLAND 20 (5PG 1T)   **WALES 0**

Nobody took much notice of the voice at the time. After all, there was a lot of celebrating to do. England, the double Grand Slammers, had just been beaten. And yet, when digesting this thumping defeat, the Welsh team and its many thousands of supporters who had travelled north with such inflated optimism would have good cause to think back to the wise words of their down-to-earth coach, Alan Davies. He had warned just after victory in Cardiff that they had far from arrived at their destination. Those who thought the route to redemption would be a short, untroubled one were rudely awakened by this performance.

True, Scotland only scored one workmanlike try and Gavin Hastings did kick goals as if his boots were fitted with radar. He landed five penalty goals, from all angles and distances. But Wales were so bereft of ideas that they never remotely threatened the Scottish try-line. They were also badly beaten in the line-outs where Cronin, Reed and Weir plucked the ball from the air with the unchallenged ease of boys picking apples in an unguarded orchard. By moving Derek Turnbull to the front on the opposition throw, Scotland also managed to cut Wales' supply-lines at source.

No ball, no contest. In all Gary Armstrong received twice as much possession as his counterpart, Robert Jones. Once again the Swansea scrum-half had no more than a few grains with which to feed his brood, starvation rations which were to take the inevitable toll on first his confidence and ultimately his place in the Welsh team.

In marked contrast to Jones' woe was the swagger with which Gavin Hastings bestrode the field. One look at his body language and you knew that Scotland were on a winner. The big man did everything, including reading the elements with the eye of an expert. Turnbull's try, which came when the Hawick flanker was driven over from a short-range line-out, ensured that the scoreboard adequately reflected the gulf between the teams.

SCOTLAND: A G Hastings (Watsonians) *(capt)*; A G Stanger (Hawick), S Hastings (Watsonians), A G Shiel (Melrose), D A Stark (Boroughmuir); C M Chalmers (Melrose), G Armstrong (Jedforest); P H Wright (Boroughmuir), K S Milne (Heriot's FP), A P Burnell (London Scottish), A I Reed (Bath), D F Cronin (London Scottish), D J Turnbull (Hawick), G W Weir (Melrose), I R Morrison (London Scottish)
Scorers *Try:* Turnbull   *Penalty Goals:* A G Hastings (5)
WALES: M A Rayer (Cardiff); I C Evans (Llanelli) *(capt)*, M R Hall (Cardiff), I S Gibbs (Swansea), W T Proctor (Llanelli); N R Jenkins (Pontypridd), R N Jones (Swansea); R L Evans (Llanelli), N Meek (Pontypool), H Williams-Jones (South Wales Police), G O Llewellyn (Neath), A H Copsey (Llanelli), E W Lewis (Llanelli), S Davies (Swansea), R E Webster (Swansea)
Referee J Dume (France)

6 March, Cardiff Arms Park
WALES 14 (3PG 1T)   IRELAND 19 (1G 3PG 1DG)

Over the last three years there have been many Irishmen in tears. As one loss followed another, they could but cry into their beer. Here the tears which streamed down the face of prop Nick Popplewell were of uncontained joy.

What Irishman cared a fig about the quality of the match itself – which rarely rose above the pitifully low – now that the sequence of 11 consecutive defeats was behind them? The glimmer of hope that had flickered against France was confirmed here to be more than just an illusion. Again the pack battled heartily but this time their sweat was not expended in vain. Scrum-half Bradley had one of his most authoritative games in an Irish shirt. His service was smooth and gave the debutant fly-half, Elwood, the perfect platform on which to show off the talent which was to so torment England a fortnight later.

Wales had little to offer. Jenkins landed only three of ten attempts at goal and again failed to get his back line on the move with any purpose or penetration. In his first game Olympic hurdler Nigel Walker had few chances to demonstrate his pace. The one Welshman who did manage to stick his head up through the cloud of mediocrity was Ieuan Evans. His second-half try stood out for its decisiveness and athleticism. He rounded the Irish defence, shrugging off tacklers as if brushing away bits of confetti, to score in the corner.

This try closed the gap to two points. But Ireland were not going to throw away the labours of their first-half work quite so easily. Clarke had dropped a goal after Jenkins' early penalty before Ireland took the game by the scruff of the neck with a finely worked try on the half-hour. Bradley's slickly delivered pass to Elwood set up the fly-half to run at the heart of the Welsh midfield. He drew two tacklers before slipping the ball to his back row. Their surge to the line was finished off by Robinson. The end was in sight.

WALES: M A Rayer (Cardiff); I C Evans (Llanelli) (*capt*), M R Hall (Cardiff), I S Gibbs (Swansea), N Walker (Cardiff); N R Jenkins (Pontypridd), R N Jones (Swansea); R L Evans (Llanelli), N Meek (Pontypool), H Williams-Jones (South Wales Police), G O Llewellyn (Neath), A H Copsey (Llanelli), E W Lewis (Llanelli), S Davies (Swansea), R E Webster (Swansea) *Replacement* A Clement (Swansea) for Evans
Scorers *Try:* Evans   *Penalty Goals:* Jenkins (3)
IRELAND: C P Clarke (Terenure Coll); R M Wallace (Garryowen), V J G Cunningham (St Mary's Coll), P P A Danaher (Garryowen), S P Geoghegan (London Irish); E P Elwood (Lansdowne), M T Bradley (Cork Const) (*capt*); N J Popplewell (Greystones), T J Kingston (Dolphin), P M Clohessy (Young Munster), P S Johns (Dungannon), M J Galwey (Shannon), P T O'Hara (Cork Const), B F Robinson (London Irish), W D McBride (Malone)
Scorers *Try:* Robinson   *Conversion:* Elwood   *Penalty Goals:* Elwood (3)
Dropped Goal: Clarke
Referee A R MacNeill (Australia)

Mick Galwey tries anxiously to shrug off the challenge of Emyr Lewis during Ireland's victory at Cardiff Arms Park. The referee is Australia's Sandy MacNeill.

6 March, Twickenham   *(Sponsored by Save & Prosper)*
ENGLAND 26 (1G 3PG 2T)   **SCOTLAND 12** (3PG 1DG)

He said he could do it, and he did it. All week Stuart Barnes had responded to the notebooks and microphones in the way few sportsmen do: he told the truth. No, he did not feel under pressure; no, he did not need good luck; and yes, the English threequarters would get a run.

And how. The Bath fly-half, called to the colours for the first time in five years at the expense of Rob Andrew, kick-started the English back line into life. The Scots may claim that the telling English scores came only after their own play-maker, Craig Chalmers – who dropped a goal before his departure – had left the field in the 24th minute with a double break of the right forearm. Influential and defensively resilient as Chalmers is, there was such an air of potency about England's play that his presence would have made little difference.

Scotland, bidding for the Triple Crown, did make a fist of it. Perhaps surprisingly, they had a decisive edge in the line-out, and with Armstrong in his customary bullish mood, England had to be ever vigilant in their fringe defence. Winterbottom, Clarke and Teague dented many a blue-shirted ball-carrier with their ferocious tackling. But this was a day to praise attack, not defence.

England's first try in the 28th minute was prosaic in comparison with what was to come. Webb and Hastings had exchanged penalty goals early on before Guscott glided over. England then struck twice within five minutes shortly after the interval. Barnes seemed to be pinned down when Morris fired a high pass to him just fractionally outside the English 22. Not so. Barnes scuttled clear before linking with Guscott on halfway. The beauty of Guscott's smooth acceleration was to be matched by the precision of his pass to Rory Underwood, which sent Underwood to the line. Rory featured again moments later when his angled run in-field drew the defence sufficiently for brother Tony to cruise around the outside. High up in the stand their mother, Anne, danced a jig of delight. And well she might.

ENGLAND: J M Webb (Bath); T Underwood (Leicester), W D C Carling (Harlequins) *(capt)*, J C Guscott (Bath), R Underwood (RAF & Leicester); S Barnes (Bath), C D Morris (Orrell); J Leonard (Harlequins), B C Moore (Harlequins), J A Probyn (Wasps), M C Bayfield (Northampton), W A Dooley (Preston Grasshoppers), M C Teague (Moseley), B B Clarke (Bath), P J Winterbottom (Harlequins)
Scorers *Tries:* Guscott, R Underwood, T Underwood   *Conversion:* Webb *Penalty Goals:* Webb (3)
SCOTLAND: A G Hastings (Watsonians) *(capt)*; A G Stanger (Hawick), S Hastings (Watsonians), A G Shiel (Melrose), D A Stark (Boroughmuir); C M Chalmers (Melrose), G Armstrong (Jedforest); P H Wright (Boroughmuir), K S Milne (Heriot's FP), A P Burnell (London Scottish), A I Reed (Bath), D F Cronin (London Scottish), D J Turnbull (Hawick), G W Weir (Melrose), I R Morrison (London Scottish) *Replacement* G P J Townsend (Gala) for Chalmers; K M Logan for S Hastings
Scorers *Penalty Goals:* A G Hastings (3)   *Dropped Goal:* Chalmers
Referee B W Stirling (Ireland)

20 March, Lansdowne Road
IRELAND 17 (2PG 2DG 1T)   ENGLAND 3 (1PG)

A trip to the bookmaker's on O'Connell Street on Thursday left no doubt as to who was going to win. England were 6-1 on: there was only one team in it. Thankfully, rugby matches are not played in smoky, down-town betting shops. And so to the famous old grey stadium on Saturday afternoon. There *was* only one team in it, and they were wearing green.

If England, and the bookies, expected, then it was Ireland who delivered. It would be tempting to paint this victory simply as one of underdog rage intimidating complacent opposition. There was a frenzied air about the Irish tackling – when Rory Underwood received his first touch, the ball had six green shirts on the end of it – but there was more than just wild energy underpinning Ireland's performance. They also had a clear sense of purpose, albeit a destructive one, as well as an assassin at fly-half pulling the trigger at just the right moment.

Elwood, in only his second international, played with the air of a veteran, time and again turning England back with his telling kicks. He also landed two penalties and two dropped goals, three of the successes coming in the second half. If Elwood emerged as a late contender for the Lions squad, so too did Clohessy, Robinson, McBride and Galwey, the latter rounding things off with a storming try just before the end.

England did not hide but neither did they cope. They didn't sweep the line-outs, a glaring failing given that they invariably got the first touch. It was no surprise therefore that control was never established at half-back. None of those pledged to retirement – Webb, Dooley and Winterbottom – will have cause to look back fondly on their contributions here.

By contrast the Irish captain, Bradley, winning his 29th cap to become his country's most-capped scrum-half, will have nothing but sweet memories. Not even the Irish will be able to embellish this tale with their customary inventiveness, for the reality was wondrous enough.

IRELAND: C P Clarke (Terenure Coll); R M Wallace (Garryowen), V J G Cunningham (St Mary's Coll), P P A Danaher (Garryowen), S P Geoghegan (London Irish); E P Elwood (Lansdowne), M T Bradley (Cork Const) (*capt*); N J Popplewell (Greystones), T J Kingston (Dolphin), P M Clohessy (Young Munster), P S Johns (Dungannon), M J Galwey (Shannon), P T O'Hara (Cork Const), B F Robinson (London Irish), W D McBride (Malone)
Scorers *Try:* Galwey   *Penalty Goals:* Elwood (2)   *Dropped Goals:* Elwood (2)
ENGLAND: J M Webb (Bath); T Underwood (Leicester), W D C Carling (Harlequins) (*capt*), J C Guscott (Bath), R Underwood (RAF & Leicester); S Barnes (Bath), C D Morris (Orrell); J Leonard (Harlequins), B C Moore (Harlequins), J A Probyn (Wasps), M C Bayfield (Northampton), W A Dooley (Preston Grasshoppers), M C Teague (Moseley), B B Clarke (Bath), P J Winterbottom (Harlequins)
Scorer *Penalty Goal:* Webb
Referee A R MacNeill (Australia)

20 March, Parc des Princes
FRANCE 26 (1G 3PG 2T)   WALES 10 (1G 1PG)

With a Championship to be won, the sun was bright in the sky and the weakest of the home countries in opposition. Spring is not the time to be slaughtering lambs but certainly there was every prospect of blood being spilled at the Parc. In the end France did take the title – their seventh in the last 13 years, albeit three of them shared – but there were to be no killing fields. Wales defended stubbornly, with Gibbs in midfield smashing men to the ground throughout. Given the result in Dublin, France had no need either to rely on points difference to settle the issue. This was the first Five Nations tournament in which such a method would have been used to decide the champions.

It was not victory in the grand style for France in this their 12th win in succession over Wales. There were only occasional flashes of the famed flamboyance. In the post-Blanco era, tries are crafted rather than magicked from nowhere. All season the most significant trait of the French team had been one of solidity, the pack providing a platform and the backs defending resolutely. Here the outstanding player was a forward, Benetton, who thundered about the field to great effect. Two tries, one in each half, were a fitting reward for him. The Agen flanker also played a crucial part in the other French try, supplying the final pass to Lafond.

Wales made six changes for this match. There was no Robert Jones or Mike Hall. The expatriate Midlander Rupert Moon won his first cap, at scrum-half, as did the hooker, Lamerton. Both thrived on the hurly-burly of the afternoon.

France had far more of the ball, due largely to the productivity of Roumat in the line-out, and led 16-3 at the interval. Walker's riposte for Wales was not scored in the manner of an Olympic hurdler: rather than sweeping majestically in from afar, he scuffed his way over in the corner.

It was not enough, however – the cockerels were already crowing over Paris.

FRANCE: J-B Lafond (Bègles); P Saint-André (Montferrand), P Sella (Agen), T Lacroix (Dax), P Hontas (Biarritz); F Mesnel (Racing Club de France), A Hueber (Toulon); L Armary (Lourdes), J-F Tordo (Nice) (*capt*), L Seigne (Merignac), A Benazzi (Agen), O Roumat (Dax), P Benetton (Agen), M Cecillon (Bourgoin), L Cabannes (Racing Club de France)
Scorers *Tries:* Benetton (2), Lafond   *Conversion:* Lafond   *Penalty Goals:* Lacroix (3)
WALES: A Clement (Swansea); I C Evans (Llanelli) (*capt*), N Davies (Llanelli), I S Gibbs (Swansea), N Walker (Cardiff); N R Jenkins (Pontypridd), R H StJ B Moon (Llanelli); R L Evans (Llanelli), A Lamerton (Llanelli), H Williams-Jones (South Wales Police), G O Llewellyn (Neath), P Davies (Llanelli), M A Perego (Llanelli), E W Lewis (Llanelli), R E Webster (Swansea) *Replacements* J D Davies (Neath) for R Evans; P Arnold (Swansea) for Perego
Scorers *Try:* Walker   *Conversion:* Jenkins   *Penalty Goal:* Jenkins
Referee O E Doyle (Ireland)

RESULTS OF INTERNATIONAL MATCHES (up to 31 March 1993)

Cap matches only.
Years for Five Nations' matches are for the second half of the season: eg 1972 means season 1971-72. Years for matches against touring teams from the Southern Hemisphere refer to the actual year of the match.
Points-scoring was first introduced in 1886, when an International Board was formed by Scotland, Ireland and Wales. Points values varied between countries until 1890, when England agreed to join the Board, and uniform values were adopted.
WC indicates a fixture played during the Rugby World Cup.

Northern Hemisphere seasons	Try	Conversion	Penalty goal	Dropped goal	Goal from mark
1890-91	1	2	2	3	3
1891-92 to 1892-93	2	3	3	4	4
1893-94 to 1904-05	3	2	3	4	4
1905-06 to 1947-48	3	2	3	4	3
1948-49 to 1970-71	3	2	3	3	3
1971-72 to 1991-92	4	2 '	3	3	3*
1992-93 onwards	5	2	3	3	–

*The goal from mark ceased to exist when free kick clause was introduced, 1977-78.

ENGLAND v SCOTLAND
Played 110   England won 54, Scotland won 39, Drawn 17

1871 Raeburn Place (Edinburgh) **Scotland** 1G 1T to 1T
1872 The Oval (London) **England** 1G 1DG 2T to 1DG
1873 Glasgow **Drawn** no score
1874 The Oval **England** 1DG to 1T
1875 Raeburn Place **Drawn** no score
1876 The Oval **England** 1G 1T to 0
1877 Raeburn Place **Scotland** 1 DG to 0
1878 The Oval **Drawn** no score
1879 Raeburn Place **Drawn** Scotland 1DG England 1G
1880 Manchester **England** 2G 3T to 1G
1881 Raeburn Place **Drawn** Scotland 1G 1T England 1DG 1T
1882 Manchester **Scotland** 2T to 0
1883 Raeburn Place **England** 2T to 1T
1884 Blackheath (London) **England** 1G to 1T
1885 No Match
1886 Raeburn Place **Drawn** no score
1887 Manchester **Drawn** 1T each
1888 No Match
1889 No Match
1890 Raeburn Place **England** 1G 1T to 0
1891 Richmond (London) **Scotland** 9-3
1892 Raeburn Place **England** 5-0
1893 Leeds **Scotland** 8-0
1894 Raeburn Place **Scotland** 6-0
1895 Richmond **Scotland** 6-3
1896 Glasgow **Scotland** 11-0

1897 Manchester **England** 12-3
1898 Powderhall (Edinburgh) **Drawn** 3-3
1899 Blackheath **Scotland** 5-0
1900 Inverleith (Edinburgh) **Drawn** 0-0
1901 Blackheath **Scotland** 18-3
1902 Inverleith **England** 6-3
1903 Richmond **Scotland** 10-6
1904 Inverleith **Scotland** 6-3
1905 Richmond **Scotland** 8-0·
1906 Inverleith **England** 9-3
1907 Blackheath **Scotland** 8-3
1908 Inverleith **Scotland** 16-10
1909 Richmond **Scotland** 18-8
1910 Inverleith **England** 14-5
1911 Twickenham **England** 13-8
1912 Inverleith **Scotland** 8-3
1913 Twickenham **England** 3-0
1914 Inverleith **England** 16-15
1920 Twickenham **England** 13-4
1921 Inverleith **England** 18-0
1922 Twickenham **England** 11-5
1923 Inverleith **England** 8-6
1924 Twickenham **England** 19-0
1925 Murrayfield **Scotland** 14-11
1926 Twickenham **Scotland** 17-9
1927 Murrayfield **Scotland** 21-13
1928 Twickenham **England** 6-0
1929 Murrayfield **Scotland** 12-6
1930 Twickenham **Drawn** 0-0
1931 Murrayfield **Scotland** 28-19
1932 Twickenham **England** 16-3

1933 Murrayfield **Scotland** 3-0
1934 Twickenham **England** 6-3
1935 Murrayfield **Scotland** 10-7
1936 Twickenham **England** 9-8
1937 Murrayfield **England** 6-3
1938 Twickenham **Scotland** 21-16
1939 Murrayfield **England** 9-6
1947 Twickenham **England** 24-5
1948 Murrayfield **Scotland** 6-3
1949 Twickenham **England** 19-3
1950 Murrayfield **Scotland** 13-11
1951 Twickenham **England** 5-3
1952 Murrayfield **England** 19-3
1953 Twickenham **England** 26-8
1954 Murrayfield **England** 13-3
1955 Twickenham **England** 9-6
1956 Murrayfield **England** 11-6
1957 Twickenham **England** 16-3
1958 Murrayfield **Drawn** 3-3
1959 Twickenham **Drawn** 3-3
1960 Murrayfield **England** 21-12
1961 Twickenham **England** 6-0
1962 Murrayfield **Drawn** 3-3
1963 Twickenham **England** 10-8
1964 Murrayfield **Scotland** 15-6
1965 Twickenham **Drawn** 3-3
1966 Murrayfield **Scotland** 6-3
1967 Twickenham **England** 27-14
1968 Murrayfield **England** 8-6

1969 Twickenham **England** 8-3
1970 Murrayfield **Scotland** 14-5
1971 Twickenham **Scotland** 16-15
1971 Murrayfield **Scotland** 26-6
Special Centenary match – non-championship
1972 Murrayfield **Scotland** 23-9
1973 Twickenham **England** 20-13
1974 Murrayfield **Scotland** 16-14
1975 Twickenham **England** 7-6
1976 Murrayfield **Scotland** 22-12
1977 Twickenham **England** 26-6
1978 Murrayfield **England** 15-0
1979 Twickenham **Drawn** 7-7
1980 Murrayfield **England** 30-18
1981 Twickenham **England** 23-17
1982 Murrayfield **Drawn** 9-9
1983 Twickenham **Scotland** 22-12
1984 Murrayfield **Scotland** 18-6
1985 Twickenham **England** 10-7
1986 Murrayfield **Scotland** 33-6
1987 Twickenham **England** 21-12
1988 Murrayfield **England** 9-6
1989 Twickenham **Drawn** 12-12
1990 Murrayfield **Scotland** 13-7
1991 Twickenham **England** 21-12
1991 Murrayfield *WC* **England** 9-6
1992 Murrayfield **England** 25-7
1993 Twickenham **England** 26-12

ENGLAND v IRELAND
Played 106   England won 61, Ireland won 37, Drawn 8

1875 The Oval (London) **England** 1G
    1DG 1T to 0
1876 Dublin **England** 1G 1T to 0
1877 The Oval **England** 2G 2T to 0
1878 Dublin **England** 2G 1T to 0
1879 The Oval **England** 2G 1DG 2T to 0
1880 Dublin **England** 1G 1T to 1T
1881 Manchester **England** 2G 2T to 0
1882 Dublin **Drawn** 2T each
1883 Manchester **England** 1G 3T to 1T
1884 Dublin **England** 1G to 0
1885 Manchester **England** 2T to 1T
1886 Dublin **England** 1T to 0
1887 Dublin **Ireland** 2G to 0
1888 No Match
1889 No Match
1890 Blackheath (London) **England** 3T
    to 0
1891 Dublin **England** 9-0
1892 Manchester **England** 7-0
1893 Dublin **England** 4-0
1894 Blackheath **Ireland** 7-5
1895 Dublin **England** 6-3
1896 Leeds **Ireland** 10-4
1897 Dublin **Ireland** 13-9
1898 Richmond (London) **Ireland** 9-6
1899 Dublin **Ireland** 6-0
1900 Richmond **England** 15-4
1901 Dublin **Ireland** 10-6

1902 Leicester **England** 6-3
1903 Dublin **Ireland** 6-0
1904 Blackheath **England** 19-0
1905 Cork **Ireland** 17-3
1906 Leicester **Ireland** 16-6
1907 Dublin **Ireland** 17-9
1908 Richmond **England** 13-3
1909 Dublin **England** 11-5
1910 Twickenham **Drawn** 0-0
1911 Dublin **Ireland** 3-0
1912 Twickenham **England** 15-0
1913 Dublin **England** 15-4
1914 Twickenham **England** 17-12
1920 Dublin **England** 14-11
1921 Twickenham **England** 15-0
1922 Dublin **England** 12-3
1923 Leicester **England** 23-5
1924 Belfast **England** 14-3
1925 Twickenham **Drawn** 6-6
1926 Dublin **Ireland** 19-15
1927 Twickenham **England** 8-6
1928 Dublin **England** 7-6
1929 Twickenham **Ireland** 6-5
1930 Dublin **Ireland** 4-3
1931 Twickenham **Ireland** 6-5
1932 Dublin **England** 11-8
1933 Twickenham **England** 17-6
1934 Dublin **England** 13-3
1935 Twickenham **England** 14-3

Scrum-half and captain Michael Bradley gets the ball away as Ireland end their 1993 International Championship on a high note against England with a thrilling 17-3 victory in Dublin. It was Ireland's first win against the English since 1987.

1936 Dublin **Ireland** 6-3
1937 Twickenham **England** 9-8
1938 Dublin **England** 36-14
1939 Twickenham **Ireland** 5-0
1947 Dublin **Ireland** 22-0
1948 Twickenham **Ireland** 11-10
1949 Dublin **Ireland** 14-5
1950 Twickenham **England** 3-0
1951 Dublin **Ireland** 3-0
1952 Twickenham **England** 3-0
1953 Dublin **Drawn** 9-9
1954 Twickenham **England** 14-3
1955 Dublin **Drawn** 6-6
1956 Twickenham **England** 20-0
1957 Dublin **England** 6-0
1958 Twickenham **England** 6-0
1959 Dublin **England** 3-0
1960 Twickenham **England** 8-5
1961 Dublin **Ireland** 11-8
1962 Twickenham **England** 16-0
1963 Dublin **Drawn** 0-0
1964 Twickenham **Ireland** 18-5
1965 Dublin **Ireland** 5-0
1966 Twickenham **Drawn** 6-6
1967 Dublin **England** 8-3
1968 Twickenham **Drawn** 9-9
1969 Dublin **Ireland** 17-15

1970 Twickenham **England** 9-3
1971 Dublin **England** 9-6
1972 Twickenham **Ireland** 16-12
1973 Dublin **Ireland** 18-9
1974 Twickenham **Ireland** 26-21
1975 Dublin **Ireland** 12-9
1976 Twickenham **Ireland** 13-12
1977 Dublin **England** 4-0
1978 Twickenham **England** 15-9
1979 Dublin **Ireland** 12-7
1980 Twickenham **England** 24-9
1981 Dublin **England** 10-6
1982 Twickenham **Ireland** 16-15
1983 Dublin **Ireland** 25-15
1984 Twickenham **England** 12-9
1985 Dublin **Ireland** 13-10
1986 Twickenham **England** 25-20
1987 Dublin **Ireland** 17-0
1988 Twickenham **England** 35-3
1988 Dublin **England** 21-10
Non-championship match
1989 Dublin **England** 16-3
1990 Twickenham **England** 23-0
1991 Dublin **England** 16-7
1992 Twickenham **England** 38-9
1993 Dublin **Ireland** 17-3

ENGLAND v WALES
Played 99   England won 39, Wales won 48, Drawn 12

1881 Blackheath (London) **England** 7G 1DG 6T to 0
1882 No Match
1883 Swansea **England** 2G 4T to 0
1884 Leeds **England** 1G 2T to 1G
1885 Swansea **England** 4T to 1G 1T
1886 Blackheath **England** 1GM 2T to 1G
1887 Llanelli **Drawn** no score
1888 No Match
1889 No Match
1890 Dewsbury **Wales** 1T to 0
1891 Newport **England** 7-3
1892 Blackheath **England** 17-0
1893 Cardiff **Wales** 12-11
1894 Birkenhead **England** 24-3
1895 Swansea **England** 14-6
1896 Blackheath **England** 25-0
1897 Newport **Wales** 11-0
1898 Blackheath **England** 14-7
1899 Swansea **Wales** 26-3
1900 Gloucester **Wales** 13-3
1901 Cardiff **Wales** 13-0
1902 Blackheath **Wales** 9-8
1903 Swansea **Wales** 21-5
1904 Leicester **Drawn** 14-14
1905 Cardiff **Wales** 25-0
1906 Richmond (London) **Wales** 16-3
1907 Swansea **Wales** 22-0
1908 Bristol **Wales** 28-18
1909 Cardiff **Wales** 8-0
1910 Twickenham **England** 11-6

1911 Swansea **Wales** 15-11
1912 Twickenham **England** 8-0
1913 Cardiff **England** 12-0
1914 Twickenham **England** 10-9
1920 Swansea **Wales** 19-5
1921 Twickenham **England** 18-3
1922 Cardiff **Wales** 28-6
1923 Twickenham **England** 7-3
1924 Swansea **England** 17-9
1925 Twickenham **England** 12-6
1926 Cardiff **Drawn** 3-3
1927 Twickenham **England** 11-9
1928 Swansea **England** 10-8
1929 Twickenham **England** 8-3
1930 Cardiff **England** 11-3
1931 Twickenham **Drawn** 11-11
1932 Swansea **Wales** 12-5
1933 Twickenham **Wales** 7-3
1934 Cardiff **England** 9-0
1935 Twickenham **Drawn** 3-3
1936 Swansea **Drawn** 0-0
1937 Twickenham **England** 4-3
1938 Cardiff **Wales** 14-8
1939 Twickenham **England** 3-0
1947 Cardiff **England** 9-6
1948 Twickenham **Drawn** 3-3
1949 Cardiff **Wales** 9-3
1950 Twickenham **Wales** 11-5
1951 Swansea **Wales** 23-5
1952 Twickenham **Wales** 8-6
1953 Cardiff **England** 8-3

1954 Twickenham **England** 9-6
1955 Cardiff **Wales** 3-0
1956 Twickenham **Wales** 8-3
1957 Cardiff **England** 3-0
1958 Twickenham **Drawn** 3-3
1959 Cardiff **Wales** 5-0
1960 Twickenham **England** 14-6
1961 Cardiff **Wales** 6-3
1962 Twickenham **Drawn** 0-0
1963 Cardiff **England** 13-6
1964 Twickenham **Drawn** 6-6
1965 Cardiff **Wales** 14-3
1966 Twickenham **Wales** 11-6
1967 Cardiff **Wales** 34-21
1968 Twickenham **Drawn** 11-11
1969 Cardiff **Wales** 30-9
1970 Twickenham **Wales** 17-13
1971 Cardiff **Wales** 22-6
1972 Twickenham **Wales** 12-3
1973 Cardiff **Wales** 25-9
1974 Twickenham **England** 16-12

1975 Cardiff **Wales** 20-4
1976 Twickenham **Wales** 21-9
1977 Cardiff **Wales** 14-9
1978 Twickenham **Wales** 9-6
1979 Cardiff **Wales** 27-3
1980 Twickenham **England** 9-8
1981 Cardiff **Wales** 21-19
1982 Twickenham **England** 17-7
1983 Cardiff **Drawn** 13-13
1984 Twickenham **Wales** 24-15
1985 Cardiff **Wales** 24-15
1986 Twickenham **England** 21-18
1987 Cardiff **Wales** 19-12
1987 Brisbane *WC* **Wales** 16-3
1988 Twickenham **Wales** 11-3
1989 Cardiff **Wales** 12-9
1990 Twickenham **England** 34-6
1991 Cardiff **England** 25-6
1992 Twickenham **England** 24-0
1993 Cardiff **Wales** 10-9

ENGLAND v FRANCE

Played 69   England won 38, France won 24, Drawn 7

1906 Paris **England** 35-8
1907 Richmond (London) **England** 41-13
1908 Paris **England** 19-0
1909 Leicester **England** 22-0
1910 Paris **England** 11-3
1911 Twickenham **England** 37-0
1912 Paris **England** 18-8
1913 Twickenham **England** 20-0
1914 Paris **England** 39-13
1920 Twickenham **England** 8-3
1921 Paris **England** 10-6
1922 Twickenham **Drawn** 11-11
1923 Paris **England** 12-3
1924 Twickenham **England** 19-7
1925 Paris **England** 13-11
1926 Twickenham **England** 11-0
1927 Paris **France** 3-0
1928 Twickenham **England** 18-8
1929 Paris **England** 16-6
1930 Twickenham **England** 11-5
1931 Paris **France** 14-13
1947 Twickenham **England** 6-3
1948 Paris **France** 15-0
1949 Twickenham **England** 8-3
1950 Paris **France** 6-3
1951 Twickenham **France** 11-3
1952 Paris **England** 6-3
1953 Twickenham **England** 11-0
1954 Paris **France** 11-3
1955 Twickenham **France** 16-9
1956 Paris **France** 14-9
1957 Twickenham **England** 9-5
1958 Paris **England** 14-0
1959 Twickenham **Drawn** 3-3
1960 Paris **Drawn** 3-3

1961 Twickenham **Drawn** 5-5
1962 Paris **France** 13-0
1963 Twickenham **England** 6-5
1964 Paris **England** 6-3
1965 Twickenham **England** 9-6
1966 Paris **France** 13-0
1967 Twickenham **France** 16-12
1968 Paris **France** 14-9
1969 Twickenham **England** 22-8
1970 Paris **France** 35-13
1971 Twickenham **Drawn** 14-14
1972 Paris **France** 37-12
1973 Twickenham **England** 14-6
1974 Paris **Drawn** 12-12
1975 Twickenham **France** 27-20
1976 Paris **France** 30-9
1977 Twickenham **France** 4-3
1978 Paris **France** 15-6
1979 Twickenham **England** 7-6
1980 Paris **England** 17-13
1981 Twickenham **France** 16-12
1982 Paris **England** 27-15
1983 Twickenham **France** 19-15
1984 Paris **France** 32-18
1985 Twickenham **Drawn** 9-9
1986 Paris **France** 29-10
1987 Twickenham **France** 19-15
1988 Paris **France** 10-9
1989 Twickenham **England** 11-0
1990 Paris **England** 26-7
1991 Twickenham **England** 21-19
1991 Paris *WC* **England** 19-10
1992 Paris **England** 31-13
1993 Twickenham **England** 16-15

ENGLAND v NEW ZEALAND
Played 16   England won 3, New Zealand won 13, Drawn 0

1905 Crystal Palace (London) **New Zealand** 15-0	1973 Twickenham **New Zealand** 9-0
1925 Twickenham **New Zealand** 17-11	1973 Auckland **England** 16-10
1936 Twickenham **England** 13-0	1978 Twickenham **New Zealand** 16-6
1954 Twickenham **New Zealand** 5-0	1979 Twickenham **New Zealand** 10-9
1963 *1* Auckland **New Zealand** 21-11	1983 Twickenham **England** 15-9
2 Christchurch **New Zealand** 9- 6	1985 *1* Christchurch **New Zealand** 18-13
New Zealand won series 2-0	2 Wellington **New Zealand** 42-15
1964 Twickenham **New Zealand** 14-0	*New Zealand won series 2-0*
1967 Twickenham **New Zealand** 23-11	1991 Twickenham *WC* **New Zealand** 18-12

ENGLAND v SOUTH AFRICA
Played 10   England won 3, South Africa won 6, Drawn 1

1906 Crystal Palace (London) **Drawn** 3-3	1972 Johannesburg **England** 18-9
1913 Twickenham **South Africa** 9-3	1984 *1* Port Elizabeth **South Africa** 33-15
1932 Twickenham **South Africa** 7-0	2 Johannesburg **South Africa** 35-9
1952 Twickenham **South Africa** 8-3	*South Africa won series 2-0*
1961 Twickenham **South Africa** 5-0	1992 Twickenham **England** 33-16
1969 Twickenham **England** 11-8	

ENGLAND v AUSTRALIA
Played 18   England won 6, Australia won 12, Drawn 0

1909 Blackheath (London) **Australia** 9-3	1976 Twickenham **England** 23-6
1928 Twickenham **England** 18-11	1982 Twickenham **England** 15-11
1948 Twickenham **Australia** 11-0	1984 Twickenham **Australia** 19-3
1958 Twickenham **England** 9-6	1987 Sydney *WC* **Australia** 19-6
1963 Sydney **Australia** 18-9	1988 *1* Brisbane **Australia** 22-16
1967 Twickenham **Australia** 23-11	2 Sydney **Australia** 28-8
1973 Twickenham **England** 20-3	*Australia won series 2-0*
1975 *1* Sydney **Australia** 16-9	1988 Twickenham **England** 28-19
2 Brisbane **Australia** 30-21	1991 Sydney **Australia** 40-15
Australia won series 2-0	1991 Twickenham *WC* **Australia** 12-6

ENGLAND v NEW ZEALAND NATIVES
Played 1   England won 1

1889 Blackheath **England** 1G 4T to 0

ENGLAND v RFU PRESIDENT'S XV
Played 1   President's XV won 1

1971 Twickenham **President's XV** 28-11

ENGLAND v ARGENTINA
Played 5   England won 3, Argentina won 1, Drawn 1

1981 *1* Buenos Aires **Drawn** 19-19	1990 *1* Buenos Aires **England** 25-12
2 Buenos Aires **England** 12-6	2 Buenos Aires **Argentina** 15-13
England won series 1-0 with 1 draw	*Series drawn 1-1*
	1990 Twickenham **England** 51-0

ENGLAND v ROMANIA
Played 2   England won 2

1985 Twickenham **England** 22-15	1989 Bucharest **England** 58-3

ENGLAND v JAPAN
Played 1 England won 1
1987 Sydney *WC* **England** 60-7

ENGLAND v UNITED STATES
Played 2 England won 2
1987 Sydney *WC* **England** 34-6   1991 Twickenham *WC* **England** 37-9

ENGLAND v FIJI
Played 3 England won 3
1988 Suva **England** 25-12   1991 Suva **England** 28-12
1989 Twickenham **England** 58-23

ENGLAND v ITALY
Played 1 England won 1
1991 Twickenham *WC* **England** 36-6

ENGLAND v CANADA
Played 1 England won 1
1992 Wembley **England** 26-13

SCOTLAND v IRELAND
Played 105 Scotland won 55, Ireland won 45, Drawn 4, Abandoned 1

1877 Belfast **Scotland** 4G 2DG 2T to 0	1903 Inverleith **Scotland** 3-0
1878 No Match	1904 Dublin **Scotland** 19-3
1879 Belfast **Scotland** 1G 1DG 1T to 0	1905 Inverleith **Ireland** 11-5
1880 Glasgow **Scotland** 1G 2DG 2T to 0	1906 Dublin **Scotland** 13-6
1881 Belfast **Ireland** 1DG to 1T	1907 Inverleith **Scotland** 15-3
1882 Glasgow **Scotland** 2T to 0	1908 Dublin **Ireland** 16-11
1883 Belfast **Scotland** 1G 1T to 0	1909 Inverleith **Scotland** 9-3
1884 Raeburn Place (Edinburgh) **Scotland** 2G 2T to 1T	1910 Belfast **Scotland** 14-0
1885 Belfast **Abandoned** Ireland 0 Scotland 1T	1911 Inverleith **Ireland** 16-10
	1912 Dublin **Ireland** 10-8
1885 Raeburn Place **Scotland** 1G 2T to 0	1913 Inverleith **Scotland** 29-14
1886 Raeburn Place **Scotland** 3G 1DG 2T to 0	1914 Dublin **Ireland** 6-0
	1920 Inverleith **Scotland** 19-0
1887 Belfast **Scotland** 1G 1GM 2T to 0	1921 Dublin **Ireland** 9-8
1888 Raeburn Place **Scotland** 1G to 0	1922 Inverleith **Scotland** 6-3
1889 Belfast **Scotland** 1DG to 0	1923 Dublin **Scotland** 13-3
1890 Raeburn Place **Scotland** 1DG 1T to 0	1924 Inverleith **Scotland** 13-8
1891 Belfast **Scotland** 14-0	1925 Dublin **Scotland** 14-8
1892 Raeburn Place **Scotland** 2-0	1926 Murrayfield **Ireland** 3-0
1893 Belfast **Drawn** 0-0	1927 Dublin **Ireland** 6-0
1894 Dublin **Ireland** 5-0	1928 Murrayfield **Ireland** 13-5
1895 Raeburn Place **Scotland** 6-0	1929 Dublin **Scotland** 16-7
1896 Dublin **Drawn** 0-0	1930 Murrayfield **Ireland** 14-11
1897 Powderhall (Edinburgh) **Scotland** 8-3	1931 Dublin **Ireland** 8-5
	1932 Murrayfield **Ireland** 20-8
1898 Belfast **Scotland** 8-0	1933 Dublin **Scotland** 8-6
1899 Inverleith (Edinburgh) **Ireland** 9-3	1934 Murrayfield **Scotland** 16-9
1900 Dublin **Drawn** 0-0	1935 Dublin **Ireland** 12-5
1901 Inverleith **Scotland** 9-5	1936 Murrayfield **Ireland** 10-4
1902 Belfast **Ireland** 5-0	1937 Dublin **Ireland** 11-4
	1938 Murrayfield **Scotland** 23-14

1939 Dublin **Ireland** 12-3
1947 Murrayfield **Ireland** 3-0
1948 Dublin **Ireland** 6-0
1949 Murrayfield **Ireland** 13-3
1950 Dublin **Ireland** 21-0
1951 Murrayfield **Ireland** 6-5
1952 Dublin **Ireland** 12-8
1953 Murrayfield **Ireland** 26-8
1954 Belfast **Ireland** 6-0
1955 Murrayfield **Scotland** 12-3
1956 Dublin **Ireland** 14-10
1957 Murrayfield **Ireland** 5-3
1958 Dublin **Ireland** 12-6
1959 Murrayfield **Ireland** 8-3
1960 Dublin **Scotland** 6-5
1961 Murrayfield **Scotland** 16-8
1962 Dublin **Scotland** 20-6
1963 Murrayfield **Scotland** 3-0
1964 Dublin **Scotland** 6-3
1965 Murrayfield **Ireland** 16-6
1966 Dublin **Scotland** 11-3
1967 Murrayfield **Ireland** 5-3
1968 Dublin **Ireland** 14-6
1969 Murrayfield **Ireland** 16-0
1970 Dublin **Ireland** 16-11

1971 Murrayfield **Ireland** 17-5
1972 No Match
1973 Murrayfield **Scotland** 19-14
1974 Dublin **Ireland** 9-6
1975 Murrayfield **Scotland** 20-13
1976 Dublin **Scotland** 15-6
1977 Murrayfield **Scotland** 21-18
1978 Dublin **Ireland** 12-9
1979 Murrayfield **Drawn** 11-11
1980 Dublin **Ireland** 22-15
1981 Murrayfield **Scotland** 10-9
1982 Dublin **Ireland** 21-12
1983 Murrayfield **Ireland** 15-13
1984 Dublin **Scotland** 32-9
1985 Murrayfield **Ireland** 18-15
1986 Dublin **Scotland** 10-9
1987 Murrayfield **Scotland** 16-12
1988 Dublin **Ireland** 22-18
1989 Murrayfield **Scotland** 37-21
1990 Dublin **Scotland** 13-10
1991 Murrayfield **Scotland** 28-25
1991 Murrayfield *WC* **Scotland** 24-15
1992 Dublin **Scotland** 18-10
1993 Murrayfield **Scotland** 15-3

SCOTLAND v WALES
Played 97   Scotland won 42, Wales won 53, Drawn 2

1883 Raeburn Place (Edinburgh)
     Scotland (3G to 1G)
1884 Newport **Scotland** 1DG 1T to 0
1885 Glasgow **Drawn** no score
1886 Cardiff **Scotland** 2G 8T to 0
1887 Raeburn Place **Scotland** 4G 8T to 0
1888 Newport **Wales** 1T to 0
1889 Raeburn Place **Scotland** 2T to 0
1890 Cardiff **Scotland** 1G 2T to 1T
1891 Raeburn Place **Scotland** 15-0
1892 Swansea **Scotland** 7-2
1893 Raeburn Place **Wales** 9-0
1894 Newport **Wales** 7-0
1895 Raeburn Place **Scotland** 5-4
1896 Cardiff **Wales** 6-0
1897 No Match
1898 No Match
1899 Inverleith (Edinburgh) **Scotland**
     21-10
1900 Swansea **Wales** 12-3
1901 Inverleith **Scotland** 18-8
1902 Cardiff **Wales** 14-5
1903 Inverleith **Scotland** 6-0
1904 Swansea **Wales** 21-3
1905 Inverleith **Wales** 6-3
1906 Cardiff **Wales** 9-3
1907 Inverleith **Scotland** 6-3
1908 Swansea **Wales** 6-5
1909 Inverleith **Wales** 5-3
1910 Cardiff **Wales** 14-0
1911 Inverleith **Wales** 32-10
1912 Swansea **Wales** 21-6
1913 Inverleith **Wales** 8-0

1914 Cardiff **Wales** 24-5
1920 Inverleith **Scotland** 9-5
1921 Swansea **Scotland** 14-8
1922 Inverleith **Drawn** 9-9
1923 Cardiff **Scotland** 11-8
1924 Inverleith **Scotland** 35-10
1925 Swansea **Scotland** 24-14
1926 Murrayfield **Scotland** 8-5
1927 Cardiff **Scotland** 5-0
1928 Murrayfield **Wales** 13-0
1929 Swansea **Wales** 14-7
1930 Murrayfield **Scotland** 12-9
1931 Cardiff **Wales** 13-8
1932 Murrayfield **Wales** 6-0
1933 Swansea **Scotland** 11-3
1934 Murrayfield **Wales** 13-6
1935 Cardiff **Wales** 10-6
1936 Murrayfield **Wales** 13-3
1937 Swansea **Scotland** 13-6
1938 Murrayfield **Scotland** 8-6
1939 Cardiff **Wales** 11-3
1947 Murrayfield **Wales** 22-8
1948 Cardiff **Wales** 14-0
1949 Murrayfield **Scotland** 6-5
1950 Swansea **Wales** 12-0
1951 Murrayfield **Scotland** 19-0
1952 Cardiff **Wales** 11-0
1953 Murrayfield **Wales** 12-0
1954 Swansea **Wales** 15-3
1955 Murrayfield **Scotland** 14-8
1956 Cardiff **Wales** 9-3
1957 Murrayfield **Scotland** 9-6
1958 Cardiff **Wales** 8-3

1959 Murrayfield **Scotland** 6-5
1960 Cardiff **Wales** 8-0
1961 Murrayfield **Scotland** 3-0
1962 Cardiff **Scotland** 8-3
1963 Murrayfield **Wales** 6-0
1964 Cardiff **Wales** 11-3
1965 Murrayfield **Wales** 14-12
1966 Cardiff **Wales** 8-3
1967 Murrayfield **Scotland** 11-5
1968 Cardiff **Wales** 5-0
1969 Murrayfield **Wales** 17-3
1970 Cardiff **Wales** 18-9
1971 Murrayfield **Wales** 19-18
1972 Cardiff **Wales** 35-12
1973 Murrayfield **Scotland** 10-9
1974 Cardiff **Wales** 6-0
1975 Murrayfield **Scotland** 12-10
1976 Cardiff **Wales** 28-6

1977 Murrayfield **Wales** 18-9
1978 Cardiff **Wales** 22-14
1979 Murrayfield **Wales** 19-13
1980 Cardiff **Wales** 17-6
1981 Murrayfield **Scotland** 15-6
1982 Cardiff **Scotland** 34-18
1983 Murrayfield **Wales** 19-15
1984 Cardiff **Scotland** 15-9
1985 Murrayfield **Wales** 25-21
1986 Cardiff **Wales** 22-15
1987 Murrayfield **Scotland** 21-15
1988 Cardiff **Wales** 25-20
1989 Murrayfield **Scotland** 23-7
1990 Cardiff **Scotland** 13-9
1991 Murrayfield **Scotland** 32-12
1992 Cardiff **Wales** 15-12
1993 Murrayfield **Scotland** 20-0

SCOTLAND v FRANCE
Played 64   Scotland won 30, France won 31, Drawn 3

1910 Inverleith (Edinburgh)
      Scotland 27-0
1911 Paris **France** 16-15
1912 Inverleith **Scotland** 31-3
1913 Paris **Scotland** 21-3
1914 No Match
1920 Paris **Scotland** 5-0
1921 Inverleith **France** 3-0
1922 Paris **Drawn** 3-3
1923 Inverleith **Scotland** 16-3
1924 Paris **France** 12-10
1925 Inverleith **Scotland** 25-4
1926 Paris **Scotland** 20-6
1927 Murrayfield **Scotland** 23-6
1928 Paris **Scotland** 15-6
1929 Murrayfield **Scotland** 6-3
1930 Paris **France** 7-3
1931 Murrayfield **Scotland** 6-4
1947 Paris **France** 8-3
1948 Murrayfield **Scotland** 9-8
1949 Paris **Scotland** 8-0
1950 Murrayfield **Scotland** 8-5
1951 Paris **France** 14-12
1952 Murrayfield **France** 13-11
1953 Paris **France** 11-5
1954 Murrayfield **France** 3-0
1955 Paris **France** 15-0
1956 Murrayfield **Scotland** 12-0
1957 Paris **Scotland** 6-0
1958 Murrayfield **Scotland** 11-9
1959 Paris **France** 9-0
1960 Murrayfield **France** 13-11
1961 Paris **France** 11-0

1962 Murrayfield **France** 11-3
1963 Paris **Scotland** 11-6
1964 Murrayfield **Scotland** 10-0
1965 Paris **France** 16-8
1966 Murrayfield **Drawn** 3-3
1967 Paris **Scotland** 9-8
1968 Murrayfield **France** 8-6
1969 Paris **Scotland** 6-3
1970 Murrayfield **France** 11-9
1971 Paris **France** 13-8
1972 Murrayfield **Scotland** 20-9
1973 Paris **France** 16-13
1974 Murrayfield **Scotland** 19-6
1975 Paris **France** 10-9
1976 Murrayfield **France** 13-6
1977 Paris **France** 23-3
1978 Murrayfield **France** 19-16
1979 Paris **France** 21-17
1980 Murrayfield **Scotland** 22-14
1981 Paris **France** 16-9
1982 Murrayfield **Scotland** 16-7
1983 Paris **France** 19-15
1984 Murrayfield **Scotland** 21-12
1985 Paris **France** 11-3
1986 Murrayfield **Scotland** 18-17
1987 Paris **France** 28-22
1987 Christchurch *WC* **Drawn** 20-20
1988 Murrayfield **Scotland** 23-12
1989 Paris **France** 19-3
1990 Murrayfield **Scotland** 21-0
1991 Paris **France** 15-9
1992 Murrayfield **Scotland** 10-6
1993 Paris **France** 11-3

SCOTLAND v NEW ZEALAND
Played 16   Scotland won 0, New Zealand won 14, Drawn 2

1905 Inverleith (Edinburgh)
      New Zealand 12-7

1935 Murrayfield **New Zealand** 18-8
1954 Murrayfield **New Zealand** 3-0

1964 Murrayfield **Drawn** 0-0
1967 Murrayfield **New Zealand** 14-3
1972 Murrayfield **New Zealand** 14-9
1975 Auckland **New Zealand** 24-0
1978 Murrayfield **New Zealand** 18-9
1979 Murrayfield **New Zealand** 20-6
1981 *1* Dunedin **New Zealand** 11-4
    2 Auckland **New Zealand** 40-15
    New Zealand won series 2-0

1983 Murrayfield **Drawn** 25-25
1987 Christchurch *WC* **New Zealand** 30-3
1990 *1* Dunedin **New Zealand** 31-16
    2 Auckland **New Zealand** 21-18
    New Zealand won series 2-0
1991 Cardiff *WC* **New Zealand** 13-6

SCOTLAND v SOUTH AFRICA
Played 8　Scotland won 3, South Africa won 5, Drawn 0

1906 Glasgow **Scotland** 6-0
1912 Inverleith **South Africa** 16-0
1932 Murrayfield **South Africa** 6-3
1951 Murrayfield **South Africa** 44-0

1960 Port Elizabeth **South Africa** 18-10
1961 Murrayfield **South Africa** 12-5
1965 Murrayfield **Scotland** 8-5
1969 Murrayfield **Scotland** 6-3

SCOTLAND v AUSTRALIA
Played 14　Scotland won 7, Australia won 7, Drawn 0

1927 Murrayfield **Scotland** 10-8
1947 Murrayfield **Australia** 16-7
1958 Murrayfield **Scotland** 12-8
1966 Murrayfield **Scotland** 11-5
1968 Murrayfield **Scotland** 9-3
1970 Sydney **Australia** 23-3
1975 Murrayfield **Scotland** 10-3
1981 Murrayfield **Scotland** 24-15

1982 *1* Brisbane **Scotland** 12-7
    2 Sydney **Australia** 33-9
    Series drawn 1-1
1984 Murrayfield **Australia** 37-12
1988 Murrayfield **Australia** 32-13
1992 *1* Sydney **Australia** 27-12
    2 Brisbane **Australia** 37-13
    Australia won series 2-0

SCOTLAND v SRU PRESIDENT'S XV
Played 1　Scotland won 1

1973 Murrayfield **Scotland** 27-16

SCOTLAND v ROMANIA
Played 6　Scotland won 4, Romania won 2

1981 Murrayfield **Scotland** 12-6
1984 Bucharest **Romania** 28-22
1986 Bucharest **Scotland** 33-18

1987 Dunedin *WC* **Scotland** 55-28
1989 Murrayfield **Scotland** 32-0
1991 Bucharest **Romania** 18-12

SCOTLAND v ZIMBABWE
Played 2　Scotland won 2

1987 Wellington *WC* **Scotland** 60-21

1991 Murrayfield *WC* **Scotland** 51-12

SCOTLAND v FIJI
Played 1　Scotland won 1

1989 Murrayfield **Scotland** 38-17

SCOTLAND v ARGENTINA
Played 1　Scotland won 1

1990 Murrayfield **Scotland** 49-3

SCOTLAND v JAPAN
Played 1　Scotland won 1

1991 Murrayfield *WC* **Scotland** 47-9

SCOTLAND v WESTERN SAMOA
Played 1   Scotland won 1

1991 Murrayfield *WC* **Scotland** 28-6

IRELAND v WALES
Played 96   Ireland won 33, Wales won 57, Drawn 6

1882 Dublin **Wales** 2G 2T to 0	1938 Swansea **Wales** 11-5
1883 No Match	1939 Belfast **Wales** 7-0
1884 Cardiff **Wales** 1DG 2T to 0	1947 Swansea **Wales** 6-0
1885 No Match	1948 Belfast **Ireland** 6-3
1886 No Match	1949 Swansea **Ireland** 5-0
1887 Birkenhead **Wales** 1DG 1T to 3T	1950 Belfast **Wales** 6-3
1888 Dublin **Ireland** 1G 1DG 1T to 0	1951 Cardiff **Drawn** 3-3
1889 Swansea **Ireland** 2T to 0	1952 Dublin **Wales** 14-3
1890 Dublin **Drawn** 1G each	1953 Swansea **Wales** 5-3
1891 Llanelli **Wales** 6-4	1954 Dublin **Wales** 12-9
1892 Dublin **Ireland** 9-0	1955 Cardiff **Wales** 21-3
1893 Llanelli **Wales** 2-0	1956 Dublin **Ireland** 11-3
1894 Belfast **Ireland** 3-0	1957 Cardiff **Wales** 6-5
1895 Cardiff **Wales** 5-3	1958 Dublin **Wales** 9-6
1896 Dublin **Ireland** 8-4	1959 Cardiff **Wales** 8-6
1897 No Match	1960 Dublin **Wales** 10-9
1898 Limerick **Wales** 11-3	1961 Cardiff **Wales** 9-0
1899 Cardiff **Ireland** 3-0	1962 Dublin **Drawn** 3-3
1900 Belfast **Wales** 3-0	1963 Cardiff **Ireland** 14-6
1901 Swansea **Wales** 10-9	1964 Dublin **Wales** 15-6
1902 Dublin **Wales** 15-0	1965 Cardiff **Wales** 14-8
1903 Cardiff **Wales** 18-0	1966 Dublin **Ireland** 9-6
1904 Belfast **Ireland** 14-12	1967 Cardiff **Ireland** 3-0
1905 Swansea **Wales** 10-3	1968 Dublin **Ireland** 9-6
1906 Belfast **Ireland** 11-6	1969 Cardiff **Wales** 24-11
1907 Cardiff **Wales** 29-0	1970 Dublin **Ireland** 14-0
1908 Belfast **Wales** 11-5	1971 Cardiff **Wales** 23-9
1909 Swansea **Wales** 18-5	1972 No Match
1910 Dublin **Wales** 19-3	1973 Cardiff **Wales** 16-12
1911 Cardiff **Wales** 16-0	1974 Dublin **Drawn** 9-9
1912 Belfast **Ireland** 12-5	1975 Cardiff **Wales** 32-4
1913 Swansea **Wales** 16-13	1976 Dublin **Wales** 34-9
1914 Belfast **Wales** 11-3	1977 Cardiff **Wales** 25-9
1920 Cardiff **Wales** 28-4	1978 Dublin **Wales** 20-16
1921 Belfast **Wales** 6-0	1979 Cardiff **Wales** 24-21
1922 Swansea **Wales** 11-5	1980 Dublin **Ireland** 21-7
1923 Dublin **Ireland** 5-4	1981 Cardiff **Wales** 9-8
1924 Cardiff **Ireland** 13-10	1982 Dublin **Ireland** 20-12
1925 Belfast **Ireland** 19-3	1983 Cardiff **Wales** 23-9
1926 Swansea **Wales** 11-8	1984 Dublin **Wales** 18-9
1927 Dublin **Ireland** 19-9	1985 Cardiff **Ireland** 21-9
1928 Cardiff **Ireland** 13-10	1986 Dublin **Wales** 19-12
1929 Belfast **Drawn** 5-5	1987 Cardiff **Ireland** 15-11
1930 Swansea **Wales** 12-7	1987 Wellington *WC* **Wales** 13-6
1931 Belfast **Wales** 15-3	1988 Dublin **Wales** 12-9
1932 Cardiff **Ireland** 12-10	1989 Cardiff **Ireland** 19-13
1933 Belfast **Ireland** 10-5	1990 Dublin **Ireland** 14-8
1934 Swansea **Wales** 13-0	1991 Cardiff **Drawn** 21-21
1935 Belfast **Ireland** 9-3	1992 Dublin **Wales** 16-15
1936 Cardiff **Wales** 3-0	1993 Cardiff **Ireland** 19-14
1937 Belfast **Ireland** 5-3	

IRELAND v FRANCE
Played 66   Ireland won 25, France won 36, Drawn 5

1909 Dublin **Ireland** 19-8	1963 Dublin **France** 24-5
1910 Paris **Ireland** 19-8	1964 Paris **France** 27-6
1911 Cork **Ireland** 25-5	1965 Dublin **Drawn** 3-3
1912 Paris **Ireland** 11-6	1966 Paris **France** 11-6
1913 Cork **Ireland** 24-0	1967 Dublin **France** 11-6
1914 Paris **Ireland** 8-6	1968 Paris **France** 16-6
1920 Dublin **France** 15-7	1969 Dublin **Ireland** 17-9
1921 Paris **France** 20-10	1970 Paris **France** 8-0
1922 Dublin **Ireland** 8-3	1971 Dublin **Drawn** 9-9
1923 Paris **France** 14-8	1972 Paris **Ireland** 14-9
1924 Dublin **Ireland** 6-0	1972 Dublin **Ireland** 24-14
1925 Paris **Ireland** 9-3	*Non-championship match*
1926 Belfast **Ireland** 11-0	1973 Dublin **Ireland** 6-4
1927 Paris **Ireland** 8-3	1974 Paris **France** 9-6
1928 Belfast **Ireland** 12-8	1975 Dublin **Ireland** 25-6
1929 Paris **Ireland** 6-0	1976 Paris **France** 26-3
1930 Belfast **France** 5-0	1977 Dublin **France** 15-6
1931 Paris **France** 3-0	1978 Paris **France** 10-9
1947 Dublin **France** 12-8	1979 Dublin **Drawn** 9-9
1948 Paris **Ireland** 13-6	1980 Paris **France** 19-18
1949 Dublin **France** 16-9	1981 Dublin **France** 19-13
1950 Paris **Drawn** 3-3	1982 Paris **France** 22-9
1951 Dublin **Ireland** 9-8	1983 Dublin **Ireland** 22-16
1952 Paris **Ireland** 11-8	1984 Paris **France** 25-12
1953 Belfast **Ireland** 16-3	1985 Dublin **Drawn** 15-15
1954 Paris **France** 8-0	1986 Paris **France** 29-9
1955 Dublin **France** 5-3	1987 Dublin **France** 19-13
1956 Paris **France** 14-8	1988 Paris **France** 25-6
1957 Dublin **Ireland** 11-6	1989 Dublin **France** 26-21
1958 Paris **France** 11-6	1990 Paris **France** 31-12
1959 Dublin **Ireland** 9-5	1991 Dublin **France** 21-13
1960 Paris **France** 23-6	1992 Paris **France** 44-12
1961 Dublin **France** 15-3	1993 Dublin **France** 21-6
1962 Paris **France** 11-0	

IRELAND v NEW ZEALAND
Played 12   Ireland won 0, New Zealand won 11, Drawn 1

1905 Dublin **New Zealand** 15-0	1976 Wellington **New Zealand** 11-3
1924 Dublin **New Zealand** 6-0	1978 Dublin **New Zealand** 10-6
1935 Dublin **New Zealand** 17-9	1989 Dublin **New Zealand** 23-6
1954 Dublin **New Zealand** 14-3	1992 *1* Dunedin **New Zealand** 24-21
1963 Dublin **New Zealand** 6-5	*2* Wellington **New Zealand** 59-6
1973 Dublin **Drawn** 10-10	*New Zealand won series 2-0*
1974 Dublin **New Zealand** 15-6	

IRELAND v SOUTH AFRICA
Played 10   Ireland won 1, South Africa won 8, Drawn 1

1906 Belfast **South Africa** 15-12	1965 Dublin **Ireland** 9-6
1912 Dublin **South Africa** 38-0	1970 Dublin **Drawn** 8-8
1931 Dublin **South Africa** 8-3	1981 *1* Cape Town **South Africa** 23-15
1951 Dublin **South Africa** 17-5	*2* Durban **South Africa** 12-10
1960 Dublin **South Africa** 8-3	*South Africa won series 2-0*
1961 Cape Town **South Africa** 24-8	

IRELAND v AUSTRALIA
Played 14   Ireland won 6, Australia won 8, Drawn 0

1927 Dublin **Australia** 5-3	2 Sydney **Ireland** 9-3
1947 Dublin **Australia** 16-3	*Ireland won series 2-0*
1958 Dublin **Ireland** 9-6	1981 Dublin **Australia** 16-12
1967 Dublin **Ireland** 15-8	1984 Dublin **Australia** 16-9
1967 Sydney **Ireland** 11-5	1987 Sydney *WC* **Australia** 33-15
1968 Dublin **Ireland** 10-3	1991 Dublin *WC* **Australia** 19-18
1976 Dublin **Australia** 20-10	1992 Dublin **Australia** 42-17
1979 *1* Brisbane **Ireland** 27-12	

IRELAND v NEW ZEALAND NATIVES
Played 1   New Zealand Natives won 1

1888 Dublin **New Zealand Natives**
4G 1T to 1G 1T

IRELAND v IRU PRESIDENT'S XV
Played 1   Drawn 1

1974 Dublin **Drawn** 18-18

IRELAND v ROMANIA
Played 1   Ireland won 1

1986 Dublin **Ireland** 60-0

IRELAND v CANADA
Played 1   Ireland won 1

1987 Dunedin *WC* **Ireland** 46-19

IRELAND v TONGA
Played 1   Ireland won 1

1987 Brisbane *WC* **Ireland** 32-9

IRELAND v WESTERN SAMOA
Played 1   Ireland won 1

1988 Dublin **Ireland** 49-22

IRELAND v ITALY
Played 1   Ireland won 1

1988 Dublin **Ireland** 31-15

IRELAND v ARGENTINA
Played 1   Ireland won 1

1990 Dublin **Ireland** 20-18

IRELAND v NAMIBIA
Played 2   Namibia won 2

1991 *1* Windhoek **Namibia** 15-6	2 Windhoek **Namibia** 26-15
Namibia won series 2-0	

IRELAND v ZIMBABWE
Played 1   Ireland won 1

1991 Dublin *WC* **Ireland** 55-11

IRELAND v JAPAN
Played 1   Ireland won 1

1991 Dublin *WC* **Ireland** 32-16

WALES v FRANCE
Played 67   Wales won 36, France won 28, Drawn 3

1908 Cardiff **Wales** 36-4	1962 Cardiff **Wales** 3-0
1909 Paris **Wales** 47-5	1963 Paris **France** 5-3
1910 Swansea **Wales** 49-14	1964 Cardiff **Drawn** 11-11
1911 Paris **Wales** 15-0	1965 Paris **France** 22-13
1912 Newport **Wales** 14-8	1966 Cardiff **Wales** 9-8
1913 Paris **Wales** 11-8	1967 Paris **France** 20-14
1914 Swansea **Wales** 31-0	1968 Cardiff **France** 14-9
1920 Paris **Wales** 6-5	1969 Paris **Drawn** 8-8
1921 Cardiff **Wales** 12-4	1970 Cardiff **Wales** 11-6
1922 Paris **Wales** 11-3	1971 Paris **Wales** 9-5
1923 Swansea **Wales** 16-8	1972 Cardiff **Wales** 20-6
1924 Paris **Wales** 10-6	1973 Paris **France** 12-3
1925 Cardiff **Wales** 11-5	1974 Cardiff **Drawn** 16-16
1926 Paris **Wales** 7-5	1975 Paris **Wales** 25-10
1927 Swansea **Wales** 25-7	1976 Cardiff **Wales** 19-13
1928 Paris **France** 8-3	1977 Paris **France** 16-9
1929 Cardiff **Wales** 8-3	1978 Cardiff **Wales** 16-7
1930 Paris **Wales** 11-0	1979 Paris **France** 14-13
1931 Swansea **Wales** 35-3	1980 Cardiff **Wales** 18-9
1947 Paris **Wales** 3-0	1981 Paris **France** 19-15
1948 Swansea **France** 11-3	1982 Cardiff **Wales** 22-12
1949 Paris **France** 5-3	1983 Paris **France** 16-9
1950 Cardiff **Wales** 21-0	1984 Cardiff **France** 21-16
1951 Paris **France** 8-3	1985 Paris **France** 14-3
1952 Swansea **Wales** 9-5	1986 Cardiff **France** 23-15
1953 Paris **Wales** 6-3	1987 Paris **France** 16-9
1954 Cardiff **Wales** 19-13	1988 Cardiff **France** 10-9
1955 Paris **Wales** 16-11	1989 Paris **France** 31-12
1956 Cardiff **Wales** 5-3	1990 Cardiff **France** 29-19
1957 Paris **Wales** 19-13	1991 Paris **France** 36-3
1958 Cardiff **France** 16-6	1991 Cardiff **France** 22-9
1959 Paris **France** 11-3	*Non-championship match*
1960 Cardiff **France** 16-8	1992 Cardiff **France** 12-9
1961 Paris **France** 8-6	1993 Paris **France** 26-10

WALES v NEW ZEALAND
Played 15   Wales won 3, New Zealand won 12, Drawn 0

1905 Cardiff **Wales** 3-0	1972 Cardiff **New Zealand** 19-16
1924 Swansea **New Zealand** 19-0	1978 Cardiff **New Zealand** 13-12
1935 Cardiff **Wales** 13-12	1980 Cardiff **New Zealand** 23-3
1953 Cardiff **Wales** 13-8	1987 Brisbane *WC* **New Zealand** 49-6
1963 Cardiff **New Zealand** 6-0	1988 *1* Christchurch **New Zealand** 52-3
1967 Cardiff **New Zealand** 13-6	2 Auckland **New Zealand** 54-9
1969 *1* Christchurch **New Zealand** 19-0	*New Zealand won series 2-0*
2 Auckland **New Zealand** 33-12	1989 Cardiff **New Zealand** 34-9
New Zealand won series 2-0	

WALES v SOUTH AFRICA
Played 7   Wales won 0, South Africa won 6, Drawn 1

1906 Swansea **South Africa** 11-0	1912 Cardiff **South Africa** 3-0

1931 Swansea **South Africa** 8-3
1951 Cardiff **South Africa** 6-3
1960 Cardiff **South Africa** 3-0

1964 Durban **South Africa** 24-3
1970 Cardiff **Drawn** 6-6

WALES v AUSTRALIA
Played 16   Wales won 8, Australia won 8, Drawn 0

1908 Cardiff **Wales** 9-6
1927 Cardiff **Australia** 18-8
1947 Cardiff **Wales** 6-0
1958 Cardiff **Wales** 9-3
1966 Cardiff **Australia** 14-11
1969 Sydney **Wales** 19-16
1973 Cardiff **Wales** 24-0
1975 Cardiff **Wales** 28-3
1978 *1* Brisbane **Australia** 18-8

2 Sydney **Australia** 19-17
Australia won series 2-0
1981 Cardiff **Wales** 18-13
1984 Cardiff **Australia** 28-9
1987 Rotorua *WC* **Wales** 22-21
1991 Brisbane **Australia** 63-6
1991 Cardiff *WC* **Australia** 38-3
1992 Cardiff **Australia** 23-6

WALES v NEW ZEALAND NATIVES
Played 1   Wales won 1

1888 Swansea **Wales** 1G 2T to 0

WALES v NEW ZEALAND ARMY
Played 1   New Zealand Army won 1

1919 Swansea **New Zealand Army** 6-3

WALES v ROMANIA
Played 2   Romania won 2

1983 Bucharest **Romania** 24-6

1988 Cardiff **Romania** 15-9

WALES v FIJI
Played 2   Wales won 2

1985 Cardiff **Wales** 40-3

1986 Suva **Wales** 22-15

WALES v TONGA
Played 2   Wales won 2

1986 Nuku'Alofa **Wales** 15-7

1987 Palmerston North *WC* **Wales** 29-16

WALES v WESTERN SAMOA
Played 3   Wales won 2, Western Samoa won 1

1986 Apia **Wales** 32-14
1988 Cardiff **Wales** 28-6

1991 Cardiff *WC* **Western Samoa** 16-13

WALES v CANADA
Played 1   Wales won 1

1987 Invercargill *WC* **Wales** 40-9

WALES v UNITED STATES
Played 1   Wales won 1

1987 Cardiff **Wales** 46-0

WALES v NAMIBIA
Played 2   Wales won 2

1990 *1* Windhoek **Wales** 18-9   *2* Windhoek **Wales** 34-30
Wales won series 2-0

WALES v BARBARIANS
Played 1   Barbarians won 1

1990 Cardiff **Barbarians** 31-24

WALES v ARGENTINA
Played 1   Wales won 1

1991 Cardiff *WC* **Wales** 16-7

FRANCE v NEW ZEALAND
Played 28   France won 5, New Zealand won 23, Drawn 0

1906 Paris **New Zealand** 38-8	1981 *1* Toulouse **New Zealand** 13-9
1925 Toulouse **New Zealand** 30-6	*2* Paris **New Zealand** 18-6
1954 Paris **France** 3-0	*New Zealand won series 2-0*
1961 *1* Auckland **New Zealand** 13-6	1984 *1* Christchurch **New Zealand** 10-9
2 Wellington **New Zealand** 5-3	*2* Auckland **New Zealand** 31-18
3 Christchurch **New Zealand** 32- 3	*New Zealand won series 2-0*
New Zealand won series 3-0	1986 Christchurch **New Zealand** 18-9
1964 Paris **New Zealand** 12-3	1986 *1* Toulouse **New Zealand** 19-7
1967 Paris **New Zealand** 21-15	*2* Nantes **France** 16-3
1968 *1* Christchurch **New Zealand** 12-9	*Series drawn 1-1*
2 Wellington **New Zealand** 9-3	1987 Auckland *WC* **New Zealand** 29-9
3 Auckland **New Zealand** 19-12	1989 *1* Christchurch **New Zealand** 25-17
New Zealand won series 3-0	*2* Auckland **New Zealand** 34-20
1973 Paris **France** 13-6	*New Zealand won series 2-0*
1977 *1* Toulouse **France** 18-13	1990 *1* Nantes **New Zealand** 24-3
2 Paris **New Zealand** 15-3	*2* Paris **New Zealand** 30-12
Series drawn 1-1	*New Zealand won series 2-0*
1979 *1* Christchurch **New Zealand** 23-9	
2 Auckland **France** 24-19	
Series drawn 1-1	

FRANCE v SOUTH AFRICA
Played 21   France won 4, South Africa won 13, Drawn 4

1913 Bordeaux **South Africa** 38-5	1971 *1* Bloemfontein **South Africa** 22-9
1952 Paris **South Africa** 25-3	*2* Durban **Drawn** 8-8
1958 *1* Cape Town **Drawn** 3-3	*South Africa won series 1-0, with 1 draw*
2 Johannesburg **France** 9-5	1974 *1* Toulouse **South Africa** 13-4
France won series 1-0, with 1 draw	*2* Paris **South Africa** 10-8
1961 Paris **Drawn** 0-0	*South Africa won series 2-0*
1964 Springs (SA) **France** 8-6	1975 *1* Bloemfontein **South Africa** 38-25
1967 *1* Durban **South Africa** 26-3	*2* Pretoria **South Africa** 33-18
2 Bloemfontein **South Africa** 16-3	*South Africa won series 2-0*
3 Johannesburg **France** 19-14	1980 Pretoria **South Africa** 37-15
4 Cape Town **Drawn** 6-6	1992 *1* Lyons **South Africa** 20-15
South Africa won series 2-1, with 1 draw	*2* Paris **France** 29-16
1968 *1* Bordeaux **South Africa** 12-9	*Series drawn 1-1*
2 Paris **South Africa** 16-11	
South Africa won series 2-0	

FRANCE v AUSTRALIA
Played 23   France won 12, Australia won 9, Drawn 2

1928 Paris **Australia** 11-8
1948 Paris **France** 13-6
1958 Paris **France** 19-0
1961 Sydney **France** 15-8
1967 Paris **France** 20-14
1968 Sydney **Australia** 11-10
1971 *1* Toulouse **Australia** 13-11
   2 Paris **France** 18-9
   Series drawn 1-1
1972 *1* Sydney **Drawn** 14-14
   2 Brisbane **France** 16-15
   France won series 1-0, with 1 draw
1976 *1* Bordeaux **France** 18-15
   2 Paris **France** 34-6
   France won series 2-0

1981 *1* Brisbane **Australia** 17-15
   2 Sydney **Australia** 24-14
   Australia won series 2-0
1983 *1* Clermont-Ferrand **Drawn** 15-15
   2 Paris **France** 15-6
   France won series 1-0, with 1 draw
1986 Sydney **Australia** 27-14
1987 Sydney *WC* **France** 30-24
1989 *1* Strasbourg **Australia** 32-15
   2 Lille **France** 25-19
   Series drawn 1-1
1990 *1* Sydney **Australia** 21-9
   2 Brisbane **Australia** 48-31
   3 Sydney **France** 28-19
   Australia won series 2-1

FRANCE v UNITED STATES
Played 5   France won 4, United States won 1

1920 Paris **France** 14-5
1924 Paris **United States** 17-3
1976 Chicago **France** 33-14

1991 *1* Denver **France** 41-9
   2 Colorado Springs **France** 10-3★
   ★Abandoned after 43 mins
   France won series 2-0

FRANCE v ROMANIA
Played 38 France won 28, Romania won 8, Drawn 2

1924 Paris **France** 59-3
1938 Bucharest **France** 11-8
1957 Bucharest **France** 18-15
1957 Bordeaux **France** 39-0
1960 Bucharest **Romania** 11-5
1961 Bayonne **Drawn** 5-5
1962 Bucharest **Romania** 3-0
1963 Toulouse **Drawn** 6-6
1964 Bucharest **France** 9-6
1965 Lyons **France** 8-3
1966 Bucharest **France** 9-3
1967 Nantes **France** 11-3
1968 Bucharest **Romania** 15-14
1969 Tarbes **France** 14-9
1970 Bucharest **France** 14-3
1971 Béziers **France** 31-12
1972 Constanza **France** 15-6
1973 Valence **France** 7-6
1974 Bucharest **Romania** 15-10

1975 Bordeaux **France** 36-12
1976 Bucharest **Romania** 15-12
1977 Clermont-Ferrand **France** 9-6
1978 Bucharest **France** 9-6
1979 Montauban **France** 30-12
1980 Bucharest **Romania** 15-0
1981 Narbonne **France** 17-9
1982 Bucharest **Romania** 13-9
1983 Toulouse **France** 26-15
1984 Bucharest **France** 18-3
1986 Lille **France** 25-13
1986 Bucharest **France** 20-3
1987 Wellington *WC* **France** 55-12
1987 Agen **France** 49-3
1988 Bucharest **France** 16-12
1990 Auch **Romania** 12-6
1991 Bucharest **France** 33-21
1991 Béziers *WC* **France** 30-3
1992 Le Havre **France** 25-6

FRANCE v NEW ZEALAND MAORIS
Played 1   New Zealand Maoris won 1

1926 Paris **New Zealand Maoris** 12-3

FRANCE v GERMANY
Played 15   France won 13, Germany won 2

1927 Paris **France** 30-5   1927 Frankfurt **Germany** 17-16

1928 Hanover **France** 14-3
1929 Paris **France** 24-0
1930 Berlin **France** 31-0
1931 Paris **France** 34-0
1932 Frankfurt **France** 20-4
1933 Paris **France** 38-17
1934 Hanover **France** 13-9

1935 Paris **France** 18-3
1936 *1* Berlin **France** 19-14
    2 Hanover **France** 6-3
    France won series 2-0
1937 Paris **France** 27-6
1938 Frankfurt **Germany** 3-0
1938 Bucharest **France** 8-5

FRANCE v ITALY
Played 17   France won 17

1937 Paris **France** 43-5
1952 Milan **France** 17-8
1953 Lyons **France** 22-8
1954 Rome **France** 39-12
1955 Grenoble **France** 24-0
1956 Padua **France** 16-3
1957 Agen **France** 38-6
1958 Naples **France** 11-3
1959 Nantes **France** 22-0

1960 Treviso **France** 26-0
1961 Chambéry **France** 17-0
1962 Brescia **France** 6-3
1963 Grenoble **France** 14-12
1964 Parma **France** 12-3
1965 Pau **France** 21-0
1966 Naples **France** 21-0
1967 Toulon **France** 60-13

FRANCE v BRITISH XVs
Played 5   France won 2, British XVs won 3

1940 Paris **British XV** 36-3
1945 Paris **France** 21-9
1945 Richmond **British XV** 27-6

1946 Paris **France** 10-0
1989 Paris **British XV** 29-27

FRANCE v NEW ZEALAND ARMY
Played 1   New Zealand Army won 1

1946 Paris **New Zealand Army** 14-9

FRANCE v ARGENTINA
Played 26   France won 21, Argentina won 4, Drawn 1

1949 *1* Buenos Aires **France** 5-0
    2 Buenos Aires **France** 12-3
    France won series 2-0
1954 *1* Buenos Aires **France** 22-8
    2 Buenos Aires **France** 30-3
    France won series 2-0
1960 *1* Buenos Aires **France** 37-3
    2 Buenos Aires **France** 12-3
    3 Buenos Aires **France** 29-6
    France won series 3-0
1974 *1* Buenos Aires **France** 20-15
    2 Buenos Aires **France** 31-27
    France won series 2-0
1975 *1* Lyons **France** 29-6
    2 Paris **France** 36-21
    France won series 2-0
1977 *1* Buenos Aires **France** 26-3
    2 Buenos Aires **Drawn** 18-18
    France won series 1-0, with 1 draw
1982 *1* Toulouse **France** 25-12

    2 Paris **France** 13-6
    France won series 2-0
1985 *1* Buenos Aires **Argentina** 24-16
    2 Buenos Aires **France** 23-15
    Series drawn 1-1
1986 *1* Buenos Aires **Argentina** 15-13
    2 Buenos Aires **France** 22-9
    Series drawn 1-1
1988 *1* Buenos Aires **France** 18-15
    2 Buenos Aires **Argentina** 18-6
    Series drawn 1-1
1988 *1* Nantes **France** 29-9
    2 Lille **France** 28-18
    France won series 2-0
1992 *1* Buenos Aires **France** 27-12
    2 Buenos Aires **France** 33-9
    France won series 2-0
1992 Nantes **Argentina** 24-20

FRANCE v CZECHOSLOVAKIA
Played 2   France won 2

1956 Toulouse **France** 28-3

1968 Prague **France** 19-6

FRANCE v FIJI
Played 3   France won 3

1964 Paris **France** 21-3
1987 Auckland *WC* **France** 31-16

1991 Grenoble *WC* **France** 33-9

FRANCE v JAPAN
Played 1   France won 1

1973 Bordeaux **France** 30-18

FRANCE v ZIMBABWE
Played 1   France won 1

1987 Auckland *WC* **France** 70-12

FRANCE v CANADA
Played 1   France won 1

1991 Agen *WC* **France** 19-13

NEW ZEALAND v SOUTH AFRICA
Played 38   New Zealand won 16, South Africa won 20, Drawn 2

1921 *1* Dunedin **New Zealand** 13-5
　　 2 Auckland **South Africa** 9-5
　　 3 Wellington **Drawn** 0-0
　　 Series drawn 1-1, with 1 draw
1928 *1* Durban **South Africa** 17-0
　　 2 Johannesburg **New Zealand** 7-6
　　 3 Port Elizabeth **South Africa** 11-6
　　 4 Cape Town **New Zealand** 13-5
　　 Series drawn 2-2
1937 *1* Wellington **New Zealand** 13-7
　　 2 Christchurch **South Africa** 13-6
　　 3 Auckland **South Africa** 17-6
　　 South Africa won series 2-1
1949 *1* Cape Town **South Africa** 15-11
　　 2 Johannesburg **South Africa** 12-6
　　 3 Durban **South Africa** 9-3
　　 4 Port Elizabeth **South Africa** 11-8
　　 South Africa won series 4-0
1956 *1* Dunedin **New Zealand** 10-6
　　 2 Wellington **South Africa** 8-3
　　 3 Christchurch **New Zealand** 17-10
　　 4 Auckland **New Zealand** 11-5
　　 New Zealand won series 3-1
1960 *1* Johannesburg **South Africa** 13-0

2 Cape Town **New Zealand** 11-3
3 Bloemfontein **Drawn** 11-11
4 Port Elizabeth **South Africa** 8-3
South Africa won series 2-1, with 1 draw
1965 *1* Wellington **New Zealand** 6-3
　　 2 Dunedin **New Zealand** 13-0
　　 3 Christchurch **South Africa** 19-16
　　 4 Auckland **New Zealand** 20-3
　　 New Zealand won series 3-1
1970 *1* Pretoria **South Africa** 17-6
　　 2 Cape Town **New Zealand** 9-8
　　 3 Port Elizabeth **South Africa** 14-3
　　 4 Johannesburg **South Africa** 20-17
　　 South Africa won series 3-1
1976 *1* Durban **South Africa** 16-7
　　 2 Bloemfontein **New Zealand** 15-9
　　 3 Cape Town **South Africa** 15-10
　　 4 Johannesburg **South Africa** 15-14
　　 South Africa won series 3-1
1981 *1* Christchurch **New Zealand** 14-9
　　 2 Wellington **South Africa** 24-12
　　 3 Auckland **New Zealand** 25-22
　　 New Zealand won series 2-1
1992 Johannesburg **New Zealand** 27-24

NEW ZEALAND v AUSTRALIA
Played 96   New Zealand won 65, Australia won 26, Drawn 5

1903 Sydney **New Zealand** 22-3
1905 Dunedin **New Zealand** 14-3
1907 *1* Sydney **New Zealand** 26-6
　　 2 Brisbane **New Zealand** 14-5
　　 3 Sydney **Drawn** 5-5
　　 New Zealand won series 2-0, with 1 draw

1910 *1* Sydney **New Zealand** 6-0
　　 2 Sydney **Australia** 11-0
　　 3 Sydney **New Zealand** 28-13
　　 New Zealand won series 2-1
1913 *1* Wellington **New Zealand** 30-5
　　 2 Dunedin **New Zealand** 25-13

93

3 Christchurch **Australia** 16-5
New Zealand won series 2-1
1914 *1* Sydney **New Zealand** 5-0
2 Brisbane **New Zealand** 17-0
3 Sydney **New Zealand** 22-7
New Zealand won series 3-0
1929 *1* Sydney **Australia** 9-8
2 Brisbane **Australia** 17-9
3 Sydney **Australia** 15-13
Australia won series 3-0
1931 Auckland **New Zealand** 20-13
1932 *1* Sydney **Australia** 22-17
2 Brisbane **New Zealand** 21-3
3 Sydney **New Zealand** 21-13
New Zealand won series 2-1
1934 *1* Sydney **Australia** 25-11
2 Sydney **Drawn** 3-3
Australia won series 1-0, with 1 draw
1936 *1* Wellington **New Zealand** 11-6
2 Dunedin **New Zealand** 38-13
New Zealand won series 2-0
1938 *1* Sydney **New Zealand** 24-9
2 Brisbane **New Zealand** 20-14
3 Sydney **New Zealand** 14-6
New Zealand won series 3-0
1946 *1* Dunedin **New Zealand** 31-8
2 Auckland **New Zealand** 14-10
New Zealand won series 2-0
1947 *1* Brisbane **New Zealand** 13-5
2 Sydney **New Zealand** 27-14
New Zealand won series 2-0
1949 *1* Wellington **Australia** 11-6
2 Auckland **Australia** 16-9
Australia won series 2-0
1951 *1* Sydney **New Zealand** 8-0
2 Sydney **New Zealand** 17-11
3 Brisbane **New Zealand** 16-6
New Zealand won series 3-0
1952 *1* Christchurch **Australia** 14-9
2 Wellington **New Zealand** 15-8
Series drawn 1-1
1955 *1* Wellington **New Zealand** 16-8
2 Dunedin **New Zealand** 8-0
3 Auckland **Australia** 8-3
New Zealand won series 2-1
1957 *1* Sydney **New Zealand** 25-11
2 Brisbane **New Zealand** 22-9
New Zealand won series 2-0
1958 *1* Wellington **New Zealand** 25-3
2 Christchurch **Australia** 6-3
3 Auckland **New Zealand** 17-8
New Zealand won series 2-1
1962 *1* Brisbane **New Zealand** 20-6
2 Sydney **New Zealand** 14-5
New Zealand won series 2-0
1962 *1* Wellington **Drawn** 9-9
2 Dunedin **New Zealand** 3-0

3 Auckland **New Zealand** 16-8
New Zealand won series 2-0, with 1 draw
1964 *1* Dunedin **New Zealand** 14-9
2 Christchurch **New Zealand** 18- 3
3 Wellington **Australia** 20-5
New Zealand won series 2-1
1967 Wellington **New Zealand** 29-9
1968 *1* Sydney **New Zealand** 27-11
2 Brisbane **New Zealand** 19-18
New Zealand won series 2-0
1972 *1* Wellington **New Zealand** 29-6
2 Christchurch **New Zealand** 30-17
3 Auckland **New Zealand** 38-3
New Zealand won series 3-0
1974 *1* Sydney **New Zealand** 11-6
2 Brisbane **Drawn** 16-16
3 Sydney **New Zealand** 16-6
New Zealand won series 2-0, with 1 draw
1978 *1* Wellington **New Zealand** 13-12
2 Christchurch **New Zealand** 22-6
3 Auckland **Australia** 30-16
New Zealand won series 2-1
1979 Sydney **Australia** 12-6
1980 *1* Sydney **Australia** 13-9
2 Brisbane **New Zealand** 12-9
3 Sydney **Australia** 26-10
Australia won series 2-1
1982 *1* Christchurch **New Zealand** 23-16
2 Wellington **Australia** 19-16
3 Auckland **New Zealand** 33-18
New Zealand won series 2-1
1983 Sydney **New Zealand** 18-8
1984 *1* Sydney **Australia** 16-9
2 Brisbane **New Zealand** 19-15
3 Sydney **New Zealand** 25-24
New Zealand won series 2-1
1985 Auckland **New Zealand** 10-9
1986 *1* Wellington **Australia** 13-12
2 Dunedin **New Zealand** 13-12
3 Auckland **Australia** 22-9
Australia won series 2-1
1987 Sydney **New Zealand** 30-16
1988 *1* Sydney **New Zealand** 32-7
2 Brisbane **Drawn** 19-19
3 Sydney **New Zealand** 30-9
New Zealand won series 2-0, with 1 draw
1989 Auckland **New Zealand** 24-12
1990 *1* Christchurch **New Zealand** 21-6
2 Auckland **New Zealand** 27-17
3 Wellington **Australia** 21-9
New Zealand won series 2-1
1991 *1* Sydney **Australia** 21-12
2 Auckland **New Zealand** 6-3
1991 Dublin *WC* **Australia** 16-6
1992 *1* Sydney **Australia** 16-15
2 Brisbane **Australia** 19-17
3 Sydney **New Zealand** 26-23
Australia won series 2-1

NEW ZEALAND v UNITED STATES
Played 2   New Zealand won 2

1913 Berkeley **New Zealand** 51-3

1991 Gloucester *WC* **New Zealand** 46-6

NEW ZEALAND v ROMANIA
Played 1   New Zealand won 1

1981 Bucharest **New Zealand** 14-6

NEW ZEALAND v ARGENTINA
Played 7   New Zealand won 6, Drawn 1

1985 *1* Buenos Aires **New Zealand** 33-20
    2 Buenos Aires **Drawn** 21-21
    New Zealand won series 1-0, with 1 draw
1987 Wellington *WC* **New Zealand**
    46-15
1989 *1* Dunedin **New Zealand** 60-9

    2 Wellington **New Zealand** 49-12
    New Zealand won series 2-0
1991 *1* Buenos Aires **New Zealand** 28-14
    2 Buenos Aires **New Zealand** 36-6
    New Zealand won series 2-0

NEW ZEALAND v ITALY
Played 2   New Zealand won 2

1987 Auckland *WC* **New Zealand** 70-6   1991 Leicester *WC* **New Zealand** 31-21

NEW ZEALAND v FIJI
Played 1   New Zealand won 1

1987 Christchurch *WC* **New Zealand** 74-13

NEW ZEALAND v CANADA
Played 1   New Zealand won 1

1991 Lille *WC* **New Zealand** 29-13

NEW ZEALAND v WORLD XVs
Played 3   New Zealand won 2, World XV won 1

1992 *1* Christchurch **World XV** 28-14
    2 Wellington **New Zealand** 54-26

    3 Auckland **New Zealand** 26-15
    New Zealand won series 2-1

SOUTH AFRICA v AUSTRALIA
Played 29   South Africa won 21, Australia won 8, Drawn 0

1933 *1* Cape Town **South Africa** 17-3
    2 Durban **Australia** 21-6
    3 Johannesburg **South Africa** 12-3
    4 Port Elizabeth **South Africa** 11-0
    5 Bloemfontein **Australia** 15-4
    South Africa won series 3-2
1937 *1* Sydney **South Africa** 9-5
    2 Sydney **South Africa** 26-17
    South Africa won series 2-0
1953 *1* Johannesburg **South Africa** 25-3
    2 Cape Town **Australia** 18-14
    3 Durban **South Africa** 18-8
    4 Port Elizabeth **South Africa** 22-9
    South Africa won series 3-1

1956 *1* Sydney **South Africa** 9-0
    2 Brisbane **South Africa** 9-0
    South Africa won series 2-0
1961 *1* Johannesburg **South Africa** 28-3
    2 Port Elizabeth **South Africa** 23-11
    South Africa won series 2-0
1963 *1* Pretoria **South Africa** 14-3
    2 Cape Town **Australia** 9-5
    3 Johannesburg **Australia** 11-9
    4 Port Elizabeth **South Africa** 22-6
    Series drawn 2-2
1965 *1* Sydney **Australia** 18-11
    2 Brisbane **Australia** 12-8
    Australia won series 2-0

1969 *1* Johannesburg **South Africa** 30-11
    2 Durban **South Africa** 16-9
    3 Cape Town **South Africa** 11-3
    4 Bloemfontein **South Africa** 19-8
    South Africa won series 4-0

1971 *1* Sydney **South Africa** 19-11
    2 Brisbane **South Africa** 14-6
    3 Sydney **South Africa** 18-6
    South Africa won series 3-0
1992 Cape Town **Australia** 26-3

SOUTH AFRICA v WORLD XVs
Played 3   South Africa won 3

1977 Pretoria **South Africa** 45-24
1989 *1* Cape Town **South Africa** 20-19

    2 Johannesburg **South Africa** 22-16
    South Africa won series 2-0

SOUTH AFRICA v SOUTH AMERICA
Played 8   South Africa won 7, South America won 1

1980 *1* Johannesburg **South Africa** 24-9
    2 Durban **South Africa** 18-9
    South Africa won series 2-0
1980 *1* Montevideo **South Africa** 22-13
    2 Santiago **South Africa** 30-16
    South Africa won series 2-0

1982 *1* Pretoria **South Africa** 50-18
    2 Bloemfontein **South America** 21-12
    Series drawn 1-1
1984 *1* Pretoria **South Africa** 32-15
    2 Cape Town **South Africa** 22-13
    South Africa won series 2-0

SOUTH AFRICA v UNITED STATES
Played 1   South Africa won 1

1981 Glenville **South Africa** 38-7

SOUTH AFRICA v NEW ZEALAND CAVALIERS
Played 4   South Africa won 3, New Zealand Cavaliers won 1

1986 *1* Cape Town **South Africa** 21-15
    2 Durban **New Zealand Cavaliers**
    19-18

    3 Pretoria **South Africa** 33-18
    4 Johannesburg **South Africa** 24-10
    South Africa won series 3-1

AUSTRALIA v UNITED STATES
Played 5   Australia won 5

1912 Berkeley **Australia** 12-8
1976 Los Angeles **Australia** 24-12
1983 Sydney **Australia** 49-3

1987 Brisbane *WC* **Australia** 47-12
1990 Brisbane **Australia** 67-9

AUSTRALIA v NEW ZEALAND MAORIS
Played 10   Australia won 4, New Zealand Maoris won 4, Drawn 2

1928 Wellington **New Zealand Maoris**
    9-8
1931 Palmerston North **Australia** 14-3
1936 Palmerston North **Australia** 31-6
1946 Hamilton **New Zealand Maoris** 20-0
1949 *1* Sydney **New Zealand Maoris**
    12-3
    2 Brisbane **Drawn** 8-8

    3 Sydney **Australia** 18-3
    Series drawn 1-1, with 1 draw
1958 *1* Brisbane **Australia** 15-14
    2 Sydney **Drawn** 3-3
    3 Melbourne **New Zealand Maoris**
    13-6
    Series drawn 1-1, with 1 draw

AUSTRALIA v FIJI
Played 15   Australia won 12, Fiji won 2, Drawn 1

1952 *1* Sydney **Australia** 15-9
    2 Sydney **Fiji** 17-15
    Series drawn 1-1
1954 *1* Brisbane **Australia** 22-19
    2 Sydney **Fiji** 18-16
    Series drawn 1-1
1961 *1* Brisbane **Australia** 24-6
    2 Sydney **Australia** 20-14
    3 Melbourne **Drawn** 3-3
    Australia won series 2-0, with 1 draw

1972 Suva **Australia** 21-19
1976 *1* Sydney **Australia** 22-6
    2 Brisbane **Australia** 21-9
    3 Sydney **Australia** 27-17
    Australia won series 3-0
1980 Suva **Australia** 22-9
1984 Suva **Australia** 16-3
1985 *1* Brisbane **Australia** 52-28
    2 Sydney **Australia** 31-9
    Australia won series 2-0

AUSTRALIA v TONGA
Played 2   Australia won 1, Tonga won 1

1973 *1* Sydney **Australia** 30-12

2 Brisbane **Tonga** 16-11
Series drawn 1-1

AUSTRALIA v JAPAN
Played 3   Australia won 3

1975 *1* Sydney **Australia** 37-7
    2 Brisbane **Australia** 50-25
    Australia won series 2-0

1987 Sydney *WC* **Australia** 42-23

AUSTRALIA v ARGENTINA
Played 9   Australia won 5, Argentina won 3, Drawn 1

1979 *1* Buenos Aires **Argentina** 24-13
    2 Buenos Aires **Australia** 17-12
    Series drawn 1-1
1983 *1* Brisbane **Argentina** 18-3
    2 Sydney **Australia** 29-13
    Series drawn 1-1
1986 *1* Brisbane **Australia** 39-19

    2 Sydney **Australia** 26-0
    Australia won series 2-0
1987 *1* Buenos Aires **Drawn** 19-19
    2 Buenos Aires **Argentina** 27-19
    Argentina won series 1-0, with 1 draw
1991 Llanelli *WC* **Australia** 32-19

AUSTRALIA v WESTERN SAMOA
Played 1   Australia won 1

1991 Pontypool *WC* **Australia** 9-3

AUSTRALIA v ITALY
Played 3   Australia won 3

1983 Rovigo **Australia** 29-7
1986 Brisbane **Australia** 39-18

1988 Rome **Australia** 55-6

AUSTRALIA v CANADA
Played 2   Australia won 2

1985 *1* Sydney **Australia** 59-3

2 Brisbane **Australia** 43-15
Australia won series 2-0

AUSTRALIA v KOREA
Played 1   Australia won 1

1987 Brisbane **Australia** 65-18

WORLD CUP WINNERS
New Zealand once: 1987
Australia once: 1991

GRAND SLAM WINNERS
England 10 times: 1913, 1914, 1921, 1923, 1924, 1928, 1957, 1980, 1991, 1992.
Wales 8 times: 1908, 1909, 1911, 1950, 1952, 1971, 1976, 1978.
France 4 times: 1968, 1977, 1981, 1987. **Scotland** 3 times: 1925, 1984, 1990.
Ireland once: 1948.

TRIPLE CROWN WINNERS
Wales 17 times: 1893, 1900, 1902, 1905, 1908, 1909, 1911, 1950, 1952, 1965, 1969, 1971, 1976, 1977, 1978, 1979, 1988. **England** 17 times: 1883, 1884, 1892, 1913, 1914, 1921, 1923, 1924, 1928, 1934, 1937, 1954, 1957, 1960, 1980, 1991, 1992. **Scotland** 10 times: 1891, 1895, 1901, 1903, 1907, 1925, 1933, 1938, 1984, 1990. **Ireland** 6 times: 1894, 1899, 1948, 1949, 1982, 1985.

INTERNATIONAL CHAMPIONSHIP WINNERS

Year	Winner	Year	Winner	Year	Winner	Year	Winner
1883	England	1911	Wales	1939	England, Ireland	1968	France
1884	England	1912	England, Ireland	1947	Wales, England	1969	Wales
1885*	—	1913	England	1948	Ireland	1970	France, Wales
1886	England, Scotland	1914	England	1949	Ireland	1971	Wales
1887	Scotland	1920	England, Scotland, Wales	1950	Wales	1972*	—
1888*	—	1921	England	1951	Ireland	1973	Quintuple tie
1889*	—	1922	Wales	1952	Wales	1974	Ireland
1890	England, Scotland	1923	England	1953	England	1975	Wales
1891	Scotland	1924	England	1954	England, France, Wales	1976	Wales
1892	England	1925	Scotland	1955	France, Wales	1977	France
1893	Wales	1926	Scotland, Ireland	1956	Wales	1978	Wales
1894	Ireland	1927	Scotland, Ireland	1957	England	1979	Wales
1895	Scotland	1928	England	1958	England	1980	England
1896	Ireland	1929	Scotland	1959	France	1981	France
1897*	—	1930	England	1960	England, France	1982	Ireland
1898*	—	1931	Wales	1961	France	1983	France, Ireland
1899	Ireland	1932	England, Wales, Ireland	1962	France	1984	Scotland
1900	Wales	1933	Scotland	1963	England	1985	Ireland
1901	Scotland	1934	England	1964	Scotland, Wales	1986	France, Scotland
1902	Wales	1935	Ireland	1965	Wales	1987	France
1903	Scotland	1936	Wales	1966	Wales	1988	Wales, France
1904	Scotland	1937	England	1967	France	1989	France
1905	Wales	1938	Scotland			1990	Scotland
1906	Ireland, Wales					1991	England
1907	Scotland					1992	England
1908	Wales					1993	France
1909	Wales						
1910	England						

Matches not completed, for various reasons

Wales have won the title outright most times, 21; England have won it 20 times, Scotland 13, Ireland 10, and France 10.

A INTERNATIONALS 1992-93

12 September 1992, Madrid
Spain 14 (2G)   Scotland A 35 (3G 3PG 1T)

Spain: F Puertas (Bayonne); J A Hermosilla (Quesos Entrepinares), J Azkargorta (Xerox Getxo), G Rivero (Pollac), P Martin (El Monte Ciencias); O Garcia (UE Santboiana), J Diaz (Xerox Getxo); J Alvarez (Dulciora El Salvador) (*capt*), F Castro (Xerox Getxo), X Alducin (Saint Jean de Luz), A Malo (UE Santboiana), M Auzmendi (UE Santboiana), J Etxebarria (Xerox Getxo), J Gutierrez (Xerox Arquitectura), E Illaregui (Saint Jean de Luz) *Replacements* U Aurrekoetxea (Xerox Getxo) for Garcia; A Gonzalez (Xerox Arquitectura) for Auzmendi; I Laskurain (Xerox Getxo) for Etxebarria
Scorers *Tries:* Azkargorta, Gutierrez   *Conversions:* Puertas (2)
Scotland A: K M Logan (Stirling County); D A Stark (Boroughmuir), G P J Townsend (Gala), I C Jardine (Stirling County), M Moncrieff (Gala); D S Wyllie (Stewart's-Melville FP), G H Oliver (Hawick); A P Burnell (London Scottish), I Corcoran (Gala), A G J Watt (Glasgow High/Kelvinside), C A Gray (Nottingham) (*capt*), A E D Macdonald (Heriot's FP), D J Turnbull (Hawick), A G Roxburgh (Kelso), G W Weir (Melrose)
Scorers *Tries:* Logan, Wyllie, Moncrieff, Roxburgh   *Conversions:* Townsend (3) *Penalty Goals:* Townsend (3)
Referee C Rouve (France)

19 December 1992, The Greenyards, Melrose
Scotland A 22 (4PG 2T)   Italy 17 (3PG 1DG 1T)

Scotland A: A G Hastings (Watsonians) (*capt*); D A Stark (Boroughmuir), G P J Townsend (Gala), S Hastings (Watsonians), M E Appleson (London Scottish); C M Chalmers (Melrose), G Armstrong (Jedforest); P M Jones (Gloucester), I Corcoran (Gala), A P Burnell (London Scottish), D F Cronin (London Scottish), G W Weir (Melrose), C D Hogg (Melrose), I R Smith (Gloucester), S J Reid (Boroughmuir)
Scorers *Tries:* S Hastings, Townsend   *Penalty Goals:* Chalmers (4)
Italy: L Troiani (L'Aquila); P Vaccari (Calvasino), I Francescato (Treviso), S Barba (Milan), Marcello Cuttitta (Milan); D Dominguez (Milan), U Casellato (Treviso); Massimo Cuttitta (Milan), C Orlandi (Piacenza), G Grespan (Rovigo), C Checchinato (Rovigo), P Raele (Rovigo), S Rigo (Treviso), M Giovanelli (Milan) (*capt*), J Gardner (Rovigo) *Replacements* M Tommasi (Milan) for Marcello Cuttitta; R Cassina (Casale) for Raele
Scorers *Try:* Checchinato   *Penalty Goals:* Dominguez (3)   *Dropped Goal:* Dominguez
Referee R McDowell (Ireland)

28 December 1992, Lansdowne Road
Ireland A 13 (1G 2PG)   Scotland A 22 (1G 3T)

Ireland A: C R Wilkinson (Malone); C S D Leahy (Wanderers), B A Walsh (Cork Const), B T Glennon (Lansdowne), N K P J Woods (Blackrock Coll); N G Malone (Oxford U), R Saunders (London Irish); P J Soden (Cork Const), M B Patton (Oxford U) (*capt*), G F Halpin (London Irish), D A Tweed (Ballymena), R A Costello (Garryowen), L M Dineen (Cork Const), K J McKee (Instonians), B Cronin (Garryowen)
Replacement P Millar (Ballymena) for Halpin
Scorers *Try:* Cronin   *Conversion:* Malone   *Penalty Goals:* Malone (2)
Scotland A: K M Logan (Stirling County); A G Stanger (Hawick), G P J Towsend (Gala), I C Jardine (Stirling County), M E Appleson (London Scottish); A G Shiel (Melrose), A D Nicol (Dundee HSFP) (*capt*); A G J Watt (Glasgow High/Kelvinside), K S Milne (Heriot's FP), P H Wright (Boroughmuir), A I Reed (Bath), D S Munro

(Glasgow High/Kelvinside), D L M McIntosh (Pontypridd), I R Morrison
(London Scottish), C D Hogg (Melrose) *Replacements* A E D Macdonald (Heriot's FP)
for Hogg; G D Wilson (Boroughmuir) for Watt
Scorers *Tries:* Stanger (2), Logan, Nicol   *Conversion:* Townsend
Referee D W Matthews (England)

15 January 1993, Leicester
England A 29 (1G 4PG 2T)   France A 17 (2G 1PG)

England A: A J Buzza (Wasps); T Underwood (Leicester), D P Hopley (Cambridge U),
J Buckton (Saracens), H Thorneycroft (Northampton); P Challinor (Harlequins),
M Dawson (Northampton); M P Hynes (Orrell), K A Dunn (Wasps), A R Mullins
(Harlequins), D Ryan (Wasps), A G Blackmore (Bristol), J P Hall (Bath) *(capt)*,
S Ojomoh (Bath), N A Back (Leicester)
Scorers *Tries:* Underwood, Thorneycroft, Hopley   *Conversion:* Challinor
Penalty Goals: Challinor (4)
France A: O Campan (Agen); P Bernat-Salles (Pau), H Couffignal (Colomiers),
M Marfaing (Toulouse), D Berty (Toulouse); A Penaud (Brive), G Accocebery (Tyrosse)
(capt); L Benezech (Racing Club de France), E Dasalmartini (Toulon), L Verge
(Bègles), H Chaffardon (Graulhet), Y Lemeur (Racing Club de France), L Loppy
(Toulon), J-J Alibert (Bègles), J-M Lhermet (Montferrand)
Scorers *Tries:* Berty, Campan   *Conversions:* Campan (2)   *Penalty Goal:* Campan
Referee J Bacigalupo (Scotland)

3 February 1993, Bath
England A 59 (4G 2PG 5T)   Italy A 0

England A: A J Buzza (Wasps); T Underwood (Leicester), S Potter (Leicester),
D P Hopley (Cambridge U), H Thorneycroft (Northampton); P Challinor (Harlequins),
M Dawson (Northampton); C Clark (Swansea), K A Dunn (Wasps), A R Mullins
(Harlequins), M Johnson (Leicester), A G Blackmore (Bristol), J P Hall (Bath) *(capt)*,
S Ojomoh (Bath), N A Back (Leicester) *Replacement* M Greenwood (Wasps) for Ojomoh
Scorers *Tries:* Underwood (2), Back (2), Potter (2), Thorneycroft, Dawson, Buzza
Conversions: Challinor (2), Buzza (2)   *Penalty Goals:* Challinor (2)
Italy A: P Dotto (Treviso); L Perziano (Treviso), M Tommasi (Milan), S Bordon
(Rovigo), L Manteri (Treviso); M Bonomi (Milan), G Faltiba (San Dona); M Dal-Sie
(San Dona), A Marengoni (Milan), F Properzi-Curti (Treviso), R Favaro (Treviso),
M Giacheri (Treviso), R Cassina (Casale), F Coppo (Treviso), D Beretta (Milan)
Replacement A Piazza (San Dona) for Marengoni
Referee G Black (Ireland)

6 February 1993, S'Hertogenbosh
Holland 12 (1G 1T)   Wales A 57 (6G 3T)

Holland: A Marcker; M M Nagtegaal, G Bos, B Wisse, J Esseveld; M Michelsen,
W Hanekom; M Tielrooy, Y Kummer *(capt)*, V Dubbeldam, P Koenen, M van Loon,
R Broers, A Seijbel, T Suring *Replacement* M Geelhoed for Broers
Scorers *Tries:* Koenen (2)   *Conversion:* Bos
Wales A: I Jones (Llanelli); S Ford (Cardiff), R Bidgood (Newport), N Davies (Llanelli)
,*(capt)*, N Walker (Cardiff); A Williams (Swansea), R Howley (Bridgend); I Buckett
(Swansea), R McBryde (Swansea), L Mustoe (Pontypool), S Roy (Cardiff), P Arnold
(Swansea), H Stone (Cardiff), M Perego (Llanelli), S Legge (South Wales Police)
Replacement A Thomas (Neath) for McBryde
Scorers *Tries:* Walker (3), Ford (2), Bidgood, Howley, Williams, Davies
Conversions: Williams (6)
Referee H Rohr (Germany)

5 March 1993, Richmond Athletic Ground
England A 66 (4G 1PG 7T)   Spain 5 (1T)

England A: P Hull (Bristol & RAF); S Hackney (Leicester), S Potter (Leicester),
D P Hopley (Cambridge U), H Thorneycroft (Northampton); P Challinor (Harlequins),
M Dawson (Northampton); C Clark (Swansea), K A Dunn (Wasps), D J Garforth
(Leicester), M Johnson (Leicester), A G Blackmore (Bristol), M Greenwood (Wasps),
D Richards (Leicester) (*capt*), S Ojomoh (Bath)
Scorers *Tries:* Hackney (4), Hull (2), Dunn, Johnson, Thorneycroft, Richards, Challinor
Conversions: Hull (4)   *Penalty Goal:* Hull
Spain: F Puertas (Bayonne) (*capt*); J Torres (Ciencias Sevilla), G Rivero (Pollac), A Mino
(Ciencias Sevilla), P Gutierrez (Arquitectura); M Sanchez (Ciencias Sevilla),
J Hernandez-Gil (Arquitectura); Jorge Gutierrez (Liceo Frances), F de la Calle
(Valladolid), R Lizarza (Atletico Berabera), A Malo (Santboiana), V Esnaola
(El Salvador), Jaime Gutierrez (Arquitectura), M Auzmendi (Santboiana), J Extebarria
(Getxo) *Replacements* J Diaz (Getxo) for Rivero; A Beloki (Getxo) for Auzmendi
Scorer *Try:* Hernandez-Gil
Referee D R Davies (Wales)

5 March 1993, Newport
Wales A 28 (1G 2PG 3T)   Ireland A 29 (1G 2PG 2DG 2T)

Wales A: I Jones (Llanelli); S Ford (Cardiff), N Davies (Llanelli) (*capt*), R Bidgood
(Newport), W Proctor (Llanelli); A Davies (Cardiff), R Howley (Bridgend); I Buckett
(Swansea), R McBryde (Swansea), L Mustoe (Pontypool), P Kawulok (Cardiff), S Roy
(Cardiff), A Reynolds (Swansea), S Legge (South Wales Police), M Budd (Cardiff)
Scorers *Tries:* Bidgood (2), Jones, Proctor   *Conversion:* A Davies
Penalty Goals: A Davies (2)
Ireland A: J E Staples (London Irish); R Carey (Dungannon), B Walsh (Cork Const),
M McCall (Bangor), N Woods (Blackrock Coll); D Humphreys (Queen's U, Belfast),
L F P Aherne (Lansdowne) (*capt*); P J Soden (Cork Const), W Mulcahy (Skerries),
P Millar (Ballymena), J Etheridge (Northampton), D Tweed (Ballymena), K Potts
(St Mary's Coll), N P Mannion (Lansdowne), L Toland (Old Crescent)
Scorers *Tries:* Staples, Humphreys, Walsh   *Conversion:* Humphreys
Penalty Goals: Humphreys (2)   *Dropped Goals:* Humphreys (2)
Referee S Piercy (England)

19 March 1993, Donnybrook, Dublin
Ireland A 18 (1G 1PG 1DG 1T)   England A 22 (2G 1PG 1T)

Ireland A: A White (St Mary's Coll); R Carey (Dungannon), B Walsh (Cork Const),
M McCall (Bangor), N Woods (Blackrock Coll); D Humphreys (Queen's U, Belfast),
L F P Aherne (Lansdowne) (*capt*); P J Soden (Cork Const), B Mulcahy (Skerries),
P Millar (Ballymena), J Etheridge (Northampton), D Tweed (Ballymena), K Potts
(St Mary's Coll), N P Mannion (Lansdowne), L Toland (Old Crescent)
Replacements S McKinty (Bangor) for Mannion; M Ridge (Blackrock Coll) for Woods
Scorers *Tries:* Walsh, Carey   *Conversion:* Humphreys   *Penalty Goal:* Humphreys
Dropped Goal: Humphreys
England A: P Hull (Bristol & RAF); S Hackney (Leicester), S Potter (Leicester),
D P Hopley (Cambridge U), H Thorneycroft (Northampton); P Challinor (Harlequins),
M Dawson (Northampton); C Clark (Swansea), K A Dunn (Wasps), D J Garforth
(Leicester), M Johnson (Leicester), A G Blackmore (Bristol), J P Hall (Bath) (*capt*),
M Greenwood (Wasps) S Ojomoh (Bath) *Replacement* N Beal (Northampton) for Hopley
Scorers *Tries:* Dawson (2), Hull   *Conversions:* Hull (2)   *Penalty Goal:* Hull
Referee R Yeman (Wales)

20 March 1993, Rubislaw, Aberdeen
Scotland A 19 (1G 4PG) France A 29 (2G 3T)

Scotland A: K M Logan (Stirling County); K R Milligan (Stewart's-Melville FP), I C Jardine (Stirling County), D S Wyllie (Stewart's-Melville FP), J Kerr (Haddington); A Donaldson (Currie), D B Millard (London Scottish); G D Wilson (Boroughmuir), M W Scott (Edinburgh Acads), S W Ferguson (Peebles), C A Gray (Nottingham) (*capt*), D S Munro (Glasgow High/Kelvinside), A E D Macdonald (Heriot's FP), I R Smith (Gloucester), D J McIvor (Edinburgh Acads)
Scorers *Try:* Logan *Conversion:* Donaldson *Penalty Goals:* Donaldson (4)
France A: J-L Sadourny (Colomiers); F Bertranck (Montferrand), P Arletaz (Perpignan), J-C Larran (Tarbes), L Arbot (Perpignan); B Bellot (Graulhet), F Galthié (Colomiers) (*capt*); L Benezech (Racing Club de France), S Morizot (Perpignan), P Gallart (Béziers), Y Lemeur (Racing Club de France), O Merle (Grenoble), L Loppy (Toulon), J-M Lhermet (Montferrand), S Dispagne (Narbonne) *Replacement* L Labit (Castres) for Bellot
Scorers *Tries:* Bertranck (2), Larran, Arbot, Galthié *Conversions:* Bellot, Labit
Referee B Campbell (England)

OTHER INTERNATIONAL MATCHES 1992-93

28 May 1992, Le Havre
FRANCE 25 (3G 1PG 1T)   ROMANIA 6 (2PG)

FRANCE: S Ougier (Toulouse); P Saint-André (Montferrand), M Marfaing (Toulouse), C Deylaud (Toulouse), S Viars (Brive); A Penaud (Brive), F Galthié (Colomiers); L Armary (Lourdes), J-P Genet (Racing Club de France), P Gallart (Beziers), J-M Cadieu (Toulouse), C Deslandes (Racing Club de France), J-F Tordo (Nice), M Cecillon (Bourgoin) *(capt)*, L Cabannes (Racing Club de France) *Replacements* D Berty (Toulouse) for Viars (36 mins); T Devergie (Nîmes) for Deslandes (53 mins)
Scorers *Tries:* Saint-André, Galthié, Cadieu, penalty try   *Conversions:* Ougier (2), Viars *Penalty Goal:* Viars
ROMANIA: V Brici (Farul); M Dumitru (Rapid Bucharest), A Lungu (Castres), N Racean (Timisoara U), G Solomie (Timisoara U); G Ignat (Steaua), T Coman (Steaua); G Leonte (Milan), G Ion (Dinamo), G Vlad (Grivita), C Cojocariu (Bayonne), T Constantin (Steaua), G Dinu (Grivita), H Dumitras (Pau) *(capt)*, I Seceleanu (CSM Sibiu)
Scorers *Penalty Goals:* Racean (2)
Referee K W McCartney (Scotland)

13 June 1992, Denver
USA 9 (2PG 1DG)   CANADA 32 (2G 4PG 2T)

USA: P Sheehy; R Schurfeld, J R Burke, M Waterman, B Tofaeono; M Gale, G Goodman; L Manga, P W Johnson, N Mottram, K R Swords *(capt)*, J Keller, R Farley, B Smoot, D Steinbauer *Replacements* M van der Molen for Keller (21 mins); V Anatoni for Tofaeono (76 mins)
Scorer *Penalty Goals:* Gale (2)   *Dropped Goal:* Gale
CANADA: D C Lougheed; P Palmer, S D Gray, J D Graf, S MacKinnon; G L Rees, C J Tynan; E A Evans, K F Svoboda, D C Jackart, N Hadley *(capt)*, I Gordon, A J Charron, C McKenzie, G I MacKinnon
Scorers *Tries:* Palmer, Gray, Tynan, Rees   *Conversions:* Rees (2) *Penalty Goals:* Rees (4)
Referee D Reardon (United States)

5 September 1992, Welford Road, Leicester
LEICESTER 11 (2PG 1T)· ENGLAND XV 18 (1G 1PG 1DG 1T)

LEICESTER: J Liley; S Hackney, S Potter, I Bates, R Underwood; J Harris, A Kardooni; G Rowntree, R Cockerill, D Garforth, M Poole, D Richards, J Wells *(capt)*, S Povoas, N Richardson
Scorers *Try:* Hackney   *Penalty Goals:* Liley (2)
ENGLAND XV: J M Webb (Bath); N J Heslop (Orrell), W D C Carling (Harlequins) *(capt)*, J C Guscott (Bath), T Underwood (Leicester); C R Andrew (Toulouse), R J Hill (Bath); M P Hynes (Orrell), B C Moore (Harlequins), J A Probyn (Wasps), N C Redman (Bath), M C Bayfield (Northampton), S Ojomoh (Bath), B B Clarke (Bath), N A Back (Leicester) *Replacements* D Pears (Harlequins) for Webb; P R de Glanville (Bath) for Heslop; M Pepper (Nottingham) for Back
Scorers *Tries:* Heslop (2)   *Conversion:* Webb   *Penalty Goal:* Webb *Dropped Goal:* Andrew
Referee E Morrison (England)

7 October 1992, Cardiff Arms Park
WALES XV 43 (4G 3T)   ITALY XV 12 (1G 1T)

Wales XV: A Clement (Swansea); I C Evans (Llanelli) (*capt*), R A Bidgood (Newport), I S Gibbs (Swansea), M R Hall (Cardiff); C J Stephens (Llanelli), R N Jones (Swansea); M Griffiths (Cardiff), G R Jenkins (Swansea), H Williams-Jones (South Wales Police), G O Llewellyn (Neath), A H Copsey (Llanelli), E W Lewis (Llanelli), S Davies (Swansea), R E Webster (Swansea) *Replacement* M A Rayer (Cardiff) for Bidgood (68 mins)
Scorers *Tries:* Clement, Evans, Stephens, Gibbs, Davies, Webster, Rayer
Conversions: Stephens (4)
Italy XV: P Vaccari (Calvisano); E Venturi (Rovigo), S Zorzi (Treviso), S Barba (Milan), Marcello Cuttitta (Milan); M Bonomi (Milan), I Francescato (Tarvisium); Massimo Cuttitta (Milan), G Pivetta (San Dona) (*capt*), G Grespan (Treviso), M Giacheri (Treviso), C Checchinato (Rovigo), R Cassina (Casale), J M Gardner (Rovigo), A Bottacchiari (L'Aquila)
Scorers *Tries:* Francescato, Marcello Cuttitta   *Conversion:* Bonomi
Referee F A Howard (England)

17 October 1992, Wembley Stadium
ENGLAND 26 (2PG 4T)   CANADA 13 (1G 2PG)

ENGLAND: J M Webb (Bath); I Hunter (Northampton), W D C Carling (Harlequins) (*capt*), J C Guscott (Bath), T Underwood (Leicester); C R Andrew (Toulouse), C D Morris (Orrell); J Leonard (Harlequins), C J Olver (Northampton), V E Ubogu (Bath), W A Dooley (Preston Grasshoppers), M C Bayfield (Northampton), D Ryan (Wasps), D Richards (Leicester), P J Winterbottom (Harlequins)
Scorers *Tries:* Hunter (2), Winterbottom, Guscott   *Penalty Goals:* Webb (2)
CANADA: D S Stewart (UBC Old Boys); S D Gray (Kats), M Williams (Meralomas), I C Stuart (Vancouver RC), D C Lougheed (Toronto Welsh); G L Rees (Oak Bay Castaways), J D Graf (UBC Old Boys); E A Evans (UBC Old Boys), K F Svoboda (Ajax Wanderers), D C Jackart (UBC Old Boys), J Knauer (Meralomas), N Hadley (UBC Old Boys) (*capt*), I Gordon (James Bay), C McKenzie (UBC Old Boys), G I MacKinnon (Ex-Britannia Lions) *Replacement* K Wirachowski for Evans (49 mins)
Scorers *Try:* Graf   *Conversion:* Rees   *Penalty Goals:* Rees (2)
Referee G Simmonds (Wales)

NATIONAL TRIAL MATCH 1993

SCOTLAND

2 January 1993, Murrayfield

Blues 29 (3G 1PG 1T) **Reds 6** (2PG)

Blues: A G Hastings (Watsonians) (*capt*); D A Stark (Boroughmuir), G P J Townsend (Gala), S Hastings (Watsonians), M E Appleson (London Scottish); C M Chalmers (Melrose), G Armstrong (Jedforest); A V Sharp (Bristol), K S Milne (Heriot's FP), P H Wright (Boroughmuir), A I Reed (Bath), D F Cronin (London Scottish), D J Turnbull (Hawick), I R Morrison (London Scottish), D L M McIntosh (Pontypridd) *Replacements* Shiel promoted from Reds for Townsend (25 mins); Weir promoted for McIntosh (half-time)
Scorers *Tries:* S Hastings, Cronin, Turnbull, McIntosh *Conversions:* A G Hastings (3) *Penalty Goal:* A G Hastings
Reds: K M Logan (Stirling County); A G Stanger (Hawick), I C Jardine (Stirling County), D S Wyllie (Stewart's-Melville FP), J Kerr (Haddington); A G Shiel (Melrose), A D Nicol (Dundee HSFP) (*capt*); A G J Watt (Glasgow High/Kelvinside), I Corcoran (Gala), A P Burnell (London Scottish), C A Gray (Nottingham), G W Weir (Melrose), D J McIvor (Edinburgh Acads), I R Smith (Gloucester), S J Reid (Boroughmuir) *Replacements* A Donaldson (Currie) for Shiel (25 mins); D S Munro (Glasgow High/Kelvinside) for Weir (half-time)
Scorer *Penalty Goals:* Wyllie (2)
Referee J M Fleming (Boroughmuir)

UNDER-21 RUGBY 1992-93

6 September 1992, Welford Road, Leicester
England U-21s 37 (3G 2PG 2T) **Italy U-21s 12** (1G 1T)

England U-21s: M Mapletoft (Rugby); J Sleightholme (Wakefield), M Dawson (Northampton), D Edwards (Loughborough U), S O'Leary (Saracens); P Grayson (Waterloo), K Bracken (Bristol U); C Clarke (Swansea U), M Regan (Bristol), S Crompton (Bath), R Bramley (Wakefield) (*capt*), R West (Gloucester), A Diprose (Loughborough U), A Morris (Sheffield), M Rennell (Bedford) *Replacement* A Handley (Waterloo) for Grayson
Scorers *Tries:* Mapletoft (2), Sleightholme, Bramley, O'Leary   *Conversions:* Mapletoft (3)   *Penalty Goals:* Grayson, Mapletoft
Italy U-21s: M Ravazzolo; M Amore, N Aldrovandi, P Residore, U Re; M Visentin, A Troncan (*capt*); P Menapace, M Alfonsetti, A Castagna, S Stocco, M David, A de Rossi, G Caione, S Falcone
Scorers *Tries:* Re, Falcone   *Conversion:* Visentin
Referee B Stirling (Ireland)

9 September 1992, Poynder Park, Kelso
Scotland U-21s 18 (6PG) **Italy U-21s 29** (1G 4PG 2T)

Scotland U-21s: M M Thomson (Stewart's-Melville FP); K R Milligan (Stewart's-Melville FP), J Smith (Kirkcaldy), D R Hamilton (Dundee HSFP), J R Jardine (Dundee HSFP); L Graham (Biggar), G G Burns (Stewart's-Melville FP); R B McNulty (Stewart's-Melville FP), S Scott (Melrose), R K Hastings (West of Scotland), S J Campbell (Dundee HSFP), M B Rudkin (Watsonians), M Waite (Dundee HSFP), A G Ness (Glasgow High/Kelvinside) (*capt*), D G Burns (Boroughmuir)
Scorer *Penalty Goals:* Thomson (6)
Italy U-21s: M Ravazzolo; S Babbo, N Aldrovandi, P Residore, M Amore; F Roselli, A Troncan (*capt*); P Menapace, T Ravasini, A Castagna, M David, S Stocco, A de Rossi, G Caione, S Falcone *Replacements* D Breviglieri for Castagna; T Signore for Caione
Scorer *Tries:* Babbo (3)   *Conversion:* Babbo   *Penalty Goals:* Babbo (4)
Referee R G Davies (Wales)

14 October 1992, Newcastle Gosforth
England U-21s 39 (3G 1PG 3T) **Ireland U-21s 28** (2G 3PG 1T)

England U-21s: M Mapletoft (Rugby); J Sleightholme (Wakefield), M Dawson (Northampton), D Edwards (Wakefield), D O'Leary (Saracens); P Burke (London Irish), K Bracken (Bristol); C Clarke (Swansea U), M Regan (Bristol), D Crompton (Bath), R Bramley (Wakefield) (*capt*), R West (Gloucester), A Diprose (Saracens), A Morris (Waterloo), M Rennell (Bedford)
Scorers *Tries:* O'Leary (2), Rennell, Mapletoft, Burke, Sleightholme   *Conversions:* Mapletoft (2), Burke   *Penalty Goal:* Burke
Ireland U-21s: I Gray (Queen's U); D Hernan (UCD), R Hunter (Northampton), S Tynan (Terenure), G McCluskey (Portadown); A McGowan (Blackrock), N Assaf (Blackrock); M Carroll (Old Belvedere), K Wood (Garryowen), P Wallace (UCC) (*capt*), G Longwell (Queen's U), B Cusack (Bective Rangers), N R Taylor (Old Crescent), L Toland (Old Crescent), S Kirkpatrick (Malone)
Scorers *Tries:* Toland, Wallace, penalty try   *Conversions:* McGowan (2)   *Penalty Goals:* McGowan (3)
Referee D Leslie (Scotland)

28 October 1992, Donnybrook, Dublin
Ireland U-21s 22 (2G 1PG 1T) **Wales U-21s 11** (2PG 1T)

Ireland U-21s: I Gray (Queen's U); S Sheehan (Garryowen), R Hunter (Northampton), S Tynan (Terenure), G McCluskey (Portadown); A McGowan (Blackrock), N Assaf (Blackrock); M Carroll (Old Belvedere), S Byrne (Blackrock), P Wallace (UCC) (*capt*), L Toland (Old Crescent), G Longwell (Queen's U), B Cusack (Bective Rangers), D Corkery (Cork Constitution), R Wilson (Instonians)
Scorers *Tries:* Wilson, McGowan, Longwell   *Conversions:* McGowan (2)   *Penalty Goal:* McGowan
Wales U-21s: D Weatherly (Swansea); J Reynolds (Neath), M Wintle (Llanelli), J Redrup (Newport), C Young (Llanelli); J Williams (Abertillery), H Harries (Cardiff); Rhys Jones (Llanelli), J Evans (Bryncoch) (*capt*), S Price (Llanharan), G Jones (Llanelli), L Harvey (Maesteg), G Taylor (Newbridge), I Callaghan (Dunvant), P Jones (Neath) *Replacements* W Morris (Aberavon) for Harries; Rhodri Jones (Llanelli) for Taylor; R Appleyard (Swansea) for Callaghan
Scorers *Try:* Reynolds   *Penalty Goals:* Williams (2)
Referee C Henderson (Scotland)

15 January 1993, Murrayfield
Scotland U-21s 3 (1PG) **Ireland U-21s 18** (1G 2PG 1T)

Scotland U-21s: M M Thomson (Stewart's-Melville FP); J W K Anderson (Loughborough U & Watsonians), D C Bain (Melrose), W M Tonkin (Currie), H R Gilmour (Heriot's FP); G M Lawrie (Heriot's FP), G G Burns (Stewart's-Melville FP); R B McNulty (Stewart's-Melville FP), D C M McGavin (Bedford), K B Scott (Hawick), S J Campbell (Dundee HSFP), M B Rudkin (Watsonians), A G Ness (Glasgow High/Kelvinside) (*capt*), N J Penny

(Stewart's-Melville FP), D G Burns (Boroughmuir)
Scorers *Penalty Goal:* Thomson
Ireland U-21s: H Carolan (Blackrock); I Gray (Queen's U), S Sexton (Greystones), R Hunter (Northampton), N Assaf (Blackrock); D Humphreys (Queen's U), B Murphy (Old Belvedere); M Carroll (Old Belvedere), S Byrne (Blackrock), P Wallace (UCC) *(capt)*, G Longwell (Queen's U), B Cusack (Bective Rangers), L Toland (Old Crescent), D Corkery (Cork Constitution), R Wilson (Instonians)
Scorers *Tries:* Longwell, Toland   *Conversion:* Carolan   *Penalty Goals:* Carolan, Humphreys
Referee G Simmonds (Wales)

5 February 1993, Parc des Sports, Dijon
France U-21s 67 (8G 2PG 1T)   **Scotland U-21s 9** (3PG)

France U-21s: P Teisseire (Toulon); A Bouyssie (Brive), H Mola (Toulouse), Y Delaigue (Toulon), F Bertranck (Montferrand); G Merceron (Cognac), S Ricco (Brive); C Soulette (Béziers), M de Rougemont (Toulon), C Califano (Toulouse), F Orsoni (Toulon), O Brouzet (Grenoble), R Sonnes (Mont de Marsan), C Moni (Nice), B de Giusti (Graulhet) *(capt)*
Scotland U-21s: M M Thomson (Stewart's-Melville FP); J W K Anderson (Loughborough U), R N C Brown (Melrose), D C Bain (Melrose), H B R Gilmour (Heriot's FP); G M Lawrie (Heriot's FP), G G Burns (Stewart's-Melville FP); R B McNulty (Stewart's-Melville FP), D C M McGavin (Bedford), K B Scott (Hawick), S J Campbell (Dundee HSFP), M B Rudkin (Watsonians), A G Ness (Glasgow High/Kelvinside) *(capt)*, N J Penny (Stewart's-Melville FP), D G Burns (Boroughmuir)
Scorers *Penalty Goals:* Thomson (3)
Referee A Condorelli (Italy)

Scott Quinnell, the outstanding forward in the match, drives on his way in the Wales Under-21 victory over Scotland at Myreside.

19 February 1993, Myreside, Edinburgh
Scotland U-21s 8 (1PG 1T) **Wales U-21s 16** (2PG 2T)

Scotland U-21s: M M Thomson (Stewart's-Melville FP); K R Milligan (Stewart's-Melville FP), R N C Brown (Melrose), W M Tonkin (Currie), G Fraser (Waterloo); D J Lee (Watsonians), G G Burns (Stewart's-Melville FP); R B McNulty (Stewart's-Melville FP), D C McGavin (Bedford) *(capt)*, G D Rigby (Stewart's-Melville FP), G W Paxton (Gala), M B Rudkin (Watsonians), M A Ballantyne (Gala), N J Penny (Stewart's-Melville FP), D G Burns (Boroughmuir)
Scorers *Try:* Rudkin   *Penalty Goal:* Thomson
Wales U-21s: P A Armstrong (Cardiff); C Bourne (Liverpool St Helen's), A J Palfrey (Cardiff), R I Lewis (Bath), A J Reynolds (Neath); J A Williams (Newport), H J Harries (Cardiff); R Jones (Llanelli), J W Evans (Bryncoch) *(capt)*, S J John (Llanelli), L I Harvey (Maesteg), P M Jones (Llanelli), R C Appleyard (Swansea), C D W Brown (Cardiff Inst), L S Quinnell (Llanelli) *Replacements* D R Evans (Llanelli) for Harvey; P J Young (Llanelli) for J W Evans
Scorers *Tries:* Appleyard, Quinnell   *Penalty Goals:* Williams (2)
Referee A Watson (Ireland)

4 April 1993, Saracens: Vauxhall National Under-21 Sevens: Semi-finals: Richmond 26, Colchester 0; Wasps 17, Bristol U 10 **Final:** Wasps 31, Richmond 14
10-11 April 1993, Sunbury: 13th London Irish Under-21 15-a-side tournament *(for the Beamish Trophy):* **Semi-finals:** West Hartlepool 3, Loughborough U 12; London Irish 10, Collegians 0
Worcester MEB Under-21 Floodlit Trophy: Semi-finals: Birmingham & Solihull 44, Newport 13; Wasps 32, Worcester 6 **Final:** Wasps 38, Birmingham & Solihull 3

1 May 1993
England U-21s 31 (2G 4PG 1T)   **French Armed Forces 3** (1PG)

England U-21s: T Stimpson (Wakefield); J Sleightholme (Wakefield), D Edwards (Wakefield), M Catt (Bath), D O'Leary (Saracens); A Handley (Waterloo), M Olsen (Llandovery); D Molloy (Wasps), M Regan (Bristol), D Crompton (Bath), R Bramley (Wakefield) *(capt)*, S Shaw (Bristol), A Diprose (Saracens), L Dallaglio (Wasps), R Hill (Salisbury)
Scorers *Tries:* Hill, Catt, Sleightholme   *Conversions:* Catt (2)   *Penalty Goals:* Catt (4)
French Armed Forces *Penalty Goal:* Bertranck
Referee J Bacigalupo (SRU)

Under-21 Divisional Championship: South & South-West 16, London & South-East 10; Midlands 23, North 37; North 11, London & South-East 17; Midlands 19, South & South-West 13; London & South-East 30, Midlands 12; South & South-West 9, North 15 **Divisional Champions:** London & South-East

ADT UNDER-21 CHAMPIONSHIP 1992-93

17 April, Twickenham
Buckinghamshire 22 (2G 1PG 1T)   Warwickshire 0

The smallest county union in the Rugby Union celebrated their first appearance at Twickenham with a decisive victory in the ADT Under-21 County Championship final. Their strong pack dominated throughout and provided a firm platform for their backs. Although Curtis in the Warwickshire centre disrupted them in the early stages with his fierce tackling, Buckinghamshire took the lead shortly before half-time with an opportunist try by Harvey, followed by a penalty goal from Braithwaite.

Buckinghamshire dominated the second half, adding tries by scrum-half Shaw and lock Robertson, Braithwaite converting both.

Divisional Rounds: London & South-East: Eastern Counties 12, Surrey 23; Hertfordshire 0, Middlesex 34; Eastern Counties 21, Hertfordshire 17; Surrey 21, Middlesex 16; Hertfordshire 3, Surrey 29; Middlesex 0, Eastern Counties 23; Hampshire 19, Army 6; Sussex 7, Kent 31; Army 29, Sussex 12; Kent 33, Hampshire 5; Army 3, Kent 6; Sussex 17, Hampshire 35 **London & South-East play off:** Surrey 27, Kent 3 **Midlands:** East Midlands 35, Notts, Lincs & Derbys 13; Notts, Lincs & Derbys 8, Leicestershire 40; Leicestershire 14, East Midlands 3; North Midlands 14, Warwickshire 32; Warwickshire 5, Staffordshire 5; Staffordshire 20, North Midlands 11 **Midlands play-off semi-finals:** Warwickshire 24, East Midlands 5; Leicestershire 23, Staffordshire 24 **Midlands play-off final:** Warwickshire 31, Staffordshire 0 **North:** Lancashire 23, Cheshire 5; Cumbria 19, Lancashire 39; Cheshire 32, Cumbria 18 (Northumberland and Durham cancelled); Yorkshire 17, Northumberland 11; Durham 10, Yorkshire 31 **North play-off:** Yorkshire 11, Lancashire 3 **South & South-West:** Berkshire 3, RAF 6; Buckinghamshire 74, Oxfordshire 3; Berkshire 8, Dorset & Wilts 18; RAF 11, Buckinghamshire 24; Dorset & Wilts 5, Buckinghamshire 46; Oxfordshire 11, Berkshire 41; Buckinghamshire 33, Berkshire 7; Dorset & Wilts 12, RAF 22; Oxfordshire 3, Dorset & Wilts 46; Cornwall 26, Devon 20; Somerset 60, Royal Navy 7; Devon 26, Cornwall 10; Royal Navy 6, Cornwall 56; Cornwall 20, Somerset 15; Gloucestershire 33, Royal Navy 7; Royal Navy 0, Devon 80; Somerset 6, Gloucestershire 22; Devon 5, Somerset 29; Gloucestershire 11, Cornwall 18 **South & South-West play-off:** Buckinghamshire 30, Cornwall 11 **Semi-finals:** Buckinghamshire 21, Yorkshire 12; Warwickshire 15, Surrey 0

FIRA REGROUPS FOR A NEW EUROPE

THE FIRA CHAMPIONSHIP 1992-93
Chris Rhys

The restructuring of the FIRA league system in 1992-93 meant that, for the first time since 1934, France did not play Romania and Italy in the championship. Although the fixtures continued as 'friendly' internationals, the three major countries found themselves in separate groups as reorganisation took place.

For the 1992-93 season, Group A was divided into two sections with France in Pool 1 and Italy and Romania in Pool 2. The top two countries in each pool go forward to a new Group A for 1993-94. The decision to split the countries for a season was taken because many believed that the break-up of the Soviet Union had resulted in a considerable falling off in the standards of the old USSR side. The FIRA committee had also decided to look at whether there were any other countries worthy of promotion to the top group.

As a consequence the season was disjointed, and many matches were one-sided. France fielded a variety of XVs, including Armed Forces, B XVs and Under-23 combinations, and Italy too resorted to fielding two separate XVs.

The most significant match of the season was probably the first game in Pool 2, in which Italy beat Romania 22-3 to establish domination of their section. Italy scored tries through Marcello Cuttitta, Checchinato and Bottachiari, with a conversion each from Troiani and Bonomi and a Bonomi penalty. Nichitean's late penalty was a consolation score for Romania.

Meanwhile in Pool 1 France, without any challenge, rattled up 11 tries against both Russia and Germany, Ironically, when the season's experiment had been prompted largely by Soviet fragmentation, it was Russia who finished runners-up to France to qualify for the top group next season.

Group A Pool 1
RESULTS

1992	*Venue*	*Result*			
11 Oct	Brussels	Belgium	11	Russia	17
18 Oct	Villeneuve sur Lot	France	76	Russia	12
25 Oct	Moscow	Russia	18	Germany	15
1 Nov	Brussels	Belgium	9	Morocco	11
15 Nov	Stuttgart	Germany	13	Belgium	10
1993					
21 Mar	Soissons	France	38	Belgium	6
17 Apr	Casablanca	Morocco	23	Germany	3
15 May	Moscow	Russia	24	Morocco	16
29 May	Casablanca	Morocco	12	France	34
30 May	Hanover	Germany	27	France	71

FINAL TABLE

	P	W	D	L	F	A	Pts
France	4	4	0	0	219	57	12
Russia	4	3	0	1	71	118	10
Morocco	4	2	0	2	62	70	8
Germany	4	1	0	3	58	122	6
Belgium	4	0	0	4	36	79	4

Group A Pool 2
RESULTS

1992	*Venue*	*Result*			
1 Oct	Rome	Italy	22	Romania	3

1993					
30 Jan	Tunis	Tunisia	8	Spain	20
14 Feb	Madrid	Spain	0	Italy	52
27 Mar	Leno	Italy	51	Tunisia	8
3 Apr	Lisbon	Portugal	13	Romania	41
17 Apr	Coimbra	Portugal	11	Italy	33
24 Apr	Tunis	Tunisia	14	Portugal	10
8 May	Bucharest	Romania	51	Tunisia	0
16 May	Lisbon	Portugal	15	Spain	37
30 May	Bucharest	Romania	33	Spain	15

FINAL TABLE

	P	W	D	L	F	A	Pts
Italy	4	4	0	0	158	22	12
Romania	4	3	0	1	128	50	10
Spain	4	2	0	2	72	108	8
Tunisia	4	1	0	3	30	132	6
Portugal	4	0	0	4	49	125	4

MATCHES OUTSIDE THE FIRA CHAMPIONSHIP 1992-93

20 February 1993, Treviso

Italy 12 (4PG)   **France 14** (2PG 1DG 1T)
Italy *Penalty Goals:* Dominquez (4)
France *Try:* Larran   *Penalty Goals:* Bertranck, Penaud   *Dropped Goal:* Penaud

20 May 1993, Dinamo Stadium, Bucharest

Romania 20 (2G 2PG)   **France 37** (4G 3PG)
Romania: D Marian; V Brici, N Fulina, N Racean, G Solomie; N Nichitean, D Neaga;
G Leonte, G Ion, D Popa, C Tudor, C Cojocariu, H Dumitras (*capt*), I Seceleanu,
T Brinza *Replacements* T Oroian for Cojocariu (59 mins); V Ionescu for Popa (64 mins);
C Gheorghe for Ion (69 mins)
Scorer *Tries:* Neaga, Leonte   *Conversions:* Nichitean (2)   *Penalty Goals:* Nichitean (2)
France: J L Sadourny (Colomiers); P Bernat-Salles (Pau), P Sella (Agen), H Couffignal

(Colomiers), S Viars (Brive); A Penaud (Brive), A Hueber (Toulon); J-M Gonzales (Bayonne), J-F Tordo (Nice) (*capt*), L Seigne (Merignac), Y Lemeur (Racing Club de France), O Roumat (Dax), L Cabannes (Racing Club de France), J M Lhermet (Montferrand), M Cecillon (Bourgoin) *Replacement* L Verge (Bègles) for Tordo (16 mins)
Scorer *Tries:* Bernat-Salles (3), Cecillon   *Conversions:* Viars (4)   *Penalty Goals:* Viars (3)
Referee B W Stirling (Ireland)

Groups B and C will continue into next season and may also include World Cup qualifying results. Group B Pool 1 comprises Andorra – who are in a midway lead – Holland, Poland, Sweden and the Czech Republic. Group B Pool 2 contains Austria, Croatia, Hungary and Slovenia. There are three Group C pools: Bulgaria, Luxembourg and Switzerland in Pool 1; Lithuania, Latvia and Moldavia in Pool 2, and Georgia, Ukraine and Khazastan-Ubekistan in Pool 3.

OTHER INTERNATIONAL TOURNAMENTS

CURRIE CUP 1992

Final: *12 September 1992, Ellis Park, Johannesburg*
Transvaal 13 (1G 2PG)   **Natal 14** (3PG 1T)

Transvaal: T van Rensburg; P Hendriks, H Fuls, J Thomson, J Small; H Le Roux, G Wright; H Rodgers, H Roberts, B Swart, L Labuschagne, K Wiese, I MacDonald, J Breedt (*capt*), F Pienaar
Scorers *Try:* Fuls   *Conversion:* van Rensburg   *Penalty Goals:* van Rensburg (2)
Natal: H Reece-Edwards; K van der Westhuizen, P Muller, R Muir, A Watson; H Honiball, R du Preez; G Harding, J Allen, L Muller, S Platford, S Atherton, A Blakeway, G Teichmann, W Bartmann (*capt*)
Scorers *Try:* Teichmann   *Penalty Goals:* Reece-Edwards (3)
Referee F Burger (SARFU)

SECTION A

	P	W	D	L	F	A	Pts
Natal	10	8	1	1	246	175	17
Transvaal	10	6	2	2	373	267	14
N Transvaal	10	5	0	5	242	218	10
W Province	10	4	0	6	205	280	8
O Free State	10	3	1	6	236	248	7
East Province	10	2	0	8	152	266	4

SECTION CENTRAL A

	P	W	D	L	F	A	Pts
W Transvaal	6	4	0	2	142	96	8
Border	6	4	0	2	114	86	8
Northern OFS	6	3	0	3	143	112	6
E Transvaal	6	1	0	5	64	169	2

SECTION CENTRAL B

	P	W	D	L	F	A	Pts
Boland	8	6	0	2	189	132	12
G West	8	6	0	2	128	77	12
Far North	8	3	1	4	158	185	7
Vaal Triangle	8	3	0	5	140	144	6
SE Transvaal	8	1	1	6	141	218	3

SECTION RURAL A

	P	W	D	L	F	A	Pts
Eastern OFS	6	5	1	0	194	92	11
Stellaland	6	4	1	1	218	76	9
SW Districts	6	4	0	2	162	105	8
North-East Cape	6	3	0	3	157	93	6
N Natal	6	2	0	4	122	144	4
Lowveld	6	1	0	5	91	154	2
North-West Cape	6	1	0	5	36	316	2

SUPER-10 TOURNAMENT

Final: *22 May 1993, Ellis Park, Johannesburg*
Transvaal 20 (1G 1PG 2T)   **Auckland 17** (2G 1PG)

Transvaal: T van Rensburg; P Hendriks, J Mulder, B Fourie, C Dirks; H Le Roux, J Roux; B Swart, U Schmidt, J Le Roux, K Wiese, H Strydom, J McDonald, D Lotter, F Pienaar (*capt*)
Scorers *Tries:* Schmidt (2), Pienaar   *Conversion:* van Rensburg
Penalty Goal: van Rensburg
Auckland: S Howarth; V Tuigamala, L Stensness, E Clarke, T Wright; G Fox, T Nu'ualita; C Dowd, S Fitzpatrick (*capt*), O Brown, R Fromont, R Brooke, B Jackson, M Jones, M Carter *Replacement* Z Brooke for Jackson
Scorers *Tries:* Stensness, Tuigamala   *Conversions:* Fox (2)   *Penalty Goal:* Fox
Referee F Burger (Western Province)

Pool A

Western Samoa 27, Queensland 19; Otago 22, Auckland 63; Queensland 21, Auckland 22; Natal 5, Western Samoa 13; Auckland 18, Western Samoa 10; Otago 13, Natal 35; Auckland 22, Natal 6; Queensland 20, Otago 8; Natal 32, Queensland 16; Western Samoa 30, Otago 20
Pool winners: Auckland

Pool B

Waikato 29, North Harbour 24; Transvaal 42, Northern Transvaal 22; New South Wales 17, Waikato 13; Transvaal 39, North Harbour 13; Northern Transvaal 45, New South Wales 20; Transvaal 30, Waikato 15; Waikato 18, Northern Transvaal 28; North Harbour 16, New South Wales 17; North Harbour 29, Northern Transvaal 14; New South Wales 3, Transvaal 10
Pool winners: Transvaal

FRENCH CLUB CHAMPIONSHIP 1993
5 June 1993, Parc des Princes

Castres 14 (2PG 1DG 1T)   **Grenoble 11** (2PG 1T)

With the return of Jacques Fouroux as an active force in French rugby, it was perhaps inevitable that the 1993 Championship final should become one of the most controversial ever played. In pure rugby terms it was a disappointingly mediocre spectacle, but while Castres and Grenoble never reached the depths of the foul-tempered 1990 final between Agen and Racing, the game and its aftermath left the balmy Paris evening tainted with ill-feeling.

The main reason for the bitter after-taste? A try awarded to Gary Whetton, the former All Black captain, playing his first season for Castres, which allowed his team to take an 11-8 lead with 12 minutes remaining. The Grenoble players, and their manager/coach Fouroux, instantly reacted strongly to the referee's decision, claiming that Franck Hueber, the replacement Grenoble scrum-half, had already touched down after claiming a 'mark' behind the goal-line. TV evidence was inconclusive, but two days later *L'Equipe* splashed a five-column photograph showing the Hueber touchdown across its front page. In the after-match turmoil Fouroux claimed victimisation by the Agen-based referee, and Grenoble requested a re-match.

Justified or not, the referee's decision remained, and will no doubt become the only memorable moment of a forgettable final. For both teams the stakes were uncommonly high: Castres had not been in a final since 1950, and Grenoble, despite an enviable record, had not won a title since 1954. Consequently they both concentrated on playing percentage rugby, a tactic in which Grenoble, with their massive pack (average weight over 17 and a half stones), appeared to have the advantage. But as happened in the semi-finals in 1992, they were once again badly let down by their kickers, who missed with seven penalty attempts.

Castres survived the initial terrible onslaught from the Grenoble forwards, intent on setting up their 16st 4lbs Polynesian centre Willy Taofifenua with the crash-ball. Regrouping as they had done all season with the reassuring presence of Whetton, they surged back to put the first points on the board with a penalty by Laurent Labit.

Grenoble replied with one of the few moments of elegance in the match, a try from Frederic Vélo from a well-placed scrum, to lead 5-3 at half-time. However, the composure of the Castrais, the unexpected resistance of their scrum, and the deft leadership of their fly-half and captain Francis Rui kept them in the match. Rui dropped a neat goal from 40 metres, then Cyril Savy at last found his range after 60 minutes to put Grenoble ahead 8-6.

The Whetton try, eight minutes later, was the turning-point, and even though in the white-hot passion of the dying minutes Grenoble were able to equalise with a penalty from Hueber, the Castres full-back Laurent Labit brought up a record personal tally of 301 points for the season with a final penalty four minutes from full-time.

Teams in the final
Castres: L Labit; J-B Bergès, A Lungu, N Combes, C Luquiaud; F Rui *(capt)*, C Tonini; L Toussaint, C Urios, T Laforgue, T Bourdet, G Whetton, J Diaz, G Pagès, A Carminati
Scorers *Try:* Whetton   *Penalty Goals:* Labit (2)   *Dropped Goal:* Rui
Grenoble: C Savy; P Meunier, W Taofifenua, F Vélo, B Bardou; P Goirand, D Mazille; P Tapie, E Ferruit, F Capdeville, O Merle, O Brouzet, G Kacala, H Chaffardon *(capt)*, D Mandic *Replacement* F Hueber for Mazille
Scorers *Try:* Vélo   *Penalty Goals:* Savy, Hueber
Referee D Salles (Perigord-Agenias)

Quarter-finals *(16 May)*
Agen 33, Brive 19; Castres 71, Narbonne 54 (game replayed: first game Castres 38, Narbonne 33; second game Castres 33, Narbonne 21); Toulon 10, Perpignan 9
Semi-finals *(29 May)*
Grenoble 21, Agen 15; Castres 17, Toulon 16

SEVENS TOURNAMENTS 1992-93

RUGBY WORLD CUP SEVENS
Murrayfield, 16-18 April 1993

Even though the tournament had some important in-built flaws, the concept of a world sevens was vindicated over three days of all-action try-feasting play at Murrayfield. The first two days, during which 24 countries competed in pools, were too much of a good thing, with try after try. Ultimately, these opening stages lacked conviction. Also, the onerous nature of the event meant that the finalists had to play five games in their pool, a further three in the final-day final pool, a semi-final and a final. That programme was ridiculous: in one sense, it meant that the winning team would be the one which had best luck with injuries. Some teams were reduced almost to a crawl on the final day because they were carrying injuries.

There was also a certain lack of conviction in the surroundings. It was very cold, the stadium was only half-built and one side of the ground was restricted to players and officials and the media area. Having said that, the parts of the ground which were finished looked magnificent and Murrayfield, when complete, will be a fabulous home for Scottish rugby.

There were also many complaints from spectators at the poor refreshment facilities. A sevens tournament is a long operation. It is essential that catering should be easily available as cheaply as possible, and long queues were a sign of poor preparation on the part of the organisers. These areas were where the tournament fell down.

By the end, England were the team left standing up, and whatever one's reservations about the shorter game, there can be no praise too high for the squad of ten heroes who battled through more favoured sides for a wonderful victory. Certainly, no man in the tournament could live up to Andrew Harriman, England's frighteningly fast wing and captain; no forwards combined the skills and pace and conviction of Tim Rodber and Chris Sheasby or the good sense in midfield of Adedeyo Adebayo. These men were well known. By the end, the rugby world also knew a little of Dave Scully, the tough Yorkshireman whose excellence at scrum-half powered the team. Scully had tackled the charging Fijian giant, Rasari, when the teams met. He hit Rasari so hard that the run was stopped, the ball rewon and an England try scored at the other end. This was recognised by the judges of the Famous Grouse Awards as the Moment of the Tournament.

For this honour it vied with a brilliant opening try in the final, against Australia, by Harriman. He blasted past David Campese and the other Australians as if the defenders were rooted to the spot. And also with a try by Willie Ofahengaue in the semi-final, in which Australia beat Ireland. The Irish played wonderfully throughout the tournament and

England's Andrew Harriman, the star of the Rugby World Cup Sevens, powers past Australia's Ryan Constable for the brilliant opening try of the final.

were beaten only in the last move of the match. But what a move. The Australians kept the ball in play for what seemed an eternity and Ofahengaue eventually scored at the posts.

The final day of action was breathtaking, with all kinds of grudge matches piling in upon each other: Western Samoa-Fiji; New Zealand-South Africa; England-Australia. The South Seas challenge, which had looked so strong over the first two days, seemed to wither in the cold of the final day, and both Samoa and Fiji bowed, but they left behind memories of their rich skills.

Among the smaller teams, the heroic Latvians played well, losing all five pool games but without embarrassing themselves. They were fêted around Edinburgh, and the occasional tries scored by the lesser-known heroes of Latvia, Holland, Taiwan and Namibia were warmly acclaimed by the crowd. Less appreciative were the followers of Scotland, Wales and France. All three played extremely poorly, especially the Scots. They had spent thousands on a global warm-up tour but their chances cooled quickly. Argentina, who won the Plate, and Japan, who won the Bowl, joined the proud Englishmen on the victory rostrum.

ENGLAND 21 (3G) **AUSTRALIA 17** (1G 2T)
ENGLAND: A Harriman (*capt*), A Adebayo, N Beal, D Scully; T Rodber, C Sheasby, L Dallaglio *Replacement* J Cassell for Rodber
Scorers *Tries:* Harriman, Dallaglio, Rodber   *Conversions:* Beal (3)
AUSTRALIA: D Campese, R Constable, M Lynagh (*capt*), S Taupeaffe; V Ofahengaue, M Burke, J Fenwicke
Scorers *Tries:* Campese, Taupeaffe, Lynagh   *Conversion:* Lynagh
Referee P Robin (France)

RESULTS

Group A: Fiji 42, Latvia 0; South Africa 28, Japan 5; Wales 33, Romania 7; Fiji 28, Japan 17; Latvia 5, Romania 22; South Africa 36, Wales 14; Fiji 40, Romania 0; Japan 7, Wales 35; Latvia 5, South Africa 47; Fiji 21, Wales 17; South Africa 38, Romania 0; Japan 21, Latvia 14; South Africa 26, Fiji 19; Wales 36, Latvia 7; Romania 15, Japan 17

	P	W	D	L	F	A	Pts
South Africa	5	5	0	0	175	43	15
Fiji	5	4	0	1	150	60	13
Wales	5	3	0	2	135	78	11
Japan	5	2	0	3	67	120	9
Romania	5	1	0	4	44	133	7
Latvia	5	0	0	5	31	168	5

Group B: New Zealand 49, Holland 7; France 22, United States 7; Ireland 21, South Korea 12; New Zealand 19, United States 5; Holland 12, South Korea 28; France 9, Ireland 17; New Zealand 19, France 5; Ireland 45, Holland 0; South Korea 26, United States 19; South Korea 14, France 0; United States 31, Holland 0; New Zealand 46, South Korea 0; France 26, Holland 14; New Zealand 24, Ireland 7; Ireland 38, United States 0

	P	W	D	L	F	A	Pts
New Zealand	5	5	0	0	157	24	15
Ireland	5	4	0	1	128	45	13
South Korea	5	3	0	2	80	98	11
France	5	2	0	3	62	71	9
United States	5	1	0	4	62	105	7
Holland	5	0	0	5	33	179	5

Group C: Australia 28, Taiwan 0; Scotland 15, Tonga 7; Argentina 17, Italy 7; Australia 7, Tonga 10; Taiwan 14, Italy 15; Scotland 10, Argentina 14; Australia 40, Italy 0; Tonga 17, Argentina 5; Taiwan 5, Scotland 36; Argentina 26, Taiwan 5; Tonga 31, Italy 7, Australia 26, Scotland 14; Tonga 52, Taiwan 0; Australia 40, Argentina 5, Scotland 21, Italy 12

	P	W	D	L	F	A	Pts
Australia	5	4	0	1	141	29	13
Tonga	5	4	0	1	117	34	13
Argentina	5	3	0	2	67	79	11
Scotland	5	3	0	2	96	64	11
Italy	5	1	0	4	41	123	7
Taiwan	5	0	0	5	24	157	5

Group D: England 40, Hong Kong 5; Western Samoa 47, Spain 0; Canada 21, Namibia 7; England 31, Spain 0; Hong Kong 19, Namibia

17; Western Samoa 28, Canada 14; Canada 35, Hong Kong 7; Namibia 26, Spain 21; Western Samoa 28, England 10; Western Samoa 47, Namibia 0; Spain 26, Hong Kong 5; England 33, Canada 0; Spain 12, Canada 5; Western Samoa 43, Hong Kong 7; England 24, Namibia 5

	P	W	D	L	F	A	Pts
W Samoa	5	5	0	0	193	31	15
England	5	4	0	1	138	38	13
Canada	5	2	0	3	75	87	9
Spain	5	2	0	3	59	114	9
Hong Kong	5	1	0	4	43	161	7
Namibia	5	1	0	4	55	132	7

PLATE: Semi-finals: Spain 10, Wales 7; Argentina 24, South Korea 0 **Final:** Argentina 19, Spain 12

BOWL: Semi-finals: Scotland 14, France 7; Japan 14, Canada 0 **Final:** Japan 33, Scotland 19

CUP: Quarter-finals

Group 1: Ireland 17, Western Samoa 0; Fiji 21, Tonga 7; Fiji 14, Western Samoa 12, Ireland 14, Tonga 12; Western Samoa 42, Tonga 7; Fiji 31, Ireland 7

	P	W	D	L	F	A	Pts
Fiji	3	3	0	0	66	26	9
Ireland	3	2	0	1	38	43	7
W Samoa	3	1	0	2	54	38	5
Tonga	3	0	0	3	26	77	3

Group 2: Australia 7, South Africa 5; England 21, New Zealand 12; England 14, South Africa 7; New Zealand 42, Australia 0; South Africa 31, New Zealand 12; Australia 21, England 12

	P	W	D	L	F	A	Pts
Australia	3	2	0	1	28	59	7
England	3	2	0	1	47	40	7
South Africa	3	1	0	2	43	35	5
New Zealand	3	1	0	2	68	52	5

CUP: Semi-finals: England 21, Fiji 7; Australia 21, Ireland 19

THE 1993 CATHAY PACIFIC-HONG KONG BANK SEVENS

Nick Cain *Rugby World & Post*

It was a year of rebuilding. Twelve months after the old Government Stadium was demolished a new steeply tiered, space-age structure with a 40,000 capacity sprang up, with almost miraculous speed, to replace it. But the rebuilding of the Hong Kong Sevens venue at Do Kon Po was small beer compared to the rebuilding needed in Western Samoa after the depradations visited on the tiny Pacific islands last year by a series of cyclones, culminating in a hurricane bearing the deceptively homely name of Val. What Val actually did was to leave a trail of destruction in its wake, wrecking the homes and livelihoods of many of Western Samoa's 150,000 inhabitants.

True to the legacy of their ancestors – the Polynesian warriors who faced all measure of adversity in crossing vast tracts of the Pacific before making landfall in the island paradise – today's Samoans are made of strong stuff. Nowhere is this more evident than on the rugby field. Given their quarter-final placing at the last World Cup and the number of Western Samoans 'adopted' currently by New Zealand for either All Black or provincial purposes, they undoubtedly produce more rugby talent per capita than any other country on earth. They proved the point in Hong Kong by deposing the champions and hot favourites, three-titles-on-the-trot Fiji, to christen the new stadium with their first-ever win at the Cathay Pacific-Hong Kong Bank-sponsored event after a highly charged final.

The tone was set by an intimidating variation on the 'Come Dancing' theme when the Samoans responded to the Fijian *cibi* with a blood-curdling rendition of their own war dance, the *manu*.

119

Fiji's Paula Bale (left), and Anatelea Aiolupo of Western Samoa compete for possession in the final of the Hong Kong Sevens, won for the first time by the Samoans, by 14-12.

In a blur of first-half action the Samoans established a 14-12 lead, Aiolupo's conversion keeping them in front as tries from Fiji's Vonolagi and Rasari were matched by Ieremia and Vaisuai. But no sooner had Vaisuai scored than he was upended by an awful challenge by Waki, which left him sidelined and the final teetering on the brink of inter-island warfare. It must be said that both sides, while a cut above anyone else in Hong Kong, are too often guilty, not only of playing the man rather than the ball, but also of making playing offside without being detected into an art form.

Despite the reassuring presence of the brilliant Waisale Serevi, who put paid to Australia in the semi-finals with a virtuoso display which included a hat-trick of tries, in the final the Fijians were the chief culprits. While Sila Vaifale and Lolagi Koko kept their composure and tackled hard but fairly for Samoa, the Fijians, Vonolagi and Waki in particular, paid the price for their indiscipline as they hardly got their hands on the ball in the scoreless second half. There is no doubt that if the six-foot-three minister-in-the-making Koko, who later pipped Serevi to the award for the tournament's Best and Fairest Player, takes up his holy orders with the same blockbusting commitment he shows on the pitch, he will be a major success.

Of the rest of the field South Africa were notable for a respectable Hong Kong debut, even if they didn't possess sufficient sevens acumen to overcome a New Zealand seven featuring Western Samoans Frank Bunce and Junior Paramore. Their fellow countrymen were too good for them in a semi-final which avenged their controversial 'overtime' defeat the previous year.

Ireland, still buzzing from their Five Nations trouncing of England, were a revelation. With Elwood calling the shots, they were very unlucky to go out to Australia when Lynagh's forward pass in extra time of their quarter-final led to Burke's winning score. Both Scotland and Wales – masquerading as a President's VII – went out at the same stage, to Samoa and Fiji respectively. While the Scots looked jaded after their sevens tour of the Southern Hemisphere the Welsh at least gave the Fijians a run for their money. So much so that, despite a 33-7 reverse, their fans broke into 'Bread of Heaven'.

They were still singing it when Danny Kaleopa, the Western Samoan captain, raised the cup with his band of teetotalling churchgoers and stated: 'There is virtually no food left, but we are rebuilding. This win has given our country the biggest boost ever.'

Pool A: Fiji 49, Malaysia 0; Namibia 38, Malaysia 7; Fiji 40, Namibia 7 **Pool B:** Canada 28, Papua New Guinea 10; Welsh President's VII 35, Papua New Guinea 2; Welsh President's VII 40, Canada 0 **Pool C:** Ireland 7, Italy 5; Italy 19, Hong Kong 14; Ireland 24, Hong Kong 0 **Pool D:** Australia 47, Singapore 5; American Eagles 42, Singapore 0; Australia 45, American Eagles 0 **Pool E:** Western Samoa 35, Thailand 0; Japan 40, Thailand 0; Western Samoa 40, Japan 7 **Pool F:** Scotland 28, Romania 5; Tonga 31, Romania 14; Scotland 10, Tonga 7 **Pool G:** South Africa 49, Sri Lanka 0; Argentina 19,

Sri Lanka 7; South Africa 28, Argentina 0 **Pool H:** New Zealand 28, Taiwan 5; Taiwan 14, South Korea 7; New Zealand 34, South Korea 0

BOWL: Final: Romania 17, Papua New Guinea 14

PLATE: Final: Tonga 38, Italy 28

CUP: Quarter-finals: Fiji 33, Welsh President's VII 7; Australia 17, Ireland 12; Western Samoa 28, Scotland 14; New Zealand 34, South Korea 0 **Semi-finals:** Fiji 17, Australia 14; Western Samoa 24, New Zealand 14 **Final:** Western Samoa 14, Fiji 12

Teams in the final
Fiji: M Rasari, S Vonolagi, F Seru, W Serevi; S Rabaka, P Bale, P Waki
Scorers *Tries:* Vonolagi, Rasari   *Conversion:* Serevi
Western Samoa: A Vaisuai, S Vaifale, A Ieremia, L Koko; J Tanu'u, A Aiolupo, B Lima
Replacement J Paramore for Vaisuai
Scorers *Tries:* Ieremia, Vaisuai   *Conversions:* Aiolupo (2)
Referee R Megson (Scotland)

THE MIDDLESEX SEVENS 1993
(Sponsored by Save & Prosper)

Wasps put on a sevens show that would have upstaged Harry Houdini. They recovered in the final from 24-5 down to perform the most extraordinary escape act in the history of the Middlesex Sevens. The north London club scored three converted tries during the last seven minutes of the nerve-racking final against Northampton to snatch victory by 26-24.

Adrian Thompson, the tactical genius of the Wasps VII, was surrounded by splendid finishers. Phil Hopley, Lawrence Dallaglio (fresh from England's triumph in the Rugby World Cup Sevens at Murrayfield), Mike Friday, Paul Volley and Laurence Scrase made effective contributions to Wasps' remarkable comeback. However, it was beefy Mike White's charge through the Northampton defence that presented Hopley with the chance to win the final with the last kick of the afternoon. The threequarter made no mistake with the conversion from in front of the posts.

On the way to their first final since 1985, Wasps disposed of both guest teams. They squashed Wellington 35-10 in the quarter-finals but an ill-tempered tie with Western Samoa went to extra time. The islanders, who had been the darlings of the 1992 event, were guilty of cynical fouls and time-wasting, and few among the crowd were disappointed to see them lose to Volley's try for Wasps in the sudden-death semi-final.

In the Plate competition for clubs knocked out in the sixth round, Richmond romped home 36-7 against Basingstoke. It was also in the Plate event that the giant-killing act of the day was seen when Reading generated one of the loudest cheers of the afternoon as they defeated Gloucester by 28-14.

RESULTS

Sixth round: London Scottish 19, Blackheath 14; Richmond 12, Northampton 19; Gloucester 5, Saracens 27; Reading 0, Harlequins 48; Wellington (NZ) 49, Rosslyn Park 12; Wasps 31, Basingstoke 0; Orrell 5, London Irish 33; Old Gaytonians 5, Western Samoa 38
Seventh round: London Scottish 12, Northampton 26; Saracens 14, Harlequins 21; Wellington 10, Wasps 35; London Irish 14, Western Samoa 17 **Semi-finals:** Northampton 26, Harlequins 5; Wasps 17, Western Samoa 12 **Final:** Wasps 26, Northampton 24

Teams in the final
Wasps: L Scrase, P Hopley, A Thompson, M Friday; M White, P Volley, L Dallaglio
Scorers *Tries:* Hopley (2), Friday, White   *Conversions:* Hopley (3)
Northampton: H Thorneycroft, F Packman, J Steele, N Knowles; M Word, P Pask, M Steffart
Scorers *Tries:* Steffart, Knowles, Word   *Conversions:* Steele (3)   *Penalty Goal:* Steele
Referee N Cousins

WINNERS

1926 **Harlequins**	1949 **Heriot's FP**	1972 **London Welsh**
1927 **Harlequins**	1950 **Rosslyn Park**	1973 **London Welsh**
1928 **Harlequins**	1951 **Richmond II**	1974 **Richmond**
1929 **Harlequins**	1952 **Wasps**	1975 **Richmond**
1930 **London Welsh**	1953 **Richmond**	1976 **Loughborough Colls**
1931 **London Welsh**	1954 **Rosslyn Park**	1977 **Richmond**
1932 **Blackheath**	1955 **Richmond**	1978 **Harlequins**
1933 **Harlequins**	1956 **London Welsh**	1979 **Richmond**
1934 **Barbarians**	1957 **St Luke's College**	1980 **Richmond**
1935 **Harlequins**	1958 **Blackheath**	1981 **Rosslyn Park**
1936 **Sale**	1959 **Loughborough Colls**	1982 **Stewart's-Melville FP**
1937 **London Scottish**	1960 **London Scottish**	1983 **Richmond**
1938 **Metropolitan Police**	1961 **London Scottish**	1984 **London Welsh**
1939 **Cardiff**	1962 **London Scottish**	1985 **Wasps**
1940 **St Mary's Hospital**	1963 **London Scottish**	1986 **Harlequins**
1941 **Cambridge U**	1964 **Loughborough Colls**	1987 **Harlequins**
1942 **St Mary's Hospital**	1965 **London Scottish**	1988 **Harlequins**
1943 **St Mary's Hospital**	1966 **Loughborough Colls**	1989 **Harlequins**
1944 **St Mary's Hospital**	1967 **Harlequins**	1990 **Harlequins**
1945 **Notts**	1968 **London Welsh**	1991 **London Scottish**
1946 **St Mary's Hospital**	1969 **St Luke's College**	1992 **Western Samoa**
1947 **Rosslyn Park**	1970 **Loughborough Colls**	1993 **Wasps**
1948 **Wasps**	1971 **London Welsh**	

Harlequins have won the title 13 times, Richmond 9 (including one by their second VII), London Welsh 8, London Scottish 7, St Mary's Hospital and Loughborough Colleges 5 each, Rosslyn Park and Wasps 4 each, Blackheath and St Luke's College (now Exeter University) twice, Barbarians, Sale, Met Police, Cardiff, Cambridge University, Notts (now Nottingham), Heriot's FP, Stewart's-Melville FP and Western Samoa once each

WORTHINGTON WELSH SEVENS 1992-93

29 August 1992, Cardiff RFC Ground, Cardiff Arms Park

Preliminary round: Cardiff 45, Pontypridd 0; Aberavon 47, Penarth 0
First round: Cardiff 45, Aberavon 5; Bridgend 24, Neath 7; Maesteg 27, Tredegar 12; Newbridge 29, Cross Keys 7; Glamorgan Wanderers 24, Pontypool 5; South Wales Police 19, Abertillery 7; Swansea 36, Ebbw Vale 14; Llanelli 21, Newport 10

Second round: Cardiff 15, Bridgend 5; Newbridge 31, Maesteg 7; South Wales Police 21, Glamorgan Wanderers 10; Swansea 22, Llanelli 17 (*aet*)
Semi-finals: Swansea 26, South Wales Police 19; Newbridge 24, Cardiff 19
Final: Newbridge 28, Swansea 24

Teams in the Final
Newbridge: D Manley, B Hayward, D Rees, S Fealey (*capt*); A Griffiths, P Crane, I Wilkinson *Replacement* S Crandon for Wilkinson
Swansea: S Davies, A Williams, M H Titley (*capt*), R N Jones; I Davies, I S Gibbs, A Reynolds
Referee C Thomas (Neath)

ENGLAND RETREAT INTO THE PACK OF EUROPEAN RUGBY

THE 1992-93 SEASON IN ENGLAND
David Hands *The Times*

A season for England which started with such unparalleled hopes proved one too far by the end. Not that the game's profile, so high after successive Grand Slams and a World Cup final appearance in 1991-92, drooped in any way, but Geoff Cooke, the national team manager, proved uncannily prophetic when he said: 'We will have to shoot ourselves in the foot not to continue being successful.' England did just that, giving away the critical score to Wales which, against an inspired defence, they could not then reclaim. The 10-9 defeat in Cardiff erased hopes of an historic third consecutive 'slam' and, at the same time, raised questions about the motivation of some older members of the side.

Success, of course, is relative. That Rugby Union in England continued to be successful could be in no doubt, not after the huge sponsorship agreed in March between the Rugby Football Union and Courage, the brewers, whose continued support of the Club Championship over the next four years will be worth over £7 million.

The League itself was a genuine contest between evergreen Bath, the holders, and Wasps, who led the way for so long until they reached the Bath Recreation Ground and fell foul of the law. Television evidence showed that Fran Clough, the Wasps centre, did not deserve to be sent off after an exchange with Jeremy Guscott – indeed, Guscott himself might have walked instead. Indeed, that incident was part of and parcel of a sorry weekend for rugby. There was embarrassment when three Harlequins players were reprimanded for wearing non-regulation studs in their Cup tie with Waterloo, and distress at the death of a Hendon player, Seamus Lavelle, during a game against Centaurs.

Rugby had already attracted criticism a month or so earlier when Steve Pilgrim, the Wasps and England B full-back, had been suspended for a year for taking part without payment in a Rugby League trial match. Earlier in the year Oldham Rugby League club had captured the services of Nigel Heslop, the Orrell wing who played in the 1991 Grand Slam England XV.

Since Heslop had also shared, as a replacement, in the 1992 Five Nations Championship, his loss underscored the cracks apparent in the England structure. As early as the October international against Canada – played at Wembley so as not to hinder the rebuilding of Twickenham's new east stand – England lacked the lustre of the previous two seasons. Playing in the redesigned national shirts, they won, but far from comfortably, upset by the abrasive Canadians as well as by the experimental ruck/maul law which proved to be a major issue all season.

The England management used the autumn internationals to look at new blood. Already one significant newcomer, Nick Beal, had been picked out for the national sevens squad, while another, Alex Snow, was invited to join the national training squad. Indeed, Beal played a leading role in the dedicated team which pulled off a remarkable triumph in the inaugural Rugby World Cup Sevens in April.

At Wembley there were debuts for Ian Hunter, Tony Underwood and Victor Ubogu, but before the international against South Africa a month later an old hand, Rory Underwood, returned from his brief international retirement. Ben Clarke, the Bath No 8, made his debut against the South Africans and Rob Andrew, England's fly-half, returned from Toulouse.

The problems of League rugby rumbled on: from the plight of the Gloucester club, which lost a dozen players before the season was barely underway, to the undignified scramble for player-registrations in early spring as players keen to remain in the First Division kept their eyes on the main chance. Amid it all were allegations of inducements which caused Danie Serfontein, the RFU president, to admit that 'illegal practices are widespread'. John Heggadon, the Saracens president, lamented that 'club loyalty as we knew it has gone out of the window', and with some justification – five leading players from his club were known to have signed provisional registration forms elsewhere as Saracens slipped towards relegation.

The second half of the season proved, in the playing sense, a lost opportunity. England A, whose 1992 summer tour to New Zealand had not proved quite as successful as might have been hoped, continued to flourish: they took the South Africans to the wire in November in a match which helped project Stuart Barnes back into the national spotlight, and were then undefeated against all-comers, although Italy and Spain proved less than adequate opposition. But they could not dislodge the sitting tenants in the Championship side save once, when Martin Johnson came in for the injured Wade Dooley.

Johnson played well in a side which hung on grimly to beat France, somewhat fortuitously, by a point. Then came defeat by Wales and demotion for Hunter and Andrew, who undoubtedly suffered through lack of First Division matchplay and, on the day, the mistakes of others. However, his loss was Barnes' gain, and the little Bath fly-half won only his ninth cap, in an international career spanning nine years, against Scotland, who came to Twickenham in search of a Triple Crown. That they left disappointed was due to the rediscovery of an England back division, sparked by Barnes, but which glossed over other imperfections in the team: in the line-out, in the scrum and in the back-row combination. All these chickens came home to roost in Dublin, where a magnificent Irish resurgence carried the day and brought a sad conclusion to the England careers of three magnificent servants – Dooley, Peter Winterbottom and Jonathan Webb.

The England team which played Scotland at Twickenham. L-R, back row: V E Ubogu (replacement), T A K Rodber (replacement), M C Teague, B B Clarke, M C Bayfield, W A Dooley, J A Probyn, J M Webb, P J Winterbottom, J Leonard, P R De Glanville (replacement); front row: C J Oliver (replacement), S Barnes, J C Guscott, B C Moore, W D C Carling (capt), T Underwood, R Underwood, C D Morris, C R Andrew (replacement), S M Bates (replacement).

ENGLISH INTERNATIONAL PLAYERS
(up to 31 March 1993)

ABBREVIATIONS

A – Australia; *Arg* – Argentina; *C* – Canada; *F* – France; *Fj* – Fiji; *I* – Ireland; *It* – Italy; *J* – Japan; *M* – Maoris; *NZ* – New Zealand; *R* – Romania; *S* – Scotland; *SA* – South Africa; *US* – United States; *W* – Wales; (C) – Centenary match v Scotland at Murrayfield, 1971 (non-championship); *P* – England v President's Overseas XV at Twickenham in RFU's Centenary season, 1970-71; (R) – Replacement. Entries in square brackets [ ] indicate appearances in the World Cup.

Note: Years given for Five Nations' matches are for second half of season; eg 1972 means season 1971-72. Years for all other matches refer to the actual year of the match. When a series has taken place, figures have been used to denote the particular matches in which players have featured. Thus 1984 *SA* 2 indicates that a player appeared in the second Test of the series.

Aarvold, C D (Cambridge U, W Hartlepool, Headingley, Blackheath) 1928 *A, W, I, F, S,* 1929 *W, I, F,* 1931 *W, S, F,* 1932 *SA, W, I, S,* 1933 *W*
Ackford, P J (Harlequins) 1988 *A,* 1989 *S, I, F, W, R, Fj,* 1990 *I, F, W, S, Arg* 3, 1991 *W, S, I, F, A, [NZ, It, F, S, A]*
Adams, A A (London Hospital) 1910 *F*
Adams, F R (Richmond) 1875 *I, S,* 1876 *S,* 1877 *I,* 1878 *S,* 1879 *S, I*
Adey, G J (Leicester) 1976 *I, F*
Adkins, S J (Coventry) 1950 *I, F, S,* 1953 *W, I, F, S*
Agar, A E (Harlequins) 1952 *SA, W, S, I, F,* 1953 *W, I*
Alcock, A (Guy's Hospital) 1906 *SA*
Alderson, F H R (Hartlepool R) 1891 *W, I, S,* 1892 *W, S,* 1893 *W*
Alexander, H (Richmond) 1900 *I, S,* 1901 *W, I, S,* 1902 *W, I*
Alexander, W (Northern) 1927 *F*
Allison, D F (Coventry) 1956 *W, I, S, F,* 1957 *W,* 1958 *W, S*
Allport, A (Blackheath) 1892 *W,* 1893 *I,* 1894 *W, I, S*
Anderson, S (Rockcliff) 1899 *I*
Anderson, W F (Orrell) 1973 *NZ* 1
Anderton, C (Manchester FW) 1889 *M*
Andrew, C R (Cambridge U, Nottingham, Wasps, Toulouse) 1985 *R, F, S, I, W,* 1986 *W, S, I, F,* 1987 *I, F, W, [J (R), US],* 1988 *S, I* 1,2, *A* 1,2, *Fj, A,* 1989 *S, I, F, W, R, Fj,* 1990 *I, F, W, S, Arg* 3, 1991 *W, S, I, F, Fj, A, [NZ, It, US, F, S, A],* 1992 *S, I, F, W, C, SA,* 1993 *F, W*
Archer, H (Bridgwater A) 1909 *W, F, I*
Armstrong, R (Northern) 1925 *W*
Arthur, T G (Wasps) 1966 *W, I*
Ashby, R C (Wasps) 1966 *I, F,* 1967 *A*
Ashcroft, A (Waterloo) 1956 *W, I, S, F,* 1957 *W, I, F, S,* 1958 *W, A, I, F, S,* 1959 *I, F, S*
Ashcroft, A H (Birkenhead Park) 1909 *A*
Ashford, W (Richmond) 1897 *W, I,* 1898 *S, W*
Ashworth, A (Oldham) 1892 *I*
Askew, J G (Cambridge U) 1930 *W, I, F*
Aslett, A R (Richmond) 1926 *W, I, F, S,* 1929 *S, F*
Assinder, E W (O Edwardians) 1909 *A, W*
Aston, R L (Blackheath) 1890 *S, I*
Auty, J R (Headingley) 1935 *S*

Bailey, M D (Cambridge U, Wasps) 1984 *SA* 1,2, 1987 *[US],* 1989 *Fj,* 1990 *I, F, S* (R)
Bainbridge, S (Gosforth, Fylde) 1982 *F, W,* 1983 *F, W, S, I, NZ,* 1984 *S, I, F, W,* 1985 *NZ* 1,2, 1987 *F, W, S, [J, US]*
Baker, D G S (OMTs) 1955 *W, I, F, S*
Baker, E M (Moseley) 1895 *W, I, S,* 1896 *W, I, S,* 1897 *W*
Baker, H C (Clifton) 1887 *W*
Bance, J F (Bedford) 1954 *S*
Barley, B (Wakefield) 1984 *I, F, W, A,* 1988 *A* 1,2, *Fj*
Barnes, S (Bristol, Bath) 1984 *A,* 1985 *R* (R), *NZ* 1,2, 1986 *S* (R), *F* (R), 1987 *I* (R), 1988 *Fj,* 1993 *S, I*
Barr, R J (Leicester) 1932 *SA, W, I*
Barrett, E I M (Lennox) 1903 *S*
Barrington, T J M (Bristol) 1931 *W, I*
Barrington-Ward, L E (Edinburgh U) 1910 *W, I, F, S*
Barron, J H (Bingley) 1896 *S,* 1897 *W, I*
Bartlett, J T (Waterloo) 1951 *W*

Bartlett, R M (Harlequins) 1957 *W, I, F, S,* 1958 *I, F, S*
Barton, J (Coventry) 1967 *I, F, W,* 1972 *F*
Batchelor, T B (Oxford U) 1907 *F*
Bates, S M (Wasps) 1989 *R*
Bateson, A H (Otley) 1930 *W, I, F, S*
Bateson, H D (Liverpool) 1879 *I*
Batson, T (Blackheath) 1872 *S,* 1874 *S,* 1875 *I*
Batten, J M (Cambridge U) 1874 *S*
Baume, J L (Northern) 1950 *S*
Baxter, J (Birkenhead Park) 1900 *W, I, S*
Bayfield, M C (Northampton) 1991 *Fj, A,* 1992 *S, I, F, W, C, SA,* 1993 *F, W, S, I*
Bazley, R C (Waterloo) 1952 *I, F,* 1953 *W, I, F, S,* 1955 *W, I, F, S*
Beaumont, W B (Fylde) 1975 *I, A* 1(R),2, 1976 *A, W, S, I, F,* 1977 *S, I, F, W,* 1978 *F, W, S, I, NZ,* 1979 *S, I, F, W, NZ,* 1980 *I, F, W, S,* 1981 *W, S, I, F, Arg* 1,2, 1982 *A, S*
Bedford, H (Morley) 1889 *M,* 1890 *S, I*
Bedford, L L (Headingley) 1931 *W, I*
Beer, I D S (Harlequins) 1955 *F, S*
Beese, M C (Liverpool) 1972 *W, I, F*
Bell, F J (Northern) 1900 *W*
Bell, H (New Brighton) 1884 *I*
Bell, J L (Darlington) 1878 *I*
Bell, P J (Blackheath) 1968 *W, I, F, S*
Bell, R W (Northern) 1900 *W, I, S*
Bendon, G J (Wasps) 1959 *W, I, F, S*
Bennett, N O (St Mary's Hospital, Waterloo) 1947 *W, S, F,* 1948 *A, W, I, S*
Bennett, W N (Bedford, London Welsh) 1975 *S, A* 1, 1976 *S* (R), 1979 *S, I, F, W*
Bennetts, B B (Penzance) 1909 *A, W*
Bentley, J (Sale) 1988 *I* 2, *A* 1
Bentley, J E (Gipsies) 1871 *S,* 1872 *S*
Berridge, M J (Northampton) 1949 *W, I*
Berry, H (Gloucester) 1910 *W, I, F, S*
Berry, J (Tyldesley) 1891 *W, I, S*
Berry, J T W (Leicester) 1939 *W, I, S*
Beswick, E (Swinton) 1882 *I, S*
Biggs, J M (UCH) 1878 *S,* 1879 *I*
Birkett, J G G (Harlequins) 1906 *S, F, SA,* 1907 *F, W, S,* 1908 *F, W, I, S,* 1910 *W, I, S,* 1911 *W, F, I, S,* 1912 *W, I, S, F*
Birkett, L (Clapham R) 1875 *S,* 1877 *I, S*
Birkett, R H (Clapham R) 1871 *S,* 1875 *S,* 1876 *S,* 1877 *I*
Bishop, C C (Blackheath) 1927 *F*
Black, B H (Blackheath) 1930 *W, I, F, S,* 1931 *W, I, S, F,* 1932 *S,* 1933 *W*
Blacklock, J H (Aspatria) 1898 *I,* 1899 *I*
Blakeway, P J (Gloucester) 1980 *I, F, W, S,* 1981 *W, S, I, F,* 1982 *I, F, W,* 1984 *I, F, W, SA* 1, 1985 *R, F, S, I*
Blakiston, A F (Northampton) 1920 *S,* 1921 *W, I, S, F,* 1922 *W, I, S, F,* 1923 *S, F,* 1924 *W, I, F, S,* 1925 *NZ, W, I, S, F*
Blatherwick, T (Manchester) 1878 *I*
Body, J A (Gipsies) 1872 *S,* 1873 *S*
Bolton, C A (United Services) 1909 *F*
Bolton, R (Harlequins) 1933 *W,* 1936 *S,* 1937 *S,* 1938 *W, I*
Bolton, W N (Blackheath) 1882 *I, S,* 1883 *W, I, S,* 1884 *W, I, S,* 1885 *I,* 1887 *I, S*
Bonaventura, M S (Blackheath) 1931 *W*
Bond, A M (Sale) 1978 *NZ,* 1979 *S, I, NZ,* 1980 *I, 1982 *I*

Bonham-Carter, E (Oxford U) 1891 *S*
Bonsor, F (Bradford) 1886 *W, I, S,* 1887 *W, S,* 1889 *M*
Boobbyer, B (Rosslyn Park) 1950 *W, I, F, S,* 1951 *W, F,* 1952 *S, I, F*
Booth, L A (Headingley) 1933 *W, I, S,* 1934 *S,* 1935 *W, I, S*
Botting, I J (Oxford U) 1950 *W, I*
Boughton, H J (Gloucester) 1935 *W, I, S*
Boyle, C W (Oxford U) 1873 *S*
Boyle, S B (Gloucester) 1983 *W, S, I*
Boylen, F (Hartlepool R) 1908 *F, W, I, S*
Bradby, M S (United Services) 1922 *I, F*
Bradley, R (W Hartlepool) 1903 *W*
Bradshaw, H (Bramley) 1892 *S,* 1893 *W, I, S,* 1894 *W, I, S*
Brain, S E (Coventry) 1984 *SA* 2, *A* (R), 1985 *R, F, S, I, W, NZ* 1,2, 1986 *W, S, I, F*
Braithwaite, J (Leicester) 1905 *NZ*
Braithwaite-Exley, B (Headingley) 1949 *W*
Brettargh, A T (Liverpool OB) 1900 *W,* 1903 *I, S,* 1904 *W, I, S,* 1905 *I, S*
Brewer, J (Gipsies) 1876 *I*
Briggs, A (Bradford) 1892 *W, I, S*
Brinn, A (Gloucester) 1972 *W, I, S*
Broadley, T (Bingley) 1893 *W, S,* 1894 *W, I, S,* 1896 *S*
Bromet, W E (Richmond) 1891 *W, I,* 1892 *W, I, S,* 1893 *W, I, S,* 1895 *W, I, S,* 1896 *I*
Brook, P W P (Harlequins) 1930 *S,* 1931 *F,* 1936 *S*
Brooke, T J (Richmond) 1968 *F, S*
Brooks, F G (Bedford) 1906 *SA*
Brooks, M J (Oxford U) 1874 *S*
Brophy, T J (Liverpool) 1964 *I, F, S,* 1965 *W, I,* 1966 *W, I, F*
Brough, J W (Silloth) 1925 *NZ, W*
Brougham, H (Harlequins) 1912 *W, I, S, F*
Brown, A A (Exeter) 1938 *S*
Brown, L G (Oxford U, Blackheath) 1911 *W, F, I, S,* 1913 *SA, W, F, I, S,* 1914 *W, I, S, F,* 1921 *W, I, S, F,* 1922 *W*
Brown, T W (Bristol) 1928 *S,* 1929 *W, I, S, F,* 1932 *S,* 1933 *W, I, S*
Brunton, J (N Durham) 1914 *W, I, S*
Brutton, E B (Cambridge U) 1886 *S*
Bryden, C C (Clapham R) 1876 *I,* 1877 *S*
Bryden, H A (Clapham R) 1874 *S*
Buckingham, R A (Leicester) 1927 *F*
Bucknall, A L (Richmond) 1969 *SA,* 1970 *I, W, S, F,* 1971 *W, I, F, S* (2[1C])
Buckton, J R D (Saracens) 1988 *A* (R), 1990 *Arg* 1,2
Budd, A (Blackheath) 1878 *I,* 1879 *S, I,* 1881 *W, S*
Budworth, R T D (Blackheath) 1890 *W,* 1891 *W, S*
Bull, A G (Northampton) 1914 *W*
Bullough, E (Wigan) 1892 *W, I, S*
Bulpitt, M P (Blackheath) 1970 *S*
Bulteel, A J (Manchester) 1876 *I*
Bunting, W L (Moseley) 1897 *I, S,* 1898 *I, S, W,* 1899 *S,* 1900 *S,* 1901 *I, S*
Burland, D W (Bristol) 1931 *W, I, F,* 1932 *I, S,* 1933 *W, I, S*
Burns, B H (Blackheath) 1871 *S*
Burton, G W (Blackheath) 1879 *S, I,* 1880 *S,* 1881 *I, W, S*
Burton, H C (Richmond) 1926 *W*
Burton, M A (Gloucester) 1972 *W, I, F, S, SA,* 1974 *F, W,* 1975 *S, A* 1,2, 1976 *A, W, S, I, F,* 1978 *F, W*
Bush, J A (Clifton) 1872 *S,* 1873 *S,* 1875 *S,* 1876 *I, S*
Butcher, C J S (Harlequins) 1984 *SA* 1,2, *A*
Butcher, W V (Streatham) 1903 *S,* 1904 *W, I, S,* 1905 *W, I, S*
Butler, A G (Harlequins) 1937 *W, I*
Butler, P E (Gloucester) 1975 *A* 1, 1976 *F*
Butterfield, J (Northampton) 1953 *F, S,* 1954 *W, NZ, I, S, F,* 1955 *W, I, F, S,* 1956 *W, I, S, F,* 1957 *W, I, F, S,* 1958 *W, A, I, F, S,* 1959 *W, I, F, S*
Byrne, J (Moseley) 1897 *W*
Byrne, J F (Moseley) 1894 *W, I, S,* 1895 *I, S,* 1896 *I,* 1897 *W, I, S,* 1898 *I, S, W,* 1899 *I*

Cain, J J (Waterloo) 1950 *W*
Campbell, D A (Cambridge U) 1937 *W, I*
Candler, P L (St Bart's Hospital) 1935 *W,* 1936 *NZ, W, I, S,* 1937 *W, I, S,* 1938 *W, S*
Cannell, L B (Oxford U, St Mary's Hospital) 1948 *F, I, 1949 W, I, F, S,* 1950 *W, I, F, S,* 1952 *SA, W,* 1953 *W,*

I, F, 1956 *I, S, F,* 1957 *W, I*
Caplan, D W N (Headingley) 1978 *S, I*
Cardus, R M (Roundhay) 1979 *F, W*
Carey, G M (Blackheath) 1895 *W, I, S,* 1896 *W, I*
Carleton, J (Orrell) 1979 *NZ,* 1980 *I, F, W, S,* 1981 *W, S, I, F, Arg* 1,2, 1982 *A, S, I, F, W,* 1983 *F, W, S, I, NZ,* 1984 *S, I, F, W, A*
Carling, W D C (Durham U, Harlequins) 1988 *F, W, S, I* 1,2, *A2, Fj, A,* 1989 *S, I, F, W, Fj,* 1990 *I, F, W, S, Arg* 1,2,3, 1991 *W, S, I, F, Fj, A,* [*NZ, It, US, F, S, A*], 1992 *S, I, F, W, C, SA,* 1993 *F, W, S, I*
Carpenter, A D (Gloucester) 1932 *SA*
Carr, R S L (Manchester) 1939 *W, I, S*
Cartwright, V H (Nottingham) 1903 *W, I, S,* 1904 *W, S,* 1905 *W, I, S, NZ,* 1906 *W, I, S, F, SA*
Catcheside, H C (Percy Park) 1924 *W, I, F, S,* 1926 *W, I,* 1927 *I, S*
Cattell, R H B (Blackheath) 1895 *W, I, S,* 1896 *W, I, S,* 1900 *W*
Cave, J W (Richmond) 1889 *M*
Cave, W T C (Blackheath) 1905 *W*
Challis, R (Bristol) 1957 *I, F, S*
Chambers, E L (Bedford) 1908 *F,* 1910 *W, I*
Chantrill, B S (Bristol) 1924 *W, I, F, S*
Chapman, C E (Cambridge U) 1884 *W*
Chapman, F E (Hartlepool) 1910 *W, I, F, S,* 1912 *W,* 1914 *W, I*
Cheesman, W I (OMTs) 1913 *SA, W, F, I*
Cheston, E C (Richmond) 1873 *S,* 1874 *S,* 1875 *I, S,* 1876 *S*
Chilcott, G J (Bath) 1984 *A,* 1986 *I, F,* 1987 *F* (R), *W,* [*J, US, W*(R)], 1988 *I* 2(R), *Fj,* 1989 *I* (R), *F, W, R*
Christopherson, P (Blackheath) 1891 *W, S*
Clark, C W H (Liverpool) 1876 *I*
Clarke, A J (Coventry) 1935 *W, I, S,* 1936 *NZ, W, I*
Clarke, B B (Bath) 1992 *SA,* 1993 *F, W, S, I*
Clarke, S J S (Cambridge U, Blackheath) 1963 *W, I, F, S, NZ* 1,2, *A,* 1964 *NZ, W, I,* 1965 *I, F, S*
Clayton, J H (Liverpool) 1871 *S*
Clements, J W (O Cranleighans) 1959 *I, F, S*
Cleveland, C R (Blackheath) 1887 *W, S*
Clibborn, W G (Richmond) 1886 *W, I, S,* 1887 *W, I, S*
Clough, F J (Cambridge U, Orrell) 1986 *I, F,* 1987 [*J*(R), *US*]
Coates, C H (Yorkshire W) 1880 *S,* 1881 *S,* 1882 *S*
Coates, V H M (Bath) 1913 *SA, W, F, I, S*
Cobby, W (Hull) 1900 *W*
Cockerham, A (Bradford Olicana) 1900 *W*
Colclough, M J (Angoulême, Wasps, Swansea) 1978 *S, I,* 1979 *NZ,* 1980 *F, W, S,* 1981 *W, S, I, F,* 1982 *A, S, I, F, W,* 1983 *F, NZ,* 1984 *S, I, F, W,* 1986 *W, S, I, F*
Coley, E (Northampton) 1929 *F,* 1932 *W*
Collins, P J (Camborne) 1952 *S, I, F*
Collins, W E (O Cheltonians) 1874 *S,* 1875 *I, S,* 1876 *I, S*
Considine, S G U (Bath) 1925 *F*
Conway, G S (Cambridge U, Rugby, Manchester) 1920 *F, I, S,* 1921 *F,* 1922 *W, I, F, S,* 1923 *W, I, S, F,* 1924 *W, I, F, S,* 1925 *NZ, W,* 1927 *W*
Cook, J G (Bedford) 1937 *S*
Cook, P W (Richmond) 1965 *I, F*
Cooke, D A (Harlequins) 1976 *W, S, I, F*
Cooke, D H (Harlequins) 1981 *W, S, I, F,* 1984 *I,* 1985 *R, F, S, I, W, NZ* 1,2
Cooke, P (Richmond) 1939 *W, I*
Coop, T (Leigh) 1892 *S*
Cooper, J G (Moseley) 1909 *A, W*
Cooper, M J (Moseley) 1973 *F, S, NZ* 2 (R), 1975 *F, W,* 1976 *A, W,* 1977 *S, I, F, W*
Coopper, S F (Blackheath) 1900 *W,* 1902 *W, I,* 1905 *W, I, S,* 1907 *W*
Corbett, L J (Bristol) 1921 *F,* 1923 *W, I,* 1924 *W, I, F, S,* 1925 *NZ, W, I, S, F,* 1927 *W, I, S, F*
Corless, B J (Coventry, Moseley) 1976 *A, I* (R), 1977 *S, I, F, W,* 1978 *F, W, S, I*
Cotton, F E (Loughborough Colls, Coventry, Sale) 1971 *S* (2[1C]), *P,* 1973 *W, I, F, S, NZ* 2, *A,* 1974 *S, I,* 1975 *I, F, W,* 1976 *A, W, S, I, F,* 1977 *S, I, F, W,* 1978 *S, I,* 1979 *NZ,* 1980 *I, F, W, S,* 1981 *W*
Coulman, M J (Moseley) 1967 *A, I, F, S, W,* 1968 *W, I, F, S*
Coulson, T J (Coventry) 1927 *W,* 1928 *A, W*
Court, E D (Blackheath) 1885 *W*
Coverdale, H (Blackheath) 1910 *F,* 1912 *I, F,* 1920 *W*

Cove-Smith, R (OMTs)1921 *S, F*, 1922 *I, F, S*, 1923 *W, I, S, F*, 1924 *W, I, S, F*, 1925 *NZ, W, I, S, F*, 1927 *W, I, S, F*,1928 *A, W, I, F, S*, 1929 *W, I*
Cowling, R J (Leicester) 1977 *S, I, F, W*, 1978 *F, NZ*, 1979 *S, I*
Cowman, A R (Loughborough Colls, Coventry) 1971 *S* (2[1C]), *P*, 1973 *W, I*
Cox, N S (Sunderland) 1901 *S*

Ben Clarke of Bath, who won his first cap in England's record 33-16 defeat of South Africa in the autumn. He went on to play in all England's Five Nations matches in 1993, and was selected for the Lions tour in May.

Cranmer, P (Richmond, Moseley) 1934 *W, I, S,* 1935 *W, I, S,* 1936 *NZ, W, I, S,* 1937 *W, I, S,* 1938 *W, I, S*
Creed, R N (Coventry) 1971 *P*
Cridlan, A G (Blackheath) 1935 *W, I, S*
Crompton, C A (Blackheath) 1871 *S*
Crosse, C W (Oxford U) 1874 *S,* 1875 *I*
Cumberlege, B S (Blackheath) 1920 *W, I, S,* 1921 *W, I, S, F,* 1922 *W*
Cumming, D C (Blackheath) 1925 *S, F*
Cunliffe, F L (RMA) 1874 *S*
Currey, F I (Marlborough N) 1872 *S*
Currie, J D (Oxford U, Harlequins, Bristol) 1956 *W, I, S, F,* 1957 *W, I, F, S,* 1958 *W, A, I, F, S,* 1959 *W, I, F, S,* 1960 *W, I, F, S,* 1961 *SA,* 1962 *W, I, F*
Cusani, D A (Orrell) 1987 *I*
Cusworth, L (Leicester) 1979 *NZ,* 1982 *F, W,* 1983 *F, W, NZ,* 1984 *S, I, F, W,* 1988 *F, W*

D'Aguilar, F B G (Royal Engineers) 1872 *S*
Dalton, T J (Coventry) 1969 *S* (R)
Danby, T (Harlequins) 1949 *W,*
Daniell, J (Richmond) 1899 *W,* 1900 *I, S,* 1902 *I, S,* 1904 *I, S*
Darby, A J L (Birkenhead Park) 1899 *I*
Davenport, A (Ravenscourt Park) 1871 *S*
Davey, J (Redruth) 1908 *S,* 1909 *W*
Davey, R F (Teignmouth) 1931 *W*
Davidson, Jas (Aspatria) 1897 *S,* 1898 *S, W,* 1899 *I, S*
Davidson, Jos (Aspatria) 1899 *W, S*
Davies, G H (Cambridge U, Coventry, Wasps) 1981 *S, I, F, Arg 1,2,* 1982 *A, S, I,* 1983 *F, W, S,* 1984 *S, SA 1,2,* 1985 *R* (R), *NZ 1,2,* 1986 *W, S, I, F*
Davies, P H (Sale) 1927 *I*
Davies, V G (Harlequins) 1922 *W,* 1925 *NZ*
Davies, W J A (United Services, RN) 1913 *SA, W, F, I, S,* 1914 *I, S, F,* 1920 *F, I, S,* 1921 *W, I, S, F,* 1922 *I, F, S,* 1923 *W, I, S, F*
Davies, W P C (Harlequins) 1953 *S,* 1954 *NZ, I,* 1955 *W, I, F, S,* 1956 *W,* 1957 *F, S,* 1958 *W*
Davis, A M (Harlequins) 1963 *W, I, S, NZ 1,2,* 1964 *NZ, W, I, F, S,* 1966 *W,* 1967 *A,* 1969 *SA,* 1970 *I, W, S*
Dawe, R G R (Bath) 1987 *I, F, W,* [US]
Dawson, E F (RIEC) 1878 *I*
Day, H L V (Leicester) 1920 *W,* 1922 *W, F,* 1926 *S*
Dean, G J (Harlequins) 1931 *I*
Dee, J M (Hartlepool R) 1962 *S,* 1963 *NZ* 1
Devitt, Sir T G (Blackheath) 1926 *I, F,* 1928 *A, W*
Dewhurst, J H (Richmond) 1887 *W, I, S,* 1890 *W*
De Glanville, P R (Bath) 1992 *SA*(R), 1993 *W*(R)
De Winton, R F C (Marlborough N) 1893 *W*
Dibble, R (Bridgwater A) 1906 *S, F, SA,* 1908 *F, W, I, S,* 1909 *A, W, F, I, S,* 1910 *S,* 1911 *W, F, S,* 1912 *W, I, S*
Dicks, J (Northampton) 1934 *W, I, S,* 1935 *W, I, S,* 1936 *S,* 1937 *I*
Dillon, E W (Blackheath) 1904 *W, I, S,* 1905 *W*
Dingle, A J (Hartlepool R) 1913 *I,* 1914 *S, F*
Dixon, P J (Harlequins, Gosforth) 1971 *P,* 1972 *W, I, F, S,* 1973 *I, F, S,* 1974 *S, I, F, W,* 1975 *I,* 1976 *F,* 1977 *S, I, F, W,* 1978 *F, S, I, NZ*
Dobbs, G E B (Devonport A) 1906 *W, I*
Doble, S A (Moseley) 1972 *SA,* 1973 *NZ 1, W*
Dobson, D D (Newton Abbot) 1902 *W, I, S,* 1903 *W, I, S*
Dobson, T H (Bradford) 1895 *S*
Dodge, P W (Leicester) 1978 *W, S, I, NZ,* 1979 *S, I, F, W,* 1980 *W, S,* 1981 *W, S, I, F, Arg 1,2,* 1982 *A, S, F, W,* 1983 *F, W, S, I, NZ,* 1985 *R, F, S, I, W, NZ 1,2*
Donnelly, M P (Oxford U) 1947 *I*
Dooley, W A (Preston Grasshoppers, Fylde) 1985 *R, F, S, I, W, NZ 2* (R), 1986 *W, S, I, F,* 1987 *F, W,* [A, US, W], 1988 *F, W, S, I 1,2, A 1,2, Fj, A,* 1989 *S, I, F, W, R, Fj,* 1990 *I, F, W, S, Arg 1,2,3,* 1991 *W, S, I, F,* [NZ, US, F, S, A], 1992 *S, I, F, W, C, SA,* 1993 *W, S, I*
Dovey, B A (Rosslyn Park) 1963 *W, I*
Down, P J (Bristol) 1909 *A*
Dowson, A O (Moseley) 1899 *S*
Drake-Lee, N J (Cambridge U, Leicester) 1963 *W, I, F, S,* 1964 *NZ, W, I,* 1965 *W*
Duckett, H (Bradford) 1893 *I, S*
Duckham, D J (Coventry) 1969 *I, F, S, W, SA,* 1970 *I, W, S, F,* 1971 *W, I, F, S* (2[1C]), *P,* 1972 *W, I, F, S,* 1973 *NZ 1, W, I, F, S, NZ 2, A,* 1974 *S, I, F, W,* 1975

I, F, W, 1976 *A, W, S*
Dudgeon, H W (Richmond) 1897 *S,* 1898 *I, S, W,* 1899 *W, I, S*
Dugdale, J M (Ravenscourt Park) 1871 *S*
Dun, A F (Wasps) 1984 *W*
Duncan, R F H (Guy's Hospital) 1922 *I, F, S*
Dunkley, P E (Harlequins) 1931 *I, S,* 1936 *NZ, W, I, S*
Duthie, J (W Hartlepool) 1903 *W*
Dyson, J W (Huddersfield) 1890 *S,* 1892 *S,* 1893 *I, S*

Ebdon, P J (Wellington) 1897 *W, I*
Eddison, J H (Headingley) 1912 *W, I, S, F*
Edgar, C S (Birkenhead Park) 1901 *S*
Edwards, R (Newport) 1921 *W, I, S, F,* 1922 *W, F,* 1923 *W,* 1924 *W, F, S,* 1925 *NZ*
Egerton, D W (Bath) 1988 *I 2, A 1, Fj* (R), *A,* 1989 *Fj,* 1990 *I, Arg 2* (R)
Elliot, C H (Sunderland) 1886 *W*
Elliot, E W (Sunderland) 1901 *W, I, S,* 1904 *W*
Elliot, W (United Services, RN) 1932 *I, S,* 1933 *W, I, S,* 1934 *W, I*
Elliott, A E (St Thomas's Hospital) 1894 *S*
Ellis, J (Wakefield) 1939 *S*
Ellis, S S (Queen's House) 1880 *I*
Emmott, C (Bradford) 1892 *W*
Enthoven, H J (Richmond) 1878 *I*
Estcourt, N S D (Blackheath) 1955 *S*
Evans, B J (Leicester) 1988 *A 2, Fj*
Evans, E (Sale) 1948 *A,* 1950 *W,* 1951 *I, F, S,* 1952 *SA, W, S, I, F,* 1953 *I, F, S,* 1954 *W, NZ, I, F,* 1956 *W, I, S, F,* 1957 *W, I, F, S,* 1958 *W, A, I, F, S*
Evans, G W (Coventry) 1972 *S,* 1973 *W* (R), *F, S, NZ 2,* 1974 *S, I, F, W*
Evans, N L (RNEC) 1932 *W, I, S,* 1933 *W, I*
Evanson, A M (Richmond) 1883 *W, I, S,* 1884 *S*
Evanson, W A D (Richmond) 1875 *S,* 1877 *S,* 1878 *S,* 1879 *S, I*
Evershed, F (Blackheath) 1889 *M,* 1890 *W, S, I,* 1892 *W, I, S,* 1893 *W, I, S*
Eyres, W C T (Richmond) 1927 *I*

Fagan, A R St L (Richmond) 1887 *I*
Fairbrother, K E (Coventry) 1969 *I, F, S, W, SA,* 1970 *I, W, S, F,* 1971 *W, I, F*
Faithfull, C K T (Harlequins) 1924 *I,* 1926 *F, S*
Fallas, H (Wakefield T) 1884 *I*
Fegan, J H C (Blackheath) 1895 *W, I, S*
Fernandes, C W L (Leeds) 1881 *I, W, S*
Fidler, J H (Gloucester) 1981 *Arg 1,2,* 1984 *SA 1,2*
Field, E (Middlesex W) 1893 *W, I*
Fielding, K J (Moseley, Loughborough Colls) 1969 *I, F, S, SA,* 1970 *I, F,* 1972 *W, I, F, S*
Finch, R T (Cambridge U) 1880 *S*
Finlan, J F (Moseley) 1967 *I, F, S, W, NZ,* 1968 *W, I,* 1969 *I, F, S, W,* 1970 *F,* 1973 *NZ* 1
Finlinson, H W (Blackheath) 1895 *W, I, S*
Finney, S (RIE Coll) 1872 *S,* 1873 *S*
Firth, F (Halifax) 1894 *W, I, S*
Fletcher, N C (OMTs) 1901 *W, I, S,* 1903 *S*
Fletcher, T (Seaton) 1897 *W*
Fletcher, W R B (Marlborough N) 1873 *S,* 1875 *S*
Fookes, E F (Sowerby Bridge) 1896 *W, I, S,* 1897 *W, I, S,* 1898 *I, W,* 1899 *I, S*
Ford, P J (Gloucester) 1964 *W, I, F, S*
Forrest, J W (United Services, RN) 1930 *W, I, F, S,* 1931 *W, I, S, F,* 1934 *I, S*
Forrest, R (Wellington) 1899 *W,* 1900 *S,* 1902 *I, S,* 1903 *I, S*
Foulds, R T (Waterloo) 1929 *W, I*
Fowler, F D (Manchester) 1878 *S,* 1879 *S*
Fowler, H (Oxford U) 1878 *S,* 1881 *W, S*
Fowler, R H (Leeds) 1877 *I*
Fox, F H (Wellington) 1890 *W, S*
Francis, T E S (Cambridge U) 1926 *W, I, F, S*
Frankcom, G P (Cambridge U, Bedford) 1965 *W, I, F, S*
Fraser, E C (Blackheath) 1875 *I*
Fraser, G (Richmond) 1902 *W, I, S,* 1903 *W, I, S*
Freakes, H D (Oxford U) 1938 *W,* 1939 *W, I*
Freeman, H (Marlborough N) 1872 *S,* 1873 *S,* 1874 *S*
French, R J (St Helens) 1961 *W, I, F, S*
Fry, H A (Liverpool) 1934 *W, I, S*
Fry, T W (Queen's House) 1880 *I, S,* 1881 *W*
Fuller, H G (Bath) 1882 *I, S,* 1883 *W, I, S,* 1884 *S*

131

Hodgson, S A M (Durham City) 1960 *W, I, F, S*, 1961 *SA, W*, 1962 *W, I, F, S*, 1964 *W*
Hofmeyr, M B (Oxford U) 1950 *W, F, S*
Hogarth, T B (Hartlepool R) 1906 *F*
Holford, G (Gloucester) 1920 *W, F*
Holland, D (Devonport A) 1912 *W, I, S*
Holliday, T E (Aspatria) 1923 *S, F*, 1925 *I, S, F*, 1926 *F, S*
Holmes, C B (Manchester) 1947 *S*, 1948 *I, F*
Holmes, E (Manningham) 1890 *S, I*
Holmes, W A (Nuneaton) 1950 *W, I, F, S*, 1951 *W, I, F, S*, 1952 *SA, S, I, F*, 1953 *W, I, F, S*
Holmes, W B (Cambridge U) 1949 *W, I, F, S*
Hook, W G (Gloucester) 1951 *S*, 1952 *SA, W*
Hooper, C A (Middlesex W) 1894 *W, I, S*
Hopley, F J V (Blackheath) 1907 *F, W*, 1908 *I*
Hordern, P C (Gloucester) 1931 *I, S, F*, 1934 *W*
Horley, C H (Swinton) 1885 *I*
Hornby, A N (Manchester) 1877 *I, S*, 1878 *S, I*, 1880 *I*, 1881 *I, S*, 1882 *I, S*
Horrocks-Taylor, J P (Cambridge U, Leicester, Middlesbrough) 1958 *W, A*, 1961 *S*, 1962 *S*, 1963 *NZ 1,2, A*, 1964 *NZ, W*
Horsfall, E L (Harlequins) 1949 *W*
Horton, A L (Blackheath) 1965 *W, I, F, S*, 1966 *F, S*, 1967 *NZ*
Horton, J P (Bath) 1978 *W, S, I, NZ*, 1980 *I, F, W, S*, 1981 *W*, 1983 *S, I*, 1984 *SA 1,2*
Horton, N E (Moseley, Toulouse) 1969 *I, F, S, W*, 1971 *I, F, S*, 1974 *S*, 1975 *W*, 1977 *S, I, F, W*, 1978 *F, W*, 1979 *S, I, F, W*, 1980 *I*
Hosen, R W (Bristol, Northampton) 1963 *NZ 1,2, A*, 1964 *F, S*, 1967 *A, I, F, S, W*
Hosking, G R d'A (Devonport Services) 1949 *W, I, F, S*, 1950 *W*
Houghton, S (Runcorn) 1892 *I*, 1896 *W*
Howard, P D (O Millhillians) 1930 *W, I, F, S*, 1931 *W, I, S, F*
Hubbard, G C (Blackheath) 1892 *W, I*
Hubbard, J C (Harlequins) 1930 *S*
Hudson, A (Gloucester) 1906 *W, I, F*, 1908 *F, W, I, S*, 1910 *F*
Hughes, G E (Barrow) 1896 *S*
Hulme, F C (Birkenhead Park) 1903 *W, I*, 1905 *W, I*
Hunt, J T (Manchester) 1882 *I, S*, 1884 *W*
Hunt, R (Manchester) 1880 *I*, 1881 *W, S*, 1882 *I*
Hunt, W H (Manchester) 1876 *S*, 1877 *I, S*, 1878 *I*
Hunter, I (Northampton) 1992 *C*, 1993 *F, W*
Huntsman, R P (Headingley) 1985 *NZ 1,2*
Hurst, A C B (Wasps) 1962 *S*
Huskisson, T F (OMTs) 1937 *W, I, S*, 1938 *W, I*, 1939 *W, I, S*
Hutchinson, F (Headingley) 1909 *F, I, S*
Hutchinson, J E (Durham City) 1906 *I*
Hutchinson, W C (RIE Coll) 1876 *S* 1877 *I*
Hutchinson, W H H (Hull) 1875 *I*, 1876 *I*
Huth, H (Huddersfield) 1879 *S*
Hyde, J P (Northampton) 1950 *F, S*
Hynes, W B (United Services, RN) 1912 *F*

Ibbitson, E D (Headingley) 1909 *W, F, I, S*
Imrie, H M (Durham City) 1906 *NZ*, 1907 *I*
Inglis, R E (Blackheath) 1886 *W, I, S*
Irvin, S H (Devonport A) 1905 *W*
Isherwood, F W (Ravenscourt Park) 1872 *S*

Jackett, E J (Leicester, Falmouth) 1905 *NZ*, 1906 *W, I, S, F, SA*, 1907 *W, I, S*, 1909 *W, F, I, S*
Jackson, A H (Blackheath) 1878 *I*, 1880 *I*
Jackson, B S (Broughton Park) 1970 *S (R), F*
Jackson, P B (Coventry) 1956 *W, I, F*, 1957 *W, I, F, S*, 1958 *W, A, F, S*, 1959 *W, I, F, S*, 1961 *S*, 1963 *W, I, F, S*
Jackson, W J (Halifax) 1894 *S*
Jacob, F (Cambridge U) 1897 *W, I, S*, 1898 *I, S, W*, 1899 *W, I*
Jacob, H P (Blackheath) 1924 *W, I, F, S*, 1930 *F*
Jacob, P G (Blackheath) 1898 *I*
Jacobs, C R (Northampton) 1956 *W, I, S, F*, 1957 *W, I, F, S*, 1958 *W, A, I, F, S*, 1960 *W, I, F, S*, 1961 *SA, W, I, F, S*, 1963 *NZ 1,2, A*, 1964 *W, I, F, S*
Jago, R A (Devonport A) 1906 *W, I, SA*, 1907 *W, I*
Janion, J P A G (Bedford) 1971 *W, I, F, S (2[1C]), P*, 1972 *W, S, SA*, 1973 *A*, 1975 *A 1,2*

Jarman, J W (Bristol) 1900 *W*
Jeavons, N C (Moseley) 1981 *S, I, F, Arg 1,2*, 1982 *A, S, I, F, W*, 1983 *F, W, S, I*
Jeeps, R E G (Northampton) 1956 *W*, 1957 *W, I, F, S*, 1958 *W, A, I, F, S*, 1959 *I*, 1960 *W, I, F, S*, 1961 *SA, W, I, F, S*, 1962 *W, I, F, S*
Jeffery, G L (Blackheath) 1886 *W, I, S*, 1887 *W, I, S*
Jennins, C R (Waterloo) 1967 *A, I, F*
Jewitt, J (Hartlepool R) 1902 *W*
Johns, W A (Gloucester) 1909 *W, F, I, S*, 1910 *W, I, F*
Johnson, M O (Leicester) 1993 *F*
Johnston, W R (Bristol) 1910 *W, I, S*, 1912 *W, I, S, F*, 1913 *SA, W, F, I, S*, 1914 *W, I, S, F*
Jones, F P (N Brighton) 1893 *S*
Jones, H A (Barnstaple) 1950 *W, I, F*
Jorden, A M (Cambridge U, Blackheath, Bedford) 1970 *F*, 1973 *I, F, S*, 1974 *F*, 1975 *W, S*
Jowett, D (Heckmondwike) 1889 *M*, 1890 *S, I*, 1891 *W, I, S*
Judd, P E (Coventry) 1962 *W, I, F, S*, 1963 *S, NZ 1,2, A*, 1964 *NZ*, 1965 *I, F, S*, 1966 *W, I, F, S*, 1967 *A, I, F, S, W, NZ*

Kayll, H E (Sunderland) 1878 *S*
Keeling, J H (Guy's Hospital) 1948 *A, W*
Keen, B W (Newcastle U) 1968 *W, I, F, S*
Keeton, G H (Leicester) 1904 *W, I, S*
Kelly, G A (Bedford) 1947 *W, I, S*, 1948 *W*
Kelly, T S (London Devonians) 1906 *W, I, S, F, SA*, 1907 *W, I, S*, 1908 *F, I, S*
Kemble, A T (Liverpool) 1885 *W, I*, 1887 *I*
Kemp, D T (Blackheath) 1935 *W*
Kemp, T A (Richmond) 1937 *W, I*, 1939 *S*, 1948 *A, W*
Kendall, P D (Birkenhead Park) 1901 *S*, 1902 *W*, 1903 *S*
Kendall-Carpenter, J MacG K (Oxford U, Bath) 1949 *I, F, S*, 1950 *W, I, F, S*, 1951 *I, F, S*, 1952 *SA, W, S*, 1953 *W, I, F, S*, 1954 *W, NZ, I, F*
Kendrew, D A (Leicester) 1930 *W, I*, 1933 *I, S*, 1934 *S*, 1935 *W, I*, 1936 *NZ, W, I*
Kennedy, R D (Camborne S of M) 1949 *I, F, S*
Kent, C P (Rosslyn Park) 1977 *S, I, F, W*, 1978 *F (R)*
Kent, T (Salford) 1891 *W, I, S*, 1892 *W, I, S*
Kershaw, C A (United Services, RN) 1920 *W, F, I, S*, 1921 *W, I, S, F*, 1922 *W, I, F, S*, 1923 *W, I, S, F*
Kewley, E (Liverpool) 1874 *S*, 1875 *S*, 1876 *I, S*, 1877 *I, S*, 1878 *S*
Kewney, A L (Leicester) 1906 *W, I, S, F*, 1909 *A, W, F, I, S*, 1911 *W, F, I, S*, 1912 *I, S*, 1913 *SA*
Key, A (O Cranleighans) 1930 *I*, 1933 *W*
Keyworth, M (Swansea) 1976 *A, W, S, I*
Kilner, B (Wakefield T) 1880 *I*
Kindersley, R S (Exeter) 1883 *W*, 1884 *S*, 1885 *W*
King, I (Harrogate) 1954 *W, NZ, I*
King, J A (Headingley) 1911 *W, F, I, S*, 1912 *W, I, S*, 1913 *SA, W, F, I, S*
King, Q E M A (Army) 1921 *S*
Kingston, P (Gloucester) 1975 *A, 1,2*, 1979 *I, F, W*
Kitching, A E (Blackheath) 1913 *I*
Kittermaster, H J (Harlequins) 1925 *NZ, W, I*, 1926 *W, I, F, S*
Knight, F (Plymouth) 1909 *A*
Knight, P M (Bristol) 1972 *F, S, SA*
Knowles, E (Millom) 1896 *S*, 1897 *S*
Knowles, T C (Birkenhead Park) 1931 *S*
Krige, J A (Guy's Hospital) 1920 *W*

Labuschagne, N A (Harlequins, Guy's Hospital) 1953 *W*, 1955 *W, I, F, S*
Lagden, R O (Richmond) 1911 *S*
Laird, H C C (Harlequins) 1927 *W, I, S*, 1928 *A, W, I, F, S*, 1929 *W, I*
Lambert, D (Harlequins) 1907 *F*, 1908 *W, F, S*, 1911 *W, F, I*
Lampkowski, M S (Headingley) 1976 *A, W, S, I*
Lapage, W N (United Services, RN) 1908 *F, W, I, S*
Larter, P J (Northampton, RAF) 1967 *A, NZ*, 1968 *W, I, F, S*, 1969 *I, F, S, W*, 1970 *I, W, S*, 1971 *W, I, F, S (2[1C]), P*, 1972 *SA*, 1973 *NZ 1, W*
Law, A F (Richmond) 1877 *S*
Law, D E (Birkenhead Park) 1927 *I*
Lawrence, Hon H A (Richmond) 1873 *S*, 1874 *S*, 1875 *I, S*
Lawrie, P W (Leicester) 1910 *S*, 1911 *S*
Lawson, R G (Workington) 1925 *I*

133

Lawson, T M (Workington) 1928 *A, W*
Leadbetter, M M (Broughton Park) 1970 *F*
Leadbetter, V H (Edinburgh Wands) 1954 *S, F*
Leake, A W R M (Harlequins) 1891 *W, I, S*
Leather, G (Liverpool) 1907 *I*
Lee, F H (Marlborough N) 1876 *S*, 1877 *I*
Lee, H (Blackheath) 1907 *F*
Le Fleming, J (Blackheath) 1887 *W*
Leonard, J (Saracens, Harlequins) 1990 *Arg* 1,2,3, 1991 *W, S, I, F, Fj, A, [NZ, It, US, F, S, A],* 1992 *S, I, F, W, C, SA,* 1993 *F, W, S, I*
Leslie-Jones, F A (Richmond) 1895 *W, I*
Lewis, A O (Bath) 1952 *SA, W, S, I, F,* 1953 *W, I, F, S,* 1954 *F*
Leyland, R (Waterloo) 1935 *W, I, S*
Linnett, M S (Moseley) 1989 *Fj*
Livesay, R O'H (Blackheath) 1898 *W,* 1899 *W*
Lloyd, R H (Harlequins) 1967 *NZ,* 1968 *W, I, F, S*
Locke, H M (Birkenhead Park) 1923 *S, F,* 1924 *W, F, S,* 1925 *W, I, S, F,* 1927 *W, I, S*
Lockwood, R E (Heckmondwike) 1887 *W, I, S,* 1889 *M,* 1891 *W, I, S,* 1892 *W, I, S,* 1893 *W, I,* 1894 *W, I*
Login, S H M (RN Coll) 1876 *I*
Lohden, F C (Blackheath) 1893 *W*
Longland, R J (Northampton) 1932 *S,* 1933 *W, S,* 1934 *W, I, S,* 1935 *W, I, S,* 1936 *NZ, W, I, S,* 1937 *W, I, S,* 1938 *W, I, S*
Lowe, C N (Cambridge U, Blackheath) 1913 *SA, W, F, I, S,* 1914 *W, I, S, F,* 1920 *W, F, I, S,* 1921 *W, I, S, F,* 1922 *W, I, F, S,* 1923 *W, I, S, F*
Lowrie, F (Wakefield T) 1889 *M,* 1890 *W*
Lowry, W M (Birkenhead Park) 1920 *F*
Lozowski, R A P (Wasps) 1984 *A*
Luddington, W G E (Devonport Services) 1923 *W, I, S, F,* 1924 *W, I, F, S,* 1925 *W, I, S, F,* 1926 *W*
Luscombe, F (Gipsies) 1872 *S,* 1873 *S,* 1875 *I, S,* 1876 *I, S*
Luscombe, J H (Gipsies) 1871 *S*
Luxmoore, A F C C (Richmond) 1900 *S,* 1901 *W*
Luya, H F (Waterloo, Headingley) 1948 *W, I, S, F,* 1949 *W*
Lyon, A (Liverpool) 1871 *S*
Lyon, G H d'O (United Services, RN) 1908 *S,* 1909 *A*

McCanlis, M A (Gloucester) 1931 *W, I*
McFadyean, C W (Moseley) 1966 *I, F, S,* 1967 *A, I, F, S, W, NZ,* 1968 *W, I*
MacIlwaine, A H (United Services, Hull & E Riding) 1912 *W, I, S, F,* 1920 *I*
Mackie, O G (Wakefield T, Cambridge U) 1897 *S,* 1898 *I*
Mackinlay, J E H (St George's Hospital) 1872 *S,* 1873 *S,* 1875 *I*
MacLaren, W (Manchester) 1871 *S*
MacLennan, R R F (OMTs) 1925 *I, S, F*
McLeod, N F (RIE Coll) 1879 *S, I*
Madge, R J P (Exeter) 1948 *A, W, I, S*
Malir, F W S (Otley) 1930 *W, I, S*
Mangles, R H (Richmond) 1897 *W, I*
Manley, D C (Exeter) 1963 *W, I, F, S*
Mann, W E (United Services, Army) 1911 *W, F, I*
Mantell, N D (Rosslyn Park) 1975 *A* 1
Markendale, E T (Manchester R) 1880 *I*
Marques, R W D (Cambridge U, Harlequins) 1956 *W, I, S, F,* 1957 *W, I, F, S,* 1958 *W, A, I, F, S,* 1959 *W, I, F, S,* 1960 *W, I, F, S,* 1961 *SA, W*
Marquis, J C (Birkenhead Park) 1900 *I, S*
Marriott, C J B (Blackheath) 1884 *W, I, S,* 1886 *W, I, S,* 1887 *I*
Marriott, E E (Manchester) 1876 *I*
Marriott, V R (Harlequins) 1963 *NZ* 1,2, *A,* 1964 *NZ*
Marsden, G H (Morley) 1900 *W, I, S*
Marsh, H (RIE Coll) 1873 *S*
Marsh, J (Swinton) 1892 *I*
Marshall, H (Blackheath) 1893 *W*
Marshall, M W (Blackheath) 1873 *S,* 1874 *S,* 1875 *I, S,* 1876 *I, S,* 1877 *I, S,* 1878 *S, I*
Marshall, R M (Oxford U) 1938 *I, S,* 1939 *W, I, S*
Martin, C R (Bath) 1985 *F, S, I, W*
Martin, N O (Harlequins) 1972 *F* (R)
Martindale, S A (Kendal) 1929 *F*
Massey, E J (Leicester) 1925 *W, I, S*
Mathias, J L (Bristol) 1905 *W, I, S, NZ*
Matters, J C (RNE Coll) 1899 *S*

Matthews, J R C (Harlequins) 1949 *F, S,* 1950 *I, F, S,* 1952 *SA, W, S, I, F*
Maud, P (Blackheath) 1893 *W, I*
Maxwell, A W (New Brighton, Headingley) 1975 *A* 1, 1976 *A, W, S, I, F,* 1978 *F*
Maxwell-Hyslop, J E (Oxford U) 1922 *I, F, S*
Maynard, A F (Cambridge U) 1914 *W, I, S*
Meikle, G W C (Waterloo) 1934 *W, I, S*
Meikle, S S C (Waterloo) 1929 *S*
Mellish, F W (Blackheath) 1920 *W, F, I, S,* 1921 *W, I*
Melville, N D (Wasps) 1984 *A,* 1985 *I, W, NZ* 1,2, 1986 *W, S, I, F,* 1988 *F, W, S, I* 1
Merriam, L P B (Blackheath) 1920 *W, F*
Michell, A T (Oxford U) 1875 *I, S,* 1876 *I*
Middleton, B B (Birkenhead Park) 1882 *I,* 1883 *I*
Middleton, J A (Richmond) 1922 *S*
Miles, J H (Leicester) 1903 *W*
Millett, H (Richmond) 1920 *F*
Mills, F W (Marlborough N) 1872 *S,* 1873 *S*
Mills, S G F (Gloucester) 1981 *Arg* 1,2, 1983 *W,* 1984 *SA* 1, *A*
Mills, W A (Devonport A) 1906 *W, I, S, F, SA,* 1907 *F, W, I, S,* 1908 *F, W*
Milman, D L K (Bedford) 1937 *W,* 1938 *W, I, S*
Milton, C H (Camborne S of M) 1906 *I*
Milton, J G (Camborne S of M) 1904 *W, I, S,* 1905 *S,* 1907 *I*
Milton, W H (Marlborough N) 1874 *S,* 1875 *I*
Mitchell, F (Blackheath) 1895 *W, I, S,* 1896 *W, I, S*
Mitchell, W G (Richmond) 1890 *W, S, I,* 1891 *W, I, S,* 1893 *S*
Mobbs, E R (Northampton) 1909 *A, W, F, I, S,* 1910 *I, F*
Moberly, W O (Ravenscourt Park) 1872 *S*
Moore, B C (Nottingham, Harlequins) 1987 *S, [A, J, W],* 1988 *F, W, S, I* 1,2, *A* 1,2, *Fj, A,* 1989 *S, I, F, W, R, Fj,* 1990 *I, F, W, S, Arg* 1,2, 1991 *W, S, I, F, Fj, A, [NZ, It, F, S, A],* 1992 *S, I, F, W, SA,* 1993 *F, W, S, I*
Moore, E J (Blackheath) 1883 *I, S*
Moore, N J N H (Bristol) 1904 *W, I, S*
Moore, P B C (Blackheath) 1951 *W*
Moore, W K T (Leicester) 1947 *W, I,* 1949 *F, S,* 1950 *I, F, S*
Mordell, R J (Rosslyn Park) 1978 *W*
Morfitt, S (W Hartlepool) 1894 *W, I, S,* 1896 *W, I, S*
Morgan, J R (Hawick) 1920 *W*
Morgan, W G D (Medicals, Newcastle) 1960 *W, I, F, S,* 1961 *SA, W, I, F, S*
Morley, A J (Bristol) 1972 *SA,* 1973 *NZ* 1, *W, I,* 1975 *S, A* 1,2
Morris, A D W (United Services, RN) 1909 *A, W, F*
Morris, C D (Liverpool St Helens, Orrell) 1988 *A,* 1989 *S, I, F, W,* 1992 *S, I, F, W, C, SA,* 1993 *F, W, S, I*
Morrison, P H (Cambridge U) 1890 *W, S, I,* 1891 *I*
Morse, S (Marlborough N) 1873 *S,* 1874 *S,* 1875 *S*
Mortimer, W (Marlborough N) 1899 *W*
Morton, H J S (Blackheath) 1909 *I, S,* 1910 *W, I*
Moss, F (Broughton) 1885 *W, I,* 1886 *W*
Mullins, A R (Harlequins) 1989 *Fj*
Mycock, J (Sale) 1947 *W, I, S, F,* 1948 *A*
Myers, E (Bradford) 1920 *I, S,* 1921 *W, I,* 1922 *W, I, F, S,* 1923 *W, I, F, S,* 1924 *W, I, F, S,* 1925 *S*
Myers, H (Keighley) 1898 *I*

Nanson, W M B (Carlisle) 1907 *F, W*
Nash, E H (Richmond) 1875 *I*
Neale, B A (Rosslyn Park) 1951 *I, F, S*
Neale, M E (Blackheath) 1912 *F*
Neame, S (O Cheltonians) 1879 *S, I,* 1880 *I, S*
Neary, A (Broughton Park) 1971 *W, I, F, S* (2[1C]), 1972 *W, I, F, S, SA,* 1973 *NZ* 1, *W, I, F, S, NZ* 2, *A,* 1974 *S, I, F, W,* 1975 *I, F, W, A* 1, 1976 *A, W, S, I, F,* 1977 *I,* 1978 *F* (R), 1979 *S, I, F, W, NZ,* 1980 *I, F, W, S*
Nelmes, B G (Cardiff) 1975 *A* 1,2, 1978 *W, S, I, NZ*
Newbold, C J (Blackheath) 1904 *W, I, S,* 1905 *W, I, S*
Newman, S C (Oxford U) 1947 *F,* 1948 *A, W*
Newton, A W (Blackheath) 1907 *S*
Newton, P A (Blackheath) 1882 *S*
Newton-Thompson, J O (Oxford U) 1947 *S, F*
Nichol, W (Brighouse R) 1892 *W, S*
Nicholas, P L (Exeter) 1902 *W*
Nicholson, B E (Harlequins) 1938 *W, I*
Nicholson, E S (Leicester) 1935 *W, I, S,* 1936 *NZ, W*

Nicholson, E T (Birkenhead Park) 1900 *W, I*
Nicholson, T (Rockcliff) 1893 *I*
Ninnes, B F (Coventry) 1971 *W*
Norman, D J (Leicester) 1932 *SA, W*
North, E H G (Blackheath) 1891 *W, I, S*
Northmore, S (Millom) 1897 *I*
Novak, M J (Harlequins) 1970 *W, S, F*
Novis, A L (Blackheath) 1929 *S, F*, 1930 *W, I, F,* 1933 *I, S*

Oakeley, F E (United Services, RN) 1913 *S,* 1914 *I, S, F*
Oakes, R F (Hartlepool R) 1897 *W, I, S,* 1898 *I, S, W,* 1899 *W, S*
Oakley, L F L (Bedford) 1951 *W*
Obolensky, A (Oxford U) 1936 *NZ, W, I, S*
Old, A G B (Middlesbrough, Leicester, Sheffield) 1972 *W, I, F, S, SA,* 1973 *NZ 2, A,* 1974 *S, I, F, W,* 1975 *I, A 2,* 1976 *S, I,* 1978 *F*
Oldham, W L (Coventry) 1908 *S,* 1909 *A*
Olver, C J (Northampton) 1990 *Arg* 3, 1991 [*US*], 1992 *C*
O'Neill, A (Teignmouth, Torquay A) 1901 *W, I, S*
Openshaw, W E (Manchester) 1879 *I*
Orwin, J (Gloucester, RAF, Bedford) 1985 *R, F, S, I, W, NZ* 1,2, 1988 *F, W, S, I* 1,2, *A* 1,2
Osborne, R R (Manchester) 1871 *S*
Osborne, S H (Oxford U) 1905 *S*
Oti, C (Cambridge U, Nottingham, Wasps) 1988 *S, I* 1, 1989 *S, I, F, W, R,* 1990 *Arg* 1,2, 1991 *Fj, A,* [*NZ, It,*] Oughtred, B (Hartlepool R) 1901 *S,* 1902 *W, I, S,* 1903 *W, I*
Owen, J E (Coventry) 1963 *W, I, F, S, A,* 1964 *NZ,* 1965 *W, I, F, S,* 1966 *I, F, S,* 1967 *NZ*
Owen-Smith, H G O (St Mary's Hospital) 1934 *W, I, S,* 1936 *NZ, W, I, S,* 1937 *W, I, S*

Page, J J (Bedford, Northampton) 1971 *W, I, F, S,* 1975 *S*
Pallant, J N (Notts) 1967 *I, F, S*
Palmer, A C (London Hospital) 1909 *I, S*
Palmer, F H (Richmond) 1905 *W*
Palmer, G V (Richmond) 1928 *I, F, S*
Palmer, J A (Bath) 1984 *SA* 1,2, 1986 *I* (R)
Pargetter, T A (Coventry) 1962 *S,* 1963 *F, NZ* 1
Parker, G W (Gloucester) 1938 *I, S*
Parker, Hon S (Liverpool) 1874 *S,* 1875 *S*
Parsons, E I (RAF) 1939 *S*
Parsons, M J (Northampton) 1968 *W, I, F, S*
Patterson, W M (Sale) 1961 *SA, S*
Pattisson, R M (Blackheath) 1883 *I, S*
Paul, J E (RIE Coll) 1875 *S*
Payne, A T (Bristol) 1935 *I, S*
Payne, C M (Harlequins) 1964 *I, F, S,* 1965 *I, F, S,* 1966 *W, I, F, S*
Payne, J H (Broughton) 1882 *S,* 1883 *W, I, S,* 1884 *I,* 1885 *W, I*
Pearce, G S (Northampton) 1979 *S, I, F, W,* 1981 *Arg* 1,2, 1982 *A, S,* 1983 *F, W, S, I, NZ,* 1984 *S, SA* 2, *A,* 1985 *R, F, S, I, W, NZ* 1,2, 1986 *W, S, I, F,* 1987 *I, F, W, S,* [*A, J, US, W*], 1988 *Fj,* 1991 [*US*]
Pears, D (Harlequins) 1990 *Arg* 1,2, 1992 *F*(R)
Pearson, A W (Blackheath) 1875 *I, S,* 1876 *I, S,* 1877 *S,* 1878 *S, I*
Peart, T G A H (Hartlepool R) 1964 *F, S*
Pease, F E (Hartlepool R) 1887 *I*
Penny, S H (Leicester) 1909 *A*
Penny, W J (United Hospitals) 1878 *I,* 1879 *S, I*
Percival, L J (Rugby) 1891 *I,* 1892 *I,* 1893 *S*
Periton, H G (Waterloo) 1925 *W,* 1926 *W, I, F, S,* 1927 *W, I, S, F,* 1928 *A, I, F, S,* 1929 *W, I, S, F,* 1930 *W, I, F, S*
Perrott, E S (O Cheltonians) 1875 *I*
Perry, D G (Bedford) 1963 *F, S, NZ* 1,2, *A* 1964 *NZ, W, I,* 1965 *W, I, F, S,* 1966 *W, I, F*
Perry, S V (Cambridge U, Waterloo) 1947 *W, I,* 1948 *A, W, I, S, F*
Peters, J (Plymouth) 1906 *S, F,* 1907 *I, S,* 1908 *W*
Phillips, C (Birkenhead Park) 1880 *S,* 1881 *I, S*
Phillips, M S (Fylde) 1958 *A, I, F, S,* 1959 *W, I, F, S,* 1960 *W, I, F, S,* 1961 *W, I, F, S, NZ* 1,2, *A,* 1964 *NZ, W, I, F, S*
Pickering, A S (Harrogate) 1907 *I*
Pickering, R D A (Bradford) 1967 *I, F, S, W,* 1968 *F, S*

Pickles, R C W (Bristol) 1922 *I, F*
Pierce, R (Liverpool) 1898 *I,* 1903 *S*
Pilkington, W N (Cambridge U) 1898 *S*
Pillman, C H (Blackheath) 1910 *W, I, F, S,* 1911 *W, F, I, S,* 1912 *W, F,* 1913 *SA, W, F, I, S,* 1914 *W, I, S*
Pillman, R L (Blackheath) 1914 *F*
Pinch, J (Lancaster) 1896 *W, I,* 1897 *S*
Pinching, W W (Guy's Hospital) 1872 *S*
Pitman, I J (Oxford U) 1922 *S*
Plummer, K C (Bristol) 1969 *W,* 1976 *S, I, F*
Poole, F O (Oxford U) 1895 *W, I, S*
Poole, R W (Hartlepool R) 1896 *S*
Pope, E B (Blackheath) 1931 *W, S, F*
Portus, G V (Blackheath) 1908 *F, I*
Poulton, R W (later Poulton Palmer) (Oxford U, Harlequins, Liverpool) 1909 *W, F, I, S,* 1910 *W,* 1911 *S,* 1912 *W, I, S,* 1913 *SA, W, F, I, S,* 1914 *W, I, S, F*
Powell, D L (Northampton) 1966 *W, I,* 1969 *I, F, S, W,* 1971 *W, I, F, S* (2[1C])
Pratten, W E (Blackheath) 1927 *S, F*
Preece, I (Coventry) 1948 *I, S, F,* 1949 *F, S,* 1950 *W, I, F, S,* 1951 *W, I, F*
Preece, P S (Coventry) 1972 *SA,* 1973 *NZ* 1, *W, I, F, S, NZ* 2, 1975 *I, F, W, A* 2, 1976 *W* (R)
Preedy, M (Gloucester) 1984 *SA* 1
Prentice, F D (Leicester) 1928 *I, F, S*
Prescott, R E (Harlequins) 1937 *W, I,* 1938 *I,* 1939 *W, I, S*
Preston, N J (Richmond) 1979 *NZ,* 1980 *I, F*
Price, H L (Harlequins) 1922 *I, S,* 1923 *W, I*
Price, J (Coventry) 1961 *I*
Price, P L A (RIE Coll) 1877 *I, S,* 1878 *S*
Price, T W (Cheltenham) 1948 *S, F,* 1949 *W, I, F, S*
Probyn, J A (Wasps, Askeans) 1988 *F, W, S, I* 1,2, *A* 1,2, *A,* 1989 *S, I, R* (R), 1990 *I, F, W, S, Arg* 1,2,3, 1991 *W, S, I, F, Fj, A,* [*NZ, It, F, S, A*], 1992 *S, I, F, W,* 1993 *F, W, S, I*
Prout, D H (Northampton) 1968 *W, I*
Pullin, J V (Bristol) 1966 *W,* 1968 *W, I, F, S,* 1969 *I, F, S, W, SA,* 1970 *I, W, S, F,* 1971 *W, I, F, S* (2[1C]), *P,* 1972 *W, I, F, S, SA,* 1973 *NZ* 1, *W, I, F, S, NZ* 2, *A,* 1974 *S, I, F, W,* 1975 *I, W* (R), *S, A* 1,2, 1976 *F*
Purdy, S J (Rugby) 1962 *S*
Pyke, J (St Helens Recreation) 1892 *W*
Pym, J A (Blackheath) 1912 *W, I, S, F*

Quinn, J P (New Brighton) 1954 *W, NZ, I, S, F*

Rafter, M (Bristol) 1977 *S, F, W,* 1978 *F, W, S, I, NZ,* 1979 *S, I, F, W, NZ,* 1980 *W* (R), 1981 *W, Arg* 1,2
Ralston, C W (Richmond) 1971 *S* (C), *P,* 1972 *W, I, F, S, SA,* 1973 *NZ* 1, *W, I, F, S, NZ* 2, *A,* 1974 *S, I, F, W,* 1975 *I, F, W, S*
Ramsden, H E (Bingley) 1898 *W, S*
Ranson, J M (Rosslyn Park) 1963 *NZ* 1,2, *A,* 1964 *W, I, F, S*
Raphael, J E (OMTs) 1902 *W, I, S,* 1905 *W, S, NZ,* 1906 *W, S, F*
Ravenscroft, J (Birkenhead Park) 1881 *I*
Rawlinson, W C W (Blackheath) 1876 *S*
Redfern, S (Leicester) 1984 *I*
Redman, N C (Bath) 1984 *A,* 1986 *S* (R), 1987 *I, S,* [*A, J, W*], 1988 *Fj,* 1990 *Arg* 1,2, 1991 *Fj,* [*It, US*]
Redmond, G F (Cambridge U) 1970 *F*
Redwood, B W (Bristol) 1968 *W, I*
Rees, G W (Nottingham) 1984 *SA* 2 (R), *A,* 1986 *I, F,* 1987 *F, W, S,* [*A, J, US, W*], 1988 *S* (R), *I* 1,2, *A* 1,2, *Fj,* 1989 *W, R* (R), *Fj* (R), 1990 *Arg* 3 (R), 1991 *Fj,* [*US*]
Reeve, J S R (Harlequins) 1929 *F,* 1930 *W, I, F, S,* 1931 *W, I, S*
Regan, M (Liverpool) 1953 *W, I, F, S,* 1954 *W, NZ, I, S, F,* 1956 *I, S, F*
Rendall, P A G (Wasps, Askeans) 1984 *W, SA* 2, 1986 *W, S,* 1987 *I, F, S,* [*A, J, W*], 1988 *F, W, S, I* 1,2, *A* 1,2, *A,* 1989 *S, I, F, W, R,* 1990 *I, F, W, S,* 1991 [*It* (R)]
Rew, H (Blackheath) 1929 *S, F,* 1930 *F, S,* 1931 *W, S, F,* 1934 *W, I, S*
Reynolds, F J (O Cranleighans) 1937 *S,* 1938 *I, S*
Reynolds, S (Richmond) 1900 *W, I, S,* 1901 *I*
Rhodes, J (Castleford) 1896 *W, I, S*
Richards, D (Leicester) 1986 *I, F,* 1987 *S,* [*A, J, US, W*], 1988 *F, W, S, I* 1, *A* 1,2, *Fj, A,* 1989 *S, I, F, W, R,* 1990 *Arg* 3, 1991 *W, S, I, F, Fj, A,* [*NZ, It, US*], 1992

Soane, F (Bath) 1893 *S*, 1894 *W, I, S*
Sobey, W H (O Millhillians) 1930 *W, F, S*, 1932 *SA, W*
Solomon, B (Redruth) 1910 *W*
Sparks, R H W (Plymouth A) 1928 *I, F, S*, 1929 *W, I, S*, 1931 *I, S, F*
Speed, H (Castleford) 1894 *W, I, S*, 1896 *S*
Spence, F W (Birkenhead Park) 1890 *I*
Spencer, J (Harlequins) 1966 *W*
Spencer, J S (Cambridge U, Headingley) 1969 *I, F, S, W, SA*, 1970 *I, W, S, F*, 1971 *W, I, S* (2[1C]), *P*
Spong, R S (O Millhillians) 1929 *F*, 1930 *W, I, F, S*, 1931 *F*, 1932 *SA, W*
Spooner, R H (Liverpool) 1903 *W*
Springman, H H (Liverpool) 1879 *S*, 1887 *S*
Spurling, A (Blackheath) 1882 *I*
Spurling, N (Blackheath) 1886 *I, S*, 1887 *W*
Squires, P J (Harrogate) 1973 *F, S, NZ* 2, *A*, 1974 *S, I, F, W*, 1975 *I, F, W, S, A* 1,2, 1976 *A, W*, 1977 *S, I, F, W*, 1978 *F, W, S, I, NZ*, 1979 *S, I, F, W*
Stafford, R C (Bedford) 1912 *W, I, S, F*
Stafford, W F H (RE) 1874 *S*
Stanbury, E (Plymouth A) 1926 *W, I, S*, 1927 *W, I, S, F*, 1928 *A, W, I, F, S*, 1929 *W, I, S, F*
Standing, G (Blackheath) 1883 *W, I*
Stanger-Leathes, C F (Northern) 1905 *I*
Stark, K J (O Alleynians) 1927 *W, I, S, F*, 1928 *A, W, I, F, S*
Starks, A (Castleford) 1896 *W, I*
Starmer-Smith, N C (Harlequins) 1969 *SA*, 1970 *I, W, S, F*, 1971 *S* (C), *P*
Start, S P (United Services, RN) 1907 *S*
Steeds, J H (Saracens) 1949 *F, S*, 1950 *I, F, S*
Steele-Bodger, M R (Cambridge U) 1947 *W, I, S, F*, 1948 *A, W, I, S, F*
Steinthal, F E (Ilkley) 1913 *W, F*
Stevens, C B (Penzance-Newlyn, Harlequins) 1969 *SA*, 1970 *I, W, S*, 1971 *P*, 1972 *W, I, F, S, SA*, 1973 *NZ* 1, *W, I, F, S, NZ* 2, *A*, 1974 *S, I, F, W*, 1975 *I, F, W, S*
Still, E R (Oxford U, Ravenscourt P) 1873 *S*
Stirling, R V (Leicester, RAF, Wasps) 1951 *W, I, F, S*, 1952 *SA, W, S, I, F*, 1953 *W, I, F, S*, 1954 *W, NZ, I, S, F*
Stoddart, A E (Blackheath) 1885 *W, I*, 1886 *W, I, S*, 1889 *M*, 1890 *W, I*, 1893 *W, S*
Stoddart, W B (Liverpool) 1897 *W, I, S*
Stokes, F (Blackheath) 1871 *S*, 1872 *S*, 1873 *S*
Stokes, L (Blackheath) 1875 *I*, 1876 *S*, 1877 *I, S*, 1878 *S*, 1879 *S, I*, 1880 *I, S*, 1881 *I, W, S*
Stone, F le S (Blackheath) 1914 *F*
Stoop, A D (Harlequins) 1905 *S*, 1906 *S, F, SA*, 1907 *F, W*, 1910 *W, I, S*, 1911 *W, F, I, S*, 1912 *W, S*
Stoop, F M (Harlequins) 1910 *S*, 1911 *F, I*, 1913 *SA*
Stout, F M (Richmond) 1897 *W, I*, 1898 *I, S, W*, 1899 *I, S*, 1903 *S*, 1904 *W, I, S*, 1905 *W, I, S*
Stout, P W (Richmond) 1898 *S, W*, 1899 *W, I, S*
Stringer, N C (Wasps) 1982 *A* (R), 1983 *NZ* (R), 1984 *SA* 1 (R), *A*, 1985 *R*
Strong, E L (Oxford U) 1884 *W, I, S*
Summerscales, G E (Durham City) 1905 *NZ*
Sutcliffe, J W (Heckmondwike) 1889 *M*
Swarbrick, D W (Oxford U) 1947 *W, I, F*, 1948 *A, W*, 1949 *I*
Swayne, D H (Oxford U) 1931 *W*
Swayne, J W R (Bridgwater) 1929 *W*
Swift, A H (Swansea) 1981 *Arg* 1,2, 1983 *F, W, S*, 1984 *SA* 2
Syddall, J P (Waterloo) 1982 *I*, 1984 *A*
Sykes, A R V (Blackheath) 1914 *F*
Sykes, F D (Northampton) 1955 *F, S*, 1963 *NZ* 2, *A*
Sykes, P W (Wasps) 1948 *F*, 1952 *S, I, F*, 1953 *W, I, F*
Syrett, R E (Wasps) 1958 *W, A, I, F*, 1960 *W, I, F, S*, 1962 *W, I, F*

Tallent, J A (Cambridge U, Blackheath) 1931 *S, F*, 1932 *SA, W*, 1935 *I*
Tanner, C C (Cambridge U, Gloucester) 1930 *S*, 1932 *SA, W, I, S*
Tarr, F N (Leicester) 1909 *A, W, F*, 1913 *S*
Tatham, W M (Oxford U) 1882 *S*, 1883 *W, I, S*, 1884 *W, I, S*
Taylor, A S (Blackheath) 1883 *W, I*, 1886 *W, I*
Taylor, E W (Rockcliff) 1892 *I*, 1893 *I*, 1894 *W, I, S*, 1895 *W, I, S*, 1896 *W, I*, 1897 *W, I, S*, 1899 *I*

Taylor, F (Leicester) 1920 *F, I*
Taylor, F M (Leicester) 1914 *W*
Taylor, H H (Blackheath) 1879 *S*, 1880 *S*, 1881 *I, W*, 1882 *S*
Taylor, J T (W Hartlepool) 1897 *I*, 1899 *I*, 1900 *I*, 1901 *W, I*, 1902 *W, I, S*, 1903 *W, I*, 1905 *S*
Taylor, P J (Northampton) 1955 *W, I*, 1962 *W, I, F, S*
Taylor, R B (Northampton) 1966 *W*, 1967 *I, F, S, W, NZ*, 1969 *F, S, W, SA*, 1970 *I, W, S, F*, 1971 *S* (2[1C])
Taylor, W J (Blackheath) 1928 *A, W, I, F, S*
Teague, M C (Gloucester, Moseley) 1985 *F* (R), *NZ* 1,2, 1989 *S, I, F, W, R*, 1990 *F, W, S*, 1991 *W, S, I, F, Fj, A, [NZ, It, F, S, A]*, 1992 *SA*, 1993 *F, W, S, I*
Teden, D E (Richmond) 1939 *W, I, S*
Teggin, A (Broughton R) 1884 *I*, 1885 *W*, 1886 *I, S*, 1887 *I, S*
Tetley, T S (Bradford) 1876 *S*
Thomas, C (Barnstaple) 1895 *W, I, S*, 1899 *I*
Thompson, P H (Headingley, Waterloo) 1956 *W, I, S, F*, 1957 *W, I, F, S*, 1958 *W, A, I, F, S*, 1959 *W, I, F, S*
Thomson, G T (Halifax) 1878 *S*, 1882 *I, S*, 1883 *W, I, S*, 1884 *I, S*, 1885 *I*
Thomson, W B (Blackheath) 1892 *W*, 1895 *W, I, S*
Thorne, J D (Bristol) 1963 *W, I, F*
Tindall, V R (Liverpool U) 1951 *W, I, F, S*
Tobin, F (Liverpool) 1871 *S*
Todd, A F (Blackheath) 1900 *I, S*
Todd, R (Manchester) 1877 *S*
Toft, H B (Waterloo) 1936 *S*, 1937 *W, I, S*, 1938 *W, I, S*, 1939 *W, I, S*
Toothill, J T (Bradford) 1890 *S, I*, 1891 *W, I*, 1892 *W, I, S*, 1893 *W, I, S*, 1894 *W, I*
Tosswill, L R (Exeter) 1902 *W, I, S*
Touzel, C J C (Liverpool) 1877 *I, S*
Towell, A C (Bedford) 1948 *F*, 1951 *S*
Travers, B H (Harlequins) 1947 *W, I*, 1948 *A, W*, 1949 *F, S*
Treadwell, W T (Wasps) 1966 *I, F, S*
Trick, D M (Bath) 1983 *I*, 1984 *SA* 1
Tristram, H B (Oxford U) 1883 *S*, 1884 *W, S*, 1885 *W*, 1887 *S*
Troop, C L (Aldershot S) 1933 *I, S*
Tucker, J S (Bristol) 1922 *W*, 1925 *NZ, W, I, S, F*, 1926 *W, I, F, S*, 1927 *W, I, S, F*, 1928 *A, W, I, F, S*, 1929 *W, I, F*, 1930 *W, I, F, S*, 1931 *W*
Tucker, W E (Blackheath) 1894 *W, I*, 1895 *W, I, S*
Tucker, W E (Blackheath) 1926 *I*, 1930 *W, I*
Turner, D P (Richmond) 1871 *S*, 1872 *S*, 1873 *S*, 1874 *S*, 1875 *I, S*
Turner, E B (St George's Hospital) 1876 *I*, 1877 *I*, 1878 *I*
Turner, G R (St George's Hospital) 1876 *S*
Turner, H J C (Manchester) 1871 *S*
Turner, M F (Blackheath) 1948 *S, F*
Turquand-Young, D (Richmond) 1928 *A, W*, 1929 *I, S, F*
Twynam, H T (Richmond) 1879 *I*, 1880 *I*, 1881 *W*, 1882 *I*, 1883 *I*, 1884 *W, I, S*

Ubogu, V E (Bath) 1992 *C, SA*
Underwood, A M (Exeter) 1962 *W, I, F, S*, 1964 *I*
Underwood, R (Leicester, RAF) 1984 *I, F, W, A*, 1985 *R, F, S, I, W*, 1986 *W, I, F*, 1987 *I, F, W, S, [A, J, W]*, 1988 *F, W, S, I* 1,2, *A* 1,2, *Fj, A*, 1989 *S, I, F, W, R, Fj*, 1990 *I, F, W, S, Arg* 3, 1991 *W, S, I, F, Fj, A, [NZ, It, US, F, S, A]*, 1992 *S, I, F, W, SA*, 1993 *F, W, S, I*
Underwood, T (Leicester) 1992 *C, SA*, 1993 *S, I*
Unwin, E J (Rosslyn Park, Army) 1937 *S*, 1938 *W, I, S*
Unwin, G T (Blackheath) 1898 *S*
Uren, R (Waterloo) 1948 *I, S, F*, 1950 *I*
Uttley, R M (Gosforth) 1973 *I, F, S, NZ* 2, *A*, 1974 *I, F, W*, 1975 *F, W, S, A* 1,2, 1977 *S, I, F, W*, 1978 *NZ*, 1979 *S*, 1980 *I, F, W, S*

Valentine, J (Swinton) 1890 *W*, 1896 *W, I, S*
Vanderspar, C H R (Richmond) 1873 *S*
Van Ryneveld, C B (Oxford U) 1949 *W, I, F, S*
Varley, H (Liversedge) 1892 *S*
Vassall, H (Blackheath) 1881 *W, S*, 1882 *I, S*, 1883 *W*
Vassall, H H (Blackheath) 1908 *I*
Vaughan, D B (Headingley) 1948 *A, W, I, S*, 1949 *I, F, S*, 1950 *W*
Vaughan-Jones, A (Army) 1932 *I, S*, 1933 *W*
Verelst, C L (Liverpool) 1876 *I*, 1878 *I*
Vernon, G F (Blackheath) 1878 *S, I*, 1880 *I, S*, 1881 *I*

Vickery, G (Aberavon) 1905 *I*
Vivyan, E J (Devonport A) 1901 *W*, 1904 *W*, *I*, *S*
Voyce, A T (Gloucester) 1920 *I*, *S*, 1921 *W*, *I*, *S*, *F*, 1922 *W*, *I*, *F*, *S*, 1923 *W*, *I*, *S*, *F*, 1924 *W*, *I*, *F*, *S*, 1925 *NZ*, *W*, *I*, *S*, *F*, 1926 *W*, *I*, *F*, *S*

Wackett, J A S (Rosslyn Park) 1959 *W*, *I*
Wade, C G (Richmond) 1883 *W*, *I*, *S*, 1884 *W*, *S*, 1885 *W*, 1886 *W*, *I*
Wade, M R (Cambridge U) 1962 *W*, *I*, *F*
Wakefield, W W (Harlequins) 1920 *W*, *F*, *I*, *S*, 1921 *W*, *I*, *S*, *F*, 1922 *W*, *I*, *F*, *S*, 1923 *W*, *I*, *S*, *F*, 1924 *W*, *I*, *F*, *S*, 1925 *NZ*, *W*, *I*, *S*, *F*, 1926 *W*, *I*, *F*, *S*, 1927 *S*, *F*
Walker, G A (Blackheath) 1939 *W*, *I*
Walker, H W (Coventry) 1947 *W*, *I*, *S*, *F*, 1948 *A*, *W*, *I*, *S*, *F*
Walker, R (Manchester) 1874 *S*, 1875 *I*, 1876 *S*, 1879 *S*, 1880 *S*
Wallens, J N S (Waterloo) 1927 *F*
Walton, E J (Castleford) 1901 *W*, *I*, 1902 *I*, *S*
Walton, W (Castleford) 1894 *S*
Ward, G (Leicester) 1913 *W*, *F*, *S*, 1914 *W*, *I*, *S*
Ward, H (Bradford) 1895 *W*
Ward, J I (Richmond) 1881 *I*, 1882 *I*
Ward, J W (Castleford) 1896 *W*, *I*, *S*
Wardlow, C S (Northampton) 1969 *SA* (R), 1971 *W*, *I*, *F*, *S* (2[1C])
Warfield, P J (Rosslyn Park, Durham U) 1973 *NZ* 1, *W*, *I*, 1975 *I*, *F*, *S*
Warr, A L (Oxford U) 1934 *W*, *I*
Watkins, J A (Gloucester) 1972 *SA*, 1973 *NZ* 1, *W*, *NZ* 2, *A*, 1975 *F*, *W*
Watkins, J K (United Services, RN) 1939 *W*, *I*, *S*
Watson, F B (United Services, RN) 1908 *S*, 1909 *S*
Watson, J H D (Blackheath) 1914 *W*, *S*, *F*
Watt, D E J (Bristol) 1967 *I*, *F*, *S*, *W*
Webb, C S H (Devonport Services, RN) 1932 *SA*, *W*, *I*, *S*, 1933 *W*, *I*, *S*, 1935 *S*, 1936 *NZ*, *W*, *I*, *S*
Webb, J M (Bristol, Bath) 1987 [*A*(R), *J*, *US*, *W*], 1988 *F*, *W*, *S*, *I* 1,2, *A* 1,2, *A*, 1989 *S*, *I*, *F*, *W*, 1991 *Fj*, *A*, [*NZ*, *It*, *F*, *S*, *A*], 1992 *S*, *I*, *F*, *W*, *C*, *SA*, 1993 *F*, *W*, *S*, *I*
Webb, J W G (Northampton) 1926 *F*, *S*, 1929 *S*
Webb, R E (Coventry) 1967 *S*, *W*, *NZ*, 1968 *I*, *F*, *S*, 1969 *I*, *F*, *S*, *W*, 1972 *I*, *F*
Webb, St L H (Bedford) 1959 *W*, *I*, *F*, *S*
Webster, J G (Moseley) 1972 *W*, *I*, *SA*, 1973 *NZ* 1, *W*, *NZ* 2, 1974 *S*, *W*, 1975 *I*, *F*, *W*
Wedge, T G (St Ives) 1907 *F*, 1909 *W*
Weighill, R H G (RAF, Harlequins) 1947 *S*, *F*, 1948 *S*, *F*
Wells, C M (Cambridge U, Harlequins) 1893 *S*, 1894 *W*, *S*, 1896 *S*, 1897 *W*, *S*
West, B R (Loughborough Colls, Northampton) 1968 *W*, *I*, *F*, *S*, 1969 *SA*, 1970 *I*, *W*, *S*
Weston, H T F (Northampton) 1901 *S*
Weston, L E (W of Scotland) 1972 *F*, *S*
Weston, M P (Richmond, Durham City) 1960 *W*, *I*, *F*, *S*, 1961 *SA*, *W*, *I*, *F*, *S*, 1962 *W*, *I*, *F*, 1963 *W*, *I*, *F*, *S*, *NZ* 1,2, *A*, 1964 *NZ*, *W*, *I*, *F*, *S*, 1965 *F*, *S*, 1966 *S*, 1968 *F*, *S*
Weston, W H (Northampton) 1933 *I*, *S*, 1934 *I*, *S*, 1935 *W*, *I*, *S*, 1936 *NZ*, *W*, *S*, 1937 *W*, *I*, *S*, 1938 *W*, *I*, *S*, 1939 *W*, *I*, *S*
Wheatley, A A (Coventry) 1937 *W*, *I*, *S*, 1938 *W*, *S*
Wheatley, H F (Coventry) 1936 *I*, 1937 *S*, 1938 *W*, *S*, 1939 *W*, *I*, *S*
Wheeler, P J (Leicester) 1975 *F*, *W*, 1976 *A*, *W*, *S*, *I*, 1977 *S*, *I*, *F*, *W*, 1978 *F*, *W*, *S*, *I*, *NZ*, 1979 *S*, *I*, *F*, *W*, *NZ*, 1980 *I*, *F*, *W*, *S*, 1981 *W*, *S*, *I*, *F*, 1982 *A*, *S*, *I*, *F*, *W*, 1983 *F*, *S*, *I*, *NZ*, 1984 *S*, *I*, *F*, *W*
White, C (Gosforth) 1983 *NZ*, 1984 *S*, *I*, *F*
White, D F (Northampton) 1947 *W*, *I*, *S*, 1948 *I*, *F*, 1951 *S*, 1952 *SA*, *W*, *S*, *I*, *F*, 1953 *W*, *I*, *S*
Whiteley, E C P (O Alleynians) 1931 *S*, *F*
Whiteley, W (Bramley) 1896 *W*
Whitley, H (Northern) 1929 *W*
Wightman, B J (Moseley, Coventry) 1959 *W*, 1963 *W*, *I*, *NZ* 2, *A*
Wigglesworth, H J (Thornes) 1884 *I*
Wilkins, D T (United Services, RN, Roundhay) 1951 *W*, *I*, *F*, *S*, 1952 *SA*, *W*, *S*, *I*, *F*, 1953 *W*, *I*, *F*, *S*
Wilkinson, E (Bradford) 1886 *W*, *I*, *S*, 1887 *W*, *S*
Wilkinson, H (Halifax) 1929 *W*, *I*, *S*, 1930 *F*
Wilkinson, H J (Halifax) 1889 *M*

Wilkinson, P (Law Club) 1872 *S*
Wilkinson, R M (Bedford) 1975 *A* 2, 1976 *A*, *W*, *S*, *I*, *F*
Willcocks, T J (Plymouth) 1902 *W*
Willcox, J G (Oxford U, Harlequins) 1961 *I*, *F*, *S*, 1962 *W*, *I*, *F*, *S*, 1963 *W*, *I*, *F*, *S*, 1964 *NZ*, *W*, *I*, *F*, *S*
William-Powlett, P B R W (United Services, RN) 1922 *S*
Williams, C G (Gloucester, RAF) 1976 *F*
Williams, C S (Manchester) 1910 *F*
Williams, J E (O Millhillians, Sale) 1954 *F*, 1955 *W*, *I*, *F*, *S*, 1956 *I*, *S*, *F*, 1965 *W*
Williams, J M (Penzance-Newlyn) 1951 *I*, *S*
Williams, P N (Orrell) 1987 *S*, [*A*, *J*, *W*]
Williams, S G (Devonport A) 1902 *W*, *I*, *S*, 1903 *I*, *S*, 1907 *I*, *S*
Williams, S H (Newport) 1911 *W*, *F*, *I*, *S*
Williamson, R H (Oxford U) 1908 *W*, *I*, *S*, 1909 *A*, *F*
Wilson, A J (Camborne S of M) 1909 *I*
Wilson, C E (Blackheath) 1898 *I*
Wilson, C P (Cambridge U, Marlborough N) 1881 *W*
Wilson, D S (Met Police, Harlequins) 1953 *F*, 1954 *W*, *NZ*, *I*, *S*, *F*, 1955 *F*, *S*
Wilson, G S (Tyldesley) 1929 *W*, *I*
Wilson, K J (Gloucester) 1963 *F*
Wilson, R P (Liverpool OB) 1891 *W*, *I*, *S*
Wilson, W C (Richmond) 1907 *I*, *S*
Winn, C E (Rosslyn Park) 1952 *SA*, *W*, *S*, *I*, *F*, 1954 *W*, *S*, *F*
Winterbottom, P J (Headingley, Harlequins) 1982 *A*, *S*, *I*, *F*, *W*, 1983 *F*, *W*, *S*, *I*, *NZ*, 1984 *S*, *F*, *W*, *SA* 1,2, 1986 *W*, *S*, *I*, *F*, 1987 *I*, *F*, *W*, [*A*, *J*, *US*, *W*], 1988 *F*, *W*, *S*, 1989 *R*, *Fj*, 1990 *I*, *F*, *W*, *S*, *Arg* 1,2,3, 1991 *W*, *S*, *I*, *F*, *A*, [*NZ*, *It*, *F*, *S*, *A*], 1992 *S*, *I*, *F*, *W*, *C*, *SA*, 1993 *F*, *W*, *S*, *I*
Wintle, T C (Northampton) 1966 *S*, 1969 *I*, *F*, *S*, *W*
Wodehouse, N A (United Services, RN) 1910 *F*, 1911 *W*, *F*, *I*, *S*, 1912 *W*, *I*, *S*, *F*, 1913 *SA*, *W*, *F*, *I*, *S*
Wood, A (Halifax) 1884 *I*
Wood, A E (Gloucester, Cheltenham) 1908 *F*, *W*, *I*
Wood, G W (Leicester) 1914 *W*
Wood, R (Liversedge) 1894 *I*
Wood, R D (Liverpool OB) 1901 *I*, 1903 *W*, *I*
Woodgate, E E (Paignton) 1952 *W*
Woodhead, E (Huddersfield) 1880 *I*
Woodruff, C G (Harlequins) 1951 *W*, *I*, *F*, *S*
Woods, S M J (Cambridge U, Wellington) 1890 *W*, *S*, *I*, 1891 *W*, *I*, *S*, 1892 *I*, *S*, 1893 *W*, *I*, 1895 *W*, *I*, *S*
Woods, T (Bridgwater) 1908 *S*
Woods, T (United Services, RN) 1920 *S*, 1921 *W*, *I*, *S*, *F*
Woodward, C R (Leicester) 1980 *I* (R), *F*, *W*, *S*, 1981 *W*, *S*, *I*, *F*, *Arg* 1,2, 1982 *A*, *S*, *I*, *F*, *W*, 1983 *I*, *NZ*, 1984 *S*, *I*, *F*, *W*
Woodward, J E (Wasps) 1952 *SA*, *W*, *S*, 1953 *W*, *I*, *F*, *S*, 1954 *W*, *NZ*, *I*, *S*, *F*, 1955 *W*, *I*, 1956 *S*
Wooldridge, C S (Oxford U, Blackheath) 1883 *W*, *I*, *S*, 1884 *W*, *I*, *S*, 1885 *I*
Wordsworth, A J (Cambridge U) 1975 *A* 1 (R)
Worton, J R B (Harlequins, Army) 1926 *W*, 1927 *W*
Wrench, D F B (Harlequins) 1964 *F*, *S*
Wright, C C G (Cambridge U, Blackheath) 1909 *I*, *S*
Wright, F T (Edinburgh Acady, Manchester) 1881 *S*
Wright, I D (Northampton) 1971 *W*, *I*, *F*, *S* (R)
Wright, J C (Met Police) 1934 *W*
Wright, J F (Bradford) 1890 *W*
Wright, T P (Blackheath) 1960 *W*, *I*, *F*, *S*, 1961 *SA*, *W*, *I*, *F*, *S*, 1962 *W*, *I*, *F*, *S*
Wright, W H G (Plymouth) 1920 *W*, *F*
Wyatt, D M (Bedford) 1976 *S* (R)

Yarranton, P G (RAF, Wasps) 1954 *W*, *NZ*, *I*, 1955 *F*, *S*
Yiend, W (Hartlepool R, Gloucester) 1889 *M*, 1892 *W*, *I*, *S*, 1893 *I*, *S*
Young, A T (Cambridge U, Blackheath, Army) 1924 *W*, *I*, *F*, *S*, 1925 *NZ*, *F*, 1926 *I*, *F*, *S*, 1927 *I*, *S*, *F*, 1928 *A*, *W*, *I*, *F*, *S*, 1929 *I*
Young, J R C (Oxford U, Harlequins) 1958 *I*, 1960 *W*, *I*, *F*, *S*, 1961 *SA*, *W*, *I*, *F*
Young, M (Gosforth) 1977 *S*, *I*, *F*, *W*, 1978 *F*, *W*, *S*, *I*, *NZ*, 1979 *S*
Young, P D (Dublin Wands) 1954 *W*, *NZ*, *I*, *S*, *F*, 1955 *W*, *I*, *F*, *S*
Youngs, N G (Leicester) 1983 *I*, *NZ*, 1984 *S*, *I*, *F*, *W*

ENGLISH INTERNATIONAL RECORDS

Both team and individual records are for official England international matches up to 31 March 1993.

TEAM RECORDS

Highest score
60 v Japan (60-7) 1987 Sydney
v individual countries
51 v Argentina (51-0) 1990 Twickenham
28 v Australia (28-19) 1988 Twickenham
26 v Canada (26-13) 1992 Wembley
58 v Fiji (58-23) 1989 Twickenham
41 v France (41-13) 1907 Richmond
38 v Ireland (38-9) 1992 Twickenham
36 v Italy (36-6) 1991 Twickenham
60 v Japan (60-7) 1987 Sydney
16 v N Zealand (16-10) 1973 Auckland
58 v Romania (58-3) 1989 Bucharest
30 v Scotland (30-18) 1980 Murrayfield
33 v S Africa (33-16) 1992 Twickenham
37 v US (37-9) 1991 Twickenham
34 v Wales (34-6) 1990 Twickenham

Biggest winning points margin
55 v Romania (58-3) 1989 Bucharest
v individual countries
51 v Argentina (51-0) 1990 Twickenham
17 v Australia { (20-3) 1973 Twickenham
{ (23-6) 1976 Twickenham
13 v Canada (26-13) 1992 Wembley
35 v Fiji (58-23) 1989 Twickenham
37 v France (37-0) 1911 Twickenham
32 v Ireland (35-3) 1988 Twickenham
30 v Italy (36-6) 1991 Twickenham
53 v Japan (60-7) 1987 Sydney
13 v N Zealand (13-0) 1936 Twickenham
55 v Romania (58-3) 1989 Bucharest
20 v Scotland (26-6) 1977 Twickenham
17 v S Africa (33-16) 1992 Twickenham
28 v US { (34-6) 1987 Sydney
{ (37-9) 1991 Twickenham
28 v Wales (34-6) 1990 Twickenham

Highest score by opposing team
42 N Zealand (15-42) 1985 Wellington
by individual countries
19 Argentina (19-19) 1981 Buenos Aires
40 Australia (15-40) 1991 Sydney
13 Canada (26-13) 1992 Wembley
23 Fiji (58-23) 1989 Twickenham
37 France (12-37) 1972 Colombes
26 Ireland (21-26) 1974 Twickenham
6 Italy (36-6) 1991 Twickenham
7 Japan (60-7) 1987 Sydney
42 N Zealand (15-42) 1985 Wellington
15 Romania (22-15) 1985 Twickenham
33 Scotland (6-33) 1986 Murrayfield
35 S Africa (9-35) 1984 Johannesburg
9 United States (37-9) 1991 Twickenham
34 Wales (21-34) 1967 Cardiff

Biggest losing points margin
27 v N Zealand (15-42) 1985 Wellington
27 v Scotland (6-33) 1986 Murrayfield
v individual countries
2 v Argentina (13-15) 1990 Buenos Aires
25 v Australia (15-40) 1991 Sydney
25 v France (12-37) 1972 Colombes
22 v Ireland (0-22) 1947 Dublin
27 v N Zealand (15-42) 1985 Wellington
27 v Scotland (6-33) 1986 Murrayfield
26 v S Africa (9-35) 1984 Johannesburg
25 v Wales (0-25) 1905 Cardiff

No defeats v Canada, Fiji, Italy, Japan, Romania or United States

Most tries by England in an international
13 v Wales 1881 Blackheath

Most tries against England in an international
8 by Wales (6-28) 1922 Cardiff

Most points by England in International Championship in a season – 118
in season 1991-92

Most tries by England in International Championship in a season – 20
in season 1913-14

INDIVIDUAL RECORDS

Most capped player
R Underwood   60   1984-93
in individual positions
Full-back
J M Webb   33   1987-93
Wing
R Underwood   60   1984-93
Centre
W D C Carling   42   1988-93
Fly-half
C R Andrew   51(52)[1]   1985-93
Scrum-half
R J Hill   29   1984-91
Prop
J A Probyn   37   1988-93
Hooker
B C Moore   45   1987-93
Lock
W A Dooley   55   1985-93
Flanker
P J Winterbottom   58   1982-93
No 8
D Richards   34   1986-92

Longest international career
G S Pearce 14 seasons 1978-79 to 1991-92

Most consecutive internationals – 36
J V Pullin 1968-75

Most internationals as captain – 35
W D C Carling 1988-93

Most points in internationals – 296
J M Webb (33 matches) 1987-93

**Most points in International
Championship in a season – 67**
J M Webb (4 matches) 1991-92

Most points in an international – 24
J M Webb v Italy 1991 Twickenham

Most tries in internationals – 36
R Underwood (60 matches) 1984-93

**Most tries in International
Championship in a season – 8**
C N Lowe (4 matches) 1913-14

Most tries in an international – 5
D Lambert v France 1907 Richmond
R Underwood v Fiji 1989 Twickenham

Most conversions in internationals – 41
J M Webb (33 matches) 1987-93

**Most conversions in International
Championship in a season – 11**
J M Webb (4 matches) 1991-92

Most conversions in an international – 8
S D Hodgkinson v Romania 1989
  Bucharest

Most dropped goals in internationals – 14
C R Andrew (52 matches) 1985-93

Most penalty goals in internationals – 67
W H Hare (25 matches) 1974-84

**Most penalty goals in International
Championship in a season – 18**
S D Hodgkinson (4 matches) 1990-91

Most penalty goals in an international – 7
S D Hodgkinson v Wales 1991 Cardiff

Most points on major tour – 56
S D Hodgkinson (4 matches) Argentina
1990
*W H Hare scored 79 points on the N American tour of 1982,
but this was not a major tour*

Most points in a tour match – 36
W N Bennett v Western Australia 1975
  Perth

Most tries in a tour match – 4
A J Morley v Western Australia 1975
  Perth
P S Preece v New South Wales 1975
  Sydney
*R E Webb scored 4 tries v Canada in 1967, and J Carleton
scored 4 against Mid-West at Cleveland in 1982, but these
were not major tours*

FINALLY, THE TROPHY GOES WEST

ADT DIVISIONAL CHAMPIONSHIP 1992

Something stirred in the west of the nation. It had been an anomaly and something of an embarrassment that the South & South-West had never won the Divisional title, and indeed, had never won more than one match in any season. At least this triumph by Stuart Barnes' men set the record straight and proved that there is enough appetite in the region to enable the Divisional team to reflect the strengths of club rugby. It was to the credit of Barnes and Keith Richardson, the coach, that they finally dragged their team from the doldrums.

There is no doubt that there are battles ahead for the credibility of the whole event, particularly since Will Carling and Peter Winterbottom pointedly missed the whole thing. Barnes himself remains unconvinced that it is a step up in class from the top level of League rugby. Nevertheless, he provided strong leadership on and off the field and if the finale was only a draw against the Midlands at Leicester (a draw was all that the South & South-West needed), it was still a triumph to savour.

Perhaps the most satisfying victory, for the team and for Barnes himself, came against London at Kingsholm. London, the favourites, were led by Rob Andrew, the stumbling-block to a place for Barnes in the England side. Indeed, the Kingsholm encounter was touted by most people as a High Noon for England fly-half play. Both players had mixed games. Andrew played a key part in his team's powerful start, which saw London lead by 17-3 at one stage. Barnes helped the South & South-West revival with a sharp break past Andrew on the way to setting up a try. Robinson, Beal and Guscott scored tries for the South & South-West; Beal showed promise throughout the Championship and took his try superbly.

In the final analysis the basis of the South & South-West victory was their ability to hold on against the experienced London front row. Clark, the Swansea prop, and Mallett were inexperienced enough at this level, but when Mallett departed early in the match he was replaced by Crompton, the young Bath man with precious little first-class rugby under his belt. All three props played splendidly, despite the presence in the opposition ranks of the formidable Leonard-Moore-Probyn combination. Hall was another to impress for the winners; in the London side, there was some clever play from Bates at scrum-half but the whole team tended to meander tactically on a poor playing surface.

London were eventually to subside even further when they lost at home to the North, one of the most surprising results in the Championship's history and a great and much-needed fillip for the game in the north. Previously, the North had disappointed and had been comfortably outsmarted by Barnes and his men in the opening round of matches. Paul Grayson, the Waterloo fly-half, maintained his promise and Tim Rodber, heavily involved in representative rugby through the season, also stood out. Yet the victory over London at the Stoop Memorial Ground was essentially a team effort and the team was certainly young enough to develop further.

The Midlands were never likely to retain the Championship. They had won with a 100 per cent record in the previous season although the event was downgraded by the absence of all of England's World Cup squad. They were comfortably defeated in the opening game when Andrew and Bates organised a London victory by 26-16. Johnson and Bayfield of the Midlands, later to team up as England's locks against France, made surprisingly little impact against a makeshift London lock partnership of Richard Langhorn and Mark Russell, both of whom are far happier in their normal position in the back row. Andrew contributed a try, a conversion and three penalty goals. There is no question that for him, at least, the Divisional Championship was essential. He was barred from Wasps' League and Cup team because a long period of re-qualification was imposed on him after his temporary move to France, where he played for Toulouse.

Johnson did revive strongly and was probably the outstanding forward on the field in the next round of matches, when the Midlands beat the North 16-13 in a game which rarely rose above the mediocre. Johnson did much of the spadework and even chipped in with a try. The Midlands were on top in the scrum but lacking in the midfield. The North's high point was a try by Tony Underwood after a move covering 65 metres. The Midlands gave their best performances in the 18-18 draw with the South & South-West at Leicester, a game of excitement if not consistent high standards. This match showed the young Midlands pack, based on the highly-promising Leicester eight, in its true light and the visitors had to dig deep for the draw, which was secured with tries by Callard at full-back and Blackmore, the towering lock from Bristol.

Andrew, with 43 points, was the leading scorer in the tournament. Both South & South-West wings, Simon Morris and Nick Beal, scored three tries. Morris scored his in the same match, against the North. He and Beal were certainly two of the best backs to emerge in the Championship.

Final Table

	P	W	D	L	F	A	Pts
South & South-West	3	2	1	0	73	51	5
Midlands	3	1	1	1	50	57	3
London	3	1	0	2	70	66	2
North	3	1	0	2	46	65	2

The North have won the Divisional Championship 4 times, London 3 times, Midlands and South & South-West once each.

The crucial match. John Hall of the South & South-West flips the ball out to Richard Hill during his team's win over London at Kingsholm.

5 December, Headingley RFC

Northern Division 9 (3PG)   **South & South-West Division 29** (2G 3T)
Northern Division: I Hunter (Harlequins); N J Heslop (Orrell), B Barley (Wakefield),
K G Simms (Liverpool St Helens) *(capt)*, R Underwood (Leicester & RAF); P Grayson
(Waterloo), C D Morris (Orrell); M Hynes (Orrell), S Mitchell (West Hartlepool),
M Whitcombe (Sale), W A Dooley (Preston Grasshoppers), P Walton (Northampton),
M Greenwood (Wasps), T A K Rodber (Northampton), M Pepper (Nottingham)
Replacements D Scully (Wakefield) for Morris; M Jackson (Fylde) for Heslop
Scorer *Penalty Goals:* Grayson (3)
South & South-West Division: J M Webb (Bath); N Beal (Northampton),
P de Glanville (Bath), J C Guscott (Bath), S Morris (Gloucester); S Barnes (Bath) *(capt)*,
R J Hill (Bath); C Clark (Swansea), K Dunn (Wasps), J Mallett (Bath), N C Redman
(Bath), A Blackmore (Bristol), J P Hall (Bath), B B Clarke (Bath), R A Robinson (Bath)
Scorers *Tries:* Morris (3), Beal (2)   *Conversions:* Webb (2)
Referee J L Bacigalupo (Scotland)

5 December, Wasps RFC

London Division 26 (1G 3PG 2T)   **Midlands Division 16** (1G 3PG)
London Division: A J Buzza (Wasps); S Pilgrim (Wasps), M Evans (Harlequins),
J Buckton (Saracens), D O'Leary (Saracens); C R Andrew (Wasps) *(capt)*, S Bates
(Wasps); J Leonard (Harlequins), B C Moore (Harlequins), J A Probyn (Wasps),
M Russell (Harlequins), R Langhorn (Harlequins), M G Skinner (Blackheath),
D Ryan (Wasps), J Cassell (Saracens)
Scorers *Tries:* Ryan, Andrew, O'Leary   *Conversion:* Andrew
Penalty Goals: Andrew (3)
Midlands Division: J Liley (Leicester); S Hackney (Leicester), S Potter (Leicester),
F Packman (Northampton), H Thorneycroft (Northampton); J Steele (Northampton),
A Kardooni (Leicester); M Linnett (Moseley), C J Olver (Northampton), D Garforth
(Leicester), M Johnson (Leicester), M C Bayfield (Northampton), P Shillingford
(Moseley), D Richards (Leicester) *(capt)*, N Back (Leicester) *Replacement* M Dawson
(Northampton) for Kardooni
Scorers *Try:* Johnson   *Conversion:* Liley   *Penalty Goals:* Liley (3)
Referee S Piercy (Yorkshire)

12 December, Waterloo RFC

Northern Division 13 (1G 2PG)   **Midlands Division 16** (2PG 2T)
Northern Division: I Hunter (Harlequins); T Underwood (Leicester), B Barley
(Wakefield), K G Simms (Liverpool St Helens) *(capt)*, R Underwood (Leicester & RAF);
P Grayson (Waterloo), D Scully (Wakefield); M Hynes (Orrell), S Mitchell
(West Hartlepool), M Whitcombe (Sale), K Westgarth (West Hartlepool), D Baldwin
(Sale), M Greenwood (Wasps), T A K Rodber (Northampton), M Pepper (Nottingham)
Scorers *Try:* T Underwood   *Conversion:* Grayson   *Penalty Goals:* Grayson (2)
Midlands Division: J Liley (Leicester); S Hackney (Leicester), S Potter (Leicester),
F Packman (Northampton), H Thorneycroft (Northampton); R Angell (Coventry),
M Dawson (Northampton); M Linnett (Moseley), C J Olver (Northampton), D Garforth
(Leicester), M Johnson (Leicester), M C Bayfield (Northampton), P Shillingford
(Moseley), D Richards (Leicester), N Back (Leicester) *Replacement* J Steele
(Northampton) for Hackney
Scorers *Tries:* Potter, Johnson   *Penalty Goals:* Steele (2)
Referee E F Morrison (Gloucestershire)

12 December, Gloucester RFC

South & South-West Division 26 (1G 3PG 2T)   **London Division 24** (1G 4PG 1T)
South & South-West Division: J M Webb (Bath); N Beal (Northampton),
P de Glanville (Bath), J C Guscott (Bath), S Morris (Gloucester); S Barnes (Bath) (*capt*),
R J Hill (Bath); C Clark (Swansea), K Dunn (Wasps), J Mallett (Bath), N C Redman
(Bath), A Blackmore (Bristol), J P Hall (Bath), B B Clarke (Bath), R A Robinson (Bath)
Replacement D Crompton (Bath) for Mallett
Scorers *Tries:* Robinson, Beal, Guscott   *Conversion:* Webb   *Penalty Goals:* Webb (3)
London Division: A J Buzza (Wasps); S Pilgrim (Wasps), F Clough (Wasps),
D P Hopley (Cambridge U), D O'Leary (Saracens); C R Andrew (Wasps) (*capt*), S Bates
(Wasps); J Leonard (Harlequins), B C Moore (Harlequins), J A Probyn (Wasps), A Snow
(Harlequins), R Langhorn (Harlequins), M G Skinner (Blackheath), D Ryan (Wasps),
J Cassell (Saracens)
Scorers *Tries:* Snow, Andrew   *Conversion:* Andrew   *Penalty Goals:* Andrew (4)
Referee G Black (Ireland)

19 December, Leicester RFC

Midlands Division 18 (1G 2PG 1T)   **South & South-West Division 18** (1G 2PG 1T)
Midlands Division: J Liley (Leicester); F Packman (Northampton), S Potter
(Leicester), I Bates (Leicester), H Thorneycroft (Northampton); R Angell (Coventry),
M Dawson (Northampton); M Linnett (Moseley), C J Olver (Northampton), D Garforth
(Leicester), M Johnson (Leicester), S Lloyd (Moseley), P Shillingford (Moseley),
D Richards (Leicester) (*capt*), N Back (Leicester) *Replacement* R Cockerill (Leicester) for
Olver
Scorers *Tries:* Richards, Potter   *Conversion:* Liley   *Penalty Goals:* Liley (2)
South & South-West Division: J Callard (Bath); N Beal (Northampton), P de Glanville
(Bath), J C Guscott (Bath), S Morris (Gloucester); S Barnes (Bath) (*capt*), R J Hill (Bath);
C Clark (Swansea), K Dunn (Wasps), V E Ubogu (Bath), N C Redman (Bath),
A Blackmore (Bristol), J P Hall (Bath), B B Clarke (Bath), R A Robinson (Bath)
Scorers *Tries:* Callard, Blackmore   *Conversion:* Callard   *Penalty Goals:* Callard, Barnes
Referee F A Howard (Liverpool/Manchester)

19 December, Harlequins RFC

London Division 20 (2G 2PG)   **Northern Division 24** (1G 4PG 1T)
London Division: A J Buzza (Wasps); S Pilgrim (Wasps), F Clough (Wasps),
D P Hopley (Cambridge U), D O'Leary (Saracens); C R Andrew (Wasps) (*capt*),
S Bates (Wasps); J Leonard (Harlequins), B C Moore (Harlequins), J A Probyn (Wasps),
A Snow (Harlequins), R Langhorn (Harlequins), M G Skinner (Blackheath), D Ryan
(Wasps), J Cassell (Saracens)
Scorers *Tries:* Skinner, Hopley   *Conversions:* Pilgrim, Andrew
Penalty Goals: Andrew (2)
Northern Division: I Hunter (Harlequins); T Underwood (Leicester), J Fletcher
(Tynedale), K G Simms (Liverpool St Helens), R Underwood (Leicester & RAF);
P Grayson (Waterloo), C D Morris (Orrell); M Hynes (Orrell), S Mitchell
(West Hartlepool), M Whitcombe (Sale), K Westgarth (West Hartlepool), D Baldwin
(Sale), A Brown (West Hartlepool), T A K Rodber (Northampton), M Greenwood
(Nottingham) *Replacements* P Hackett (Waterloo) for Mitchell; J Mallinder (Sale) for
Fletcher
Scorers *Tries:* Brown, R Underwood   *Conversion:* Grayson   *Penalty Goals:* Grayson (4)
Referee J Dume (France)

MAULING DEAN DRAGS ALONG THE YOUNG TIGERS OF TWICKENHAM

PILKINGTON CUP 1992-93
Michael Austin

1 May, Twickenham
Harlequins 16 (1G 3PG)   **Leicester 23** (2G 2PG 1DG)

After the high drama of the two previous finals extending into extra time, a disappointing match blemished 1992-93, though not from Leicester's viewpoint. They won the Cup for the first time in 12 years to cast aside two interim losing appearances at Twickenham. Coached by Ian Smith, their former long-serving flanker, Leicester won their first trophy since the League title five years earlier and confirmed the swift development of a young pack, and especially a front row with an average age of less than 24.

The sunlit match was imperfect, partly because of defensive restraints and an unyielding insistence to punt speculatively, which betrayed exactly how much was at stake for two sides intent on challenging the domination of Bath. A capacity crowd of 54,000, including 14,000 from Leicester, saw Harlequins stay in contention, but only through the perfect goal-kicking of Challinor, who landed all of his four attempts. In contrast, Liley again suffered the big-match nerves that had afflicted him previously and missed two eminently kickable penalty goals in the game's formative stages. To win, Leicester also had to survive a rigorous examination from the Harlequins pack.

Boot and blunder was the general theme but two Leicester forwards, Richards and Back, rose above the shortcomings. Richards, a powerful mauler, made a significant contribution in the loose and Back, the openside flanker, launched a 65-yard diagonal kick to confirm the depth of his talents, which England have yet to acknowledge. The unassuming Wells, in his last game as captain after two seasons, also played mightily.

Even so, Leicester's scrummage was unstable, they were short of line-out power towards the back and the kicking of Kardooni and Harris, like that of Liley, lacked precision. Neither of the Underwood brothers was given a run, and Harlequins too had cause to regret their unwillingness to spread the ball to the wings. This was especially poignant because Madderson, playing in only his fourth senior match, looked lively when in rare possession, notably when he made a long run skilfully supported by Winterbottom, in his final club game, and Sheasby.

Harlequins spun the ball along the threequarter line only when facing defeat, and were a pale imitation of the side beaten in the final by Bath the previous season. They suffered a psychological blow with the withdrawal of Moore, through a groin injury, on the morning of the match.

This brought in Killick, who had played in 75 senior games spanning six years. His accurate throwing helped Harlequins to share the line-out, in which Langhorn impressed. But it was Snow who won the ball in the build-up to their tenth-minute try. Challinor hoisted a high kick which fell near the posts, Russell tried to barge his way over and made the ball available for Glenister to score a blindside try from a ruck. Challinor converted.

Leicester trailed 13-10 at half-time but victory was the prize for subsequent long spells of domination. Potter began their scoring with a powerful run and an outrageous dummy following an elusive dash from defence by Liley and the support of Kardooni, Harris and Back, who provided the scoring pass. From 7-7 after 18 minutes, Harlequins profited from two penalty goals by Challinor either side of a dropped goal from Harris. Liley's first penalty goal after 44 minutes regained equality for Leicester, and six minutes later a well-rehearsed tapped penalty move heralded victory. Cockerill acted as pivot and Leicester's forwards ran at all angles as decoys for Johnson, standing deep and undetected, to build enough impetus to plough through with barely a hand laid on him.

Liley's conversion took Leicester 20-13 ahead and foreshadowed

Martin Johnson scores for the Tigers in their 23-16 Cup final victory. Kent Bray of Harlequins is powerless to stop him.

147

tense final minutes in which Challinor landed a third penalty goal and Liley responded to seal the match with a minute remaining. Victory for Leicester was not as convincing as their 23-0 League win over Harlequins, but all the sweeter for their burgeoning side.

Harlequins: K A Bray; C S Madderson, W D C Carling, G J Thompson, J R Alexander; A P Challinor, R J Glenister; J Leonard, N Killick, A R Mullins, A C W Snow, R S R Langhorn, M P Russell, C M A Sheasby, P J Winterbottom (*capt*)
Scorers *Try:* Glenister   *Conversion:* Challinor   *Penalty Goals:* Challinor (3)
Leicester: J G Liley; T Underwood, S Potter, I Bates, R Underwood; J C Harris, A Kardooni; G C Rowntree, R Cockerill, D J Garforth, M O Johnson, M D Poole, J M Wells (*capt*), D Richards, N A Back
Scorers *Tries:* Potter, Johnson   *Conversions:* Liley (2)   *Penalty Goals:* Liley (2)
Dropped Goal: Harris
Referee A J Spreadbury (Somerset Society)

The semi-finals could not have been more contrasting. Leicester overpowered Northampton 28-6 before a capacity crowd at Welford Road in a live televised match while Harlequins, managed by Jamie Salmon, squeezed past Wasps 14-13 through a late try by Thompson.

Leicester's was a comprehensive victory, a triumph for diligent preparation, self-belief and team-work, bound together by Tony Russ, the club's director of coaching. They scored tries through Richards, Back and Boyle, a replacement, who ran in the final score after Northampton had been hit by a volley of 23 points before half-time.

Their tightest match en route to Twickenham was against London Scottish in the third round at Richmond, where a 20-11 win was the prelude to a 28-3 victory at Nottingham. Wells, a part-time farmer, jokingly suggested that their success could be attributed to lean meat – venison in red wine which he had provided for a players' supper two days earlier. With better goal-kicking from Liley at the quarter-final stage, Leicester would have broken the competition record win. They scored 76 points without reply from Exeter but Liley converted only four of the 13 tries, three of them from Tony Underwood.

Harlequins ran in 12 tries, including a hat-trick from Glenister, in their third-round drubbing of Blackheath. After beating Wakefield, they endured tougher times at Waterloo, where home officials accused them of using illegal, longer Rugby League-type studs, and of foul play. Moore, Leonard and Snow were instructed to change their footwear by Stewart Piercy, the referee.

Waterloo, whose back division had an average age of 21, provided the competition's shock result when eliminating Bath 9-8. Barnes, the catalyst in so many outstanding Bath performances, was absent, playing for the Barbarians against Australia. Jack Rowell, the Bath coach, said: 'We missed him, but Waterloo were highly committed, very lively and tackled their hearts out.' An 8-3 win over Orrell in the fourth round illustrated Waterloo's mettle, which almost promoted them into the

First Division of the Courage Clubs Championship. Underdogs had done some barking at the door but the days of sides bridging six or seven leagues to achieve surprise wins are heavily numbered as the higher-placed clubs become more 'professional'. Tynedale and Tabard were the only teams from outside the top four leagues to reach the third round. Tabard's win at Brixham illustrated that style is as important as power on these august Cup occasions. Ten supporters sailed on two yachts from the Hamble to the Devon fishing town, and around 300 more enjoyed pre-match cocktails on board. Two tries gave Tabard an 18-16 win. Their eventual reward was a home draw against Northampton, who beat brave opposition 50-13. Tynedale, narrowly eliminated at Morley, had defeated Sheffield, confirming their habit of upsetting senior opponents. The previous season, they toppled Wakefield.

The mantle of possible giant-killers passed to Exeter and Redruth, fourth-round qualifiers for the first time after beating London Welsh. As luck would have it, they met each other, and Exeter's narrow win sent them along the rocky road to Leicester.

Bath, Bristol and Gloucester were knocked out in the third round, a stimulant for the South and South-West to win the ADT Divisional Championship the following month. Performances of special merit belonged to West Hartlepool, who beat London Irish before losing at home to Wasps, and to Moseley. They kept a Cup run and a successful battle against relegation ticking over simultaneously.

Over the years, the competition has offered a quirk or two and Moseley's win over Harrogate at The Reddings provided another. A try by Parry, the Moseley flanker, made the difference but it was scored during confusion over the use of floodlights. Harrogate, forced into an early kick-off because of their lack of experience under artificial light, nevertheless found themselves under the electric glare when visibility became poor. The lights were turned off at Harrogate's request, Parry scored in the gloom and they were switched back on for the rest of the match.

The competition included nine newcomers, who increased the total participants to 218 in 22 seasons. They were Amber Valley, Horsham, Leamington, Macclesfield, Old Blues, Penrith, Sedgley Park, Tiverton and Westcombe Park, who were among those benefiting from Pilkington's sponsorship in the second season of a second three-year agreement, worth £1 million over that time-span.

RESULTS

First Round

Amber Valley 3, Hereford 6; Askeans 24, Ruislip 0; Berry Hill 24, Salisbury 10; Bradford & Bingley 23, Aspatria 9; Bridgwater & Alb 20, Old Alleynians 17; Brixham 16, Tabard 18; Camborne 11, Redruth 24; Chesterfield 8, Worcester 13; Clifton 43, Horsham 10; Exeter 30, Newbury 6; Harrogate 25, Leamington 15; High Wycombe 17, Old Colfeians 0; Lichfield 52, Penrith 3; London Welsh 31, Havant 8; Lydney 13, Basingstoke 6;

Sedgley Park 6, Leeds 20; Sheffield 17, Liverpool St Helens 14; Sudbury 19, North Walsham 12; Tiverton 21, Henley 30; Towcestrians 15, Macclesfield 10; Tynedale 39, Hartlepool Rovers 16; Vale of Lune 3, Otley 46; Vipers 5, Broughton Park 15; Westcombe Park 7, Old Blues 18.

Second Round

Bedford 21, Askeans 12; Bridgwater & Alb 3, Redruth 7; Coventry 34, Hereford 15; Exeter 15, Berry Hill 13; Fylde 21, Leeds 6; Henley 18, London Welsh 40; Lichfield 8, Waterloo 39; Lydney 6, Clifton 9; Morley 39, Broughton Park 17; Moseley 16, Harrogate 12; Old Blues 3, Blackheath 27; Otley 8, Sale 14; Richmond 37, Sudbury 15; Rosslyn Park 49, Plymouth Albion 3; Tabard 14, High Wycombe 9; Towcestrians 8, Newcastle Gosforth 36; Tynedale 21, Sheffield 14; Wakefield 31, Bradford & Bingley 9; Worcester 15, Nottingham 39.

Third Round

Clifton 3, Exeter 19; Coventry 14, Nottingham 28; Morley 10, Tynedale 6; Moseley 19, Fylde 6; Newcastle Gosforth 13, Gloucester 10; Orrell 20, Sale 3; Redruth 16, London Welsh 7; Richmond 22, Wakefield 25; Rosslyn Park 10, Wasps 37; Rugby 27, Bedford 14; Tabard 13, Northampton 50; Saracens 20, Bristol 15; Waterloo 9, Bath 8; West Hartlepool 13, London Irish 8; London Scottish 11, Leicester 20; Harlequins 72, Blackheath 3.

Fourth Round

Harlequins 47, Wakefield 18; Northampton 33, Newcastle Gosforth 3; Nottingham 3, Leicester 28; Redruth 3, Exeter 8; Rugby 5, Moseley 11; Wasps 18, Saracens 17; Waterloo 8, Orrell 3; West Hartlepool 21, Morley 3.

Quarter-finals

Leicester 76, Exeter 0; Northampton 37, Moseley 15; Waterloo 14, Harlequins 21; West Hartlepool 9, Wasps 15.

Semi-finals

Leicester 28, Northampton 6; Wasps 13, Harlequins 14.

Previous finals *(all at Twickenham)*

1972 Gloucester 17 Moseley 6
1973 Coventry 27 Bristol 15
1974 Coventry 26 London Scottish 6
1975 Bedford 28 Rosslyn Park 12
1976 Gosforth 23 Rosslyn Park 14
1977 Gosforth 27 Waterloo 11
1978 Gloucester 6 Leicester 3
1979 Leicester 15 Moseley 12
1980 Leicester 21 London Irish 9
1981 Leicester 22 Gosforth 15
1982 Gloucester 12 Moseley 12
      (title shared)
1983 Bristol 28 Leicester 22
1984 Bath 10 Bristol 9
1985 Bath 24 London Welsh 15
1986 Bath 25 Wasps 17
1987 Bath 19 Wasps 12
1988 Harlequins 28 Bristol 22
1989 Bath 10 Leicester 6
1990 Bath 48 Gloucester 6
1991 Harlequins 25, Northampton 13
      (aet)
1992 Harlequins 12, Bath 15 *(aet)*

COUNTY CUP WINNERS 1992-93

Berkshire	**Reading**
Buckinghamshire	**High Wycombe**
Cheshire	**Winnington Park**
Cornwall	**Redruth**
Cumbria	**Aspatria**
Dorset/Wilts	**Wimborne**
Devon	**Exeter**
Durham	**Stockton**
Eastern Counties	**Sudbury**
East Midlands	**Kettering**
Gloucestershire	**Stroud**
Hampshire	**Basingstoke**
Hertfordshire	**Tabard**
Kent	**Westcombe Park**
Lancashire	**Waterloo**
Leicestershire	**Syston**
Middlesex	**Ruislip**
North Midlands	**Birmingham-Solihull**
Northumberland	**Newcastle G & Tyne-dale** *(trophy shared)*
Notts, Lincs & Derbys	**Scunthorpe**
Oxfordshire	**Henley**
Somerset	**Bridgwater**
Staffordshire	**Stoke-on-Trent**
Surrey	**Old Mid-Whitgift**
Sussex	**Worthing**
Warwickshire	**Broadstreet**
Yorkshire	**Otley**

BATH STAND ABOVE THE PANIC
AND STAY CHAMPIONS

THE COURAGE LEAGUES 1992-93

There was always an element of panic about the operation of the top divisions in the Courage Leagues. With each division being reduced to ten clubs for the 1993-94 season in order to provide for home and away fixtures, there were four clubs to be relegated from Division 1, no fewer than seven from Division 2; when you reached down as far as Divisions 4 North and South, you had to win the division in order to escape what amounted to relegation to the new Division 5 for 1993-94.

It made for frenetic action and also meant that teams who enjoyed a relatively good season were relegated. Take West Hartlepool. Their courageous promotion push in 1991-92 availed them nothing – they appeared last season in Division 1, from which four teams were to be relegated. They may be something of an outpost but they coped splendidly in the top division. They won three games, including a glorious effort away at Gloucester; they came perilously close to winning at least twice more and generally did enough to keep their flag flying in the top flight – had it not been for the four-down trapdoor. For long periods of the season, giants such as Gloucester and Orrell were in relegation trouble.

Bath never panicked. They were taken to the limit by Wasps, who shrugged off the loss of some key players and, even though they had nothing like the scoring power or star quality of Bath, were still there at the end. To win the title on points difference. Bath had to win at Saracens on the last weekend, and even though they were already relegated, Saracens put up mighty opposition. Near the end, Bath were trailing. No panic. They came storming back and deservedly claimed yet another title – they did not win the double (they were sensationally knocked out of the Cup at Waterloo when their two great engines, Stuart Barnes and Ben Clarke, were missing) so the season, by their standards, was a relative failure.

Newcastle Gosforth proudly take their place in the top flight for the new season but famous names such as Rosslyn Park, Coventry and Bedford subside to Division 3. Otley, ruling the roost in their part of Yorkshire despite the emergence of the newly-created Leeds club, won Division 3 and Harrogate and Sudbury rose from Divisions 4 North and South respectively. The tensions and demands on the players will grow ever stronger now that an 18-match programme is instituted for the top divisions. The Courage Leagues as a whole remain an outstanding success, reflected by the decision of Courage renew their sponsorship with a massive £7 million. It is a sign of the company's confidence and also of the stature of the whole leagues operation in England.

Courage League champions Bath savour their success after beating Saracens on the last League Saturday.

NATIONAL DIVISION

National 1

	P	W	D	L	F	A	Pts
Bath	12	11	0	1	355	97	22
Wasps	12	11	0	1	186	118	22
Leicester	12	9	0	3	220	116	18
Northampton	12	8	0	4	215	150	16
Gloucester	12	6	0	6	173	151	12
Bristol	12	6	0	6	148	169	12
L Irish	12	6	0	6	175	223	12
Harlequins	12	5	1	6	197	187	11
Orrell	12	5	0	7	175	183	10
L Scottish	12	3	1	8	192	248	7
Saracens	12	3	0	9	137	180	6
W Hartlepool	12	3	0	9	149	236	6
Rugby	12	1	0	11	104	368	2

National 2

	P	W	D	L	F	A	Pts
Newcastle Gos	12	10	0	2	241	106	20
Waterloo	12	10	0	2	228	138	20
Wakefield	12	8	1	3	186	123	17
Nottingham	12	8	0	4	249	145	16
Sale	12	7	1	4	237	102	15
Moseley	12	6	2	4	184	150	14
Bedford	12	6	2	4	186	183	14
Rosslyn Pk	12	5	0	7	209	199	10
Richmond	12	5	0	7	202	196	10
Blackheath	12	4	2	6	142	231	10
Coventry	12	3	0	9	192	236	6
Fylde	12	0	3	9	108	290	3
Morley	12	0	1	11	107	372	1

National 3

	P	W	D	L	F	A	Pts
Otley	11	8	1	2	274	118	17
Havant	11	8	1	2	185	93	17
Exeter	11	8	1	2	247	169	17
Redruth	11	7	2	2	175	125	16
Sheffield	11	7	0	4	208	134	14
Leeds	11	7	0	4	228	220	14
Liverpool SH	11	5	0	6	203	130	10
Clifton	11	4	2	5	206	175	10
Aspatria	11	3	1	7	170	308	7
Askeans	11	3	0	8	132	300	6
Broughton Pk	11	2	0	9	136	217	4
Plymouth A	11	0	0	11	130	305	0

National 4 North*

	P	W	D	L	F	A	Pts
Harrogate	12	10	1	1	363	115	21
Rotherham	12	10	1	1	259	123	21
Preston Grass	12	8	0	4	157	135	16
Stoke-on-Trent	12	7	0	5	193	168	14
Lichfield	12	6	1	5	221	224	13
Kendal	12	6	0	6	182	189	12
Walsall	12	6	0	6	160	192	12
Durham C	12	6	0	6	179	219	12
Stourbridge	12	5	1	6	161	144	11
Winnington Pk	12	5	1	6	167	165	11
Hereford	12	2	2	8	147	216	6
Nuneaton	12	2	0	10	138	269	4
Towcestrians	12	1	1	10	118	286	3

All teams bar champions to National Division 5 for 1993-94

National 4 South

	P	W	D	L	F	A	Pts
Sudbury	12	11	1	0	337	130	23
L Welsh	12	10	0	2	353	170	20
Lydney	12	8	0	4	187	170	16
Camborne	12	7	1	4	180	168	15
Basingstoke	12	7	0	5	192	145	14
Southend	12	6	1	5	196	189	13
Berry Hill	12	4	3	5	187	216	11
High Wycombe	12	5	0	7	196	159	10
Met Police	12	4	1	7	201	207	9
Weston-s-Mare	12	4	1	7	154	226	9
N Walsham	12	4	0	8	125	209	8
Maidstone	12	2	0	10	122	306	4
Thurrock	12	2	0	10	147	295	2

NORTH DIVISION

North 1

	P	W	D	L	F	A	Pts
Bradford & B	12	11	1	0	324	106	23
Tynedale	12	9	0	3	323	111	18
Wharfedale	12	7	0	5	216	208	14
Sandal	12	6	1	5	205	129	13
Middlesbrough	12	6	1	5	185	160	13
Hull Ionians	12	6	0	6	206	208	12
Widnes	12	6	0	6	164	175	12
Stockton	12	6	0	6	138	160	12
Hartlepool R	12	5	0	7	161	182	8
Wigton	12	3	1	8	121	220	7
Vale of Lune	12	3	1	8	167	291	7
Northern	12	3	1	8	124	276	7
Lymm	12	4	0	8	133	244	6

North 2

	P	W	D	L	F	A	Pts
Manchester	12	10	0	2	302	103	20
Huddersfield	12	10	0	2	247	111	20
York	12	9	0	3	295	106	18
W Pk Bramhope	12	9	0	3	270	97	18
O Crossleyans	12	9	0	3	222	144	18
Alnwick	12	8	0	4	196	152	14
West Pk St H	12	7	0	5	207	179	14
Northwich	12	4	0	8	145	235	8
Wigan	12	4	0	8	124	229	6
Birkenhead Pk	12	3	0	9	120	246	6
Carlisle	12	3	0	9	127	275	6

Wasps skipper Dean Ryan and Richard Kinsey (No 4) dispute a line-out with Matt Poole (left), Darren Garforth and Dean Richards of Leicester. Wasps won the match 14-13.

Halifax	12	2	0	10	153	265	4
Sandbach	12	0	0	12	64	363	0

North-West 1

	P	W	D	L	F	A	Pts
Macclesfield	12	12	0	0	310	68	24
New Brighton	12	9	1	2	243	103	19
Merseyside Pol	12	9	0	3	180	84	18
St Edward's OB	12	7	1	4	165	148	15
Ashton-on-Mers	12	6	1	5	106	111	13
Caldy	12	7	0	5	184	217	12
Chester	12	5	0	7	215	159	10
Cockermouth	12	5	0	7	112	186	10
Blackburn	12	4	0	8	165	183	8
Davenport	12	5	0	7	131	197	8
Sedgley Pk	12	4	0	8	149	188	6
Wirral	12	2	0	10	85	243	4
Egremont	12	1	1	10	111	292	2

North-West 2

	P	W	D	L	F	A	Pts
Oldershaw	12	10	0	2	244	105	20
K Lonsdale	12	9	0	3	196	162	18
O Salians	11	8	0	3	169	81	16
O Aldwinians	12	7	1	4	174	105	15
Netherhall	12	7	0	5	160	136	14
Ormskirk	11	6	1	4	236	144	13
Wilmslow	11	6	0	5	135	149	12
Vagabonds	9	5	0	4	119	95	10
Warrington	12	5	0	7	117	203	10
Rochdale	12	4	0	8	81	177	8
Rossendale	12	4	0	8	102	162	4
Workington	12	2	0	10	102	216	4
S Liverpool	12	1	0	11	101	241	0

Cumbria/Lancs North

	P	W	D	L	F	A	Pts
Penrith	12	9	0	3	226	103	18
Windermere	12	8	1	3	287	128	17
Calder Vale	12	8	1	3	201	115	17
Oldham	12	7	2	3	172	158	16
St Benedict's	12	7	0	5	175	137	14
Moresby	12	7	0	5	190	156	14
Metrovick	12	6	2	4	160	144	14
Furness	12	6	1	5	140	134	13
Vickers	12	5	1	6	147	214	11
Tyldesley	12	3	1	8	148	169	7
Upper Eden	12	3	0	9	153	223	6
De La Salle	12	2	0	10	109	260	4
Keswick	12	2	1	9	116	293	3

Cumbria

	P	W	D	L	F	A	Pts
Smith Bros	8	8	0	0	153	76	14
British Steel	8	7	0	1	131	41	12
Creighton	8	5	0	3	110	79	10
Carnforth	8	3	1	4	97	137	7
Millom	8	4	0	4	86	101	6
Whitehaven	8	3	0	5	73	121	6
Ambleside	8	2	0	6	101	158	4
Green Garth	8	1	1	6	56	130	3
Silloth	8	2	0	6	33	88	0

Lancashire North 1

	P	W	D	L	F	A	Pts
Fleetwood	13	12	0	1	438	108	24
Burnage	13	11	0	2	261	111	22
Bolton	13	10	0	3	227	183	20
Chorley	13	8	0	5	158	161	16
Bury	13	7	1	5	199	170	15
Thornton Clev	13	8	0	5	215	158	14
Blackpool	13	6	0	7	198	199	12
Broughton	13	5	1	7	137	216	11
Colne & Nelson	13	5	1	7	162	252	11
O Bedians	13	4	1	8	115	199	9
Ashton-U-Lyne	13	5	0	8	92	187	6
Marple	13	3	0	10	116	246	6
Littleborough	13	4	0	9	128	215	4
Heaton Moor	13	0	2	11	91	206	2

Lancashire North 2

	P	W	D	L	F	A	Pts
Clitheroe	8	7	0	1	197	57	14
Dukinfield	8	7	0	1	212	74	14
N Manchester	8	4	0	4	86	87	6
Lostock	7	1	0	6	39	185	2
Agecroft	7	0	0	7	40	193	0

Cheshire/Lancs South

	P	W	D	L	F	A	Pts
Ruskin Pk	11	10	1	0	233	85	21
Kersal	9	8	0	1	158	69	16
O Parkonians	10	7	0	3	173	93	14
Aspull	10	6	1	3	181	129	13
Crewe & N'wich	10	6	0	4	149	102	12
Leigh	10	5	0	5	159	121	10
Liverpool Coll	11	4	0	7	153	159	8
Newton-le-W	9	3	0	6	73	166	6
St Mary's OB	10	2	1	7	78	144	5
Eagle	10	1	1	8	74	148	3
Southport	9	2	0	7	90	213	2
Douglas (I of M)	7	1	0	6	70	216	2

Cheshire

	P	W	D	L	F	A	Pts
O Anselmians	10	8	0	2	348	98	16
Wallasey	10	7	0	3	201	90	14
Congleton	10	7	0	3	193	147	14
Bowdon	10	7	0	3	154	146	14
Port Sunlight	10	6	0	4	222	107	12
Prenton	10	5	0	5	114	90	8

	P	W	D	L	F	A	Pts
Hoylake	10	5	0	5	132	142	8
Shell Stanlow	10	3	0	7	89	210	4
Holmes Chapel	10	3	0	7	86	234	4
Moore	10	2	0	8	61	217	2
Helsby	10	2	0	8	84	260	0

Lancashire South

	P	W	D	L	F	A	Pts
Sefton	9	8	0	1	214	71	16
Eccles	9	8	0	1	174	79	16
Manchester YMCA	9	6	1	2	160	92	13
Birchfield	9	5	0	4	134	95	10
Halton	9	3	1	5	96	186	7
Vulcan	9	5	0	4	152	112	6
Didsbury TOC H	9	4	1	4	77	93	5
Mossley Hill	9	2	1	6	104	180	5
Hightown	9	1	1	7	85	165	1
Lucas	9	0	1	8	69	276	1

North-East 1

	P	W	D	L	F	A	Pts
Bridlington	12	10	0	2	284	110	20
Blaydon	12	8	2	2	307	92	18
Selby	12	7	1	4	179	135	15
O Brodleians	12	7	0	5	168	152	14
Morpeth	12	7	0	5	152	138	14
Novocastrians	12	5	3	4	148	129	13
Keighley	12	6	0	6	153	117	12
Redcar	12	5	1	6	121	199	9
Pontefract	12	4	1	7	153	154	7
Gateshead Fell	12	3	1	8	119	277	7
Thornensians	12	2	1	9	95	242	5
Roundhegians	12	6	2	4	142	145	2
Bramley	12	2	0	10	116	321	2

North-East 2

	P	W	D	L	F	A	Pts
Doncaster	12	11	0	1	294	39	22
Driffield	12	9	2	1	265	76	20
Hull	12	9	1	2	280	88	19
Cleckheaton	12	9	1	2	260	88	19
Horden	12	7	0	5	259	156	14
Blyth	12	6	0	6	157	228	12
Ripon	12	5	0	7	183	205	10
Ashington	12	5	0	7	161	244	10
Westoe	12	4	0	8	147	176	8
Acklam	12	4	0	8	84	247	6
Rockcliff	12	3	0	9	90	277	6
Beverley	12	2	0	10	112	226	4
Bishop Auck	12	2	0	10	121	386	4

Durham & Northumberland

	P	W	D	L	F	A	Pts
Whitby	12	10	0	2	261	107	20
Darlington	12	9	0	3	251	126	18
W Hart TDSOB	12	7	2	3	157	134	16

	P	W	D	L	F	A	Pts
Ryton	12	7	1	4	187	105	15
Mowden Pk	12	7	0	5	185	130	14
Guisborough	12	7	0	5	130	139	14
Sunderland	12	6	0	6	161	155	12
Seaham	12	6	0	6	169	180	12
Percy Pk	12	5	1	6	210	207	11
Darlington RA	12	4	0	8	115	194	8
Consett	12	3	0	9	111	190	6
Hartlepool	12	3	0	9	101	186	6
Seghill	12	2	0	10	112	297	4

Durham & Northumberland 2

	P	W	D	L	F	A	Pts
N Durham	12	10	0	2	197	105	20
N Shields	12	8	1	3	228	59	17
Wallsend	12	8	2	2	161	114	16
Chester-le-S	12	7	1	4	131	102	15
Houghton	12	7	0	5	207	180	14
Medicals	12	8	0	4	159	134	12
Ponteland	12	6	0	6	143	132	12
Wensleydale	12	5	1	6	120	93	11
Seaton Carew	12	5	0	7	136	190	10
Winlaton	12	4	0	8	122	140	8
S Tyneside Coll	12	3	1	8	95	256	7
Billingham	12	3	0	9	104	199	4
Barnard Castle	12	1	0	11	71	265	0

Durham & Northumberland 3

	P	W	D	L	F	A	Pts
N Aycliffe	10	9	0	1	256	103	16
Hart BBOB	11	7	2	2	215	165	16
Richmondshire	10	7	0	3	289	80	14
Sedgefield	10	7	0	3	232	113	14
Prudhoe	10	6	1	3	127	89	13
Jarrovians	10	5	0	5	182	110	10
Wearside	10	5	0	5	170	145	8
Washington	10	4	0	6	100	242	8
Hartlepool Ath	9	0	2	7	70	165	2
Durham CS	10	2	0	8	115	264	2
Shildon	10	0	1	9	46	381	1

Yorkshire 1

	P	W	D	L	F	A	Pts
Goole	12	10	0	2	285	84	20
Bradford Salem	12	10	0	2	253	129	20
Sheffield Oaks	12	10	0	2	201	108	20
Wheatley Hills	12	9	0	3	260	108	18
Leodiensians	12	9	0	3	200	134	18
N Ribblesdale	12	8	0	4	183	105	14
Malton & Nort	12	5	0	7	228	177	10
Yarnbury	12	5	0	7	180	230	10
Pocklington	12	4	1	7	164	158	9
O Otliensians	12	3	0	9	126	255	6
Hemsworth	12	2	1	9	124	231	5
York RI	12	2	0	10	157	335	4
Castleford	12	0	0	12	49	395	0

Yorkshire 2

	P	W	D	L	F	A	Pts
Wath	12	12	0	0	245	75	22
Ilkley	12	10	0	2	383	57	20
O Modernians	12	9	0	3	172	121	18
Barnsley	12	8	0	4	268	113	16
Northallerton	12	6	1	5	117	153	13
Scarborough	12	6	1	5	117	181	13
H'field YMCA	12	5	1	6	123	171	11
Moortown	12	4	1	7	120	173	9
Sheffield Tigers	12	4	0	8	133	159	8
Dinnington	12	4	0	8	160	240	8
W Leeds	12	4	0	8	105	241	8
Leeds CSSA	12	2	0	10	137	286	4
Knottingley	12	2	0	10	67	222	2

Yorkshire 3

	P	W	D	L	F	A	Pts
Hessle	12	11	1	0	317	89	23
Halifax Vands	12	10	1	1	213	108	21
Hullensians	12	8	0	4	153	119	16
Heath	12	7	0	5	146	106	14
Wetherby	12	6	1	5	179	147	13
Wibsey	12	6	1	5	204	174	13
Aireborough	12	6	1	5	140	104	11
Rodillians	12	5	1	6	119	142	11
O Rishworthians	12	4	1	7	107	165	9
Leeds Corinths	12	4	0	8	119	243	8
Marist	12	3	1	8	123	228	7
Burley	12	2	1	9	114	186	3
Baildon	12	1	1	10	65	193	3

Yorkshire 4

	P	W	D	L	F	A	Pts
Ossett	12	12	0	0	234	47	24
Leeds YMCA	12	9	0	3	217	86	18
De La Salle	12	8	1	3	215	108	17
Phoenix Pk	12	8	1	3	186	107	17
Skipton	12	7	0	5	216	102	14
Mosborough	12	7	0	5	192	119	14
Danum Phoenix	12	6	1	5	186	127	13
Hornsea	12	7	0	5	184	152	10
BP Chemicals	12	4	0	8	123	203	8
Castle Coll	12	3	1	8	130	203	7
Withernsea	12	3	0	9	93	178	6
Yorks Main	12	1	0	11	46	325	0
Yorkshire CW	12	1	0	11	48	344	0

Yorkshire 5

	P	W	D	L	F	A	Pts
Knaresborough	9	9	0	0	219	42	18
Rowntrees	9	7	1	1	178	54	15
Stocksbridge	9	7	0	2	112	51	14
Rawmarsh	9	5	0	4	163	64	10
Adwick-le-St	8	4	1	3	134	71	9

St James	8	4	0	4	88	175	8
Garforth	9	3	0	6	84	121	6
New Earswick	8	2	0	6	68	174	4
Armthorpe Mark	8	1	0	7	34	178	2
Leger	9	0	0	9	44	194	0

SOUTH & SOUTH-WEST DIVISION

South-West 1

	P	W	D	L	F	A	Pts
Reading	12	11	0	1	267	99	22
Henley	12	9	0	3	312	143	18
Newbury	12	8	1	3	251	158	17
St Ives	12	7	0	5	167	147	14
Maidenhead	12	6	1	5	153	214	13
Cheltenham	12	6	0	6	221	197	12
Salisbury	12	6	0	6	180	188	12
Sherborne	12	5	1	6	182	171	11
Cinderford	12	5	0	7	170	269	10
Brixham	12	4	0	8	207	217	8
Torquay	12	4	0	8	117	263	8
Gordon League	12	3	1	8	162	201	7
Penryn	12	2	0	10	140	262	4

South-West 2

	P	W	D	L	F	A	Pts
Stroud	12	11	0	1	290	129	22
Barnstaple	12	9	1	2	201	123	19
Bridgwater & A	12	9	0	3	243	114	18
Matson	12	9	0	3	209	97	18
Banbury	12	7	0	5	199	172	14
Taunton	12	6	0	6	182	192	12
Aylesbury	12	5	0	7	100	205	10
Combe Down	12	4	1	7	191	201	9
Oxford	12	4	1	7	200	298	9
Clevedon	12	4	0	8	157	180	8
Windsor	12	4	0	8	156	214	8
Marlow	12	3	0	9	150	191	6
O Culverhays	12	1	1	10	88	250	3

Southern Counties

	P	W	D	L	F	A	Pts
Swanage & W	12	9	2	1	251	96	20
Dorchester	12	9	2	1	198	115	20
Bournemouth	12	9	0	3	235	95	18
Bracknell	12	8	1	3	198	95	17
Olney	12	8	1	3	218	129	17
Wimborne	12	8	0	4	172	95	16
Bicester	12	7	0	5	166	131	14
Abbey	12	5	0	7	121	187	10
Chippenham	12	4	0	8	164	144	8
Slough	12	3	0	9	128	234	6
Bletchley	12	3	0	9	119	244	6
Redingensians	12	1	0	11	82	229	2
Grove	12	1	0	11	59	317	2

Western Counties

	P	W	D	L	F	A	Pts
Gloucester OB	12	12	0	0	321	86	24
Launceston	12	11	0	1	317	75	22
Okehampton	12	9	0	3	223	172	18
Penzance N'lyn	12	8	0	4	314	129	16
Spartans	12	7	0	5	208	141	14
Wiveliscombe	12	6	0	6	183	200	12
Bideford	12	5	0	7	167	175	10
Drybrook	12	5	0	7	169	198	10
Tiverton	12	5	0	7	170	208	10
Avonmouth	12	5	0	7	137	187	10
Crediton	12	3	0	9	163	232	6
Plymouth CS	12	2	0	10	117	349	4
Devon & Corn Pol	12	0	0	12	95	432	0

Cornwall & Devon

	P	W	D	L	F	A	Pts
Devonport Servs	12	12	0	0	301	98	24
Exmouth	12	8	0	4	226	174	16
Teignmouth	12	7	1	4	205	137	15
Truro	12	7	1	4	186	146	15
South Molton	12	6	2	4	215	215	14
Sidmouth	12	6	1	5	175	169	13
Liskeard-Looe	12	6	1	5	174	173	13
Newquay Horns	12	5	1	6	152	148	11
Ivybridge	12	5	0	7	214	217	10
Hayle	12	4	1	7	137	175	9
Bude	12	3	2	7	117	150	8
Exeter Saras	12	1	2	9	98	228	4
Saltash	12	2	0	10	143	313	4

Glos & Somerset

	P	W	D	L	F	A	Pts
O Patesians	12	11	0	1	307	94	22
Keynsham	12	10	1	1	276	89	21
Dings Crus	12	6	3	3	194	128	15
Whitehall	12	7	1	4	207	152	15
North Bristol	12	7	1	4	179	130	15
Oldfield OB	12	7	0	5	180	177	14
Frome	12	7	0	5	183	182	14
O Redcliffians	12	6	0	6	183	156	12
Thornbury	12	4	1	7	135	273	9
Bristol Harl	12	3	1	8	127	194	7
Coney Hill	12	3	1	8	153	221	7
Cirencester	12	1	1	10	104	331	3
O Sulians	12	1	0	11	160	261	2

Cornwall 1

	P	W	D	L	F	A	Pts
Veor	8	7	0	1	164	63	14
Falmouth	8	6	0	2	175	80	12
St Austell	8	6	0	2	190	98	12
Bodmin	8	5	0	3	101	71	10
Illogan Pk	8	3	1	4	65	67	7
Stithians	8	3	0	5	89	137	6
St Just	8	2	1	5	98	152	5
Redruth Albany	8	2	0	6	119	249	4
Camborne SoM	8	1	0	7	94	178	2

Cornwall 2

	P	W	D	L	F	A	Pts
Helston	10	9	0	1	312	101	18
Wadebridge Cam	10	7	0	3	190	75	14
St Agnes	10	7	0	3	201	175	14
St Day	10	4	0	6	177	201	8
Lankelly Fowey	10	2	1	7	100	215	5
Roseland	10	0	1	9	69	282	1

Devon 1

	P	W	D	L	F	A	Pts
Paignton*	12	10	1	1	239	74	21
Honiton	12	9	0	3	296	128	18
Kingsbridge	12	8	2	2	264	119	18
Newton Abbot	12	9	0	3	172	81	18
Tavistock	12	7	0	5	218	136	14
O Plymothians	12	7	0	5	207	179	14
Topsham*	12	6	0	6	297	184	12
Ilfracombe	12	6	0	6	151	195	12
O Technicians	12	5	0	7	133	118	10
O Public Oaks	12	4	2	6	151	143	10
Jesters	12	1	1	10	74	269	3
Cullompton	12	1	1	10	82	299	3
Plymouth Arg	12	1	1	10	80	439	3

*Paignton v Topsham game postponed – council declared pitch unfit.

Devon 2

	P	W	D	L	F	A	Pts
Dartmouth	13	12	0	1	467	50	24
Withycombe†	13	12	0	1	378	41	24
Totnes*	13	11	0	2	375	164	22
Torrington*	13	9	0	4	293	276	18
Prince Rock	13	8	1	4	191	143	17
N Tawton	13	8	0	5	247	234	16
St Columba	13	8	0	5	153	156	16
Plymstock	13	6	0	7	144	185	12
Tamar Saracens	13	4	1	8	124	260	9
Salcombe	13	4	0	9	195	244	8
Plymouth YMCA	13	2	1	10	131	356	5
Plympton†	13	2	1	10	100	331	5
Devonport HSOB	13	2	0	11	107	259	4
Victoria	13	1	0	12	108	314	2

*Totnes v Torrington postponed.
†Plympton defaulted; Withycombe w/o.

Gloucester 1

	P	W	D	L	F	A	Pts
St Mary's OB	12	10	0	2	229	88	20
Bream	12	9	0	3	295	99	18
Cleve	12	9	0	3	246	117	18

Frampton Cott	12	7	1	4	139	135	15
Longlevens	12	7	0	5	197	134	14
Cheltenham N	12	6	1	5	262	151	13
Ashley Down OB	12	6	0	6	161	192	12
O Richians	12	6	0	6	134	168	12
Saintbridge	12	5	1	6	184	177	11
O Cryptians	12	4	1	7	167	224	9
Brockworth	12	3	2	7	132	161	8
Widden OB	12	1	2	9	77	290	4
Bristol Sara	12	1	0	11	104	391	2

Gloucester 2

	P	W	D	L	F	A	Pts
Stow-on-the-W	12	11	0	1	339	115	22
Painswick	12	8	2	2	204	93	18
O Bristolians	12	8	1	3	219	118	17
Cheltenham Sara	12	7	0	5	151	136	14
Chosen Hill FP	12	6	1	5	179	148	13
Tredworth	12	6	0	6	201	157	12
Hucclecote	12	6	0	6	144	152	12
Chipping Sod	12	5	1	6	120	163	11
Bristol Tel	12	5	1	6	83	137	11
Cheltenham CS	12	5	0	7	135	216	10
Cotham Park	12	4	1	7	158	202	9
Barton Hill	12	1	2	9	86	262	4
Cainscross	12	1	1	10	151	271	3

Gloucester 3

	P	W	D	L	F	A	Pts
Dursley	12	10	0	2	329	129	20
Tetbury	12	9	1	2	334	132	19
O Elizabeth	12	8	1	3	223	121	17
Bishopston	12	7	2	3	268	114	16
Kingswood	12	8	0	4	210	132	16
Broad Plain	12	8	0	4	218	166	16
Gloucester CS	12	6	1	5	231	130	13
Westbury-on-S	12	6	0	6	149	128	12
Bristol Aero	12	4	0	8	136	250	8
O Colstonians	12	3	1	8	132	201	7
Gloucester AB	12	3	0	9	79	218	6
Southmead	12	2	0	10	83	267	4
Tewkesbury	12	1	0	11	68	472	2

Gloucester 4

	P	W	D	L	F	A	Pts
Smiths (Ind)	12	10	1	1	323	83	21
Aretians	12	10	0	2	370	102	20
Newent	12	7	0	5	202	175	14
Pilning	12	6	1	5	155	146	13
Dowty	12	3	1	8	138	176	7
Minchinhampton	12	3	0	9	95	201	6
Wotton-u-Edge	12	1	1	10	57	457	3

Somerset 1

	P	W	D	L	F	A	Pts
Hornets	12	12	0	0	428	53	24
Walcot OB	12	10	0	2	264	85	20
Midsomer N	12	10	0	2	241	101	20
Wellington	12	8	1	3	195	162	17
Wells	12	7	0	5	228	195	14
Imperial	12	7	0	5	161	160	14
St B'dette's OB	12	6	0	6	203	158	12
Yeovil	12	5	0	7	136	160	10
Minehead Barbs	12	4	0	8	126	188	8
Yatton	12	3	1	8	150	249	7
Stothert & Pitt	12	3	0	9	143	283	6
Gordano	12	2	0	10	120	249	4
Westland	12	0	0	12	66	418	0

Somerset 2

	P	W	D	L	F	A	Pts
N Petherton	12	11	0	1	339	66	22
Chard	12	10	0	2	271	82	20
Tor	12	8	2	2	345	139	18
Winscombe	12	7	0	5	206	144	14
Blagdon	12	6	1	5	206	132	13
Bath Saracens*	12	6	0	6	164	204	12
Avonvale	12	6	0	6	143	201	12
Crewkerne	12	5	1	6	221	136	11
Bath O Edwards	12	5	1	6	146	147	11
Backwell	12	5	1	6	185	227	11
Avon	12	4	2	6	185	197	10
Castle Cary	12	1	0	11	72	385	2
Burnham-o-Sea	12	0	0	12	58	481	0

Formerly Bath Civil Service.

Somerset 3

	P	W	D	L	F	A	Pts
Chew Valley	12	11	1	0	370	42	23
O Ashtonians	12	9	1	2	295	63	19
Cheddar Valley	12	9	0	3	223	101	18
St Brendan's OB	12	4	1	7	133	286	9
Aller	12	4	0	8	107	218	8
Morganians	12	2	0	10	56	240	4
South-West Gas	12	1	1	10	54	288	3

Berks/Dorset/Wilts 1

	P	W	D	L	F	A	Pts
Wootton Bass	12	11	0	1	324	112	22
Swindon	12	10	2	0	286	78	22
Swindon Coll	12	8	0	4	241	129	16
Devizes	12	6	2	4	196	116	14
Melksham	12	6	1	5	147	192	13
Aldermaston	12	6	0	6	119	173	12
Lytchett Minst	12	5	1	6	158	145	11
Corsham	12	5	1	6	132	139	11
Bradford-on-A	12	5	1	6	159	207	11
Weymouth	12	5	0	7	143	149	10
N Dorset	12	4	1	7	142	207	9
Puddletown	12	1	1	10	110	308	3
Bournemouth U*	12	1	0	11	83	285	2

Formerly Bournemouth Poly.

Berks/Dorset/Wilts 2

	P	W	D	L	F	A	Pts
Supermarine	12	11	0	1	290	83	22
Marlborough	12	10	1	1	325	95	21
Thatcham	12	10	0	2	226	87	20
Blandford	12	7	1	4	208	165	15
Calne	12	6	2	4	182	132	14
Tadley	12	6	1	5	184	176	13
Bridport	12	6	0	6	178	204	12
Trowbridge	12	5	1	6	191	174	11
Oakmedians	12	5	0	7	114	191	10
Warminster	12	4	1	7	189	229	9
Hungerford	12	3	1	8	75	154	7
Minety	12	1	0	11	77	311	2
Berkshire SH	12	0	0	12	101	339	0

Berks/Dorset/Wilts 3

	P	W	D	L	F	A	Pts
Poole	10	9	0	1	210	62	18
Westbury	10	8	0	2	285	82	16
Portcastrians	10	6	0	4	257	112	12
Colerne	10	4	0	6	134	151	8
Amesbury	10	2	0	8	132	271	4
Plessey Christ*	10	1	0	9	50	390	2

*Christchurch RFC for 1993-94.

Bucks & Oxon 1

	P	W	D	L	F	A	Pts
Oxford Mara	12	11	0	1	402	77	22
Chiltern*	12	11	0	1	262	86	22
Oxford OB	12	9	0	3	300	133	18
Chinnor	12	8	0	4	215	141	16
Witney	12	8	0	4	159	87	16
Drifters	12	6	1	5	140	120	13
Pennanians	12	5	1	6	168	190	11
Beaconsfield	12	5	0	7	166	232	10
Abingdon	12	3	2	7	143	266	8
Chesham	12	3	0	9	139	231	6
Milton Keynes	12	2	2	8	76	204	6
Buckingham	12	2	0	10	176	351	4
Wheatley	12	1	2	9	62	290	4

Amersham & Chiltern for 1993-94.

Bucks & Oxon 2

	P	W	D	L	F	A	Pts
Littlemore	14	12	0	2	436	98	24
Chipping Norton	14	12	0	2	312	128	24
Thames Valley Pol	14	9	1	4	220	150	19
Gosford All Blacks	14	9	0	5	224	121	18
Harwell	14	5	0	9	117	343	10
Cholsey	14	4	1	9	169	280	9
Phoenix	14	4	0	10	178	250	8
Didcot	14	0	0	14	100	386	0

LONDON DIVISION

London 1

	P	W	D	L	F	A	Pts
Tabard	12	10	1	1	230	127	21
Ealing	12	10	0	2	212	118	20
Sutton & Epsom	12	6	3	3	177	145	15
Streatham-Croy	12	6	2	4	169	138	14
Guildford & G	12	7	0	5	185	168	14
Eton Manor	12	6	2	4	156	147	14
Barking	12	6	1	5	183	171	13
O Colfeians	12	5	2	5	198	203	12
O Mid Whitgift	12	5	0	7	197	185	10
O Alleynian	12	5	0	7	183	186	10
Dorking	12	2	1	9	111	230	5
O Gaytonians	12	1	2	9	169	245	4
Sidcup	12	2	0	10	134	241	4

London 2 North

	P	W	D	L	F	A	Pts
Harlow	12	11	1	0	327	124	23
Cheshunt	12	8	1	3	238	167	17
Ruislip	12	8	0	4	163	110	16
Woodford	12	8	0	4	209	180	16
Finchley	12	8	0	4	196	140	14
Norwich	12	6	2	4	182	131	14
Bp's Stortford	12	7	0	5	176	131	14
Cambridge	12	5	1	6	109	141	11
Chingford	12	4	0	8	121	182	8
Upper Clapton	12	3	0	9	125	164	6
O Edwardians	12	2	1	9	110	319	5
Lensbury	12	4	0	8	127	193	2
Ipswich	12	1	0	11	100	252	2

London 2 South

	P	W	D	L	F	A	Pts
Camberley	12	10	2	0	241	94	22
Westcombe Pk	12	9	1	2	279	135	19
Esher	12	7	0	5	201	189	14
KCS OB	12	7	0	5	170	176	14
O Juddian	12	6	1	5	274	299	13
O Blues	12	6	0	6	269	141	12
O Reigatian	12	6	0	6	242	165	12
Charlton Pk	12	6	0	6	238	182	10
Worthing	12	5	0	7	178	228	10
Thanet Wands	12	5	0	7	182	234	10
Lewes	12	5	0	7	134	226	10
Gravesend	12	3	0	9	146	218	6
US Portsmouth	12	1	0	11	110	390	2

London 3 North-East

	P	W	D	L	F	A	Pts
Brentwood	12	10	0	2	266	102	20
Rochford	12	10	0	2	210	129	20
Romford & G Pk	12	9	1	2	340	91	19
Colchester	12	8	0	4	203	98	16

	P	W	D	L	F	A	Pts
Campion	12	8	0	4	167	139	16
Basildon	12	7	0	5	159	146	14
Woodbridge	12	5	1	6	172	144	11
Braintree	12	5	1	6	147	130	11
Chelmsford	12	5	1	6	187	192	11
Westcliff	12	5	0	7	163	140	10
Saffron Walden	12	2	0	10	80	265	4
Canvey Island	12	2	0	10	77	294	4
Cantabrigian	12	0	0	12	65	366	0

London 3 North-West

	P	W	D	L	F	A	Pts
O Verulamians	12	11	0	1	312	108	22
Letchworth	12	11	0	1	268	102	22
Staines	12	9	0	3	252	129	18
O Elizabethans	12	7	1	4	168	128	15
Welwyn	12	6	0	6	141	125	12
O Merchant Ts	12	6	0	6	191	196	12
Fullerians	12	5	1	6	177	203	11
Grasshoppers	12	5	0	7	172	168	10
Kingsburians	12	5	0	7	165	196	10
O Albanians	12	4	1	7	135	171	9
Hertford	12	4	1	7	141	187	9
O Millhillians	12	2	0	10	77	274	4
Harpenden	12	1	0	11	109	321	2

London 3 South-East

	P	W	D	L	F	A	Pts
Horsham	12	10	1	1	304	114	21
Brighton	12	9	1	2	202	121	19
O Beccehamian	12	8	1	3	171	147	17
Hove	12	8	0	4	204	160	16
Beckenham	12	7	0	5	172	101	14
E Grinstead	12	6	0	6	171	148	12
Gillingham Anc	12	5	0	7	156	153	10
Erith	12	5	0	7	94	142	10
Tunbridge W	12	5	0	7	128	207	10
Chichester	12	4	1	7	133	218	9
O Brockleians	12	4	0	8	198	137	8
Dartfordians	12	4	0	8	161	238	8
Crawley	12	1	0	11	69	277	2

London 3 South-West

	P	W	D	L	F	A	Pts
O Wimbledon	12	12	0	0	353	67	24
Warlingham	12	8	1	3	203	111	17
Cranleigh	12	7	1	4	127	116	15
O Walcountians	12	7	1	4	173	175	15
Purley	12	6	2	4	199	154	14
Guy's Hosp	12	6	1	5	192	158	13
Eastleigh	12	5	1	6	156	175	11
Winchester	12	4	2	6	138	203	10
O Emanuel	12	5	0	7	144	210	10
Alton	12	5	0	7	193	193	8
Millbrook	12	3	1	8	121	242	7
Portsmouth	12	3	0	9	125	188	6
Jersey	12	2	0	10	115	254	4

Eastern Counties 1

	P	W	D	L	F	A	Pts
Bury St Edmunds	12	10	0	2	301	79	20
Shelford	12	9	0	3	256	148	18
Newmarket	12	8	1	3	247	126	17
Maldon	12	7	1	4	234	147	15
West Norfolk	12	8	2	2	255	107	14
Ely	12	7	0	5	249	135	14
Lowestoft & Yar	12	7	0	5	207	148	14
Upminster	12	4	0	8	156	175	8
Bancroft	12	4	0	8	160	215	8
Wanstead	12	4	0	8	113	204	8
Ravens	12	5	0	7	148	265	8
Crusaders	12	3	0	9	91	283	4
Met P Chigwell	12	0	0	12	34	494	0

Eastern Counties 2

	P	W	D	L	F	A	Pts
Wymondham	12	12	0	0	440	61	24
Harwich & Dov	12	9	1	2	323	52	19
Diss	12	9	0	3	236	75	16
Thames Sports	12	7	1	4	139	158	15
O Palmerians	12	8	1	3	102	136	15
Thetford	12	7	0	5	173	169	14
Holt	12	7	0	5	141	154	10
E London	12	5	0	7	116	197	10
O Bealonians	12	4	0	8	90	242	8
Ipswich YMCA	12	3	0	9	95	167	6
Lakenham Hewett	12	2	0	10	112	264	4
S Wood Ferrers	12	2	1	9	112	230	3
Redbridge	12	1	0	11	88	311	2

Eastern Counties 3

	P	W	D	L	F	A	Pts
Loughton	12	12	0	0	298	111	24
Clacton	12	9	0	3	308	153	18
O Cooperians	12	9	0	3	192	113	16
Ilford Wands	12	9	0	3	204	107	14
Fakenham	12	6	0	6	171	136	12
Stowmarket	12	6	0	6	158	146	12
Beccles	12	6	0	6	177	182	12
Southwold	12	5	0	7	166	150	8
Haverhill	12	6	0	6	214	150	6
London Hosp	12	4	0	8	205	200	6
Wisbech	12	3	0	9	92	242	4
O Brentwoods	12	2	0	10	79	525	4
Dereham	12	1	0	11	98	319	2

Eastern Counties 4

	P	W	D	L	F	A	Pts
Felixstowe	11	10	1	0	208	70	19
Thurston	11	8	1	2	236	79	17
Hadleigh	11	8	1	2	209	130	15
Ongar	11	6	1	4	186	144	13
Billericay	11	6	0	5	198	163	12
Burnham-on-C	11	4	2	5	254	160	10
Essex Police	11	6	2	3	124	189	10

Brightlingsea	11	5	1	5	165	152	9
March	11	4	0	7	137	165	8
Witham	11	2	0	9	109	195	4
Swaffham	11	1	1	9	82	274	3
Norwich Union	11	1	0	10	73	331	2
Stanford							

O Ashmoleans	10	5	0	5	169	178	10
Royston	10	4	0	6	103	269	8
Hatfield	10	2	0	8	88	257	4
Watford	10	2	1	7	82	176	3
QEII Hosp	10	1	0	9	56	279	2
O Stanfordians	10	0	1	9	40	242	1

Eastern Counties 5

	P	W	D	L	F	A	Pts
May & Baker	8	8	0	0	379	18	16
Broadland	8	6	0	2	295	56	12
Leiston	8	6	0	2	159	97	12
Burwell	8	4	0	4	91	164	8
Sawston	8	3	1	4	68	113	7
Mersea Island	8	3	0	5	123	159	4
Mayfield OB	8	3	0	5	102	178	4
Chigwell	8	1	1	6	56	196	1
Mistley	8	1	0	7	44	351	0
Watton							
Essex U							

Hampshire 1

	P	W	D	L	F	A	Pts
Southampton	11	10	0	1	142	60	20
Gosport	11	9	0	2	216	76	18
Farnborough	11	8	0	3	161	103	16
Tottonians	11	6	1	4	110	92	13
New Milton	11	7	0	4	174	139	12
Andover	11	5	1	5	179	106	11
Sandown & S	11	5	0	6	119	164	10
Fareham Hs	11	4	1	6	81	158	9
Petersfield	11	4	0	7	113	153	8
Isle of Wight	11	3	1	7	113	193	7
Guernsey	11	3	0	8	106	172	6
Esso	11	0	0	11	93	200	0

Hampshire 2

	P	W	D	L	F	A	Pts
Trojans	10	10	0	0	368	37	20
Romsey	10	8	0	2	262	108	14
Alresford	10	7	0	3	182	152	14
AC Delco	10	6	1	3	222	114	13
Overton	10	6	1	3	160	109	13
Fordingbridge	10	4	1	5	134	134	9
Ventnor	10	4	1	5	135	125	7
Ellingham	10	3	1	6	87	178	7
Nomads	10	3	0	7	107	201	6
Waterlooville	10	1	0	9	54	313	2
Basingstoke Ws	10	0	1	9	59	304	1

Hertfordshire 1

	P	W	D	L	F	A	Pts
Barnet	10	10	0	0	370	48	20
Tring	10	9	0	1	241	88	18
Bacavians	10	7	1	2	172	98	13
Datchworth	10	6	0	4	180	127	12
St Albans	10	7	1	2	280	64	11

Herts/Middlesex 1

	P	W	D	L	F	A	Pts
O Meadonians	12	10	2	0	162	88	22
L New Zealand	12	8	3	1	183	68	19
Centaurs	12	7	0	5	258	169	14
Hendon	11	7	0	4	128	94	14
Haringey	12	8	0	4	165	142	14
Antlers	12	5	1	6	160	184	11
Uxbridge	11	5	0	6	99	116	10
Harrow	12	5	0	7	120	154	10
St Mary's Hosp	12	5	0	7	156	222	10
Hemel Hempstead	12	4	0	8	169	191	8
Hitchin	12	3	1	8	175	184	7
Twickenham	12	4	1	7	145	197	7
Stevenage	12	2	0	10	68	241	4

Kent 1

	P	W	D	L	F	A	Pts
Canterbury	12	11	0	1	289	79	22
Sevenoaks	12	10	1	1	339	104	21
Park House	12	10	0	2	254	117	20
O Dunstonians	12	7	1	4	219	143	15
Snowdon CW	12	6	0	6	126	189	12
Met Police Hayes	12	5	2	5	120	203	12
Bromley	12	5	1	6	214	196	11
Medway	12	5	1	6	177	217	11
Betteshanger	12	5	0	7	136	153	10
New Ash Green	12	5	0	7	194	214	10
Sheppey	12	5	0	7	157	194	10
Tonbridge	12	1	0	11	103	264	2
Sittingbourne	12	0	0	12	82	337	0

Kent 2

	P	W	D	L	F	A	Pts
Thames Poly	12	10	1	1	218	94	21
Nat West Bank	12	9	2	1	213	114	20
Folkestone	12	9	1	2	220	129	19
O Shooters	12	9	0	3	247	85	18
Ashford	12	7	0	5	145	138	14
O Elthamians	12	6	0	6	181	119	12
Dover	12	5	1	6	143	194	11
Deal	12	5	0	7	121	176	10
Midland Bank	12	4	1	7	166	182	9
Vigo	12	4	0	8	131	127	8
Bexley	12	4	0	8	74	164	8
Linton	12	3	0	9	104	181	6
O Gravesends	12	0	0	12	108	368	0

Kent 3

	P	W	D	L	F	A	Pts
Cranbrook	9	7	0	2	203	80	14
Lloyds Bank	9	6	0	3	128	105	12
STC Footscray	9	6	0	3	86	73	12
O Williamsonians	9	5	0	4	111	80	10
Orpington	9	4	1	4	89	98	9
Citizens	9	4	1	4	100	110	9
Whitstable	9	4	0	5	125	122	8
Kent Police	9	3	1	5	106	124	7
O Olavians	9	2	1	6	56	116	5
Greenwich	9	2	0	7	88	184	4

Kent 4

	P	W	D	L	F	A	Pts
Lordswood	10	9	0	1	291	64	18
Darenth Valley	10	8	0	2	241	102	16
Edenbridge	10	6	0	4	98	74	12
Westerham	10	5	0	5	141	125	10
Centurians	10	2	0	8	103	236	2
E Peckham	10	0	0	10	41	314	0

Middlesex 1

	P	W	D	L	F	A	Pts
Hampstead	12	11	0	1	371	71	22
Mill Hill	12	10	1	1	343	107	21
Roxeth M OB	12	9	0	3	192	120	18
O Haberdashers	12	8	0	4	221	101	16
Wembley	12	8	0	4	196	138	16
Civil Service	12	6	1	5	160	138	13
O Abbots	12	5	1	6	155	179	11
Hackney	12	5	1	6	100	166	9
Sudbury Court	12	4	0	8	105	140	8
H'smith & Fulham	12	4	0	8	104	246	8
O Isleworths	12	3	0	9	121	184	6
O Grammarians	12	2	0	10	89	251	2
Orleans FP	12	1	0	11	78	411	0

Middlesex 2

	P	W	D	L	F	A	Pts
O Hamptonians	12	11	0	1	266	107	22
O Actonians	12	10	0	2	181	117	20
Barclays Bank	12	7	1	4	189	116	15
O Paulines	12	7	0	5	196	114	14
Belsize Pk	12	5	1	6	138	135	11
Osterley	12	3	3	6	146	158	9
HAC	12	6	1	5	145	186	9
Feltham	12	5	0	7	145	188	8
Thamesians	12	4	0	8	115	169	8
L Cornish	12	6	2	4	204	177	7
Enfield Ignats	12	3	3	6	124	118	7
O Tottonians	12	3	1	8	78	206	5
St Bart's Hosp	12	2	0	10	115	293	2

Middlesex 3

	P	W	D	L	F	A	Pts
Pinner & Grams	9	7	0	2	138	52	14
Hayes	9	6	0	3	167	93	12
B of England	9	8	0	1	146	85	12
UCS OB	9	6	0	3	160	116	12
St Nicholas OB	9	5	0	4	170	114	10
Northolt	9	5	0	4	102	74	10
Quintin	8	2	0	6	61	138	4
Royal Free Hosp	9	3	0	6	84	179	2
L French	8	2	0	6	75	132	0
Meadhurst	9	0	0	9	37	198	0

Middlesex 4

	P	W	D	L	F	A	Pts
L Nigerians	8	8	0	0	240	54	16
L Exiles	8	7	0	1	249	82	14
Southgate	8	5	0	3	182	123	10
Kodak	8	3	0	5	121	125	6
Middlesex Hosp	7	34	0	4	91	161	6
GWR	7	3	1	3	52	93	5
U Coll	5	2	0	3	84	73	4
British Airways	8	1	0	7	27	168	2
St George's H	7	0	1	6	32	201	1

Surrey 1

	P	W	D	L	F	A	Pts
O Guildfords	12	11	0	1	411	60	22
Wimbledon	12	11	0	1	267	64	22
U Vandals	12	9	0	3	152	74	18
O Whitgiftians	12	9	0	3	194	125	18
Kingston	12	5	1	6	104	111	11
John Fisher OB	12	5	1	6	153	192	11
Raynes Pk	12	5	0	7	138	172	10
Shirley Wands	12	4	1	7	128	197	9
O Rutlishians	12	4	1	7	133	231	9
O Reedonians	12	3	2	7	140	187	8
Mitcham	12	2	2	8	98	300	6
Effingham	12	2	1	9	100	244	5
Cobham	12	3	1	8	107	180	3

Surrey 2

	P	W	D	L	F	A	Pts
Barnes Harrods	12	12	0	0	268	95	22
Chobham	12	9	0	3	277	124	18
Merton	12	9	0	3	217	110	18
O Haileys	12	7	0	5	160	158	14
Char X/West H	12	6	1	5	274	192	13
O Cranleighians	12	5	1	6	158	142	11
Bec OB	12	5	1	6	148	151	11
Reigate & Red	12	5	1	6	153	182	11
Law Society	12	5	0	7	176	163	10
Farnham	12	4	1	7	159	209	9
O Tiffinians	12	3	1	8	135	223	7
Wandsworthians	12	2	1	9	75	264	5
O Bevonians	12	2	1	9	97	297	5

Surrey 3

	P	W	D	L	F	A	Pts
O Caterhamians	10	9	0	1	375	65	18
Chipstead	10	8	0	2	148	95	16
Battersea Irons	10	7	0	3	213	133	14
Woking	10	5	1	4	183	117	11
O Pelhamians	10	5	1	4	142	106	11
O Suttonians	10	5	0	5	179	125	10
London Fire Br	10	5	0	5	160	120	10
R Holloway Coll	10	3	0	7	91	147	6
Old Freemans	10	3	0	7	91	262	6
King's Coll H	10	2	0	8	112	302	4
Croydon	10	2	0	8	69	291	4
Shene OGs							

Surrey 4

	P	W	D	L	F	A	Pts
Haslemere	9	9	0	0	338	63	18
Lightwater	9	7	0	2	188	48	14
London Media	9	7	0	2	206	92	14
Oxted	9	5	1	3	152	82	11
O Johnians	9	5	0	4	163	74	10
Surrey Police	9	4	1	4	133	148	9
Egham	9	4	0	5	110	115	8
Racal-Decca	9	2	0	7	115	214	4
Economicals	9	1	0	8	53	424	2
O Epsomians	9	0	0	9	32	230	0
Surrey U							

Sussex 1

	P	W	D	L	F	A	Pts
Haywards Heath	11	11	0	0	365	82	22
Hastings & Bex	11	9	1	1	228	100	19
H'field & Wald	11	8	0	3	215	107	16
Bognor	11	7	0	4	218	134	14
Uckfield	11	7	0	4	152	109	14
Seaford	11	6	0	5	156	131	12
Eastbourne	11	5	0	6	146	176	10
Burgess Hill	11	4	1	6	170	196	9
Crowborough	11	4	0	7	97	177	8
O Brightonians	11	3	0	8	133	204	6
Hellingly	11	1	0	10	54	320	2
St Francis	11	0	0	11	72	270	0

Sussex 2

	P	W	D	L	F	A	Pts
BA Wingspan	7	7	0	0	196	25	14
Ditchling	7	6	0	1	164	53	12
Pulborough	7	4	0	3	185	89	8
Newick	7	4	0	3	60	100	8
Sunallon	7	3	0	4	46	85	6
Sussex Police	7	2	0	5	45	115	4
Plumpton	7	2	0	5	85	215	4
Midhurst	7	0	0	7	52	151	0

MIDLANDS DIVISION

Midlands 1

	P	W	D	L	F	A	Pts
B'ham S'hull	13	11	1	1	250	107	23
Barker's Butts	13	10	1	2	255	128	21
Leamington	13	9	0	4	235	218	18
Syston	13	7	2	4	224	114	16
Camp Hill	13	7	0	6	137	204	14
Bedworth	13	6	1	6	202	152	13
Derby	13	6	1	6	189	170	13
Wolverhampton	13	6	0	7	174	126	12
Westleigh	13	6	0	7	129	167	12
Leighton Buzz	13	6	0	7	143	209	12
Mansfield	13	5	1	7	130	161	11
Newark	13	4	0	9	111	248	8
Paviors	13	2	1	10	104	168	5
Vipers	13	1	2	10	118	229	4

Midlands 2

	P	W	D	L	F	A	Pts
Burton	11	10	1	0	209	74	21
Worcester	11	9	0	2	188	89	18
Bedford Ath	11	8	1	2	194	91	17
Stockwood Pk	11	6	1	4	133	168	13
Keresley	11	6	0	5	145	151	12
Broad St	11	5	1	5	169	127	11
Peterborough	11	5	0	6	135	133	10
Stafford	11	5	0	6	141	154	10
Whitchurch	11	4	0	7	156	130	8
Matlock	11	2	0	9	102	167	4
Moderns	11	2	0	9	64	206	4
Biggleswade	11	2	0	9	101	247	4

Midlands East 1

	P	W	D	L	F	A	Pts
Belgrave	12	11	0	1	245	77	22
Hinckley	12	10	1	1	296	119	21
Ampthill	12	8	0	4	204	200	16
Stoneygate	12	6	2	4	251	108	14
Scunthorpe	12	6	2	4	234	155	14
Chesterfield	12	6	1	5	151	187	13
Amber Valley	12	4	3	5	148	125	11
Stewart's & L	12	5	1	6	123	196	11
Spalding	12	6	0	6	156	196	10
Luton	12	3	3	6	147	144	9
Mellish	12	2	2	8	97	241	4
W Bridgford	12	2	0	10	121	288	4
Dronfield	12	1	1	10	84	262	1

Midlands West 1

	P	W	D	L	F	A	Pts
Willenhall	12	9	0	3	183	97	18
Newbold	12	7	2	3	163	87	16
O Leamingtons	12	7	1	4	168	156	15
Bromsgrove	12	7	0	5	188	103	14

Ludlow	12	6	2	4	157	129	14
O Longtonians	12	6	0	6	110	186	12
Dudley	12	5	1	6	152	119	11
Leek	12	5	1	6	130	148	11
Sutton Cold	12	5	1	6	138	204	11
King's Norton	12	5	0	7	147	128	10
O Halesonians	12	5	0	7	120	165	10
Newcastle	12	3	3	6	92	113	9
O Yardleians	12	2	1	9	132	245	5

Midlands East 2

	P	W	D	L	F	A	Pts
Kettering	13	12	0	1	351	66	24
Northampton BB	13	11	0	2	264	87	22
Long Buckby	13	10	1	2	357	116	21
S Leicester	13	8	0	5	171	178	16
Worksop	13	7	0	6	205	149	14
Lincoln	13	8	0	5	152	148	14
Wellingborough	13	6	1	6	191	192	13
Coalville	13	6	1	6	88	164	13
Kesteven	13	3	2	8	129	302	8
Lutterworth	13	3	1	9	144	199	7
Stamford	13	4	1	8	102	215	7
M Rasen & L	13	3	1	9	139	269	7
Southwell	13	3	0	10	146	248	6
Glossop	13	3	0	10	96	237	6

Midlands West 2

	P	W	D	L	F	A	Pts
Nuneaton OE	12	11	1	0	245	82	23
Aston OE	12	11	0	1	277	92	22
Selly Oak	12	9	1	2	274	90	19
O Laurentians	12	8	1	3	270	96	17
Stratford-on-A	12	6	1	5	126	133	13
Shrewsbury	12	6	1	5	145	207	13
Kenilworth	12	6	0	6	177	204	12
Dixonians	12	5	1	6	135	140	11
Tamworth	12	4	1	7	158	198	9
W Midlands Pol	12	3	1	8	90	165	5
Woodrush	12	2	1	9	108	209	5
Coventry Welsh	12	2	1	9	105	218	5
Handsworth	12	0	0	12	67	359	0

East Midlands/Leics 1

	P	W	D	L	F	A	Pts
Kibworth	12	12	0	0	320	116	24
Loughborough	12	10	0	2	238	138	20
Northampton MO	12	9	0	3	221	122	18
Northampton OS	12	8	1	3	306	156	17
Market Bos	12	7	1	4	241	124	15
Oadby Wygges	12	6	0	6	159	130	12
St Neots	12	5	1	6	184	161	11
O Bosworthians	12	5	0	7	173	221	10
Melton Mowbray	12	4	1	7	143	173	9
Huntingdon	12	4	1	7	131	225	9
Aylestone St J	12	3	0	9	103	227	6

Brackley	12	2	0	10	203	272	4
St Ives	12	0	1	11	84	441	1

East Midland/Leics 2

	P	W	D	L	F	A	Pts
Daventry	11	8	1	2	172	82	17
Dunstablians	11	8	0	3	215	131	16
Wigston	11	8	0	3	173	113	16
Oakham	11	7	1	3	180	97	15
Rushden & High	11	6	1	4	162	115	13
Bedford Queens	11	6	0	5	178	111	12
Aylestonians	11	5	1	5	149	175	11
Birstall	11	4	1	6	155	142	9
Wellingbro OG	11	3	2	6	135	165	8
O Ashbeians	11	3	2	6	103	168	8
Northampton Cas	11	3	0	8	130	185	6
New Parks OB	11	0	1	10	75	353	1

East Midlands/Leics 3

	P	W	D	L	F	A	Pts
O Northamptons	12	12	0	0	504	50	24
Bugbrooke	12	11	0	1	584	75	22
Bedford Swifts	12	9	0	3	326	172	18
Westwood	12	7	1	4	313	169	15
Oundle	12	7	1	4	205	187	15
Anstey	12	6	2	4	251	104	14
Colworth House	12	7	1	4	325	180	13
Deepings	12	5	2	5	183	254	12
O Newtonians	12	4	1	7	130	206	9
Shepshed	12	3	0	9	87	457	6
W Leicester	12	2	0	10	88	366	4
O Wellings	12	1	0	11	75	388	2
Burbage	12	0	0	12	63	508	0

East Midlands/Leics 4

	P	W	D	L	F	A	Pts
Kempston	8	7	1	0	267	23	15
Corby	8	7	1	0	262	27	15
Vauxhall Mots	8	6	0	2	199	82	12
Littlehey	8	4	0	4	125	75	8
Northampton H	8	4	0	4	130	118	8
Potton	8	3	0	5	66	205	6
Thorney	8	2	0	6	60	170	4
Clapham T	8	2	0	6	56	225	4
Braunstone T	8	0	0	8	13	253	0

North Midlands 1

	P	W	D	L	F	A	Pts
Newport	12	11	0	1	382	81	22
Five Ways OE	12	11	0	1	252	70	22
Luctonians	12	10	0	2	400	76	20
Pershore	12	6	0	6	188	159	12
Telford	12	6	0	6	196	178	12
Evesham	12	6	1	5	170	153	11
Veseyans	12	6	1	5	141	141	11
O Centrals	12	5	0	7	154	181	10

Warley	12	4	0	8	143	155	8
O Griffinians	12	5	0	7	188	212	8
Bridgnorth	12	3	0	9	92	338	6
Redditch	12	2	0	10	98	360	4
Ross-on-Wye	12	2	0	10	102	427	2

North Midlands 2

	P	W	D	L	F	A	Pts
Droitwich	12	11	0	1	248	133	22
Kidderminster	12	10	1	1	244	91	21
Edwardians	12	10	0	2	291	39	20
Erdington	12	8	1	3	260	91	17
Birmingham CO	12	8	1	3	259	116	17
Malvern	12	6	1	5	278	145	13
Market Drayton	12	5	0	7	201	197	10
Bournville	12	5	0	7	125	260	10
O Moseleians	12	4	0	8	169	278	8
Bromyard	12	3	1	8	132	192	7
Tenbury	12	2	1	9	96	216	5
Kynoch	12	2	0	10	92	364	4
Birchfield	12	1	0	11	95	368	2

North Midlands 3

	P	W	D	L	F	A	Pts
B'ham Welsh	11	10	0	1	296	112	20
O Saltleians	11	9	0	2	217	99	18
Birmingham CS	11	8	1	2	250	80	17
Upton-on-S	11	7	1	3	163	113	15
Yardley & Dist	11	6	1	4	137	75	13
Bishop's Castle	11	6	0	5	165	77	12
Bewdley	11	4	1	6	191	131	9
Oswestry	11	4	0	7	117	151	8
Ledbury	11	4	0	7	129	189	8
Witton	11	4	0	7	129	221	8
West Mercia Pol	11	2	0	9	84	243	4
Thimblemill	11	0	0	11	21	408	0

Notts/Lincs/Derbys 1

	P	W	D	L	F	A	Pts
Grimsby	11	9	1	1	239	112	19
Ilkeston	11	9	0	2	332	122	18
Sleaford	11	9	0	2	225	100	18
Nottingham Cas	11	7	1	3	166	131	15
Ashbourne	11	7	0	4	200	104	14
Bakewell Manns	11	7	0	4	195	130	14
Long Eaton	11	5	0	6	153	171	10
Keyworth	11	4	0	7	130	174	6
All Spartans	11	2	1	8	103	196	5
E Retford	11	2	0	9	76	293	4
Nottinghamians	11	1	0	10	89	238	2
Notts Cons	11	2	1	8	70	241	1

Notts/Lincs/Derbys 2

	P	W	D	L	F	A	Pts
E Leake	12	11	0	1	281	95	22
Meden Vale	12	9	0	3	250	112	18
Leesbrook	12	8	1	3	181	117	17
Rolls Royce	12	8	0	4	238	145	16
Buxton	12	8	0	4	242	124	14
Boston	12	6	1	5	170	181	13
Melbourne	12	7	0	5	223	144	12
Boots Ath	12	5	1	6	103	128	11
Ashfield Swans	12	5	0	7	148	181	10
N Kesteven	12	5	1	6	235	195	9
Belper	12	3	0	9	112	288	4
Tupton	12	1	0	11	128	365	2
Cleethorpes	12	0	0	12	118	400	0

Notts/Lincs/Derbys 3

	P	W	D	L	F	A	Pts
Bingham	11	10	0	1	229	97	20
Stamford Coll	11	9	0	2	226	76	18
Gainsborough	11	9	0	2	186	106	18
Barton & Dist	11	7	0	4	110	99	14
Ollerton & Bev	11	6	0	5	175	164	12
Hope Valley	11	5	0	6	252	141	10
Bourne	11	5	0	6	146	169	10
Skegness	11	5	0	6	123	184	10
Derby Coll	11	4	0	7	123	169	8
Yarborough Bees	11	3	0	8	114	228	6
Bolsover	11	2	0	9	31	133	4
Rainworth	11	1	0	10	58	207	2

Notts/Lincs/Derbys 4

	P	W	D	L	F	A	Pts
Cotgrave	10	9	0	1	263	68	18
Horncastle	10	7	0	3	193	106	14
Sutton Bonn Sc	10	6	0	4	225	105	12
Castle Don	10	4	0	6	145	152	8
Whitwell	10	4	0	6	132	193	8
Bilsthorpe	10	0	0	10	37	371	0

Staff/Warwicks 1

	P	W	D	L	F	A	Pts
O Coventrians	12	11	1	0	345	54	23
Manor Pk	12	10	1	1	341	117	21
Dunlop	12	9	0	3	244	109	16
Trentham	12	8	0	4	261	161	16
Coventry Sara	12	7	0	5	213	111	14
O Wheatleyans	12	7	0	5	254	154	14
Trinity Guild	12	7	0	5	337	160	12
GEC St Leonards	12	5	0	7	154	255	10
GEC Coventry	12	5	0	7	141	176	8
Eccleshall	12	5	0	7	158	224	8
Linley	12	1	0	11	68	441	2
Wednesbury	12	1	0	11	56	353	0
Uttoxeter	12	1	0	11	53	362	0

Staffs/Warwicks 2

	P	W	D	L	F	A	Pts
Stoke OB	12	12	0	0	362	81	24
Southam	12	11	0	1	371	94	22
Silhillians	12	10	0	2	250	97	20
Pinley	12	8	0	4	227	159	16
Rugby St A	12	7	1	4	173	134	15
Earlsdon	12	6	0	6	189	136	12
Spartans	12	7	0	5	167	123	12
Berkswell & B	12	5	1	6	165	122	11
Cannock	12	4	0	8	123	337	8
Coventrians	12	3	0	9	118	191	6
O Oaks	12	2	1	9	106	236	5
Rubery Owen	12	1	1	10	72	273	3
Rugeley	12	0	0	12	39	413	0

Staffs/Warwicks 3

	P	W	D	L	F	A	Pts
Atherstone	11	10	0	1	283	64	20
Harbury	11	8	1	2	184	61	17
Warwick	11	8	0	3	221	156	'16
O Warwickians	11	7	0	4	219	142	14
Shipston-on-S	11	6	1	4	231	111	13
Standard	11	5	1	5	116	160	9
Wheaton Aston	11	4	0	7	113	145	8
Michelin	11	4	0	7	92	212	8
Alcester	11	3	1	7	85	100	7
Wulfrun	11	3	1	7	119	195	7
Claverdon	11	3	0	8	162	225	6
Coventry Tech	11	2	1	8	82	348	5

Staffs/Warwicks 4

	P	W	D	L	F	A	Pts
Warwicks Pol	9	9	0	0	324	31	18
Burntwood	9	8	0	1	296	61	16
Shottery	9	6	1	2	194	77	13
Rugby Welsh	9	6	0	3	204	105	12
Stone	9	4	1	4	230	154	9
Bloxwich	9	3	2	4	65	121	8
Coventry PO	9	3	0	6	94	113	6
Ford	9	3	0	6	104	145	6
Jaguar (Cov)	9	0	0	9	35	261	0
Cheadle	9	1	0	8	18	370	0

BORING ROSES MATCH FAILS TO STIR THE BLOOD OR THE CROWD

ADT COUNTY CHAMPIONSHIP 1992-93
Mick Cleary *The Observer*

17 April, Twickenham
Lancashire 9 (3PG)   **Yorkshire 6** (2PG)

What a way to go. The ADT County Championship went out with a whimper at Twickenham in front of the lowest crowd, 18,700, for a few years. Several thousand of those were schoolchildren who had been admitted free. There were two theories behind the relatively poor turn-out. One was that the spectators had looked into the tea-leaves and seen what a wretched game it was going to be. The second reason was more prosaic but far more substantial: for only the second time in five years Cornwall had not made the final and so Twickenham was deprived of the annual invasion of the Duchy's splendid followers.

They didn't miss much, and if ever a game summed up the uncertainty and malaise that has afflicted the County Championship in the last few years, then this was it. The match lacked shape and direction. So, too, does the tournament. Loud as the objections from the county stalwarts might be, the Championship has ceased to have any impact on the highest playing levels in the country. Quite rightly, then, this was the last year of its outmoded format. Next season Courage Division 1 and 2 fixtures will coincide with the Championship, and therefore none of those players will be eligible.

Here Lancashire had seven Orrell players in their ranks, none of whom will be there next season. Last year they were deprived of their Orrell contingent because of a rescheduled League fixture. Victory then was enhanced by another one here, giving Lancashire their 16th County title and so extending the record they had held jointly with Gloucestershire.

This was the 100th Championship Roses match and few can so singularly have failed to stir the blood. Not even the weather could be blamed, for conditions were nigh on perfect. Lancashire had enough possession to have made sure of victory long before they did, but there was only one decent threequarter movement in the entire match. Even though Handley and Saverimutto were the more accomplished pairing at half-back, Lancashire had only Ainscough's penalty goal on the scoreboard at half-time. Yorkshire did better in the second half. However, the only men to score points after the interval were the goal-kickers, and Ainscough's two penalty goals were matched by a brace from Liley.

Mike Kenrick of Sale on the burst for Lancashire in the 1993 County Championships final. This was his second successive year on the winning side: in 1992 he captained Lancashire to victory.

TEAMS IN THE FINAL

Lancashire (*Orrell unless stated*): S Taberner; P Hamer, G Ainscough, S Langford,
S Bromley (Rugby); A Handley (Waterloo), C Saverimutto (Waterloo); J Russell
(Broughton Park), G French (Liverpool St Helens), D Southern (*capt*), C Cusani,
N Allott (Waterloo), P Manley, M Kenrick (Sale), N Ashurst
Scorer *Penalty Goals:* Ainscough (3)
Yorkshire (*Wakefield unless stated*): R Thompson; J Eagle (Leeds), D Edwards,
P Johnson (Leeds), J Sleightholme; R Liley, A Crowley (Bradford & Bingley);
M Vincent, T Garnett, S Rice (Otley), I Carroll, D Baldwin (Sale), S Tipping (Otley),
C Vyvyan (Upper Wharfedale), P Buckton (Waterloo) (*capt*)
Scorer *Penalty Goals:* Liley (2)
Referee E Morrison (Bristol Society)

TEAMS IN THE SEMI-FINALS

20 February, Redruth RFC
Cornwall 3 (1PG)   **Yorkshire 20** (2G 2PG)

Cornwall: K Thomas (Redruth); A Mead (Redruth), C Laity (Cardiff), M Brain
(Clifton), M Chatterton (Exeter); D Chapman (Camborne), I Sanders (Bath); A Ellery
(Redruth), G Dawe (Bath) (*capt*), J May (Redruth), M Addinall (Penryn), M Wesson
(Penzance & Newlyn), A Cook (Redruth), J Polglase (Camborne), M Haag (Bath)
Replacements J Pearce (St Ives) for May (32 mins); D Weeks (Camborne) for Chatterton
(62 mins)
Scorer *Penalty Goal:* Chapman
Yorkshire (*Wakefield unless stated*): R Thompson; J Sleightholme, D Edwards, P Johnson
(Leeds), J Eagle (Leeds); R Liley, A Crowley (Bradford & Bingley); J Woodthorpe
(Harrogate), T Garnett, S Rice (Otley), S Tipping (Otley), I Carroll, D Baldwin (Sale),
P Buckton (Waterloo) (*capt*), C Vyvyan (Upper Wharfedale)
Scorers *Tries:* Tipping, Crowley   *Conversions:* Liley (2)   *Penalty Goals:* Liley (2)
Referee K Ricketts (Hampshire)

Lancashire 17 (4PG 1T)   **Middlesex 11** (2PG 1T)

Lancashire (*Orrell unless stated*): S Taberner; S Bromley (Rugby), S Langford,
G Ainscough, P Hamer; A Handley (Waterloo), C Saverimutto (Waterloo); J Russell
(Broughton Park), G French (Liverpool St Helens), D Southern (*capt*), S Gallagher,
R Kimmins, N Allott (Waterloo), N Ashurst, M Kenrick (Sale)
Scorers *Try:* Hamer   *Penalty Goals:* Ainscough (4)
Middlesex (*Harlequins unless stated*): K Bray; M Wedderburn, A Lee (Saracens),
R Lozowski (Wasps), M Hutton (Richmond); P Challinor, C Luxton (Richmond);
M Hobley (*capt*), G Botterman (Saracens), S Wilson, C Tarbuck (Saracens), L Adamson
(Saracens), J Fowler (Rosslyn Park), A Fox, C Sheasby
Scorers *Try:* Tarbuck   *Penalty Goals:* Challinor (2)

DIVISIONAL ROUNDS

Area North

League 1

Cumbria	5	Yorkshire	31
Lancashire	29	Northumberland	11
Northumberland	29	Cumbria	3
Yorkshire	16	Lancashire	23

| Lancashire | 20 | Cumbria | 0 |
| Northumberland | 11 | Yorkshire | 27 |

	P	W	D	L	F	A	Pts
Lancashire	3	3	0	0	72	27	6
Yorkshire	3	2	0	1	74	39	4
Northumberland	3	1	0	2	51	59	2
Cumbria	3	0	0	3	8	80	0

League 2

North Midlands	3	Durham	10
Warwickshire	16	Leicestershire	12
Durham	20	Warwickshire	3
Leicestershire	11	North Midlands	6
North Midlands	12	Warwickshire	39
Durham	17	Leicestershire	10

	P	W	D	L	F	A	Pts
Durham	3	3	0	0	47	16	6
Warwickshire	3	2	0	1	58	44	4
Leicestershire	3	1	0	2	33	39	2
North Midlands	3	0	0	3	21	60	0

League 3

Notts, Lincs & Derbys	11	Staffordshire	8
Cheshire	60	East Midlands	3
East Midlands	8	Notts, Lincs & Derbys	40
Staffordshire	9	Cheshire	23
Cheshire	18	Notts, Lincs & Derbys	3
East Midlands	26	Staffordshire	22

	P	W	D	L	F	A	Pts
Cheshire	3	3	0	0	101	15	6
Notts, Lincs & Derbys	3	2	0	1	54	34	4
East Midlands	3	1	0	2	37	122	2
Staffordshire	3	0	0	3	39	60	0

Area South
League 1

Cornwall	15	Middlesex	14
Hampshire	18	Surrey	6
Surrey	8	Cornwall	9
Middlesex	29	Hampshire	10
Hampshire	9	Cornwall	12
Surrey	8	Middlesex	54

	P	W	D	L	F	A	Pts
Cornwall	3	3	0	0	36	31	6
Middlesex	3	2	0	1	97	33	4

Hampshire	3	1	0	2	37	47	2
Surrey	3	0	0	3	22	81	0

League 2

Hertfordshire	6	Kent	29
Devon	19	Gloucestershire	21
Gloucestershire	36	Hertfordshire	5
Kent	22	Devon	5
Devon	15	Hertfordshire	13
Gloucestershire	19	Kent	17

	P	W	D	L	F	A	Pts
Gloucestershire	3	3	0	0	76	41	6
Kent	3	2	0	1	68	30	4
Devon	3	1	0	2	39	56	2
Hertfordshire	3	0	0	3	24	80	0

League 3

Sussex	38	Berkshire	5
Dorset & Wilts	23	Buckinghamshire	8
Buckinghamshire	19	Sussex	12
Berkshire	14	Dorset & Wilts	27
Dorset & Wilts	15	Sussex	6
Buckinghamshire	22	Berkshire	6

	P	W	D	L	F	A	Pts
Dorset & Wilts	3	3	0	0	65	28	6
Buckinghamshire	3	2	0	1	49	41	4
Sussex	3	1	0	2	56	39	2
Berkshire	3	0	0	3	25	87	0

League 4

Oxfordshire	24	Eastern Counties	21
Eastern Counties	13	Somerset	11
Somerset	35	Oxfordshire	11

	P	W	D	L	F	A	Pts
Somerset	2	1	0	1	46	24	2
Eastern Counties	2	1	0	1	34	35	2
Oxfordshire	2	1	0	1	35	56	2

ENGLISH COUNTY CHAMPIONS 1889-1993

FIRST SYSTEM

1889 **Yorkshire,** undefeated, declared champions by RU (scored 18G 17T to 1G 3T)

1890 **Yorkshire,** undefeated, declared champions (scored 10G 16T to 2G 4T)

SECOND SYSTEM

1891	**Lancashire** champions.	Group Winners — Yorkshire, Surrey, Gloucestershire.
1892	**Yorkshire** champions.	Group Winners — Lancashire, Kent, Midlands.
1893	**Yorkshire** champions.	Group Winners — Cumberland, Devon, Middlesex.
1894	**Yorkshire** champions.	Group Winners — Lancashire, Gloucestershire, Midlands.
1895	**Yorkshire** champions.	Group Winners — Cumberland, Devon, Midlands.

THIRD SYSTEM

	Champions	*Runners-up*	*Played at*
1896	**Yorkshire**	Surrey	Richmond
1897	**Kent**	Cumberland	Carlisle
1898	**Northumberland**	Midlands	Coventry
1899	**Devon**	Northumberland	Newcastle
1900	**Durham**	Devon	Exeter
1901	**Devon**	Durham	W Hartlepool
1902	**Durham**	Gloucestershire	Gloucester
1903	**Durham**	Kent	W Hartlepool
1904	**Kent**	Durham	Blackheath (2nd meeting)
1905	**Durham**	Middlesex	W Hartlepool
1906	**Devon**	Durham	Exeter
1907	**Devon** and **Durham** joint champions after drawn games at W Hartlepool and Exeter		
1908	**Cornwall**	Durham	Redruth
1909	**Durham**	Cornwall	W Hartlepool
1910	**Gloucestershire**	Yorkshire	Gloucester
1911	**Devon**	Yorkshire	Headingley
1912	**Devon**	Northumberland	Devonport
1913	**Gloucestershire**	Cumberland	Carlisle
1914	**Midlands**	Durham	Leicester
1920	**Gloucestershire**	Yorkshire	Bradford

FOURTH SYSTEM

	Champions	*Runners-up*	*Played at*
1921	**Gloucestershire (31)**	Leicester (4)	Gloucester
1922	**Gloucestershire (19)**	N Midlands (0)	Birmingham
1923	**Somerset (8)**	Leicester (6)	Bridgwater
1924	**Cumberland (14)**	Kent (3)	Carlisle
1925	**Leicestershire (14)**	Gloucestershire (6)	Bristol
1926	**Yorkshire (15)**	Hampshire (14)	Bradford
1927	**Kent (22)**	Leicestershire (12)	Blackheath
1928	**Yorkshire (12)**	Cornwall (8)	Bradford
1929	***Middlesex (9)**	Lancashire (8)	Blundellsands
1930	**Gloucestershire (13)**	Lancashire (7)	Blundellsands
1931	**Gloucestershire (10)**	Warwickshire (9)	Gloucester
1932	**Gloucestershire (9)**	Durham (3)	Blaydon
1933	**Hampshire (18)**	Lancashire (7)	Boscombe
1934	**E Midlands (10)**	Gloucester (0)	Northampton
1935	**Lancashire (14)**	Somerset (0)	Bath
1936	**Hampshire (13)**	Northumberland (6)	Gosforth
1937	**Gloucestershire (5)**	E Midlands (0)	Bristol
1938	**Lancashire (24)**	Surrey (12)	Blundellsands
1939	**Warwickshire (8)**	Somerset (3)	Weston
1947	**†Lancashire (14)**	Gloucestershire (3)	Gloucester
1948	**Lancashire (5)**	E Counties (0)	Cambridge
1949	**Lancashire (9)**	Gloucestershire (3)	Blundellsands
1950	**Cheshire (5)**	E Midlands (0)	Birkenhead Park
1951	**E Midlands (10)**	Middlesex (0)	Northampton
1952	**Middlesex (9)**	Lancashire (6)	Twickenham
1953	**Yorkshire (11)**	E Midlands (3)	Bradford
1954	**Middlesex (24)**	Lancashire (6)	Blundellsands
1955	**Lancashire (14)**	Middlesex (8)	Twickenham

1956	**Middlesex** (13)	Devon (9)	Twickenham
1957	**Devon** (12)	Yorkshire (3)	Plymouth
1958	**Warwickshire** (16)	Cornwall (8)	Coventry
1959	**Warwickshire** (14)	Gloucestershire (9)	Bristol
1960	**Warwickshire** (9)	Surrey (6)	Coventry
1961	o**Cheshire** (5)	Devon (3)	Birkenhead Park
1962	**Warwickshire** (11)	Hampshire (6)	Twickenham
1963	**Warwickshire** (13)	Yorkshire (10)	Coventry
1964	**Warwickshire** (8)	Lancashire (6)	Coventry
1965	**Warwickshire** (15)	Durham (9)	Hartlepool
1966	**Middlesex** (6)	Lancashire (0)	Blundellsands
1967	****Surrey and Durham**		
1968	**Middlesex** (9)	Warwickshire (6)	Twickenham
1969	**Lancashire** (11)	Cornwall (9)	Redruth
1970	**Staffordshire** (11)	Gloucestershire (9)	Burton-on-Trent
1971	**Surrey** (14)	Gloucestershire (3)	Gloucester
1972	**Gloucestershire** (11)	Warwickshire (6)	Coventry
1973	**Lancashire** (17)	Gloucestershire (12)	Bristol
1974	**Gloucestershire** (22)	Lancashire (12)	Blundellsands
1975	**Gloucestershire** (13)	E Counties (9)	Gloucester
1976	**Gloucester** (24)	Middlesex (9)	Richmond
1977	**Lancashire** (17)	Middlesex (6)	Blundellsands
1978	**N Midlands** (10)	Gloucestershire (7)	Moseley
1979	**Middlesex** (19)	Northumberland (6)	Twickenham
1980	**Lancashire** (21)	Gloucestershire (15)	Vale of Lune
1981	**Northumberland** (15)	Gloucestershire (6)	Gloucester
1982	**Lancashire** (7)	North Midlands (3)	Moseley

FIFTH SYSTEM

	Champions	Runners-up	Played at
1983	**Gloucestershire** (19)	Yorkshire (7)	Bristol
1984	**Gloucestershire** (36)	Somerset (18)	Twickenham
1985	**Middlesex** (12)	Notts, Lincs and Derbys (9)	Twickenham

SIXTH SYSTEM

	Champions	Runners-up	Played at
1986	**Warwickshire** (16)	Kent (6)	Twickenham
1987	**Yorkshire** (22)	Middlesex (11	Twickenham
1988	**Lancashire** (23)	Warwickshire (18)	Twickenham
1989	**Durham** (13)	Cornwall (9)	Twickenham
1990	**Lancashire** (32)	Middlesex (9)	Twickenham
1991	**Cornwall** (29	Yorkshire (20) (aet)	Twickenham
1992	**Lancashire** (9)	Cornwall (6)	Twickenham
1993	**Lancashire** (9)	Yorkshire (6)	Twickenham

*After a draw at Twickenham.   †After a draw, 8-8, at Blundellsands.   oAfter a draw 0-0, at Plymouth.
**Surrey and Durham drew 14 each at Twickenham and no score at Hartlepool and thus became joint champions. Lancashire have won the title 16 times, Gloucestershire 15, Yorkshire 12, Warwickshire 9, Middlesex 8, Durham 8 (twice jointly), Devon 7 (once jointly), Kent 3 times, Hampshire, East Midlands, Cheshire, Northumberland and Cornwall twice each, Surrey twice (once jointly), and Midlands (3rd System), Somerset, Cumberland, Leicestershire, Staffordshire and North Midlands once each.

PROVINCIAL INSURANCE CUP 1992-93

Brendan Gallagher *The Daily Telegraph*

3 April 1993, Twickenham
Fleetwood 13 (1DG 2T)   **Hitchin 7** (1G)

Fleetwood became the first Lancashire club to appear in a Twickenham Cup final when they won the RFU Junior Clubs knock-out competition, the last to be sponsored by Provincial Insurance. Fleetwood, doughty Cup fighters throughout their arduous campaign, were worthy winners with tries from wing Mark Wilkinson and flanker Dave Berry, a master chef with the Household Cavalry.

Steve Burnage, an outstanding performer over the years with both Orrell and Fylde, dropped a goal for Fleetwood, while Hitchin captain David Marshall scored a well-deserved consolation try, converted by centre Les Jeffries. It wasn't a classic but Cup finals at all levels are often tight, tense affairs. An enthusiastic crowd of 7,500 enjoyed the occasion immensely, as did the players.

Victory was particularly sweet for Fleetwood scrum-half John Wright, who gave up a County final place with Lancashire the previous season on a matter of principle. The game also featured two of the oldest players ever to appear at headquarters. Hitchin lock Roger Cobley, aged 43, is a veteran of 23 seasons whereas Fleetwood prop Bob Gawne, 41, took up the game only six years ago.

Fleetwood's road to Twickenham included early victories over Thornton Cleveleys, Smith Brothers and Tyldesley before they beat Old Modernians 14-5 in the fourth round. Three consecutive away wins, against Wath upon Dearne (11-3), Windermere (9-5) and Old Northamptonians (17-12) took them to the semi-final stage at Moseley, where they defeated Tredworth 25-5.

Hitchin progressed smoothly until the sixth round, when they encountered serious resistance from Hertfordshire rivals Barnet, coming through to win 10-0. Another derby victory, 8-0 against Datchworth, followed in the quarter-finals. They booked their Cup final place with a 19-10 win over Kidderminster Carolians at Nuneaton.

Teams in the final
Fleetwood: M Hill; P Seed, A Crowther, S Fearn, M Wilkinson; S Burnage, J Wright; R Gawne, W Baxter (*capt*), M Pilkington, A Burman, P Hanley, S Merrick, D Berry, I Cameron
Scorers *Tries:* Wilkinson, Berry   *Dropped Goal:* Burnage
Hitchin: C Lee; V Donnelly, L Jeffries, A Smith, R Simon; A Forrest, R Owen; P Joyce, I Callicott, P Tasko, D Marshall (*capt*), R Cobley, P Broadhurst, D Thompson, B James
Scorers *Try:* Marshall   *Conversion:* Jeffries
Referee R Quittenton (Sussex Society)

Fleetwood flanker Dave Berry touches down for a try in their 13-7 victory over Hitchin in the final.

RESULTS

Third Round Draw

London Division: Region 1 – Eastern Counties, Herts, Middlesex Essex Police 5, Tring 32; Bank of England 6, London Cornish 20; Old Ashmoleans 16, Osterley 3; Fakenham 55, Witham 7; Old Actonians 18, Hitchin 24; Belsize Park 3, Barnet 28; Datchworth 31, Ilford Wanderers 0; Barclays Bank 10, Old Cooperians 14 *Region 2 – Hampshire, Surrey, Kent and Sussex* Chipstead 16, Haslemere 17; Seaford 11, Linton 8; Crowborough 10, Cranbrook 8; Old Caterhamians 10, Battersea Ironsides 3; Trojans 13, STC Footscray 0; Andover 27, Old Gravesendians 10; Old Pelhamians 21,

Old Williamsonian 16; Hellingly 13, Old Freemans 3

Midland Division: Region 1 – North Midland, Staffs, Warwicks Old Centrals 6, Erdington 3; Stoke Old Boys 18, Pinley 0; Linley 12, Droitwich 27; Berkswell & Balsall 8, Silhillians 5; Tenbury 21, Malvern 24; Southam 0, Kidderminster 18; Edwardian 32, Coventrians 0 *Region 2 – East Midlands, Leics, Notts, Lincs & Derbys* Ashfield Swans 22, Leesbrook Asterdale 23; Tupton 6, Market Bosworth 59; Bugbrooke 17, Old Northamptonians 18; Wigston 23, Daventry 9; Colworth House 49, Horncastle 7; Meden Vale 13, Loughborough 12; Rolls Royce 21, Bedford Swifts 10; Oadby

Wyggestonians 14, Melbourne 8
South-West Division: Region 1 – Berks,
Bucks, Dorset & Wilts, Oxon Tadley 23,
Blandford 10; Beaconsfield 35, Chipping
Norton 0; Bradford on Avon 18, Gosford
All Blacks 13; Bracknell 13, Bridport 17;
Littlemore 18, Aldermaston 3 *Region 2 –*
Cornwall, Devon, Glos and Somerset
Gordano 13, Withycombe 3; Stithians 3,
Tavistock 6; Tredworth 42, St Day 0;
Gloucester Civil Service 14, Kingsbridge
3; Helston 13, Hucclecote Old Boys 19;
Old Public Oaks 6, Stow on the Wold 10;
Cheltenham Saracens 9, Chipping
Sodbury 24; Chosen Hill FP 34,
Salcombe 3; Imperial 27, Bath Old
Edwardians 0; Yeovil 38, Cheltenham CS
7; North Petherton 40, Illogan Park 5
North Division Region 1 – Durham,
Northumberland, Yorks Phoenix Park 12,
Ponteland 5; West Leeds 10, Moortown 8;
Danum Phoenix 10, Stanley Rodillians 58;
Whitby 49, Knaresborough 9; South
Tyneside College 17, Wath upon Dearne
41; Old Modernians 48, Sheffield Tigers
10; Chester le Street 13, Northallerton 8;
Baildon 17, Seghill 18 *Region 2 –*
Cheshire, Cumbria, Lancs Sefton 6,
Metrovick 11; Upper Eden 18, Bolton 20;
Burnage 23, Didsbury Toc H 5; Vickers
29, Chorley 10; British Steel 12,
Birchfield 8; Windermere 23, Calder Vale
12; St Benedicts 8, Old Anselmians 13;
Tyldesley 3, Fleetwood 20

Fourth Round
London Division: Barnet 13, Old
Ashmoleans 5; Hellingly 11, Seaford 18;
Crowborough 12, Andover 5; Trojans 14,
Fakenham 13; Datchworth 14,
Haslemere 0; Tring 20, Old
Caterhamians 8; Old Pelhamians 5,
Hitchin 12; London Cornish 37, Old
Cooperians 10
Midland Division: Old Northamptonians
19, Leesbrook Asterdale 16; Edwardian
6, Wigston 8; Cannock 0, Kidderminster
30; Meden Vale 16, Stoke Old Boys 23;
Malvern 13, Market Bosworth 5; Oadby
Wyggestonians 6, Droitwich 8; Old
Centrals 13, Colworth House 10;
Berkswell & Balsall 11, Rolls Royce 8
South-West Division: Chipping Sodbury
7, Hucclecote Old Boys 5; Tavistock 12,
Tadley 9; Chosen Hill FP 22,
Beaconsfield 11; Stow on the Wold 27,

Yeovil 0; Bridport 0, Bradford on Avon 5;
Gloucester Civil Service 0, Tredworth 11;
Gordano 5, Imperial 12; Littlemore 10,
North Petherton 0
North Division: Phoenix Park 14, British
Steel 13; Seghill 15, Bolton 14; Metrovick
3, Wath upon Dearne 16; Windermere
55, Burnage 0; Fleetwood 14, Old
Modernians 5; Stanley Rodillians 8, Old
Anselmians 33; Chester le Street 15, West
Leeds 21; Whitby 14, Vickers 6

Fifth Round
London Division: Barnet 32,
Crowborough 0; Datchworth 10, London
Cornish 0; Seaford 8, Hitchin 38; Trojans
7, Tring 13
South-West Division: Tredworth 22,
Littlemore 0; Stow on the Wold 30,
Imperial 10; Chipping Sodbury 15,
Tavistock 8; Bradford on Avon 19,
Chosen Hill FP 21
Midland Division: Malvern 13, Old
Northamptonians 15; Berkswell & Balsall
8, Kidderminster Carolians 11; Old
Centrals 11, Droitwich 0; Stoke Old Boys
0, Wigston 3
North Division: Wath upon Dearne 3,
Fleetwood 11; Windermere 20, Whitby
13; Old Anselmians 32, West Leeds 3;
Seghill 5, Phoenix Park 12

Sixth Round
North & Midlands: Old Centrals 11,
Kidderminster Carolians 18; Old
Anselmians 47, Wigston 24; Windermere
5, Fleetwood 9; Phoenix Park 9, Old
Northamptonians 11
London & South-West: Chipping Sodbury
0, Stow on the Wold 7; Datchworth 5,
Tring 0; Hitchin 10, Barnet 0; Tredworth
25, Chosen Hill FP 12

Quarter-finals
North & Midlands: Old Anselmians 9,
Kidderminster Carolians 15; Old
Northamptonians 12, Fleetwood 17
London & South-West: Tredworth 5, Stow
on the Wold 0; Hitchin 8, Datchworth 0

Semi-finals
Fleetwood 25, Tredworth 5;
Kidderminster Carolians 10, Hitchin 19

Final
Fleetwood 13, Hitchin 7

BARBARIANS TAKE THE ENTERTAINING ROUTE THROUGH ANOTHER AMICABLE SEASON

THE BARBARIANS 1992-93
Geoff Windsor-Lewis

The Barbarians won four of their six matches, averaging 40 points per match and thus raising the total donated to youth rugby by the club sponsors, Scottish Amicable, to £38,950. Scottish Amicable, under the Amicable Gesture, made their donation based on £300 for every try scored by the Barbarians. The money will be handed on to the Home Unions to provide essential training equipment for junior rugby, including, so far, more than 2,500 rugby balls, and also scrummaging machines and tackle bags.

The season began at Newport, where the Barbarians won a superb match in style, scoring eight tries to three. This was high-value entertainment. The outstanding personality in the match was undoubtedly Craig Chalmers, the Scottish fly-half. His all-round ability and astute eye for the gap created many of the attacking moves produced by the Barbarians. Among the try-scoring was a hat-trick by Derek Stark, the pacy Scotland wing; it was rounded off by Ian Smith, captain for the match. He scored the eighth and last try just before the end. The notable efforts of David Waters and Mark Yeandle kept Newport in the game, but eventually the home side were outpaced.

The highlight of the season was the encounter with the Australians in the final match of their tour to Ireland and Wales. The Barbarians had picked a strong team in which, it was hoped, the pack would supply enough ball for the threequarters to attack the Wallabies out wide. Overall, the game was of a high standard but in the end the superior organisation of the world champions' forwards was the decisive factor. Twice in an exciting second half, when the Barbarians threatened to get back into the match, the Australian forwards produced their long driving maul, scattering opponents in front of them and scoring on each occasion.

Barnes opened the scoring for the Barbarians with a penalty goal but then Little burst through the centre to put Horan over for the first of the Wallabies' three tries.

Perhaps the best move of the day came next. It started from a line-out inside the Barbarians' half when Mick Skinner burst through and sent the ball back. Stuart Barnes burst up to accelerate through a small gap. He fed Will Carling and the ball flowed through Scott Gibbs and Mike Rayer, who created the space for Ian Hunter to score a memorable try of the highest standard.

The Barbarians began the second half with a burst of attack. They then won a scrum close to the Australian line and Ben Clarke made

178

ground for Ian Jones to score. Next Roebuck kicked his third penalty and Crowley scored for the Wallabies after their rolling maul. The match continued to boil. Carling caught Campese behind his own line and eventually Jeff Probyn scored a popular try from a free kick under the Wallaby posts. Rayer converted, and with ten minutes to go the Barbarians were within three points.

However, a famous victory was not to be as the world champions quickly rediscovered the game and Phil Kearns, a popular stand-in captain, scored the vital last try from another maul and sealed the day for a well-earned Australian victory.

The annual Christmas match at Leicester gave the club side their first victory for three years. A strong and effective Leicester pack, in which Dean Richards and Neil Back thoroughly enjoyed themselves, denied the Barbarians a plentiful supply of ball, enabling the Leicester outsides to indulge themselves. John Liley, John Wells and Rory Underwood ran in tries for Leicester before half-time. The last try by the home side was perhaps the highlight of the afternoon. Tony Underwood ran from his own line and linked with brother Rory. Liley took up the move down the left-hand touchline, and perfectly timed his pass to the young Underwood. Tony went on to score in a move which had gone from goal-line to goal-line.

The Barbarians started in great style against East Midlands and were soon in a dominant position, eventually winning with an astonishing six goals and seven tries. A patchy defence allowed the East Midlands into the game for a contest that did not quite come up to standard. Simon Geoghegan led the way with four tries, and the popular Lee Adamson of Saracens, playing his first match for the Barbarians, celebrated with a try. Wilkinson ran 70 metres for the East Midlands' fifth try. The Moon brothers, Richard and Rupert, found themselves on the same side for the first time in their lives.

On a glorious Easter Saturday afternoon, the Barbarians quickly settled into their stride against a young Cardiff team and were greatly helped by David McIvor and Ken Leahy, outstanding in the loose. The Bridgend half-backs, Robert Howley and Luc Evans, began to dictate the course of the game. Jon Sleightholme, Rees and Evans had scored tries by half-time. Jerry Guscott, captaining the Barbarians, then shredded the Cardiff defence with a devastating change of pace, enabling Alex Moore to touch down. Although Cardiff came back at the beginning of the second half, tries from Rees and Moore put the visitors further ahead, and while Cardiff slowly closed, the Barbarians always had enough in hand.

An old favourite, Jean-Baptiste Lafond, and Argentinian Fabio Gomez were both instrumental in a convincing victory against Swansea on Easter Monday. In an even first half the standard of tackling was high, and several promising moves were stopped at the death. All but five of the points were scored after the interval. At one stage the

Barbarians pulled away to a 19-point lead, but could not always finish off the many moves initiated by Luc Evans and Fabio Gomez. Lafond scored a hat-trick of tries and was joined on the scoreboard by Graham Dawe, captaining the Barbarians with his usual West Country spirit, Huw Williams-Jones and Lee Adamson.

So for the second consecutive year the Barbarians won both their matches on the Easter tour. There has been much recent comment about the tour, which dates back to 1901 and is very much part of the Barbarian tradition in South Wales. In spite of League and Cup difficulties, both Cardiff and Swansea want to continue the tradition, and perhaps, when all is considered, the enjoyment of the players is paramount. There is little doubt that the Barbarian players do enjoy the weekend, and if standards are not as high on the playing field as was once the case, there is little wrong with the current spirit and enjoyment both on and off the field. On this tour players from eight different countries came together for a weekend which, it is hoped, all will remember fondly.

RESULTS 1992-93

Played 8   Won 5   Lost 3   Drawn 0   *Points for 295 (22G 4PG 1DG 27T)
Points against 261 (25G 13PG 2DG 9T)

1992

3-6 June	***Tour to Russia** Krasny Yar 32 (4G 2T), Barbarians 21 (1G 4PG 1DG) CIS 23 (1G 2PG 1DG 2T), Barbarians 27 (3G 3PG)
3 Nov	**Beat Newport** at Rodney Parade 48 (4G 4T) to 23 (1G 1PG 1DG 2T)
28 Nov	**Lost to Australia** at Twickenham 20 (1G 1PG 2T) to 30 (3G 3PG)
28 Dec	**Lost to Leicester** at Welford Road 23 (1PG 4T) to 41 (4G 1PG 2T)
1993	
10 Mar	**Beat East Midlands** at Franklins Gardens, Northampton 77 (6G 7T) to 59 (7G 2T)
10 Apr	**Beat Cardiff** at Cardiff Arms Park 36 (3G 3T) to 34 (3G 1PG 2T)
12 Apr	**Beat Swansea** at St Helen's, Swansea 36 (3G 3T) to 26 (3G 1T)

*The Russian tour took place under the old scoring values (4 points for a try): points for 55 (5G 2PG 1DG 4T); against 48 (4G 7PG 1DG). From 1 September 1992, when new scoring values became applicable (5 points for a try), their results were: points for 240 (17G 2PG 23T); against 213 (21G 6PG 1DG 9T).

PLAYERS 1992-93

Abbreviations: *RT1* – Russian Tour v Krasny Yar; *RT2* – Russian Tour v CIS (Moscow); *N* – Newport; *A* – Australia; *L* – Leicester; *EM* – East Midlands; *SW1* – Cardiff; *SW2* – Swansea; (R) – Replacement; * – New Barbarian

Full-backs: *S Pilgrim (Wasps) [*RT1*]; J-B Lafond (Bègles & France) [*RT1*(R), *RT2*, *L* (centre), *SW2*]; *J E Staples (London Irish & Ireland) [*N*]; M A Rayer (Cardiff & Wales) [*A*]; A G Hastings (Watsonians & Scotland) [*L*]; I Hunter (Northampton & England) [*EM*, *A* (wing ¾)]; *G Rees (Oak Bay Castaways & Canada) [*SW1*, *SW2* (centre)]

Threequarters: *A Moore (Edinburgh Acads) [*RT1*, *RT2*, *SW1*]; J-M Lafond (Racing Club de France) [*RT1*, *RT2*, *L*]; *S P Geoghegan (London Irish & Ireland) [*N*, *EM*]; *D M Stark (Boroughmuir & Scotland) [*N*]; T Underwood (Leicester & England) [*A*]; H S Thorneycroft (Northampton) [*L*, *SW2*]; R Wallace (Garryowen & Ireland) [*EM*]; *J Sleightholme (Wakefield) [*SW1*, *SW2*]; D Charvet (Toulouse & France) [*RT1*, *RT2*]; R R W Maclean (Moseley) [*RT1*]; R Bidgood (Newport & Wales) [*RT2*]; D M Curtis (London Irish & Ireland) [*N*]; *P P A Danaher (Garryowen & Ireland) [*N*]; W D C Carling (Harlequins & England) [*A*]; I S Gibbs (Swansea & Wales) [*A*]; *L F Walker (Randwick & Australia) [*L*]; *F S Packman (Northampton) [*EM*]; H Woodland (Neath) [*EM*]; J C Guscott (Bath & England) [*SW1*]; *C Glasgow (Heriot's FP) [*SW1*, *SW2*]

Half-backs: D Pears (Harlequins & England) [*RT1*]; S M Bates (Wasps) [*RT1*, *L*]; *A Williams (Swansea) [*RT2*]; R J Hill (Bath & England) [*RT2*]; C M Chalmers (Melrose & Scotland) [*N*, *L*]; *C D Morris (Orrell & England) [*N*]; S Barnes (Bath & England) [*A*]; R N Jones (Swansea & Wales) [*A*]; A Davies (Cardiff & Wales) [*EM*]; R H StJ B Moon (Llanelli) [*EM*]; R H Q B Moon (Rosslyn Park) [*EM*(R)]; * I L Evans (Bridgend) [*SW1*, *SW2*]; *R Howley (Bridgend) [*SW1*]; E F Gomez (Amatori, Milan & Argentina)

Forwards: M S Linnett (Moseley & England) [*RT1*, *RT2*, *L*, *EM*, *SW2*]; P John (Pontypridd) [*RT1*]; *M Hobley (Harlequins) [*RT1*]; A E D Macdonald (Heriot's FP) [*RT1*]; N C Redman (Bath & England) [*RT1*, *RT2*]; D J Pegler (Wasps) [*RT1*]; *S Davies (Swansea & Wales) [*RT1*, *RT2*]; *D J Turnbull (Hawick & Scotland) [*RT1*, *RT2*]; R A Robinson (Bath & England) [*RT1*(R), *RT2*]; M Hayashi (Oxford U & Japan) [*RT1*(R), *RT2*]; N Meek (Pontypool & Wales) [*RT2*, *A*, *EM*, *SW1*, *SW2*(R)]); S Dear (Harlequins) [*RT2*]; M Griffiths (Cardiff & Wales) [*N*]; R G R Dawe (Bath & England) [*N*, *SW2*]; *R Keast (Redruth) [*N*]; D F Cronin (London Scottish & Scotland) [*N*, *L*]; R Goodey (Pontypool) [*N*]; M G Skinner (Blackheath & England) [*N*, *A*]; I R Smith (Gloucester & Scotland) [*N*, *A*]; *G W Weir (Melrose & Scotland) [*N*, *EM*]; N J Popplewell (Greystones & Ireland) [*A*]; J A Probyn (Wasps & England) [*A*, *L*]; I D Jones (North Harbour & New Zealand) [*A*]; *N Hadley (UBC Old Boys & Canada) [*A*]; B B Clarke (Bath & England) [*A*]; C J Olver (Northampton & England) [*L*]; S J Lloyd (Moseley) [*L*, *EM*, *SW1*, *SW2*]; T A K Rodber (Northampton & England) [*L*, *EM*]; *E W Peters (Cambridge U) [*L*]; L Cabannes (Racing Club de France & France) [*L*]; H Williams-Jones (South Wales Police & Wales) [*EM*, *SW2*]; *R L Adamson (Saracens) [*EM*, *SW1*, *SW2*]; N A Back (Leicester) [*EM*]; *R Shaw (Bridgend) [*SW1*, *SW2*(R)]; *J Davies (Neath) [*SW1*]; *K Leahy (Dublin Wanderers & Ireland) [*SW1*, *SW2*]; *T Coker (Harlequins & Australia) [*SW1*]; *D McIvor (Edinburgh Acads) [*SW1*, *SW2*]; *G Adams (Bath) [*SW2*]

OXFORD'S PEDIGREE COUNTS FOR NOTHING WITH LIGHT BLUE HEROES

THE VARSITY MATCH 1992
(for the Bowring Bowl)

8 December, Twickenham
Oxford University 11 (1PG 1DG 1T)
Cambridge University 19 (1G 2PG 2DG)

There was yet another packed house at Twickenham – 54,000 crammed in to the partly-rebuilt stadium. However, the neutrals in this army had to rely on other pursuits for final fulfilment of their day because it was not an outstanding match. As ever it was desperately hard-fought and occasionally exciting, but not vintage.

It was a marvellous day for Cambridge: many seasoned observers indicated beforehand that Oxford had more pedigree, and that certainly seemed to be borne out as Oxford dominated the early stages and quite clearly deserved to be ahead. But Cambridge stuck to it. Their pack eventually warmed up, gained parity and, as the match wore on, gained something of a stranglehold. That diverted Oxford from their tactical plan, established Cambridge and gave the match to the Light Blues.

Cambridge found an inspirational figure in Peters, their rangy captain, and their hard-working pack made up in the loose for what they lacked in the tight play. Oxford had enough big guns in the pack and a talented fly-half in Malone, later to play for Ireland. But du Toit was nothing like as effective at scrum-half as he had been in the 1991 match, and the Dark Blues gradually lost the plot, a frustrating matter for Patton, a fine Oxford captain.

Oxford had ample cause to rue their lack of finishing in the early stages when they were in control – despite all their pressure it was Cambridge who took the lead when Lloyd Davies, brother of Blues Adrian and Graham, dropped a neat goal. Malone did put Oxford in front with a drop and a penalty but Flood, the clever Cambridge centre, scored the third dropped goal of the match to level it at 6-6 by half-time.

Davies kicked a Cambridge penalty goal within the first three minutes of the second half but then Oxford gave a brief flash of their true capability with a splendidly-worked try. Nasser, Oxford's Australian international back-row man, picked up at the back of a scrum, fed du Toit in a well-timed, pre-planned move down the blindside, and Spence came down the wing for the try.

Cambridge reacted strongly. Davies put them back in the lead with another penalty and Batstone scored a crucial try, sent on his way by Price and de Maid after a strong burst by Peters. The conversion took Cambridge more than one score ahead and to safety.

A typical Varsity tackle. Oxford's Chad Lion-Cachet hammers Kevin Price to stop a Cambridge move at Twickenham.

Oxford University: M T Joy (Marling GS, Stroud & Keble); A E Lumsden (Alfred Sutton, Reading & St Cross), K P Street (King Henry VIII, Coventry & Christ Church), D P O'Mahony (CBC, Cork & Keble), D O Spence (St Andrew's, Johannesburg & Keble); N G Malone (Methodist Coll, Belfast & Keble), S F du Toit (Paul Roos Gymnasium, Stellenbosch & Christ Church); I M Buckett (Holywell HS & University), M B Patton (Campbell Coll, Belfast & St Catherine's) (*capt*), A D Williams (Fishguard HS & St Anne's), D R Evans (Bro Myrddin CS, Carmarthen & St Anne's), J B B Daniell (Wanganui Coll & St Catherine's), B P Nasser (St Joseph's, Brisbane & Keble), B G O'Mahony (PBC, Cork & Keble), C C Lion-Cachet (Pretoria HS & Keble) *Replacement* D S Currie (RGS High Wycombe & Templeton) for Lumsden (79 mins)
Scorers *Try:* Spence *Penalty Goal:* Malone *Dropped Goal:* Malone
Cambridge University: L Davies (Pencoed CS & St Edmund's); S A Burns (St Dunstan's Coll & Magdalene), D P Hopley (Harrow & Hughes Hall), J P Flood (Stonyhurst & St Edmund's), G R D Batstone (Epsom Coll & Downing); K L Price (Aberdare CS & St Edmund's), M W de Maid (St Mary's HS, Cardiff & Hughes Hall); D R Perrett (Perse & Jesus), A J G Read (RGS High Wycombe & Hughes Hall), P G Callow (Oakham & Fitzwilliam), D J Bickle (Nower Hill HS & Hughes Hall), D P A Dix (Shore, Sydney & Hughes Hall), M B Duthie (Backwell CS & Queens'), E W Peters (Brentwood & Hughes Hall) (*capt*), R H J Jenkins (Oundle & Downing)
Scorers *Try:* Batstone *Conversion:* Davies *Penalty Goals:* Davies (2)
Dropped Goals: Davies, Flood
Referee E F Morrison (Bristol)

---

8 December, Stoop Memorial Ground

Oxford University Under-21s 10 (2T) **Cambridge University Under-21s 31** (1G 3PG 3T)
Oxford University Under-21s: J Osborne (Christ Church); N Johnson (St Anne's), T Watson (St Edmund Hall), M Woodfine (St Edmund Hall) (*capt*), J Bursell (New); M Hutchings (St Hugh's), C Squire (St Catherine's); A Bryce (Keble), T Bennett-Britton (Oriel), B Cordery (Pembroke), R Paul (Keble), R Yeabsley (Keble), M Freer (Keble), A Bridgwood (Keble), R Bhagobati (University)
Scorers *Tries:* Watson, Bursell
Cambridge University Under-21s: T Walton (Downing); G Curran (St Catharine's), W Thompson (Magdalene), G Hodgson (Jesus) (*capt*), S Brown (Fitzwilliam); A Kennedy (St John's), D Maslen (Girton); P Kay (St Catharine's), J Edwards (St Catharine's), T Hughes (Trinity), J Motts (Robinson), A McCracken (Downing), G Howard (Downing), R Calvert (Pembroke), E Rollitt (Magdalene)
Scorers *Tries:* McCracken, Brown, Thompson, Rollitt *Conversion:* Thompson
Penalty Goals: Thompson (2), Kennedy
Referee K Ricketts (Hampshire)

1 December, Grange Road, Cambridge

Cambridge University LX Club 3 (1PG) **Oxford University Greyhounds 7** (1G)
Cambridge University LX Club: S Phillips (St Edmund's); A Boyd (Jesus), R Davidson (Sidney Sussex), W Thompson (Magdalene), N Murphy (Emmanuel); D Wright (Magdalene) (*capt*), A Nickalls (St Edmund's); J Priestley (Hughes Hall), T Keith-Roach (Jesus), D Doran (Hughes Hall), L Longstaff (Downing), T Dower (St John's), P Irons (Hughes Hall), H Jones (Caius), A McCracken (Downing)
Scorer *Penalty Goal:* Thompson
Oxford University Greyhounds: D Currie (Templeton); R Sennitt (St Edmund Hall), T Watson (St Edmund Hall), V Nairac (Hertford), R Morgan (St Anne's); E Rayner (Oriel), P Miles (Keble); R Tice (Wycliffe), M Humphreys (Brasenose) (*capt*), A McConville (St Anne's), R Underhill (Green), P Coveney (Templeton), C Keey (Keble), A Bridgwood (Keble), C McMullen (St Peter's)
Scorers *Try:* Currie *Conversion:* Rayner
Referee J Wilson (Hertfordshire)

18 November, Iffley Road, Oxford
Oxford University 26 (3G 1T) **Major Stanley's XV 20** (4T)

25 November, Grange Road, Cambridge
Cambridge University 19 **M R Steele-Bodger's XV 27**

3 December, Iffley Road, Oxford
Oxford University Whippets 17 **Cambridge University LX Club II 0**

VARSITY MATCH RESULTS

111 Matches played   Oxford 47 wins   Cambridge 51 wins   13 Draws

*Match played at Oxford 1871-72; Cambridge 1872-73; The Oval 1873-74 to 1879-80; Blackheath 1880-81 to 1886-87; Queen's Club 1887-88 to 1920-21; then Twickenham.   *At this date no match could be won unless a goal was scored.*

Year	Winner	Score	Year	Winner	Score
1871-72	Oxford	1G 1T to 0	1936-37	Cambridge	2T (6) to 1G (5)
1872-73	Cambridge	1G 2T to 0	1937-38	Oxford	1G 4T (17) to 1DG (4)
1873-74	Drawn	1T each	1938-39	Cambridge	1G 1PG (8) to 2PG (6)
1874-75*	Drawn	Oxford 2T to 0	1939-45	*War-time series*	
1875-76	Oxford	1T to 0	1945-46	Cambridge	1G 2T (11) to 1G 1PG (8)
1876-77	Cambridge	1G 2T to 0	1946-47	Oxford	1G 1DG 2T (15) to 1G (5)
1877-78	Oxford	2T to 0	1947-48	Cambridge	2PG (6) to 0
1878-79	Drawn	No score	1948-49	Oxford	1G 1DG 2T (14) to 1G 1PG (8)
1879-80	Cambridge	1G 1DG to 1DG	1949-50	Oxford	1T (3) to 0
1880-81	Drawn	1T each	1950-51	Oxford	1G 1PG (8) to 0
1881-82	Oxford	2G 1T to 1G	1951-52	Oxford	2G 1T (13) to 0
1882-83	Oxford	1T to 0	1952-53	Cambridge	1PG 1T (6) to 1G (5)
1883-84	Oxford	3G 4T to 1G	1953-54	Drawn	Oxford 1PG 1T (6)
1884-85	Oxford	3G 1T to 1T			Cambridge 2PG (6)
1885-86	Cambridge	2T to 0	1954-55	Cambridge	1PG(3) to 0
1886-87	Cambridge	3T to 0	1955-56	Oxford	1PG 2T (9) to 1G (5)
1887-88	Cambridge	1DG 2T to 0	1956-57	Cambridge	1G 1PG 1DG 1T (14) to
1888-89	Cambridge	1G 2T to 0			2PG 1T (9)
1889-90	Oxford	1G 1T to 0	1957-58	Oxford	1T (3) to 0
1890-91	Drawn	1G each	1958-59	Cambridge	1G 1PG 3T (17) to 1PG 1T (6)
1891-92	Cambridge	2T to 0	1959-60	Oxford	3PG (9) to 1PG (3)
1892-93	Drawn	No score	1960-61	Cambridge	2G 1T (13) to 0
1893-94	Oxford	1T to 0	1961-62	Cambridge	1DG 2T (9) to 1DG (3)
1894-95	Drawn	1G each	1962-63	Cambridge	1G 1PG 1DG 1T (14) to 0
1895-96	Cambridge	1G to 0	1963-64	Cambridge	2G 1PG 2T (19) to
1896-97	Oxford	1G 1DG to 1G 1T			1G 1PG 1DG (11)
1897-98	Oxford	2T to 0	1964-65	Oxford	2G 1PG 2T (19) to 1PG 1GM (6)
1898-99	Cambridge	1G 2T to 0	1965-66	Drawn	1G (5) each
1899-1900	Cambridge	2G 4T to 0	1966-67	Oxford	1G 1T (8) to 1DG 1T (6)
1900-01	Oxford	2G to 1G 1T	1967-68	Cambridge	1T 1PG (6) to 0
1901-02	Oxford	1G 1T to 0	1968-69	Cambridge	1T 1PG 1DG (9) to 2T (6)
1902-03	Drawn	1G 1T each	1969-70	Oxford	3PG (9) to 2PG (6)
1903-04	Oxford	3G 1T to 2G 1T	1970-71	Oxford	1G 1DG 2T (14) to 1PG (3)
1904-05	Cambridge	3G to 2G	1971-72	Oxford	3PG 3T (21) to 1PG (3)
1905-06	Cambridge	3G (15) to 2G 1T (13)	1972-73	Cambridge	1G 1PG 1DG 1T (16) to
1906-07	Oxford	4T (12) to 1G 1T (8)			2PG (6)
1907-08	Oxford	1G 4T (17) to 0	1973-74	Cambridge	1PG 1DG 2T (14) to
1908-09	Drawn	1G (5) each			1G 2PG (12)
1909-10	Oxford	4G 5T (35) to 1T (3)	1974-75	Cambridge	1G 2PG 1T (16) to 5PG (15)
1910-11	Oxford	4G 1T (23) to 3G 1T (18)	1975-76	Cambridge	2G 5PG 1DG 1T (34) to
1911-12	Oxford	2G 3T (19) to 0			3PG 1DG (12)
1912-13	Cambridge	2G (10) to 1T (3)	1976-77	Cambridge	1G 3PG (15) to 0
1913-14	Cambridge	1DG 3T (13) to 1T (3)	1977-78	Oxford	4PG 1T (16) to 2PG 1T (10)
1914-18	*No matches*		1978-79	Cambridge	2G 3PG 1T (25) to
1919-20	Cambridge	1PG 1DG (7) to 1G (5)			1PG 1T (7)
1920-21	Oxford	1G 4T (17) to 1G 3T (14)	1979-80	Oxford	2PG 1DG (9) to 1PG (3)
1921-22	Oxford	1G 2T (11) to 1G (5)	1980-81	Cambridge	3PG 1T (13) to 3PG (9)
1922-23	Cambridge	3G 2T (21) to 1G 1T (8)	1981-82	Cambridge	3PG (9) to 2PG (6)
1923-24	Oxford	3G 2T (21) to 1G 1PG 2T (14)	1982-83	Cambridge	3PG 1DG 2T (20) to
1924-25	Oxford	1G 2T (11) to 2T (6)			1G 1PG 1T (13)
1925-26	Cambridge	3G 6T (33) to 1T (3)	1983-84	Cambridge	4PG 2T (20) to 3PG (9)
1926-27	Cambridge	3G 5T (30) to 1G (5)	1984-85	Cambridge	4G 2T (32) to 2PG (6)
1927-28	Cambridge	2G 2PG 2T (22) to 1G 3T (14)	1985-86	Oxford	1PG 1T (7) to 2PG (6)
1928-29	Cambridge	1G 3T (14) to	1986-87	Oxford	3PG 2DG (15) to 1PG 1DG 1T (10)
		1PG 1DG 1T (10)	1987-88	Cambridge	1DG 3T (15) to 2PG 1T (10)
1929-30	Oxford	1G 1DG (9) to 0	1988-89	Oxford	2G 1DG 3T (27) to 1DG 1T (7)
1930-31	Drawn	Oxford 1PG (3)	1989-90	Cambridge	2G 2PG 1T (22) to
		Cambridge 1T (3)			1G 1PG (13)
1931-32	Oxford	1DG 2T (10) to 1T (3)	1990-91	Oxford	2G 2PG 1DG (21) to 1G 2PG (12)
1932-33	Oxford	1G 1T (8) to 1T (3)	1991-92	Cambridge	2PG 1DG 2T (17) to
1933-34	Oxford	1G (5) to 1T (3)			1DG 2T (11)
1934-35	Cambridge	2G 1PG 1DG 4T (29) to	1992-93	Cambridge	1G 2PG 2DG (19) to
		1DG (4)			1PG 1DG 1T (11)
1935-36	Drawn	No score			

THE WAR-TIME MATCHES

Year	Winner	Score	Year	Winner	Score
1939-40	Oxford	1G 1DG 2T (15) to 1T (3) (at Cambridge)		Cambridge	2G 1T (13) to 0 (at Cambridge)
	Cambridge	1G 1T (14) to 2G 1T (13) (at Oxford)	1941-42	Cambridge	1PG 2T (9) to 1PG 1T (6) (at Cambridge)
1940-41	Cambridge	1G 2T (11) to 1G 1DG (9) (at Oxford)		Cambridge	1G 2PG 2T (17) to 1G 1T (8) (at Oxford)

1942-43	**Cambridge**	1G 1DG (9) to 0 (at Oxford)		**Oxford**	2T (6) to 1G (5)
	Cambridge	2G 2T (16) to			(at Oxford)
		1T (3) (at Cambridge)	1944-45	Drawn	1T (3) each (at Oxford)
1943-44	**Cambridge**	2G 1T (13) to		**Cambridge**	2G 2T (16) to
		1DG (4) (at Cambridge)			1DG (4) (at Cambridge)

OXFORD and CAMBRIDGE BLUES 1872-1992

(Each year indicates a separate appearance, and refers to the first half of the season. Thus 1879 refers to the match played in the 1879-80 season.) (R) indicates an appearance as a replacement.

OXFORD

Abbott, J S	1954-55	Boobbyer, B	1949-50-51	Carey, W J	1894-95-96-97
Abell, G E B	1923-24-25-26	Booker, J L	1880	Carlyon, H B	1871
Adamson, J A	1928-29-31	Booth, J L	1956	Carroll, B M	1970-71
Adcock, J R L	1961	Bos, F H ten	1958-59-60	Carroll, P R	1968-69-70
Aitken, G G	1922-24	Boswell, J D	1885-86-87	Carter, C R	1885
Aldridge, J E	1888	Botfield, A S G	1871	Cartwright, V H	1901-02-03-04
Alexander, H	1897-98	Botting, I J	1949-50	Cass, T	1961
Alexander, P C	1930	Bourdillon, H	1873-74-75	Castens, H H	1886-87
Allaway, R C P	1953-54-55	Bourns, C	1903	Cattell, R H B	1893
Allen, C P	1881-82-83	Bowers, J B	1932-34	Cave, H W	1881
Allen, T	1909	Boyce, A W	1952-53	Cawkwell, G L	1946-47
Allen, W C	1910	Boyd, A de H	1924	Chadwick, A J	1898-99
Allison, M G	1955	Boyd, E F	1912	Chambers, J C	1921
Almond, R G P	1937	Boyle, D S	1967-68-69	Champain, F H B	1897-98-99
Ashby, C J	1973	Brace, D O	1955-56	Champneys, F W	1874-75-76
Asher, A G G	1881-82-83-84	Bradby, G F	1882-85	Charles, A E S	1932
Asquith, P R	1974	Bradford, C C	1887	Cheesman, W I	1910-11
Atkinson, C C	1876	Branfoot, E P	1878-79	Cheyne, H	1903-04
		Bray, C N	1979	Chislett, J	1986-87
Back, A	1878	Bray, K A	1989	Cholmondeley, F G	1871-73
Badenoch, D F	1971	Bremridge, H	1876-77	Christopherson, P	1886-87-88
Baden-Powell, F S	1873	Brett, J A	1935-36-37	Clark, R B	1978-79
Baggaley, J C	1953-54	Brett, P V	1978	Clarke, E J D	1973
Bain, D McL	1910-11-12-13	Brewer, R J	1965	Clarke, I A	1913
Bainbrigge, J H	1874-76-77	Brewer, T J	1951	Clauss, P R	1889-90-91
Baird, J S	1966-67	Bridge, D J W	1946-47-48	Clements, B S	1975
Baiss, R S H	1894-95	Brierley, H	1871	Cleveland, C R	1885-86
Baker, C D	1891-93	Britton, R B	1963-64	Cochran, P C	1889-91
Baker, D G S	1951-52	Bromet, W E	1889	Cohen, B A	1884
Baker, E M	1893-94-95-96	Brooks, A W	1980-81-82	Coker, J B H	1965
Baker, P	1980(R)	Brooks, M J	1873	Coker, T	1988-89
Baker, R T	1968	Brooks, W	1872	Cole, B W	1945
Balfour, E R	1893-94-95	Broster, L R	1912	Coleman, D J	1982-83
Bannerman, J MacD	1927-28	Broughton, R C	1965	Coles, D G G	1937-38
Barclay, S L	1990-91	Brown, L G	1910-11-12	Coles, P	1884-85-86
Barker, A C	1966-67	Brown, M E O	1988	Coles, S C	1954-56-57
Barnes, S	1981-82-83	Brunskill, R F	1873-74	Collingwood, J A	1961-62
Barr, D C A	1980	Bryan, T A	1975-76-77	Colville, A H	1892-93
Barry, C E	1897-98-99	Bryer, L W	1953	Conway-Rees, J	1891-92-93
Barry, D M	1968-69-70	Buchanan, F G	1909-10	Cook, D J	1988(R)-89
Barwick, W M	1880-81	Buckett, I M	1992	Cooke, J L	1968-69
Bass, R G	1961	Bucknall, A L	1965-66	Cooke, P	1936-37
Batchelor, T B	1906	Budge, K J	1977-78-79	Cooke, W R	1976
Bateson, H D	1874-75-77	Budworth, R T D	1887-88-89	Cookson, G H F	1891-92
Baxter, T J	1958-59	Bullard, G L	1950-51	Cooper, A H	1951
Beamish, S H	1971	Bullock, H	1910-11	Cooper, M McG	1934-35-36
Beare, A	1982	Bulpett, C W L	1871	Cooper, R A	1937
Bedford, T P	1965-66-67	Burnet, P J	1960	Cooper, R M	1946
Behn, A R	1968-69	Burrow, K C	1933	Cornish, W H	1876
Bell, D L	1970	Burse, R M	1974	Couper, T	1899-1900
Benson, E T	1928	Bush, A	1934	Court, E D	1882-83
Bentley, P J	1960	Bussell, J G	1903-04	Cousins, F C	1885-86
Berkeley, W V	1924-25-26	Butcher, W M	1954	Coutts, I D F	1951
Berry, C W	1883-84	Butler, F E R	1959-60	Coventry, R G T	1889-90-91
Bettington, R H B	1920-22	Button, E L	1936	Cowen, T J	1938
Bevan, J H	1946	Byers, R M	1926	Cowlishaw, F I	1890-91
Bibby, A J	1980-81			Cox, G V	1878
Binham, P A	1971	Caccia, H A	1926	Cozens-Hardy, B	1904-05-06
Birrell, H B	1953	Cadell, P R	1890	Crabbie, J E	1898-99-1900-01
Black, B H	1929	Cairns, A G	1899-1900-01	Craig, F J R	1963-64-65
Blair, A S	1884	Calcraft, W J	1986-87	Crane, C M	1985-86-87
Blencowe, L C	1907-08	Cameron, A J	1988	Cranmer, P	1933-34
Bloxham, C T	1934-35-36-37	Campbell, E	1919-20-21	Crawfurd, J W F A	1900
Blyth, P H	1885-86	Campbell, W	1987	Creese, N A H	1951
Bolton, W H	1873-74-75	Cannell, L B	1948-49-50	Cridlan, A G	1928-29-30
Bonham-Carter, C R	1990	Cardale, C F	1929-30	Croker, J R	1966-67
Bonham-Carter, E	1890-91	Carey, G M	1891-92-94	Crole, G B	1913-19

Wilson, J	1967-68	Winn, R R	1953	Wordsworth, C R	1922-23-24
Wilson, J H G	1888-89-90	Witney, N K J	1970-71	Wordsworth, C W	1902
Wilson, N G C	1967	Wix, R S	1904-05-06-07	Wordsworth, J R	1885
Wilson, R W	1956	Wood, A E	1904	Wray, M O	1933-34
Wilson, S	1963-64	Wood, D E	1952-53	Wyatt, D M	1981
Wilson, S E	1890	Wood, G F	1919	Wydell, H A	1951
Wilson, W G	1887	Woodhead, P G	1974	Wynter, E C C	1947
Wimperis, E J	1951	Woodrow, D K	1978-79-80		
Winn, C E	1950	Wooldridge, C S	1882	Young, J R C	1957-58

CAMBRIDGE

Aarvold, C D	1925-26-27-28	Berman, J V	1966	Carey, G V	1907-08
Ackford, P J	1979	Berry, S P	1971	Carpmael, W P	1885
Adams, G C A	1929	Bevan, G A J	1951	Carris, H E	1929
Adams, H F S	1884-85	Bevan, J A	1877-80	Carter, C P	1965
Agnew, C M	1875-76	Bevan, W	1887	Cave, J W	1887-88
Agnew, G W	1871-72-73	Bickle, D J	1992	Cave, W T C	1902-03-04
Agnew, W L	1876-77-78	Biddell, C W	1980-81	Chadwick, W O	1936-37-38
Albright, G S	1877	Biggar, M A	1971	Chalmers, P S	1979
Alderson, F H R	1887-88	Bird, D R J	1958-59	Chambers, E L	1904
Alexander, E P	1884-85-86	Birdwood, C R B	1932	Chapman, C E	1881-84
Alexander, J W	1905-06	Bishop, C C	1925	Chapman, E S	1879-80
Allan, C J	1962	Black, M A	1897-98	Chapman, G M	1907-08-09
Allan, J L F	1956	Blair, P C B	1910-11-12-13	Chapman, J M	1873
Allchurch, T J	1980-81	Blake, W H	1875	Chapple, M A	1991
Allen, A D	1925-26-27	Boggon, R P	1956	Chilcott, E W	1883
Allen, D B	1975	Bole, E	1945-46-47	Child, H H	1875-76
Allen, J	1875-76	Bonham-Carter, J	1873	Clarke, B D F	1978
Anderson, W T	1931-32	Booth, A H	1989-90	Clarke, S J S	1962-63
Andrew, C R	1982-83-84	Bordass, J H	1923-24	Clayton, H R	1876-77-78
Anthony, A J	1967	Borthwick, T J L	1985	Clayton, J R W	1971
Archer, G M D	1950-51	Boughton-Leigh, C E W	1878	Clements, J W	1953-54-55
Arthur, T G	1962	Boulding, P V	1975-76	Clifford, P H	1876-77-78
Ashcroft, A H	1908-09	Bowcott, H M	1927-28	Clough, F J	1984-85-86-87
Ashford, C L	1929	Bowcott, J E	1933	Coates, C H	1877-78-79
Ashworth, J	1988-89	Bowen, R W	1968	Coates, V H M	1907
Askew, J G	1929-30-31	Bowhill, J W	1888-89	Cobby, W	1900
Asquith, J P K	1953	Bowman, J H	1933-34	Cock, T A	1899
Aston, R L	1889-90	Boyd, C W	1909	Cocks, F W	1935
Atkinson, M L	1908-09	Boyd-Moss, R J	1980-81-82	Coghlan, G B	1926-27-28
Attfield, S J W	1982-84	Brandram, R A	1896	Cohen, A S	1922
		Brash, J C	1959-60-61	Colbourne, G L	1883
Back, F F	1871-72	Brathwaite, G A	1934	Coley, M	1964
Bailey, G H	1931	Breakey, J N F	1974-75(R)-77	Collett, G F	1898
Bailey, M D	1982-83-84-85	Bree-Frink, F C	1888-89-90	Collier, R B	1960-61
Bailey, R C	1982-83	Briggs, P D	1962	Collin, T	1871
Balding, I A	1961	Bromet, E	1887-88	Collins, W O H	1931
Balfour, A	1896-97	Brook, P W P	1928-29-30-31	Collis, W R F	1919-20
Bance, J F	1945	Brookstein, R	1969	Collison, L H	1930
Bannerman, C M	1990	Brooman, R J	1977-78	Combe, P H	1984-85
Barker, R E	1966	Browell, H H	1877-78	Considine, W C D	1919
Barlow, C S	1923-24-25-26	Brown, A C	1920-21	Conway, G S	1919-20-21
Barlow, R M M	1925	Brown, S L	1975-76	Cook, D D B	1920-21
Barrow, C	1950	Browning, O C	1934	Cook, S	1920-21
Barter, A F	1954-55-56	Bruce Lockhart, J H	1910	Cooke, S J	1981
Bartlett, R M	1951	Bruce Lockhart, L	1945-46	Cooper, H S	1881
Bateman-Champain, P J C	1937	Bruce Lockhart, R B	1937-38	Cooper, P T	1927-28
Bates, C S	1991	Brutton, E B	1883-85-86	Cope, W	1891
Batstone, G R D	1992	Bryant, S S	1988	Corry, T M	1966
Batten, J M	1871-72-73-74	Bryce, R D H	1965	Cosh, N J	1966
Batty, P A	1919-20	Bull, H A	1874-75	Covell, G A B	1949
Baxter, R	1871-72-73	Bunting, W L	1894-95	Cove-Smith, R	1919-20-21
Baxter, W H B	1912-13	Burns, S A	1992	Cox, F L	1879
Bealey, R J	1874	Burt-Marshall, J	1905	Craig, H J	1891
Beard, P L	1987	Burton, B C	1882-83	Craigmile, H W C	1920
Bearne, K R F	1957-58-59	Bush, J D	1983	Crichton-Miller, D	1928
Beazley, T A G	1971	Bussey, W M	1960-61-62	Crothers, G	1977(R)
Bedell-Sivright, D R		Butler, E T	1976-77-78	Crow, W A M	1961-62
	1899-1900-01-02	Buzza, A J	1988-89	Cullen, J C	1980-81-82
Bedell-Sivright, J V				Cumberlege, B S	1910-11-12-13
	1900-01-02-03	Cake, J J	1988	Cumberlege, R F	1897
Beer, I D S	1952-53-54	Callow, P G	1992	Cumming, D C	1922-23-24
Bell, D S	1989	Campbell, D A	1936	Currie, W C	1905
Bell, R W	1897-98-99	Campbell, H H	1946	Cushing, A	1986
Bell, S P	1894-95-96	Campbell, J A	1897-98-99		
Bennett, G M	1897-98	Campbell, J D	1927	Dalgleish, K J	1951-52-53
Bennett, R J	1981	Campbell, J J	1973-74	Dalton, E R	1872-73-74
Benthall, E C	1912	Campbell, R C C	1907	Dalton, W L T	1875-76
Beringer, F R	1951-52	Candler, P L	1934	Daniell, J	1898-99-1900
Beringer, G G	1975-76	Cangley, B T G	1946	Darby, A J L	1896-97-98

191

Rigby, J C A	1982
Riley, H	1871-72-73
Risman, M A	1987(R)
Ritchie, W T	1903-04
Robbie, J C	1977-78
Roberts, A F	1901-02
Roberts, A J R	1901-02
Roberts, J	1952-53-54
Roberts, J	1927-28
Roberts, S N J	1983
Robertson, A J	1990
Robertson, D D	1892
Robertson, I	1967
Robinson, A	1886-87
Robinson, B F	1891-92-93
Robinson, J J	1892
Robinson, N J	1990
Robinson, P J	1962
Rocyn-Jones, D N	1923
Roden, W H	1936-37
Rodgers, A K	1968-69-70
Roffey, D B	1874-75
Rose, H	1872
Rose, W M H	1979-80-81
Rosser, D W A	1962-63-64
Rosser, M F	1972-73
Ross-Skinner, W M	1924
Rotherham, A	1890-91
Rottenburg, H	1898
Rowell, W I	1890
Ryan, C J	1966
Ryan, P H	1952-53
Ryder, D C D	1921-23
Sagar, J W	1899-1900
Salmon, W B	1883
Sample, C H	1882-83-84
Sample, H W	1884
Sanderson, A B	1901
Saunders-Jacobs, S M	1929
Saville, C D	1967-68-69-70
Sawyer, B T C	1910
Saxon, K R J	1919-21
Scholfield, J A	1909-10
Schwarz, R O	1893
Scotland, K J F	1958-59-60
Scott, A W	1945-48
Scott, C T	1899
Scott, J M	1927
Scott, M T	1885-86-87
Scott, R R F	1957
Scott, W B	1923-24
Scott, W M	1888
Scoular, J G	1905-06
Seddon, E R H	1921
Shackleton, I R	1968-69-70
Shaw, P A V	1977
Sheasby, C M A	1990-91
Shepherd, J K	1950
Sherrard, P	1938
Shipsides, J	1970
Shirer, J A	1885
Silk, D R W	1953-54
Sim, R G	1966-67
Simms, K G	1983-84-85
Simms, N J	1989
Simpson, C P	1890
Simpson, F W	1930-31
Sisson, J P	1871
Skinner, R C O	1970-71
Slater, K J P	1964
Smallwood, A M	1919
Smeddle, R W	1928-29-30-31
Smith, A F	1873-74
Smith, A R	1954-55-56-57
Smith, H K P	1920
Smith, H Y L	1878-79-80-81
Smith, J	1889
Smith, J J E	1926
Smith, J M	1972
Smith, J V	1948-49-50
Smith, K P	1919
Smith, M A	1966-67
Smith, P K	1970

Smith, S R	1958-59
Smith, S T	1982-83
Sobey, W H	1925-26
Spencer, J S	1967-68-69
Spicer, N	1901-02
Spray, K A N	1946-47
Sprot, A	1871
Stauton, H	1891
Stead, R J	1977
Steeds, J H	1938
Steel, D Q	1877
Steele, H K	1970
Steele, J T	1879-80
Steele-Bodger, M R	1945-46
Stevenson, H J	1977(R)-79
Stevenson, L E	1884-85
Steward, R	1875-76
Stewart, A A	1975-76
Stewart, J R	1935
Stileman, W M C	1985
Stokes, R R	1921
Stone, R J	1901
Storey, E	1878-79-80
Storey, L H T	1909
Storey, T W P	1889-90-91-92
Stothard, N A	1979
Style, H B	1921
Surtees, A A	1886
Sutherland, J F	1908
Sutton, A J	1987-88
Swanson, J C	1938
Swayne, F G	1884-85-86
Symington, A W	1911-12-13
Synge, J S	1927
Tait, J G	1880-82
Talbot, S C	1900
Tallent, J A	1929-30-31
Tanner, C C	1930
Tarrant, J M	1990
Tarsh, D N	1955
Taylor, A S	1879-80-81
Taylor, D G	1982
Taylor, H B J	1894-96
Taylor, W J	1926
Templer, J L	1881-82
Thomas, B E	1960-61-62
Thomas, D R	1972-73-74
Thomas, H W	1912
Thomas, J	1945
Thomas, M D C	1986-87
Thomas, N B	1966
Thomas, R C C	1949
Thomas, T J	1895-96
Thomas, W H	1886-87
Thompson, M J M	1950
Thompson, R	1890
Thompson, R V	1948-49
Thorman, W H	1890
Thorne, C	1911
Thornton, J F	1976-78-79
Threlfall, R	1881-83
Timmons, F J	1983
Todd, A F	1893-94-95
Todd, T	1888
Topping, N P	1986-87
Touzel, C J C	1874-75-76
Tredwell, J R	1968
Trethewy, A	1888
Trubshaw, A R	1919
Tucker, W E	1892-93-94
Tucker, W E	1922-23-24-25
Tudsbery, F C T	1907-08
Tunningley, A J	1988(R)
Turnbull, B R	1924-25
Turner, J A	1956
Turner, J M P C	1985
Turner, M F	1946
Tyler, R H	1978-79-80
Umbers, R H	1954
Underwood, T	1990-91
Ure, C McG	1911

Valentine, G E	1930
Van Schalkwijk, J	1906
Vaughan, G P	1949
Vaux, J G	1957
Vickerstaff, M	1988
Vincent, C A	1913
Vivian, J M	1976
Vyvyan, C B	1987-88
Wace, H	1873-74
Waddell, G H	1958-60-61
Wade, M R	1958-59-60-61
Wainwright, J F	1956
Wainwright, M A	1980
Wainwright, R I	1986-87-88
Wakefield, W W	1921-22
Walker, A W	1929-30
Walker, D R	1980-81
Walker, E E	1899-1900
Walker, R M	1963
Walkey, J R	1902
Wallace, W M	1912-13
Waller, G S	1932
Wallis, H T	1895-96
Ward, R O C	1903
Ware, C H	1882
Warfield, P J	1974
Warlow, S	1972-74
Waters, F H	1927-28-29
Waters, J B	1902-03-04
Watherston, J G	1931
Watson, C F K	1919-20
Watt, J R	1970
Webb, G K M	1964-65
Webster, A P	1971
Wells, C M	1891-92
Wells, T U	1951
Weston, M T	1958-59-60
Wheeler, P J F	1951-52-53
White, J B	1922
White, W N	1947
Whiteway, S E A	1893
Wiggins, C E M	1928
Wiggins, C M	1964
Wilby, J B	1989
Wilkinson, R M	1971-72-73
Will, J G	1911-12-13
Williams, A G	1926-27
Williams, C C U	1950
Williams, C H	1930
Williams, C R	1971-72-73
Williams, D B	1973
Williams, E J H	1946
Williams, H A	1876
Williams, J M	1949
Williams, L T	1874-75
Williams, N E	1950
Williams, P T	1888-89
Williamson, I S	1972
Williamson, P R	1984
Willis, H	1949-50-51
Wilson, A H	1911-12-13
Wilson, C P	1877-78-79-80
Wilson, C W	1936
Winthrop, W Y	1871
Wintle, T C	1960-61
Withyman, T A	1985-86
Wood, G E	1974-75-76
Wood, G E C	1919
Woodall, B J C	1951
Woodroffe, O P	1952
Woods, S M J	1888-89-90
Wooller, W	1933-34-35
Wordley, S A	1988-89
Wordsworth, A J	1973-75
Wotherspoon, W	1888-89
Wrench, D F B	1960
Wright, C C G	1907-08
Wrigley, P T	1877-78-79-80
Wyles, K T	1985-86
Wynne, E H	1887
Yetts, R M	1879-80-81
Young, A B S	1919-20
Young, A T	1922-23-24

Young, J S	1935	Young, P D	1949	Young, W B	1935-36-37
Young, J V	1906	Young, S K	1974		

VARSITY MATCH REFEREES

(From 1881, when referees first officiated at the match. Prior to this date, the match was controlled by a pair of umpires elected by the Universities.) Each year indicates a separate appearance, and refers to the first half of the season. Thus 1881 refers to the match played in the 1881-82 season.

Allan, M A	1933-34	Freethy, A E	1923-25-27-29-31-32	Murdoch, W C W	1952
Ashmore, H L	1891-92-93-95-96	Gadney, C H	1935-36-37-38-45-47	Norling, C	1977-78-81-88-89
Bean, A S	1948-49	Gillespie, J I	1905	Pattinson, K A	1974
Bolton, W N	1882	Harnett, G H		Potter-Irwin, F C	1909-11-13-19
Boundy, L M	1958		1897-98-99-1900-01-02	Prideaux, L	1984
Burnett, D I H	1980-82	Hill, G R	1883-84-86-87-88-89-90	Quittenton, R C	1985-87
Burrell, R P	1963	Hosie, A M	1979	Sanson, N R	1976
Clark, K H	1973	Howard, F A	1986	Sturrock, J C	1921
Cooper, Dr P F	1951-53	Jeffares, R W	1930	Taylor, H H	1881
Crawford, S H	1920	John, K S	1956-67	Titcombe, M H	1969
Currey, F I	1885	Johnson, R F	1972	Trigg, J A F	1983
Dallas, J D	1910-12	Jones, T	1950	Vile, T H	1922-24-26-28
D'Arcy, D P	1968	Lamb, Air Cdre G C	1970	Walters, D G	
David, I	1954-55	Lambert, N H	1946		1957-60-61-62-64-65-66
Doyle, O E	1990	Lawrence, Capt H D	1894	Welsby, A	1975
Evans, G	1907	Lewis, R	1971	Williams, R C	1959
Findlay, J C	1904-08	Marsh, F W	1906	Williams, T	1903
Fleming, J M	1991	Morrison, E F	1992		

WORLD STUDENTS CUP 1992

Brendan Gallagher *Daily Telegraph*

30 June to 19 July 1992, Italy and Sicily

France, surprising many with their power, organisation and discipline, were worthy winners of the second World Students Cup when they comprehensively defeated holders New Zealand in the final at Rovigo.

The French remained cool in the heat of battle, especially against New Zealand, when the stakes were highest. They did not concede silly penalties and were never tempted into violence or retaliation up front. The presence of the French Federation's president, Bernard Lapasset, was probably no coincidence, and during the post-match celebrations M Lapasset again repeated the message that disciplined rugby is usually winning rugby.

Against New Zealand, Laurent Mazas landed three well-struck dropped goals, Thierry Lacroix and Pascal Fauthoux kicked a penalty apiece and Fauthoux converted Marin's pushover try, a score that epitomised France's forward domination and had French rugby director Robert Paparemborde purring with pleasure in the stands. New Zealand, who had endured the worst of the travel arrangements during a gruelling three weeks, enjoyed their best moments in the first half but faded after the break. Centre John Leslie scored their try, full-back Danny Love adding a conversion and a penalty.

After the disappointment of failing to win the inaugural competition on their own soil four years earlier, France selected their strongest possible squad, full internationals Serge Simon, Sebastien Conchy and Thierry Lacroix playing prominent roles. The controversial Simon captained the side with hitherto unsuspected maturity, Conchy was the perfect link-man and Lacroix was the competition's outstanding back.

After a comfortable passage through their pool, France beat England 9-6 in a tense quarter-final, resisting a spirited second-half revival from the English, for whom flanker Martin Pepper, lock Alex Snow and scrum-half Steve Douglas impressed. A 17-hour transit from Cagliari to L'Aquila saw an exhausted France struggle against Italy in their semi-final, where a massive 65-yard penalty from Thierry Lacroix in injury-time was needed to ensure a 25-21 victory.

Three hundred miles away in Castellammare di Stabia, New Zealand were distinctly flattered by their 21-9 semi-final win over Argentina, well captained throughout by Pumas No 8 Pablo Camerlinckx. The Kiwis had produced their best performance in a 53-7 quarter-final win against Ireland, in which the arrival of fly-half Lee Stensness from the New Zealand XV's series against England B heralded an eight-try romp.

Elsewhere, Wales missed out on a quarter-final place by slipping up against Romania in their pool game and Scotland's popular squad competed bravely before falling victim to Argentina's scrummaging power. South Africa Students became the first representative team from that country to return to the international scene, but inevitably struggled in a tough pool which included England and Argentina. Consolation came from a multitude of lessons learned and friendships made.

The competition's organisation was entrusted to CUSI, an Italian student body with absolutely no experience of rugby and the needs of rugby players. Happily, the enthusiasm and goodwill of Italy's growing rugby fraternity overcame this disadvantage, but it was a close call. New Zealand and Australia (joint bid), South Africa, Argentina and Japan all want to stage the 1996 competition, so the World Students Cup seems certain to expand still further.

FINAL 19 July, Rovigo

France 21 (1G 2PG 3DG)   **New Zealand 9** (1G 1PG)

France: O Campan (Agen); P Fauthoux (Racing Club de France), B Daguere (Biarritz), T Lacroix (Dax), P Lacroix (Dax); L Mazas (Colomiers), J-P Saffore (IRCF); S Simon (Bègles) (*capt*), S Morizot (USAP), P Voisin (Racing Club de France), P Pelous (Brive), Y Lemeur (ACBB), P Pueyo (Lourdes), S Conchy (Bègles), O Marin (Stade Toulousain)
Scorers *Try:* Marin   *Conversion:* Fauthoux   *Penalty Goals:* T Lacroix, Fauthoux
Dropped Goals: Mazas (3)

New Zealand: D Love (Massey U); J Wright (Otago U), J Leslie (Otago U), S Cottrell (Harlequins) (*capt*), P Alston; L Stensness (Massey U), J Hewlett (Auckland U); M Otai (Massey U), N Mantell (Auckland U), T Donnelly (Auckland U), B Timmins (Otago U), D Coleman (Massey U), S Surridge (Auckland U), T Hunt (Otago U), J Campbell (Otago U)
Scorers *Try:* Leslie   *Conversion:* Love   *Penalty Goal:* Love
Referee W D Bevan (WRU)

GROUP MATCHES

Pool A (Rovigo, Treviso and Padova): Italy 8, CIS 13; Ireland 74, Germany 3; Italy 100, Germany 0; Ireland 35, CIS 16; Italy 17, Ireland 6; CIS 46, Germany 9
Pool B (Genova): France 57, Spain 3; Scotland 21, Japan 16; Scotland 25, Spain 4; France 34, Japan 25; France 38, Scotland 15; Japan 6, Spain 23
Pool C (Naples): England 91, Taiwan 6; South Africa 6, Argentina 15; South Africa 108, Taiwan 0; England 6, Argentina 9; South Africa 13, England 20; Argentina 95, Taiwan 0
Pool D (Catania): New Zealand 22, Romania 10; Wales 49, Holland 7; New Zealand 118, Holland 3; Wales 6, Romania 21; New Zealand 15, Wales 7
Quarter-finals (Cagliari): Italy 27, Romania 7; Argentina 27, Scotland 18; France 9, England 6; New Zealand 53, Ireland 7
Semi-finals: Italy 21, France 25 (L'Aquila); Argentina 9, New Zealand 21 (Castellammare di Stabia)
Third place play-off (Rovigo): Argentina 21, Italy 8

STUDENT RUGBY AT THE CROSSROADS

RUGBY IN THE STUDENT SECTOR 1992-93
Harry Townsend

The introduction of more teams to UAU rugby breathed new life into a competition that had almost become the preserve of the few (Loughborough, Durham, Bristol, Swansea, Cardiff). Although Loughborough and Durham won through again, they were pushed hard as five newcomers – Cardiff Institute, West London Institute, Charing Cross/Westminster Hospital, Edinburgh and Aberdeen – reached the last eight, and with the dissolution of the BSSA (ex BPSA, or Polytechnics to you and me) and BCSA (British Colleges) on 1 August, a further 68 Institutes of Higher Education (IHEs) have already joined the UAU to make a total of 135 participating IHEs next season. That means more than 10,000 young players.

Peter Drewett, the RFU technical administrator (higher education), has been in post for two terms of a two-year appointment. Meetings have already been convened to discuss the structure of student rugby over the next decade, and there will be an October conference for everybody involved with student sport in a coaching, administrative or supporting role. The strain on UAU administration in the coming season will be maintained for a further year while the exciting prospect of student leagues is discussed and offered for sponsorship, without which they could not proceed.

The regional stages of the UAU competition are likely to be in three groupings, IHEs fielding more than 26 teams with at least 20 core sports, those with 15 to 20, and those with less than 15. Each grouping would get proportional allocations of places for a probable 64-team first round, although there would inevitably be exceptions. A real structure is vital, for all standards and all institutions.

The RFU could take on more of the financial burden of competitive grass-roots student rugby. It does this completely for the England Students team, which carries the banner for student rugby with the Student World Cup the highest prize. Yet this tournament has been mishandled by many unions, who do not realise its potential, and unless the New Zealand, South African or Japanese RFUs take the 1996 tournament on board, there could be a real fiasco.

Ten thousand student players are our prize: their structured rugby future must be assured.

Representative matches: Wales Students 6, Australia 37 (Bridgend); Scotland Students 7, Oxford U 19 (Boroughmuir); England Students 20, France Students 9 (Cambridge U); Scotland Students 13, Irish Students 49 (Duddington); Wales Students 21, England Students 13 (Llanelli); England Students 71, Scotland Students 20 (Basingstoke); France Students 37, Wales Students 11 (Nantes); Ireland Students 19, England Students 6 (Old Belvedere); English Universities 52, Scottish Universities 13 (London Welsh); Welsh

Universities 8, English Universities 34 (Newbridge); Irish Universities 8, English Universities 44 (Dublin); Welsh Universities 18, Scottish Universities 18 (Edinburgh); Welsh Universities 20, Irish Universities 18 (Cross Keys); Irish Colleges 20, British Colleges 19 (Cork).

COMMERCIAL UNION UAU CHAMPIONSHIP 1992-93

17 March, Twickenham
Loughborough University 25 (2G 2PG 1T)
Bristol University 18 (1G 2PG 1T)

Bristol might be counted somewhat lucky to have reached the final. They lost their opening two group matches and qualified for the play-off round only on points difference, but when they got to Twickenham they combined with perennial finalists Loughborough to make this one of the truly memorable finals.

Loughborough, seven times champions in the last nine seasons, had scored 337 against 56 in their eight matches before the final. Only West London Institute, in the semi-final, had provided any real opposition before going down 24-11. But Bristol, fired by scrum-half Kyran Bracken, shook them rigid by snatching a 12-0 lead with tries by Nolan (converted by Chris John) and Bracken himself.

However, Loughborough bounced back. Tomlinson scored a try, and converted it; then flanker Metcalf dived on to a loose ball from a line-out to level the scores at 12-12, and all this in the opening 30 minutes. The second half (two penalty goals by John to two by Tomlinson) might sound dull, but not a bit of it: Bracken and John at half-back, Singer, a thrusting full-back, and Nolan, sparkling in the centre, stretched Loughborough to their limits, only the strength of their pack and devastating tackling keeping them in the game at times. But the longer the game continued, the more Bristol relied on the magic of Bracken as he toiled behind a tiring pack in which No 8 Kurt Seecharan proved his ablest ally as he channelled and protected their scraps of possession.

It was left to John to equalise for Bristol with the last kick of normal time, a superb pressure kick in the swirling Twickenham wind. Extra time was torture for tiring limbs. Bristol were completely dominated in scrum and line-out, yet Loughborough scarcely got into the Bristol 22 until the final minute, when they were awarded a scrum almost on the line. The scrum had to be reset, and it was in overtime, with the crowd willing the referee to blow for no side, that a mighty Loughborough shove allowed No 8 Tony Diprose to score a pushover try which Tomlinson converted.

What a match, and what an advertisement for rugby – and for student rugby above all. It was full of passion and sportsmanship; it raised the profile of the game and deserved the sort of audience figures that *Rugby Special* receives.

Bristol's Kyran Bracken finds the Loughborough defence in determined mood during the 1993 UAU final at Twickenham. It was an exciting match in a competition growing vastly in numbers.

Loughborough University: N Stork; M Nicholson, P Bingham, R Tomlinson,
M Dawson; G Williams, R Stone; G Reynolds, C Johnson, D Lockyer, M Wright,
D Jones, A Metcalf, N Richardson (*capt*), A Diprose
Scorers *Tries:* Tomlinson, Metcalf, Diprose   *Conversions:* Tomlinson (2)
Penalty Goals: Tomlinson (2)
Bristol University: M Singer; T Dalwood, M Nolan, M Jones, A Robertson; C John,
K Bracken; I Murray, J Binks (*capt*), A Reuben, O Johnson, J Nakhorn, G Bulstrode,
A Maynard, K Seecharan
Scorers *Tries:* Nolan, Bracken   *Conversion:* John   *Penalty Goals:* John (2)
Referee D Matthews (Liverpool)

Loughborough have won the title 25 times, Durham 8, Liverpool and Swansea 7, Bristol 5, Cardiff and Manchester 4, Bangor and UWIST 2, Aberystwyth, Birmingham, Leeds and Newcastle once each.

Second XV final: Cardiff Institute 28, Liverpool 13
Third XV final: Loughborough 39, Newcastle 17

It seemed as though a breath of fresh air was about to sweep through UAU rugby with the addition of new teams as the 'universitisation' of more than 70 IHEs began. Additionally, an entire new group was added with the inclusion of the Scottish universities, and overnight, it seemed, we were faced with the prospect of the overthrow of the established power-base of UAU rugby. It was almost realised: five of the last eight were in their first season of UAU rugby, and although Charing Cross/Westminster Hospital (to Bristol), Edinburgh (to Durham) and Aberdeen (to Loughborough) fell at this hurdle, West London Institute defeated Cardiff Institute to pose the only real threat experienced by Loughborough, to whom they lost 24-11 in the semi-final.

These new challengers introduced real strength in depth to the competition, and scores in the 50s and above were now commonplace. Cardiff Institute swept aside their fellow Welsh opposition by 73-15, 57-31, 67-7 and 56-8 (against regular finalists and group runners-up Swansea, no less, who lost only 22-19 away to Durham in the challenge round) and then Essex, 108-3 in the challenge round. West London Institute notched up 94-0, 66-3 and 124-3, with two other opponents prudently scratching. But to even it up, Loughborough dominated their own group 58-3, 47-8, 55-8 (against group runners-up Birmingham), 39-3 and 48-0. Keele are also gaining credibility. They were undefeated in their eight-team group, and then beat Leeds 35-6 before losing 11-8 to Aberdeen. The old guard came through in the end, but only just.

GROUP TABLES

The top three from Groups A to D and the top four from Group E to H go forward to the play-off round. The top two from the Scottish competition, Edinburgh and Aberdeen, go direct to the challenge round.

SOUTHERN DIVISION

Group A South-West

	P	W	D	L	F	A	Pts
Exeter	4	3	0	1	67	32	6

Group B South Central

	P	W	D	L	F	A	Pts
Charing X/WH	5	5	0	1	132	40	10

	P	W	D	L	F	A	Pts
Bath	4	3	0	1	65	54	6
Bristol	4	2	0	2	86	34	4
Cranfield	4	2	0	2	38	49	4
Southampton	4	0	0	4	25	112	0

Group C South-East North

	P	W	D	L	F	A	Pts
Essex	3	3	0	0	45	21	6
UCL	3	1	1	1	45	15	3
QMWC	3	1	1	1	30	34	3
Middlesex	3	0	0	3	19	69	0

	P	W	D	L	F	A	Pts
Reading	5	4	0	1	108	36	8
Imperial	5	3	0	2	85	74	6
RHNBC	5	1	1	3	35	103	3
King's	5	0	1	4	33	71	1

Group D South-East South

	P	W	D	L	F	A	Pts
W London In	5	5	0	0	284	6	10
Kent	5	4	0	1	92	135	8
City	5	3	0	2	106	115	6
LSE	5	2	0	3	80	73	4
Surrey	5	1	0	4	47	192	2
Sussex	5	0	0	5	34	122	0

WELSH DIVISION
Group E Wales

	P	W	D	L	F	A	Pts
Cardiff Inst	5	5	0	0	253	61	10
Swansea	5	4	0	1	121	107	8
UWCC	5	3	0	2	117	105	6
UWCM	5	2	0	3	91	90	4
Glamorgan	5	1	0	4	96	166	2
Aberyswyth	5	0	0	5	49	198	0

MIDLANDS DIVISION
Group F Midlands

	P	W	D	L	F	A	Pts
Loughborough	5	5	0	0	247	22	10
Birmingham	5	4	0	1	123	80	8
Nottingham	5	2	0	3	32	91	4
Oxford/Brks	5	2	0	3	46	132	4
Warwick	5	1	0	4	50	93	2
Leicester	5	1	0	4	36	116	2

NORTHERN DIVISION
Group G North-East

	P	W	D	L	F	A	Pts
Durham	4	4	0	0	186	31	8
Newcastle	4	3	0	1	111	73	6
Sheffield	4	2	0	2	88	76	4
Leeds	4	2	0	2	46	129	4
Hull	4	0	0	4	23	145	0

Group H North-West

	P	W	D	L	F	A	Pts
Keele	7	7	0	0	170	43	14
Liverpool	7	6	0	1	185	69	12
Manchester	7	4	0	3	132	108	8
UMIST	7	4	0	3	118	109	8
Lancaster	7	3	0	4	92	98	6
Salford	7	2	0	5	77	76	4
Chester	6	0	0	6	44	153	0
Bradford	6	0	0	6	57	219	0

Play-off round: Durham w/o UMIST; Swansea 30, Manchester 0; Newcastle 18, UWCC 26; Keele 35, Leeds 6; Loughborough 42, UWCM 11; Liverpool 5, Sheffield 11; Charing Cross/Westminster Hosp 34, City 17; Birmingham 15, Bath 3; Exeter 63, QMWC 0; Kent 3, Bristol 27; West London Inst 34, Imperial 3; Reading 21, UCL 5; Cardiff Inst w/o Nottingham; Essex 5, Oxford/Brookes 0

Challenge round: Durham 22, Swansea 19; Edinburgh 11, UWCC 5; Keele 8, Aberdeen 11; Loughborough 21, Sheffield 6; Charing Cross/Westminster Hosp 38, Birmingham 16; Exeter 14, Bristol 17; West London Inst 26, Reading 3; Cardiff Inst 106, Essex 3

Quarter-finals: Durham 43, Edinburgh 0; Aberdeen 6, Loughborough 51; Charing Cross/Westminster Hosp 14, Bristol 22; West London Inst 14, Cardiff Inst 4

Semi-finals: Durham 13, Bristol 20; Loughborough 24, West London Inst 11

COMMERCIAL UNION UAU Seven-a-side Tournament
7 March 1993, Aston University
Quarter-finals: Bangor 0, Warwick 12; Stirling 0, Bristol 47; Reading 0, Exeter 43; Bath 38, UCL 7 **Semi-finals:** Warwick 14, Bristol 19; Exeter 28, Bath 12
Final: Bristol 35, Exeter 7
Plate final: Trinity and All Saints 0, Nottingham 35

BRITISH STUDENT SPORT ASSOCIATION CUP 1993

10 March 1993, Rugby RFC
Sheffield Hallam University 14 (3PG 1T)
University of Northumbria 13 (1PG 2T)

A rerun of the 1992 BPSA (Polytechnics) final between teams better recognised under their old guises (Sheffield Poly and Newcastle Poly) brought the same result in the one and only year of the BSSA Cup competition.

Sheffield Hallam stuck loyally to their regular team, with Waterloo scrum-half Saverimutto and England Under-21 flanker Morris volunteers on the bench.

The stronger Northumbria pack dominated the early exchanges. Hooker Hayes drove over for the opening try from a maul following a line-out and although Gallagher countered for Sheffield with a penalty, a blindside break on the Sheffield 22 by scrum-half Eley was continued by prop Bowen for a second Northumbria try. Jervis added a penalty before two by Gallagher for Sheffield closed the gap to 13-9 at half-time.

The more innovative Sheffield backs finally clinched the match with ten minutes remaining. Full-back Judds came into the line to feed the ball back in to Slater, and although both teams had chances in the closing stages, Sheffield Hallam hung on for a 100 per cent BSSA record.

Sheffield Hallam University: S Judds; M Gallagher, M Old, S Slater, M Leppard (*capt*); A Parker, A Hanson; S Henry, R Wright, R Williams, G Davies, P Howse, I Kierney, M Pinder, D Tether
Scorers *Try:* Slater *Penalty Goals:* Gallagher (3)
University of Northumbria: J Miller; M Bush, S Grzonka, D Stirrett, N Hanna; S Jervis, J Eley; M Long, D Hayes, S Bowen (*capt*), C Heseltine, M Smith, M Curry, D Blyth, B Naylor
Scorers *Tries:* Hayes, Bowen *Penalty Goal:* Jervis

First round proper: Leeds Metropolitan 3, Sheffield Hallam 13; Manchester Metropolitan 13, Harper Adams 8; RAC beat St Mary's; Northumbria 31, De Montfort (Leicester) 10; Westminster 13, Bournemouth 10; Portsmouth w/o North London; Roehampton 21, Plymouth 13; Liverpool John Moores beat Birmingham

Quarter-finals: Sheffield Hallam 37, Manchester Metropolitan 18; RAC 24, Westminster 5; Liverpool John Moores 3, Northumbria 56; Portsmouth 0, Roehampton 13

Semi-finals: Sheffield Hallam 15, RAC 9; Northumbria 8, Roehampton 0

Second XV final: Sheffield Hallam U 18, Coventry 14
Third XV final: Portsmouth 16, UCE Birmingham 14

BSSA Seven-a-side Tournament
28 April 1993, Coventry
Semi-finals: De Montfort (Leicester) 33, Derby 12; Sheffield Hallam 21, Coventry 12
Final: De Montfort (Leicester) 34, Sheffield Hallam 7

SESSA CUP
1st XV final: Roehampton 16, St Mary's 8
2nd XV final: Portsmouth 2nd XV 19, Royal School of Mines 0
3rd XV final: Portsmouth 3rd XV 29, Westminster 0

BRITISH COLLEGES (BCSA) CUP
Quarter-finals: St Martin's 21, North Cheshire 20; Gwent w/o Edge Hill; Cheltenham & Gloucester 36, St John's, York 3; St Mary's beat Christ Church, Canterbury
Semi-finals: St Mary's 38, St Martin's 15; Cheltenham & Gloucester 32, Gwent 15
Final: St Mary's 26, Cheltenham & Gloucester 3
Plate final: Cardinal Newman 27, Bradford & Ilkley 6

HOSPITALS CHALLENGE CUP

Paul Nelson *The Sunday Times*

10 March, Old Deer Park
Charing Cross/Westminster Hospital 16 (2PG 2T)
St Mary's Hospital 9 (2PG 1DG)

Two remarkable events occurred in the 106th Hospitals Cup tournament. Not only did St Mary's, unbeaten for almost seven years, lose a game, but the competition began to show signs of halting its long, gradual decline. At one time the domain of internationals and British Lions, in 1993 the tournament again featured a healthy sprinkling of first-class players, two of whom were instrumental in securing the Cup for the combined Charing Cross/Westminster side for the first time. David Clift, the former Liverpool St Helens fly-half and captain, and Mike Hutton, a centre for semi-finalists Middlesex in the County Championship, ran with such pace and power that few defenders could cope.

The only way to stop the Charing Cross/Westminister backs, who defied a snowstorm to sweep Kings' aside 48-0 in an extraordinary semi-final performance, appeared to be to deny them the ball. Here lay the hopes of St Mary's in an entertaining, fiercely contested final.

Despite fielding five of the pack from the previous year's final, however, St Mary's were unable to monopolise possession, and although their threequarters defended tirelessly, Charing Cross/Westminster eventually worked both wings over to clinch the game with excellent tries. A break by Clift put Gary Sinclair in at the corner and Chris Swartz wrapped up matters with the second try after a superb four-man move.

Buoyed by the high standard of the competition, the United Hospitals club voted to continue staging the world's oldest tournament, despite the likelihood that hospital mergers will reduce the number of participants. Proposals to use the Cup to launch a competition for medical schools nationwide were also being considered.

Charing Cross/Westminster: A Redman; G Sinclair, G O'Driscoll, M Hutton, C Swartz; D Clift (*capt*), E Rowe; I Josephs, A Dalrymple, A Norrish, H Lewis, B Whitehouse, M Jeffrey, J Hickey, R Walker
Scorers *Tries:* Sinclair, Swartz *Penalty Goals:* Clift (2)
St Mary's: D Abrams; R Wintle, A Morgan, J Waters, C Boos; S Berry, C Wright (*capt*); N Hunt, L O'Hara, J Reid, P Tooze-Hobson, M Tremelling, J Torkington, C Langrish, M Crowther
Scorers *Penalty Goals:* Berry (2) *Dropped Goal:* Morgan
Referee J Burtenshaw (London Society)

First Round: Bart's 10, Royal Free 3; King's 15, St George's 3
Second Round: Bart's 0, St Mary's 27; St Thomas's 0, The London 18; Charing Cross/Westminster 10, Guy's 6; King's 26, UCH/Middlesex 3
Semi-finals: St Mary's 23, The London 0; Charing Cross/Westminster 48, King's 0

St Mary's have won the cup 31 times, Guy's 30, St Thomas's 17, The London 11, St Bartholomew's 9, St George's and Westminster 3 times each and Middlesex and Charing Cross/Westminster once each.

THE AIRMEN'S HAPPY ANNIVERSARY

THE SERVICES 1992-93
John Mace   *Daily Telegraph*

Inter-Services Tournament

The Royal Navy, Army and RAF began their seasons early to prepare for their fixtures with the New Zealand Combined Services in November and December. Predictably, the tourists proved too strong for all three and, like their 1985 predecessors, won all their seven matches. However, lessons were learned and the services' coaching organisations have since reassessed their aims and structure.

The Inter-Services Tournament also benefited from the New Zealanders' influence because each side attempted to play purposeful running rugby. Although they only just scraped home against the Army, the RAF won the title. This was a timely contribution to the service's 75th anniversary celebrations. Sadly, despite thorough planning and much hard work, the Navy did not realise their potential in either match and have now recorded only one tournament victory in six seasons.

A crowd of more than 12,000, including Prince Edward, watched the Army outplay the Navy, who started as marginal favourites. The Army forwards, with Tim Rodber, Gareth James and Mike Watson outstanding, won lots of possession and their half-backs, Dave Williams and Andy Deans, also made telling contributions. The Navy began well and even led 13-8 at one point, but were unable to sustain their momentum, whereas the Army grew stronger as the game progressed. Army tries either side of half-time proved a watershed in the Navy's fortunes.

In the second match the RAF defended resolutely and absorbed heavy pressure from the Army to win a disjointed but exciting game. They owed much to their willingness to run from deep positions and to their fly-half, Paul Hull, who frequently kicked them out of trouble and also had a hand in each of their three tries, two of which were scored by Rory Underwood. Above all they took their chances while the Army squandered several try-scoring opportunities, any one of which would have given them the title.

The RAF's victory in the final game was decisive, and although the Navy again had the better of the early exchanges they were unable to score and the RAF took control to build up a 23-point lead. Their durable locks, Brian Richardson and Dick Burn, dominated the line-outs, their back row of Chris Morgan, Darren Watkins and Chris Moore foraged effectively and their solid scrummaging caused the Navy problems. The whole side again tackled tenaciously, and with shrewd use of possession by half-backs Steve Worrall and Paul Hull, their talented backs launched some impressive handling attacks, even though the ball would not run for Rory Underwood. Only determined

Navy defence kept the score down and to their credit, with Iain Dixon, Bob Armstrong and Ian Russell prominent they rallied in the final quarter to score a consolation try.

Steve Worrall's 22nd inter-service match appearance put him one ahead of Rory Underwood for the RAF and equal with the Army's Andy Hoon and the late Norman Bruce in the tri-service list. He hopes to be back next season to claim the record.

13 March, Twickenham
Royal Navy 15 (1G 1PG 1T)   **Army 37** (3G 2DG 2T)
for the Willis Corroon Trophy

Royal Navy: POMEA K Bethwaite (HMS Neptune); Lt E Gibbs (HMS Splendid), AB(S) D Sibson (HMS Dryad), Lt R Bigland (HMS Seahawk), LS L Oman

Steve Worrall, the long-serving RAF scrum-half, celebrates the RAF victory over the Navy at Twickenham by flourishing the Windsor Life Trophy.

(HMS Cambridge); Mne J Kaye (RM Poole), Lt C Read (HMS Seahawk);
Capt M Dunham RM (RMA Sandhurst), POPT M Clay (HMS Temeraire),
LS N Bartlett (HMS Heron), Lt C Palmer RM (Cdo Log Regt RM), Cpl S Trench
(CTC RM), Mne R Armstrong (42 Cdo RM), POPT S Jones (BRNC Dartmouth),
Lt C Dixon RM (DNR London) *(capt)*
Scorers *Tries:* Palmer, Sibson *Conversion:* Bethwaite *Penalty Goal:* Bethwaite
Army: Lt H Graham (RHA); S/Sgt J Simon (REME), Capt A Glasgow (RE),
S/Sgt C Spowart (APTC), S/Sgt E Atkins (Royal Signals); Capt A Deans (AGC) *(capt)*,
Cpl D Williams (RRW); Lt S Stewart (DWR), Capt J Brammer (RE), Bdr J Fowers
(RHA), 2/Lt D Dahinten (RHA), Capt T Swan (RAMC), 2/Lt T Rodber
(Green Howards), Lt G James (RRW), Cpl M Watson (REME) *Replacement* Sgt D Coghlan
(RHA) for Stewart
Scorers *Tries:* Atkins, Brammer, Deans, Watson (2) *Conversions:* Graham, Spowart (2)
Dropped Goals: Deans, Spowart
Referee B Campsall (Yorkshire Society)

24 March, Twickenham
Army 17 (2G 1PG) **Royal Air Force 20** (1G 1PG 2T)
for the Windsor Life Challenge Cup

Army: Lt H Graham (RHA); S/Sgt J Simon (REME), Capt A Glasgow (RE),
S/Sgt C Spowart (APTC), S/Sgt E Atkins (Royal Signals); Capt A Deans (AGC) *(capt)*,
Cpl D Williams (RRW); Sgt D Coghlan (RHA), Capt J Brammer (RE), Bdr J Fowers
(RHA), 2/Lt D Dahinten (RHA), Capt T Swan (RAMC), 2/Lt T Rodber
(Green Howards), Lt G James (RRW), Cpl M Watson (REME)
Scorers *Tries:* Glasgow, Rodber *Conversions:* Spowart (2) *Penalty Goal:* Spowart
Royal Air Force: Cpl S Lazenby (Brize Norton); Cpl S Crossland (Locking), Cpl S Roke
(St Athan), SAC G Sharp (Benson), Flt Lt R Underwood (Wyton); Cpl P Hull
(Lyneham), Sgt S Worrall (Cottesmore) *(capt)*; Sgt D Robson (Odiham), Sgt S Collins
(Innsworth), Cpl A Billett (St Athan), Flt Lt R Burn (Lossiemouth), Sgt B Richardson
(Rudloe Manor), Cpl C Morgan (Laarbruch), Fg Off D Watkins (Brize Norton),
Flt Lt C Moore (Oakhanger)
Scorers *Tries:* Underwood (2), Watkins *Conversion:* Hull *Penalty Goal:* Hull
Referee R C Rees (London Society)

31 March, Twickenham
Royal Navy 7 (1G) **Royal Air Force 23** (2G 3PG)
for the Windsor Life Challenge Trophy

Royal Navy: POMEA K Bethwaite (HMS Neptune); Lt E Gibbs (HMS Splendid),
AB(S) D Sibson (HMS Dryad), Lt R Bigland (HMS Seahawk), LS L Oman
(HMS Cambridge); Mne J Kaye (RM Poole), S/Lt I Torpey (HMS Temeraire);
Capt M Dunham RM (RMA Sandhurst), POPT M Clay (HMS Temeraire),
LS N Bartlett (HMS Heron), LPT I Russell (HMS Ambuscade), Cpl S Trench
(CTC RM), Mne R Armstrong (42 Cdo RM), Lt C Dixon RM (DNR London) *(capt)*,
Lt C Palmer RM (Cdo Log Regt RM) *Replacement* LWEM S Burns (HMS Collingwood)
for Bartlett
Scorers *Try:* Palmer *Conversion:* Oman
Royal Air Force: Cpl S Lazenby (Brize Norton); Cpl S Crossland (Locking), Cpl S Roke
(St Athan), SAC G Sharp (Benson), Flt Lt R Underwood (Wyton); Cpl P Hull
(Lyneham), Sgt S Worrall (Cottesmore) *(capt)*; Sgt D Robson (Odiham), Sgt S Collins
(Innsworth), Cpl A Billett (St Athan), Flt Lt R Burn (Lossiemouth), Sgt B Richardson
(Rudloe Manor), Cpl C Morgan (Laarbruch), Fg Off D Watkins (Brize Norton),
Flt Lt C Moore (Oakhanger) *Replacement* Cpl M Cooke (Wyton) for Lazenby
Scorers *Tries:* Worrall, penalty try *Conversions:* Hull (2) *Penalty Goals:* Hull (3)
Referee A M W Reay (Bristol Society)

Inter-Services Tournament Champions

The Army have won the Tournament outright 28 times, the Royal Navy 16 times and the Royal Air Force 13 times. The Army and the Royal Air Force have shared it on 2 occasions and there have been 9 triple ties.

1920 **RN**	1949 **Army and RAF**	1972 **Army**
1921 **RN**	1950 **Army**	1973 **RN**
1922 **RN**	1951 **RN**	1974 **RN**
1923 **RAF**	1952 **Army**	1975 Triple Tie
1924 Triple Tie	1953 **Army**	1976 **Army**
1925 **Army and RAF**	1954 Triple Tie	1977 **RN**
1926 **Army**	1955 **RAF**	1978 Triple Tie
1927 **RN**	1956 Triple Tie	1979 **RAF**
1928 **Army**	1957 **Army**	1980 **Army**
1929 **Army**	1958 **RAF**	1981 RN
1930 **Army**	1959 **RAF**	1982 **RAF**
1931 **RN**	1960 **Army**	1983 **Army**
1932 **Army**	1961 **RN**	1984 Triple Tie
1933 **Army**	1962 **RAF**	1985 **RAF**
1934 **Army**	1963 **Army**	1986 **RAF**
1935 Triple Tie	1964 **Army**	1987 **RN**
1936 **Army**	1965 **Army**	1988 **Army**
1937 **Army**	1966 **RN**	1989 **Army**
1938 RN	1967 **Army**	1990 **Army**
1939 **RN**	1968 **Army**	1991 **RAF**
1946 **Army**	1969 **Army**	1992 Triple Tie
1947 RAF	1970 **RN**	1993 **RAF**
1948 Triple Tie	1971 **RAF**	

Royal Navy v Army The Royal Navy have won 31, the Army 42, and 3 matches have been drawn (including matches before 1920) **Royal Navy v Royal Air Force** The Royal Navy have won 37, the Royal Air Force 27, and 4 matches have been drawn **Army v Royal Air Force** The Army have won 38, the Royal Air Force 22, and 8 matches have been drawn

Other Competitions

Inter-Services Under-21 Tournament
Army 11, RAF 6; RN 3, RAF 24; RN 0, Army 27 **Winners:** Army

Inter-Services Colts (under-19) Tournament
RN 3, Army 9; RN 5, RAF 24; Army 21, RAF 12 **Winners:** Army

Combined Services Matches
Senior: Combined Services 3, British Police 15 (*for the Securicor Trophy*)
Under-21: Combined Services 14, Irish Exiles 12; Combined Services 12, Welsh Exiles 26; Combined Services 17, England Students 32; Combined Services 28, Nottingham University 10
Colts (under-19): Combined Services 8, Cardiff and District 58; Combined Services 28, Ogmore and District 39

Individual Service Competitions
ROYAL NAVY
Inter-Command match: Royal Marines 44, Naval Air Command 0
Inter-Unit Cup: HMS Nelson 19, HMS Neptune 10
Inter-Unit Sevens: HMS Nelson 29, HMS Dolphin 10
ARMY
Inter Corps Merit Table: Division 1 winners: Royal Signals **Division 2 winners:** Royal

Army Ordnance Corps
Major Units Cup: 7th Parachute Regiment Royal Horse Artillery 20, 7th Signal Regiment 11
Minor Units Cup: 12th Armoured Workshop REME 3, 3rd Field Workshop REME 5
Inter-Unit Sevens: 1st Battalion Royal Regiment of Wales 29, 2nd Signal Regiment 14
RAF
Inter-Command matches: Strike Command 16, Support Command 23; Strike Command 15, RAF Germany 15; Support Command 14, RAF Germany 11; RAF Germany 3, BAOR 13
Inter-Station Cup: RAF Cottesmore 22, RAF Wyton 27
Inter-Station Shield: RAF Aldergrove 30, RAF Marham 5
Inter-Station Sevens: RAF Brize Norton 19, RAF St Athan 12

New Zealand Combined Services Tour of England

The 1992 New Zealand Combined Services (which includes their police) won all seven matches and proved themselves admirable ambassadors for their country and individual services. The squad contained several players with provincial experience, including their influential captain Steve Hansen, plus some talented youngsters who developed as the tour progressed. They were managed by Commander Mike Franklin and coached by Otago's Gordon Hunter.

Supremely fit, they played enterprising rugby and their outstanding ability to keep the ball alive was augmented by a willingness to attack from anywhere. The side were particularly adept at tying in the opposition and exploiting the resulting space with direct running and speedy, accurate passing and the ferocity of their tackling epitomised their policy of pressurising the opposition at all times. They scored 228 points, including 30 tries, and conceded only 57 points and 3 tries; an accurate reflection of their ability and determination.

Cornwall, playing with typical fervour, were the only side to run them close, although the British Combined Services and Police dominated the first 30 minutes of their match before succumbing to the visitors' non-stop handling game. On their next visit the New Zealanders should be given two stronger civilian fixtures while the British Police, and British Combined Services and Police, must field more of their many internationals if they hope to compensate for the cohesion the tourists are able to develop.

MATCH DETAILS

DATE	OPPONENTS	VENUE	RESULT
22 Nov 1992	Hampshire	Havant	W 33-9
25 Nov	Royal Navy	Devonport	W 28-6
29 Nov	Cornwall	Redruth	W 13-6
2 Dec	British Police	Northampton	W 25-3
7 Dec	Royal Air Force	Brize Norton	W 36-0
10 Dec	Army	Aldershot	W 54-10
15 Dec	British Combined Services & Police	Imber Court	W 39-23

IRELAND PROMISE WELL: ENGLAND STRUGGLE ON

SCHOOLS RUGBY 1992-93
Michael Stevenson

When England Schools 18 Group crossed to Belfast in mid-April they needed victory to avoid an unaccustomed whitewash, while Ireland's eyes were firmly fixed on the Junior Triple Crown. It was a close contest but Ireland, scoring two tries to one, fully deserved their 13-8 win and the reassuring knowledge that their schools' side has looked good for a number of years. Ireland struck first. No 8 Millar broke crisply and put the right wing, Topping, in for a good try; Hickie, his colleague on the left wing, sealed the match with a break and a chip-and-chase try before fly-half Campion added a second-half penalty after a fluent attack had ended in a try for the England right wing, Morgan.

The season opened inauspiciously for England, prior to their final trial, with a visit to Pembroke, where Welsh Schools, who had already played two matches, edged them out by a single point, 8-7, echoing the dramatic experience of their seniors at Cardiff. Wales had already narrowly beaten Scotland at Murrayfield (5-3) and showed considerable improvement at Pembroke. Oldham in the back row and hooker Greening laboured mightily to keep Wales' lead down to 8-0 at half-time, but it seemed insufficient for victory. Evans, with a penalty, and Hawkins, with a try made by No 8 Wareham, were Wales' points-scorers. England were unlucky to lose their fly-half, Binns, and full-back, Ashforth, both from Bradford GS, but their replacements, Weston of Durham and Blyth of Rugby, contributed their side's points: Blyth scored a try and Weston a conversion. England, trailing by that crucial single point, had much the better of the late play, but brave Welsh defence kept them out for a victory that Wales just about deserved.

England's season was dominated by injuries to members of their squad and only in the second halves of the games against Wales and Ireland did the side's performance approach its potential. The pack consistently struggled to win good possession and the delivery of the ball from half-back was very variable.

Japan High Schools toured England during March and won four matches, losing only to London Colts at Wasps, 26-15. The tour opened with a narrow 15-14 victory over Yorkshire Schools, and after the setback in London the final matches were against Devon and Cornwall (27-8), Gloucestershire Schools (28-24) and England 18 Group A at Castlecroft (20-17), which was a wonderful climax to an excellent tour.

For any side to remain unbeaten in a season requires skill, great spirit and, usually, a soupçon of good luck. *Bradford GS* came within a sliver

Royal GS scrum-half Machell clears the ball in the Daily Mail *Under-18 Schools Cup.*

of achieving this distinction in successive seasons before they went down narrowly to *Woodhouse Grove* (17-12) in their penultimate match of the season. Bradford were without the services of their England backs, Binns and Ashforth, but were loud in their praise of a superb display by the winners, who lost only to King Edward VII, Lytham (11-10) and Mount St Mary's (10-3) in winning 17 out of 19 matches played. Bradford's showing was the more remarkable in the light of their domination of the admirable *Daily Mail* Under-18 Cup, which they won for the second successive year, beating Warwick (43-10) in the semi-final and RGS Guildford (75-17) at Twickenham in the final. Remarkably, 14 of their side gained representative honours, four (Binns, Ellison, Ashforth and Ions) representing England at 18 Group level.

The season was a tribute to their dedicated and shrewd coach, Geoff Wappett, and his efficient squad system. Perhaps their most commendable victory was against Birkenhead School (18-10), for which only three first-choice players were available. Their final record was P25, W24, L1, points for 1,292, against 203. As one experienced and intelligent school coach put it, 'Bradford simply are the best school side that I have ever seen.' In the *Daily Mail* Under-15 Cup final, *King Edward's, Birmingham,* met *St Benedict's, Ealing,* whom they defeated 11-10 in a vastly more even contest than the Bradford versus Warwick Under-18 match.

The ever-popular Ulster Bank Schools' Cup was won by the hot favourites, Campbell College, their 20th success in the competition. In the final they stormed to victory over Dalriada (46-13), whose defence did not cope with the pace and thrust of the Campbell backs. In fact Dalriada led uneasily at half-time by 13-10, but, inspired by the speed and skill of their captain and full-back, Turtle, Campbell seemed invincible in a masterful second-half display.

Durham, entertaining Sevenoaks late in the season, needed a late penalty to snatch a 16-14 victory, which preserved their second successive unbeaten record. They scored 611 points to 104 conceded. Their wins against Glenalmond (54-0), Edinburgh Academy (43-0) and Ampleforth (33-18) were by record margins, but as pressure mounted towards the term's end, they were relieved to see off St Peter's, York (15-10) and RGS Newcastle (15-8). Their second XV was also unbeaten.

It was *Oakham's* ambition to celebrate the school's centenary with an unbeaten season, and they came creditably close to achieving that aim with 11 wins from 13 matches, stumbling only against Trent and Bedford Modern. These setbacks were offset by good wins against Oundle, Uppingham and Stowe. *Trent College* enjoyed an outstanding season, winning all 13 matches played with a points tally of 398 scored to 83 conceded, although they were relieved to emerge with an 8-5 win against Warwick. More typical were their victories against Nottingham HS (39-11), Denstone (26-0) and Worksop (36-3).

No school experienced a more curious winter than *Monmouth.* They scored 465 points, conceding 183, in winning their first 11 matches, including a 106-0 defeat of Wycliffe; they then lost their final four games but will remember with pride their previous double against Christ College, Brecon (17-12) and Llandovery (23-17). In the latter match the lead changed hands seven times in the second half. Their distinguished and long-serving coach, Rod Sealy, retired at the season's close.

Further south, *Kelly College* again prospered, with a two-year record of 25 wins from 26 matches and victory in the Devon Cup final, in which they beat Kingsbridge 22-5 after accounting for Blundell's in an earlier round. Their one defeat this winter was compensated for by a wonderful showing in the sevens game, the high spot of which was a 22-14 victory in the Millfield Sevens final against the home school.

Bolton School have, in the past, been more famed for soccer than rugby, which makes their excellent record this winter the more admirable. They won all 16 games played and scored over 300 points, conceding only 75. They would probably cite as their most prestigious win the 22-15 victory against Widnes Sixth Form College, but they also defeated Cowley HS and St Anselm's. Yet another school to feel the chill wind of Bradford's power was *King's, Macclesfield.* They carried an unbeaten record over the Pennines and creditably held Bradford to 12-3 at half-time; but as is so often the case the stronger side dominated the second half and King's lost 41-3. They still enjoyed one of their most successful seasons in recent years (P19, W15, D2, L2). Their coach and inspiration, Reg Davenport, is standing down before next season in favour of Paul Halewood.

A mixed bag of form made pre-eminence difficult on the Scottish circuit. *Dollar Academy,* unbeaten last season, had not lost this year until they met Loretto; but they went down 5-3 and then lost to Merchiston Castle and Hutcheson's GS. *Loretto* enjoyed good wins early in the new year against Regent House (18-13) and King's, Tynemouth (41-3), but were disappointed to lose 16-18 to Stewart's-Melville, having led 16-6. Their record was P15, W13, L2.

With 12 wins, a draw and one defeat to report, *Pangbourne* must go back 30 years to find a comparably successful season. They scored 403 points and conceded 97, and their colts side was unbeaten. It is a guide to their style of play that 26 tries were scored by the wings (Tingey 11 and Everett 15), and no victories will have given greater pleasure than those against Dauntsey's (26-3), Marlborough (18-13), Reigate (28-10), Abingdon (13-6) and Stowe (42-0).

After a comfortable 21-7 semi-final victory over Christ College, Brecon, *King's, Canterbury* triumphed in the Shell Rosslyn Park Festival Sevens final, defeating Blundell's by 21-17. *Blundell's* had put out the holders, Wellington College, at the quarter-final stage and accounted for Cheltenham, 19-7, in the semi-finals. Gardner (two) and Orsler scored tries for the winners and Garrett, Coad and Clifford-Jones for Blundell's, but the King's captain, Craddock, converted all three and Stormonth, for Blundell's, only one of three difficult chances.

It was King's, Canterbury's first Rosslyn Park success but, in contrast, *Millfield* won the Open Competition for a record sixth time. They sailed confidently through their run-up to the final, beating Brynteg (26-10), St Cyres (24-0) and Eltham – who had earlier eliminated the holders, Llandovery – (29-5). In the final, they met a young *Strade* side that had beaten Ampleforth (17-12) and Bradford GS (17-10), before a 28-10 semi-final win over RGS Newcastle. In a curiously one-sided final, Millfield ran in six tries, including a hat-trick for their fast wing, Adam Jones. Matt Jones contributed five conversions to their 40-5 victory.

The following players took part in the 18 Group international matches. Countries played against are shown in square brackets.
Abbreviations: *E* – England, *F* – France, *I* – Ireland, *S* – Scotland, *W* – Wales, (R) – Replacement

ENGLAND

Full-backs: R Ashworth (Bradford GS) [*F, I, W*]; A Blyth (Rugby) [*S, W*(R)]
Threequarters: T Morgan (Clifton) [*F, I, S*]; M Denney (Bedford Modern) [*F, I, S, W*]; A Blyth (Rugby) [*F, I*]; T Beim (Cheltenham) [*F, I, S*]; J Ellison (Bradford GS) [*I*(R)], G Truelove (Durham) [*S, W*]; G Anderton (King Edward VII, (Lytham) [*W*]
Half-backs: S Binns (Bradford GS) [*F, I, W*]; R Weston (Durham) [*S, W*(R)]; P Harvey (Durham) [*S, W*]; D Malone (Sharnebrook US) [*F, I*]
Forwards: A Ozdemir (Hurstpierpoint) [*F, I, S, W*]; C Dawson-Walker (Worth) [*F, I*]; P Greening (Chosen Hill) [*S, W*]; D Bell (Colston's) [*F, I, S*]; J Smith (Duchess HS) [*W*]; R Fidler (Cheltenham) [*F, I, S, W*]; D Bailey (Widnes VI FC) [*F, S, W*]; D Cook (Hymers) [*I*]; B Wade (Airedale & Wharfedale College) [*F, I, S*]; J Ions (Bradford GS) [*I, S*]; N Oldham (Eastbourne) [*W*]; M Brookes (Trent) [*F, I, W*]; G Mitchell (Haileybury) [*F, S*]; M Orsler (King's, Canterbury) [*W*]
Ions was captain against Scotland; Denney in the other three matches

IRELAND

Full-back: J Cunningham (Bangor GS) [*E, S, W*]
Threequarters: J Topping (Ballymena Academy) [*E, S, W*]; G Brennan (PB Bray) [*E, S, W*]; R McIlreavy (Wesley College) [*E, S, W*]; D Hickie (St Mary's College) [*E, S, W*]; A Turtle (Campbell College) [*W*(R)]
Half-backs: F Campion (St Mary's College) [*E, S, W*]; C McGuinness (St Mary's College) [*E, S, W*]
Forwards: S Waterworth (Methodist College, Belfast) [*E, S, W*]; C Egan (Terenure College) [*E, S, W*]; B O'Doherty-Campbell (Terenure College) [*E, S, W*]; R Powell (King's Hospital) [*E, S, W*]; J Ryan (Blackrock College) [*E, S, W*]; K Dawson (Bangor GS) [*E, S, W*]; E Miller (Wesley College) [*E, S, W*]; T O'Connell (PBC Cork) [*E, W*]; A Bermingham (St Munchin's College) [*S, W*(R)]
O'Connell was captain against England and Wales; McGuinness against Ireland

SCOTLAND

Full-backs: K Baillie (Hutchesons' GS) [*F, I, W*]; M Doherty (Glenalmond) [*E*]
Threequarters: C Brims (Fettes) [*E, F, I, W*]; A McGregor (Stewart's-Melville) [*E, F, I, W*]; C Murray (Knox Academy) [*E, F, I*]; M Burt (Loretto) [*F*(R), *W*]; D Ablett (Boroughmuir HS) [*E, I*]; C Lawson (Galashiels Academy) [*F, I*(R), *W*]
Half-backs: M Hose (Stranraer Academy) [*E, F, I, W*]; P Simpson (Balwearie HS) [*E, I*]; J Weston (Merchiston Castle) [*F, W*]
Forwards: S Lithgow (Merchiston Castle) [*E, I*]; C Docherty (Marr College) [*E, I*]; G Bulloch (Hutchesons' GS) [*F, W*]; D Grant (Dollar Academy) [*E, F, I, W*]; C Flockhart (Stewart's-Melville) [*F, I*(R), *W*]; G Perrett (Bearsden Academy) [*E, F*(R), *I*]; C Rutherford (Merchiston Castle) [*E, F, I, W*]; T McVie (Edinburgh Academy) [*F, W*]; K Hamilton (Stewart's-Melville) [*E, F, I, W*]; G Dall (George Heriot's) [*E, I*]; D McLeish (Kelso HS) [*E, I, W*]; N Gallagher (Berwickshire HS) [*F, I*(R), *W*]; G Burton (Strathallan) [*I*(R)]; J McIntosh (George Watson's) [*E*(R)), *I*(R)]; B Stewart (Edinburgh Academy) [*F*(R)]
Dall was captain against England and Ireland; Murray against France; Rutherford against Wales

WALES

Full-back: M Evans (Bassaleg CS) [*E, F, I, S*]
Threequarters: C Wilkins (Glan Hafren) [*E, F, I, S*]; R Jones (Millfield) [*E, F, I*]; J Funell (Neath College) [*S*]; G Jones (Neath College) [*E, F, I, S*]; D Drew (Christ College, Brecon) [*E, F, I, S*]; N Walne (Caerleon CS) [*I*(R)]; P Evans (Neath College) [*I*(R)]; S Lonergan (Monmouth) [*I*(R)]
Half-backs: L Davies (Swansea College) [*E, F, I, S*]; D Hawkins (Neath College) [*E, F, I, S*]
Forwards: D Morris (Neath College) [*E, F, I, S*]; J Power (Neath College) [*E, F, I, S*]; B Evans (St Martin's CS) [*E, F, I, S*]; C Quinnell (Llandovery) [*E, F, I*]; Noel Thomas (Maesteg CS) [*E, F, I, S*]; S Ford (Neath College) [*S*]; Nathan Thomas (Llandovery) [*E, F, I, S*]; M Williams (Coed y Lan CS) [*E, F, I, S*]; M Wareham (Maesteg CS) [*E, F, I*]; A Cummings (Coed y Lan CS) [*S*]
Morris was captain against Scotland; Richard Jones in the other three matches

MATCH DETAILS 1992-93 (18 Group)

19 December 1992, Stade Pierre-Antoine, Castres

FRANCE 37 (4G 3PG)   **SCOTLAND 5** (1T)
FRANCE *Tries:* Malie, Viars, Bordesoule, penalty try   *Conversions:* Peclier (4)
Penalty Goals: Peclier (3)
SCOTLAND *Try:* Burt
Referee M Etxebeste (Spain)

4 January 1993, Goldenacre, Edinburgh

SCOTLAND 3 (1PG)   **WALES 5** (1T)
SCOTLAND *Penalty Goal:* Hose
WALES *Try:* Drew
Referee D Gillet (France)

24 February 1993, Pembroke

WALES 8 (1PG 1T)   **ENGLAND 7** (1G)
WALES *Try:* Hawkins   *Penalty Goal:* Davies
ENGLAND *Try:* Blyth   *Conversion:* Weston
Referee R S Clarke (Scotland)

13 March 1993, Stade d'Aubenas

FRANCE 26 (1G 3PG 2T)   **WALES 16** (1G 2PG 1DG)
FRANCE *Tries:* Bergez, Macurdy, Nadau   *Conversion:* Jechoux
Penalty Goals: Jechoux (3)
WALES *Try:* Drew   *Conversion:* Davies   *Penalty Goals:* Davies (2)
Dropped Goal: Davies
Referee J L Bacugalupo (Scotland)

3 April 1993, Castlecroft, Wolverhampton

ENGLAND 3 (1PG)   **SCOTLAND 10** (1G 1PG)
ENGLAND *Penalty Goal:* Weston
SCOTLAND *Try:* Murray   *Conversion:* Doherty   *Penalty Goal:* Hose
Referee G Crothers (Ireland)

6 April 1993, Ebbw Vale

WALES 0   IRELAND 8 (1PG 1T)
IRELAND *Try:* Bermingham   *Penalty Goal:* Campion
Referee C Rees (England)

7 April 1993, Camborne

ENGLAND 9 (3PG)   **FRANCE 22** (2G 1DG 1T)
ENGLAND *Penalty Goals:* Ashforth (3)
Referee C Thomas (Wales)

10 April 1993, Balgray, Glasgow

SCOTLAND 9 (3PG)   **IRELAND 21** (1G 3PG 1T)
SCOTLAND *Penalty Goals:* Hose (3)
IRELAND *Tries:* Cunningham, Hickie   *Conversion:* Campion
Penalty Goals: Campion (3)
Referee S W Piercy (England)

14 April 1993, Ravenhill, Belfast

IRELAND 13 (1PG 2T)   **ENGLAND 8** (1PG 1T)
IRELAND *Tries:* Topping, Hickie   *Penalty Goal:* Campion
ENGLAND *Try:* Morgan   *Penalty Goal:* Ashforth
Referee E Murray (Scotland)

GIANT FRENCHMEN MAINTAIN DOMINANCE

COLTS AND YOUTH RUGBY 1992-93
Michael Stevenson

England Colts have beaten French Juniors only once, and a second victory this spring at Nice would have given them a Grand Slam and a wonderful climax to a season of considerable success and steady improvement. But it was not to be, and France, possessors of a giant pack, proved far too fast and strong, racing away with the game to win by 52-13. England were 21 points down after 17 minutes and, despite tries from their promising wing, Naylor, and No 8 Vander, plus a penalty by full-back Ufton, they were seldom on terms with their formidable opponents, who scored two second-half tries from interceptions and finished in total control.

The match was a personal triumph for Dourthe, the French full-back, whose father, Claude, played for France in the 60s and 70s. He contributed 22 points, comprising a try, three penalties and four conversions.

England's first international match resulted in a 23-13 victory over Italy Juniors, having trailed by ten points at half-time, and a spirited win against Welsh Youth (17-16) and Scotland Under-19s (28-3) followed.

Welsh Youth opened their representative season with two matches for which caps were not awarded, losing to Welsh Schools (17-6) and the Lupi Provincial XV in Rome (20-15) during a short tour of Italy. From Rome they flew to Milan, where there was opportunity for training, coaching and reappraisal, which bore fruit in the form of an excellent 33-6 win against Italy Youth. Only the captain, Williams, and Prendiville had already won Youth caps, so 16 players, including three replacements, gained their first caps.

Their next match was against French Juniors at St Helen's, Swansea, where the visitors were extended in their 21-17 victory, followed by the single-point defeat by England at Bath (17-16). Their record was P5 W1 L4, points for 91, against 87.

The Divisional Championship at Castlecroft in January was won for the third time in succession by London, who defeated the North by 21-14. They had beaten the South-West (35-15) and the North had defeated the Midlands (37-9) in the preliminary matches.

A 45-strong squad was selected after the Divisional matches but was reduced to 27 following the final trial. It included nine of the England 18 Group side that had won the Grand Slam in the previous season: Gomarsall, Ufton, Shepherd, Allen, Tempest, Perkins, Archer, Leach and Yates. The next stage in preparation for the coming international campaign was the two matches between 'England' and the joint divisions. They augured well for the coming season: London and the South-West were demolished 73-8 at Bath, the wings, Naylor and Dontoh, both contributing hat-tricks of tries from the 13 scored. Ufton kicked four conversions. After this match, Dale, the Sudbury lock who had impressed in adversity for the losers, was added to the England squad.

Injuries to Leach and Archer disrupted the 'England' team for the next match, against the North & Midlands, but it was won comfortably enough (27-3); Port and Burrows, both from Cumbria, and Cudleigh of the North Midlands were added to the squad, which was reduced again to 21 for the opening match against Loughborough University Freshers. Loughborough Freshers, strong and talented this year, won narrowly. There was plenty of promise apparent in England's showing, and they lost by a single point (13-12).

The Colts' County Championship threw up thoroughly worthy but perhaps surprising winners in Somerset, after Yorkshire's form had clearly suggested that they were the strongest side. Somerset's success was squarely based on their pack, with the props, McCarthy of Bath and Tempest of Bristol, most impressive. They beat Durham (12-7) before registering a runaway win over Surrey (43-21) to earn a place in the final at Twickenham.

Yorkshire had seen off East Midlands 27-3, their fast wing, Roclawski of West Park, Bramhope, contributing his second successive hat-trick of tries to add to the four successive hat-tricks by his fellow wing, Scales of Otley. Kent had reached the semi-final stage through a 10-5 win over North Midlands at Blackheath, but they were no match for Yorkshire, who sailed through their semi-final to win by 30-16.

The key to the final was the excellence of Somerset's tackling, which managed to repel Yorkshire's initial onslaught. The first points came from a penalty by Somerset's excellent full-back, Kennard. After he kicked another, a try by Breden who, remarkably, scored a try in every match, stretched Somerset's lead. Yorkshire struck back with a try by Brotherton, which Hale converted, but a dropped goal from Pritchard prevented any chance of a Yorkshire resurgence, and Somerset won deservedly by 14-7.

Newfoundland Colts, who toured England before Christmas, chose a very demanding itinerary of six games in eight days. At home, however, they can play as many as eight matches in four days during the Canadian Championships, and the tour schedule did not present any problems. They experienced mixed fortunes, losing narrowly to London Irish Colts in their first match (15-11), and decisively to Epsom College (53-13), when they included a number of their less experienced players. These setbacks made a convincing 35-16 victory over Thurrock Colts all the more satisfying.

When Northampton Colts received their team of the month award from *Rugby World & Post* in May, they had lost only one match, to Orrell, and had 24 wins from 25 matches to report, with a points tally of 967 scored to 133 conceded. They have an immensely demanding fixture list, which makes their wonderful record the more impressive. They registered doubles against both Coventry and Leicester and trounced Wasps Colts 54-17. Price reached the final England trial and Vollands, Wilson, Seeley and Thompson all represented the Midlands.

North of the Border, Kelso Harlequins enjoyed a superb season and close to their Digital Cup final against Stirling County they were still unbeaten.

Cheltenham's wonderful run of 14 consecutive wins ended when they met Stourbridge and lost 22-17, but it was still their most successful season ever. Cardiff Colts slipped up early in the season, losing to Leicester (27-13) and Llandaff North (16-0), but then embarked on an unbeaten run of 16 matches. Bishop's Stortford Colts stumbled just once, losing to Fullerians 12-6 in the semi-final of the Hertfordshire Cup. They won 15 of the 16 games played with a points tally of 491 scored to 96 conceded. Predictably, they did well at representative level and five of their side played for Hertfordshire. Outstanding for Bishop's Stortford was their Australian No 8, Harnett.

The following players took part in the Colts/Youth international matches. Countries played against are shown in square brackets.
Abbreviations: *E* – England, *F* – France, *I* – Ireland, *It* – Italy, *S* – Scotland, *Sp* – Spain, *W* – Wales, (R) – Replacement

ENGLAND
Full-backs: J Ufton (Old Whitgiftians) [*F, It, S, W*]; B Kennard (Bath) [*F*(R)]
Threequarters: J Naylor (Old Crossleyans) [*F, It, S, W*]; A Peacock (Orrell) [*F, It, S, W*]; J Shepherd (Morley) [*F, It, S, W*]; N Dontoh (Richmond) [*F, It, S, W*]; M Allen (Loughborough Students) [*It*(R)]
Half-backs: T Knowles (Durham City) [*F, It, S, W*]; A Gomarsall (Wasps) [*F, It, S, W*]; M Chudleigh (Mosley) [*F*(R)]
Forwards: S Sparks (Blyth) [*F, It, S, W*]; S Perkin (St Ives) [*F, It, S, W*]; N McCarthy (Bath) [*F, It, S, W*]; N Tempest (Bristol) [*W,* (R)]; S Kneale (Morley & West Hartlepool) [*F*(R)]; E Raine (Leicester) [*F, It, S, W*]; G Archer (Durham City) [*F, S, W*]; A Bailey (Saracens) [*It*]; M Bowman (Wigton) [*F*(R), *S, W*]; K Yates (Otley) [*F, It, S, W*]; A Vander (Haywards Heath) [*F, It, S, W*]; R Port (Cardiff)[*It*]; R Leach (Durham University) [*F*]
Gomarsall was captain in all four matches

IRELAND
Under-18 (*against Scotland Under-18*)
Full-back: B Roche (Highfield)
Threequarters: D Batch (Carrickfergus), R Larkin (Curragh), G Foley (Sligo), B Everett (Nenagh-Ormond)
Half-backs: C Burke (Clonmel), T Tierney (Richmond)
Forwards: R Thomas (Cork Constitution), R McGarrigle (Limavady), L Johnston (Dromore), E Gannon (Ballina), L Moore (Limavady), E McEntee (Naas), A Quinlan (Clanwilliam), I Dillon (Young Munster)
Quinlan was captain

SCOTLAND
Under-18
Full-back: G Tosh (Dundee HSFP) [*I, Sp*]
Threequarters: C MacRobert (Stirling County) [*I, Sp*]; M Plumb (Currie) [*I, Sp*]; R Laing (Kelso Harlequins) [*I, Sp*]; C Wilson (Aberdeen GSFP) [*I, Sp*]

Half-backs: C Richards (Jed Thistle) [*I, Sp*]; D Paterson (Gala Wanderers) [*I, Sp*]
Forwards: M McCluskie (Musselburgh) [*I*]; J Smith (Aberdeen GSFP) [*Sp*]; P Cranston (Hawick PSA) [*I, Sp*]; E Johnston (Gala Wanderers) [*I, Sp*]; S Murray (Preston Lodge FP) [*I, Sp*]; C Roemmele (Aberdeen GSFP) [*I, Sp*]; F Wilson (Aberdeen U) [*I, Sp*]; G Blaikie (Penicuik) [*Sp*]; P Littlefield (Edinburgh U) [*I*]; G Brown (Gala Wanderers) [*Sp*]; S Laurie (Selkirk YC) [*I*]; C Hunter (Livingston) [*Sp*(R)]
Plumb was captain in both matches

Under-19
Full-backs: I Leighton (Melrose) [*E, W*]; C A Murray (Haddington) [*W*(R)]
Threequarters: H Gilmour (Heriot's) [*E, W*]; R Brown (Melrose) [*E*]; P Flockhart (Stewart's-Melville) [*E, W*]; C Dalgleish (Gala) [*E, W*]; D Hodge (Durham U) [*W*]
Half-backs: D Lee (Watsonians) [*E*]; B Easson (Dundee HSFP) [*W*]; M Dungait (Morpeth) [*E, W*]
Forwards: A Binnie (Heriot's) [*E*]; M McCluskie (Musselburgh) [*W*]; D Cunningham (Haddington) [*E, W*]; L Graham (Boroughmuir) [*E, W*]; I Elliot (Hawick) [*E, W*]; P Jennings (Boroughmuir) [*E, W*]; J Whittaker (Nottingham) [*E, W*]; J Healy (Hutcheson's/Aloysians) [*E, W*]; S Logan (Livingston) [*E*]; D Thompson (Hutcheson's/Aloysians) [*W*]; D Clark (Royal High) [*W*(R)]
Flockhart was captain in both matches

WALES
Welsh Youth
Full-backs: S Jones (Llangennech) [*F, It*]; D Heath (Camarthen Athletic) [*E*]
Threequarters: N John (Cardiff) [*E, F, It*]; S Prendiville (Llangennech) [*F, It*]; S Webley (Blackwood) [*E, F, It*]; L Morgan (Maesteg) [*E, F, It*]; A Howells (Maesteg) [*It*(R)]; G Thomas (Pencoed) [*E, F*(R)]
Half-backs: L Griffiths (Pencoed) [*E, F, It*]; J Hewlett (Cardiff) [*E, F, It*]
Forwards: S Ohlsson (Pontarddulais) [*E, F, It*]; B Williams (Llanelli) [*E, F, It*]; A Griffiths (Llandybie) [*E, F, It*]; S Mellalieu (Dunvant) [*E, F, It*]; S Martin (Neath Colts) [*E, F, It*]; M Popple (Rumney/Cardiff Harlequins) [*It*]; G John (Treorchy) [*E, F, It*]; C Morgan (Swansea) [*F, It*]; A Moore (Wrexham) [*E, F, It*(R)]; R Morris (Neath Colts) [*E, It*(R)]
Williams was captain in all three matches

Under-19 (*against Scotland Under-19*)
Full-back: J Thomas (Llanelli)
Threequarters: O Thomas (Cardiff), S Webley (Blackwood), Stephen John (Cardiff), C Moir (Llanelli)
Half-backs: J Strange (Ebbw Vale), J Hewlett (Cardiff)
Forwards: C Loader (Swansea), B Williams (Llanelli), Spencer John (Llanelli), S Mellalieu (Dunvant), S Martin (Neath Colts), C Mills (Cardiff), M Williams (Pontypridd), A Moore (Wrexham)
Hewlett was captain

MATCH DETAILS 1992-93

27 February 1993, Parabiago, Milan

ITALY YOUTH 6 (2PG)   **WELSH YOUTH 33** (2G 2PG 1DG 2T)
ITALY *Penalty Goals:* Ziliotti (2)
WALES *Tries:* Jones, Webley, Hewlett, L Griffiths   *Conversions:* L Griffiths (2)
Penalty Goals: L Griffiths (2)   *Dropped Goal:* L Griffiths
Referee H Rohr (Germany)

13 March 1993, United Services Ground, Portsmouth

ENGLAND COLTS 23 (1G 2PG 2T)   **ITALY YOUTH 13** (1G 2PG)
ENGLAND *Tries:* Naylor (2), Shepherd   *Conversion:* Ufton   *Penalty Goals:* Ufton (2)
ITALY *Try:* Mazzariol   *Conversion:* Pilat   *Penalty Goals:* Pilat (2)
Referee W W Calder (Scotland)

13 March 1993, Swansea

WELSH YOUTH 21 (1G 3PG 1T)   **FRANCE JUNIORS 27** (2G 1PG 2T)
WALES *Tries:* Morgan (2)   *Conversion:* L Griffiths   *Penalty Goals:* L Griffiths (3)
FRANCE *Tries:* Paillat (2), Sudre, Bracou   *Conversions:* Brieule (2)   *Penalty Goal:* Brieule
Referee S Lander (England)

27 March 1993, Bath

ENGLAND COLTS 17 (2G 1PG)   **WELSH YOUTH 16** (1PG 1DG 2T)
ENGLAND *Tries:* Naylor, Shepherd   *Conversions:* Ufton (2)   *Penalty Goal:* Gomarsall
WALES *Tries:* John, Ohlsson   *Penalty Goal:* L Griffiths   *Dropped Goal:* L Griffiths
Referee D Mene (France)

3 April 1993, Madrid

SPAIN 32   **SCOTLAND UNDER-18 28** (2G 3PG 1T)
SCOTLAND *Tries:* MacRobert (2), Tosh   *Conversions:* Tosh (2)   *Penalty Goals:* Tosh (3)

10 April 1993, Millbrae

SCOTLAND UNDER-19 3 (1DG)   **ENGLAND COLTS 28** (1G 1PG 1DG 3T)
SCOTLAND *Dropped Goal:* Lee
ENGLAND *Tries:* Dontoh, Knowles, Yates (2)   *Conversion:* Ufton   *Penalty Goal:* Ufton
Dropped Goal: Ufton
Referee R Duhau (France)

10 April 1993, Millbrae

SCOTLAND UNDER-18 20 (2G 2PG)   **IRELAND UNDER-18 14** (2G)
SCOTLAND *Tries:* MacRobert (2)   *Conversions:* Tosh (2)   *Penalty Goals:* Tosh (2)
IRELAND *Tries:* Roche, penalty try   *Conversions:* Roche (2)
Referee D Haladjian (France)

23 April 1993, National Stadium, Cardiff

WALES UNDER-19 20 (1G 1PG 2T)   **SCOTLAND UNDER-19 3** (1PG)
WALES *Tries:* Hewlett, S John, Strange   *Conversion:* Strange   *Penalty Goal:* Strange
SCOTLAND *Penalty Goal:* Easson
Referee A Spreadbury (England)

24 April 1993, Nice

FRANCE JUNIORS 52 (4G 3PG 3T)   **ENGLAND COLTS 13** (1PG 2T)
FRANCE *Tries:* Falda (2), Pascal, Paillat, Bonnet, Betsen, Dourthe
Conversions: Dourthe (4)   *Penalty Goals:* Dourthe (3)
ENGLAND *Tries:* Naylor, Vander   *Penalty Goal:* Ufton
Referee C Giacomelli (Italy)

TRANSITIONAL SCOTLAND TREAD THE MIDDLE OF THE ROAD

THE 1992-93 SEASON IN SCOTLAND
Bill McMurtrie *Glasgow Herald*

Scotland won their two home matches in the Five Nations' Championship and lost their two away games. Unembellished by detail, it would seem a middle-of-the-road season, but the final result was more than widely expected, and less than deserved. It was a season of change, with a new captain and four new caps chosen for the opening international as well as other recasting. Scotland, unlike the other Championship contestants, did not have the benefit of an early-season international. The modernisation of Murrayfield meant that only the internationals against Ireland and Wales could be fitted into the scheme.

Gavin Hastings took over as captain from David Sole, who had retired from rugby after the 1992 tour in Australia. The appointment was made for the season, and announced a month before the January game against Ireland – the first time Scotland's selectors had shown such confidence in one man to name him as captain for the duration – but Hastings had to take over a much-changed team. Only Tony Stanger, Scott Hastings, Chalmers, Doddie Weir and Damian Cronin remained from the second Test against the Wallabies. Derek Stark, Iain Morrison, Andy Reed and Alan Sharp were named as new caps. True, Paul Burnell and Gary Armstrong, who had missed the Australian tour, were back. So was Gavin Hastings himself, who had pulled out of the team the night before the second Test. Alan Watt, the Glasgow High/Kelvinside forward who had been capped at tight head in the 1991 World Cup match against Zimbabwe, was restored as left lock against Ireland.

On the day the Scottish forwards proved themselves. The line-out game was especially heartening. Cronin found a new lease of life, Reed had a notable debut and Weir's move to No 8 was a bonus. Not for many a year had Scotland had such line-out security. They won 15-3, Stark scoring a debut try and Stanger his 15th international try.

Not unnaturally, the team was unchanged for the Paris international, but fate conspired again to upset the front-row plans. Watt fell ill, and Peter Wright, the Boroughmuir prop who had been capped as tight head in Australia, was recalled, though out of position on the left. So well did he adjust, uninhibited by any opponent, that he was chosen for the Lions' tour to New Zealand, as were his four colleagues among Scotland's tight forwards. Morrison, Scotland's new openside wing forward, had an equally productive campaign, though without recognition by the Lions' selectors.

Scotland's losing run in Paris continued with an 11-3 defeat – they have not won there since 1969, before France moved base from Colombes to Parc des Princes – but they returned to their winning ways back home with victory against Wales at Murrayfield. A Derek Turnbull try was all that Scotland could add to five penalty goals by Gavin Hastings, but the memory had to stretch into the dim past to recall when Scotland's forwards had last been so dominant in an international match.

And so to Twickenham. As so often in the past, however, the Scots stumbled at that final hurdle. The bubble was burst when Craig Chalmers broke an arm midway through the first half immediately after he had put his side 6-3 up with a dropped goal. It was, instead, Stuart Barnes' day, as England won 26-9. Scotland have won only five of their 36 Twickenham internationals, and only once in nine attempts have they taken the Triple Crown there.

As preparation for the Championship, Scotland played three A internationals – against Spain in Madrid, Italy at Melrose, and Ireland A at Lansdowne Road – and won them all. The Italians, though, proved they deserved a full international in the future (the Scots won by only 22-17). Captained by Andy Nicol from scrum-half, Scotland A had to pull back from a 0-13 deficit early in the second half to beat the Irish by 22-13. In their other A international, after their Championship season was over, the Scots lost 19-29 to the French in Aberdeen.

Also on the international field, Scotland undertook their most extensive Under-21 programme to date with matches against Italy, Ireland, France and Wales. The Scots lost them all, including a severe drubbing by France by 67-9 in Dijon. A wing from Montferrand, Fabien Bertranck, scored two of the nine French tries in that match, and he repeated the dose in the A international a month later in Aberdeen.

In domestic rugby Borderers reigned almost supreme. The South took the McEwan's Inter-District title as well as its Under-18 equivalent, and Melrose retained the National League Championship for the third year in four. Edinburgh broke the mould with a clean sweep in the Under-21 district series.

Gala proved to be dominant club in the Border sevens, winning their own tournament as well as those at Selkirk, Jedforest and Langholm. On the way to their Selkirk success Gala eliminated the first draft of England's seven preparing for what was to turn out to be victory in the Rugby World Cup Sevens at Murrayfield. In the final of their own tournament Gala beat Edinburgh Borderers (a draft version of Scotland's seven). A week later Scotland's seven, stronger this time and wearing the Co-optimists' colours, won the prestigious Melrose tournament.

DOMINATION OF TELFER'S NURSERYMEN

McEWAN'S NATIONAL LEAGUE REVIEW

Melrose, otherwise known as Jim Telfer's rugby nursery, retained the McEwan's National League title for the third time in four years, and they did it with plenty to spare, five points clear of Edinburgh Academ-

The Scotland team which played England at Twickenham. L-R, back row: S R Hilditch (touch-judge), B W Stirling (referee), D B Millard (replacement), D J Turnbull, I R Morrison, D F Cronin, A I Reed, G W Weir, A G Stanger, P H Wright, K S Milne, A P Burnell, C D Hogg (replacement), O E Doyle (touch-judge); front row: G R Isaac (replacement), G P J Townsend (replacement), C M Chalmers, A G Shiel, G Armstrong, A G Hastings (capt), S Hastings, D A Stark, K M Logan (replacement), I Corcoran (replacement).

icals and Gala. Adding to their kudos, Melrose also won the Bank of Scotland Border League championship for the fourth successive year. It has been a notable era in the club's 116-year history.

Telfer, the coach who had a hand in Scotland's 1984 and 1990 Grand Slams, has guided Melrose to the titles without a core of hard-bitten warriors. He has a highly successful young team with an average age of about 22. Even so, Melrose are well blessed with experience in their ranks. Craig Chalmers, Graham Shiel, Doddie Weir and Carl Hogg, none older than 24, are all international players.

Only Stirling County beat Melrose in the course of the National League programme. The 13-9 defeat at Bridgehaugh early in the season gave the champions' challengers a scent for the chase. That result left Gala and Jedforest as joint leaders. A week later, however, Jed were out on their own as Edinburgh Academicals beat Gala 33-20 at Raeburn Place. Seven days after that Jed, too, were back down in the pack, beaten 27-10 by Boroughmuir at Meggetland.

Melrose continued unhindered after the Stirling defeat. The following week the champions saw off Hawick by 20-14. Victories followed against Kelso by 50-13 at Poynder Park and Dundee HSFP by 46-6 at the Greenyards. Hogg, the back-row forward capped in Scotland's two Tests against Australia in 1992, scored three tries against Kelso and followed up with one against Dundee. Thereafter Melrose were untroubled apart from a narrow 19-16 win against Jed at Riverside Park, a match in which Chalmers had two crucial dropped goals, and in their next game, unexpectedly early, Melrose retained the titled by beating Currie 16-7 at the Greenyards. The champions were helped that day when their two remaining rivals slipped: Gala lost 13-16 at Dundee, a result that could not save the Tayside club from the drop, and Edinburgh Academicals drew with relegation-threatened Selkirk.

Parker, the former Hearts footballer now enjoying a new lease of life as wing and occasional scrum-half for Melrose, scored 118 of the champions' 326 League points, including four tries, a figure matched by three forwards, Robbie Brown, Hogg and Weir.

Gala hung in with Melrose until the new year. Even after Gala's 9-9 draw at Hawick it seemed that the League season would have the ideal ending, with the top two meeting at Netherdale in a head-to-head championship decider, but Dundee had other ideas. Edinburgh Academicals lost to Melrose 0-14 at the Greenyards on the second League Saturday, and the city club stumbled unexpectedly in November, beaten 26-16 by Kelso at Poynder Park. Jed, one-time outright leaders, lost six of their next seven League matches, although they stopped the rot with a 50-5 Myreside victory over Watsonians (without both Hastings brothers).

Glasgow High/Kelvinside and Dundee dropped down after a relegation contest that went to the last day. Stirling had to beat Boroughmuir at Bridgehaugh to survive – and they did – but GHK let a 13-0 lead slide to a 30-18 defeat by Currie at Malleny Park. GHK were an enigma. Their League programme included wins against Dundee by 41-0, Heriot's by 56-13, and Hawick by 39-0, the heaviest defeat suffered by Hawick in 20 years of League rugby. The Glasgow club, however, won just one other match.

Musselburgh led all the way in the Second Division until the final day, but they then lost out on points difference in a three-way tie because of a defeat by Stewart's-Melville FP in Inverleith. Stewart's-Melville went up as runners-up to West of Scotland. Only Stewartry and Duns went through their League programmes with maximum points, each earning promotion for the second successive year. Stewartry won the Fourth Division and Duns the Sixth, and the latter set a record for the championship's 20 seasons by running up 585 points.

Ross High also broke a League record. Needing a huge win to have any hope of promotion, the Tranent club beat Strathmore 127-3 and went up to the Sixth Division as runners-up to Allan Glen's, Holy Cross missing out in a three-way tie.

McEWAN'S NATIONAL LEAGUE 1992-93

Division 1	P	W	D	L	F	A	Pts
Melrose	13	12	0	1	326	134	24
Edinburgh Acs	13	9	1	3	265	155	19
Gala	13	9	1	3	275	171	19
Currie	13	8	0	5	218	242	16
Jedforest	13	7	0	6	206	185	14
Boroughmuir	11	6	0	5	208	162	12
Hawick	12	5	1	6	197	199	11
Heriot's FP	13	5	0	8	295	285	10
Stirling County	13	5	0	8	179	208	10
Watsonians	13	5	0	8	196	277	10
Kelso	13	5	0	8	211	245	10
Selkirk	13	4	1	8	194	316	9
Glasgow H/K	13	4	0	9	291	255	8
Dundee HSFP	12	3	0	9	142	269	6

Previous champions: Hawick 10 times, 1973-74 to 1977-78, 1981-82, 1983-84 to 1986-87; Gala 3 times, 1979-80, 1980-81, 1982-83; Kelso twice, 1987-88, 1988-89; Melrose twice, 1989-90, 1991-92; Heriot's FP 1979-80; Boroughmuir 1990-91.

Division 2	P	W	D	L	F	A	Pts
W of Scotland	13	11	0	2	377	156	22
Stewart's-Mel	13	11	0	2	354	156	22
Musselburgh	13	11	0	2	283	124	22
Glasgow Acs	13	8	1	4	331	208	17
Clarkston	13	7	1	5	267	173	15
Ayr	13	7	0	6	165	210	14
Peebles	13	6	1	6	150	178	13
Preston Lodge	13	5	2	6	204	205	12
Kirkcaldy	13	5	1	7	233	234	11
Grangemouth	13	4	0	9	189	261	8
Edinburgh W	13	4	0	9	176	253	8
Wigtownshire	13	3	2	8	160	294	8
Dunfermline	13	2	2	9	141	322	6
Kilmarnock	13	2	0	11	120	376	4

Division 3	P	W	D	L	F	A	Pts
Haddington	13	10	0	3	346	94	20
Biggar	13	10	0	3	307	123	20
Hutchesons'/Al	13	10	0	3	257	146	20
Hillhead/J	13	7	0	6	199	194	14
Howe of Fife	13	6	2	5	190	188	14
Langholm	13	7	0	6	144	190	14
Portobello FP	13	6	0	7	221	177	12
Dumfries	13	6	0	7	242	241	12
Royal High	13	5	1	7	171	226	11
Corstorphine	13	5	1	7	173	232	11
Perthshire	13	5	0	8	186	186	10
Gordonians	13	5	0	8	220	242	10
Morgan FP	13	5	0	8	169	231	10
St Boswells	13	2	0	11	125	480	4

Division 4	P	W	D	L	F	A	Pts
Stewartry	13	13	0	0	295	96	26
East Kilbride	13	12	0	1	309	125	24
Dalziel HSFP	13	9	0	4	182	143	18
Trinity Acs	13	8	0	4	258	144	16
Aberdeen GSFP	12	7	0	5	331	165	14
Leith Acs	13	7	0	6	218	276	14
Cartha QP	13	5	0	8	132	163	10
Highland	12	5	0	7	145	179	10

	P	W	D	L	F	A	Pts
Edinburgh U	13	5	0	8	174	211	10
Cambuslang	12	5	0	7	151	234	10
Alloa	13	4	0	9	185	220	8
Livingston	13	4	0	9	142	222	8
Linlithgow	13	4	0	9	132	222	8
Lismore	13	1	0	12	141	395	2

Division 5

	P	W	D	L	F	A	Pts
Ardrossan Acs	12	11	0	1	255	97	22
North Berwick	13	10	0	3	277	125	20
Clydebank	13	8	0	5	240	174	16
Falkirk	12	8	0	4	176	126	16
Irvine	13	7	1	5	214	115	15
Glenrothes	13	6	2	5	182	158	14
Hillfoots	13	6	0	7	164	169	12
Aberdeenshire	12	6	0	6	189	199	12
Penicuik	12	5	0	7	155	193	10
Madras FP	13	5	0	8	152	224	10
Paisley	13	5	0	8	174	255	10
Lenzie	13	4	1	8	182	218	9
Waysiders	13	3	2	8	151	200	8
Moray	13	2	0	11	138	396	4

Division 6

	P	W	D	L	F	A	Pts
Duns	13	13	0	0	585	111	26
Berwick	13	10	0	3	312	96	20
Marr	13	8	0	5	245	107	16
Harris FP	13	8	0	5	207	158	16
Forrester FP	13	7	0	6	218	217	14
Greenock W	13	6	0	7	167	197	12

	P	W	D	L	F	A	Pts
Lasswade	13	6	0	7	170	186	12
Earlston	12	6	0	6	177	237	12
Dunbar	13	6	0	7	126	263	12
Murrayfield	13	6	0	7	151	309	12
St Andrews U	13	5	0	8	216	236	10
Cumbernauld	12	5	0	7	126	219	10
Broughton FP	13	3	0	10	112	286	6
Drumpellier*	13	1	0	12	116	406	2

Drumpellier and Waysiders to amalgamate for 1993-94.

Division 7

	P	W	D	L	F	A	Pts
Allan Glen's	13	11	0	2	420	92	22
Ross High	13	11	0	2	392	113	22
Holy Cross	13	10	2	1	301	97	22
Whitecraigs	13	10	0	3	214	157	20
Waid FP	13	8	0	5	260	176	16
RAF Kinloss	12	7	0	5	212	144	14
Montrose	13	6	1	6	178	181	13
Hyndland FP	13	6	1	6	160	182	13
Panmure	12	4	2	6	183	185	10
Garnock	13	4	0	9	118	198	8
Stirling U	13	4	0	9	109	277	8
Walkerburn	13	4	0	9	118	373	8
Carnoustie FP	13	1	0	12	125	274	2
Strathmore	13	1	0	12	73	414	2

District League Champions (*promoted to Division 7*):
Glasgow: Annan
Edinburgh: Dalkeith
North & Midlands: Aberdeen U

BANK OF SCOTLAND BORDER LEAGUE

	P	W	D	L	F	A	Pts
Melrose	10	10	0	0	313	105	20
Gala	11	8	1	2	294	122	17
Hawick	11	6	1	4	234	131	13
Jedforest	9	6	0	3	194	101	12
Selkirk	12	4	0	8	181	309	8
Kelso	11	2	0	9	147	274	4
Langholm	10	0	0	10	55	376	0

McEWAN'S DISTRICT CHAMPIONSHIP

	P	W	D	L	F	A	Pts
South	4	3	0	1	60	33	6
Edinburgh	4	2	1	1	93	69	5
North & Midlands	4	2	0	2	60	101	4
Glasgow	4	1	1	2	44	59	3
Exiles	4	1	0	3	57	52	2

McEWAN'S DISTRICT CHAMPIONSHIP 1992-93

21 November, Goldenacre
Edinburgh 13 (1G 2PG)   **Glasgow 13** (1G 1PG 1DG)

Edinburgh: A G Hastings (Watsonians) (*capt*); A Moore (Edinburgh Acads), J Kerr (Haddington), D S Wyllie (Stewart's-Melville FP), D Macrae (Boroughmuir); A Donaldson (Currie), D W Patterson (Edinburgh Acads); G D Wilson (Boroughmuir), K S Milne (Heriot's FP), D J Wilson (Edinburgh Acads), S A Aitken (Watsonians), M J McVie (Edinburgh Acads), B W Ward (Currie), J Robertson (Heriot's FP), S J Reid (Boroughmuir)
Scorers *Try:* Patterson   *Conversion:* Donaldson   *Penalty Goals:* Hastings, Donaldson
Glasgow: D N Barrett (West of Scotland); R A G Porter (Edinburgh Acads), C T Simmers (Edinburgh Acads),

I C Jardine (Stirling County), K M Logan (Stirling County); G M Breckenridge (Glasgow High/Kelvinside), F H Stott (West of Scotland); A G J Watt (Glasgow High/Kelvinside), K D McKenzie (Stirling County), G B Robertson (Stirling County), E J Murphy (Glasgow High/Kelvinside), D S Munro (Glasgow High/Kelvinside), F D Wallace (Glasgow High/Kelvinside) (*capt*), G T Mackay (Glasgow Acads), J Brough (Stirling County) *Replacement* D R McKee (West of Scotland) for Simmers
Scorers *Try:* Logan *Conversion:* Barrett *Penalty Goal:* Breckenridge *Dropped Goal:* Breckenridge
Referee I C Henderson (Kelso)

21 November, Mayfield, Dundee
North & Midlands 3 (1PG) **South 26** (3G 1T)

North & Midlands: S A D Burns (Edinburgh Acads) (*capt*); D J McLaughlin (Alloa), P R Rouse (Dundee HSFP), J W Thomson (Kirkcaldy), J F Swanson (Edinburgh Acads); B R Easson (Dundee HSFP), A E Milne (Boroughmuir); J J Manson (Dundee HSFP), M W Scott (Edinburgh Acads), D Herrington (Dundee HSFP) S J Campbell (Dundee HSFP), B M Bell (Highland), D J McIvor (Edinburgh Acads), D H Mitchell (Dunfermline), J G Mathieson (Morgan Academy FP) *Replacements* D R Milne (Dundee HSFP) for McIvor; J Kerr (Gordonians) for A E Milne
Scorer *Penalty Goal:* Easson
South: G J Aitchison (Kelso); A G Stanger (Hawick), S A Nichol (Selkirk), A G Shiel (Melrose), M Moncrieff (Gala); C M Chalmers (Melrose) (*capt*), G Armstrong (Jedforest); G R Isaac (Gala), J A Hay (Hawick), S W Ferguson (Peebles), R R Brown (Melrose), G W Weir (Melrose), D J Turnbull (Hawick), J P Amos (Gala), R M Kirkpatrick (Jedforest) *Replacement* S McGauchie (Selkirk) for Stanger
Scorers *Tries:* Armstrong, Chalmers, Ferguson, Weir *Conversions:* Chalmers (3)
Referee J L Bacigalupo (Edinburgh Wanderers)

28 November, Hughenden
Glasgow 9 (3PG) **South 7** (1G)

Glasgow: D N Barrett (West of Scotland); R A G Porter (Edinburgh Acads), C T Simmers (Edinburgh Acads), I C Jardine (Stirling County), K M Logan (Stirling County); G M Breckenridge (Glasgow High/Kelvinside), F H Stott (West of Scotland); A G J Watt (Glasgow High/Kelvinside), K D McKenzie (Stirling County), G B Robertson (Stirling County), E J Murphy (Glasgow High/Kelvinside), D S Munro (Glasgow High/Kelvinside), G T Mackay (Glasgow Acads), B Ireland (Stirling County), F D Wallace (Glasgow High/Kelvinside) (*capt*)
Scorer *Penalty Goals:* Barrett (3)
South: A C Redpath (Melrose); A G Stanger (Hawick), S A Nichol (Selkirk), A G Shiel (Melrose), I Tukalo (Selkirk); G P J Townsend (Gala), G H Oliver (Hawick); G R Isaac (Gala), I Corcoran (Gala) (*capt*), H A Hunter (Gala), R R Brown (Melrose), G W Weir (Melrose), D J Turnbull (Hawick), J P Amos (Gala), C D Hogg (Melrose) *Replacement* N A McIlroy (Jedforest) for Hunter
Scorers *Try:* Tukalo *Conversion:* Townsend
Referee R J Megson (Edinburgh Wanderers)

28 November, Countesswells, Aberdeen
North & Midlands 18 (1G 2PG 1T) **Edinburgh 45** (4G 4PG 1T)

North & Midlands: S A D Burns (Edinburgh Acads) (*capt*); D J McLaughlin (Alloa), P R Rouse (Dundee HSFP), R J S Shepherd (Edinburgh Acads), J F Swanson (Edinburgh Acads); B R Easson (Dundee HSFP), A D Nicol (Dundee HSFP); J J Manson (Dundee HSFP), M W Scott (Edinburgh Acads), D Herrington (Dundee HSFP), S J Campbell (Dundee HSFP), B M Bell (Highland), D J McIvor (Edinburgh Acads), D H Mitchell (Dunfermline), J G Mathieson (Morgan Academy FP)
Scorers *Tries:* McIvor, Rouse *Conversion:* Easson *Penalty Goals:* Easson (2)
Edinburgh: A G Hastings (Watsonians) (*capt*); I C Glasgow (Heriot's FP), S Hastings (Watsonians), D S Wyllie (Stewart's-Melville FP), D Macrae (Boroughmuir); A Donaldson (Currie), D W Patterson (Edinburgh Acads); G D Wilson (Boroughmuir), K S Milne (Heriot's FP), P H Wright (Boroughmuir), M B Rudkin (Watsonians), A E D Macdonald (Heriot's FP), S A Aitken (Watsonians), J Robertson (Heriot's FP), S J Reid (Boroughmuir)
Scorers *Tries:* Glasgow, A G Hastings, S Hastings, Macrae, Milne *Conversions:* Donaldson (4)
Penalty Goals: Donaldson (4)
Referee W W Calder (Selkirk)

2 December, Richmond
Exiles 17 (2G 1PG) **Glasgow 7** (1G)

Exiles (*London Scottish unless stated*): M E Appleson; N J Grecian, F J Harrold, M S Sly, D W Caskie (Gloucester); R I Cramb (*capt*), D B Millard; A V Sharp (Bristol), L M Mair, A P Burnell, D F Cronin, A I Reed (Bath), N G Provan, I R Morrison, D L M McIntosh (Pontypridd)
Scorers *Tries:* Millard, Appleson *Conversions:* Grecian (2) *Penalty Goal:* Grecian
Glasgow: D N Barrett (West of Scotland); R A G Porter (Edinburgh Acads), C T Simmers (Edinburgh Acads), I C Jardine (Stirling County), K M Logan (Stirling County); G M Breckenridge (Glasgow High/Kelvinside), F H Stott (West of Scotland); J T Gibson (Stirling County), K D McKenzie, A G J Watt (Glasgow High/Kelvinside), E J Murphy (Glasgow High/Kelvinside), D S Munro (Glasgow High/Kelvinside), F D Wallace (Glasgow High/Kelvinside) (*capt*), B Ireland (Stirling County), J Brough (Stirling County) *Replacement* S Blair (West of Scotland) for Watt
Scorers *Try:* Porter *Conversion:* Barrett
Referee D Leslie (Hamilton Academicals)

5 December, Burnbrae
Glasgow 15 (1G 1PG 1T) **North & Midlands 22** (1G 5PG)

Glasgow: D N Barrett (West of Scotland); R A G Porter (Edinburgh Acads), C T Simmers (Edinburgh Acads), I C Jardine (Stirling County), K M Logan (Stirling County); G M Breckenridge (Glasgow High/Kelvinside), F H Stott (West of Scotland); J T Gibson (Stirling County), K D McKenzie (Stirling County), G B Robertson (Stirling County),

227

M Norval (Stirling County), D S Munro (Glasgow High/Kelvinside), W H Malcolm (Glasgow High/Kelvinside), B Ireland (Stirling County), F D Wallace (Glasgow High/Kelvinside) (*capt*)
Scorers *Tries:* Porter, Logan   *Conversion:* Barrett   *Penalty Goal:* Barrett
North & Midlands: S A D Burns (Edinburgh Acads) (*capt*); M A Cousin (Dundee HSFP), P R Rouse (Dundee HSFP), R J S Shepherd (Edinburgh Acads), J F Swanson (Edinburgh Acads); B R Easson (Dundee HSFP), A D Nicol (Dundee HSFP); J J Manson (Dundee HSFP), M W Scott (Edinburgh Acads), D Herrington (Dundee HSFP), S J Campbell (Dundee HSFP), B M Bell (Highland), D J McIvor (Edinburgh Acads), D H Mitchell (Dunfermline), J G Mathieson (Morgan Academy FP)
Scorers *Try:* Cousin   *Conversion:* Easson   *Penalty Goals:* Easson (5)
Referee R S Clark (Stewart's-Melville FP)

5 December, Mansfield Park, Hawick
South 8 (1PG 1T)   **Exiles 6** (2PG)

South: G J Aitchison (Kelso); M Moncrieff (Gala), G P J Townsend (Gala), A G Shiel (Melrose), I Tukalo (Selkirk); C M Chalmers (Melrose), G Armstrong (Jedforest); G R Isaac (Gala), I Corcoran (Gala) (*capt*), H A Hunter (Gala), R R Brown (Melrose), G W Weir (Melrose), D J Turnbull (Hawick), J P Amos (Gala), C D Hogg (Melrose)
Scorers *Try:* Moncrieff   *Penalty Goal:* Aitchison
Exiles (*London Scottish unless stated*): M E Appleson; N J Grecian, F J Harrold, M S Sly, D W Caskie (Gloucester); R I Cramb (*capt*), D B Millard; A V Sharp (Bristol), L M Mair, A P Burnell, D F Cronin, A I Reed (Bath), N Provan, I R Morrison, D L M McIntosh (Pontypridd)
Scorer *Penalty Goals:* Grecian (2)
Referee J M Fleming (Boroughmuir)

9 December, Meggetland
Edinburgh 20 (2G 2PG)   **Exiles 19** (1G 4PG)

Edinburgh: A G Hastings (Watsonians) (*capt*); J Kerr (Haddington), S Hastings (Watsonians), D S Wyllie (Stewart's-Melville FP), I C Glasgow (Heriot's FP); A Donaldson (Currie), D W Patterson (Edinburgh Acads); D J Wilson (Edinburgh Acads), C B Brown (Boroughmuir), P H Wright (Boroughmuir), M D Rudkin (Watsonians), A E D Macdonald (Heriot's FP), S A Aitken (Watsonians), J Robertson (Heriot's FP), S J Reid (Boroughmuir)
Replacement B Hay-Smith (Edinburgh Acads) for Glasgow
Scorers *Tries:* A G Hastings, S Hastings   *Conversions:* Donaldson (2)   *Penalty Goals:* Donaldson (2)
Exiles (*London Scottish unless stated*): M E Appleson; W L Renwick, F J Harrold, M S Sly, D W Caskie (Gloucester); R I Cramb (*capt*), D B Millard; A V Sharp (Bristol), B W Gilchrist, A P Burnell, D F Cronin, A I Reed (Bath), I R Morrison, I R Smith (Gloucester), D L M McIntosh (Pontypridd) *Replacement* M Hamilton (Leicester) for Renwick
Scorers *Try:* Gilchrist   *Conversion:* Sly   *Penalty Goals:* Appleson (4)
Referee K W McCartney (Hawick) *replaced by* L D Crerar (Glasgow High/Kelvinside) at half-time.

12 December, Franklins Gardens, Northampton
Exiles 15 (1G 1PG 1T)   **North & Midlands 17** (2G 1PG)

Exiles (*London Scottish unless stated*): M E Appleson; M S Sly, F J Harrold, R McNaughton (Northampton), D W Caskie (Gloucester); R I Cramb (*capt*), D B Millard; A V Sharp (Bristol), L M Mair, A P Burnell, D F Cronin, A I Reed (Bath), N G Provan, C I M Dixon, C Brown
Scorers *Tries:* Appleson, McNaughton   *Conversion:* Sly   *Penalty Goal:* Sly
North & Midlands: S A D Burns (Edinburgh Acads) (*capt*); M A Cousin (Dundee HSFP), P R Rouse (Dundee HSFP), R J S Shepherd (Edinburgh Acads), J F Swanson (Edinburgh Acads); B R Easson (Dundee HSFP), A D Nicol (Dundee HSFP); J J Manson (Dundee HSFP), M W Scott (Edinburgh Acads), D Herrington (Dundee HSFP), S J Campbell (Dundee HSFP), B M Bell (Highland), D J McIvor (Edinburgh Acads), D H Mitchell (Dunfermline), J G Mathieson (Morgan Academy FP) *Replacement* W D Anderson (Kirkcaldy) for Manson
Scorers *Tries:* Nicol (2)   *Conversions:* Easson (2)   *Penalty Goal:* Easson
Referee C B Muir (Langholm)

12 December, The Greenyards, Melrose
South 19 (1G 4PG)   **Edinburgh 15** (1G 1PG 1T)

South: G J Aitchison (Kelso); A G Stanger (Hawick), G P J Townsend (Gala), A G Shiel (Melrose), I Tukalo (Selkirk); C M Chalmers (Melrose), G Armstrong (Jedforest); G R Isaac (Gala), I Corcoran (Gala) (*capt*), H A Hunter (Gala), R R Brown (Melrose), G W Weir (Melrose), D J Turnbull (Hawick), J P Amos (Gala), C D Hogg (Melrose)
Replacement S A Nichol (Selkirk) for Stanger
Scorers *Try:* Stanger   *Conversion:* Chalmers   *Penalty Goals:* Chalmers (4)
Edinburgh: A G Hastings (Watsonians) (*capt*); J Kerr (Haddington), S Hastings (Watsonians), D S Wyllie (Stewart's-Melville FP), K R Milligan (Stewart's-Melville FP); A Donaldson (Currie), D W Patterson (Edinburgh Acads); D J Wilson (Edinburgh Acads), C B Brown (Boroughmuir), P H Wright (Boroughmuir), M D Rudkin (Watsonians), A E D Macdonald (Heriot's FP), S A Aitken (Watsonians), J Robertson (Heriot's FP), D T H Jackson (Edinburgh Acads)
Scorers *Tries:* Kerr (2)   *Conversion:* Donaldson   *Penalty Goal:* Donaldson
Referee A J Spreadbury (England)

SCOTTISH INTERNATIONAL PLAYERS
(up to 31 March 1993)

ABBREVIATIONS

A – Australia; *Arg* – Argentina; *E* – England; *F* – France; *Fj* – Fiji; *I* – Ireland; *J* – Japan; *NZ* – New Zealand; *R* – Romania; *SA* – South Africa; *W* – Wales; *WS* – Western Samoa; *Z* – Zimbabwe; (C) – Centenary match v England at Murrayfield, 1971 (non-championship); P – Scotland v President's Overseas XV at Murrayfield in SRU's Centenary season, 1972-73; (R) Replacement. Entries in square brackets [ ] indicate appearances in the World Cup.

Note: Years given for Five Nations' matches are for second half of season; eg 1972 means season 1971-72. Years for all other matches refer to the actual year of the match. When a series has taken place, figures have been used to denote the particular matches in which players have featured. Thus 1981 *NZ* 1,2 indicates that a player appeared in the first and second Tests of the series. The abandoned game with Ireland at Belfast in 1885 is now included as a cap-match.

Abercrombie, C H (United Services) 1910 *I, E,* 1911 *F, W,* 1913 *F, W*
Abercrombie, J G (Edinburgh U) 1949 *F, W, I,* 1950 *F, W, I, E*
Agnew, W C C (Stewart's Coll FP) 1930 *W, I*
Ainslie, R (Edinburgh Inst FP) 1879 *I, E,* 1880 *I, E,* 1881 *E,* 1882 *I, E*
Ainslie, T (Edinburgh Inst FP) 1881 *E,* 1882 *I, E,* 1883 *W, I, E,* 1884 *W, I, E,* 1885 *W, I*1,2
Aitchison, G R (Edinburgh Wands) 1883 *I*
Aitchison, T G (Gala) 1929 *W, I, E*
Aitken, A I (Edinburgh Inst FP) 1889 *I*
Aitken, G G (Oxford U) 1924 *W, I, E,* 1925 *F, W, I, E,* 1929 *F*
Aitken, J (Gala) 1977 *E, I, F,* 1981 *F, W, E, I, NZ*1,2, *R, A,* 1982 *E, I, F, W,* 1983 *F, W, E, NZ,*1984 *W, E, I, F, R*
Aitken, R (London Scottish) 1947 *W*
Allan, B (Glasgow Acads) 1881 *I*
Allan, J (Edinburgh Acads) 1990 *NZ*1, 1991 *W, I, R, [J, I, WS, E, NZ]*
Allan, J (Melrose) 1952 *F, W, I,* 1953 *W*
Allan, J L F (Cambridge U) 1957 *I, E*
Allan, J W (Melrose) 1927 *F,* 1928 *I,* 1929 *F, W, I, E,* 1930 *F, E,* 1931 *F, W, I, E,* 1932 *SA, W, I,* 1934 *I, E*
Allan, R C (Hutchesons' GSFP) 1969 *I*
Allardice, W D (Aberdeen GSFP) 1947 *A,* 1948 *F, W, I,* 1949 *F, W, I, E*
Allen, H W (Glasgow Acads) 1873 *E*
Anderson, A H (Glasgow Acads) 1894 *I*
Anderson, D G (London Scottish) 1889 *I,* 1890 *W, I, E,* 1891 *W, E,* 1892 *W, E*
Anderson, E (Stewart's Coll FP) 1947 *I, E*
Anderson, J W (W of Scotland) 1872 *E*
Anderson, T (Merchiston) 1882 *I*
Angus, A W (Watsonians) 1909 *W,* 1910 *F, W, E,* 1911 *W, I,* 1912 *F, W, I, E, SA,* 1913 *F, W,* 1914 *E,* 1920 *F, W, I, E*
Anton, P A (St Andrew's U) 1873 *E*
Armstrong, G (Jedforest) 1988 *A,* 1989 *W, E, I, F, Fj, R,* 1990 *I, F, W, E, NZ* 1,2, *Arg,* 1991 *F, W, E, I, R, [J, I, WS, E, NZ],* 1993 *I, F, W, E*
Arneil, R J (Edinburgh Acads, Leicester and Northampton) 1968 *I, E, A,*1969 *F, W, I, E, SA,* 1970 *F, W, I, E, A,* 1971 *F, W, I, E*(2[1C]), 1972 *F, W, E, NZ*
Arthur, A (Glasgow Acads) 1875 *E,* 1876 *E*
Arthur, J W (Glasgow Acads) 1871 *E,* 1872 *E*
Asher, A G G (Oxford U) 1882 *I,* 1884 *W, I, E,* 1885 *W,* 1886 *I, E*
Auld, W (W of Scotland) 1889 *W,* 1890 *W*
Auldjo, L J (Abertay) 1878 *E*

Bain, D McL (Oxford U) 1911 *E,* 1912 *F, W, E, SA,* 1913 *F, W, I, E,* 1914 *W, I*
Baird, G R T (Kelso) 1981 *A,* 1982 *E, I, F, W, A* 1,2, 1983 *I, F, W, E, NZ,* 1984 *W, E, I, F, A,* 1985 *I, W, E,* 1986 *F, W, E, I, R,* 1987 *E,* 1988 *I*
Balfour, A (Watsonians) 1896 *W, I, E,* 1897 *E*
Balfour, L M (Edinburgh Acads) 1872 *E*
Bannerman, E M (Edinburgh Acads) 1872 *E,* 1873 *E*
Bannerman, J M (Glasgow HSFP) 1921 *F, W, I, E,* 1922 *F, W, I, E,* 1923 *F, W, I, E,* 1924 *F, W, I, E,* 1925 *F, W, I, E,* 1926 *F, W, I, E,* 1927 *F, W, I, E, A,* 1928

F, W, I, E, 1929 *F, W, I, E*
Barnes, I A (Hawick) 1972 *W,* 1974 *F* (R), 1975 *E* (R), *NZ,* 1977 *I, F, W*
Barrie, R W (Hawick) 1936 *E*
Bearne, K R F (Cambridge U, London Scottish) 1960 *F, W*
Beattie, J A (Hawick) 1929 *F, W,* 1930 *W,* 1931 *F, W, I, E,* 1932 *SA, W, I, E,* 1933 *W, E, I,* 1934 *I, E,* 1935 *W, I, E, NZ,* 1936 *W, I, E*
Beattie, J R (Glasgow Acads) 1980 *I, F, W, E,* 1981 *F, W, E, I,* 1983 *F, W, E, NZ,* 1984 *F* (R), *R, A,* 1985 *I,* 1986 *F, W, E, I, R,* 1987 *I, F, W, E*
Bedell-Sivright, D R (Cambridge U, Edinburgh U) 1900 *W,* 1901 *W, I, E,* 1902 *W, I, E,* 1903 *W, I,* 1904 *W, I, E,* 1905 *NZ,* 1906 *W, I, E, SA,* 1907 *W, I, E,* 1908 *W, I*
Bedell-Sivright, J V (Cambridge U) 1902 *W*
Begbie, T A (Edinburgh Wands) 1881 *I, E*
Bell, D L (Watsonians) 1975 *I, F, W, E*
Bell, J A (Clydesdale) 1901 *W, I, E,* 1902 *W, I, E*
Bell, L H I (Edinburgh Acads) 1900 *E,* 1904 *W, I*
Berkeley, W V (Oxford U) 1926 *F,* 1929 *F, W, I*
Berry, C W (Fettesian-Lorettonians) 1884 *I, E,* 1885 *W, I* 1, 1887 *I, W, E,* 1888 *W, I*
Bertram, D M (Watsonians) 1922 *F, W, I, E,* 1923 *F, W, I, E,* 1924 *W, I, E*
Biggar, A G (London Scottish) 1969 *SA,* 1970 *F, I, E, A,* 1971 *F, W, I, E* (2[1C]), 1972 *F, W*
Biggar, M A (London Scottish) 1975 *I, F, W, E,* 1976 *W, E, I,* 1977 *I, F, W,* 1978 *I, F, W, E, NZ,* 1979 *W, E, I, F, NZ,* 1980 *I, F, W, E*
Birkett, G A (Harlequins, London Scottish) 1975 *NZ*
Bishop, J M (Glasgow Acads) 1893 *I*
Bisset, A A (RIE Coll) 1904 *W*
Black, A W (Edinburgh U) 1947 *F, W,* 1948 *E,* 1950 *W, I, E*
Black, W P (Glasgow HSFP) 1948 *F, W, I, E,* 1951 *E*
Blackadder, W F (W of Scotland) 1938 *E*
Blaikie, C F (Heriot's FP) 1963 *I, E,* 1966 *E,* 1968 *A,* 1969 *F, W, I, E*
Blair, P C B (Cambridge U) 1912 *SA,* 1913 *F, W, I, E*
Bolton, W H (W of Scotland) 1876 *E*
Borthwick, J B (Stewart's Coll FP) 1938 *W, I*
Bos, F H ten (Oxford U, London Scottish) 1959 *E,* 1960 *F, W, SA,* 1961 *F, SA, W, I, E,* 1962 *F, W, I, E,* 1963 *F, W, I, E*
Boswell, J D (W of Scotland) 1889 *W, I,* 1890 *W, I, E,* 1891 *W, E,* 1892 *W, I, E,* 1893 *I, E,* 1894 *I, E*
Bowie, T C (Watsonians) 1913 *I, E,* 1914 *I, E*
Boyd, G M (Glasgow HSFP) 1926 *E*
Boyd, J L (United Services) 1912 *E, SA*
Boyle, A C W (London Scottish) 1963 *F, W, I*
Boyle, A H W (St Thomas's Hospital, London Scottish) 1966 *A,* 1967 *F, NZ,* 1968 *F, W, I*
Brash, J C (Cambridge U) 1961 *E*
Breakey, R W (Gosforth) 1978 *E*
Brewis, N T (Edinburgh Inst FP) 1876 *E,* 1878 *E,* 1879 *I, E,* 1880 *I, E*
Brewster, A K (Stewart's-Melville FP) 1977 *E,* 1980 *I, F,* 1986 *E, I, R*
Brown, A H (Heriot's FP) 1928 *E,* 1929 *F, W*
Brown, A R (Gala) 1971 *E* (2[1C]), 1972 *F, W, E*
Brown, C H C (Dunfermline) 1929 *E*
Brown, D I (Cambridge U) 1933 *W, E, I*
Brown, G L (W of Scotland) 1969 *SA,* 1970 *F, W* (R),

229

Dalgleish, K J (Edinburgh Wands, Cambridge U) 1951 *I, E*, 1953 *F, W*
Dallas, J D (Watsonians) 1903 *E*
Davidson, J A (London Scottish, Edinburgh Wands) 1959 *E*, 1960 *I, E*
Davidson, J N G (Edinburgh U) 1952 *F, W, I, E*, 1953 *F, W*, 1954 *F*
Davidson, J P (RIE Coll) 1873 *E*, 1874 *E*
Davidson, R S (Royal HSFP) 1893 *E*
Davies, D S (Hawick) 1922 *F, W, I, E*, 1923 *F, W, I, E*, 1924 *F, E*, 1925 *W, I, E*, 1926 *F, W, I, E*, 1927 *F, W, I*
Dawson, J C (Glasgow Acads) 1947 *A*, 1948 *F, W*, 1949 *F, W, I*, 1950 *F, W, I, E*, 1951 *F, W, I, E, SA*, 1952 *F, W, I, E*, 1953 *E*
Deans, C T (Hawick) 1978 *F, W, E, NZ*, 1979 *W, E, I, F, NZ*, 1980 *I, F*, 1981 *F, W, E, I, NZ* 1,2, *R, A*, 1982 *E, I, F, W, A* 1,2, 1983 *I, F, W, E, NZ*, 1984 *W, E, I, F, A*, 1985 *I, F, W, E*, 1986 *F, W, E, I, R*, 1987 *I, F, W, E, [F, Z, R, NZ]*
Deans, D T (Hawick) 1968 *E*
Deas, D W (Heriot's FP) 1947 *F, W*
Dick, L G (Loughborough Colls, Jordanhill, Swansea) 1972 *W* (R), *E*, 1974 *W, E, I, F*, 1975 *I, F, W, E, NZ, A*, 1976 *F*, 1977 *E*
Dick, R C S (Cambridge U, Guy's Hospital) 1934 *W, I, E*, 1935 *W, I, E, NZ*, 1936 *W, I, E*, 1937 *W*, 1938 *W, I, E*
Dickson, G (Gala) 1978 *NZ*, 1979 *W, E, I, F, NZ*, 1980 *W*, 1981 *F*, 1982 *W* (R)
Dickson, M R (Edinburgh U) 1905 *I*
Dickson, W M (Blackheath, Oxford U) 1912 *F, W, E, SA*, 1913 *F, W, I*
Dobson, J (Glasgow Acads) 1911 *E*, 1912 *F, W, I, E, SA*
Dobson, J D (Glasgow Acads) 1910 *I*
Dobson, W G (Heriot's FP) 1922 *W, I, E*,
Docherty, J T (Glasgow HSFP) 1955 *F, W*, 1956 *E*, 1958 *F, W, A, I, E*
Dods, F P (Edinburgh Acads) 1901 *I*
Dods, J H (Edinburgh Acads) 1895 *W, I, E*, 1896 *W, I, E*, 1897 *I, E*
Dods, P W (Gala) 1983 *I, F, W, E, NZ*, 1984 *W, E, I, F, R, A*, 1985 *I, F, W, E*, 1989 *W, E, I, F*, 1991 *I*(R), *R, [Z, NZ*(R)]
Donald, D G (Oxford U) 1914 *W, I*
Donald, R L H (Glasgow HSFP) 1921 *W, I, E*
Donaldson, W P (Oxford U, W of Scotland) 1893 *I*, 1894 *I*, 1895 *E*, 1896 *I, E*, 1899 *F*
Don-Wauchope, A R (Fettesian-Lorettonians) 1881 *E*, 1882 *E*, 1883 *W*, 1884 *W, I, E*, 1885 *W, I* 1,2, 1886 *W, I, E*, 1888 *I*
Don-Wauchope, P H (Fettesian-Lorettonians) 1885 *I* 1,2, 1886 *W*, 1887 *I, W, E*
Dorward, A F (Cambridge U, Gala) 1950 *F*, 1951 *SA*, 1952 *W, I, E*, 1953 *F, W, E*, 1955 *F*, 1956 *I, E*, 1957 *F, W, I, E*
Dorward, T F (Gala) 1938 *W, I, E*, 1939 *I, E*
Douglas, G (Jedforest) 1921 *W*
Douglas, J (Stewart's Coll FP) 1961 *F, SA, W, I, E*, 1962 *F, W, I, E*, 1963 *F, W, I*
Douty, P S (London Scottish) 1927 *A*, 1928 *F, W*
Drew, D (Glasgow Acads) 1871 *E*, 1876 *E*
Druitt, W A H (London Scottish) 1936 *W, I, E*
Drummond, A H (Kelvinside Acads) 1938 *W, I*
Drummond, C W (Melrose) 1947 *F, W, I, E*, 1948 *F, I, E*, 1950 *F, W, I, E*
Drybrough, A S (Edinburgh Wands, Merchistonians) 1902 *I*, 1903 *I*
Dryden, R H (Watsonians) 1937 *E*
Drysdale, D (Heriot's FP) 1923 *F, W, I, E*, 1924 *F, W, I, E*, 1925 *F, W, I, E*, 1926 *F, W, I, E*, 1927 *F, W, I, E, A*, 1928 *F, W, I, E*, 1929 *F*
Duff, P L (Glasgow Acads) 1936 *W, I*, 1938 *W, I, E*, 1939 *W*
Duffy, H (Jedforest) 1955 *F*
Duke, A (Royal HSFP) 1888 *W, I*, 1889 *W, I*, 1890 *W, I*
Duncan, A W (Edinburgh U) 1901 *W, I, E*, 1902 *W, I, E*
Duncan, D D (Oxford U) 1920 *F, W, I, E*
Duncan, M D F (W of Scotland) 1986 *F, W, E, R*, 1987 *I, F, W, E, [F, Z, R, NZ]*, 1988 *I, F, W, E, A*, 1989 *W*
Duncan, M M (Fettesian-Lorettonians) 1888 *W*
Dunlop, J W (W of Scotland) 1875 *E*

Dunlop, Q (W of Scotland) 1971 *E* (2[1C])
Dykes, A S (Glasgow Acads) 1932 *E*
Dykes, J C (Glasgow Acads) 1922 *F, E*, 1924 *I*, 1925 *F, W, I*, 1926 *F, W, I, E*, 1927 *F, W, I, E, A*, 1928 *F, I*, 1929 *F, W, I*
Dykes, J M (Clydesdale, Glasgow HSFP) 1898 *I, E*, 1899 *W, E*, 1900 *W, I*, 1901 *W, I, E*, 1902 *E*

Edwards, D B (Heriot's FP) 1960 *I, E, SA*
Edwards, N G B (Harlequins) 1992 *E, I, F, W, A* 1
Elgie, M K (London Scottish) 1954 *NZ, I, E, W*, 1955 *F, W, I, E*
Elliot, C (Langholm) 1958 *E*, 1959 *F*, 1960 *F*, 1963 *E*, 1964 *F, NZ, W, I, E*, 1965 *F, W, I*
Elliot, M (Hawick) 1895 *W*, 1896 *E*, 1897 *I, E*, 1898 *I, E*
Elliot, T (Gala) 1905 *E*
Elliot, T (Gala) 1955 *W, I, E*, 1956 *F, W, I, E*, 1957 *F, W, I, E*, 1958 *W, A, I*
Elliot, T G (Langholm) 1968 *W, A*, 1969 *F, W*, 1970 *E*
Elliot, W I D (Edinburgh Acads) 1947 *F, W, E, A*, 1948 *F, W, I, E*, 1949 *F, W, I, E*, 1950 *F, W, I, E*, 1951 *F, W, I, E, SA*, 1952 *F, W, I, E*, 1954 *NZ, I, E, W*
Emslie, W D (Royal HSFP) 1930 *F*, 1932 *I*
Evans, H L (Edinburgh U) 1885 *I* 1,2
Ewart, E N (Glasgow Acads) 1879 *E*, 1880 *I, E*

Fahmy, Dr E C (Abertillery) 1920 *F, W, I, E*
Fasson, F H (London Scottish, Edinburgh Wands) 1900 *W*, 1901 *W, I*, 1902 *W, E*
Fell, A N (Edinburgh U) 1901 *W, I, E*, 1902 *W, E*, 1903 *W, E*
Ferguson, J H (Gala) 1928 *W*
Ferguson, W G (Royal HSFP) 1927 *A*, 1928 *F, W, I, E*
Fergusson, E A J (Oxford U) 1954 *F, NZ, I, E, W*
Finlay, A B (Edinburgh Acads) 1875 *E*
Finlay, J F (Edinburgh Acads) 1871 *E*, 1872 *E*, 1874 *E*, 1875 *E*
Finlay, N J (Edinburgh Acads) 1875 *E*, 1876 *E*, 1878 *E*, 1879 *I, E*, 1880 *I, E*, 1881 *I, E*
Finlay, R (Watsonians) 1948 *E*
Fisher, A T (Waterloo, Watsonians) 1947 *I, E*
Fisher, C D (Waterloo) 1975 *NZ, A*, 1976 *W, E, I*
Fisher, D (W of Scotland) 1893 *I*
Fisher, J P (Royal HSFP, London Scottish) 1963 *E*, 1964 *F, NZ, W, I, E*, 1965 *F, W, I, E, SA*, 1966 *F, W, I, E, A*, 1967 *F, W, I, E, NZ*, 1968 *F, W, I, E*
Fleming, C J N (Edinburgh Wands) 1896 *I, E*, 1897 *I*
Fleming, G R (Glasgow Acads) 1875 *E*, 1876 *E*
Fletcher, H N (Edinburgh U) 1904 *E*, 1905 *W*
Flett, A B (Edinburgh U) 1901 *W, I, E*, 1902 *W, I*
Forbes, J L (Watsonians) 1905 *W*, 1906 *I, E*
Ford, D St C (United Services, RN) 1930 *I, E*, 1931 *E*, 1932 *W, I*
Ford, J R (Gala) 1893 *I*
Forrest, J E (Glasgow Acads) 1932 *SA*, 1935 *E, NZ*
Forrest, J G S (Cambridge U) 1938 *W, I, E*
Forrest, W T (Hawick) 1903 *W, I, E*, 1904 *W, I, E*, 1905 *W, I*
Forsayth, H H (Oxford U) 1921 *F, W, I, E*, 1922 *W, I, E*
Forsyth, I W (Stewart's Coll FP) 1972 *NZ*, 1973 *F, W, I, E, P*
Forsyth, J (Edinburgh U) 1871 *E*
Foster, R A (Hawick) 1930 *W*, 1932 *SA, I, E*
Fox, J (Gala) 1952 *F, W, I, E*
Frame, J N M (Edinburgh U, Gala) 1967 *NZ*, 1968 *F, W, I, E*, 1969 *W, I, E, SA*, 1970 *F, W, I, E, A*, 1971 *F, W, I, E* (2[1C]), 1972 *F, W, E*, 1973 *P* (R)
France, C (Kelvinside Acads) 1903 *I*
Fraser, C F P (Glasgow U) 1888 *W*, 1889 *W*
Fraser, J W (Edinburgh Inst FP) 1881 *E*
Fraser, R (Cambridge U) 1911 *F, W, I, E*
French, J (Glasgow Acads) 1886 *W*, 1887 *I, W, E*
Frew, A (Edinburgh U) 1901 *W, I, E*
Frew, G M (Glasgow HSFP) 1906 *SA*, 1907 *W, I, E*, 1908 *W, I, E*, 1909 *W, I, E*, 1910 *F, W, I*, 1911 *I, E*
Friebe, J P (Glasgow HSFP) 1952 *E*
Fulton, A K (Edinburgh U, Dollar Acads) 1952 *F*, 1954 *F*
Fyfe, K C (Cambridge U, Sale, London Scottish) 1933 *W, E*, 1934 *E*, 1935 *W, I, E, NZ*, 1936 *W, E*, 1939 *I*

Gallie, G H (Edinburgh Acads) 1939 *W*
Gallie, R A (Glasgow Acads) 1920 *F, W, I, E,* 1921 *F, W, I, E*
Gammell, W B B (Edinburgh Wands) 1977 *I, F, W,* 1978 *W, E*
Geddes, I C (London Scottish) 1906 *SA,* 1907 *W, I, E,* 1908 *W, E*
Geddes, K I (London Scottish) 1947 *F, W, I, E*
Gedge, H T S (Oxford U, London Scottish, Edinburgh Wands) 1894 *W, I, E,* 1896 *E,* 1899 *W, E*
Gedge, P M S (Edinburgh Wands) 1933 *I*
Gemmill, R (Glasgow HSFP) 1950 *F, W, I, E,* 1951 *F, W, I*
Gibson, W R (Royal HSFP) 1891 *I, E,* 1892 *W, I, E,* 1893 *W, I, E,* 1894 *W, I, E,* 1895 *W, I, E*
Gilbert-Smith, D S (London Scottish) 1952 *E*
Gilchrist, J (Glasgow Acads) 1925 *F*
Gill, A D (Gala) 1973 *P,* 1974 *W, E, I, F*
Gillespie, J I (Edinburgh Acads) 1899 *E,* 1900 *W, E,* 1901 *W, I, E,* 1902 *W, I,* 1904 *I, E*
Gillies, A C (Watsonians) 1924 *W, I, E,* 1925 *F, W, E,* 1926 *F, W,* 1927 *F, W, I, E*
Gilray, C M (Oxford U, London Scottish) 1908 *E,* 1909 *W, E,* 1912 *I*
Glasgow, R J C (Dunfermline) 1962 *F, W, I, E,* 1963 *I, E,* 1964 *I, E,* 1965 *W, I*
Glen, W S (Edinburgh Wands) 1955 *W*
Gloag, L G (Cambridge U) 1949 *F, W, I, E*
Goodfellow, J (Langholm) 1928 *W, I, E*
Goodhue, F W J (London Scottish) 1890 *W, I, E,* 1891 *W, I, E,* 1892 *W, I, E*
Gordon, R (Edinburgh Wands) 1951 *W,* 1952 *F, W, I, E,* 1953 *W*
Gordon, R E (Royal Artillery) 1913 *F, W, I*
Gordon, R J (London Scottish) 1982 *A 1,2*
Gore, A C (London Scottish) 1882 *I*
Gossman, B M (W of Scotland) 1980 *W,* 1983 *F, W*
Gossman, J S (W of Scotland) 1980 *E* (R)
Gowans, J J (Cambridge U, London Scottish) 1893 *W,* 1894 *W, E,* 1895 *W, I, E,* 1896 *I, E*
Gowland, G C (London Scottish) 1908 *W,* 1909 *W, E,* 1910 *F, W, I, E*
Gracie, A L (Harlequins) 1921 *F, W, I, E,* 1922 *F, W, I, E,* 1923 *F, W, I, E,* 1924 *F*
Graham, I N (Edinburgh Acads) 1939 *I, E*
Graham, J (Kelso) 1926 *I, E,* 1927 *F, W, I, E, A,* 1928 *F, W, I, E,* 1930 *I, E,* 1932 *SA, W*
Graham, J H S (Edinburgh Acads) 1876 *E,* 1877 *I, E,* 1878 *E,* 1879 *I, E,* 1880 *I, E,* 1881 *I, E*
Grant, D (Hawick) 1965 *F, E, SA,* 1966 *F, W, I, E, A,* 1967 *F, W, I, E, NZ,* 1968 *F*
Grant, D M (East Midlands) 1911 *W, I*
Grant, M L (Harlequins) 1955 *F,* 1956 *F, W,* 1957 *F*
Grant, T O (Hawick) 1960 *I, E, SA,* 1964 *F, NZ, W*
Grant, W St C (Craigmount) 1873 *E,* 1874 *E*
Gray, C A (Nottingham) 1989 *W, E, I, F, Fj, R,* 1990 *I, F, W, E, NZ 1,2, Arg,* 1991 *F, W, E, I, [J, I, WS, E, NZ]*
Gray, D (W of Scotland) 1978 *E,* 1979 *I, F, NZ,* 1980 *I, F, W, E,* 1981 *F*
Gray, G L (Gala) 1935 *NZ,* 1937 *W, I, E*
Gray, T (Northampton, Heriot's FP) 1950 *E,* 1951 *F, E,* 1952 *F, W*
Greenlees, H D (Leicester) 1927 *A,* 1928 *F, W,* 1929 *I, E,* 1930 *E*
Greenlees, J R C (Cambridge U, Kelvinside Acads) 1900 *I,* 1902 *W, I, E,* 1903 *W, I, E*
Greenwood, J T (Dunfermline and Perthshire Acads) 1952 *F,* 1955 *F, W, I, E,* 1956 *F, W, I, E,* 1957 *F, W, E,* 1958 *F, W, A, I, E,* 1959 *F, W, I*
Greig, A (Glasgow HSFP) 1911 *I*
Greig, L L (Glasgow Acads, United Services) 1905 *NZ,* 1906 *SA,* 1907 *W,* 1908 *W, I*
Greig, R C (Glasgow Acads) 1893 *W,* 1897 *I*
Grieve, C F (Oxford U) 1935 *W,* 1936 *E*
Grieve, R M (Kelso) 1935 *W, I, E, NZ,* 1936 *W, I, E*
Gunn, A W (Royal HSFP) 1912 *F, W, I, SA,* 1913 *F*

Hamilton, A S (Headingley) 1914 *W,* 1920 *F*
Hamilton, H M (W of Scotland) 1874 *E,* 1875 *E*
Hannah, R S M (W of Scotland) 1971 *I*
Harrower, P R (London Scottish) 1885 *W*
Hart, J G M (London Scottish) 1951 *SA*
Hart, T M (Glasgow U) 1930 *W, I*
Hart, W (Melrose) 1960 *SA*

Harvey, L (Greenock Wands) 1899 *I*
Hastie, A J (Melrose) 1961 *W, I, E,* 1964 *I, E,* 1965 *E, SA,* 1966 *F, W, I, E, A,* 1967 *F, W, I, NZ,* 1968 *F, W*
Hastie, I R (Kelso) 1955 *F,* 1958 *F, E,* 1959 *F, W, I*
Hastie, J D H (Melrose) 1938 *W, I, E*
Hastings, A G (Cambridge U, Watsonians, London Scottish) 1986 *F, W, E, I, R,* 1987 *I, F, W, E, [F, Z, R, NZ],* 1988 *I, F, W, E, A,* 1989 *Fj, R,* 1990 *I, F, W, E, NZ* 1,2, *Arg,* 1991 *F, W, E, I, [J, I, WS, E, NZ],* 1992 *E, I, F, W, A* 1, 1993 *I, F, W, E*
Hastings, S (Watsonians) 1986 *F, W, E, I, R,* 1987 *I, F, W, [R],* 1988 *I, F, W, A,* 1989 *W, E, I, F, Fj, R,* 1990 *I, F, W, E, NZ* 1,2, *Arg,* 1991 *F, W, E, I, [J, Z, I, WS, E, NZ],* 1992 *E, I, F, W, A* 1,2, 1993 *I, F, W, E*
Hay, B H (Boroughmuir) 1975 *NZ, A,* 1976 *F,* 1978 *I, F, W, E, NZ,* 1979 *W, E, I, F, NZ,* 1980 *I, F, W, E,* 1981 *F, W, E, I, NZ* 1,2
Hay-Gordon, J R (Edinburgh Acads) 1875 *E,* 1877 *I, E*
Hegarty, C B (Hawick) 1978 *I, F, W, E*
Hegarty, J J (Hawick) 1951 *F,* 1953 *F, W, I, E,* 1955 *F*
Henderson, B C (Edinburgh Wands) 1963 *E,* 1964 *F, I, E,* 1965 *F, W, I, E,* 1966 *F, W, I, E*
Henderson, F W (London Scottish) 1900 *W, I,*
Henderson, I C (Edinburgh Acads) 1939 *I, E,* 1947 *F, W, E, A,* 1948 *I, E*
Henderson, J H (Oxford U, Richmond) 1953 *F, W, I, E,* 1954 *F, NZ, I, E, W*
Henderson, J M (Edinburgh Acads) 1933 *W, E, I*
Henderson, J Y M (Watsonians) 1911 *E*
Henderson, M M (Dunfermline) 1937 *W, I, E*
Henderson, N F (London Scottish) 1892 *I*
Henderson, R G (Newcastle Northern) 1924 *I, E*
Hendrie, K G P (Heriot's FP) 1924 *F, W, I*
Hendry, T L (Clydesdale) 1893 *W, I, E,* 1895 *I*
Henriksen, E H (Royal HSFP) 1953 *I*
Hepburn, D P (Woodford) 1947 *A,* 1948 *F, W, I, E,* 1949 *F, W, I, E*
Heron, G (Glasgow Acads) 1874 *E,* 1875 *E*
Hill, C C P (St Andrew's U) 1912 *F, I*
Hinshelwood, A J W (London Scottish) 1966 *F, W, I, E, A,* 1967 *F, W, I, E, NZ,* 1968 *F, W, I, E, A,* 1969 *F, W, I, SA,* 1970 *F, W*
Hodgson, C G (London Scottish) 1968 *I, E*
Hogg, C D (Melrose) 1992 *A* 1,2
Hogg, C G (Boroughmuir) 1978 *F* (R), *W* (R)
Holms, W F (RIE Coll) 1886 *W, E,* 1887 *I, E,* 1889 *W, I*
Horsburgh, G B (London Scottish) 1937 *W, I, E,* 1938 *W, I, E,* 1939 *W, I, E*
Howie, D D (Kirkcaldy) 1912 *F, W, I, E, SA,* 1913 *F, W*
Howie, R A (Kirkcaldy) 1924 *F, W, I, E,* 1925 *W, I, E*
Hoyer-Millar, G C (Oxford U) 1953 *I*
Huggan, J L (London Scottish) 1914 *E*
Hume, J (Royal HSFP) 1912 *F,* 1920 *F,* 1921 *F, W, I, E,* 1922 *F*
Hume, J W G (Oxford U, Edinburgh Wands) 1928 *I,* 1930 *F*
Hunter, F (Edinburgh U) 1882 *I*
Hunter, I G (Selkirk) 1984 *I* (R), 1985 *F* (R), *W, E*
Hunter, J M (Cambridge U) 1947 *F*
Hunter, M D (Glasgow High) 1974 *F*
Hunter, W J (Hawick) 1964 *F, NZ, W,* 1967 *F, W, I, E*
Hutchison, W R (Glasgow HSFP) 1911 *E*
Hutton, A H M (Dunfermline) 1932 *I*
Hutton, J E (Harlequins) 1930 *E,* 1931 *F*

Inglis, H M (Edinburgh Acads) 1951 *F, W, I, E, SA,* 1952 *W, I*
Inglis, J M (Selkirk) 1952 *E*
Inglis, W M (Cambridge U, Royal Engineers) 1937 *W, I, E,* 1938 *W, I, E*
Innes, J R S (Aberdeen GSFP) 1939 *W, I, E,* 1947 *A,* 1948 *F, W, I, E*
Ireland, J C H (Glasgow HSFP) 1925 *W, I, E,* 1926 *F, W, I, E,* 1927 *F, W, I, E*
Irvine, A R (Heriot's FP) 1972 *NZ,* 1973 *F, W, I, E, P,* 1974 *W, E, I, F,* 1975 *I, F, W, E, NZ, A,* 1976 *F, W, E, I,* 1977 *E, I, F, W,* 1978 *I, F, E, NZ,* 1979 *W, E, I, F, NZ,* 1980 *I, F, W, E,* 1981 *F, W, E, I, NZ* 1,2, *R, A,* 1982 *E, I, F, W, A* 1,2
Irvine, D R (Edinburgh Acads) 1878 *E,* 1879 *I, E*
Irvine, R W (Edinburgh Acads) 1871 *E,* 1872 *E,* 1873 *E,* 1874 *E,* 1875 *E,* 1876 *E,* 1877 *I, E,* 1878 *E,* 1879 *I, E,* 1880 *I, E*

Irvine, T W (Edinburgh Acads) 1885 *I* 1,2, 1886 *W*, *I*, *E*, 1887 *I*, *W*, *E*, 1888 *W*, *I*, 1889 *I*

Jackson, K L T (Oxford U) 1933 *W*, *E*, *I*, 1934 *W*
Jackson, T G H (Army) 1947 *F*, *W*, *E*, *A*, 1948 *F*, *W*, *I*, *E*, 1949 *F*, *W*, *I*, *E*
Jackson, W D (Hawick) 1964 *I*, 1965 *E*, *SA*, 1968 *A*, 1969 *F*, *W*, *I*, *E*
Jamieson, J (W of Scotland) 1883 *W*, *I*, *E*, 1884 *W*, *I*, *E*, 1885 *W*, *I* 1,2
Jeffrey, J (Kelso) 1984 *A*, 1985 *I*, *E*, 1986 *F*, *W*, *E*, *I*, *R*, 1987 *I*, *F*, *W*, *E*, [*F*, *Z*, *R*], 1988 *I*, *W*, *A*, 1989 *W*, *E*, *I*, *F*, *Fj*, *R*, 1990 *I*, *F*, *W*, *E*, *NZ* 1,2, *Arg*, 1991 *F*, *W*, *E*, *I*, [*J*, *I*, *WS*, *E*, *NZ*]
Johnston, D I (Watsonians) 1979 *NZ*, 1980 *I*, *F*, *W*, *E*, 1981 *R*, *A*, 1982 *E*, *I*, *F*, *W*, *A* 1,2, 1983 *I*, *F*, *W*, *NZ*, 1984 *W*, *E*, *I*, *F*, *R*, 1986 *F*, *W*, *E*, *I*, *R*
Johnston, H H (Edinburgh Collegian FP) 1877 *I*, *E*
Johnston, J (Melrose) 1951 *SA*, 1952 *F*, *W*, *I*, *E*
Johnston, W C (Glasgow HSFP) 1922 *F*
Johnston, W G S (Cambridge U) 1935 *W*, *I*, 1937 *W*, *I*, *E*
Jones, P M (Gloucester) 1992 *W*(R)
Junor, J E (Glasgow Acads) 1876 *E*, 1877 *I*, *E*, 1878 *E*, 1879 *E*, 1881 *I*

Keddie, R R (Watsonians) 1967 *NZ*
Keith, G J (Wasps) 1968 *F*, *W*
Keller, D H (London Scottish) 1949 *F*, *W*, *I*, *E*, 1950 *F*, *W*, *I*
Kelly, R F (Watsonians) 1927 *A*, 1928 *F*, *W*, *E*
Kemp, J W Y (Glasgow HSFP) 1954 *W*, 1955 *F*, *W*, *I*, *E*, 1956 *F*, *W*, *I*, *E*, 1957 *F*, *W*, *I*, *E*, 1958 *F*, *W*, *A*, *I*, *E*, 1959 *F*, *W*, *I*, *E*, 1960 *F*, *W*, *I*, *E*, *SA*
Kennedy, A E (Watsonians) 1983 *NZ*, 1984 *W*, *E*, *A*
Kennedy, F (Stewart's Coll FP) 1920 *F*, *W*, *I*, *E*, 1921 *E*
Kennedy, N (W of Scotland) 1903 *W*, *I*, *E*
Ker, A B M (Kelso) 1988 *W*, *E*
Ker, H T (Glasgow Acads) 1887 *I*, *W*, *E*, 1888 *I*, 1889 *W*, 1890 *I*, *E*
Kerr, D S (Heriot's FP) 1923 *F*, *W*, 1924 *F*, 1926 *I*, *E*, 1927 *W*, *I*, *E*, 1928 *I*, *E*
Kerr, G C (Old Dunelmians, Edinburgh Wands) 1898 *I*, *E*, 1899 *I*, *W*, *E*, 1900 *W*, *I*, *E*
Kerr, J M (Heriot's FP) 1935 *NZ*, 1936 *I*, *E*, 1937 *W*, *I*
Kerr, W (London Scottish) 1953 *E*
Kidston, D W (Glasgow Acads) 1883 *W*, *E*
Kidston, W H (W of Scotland) 1874 *E*
Kilgour, I J (RMC Sandhurst) 1921 *F*
King, J H F (Selkirk) 1953 *F*, *W*, *E*, 1954 *E*
Kininmonth, P W (Oxford U, Richmond) 1949 *F*, *W*, *I*, *E*, 1950 *F*, *W*, *I*, *E*, 1951 *F*, *W*, *I*, *E*, *SA*, 1952 *F*, *W*, *I*, 1954 *F*, *NZ*, *I*, *E*, *W*
Kinnear, R M (Heriot's FP) 1926 *F*, *W*, *I*
Knox, J (Kelvinside Acads) 1903 *W*, *I*, *E*
Kyle, W E (Hawick) 1902 *W*, *I*, *E*, 1903 *W*, *I*, *E*, 1904 *W*, *I*, *E*, 1905 *W*, *I*, *E*, *NZ*, 1906 *W*, *I*, *E*, 1908 *E*, 1909 *W*, *I*, *E*, 1910 *W*

Laidlaw, A S (Hawick) 1897 *I*
Laidlaw, F A L (Melrose) 1965 *F*, *W*, *I*, *E*, *SA*, 1966 *F*, *W*, *I*, *E*, *A*, 1967 *F*, *W*, *I*, *E*, *NZ*, 1968 *F*, *W*, *I*, *A*, 1969 *F*, *W*, *I*, *E*, *SA*, 1970 *F*, *W*, *I*, *E*, *A*, 1971 *F*, *W*, *I*
Laidlaw, R J (Jedforest) 1980 *I*, *F*, *W*, *E*, 1981 *F*, *W*, *E*, *I*, *NZ* 1,2, *R*, *A*, 1982 *E*, *I*, *F*, *W*, *A* 1,2, 1983 *I*, *F*, *W*, *E*, *NZ*, 1984 *W*, *E*, *I*, *F*, *R*, *A*, 1985 *I*, *F*, 1986 *F*, *W*, *E*, *I*, *R*, 1987 *I*, *F*, *W*, *E*, [*F*, *R*, *NZ*], 1988 *I*, *F*, *W*, *E*
Laing, A D (Royal HSFP) 1914 *W*, *I*, *E*, 1920 *F*, *W*, *I*, 1921 *F*
Lambie, I K (Watsonians) 1978 *NZ* (R), 1979 *W*, *E*, *NZ*
Lambie, L B (Glasgow HSFP) 1934 *W*, *I*, *E*, 1935 *W*, *I*, *E*, *NZ*
Lamond, G A W (Kelvinside Acads) 1899 *W*, *E*, 1905 *E*
Lang, D (Paisley) 1876 *E*, 1877 *I*
Langrish, R W (London Scottish) 1930 *F*, 1931 *F*, *W*, *I*
Lauder, W (Neath) 1969 *I*, *E*, *SA*, 1970 *F*, *W*, *I*, *A*, 1973 *F*, 1974 *W*, *E*, *I*, *F*, 1975 *I*, *F*, *NZ*, *A*, 1976 *F*, 1977 *E*
Laughland, I H P (London Scottish) 1959 *F*, 1960 *F*, *W*, *I*, *E*, 1961 *SA*, *W*, *I*, *E*, 1962 *F*, *W*, *I*, *E*, 1963 *F*, *W*, *I*, 1964 *F*, *NZ*, *W*, *I*, *E*, 1965 *F*, *W*, *I*, *E*, *SA*, 1966 *F*, *W*, *I*, *E*, 1967 *E*
Lawrie, J R (Melrose) 1922 *F*, *W*, *I*, *E*, 1923 *F*, *W*, *I*,

E, 1924 *W*, *I*, *E*
Lawrie, K G (Gala) 1980 *F* (R), *W*, *E*
Lawson, A J M (Edinburgh Wands, London Scottish) 1972 *F* (R), *E*, 1973 *F*, 1974 *W*, *E*, 1976 *E*, *I*, 1977 *E*, 1978 *NZ*, 1979 *W*, *E*, *I*, *F*, *NZ*, 1980 *W* (R)
Lawther, T H B (Old Millhillians) 1932 *SA*, *W*
Ledingham, G A (Aberdeen GSFP) 1913 *F*
Lees, J B (Gala) 1947 *I*, *A*, 1948 *F*, *W*, *E*
Leggatt, H T O (Watsonians) 1891 *W*, *I*, *E*, 1892 *W*, *I*, 1893 *W*, *E*, 1894 *I*, *E*
Lely, W G (Cambridge U, London Scottish) 1909 *I*
Leslie, D G (Dundee HSFP, W of Scotland, Gala) 1975 *I*, *F*, *W*, *E*, *NZ*, *A*, 1976 *F*, *W*, *E*, *I*, 1978 *NZ*, 1980 *E*, 1981 *F*, *I*, *NZ* 1,2, *R*, *A*, 1982 *E*, 1983 *I*, *F*, *W*, *E*, 1984 *W*, *E*, *I*, *F*, *R*, 1985 *F*, *W*, *E*
Liddell, E H (Edinburgh U) 1922 *F*, *W*, *I*, 1923 *F*, *W*, *I*, *E*
Lind, H (Dunfermline) 1928 *I*, 1931 *F*, *W*, *I*, *E*, 1932 *SA*, *W*, *E*, 1933 *W*, *E*, *I*, 1934 *W*, *I*, *E*, 1935 *I*, 1936 *E*
Lindsay, A B (London Hospital) 1910 *I*, 1911 *I*
Lindsay, G C (London Scottish) 1884 *W*, 1885 *I* 1, 1887 *W*, *E*
Lindsay-Watson, R H (Hawick) 1909 *I*
Lineen, S R P (Boroughmuir) 1989 *W*, *E*, *I*, *F*, *Fj*, *R*, 1990 *I*, *F*, *W*, *E*, *NZ* 1,2, *Arg*, 1991 *F*, *W*, *E*, *I*, *R*, [*J*, *Z*, *I*, *E*, *NZ*], 1992 *E*, *I*, *F*, *W*, *A* 1,2
Little, A W (Hawick) 1905 *W*
Logan, K M (Stirling County) 1992 *A* 2, 1993 *E*(R)
Logan, W R (Edinburgh U, Edinburgh Wands) 1931 *E*, 1932 *SA*, *W*, *I*, 1933 *W*, *E*, *I*, 1934 *W*, *I*, *E*, 1935 *W*, *I*, *E*, *NZ*, 1936 *W*, *I*, *E*, 1937 *W*, *I*, *E*
Lorraine, H D B (Oxford U) 1933 *W*, *E*, *I*
Loudoun-Shand, E G (Oxford U) 1913 *E*
Lowe, J D (Heriot's FP) 1934 *W*
Lumsden, I J M (Bath, Watsonians) 1947 *F*, *W*, *A*, 1949 *F*, *W*, *I*, *E*
Lyall, G G (Gala) 1947 *A*, 1948 *F*, *W*, *I*, *E*
Lyall, W J C (Edinburgh Acads) 1871 *E*

Mabon, J T (Jedforest) 1898 *I*, *E*, 1899 *I*, 1900 *I*
Macarthur, J P (Waterloo) 1932 *E*
MacCallum, J C (Watsonians) 1905 *E*, *NZ*, 1906 *W*, *I*, *E*, *SA*, 1907 *W*, *I*, *E*, 1908 *W*, *I*, *E*, 1909 *W*, *I*, *E*, 1910 *F*, *W*, *I*, *E*, 1911 *F*, *I*, *E*, 1912 *F*, *W*, *I*, *E*
McClung, T (Edinburgh Acads) 1956 *I*, *E*, 1957 *W*, *I*, *E*, 1959 *F*, *W*, *I*, 1960 *W*
McClure, G B (W of Scotland) 1873 *E*
McClure, J H (W of Scotland) 1872 *E*
McCowan, D (W of Scotland) 1880 *I*, *E*, 1881 *I*, *E*, 1882 *I*, *E*, 1883 *I*, *E*, 1884 *I*, *E*
McCowat, R H (Glasgow Acads) 1905 *I*
McCrae, I G (Gordonians) 1967 *E*, 1968 *I*, 1969 *F* (R), *W*, 1972 *F*, *NZ*
McCrow, J W S (Edinburgh Acads) 1921 *I*
McDonald, C (Jedforest) 1947 *A*
Macdonald, D C (Edinburgh U) 1953 *F*, *W*, 1958 *I*, *E*
Macdonald, D S M (Oxford U, London Scottish, W of Scotland) 1977 *E*, *I*, *F*, *W*, 1978 *I*, *W*, *E*
Macdonald, J D (London Scottish, Army) 1966 *F*, *W*, *I*, *E*, 1967 *F*, *W*, *I*, *E*
Macdonald, J M (Edinburgh Wands) 1911 *W*
Macdonald, J S (Edinburgh U) 1903 *E*, 1904 *W*, *I*, *E*, 1905 *W*
Macdonald, K R (Stewart's Coll FP) 1956 *F*, *W*, *I*, 1957 *W*, *I*, *E*
Macdonald, R (Edinburgh U) 1950 *F*, *W*, *I*, *E*
McDonald, W A (Glasgow U) 1889 *W*, 1892 *I*, *E*
Macdonald, W G (London Scottish) 1969 *I* (R)
Macdougall, J B (Greenock Wands, Wakefield) 1913 *F*, 1914 *I*, 1921 *F*, *I*, *E*
McEwan, M C (Edinburgh Acads) 1886 *E*, 1887 *I*, *W*, *E*, 1888 *W*, *I*, 1889 *W*, *I*, 1890 *W*, *I*, *E*, 1891 *W*, *I*, *E*, 1892 *E*
MacEwan, N A (Gala, Highland) 1971 *F*, *W*, *I*, *E* (2[1C]), 1972 *F*, *W*, *E*, *NZ*, 1973 *F*, *W*, *I*, *E*, *P*, 1974 *W*, *E*, *I*, *F*, 1975 *W*, *E*
McEwan, W M C (Edinburgh Acads) 1894 *W*, *E*, 1895 *W*, *E*, 1896 *W*, *I*, *E*, 1897 *I*, *E*, 1898 *I*, *E*, 1889 *I*, *W*, *E*, 1900 *W*, *E*
MacEwen, R K G (Cambridge U, London Scottish) 1954 *F*, *NZ*, *I*, *W*, 1956 *F*, *W*, *I*, *E*, 1957 *F*, *W*, *I*, *E*, 1958 *W*
Macfarlan, D J (London Scottish) 1883 *W*, 1884 *W*, *I*, *E*, 1886 *W*, *I*, 1887 *I*, 1888 *I*

McFarlane, J L H (Edinburgh U) 1871 *E*, 1872 *E*, 1873 *E*
McGaughey, S K (Hawick) 1984 *R*
McGeechan, I R (Headingley) 1972 *NZ*, 1973 *F, W, I, E, P*, 1974 *W, E, I, F*, 1975 *I, F, W, E, NZ, A*, 1976 *F, W, E, I*, 1977 *E, I, F, W*, 1978 *I, F, W, NZ*, 1979 *W, E, I, F*
McGlashan, T P L (Royal HSFP) 1947 *F, I, E*, 1954 *F, NZ, I, E, W*
MacGregor, D G (Watsonians, Pontypridd) 1907 *W, I, E*
MacGregor, G (Cambridge U) 1890 *W, I, E*, 1891 *W, I, E*, 1893 *W, I, E*, 1894 *W, I, E*, 1896 *E*
MacGregor, I A A (Hillhead HSFP, Llanelli) 1955 *I, E*, 1956 *F, W, I, E*, 1957 *F, W, I*
MacGregor, J R (Edinburgh U) 1909 *I*
McGuinness, G M (W of Scotland) 1982 *A* 1,2, 1983 *I*, 1985 *I, F, W, E*
McHarg, A F (W of Scotland, London Scottish) 1968 *I, E, A*, 1969 *F, W, I, E*, 1971 *F, W, I, E* (2[1C]), 1972 *F, E, NZ*, 1973 *F, W, I, E, P*, 1974 *W, E, I, F*, 1975 *I, F, W, E, NZ, A*, 1976 *F, W, E, I*, 1977 *E, I, F, W*, 1978 *I, F, W, NZ*, 1979 *W, E*
McIndoe, F (Glasgow Acads) 1886 *W, I*
MacIntyre, I (Edinburgh Wands) 1890 *W, I, E*, 1891 *W, I, E*
McIvor, D J (Edinburgh Acads) 1992 *E, I, F, W*
Mackay, E B (Glasgow Acads) 1920 *W*, 1922 *E*
McKeating, E (Heriot's FP) 1957 *F, W*, 1961 *SA, W, I, E*
McKendrick, J G (W of Scotland) 1889 *I*
Mackenzie, A D G (Selkirk) 1984 *A*
Mackenzie, C J G (United Services) 1921 *E*
Mackenzie, D D (Edinburgh U) 1947 *W, I, E*, 1948 *F, W, I*
Mackenzie, D K A (Edinburgh Wands) 1939 *I, E*
Mackenzie, J M (Edinburgh U) 1905 *NZ*, 1909 *W, I, E*, 1910 *W, I, E*, 1911 *W, I*
Mackenzie, R C (Glasgow Acads) 1877 *I, E*, 1881 *I, E*
Mackie, G Y (Highland) 1975 *A*, 1976 *F, W*, 1978 *F*
MacKinnon, A (London Scottish) 1898 *I, E*, 1899 *I, W, E*, 1900 *E*
Mackintosh, C E W C (London Scottish) 1924 *F*
Mackintosh, H S (Glasgow U, W of Scotland) 1929 *F, W, I, E*, 1930 *F, W, I, E*, 1931 *F, W, I, E*, 1932 *SA, W, I, E*
MacLachlan, L P (Oxford U, London Scottish) 1954 *NZ, I, E, W*
Maclagan, W E (Edinburgh Acads) 1878 *E*, 1879 *I, E*, 1880 *I, E*, 1881 *I, E*, 1882 *I, E*, 1883 *W, I, E*, 1884 *W, I, E*, 1885 *W, I* 1,2, 1887 *I, E*, 1888 *W, I*, 1890 *W, I, E*
McLaren, A (Durham County) 1931 *F*
McLaren, E (London Scottish, Royal HSFP) 1923 *F, W, I, E*, 1924 *F*
McLauchlan, J (Jordanhill) 1969 *E, SA*, 1970 *F, W*, 1971 *F, W, I, E* (2[1C]), 1972 *F, W, E, NZ*, 1973 *F, W, I, E, P*, 1974 *W, E, I, F*, 1975 *I, F, W, E, NZ, A*, 1976 *F, W, E, I*, 1977 *W*, 1978 *I, F, W, E, NZ*, 1979 *W, E, I, F, NZ*
McLean, D I (Royal HSFP) 1947 *I, E*
Maclennan, W D (Watsonians) 1947 *F, I*
MacLeod, D A (Glasgow U) 1886 *I, E*
MacLeod, G (Edinburgh Acads) 1878 *E*, 1882 *I*
McLeod, H F (Hawick) 1954 *F, NZ, I, E, W*, 1955 *F, W, I, E*, 1956 *F, W, I, E*, 1957 *F, W, I, E*, 1958 *F, W, A, I, E*, 1959 *F, W, I, E*, 1960 *F, W, I, E, SA*, 1961 *F, SA, W, I, E*, 1962 *F, W, I, E*
MacLeod, K G (Cambridge U) 1905 *NZ*, 1906 *W, I, E, SA*, 1907 *W, I, E*, 1908 *I, E*
MacLeod, L M (Cambridge U) 1904 *W, I, E*, 1905 *W, I, NZ*
Macleod, W M (Fettesian-Lorettonians, Edinburgh Wands) 1886 *W, I*
McMillan, K H D (Sale) 1953 *F, W, I, E*
MacMillan, R G (London Scottish) 1887 *W, I, E*, 1890 *W, I, E*, 1891 *W, E*, 1892 *W, I, E*, 1893 *W, E*, 1894 *W, I, E*, 1895 *W, I, E*, 1897 *I, E*
MacMyn, D J (Cambridge U, London Scottish) 1925 *F, W, I, E*, 1926 *F, W, I, E*, 1927 *E, A*, 1928 *F*
McNeil, A S B (Watsonians) 1935 *I*
McPartlin, J J (Harlequins, Oxford U) 1960 *F, W*, 1962 *F, W, I, E*
Macphail, J A R (Edinburgh Acads) 1949 *E*, 1951 *SA*

Macpherson, D G (London Hospital) 1910 *I, E*
Macpherson, G P S (Oxford U, Edinburgh Acads) 1922 *F, W, I, E*, 1924 *W, E*, 1925 *F, W, E*, 1927 *F, W, I, E*, 1928 *F, W, E*, 1929 *I, E*, 1930 *F, W, I, E*, 1931 *W, E*, 1932 *SA, E*
Macpherson, N C (Newport, Mon) 1920 *W, I, E*, 1921 *F, E*, 1923 *I, E*
McQueen, S B (Waterloo) 1923 *F, W, I, E*
Macrae, D J (St Andrews U) 1937 *W, I, E*, 1938 *W, I, E*, 1939 *W, I, E*
Madsen, D F (Gosforth) 1974 *W, E, I, F*, 1975 *I, F, W, E*, 1976 *F, W*, 1977 *E, I, F, W*, 1978 *I*
Mair, N G R (Edinburgh U) 1951 *F, W, I, E*
Maitland, G (Edinburgh Inst FP) 1885 *W, I* 2
Maitland, R (Edinburgh Inst FP) 1881 *E*, 1882 *I, E*, 1884 *W*, 1885 *W*
Maitland, R P (Royal Artillery) 1872 *E*
Malcolm, A G (Glasgow U) 1888 *I*
Marsh, J (Edinburgh Inst FP) 1889 *W, I*
Marshall, A (Edinburgh Acads) 1875 *E*
Marshall, G R (Selkirk) 1988 *A* (R), 1989 *Fj*, 1990 *Arg*, 1991 [*Z*]
Marshall, J C (London Scottish) 1954 *F, NZ, I, E, W*
Marshall, K W (Edinburgh Acads) 1934 *W, I, E*, 1935 *W, I, E*, 1936 *W*, 1937 *E*
Marshall, T R (Edinburgh Acads) 1871 *E*, 1872 *E*, 1873 *E*, 1874 *E*
Marshall, W (Edinburgh Acads) 1872 *E*
Martin, H (Edinburgh Acads, Oxford U) 1908 *W, I, E*, 1909 *W, E*
Masters, W H (Edinburgh Inst FP) 1879 *I*, 1880 *I, E*
Maxwell, F T (Royal Engineers) 1872 *E*
Maxwell, G H H P (Edinburgh Acads, RAF, London Scottish) 1913 *I, E*, 1914 *W, I, E*, 1920 *W, E*, 1921 *F, W, I, E*, 1922 *F, E*
Maxwell, J M (Langholm) 1957 *I*
Mein, J (Edinburgh Acads) 1871 *E*, 1872 *E*, 1873 *E*, 1874 *E*, 1875 *E*
Melville, C L (Army) 1937 *W, I, E*
Menzies, H F (W of Scotland) 1893 *W, I*, 1894 *W, E*
Methuen, A (London Scottish) 1889 *W, I*
Michie, E J S (Aberdeen U, Aberdeen GSFP) 1954 *F, NZ, I, E*, 1955 *W, I, E*, 1956 *F, W, I, E*, 1957 *F, W, I, E*
Millar, J N (W of Scotland) 1892 *W, I, E*, 1893 *W*, 1895 *I, E*
Millar, R K (London Scottish) 1924 *I*
Millican, J G (Edinburgh U) 1973 *W, I, E*
Milne, C J B (Fettesian-Lorettonians, W of Scotland) 1886 *W, I, E*
Milne, D F (Heriot's FP) 1991 [*J*(R)]
Milne, I G (Heriot's FP, Harlequins) 1979 *I, F, NZ*, 1980 *I, F*, 1981 *NZ* 1,2, *R, A*, 1982 *E, I, F, W, A* 1,2, 1983 *I, F, W, E, NZ*, 1984 *W, E, I, F, A*, 1985 *F, W, E*, 1986 *F, W, E, I, R*, 1987 *I, F, W, E, [F, Z, NZ]*, 1988 *A*, 1989 *W*, 1990 *NZ* 1,2
Milne, K S (Heriot's FP) 1989 *W, E, I, F, Fj, R*, 1990 *I, F, W, E*, 1990 *NZ* 2, *Arg*, 1991 *F, W*(R), *E, [Z]*, 1992 *E, I, F, W, A* 1, 1993 *I, F, W, E*
Milne, W M (Glasgow Acads) 1904 *I, E*, 1905 *W, I*
Milroy, E (Watsonians) 1910 *W*, 1911 *E*, 1912 *W, I, E, SA*, 1913 *F, W, I, E*, 1914 *I, E*
Mitchell, G W E (Edinburgh Wands) 1967 *NZ*, 1968 *F, W*
Mitchell, J G (W of Scotland) 1885 *W, I* 1,2
Moncreiff, F J (Edinburgh Acads) 1871 *E*, 1872 *E*, 1873 *E*
Monteith, H G (Cambridge U, London Scottish) 1905 *E*, 1906 *W, I, E, SA*, 1907 *W, I*, 1908 *E*
Monypenny, D B (London Scottish) 1899 *I, W, E*
Moodie, A R (St Andrew's U) 1909 *E*, 1910 *F*, 1911 *F*
Moore, A (Edinburgh Acads) 1990 *NZ* 2, *Arg*, 1991 *F, W, E*
Morgan, D W (Stewart's-Melville FP) 1973 *W, I, E, P*, 1974 *I, F*, 1975 *I, F, W, E, NZ, A*, 1976 *F, W*, 1977 *I, F, W*, 1978 *I, F, W, E*
Morrison, I R (London Scottish) 1993 *I, F, W, E*
Morrison, M C (Royal HSFP) 1896 *W, I, E*, 1897 *I, E*, 1898 *I, E*, 1899 *I, W, E*, 1900 *W, E*, 1901 *W, I, E*, 1902 *W, I, E*, 1903 *W, I*, 1904 *W, I, E*
Morrison, R H (Edinburgh U) 1886 *W, I, E*
Morrison, W H (Edinburgh Acads) 1900 *W*
Morton, D S (W of Scotland) 1887 *I, W, E*, 1888 *W, I*, 1889 *W, I*, 1890 *I, E*

Mowat, J G (Glasgow Acads) 1883 *W, E*
Muir, D E (Heriot's FP) 1950 *F, W, I, E*, 1952 *W, I, E*
Munnoch, N M (Watsonians) 1952 *F, W, I*
Munro, P (Oxford, London Scottish) 1905 *W, I, E,
NZ*, 1906 *W, I, E, SA*, 1907 *I, E*, 1911 *F, W, I*
Munro, R (St Andrews U) 1871 *E*
Munro, S (Ayr, W of Scotland) 1980 *I, F*, 1981 *F, W,
E, I, NZ* 1,2, *R*, 1984 *W*
Munro, W H (Glasgow HSFP) 1947 *I, E*
Murdoch, W C W (Hillhead HSFP) 1935 *E, NZ*, 1936
W, I, 1939 *E*, 1948 *F, W, I, E*
Murray, G M (Glasgow Acads) 1921 *I*, 1926 *W*
Murray, H M (Glasgow U) 1936 *W, I*
Murray, K T (Hawick) 1985 *I, F, W*
Murray, R O (Cambridge U) 1935 *W, E*
Murray, W A K (London Scottish) 1920 *F, I*, 1921 *F*

Napier, H M (W of Scotland) 1877 *I, E*, 1878 *E*, 1879
I, E
Neill, J B (Edinburgh Acads) 1963 *E*, 1964 *F, NZ, W,
I, E*, 1965 *F*
Neill, R M (Edinburgh Acads) 1901 *E*, 1902 *I*
Neilson, G T (W of Scotland) 1891 *W, I, E*, 1892 *W, E,
1893 W*, 1894 *W, I*, 1895 *W, I, E*, 1896 *W, I, E*
Neilson, J A (Glasgow Acads) 1878 *E*, 1879 *E*
Neilson, R T (W of Scotland) 1898 *I, E*, 1899 *I, W,
1900 I, E*
Neilson, T (W of Scotland) 1874 *E*
Neilson, W (Merchiston, Cambridge U, London Scot-
tish) 1891 *W, E*, 1892 *W, I, E*, 1893 *I, E*, 1894 *E*, 1895
W, I, E, 1896 *I*, 1897 *I, E*
Neilson, W G (Merchistonians) 1894 *E*
Nelson, J B (Glasgow Acads) 1925 *F, W, I, E*, 1926 *F,
W, I, E*, 1927 *F, W, I, E*, 1928 *I, E*, 1929 *F, W, I, E*,
1930 *F, W, I, E*, 1931 *F, W, I*
Nelson, T A (Oxford U) 1898 *E*
Nichol, J A (Royal HSFP) 1955 *W, I, E*
Nicol, A D (Dundee HSFP) 1992 *E, I, F, W, A* 1,2
Nimmo, C S (Watsonians) 1920 *E*

Ogilvy, C (Hawick) 1911 *I, E*, 1912 *I*
Oliver, G H (Hawick) 1987 *[Z]*, 1990 *NZ* 2 (R), 1991
[Z]
Oliver, G K (Gala) 1970 *A*
Orr, C E (W of Scotland) 1887 *I, E, W*, 1888 *W, I*, 1889
W, I, 1890 *W, I, E*, 1891 *W, I, E*, 1892 *W, I, E*
Orr, H J (London Scottish) 1903 *W, I, E*, 1904 *W, I*
Orr, J E (W of Scotland) 1889 *I*, 1890 *W, I, E*, 1891 *W,
I, E*, 1892 *W, I, E*, 1893 *I, E*
Orr, J H (Edinburgh City Police) 1947 *F, W*
Osler, F L (Edinburgh U) 1911 *F, W*

Park, J (Royal HSFP) 1934 *W*
Paterson, D S (Gala) 1969 *SA*, 1970 *I, E, A*, 1971 *F, W,
I, E* (2[1C]), 1972 *W*
Paterson, G Q (Edinburgh Acads) 1876 *E*
Paterson, J R (Birkenhead Park) 1924 *F, W, I, E*, 1926
F, W, I, E, 1927 *F, W, I, E, A*, 1928 *F, W, I, E*, 1929
F, W, I, E
Patterson, D (Hawick) 1896 *W*
Pattullo, G L (Panmure) 1920 *F, W, I, E*
Paxton, I A M (Selkirk) 1981 *NZ* 1,2, *R, A*, 1982 *E, I,
F, W, A* 1,2, 1983 *I, E, NZ*, 1984 *W, E, I, F*, 1985 *I* (R),
F, W, E, 1986 *W, E, I, R*, 1987 *I, F, W, E*, *[F, Z, R,
NZ]*, 1988 *I, E, A*
Paxton, R E (Kelso) 1982 *I, A* 2 (R)
Pearson, J (Watsonians) 1909 *I, E*, 1910 *F, W, I, E*,
1911 *F*, 1912 *F, W, SA*, 1913 *I, E*
Pender, I M (London Scottish) 1914 *E*
Pender, N E K (Hawick) 1977 *I*, 1978 *F, W, E*
Penman, W M (RAF) 1939 *I*
Peterkin, W A (Edinburgh U) 1881 *E*, 1883 *I*, 1884 *W,
I, E*, 1885 *W, I* 1,2
Petrie, A G (Royal HSFP) 1873 *E*, 1874 *E*, 1875 *E*,
1876 *E*, 1877 *I, E*, 1878 *E*, 1879 *I, E*, 1880 *I, E*
Philp, A (Edinburgh Inst FP) 1882 *E*
Pocock, E I (Edinburgh Wands) 1877 *I, E*
Pollock, J A (Gosforth) 1982 *W*, 1983 *E, NZ*, 1984 *E*
(R), *I, F, R*, 1985 *F*
Polson, A H (Gala) 1930 *E*
Purdie, W (Jedforest) 1939 *W, I, E*
Purves, A B H L (London Scottish) 1906 *W, I, E, SA*,
1907 *W, I, E*, 1908 *W, I, E*
Purves, W D C L (London Scottish) 1912 *F, W, I, SA*,
1913 *I, E*

Rea, C W W (W of Scotland, Headingley) 1968 *A*, 1969
F, W, I, SA, 1970 *F, W, I, A*, 1971 *F, W, E* (2[1C])
Reed, A I (Bath) 1993 *I, F, W, E*
Reid, C (Edinburgh Acads) 1881 *I, E*, 1882 *I, E*, 1883
W, I, E, 1884 *W, I, E*, 1885 *W, I* 1,2, 1886 *W, I, E*, 1887
I, W, E, 1888 *W, I*
Reid, J (Edinburgh Wands) 1874 *E*, 1875 *E*, 1876 *E*,
1877 *I, E*
Reid, J M (Edinburgh Acads) 1898 *I, E*, 1899 *I*
Reid, M F (Loretto) 1883 *I, E*
Reid-Kerr, J (Greenock Wand) 1909 *E*
Relph, W K L (Stewart's Coll FP) 1955 *F, W, I, E*
Renny-Tailyour, H W (Royal Engineers) 1872 *E*
Renwick, J M (Hawick) 1972 *W, E, NZ*, 1973 *F,
1974 W, E, I, F*, 1975 *I, F, W, E, NZ, A*, 1976 *F, W,
E*(R), 1977 *I, F, W*, 1978 *I, F, W, E, NZ*, 1979 *W, E,
I, F, NZ*, 1980 *I, F, W, E*, 1981 *F, W, E, I, NZ* 1,2, *R,
A*, 1982 *E, I, F, W*, 1983 *I, F, W, E*, 1984 *R*
Renwick, W L (London Scottish) 1989 *R*
Renwick, W N (London Scottish, Edinburgh Wands)
1938 *E*, 1939 *W*
Ritchie, G (Merchistonians) 1871 *E*
Ritchie, G F (Dundee HSFP) 1932 *E*
Ritchie, J M (Watsonians) 1933 *W, E, I*, 1934 *W, I, E*
Ritchie, W T (Cambridge U) 1905 *I, E*
Robb, G H (Glasgow U) 1881 *I*, 1885 *W*
Roberts, G (Watsonians) 1938 *W, I, E*, 1939 *W, E*
Robertson, A H (W of Scotland) 1871 *E*
Robertson, A W (Edinburgh Acads) 1897 *E*
Robertson, D (Edinburgh Acads) 1875 *E*
Robertson, D D (Cambridge U) 1893 *W*
Robertson, I (London Scottish, Watsonians) 1968 *E,
1969 E, SA*, 1970 *F, W, I, E, A*
Robertson, I P M (Watsonians) 1910 *F*
Robertson, J (Clydesdale) 1908 *E*
Robertson, K W (Melrose) 1978 *NZ*, 1979 *W, E, I, F,
NZ*, 1980 *W, E*, 1981 *F, W, E, I, F, R, A*, 1982 *E, I, F,
A* 1,2, 1983 *I, F, W, E*, 1984 *E, I, F, R*, 1985 *I, F,
W, E*, 1986 *I*, 1987 *F* (R), *W, E*, *[F, Z, NZ]*, 1988 *E, A*,
1989 *E, I, F*
Robertson, L (London Scottish, United Services) 1908
E, 1911 *W*, 1912 *W, I, E, SA*, 1913 *W, I, E*
Robertson, M A (Gala) 1958 *F*
Robertson, R D (London Scottish) 1912 *F*
Robson, A (Hawick) 1954 *F*, 1955 *F, W, I, E*, 1956 *F,
W, I, E*, 1957 *F, W, I, E*, 1958 *W, A, I, E*, 1959 *F, W,
I, E*, 1960 *F*
Rodd, J A T (United Services, RN, London Scottish)
1958 *F, W, A, I, E*, 1960 *F, W*, 1962 *F*, 1964 *F, NZ, W*,
1965 *F, W, I*
Rogerson, J (Kelvinside Acads) 1894 *W*
Roland, E T (Edinburgh Acads) 1884 *I, E*
Rollo, D M D (Howe of Fife) 1959 *E*, 1960 *F, W, I, E,
SA*, 1961 *F, SA, W, I, E*, 1962 *F, W, E*, 1963 *F, W, I,
E*, 1964 *F, NZ, W, I, E*, 1965 *F, W, I, E, SA*, 1966 *F,
W, I, E, A*, 1967 *F, W, E, NZ*, 1968 *F, W, I*
Rose, D M (Jedforest) 1951 *F, W, I, E, SA*, 1953 *F, W*
Ross, A (Kilmarnock) 1924 *F, W*
Ross, A (Royal HSFP) 1905 *W, I, E*, 1909 *W, I*
Ross, A R (Edinburgh U) 1911 *W*, 1914 *W, I, E*
Ross, E J (London Scottish) 1904 *W*
Ross, G T (Watsonians) 1954 *NZ, I, E, W*
Ross, I A (Hillhead HSFP) 1951 *F, W, I, E*
Ross, J (London Scottish) 1901 *W, I, E*, 1902 *W*, 1903
E
Ross, K I (Boroughmuir FP) 1961 *SA, W, I, E*, 1962 *F,
W, I, E*, 1963 *F, W, E*
Ross, W A (Hillhead HSFP) 1937 *W, E*
Rottenburg, H (Cambridge U, London Scottish) 1899
W, E, 1900 *W, I, E*
Roughead, W N (Edinburgh Acads, London Scottish)
1927 *A*, 1928 *F, W, I, E*, 1930 *I, E*, 1931 *F, W, I, E*,
1932 *W*
Rowan, N A (Boroughmuir) 1980 *W, E*, 1981 *F, W, E,
I*, 1984 *R*, 1985 *I*, 1987 *[R]*, 1988 *I, F, W, E*
Rowand, R (Glasgow HSFP) 1930 *F, W*, 1932 *E*, 1933
W, E, I, 1934 *W*
Roy, A (Waterloo) 1938 *W, I, E*, 1939 *W, I, E*
Russell, W L (Glasgow Acads) 1905 *NZ*, 1906 *W, I, E*
Rutherford, J Y (Selkirk) 1979 *W, E, I, F, NZ*, 1980 *I,
F, E*, 1981 *F, W, E, I, NZ* 1,2, *A*, 1982 *E, I, F, W, A*
1,2, 1983 *E, NZ*, 1984 *W, E, I, F, R*, 1985 *I, F, W, E*,
1986 *F, W, E, I, R*, 1987 *I, F, W, E, [F]*

Sampson, R W F (London Scottish) 1939 *W*, 1947 *W*
Sanderson, G A (Royal HSFP) 1907 *W, I, E*, 1908 *I*
Sanderson, J L P (Edinburgh Acads) 1873 *E*
Schulze, D G (London Scottish) 1905 *E*, 1907 *I, E*, 1908 *W, I, E*, 1909 *W, I, E*, 1910 *W, I, E*, 1911 *W*
Scobie, R M (Royal Military Coll) 1914 *W, I, E*
Scotland, K J F (Heriot's FP, Cambridge U, Leicester) 1957 *F, W, I, E*, 1958 *E*, 1959 *F, W, I, E*, 1960 *F, W, I, E*, 1961 *F, SA, W, I, E*, 1962 *F, W, I, E*, 1963 *F, W, I, E*, 1965 *F*
Scott, D M (Langholm, Watsonians) 1950 *I, E*, 1951 *W, I, E, SA*, 1952 *F, W, I*, 1953 *F*
Scott, J M B (Edinburgh Acads) 1907 *E*, 1908 *W, I, E*, 1909 *W, I, E*, 1910 *F, W, I, E*, 1911 *F, W, I*, 1912 *W, I, E, SA*, 1913 *W, I, E*
Scott, J S (St Andrews U) 1950 *E*
Scott, J W (Stewart's Coll FP) 1925 *F, W, I, E*, 1926 *F, W, I, E*, 1927 *F, W, I, E, A*, 1928 *F, W, E*, 1929 *E*, 1930 *F*
Scott, M (Dunfermline) 1992 *A 2*
Scott, R (Hawick) 1898 *I*, 1900 *I, E*
Scott, T (Langholm, Hawick) 1896 *W*, 1897 *I, E*, 1898 *I, E*, 1899 *I, W, E*, 1900 *W, I, E*
Scott, T M (Hawick) 1893 *E*, 1895 *W, I, E*, 1896 *W, E*, 1897 *I, E*, 1898 *I, E*, 1900 *W, I*
Scott, W P (W of Scotland) 1900 *I, E*, 1902 *I, E*, 1903 *W, I, E*, 1904 *W, I, E*, 1905 *W, I, E, NZ*, 1906 *W, I, E, SA*, 1907 *W, I, E*
Scoular, J G (Cambridge U) 1905 *NZ*, 1906 *W, I, E, SA*
Selby, J A R (Watsonians) 1920 *W, I*
Shackleton, J A P (London Scottish) 1959 *E*, 1963 *F, W*, 1964 *NZ, W*, 1965 *I, SA*
Sharp, G (Stewart's FP, Army) 1960 *F*, 1964 *F, NZ, W*
Shaw, G D (Sale) 1935 *NZ*, 1936 *W*, 1937 *W, I, E*, 1939 *I*
Shaw, I (Glasgow HSFP) 1937 *I*
Shaw, J N (Edinburgh Acads) 1921 *W, I*
Shaw, R W (Glasgow HSFP) 1934 *W, I, E*, 1935 *W, I, E, NZ*, 1936 *W, I, E*, 1937 *W, I, E*, 1938 *W, I, E*, 1939 *W, I, E*
Shedden, D (W of Scotland) 1972 *NZ*, 1973 *F, W, I, E, P*, 1976 *W, E, I*, 1977 *I, F, W*, 1978 *I, F, W*
Shiel, A G (Melrose) 1991 *[I(R), WS]*, 1993 *I, F, W, E*
Shillinglaw, R B (Gala, Army) 1960 *I, E, SA*, 1961 *F, SA*
Simmers, B M (Glasgow Acads) 1965 *F, W*, 1966 *A*, 1967 *F, W, I*, 1971 *F (R)*
Simmers, W M (Glasgow Acads) 1926 *W, I, E*, 1927 *F, W, I, E, A*, 1928 *F, W, I, E*, 1929 *F, W, I, E*, 1930 *F, W, I, E*, 1931 *F, W, I, E*, 1932 *SA, W, I, E*
Simpson, J W (Royal HSFP) 1893 *I, E*, 1894 *W, I, E*, 1895 *W, I, E*, 1896 *W, I*, 1897 *E*, 1899 *W, E*
Simpson, R S (Glasgow Acads) 1923 *I*
Simson, E D (Edinburgh U, London Scottish) 1902 *E*, 1903 *W, I, E*, 1904 *W, I, E*, 1905 *W, I, E, NZ*, 1906 *W, I, E*, 1907 *W, I, E*
Simson, J T (Watsonians) 1905 *NZ*, 1909 *W, I, E*, 1910 *F, W*, 1911 *I*
Simson, R F (London Scottish) 1911 *E*
Sloan, A T (Edinburgh Acads) 1914 *W*, 1920 *F, W, I, E*, 1921 *F, W, I, E*
Sloan, D A (Edinburgh Acads, London Scottish) 1950 *F, W, E*, 1951 *W, I, E*, 1953 *F*
Sloan, T (Glasgow Acads, Oxford U) 1905 *NZ*, 1906 *W, SA*, 1907 *W, E*, 1908 *W*, 1909 *I*
Smeaton, P W (Edinburgh Acads) 1881 *I*, 1883 *I, E*
Smith, A R (Oxford U) 1895 *W, I, E*, 1896 *W, I*, 1897 *I, E*, 1898 *I, E*, 1900 *I, E*
Smith, A R (Cambridge U, Gosforth, Ebbw Vale, Edinburgh Wands) 1955 *W, I, E*, 1956 *F, W, I, E*, 1957 *F, W, I, E*, 1958 *F, W, A, I*, 1959 *F, W, I, E*, 1960 *F, W, I, E, SA*, 1961 *F, SA, W, I, E*, 1962 *F, W, I, E*
Smith, D W C (London Scottish) 1949 *F, W, I, E*, 1950 *F, W, I*, 1953 *I*
Smith, E R (Edinburgh Acads) 1879 *I*
Smith, G K (Kelso) 1957 *I, E*, 1958 *F, W, A*, 1959 *F, W, I, E*, 1960 *F, W, I, E*, 1961 *F, SA, W, I, E*
Smith, H O (Watsonians) 1895 *W*, 1896 *W, I, E*, 1898 *I, E*, 1899 *W, I, E*, 1900 *E*, 1902 *E*
Smith, I R (Gloucester) 1992 *E, I, W, A 1,2*
Smith, I S (Oxford U, Edinburgh U) 1924 *W, I, E*, 1925 *F, W, I, E*, 1926 *F, W, I, E*, 1927 *F, I, E*, 1929 *F, W, I, E*, 1930 *F, W, I*, 1931 *F, W, I, E*, 1932 *SA, W, I, E*,

1933 *W, E, I*
Smith, I S G (London Scottish) 1969 *SA*, 1970 *F, W, I, E*, 1971 *F, W, I*
Smith, M A (London Scottish) 1970 *W, I, E, A*
Smith, R T (Kelso) 1929 *F, W, I, E*, 1930 *F, W, I*
Smith, S H (Glasgow Acads) 1877 *I*, 1878 *E*
Smith, T J (Gala) 1983 *E, NZ*, 1985 *I, F*
Sole, D M B (Bath, Edinburgh Acads) 1986 *F, W*, 1987 *I, F, W, E, [F, Z, R, NZ]*, 1988 *I, F, W, E, A*, 1989 *W, E, I, F, Fj, R*, 1990 *I, F, W, E, NZ 1,2, Arg*, 1991 *F, W, E, I, R, [J, I, WS, E, NZ]*, 1992 *E, I, F, W, A 1,2*
Somerville, D (Edinburgh Inst FP) 1879 *I*, 1882 *I*, 1883 *W, I, E*, 1884 *W*
Speirs, L M (Watsonians) 1906 *SA*, 1907 *W, I, E*, 1908 *W, I, E*, 1910 *F, W, E*
Spence, K M (Oxford U) 1953 *I*
Spencer, E (Clydedale) 1898 *I*
Stagg, P K (Sale) 1965 *F, W, E, SA*, 1966 *F, W, I, E, A*, 1967 *F, W, I, E, NZ*, 1968 *F, W, I, E, A*, 1969 *F, W, I (R), SA*, 1970 *F, W, I, E, A*
Stanger, A G (Hawick) 1989 *Fj, R*, 1990 *I, F, W, E, NZ 1,2, Arg*, 1991 *F, W, E, I, R, [J, Z, I, WS, E, NZ]*, 1992 *E, I, F, W, A 1,2*, 1993 *I, F, W, E*
Stark, D A (Boroughmuir) 1993 *I, F, W, E*
Steele, W C C (Langholm, Bedford, RAF, London Scottish) 1969 *E*, 1971 *F, W, I, E* (2[1C]), 1972 *F, W, E, NZ*, 1973 *F, W, I, E*, 1975 *I, F, W, E, NZ* (R), 1976 *W, E, I*, 1977 *E*
Stephen, A E (W of Scotland) 1885 *W*, 1886 *I*
Steven, P D (Heriot's FP) 1984 *A*, 1985 *F, W, E*
Steven, R (Edinburgh Wands) 1962 *I*
Stevenson, A K (Glasgow Acads) 1922 *F*, 1923 *F, W, E*
Stevenson, A M (Glasgow U) 1911 *F*
Stevenson, G D (Hawick) 1956 *E*, 1957 *F, W, I, E*, 1958 *F, W, A, I, E*, 1959 *W, I, E*, 1960 *W, I, E, SA*, 1961 *F, SA, W, I, E*, 1963 *F, W, I*, 1964 *E*, 1965 *F*
Stevenson, H J (Edinburgh Acads) 1888 *W, I*, 1889 *W, I*, 1890 *W, I, E*, 1891 *W, I, E*, 1892 *W, I, E*, 1893 *I, E*
Stevenson, L E (Edinburgh U) 1888 *W*
Stevenson, R C (London Scottish) 1897 *I, E*, 1898 *E*, 1899 *I, W, E*
Stevenson, R C (St Andrews U) 1910 *F, I, E*, 1911 *F, W, I*
Stevenson, W H (Glasgow Acads) 1925 *F*
Stewart, A K (Edinburgh U) 1874 *E*, 1876 *E*
Stewart, A M (Edinburgh Acads) 1914 *W*
Stewart, C A R (W of Scotland) 1880 *I, E*
Stewart, C E B (Kelso) 1960 *W*, 1961 *F*
Stewart, J (Glasgow HSFP) 1930 *F*
Stewart, J L (Edinburgh Acads) 1921 *I*
Stewart, M S (Stewart's Coll FP) 1932 *SA, W, I*, 1933 *W, E, I*, 1934 *W, I, E*
Stewart, W A (London Hospital) 1913 *F, W, I*, 1914 *W*
Steyn, S S L (Oxford U) 1911 *E*, 1912 *I*
Strachan, G M (Jordanhill) 1971 *E* (C) (R), 1973 *W, I, E, P*
Stronach, R S (Glasgow Acads) 1901 *W, E*, 1905 *W, I, E*
Stuart, C D (W of Scotland) 1909 *I*, 1910 *F, W, I, E*, 1911 *I, E*
Stuart, L M (Glasgow HSFP) 1923 *F, W, I, E*, 1924 *F*, 1928 *E*, 1930 *I, E*
Suddon, N (Hawick) 1965 *W, I, E, SA*, 1966 *A*, 1968 *E, A*, 1969 *F, W, I*, 1970 *I, E, A*
Sutherland, W R (Hawick) 1910 *W, E*, 1911 *F, E*, 1912 *F, W, E, SA*, 1913 *F, W, I, E*, 1914 *W*
Swan, J S (Army, London Scottish, Leicester) 1953 *E*, 1954 *F, NZ, I, E, W*, 1955 *F, W, I, E*, 1956 *F, W, I, E*, 1957 *F, W*, 1958 *F*
Swan, M W (Oxford U, London Scottish) 1958 *F, W, A, I, E*, 1959 *F, W, I*
Sweet, J B (Glasgow HSFP) 1913 *E*, 1914 *I*
Symington, A W (Cambridge U) 1914 *W, E*

Tait, A V (Kelso) 1987 *[F(R), Z, R, NZ]*, 1988 *I, F, W, E*
Tait, J G (Edinburgh Acads) 1880 *I*, 1885 *I 2*
Tait, P W (Royal HSFP) 1935 *E*
Taylor, E G (Oxford U) 1927 *W, A*
Taylor, R C (Kelvinside-West) 1951 *W, I, E, SA*
Telfer, C M (Hawick) 1968 *A*, 1969 *F, W, I, E*, 1972 *F, W, E*, 1973 *W, I, E, P*, 1974 *W, E, I*, 1975 *A*, 1976 *F*
Telfer, J W (Melrose) 1964 *F, NZ, W, I, E*, 1965 *F, W, I*, 1966 *F, W, I, E*, 1967 *W, I, E*, 1968 *E, A*, 1969 *F, W,*

SCOTTISH INTERNATIONAL RECORDS

Both team and individual records are for official Scotland international matches, up to 31 March 1993.

TEAM RECORDS

Highest score
60 v Zimbabwe (60-21) 1987 Wellington

v individual countries
46 v Argentina (49-3) 1990 Murrayfield
24 v Australia (24-15) 1981 Murrayfield
33 v England (33-6) 1986 Murrayfield
38 v Fiji (38-17) 1989 Murrayfield
31 v France (31-3) 1912 Inverleith
37 v Ireland (37-21) 1989 Murrayfield
47 v Japan (47-9) 1991 Murrayfield
25 v N Zealand (25-25) 1983 Murrayfield
55 v Romania (55-28) 1987 Dunedin
10 v S Africa (10-18) 1960 Port Elizabeth
35 v Wales (35-10) 1924 Inverleith
28 v W Samoa (28-6) 1991 Murrayfield
60 v Zimbabwe (60-21) 1987 Wellington

Biggest winning points margin
46 v Argentina (49-3) 1990 Murrayfield

v individual countries
46 v Argentina (49-3) 1990 Murrayfield
 9 v Australia (24-15) 1981 Murrayfield
27 v England (33-6) 1986 Murrayfield
21 v Fiji (38-17) 1989 Murrayfield
28 v France (31-3) 1912 Inverleith
23 v Ireland (32-9) 1984 Dublin
38 v Japan (47-9) 1991 Murrayfield
No win v N Zealand
32 v Romania (32-0) 1989 Murrayfield
 6 v S Africa (6-0) 1906 Glasgow
25 v Wales (35-10) 1924 Inverleith
22 v W Samoa (28-6) 1991 Murrayfield
39 v Zimbabwe $\begin{cases} (60\text{-}21) \ 1987 \ \text{Wellington} \\ (51\text{-}12) \ 1991 \ \text{Murrayfield} \end{cases}$

Highest score by opposing team
44 S Africa (0-44) 1951 Murrayfield

by individual countries
 3 Argentina (49-3) 1990 Murrayfield
37 Australia $\begin{cases} (12\text{-}37) \ 1984 \ \text{Murrayfield} \\ (13\text{-}37) \ 1992 \ \text{Brisbane} \end{cases}$
30 England (18-30) 1980 Murrayfield
17 Fiji (38-17) 1989 Murrayfield
28 France (22-28) 1987 Parc de Princes
26 Ireland (8-26) 1953 Murrayfield
 9 Japan (47-9) 1991 Murrayfield
40 N Zealand (15-40) 1981 Auckland

28 Romania $\begin{cases} (22\text{-}28) \ 1984 \ \text{Bucharest} \\ (55\text{-}28) \ 1987 \ \text{Dunedin} \end{cases}$
44 S Africa (0-44) 1951 Murrayfield
35 Wales (12-35) 1972 Cardiff
 6 W Samoa (28-6) 1991 Murrayfield
21 Zimbabwe (60-21) 1987 Wellington

Biggest losing points margin
44 v S Africa (0-44) 1951 Murrayfield

v individual countries
25 v Australia (12-37) 1984 Murrayfield
20 v England (6-26) 1977 Twickenham
20 v France (3-23) 1977 Parc des Princes
21 v Ireland (0-21) 1950 Dublin
27 v N Zealand (3-30) 1987 Christchurch
 6 v Romania $\begin{cases} (22\text{-}28) \ 1984 \ \text{Bucharest} \\ (12\text{-}18) \ 1991 \ \text{Bucharest} \end{cases}$
44 v S Africa (0-44) 1951 Murrayfield
23 v Wales (12-35) 1972 Cardiff
No defeat v Argentina, Fiji, Japan, Western Samoa or Zimbabwe

---

Most tries by Scotland in an international
12 v Wales 1887 Raeburn Place (Edinburgh)

Most tries against Scotland in an international
9 by S Africa (0-44) 1951 Murrayfield

Most points by Scotland in International Championship in a season – 86
in season 1983-84

Most tries by Scotland in International Championship in a season – 17
in season 1924-25

INDIVIDUAL RECORDS

Most capped player
J M Renwick 52 1972-84
C T Deans 52 1978-87

in individual positions
Full-back
A R Irvine 47(51)[1] 1972-82
Wing
I Tukalo 37 1985-92
Centre
J M Renwick 51(52)[2] 1972-84
Fly-half
J Y Rutherford 42 1979-87
Scrum-half
R J Laidlaw 47 1980-88
Prop
A B Carmichael 50 1967-78
Hooker
C T Deans 52 1978-87
Lock
A J Tomes 48 1976-87
Flanker
J Jeffrey 40 1984-91
No 8
D B White 29(41)[3] 1982-92
[1]*Irvine played 4 matches as a wing*
[2]*Renwick played once, as a replacement, on the wing*
[3]*White won 5 caps as a flanker and 7 as a lock*

Longest international career
W C W Murdoch 14 seasons 1935-48

Most consecutive Tests – 49
A B Carmichael 1967-78

Most internationals as captain – 25
D M B Sole 1989-92

Most points in internationals – 424
A G Hastings (45 matches) 1986-93

Most points in International Championship in a season – 52
A G Hastings (4 matches) 1985-86

Most points in an international – 27
A G Hastings v Romania 1987 Dunedin

Most tries in internationals – 24
I S Smith (32 matches) 1924-33

Most tries in International Championship in a season – 8
I S Smith (4 matches) 1924-25

Most tries in an international – 5
G C Lindsay v Wales 1887 Raeburn Place (Edinburgh)

Most conversions in internationals – 60
A G Hastings (45 matches) 1986-93

Most conversions in International Championship in a season – 8
P W Dods (4 matches) 1983-84

Most conversions in an international – 8
A G Hastings v Zimbabwe 1987 Wellington
A G Hastings v Romania 1987 Dunedin

Most dropped goals in internationals – 12
J Y Rutherford (42 matches) 1972-82

Most penalty goals in internationals – 88
A G Hastings (45 matches) 1986-93

Most penalty goals in International Championship in a season – 14
A G Hastings (4 matches) 1985-86

Most penalty goals in an international – 6
A G Hastings v France 1986 Murrayfield

Most points on major tour – 58
P W Dods (4 matches) N Zealand 1990
C D R Mair scored 100 points in the Far East in 1977, but this was not on a major tour

Most points in a tour match – 24
D W Morgan v Wellington 1975 Wellington, NZ
A R Irvine v King Country 1981 Taumarunui, NZ
A R Irvine v Wairarapa-Bush 1981 Masterton, NZ
P W Dods scored 43 points v Alberta in 1985, but this was not on a major tour

Most tries in a tour match – 3
A R Smith v Eastern Transvaal 1960 Springs, SA
K R F Bearne scored 5 tries v Ontario U in 1964, A J W Hinshelwood scored 5 v Quebec in 1964, and D E W Leckie scored 5 v Goshawks (Zimbabwe) in 1988, but these were not on a major tour

IRELAND'S LONG LANE REACHES THE LONG-AWAITED TURNING-POINT

THE 1992-93 SEASON IN IRELAND
Sean Diffley *Irish Independent*

It was the most extraordinary of seasons. Ireland lost their 11th game in succession, an all-time record; their coach, Ciaran Fitzgerald, resigned in total despair after the reverse against the touring Australians. And then, clueless and shattered against Scotland and France in the Five Nations Championship, they glimpsed the bottom of the abyss, the Dante's Inferno of Irish rugby.

The criticism was virulent. One Sunday newspaper had a banner heading which demanded that 'Noel Murphy Must Resign'. The manager bore the brunt of the criticism. Fitzgerald's successor as coach, Gerry Murphy, was permitted a newcomer's settling-in period. Irish rugby had never before witnessed such disenchantment among the followers and such indifferent play by the national team.

And while the spate of venomous criticism often went well over the top there was some substance to the complaints about inconsistent selections. Mick Galwey, for instance, wasn't in the side that opened against Scotland at Murrayfield in mid-January; Eric Elwood was introduced only as a desperate afterthought and Noel Murphy's partiality for a patently unfit Neil Francis was strange, to say the least.

But was there something basically unsound, all of a sudden, about Irish rugby? Nobody could quite make up their minds. Andy Leslie, on a three-month advisory coaching course that lasted until just up to the start of the Five Nations tournament, added his advice. And apart from the former All Blacks captain there was the official assistance of one of the IRFU development officers, the one and only Willie Anderson, who worked hard on continuity play with the forwards at squad training sessions. The strange aspect was that at Insurance Corporation All-Ireland League level the standard and intensity of the matches was excellent. Why could not the commitment be translated into the activities of the national side?

Of course, it's a very long lane that has no turning. The long-suffering Noel Murphy kept harping away at what he called 'the sound heart of Irish rugby – the game needs Ireland at their traditional best, and it will all come right soon'. And it did. In Wales. And not, notably, at the National Stadium in Cardiff, but on the night before in the A international in Newport. It was there, under the Rodney Parade lights and before a crowd expecting something special from a highly rated Welsh side, that a significant Irish performance recaptured the glories of yesteryear. The old virtues returned and there is no doubt that the full Irish team, watching the display, were suddenly primed to repeat the feat the following day.

The Ireland team which beat England at Lansdowne Road. L-R, back row: B T Glennon (replacement), E P Elwood, P M Clohessy, W D McBride, B F Robinson, M J Galwey, P S Johns, P T O'Hara, S P Geoghegan, N P J Francis (replacement), J N Murphy (replacement), R Saunders (replacement); front row: N J Popplewell, V J G Cunningham, P P A Danaher, M T Bradley (capt), C A Quaid (IRFU president), T J Kingston, C P Clarke, R M Wallace.

The following day Ireland won a full international match at last and there were tears in Irish eyes after that. It was there that the cool experience of Michael Bradley was so much in evidence, the dash of the forwards and the quite astonishing maturity of the new fly-half, Eric Elwood.

But England, two weeks later, would surely be a very different matter? Well, it wasn't. Again the traditional virtues, plus the maturity, again, of Elwood and the dashing defence of all, brought about the shock of the season. Two wins out of four – it was suddenly the stuff of fairy stories with happy endings. There was, certainly, dismay that only two players, Nick Popplewell and Mick Galwey, were chosen for the Lions. Ireland certainly did not expect a whole raft of suddenly elevated players after the England match, but there was a feeling that the form in the Five Nations, hitherto the criterion for selection of the Lions, was, like so many of the better aspects of the game, being summarily jettisoned. Richard Wallace and Vincent Cunningham were subsequently added to the touring party when injury struck.

On the domestic level the All-Ireland Leagues continued for the third season to be dominated by Munster clubs. Young Munster followed in the footsteps of Cork Constitution and Garryowen as the First Division champions. Once again the decider took place on the very last day, with Young Munster and the Dublin side, St Mary's College, attracting a crowd of just over 18,000 to Lansdowne Road to see Munster win by a late penalty goal.

Ulster, once again, was the dominant province, taking the Inter-Provincial title for the eighth successive season.

WINNERS OF PROVINCIAL TOURNAMENTS

LEINSTER
Senior Cup: St Mary's College **Senior League:** Old Belvedere **Schools Senior Cup:** Terenure College **Schools Junior Cup:** Blackrock College

ULSTER
Senior Cup: Dungannon **Senior League:** Malone **Schools Senior Cup:** Campbell **Schools Medallion:** Campbell

MUNSTER
Senior Cup: Garryowen **Senior League:** Sunday's Well **Schools Senior Cup:** PB Cork **Schools Junior Cup:** St Munchin's

CONNACHT
Senior Cup: Corinthians **Senior League:** Ballina **Schools Senior Cup:** St Joseph Galway **Schools Junior Cup:** Garbally College

INSURANCE CORPORATION ALL-IRELAND LEAGUE

Division 1

	P	W	D	L	F	A	Pts
Young Munster	8	6	1	1	114	89	13
Cork Const	8	6	0	2	166	128	12
St Mary's Coll	8	5	1	1	170	94	11
Greystones	8	4	1	3	132	132	9
Old Wesley	8	4	0	4	107	151	8
Dungannon	8	3	0	5	144	172	6
Shannon	8	2	1	5	85	86	5
Garryowen	8	2	0	6	132	144	4
Ballymena	8	2	0	6	97	151	2

Division 2

	P	W	D	L	F	A	Pts		P	W	D	L	F	A	Pts
Lansdowne	9	9	0	0	209	118	18	Instonians	9	5	0	4	124	126	10
Wanderers	9	7	0	2	168	121	14	Old Crescent	9	3	0	6	130	166	6
Blackrock Coll	9	6	1	2	149	95	13	Galwegians	9	1	2	6	97	143	4
Dolphin	9	5	0	4	133	124	10	Bangor	9	1	1	7	112	174	3
Terenure Coll	9	5	0	4	123	121	10	Clontarf	9	1	0	8	86	143	2

The All-Ireland Insurance Corporation League is being extended for the 1993-94 season to include all 47 Irish senior clubs in four divisions. Division 2 includes the 1992-93 champion clubs from the four provincial leagues and the composition of Divisions 3 and 4 is determined by the clubs' final positions in the provincial leagues.

Division 1
*Blackrock College
 Cork Constitution
 Dungannon
 Garryowen
 Greystones
*Lansdowne
 Old Wesley
 Shannon
 St Mary's College
*Wanderers
 Young Munster
Promoted from Division 2

Division 2
 Ballina
 Ballymena
 Bangor
 Dolphin
 Galwegians
 Instonians
 Malone
 Old Belvedere
 Old Crescent
 Sunday's Well
 Terenure College
Ballymena are relegated from Division 1. 1992-93 provincial champions Ballina (Connacht), Malone (Ulster), Old Belvedere (Leinster), Sunday's Well (Munster).

Division 3
 Athlone
 Bective Rangers
 City of Derry
 Clontarf
 Collegians
 De La Salle Palmerston
 Galway Corinthians
 Highfield
 NIFC
 Portadown
 Sligo
 University Coll, Cork
 University Coll, Dublin

Division 4
 Ards
 Armagh
 Ballinasloe
 Bohemians
 CIYMS
 Dublin U
 Monkstown
 Queen's U, Belfast
 Skerries
 University College, Galway
 Waterpark
 Westport

INTER-PROVINCIAL TOURNAMENT 1992

12 September, London Irish RFC

Exiles 19 (1G 4PG)   **Munster 13** (1G 2PG)
Exiles: J E Staples (London Irish) *(capt)*; S P Geoghegan (London Irish), D Curtis (London Irish), D Dooley (Saracens), M Corcoran (London Irish); B Wellens (Orrell), R Saunders (London Irish); N Donovan (London Irish), J McFarland (London Irish), G F Halpin (London Irish), M Keenan (London Irish), J Etheridge (Northampton), D Cleary (Orrell), P Collins (London Irish), D Kelly (Manchester) *Replacement* D Lynagh (Paris U) for Wellens
Scorers *Try:* Keenan   *Conversion:* Corcoran   *Penalty Goals:* Corcoran (4)
Munster: C Haly (Cork Const); R M Wallace (Garryowen), B Walsh (Cork Const), D J Clarke (Dolphin), W O'Shea (Shannon); D Larkin (Garryowen), O Kiely (Shannon); J J Fitzgerald (Young Munster), T J Kingston (Dolphin) *(capt)*, P McCarthy (Cork Const), M J Galwey (Shannon), R Costello (Garryowen), P O'Hara (Cork Const), B O'Mahony (UC, Cork), G Earls (Young Munster) *Replacements* G O'Sullivan (Highfield) for Larkin; P Wallace (UC Cork) for Fitzgerald; D O'Mahony (UC Cork) for Kiely
Scorers *Try:* Costello   *Conversion:* O'Sullivan   *Penalty Goals:* O'Sullivan (2)
Referee B W Stirling

22 September, Donnybrook, Dublin

Leinster 16 (2PG 2T) **Exiles 14** (3PG 1T)
Leinster: C Clarke (Terenure Coll); D O'Brien (Clontarf), M Ridge (Blackrock Coll), V J G Cunningham
(St Mary's Coll), N Woods (Blackrock Coll); P Hennebry (Terenure), L F P Aherne (Lansdowne); N J Popplewell
(Greystones) (*capt*), J J Murphy (Greystones), D Dowling (St Mary's Coll), B J Rigney (Greystones),
J O'Callaghan (Wanderers), K Leahy (Wanderers), P Lawlor (Bective Rangers), R Love (Old Wesley) *Replacements*
R Finnegan (Lansdowne) for Leahy; S Byrne (Blackrock) for Finnegan
Scorers *Tries:* Woods, Popplewell *Penalty Goals:* Woods (2)
Exiles: J E Staples (London Irish) (*capt*); S P Geoghegan (London Irish), D Dooley (Saracens), D Curtis (London Irish),
M Corcoran (London Irish); D Lynagh (Paris U), R Saunders (London Irish); D Donovan (London Irish), J McFarland
(London Irish), G F Halpin (London Irish), J Etheridge (Northampton), M Keenan (London Irish), D Cleary (Orrell),
K Hickey (Coventry), D Kelly (Manchester)
Scorer *Try:* Corcoran *Penalty Goals:* Corcoran (3)
Referee S R Hilditch

28 November, Thomond Park, Limerick

Munster 11 (2PG 1T) **Ulster 12** (3PG 1DG)
Munster: C Haly (Cork Const); R M Wallace (Garryowen), P P A Danaher (Garryowen) (*capt*), B Walsh (Cork Const),
P Murray (Shannon); J Galvin (Shannon), B Tobin (Young Munster); P McCarthy (Cork Const), P Kenny (Shannon),
P Clohessy (Young Munster), M J Galwey (Shannon), R Costello (Garryowen), G Clohessy (Young Munster), B Cronin
(Garryowen), E Halvey (Shannon) *Replacement* L Dineen (Cork Const) for Cronin
Scorers *Try:* Cronin *Penalty Goals:* Haly (2)
Ulster: C Wilkinson (Malone); R Carey (Dungannon), W Harbinson (Malone), M Field (Malone), T Howe
(Dungannon); P Russell (Instonians), A Matchett (Ballymena); D Elliott (Bangor), S Smith (Ballymena), G Bell
(Instonians), G Longwell (Queen's U), D Tweed (Ballymena), S McKinty (Bangor), B Robinson (London Irish),
D McBride (Malone) (*capt*) *Replacements* A Adair (Instonians) for Smith; D Humphreys (Queen's U) for Russell
Scorers *Penalty Goals:* Russell, Humphreys (2) *Dropped Goal:* Humphreys
Referee O E Doyle

28 November, Sportsground, Galway

Connacht 28 (2G 3PG 1T) **Leinster 9** (3PG)
Connacht: A White (St Mary's Coll); C Leahy (Wanderers), M Cosgrave (Wanderers) (*capt*), S Carty (Galwegians),
G Curley (Athlone); E Elwood (Lansdowne), K Lawless (Clontarf); T P J Clancy (Lansdowne), W Mulcahy (Skerries),
D Henshaw (Athlone), T Coughlin (St Mary's Coll), S Jameson (St Mary's Coll), S Moran (Blackrock Coll), K Devlin
(St Mary's Coll), N P Mannion (Lansdowne)
Scorers *Tries:* Mulcahy (2), Curley *Conversions:* White (2) *Penalty Goals:* White (3)
Leinster: C O'Shea (Lansdowne); J Sexton (Lansdowne), M Ridge (Blackrock), V J G Cunningham (St Mary's Coll)
(*capt*), N Woods (Blackrock Coll); A McGowan (Blackrock Coll), L F P Aherne (Lansdowne); H Hurley (Old Wesley),
J J Murphy (Greystones), D Dowling (St Mary's Coll), M O'Neill (Blackrock Coll), J O'Callaghan (Wanderers),
K Leahy (Wanderers), R Love (Old Wesley), P Lawlor (Bective Rangers)
Scorer *Penalty Goals:* McGowan (3)
Referee R McDowell

5 December, Ravenhill, Belfast

Ulster 19 (2G 1T) **Connacht 6** (2PG)
Ulster: C Wilkinson (Malone); R Carey (Dungannon), W Harbinson (Malone), M Field (Malone), T Howe
(Dungannon); P Russell (Instonians), A Matchett (Ballymena); D Elliott (Bangor), J McDonald (Malone), G Bell
(Instonians), P Johns (Dungannon), D Tweed (Ballymena), S McKinty (Bangor), B Robinson (London Irish),
D McBride (Malone) (*capt*)
Scorers *Tries:* Field, Tweed, Howe *Conversions:* Russell (2)
Connacht: A White (St Mary's Coll); C Leahy (Wanderers), M Cosgrave (Wanderers) (*capt*), S Carty (Galwegians),
G Curley (Athlone); E Elwood (Lansdowne), K Lawless (Clontarf); T P J Clancy (Lansdowne), W Mulcahy (Skerries),
D Henshaw (Athlone), T Coughlin (St Mary's Coll), S Jameson (St Mary's Coll), S Moran (Blackrock Coll),
N P Mannion (Lansdowne), K Devlin (St Mary's Coll)
Scorer *Penalty Goals:* White (2)
Referee B Smith

5 December, Donnybrook, Dublin

Leinster 21 (1G 3PG 1T) **Munster 20** (2G 2DG)
Leinster: C O'Shea (Lansdowne); J Sexton (Lansdowne), V J G Cunningham (St Mary's Coll), C Younger
(Terenure Coll), N Woods (Blackrock Coll); P Hennebry (Terenure Coll), A Rolland (Blackrock Coll);
N J Popplewell (Greystones) (*capt*), J J Murphy (Greystones), D Dowling (St Mary's Coll), D Bursey (Old Wesley),
J O'Callaghan (Wanderers), C Pim (Old Wesley), R Love (Old Wesley), P Lawlor (Bective Rangers) *Replacements*
A McKeen (Lansdowne) for Dowling; L F P Aherne (Lansdowne) for Rolland
Scorers *Tries:* Pim, Cunningham *Conversion:* Woods *Penalty Goals:* O'Shea (2), Woods
Munster: P Murray (Shannon) (*capt*); W O'Shea (Shannon), B Walsh (Cork Const), P P A Danaher (Garryowen),
R Wallace (Garryowen); J Galvin (Shannon), M Bradley (Cork Const); P McCarthy (Cork Const), P Kenny
(Shannon), P Clohessy (Young Munster), E O'Sullivan (Old Crescent), R Costello (Garryowen), L Dineen
(Cork Const), E Halvey (Shannon), M J Galwey (Shannon) *Replacement* D Larkin (Garryowen) for Galvin

Scorers *Tries:* Galvin, Walsh   *Conversions:* O'Shea (2)   *Dropped Goals:* Galvin, Larkin
Referee A Watson

12 December, Roehampton, London

Exiles 13 (1G 2PG)   **Ulster 16** (1G 2PG 1DG)
Exiles: J E Staples (London Irish) (*capt*); S Geoghegan (London Irish), D Curtis (London Irish), D Dooley (Saracens), M Corcoran (London Irish); B Wellens (Orrell), R Saunders (London Irish); N Donovan (London Irish), J McFarland (London Irish), G Halpin (London Irish), J Etheridge (Northampton), M Keenan (London Irish), D Cleary (Orrell), A Verling (London Irish), D Kelly (Manchester)
Scorers *Try:* Verling   *Conversion:* Corcoran   *Penalty Goals:* Corcoran (2)
Ulster: C Wilkinson (Malone); R Carey (Dungannon), M Field (Malone), W Harbinson (Malone), T Howe (Dungannon); P Russell (Instonians), A Matchett (Ballymena); D Elliott (Bangor), S J Smith (Ballymena), G Bell (Instonians), D Tweed (Ballymena), P Johns (Dungannon), S McKinty (Bangor), B Robinson (London Irish), D McBride (Malone) (*capt*) *Replacement* G Longwell (Queen's U) for Robinson
Scorers *Try:* Harbinson   *Conversion:* Russell   *Penalty Goals:* Russell (2)   *Dropped Goal:* Russell
Referee D Lamont

12 December, Musgrave Park, Cork

Munster 20 (2G 2PG)   **Connacht 10** (1G 1PG)
Munster: P Murray (Shannon) (*capt*); W O'Shea (Shannon), B Walsh (Cork Const), P P A Danaher (Garryowen), R Wallace (Garryowen); D Larkin (Garryowen), M T Bradley (Cork Const); P McCarthy (Cork Const), P Kenny (Shannon), P Clohessy (Young Munster), M J Galwey (Shannon), R Costello (Garryowen), L Dineen (Cork Const), E Halvey (Shannon), B Cronin (Garryowen) *Replacement* P Soden (Cork Const) for Clohessy
Scorers *Tries:* O'Shea, Halvey   *Conversions:* O'Shea (2)   *Penalty Goals:* O'Shea (2)
Connacht: A White (St Mary's Coll); C Leahy (Wanderers), M Cosgrave (Wanderers) (*capt*), S Carty (Galwegians), G Curley (Athlone); E Elwood (Lansdowne), K Lawless (Clontarf); T P J Clancy (Lansdowne), W Mulcahy (Skerries), D Henshaw (Athlone), S Moran (Blackrock Coll), T Coughlin (St Mary's Coll), P Brady (Wanderers), K Devlin (St Mary's Coll), N P Mannion (Lansdowne) *Replacements* B Comerford (Athlone) for Lawless; E Walsh (Dolphin) for Brady
Scorers *Try:* Coughlin   *Conversion:* White   *Penalty Goal:* White
Referee A Lewis

19 December, Ravenhill, Belfast

Ulster 12 (3PG 1DG)   **Leinster 8** (1PG 1T)
Ulster: C Wilkinson (Malone); R Carey (Dungannon), W Harbinson (Malone), M Field (Malone), T Howe (Dungannon); P Russell (Instonians), A Matchett (Ballymena), M T Bradley (Ballymena); D Elliott (Bangor), S J Smith (Ballymena), G Bell (Instonians), P Johns (Dungannon), D Tweed (Ballymena), C Darragh (NIFC), S McKinty (Bangor), D McBride (Malone) (*capt*) *Replacement* B McKibbin (Instonians) for Elliott
Scorer *Penalty Goals:* Russell (3)
Leinster: C O'Shea (Lansdowne); B Glennon (Lansdowne), V J G Cunningham (St Mary's Coll), C Younger (Terenure Coll), N Woods (Blackrock Coll); P Hennebry (Terenure), A Rolland (Blackrock); H Hurley (Old Wesley), J J Murphy (Greystones) (*capt*), A McKeen (Lansdowne), J O'Callaghan (Wanderers), D Bursey (Old Wesley), C Pim (Old Wesley), P Lawlor (Bective Rangers), R Love (Old Wesley) *Replacements* M Mahon (Wanderers) for Younger; L F P Aherne (Lansdowne) for Rolland
Scorer *Try:* O'Shea   *Penalty Goal:* O'Shea
Referee D McHugh

19 December, Sportsground, Galway

Connacht 12 (4PG)   **Exiles 17** (2G 1PG)
Connacht: A White (St Mary's Coll); C Leahy (Wanderers), M Cosgrave (Wanderers) (*capt*), S Carty (Galwegians), G Curley (Athlone); E Elwood (Lansdowne), B Comerford (Athlone); T P J Clancy (Lansdowne), W Mulcahy (Skerries), D Henshaw (Athlone), S Moran (Blackrock Coll), T Coughlin (St Mary's Coll), E Walsh (Dolphin), N P Mannion (Lansdowne), K Devlin (St Mary's Coll)
Scorer *Penalty Goals:* White (4)
Exiles: J E Staples (London Irish) (*capt*); S P Geoghegan (London Irish), D Dooley (Saracens), D Curtis (London Irish), M Corcoran (London Irish); B Wellens (Orrell), R Saunders (London Irish); N Donovan (London Irish), J McFarland (London Irish), G Halpin (London Irish), J Etheridge (Northampton), M Keenan (London Irish), D Cleary (Orrell), A Verling (London Irish), D Kelly (Manchester)
Scorers *Tries:* Corcoran, Staples   *Conversions:* Corcoran (2)   *Penalty Goal:* Corcoran
Referee G Black

Final Table

	P	W	D	L	F	A	Pts
Ulster	4	4	0	0	59	38	8
Exiles	4	2	0	2	63	57	4
Leinster	4	2	0	2	54	74	4
Connacht	4	1	0	3	56	65	2
Munster	4	1	0	3	64	62	2

IRISH INTERNATIONAL PLAYERS
(up to 31 March 1993)

ABBREVIATIONS

A – Australia; *Arg* – Argentina; *C* – Canada; *E* – England; *F* – France; *It* – Italy; *J* – Japan; *M* – Maoris; *Nm* – Namibia; *NZ* – New Zealand; *R* – Romania; *S* – Scotland; *SA* – South Africa; *Tg* – Tonga; *W* – Wales; *WS* – Western Samoa; *Z* – Zimbabwe; *P* – Ireland v IRFU President's XV at Lansdowne Road in IRFU centenary season, 1974-75; (R) – Replacement. Entries in square brackets [ ] indicate appearances in the World Cup. NIFC – North of Ireland Football Club; CIYMS – Church of Ireland Young Men's Society; KCH – King's College Hospital

Note: Years given for Five Nations' matches are for second half of season; eg 1972 means season 1971-72. Years for all other matches refer to the actual year of the match. When a series has taken place, figures have been used to denote the particular matches in which players have featured. Thus 1981 *SA* 2 indicates that a player appeared in the second Test of the series. The abandoned game with Scotland at Belfast in 1885 is now included as a cap match.

NB – The second of Ireland's two matches against France in 1972 was a non-championship match.

Abraham, M (Bective Rangers) 1912 *E, S, W, SA*, 1914 *W*
Adams, C (Old Wesley) 1908 *E*, 1909 *E, F*, 1910 *F*, 1911 *E, S, W, F*, 1912 *S, W, SA*, 1913 *W, F*, 1914 *F, E, S*
Agar, R D (Malone) 1947 *F, E, S, W*, 1948 *F*, 1949 *S, W*, 1950 *F, E , W*
Agnew, P J (CIYMS) 1974 *F* (R), 1976 *A*
Ahearne, T (Queen's Coll, Cork) 1899 *E*
Aherne, L F P (Dolphin, Lansdowne) 1988 *E* 2, *WS, It*, 1989 *F, W, E, S, NZ*, 1990 *E, S, F, W* (R), 1992 *E, S, F, A*
Alexander, R (NIFC, Police Union) 1936 *E, S, W*, 1937 *E, S, W*, 1938 *E, S*, 1939 *E, S, W*
Allen, C E (Derry, Liverpool) 1900 *E, S, W*, 1901 *E, S, W*, 1903 *S, W*, 1904 *E, S, W*, 1905 *E, S, W, NZ*, 1906 *E, S, W, SA*, 1907 *S, W*
Allen, G G (Derry, Liverpool) 1896 *E, S, W*, 1897 *E, S*, 1898 *E, S*, 1899 *E, W*
Allen, T C (NIFC) 1885 *E, S* 1
Allen, W S (Wanderers) 1875 *E*
Allison, J B (Edinburgh U) 1899 *E, S*, 1900 *E, S, W*, 1901 *E, S, W*, 1902 *E, S, W*, 1903 *S*
Anderson, F E (Queen's U, Belfast, NIFC) 1953 *F, E, S, W*, 1954 *NZ, F, E, S, W*, 1955 *F, E, S, W*
Anderson, H J (Old Wesley) 1903 *E, S*, 1906 *E, S*
Anderson, W A (Dungannon) 1984 *A*, 1985 *S, F, W, E*, 1986 *F, S, R*, 1987 *E, S, F, W*, [*W, C, Tg, A*], 1988 *S, F, W, E* 1,2, 1989 *F, W, E, NZ*, 1990 *E, S*
Andrews, G (NIFC) 1875 *E*, 1876 *E*
Andrews, H W (NIFC) 1888 *M*, 1889 *S, W*
Archer, A M (Dublin U, NIFC) 1879 *S*
Arigho, J E (Lansdowne) 1928 *F, E, W*, 1929 *F, E, S, W*, 1930 *F, E, S, W*, 1931 *F, E, S, W*, 1903 *S*
Armstrong, W K (NIFC) 1960 *SA*, 1961 *E*
Arnott, D T (Lansdowne) 1876 *E*
Ash, W H (NIFC) 1875 *E*, 1876 *E*, 1877 *S*
Aston, H R (Dublin U) 1908 *E, W*
Atkins, A P (Bective Rangers) 1924 *F*
Atkinson, J M (NIFC) 1927 *F, A*
Atkinson, J R (Dublin U) 1882 *W, S*

Bagot, J C (Dublin U, Lansdowne) 1879 *S, E*, 1880 *E, S*, 1881 *S*
Bailey, A H (UC Dublin, Lansdowne) 1934 *W*, 1935 *E, S, W, NZ*, 1936 *E, S, W*, 1937 *E, S, W*, 1938 *E, S*
Bailey, N (Northampton) 1952 *E*
Bardon, M E (Bohemians) 1934 *E*
Barlow, M (Wanderers) 1875 *E*
Barnes, R J (Dublin U, Armagh) 1933 *W*
Barr, A (Methodist Coll, Belfast) 1898 *W*, 1899 *S*, 1901 *E, S*
Barry, N J (Garryowen) 1991 *Nm*2(R)
Beamish, C E St J (RAF, Leicester) 1933 *W, S*, 1934 *S, W*, 1935 *E, S, W, NZ*, 1936 *E, S, W*, 1938 *W*
Beamish, G R (RAF, Leicester) 1925 *E, S, W*, 1928 *F, E, S, W*, 1929 *F, E, S, W*, 1930 *F, E, S, W*, 1931 *F, E, S, W, SA*, 1932 *E, S, W*, 1933 *E, W, S*
Beatty, W J (NIFC, Richmond) 1910 *F*, 1912 *F, W*
Becker, V A (Lansdowne) 1974 *F, W*
Beckett, G G P (Dublin U) 1908 *E, S, W*

Bell, R J (NIFC) 1875 *E*, 1876 *E*
Bell, W E (Belfast Collegians) 1953 *F, E, S, W*
Bennett, F (Belfast Collegians) 1913 *S*
Bent, G C (Dublin U) 1882 *W, E*
Berkery, P J (Lansdowne) 1954 *W*, 1955 *W*, 1956 *S, W*, 1957 *F, E, S, W*, 1958 *A, E, S*
Bermingham, J J C (Blackrock Coll) 1921 *E, S, W, F*
Blackham, J C (Queen's Coll, Cork) 1909 *S, W, F*, 1910 *E, S, W*
Blake-Knox, S E F (NIFC) 1976 *E, S*, 1977 *F* (R)
Blayney, J J (Wanderers) 1950 *S*
Bond, A T W (Derry) 1894 *S, W*
Bornemann, W W (Wanderers) 1960 *E, S, W, SA*
Bowen, D St J (Cork Const) 1977 *W, E, S*
Boyd, C A (Dublin U) 1900 *S*, 1901 *S, W*
Boyle, C V (Dublin U) 1935 *NZ*, 1936 *E, S, W*, 1937 *E, S, W*, 1938 *W*, 1939 *W*
Brabazon, H M (Dublin U) 1884 *E*, 1885 *S* 1, 1886 *E*
Bradley, M J (Dolphin) 1920 *W, F*, 1922 *E, S, W, F*, 1923 *E, S, W, F*, 1925 *F, S, W*, 1926 *F, E, S, W*, 1927 *F, W*
Bradley, M T (Cork Constitution) 1984 *A*, 1985 *S, F, W, E*, 1986 *F, W, E, S, R*, 1987 *E, S, F, W*, [*W, C, Tg, A*], 1988 *S, F, W, E* 1, 1990 *W*, 1992 *NZ* 1,2, 1993 *S, F, W, E*
Bradshaw, G (Belfast Collegians) 1903 *W*
Bradshaw, R M (Wanderers) 1885 *E, S* 1,2
Brady, A M (UC Dublin, Malone) 1966 *S*, 1968 *E, S, W*
Brady, J A (Wanderers) 1976 *E, S*
Brady, J (CIYMS) 1951 *S, W*, 1953 *F, E, S, W*, 1954 *W*, 1956 *W*, 1957 *F, E, S, W*
Bramwell, T (NIFC) 1928 *F*
Brand, T N (NIFC) 1924 *NZ*
Brennan, J I (CIYMS) 1957 *S, W*
Bresnihan, F P K (UC Dublin, Lansdowne, London Irish) 1966 *E, W*, 1967 *A* 1, *E, S, W, F*, 1968 *F, E, S, W, A*, 1969 *F, E, S, W*, 1970 *SA, F, E, S, W*, 1971 *F, E, S, W*
Brett, J T (Monkstown) 1914 *W*
Bristow, J R (NIFC) 1879 *E*
Brophy, N H (Blackrock Coll, UC Dublin, London Irish) 1957 *F, E*, 1959 *E, S, W, F*, 1960 *F, SA*, 1961 *S, W*, 1962 *S, W*, 1963 *E, W*, 1967 *E, S, W, F, A* 2
Brown, E L (Instonians) 1958 *F*
Brown, G S (Monkstown, United Services) 1912 *S, W, SA*
Brown, H (Windsor) 1877 *E*
Brown, T (Windsor) 1877 *E, S*
Brown, W H (Dublin U) 1899 *E*
Brown, W J (Malone) 1970 *SA, F, S, W*
Brown, W S (Dublin U) 1893 *S, W*, 1894 *E, S, W*
Browne, A W (Dublin U) 1951 *SA*
Browne, D (Blackrock Coll) 1920 *F*
Browne, H C (United Services and RN) 1929 *E, S, W*
Browne, W F (United Services and Army) 1925 *E, S, W*, 1926 *S, W*, 1927 *F, E, S, W, A*, 1928 *E, S*
Browning, D R (Wanderers) 1881 *E, S*
Bruce, S A M (NIFC) 1883 *E, S*, 1884 *E*
Brunker, A A (Lansdowne) 1895 *E, W*
Bryant, C H (Cardiff) 1920 *E, S*
Buchanan, A McM (Dublin U) 1926 *E, S, W*, 1927 *S,*

W, A
Buchanan, J W B (Dublin U) 1882 *S*, 1884 *E, S*
Buckley, J H (Sunday's Well) 1973 *E, S*
Bulger, L Q (Lansdowne) 1896 *E, S, W*, 1897 *E, S,* 1898 *E, S, W*
Bulger, M J (Dublin U) 1888 *M*
Burges, J H (Rosslyn Park) 1950 *F, E*
Burgess, R B (Dublin U) 1912 *SA*
Burkitt, J C S (Queen's Coll, Cork) 1881 *E*
Burns, I J (Wanderers) 1980 *E* (R)
Butler, L G (Blackrock Coll) 1960 *W*
Butler, N (Bective Rangers) 1920 *E*
Byers, R M (NIFC) 1928 *S, W*, 1929 *E, S, W*
Byrne, E M J (Blackrock Coll) 1977 *S, F*, 1978 *F, W, E, NZ*
Byrne, N F (UC Dublin) 1962 *F*
Byrne, S J (UC Dublin, Lansdowne) 1953 *S, W*, 1955 *F*
Byron, W G (NIFC) 1896 *E, S, W*, 1897 *E, S*, 1898 *E, S, W*, 1899 *E, S, W*

Caddell, E D (Dublin U, Wanderers) 1904 *S*, 1905 *E, S, W, NZ*, 1906 *E, S, W, SA*, 1907 *E, S*, 1908 *S, W*
Cagney, S J (London Irish) 1925 *W*, 1926 *F, E, S, W*, 1927 *F*, 1928 *E, S, W*, 1929 *F, E, S, W*
Callan, C P (Lansdowne) 1947 *F, E, S, W*, 1948 *F, E, S, W*, 1949 *F, E*
Cameron, E D (Bective Rangers) 1891 *S, W*
Campbell, C E (Old Wesley) 1970 *SA*
Campbell, E F (Monkstown) 1899 *S, W*, 1900 *E, W*
Campbell, S B B (Derry) 1911 *E, S, W, F*, 1912 *F, E, S, W, SA*, 1913 *E, S, F*
Campbell, S O (Old Belvedere) 1976 *A*, 1979 *A 1,2*, 1980 *E, S, F, W*, 1981 *F, W, E, S, SA* 1, 1982 *W, E, S, F*, 1983 *S, F, W, E*, 1984 *F, W*
Canniffe, D M (Lansdowne) 1976 *W, E*
Cantrell, J L (UC Dublin, Blackrock Coll) 1976 *A, F, W, E, S*, 1981 *S, SA 1,2, A*
Carey, R W (Dungannon) 1992 *NZ 1,2*
Carpendale, M J (Monkstown) 1886 *S*, 1887 *W*, 1888 *W, S*
Carr, N J (Ards) 1985 *S, F, W, E*, 1986 *W, E, S, R*, 1987 *E, S, W*
Carroll, C (Bective Rangers) 1930 *F*
Carroll, R (Lansdowne) 1947 *F*, 1950 *S, W*
Casement, B N (Dublin U) 1875 *E*, 1876 *E*, 1879 *E*
Casement, F (Dublin U) 1906 *E, S, W*
Casey, J C (Young Munster) 1930 *S*, 1932 *E*
Casey, P J (UC Dublin, Lansdowne) 1963 *F, E, S, W, NZ*, 1964 *E, S, W, F*, 1965 *F, E, S*
Chambers, J (Dublin U) 1886 *E, S*, 1887 *E, S, W*
Chambers, R R (Instonians) 1951 *F, E, S, W*, 1952 *F, W*
Clancy, T P J (Lansdowne) 1988 *W, E* 1,2, *WS, It*, 1989 *F, W, E, S*
Clarke, C P (Terenure Coll) 1993 *F, W, E*
Clarke, D J (Dolphin) 1991 *W, Nm* 1,2, [*J, A*], 1992 *NZ* 2(R)
Clarke, J A B (Bective Rangers) 1922 *S, W, F*, 1923 *F*, 1924 *E, S, W*
Clegg, R J (Bangor) 1973 *F*, 1975 *E, S, F, W*
Clifford, J T (Young Munster) 1949 *F, E, S, W*, 1950 *F, E, S, W*, 1951 *F, E, S, W, SA*, 1952 *F, S, W*
Clinch, A D (Dublin U, Wanderers) 1892 *S*, 1893 *W*, 1895 *E, S, W*, 1896 *E, S, W*, 1897 *E, S*
Clinch, J D (Wanderers, Dublin U) 1923 *W*, 1924 *F, E, S, W, NZ*, 1925 *F, E, S*, 1926 *E, S, W*, 1927 *F*, 1928 *F, E, S, W*, 1929 *F, E, S, W*, 1930 *F, E, S, W*, 1931 *F, E, S, W, SA*
Clohessy, P M (Young Munster) 1993 *F, W, E*
Clune, J J (Blackrock Coll) 1912 *SA*, 1913 *W, F*, 1914 *F, E, W*
Coffey, J J (Lansdowne) 1900 *E*, 1901 *W*, 1902 *E, S, W*, 1903 *E, S, W*, 1905 *E, S, W, NZ*, 1906 *E, S, W, SA*, 1907 *E*, 1908 *W*, 1910 *F*
Cogan, W St J (Queen's Coll, Cork) 1907 *E, S*
Collier, S R (Queen's Coll, Belfast) 1883 *S*
Collins, P C (Lansdowne, London Irish) 1987 [*C*], 1990 *S* (R)
Collis, W R F (KCH, Harlequins) 1924 *F, W, NZ*, 1925 *F, E, S*, 1926 *F*
Collis, W S (Wanderers) 1884 *W*
Collopy, G (Bective Rangers) 1891 *S*, 1892 *S*
Collopy, R (Bective Rangers) 1923 *E, S, W, F*, 1924 *F, E, S, W, NZ*, 1925 *F, E, S, W*
Collopy, W P (Bective Rangers) 1914 *F, E, S, W*, 1921

E, S, W, F, 1922 *E, S, W, F*, 1923 *S, W, F*, 1924 *F, E, S, W*
Combe, A (NIFC) 1875 *E*
Condon, H C (London Irish) 1984 *S* (R)
Cook, H G (Lansdowne) 1884 *W*
Coote, P B (RAF, Leicester) 1933 *S*
Corcoran, J C (London Irish) 1947 *A*, 1948 *F*
Corken, T S (Belfast Collegians) 1937 *E, S, W*
Corley, H H (Dublin U, Wanderers) 1902 *E, S, W*, 1903 *E, S, W*, 1904 *E, S*
Cormac, H S T (Clontarf) 1921 *E, S, W*
Costello, P (Bective Rangers) 1960 *F*
Costello, R A (Garryowen) 1993 *S*
Cotton, J (Wanderers) 1889 *W*
Coulter, H H (Queen's U, Belfast) 1920 *E, S, W*
Courtney, A W (UC Dublin) 1920 *S, W, F*, 1921 *E, S, W, F*
Cox, H L (Dublin U) 1875 *E*, 1876 *E*, 1877 *E, S*
Craig, R G (Queen's U, Belfast) 1938 *S, W*
Crawford, E C (Dublin U) 1885 *E, S* 1
Crawford, W E (Lansdowne) 1920 *E, S, W, F*, 1921 *E, S, W, F*, 1922 *E, S*, 1923 *E, S, W, F*, 1924 *F, E, W, NZ*, 1925 *F, E, S, W*, 1926 *F, E, S, W*, 1927 *F, E, S, W*
Crean, T J (Wanderers) 1894 *E, S, W*, 1895 *E, S, W*, 1896 *E, S, W*
Crichton, R Y (Dublin U) 1920 *E, S, W, F*, 1921 *F*, 1922 *E*, 1923 *W, F*, 1924 *F, E, S, W, NZ*, 1925 *E, S*
Croker, E W D (Limerick) 1878 *E*
Cromey, G E (Queen's U, Belfast) 1937 *E, S, W*, 1938 *E, S, W*, 1939 *E, S, W*
Cronyn, A P (Dublin U, Lansdowne) 1875 *E*, 1876 *E*, 1880 *S*
Crossan, K D (Instonians) 1982 *S*, 1984 *F, W, E, S*, 1985 *S, F, W, E*, 1986 *E, S, R*, 1987 *E, S, F, W*, [*W, C, Tg, A*], 1988 *S, F, W, E* 1, *WS, It*, 1989 *W, S, NZ*, 1990 *E, S, F, W, Arg*, 1991 *E, S*, *Nm* 2, [*Z, J, S*], 1992 *W*
Crowe, J F (UC Dublin) 1974 *NZ*
Crowe, L (Old Belvedere) 1950 *E, S, W*
Crowe, M P (Lansdowne) 1929 *W*, 1930 *E, S, W*, 1931 *F, S, W, SA*, 1932 *S, W*, 1933 *W, S*, 1934 *E*
Crowe, P M (Blackrock Coll) 1935 *E*, 1938 *E*
Cullen, T J (UC Dublin) 1949 *F*
Cullen, W J (Monkstown and Manchester) 1920 *E*
Culliton, M G (Wanderers) 1959 *E, S, W, F*, 1960 *E, S, W, F, SA*, 1961 *E, S, W, F*, 1962 *S, F*, 1964 *E, S, W, F*
Cummins, W E A (Queen's Coll, Cork) 1879 *S*, 1881 *E*, 1882 *E*
Cunningham, D McC (NIFC) 1923 *E, S, W*, 1925 *F, E, W*
Cunningham, M J (UC Cork) 1955 *F, E, S, W*, 1956 *F, S, W*
Cunningham, V J G (St Mary's Coll) 1988 *E* 2, *It* 1990 *Arg* (R), 1991 *Nm* 1,2, [*Z, J*(R)], 1992 *NZ* 1,2, *A*, 1993 *S, F, W, E*
Cunningham, W A (Lansdowne) 1920 *W*, 1921 *E, S, W, F*, 1922 *E*, 1923 *S, W*
Cuppaidge, J L (Dublin U) 1879 *E*, 1880 *E, S*
Currell, J (NIFC) 1877 *S*
Curtis, A B (Oxford U) 1950 *F, E, S*
Curtis, D M (London Irish) 1991 *W, E, S, Nm* 1,2, [*Z, J, S, A*], 1992 *W, E, S*(R), *F*
Cuscaden, W A (Dublin U, Bray) 1876 *E*
Cussen, D J (Dublin U) 1921 *E, S, W, F*, 1922 *E*, 1923 *E, S, W, F*, 1926 *F, E, S, W*, 1927 *F, E*

Daly, J C (London Irish) 1947 *F, E, S, W*, 1948 *E, S, W*
Daly, M J (Harlequins) 1938 *E*
Danaher, P P A (Lansdowne, Garryowen) 1988 *S, F, W, WS, It*, 1989 *F, NZ* (R), 1990 *F*, 1992 *S, F, NZ* 1, *A*, 1993 *S, F, W, E*
Dargan, M J (Old Belvedere) 1952 *S, W*
Davidson, C T (NIFC) 1921 *F*
Davidson, I G (NIFC) 1899 *E*, 1900 *S, W*, 1901 *E, S, W*, 1902 *E, S, W*
Davidson, J C (Dungannon) 1969 *F, E, S, W*, 1973 *NZ*, 1976 *NZ*
Davies, F E (Lansdowne) 1892 *S, W*, 1893 *E, S, W*
Davis, J L (Monkstown) 1898 *E, S*
Davis, W J N (Edinburgh U, Bessbrook) 1890 *S, W, E*, 1891 *E, S, W*, 1892 *E, S*, 1895 *S*
Davison, W (Belfast Academy) 1887 *W*
Davy, E O'D (UC Dublin, Lansdowne) 1925 *W*, 1926

F, E, S, W, 1927 F, E, S, W, A, 1928 F, E, S, W, 1929
F, E, S, W, 1930 F, E, S, W, 1931 F, E, S, W, SA, 1932
E, S, W, 1933 E, W, S, 1934 E
Dawson, A R (Wanderers) 1958 A, E, S, W, F, 1959 E,
S, W, F, 1960 F, SA, 1961 E, S, W, F, SA, 1962 S, F,
W, 1963 F, E, S, W, NZ, 1964 E, S, F
Dean, P M (St Mary's Coll) 1981 SA 1,2, A, 1982 W, E,
S, F, 1984 A, 1985 S, F, W, E, 1986 F, W, R, 1987 F,
S, F, W, [W, A], 1988 S, F, W, E 1,2, WS, It, 1989 F,
W, E, S
Deane, E C (Monkstown) 1909 E
Deering, M J (Bective Rangers) 1929 W
Deering, S J (Bective Rangers) 1935 E, S, W, NZ, 1936
E, S, W, 1937 E, S
Deering, S M (Garryowen, St Mary's Coll) 1974 W,
1976 F, W, E, S, 1977 W, E, 1978 NZ
de Lacy, H (Harlequins) 1948 E, S
Delaney, M G (Bective Rangers) 1895 W
Dennison, S P (Garryowen) 1973 F, 1975 E, S
Dick, C J (Ballymena) 1961 W, F, SA, 1962 W, 1963 F,
E, S, W
Dick, J S (Queen's U, Belfast) 1962 E
Dick, J S (Queen's U, Cork) 1887 E, S, W
Dickson, J A N (Dublin U) 1920 E, W, F
Doherty, A E (Old Wesley) 1974 P (R)
Doherty, W D (Guy's Hospital) 1920 E, S, W, 1921 E,
S, W, F
Donaldson, J A (Belfast Collegians) 1958 A, E, S, W
Donovan, T M (Queen's Coll, Cork) 1889 S
Dooley, J F (Galwegians) 1959 E, S, W
Doran, B R W (Lansdowne) 1900 S, W, 1901 E, S, W,
1902 E, S, W
Doran, E F (Lansdowne) 1890 S, W
Doran, G P (Lansdowne) 1899 S, W, 1900 E, S, 1902
S, W, 1903 W, 1904 E
Douglas, A C (Instonians) 1923 F, 1924 E, S, 1927 A,
1928 S
Downing, A J (Dublin U) 1882 W
Dowse, J C A (Monkstown) 1914 F, S, W
Doyle, J A P (Greystones) 1984 E, S
Doyle, J T (Bective Rangers) 1935 W
Doyle, M G (Blackrock Coll, UC Dublin, Cambridge
U, Edinburgh Wands) 1965 F, E, S, W, SA, 1966 F, E,
S, W, 1967 A 1, E, S, W, F A 2, 1968 F, E, S, W, A
Doyle, T J (Wanderers) 1968 E, S, W
Duggan, A T A (Lansdowne) 1963 NZ, 1964 F, 1966
W, 1967 A 1, S, W, A 2, 1968 F, E, S, W, 1969 F, E, S,
W, 1970 SA, F, E, S, W, 1971 F, E, S, W, 1972 F 2
Duggan, W (UC Cork) 1920 S, W
Duggan, W P (Blackrock Coll) 1975 E, S, F, W, 1976
A, F, W, S, NZ, 1977 W, E, S, F, 1978 S, F, W, E, NZ,
1979 E, S, A 1,2, 1980 E, 1981 F, W, E, S, SA 1,2, A,
1982 W, F, S, 1983 S, F, W, E, 1984 F, W, E, S
Duncan, W R (Malone) 1984 W, E
Dunlea, J (Lansdowne) 1989 W, E, S
Dunlop, R (Dublin U) 1889 W, 1890 S, W, E, 1891 E,
S, W, 1892 E, S, 1893 W, 1894 W
Dunn, P E F (Bective Rangers) 1923 S
Dunn, T B (NIFC) 1935 NZ
Dunne, M J (Lansdowne) 1929 F, E, S, 1930 F, E, S,
W, 1932 E, S, W, 1933 E, W, S, 1934 E, S, W
Dwyer, P J (UC Dublin) 1962 W, 1963 F, NZ, 1964 S,
W

Edwards, H G (Dublin U) 1877 E, 1878 E
Edwards, R W (Malone) 1904 W
Edwards, T (Lansdowne) 1888 M, 1890 S, W, E, 1892
W, 1893 W
Edwards, W V (Malone) 1912 F, E
Egan, J D (Bective Rangers) 1922 S
Egan, J T (Cork Constitution) 1931 F, E, SA
Egan, M S (Garryowen) 1893 E, 1895 S
Ekin, W (Queen's Coll, Belfast) 1888 W, S
Elliott, W R J (Bangor) 1979 S
Elwood, E P (Lansdowne) 1993 W, E
English, M A F (Lansdowne, Limerick Bohemians)
1958 W, F, 1959 E, S, F, 1960 E, S, 1961 S, W, F, 1962
F, W, 1963 E, S, W, NZ
Ennis, F N G (Wanderers) 1979 A 1 (R)
Ensor, A H (Wanderers) 1973 W, F, 1974 F, W, E, S,
P, NZ, 1975 E, S, F, W, 1976 A, F, W, E, NZ, 1977 E,
1978 S, F, W, E
Entrican, J C (Queen's U, Belfast) 1931 S

Fagan, G L (Kingstown School) 1878 E
Fagan, W B C (Wanderers) 1956 F, E, S
Farrell, J L (Bective Rangers) 1926 F, E, S, W, 1927 F,
E, S, W, A, 1928 F, E, S, W, 1929 F, E, S, W, 1930 F,
E, S, W, 1931 F, E, S, W, SA, 1932 E, S, W
Feddis, N (Lansdowne) 1956 E
Feighery, C F P (Lansdowne) 1972 F 1, E, F 2
Feighery, T A O (St Mary's Coll) 1977 W, E
Ferris, H H (Queen's Coll, Belfast) 1901 W
Ferris, J H (Queen's Coll, Belfast) 1900 E, S, W
Finlay, J E (Queen's Coll, Belfast) 1913 E, S, W, 1920
E, S, W
Finlay, W (NIFC) 1876 E, 1877 E, S, 1878 E, 1879 S,
E, 1880 S, 1882 S
Finn, M C (UC Cork, Cork Constitution) 1979 E, 1982
W, E, S, F, 1983 S, F, W, E, 1984 E, S, A, 1986 F, W
Finn, R G A (UC Dublin) 1977 F
Fitzgerald, C C (Glasgow U, Dungannon) 1902 E, 1903
E, S
Fitzgerald, C F (St Mary's Coll) 1979 A 1,2, 1980 E, S,
F, W, 1982 W, E, S, F, 1983 S, F, W, E, 1984 F, W, A,
1985 S, F, W, E, 1986 F, W, E, S
Fitzgerald, D C (Lansdowne, De La Salle Palmerston)
1984 E, S, 1986 W, E, S, R, 1987 E, S, F, W, [W, C,
A], 1988 S, F, W, E 1, 1989 NZ (R), 1990 E, S, F, W,
Arg, 1991 F, W, E, S, Nm 1,2, [Z, S, A], 1992 W, S(R)
Fitzgerald, J (Wanderers) 1884 W
Fitzgerald, J J (Young Munster) 1988 S, F, 1990 S,
F, W, 1991 F, W, E, S, [J]
Fitzgibbon, M J J (Shannon) 1992 W, E, S, F, NZ 1,2
Fitzpatrick, M P (Wanderers) 1978 S, 1980 S, F, W,
1981 F, W, E, S, A, 1985 F (R)
Fletcher, W W (Kingstown) 1882 W, S, 1883 E
Flood, R S (Dublin U) 1925 W
Flynn, M K (Wanderers) 1959 F, 1960 F, 1962 E, S, F,
W, 1964 E, S, W, F, 1965 F, E, S, W, SA, 1966 F, E,
S, 1972 F 1, E, F 2, 1973 NZ
Fogarty, T (Garryowen) 1891 W
Foley, B O (Shannon) 1976 F, E, 1977 W (R), 1980 F,
W, 1981 F, E, S, SA, 1,2, A
Forbes, R E (Malone) 1907 E
Forrest, A J (Wanderers) 1880 E, S, 1881 E, S, 1882
W, E, 1883 E, 1885 S 2
Forrest, E G (Wanderers) 1888 M, 1889 S, W, 1890 S,
E, 1891 E, 1893 S, 1894 E, S, W, 1895 W, 1897 E, S
Forrest, H (Wanderers) 1893 S, W
Fortune, J J (Clontarf) 1963 NZ, 1964 E
Foster, A R (Derry) 1910 E, S, F, 1911 E, S, W, F,
1912 F, E, S, W, 1914 E, S, W, 1921 E, S, W
Francis, N P J (Blackrock Coll, London Irish) 1987
[Tg, A], 1988 WS, It, 1989 S, 1990 E, F, W, 1991 E, S,
Nm 1,2, [Z, J, S, A], 1992 W, E, S, 1993 F
Franks, J G (Dublin U) 1898 E, S, W
Frazer, E F (Bective Rangers) 1891 S, 1892 S
Freer, A E (Lansdowne) 1901 E, S, W
Fulton, J (NIFC) 1895 S, W, 1896 E, S, W, 1897 E, 1898 W,
1899 E, 1900 W, 1901 E, 1902 E, S, W, 1903 E, S, W,
1904 E, S
Furlong, J N (UC Galway) 1992 NZ 1,2

Gaffikin, W (Windsor) 1875 E
Gage, J H (Queen's U, Belfast) 1926 S, W, 1927 S, W
Galbraith, E (Dublin U) 1875 E
Galbraith, H T (Belfast Acad) 1890 W
Galbraith, R (Dublin U) 1875 E, 1876 E, 1877 E
Galwey, M J (Shannon) 1991 F, W, Nm 2(R), [J], 1992
E, S, F, NZ 1,2, A, 1993 F, W, E
Ganly, J B (Monkstown) 1927 F, E, S, W, A, 1928 F,
E, S, W, 1929 F, S, 1930 F
Gardiner, F (NIFC) 1900 E, S, 1901 E, W, 1902 E, S,
W, 1903 E, W, 1904 E, S, W, 1906 E, S, W, 1907 S, W,
1908 S, W, 1909 E, S, F
Gardiner, J B (NIFC) 1923 E, S, W, F, 1924 F, E, S,
W, NZ, 1925 F, E, S, W
Gardiner, S (Belfast Albion) 1893 E, S
Gardiner, W (NIFC) 1892 E, S, 1893 E, S, W, 1894 E,
S, W, 1895 E, S, W, 1896 E, S, W, 1897 E, S, 1898 W
Garry, M G (Bective Rangers) 1909 E, S, W, F, 1911
E, S, W
Gaston, J T (Dublin U) 1954 NZ, F, E, S, W, 1955 W,
1956 F, E
Gavin, T J (Moseley, London Irish) 1949 F, E
Geoghegan, S P (London Irish) 1991 F, W, E, S, Nm
1, [Z, S, A], 1992 E, S, F, A, 1993 S, F, W, E

Gibson, C M H (Cambridge U, NIFC) 1964 *E, S, W, F*, 1965 *F, E, S, W, SA*, 1966 *F, E, S, W*, 1967 *A* 1, *E, S, W, F, A* 2, 1968 *E, S, W, A*, 1969 *E, S, W*, 1970 *SA, F, E, S, W*, 1971 *F, E, S, W*, 1972 *F* 1, *E, F* 2, 1973 *NZ, E, S, W, F*, 1974 *F, W, E, S, P*, 1975 *E, S, F, W*, 1976 *A, F, W, E, S, NZ*, 1977 *W, E, S, F*, 1978 *F, W, E, NZ*, 1979 *S, A* 1,2
Gibson, M E (Lansdowne, London Irish) 1979 *F, W, E, S*, 1981 *W* (R), 1986 *R*, 1988 *S, F, W, E* 2
Gifford, H P (Wanderers) 1890 *S*
Gillespie, J C (Dublin U) 1922 *W, F*
Gilpin, F G (Queen's U, Belfast) 1962 *E, S, F*
Glass, D C (Belfast Collegians) 1958 *F*, 1960 *W*, 1961 *W, SA*
Glennon, B T (Lansdowne) 1993 *F*(R)
Glennon, J J (Skerries) 1980 *E, S*, 1987 *E, S, F*, [*W*(R)]
Godfrey, R P (UC Dublin) 1954 *S, W*
Goodall, K G (City of Derry, Newcastle U) 1967 *A* 1, *E, S, W, F, A* 2, 1968 *F, E, S, W, A*, 1969 *F, E, S*, 1970 *SA, F, E, S, W*
Gordon, A (Dublin U) 1884 *S*
Gordon, T G (NIFC) 1877 *E, S*, 1878 *E*
Gotto, R P C (NIFC) 1906 *SA*
Goulding, W J (Cork) 1879 *S*
Grace, T O (UC Dublin, St Mary's Coll) 1972 *F* 1, *E*, 1973 *NZ, E, S, W*, 1974 *E, S, P, NZ*, 1975 *E, S, F, W*, 1976 *A, F, W, E, S, NZ*, 1977 *W, E, S, F*, 1978 *S*
Graham, R I (Dublin U) 1911 *F*
Grant, E L (CIYMS) 1971 *F, E, S, W*
Grant, P J (Bective Rangers) 1894 *S, W*
Graves, C R A (Wanderers) 1934 *E, S, W*, 1935 *E, S, W, NZ*, 1936 *E, S, W*, 1937 *E, S*, 1938 *E, S, W*
Gray, R D (Old Wesley) 1923 *E, S*, 1925 *F*, 1926 *F*
Greene, E H (Dublin U, Kingstown) 1882 *W*, 1884 *W*, 1885 *E, S* 2, 1886 *E*
Greer, R (Kingstown) 1876 *E*
Greeves, T J (NIFC) 1907 *E, S, W*, 1909 *W, F*
Gregg, R J (Queen's U, Belfast) 1953 *F, E, S, W*, 1954 *F, E, S*
Griffin, C S (London Irish) 1951 *F, E*
Griffin, J L (Wanderers) 1949 *S, W*
Griffiths, W (Limerick) 1878 *E*
Grimshaw, C (Queen's U, Belfast) 1969 *E* (R)
Guerin, B N (Galwegians) 1956 *S*
Gwynn, A P (Dublin U) 1895 *W*
Gwynn, L H (Dublin U) 1893 *S*, 1894 *E, S, W*, 1897 *S*, 1898 *E, S*

Hakin, R F (CIYMS) 1976 *W, S, NZ*, 1977 *W, E, F*
Hall, R O N (Dublin U) 1884 *W*
Hall, W H (Instonians) 1923 *E, S, W, F*, 1924 *F, S*
Hallaran, C F G T (Royal Navy) 1921 *E, S, W*, 1922 *E, S, W*, 1923 *E, F*, 1924 *F, E, S, W*, 1925 *F*, 1926 *F, E*
Halpin, G F (Wanderers, London Irish) 1990 *E*, 1991 [*7*], 1992 *E, S, F*
Halpin, T (Garryowen) 1909 *S, W, F*, 1910 *E, S, W*, 1911 *E, S, W, F*, 1912 *F, E, S*
Hamilton, A J (Lansdowne) 1884 *W*
Hamilton, G F (NIFC) 1991 *F, W, E, S, Nm* 2, [*Z, 7, S, A*], 1992 *A*
Hamilton, R L (NIFC) 1926 *F*
Hamilton, R W (Wanderers) 1893 *W*
Hamilton, W J (Dublin U) 1877 *E*
Hamlet, G T (Old Wesley) 1902 *E, S, W*, 1903 *E, S, W*, 1904 *S, W*, 1905 *E, S, W, NZ*, 1906 *SA*, 1907 *E, S, W*, 1908 *E, S, W*, 1909 *E, S, W, F*, 1910 *E, S, F*, 1911 *E, S, W, F*
Hanrahan, C J (Dolphin) 1926 *S, W*, 1927 *E, S, W, A*, 1928 *F, E, S*, 1929 *F, E, S, W*, 1930 *F, E, S, W*, 1931 *F*, 1932 *S, W*
Harbison, H T (Bective Rangers) 1984 *W* (R), *E, S*, 1986 *R*, 1987 *E, S, F, W*
Hardy, G G (Bective Rangers) 1962 *S*
Harman, G R A (Dublin U) 1899 *E, W*
Harper, J (Instonians) 1947 *F, E, S*
Harpur, T G (Dublin U) 1908 *E, S, W*
Harrison, T (Cork) 1879 *S*, 1880 *S*, 1881 *E*
Harvey, F M W (Wanderers) 1907 *W*, 1911 *F*
Harvey, G A D (Wanderers) 1903 *E, S*, 1904 *W*, 1905 *E, S*
Harvey, T A (Dublin U) 1900 *W*, 1901 *S*, 1902 *E, S, W*, 1903 *E, W*
Haycock, P P (Terenure Coll) 1989 *E*
Headon, T A (UC Dublin) 1939 *S, W*

Healey, P (Limerick) 1901 *E, S, W*, 1902 *E, S, W*, 1903 *E, S, W*, 1904 *S*
Heffernan, M R (Cork Constitution) 1911 *E, S, W, F*
Hemphill, R (Dublin U) 1912 *F, E, S, W*
Henderson, N J (Queen's U, Belfast, NIFC) 1949 *S, W*, 1950 *F*, 1951 *F, E, S, W, SA*, 1952 *F, S, W, E*, 1953 *F, E, S, W*, 1954 *NZ, F, E, S, W*, 1955 *F, E, S, W*, 1956 *S, W*, 1957 *F, E, S, W*, 1958 *A, E, S, W, F*, 1959 *E, S, W, F*
Henebrey, G J (Garryowen) 1906 *E, S, W, SA*, 1909 *W, F*
Heron, A G (Queen's Coll, Belfast) 1901 *E*
Heron, J (NIFC) 1877 *S*, 1879 *E*
Heron, W T (NIFC) 1880 *E, S*
Herrick, R W (Dublin U) 1886 *S*
Heuston, F S (Kingstown) 1882 *W*, 1883 *E, S*
Hewitt, D (Queen's U, Belfast, Instonians) 1958 *A, E, S, F*, 1959 *S, W, F*, 1960 *E, S, W, F*, 1961 *E, S, W, F*, 1962 *S, F*, 1965 *W*
Hewitt, F S (Instonians) 1924 *W, NZ*, 1925 *F, E, S*, 1926 *E, S, W*
Hewitt, J A (NIFC) 1981 *SA* 1 (R), 2 (R)
Hewitt, T R (Queen's U, Belfast) 1924 *W, NZ*, 1925 *F, E, S*, 1926 *F, E, S, W*
Hewitt, V A (Instonians) 1935 *S, W, NZ*, 1936 *E, S, W*
Hewitt, W J (Instonians) 1954 *E*, 1956 *S*, 1959 *W*, 1961 *SA*
Hewson, F T (Wanderers) 1875 *E*
Hickie, D J (St Mary's Coll) 1971 *F, E, S, W*, 1972 *F* 1, *E*
Higgins, J A D (Civil Service) 1947 *S, W, A*, 1948 *F, S, W*
Higgins, W W (NIFC) 1884 *E, S*
Hillary, M F (UC Dublin) 1952 *E*
Hingerty, D J (UC Dublin) 1947 *F, E, S, W*
Hinton, W P (Old Wesley) 1907 *W*, 1908 *E, S, W*, 1909 *E, S*, 1910 *E, S, W, F*, 1911 *E, S, W*, 1912 *F, E, W*
Hipwell, M L (Terenure Coll) 1962 *E, S*, 1968 *F, A*, 1969 *F* (R), *S* (R), *W*, 1971 *F, E, S, W*, 1972 *F* 2
Hobbs, T H M (Dublin U) 1884 *S*, 1885 *E*
Hobson, E W (Dublin U) 1876 *E*
Hogan, P (Garryowen) 1992 *F*
Hogg, W (Dublin U) 1885 *S* 2
Holland, J J (Wanderers) 1981 *SA* 1,2, 1986 *W*
Holmes, G W (Dublin U) 1912 *SA*, 1913 *E, S*
Holmes, L J (Lisburn) 1889 *S, W*
Hooks, K J (Queen's U, Belfast, Ards, Bangor) 1981 *S*, 1989 *NZ*, 1990 *F, W, Arg*, 1991 *F*
Horan, A K (Blackheath) 1920 *E, W*
Houston, D J (Oxford U, London Irish) 1961 *SA*, 1964 *S, W*, 1965 *F, E, SA*
Hughes, R W (NIFC) 1878 *E*, 1880 *E, S*, 1881 *S*, 1882 *E, S*, 1883 *E, S*, 1884 *E, S*, 1885 *E*, 1886 *E*
Hunt, E W F de Vere (Army, Rosslyn Park) 1930 *F*, 1932 *E, S, W*, 1933 *E*
Hunter, D V (Dublin U) 1885 *S* 2
Hunter, L (Civil Service) 1968 *W, A*
Hunter, W R (CIYMS) 1962 *E, S, W, F*, 1963 *F, E, S*, 1966 *F, E, S*
Hutton, S A (Malone) 1967 *S, W, F, A* 2

Ireland, J (Windsor) 1876 *E*, 1877 *E*
Irvine, H A S (Collegians) 1901 *S*
Irwin, D G (Queen's U, Belfast, Instonians) 1980 *F, W*, 1981 *F, W, E, S, SA* 1,2, 1982 *W*, 1983 *S, F, W, E*, 1984 *F, W*, 1987 [*Tg, A*(R)], 1989 *F, W, E, S, NZ*, 1990 *E, S*
Irwin, J W S (NIFC) 1938 *E, S*, 1939 *E, S, W*
Irwin, S T (Queen's Coll, Belfast) 1900 *E, S, W*, 1901 *E, W*, 1902 *E, S, W*, 1903 *S*

Jack, H W (UC Cork) 1914 *S, W*, 1921 *W*
Jackson, A R V (Wanderers) 1911 *E, S, W, F*, 1913 *W, F*, 1914 *F, E, S, W*
Jackson, F (NIFC) 1923 *E*
Jackson, H W (Dublin U) 1877 *E*
Jameson, J S (Lansdowne) 1888 *M*, 1889 *S, W*, 1891 *W*, 1892 *E, W*, 1893 *S*
Jeffares, E W (Wanderers) 1913 *E, S*
Johns, P S C (Dublin U, Dungannon) 1990 *Arg*, 1992 *NZ* 1,2 *A*, 1993 *S, F, W, E*
Johnston, J (Belfast Acad) 1881 *S*, 1882 *S*, 1884 *S*, 1885 *S* 1,2, 1886 *E*, 1887 *E, S, W*
Johnston, M (Dublin U) 1880 *E, S*, 1881 *E, S*, 1882 *E*, 1884 *E, S*, 1886 *E*

McFarland, B A T (Derry) 1920 *S, W, F,* 1922 *W*
McGann, B J (Lansdowne) 1969 *F, E, S, W,* 1970 *SA, F, E, S, W,* 1971 *F, E, S, W,* 1972 *F* 1, *E, F* 2, 1973 *NZ, E, S, W,* 1976 *F, W, E, S, NZ*
McGown, T M W (NIFC) 1899 *E, S,* 1901 *S*
McGrath, D G (UC Dublin, Cork Const) 1984 *S,* 1987 *[W, C, Tg, A]*
McGrath, N F (Oxford U, London Irish) 1934 *W*
McGrath, P J (UC Cork) 1965 *E, S, W, SA,* 1966 *F, E, S, W,* 1967 *A* 1, *A* 2
McGrath, R J M (Wanderers) 1977 *W, E, F* (R), 1981 *SA* 1,2, *A,* 1982 *W, E, S, F,* 1983 *S, F, W, E,* 1984 *F, W*
McGrath, T (Garryowen) 1956 *W,* 1958 *F,* 1960 *E, S, W, F,* 1961 *SA*
McGuire, E P (UC Galway) 1963 *E, S, W, NZ,* 1964 *E, S, W, F*
MacHale, S (Lansdowne) 1965 *F, E, S, W, SA,* 1966 *F, E, S, W,* 1967 *S, W, F*
McIldowie, G (Malone) 1906 *SA,* 1910 *E, S, W*
McIlrath, J A (Ballymena) 1976 *A, F, NZ,* 1977 *W, E*
McIlwaine, E H (NIFC) 1895 *S, W*
McIlwaine, E N (NIFC) 1875 *E,* 1876 *E*
McIlwaine, J E (NIFC) 1897 *E, S,* 1898 *E, S, W,* 1899 *E, W*
McIntosh, L M (Dublin U) 1884 *S*
MacIvor, C V (Dublin U) 1912 *F, E, S, W,* 1913 *E, S, F*
McKay, J W (Queen's U, Belfast) 1947 *F, E, S, W, A,* 1948 *F, E, S, W,* 1949 *F, E, S, W,* 1950 *F, E, S, W,* 1951 *F, E, S, W, SA,* 1952 *F*
McKee, W D (NIFC) 1947 *A,* 1948 *F, E, S, W,* 1949 *F, E, S, W,* 1950 *F, E,* 1951 *SA*
McKelvey, J M (Queen's U, Belfast) 1956 *F, E*
McKibbin, A R (Instonians, London Irish) 1977 *W, E, S,* 1978 *S, F, W, E, NZ,* 1979 *F, W, E, S,* 1980 *E, S*
McKibbin, C H (Instonians) 1976 *S* (R)
McKibbin, D (Instonians) 1950 *F, E, S, W,* 1951 *F, E, S, W*
McKibbin, H R (Queen's U, Belfast) 1938 *W,* 1939 *E, S, W*
McKinney, S A (Dungannon) 1972 *F* 1, *E, F* 2, 1973 *W, F,* 1974 *F, E, S, P, NZ,* 1975 *E, S,* 1976 *A, F, W, E, S, NZ,* 1977 *W, E, S,* 1978 *S* (R), *F, W, E*
McLaughlin, J H (Derry) 1887 *E, S,* 1888 *W, S*
McLean, R E (Dublin U) 1881 *S,* 1882 *W, E, S,* 1883 *E, S,* 1884 *E, S,* 1885 *E, S* 1
Mclear, B (Cork County, Monkstown) 1905 *E, S, W, NZ,* 1906 *E, S, W, SA,* 1907 *E, S, W*
McLennan, A C (Wanderers) 1977 *F,* 1978 *S, F, W, E, NZ,* 1979 *F, W, E, S,* 1980 *E, F,* 1981 *F, W, E, S, SA* 1,2
McLoughlin, F M (Northern) 1976 *A*
McLoughlin, G A J (Shannon) 1979 *W, F, E, S, A* 1,2, 1980 *E,* 1981 *SA* 1,2, 1982 *W, E, S, F,* 1983 *S, F, W, E,* 1984 *F*
McLoughlin, R J (UC Dublin, Blackrock Coll, Gosforth) 1962 *E, S, F,* 1963 *E, S, W, NZ,* 1964 *E, S,* 1965 *F, E, S, W, SA,* 1966 *F, E, S, W,* 1971 *F, E, S, W,* 1972 *F* 1, *E, F* 2, 1973 *NZ, E, S, W, F,* 1974 *F, W, E, S, P, NZ,* 1975 *E, S, F, W*
McMahon, L B (Blackrock Coll, UC Dublin) 1931 *E, SA,* 1933 *E,* 1934 *E,* 1936 *E, S, W,* 1937 *E, S, W,* 1938 *E, S*
McMaster, A W (Ballymena) 1972 *F* 1, *E, F* 2, 1973 *NZ, E, S, W, F,* 1974 *F, E, S, P,* 1975 *F, W,* 1976 *A, F, W, NZ*
McMordie, J (Queen's Coll, Belfast) 1886 *S*
McMorrow, A (Garryowen) 1951 *W*
McMullen, A R (Cork) 1881 *E, S*
McNamara, V (UC Cork) 1914 *E, S, W*
McNaughton, P P (Greystones) 1978 *S, F, W, E,* 1979 *F, W, E, S, A* 1,2, 1980 *E, S, F, W,* 1981 *F*
MacNeill, H P (Dublin U, Oxford U, Blackrock Coll, London Irish) 1981 *F, W, E, S, A,* 1982 *W, E, S, F,* 1983 *S, F, W, E,* 1984 *F, W, E, A,* 1985 *S, F,* 1986 *F, W, E, S, R,* 1987 *E, S, F, W, [W, C, Tg, A],* 1988 *S*(R), *E* 1,2
MacSweeney, D A (Blackrock Coll) 1955 *S*
McVicker, H (Army, Richmond) 1927 *E, S, W, A,* 1928 *F*
McVicker, J (Collegians) 1924 *F, E, S, W, NZ,* 1925 *F, E, S, W,* 1926 *F, E, S, W,* 1927 *F, E, S, W, A,* 1928 *W,* 1930 *F*
McVicker, S (Queen's U, Belfast) 1922 *E, S, W, F*
Madden, M N (Sunday's Well) 1955 *E, S, W*

Magee, J T (Bective Rangers) 1895 *E, S*
Magee, A M (Louis) (Bective Rangers, London Irish) 1895 *E, S, W,* 1896 *E, S, W,* 1897 *E, S,* 1898 *E, S, W,* 1899 *E, S, W,* 1900 *E, S, W,* 1901 *E, S, W,* 1902 *E, S, W,* 1903 *E, S, W,* 1904 *W*
Maginiss, R M (Dublin U) 1875 *E,* 1876 *E*
Magrath, R M (Cork Constitution) 1909 *S*
Maguire, J F (Cork) 1884 *S*
Mahoney, J (Dolphin) 1923 *E*
Malcolmson, G L (RAF, NIFC) 1935 *NZ,* 1936 *E, S, W,* 1937 *E, S, W*
Malone, N G (Oxford U) 1993 *S, F*
Mannion, N P (Corinthians, Lansdowne, Wanderers) 1988 *WS, It,* 1989 *F, W, E, S, NZ,* 1990 *E, S, F, W, Arg,* 1991 *Nm* 1(R),2, *[J],* 1993 *S*
Marshall, B D E (Queen's U, Belfast) 1963 *E*
Massey-Westropp, R H (Limerick, Monkstown) 1886 *E*
Matier, R N (NIFC) 1878 *E,* 1879 *S*
Matthews, P M (Ards, Wanderers) 1984 *A,* 1985 *S, F, W, E,* 1986 *R,* 1987 *E, S, F, W, [W, Tg, A],* 1988 *S, F, W, E* 1,2, *WS, It,* 1989 *F, W, E, S, NZ,* 1990 *E, S,* 1991 *F, W, E, S, Nm* 1, *[Z, S, A],* 1992 *W, E, S*
Mattsson, J (Wanderers) 1948 *E*
Mayne, R B (Queen's U, Belfast) 1937 *W,* 1938 *E, W,* 1939 *E, S*
Mayne, R H (Belfast Academy) 1888 *W, S*
Mayne, T (NIFC) 1921 *E, S, F*
Mays, K M A (UC Dublin) 1973 *NZ, E, S, W*
Meares, A W D (Dublin U) 1899 *S, W,* 1900 *E, W*
Megaw, J (Richmond, Instonians) 1934 *W,* 1938 *E*
Millar, A (Kingstown) 1880 *E, S,* 1883 *E*
Millar, H J (Monkstown) 1904 *W,* 1905 *E, S, W*
Millar, S (Ballymena) 1958 *F,* 1959 *E, S, W, F,* 1960 *E, S, W, F, SA,* 1961 *E, S, W, F, SA,* 1962 *E, S, F,* 1963 *F, E, S, W,* 1964 *F,* 1968 *F, E, S, W, A,* 1969 *F, E, S, W,* 1970 *SA, F, E, S, W*
Millar, W H J (Queen's U, Belfast) 1951 *E, S, W,* 1952 *S, W*
Miller, F H (Wanderers) 1886 *S*
Milliken, R A (Bangor) 1973 *E, S, W, F,* 1974 *F, W, E, S, P, NZ,* 1975 *E, S, F, W*
Millin, T J (Dublin U) 1925 *W*
Minch, J B (Bective Rangers) 1912 *SA,* 1913 *E, S,* 1914 *E, S*
Moffat, J (Belfast Academy) 1888 *W, S, M,* 1889 *S,* 1890 *S, W,* 1891 *S*
Moffatt, J E (Old Wesley) 1904 *S,* 1905 *E, S, W*
Moffett, J W (Ballymena) 1961 *E, S*
Molloy, M G (UC Galway, London Irish) 1966 *F, E,* 1967 *A* 1, *E, S, W, F, A* 2, 1968 *F, E, S, W, A,* 1969 *F, E, S, W,* 1970 *F, E, S, W,* 1971 *F, E, S, W,* 1973 *F,* 1976 *A*
Moloney, J J (St Mary's Coll) 1972 *F* 1, *E, F* 2, 1973 *NZ, E, S, W, F,* 1974 *F, W, E, S, P, NZ,* 1975 *E, S, F, W,* 1976 *S,* 1978 *S, F, W, E,* 1979 *A* 1,2, 1980 *S, W*
Moloney, L A (Garryowen) 1976 *W*(R), *S,* 1978 *S* (R), *NZ*
Molony, J U (UC Dublin) 1950 *S*
Monteith, J D E (Queen's U, Belfast) 1947 *E, S, W*
Montgomery, A (NIFC) 1895 *S*
Montgomery, F P (Queen's U, Belfast) 1914 *E, S, W*
Montgomery, R (Cambridge U) 1887 *E, S, W,* 1891 *E,* 1892 *W*
Moore, C M (Dublin U) 1887 *S,* 1888 *W, S*
Moore, D F (Wanderers) 1883 *E, S,* 1884 *E, W*
Moore, F W (Wanderers) 1884 *W,* 1885 *E, S* 2, 1886 *S*
Moore, H (Windsor) 1876 *E,* 1877 *S*
Moore, H (Queen's U, Belfast) 1910 *S,* 1911 *W, F,* 1912 *F, E, S, W, SA*
Moore, T A P (Highfield) 1967 *A* 2, 1973 *NZ, E, S, W, F,* 1974 *F, W, E, S, P, NZ*
Moore, W D (Queen's Coll, Belfast) 1878 *E*
Moran, F G (Clontarf) 1936 *E,* 1937 *E, S, W,* 1938 *S, W,* 1939 *E, S, W*
Morell, H B (Dublin U) 1881 *E, S,* 1882 *W, E*
Morgan, G J (Clontarf) 1934 *E, S, W,* 1935 *E, S, W, NZ,* 1936 *E, S, W,* 1937 *E, S, W,* 1938 *E, S, W,* 1939 *E, S, W*
Moriarty, C C H (Monkstown) 1899 *W*
Moroney, J C M (Garryowen) 1968 *W, A,* 1969 *F, E, S, W*
Moroney, R J M (Lansdowne) 1984 *F, W,* 1985 *F*
Moroney, T A (UC Dublin) 1964 *W,* 1967 *A* 1, *E*
Morphy, E McG (Dublin U) 1908 *E*

Morris, D P (Bective Rangers) 1931 *W*, 1932 *E*, 1935 *E*, *S, W, NZ*
Morrow, J W R (Queen's Coll, Belfast) 1882 *S*, 1883 *E*, *S*, 1884 *E*, *W*, 1885 *S* 1,2, 1886 *E*, *S*, 1888 *S*
Morrow, R D (Bangor) 1986 *F, E, S*
Mortell, M (Bective Rangers, Dolphin) 1953 *F, E, S*, *W*, 1954 *NZ, F, E, S, W*
Morton, W A (Dublin U) 1888 *S*
Moyers, L W (Dublin U) 1884 *W*
Moylett, M M F (Shannon) 1988 *E* 1
Mulcahy, W A (UC Dublin, Bective Rangers, Bohemians) 1958 *A, E, S, W, F*, 1959 *E, S, W, F*, 1960 *E, S, W, SA*, 1961 *E, S, W, SA*, 1962 *E, S, F, W*, 1963 *F, E, S, W, NZ*, 1964 *E, S, W, F*, 1965 *F, E, S, W, SA*
Mullan, B (Clontarf) 1947 *F, E, S, W*, 1948 *F, E, S, W*
Mullane, J P (Limerick Bohemians) 1928 *W*, 1929 *F*
Mullen, K D (Old Belvedere) 1947 *F, E, S, W, A*, 1948 *F, E, S, W*, 1949 *F, E, S, W*, 1950 *F, E, S, W*, 1951 *F, E, S, W, SA*, 1952 *F, S, W*
Mulligan, A A (Wanderers) 1956 *F, E*, 1957 *F, E, S, W*, 1958 *A, E, S, F*, 1959 *E, S, W, F*, 1960 *E, S, W, F, SA*, 1961 *W, F, SA*
Mullin, B J (Dublin U, Oxford U, Blackrock Coll, London Irish) 1984 *A*, 1985 *S, W, E*, 1986 *F, W, E, S, R*, 1987 *E, S, F, W*, [*W, C, Tg, A*], 1988 *S, F, W, E* 1,2, *WS, It*, 1989 *F, W, E, S, NZ*, 1990 *E, S, W, Arg*, 1991 *F, W, E, S, Nm* 1,2, [*J, S, A*], 1992 *W, E, S*
Murphy, C J (Lansdowne) 1939 *E, S, W*, 1947 *F, E*
Murphy, J G M W (London Irish) 1951 *SA*, 1952 *S, W, E*, 1954 *NZ*, 1958 *W*
Murphy, J J (Greystones) 1981 *SA* 1, 1982 *W* (R), 1984 *S*
Murphy, J N (Greystones) 1992 *A*
Murphy, K J (Cork Constitution) 1990 *E, S, F, W, Arg*, 1991 *F, W* (R), *S* (R), 1992 *S, F, NZ* 2 (R)
Murphy, N A A (Cork Constitution) 1958 *A, E, S, W, F*, 1959 *E, S, W, F*, 1960 *E, S, W, F, SA*, 1961 *E, S, W*, 1962 *E, S, W, F*, 1963 *NZ*, 1964 *E, S, W, F*, 1965 *F, E, S, W, SA*, 1966 *F, E, S, W*, 1967 *A* 1, *E, S, W, F*, 1969 *F, E, S, W*
Murphy, N F (Cork Constitution) 1930 *E, W*, 1931 *F, E, S, W, SA*, 1932 *E, S, W*, 1933 *E*
Murphy-O'Connor, J (Bective Rangers) 1954 *E*
Murray, H W (Dublin) 1877 *S*, 1878 *E*, 1879 *E*
Murray, J B (UC Dublin) 1963 *F*
Murray, P F (Wanderers) 1927 *F*, 1929 *F, E, S*, 1930 *F, E, S, W*, 1931 *F, E, S, W, SA*, 1932 *E, S, W*, 1933 *E, W, S*
Murtagh, C W (Portadown) 1977 *S*
Myles, J (Dublin U) 1875 *E*

Nash, L C (Queen's Coll, Cork) 1889 *S*, 1890 *W, E*, 1891 *E, S, W*
Neely, M R (Collegians) 1947 *F, E, S, W*
Neill, H J (NIFC) 1885 *E, S* 1,2, 1886 *S*, 1887 *E, S, W*, 1888 *W, S*
Neill, J McF (Instonians) 1926 *F*
Nelson, J E (Malone) 1947 *A*, 1948 *E, S, W*, 1949 *F, E, S, W*, 1950 *F, E, S, W*, 1951 *F, E, W*, 1954 *F*
Nelson, R (Queen's Coll, Belfast) 1882 *E, S*, 1883 *S*, 1886 *S*
Nesdale, T J (Garryowen) 1961 *F*
Neville, W C (Dublin U) 1879 *S, E*
Nicholson, P C (Dublin U) 1900 *E, S, W*
Norton, G W (Bective Rangers) 1949 *F, E, S, W*, 1950 *F, E, S, W*, 1951 *F, E, S*
Notley, J R (Wanderers) 1952 *F, S*

O'Brien, B (Derry) 1893 *S, W*
O'Brien, B A P (Shannon) 1968 *F, E, S*
O'Brien, D J (London Irish, Cardiff, Old Belvedere) 1948 *E, S, W*, 1949 *F, E, S, W*, 1950 *F, E, S, W*, 1951 *F, E, S, W, SA*, 1952 *F, S, W, E*
O'Brien, K A (Broughton Park) 1980 *E*, 1981 *SA* 1 (R), 2
O'Brien-Butler, P E (Monkstown) 1897 *S*, 1898 *E, S*, 1899 *S, W*, 1900 *E*
O'Callaghan, C T (Carlow) 1910 *W, F*, 1911 *E, S, W, F*, 1912 *F*
O'Callaghan, M P (Sunday's Well) 1962 *W*, 1964 *E, F*
O'Callaghan, P (Dolphin) 1967 *A* 1, *E, A* 2, 1968 *F, E, S, W*, 1969 *F, E, S, W*, 1970 *SA, F, E, S, W*, 1976 *F, W, E, S, NZ*
O'Connell, P (Bective Rangers) 1913 *W, F*, 1914 *F, E, S, W*
O'Connell, W J (Lansdowne) 1955 *F*

O'Connor, H S (Dublin U) 1957 *F, E, S, W*
O'Connor, J (Garryowen) 1895 *S*
O'Connor, J H (Bective Rangers) 1888 *M*, 1890 *S, W, E*, 1891 *E, S*, 1892 *E, W*, 1893 *E, S*, 1894 *E, S, W*, 1895 *E*, 1896 *E, S, W*
O'Connor, J J (Garryowen) 1909 *F*
O'Connor, J J (UC Cork) 1933 *S*, 1934 *E, S, W*, 1935 *E, S, W, NZ*, 1936 *S, W*, 1938 *S*
O'Connor, P J (Lansdowne) 1887 *W*
Odbert, R V M (RAF) 1928 *F*
O'Donnell, R C (St Mary's Coll) 1979 *A* 1,2, 1980 *S, F, W*
O'Donoghue, P J (Bective Rangers) 1955 *F, E, S, W*, 1956 *W*, 1957 *F, E*, 1958 *A, E, S, W*
O'Driscoll, B J (Manchester) 1971 *F* (R), *E, S, W*
O'Driscoll, J B (London Irish, Manchester) 1978 *S*, 1979 *A* 1,2, 1980 *E, S, F, W*, 1981 *F, W, E, S, SA* 1,2, *A*, 1982 *W, E, S, F*, 1983 *S, F, W, E*, 1984 *F, W, E, S*
O'Flanagan, K P (London Irish) 1947 *A*
O'Flanagan, M (Lansdowne) 1948 *S*
O'Hanlon, B (Dolphin) 1947 *E, S, W*, 1948 *F, E, S, W*, 1949 *F, E, S, W*, 1950 *F*
O'Hara, P T J (Sunday's Well, Cork Const) 1988 *WS* (R), 1989 *F, W, E, NZ*, 1990 *E, S, F, W*, 1991 *Nm* 1, [*J*], 1993 *F, W, E*
O'Leary, A (Cork Constitution) 1952 *S, W, E*
O'Loughlin, D B (UC Cork) 1938 *E, S, W*, 1939 *E, S, W*
O'Meara, J A (UC Cork, Dolphin) 1951 *F, E, S, W, SA*, 1952 *F, S, W, E*, 1953 *F, E, S, W*, 1954 *NZ, F, E, S*, 1955 *F, E*, 1956 *S, W*, 1958 *W*
O'Neill, H O'H (Queen's U, Belfast, UC Cork) 1930 *E, S, W*, 1933 *E, S, W*
O'Neill, J B (Queen's U, Belfast) 1920 *S*
O'Neill, W A (UC Dublin, Wanderers) 1952 *E*, 1953 *F, E, S, W*, 1954 *NZ*
O'Reilly, A J F (Old Belvedere, Leicester) 1955 *F, E, S, W*, 1956 *F, E, S, W*, 1957 *F, E, S, W*, 1958 *A, E, S, W, F*, 1959 *E, S, W, F*, 1960 *E*, 1961 *E, F, SA*, 1963 *F, S, W*, 1970 *E*
Orr, P A (Old Wesley) 1976 *F, W, E, S, NZ*, 1977 *W, E, S, F*, 1978 *S, F, W, E, NZ*, 1979 *F, W, E, S, A* 1,2, 1980 *E, S, W, F*, 1981 *F, W, E, S, SA* 1,2, *A*, 1982 *W, E, S, F*, 1983 *S, F, W, E, S, A*, 1985 *S, F, W, E*, 1986 *F, S, R*, 1987 *E, S, F, W*, [*W, C, A*]
O'Sullivan, A C (Dublin U) 1882 *S*
O'Sullivan, J M (Limerick) 1884 *S*, 1887 *S*
O'Sullivan, P J A (Galwegians) 1957 *F, E, S, W*, 1959 *E, S, W, F*, 1960 *SA*, 1961 *E, S*, 1962 *F, W*, 1963 *F, NZ*
O'Sullivan, W (Queen's Coll, Cork) 1895 *S*
Owens, R H (Dublin U) 1922 *E, S*

Parfrey, P (UC Cork) 1974 *NZ*
Parke, J C (Monkstown) 1903 *W*, 1904 *E, S, W*, 1905 *W, NZ*, 1906 *E, S, W, SA*, 1907 *E, S, W*, 1908 *E, S, W*, 1909 *E, S, W, F*
Parr, J S (Wanderers) 1914 *F, E, S, W*
Patterson, C S (Instonians) 1978 *NZ*, 1979 *F, W, E, S, A* 1,2, 1980 *E, S, F, W*
Patterson, R d'A (Wanderers) 1912 *F, S, W, SA*, 1913 *E, S, W, F*
Payne, C T (NIFC) 1926 *E*, 1927 *F, E, S, A*, 1928 *F, E, S, W*, 1929 *F, E, W*, 1930 *F, E, S, W*
Pedlow, A C (CIYMS) 1953 *W*, 1954 *NZ, F, E*, 1955 *F, W*, 1956 *F, E, S, W*, 1957 *F, E, W*, 1958 *A, E, S, W, F*, 1959 *E, S, W, F, SA*, 1961 *S*, 1962 *W*, 1963 *F*
Pedlow, J (Bessbrook) 1882 *S*, 1884 *W*
Pedlow, R (Bessbrook) 1891 *W*
Pedlow, T B (Queen's Coll, Belfast) 1889 *S, W*
Peel, T (Limerick) 1892 *E, S, W*
Peirce, W (Cork) 1881 *E*
Phipps, G C (Army) 1950 *E, W*, 1952 *F, W, E*
Pike, T O (Lansdowne) 1927 *E, S, W, A*, 1928 *F, E, S, W*
Pike, V J (Lansdowne) 1931 *E, S, W, SA*, 1932 *E, S, W*, 1933 *E, S, W*, 1934 *E, S, W*
Pike, W W (Kingstown) 1879 *E*, 1881 *E, S*, 1882 *E*, 1883 *S*
Pinion, G (Belfast Collegians) 1909 *E, S, W, F*
Piper, O J S (Cork Constitution) 1909 *E, S, W, F*, 1910 *E, S, W, F*
Polden, S E (Clontarf) 1913 *W, F*, 1914 *F*, 1920 *F*
Popham, I (Cork Constitution) 1922 *S, W, F*, 1923 *F*

Popplewell, N J (Greystones) 1989 *NZ*, 1990 *Arg*, 1991 *Nm* 1,2, [*Z, S, A*], 1992 *W, E, S, F, NZ* 1,2, *A*, 1993 *S, F, W, E*
Potterton, H N (Wanderers) 1920 *W*
Pratt, R H (Dublin U) 1933 *E, W, S*, 1934 *E, S*
Price, A H (Dublin U) 1920 *S, F*
Pringle, J C (NIFC) 1902 *S, W*
Purcell, N M (Lansdowne) 1921 *E, S, W, F*
Purdon, H (NIFC) 1879 *S, E*, 1880 *E*, 1881 *E, S*
Purdon, W B (Queen's Coll, Belfast) 1906 *E, S, W*
Purser, F C (Dublin U) 1898 *E, S, W*

Quinlan, S V J (Blackrock Coll) 1956 *F, E, W*, 1958 *W*
Quinn, B T (Old Belvedere) 1947 *F*
Quinn, F P (Old Belvedere) 1981 *F, W, E*
Quinn, J P (Dublin U) 1910 *E, S*, 1911 *E, S, W, F*, 1912 *E, S, W*, 1913 *E, W, F*, 1914 *F, E, S*
Quinn, K (Old Belvedere) 1947 *F, A*, 1953 *F, E, S*
Quinn, M A M (Lansdowne) 1973 *F*, 1974 *F, W, E, S, P, NZ*, 1977 *S, F*, 1981 *SA* 2
Quirke, J M T (Blackrock Coll) 1962 *E, S*, 1968 *S*

Rainey, P I (Ballymena) 1989 *NZ*
Rambaut, D F (Dublin U) 1887 *E, S, W*, 1888 *W*
Rea, H H (Edinburgh U) 1967 *A* 1, 1969 *F*
Read, H M (Dublin U) 1910 *E, S*, 1911 *E, S, W, F*, 1912 *F, E, S, W, SA*, 1913 *E, S*
Rearden, J V (Cork Constitution) 1934 *E, S*
Reid, C (NIFC) 1899 *S, W*, 1900 *E*, 1903 *W*
Reid, J L (Richmond) 1934 *S, W*
Reid, P J (Garryowen) 1947 *A*, 1948 *F, E, W*
Reid, T E (Garryowen) 1953 *E, S, W*, 1954 *NZ, F*, 1955 *E, S*, 1956 *F, E*, 1957 *F, E, S, W*
Reidy, C J (London Irish) 1937 *W*
Reidy, G F (Dolphin, Lansdowne) 1953 *W*, 1954 *F, E, S, W*
Richey, H A (Dublin U) 1889 *W*, 1890 *S*
Ridgeway, E C (Wanderers) 1932 *S, W*, 1935 *E, S, W*
Rigney, B J (Greystones) 1991 *F, W, E, S, Nm* 1, 1992 *F, NZ* 1(R),2
Ringland, T M (Queen's U, Belfast, Ballymena) 1981 *A*, 1982 *W, E, F*, 1983 *S, F, W, E*, 1984 *F, W, E, S, A*, 1985 *S, F, W, E*, 1986 *F, W, E, S, R*, 1987 *E, S, F, W*, [*W, C, Tg, A*], 1988 *S, F, W, E* 1
Riordan, W F (Cork Constitution) 1910 *E*
Ritchie, J S (London Irish) 1956 *F, E*
Robb, C G (Queen's Coll, Belfast) 1904 *E, S, W*, 1905 *NZ*, 1906 *S*
Robbie, J C (Dublin U, Greystones) 1976 *A, F, NZ*, 1977 *S, F*, 1981 *F, W, E, S*
Robinson, B F (Ballymena, London Irish) 1991 *F, W, E, S, Nm* 1,2, [*Z, S, A*], 1992 *W, E, S, F, NZ* 1,2, *A*, 1993 *W, E*
Robinson, T T H (Wanderers) 1904 *E, S*, 1905 *E, S, W, NZ*, 1906 *SA*, 1907 *E, S, W*
Roche, J (Wanderers) 1890 *S, W, E*, 1891 *E, S, W*, 1892 *W*
Roche, R E (UC Galway) 1955 *E, S*, 1957 *S, W*
Roche, W J (UC Cork) 1920 *E, S, F*
Roddy, P J (Bective Rangers) 1920 *S, F*
Roe, R (Lansdowne) 1952 *F*, 1953 *F, E, S, W*, 1954 *F, E, S, W*, 1955 *F, E, S, W*, 1956 *F, E, S, W*, 1957 *F, E, S, W*
Rolland, A C (Blackrock Coll) 1990 *Arg*
Rooke, C V (Dublin U) 1891 *E, W*, 1892 *E, S, W*, 1893 *E, S, W*, 1894 *E, S, W*, 1895 *E, S, W*, 1896 *E, S, W*, 1897 *E, S*
Ross, D J (Belfast Academy) 1884 *E*, 1885 *S* 1,2, 1886 *E, S*
Ross, G R P (CIYMS) 1955 *W*
Ross, J F (NIFC) 1886 *S*
Ross, J P (Lansdowne) 1885 *E, S* 1,2, 1886 *E, S*
Ross, N G (Malone) 1927 *F, E*
Ross, W McC (Queen's U, Belfast) 1932 *E, S, W*, 1933 *E, W, S*, 1934 *E, S, W*, 1935 *NZ*
Russell, J (UC Cork) 1931 *F, E, S, W, SA*, 1933 *E, W, S*, 1934 *E, S, W*, 1935 *E, S, W*, 1936 *E, S, W*, 1937 *E, S*
Russell, P (Instonians) 1990 *E*, 1992 *NZ* 1,2, *A*
Rutherford, W G (Tipperary) 1884 *E, S*, 1885 *E, S* 1, 1886 *E*, 1888 *W*
Ryan, E (Dolphin) 1937 *W*, 1938 *E, S*
Ryan, J (Rockwell Coll) 1897 *E*, 1898 *E, S, W*, 1899 *E, S, W*, 1900 *S, W*, 1901 *E, S, W*, 1902 *E*, 1904 *E*
Ryan, J G (UC Dublin) 1939 *E, S, W*

Ryan, M (Rockwell Coll) 1897 *E, S*, 1898 *E, S, W*, 1899 *E, S, W*, 1900 *E, S, W*, 1901 *E, S, W*, 1903 *E*, 1904 *E, S*

Saunders, R (London Irish) 1991 *F, W, E, S, Nm* 1,2, [*Z, J, S, A*], 1992 *W*
Sayers, H J M (Lansdowne) 1935 *E, S, W*, 1936 *E, S, W*, 1938 *W*, 1939 *E, S, W*
Schute, F (Wanderers) 1878 *E*, 1879 *E*
Schute, F G (Dublin U) 1912 *SA*, 1913 *E, S*
Scott, D (Malone) 1961 *F, SA*, 1962 *S*
Scott, R D (Queen's U, Belfast) 1967 *E, F*, 1968 *F, E, S*
Scovell, R H (Kingstown) 1883 *E*, 1884 *E*
Scriven, G (Dublin U) 1879 *S, E*, 1880 *E, S*, 1881 *E*, 1882 *S*, 1883 *E, S*
Sealy, J (Dublin U) 1896 *E, S, W*, 1897 *S*, 1899 *E, S, W*, 1900 *E, S*
Sexton, J F (Dublin U, Lansdowne) 1988 *E* 2, *WS, It*, 1989 *F*
Sexton, W J (Garryowen) 1984 *A*, 1988 *S, E* 2
Shanahan, T (Lansdowne) 1885 *E, S* 1,2, 1886 *E*, 1888 *S, W*
Shaw, G M (Windsor) 1877 *S*
Sheehan, M D (London Irish) 1932 *E*
Sherry, B F (Terenure Coll) 1967 *A* 1, *E, S, A* 2, 1968 *F, E*
Sherry, M J A (Lansdowne) 1975 *F, W*
Siggins, J A E (Belfast Collegians) 1931 *F, E, S, W, SA*, 1932 *E, S, W*, 1933 *E, W, S*, 1934 *E, S, W*, 1935 *E, S, W, NZ*, 1936 *E, S, W*, 1937 *E, S, W*
Slattery, J F (UC Dublin, Blackrock Coll) 1970 *SA, F, E, S, W*, 1971 *F, E, S, W*, 1972 *F* 1, *E, F* 2, 1973 *NZ, E, S, W, F*, 1974 *F, W, E, S, P, NZ*, 1975 *E, S, F, W*, 1976 *A*, 1977 *S, F*, 1978 *S, F, W, E, NZ*, 1979 *F, W, E, S, A* 1,2, 1980 *E, S, F, W*, 1981 *F, W, E, S, SA* 1,2, *A*, 1982 *W, E, S, F*, 1983 *S, F, W, E*, 1984 *F*
Smartt, F N B (Dublin U) 1908 *E, S*, 1909 *E*
Smith, B A (Oxford U, Leicester) 1989 *NZ*, 1990 *S, F, W, Arg*, 1991 *F, W, E, S*
Smith, J H (London Irish) 1951 *F, E, S, W, SA*, 1952 *F, S, W, E*, 1954 *NZ, W, F*
Smith, R E (Lansdowne) 1892 *E*
Smith, S J (Ballymena) 1988 *E* 2, *WS, It*, 1989 *F, W, E, S, NZ*, 1990 *E*, 1991 *F, W, E, S, Nm* 1,2, [*Z, S, A*], 1992 *W, E, S, F, NZ* 1,2, 1993 *S*
Smithwick, F F S (Monkstown) 1898 *S, W*
Smyth, J T (Queen's U, Belfast) 1920 *F*
Smyth, P J (Belfast Collegians) 1911 *E, S, F*
Smyth, R S (Dublin U) 1903 *E, S*, 1904 *E*
Smyth, T (Malone, Newport) 1908 *E, S, W*, 1909 *E, S, W*, 1910 *E, S, W, F*, 1911 *E, S, W*, 1912 *E*
Smyth, W S (Belfast Collegians) 1910 *W, F*, 1920 *E*
Solomons, B A H (Dublin U) 1908 *E, S, W*, 1909 *E, S, W, F*, 1910 *E, S, W*
Spain, A W (UC Dublin) 1924 *NZ*
Sparrow, W (Dublin U) 1893 *W*, 1894 *E*
Spillane, B J (Bohemians) 1985 *S, F, W, E*, 1986 *F, W, E*, 1987 *F, W*, [*W, C, A(R)*], 1989 *E* (R)
Spring, D E (Dublin U) 1978 *S, NZ*, 1979 *S*, 1980 *S, F, W*, 1981 *W*
Spring, R M (Lansdowne) 1979 *F, W, E*
Spunner, H F (Wanderers) 1881 *E, S*, 1884 *W*
Stack, C R R (Dublin U) 1889 *S*
Stack, G H (Dublin U) 1875 *E*
Staples, J E (London Irish) 1991 *W, E, S, Nm* 1,2, [*Z, J, S, A*], 1992 *W, E, NZ* 1,2, *A*
Steele, H W (Ballymena) 1976 *E*, 1977 *F*, 1978 *F, W, E*, 1979 *F, W, E, A* 1,2
Stephenson, G V (Queen's U, Belfast, London Hosp) 1920 *F*, 1921 *E, S, W, F*, 1922 *E, S, W, F*, 1923 *E, S, W, F*, 1924 *F, E, S, W, NZ*, 1925 *F, E, S, W*, 1926 *F, E, S, W*, 1927 *F, E, S, W, A*, 1928 *F, E, S, W*, 1929 *F, E, W*, 1930 *F, E, S, W*
Stephenson, H W V (United Services) 1922 *S, W, F*, 1924 *F, E, S, W, NZ*, 1925 *F, E, S, W*, 1927 *A*, 1928 *E*
Stevenson, J (Dungannon) 1888 *M*, 1889 *S*
Stevenson, J B (Instonians) 1958 *A, E, S, W, F*
Stevenson, R (Dungannon) 1887 *E, S, W*, 1888 *M*, 1889 *S, W*, 1890 *S, W, E*, 1891 *W*, 1892 *W*, 1893 *E, S, W*
Stevenson, T H (Belfast Acad) 1895 *E, W*, 1896 *E, S, W*, 1898 *E, S*
Stewart, A L (NIFC) 1913 *W, F*, 1914 *F*
Stewart, W J (Queen's U, Belfast, NIFC) 1922 *F*, 1924 *S*, 1928 *F, E, S, W*, 1929 *F, E, S, W*

IRISH INTERNATIONAL RECORDS

Both team and individual records are for official Ireland international matches up to 31 March 1993.

TEAM RECORDS

Highest score
60 v Romania (60-0) 1986 Dublin
v individual countries
20 v Argentina (20-18) 1990 Dublin

27 v Australia (27-12) 1979 Brisbane
46 v Canada (46-19) 1987 Dunedin
26 v England (26-21) 1974 Twickenham

25 v France $\begin{cases} \text{(25-5) 1911 Cork} \\ \text{(25-6) 1975 Dublin} \end{cases}$
31 v Italy (31-15) 1988 Dublin
32 v Japan (32-16) 1991 Dublin
15 v Namibia (15-26) 1991 Windhoek
21 v N Zealand (21-24) 1992 Dunedin
60 v Romania (60-0) 1986 Dublin
15 v S Africa (15-23) 1981 Cape Town
26 v Scotland (26-8) 1953 Murrayfield
32 v Tonga (32-9) 1987 Brisbane

21 v Wales $\begin{cases} \text{(21-24) 1979 Cardiff} \\ \text{(21-7) 1980 Dublin} \\ \text{(21-9) 1985 Cardiff} \\ \text{(21-21) 1991 Cardiff} \end{cases}$
49 v W Samoa (49-22) 1988 Dublin
55 v Zimbabwe (55-11) 1991 Dublin

Biggest winning points margin
60 v Romania (60-0) 1986 Dublin
v individual countries
 2 v Argentina (20-18) 1990 Dublin
15 v Australia (27-12) 1979 Brisbane
27 v Canada (46-19) 1987 Dunedin
22 v England (22-0) 1947 Dublin
24 v France (24-0) 1913 Cork
16 v Italy (31-15) 1988 Dublin
16 v Japan (32-16) 1991 Dublin
No win v Namibia
No win v N Zealand
60 v Romania (60-0) 1986 Dublin
 3 v S Africa (9-6) 1965 Dublin
21 v Scotland (21-0) 1950 Dublin
23 v Tonga (32-9) 1987 Brisbane
16 v Wales (19-3) 1925 Belfast
27 v W Samoa (49-22) 1988 Dublin
44 v Zimbabwe (55-11) 1991 Dublin

Highest score by opposing team
59 N Zealand (6-59) 1992 Wellington
by individual countries
18 Argentina (20-18) 1990 Dublin
42 Australia (17-42) 1992 Dublin
19 Canada (46-19) 1987 Dunedin
38 England (9-38) 1992 Twickenham
44 France (12-44) 1992 Paris
15 Italy (31-15) 1988 Dublin
16 Japan (32-16) 1991 Dublin
26 Namibia (15-26) 1991 Windhoek
59 N Zealand (6-59) 1992 Wellington
 0 Romania (60-0) 1986 Dublin
38 S Africa (0-38) 1912 Dublin
37 Scotland (21-37) 1989 Murrayfield
 9 Tonga (32-9) 1987 Brisbane
34 Wales (9-34) 1976 Dublin

22 W Samoa (49-22) 1988 Dublin
11 Zimbabwe (55-11) 1991 Dublin

Biggest losing points margin
53 v N Zealand (6-59) 1992 Wellington
v individual countries
25 v Australia (17-42) 1992 Dublin
32 v England (3-35) 1988 Twickenham
32 v France (12-44) 1992 Paris
11 v Namibia (15-26) 1991 Windhoek
53 v N Zealand (6-59) 1992 Wellington
38 v S Africa (0-38) 1912 Dublin
23 v Scotland (9-32) 1984 Dublin
29 v Wales (0-29) 1907 Cardiff
No defeats v Argentina, Canada, Italy, Japan, Romania, Tonga, W Samoa or Zimbabwe

---

Most tries by Ireland in an international
10 v Romania (60-0) 1986 Dublin

Most tries against Ireland in an international
10 by S Africa (0-38) 1912 Dublin

Most points by Ireland in International Championship in a season – 71
in season 1982-83

Most tries by Ireland in International Championship in a season – 12
in seasons 1927-28 and 1952-53

INDIVIDUAL RECORDS

Most capped player
C M H Gibson   69   1964-79
in individual positions
Full-back
T J Kiernan   54   1960-73
Wing
K D Crossan   41   1982-92
Centre
B J Mullin   45[1]   1984-92
Fly-half
J W Kyle   46   1947-58
Scrum-half
M T Bradley   29   1984-93
Prop
P A Orr   58   1976-87
Hooker
K W Kennedy   45   1965-75

Lock
W J McBride   63   1962-75
Flanker
J F Slattery   61   1970-84
No 8
W P Duggan   39(41)² 1975-84
¹*C M H Gibson won 40 caps as a centre, 25 at fly-half and 4 as a wing*
²*Duggan won 39 caps at No 8 and 2 as a flanker*

Longest international career
A J F O'Reilly 16 seasons 1955-70
C M H Gibson 16 seasons 1964-79
Gibson's career ended during a Southern Hemisphere season

Most consecutive Tests – 52
W J McBride 1964-75

Most internationals as captain – 24
T J Kiernan   1963-73

Most points in internationals – 308
M J Kiernan (43 matches) 1982-91

Most points in International Championship in a season – 52
S O Campbell (4 matches) 1982-83

Most points in an international – 23
R P Keyes v Zimbabwe 1991 Dublin

Most tries in internationals – 15
B J Mullin (45 matches) 1984-92

Most tries in International Championship in a season – 5
J E Arigho (3 matches) 1927-28

Most tries in an international – 4
B F Robinson v Zimbabwe 1991 Dublin

Most conversions in internationals – 40
M J Kiernan (43 matches) 1982-91

Most conversions in International Championship in a season – 7
R A Lloyd (4 matches) 1912-13

Most conversions in an international – 7
M J Kiernan v Romania 1986 Dublin

Most dropped goals in internationals – 7
R A Lloyd (19 matches) 1910-20
S O Campbell (22 matches) 1976-84

Most penalty goals in internationals – 62
M J Kiernan (43 matches) 1982-91

Most penalty goals in International Championship in a season – 14
S O Campbell (4 matches) 1982-83

Most penalty goals in an international – 6
S O Campbell v Scotland 1982 Dublin

Most points for Ireland on overseas tour – 60
S O Campbell (5 appearances) 1979 Australia
M J Kiernan scored 65 points in Japan 1985, but this was not on a major tour

Most points in any match on tour – 19
A J P Ward v Australian Capital Territory 1979 Canberra
S O Campbell v Australia 1979 Brisbane
M J Kiernan scored 25 points in the second match against Japan 1985, but this was not on a major tour

Most tries in any match on tour – 3
A T A Duggan v Victoria 1967 Melbourne
J F Slattery v SA President's XV 1981 East London
M J Kiernan v Gold Cup XV 1981 Oudtshoorn, SA
T M Ringland scored 3 tries v Japan at Osaka 1985, but this was not on a major tour

CLUB'S REBELLION SHOCKS WRU IN A YEAR OF FRUSTRATION

THE 1992-93 SEASON IN WALES
John Billot *Western Mail*

Victory over England was but a candle in the dark and the game in Wales quickly plunged back into controversy and turmoil. The great rebellion by the majority of the 212 WRU member clubs, reacting to what they viewed as mismanagement, resulted in an unprecedented vote of no confidence in the general committee at a special general meeting in Port Talbot on Sunday 4 April 1993. It was indeed the crack of doom for the men at the helm of Welsh rugby. The general committee, which had banned the media from attendance, left the meeting, which continued for some three hours in their absence. It was decided, until new elections could be rushed through, that the affairs of the WRU should be conducted by the professional staff, headed up by two trustees, Graham Tregidon and Hermas Evans, together with the only elected member, Glanmor Griffiths. He had resigned as hon. treasurer in December, but was asked to stand again and reinstated.

There had been a bitter personality clash between WRU secretary Denis Evans and Griffiths, and the WRU had taken Griffiths to the High Court to prevent him communicating with the clubs to explain his decision, and to recover official documents relating to committee meetings. However, the injunction was discharged on appeal with costs against the WRU. It was a messy business and became even more involved. After confirming that the trustees would work with Griffiths, Tregidon then changed his mind and the treasurer was excluded from immediate WRU business. This situation was hurriedly revised again after Tregidon was asked to leave on arriving to chair a meeting, where he was reminded that he had been voted out of office by the SGM and instructed to work in conjunction with Griffiths in a caretaker composite. The clubs' militancy was making itself felt: those who ignored them would receive sharp reminders.

Selwyn Walters (Lampeter RFC), chairman of District G clubs, who proposed the no-confidence motion, explained, 'The clubs have made sure they will be asserting greater control on what goes on in the workings of the WRU. We don't take glory out of what has happened because it is very sad that it ever came to this.' The leaking of the Pugh Report regarding the Welsh involvement on and off the field in the 1989 South African centenary rugby celebrations incurred the resentment of clubs which had been kept in the dark about the revelations. This led to Terry Vaux deciding not to offer himself as the next WRU president. 'Opinion against me is entrenched and will not shift, no matter how often I tell the truth,' he said. Eight of the nine WRU districts had expressed opposition to him.

257

The Wales team which beat England at Cardiff. L-R, back row: R H St J B Moon (replacement), R W Webster, S Davies, A H Copsey, G O Llewellyn, E W Lewis, R L Evans, N Meek, H Williams-Jones, P A Kawulok (replacement); front row: I S Gibbs, M R Hall, W T Proctor, I C Evans (capt), R N Jones, M A Rayer, N R Jenkins.

It can only be hoped that from all this upheaval will emerge a new era of frankness and communication. The clubs are of paramount importance to the game, while schools and youth rugby must be encouraged to maximum advantage. In reshaping the structure of the WRU, the clubs' interests must be safeguarded before personalities. This, above all else, is obvious after Bloody Sunday at Port Talbot.

On the playing side, it was a melancholy season. A commendable defensive operation shocked England at Cardiff and that was the single episode that brought a measure of pride and undisguised pleasure. Most people considered it a freak result and a misguiding influence. Selection involved a policy of continuity so, after deliberating for seven hours following the Murrayfield defeat, just one change was made, on the wing. The lessons of failure were cast aside and defeat by Ireland was the ultimate humiliation. It exploded the misplaced faith in continuity. Changes were made for Paris, a match too late; and, in the case of scrum-half, many suggested a season too late. It was a point to ponder.

The Welsh forwards were still a long way short of making a sustained impact. There was predictability at half-back and perhaps the reluctance to run the ball fast and wide had its roots in the absence of a speedy openside forward to reach the point of breakdown. There seemed too much emphasis on safety first. Lack of vision in selection was a worrying aspect. However, amid disappointments, and even some despondency, Llanelli left us all with many fragrant memories with their adventure and, above all, style. Amen to that.

ANOTHER DROP OF TROUBLE

SWALEC CUP 1992-93
John Billot   *Western Mail*

8 May, Cardiff Arms Park
Llanelli 21 (1G 2PG 1DG 1T)   **Neath 18** (1G 2PG 1T)

Controversy was never far from the surface in Welsh rugby during the season and never more so than in this Cup final. It would be the under-statement of the decade to observe that Neath were less than happy with referee Gareth Simmonds as Llanelli stole the decision with a dropped goal 16 minutes from the end. Most critics anticipated a comfortable eighth Cup conquest and a third in a row for the super Scarlets to complete a unique Cup and Heineken League double.

Neath did not see it that way, however, and the scores were tied at 18-18 when Llanelli launched quick passing from a free kick. The ball was worked across to Emyr Lewis, standing among his centres, and the No 8 fired over that startling drop shot. 'I never dropped a goal before – or even attempted one,' he reflected. But was it valid? Furious Neath

Ieuan Evans scores the second of his two tries for Llanelli in the Welsh Cup final, to the delight of team-mate Colin Stephens.

accused the referee of an enormous blunder. Under the changed laws, a dropped goal cannot be scored from a free kick without intervention by the opposition.

Neath coach Leighton Davies said: 'Players make mistakes and referees make mistakes. It is unfortunate that it should happen on this occasion.' However, Ken Rowlands, the WRU referees' development officer, supported the decision after watching video recordings, stressing that it appeared that Neath tacklers *had* made interventionary contact, and Simmonds himself was happy with his handling of the incident – though only after he had seen the video. Neath, surprising everyone, and Llanelli in particular, with their stubborn resistance, also suffered in some other refereeing decisions. The Gnoll battlers thoroughly deserved to take the match into extra time.

Ieuan Evans scored both the Llanelli tries, setting an aggregate Cup record of 41 tries. Colin Stephens converted one and kicked two penalty goals before that drop shot sailed over. Neath, whose skipper Gareth Llewellyn was chosen as Man of the Match, recovered from 12-3 down as Steve Bowling and Adrian Varney crossed the try-line, Thorburn converting one and kicking two penalty goals.

Llanelli: I Jones; I C Evans, N Boobyer, N G Davies, W T Proctor; C J Stephens, R H St J B Moon (*capt*); R L Evans, A E Lamerton, D Joseph, P T Davies, A H Copsey, M A Perego, E W Lewis, L Jones
Scorers *Tries:* I C Evans (2) *Conversion:* Stephens *Penalty Goals:* Stephens (2)
Dropped Goal: Lewis
Neath: P H Thorburn; J Reynolds, H Woodland, A Donovan, S Bowling; M McCarthy, R Jones; B Williams, A Thomas, J D Davies, G D Llewellyn, G O Llewellyn (*capt*), M S Morris, S Williams, A Varney
Scorers *Tries:* Bowling, Varney *Conversion:* Thorburn *Penalty Goals:* Thorburn (2)
Referee G Simmonds (Cardiff)

Swansea were doomed to April disasters, losing five successive games, among them the Cup semi-final, 29-18 to Llanelli at Cardiff RFC ground. It was a repeat clash of the previous season's final and provided the Scarlets with their fifth Cup success in six meetings with the Swansea team. The Llanelli back row exerted a commanding influence while the line-out supremacy of Phil Davies and Copsey was another decisive factor. There were tries from Ian Jones, Ieuan Evans and Proctor and 14 points from Colin Stephens from a conversion and four penalty goals. Swansea, trailing 29-6 with just two penalty goals by Aled Williams, struck defiantly for two late tries, one by Simon Davies and the other from Webster, and one conversion by Williams.

Neath too had to stage a recovery in the other semi-final after Bridgend led 15-13 at half-time at Stradey Park. But this revival was emphatic and compelling as the Neath pack took charge to batter Bridgend into 33-15 submission. Neath have the 'Indian sign' on the Brewery Field team, having conceded just one defeat in their last 13 encounters and, despite the jolt of seeing Robert Howley snap up two tries for Bridgend, they were in no mood to surrender tactical control. With the Llewellyn brothers, Gareth and Glyn, dominating the line-out, Neath applied relentless pressure and there were tries for James Reynolds (two), Bowling, Thorburn and McCarthy. Thorburn converted one and kicked two penalty goals. Luc Evans converted one of Howley's tries and added a penalty goal.

In the quarter-finals, Newport were unhappy with the referee's decision that gave Bridgend an 18-16 victory in the fourth minute of injury time with a penalty goal by Luc Evans. But there were no complaints from Pontypridd, comprehensively turned over for a seventh time in the Cup by Llanelli by 24-6, while Neath knocked out stubborn Cross Keys 24-15. Swansea could manage just one try in taking Bonymaen's ground record by 13-0. Skipper Stuart Davies scored the try, and praised the losers for their combative spirit on their first appearance in the quarter-final stage.

In the sixth round, Pontypridd won 21-18 at Pontypool through a dropped goal by Neil Jenkins two minutes from the end. Cross Keys went through on their try-count in a 10-10 draw at Dunvant. Ieuan Evans scored four tries as Llanelli overwhelmed Newbridge 67-3 and giant-killers St Peter's failed 18-13 against Bonymaen on goal-kicks, five of them penalty goals by Simon Morris.

It was the fifth round that saw the most sensational result in the 22 years of the Cup. St Peter's, the junior club from the suburbs of Cardiff and struggling near the bottom of Heineken Division 3, defeated Cardiff, the Division 1 leaders, 16-14 to steal the Arms Park ground record. The shocked losers had ignored the golden rule of Cup rugby – select the strongest team – and stood down nine of the players who had figured in the side that toppled Maesteg in the previous round. Andy Edwards kicked St Peter's three penalty goals and converted the try by Gareth Snook.

The fourth round also brought a surprise for a major club as Aberavon made an undignified exit, 9-5, at Fleur de Lys. Jim Egan kicked the Monmouthshire League Division 3 club to victory in their centenary season with three penalty goals. It was a round of success for the smaller clubs as Talywain toppled Ebbw Vale 16-15, Tenby United won 19-16 at Penarth, Glamorgan Wanderers went out 13-3 at Trimsaran and Bonymaen accounted for Abertillery 23-8.

RESULTS

Third Round

Abercarn 27, Pontyclun 7; Amman Utd 22, Beddau 8; Blackwood 20, Garndiffaith 5; Bonymaen 47, Penygroes 22; BSC (Port Talbot) 3, Pyle 23; Builth Wells 11, Mountain Ash 6; Caerphilly 48, Morriston 8; Cardiff Inst of Ed 12, Cefn Coed 11; Cardigan 13, St Peter's 19; Carmarthen 15, Ystrad Rhondda 21; Cefn Cribbwr 3, Pentyrch 10; Cwmavon 13, Pencoed 20; Cwmgwrach 23, Haverfordwest 7; Furnace Utd 3, †Colwyn Bay 3; Glynneath 10, Risca 6; Gorseinon 11, RTB (Ebbw Vale) 18; Hendy 6, Fleur de Lys 8; Kenfig Hill 51, Ruthin 3; Kidwelly 14, Croesyceiliog 13; Lampeter Town 10, Aberavon Quins 11; Llandaff 3, Abercynon 8; Llanhilleth 14, Ystradgynlais 52; Merthyr 6, Blaenau

Gwent 22; Newport HSOB 22, Treorchy 0; Newport Saracens 0, Llantrisant 48; Oakdale 8, Monmouth 0; Ogmore Vale 3, Pontypool Utd 28; Old Penarthians 29, Usk 0; Pill Harriers 9, Tumble 14; Pontarddulais 37, Cilfynydd 15; Rhyl 12, Treherbert 21; Rumney 10, Senghenydd 27; St Alban's 25, Bridgend Ath 20; Tonyrefail 13, Wrexham 3; Tredegar Ironsides 12, Trimsaran 13; Vardre 17, New Dock Stars 14; Ynysybwl 36, Hirwaun 13

Fourth Round

Aberavon Quins 5, Neath 31; Amman Utd 6, Newport 8; Blaina 9, Pontypool 17; Bonymaen 23, Abertillery 8; Bridgend 30, Pentyrch 3; Builth Wells 28, Vardre 11; Caerphilly 17, Cardiff HSOB Quins 18; Cardiff 55, Maesteg 3; Cross Keys 27, Old Penarthians 10; Cwmgwrach 11, Newport HSOB 3; Fleur de Lys 9, Aberavon 5; Kenfig Hill 25, Kidwelly 7; Llanelli 54, St Alban's 3; Llanharan 9, Tondu 17; Llantrisant 10, Newbridge 25; Narberth 8, St Peter's 22; Oakdale 3, Dunvant 14; Penarth 16, Tenby Utd 19; Pontarddulais 10, Pontypridd 39; Pontypool Utd 34, Blaenau Gwent 8; Pyle 31, Senghenydd 18; RTB (Ebbw Vale) 3, Colwyn Bay 12; SW Police 57, Cardiff Inst of Ed 12; Swansea 75, Abercynon 0; Talywain 16, Ebbw Vale 15; Tonyrefail 13, Treherbert 12; Tredegar 25, Glynneath 7; Trimsaran 13, Glamorgan Wands 3; Tumble 19, Blackwood 15; Ynysybwl 13, Pencoed 20; Ystradgynlais 0, Llandovery 10; Ystrad Rhondda 9, Abercarn 11

Fifth Round

Abercarn 3, Talywain 18; Cardiff 14, St Peter's 16; Cardiff HSOB Quins 20, Builth Wells 13; Colwyn Bay 0, Pontypool 18; Cwmgwrach 14, Cross Keys 23; Fleur de Lys 0, Bridgend 12; Kenfig Hill 6, Llanelli 17; Llandovery 15, Tondu 12; Pontypool Utd 0, Newport 10; Pontypridd 62, Pencoed 0; Pyle 10, Neath 20; Tenby

Utd 6, Swansea 22; Tonyrefail 6, Dunvant 12; Tredegar 0, SW Police 21; Trimsaran 10, Bonymaen 20; Tumble 3, Newbridge 11

Sixth Round

Bridgend 41, Llandovery 0; Dunvant 10, *Cross Keys 10; Llanelli 67, Newbridge 3; Neath 30, Talywain 7; Newport 27, Cardiff HSOB Quins 11; Pontypool 18, Pontypridd 21; SW Police 11, Swansea 27; St Peter's 13, Bonymaen 18

Seventh Round

Bonymaen 0, Swansea 13; Bridgend 18, Newport 16; Llanelli 24, Pontypridd 6; Neath 24, Cross Keys 15

Semi-finals

Llanelli 29 Swansea 18
(at Cardiff RFC ground)
Neath 33 Bridgend 15
(at Stradey Park)
FINAL *(at Cardiff Arms Park)*
Llanelli 21 Neath 18

Previous finals
(all at Cardiff Arms Park)
1972	Neath 15	Llanelli 9
1973	Llanelli 30	Cardiff 7
1974	Llanelli 12	Aberavon 10
1975	Llanelli 15	Aberavon 6
1976	Llanelli 15	Swansea 4
1977	Newport 16	Cardiff 15
1978	Swansea 13	Newport 9
1979	Bridgend 18	Pontypridd 12
1980	Bridgend 15	Swansea 9
1981	Cardiff 14	Bridgend 6
1982*	Cardiff 12	Bridgend 12
1983	Pontypool 18	Swansea 6
1984	Cardiff 24	Neath 19
1985	Llanelli 15	Cardiff 14
1986	Cardiff 28	Newport 21
1987	Cardiff 16	Swansea 15
1988	Llanelli 28	Neath 13
1989	Neath 14	Llanelli 13
1990	Neath 16	Bridgend 10
1991	Llanelli 24	Pontypool 9
1992	Llanelli 16	Swansea 7

Winners on 'most tries' rule
†*Winners as away team*

LLANELLI SMASH THE RECORDS
THE HEINEKEN LEAGUES 1992-93

No records were unassailable as Llanelli, in dynamic form, captured the Heineken League First Division title for the first time. In fact, having eclipsed all other records, they were left with only their own high marks to improve, and they did that twice in a season of unforgettable success. There were challenges from the holders, Swansea, long-time leaders, and resurgent Cardiff; but only Swansea and Bridgend defeated them; and after the 18-8 reverse at the Brewery Field on 2 January it was triumph all the way.

Newport's record of 83 League tries was shattered as the Scarlets posted an amazing total of 136 tries in 22 games, an average of just over six per match. There were 11 against Newport in a 79-10 score that inflicted an unprecedented annihilation at Rodney Parade. This new mark was exceeded with 14 tries when Maesteg disintegrated 82-13, and next it was humiliation for South Wales Police, by 93-0, as they were helpless to prevent 15 tries. In the Maesteg match, Ieuan Evans, who became Welsh Player of the Year, crossed for a League record six tries. He and fellow Llanelli wing Wayne Proctor set League records with 20 tries each.

Had there been relegation in the previous season, Cardiff would have taken the dreaded tumble. Now they found themselves transformed into runners-up; an almost magical metamorphosis under the sagacious control of coaching supremo Alex Evans, forwards coach to the 1984 Grand Slam Wallabies in the UK. Adrian Davies was a significant figure at fly-half. He finished with a League record aggregate of 264 points. Swansea inexplicably crumbled in April, losing their last five fixtures, including matches against the Barbarians and Llanelli in the Cup semi-final. In that sequence there was a 12-6 defeat at Aberavon. It nailed the lid on their hopes of retaining the title.

The increased number of teams in each division (12 as opposed to ten last season) found general favour, although a few of the leading clubs expressed the view that it imposed additional pressure on players and called for a reduction. Perhaps the fact that prize-money was substantially lower had some bearing on this. However, with midweek rugby in Wales destroyed by the League system, there was a strong groundswell of opinion that meaningful Saturday rugby must be preserved at all costs. The national team is a product of club rugby and clubs must never be disadvantaged.

Dunvant and Cross Keys were promoted to replace Maesteg and South Wales Police. Dunvant's rise from Swansea and District League status some 15 years ago was astonishing and, as Second Division champions, defeated only once (by Llanharan, 12-3), Dunvant became the first small club to join the illustrious names in the top rank. Their 15 consecutive victories was a League record. Cross Keys went up because they had a superior try-count to Llanharan. Veteran Benny Jones, the former Pontypool fly-half, was an inspiring coaching organiser for the Keys.

Treorchy lost only to St Peter's in winning the Third Division title and went up together with Mountain Ash, replacing relegated Tredegar and Blaina. Tondu were the Fourth Division champions, pipping Ystrad-gynlais for top spot on their try-count, and those two replaced Rumney and Wrexham in Division 3. Four new teams came in after winning their play-offs. They are Caerphilly, Oakdale, Pyle and Whitland.

HEINEKEN LEAGUES

Division 1

	P	W	D	L	F	A	Pts
Llanelli	22	19	1	2	901	254	39
Cardiff	22	18	0	4	636	260	36
Swansea	22	17	0	5	548	326	34
Neath	22	13	0	9	448	359	26
Pontypridd	22	11	2	9	400	353	24
Bridgend	22	11	1	10	402	400	23
Newport	22	11	0	11	513	512	22
Pontypool	22	10	0	12	489	508	20
Aberavon	22	7	0	15	271	501	14
Newbridge	22	6	0	16	258	536	12
Maesteg	22	3	1	18	278	632	7
SW Police	22	3	1	18	243	746	7

Division 2

	P	W	D	L	F	A	Pts
Dunvant	22	21	0	1	478	134	42
Cross Keys	22	16	1	5	474	268	33
Llanharan	22	16	1	5	435	202	33
Narberth	22	15	1	6	358	209	31
Tenby Utd	22	12	1	9	432	234	25
Glam Wands	22	11	0	11	357	409	22
Abertillery	22	11	0	11	366	355	22
Llandovery	22	7	0	15	285	345	14
Penarth	22	7	0	15	245	546	14
Ebbw Vale	22	7	0	15	183	355	14
Tredegar	22	3	2	17	200	406	8
Blaina	22	3	0	19	199	549	6

Division 3

	P	W	D	L	F	A	Pts
Treorchy	22	19	2	1	500	189	40
Mountain Ash	22	16	1	5	383	227	33
Abercynon	22	12	1	9	339	276	25
Blackwood	22	11	0	11	382	389	22
Tumble	22	11	0	11	322	358	22
Pontypool Utd	22	11	0	11	338	298	22
Bonymaen	22	10	1	11	412	316	21
Kenfig Hill	22	9	2	11	359	386	20
St Peter's	22	8	1	13	316	440	17
Aberavon Q	22	7	1	14	274	314	15
Rumney	22	7	1	14	248	420	15
Wrexham	22	6	0	16	215	475	12

Division 4

	P	W	D	L	F	A	Pts
Tondu	22	19	0	3	537	193	38
Ystradgynlais	22	19	0	3	516	215	38
Builth Wells	22	17	1	4	402	206	35

Cardiff Q	22	14	1	7	496	326	29
Carmarthen	22	10	1	11	353	378	21
Kidwelly	22	10	1	11	288	363	21
Vardre	22	9	1	12	380	330	19
Garndiffaith	22	8	1	13	313	380	17
Cilfynydd	22	8	0	14	299	359	16
Ruthin	22	4	3	15	254	529	11
Cardigan	22	5	1	16	202	417	11
Colwyn Bay	22	3	2	17	164	508	8

FEEDER LEAGUES
JEWSONS PEMBROKESHIRE CHAMPIONSHIP

	P	W	D	L	Pts
Whitland	18	17	0	1	34
Haverfordwest	18	14	1	3	29
Aberystwyth	18	11	0	7	22
Milford Haven	18	10	1	7	21
Neyland	18	10	1	7	21
Pembroke	18	8	0	10	16
Fishguard	18	6	1	11	13
Llangwm	18	5	2	11	12
Pembroke DQ	18	4	2	12	10
St David's	18	1	0	17	2

WISTECH CENTRAL GLAMORGAN LEAGUE

Division 1	P	W	D	L	Pts
Pyle	18	18	0	0	36
Porthcawl	18	12	1	5	25
Bridgend Ath	18	11	1	6	23
Nantyffyllon	18	10	1	7	21
Neath Athletic	18	8	0	10	16
Bridgend Sports	18	7	1	10	15
Cefn Cribbwr	18	7	0	11	14
Maesteg Celtic	18	7	0	11	14
British Steel	18	7	0	11	13
Pontycymmer	18	1	0	17	2

Division 2 finishing order: Tonmawr, Nantymoel, Taibach, Cwmavon, Briton Ferry, Aberavon Green Stars, Maesteg Quins, Blaengarw, Ogmore Vale

WEST WALES WELSH BREWERS CHAMPIONSHIP

Section A	P	W	D	L	Pts
Felinfoel	18	15	2	1	32
Trimsaran	18	14	1	3	29
Seven Sisters	18	11	1	6	23
Glynneath	18	11	1	6	23
Carmarthen Ath	18	10	3	5	23

Pontarddulais	18	9	0	9	18
Amman Utd	18	8	2	8	18
Pontyberem	18	5	0	13	10
Waunarlwydd	18	1	0	17	2
Bryncoch	18	1	0	17	2

Section B finishing order: Cwmgwrach, Morriston, Llandybie, Ammanford, Abercrave, New Dock Stars, Brynamman, Gorseinon, Bynea, Newcastle Emlyn **Division B finishing order:** Hendy, Llandeilo, Resolven, Furnace Utd, Gowerton, Llangennech, Loughor, Laugharne, Penclawdd, Cwmgorse **Section C finishing order:** Penygroes, Skewen, Ystalyfera, Mumbles, Lampeter Town, Burry Port, Cwmllynfell, Cefneithin, Tonna, Tycroes **Division C finishing order:** Glais, Alltwen, Crynant, Swansea Uplands, Trebanos, Llanelli Wands, Pontardawe, Llanybydder, BP Llandarcy, Pontyates

EAST DISTRICT CHAMPIONSHIP
Division 1 (*S A Brain Cup*)

	P	W	D	L	Pts
Cardiff Inst	16	14	1	1	29
Old Penarthians	16	13	0	3	26
Pencoed	16	11	0	5	22
Rhiwbina	16	10	0	6	20
Old Illtydians	15	8	0	7	16
Pentyrch	15	5	1	9	11
Llandaff	16	5	0	11	10
Taff's Well	16	4	0	12	8
Heol-y-Cyw	16	0	0	16	0

Division 2 (*Labatt Trophy*) **finishing order:** Llandaff North, Pontyclun, Barry, Cowbridge, St Joseph's, Dinas Powys, Llantwit Major, Llanishen, Cardiff U

TENNENTS MID-DISTRICT CHAMPIONSHIP
Division 1

	P	W	D	L	F	A	Pts
Caerphilly*	11	10	1	0	308	108	21
Tonyrefail	12	8	1	3	230	129	17
Llantrisant	11	6	1	4	202	164	13
Nelson	12	6	1	5	190	225	13
Merthyr	12	4	0	8	148	246	8
Senghenydd	12	2	1	9	152	239	5
Beddau	12	2	1	9	110	229	5

Caerphilly promoted to Heineken National League Division 4 for 1993-94

Division 2 finishing order: Ystrad Rhondda, Ynsylbwl, Hirwaun, Aberaman, Gilfach Goch, Tylorstown, Llantwit Fardre **Division 3 finishing order:** Brecon, Treherbert, Penygraig, Cefn Coed, Bargoed, Rhydyfelin

ALLBRIGHT BITTER MONMOUTHSHIRE LEAGUE

	P	W	D	L	Pts
Oakdale	18	17	0	1	34
Blaenau Gwent	18	13	1	4	27
Bedwas	17	10	1	6	21
Tredegar Irons	17	10	0	7	20
Rhymney	18	7	1	10	15
Newport Saras	18	7	1	10	15
Abergavenny*	17	6	0	11	14
Pill Harriers	18	6	2	10	14
Cwmbran	18	5	1	12	11
Croesyceiliog	17	3	1	13	7

Two points awarded to Abergavenny v Croesyceiliog

Division 2 finishing order: Abercarn, Talywain, NHOB, Chepstow, Brynmawr, Llanhilleth, Risca, Machen, Caldicot, Trinant **Division 3 finishing order:** Fleur de Lys, Monmouth, RTB, Nantyglo, Crumlin, Usk, Blaenavon, Ynysddu

NORTH WALES (DAVID McLEAN) LEAGUE

	P	W	D	L	Pts
Mold*	21	20	0	1	40
Newtown	22	20	0	2	40
Dolgellau	22	16	0	6	32
Pwllheli	22	15	1	6	31
Llandudno	22	14	0	8	28
Welshpool	22	11	1	10	23
Rhyl	20	11	0	9	22
Caernarfon	22	7	1	14	15
Denbigh	22	6	1	15	13
Bangor U	22	3	0	19	6
Bangor	22	3	0	19	6
Bangor Normal Coll	20	0	0	20	0

Mold won on points difference of +800.

WELSH INTERNATIONAL PLAYERS
(up to 31 March 1993)

ABBREVIATIONS

A – Australia; *Arg* – Argentina; *Bb* – Barbarians; *C* – Canada; *E* – England; *F* – France; *Fj* – Fiji; *I* – Ireland; *M* – Maoris; *Nm* – Namibia; *NZ* – New Zealand; *NZA* – New Zealand Army; *R* – Romania; *S* – Scotland; *SA* – South Africa; *Tg* – Tonga; *US* – United States; *WS* – Western Samoa; (R) – Replacement. Entries in square brackets [ ] indicate appearances in the World Cup.

Note: Years given for Five Nations' matches are for second half of season; eg 1972 means season 1971-72. Years for all other matches refer to the actual year of the match. When a series has taken place, figures have been used to denote the particular matches in which players have featured. Thus 1969 *NZ* 2 indicates that a player appeared in the second Test of the series.

Ackerman, R A (Newport, London Welsh) 1980 *NZ*, 1981 *E, S, A,* 1982 *I, F, E, S,* 1983 *S, I, F, R,* 1984 *S, I, F, E, A,* 1985 *S, I, F, E, Fj*
Alexander, E P (Llandovery Coll, Cambridge U) 1885 *S,* 1886 *E, S,* 1887 *E, I*
Alexander, W H (Llwynypia) 1898 *I, E,* 1899 *E, S, I,* 1901 *S, I*
Allen, A G (Newbridge) 1990 *F, E, I*
Allen, C P (Oxford U, Beaumaris) 1884 *E, S*
Andrews, F (Pontypool) 1912 *SA,* 1913 *E, S, I*
Andrews, F G (Swansea) 1884 *E, S*
Andrews, G E (Newport) 1926 *E, S,* 1927 *E, F, I*
Anthony, L (Neath) 1948 *E, S, F*
Arnold, P (Swansea) 1990 *Nm* 1,2, *Bb,* 1991 *E, S, I, F*1, *A,* [*Arg, A*], 1993 *F*(R)
Arnold, W R (Swansea) 1903 *S*
Arthur, C S (Cardiff) 1888 *I, M,* 1891 *E*
Arthur, T (Neath) 1927 *S, F, I,* 1929 *E, S, F, I,* 1930 *E, S, I, F,* 1931 *E, S, F, I, SA,* 1933 *E, S*
Ashton, C (Aberavon) 1959 *E, S, I,* 1960 *E, S, I,* 1962 *I*
Attewell, S L (Newport) 1921 *E, S, F*

Badger, O (Llanelli) 1895 *E, S, I,* 1896 *E*
Baker, A (Neath) 1921 *I,* 1923 *E, S, F, I*
Baker, A M (Newport) 1909 *S, F,* 1910 *S*
Bancroft, J (Swansea) 1909 *E, S, F, I,* 1910 *F, E, S, I,* 1911 *E, F, I,* 1912 *E, S, I,* 1913 *I,* 1914 *E, S, F*
Bancroft, W J (Swansea) 1890 *S, E, I,* 1891 *E, S, I,* 1892 *E, S, I,* 1893 *E, S, I,* 1894 *E, S, I,* 1895 *E, S, I,* 1896 *E, S, I,* 1897 *E,* 1898 *I, E,* 1899 *E, S, I,* 1900 *E, S, I,* 1901 *E, S, I*
Barlow, T M (Cardiff) 1884 *I*
Barrell, R J (Cardiff) 1929 *S, F, I,* 1933 *I*
Bartlett, J D (Llanelli) 1927 *S,* 1928 *E, S*
Bassett, A (Cardiff) 1934 *I,* 1935 *E, S, I,* 1938 *E, S*
Bassett, J A (Penarth) 1929 *E, S, F, I,* 1930 *E, S, I,* 1931 *E, S, F, I, SA,* 1932 *E, S, I*
Bateman, A G (Neath) 1990 *S, I, Nm* 1,2
Bayliss, G (Pontypool) 1933 *S*
Bebb, D I E (Carmarthen TC, Swansea) 1959 *E, S, I, F,* 1960 *E, S, I, F, SA,* 1961 *E, S, I, F,* 1962 *E, S, F, I,* 1963 *E, F, NZ,* 1964 *E, S, F, SA,* 1965 *E, S, I, F,* 1966 *F, A,* 1967 *S, I, F, E*
Beckingham, G (Cardiff) 1953 *E, S,* 1958 *F*
Bennett, I (Aberavon) 1937 *I*
Bennett, P (Cardiff Harlequins) 1891 *E, S,* 1892 *S, I*
Bennett, P (Llanelli) 1969 *F* (R), 1970 *SA, S, F,* 1972 *S* (R), *NZ,* 1973 *E, S, I, F, A,* 1974 *S, I, F, E,* 1975 *S* (R), *I,* 1976 *E, S, I, F,* 1977 *I, F, E, S,* 1978 *E, S, I, F*
Bergiers, R T E (Cardiff Coll of Ed, Llanelli) 1972 *E, S, F, NZ,* 1973 *E, S, I, F, A,* 1974 *E,* 1975 *I*
Bevan, G W (Llanelli) 1947 *E*
Bevan, J A (Cambridge U) 1881 *E*
Bevan, J C (Cardiff, Cardiff Coll of Ed) 1971 *E, S, I, F,* 1972 *E, S, F, NZ,* 1973 *E, S*
Bevan, J D (Aberavon) 1975 *F, E, S, A*
Bevan, S (Swansea) 1904 *I*
Beynon, B (Swansea) 1920 *E, S*
Beynon, G E (Swansea) 1925 *F, I*
Bidgood, R A (Newport) 1992 *S*
Biggs, N W (Cardiff) 1888 *M,* 1889 *I,* 1892 *I,* 1893 *E, S, I,* 1894 *E, I*
Biggs, S H (Cardiff) 1895 *E, S,* 1896 *S,* 1897 *E,* 1898 *I, E,* 1899 *S, I,* 1900 *I*

Birch, J (Neath) 1911 *S, F*
Birt, F W (Newport) 1911 *E, S,* 1912 *E, S, I, SA,* 1913 *E*
Bishop, D J (Pontypool) 1984 *A*
Bishop, E H (Swansea) 1889 *S*
Blackmore, J H (Abertillery) 1909 *E*
Blackmore, S W (Cardiff) 1987 *I,* [*Tg* (R), *C, A*]
Blake, J (Cardiff) 1899 *E, S, I,* 1900 *E, S, I,* 1901 *E, S, I*
Blakemore, R E (Newport) 1947 *E*
Bland, A F (Cardiff) 1887 *E, S, I,* 1888 *S, I, M,* 1890 *S, E, I*
Blyth, L (Swansea) 1951 *SA,* 1952 *E, S*
Blyth, W R (Swansea) 1974 *E,* 1975 *S* (R), 1980 *F, E, S, I*
Boon, R W (Cardiff) 1930 *S, F,* 1931 *E, S, F, I, SA,* 1932 *E, S, I,* 1933 *E, I*
Booth, J (Pontymister) 1898 *I*
Boots, J G (Newport) 1898 *I, E,* 1899 *I,* 1900 *E, S, I,* 1901 *E, S, I,* 1902 *E, S, I,* 1903 *E, S, I,* 1904 *E*
Boucher, A W (Newport) 1892 *E, S, I,* 1894 *E,* 1895 *E, S, I,* 1896 *E, I,* 1897 *E*
Bowcott, H M (Cardiff, Cambridge U) 1929 *S, F, I,* 1930 *E,* 1931 *E, S,* 1933 *E, I*
Bowdler, F A (Cross Keys) 1927 *A,* 1928 *E, S, I, F,* 1929 *E, S, F, I,* 1930 *E,* 1931 *SA,* 1932 *E, S, I,* 1933 *I*
Bowen, B (S Wales Police, Swansea) 1983 *R,* 1984 *S, I, F, E,* 1985 *Fj,* 1986 *E, S, I, F, Fj, Tg, WS,* 1987 [*C, E, NZ*], *US,* 1988 *E, S, I, F, WS,* 1989 *S, I*
Bowen, C A (Llanelli) 1896 *E, S, I,* 1897 *E*
Bowen, D H (Llanelli) 1883 *E,* 1886 *E, S,* 1887 *E*
Bowen, G E (Swansea) 1887 *S, I,* 1888 *S, I*
Bowen, W (Swansea) 1921 *S, F,* 1922 *E, S, I, F*
Bowen, Wm A (Swansea) 1886 *E, S,* 1887 *E, S, I,* 1888 *M,* 1889 *S, I,* 1890 *S, E, I,* 1891 *E, S*
Brace, D O (Llanelli, Oxford U) 1956 *E, S, I, F,* 1957 *E,* 1960 *S, I, F,* 1961 *I*
Braddock, K J (Newbridge) 1966 *A,* 1967 *S, I*
Bradshaw, K (Bridgend) 1964 *E, S, I, F, SA,* 1966 *E, S, I, F*
Brewer, T J (Newport) 1950 *E,* 1955 *E, S*
Brice, A B (Aberavon) 1899 *E, S, I,* 1900 *E, S, I,* 1901 *E, S, I,* 1902 *E, S, I,* 1903 *E, S, I,* 1904 *E, S, I*
Bridges, C J (Neath) 1990 *Nm* 1,2, *Bb,* 1991 *E*(R), *I, F*1, *A*
Bridie, R H (Newport) 1882 *I*
Britton, G R (Newport) 1961 *S*
Broughton, A S (Treorchy) 1927 *A,* 1929 *S*
Brown, A (Newport) 1921 *I*
Brown, J (Cardiff) 1925 *I*
Brown, J A (Cardiff) 1907 *E, S, I,* 1908 *E, S, F,* 1909 *E*
Brown, M (Pontypool) 1983 *R,* 1986 *E, S, Fj* (R), *Tg, WS*
Bryant, D J (Bridgend) 1988 *NZ* 1,2, *WS, R,* 1989 *S, I, F, E*
Buchanan, A (Llanelli) 1987 [*Tg, E, NZ, A*], 1988 *I*
Burcher, D H (Newport) 1977 *I, F, E, S*
Burgess, R C (Ebbw Vale) 1977 *I, F, E, S,* 1981 *I, F,* 1982 *F, E, S*
Burnett, R (Newport) 1953 *E*
Burns, J (Pontymister) 1927 *F, I*
Bush, P F (Cardiff) 1905 *NZ,* 1906 *E, SA,* 1907 *I,* 1908 *E, S,* 1910 *S, I*
Butler, E T (Pontypool) 1980 *F, E, S, I, NZ* (R), 1982 *S,* 1983 *E, S, I, F, R,* 1984 *S, I, F, E, A*

267

Edwards, A B (London Welsh, Army) 1955 *E, S*
Edwards, B O (Newport) 1951 *I*
Edwards, D (Glynneath) 1921 *E*
Edwards, G O (Cardiff, Cardiff Coll of Ed) 1967 *F, E,
NZ,* 1968 *E, S, I, F,* 1969 *S, I, F, E, NZ* 1,2, *A,* 1970
SA, S, E, I, F, 1971 *E, S, I, F,* 1972 *E, S, F, NZ,* 1973
E, S, I, F, A, 1974 *S, I, F,* 1975 *F, E, S, I, A,* 1976
E, S, I, F, 1977 *I, F, E, S,* 1978 *E, S, I, F*
Eidman, I H (Cardiff) 1983 *S, R,* 1984 *I, F, E, A,* 1985
S, I, Fj, 1986 *E, S, I, F*
Elliott, J E (Cardiff) 1894 *I,* 1898 *I, E*
Elsey, W J (Cardiff) 1895 *E*
Emyr, Arthur (Swansea) 1989 *E, NZ,* 1990 *F, E, S, I,
Nm* 1,2, 1991 *F* 1,2, *[WS, Arg, A]*
Evans, A C (Pontypool) 1924 *E, I, F*
Evans, B (Swansea) 1933 *S*
Evans, B (Llanelli) 1933 *E, S,* 1936 *E, S, I,* 1937 *E*
Evans, B S (Llanelli) 1920 *E,* 1922 *E, S, I, F*
Evans, C (Pontypool) 1960 *E*
Evans, D (Penygraig) 1896 *S, I,* 1897 *E,* 1898 *E*
Evans, D B (Swansea) 1926 *E*
Evans, D D (Cheshire, Cardiff U) 1934 *E*
Evans, D P (Llanelli) 1960 *SA*
Evans, D W (Neath) 1889 *S, I,* 1890 *E, I,* 1891 *E*
Evans, D W (Oxford U, Cardiff) 1989 *F, E, NZ,* 1990
F, E, S, I, Bb, 1991 *A(R), F2(R), [A(R)]*
Evans, E (Llanelli) 1937 *E,* 1939 *S, I*
Evans, F (Llanelli) 1921 *S*
Evans, G (Cardiff) 1947 *E, S, F, I, A,* 1948 *E, S, F, I,*
1949 *E, S, I*
Evans, G (Maesteg) 1981 *S* (R), *I, F, A,* 1982 *I, F, E,
S,* 1983 *F, R*
Evans, G L (Newport) 1977 *F* (R), 1978 *F, A* 2 (R)
Evans, I (London Welsh) 1934 *S, I*
Evans, I (Swansea) 1922 *E, S, I, F*
Evans, I C (Llanelli) 1987 *F, E, S, I, [I, C, E, NZ, A],*
1988 *E, S, I, F, NZ* 1,2, 1989 *I, F, E,* 1991 *E, S, I, F1,
A, F2, [WS, Arg, A],* 1992 *I, F, E, S, A,* 1993 *E, S, I, F*
Evans, I L (Llanelli) 1991 *F2(R)*
Evans, J (Llanelli) 1896 *S, I,* 1897 *E*
Evans, J (Blaina) 1904 *I*
Evans, J (Pontypool) 1907 *E, S, I*
Evans, J D (Cardiff) 1958 *I, F*
Evans, J E (Llanelli) 1924 *S*
Evans, J R (Newport) 1934 *E*
Evans, O J (Cardiff) 1887 *E, S,* 1888 *S, I*
Evans, P D (Llanelli) 1951 *E, F*
Evans, R (Cardiff) 1889 *S*
Evans, R (Bridgend) 1963 *S, I, F*
Evans, R L (Llanelli) 1993 *E, S, I, F*
Evans, R T (Newport) 1947 *F, I,* 1950 *E, S, I, F,* 1951
E, S, I, F
Evans, S (Swansea, Neath) 1985 *F, E,* 1986 *Fj, Tg,
WS,* 1987 *F, E, [I, Tg]*
Evans, T (Swansea) 1924 *I*
Evans, T G (London Welsh) 1970 *SA, S, E, I,* 1972 *E,
S, F*
Evans, T H (Llanelli) 1906 *I,* 1907 *E, S, I,* 1908 *I, A,*
1909 *E, S, F, I,* 1910 *F, E, S, I,* 1911 *E, S, F, I*
Evans, T P (Swansea) 1975 *F, E, S, I, A,* 1976 *E, S, I,
F,* 1977 *I*
Evans, V (Neath) 1954 *I, F, S*
Evans, W (Llanelli) 1958 *A*
Evans, W F (Rhymney) 1882 *I,* 1883 *S*
Evans, W G (Brynmawr) 1911 *I*
Evans, W H (Llwynypia) 1914 *E, S, F, I*
Evans, W J (Pontypool) 1947 *S*
Evans, W R (Bridgend) 1958 *A, E, S, I, F,* 1960 *SA,*
1961 *E, S, I, F,* 1962 *E, S, I*
Everson, W A (Newport) 1926 *S*

Faulkner, A G (Pontypool) 1975 *F, E, S, I, A,* 1976 *E,
S, I, F,* 1978 *E, S, I, F, A* 1,2, *NZ,* 1979 *S, I, F*
Faull, J (Swansea) 1957 *I, F,* 1958 *A, E, S, I, F,* 1959
E, S, I, 1960 *E, F*
Fauvel, T J (Aberavon) 1988 *NZ* 1 (R)
Fear, A G (Newport) 1934 *S, I,* 1935 *S, I*
Fender, N H (Cardiff) 1930 *I, F,* 1931 *E, S, F, I*
Fenwick, S P (Bridgend) 1975 *F, E, S, A,* 1976 *E, S, I,
F,* 1977 *I, F, E, S,* 1978 *E, S, I, F, A* 1,2, *NZ,* 1979 *S,
I, F, E,* 1980 *F, E, S, I, NZ,* 1981 *E, S*
Finch, E (Llanelli) 1924 *F, NZ,* 1925 *F, I,* 1926 *F,* 1927
A, 1928 *I*
Finlayson, A A J (Cardiff) 1974 *I, F, E*

Fitzgerald, D (Cardiff) 1894 *S, I*
Ford, F J V (Welch Regt, Newport) 1939 *E*
Ford, I (Newport) 1959 *E, S*
Ford, S P (Cardiff) 1990 *I, Nm* 1,2, *Bb,* 1991 *E, S, I, A*
Forward, A (Pontypool, Mon Police) 1951 *S, SA,* 1952
E, S, I, F
Fowler, I J (Llanelli) 1919 *NZA*
Francis, D G (Llanelli) 1919 *NZA,* 1924 *S*
Francis, P (Maesteg) 1987 *S*

Gabe, R T (Cardiff, Llanelli) 1901 *I,* 1902 *E, S, I,* 1903
E, S, I, 1904 *E, S, I,* 1905 *E, S, I, NZ,* 1906 *E, I, SA,*
1907 *E, S, I,* 1908 *E, S, F, I*
Gale, N R (Swansea, Llanelli) 1960 *I,* 1963 *E, S, I, NZ,*
1964 *E, S, I, F, SA,* 1965 *E, S, I, F,* 1966 *E, S, I, F,
A,* 1967 *E, NZ,* 1968 *E,* 1969 *NZ* 1 (R), 2, *A*
Gallacher, I S (Llanelli) 1970 *F*
Garrett, R M (Penarth) 1888 *M,* 1889 *S,* 1890 *S, E, I,*
1891 *S, I,* 1892 *E*
Geen, W P (Oxford U, Newport) 1912 *SA,* 1913 *E, I*
George, E E (Pontypridd, Cardiff) 1895 *S, I,* 1896 *E*
George, G M (Newport) 1991 *E, S*
Gething, G I (Neath) 1913 *F*
Gibbs, I S (Neath, Swansea) 1991 *E, S, I, F1, A, F2,
[WS, Arg, A],* 1992 *I, F, E, S, A,* 1993 *E, S, I, F*
Gibbs, R A (Cardiff) 1906 *S, I,* 1907 *E, S,* 1908 *E, S,
F, I,* 1910 *F, E, S, I,* 1911 *E, S, F, I*
Giles, R (Aberavon) 1983 *E, NZ, Fj* (R), 1987 *[C]*
Girling, B E (Cardiff) 1881 *E*
Goldsworthy, S J (Swansea) 1884 *I,* 1885 *E, S*
Gore, J H (Blaina) 1924 *I, F, NZ,* 1925 *E*
Gore, W (Newbridge) 1947 *S, F, I*
Gould, A J (Newport) 1885 *E, S,* 1886 *E, S,* 1887 *E, S,
I,* 1888 *S,* 1889 *I,* 1890 *S, E, I,* 1892 *E, S, I,* 1893 *E, S,
I,* 1894 *E, S,* 1895 *E, S, I,* 1896 *E, S, I,* 1897 *E*
Gould, G H (Newport) 1892 *I,* 1893 *S, I*
Gould, R (Newport) 1882 *I,* 1883 *E, S,* 1884 *E, S, I,*
1885 *E, S,* 1886 *E,* 1887 *E, S*
Graham, T C (Newport) 1890 *I,* 1891 *S, I,* 1892 *E, S,*
1893 *E, S, I,* 1894 *E, S,* 1895 *E, S*
Gravell, R W R (Llanelli) 1975 *F, E, S, I, A,* 1976 *E,
S, I, F,* 1978 *E, S, I, F, A* 1,2, *NZ,* 1979 *S, I,* 1981 *I,
F,* 1982 *F, E*
Gray, A J (London Welsh) 1968 *E, S*
Greenslade, D (Newport) 1962 *S*
Greville, H G (Llanelli) 1947 *A*
Griffin, Dr J (Edinburgh U) 1883 *S*
Griffiths, C (Llanelli) 1979 *E* (R)
Griffiths, D (Llanelli) 1888 *M,* 1889 *I*
Griffiths, G (Llanelli) 1889 *I*
Griffiths, G M (Cardiff) 1953 *E, S, I, F, NZ,* 1954 *I, F,
S,* 1955 *I, F,* 1957 *E, S*
Griffiths, J L (Llanelli) 1988 *NZ* 2, 1989 *S*
Griffiths, M (Bridgend, Cardiff) 1988 *WS, R,* 1989 *S,
I, F, E, NZ,* 1990 *F, E, Nm* 1,2, *Bb,* 1991 *F1, F2, [WS,
Arg, A],* 1992 *I, F, E, S, A*
Griffiths, V M (Newport) 1924 *S, I, F*
Gronow, B (Bridgend) 1910 *F, E, S, I*
Gwilliam, J A (Cambridge U, Newport) 1947 *A,* 1948 *I,*
1949 *E, S, I, F,* 1950 *E, S, I, F,* 1951 *E, S, I, SA,* 1952
E, S, I, F, 1953 *E, I, F, NZ,* 1954 *E*
Gwynn, D (Swansea) 1883 *E,* 1887 *S,* 1890 *E, I,* 1891
E, S
Gwynn, W H (Swansea) 1884 *E, S, I,* 1885 *E, S*

Hadley, A M (Cardiff) 1983 *R,* 1984 *S, I, F, E,* 1985 *F,
E, Fj,* 1986 *E, S, I, F, Fj, Tg,* 1987 *S* (R), *I, [I, Tg, C,
E, NZ, A],* 1988 *E, S, I, F*
Hall, I (Aberavon) 1967 *NZ,* 1970 *SA, S, E,* 1971 *S,*
1974 *S, I, F*
Hall, M R (Cambridge U, Bridgend, Cardiff) 1988 *NZ*
1 (R) 2, *WS, R,* 1989 *S, I, F, E, NZ,* 1990 *F, E, S,* 1991
A, F2, [WS, Arg, A], 1992 *I, F, E, S, A,* 1993 *E, S, I*
Hall, W H (Bridgend) 1988 *WS*
Hancock, F E (Cardiff) 1884 *I,* 1885 *E, S,* 1886 *S*
Hannan, J (Newport) 1888 *M,* 1889 *S, I,* 1890 *S, E, I,*
1891 *E,* 1892 *E, S, I,* 1893 *E, S, I,* 1894 *E, S, I,* 1895
E, S, I
Harding, A F (London Welsh) 1902 *E, S, I,* 1903 *E, S,
I,* 1904 *E, S, I,* 1905 *E, S, I, NZ,* 1906 *E, S, I, SA,*
1907 *I,* 1908 *E, S*
Harding, G F (Newport) 1881 *E,* 1882 *I,* 1883 *E, S*
Harding, R (Swansea, Cambridge U) 1923 *E, S, F, I,*
1924 *I, F, NZ,* 1925 *F, I,* 1926 *E, I, F,* 1927 *E, S, F,*

269

Jones, R (Swansea) 1927 *A*, 1928 *F*
Jones, R B (Cambridge U) 1933 *E*, *S*
Jones, R E (Coventry) 1967 *F, E*, 1968 *S, I, F*
Jones, R N (Swansea) 1986 *E, S, I, F, Fj, Tg, WS*, 1987 *F, E, S, I, [I, Tg, E, NZ, A],* US, 1988 *E, S, I, F, NZ* 1, *WS, R*, 1989 *I, F, E, NZ*, 1990 *F, E, S, I*, 1991 *E, S, F2, [WS, Arg, A]*, 1992 *I, F, E, S, A*, 1993 *E, S, I*
Jones, S T (Pontypool) 1983 *S, I, F, R*, 1984*S*, 1988 *E, S, F, NZ* 1,2
Jones, Tom (Newport) 1922 *E, S, I, F*, 1924 *E, S*
Jones, T B (Newport) 1882 *I*, 1883 *E, S*, 1884 *S*, 1885 *E, S*
Jones, W (Cardiff) 1898 *I, E*
Jones, W (Mountain Ash) 1905 *I*
Jones, W I (Llanelli, Cambridge U) 1925 *E, S, F, I*
Jones, W J (Llanelli) 1924 *I*
Jones, W K (Cardiff) 1967 *NZ*, 1968 *E, S, I, F*
Jones-Davies, T E (London Welsh) 1930 *E, I*, 1931 *E, S*
Jordan, H M (Newport) 1885 *E, S*, 1889 *S*
Joseph, W (Swansea) 1902 *E, S, I*, 1903 *E, S, I*, 1904 *E, S*, 1905 *E, S, I, NZ*, 1906 *E, S, I, SA*
Jowett, W F (Swansea) 1903 *E*
Judd, S (Cardiff) 1953 *E, S, I, F, NZ*, 1954 *E, F, S*, 1955 *E, S*
Judson, J H (Llanelli) 1883 *E, S*

Kedzlie, Q D (Cardiff) 1888 *S, I*
Keen, L (Aberavon) 1980 *F, E, S, I*
Knight, P (Pontypridd) 1990 *Nm* 1,2, *Bb*(R), 1991 *E, S*
Knill, F M D (Cardiff) 1976 *F* (R)

Lamerton, A E H (Llanelli) 1993 *F*
Lane, S M (Cardiff) 1978 *A* 1 (R), 2, 1979 *I* (R), 1980 *S, I*
Lang, J (Llanelli) 1931 *F, I*, 1934 *S, I*, 1935 *E, S, I, NZ*, 1936 *E, S, I*, 1937 *E*
Lawrence, S (Bridgend) 1925 *S, I*, 1926 *S, I, F*, 1927 *E*
Law, V J (Newport) 1939 *I*
Legge, W S G (Newport) 1937 *I*, 1938 *I*
Leleu, J (London Welsh, Swansea) 1959 *E, S*, 1960 *F, SA*
Lemon, A (Neath) 1929 *I*, 1930 *S, I, F*, 1931 *E, S, F, I, SA*, 1932 *E, S, I*, 1933 *I*
Lewis, A J L (Ebbw Vale) 1970 *F*, 1971 *E, I, F*, 1972 *E, S, F*, 1973 *E, S, I, F*
Lewis, A R (Abertillery) 1966 *E, S, I, F, A*, 1967 *I*
Lewis, B R (Swansea, Cambridge U) 1912 *I*, 1913 *I*
Lewis, C P (Llandovery Coll) 1882 *I*, 1883 *E, S*, 1884 *E, S*
Lewis, D H (Cardiff) 1886 *E, S*
Lewis, E J (Llandovery) 1881 *I*
Lewis, E W (Llanelli) 1991 *I, F*1, *A, F*2, *[WS, Arg, A]*, 1992 *I, F, S, A*, 1993 *E, S, I, F*
Lewis, G W (Richmond) 1960 *E, S*
Lewis, H (Swansea) 1913 *S, F, I*, 1914 *E*
Lewis, J G (Llanelli) 1887 *I*
Lewis, J M C (Cardiff, Cambridge U) 1912 *E*, 1913 *S, F, I*, 1914 *E, S, F, I*, 1921 *I*, 1923 *E, S*
Lewis, J R (S Glam Inst, Cardiff) 1981 *E, S, I, F*, 1982 *F, E, S*
Lewis, M (Treorchy) 1913 *F*
Lewis, P I (Llanelli) 1984 *A*, 1985 *S, I, F, E*, 1986 *E, S, I*
Lewis, T W (Cardiff) 1926 *E*, 1927 *E, S*
Lewis, W (Llanelli) 1925 *F*
Lewis, W H (London Welsh, Cambridge U) 1926 *I*, 1927 *E, F, I, A*, 1928 *F*
Llewelyn, D B (Newport, Llanelli) 1970 *SA, S, E, I, F*, 1971 *E, S, I, F*, 1972 *E, S, F, NZ*
Llewellyn, G D (Neath) 1990 *Nm* 1,2, *Bb*, 1991 *E, S, I, F*1, *A, F*2
Llewellyn, G O (Neath) 1989 *NZ*, 1990 *E, S, I*, 1991 *E, S, A*(R), 1992 *I, F, E, S, A*, 1993 *E, S, I, F*
Llewellyn, P D (Swansea) 1973 *I, F, A*, 1974 *S, E*
Llewellyn, W (Llwynypia) 1899 *E, S, I*, 1900 *E, S, I*, 1901 *E, S, I*, 1902 *E, S, I*, 1903 *I*, 1904 *E, S, I*, 1905 *E, S, I, NZ*
Lloyd, D J (Bridgend) 1966 *E, S, I, F, A*, 1967 *S, I, F, E*, 1968 *S, I, F*, 1969 *S, I, F, E, NZ* 1, *A*, 1970 *F*, 1972 *E, S, F*, 1973 *E, S*
Lloyd, E (Llanelli) 1895 *S*
Lloyd, G L (Newport) 1896 *I*, 1899 *S, I*, 1900 *E, S*, 1901 *E, S*, 1902 *S, I*, 1903 *E, S, I*

Lloyd, P (Llanelli) 1890 *S, E*, 1891 *E, I*
Lloyd, R A (Pontypool) 1913 *S, F, I*, 1914 *E, S, F, I*
Lloyd, T (Maesteg) 1953 *I, F*
Lloyd, T C (Neath) 1909 *F*, 1913 *F, I*, 1914 *E, S, F, I*
Lockwood, T W (Newport) 1887 *E, S, I*
Long, E C (Swansea) 1936 *E, S, I*, 1937 *E, S*, 1939 *S, I*
Lyne, H S (Newport) 1883 *S*, 1884 *E, S, I*, 1885 *E*

McCall, B E W (Welch Regt, Newport) 1936 *E, S, I*
McCarley, A (Neath) 1938 *E, S, I*
McCutcheon, W M (Swansea) 1891 *S*, 1892 *E, S*, 1893 *E, S, I*, 1894 *E*
Maddock, H T (London Welsh) 1906 *E, S, I*, 1907 *E, S*, 1910 *F*
Maddocks, K (Neath) 1957 *E*
Main, D R (London Welsh) 1959 *E, S, I, F*
Mainwaring, H J (Swansea) 1961 *F*
Mainwaring, W T (Aberavon) 1967 *S, I, F, E, NZ*, 1968 *E*
Major, W C (Maesteg) 1949 *F*, 1950 *S*
Male, B O (Cardiff) 1921 *F*, 1923 *S*, 1924 *S, I*, 1927 *E, S, F, I*, 1928 *S, I, F*
Manfield, L (Mountain Ash, Cardiff) 1939 *S, I*, 1947 *A*, 1948 *E, S, F, I*
Mann, B B (Cardiff) 1881 *E*
Mantle, J T (Loughborough Colls, Newport) 1964 *E, SA*
Margrave, F L (Llanelli) 1884 *E, S*
Marsden-Jones, D (Cardiff) 1921 *E*, 1924 *NZ*
Martin, A J (Aberavon) 1973 *A*, 1974 *S, I*, 1975 *F, E, S, I, A*, 1976 *E, S, I, F*, 1977 *I, F, E, S*, 1978 *E, S, I, F, A* 1,2, *NZ*, 1979 *S, I, F, E*, 1980 *F, E, S, I, NZ*, 1981 *I, F*
Martin, W J (Newport) 1912 *I, F*, 1919 *NZA*
Mason, J (Pontypridd) 1988 *NZ* 2 (R)
Mathews, Rev A A (Lampeter) 1886 *S*
Mathias, R (Llanelli) 1970 *F*
Matthews, C (Bridgend) 1939 *I*
Matthews, J (Cardiff) 1947 *E, A*, 1948 *E, S, F*, 1949 *E, S, I, F*, 1950 *E, S, I, F*, 1951 *E, S, I, F*
May, P S (Llanelli) 1988 *E, S, I, F, NZ* 1,2, 1991 *[WS]*
Meek, N N (Pontypool) 1993 *E, S, I*
Meredith, A (Devonport Services) 1949 *E, S, I*
Meredith, B V (St Luke's Coll, London Welsh, Newport) 1954 *I, F, S*, 1955 *E, S, I, F*, 1956 *E, S, I, F*, 1957 *E, S, I, F*, 1958 *A, E, S, I, F*, 1959 *E, S, I, F*, 1960 *E, S, F, SA*, 1961 *E, S, I, F*, 1962 *E, S, F, I*
Meredith, C C (Neath) 1953 *S, NZ*, 1954 *E, I, F, S*, 1955 *E, S, I, F*, 1956 *E, I*, 1957 *E, S*
Meredith, J (Swansea) 1888 *S, I*, 1890 *S, E*
Merry, A E (Pill Harriers) 1912 *I, F*
Michael, G (Swansea) 1923 *E, S, F*
Michaelson, R C B (Aberavon, Cambridge U) 1963 *E*
Miller, F (Mountain Ash) 1896 *I*, 1900 *E, S, I*, 1901 *E, S, I*
Mills, F M (Swansea, Cardiff) 1892 *E, S, I*, 1893 *E, S, I*, 1894 *E, S, I*, 1895 *E, S, I*, 1896 *E*
Moon, R H StJ B (Llanelli) 1993 *F*
Moore, W J (Bridgend) 1933 *I*
Morgan, C H (Llanelli) 1957 *I, F*
Morgan, C I (Cardiff) 1951 *I, F, SA*, 1952 *E, S, I*, 1953 *S, I, F, NZ*, 1954 *E, I, S*, 1955 *E, S, I, F*, 1956 *E, S, I, F*, 1957 *E, S, I, F*, 1958 *E, S, I, F*
Morgan, D (Swansea) 1885 *S*, 1886 *E, S*, 1887 *E, S, I*, 1889 *I*
Morgan, D (Llanelli) 1895 *I*, 1896 *E*
Morgan, D R R (Llanelli) 1962 *E, S, F, I*, 1963 *E, S, I, F, NZ*
Morgan, E (Llanelli) 1920 *I*, 1921 *E, S, F*
Morgan, Edgar (Swansea) 1914 *E, S, F, I*
Morgan, E T (London Welsh) 1902 *E, S, I*, 1903 *I*, 1904 *E, S, I*, 1905 *E, S, I, NZ*, 1906 *E, S, I, SA*, 1908 *F*
Morgan, F L (Llanelli) 1938 *E, S, I*, 1939 *E*
Morgan, H J (Abertillery) 1958 *E, S, I, F*, 1959 *I, F*, 1960 *E*, 1961 *E, S, I, F*, 1962 *E, S, F, I*, 1963 *S, I, F*, 1965 *E, S, I, F*, 1966 *E, S, I, F, A*
Morgan, H P (Newport) 1956 *E, S, I, F*
Morgan, I (Swansea) 1908 *A*, 1909 *E, S, F, I*, 1910 *F, E, S, I*, 1911 *E, F, I*, 1912 *S*
Morgan, J L (Llanelli) 1912 *SA*, 1913 *E*
Morgan, M E (Swansea) 1938 *E, S, I*, 1939 *E*
Morgan, N (Newport) 1960 *S, I, F*
Morgan, P E J (Aberavon) 1961 *E, S, F*
Morgan, P J (Llanelli) 1980 *S* (R), *I, NZ* (R), 1981 *I*

Ramsey, S H (Treorchy) 1896 E, 1904 E
Randell, R (Aberavon) 1924 I, F
Raybould, W H (London Welsh, Cambridge U, Newport) 1967 S, I, F, E, NZ, 1968 I, F, 1970 SA, E, I, F (R)
Rayer, M A (Cardiff) 1991 [WS(R)], Arg, A(R)], 1992 E(R), A, 1993 E, S, I
Rees, Aaron (Maesteg) 1919 NZA
Rees, Alan (Maesteg) 1962 E, S, F
Rees, A M (London Welsh) 1934 E, 1935 E, S, I, NZ, 1936 E, S, I, 1937 E, S, I, 1938 E, S
Rees, B I (London Welsh) 1967 S, I, F
Rees, C F W (London Welsh) 1974 I, 1975 A, 1978 NZ, 1981 F, A, 1982 I, F, E, S, 1983 E, S, I, F
Rees, D (Swansea) 1968 S, I, F
Rees, Dan (Swansea) 1900 E, 1903 E, S, 1905 E, S
Rees, E B (Swansea) 1919 NZA
Rees, H (Cardiff) 1937 S, I, 1938 E, S, I
Rees, H E (Neath) 1979 S, I, F, E, 1980 F, E, S, I, NZ, 1983 E, S, I, F
Rees, J (Swansea) 1920 E, S, F, I, 1921 E, S, I, 1922 E, 1923 E, F, I, 1924 E
Rees, J I (Swansea) 1934 E, S, I, 1935 S, NZ, 1936 E, S, I, 1937 E, S, I, 1938 E, S, I
Rees, L M (Cardiff) 1933 I
Rees, P (Llanelli) 1947 F, I
Rees, P M (Newport) 1961 E, S, I, 1964 I
Rees, T (Newport) 1935 S, I, NZ, 1936 E, S, I, 1937 E, S
Rees, T A (Llandovery) 1881 E
Rees, T E (London Welsh) 1926 I, F, 1927 A, 1928 E
Rees-Jones, G R (Oxford U, London Welsh) 1934 E, S, 1935 I, NZ, 1936 E
Reeves, F (Cross Keys) 1920 F, I, 1921 E
Reynolds, A (Swansea) 1990 Nm 1,2(R), 1992 A(R)
Rhapps, J (Penygraig) 1897 E
Rice-Evans, W (Swansea) 1890 S, 1891 E, S
Richards, B (Swansea) 1960 F
Richards, C (Pontypool) 1922 E, S, I, F, 1924 I
Richards, D S (Swansea) 1979 F, E, 1980 F, E, S, I, NZ, 1981 E, S, I, F, 1982 I, F, 1983 E, S, I, R (R)
Richards, E G (Cardiff) 1927 S
Richards, E S (Swansea) 1885 E, 1887 S
Richards, H D (Neath) 1986 Tg (R), 1987 [Tg, E (R), NZ]
Richards, I (Cardiff) 1925 E, S, F
Richards, K H L (Bridgend) 1960 SA, 1961 E, S, I, F
Richards, M C R (Cardiff) 1968 I, F, 1969 S, I, F, E, NZ 1,2, A
Richards, R (Aberavon) 1913 S, F, I
Richards, R (Cross Keys) 1956 F
Richards, T L (Maesteg) 1923 I
Richardson, S J (Aberavon) 1978 A 2 (R), 1979 E
Rickards, A R (Cardiff) 1924 F
Ring, J (Aberavon) 1921 E
Ring, M G (Cardiff, Pontypool) 1983 E, 1984 A, 1985 S, I, F, 1987 I, [I, Tg, A], US, 1988 E, S, I, F, NZ 1,2, 1989 NZ, 1990 F, E, S, I, Nm 1,2, Bb, 1991 E, S, I, F1,2, [WS, Arg, A]
Ringer, P (Ebbw Vale, Llanelli) 1978 NZ, 1979 S, I, F, E, 1980 F, E, NZ
Roberts, C (Neath) 1958 I, F
Roberts, D E A (London Welsh) 1930 E
Roberts, E (Llanelli) 1886 E, 1887 I
Roberts, E J (Llanelli) 1888 S, I, 1889 I
Roberts, G J (Cardiff) 1985 F (R), E, 1987 [I, Tg, C, E, A]
Roberts, H M (Cardiff) 1960 SA, 1961 E, S, I, F, 1962 S, F, 1963 I
Roberts, J (Cardiff) 1927 E, S, F, I, A, 1928 E, S, I, F, 1929 E, S, F, I
Roberts, M G (London Welsh) 1971 E, S, I, F, 1973 I, F, 1975 S, 1979 E
Roberts, T (Newport, Risca) 1921 S, F, I, 1922 E, S, I, F, 1923 E, S
Roberts, W (Cardiff) 1929 E
Robins, J D (Birkenhead Park) 1950 E, S, I, F, 1951 E, S, I, F, 1953 E, I, F
Robins, R J (Pontypridd) 1953 S, 1954 F, S, 1955 E, S, I, F, 1956 E, F, 1957 E, S, I, F
Robinson, I R (Cardiff) 1974 F, E
Rocyn-Jones, D N (Cambridge U) 1925 I
Roderick, W B (Llanelli) 1884 I
Rosser, M A (Penarth) 1924 S, F

Rowland, E M (Lampeter) 1885 E
Rowlands, C F (Aberavon) 1926 I
Rowlands, D C T (Pontypool) 1963 E, S, I, F, NZ, 1964 E, S, I, F, SA, 1965 E, S, I, F
Rowlands, G (RAF, Cardiff) 1953 NZ, 1954 E, F, 1956 F
Rowlands, K A (Cardiff) 1962 F, I, 1963 I, 1965 I, F
Rowles, G R (Penarth) 1892 E
Russell, S (London Welsh) 1987 US

Samuel, D (Swansea) 1891 I, 1893 I
Samuel, F (Mountain Ash) 1922 S, I, F
Samuel, J (Swansea) 1891 I
Scourfield, T (Torquay) 1930 F
Scrine, G F (Swansea) 1899 E, S, 1901 I
Shanklin, J L (London Welsh) 1970 F, 1972 NZ, 1973 I, F
Shaw, G (Neath) 1972 NZ, 1973 E, S, I, F, A, 1974 S, I, F, E, 1977 I, F
Shaw, T W (Newbridge) 1983 R
Shea, J (Newport) 1919 NZA, 1920 E, S, 1921 E
Shell, R C (Aberavon) 1973 A (R)
Simpson, H J (Cardiff) 1884 E, S, I
Skrimshire, R T (Newport) 1899 E, S, I
Skym, A (Llanelli) 1928 E, S, I, F, 1930 E, S, I, F, 1931 E, S, F, I, SA, 1932 E, S, I, 1933 E, S, I, 1935 E
Smith, J S (Cardiff) 1884 E, I, 1885 E
Sparks, B (Neath) 1954 I, 1955 E, F, 1956 E, S, I, 1957 S
Spiller, W J (Cardiff) 1910 S, I, 1911 E, S, F, I, 1912 E, F, SA, 1913 E
Squire, J (Newport, Pontypool) 1977 I, F, 1978 E, S, I, F, A 1, NZ, 1979 S, I, F, E, 1980 F, E, S, I, NZ, 1981 E, S, I, F, A, 1982 I, F, E, 1983 E, S, I, F
Stadden, W J W (Cardiff) 1884 I, 1886 E, S, 1887 I, 1888 S, M, 1890 S, E
Stephens, C J (Llanelli) 1992 I, F, E, A
Stephens, G (Neath) 1912 E, S, I, F, SA, 1913 E, S, F, I, 1919 NZA
Stephens, I (Bridgend) 1981 E, S, I, F, A, 1982 I, F, E, S, 1984 I, F, E, A
Stephens, Rev J G (Llanelli) 1922 E, S, I, F
Stephens, J R G (Neath) 1947 E, S, F, I, 1948 I, 1949 S, I, F, 1951 F, SA, 1952 E, S, I, F, 1953 E, S, I, F, NZ, 1954 E, I, 1955 E, S, I, F, 1956 S, I, F, 1957 E, S, I, F
Stock, A (Newport) 1924 F, NZ, 1926 E, S
Stone, P (Llanelli) 1949 F
Strand-Jones, J (Llanelli) 1902 E, S, I, 1903 E, S
Summers, R H B (Haverfordwest) 1881 E
Sutton, S (Pontypool, S Wales Police) 1982 F, E, 1987 F, E, S, I, [C, NZ, A]
Sweet-Escott, R B (Cardiff) 1891 S, 1894 I, 1895 I

Tamplin, W E (Cardiff) 1947 S, F, I, A, 1948 E, S, F
Tanner, H (Swansea, Cardiff) 1935 NZ, 1936 E, S, I, 1937 E, S, I, 1938 E, S, I, 1939 E, S, I, 1947 E, S, F, I, 1948 E, S, F, I, 1949 E, S, F
Tarr, D J (Swansea, Royal Navy) 1935 NZ
Taylor, A R (Cross Keys) 1937 I, 1938 I, 1939 E
Taylor, C G (Ruabon) 1884 E, S, I, 1885 E, S, 1886 E, S, 1887 E, I
Taylor, J (London Welsh) 1967 S, I, F, E, NZ, 1968 I, F, 1969 S, I, F, E, NZ 1 A, 1970 F, 1971 E, S, I, F, 1972 E, S, F, NZ, 1973 E, S, I, F
Thomas, A (Newport) 1963 NZ, 1964 E
Thomas, A G (Swansea, Cardiff) 1952 E, S, I, F, 1953 S, I, F, 1954 E, I, F, 1955 I, S, I, F
Thomas, Bob (Swansea) 1900 E, S, I, 1901 E
Thomas, Brian E (Neath, Cambridge U) 1963 E, S, I, F, NZ, 1964 E, S, I, F, SA, 1965 E, 1966 E, S, I, 1967 NZ, 1969 S, I, F, E, NZ 1,2
Thomas, C (Bridgend) 1925 E, S
Thomas, C J (Newport) 1888 I, M, 1889 S, I, 1890 S, E, I, 1891 E, I
Thomas, D (Aberavon) 1961 I
Thomas, D (Llanelli) 1954 I
Thomas, Dick (Mountain Ash) 1906 SA, 1908 F, I, 1909 S
Thomas, D J (Swansea) 1904 E, 1908 A, 1910 E, S, I, 1911 E, S, F, I, 1912 E
Thomas, D J (Swansea) 1930 S, I, 1932 E, S, I, 1933 E, S, 1934 E, 1935 E, S, I
Thomas, D L (Neath) 1937 E
Thomas, E (Newport) 1904 S, I, 1909 S, F, I, 1910 F

273

Thomas, **G** (Llanelli) 1923 *E, S, F, I*
Thomas, **G** (Newport) 1888 *M*, 1890 *I*, 1891 *S*
Thomas, **H** (Llanelli) 1912 *F*
Thomas, **H** (Neath) 1936 *E, S, I*, 1937 *E, S, I*
Thomas, **H W** (Swansea) 1912 *SA*, 1913 *E*
Thomas, **I** (Bryncethin) 1924 *E*
Thomas, **L C** (Cardiff) 1885 *E, S*
Thomas, **M C** (Newport, Devonport Services) 1949 *F*,
1950 *E, S, I, F*, 1951 *E, S, I, F, SA*, 1952 *E, S, I, F*,
1953 *E*, 1956 *E, S, I, F*, 1957 *E, S*, 1958 *E, S, I, F*,
1959 *I, F*
Thomas, **M G** (St Bart's Hospital) 1919 *NZA*, 1921 *S*,
F, I, 1923 *F*, 1924 *E*
Thomas, **R** (Pontypool) 1909 *F, I*, 1911 *S, F*, 1912 *E*,
S, SA, 1913 *E*
Thomas, **R C C** (Swansea) 1949 *F*, 1952 *I, F*, 1953 *S*,
I, F, NZ, 1954 *E, I, F, S*, 1955 *S, I*, 1956 *E, S, I*, 1957
E, 1958 *A, E, S, I, F*, 1959 *E, S, I, F*
Thomas, **R L** (London Welsh) 1889 *S, I*, 1890 *I*, 1891
E, S, I, 1892 *E*
Thomas, **S** (Llanelli) 1890 *S, E*, 1891 *I*
Thomas, **W D** (Llanelli) 1966 *A*, 1968 *S, I, F*, 1969 *E*,
NZ 2, *A*, 1970 *SA, S, E, I, F*, 1971 *E, S, I, F*, 1972 *E*,
S, F, NZ, 1973 *E, S, I, F*, 1974 *E*
Thomas, **W G** (Llanelli, Waterloo, Swansea) 1927 *E*,
S, F, I, 1929 *E*, 1931 *E, S, SA*, 1932 *E, S, I*, 1933 *E*,
S, I
Thomas, **W H** (Llandovery Coll, Cambridge U) 1885
S, 1886 *E, S*, 1887 *E, S*, 1888 *S, I*, 1890 *E, I*, 1891 *S, I*
Thomas, **W J** (Cardiff) 1961 *F*, 1963 *F*
Thomas, **W L** (Newport) 1894 *S*, 1895 *E, I*
Thomas, **W T** (Abertillery) 1930 *E*
Thompson, **J F** (Cross Keys) 1923 *E*
Thorburn, **P H** (Neath) 1985 *F, E, Fj*, 1986 *E, S, I, F*,
1987 *F*, [*I, Tg, C, E, NZ, A*], *US*, 1988 *S, I, F, WS, R*
(R), 1989 *S, I, F, E, NZ*, 1990 *F, E, S, I, Nm* 1,2, *Bb*,
1991 *E, S, I, F1, A*
Titley, **M H** (Bridgend, Swansea) 1983 *R*, 1984 *S, I, F*,
E, A, 1985 *S, I, Fj*, 1986 *F, Fj, Tg, WS*, 1990 *F, E*
Towers, **W H** (Swansea) 1887 *I*, 1888 *M*
Travers, **G** (Pill Harriers) 1903 *E, S, I*, 1905 *E, S, I*,
NZ, 1906 *E, S, I, SA*, 1907 *E, S, I*, 1908 *E, S, F, I, A*,
1909 *E, S, I*, 1911 *S, F, I*
Travers, **W H** (Newport) 1937 *S, I*, 1938 *E, S, I*, 1939
E, S, I, 1949 *E, S, I, F*
Treharne, **E** (Pontypridd) 1881 *E*, 1883 *E*
Trew, **W J** (Swansea) 1900 *E, S, I*, 1901 *E, S*, 1903 *S*,
1905 *S*, 1906 *S*, 1907 *E, S*, 1908 *E, S, F, I, A*, 1909 *E*,
S, F, I, 1910 *F, E, S*, 1911 *E, S, F, I*, 1912 *S*, 1913 *S, F*
Trott, **R F** (Cardiff) 1948 *E, S, F, I*, 1949 *E, S, I, F*
Truman, **W H** (Llanelli) 1934 *E*, 1935 *E*
Trump, **L C** (Newport) 1912 *E, S, I, F*
Turnbull, **B R** (Cardiff) 1925 *I*, 1927 *E, S*, 1928 *E, F*,
1930 *S*
Turnbull, **M J L** (Cardiff) 1933 *E, I*
Turner, **P** (Newbridge) 1989 *I* (R), *F, E*

Uzzell, **H** (Newport) 1912 *E, S, I, F*, 1913 *S, F, I*, 1914
E, S, F, I, 1920 *E, S, F, I*
Uzzell, **J R** (Newport) 1963 *NZ*, 1965 *E, S, I, F*

Vickery, **W E** (Aberavon) 1938 *E, S, I*, 1939 *E*
Vile, **T H** (Newport) 1908 *E, S*, 1910 *I*, 1912 *I, F, SA*,
1913 *E*, 1921 *S*
Vincent, **H C** (Bangor) 1882 *I*

Wakeford, **J D M** (S Wales Police) 1988 *WS, R*
Waldron, **R** (Neath) 1965 *E, S, I, F*
Walker, **N** (Cardiff) 1993 *I, F*
Waller, **P D** (Newport) 1908 *A*, 1909 *E, S, F, I*, 1910 *F*
Walters, **N** (Llanelli) 1902 *E*
Wanbon, **R** (Aberavon) 1968 *E*
Ward, **W S** (Cross Keys) 1934 *S, I*
Warlow, **J** (Llanelli) 1962 *I*
Waters, **D R** (Newport) 1986 *E, S, I, F*
Waters, **K** (Newbridge) 1991 [*WS*]
Watkins, **D** (Newport) 1963 *E, S, I, F, NZ*, 1964 *E, S*,
I, F, SA, 1965 *E, S, I, F*, 1966 *E, S, I, F*, 1967 *I, F, E*
Watkins, **E** (Neath) 1924 *E, S, I, F*
Watkins, **E** (Blaina) 1926 *S, I, F*
Watkins, **E** (Cardiff) 1935 *NZ*, 1937 *S, I*, 1938 *E, S, I*,
1939 *E, S*
Watkins, **H** (Llanelli) 1904 *S, I*, 1905 *E, S, I*, 1906 *E*
Watkins, **I J** (Ebbw Vale) 1988 *E* (R), *S, I, F, NZ* 2, *R*,

1989 *S, I, F, E*
Watkins, **L** (Oxford U, Llandaff) 1881 *E*
Watkins, **M J** (Newport) 1984 *I, F, E, A*
Watkins, **S J** (Newport, Cardiff) 1964 *S, I, F*, 1965 *E*,
S, I, F, 1966 *E, S, I, F, A*, 1967 *S, I, F, E, NZ*, 1968
E, S, 1969 *S, I, F, E, NZ* 1, 1970 *E, I*
Watkins, **W R** (Newport) 1959 *F*
Watts, **D** (Maesteg) 1914 *E, S, F, I*
Watts, **J** (Llanelli) 1907 *E, S, I*, 1908 *E, S, F, I, A*,
1909 *S, F, I*
Watts, **W** (Llanelli) 1914 *E*
Watts, **W H** (Newport) 1892 *E, S, I*, 1893 *E, S, I*, 1894
E, S, I, 1895 *E, I*, 1896 *E*
Weaver, **D** (Swansea) 1964 *E*
Webb, **J** (Abertillery) 1907 *S*, 1908 *E, S, F, I, A*, 1909
E, S, F, I, 1910 *F, E, S, I*, 1911 *E, S, F, I*, 1912 *E, S*
Webb, **J E** (Newport) 1888 *M*, 1889 *S*
Webbe, **G M C** (Bridgend) 1986 *Tg* (R), *WS*, 1987 *F*,
E, S, [*Tg*], *US*, 1988 *F* (R), *NZ* 1, *R*
Webster, **R E** (Swansea) 1987 [*A*], 1990 *Bb*, 1991 [*Arg*,
A], 1992 *I, F, E, S, A*, 1993 *E, S, I, F*
Wells, **G T** (Cardiff) 1955 *E, S*, 1957 *I, F*, 1958 *A, E, S*
Westacott, **D** (Cardiff) 1906 *I*
Wetter, **H** (Newport) 1912 *SA*, 1913 *E*
Wetter, **J J** (Newport) 1914 *S, F, I*, 1920 *E, S, F, I*,
1921 *E*, 1924 *I, NZ*
Wheel, **G A D** (Swansea) 1974 *I, E* (R), 1975 *F, E, I*,
A, 1976 *E, S, I, F*, 1977 *I, E, S*, 1978 *E, S, I, F, A* 1,2,
NZ, 1979 *S, I*, 1980 *F, E, S, I*, 1981 *E, S, I, F, A*,
1982 *I*
Wheeler, **P J** (Aberavon) 1967 *NZ*, 1968 *E*
Whitefoot, **J** (Cardiff) 1984 *A* (R), 1985 *S, I, F, E, Fj*,
1986 *E, S, I, F, Fj, Tg, WS*, 1987 *F, E, S, I*, [*I, C*]
Whitfield, **J** (Newport) 1919 *NZA*, 1920 *E, S, F, I*,
1921 *E*, 1922 *E, S, I, F*, 1924 *S, I*
Whitson, **G K** (Newport) 1956 *F*, 1960 *S, I*
Williams, **A** (Bridgend) 1990 *Nm* 2(R)
Williams, **B** (Llanelli) 1920 *S, F, I*
Williams, **B L** (Cardiff) 1947 *E, S, F, I, A*, 1948 *E, S*,
F, I, 1949 *E, S, I*, 1951 *I, SA*, 1952 *S*, 1953 *E, S, I, F*,
NZ, 1954 *S*, 1955 *E*
Williams, **B R** (Neath) 1990 *S, I, Bb*, 1991 *E, S*
Williams, **C** (Llanelli) 1924 *NZ*, 1925 *E*
Williams, **C** (Aberavon, Swansea) 1977 *E, S*, 1980 *F*,
E, S, I, NZ, 1983 *E*
Williams, **C D** (Cardiff, Neath) 1955 *F*, 1956 *F*
Williams, **D** (Ebbw Vale) 1963 *E, S, I, F*, 1964 *E, S, I*,
F, SA, 1965 *E, S, I, F*, 1966 *E, S, I, A*, 1967 *F, E, NZ*,
1968 *E*, 1969 *S, I, F, E, NZ* 1,2, *A*, 1970 *SA, S, E, I*,
1971 *E, S, I, F*
Williams, **D B** (Newport, Swansea) 1978 *A* 1, 1981 *E, S*
Williams, **E** (Neath) 1924 *NZ*, 1925 *F*
Williams, **E** (Aberavon) 1925 *E, S*
Williams, **F L** (Cardiff) 1929 *S, F, I*, 1930 *E, S, I, F*,
1931 *F, I, SA*, 1932 *E, S, I*, 1933 *I*
Williams, **G** (Aberavon) 1936 *E, S, I*
Williams, **G** (London Welsh) 1950 *I, F*, 1951 *E, S, I*,
F, SA, 1952 *E, S, I, F*, 1953 *NZ*, 1954 *E*
Williams, **G** (Bridgend) 1981 *I, F*, 1982 *E* (R), *S*
Williams, **G P** (Bridgend) 1980 *NZ*, 1981 *E, S, A*,
1982 *I*
Williams, **J** (Blaina) 1920 *E, S, F, I*, 1921 *S, F, I*
Williams, **J F** (London Welsh) 1905 *I, NZ*, 1906 *S, SA*
Williams, **J J** (Llanelli) 1973 *F* (R), *A*, 1974 *S, I, F, E*,
1975 *F, E, S, I, A*, 1976 *E, S, I, F*, 1977 *I, F, E, S*,
1978 *E, S, I, F, A* 1,2, *NZ*, 1979 *S, I, F, E*
Williams, **J L** (Cardiff) 1906 *SA*, 1907 *E, S, I*, 1908
E, S, I, A, 1909 *E, S, F, I*, 1910 *I*, 1911 *E, S, F, I*
Williams, **J P R** (London Welsh, Bridgend) 1969 *S, I*,
F, E, NZ 1,2, *A*, 1970 *SA, S, E, I, F*, 1971 *E, S, I, F*,
1972 *E, S, F, NZ*, 1973 *E, S, I, F, A*, 1974 *S, I, F*, 1975
F, E, S, I, A, 1976 *E, S, I, F*, 1977 *I, F, E, S*, 1978 *E*,
S, I, F, A 1,2, *NZ*, 1979 *S, I, F, E*, 1980 *NZ*, 1981 *E, S*
Williams, **L** (Llanelli, Cardiff) 1947 *E, S, F, I, A*, 1948
I, 1949 *E*
Williams, **L H** (Cardiff) 1957 *S, I, F*, 1958 *E, S, I, F*,
1959 *E, S, I*, 1961 *F, I*, 1962 *E, S*
Williams, **M** (Newport) 1923 *F*
Williams, **O** (Bridgend) 1990 *Nm* 2
Williams, **O** (Llanelli) 1947 *E, S, A*, 1948 *E, S, F, I*
Williams, **R** (Llanelli) 1954 *S*, 1957 *F*, 1958 *A*
Williams, **R D G** (Newport) 1881 *E*
Williams, **R F** (Cardiff) 1912 *SA*, 1913 *E, S*, 1914 *I*
Williams, **R H** (Llanelli) 1954 *I, F, S*, 1955 *S, I, F*,

1956 *E, S, I,* 1957 *E, S, I, F,* 1958 *A, E, S, I, F,* 1959 *E, S, I, F,* 1960 *E*
Williams, S (Llanelli) 1947 *E, S, F, I,* 1948 *S, F*
Williams, S A (Aberavon) 1939 *E, S, I*
Williams, T (Pontypridd) 1882 *I*
Williams, T (Swansea) 1888 *S, I*
Williams, T (Swansea) 1912 *I,* 1913 *F,* 1914 *E, S, F, I*
Williams, Tudor (Swansea) 1921 *F*
Williams, T G (Cross Keys) 1935 *S, I, NZ,* 1936 *E, S, I,* 1937 *S, I*
Williams, W A (Crumlin) 1927 *E, S, F, I*
Williams, W A (Newport) 1952 *I, F,* 1953 *E*
Williams, W E O (Cardiff) 1887 *S, I,* 1889 *S,* 1890 *S, E*
Williams, W H (Pontymister) 1900 *E, S, I,* 1901 *E*
Williams, W O G (Swansea, Devonport Services) 1951 *F, SA,* 1952 *E, S, I, F,* 1953 *E, S, I, F, NZ,* 1954 *E, I, F, S,* 1955 *E, S, I, F,* 1956 *E, S, I*
Williams, W P J (Neath) 1974 *I, F*
Williams-Jones, H (S Wales Police) 1989 *S*(R), 1990 *F*(R), *I,* 1991 *A,* 1992 *S, A,* 1993 *E, S, I, F*
Willis, W R (Cardiff) 1950 *E, S, I, F,* 1951 *E, S, I, F, SA,* 1952 *E, S,* 1953 *S, NZ,* 1954 *E, I, F, S,* 1955 *E, S, I, F*

Wiltshire, M L (Aberavon) 1967 *NZ,* 1968 *E, S, F*
Windsor, R W (Pontypool) 1973 *A,* 1974 *S, I, F, E,* 1975 *F, E, S, I, A,* 1976 *E, S, I, F,* 1977 *I, F, E, S,* 1978 *E, S, I, F, A* 1,2, *NZ,* 1979 *S, I, F*
Winfield, H B (Cardiff) 1903 *I,* 1904 *E, S, I,* 1905 *NZ,* 1906 *E, S, I,* 1907 *S, I,* 1908 *E, S, F, I, A*
Winmill, S (Cross Keys) 1921 *E, S, F, I*
Wintle, R V (London Welsh) 1988 *WS*(R)
Wooller, W (Sale, Cambridge U, Cardiff) 1933 *E, S, I,* 1935 *E, S, I, NZ,* 1936 *E, S, I,* 1937 *E, S, I,* 1938 *S, I,* 1939 *E, S, I*
Wyatt, M A (Swansea) 1983 *E, S, I, F,* 1984 *A,* 1985 *S, I,* 1987 *E, S, I*

Young, D (Swansea, Cardiff) 1987 [*E, NZ*], *US,* 1988 *E, S, I, F, NZ* 1,2, *WS, R,* 1989 *S, NZ,* 1990 *F*
Young, G A (Cardiff) 1886 *E, S*
Young, J (Harrogate, RAF, London Welsh) 1968 *S, I, F,* 1969 *S, I, F, E, NZ* 1, 1970 *E, I, F,* 1971 *E, S, I, F,* 1972 *E, S, F, NZ,* 1973 *E, S, I, F*

WELSH INTERNATIONAL RECORDS

Both team and individual records are for official Welsh international matches up to 31 March 1993.

TEAM RECORDS

Highest score
49 v France (49-14) 1910 Swansea
v individual countries
16 v Argentina (16-7) 1991 Cardiff
28 v Australia (28-3) 1975 Cardiff
40 v Canada (40-9) 1987 Invercargill
34 v England (34-21) 1967 Cardiff
49 v France (49-14) 1910 Swansea
40 v Fiji (40-3) 1985 Cardiff
34 v Ireland (34-9) 1976 Dublin
34 v Namibia (34-30) 1990 Windhoek
16 v N Zealand (16-19) 1972 Cardiff
 9 v Romania (9-15) 1988 Cardiff
35 v Scotland (35-12) 1972 Cardiff
 6 v S Africa (6-6) 1970 Cardiff
29 v Tonga (29-16) 1987 Palmerston North
46 v United States (46-0) 1987 Cardiff
32 v W Samoa (32-14) 1986 Apia

Biggest winning points margin
46 v United States (46-0) 1987 Cardiff
v individual countries
 9 v Argentina (16-7) 1991 Cardiff
25 v Australia (28-3) 1975 Cardiff
31 v Canada (40-9) 1987 Invercargill
25 v England (25-0) 1905 Cardiff
42 v France (47-5) 1909 Colombes
37 v Fiji (40-3) 1985 Cardiff
29 v Ireland (29-0) 1907 Cardiff
 9 v Namibia (18-9) 1990 Windhoek

 5 v N Zealand (13-8) 1953 Cardiff
23 v Scotland (35-12) 1972 Cardiff
13 v Tonga (29-16) 1987 Palmerston North
46 v United States (46-0) 1987 Cardiff
22 v W Samoa (28-6) 1988 Cardiff
No wins v Romania or South Africa

Highest score by opposing team
63 Australia (6-63) 1991 Brisbane
v individual countries
 7 Argentina (16-7) 1991 Cardiff
63 Australia (6-63) 1991 Brisbane
 9 Canada (40-9) 1987 Invercargill
34 England (6-34) 1990 Twickenham
36 France (3-36) 1991 Paris
15 Fiji (22-15) 1986 Suva
21 Ireland { (24-21) 1979 Cardiff
(7-21) 1980 Dublin
(9-21) 1985 Cardiff
(21-21) 1991 Cardiff
30 Namibia (34-30) 1990 Windhoek
54 N Zealand (9-54) 1988 Auckland
24 Romania (6-24) 1983 Bucharest
35 Scotland (10-35) 1924 Inverleith
24 S Africa (3-24) 1964 Durban
16 Tonga (29-16) 1987 Palmerston North
 0 United States (46-0) 1987 Cardiff
16 W Samoa (13-16) 1991 Cardiff

Biggest losing points margin
57 v Australia (6-63) 1991 Brisbane
v individual countries
57 v Australia (6-63) 1991 Brisbane
28 v England (6-34) 1990 Twickenham
33 v France (3-36) 1991 Paris
16 v Ireland (3-19) 1925 Belfast
49 v N Zealand (3-52) 1988 Christchurch
18 v Romania (6-24) 1983 Bucharest
25 v Scotland (10-35) 1924 Inverleith
21 v S Africa (3-24) 1964 Durban
3 v W Samoa (13-16) 1991 Cardiff
No defeats v Argentina, Canada, Fiji, Namibia, Tonga or United States

Most tries by Wales in an international
11 v France (47-5) 1909 Colombes

Most tries against Wales in an international
13 by England 1881 Blackheath

Most points by Wales in International Championship in a season – 102
in season 1975-76

Most tries by Wales in International Championship in a season – 21
in season 1909-10

INDIVIDUAL RECORDS

Most capped player
J P R Williams 55 1969-81
in individual positions
Full-back
J P R Williams 54(55)[1] 1969-81
Wing
K J Jones 44[2] 1947-57
Centre
S P Fenwick 30[3] 1975-81
Fly-half
C I Morgan 29[3] 1951-58
Scrum-half
G O Edwards 53 1967-78
Prop
G Price 41 1975-83
Hooker
B V Meredith 34 1954-62

Lock
A J Martin 34 1973-81
R L Norster 34 1982-89
Flanker
W D Morris 32(34)[4] 1967-74
No 8
T M Davies 38 1969-76

[1]*Williams won one cap as a flanker*
[2]*T G R Davies, 46 caps, won 35 as a wing, 11 as a centre*
[3]*M G Ring, 32 caps, won 27 at centre, 4 at fly-half and 1 as a full-back. P Bennett, 29 caps, played 25 times as a fly-half*
[4]*Morris won his first two caps as a No 8*

Longest international career
W J Trew
14 seasons 1899-1900 to 1912-13
T H Vile
14 seasons 1907-08   to 1920-21
H Tanner
14 seasons 1935-36   to 1948-49

Most consecutive Tests – 53★
G O Edwards 1967-78
★*entire career*

Most internationals as captain – 18
A J Gould 1889-97

Most points in internationals – 304
P H Thorburn (37 matches) 1985-91

Most points in International Championship in a season – 52
P H Thorburn (4 matches) 1985-86

Most points in an international – 21
P H Thorburn v Barbarians 1990 Cardiff

Most tries in internationals – 20
G O Edwards (53 matches) 1967-78
T G R Davies (46 matches) 1966-78

Most tries in International Championship in a season – 6
R A Gibbs (4 matches) 1907-08
M C R Richards (4 matches) 1968-69

Most tries in an international – 4
W M Llewellyn* v England 1899 Swansea
R A Gibbs v France 1908 Cardiff
M C R Richards v England 1969 Cardiff
I C Evans v Canada 1987 Invercargill
on first appearance

Most conversions in internationals – 43
P H Thorburn (37 matches) 1985-91

**Most conversions in International
Championship in a season – 11**
J Bancroft (4 matches) 1908-09

Most conversions in an international – 8
J Bancroft v France 1910 Swansea

Most dropped goals in internationals – 13
J Davies (27 matches) 1985-88

Most penalty goals in internationals – 70
P H Thorburn (37 matches) 1985-91

**Most penalty goals in International
Championship in a season – 16**
P H Thorburn (4 matches) 1985-86

Most penalty goals in an international – 6
G Evans v France 1982 Cardiff

Most points on major overseas tour – 64
M Rayer (3 matches) Namibia 1990

Most points in a tour match – 28
M Rayer v N Region 1990 Namibia
*P Bennett scored 34 points v Japan in Tokyo in 1975, but
this was not on a major tour*

Most tries in a tour match – 3
M C R Richards v Otago 1969 Dunedin,
    NZ
S Fealey v Welwitschia 1990 Swakop-
    mund, Namibia
Several others have scored 3 in matches on non-major tours

THE FIVE NATIONS CHAMPIONS SPEAK FOR THEIR SPORT

THE 1992-93 SEASON IN FRANCE
Bob Donahue *International Herald Tribune*

You could never let your attention wander from France this season: not just because France won the first Five Nations Championship trophy – although winning the Championship is always a big achievement – but because of the angry gloom that darkened the season from start to finish. Maybe this discontent was a purely French matter, a passing Gallic mood. Or maybe it reflects on the game at large.

Since Championship play resumed in 1947 after the war, the French have earned 227 Championship points, the Welsh 217, the English 188, the Irish 155, the Scots 149 (the total is 4 points short of 940 because two matches were missed in 1972). And France have scored 329 tries, Wales 296, England 243, Scotland 218, Ireland 216.

The French are uncontestably the leading Northern Hemisphere rugby power of the modern era. It was appropriate that they should represent the hemisphere in 1987 in the final of the first World Cup. Appropriate, too, that they should now take the first Five Nations trophy.

One might think that this fine record would instil an underlying confidence in French hearts, a sage disposition to shrug off occasional adversity and get on with striving to be world class. But no. Home defeats against South Africa and Argentina early in the season were greeted like ominous calamities.

The rather listless performance against Naas Botha's boring Springboks in Lyons was followed in Paris by emphatic French victory in the Second Test. It was an historic First Test defeat of South Africa in France, yet it caused little pleasure. Anyway, underestimated Argentina soon won an historic First Test victory in France themselves with seven penalty goals against three French tries, whereupon the French rugby establishment pretty much blew apart.

Robert Paparemborde, vice-president and lurking opposition leader, announced that he was sacking the coaches, Pierre Berbizier and Christophe Mombet. President Bernard Lapasset, by no means secure at the helm, called an emergency committee meeting to defeat Paparemborde, who withdrew as general manager of the various national squads. Jacques Fouroux continued to await his hour.

There are simple explanations to advance for the patchy start to the international season. The French are never at their best in October and November, and the 12 months from mid-July 1991 to mid-July 1992 had seen a French record of 14 Tests played. Three more Tests in the autumn were overtime labour for some of the players.

France used 38 men in the ten tests of 1992, 14 of them new caps. Berbizier had been trying to build a squad for the 1995 World Cup.

The France team which played Ireland at Lansdowne Road. L-R, back row: L Seigne, J-F Tordo (capt), L Armary, L Cabannes, P Benetton, M Cecillon, A Benazzi, O Roumat; front row: P Saint-André, P Sella, A Hueber, D Camberabero, T Lacroix, J-B Lafond, P Hontas.

Now Paparemborde's failed coup resulted in a revival of old-fashioned rule by selection committee, with Guy Laporte in the chair. Berbizier was no longer running the show alone, and Laporte's mandate from Lapasset was clear: forget 1995 and get me some wins in the Championship.

Out went Alain Penaud, France's young equivalent of Stuart Barnes, and back in came Didier Camberabero to face England. Whereas the team against Argentina had boasted 217 previous caps (83 of them belonging to Philippe Sella alone), the total against Wales by the end of the Championship was 407 caps (88 for Sella). Rebuilding for 1995 had been put off to the summer tour of South Africa.

At Twickenham, lo and behold, France almost won. The aim was simply not to look ridiculous. Bad luck with the posts cost a Grand Slam, as it later turned out, but hardly anyone talked about luck. There was great relief to have done well (and also an intriguing question: why, since 1980, have France fared better against England at Twickenham than at home in Paris?).

French luck turned, and the Scots, with less self-belief than they deserved, managed to lose in Paris as usual. Defence (France's included) was by now emerging as the salient feature of the 1993 Championship. But French opinion, resolutely liverish, was scandalised that Jeff Tordo's team should score only one try at the Parc des Princes. Players and officials promised to do much better in Dublin. Alas, a 21-6 victory against the Irish and the elements (including Sella's 27th Test try), did no good.

All of this helps to explain why the Parc des Princes crowd whistled derisively near the end of the Welsh match in Paris. Winning, even winning comfortably, was not enough. Where was French flair?

Hand-wringers at the sickbed of rugby moaned about semi-professionalism; about win-at-all-costs tactics that kill off flair; about too heavy demands on senior players; about the insufferable and never-ending cat-fight for power in the upper reaches of the Federation; about the law changes; about the Southern Hemisphere powers being streets ahead of Europe.

Amid all the noise, quiet discipline was one key to France's first success in the Championship since 1989. A little bit more of it, enough to have averted just one of Jonathan Webb's three penalty goals, could have meant a French Grand Slam.

Abdel Benazzi at lock and flanker Philippe Benetton were the revelations of the season, but problems remained at Nos 8, 9, 10, 11, and 15. Two old-style props did well in the Championship but seemed unsuited to the Australian era. Tordo, whose captaincy began against Argentina, looked a serviceable hooker, but needed to learn to throw in at the line-out so as to free up his scrum-half. Rebuilding in 1975 in South Africa cost painful defeats there but produced the great French team of 1976 and 1977. Will history repeat itself in 1993-94?

FRENCH INTERNATIONAL PLAYERS
(up to 31 March 1993)

ABBREVIATIONS

A – Australia; *Arg* – Argentina; *B* – British Forces and Home Union Teams; *C* – Canada; *Cz* – Czechoslovakia; *E* – England; *Fj* – Fiji; *G* – Germany; *I* – Ireland; *It* – Italy; *J* – Japan; *K* – New Zealand Services; *M* – Maoris; *NZ* – New Zealand; *R* – Romania; *S* – Scotland; *SA* – South Africa; *US* – United States of America; *W* – Wales; *Z* – Zimbabwe; (R) – Replacement. Entries in square brackets [ ] indicate appearances in the World Cup.

Club Abbreviations: ASF – Association Sportive Française; BEC – Bordeaux Etudiants Club; CASG – Club Athlétique des Sports Généraux; PUC – Paris Université Club; RCF – Racing Club de France; SB – Stade Bordelais; SBUC – Stade Bordelais Université Club; SCUF – Sporting Club Universitaire de France; SF – Stade Français; SOE – Stade Olympien des Etudiants; TOEC – Toulouse Olympique Employés Club.

Note: Years given for Five Nations' matches are for second half of season, eg 1972 refers to season 1971-72. Years for all other matches refer to the actual year of the match. When a series has taken place, or more than one match has been played against a country in the same year, figures have been used to denote the particular matches in which players have featured. Thus 1967 *SA* 2,4 indicates that a player appeared in the second and fourth Tests of the 1967 series against South Africa. This list includes only those players who have appeared in FFR International Matches '*donnant droit au titre d'international*'.

Abadie, A (Pau) 1964 *I*
Abadie, A (Graulhet) 1965 *R*, 1967 *SA* 1,3,4, *NZ*, 1968 *S*, *I*
Abadie, L (Tarbes) 1963 *R*
Aguerre, R (Biarritz O) 1979 *S*
Aguilar, D (Pau) 1937 *G*
Aguirre, J-M (Bagnères) 1971 *A* 2, 1972 *S*, 1973 *W*, *I*, *J*, *R*, 1974 *I*, *W*, *Arg* 2, *R*, *SA* 1, 1976 *W* (R), *E*, *US*, *A* 2, *R*, 1977 *W*, *E*, *S*, *I*, *Arg* 1,2, *NZ* 1,2, *R*, 1978 *E*, *S*, *I*, *W*, *R*, 1979 *I*, *W*, *E*, *S*, *NZ* 1,2, *R*, 1980 *W*, *I*
Ainciart, E (Bayonne) 1933 *G*, 1934 *G*, 1935 *G*, 1937 *G*, *It*, 1938 *G* 1
Albaladejo, P (Dax) 1954 *E*, *It*, 1960 *W*, *I*, *It*, *R*, 1961 *S*, *SA*, *E*, *W*, *I*, *NZ* 1,2, *A*, 1962 *S*, *E*, *W*, *I*, 1963 *S*, *I*, *E*, *W*, *It*, 1964 *S*, *NZ*, *W*, *It*, *I*, *SA*, *Fj*
Alvarez, A-J (Tyrosse) 1945 *B* 2, 1946 *B*, *I*, *K*, *W*, 1947 *S*, *I*, *W*, *E*, 1948 *I*, *A*, *S*, *W*, *E*, 1949 *I*, *E*, *W*, 1951 *S*, *E*, *W*
Amand, H (SF) 1906 *NZ*
Ambert, A (Toulouse) 1930 *S*, *I*, *E*, *G*, *W*
Amestoy, J-B (Mont-de-Marsan) 1964 *NZ*, *E*
André, G (RCF) 1913 *SA*, *E*, *W*, *I*, 1914 *I*, *W*, *E*
Andrieu, M (Nîmes) 1986 *Arg* 2, *NZ* 1, *R* 2, *NZ* 2, 1987 [*R*, *Z*], *R*, 1988 *E*, *S*, *I*, *W*, *Arg* 1,2,3,4, *R*, 1989 *I*, *W*, *E*, *S*, *NZ* 2, *B*, *A* 2, 1990 *W*, *E*, *I*(R)
Anduran, J (SCUF) 1910 *W*
Araou, R (Narbonne) 1924 *R*
Arcalis, R (Brive) 1950 *S*, *I*, 1951 *I*, *E*, *W*
Arino, M (Agen) 1962 *R*
Aristouy, P (Pau) 1948 *S*, 1949 *Arg* 2, 1950 *S*, *I*, *E*, *W*
Armary, L (Lourdes) 1987 [*R*], *R*, 1988 *S*, *I*, *W*, *Arg* 3,4, *R*, 1989 *W*, *S*, *A* 1,2, 1990 *W*, *E*, *S*, *I*, *A* 1,2,3, *NZ* 1, 1991 *W*2, 1992 *S*, *I*, *R*, *Arg* 1,2, *SA* 1,2, *Arg*, 1993 *E*, *S*, *I*, *W*
Arnal, J-M (RCF) 1914 *I*, *W*
Arnaudet, M (Lourdes) 1964 *I*, 1967 *It*, *W*
Arotca, R (Bayonne) 1938 *R*
Arrieta, J (SF) 1953 *E*, *W*
Arthapignet, P (see Harislur-Arthapignet)
Astre, R (Béziers) 1971 *R*, 1972 *I* 1, 1973 *E* (R), 1975 *E*, *S*, *I*, *SA* 1,2, *Arg* 2, 1976 *A* 2, *R*
Augé, J (Dax) 1929 *S*, *W*
Augras-Fabre, L (Agen) 1931 *I*, *S*, *W*
Averous, J-L (La Voulte) 1975 *S*, *I*, *SA* 1,2, 1976 *I*, *W*, *E*, *US*, *A* 1,2, *R*, 1977 *W*, *E*, *S*, *I*, *Arg* 1, *R*, 1978 *E*, *S*, *I*, 1979 *NZ* 1,2, 1980 *E*, *S*, 1981 *A* 2
Azarete, J-L (Dax, St Jean-de-Luz) 1969 *W*, *R*, 1970 *S*, *I*, *W*, *R*, 1971 *S*, *I*, *E*, *SA* 1,2, *A* 1, 1972 *E*, *W*, *I* 2, *A* 1, *R*, 1973 *NZ*, *W*, *I*, *R*, 1974 *I*, *R*, *SA* 1,2, 1975 *W*

Bader, E (Primevères) 1926 *M*, 1927 *I*, *S*
Badin, C (Chalon) 1973 *W*, 1975 *Arg* 1
Baillette, M (Perpignan) 1925 *I*, *NZ*, *S*, 1926 *W*, *M*, 1927 *I*, *W*, *G* 2, 1929 *G*, 1930 *S*, *I*, *E*, *G*, 1931 *I*, *S*, *E*, 1932 *G*
Baladie, G (Agen) 1945 *B* 1,2, *W*, 1946 *B*, *I*, *K*
Ballarin, J (Tarbes) 1924 *E*, 1925 *NZ*, *S*

Baquey, J (Toulouse) 1921 *I*
Barbazanges, A (Roanne) 1932 *G*, 1933 *G*
Barrau, M (Beaumont, Toulouse) 1971 *S*, *E*, *W*, 1972 *E*, *W*, *A* 1,2, 1973 *S*, *NZ*, *E*, *I*, *J*, *R*, 1974 *I*, *S*
Barrère, P (Toulon) 1929 *G*, 1931 *W*
Barrière, R (Béziers) 1960 *R*
Barthe, E (SBUC) 1925 *W*, *E*
Barthe, J (Lourdes) 1954 *Arg* 1,2, 1955 *S*, 1956 *I*, *W*, *It*, *E*, *Cz*, 1957 *S*, *I*, *E*, *W*, *R* 1,2, 1958 *S*, *E*, *A*, *W*, *It*, *I*, *SA* 1,2, 1959 *S*, *E*, *It*, *W*
Basauri, R (Albi) 1954 *Arg* 1
Bascou, P (Bayonne) 1914 *E*
Basquet, G (Agen) 1945 *W*, 1946 *B*, *I*, *K*, *W*, 1947 *S*, *I*, *W*, *E*, 1948 *I*, *A*, *S*, *W*, *E*, 1949 *S*, *I*, *E*, *W*, *Arg* 1, 1950 *S*, *I*, *E*, *W*, 1951 *S*, *I*, *E*, *W*, 1952 *S*, *I*, *SA*, *W*, *E*, *It*
Bastiat, J-P (Dax) 1969 *R*, 1970 *S*, *I*, *W*, 1971 *S*, *I*, *SA* 2, 1972 *S*, *A* 1, 1973 *E*, 1974 *Arg* 1,2, *SA* 2, 1975 *W*, *Arg* 1,2, *R*, 1976 *S*, *I*, *W*, *E*, *A* 1,2, *R*, 1977 *W*, *E*, *S*, *I*, 1978 *E*, *S*, *I*, *W*
Baudry, N (Montferrand) 1949 *S*, *I*, *W*, *Arg* 1,2
Baulon, R (Vienne, Bayonne) 1954 *S*, *NZ*, *W*, *E*, *It*, 1955 *I*, *E*, *W*, *It*, 1956 *S*, *I*, *W*, *It*, *E*, *Cz*, 1957 *S*, *I*, *It*
Baux, J-P (Lannemezan) 1968 *NZ* 1,2, *SA* 1,2
Bavozet, J (Lyon) 1911 *S*, *E*, *W*
Bayard, J (Toulouse) 1923 *S*, *W*, *E*, 1924 *W*, *R*, *US*
Bayardon, J (Chalon) 1964 *S*, *NZ*, *E*
Beaurin-Gressier, C (SF) 1907 *E*, 1908 *E*
Bégu, J (Dax) 1982 *Arg* 2 (R), 1984 *E*, *S*
Béguerie, C (Agen) 1979 *NZ* 1
Beguet, L (RCF) 1922 *I*, 1923 *S*, *W*, *E*, *I*, 1924 *S*, *I*, *E*, *R*, *US*
Behoteguy, A (Bayonne, Cognac) 1923 *E*, 1924 *S*, *I*, *E*, *W*, *R*, *US*, 1926 *E*, 1927 *E*, *G* 1,2, 1928 *A*, *I*, *E*, *G*, *W*, 1929 *S*, *W*, *E*
Behoteguy, H (RCF, Cognac) 1923 *W*, 1928 *A*, *I*, *E*, *G*, *W*
Belascain, C (Bayonne) 1977 *R*, 1978 *E*, *S*, *I*, *W*, *R*, 1979 *I*, *W*, *E*, *S*, 1982 *W*, *E*, *S*, *I*, 1983 *E*, *S*, *I*, *W*
Belletante, G (Nantes) 1951 *I*, *E*, *W*
Benazzi, A (Agen) 1990 *A* 1,2,3, *NZ* 1,2, 1991 *E*, *US*1(R),2, [*R*, *Fj*, *C*], 1992 *SA* 1(R),2, *Arg*, 1993 *E*, *S*, *I*, *W*
Bénésis, R (Narbonne) 1969 *W*, *R*, 1970 *S*, *I*, *W*, *E*, *R*, 1971 *S*, *I*, *E*, *W*, *A* 2, *R*, 1972 *S*, *I* 1, *E*, *W*, *I* 2, *A* 1, *R*, 1973 *NZ*, *E*, *W*, *I*, *J*, *R*, 1974 *I*, *W*, *E*, *S*
Benetière, J (Roanne) 1954 *I*, *Arg* 1
Benetton, P (Agen) 1989 *B*, 1990 *NZ* 2, 1991 *US*2, 1992 *Arg* 1,2(R), *SA* 1(R),2, *Arg*, 1993 *E*, *S*, *I*, *W*
Berbizier, P (Lourdes, Agen) 1981 *S*, *I*, *W*, *E*, *NZ* 1,2, 1982 *I*, *R*, 1983 *S*, *I*, 1984 *S* (R), *NZ* 1,2, 1985 *Arg* 1,2, 1986 *S*, *I*, *W*, *E*, *R* 1, *Arg* 1, *A*, *NZ* 1, *R* 2, *NZ* 2,3, 1987 *W*, *E*, *S*, *I*, [*S*, *R*, *Fj*, *A*, *NZ*], *R*, 1988 *E*, *S*, *I*, *W*, *Arg* 1,2, 1989 *I*, *W*, *E*, *S*, *NZ* 1,2, *B*, *A* 1, 1990 *W*, *E*, 1991 *S*, *I*, *W*1, *E*
Berejnoi, J-C (Tulle) 1963 *R*, 1964 *S*, *W*, *It*, *I*, *SA*, *Fj*, *R*, 1965 *S*, *I*, *E*, *W*, *It*, *R*, 1966 *S*, *I*, *E*, *W*, *It*, *R*, 1967 *S*, *A*, *E*, *It*, *W*, *I*, *R*

Berges, B (Toulouse) 1926 *I*
Berges-Cau, R (Lourdes) 1976 *E* (R)
Bergese, F (Bayonne) 1936 *G* 2, 1937 *G*, *It*, 1938 *G* 1, *R*, *G* 2
Bergougnan, Y (Toulouse) 1945 *B* 1, *W*, 1946 *B*, *I*, *K*, *W*, 1947 *S*, *I*, *W*, *E*, 1948 *S*, *W*, *E*, 1949 *S*, *E*, *Arg* 1,2
Bernard, R (Bergerac) 1951 *S*, *I*, *E*, *W*
Bernat-Salles, P (Pau) 1992 *Arg*
Bernon, J (Lourdes) 1922 *I*, 1923 *S*
Bérot, J-L (Toulouse) 1968 *NZ* 3, *A*, 1969 *S*, *I*, 1970 *E*, *R*, 1971 *S*, *I*, *E*, *W*, *SA* 1,2, *A* 1,2, *R*, 1972 *S*, *I* 1, *E*, *W*, *A* 1, 1974 *I*
Bérot, P (Agen) 1986 *R* 2, *NZ* 2,3, 1987 *W*, *E*, *S*, *I*, *R*, 1988 *E*, *S*, *I*, *Arg* 1,2,3,4, *R*, 1989 *S*, *NZ* 1,2
Bertrand, P (Bourg) 1951 *I*, *E*, *W*, 1953 *S*, *I*, *E*, *W*, *It*
Bertranne, R (Bagnères) 1971 *E*, *W*, *SA* 2, *A* 1,2, 1972 *S*, *I* 1, 1973 *NZ*, *E*, *J*, *R*, 1974 *I*, *W*, *E*, *S*, *Arg* 1,2, *R*, *SA* 1,2, 1975 *W*, *E*, *S*, *I*, *SA* 1,2, *Arg* 1,2, *R*, 1976 *S*, *I*, *W*, *E*, *US*, *A* 1,2, *R*, 1977 *W*, *E*, *S*, *I*, *Arg* 1,2, *NZ* 1,2, *R*, 1978 *E*, *S*, *I*, *W*, *R*, 1979 *I*, *W*, *E*, *S*, *R*, 1980 *W*, *E*, *S*, *I*, *SA*, *R*, 1981 *S*, *I*, *W*, *E*, *R*, *NZ* 1,2
Berty, D (Toulouse) 1990 *NZ* 2, 1992 *R*(R)
Besset, E (Grenoble) 1924 *S*
Besset, L (SCUF) 1914 *W*, *E*
Besson, M (CASG) 1924 *I*, 1925 *I*, *E*, 1926 *S*, *W*, 1927 *I*
Besson, P (Brive) 1963 *S*, *I*, *E*, 1965 *R*, 1968 *SA* 1
Bianchi, J (Toulon) 1986 *Arg* 1
Bichindaritz, J (Biarritz O) 1954 *It*, *Arg* 1,2
Bidart, L (La Rochelle) 1953 *W*
Biemouret, P (Agen) 1969 *E*, *W*, 1970 *I*, *W*, *E*, 1971 *W*, *SA* 1,2, *A* 1, 1972 *E*, *W*, *I* 2, *A* 2, *R*, 1973 *S*, *NZ*, *E*, *W*, *I*
Biénès, R (Cognac) 1950 *S*, *I*, *E*, *W*, 1951 *S*, *I*, *E*, *W*, 1952 *S*, *I*, *SA*, *W*, *E*, *It*, 1953 *S*, *I*, *E*, 1954 *S*, *I*, *NZ*, *W*, *E*, *Arg* 1,2, 1956 *S*, *I*, *W*, *It*, *E*
Bigot, C (Quillan) 1930 *S*, *E*, 1931 *I*, *S*
Bilbao, L (St Jean de Luz) 1978 *I*, 1979 *I*
Billac, E (Bayonne) 1920 *S*, *E*, *W*, *I*, *US*, 1921 *S*, *W*, 1922 *W*, 1923 *E*
Billière, M (Toulouse) 1968 *NZ* 3
Bioussa, A (Toulouse) 1924 *W*, *US*, 1925 *I*, *NZ*, *S*, *E*, 1926 *S*, *I*, *E*, 1928 *E*, *G*, *W*, 1929 *I*, *S*, *W*, *E*, 1930 *S*, *I*, *E*, *G*, *W*
Bioussa, C (Toulouse) 1913 *W*, *I*, 1914 *I*
Biraben, M (Dax) 1920 *W*, *I*, *US*, 1921 *S*, *W*, *E*, *I*, 1922 *S*, *E*, *I*
Blain, A (Carcassonne) 1934 *G*
Blanco, S (Biarritz O) 1980 *SA*, *R*, 1981 *S*, *W*, *E*, *A* 1, 2, *R*, *NZ* 1,2, 1982 *W*, *E*, *S*, *I*, *R*, *Arg* 1,2, 1983 *E*, *S*, *I*, *W*, 1984 *I*, *W*, *E*, *S*, *NZ* 1,2, *R*, 1985 *E*, *S*, *I*, *W*, *Arg* 1,2, 1986 *S*, *I*, *W*, *E*, *R* 1, *Arg* 2, *A*, *NZ* 1, *R* 2, *NZ* 2,3, 1987 *W*, *E*, *S*, *I*, [*S*, *R*, *Fj*, *A*, *NZ*], *R*, 1988 *E*, *S*, *I*, *W*, *Arg* 1,2,3,4, *R*, 1989 *I*, *W*, *E*, *S*, *NZ* 1,2, *B*, *A* 1, 1990 *E*, *S*, *I*, *A* 1,2,3, *NZ* 1,2, 1991 *S*, *I*, *W*1, *E*, *R*, *US*1,2, *W*2, [*R*, *Fj*, *C*, *E*]
Blond, J (SF) 1935 *G*, 1936 *G* 2, 1937 *G*, 1938 *G* 1, *R*, *G* 2
Blond, X (RCF) 1990 *A* 3, 1991 *S*, *I*, *W*1, *E*
Boffelli, V (Aurillac) 1971 *A* 2, *R*, 1972 *S*, *I* 1, 1973 *J*, *R*, 1974 *I*, *W*, *E*, *S*, *Arg* 1,2, *R*, *SA* 1,2, 1975 *W*, *S*, *I*
Bonal, J-M (Toulouse) 1968 *E*, *W*, *Cz*, *NZ* 2,3, *SA* 1, 2, *R*, 1969 *S*, *I*, *E*, *R*, 1970 *W*, *E*
Bonamy, R (SB) 1928 *A*, *I*
Boniface, A (Mont-de-Marsan) 1954 *I*, *NZ*, *W*, *E*, *It*, *Arg* 1,2, 1955 *S*, *I*, 1956 *S*, *I*, *W*, *It*, *Cz*, 1957 *S*, *I*, *W*, *R* 2, 1958 *S*, *E*, 1959 *E*, 1961 *NZ* 1,3, *A*, *R*, 1962 *E*, *W*, *I*, *It*, *R*, 1963 *S*, *I*, *E*, *W*, *It*, *R*, 1964 *S*, *NZ*, *E*, *W*, *It*, 1965 *W*, *It*, *R*, 1966 *S*, *I*, *E*, *W*
Boniface, G (Mont-de-Marsan) 1960 *W*, *I*, *It*, *R*, *Arg* 1, 2,3, 1961 *S*, *SA*, *E*, *W*, *It*, *I*, *NZ* 1,2,3, *R*, 1962 *R*, 1963 *S*, *I*, *E*, *W*, *It*, *R*, 1964 *S*, 1965 *S*, *I*, *E*, *W*, *It*, *R*, 1966 *S*, *I*, *E*, *W*
Bonnes, E (Narbonne) 1924 *W*, *R*, *US*
Bonneval, E (Toulouse) 1984 *NZ* 2 (R), 1985 *W*, *Arg* 1, 1986 *W*, *E*, *Arg* 1,2, *A*, *R* 2, *NZ* 2,3, 1987 *W*, *E*, *S*, *I*, [*Z*], 1988 *E*
Bonnus, F (Toulon) 1950 *S*, *I*, *E*, *W*
Bonnus, M (Toulon) 1937 *It*, 1938 *G* 1, *R*, *G* 2, 1940 *B*
Bontemps, D (La Rochelle) 1968 *SA* 2
Borchard, G (RCF) 1908 *E*, 1909 *E*, *W*, *I*, 1911 *I*
Borde, F (RCF) 1920 *I*, *US*, 1921 *S*, *W*, *E*, 1922 *S*, *W*, 1923 *S*, *I*, 1924 *E*, 1925 *I*, 1926 *E*
Bordenave, L (Toulon) 1948 *A*, *S*, *W*, *E*, 1949 *S*
Boubée, J (Tarbes) 1921 *S*, *E*, *I*, 1922 *E*, *W*, 1923 *E*, *I*,

1925 *NZ*, *S*
Boudreaux, R (SCUF) 1910 *W*, *S*
Bouet, D (Dax) 1989 *NZ* 1,2, *B*, *A* 2, 1990 *A* 3
Bouguyon, G (Grenoble) 1961 *SA*, *E*, *W*, *It*, *I*, *NZ* 1,2, 3, *A*
Boujet, C (Grenoble) 1968 *NZ* 2, *A* (R), *SA* 1
Bouquet, J (Bourgoin, Vienne) 1954 *S*, 1955 *E*, 1956 *S*, *I*, *W*, *It*, *E*, *Cz*, 1957 *S*, *E*, *W*, *R* 2, 1958 *S*, *E*, 1959 *S*, *It*, *W*, *I*, 1960 *S*, *E*, *W*, *I*, *R*, 1961 *S*, *SA*, *E*, *W*, *It*, *I*, *R*, 1962 *S*, *E*, *W*, *I*
Bourdeu, J R (Lourdes) 1952 *S*, *I*, *SA*, *W*, *E*, *It*, 1953 *S*, *I*, *E*
Bourgarel, R (Toulouse) 1969 *R*, 1970 *S*, *I*, *E*, *R*, 1971 *W*, *SA* 1,2, 1973 *E*
Bourguignon, G (Narbonne) 1988 *Arg* 3, 1989 *I*, *E*, *B*, *A* 1, 1990 *R*
Bousquet, A (Béziers) 1921 *E*, *I*, 1924 *R*
Bousquet, B (Albi) 1926 *M*, 1927 *I*, *S*, *W*, *E*, *G* 1, 1929 *W*, *E*, 1930 *W*
Boyau, M (SBUC) 1912 *I*, *S*, *W*, *E*, 1913 *W*, *I*
Boyer, P (Toulon) 1935 *G*
Branca, G (SF) 1928 *S*, 1929 *I*, *S*
Branlat, A (RCF) 1906 *NZ*, *E*, 1908 *W*
Brejassou, R (Tarbes) 1952 *S*, *I*, *SA*, *W*, *E*, 1953 *W*, *E*, 1954 *S*, *I*, *NZ*, 1955 *S*, *I*, *E*, *W*, *It*
Brethes, R (St Sever) 1960 *Arg* 2
Bringeon, A (Biarritz O) 1925 *W*
Brun, G (Vienne) 1950 *E*, *W*, 1951 *S*, *E*, *W*, 1952 *S*, *I*, *SA*, *W*, *E*, *It*, 1953 *E*, *W*, *It*
Bruneau, M (SBUC) 1910 *W*, *E*, 1913 *SA*, *E*
Brunet, Y (Perpignan) 1975 *SA* 1, 1977 *Arg* 1
Buchet, E (Nice) 1980 *R*, 1982 *E*, *R* (R), *Arg* 1,2
Buisson, H (see Empereur-Buisson)
Buonomo, Y (Béziers) 1971 *A* 2, *R*, 1972 *I* 1
Burgun, M (RCF) 1909 *I*, 1910 *W*, *S*, *I*, 1911 *S*, *E*, 1912 *I*, *S*, 1913 *S*, *E*, 1914 *E*
Bustaffa, D (Carcassonne) 1977 *Arg* 1,2, *NZ* 1,2, 1978 *W*, *R*, 1980 *W*, *E*, *S*, *SA*, *R*
Buzy, C-E (Lourdes) 1946 *K*, *W*, 1947 *S*, *I*, *W*, *E*, 1948 *I*, *A*, *S*, *W*, *E*, 1949 *S*, *I*, *E*, *W*, *Arg* 1,2

Cabanier, J-M (Montauban) 1963 *R*, 1964 *S*, *Fj*, 1965 *S*, *I*, *W*, *It*, *R*, 1966 *S*, *I*, *E*, *W*, *It*, *R*, 1967 *S*, *A*, *E*, *It*, *W*, *I*, *SA* 1,3, *NZ*, *R*, 1968 *S*, *I*
Cabannes, L (RCF) 1990 *NZ* 2(R), 1991 *S*, *I*, *W*1, *E*, *US*2, [*R*, *Fj*, *C*, *E*], 1992 *W*, *E*, *S*, *I*, *R*, *Arg* 2, *SA* 1,2, 1993 *E*, *S*, *I*, *W*
Cabrol, H (Béziers) 1972 *A* 1 (R), *A* 2, 1973 *J*, 1974 *SA* 2
Cadenat, J (SCUF) 1910 *S*, *E*, 1911 *W*, *I*, 1912 *W*, *E*, 1913 *I*
Cadieu, J-M (Toulouse) 1991 *R*, *US*1, [*R*, *Fj*, *C*, *E*], 1992 *W*, *I*, *R*, *Arg* 1,2, *SA* 1
Cahuc, F (St Girons) 1922 *S*
Cals, R (RCF) 1938 *G* 1
Calvo, G (Lourdes) 1961 *NZ* 1,3
Camberabero, D (La Voulte, Béziers) 1982 *R*, *Arg* 1,2, 1983 *E*, *W*, 1987 [*R*(R), *Z*, *Fj*(R), *A*, *NZ*], 1988 *I*, 1989 *B*, *A* 1, 1990 *W*, *S*, *I*, *R*, *A* 1,2,3, *NZ* 1,2, 1991 *S*, *I*, *W*1, *E*, *R*, *US*1,2, *W*2, [*R*, *Fj*, *C*], 1993 *E*, *S*, *I*
Camberabero, G (La Voulte) 1961 *NZ* 3, 1962 *R*, 1964 *R*, 1967 *A*, *E*, *It*, *W*, *I*, *SA* 1,3,4, 1968 *S*, *E*, *W*
Camberabero, L (La Voulte) 1964 *R*, 1965 *S*, *I*, 1966 *E*, *W*, 1967 *A*, *E*, *It*, *W*, *I*, 1968 *S*, *E*, *W*
Cambré, T (Oloron) 1920 *E*, *W*, *I*, *US*
Camel, A (Toulouse) 1928 *S*, *A*, *I*, *E*, *G*, *W*, 1929 *W*, *E*, *G*, 1930 *S*, *I*, *E*, *G*, *W*, 1935 *G*
Camel, M (Toulouse) 1929 *S*, *W*, *E*
Camicas, F (Tarbes) 1927 *G* 2, 1928 *S*, *I*, *E*, *G*, *W*, 1929 *I*, *S*, *W*, *E*
Camo, E (Villeneuve) 1931 *I*, *S*, *W*, *E*, *G*, 1932 *G*
Campaes, A (Lourdes) 1965 *W*, 1967 *NZ*, 1968 *S*, *I*, *E*, *W*, *Cz*, *NZ* 1,2, *A*, 1969 *S*, *W*, 1972 *R*, 1973 *NZ*
Cantoni, J (Béziers) 1970 *W*, *R*, 1971 *S*, *I*, *E*, *W*, *SA* 1, 2, *A* 1, *R*, 1972 *S*, *I* 1, 1973 *S*, *NZ*, *W*, *I*, 1975 *W* (R)
Capdouze, J (Pau) 1964 *SA*, *Fj*, *R*, 1965 *S*, *I*, *E*
Capendeguy, J-M (Begles) 1967 *NZ*, *R*
Capitani, P (Toulon) 1954 *Arg* 1,2
Capmau, J-L (Toulouse) 1914 *E*
Carabignac, G (Agen) 1951 *S*, *I*, 1952 *SA*, *W*, *E*, 1953 *S*, *I*
Carbonne, J (Perpignan) 1927 *W*
Carminati, A (Béziers) 1986 *R* 2, *NZ* 2, 1987 [*R*, *Z*], 1988 *I*, *W*, *Arg* 1,2, 1989 *I*, *W*, *S*, *NZ* 1(R),2, *A* 2, 1990 *S*

Caron, L (Lyon O, Castres) 1947 *E*, 1948 *I*, *A*, *W*, *E*, 1949 *S*, *I*, *E*, *W*, *Arg* 1
Carpentier, M (Lourdes) 1980 *E*, *SA*, *R*, 1981 *S*, *I*, *A* 1, 1982 *E*, *S*
Carrère, C (Toulon) 1966 *R*, 1967 *S*, *A*, *E*, *W*, *I*, *SA* 1, 3,4, *NZ*, *R*, 1968 *S*, *I*, *E*, *W*, *Cz*, *NZ* 3, *A*, *R*, 1969 *S*, *I*, 1970 *S*, *I*, *W*, *E*, 1971 *E*, *W*
Carrère, J (Vichy, Toulon) 1956 *S*, 1957 *E*, *W*, *R* 2, 1958 *S*, *SA* 1,2, 1959 *I*
Carrère, R (Mont-de-Marsan) 1953 *E*, *It*
Casaux, L (Tarbes) 1959 *I*, *It*, 1962 *S*
Cassagne, P (Pau) 1957 *It*
Cassayet-Armagnac, A (Tarbes, Narbonne) 1920 *S*, *E*, *W*, *US*, 1921 *W*, *E*, *I*, 1922 *S*, *E*, *W*, 1923 *S*, *W*, *E*, *I*, 1924 *S*, *E*, *W*, *R*, *US*, 1925 *I*, *NZ*, *S*, *W*, 1926 *S*, *I*, *E*, *W*, *M*, 1927 *I*, *S*, *W*
Cassiède, M (Dax) 1961 *NZ* 3, *A*, *R*
Castets, J (Toulon) 1923 *W*, *E*, *I*
Caujolle, J (Tarbes) 1909 *E*, 1913 *SA*, *E*, 1914 *W*, *E*
Caunègre, R (SB) 1938 *R*, *G* 2
Caussade, A (Lourdes) 1978 *R*, 1979 *I*, *W*, *E*, *NZ* 1,2, *R*, 1980 *W*, *E*, *S*, 1981 *S* (R), *I*
Caussarieu, G (Pau) 1929 *I*
Cayrefourcq, E (Tarbes) 1921 *E*
Cazals, P (Mont-de-Marsan) 1961 *NZ* 1, *A*, *R*
Cazenave, A (Pau) 1927 *E*, *G* 1, 1928 *S*, *A*, *G*
Cazenave, F (RCF) 1950 *E*, 1952 *S*, 1954 *I*, *NZ*, *W*, *E*
Cecillon, M (Bourgoin) 1988 *I*, *W*, *Arg* 2,3,4, *R*, 1989 *I*, *E*, *NZ* 1,2, *A* 1, 1991 *S*, *I*, *E* (R), *R*, *US*1, *W*2, [*E*], 1992 *W*, *E*, *S*, *I*, *R*, *Arg* 1,2, *SA* 1,2, 1993 *E*, *S*, *I*, *W*
Celaya, M (Biarritz O, SBUC) 1953 *E*, *W*, *It*, 1954 *I*, *E*, *It*, *Arg* 1,2, 1955 *S*, *I*, *E*, *W*, *It*, 1956 *S*, *I*, *W*, *It*, *E*, *Cz*, 1957 *S*, *I*, *E*, *W*, *R* 2, 1958 *S*, *E*, *A*, *W*, *It*, 1959 *S*, *E*, 1960 *S*, *E*, *W*, *I*, *R*, *Arg* 1,2,3, 1961 *S*, *SA*, *E*, *W*, *It*, *I*, *NZ* 1,2,3, *A*, *R*
Celhay, M (Bayonne) 1935 *G*, 1936 *G* 1, 1937 *G*, *It*, 1938 *G* 1, 1940 *B*
Cessieux, N (Lyon) 1906 *NZ*
Cester, E (TOEC, Valence) 1966 *S*, *I*, *E*, 1967 *W*, 1968 *S*, *I*, *E*, *W*, *Cz*, *NZ* 1,3, *A*, *SA* 1,2, *R*, 1969 *S*, *I*, *E*, *W*, 1970 *S*, *I*, *W*, *E*, 1971 *A* 1, 1972 *R*, 1973 *S*, *NZ*, *W*, *I*, *J*, *R*, 1974 *I*, *W*, *E*, *S*
Chaban-Delmas, J (CASG) 1945 *B* 2
Chabowski, H (Nice, Bourgoin) 1985 *Arg* 2, 1986 *R* 2, *NZ* 2, 1989 *B*(R)
Chadebech, P (Brive) 1982 *R*, *Arg* 1,2, 1986 *S*, *I*
Champ, E (Toulon) 1985 *Arg* 1,2, 1986 *I*, *W*, *E*, *R* 1, *Arg* 1,2, *A*, *NZ* 1, *R* 2, *NZ* 2,3, 1987 *W*, *E*, *S*, *I*, [*S*, *R*, *Fj*, *A*, *NZ*], *R*, 1988 *E*, *S*, *Arg* 1,3,4, *R*, 1989 *W*, *S*, *A* 1,2, 1990 *W*, *E*, *NZ* 1, 1991 *R*, *US*1, [*R*, *Fj*, *C*, *E*]
Chapuy, L (SF) 1926 *S*
Charpentier, G (SF) 1911 *E*, 1912 *W*, *E*
Charton, P (Montferrand) 1940 *B*
Charvet, D (Toulouse) 1986 *W*, *E*, *R* 1, *Arg* 1, *A*, *NZ* 1,3, 1987 *W*, *E*, *S*, *I*, [*S*, *R*, *Z*, *Fj*, *A*, *NZ*], *R*, 1989 *E*(R), 1990 *W*, *E*, 1991 *S*, *I*
Chassagne, J (Montferrand) 1938 *G* 1
Chatau, A (Bayonne) 1913 *SA*
Chaud, E (Toulon) 1932 *G*, 1934 *G*, 1935 *G*
Chenevay, C (Grenoble) 1968 *SA* 1
Chevallier, B (Montferrand) 1952 *S*, *I*, *SA*, *W*, *E*, *It*, 1953 *E*, *W*, *It*, 1954 *S*, *I*, *NZ*, *W*, *Arg* 1, 1955 *S*, *I*, *E*, *W*, *It*, 1956 *S*, *I*, *W*, *It*, *E*, *Cz*, 1957 *S*
Chiberry, J (Chambéry) 1955 *It*
Chilo, A (RCF) 1920 *S*, *W*, 1925 *I*, *NZ*
Cholley, G (Castres) 1975 *E*, *S*, *I*, *SA* 1,2, *Arg* 1,2, *R*, 1976 *S*, *I*, *W*, *E*, *A* 1,2, *R*, 1977 *W*, *E*, *S*, *I*, *Arg* 1,2, *NZ* 1,2, *R*, 1978 *E*, *S*, *I*, *W*, *R*, 1979 *I*, *S*
Choy, J (Narbonne) 1930 *S*, *I*, *E*, *G*, *W*, 1931 *I*, 1933 *G*, 1934 *G*, 1935 *G*, 1936 *G* 2
Cimarosti, J (Castres) 1976 *US* (R)
Clady, A (Lezignan) 1929 *G*, 1931 *I*, *S*, *E*, *G*
Clarac, H (St Girons) 1938 *G* 1
Claudel, R (Lyon) 1932 *G*, 1934 *G*
Clauzel, F (Béziers) 1924 *E*, *W*, 1925 *W*
Clavé, J (Agen) 1936 *G* 2, 1938 *R*, *G* 2
Claverie, H (Lourdes) 1954 *NZ*, *W*
Clément, G (RCF) 1931 *W*
Clément, J (RCF) 1921 *S*, *W*, *E*, 1922 *S*, *E*, *W*, *I*, 1923 *S*, *W*, *I*
Clemente, M (Oloron) 1978 *R*, 1980 *S*, *I*
Cluchague, L (Biarritz O) 1924 *S*, 1925 *E*
Coderc, J (Chalon) 1932 *G*, 1933 *G*, 1934 *G*, 1935 *G*, 1936 *G* 1

Codorniou, D (Narbonne) 1979 *NZ* 1,2, *R*, 1980 *W*, *E*, 1981 *S*, *W*, *E*, *A* 2, 1983 *E*, *S*, *I*, *W*, *A* 1,2, *R*, 1984 *I*, *W*, *E*, *S*, *NZ* 1,2, *R*, 1985 *E*, *S*, *I*, *W*, *Arg* 1,2
Coeurveille, C (Agen) 1992 *Arg* 1(R),2
Cognet, L (Montferrand) 1932 *G*, 1936 *G* 1,2, 1937 *G*, *It*
Colombier, J (St Junien) 1952 *SA*, *W*, *E*
Colomine, G (Narbonne) 1979 *NZ* 1
Combe, J (SF) 1910 *S*, *E*, *I*, 1911 *S*
Combes, G (Fumel) 1945 *B* 2
Communeau, M (SF) 1906 *NZ*, *E*, 1907 *E*, 1908 *E*, *W*, 1909 *E*, *W*, *I*, 1910 *S*, *E*, *I*, 1911 *S*, *E*, *I*, 1912 *I*, *S*, *W*, *E*, 1913 *SA*, *E*, *W*
Condom, J (Boucau, Biarritz O) 1982 *R*, 1983 *E*, *S*, *I*, *W*, *A* 1,2, *R*, 1984 *I*, *W*, *E*, *S*, *NZ* 1,2, *R*, 1985 *E*, *S*, *I*, *W*, *Arg* 1,2, 1986 *S*, *I*, *W*, *E*, *R* 1, *Arg* 1,2, *NZ* 1, *R* 2, *NZ* 2,3, 1987 *W*, *E*, *S*, *I*, [*S*, *R*, *Z*, *A*, *NZ*], *R*, 1988 *E*, *S*, *W*, *Arg* 1,2,3,4, *R*, 1989 *I*, *W*, *E*, *S*, *NZ* 1,2, *A* 1, 1990 *I*, *R*, *A* 2,3(R)
Conilh de Beyssac, J-J (SBUC) 1912 *I*, *S*, 1914 *I*, *W*, *E*
Constant, G (Perpignan) 1920 *W*
Coscolla, G (Béziers) 1921 *S*, *W*
Costantino, J (Montferrand) 1973 *R*
Costes, F (Montferrand) 1979 *E*, *S*, *NZ* 1,2, *R*, 1980 *W*, *I*
Coulon, E (Grenoble) 1928 *S*
Courtiols, M (Bègles) 1991 *R*, *US*1, *W*2
Crabos, R (RCF) 1920 *S*, *E*, *W*, *I*, *US*, 1921 *S*, *W*, *E*, *I*, 1922 *S*, *E*, *W*, *I*, 1923 *S*, *I*, 1924 *S*, *I*
Crampagne, J (Begles) 1967 *SA* 4
Crancee, R (Lourdes) 1960 *Arg* 3, 1961 *S*
Crauste, M (RCF, Lourdes) 1957 *R* 1,2, 1958 *S*, *E*, *A*, *W*, *It*, 1959 *E*, *It*, *W*, *I*, 1960 *S*, *E*, *W*, *I*, *It*, *R*, *Arg* 1, 3, 1961 *S*, *SA*, *E*, *W*, *It*, *I*, *NZ* 1,2,3, *A*, *R*, 1962 *S*, *E*, *W*, *I*, *It*, *R*, 1963 *S*, *I*, *E*, *W*, *It*, *R*, 1964 *S*, *NZ*, *E*, *W*, *It*, *I*, *SA*, *Fj*, *R*, 1965 *S*, *I*, *E*, *W*, *It*, *R*, 1966 *S*, *I*, *E*, *W*, *It*
Cremaschi, M (Lourdes) 1980 *R*, 1981 *R*, *NZ* 1,2, 1982 *W*, *S*, 1983 *A* 1,2, *R*, 1984 *I*, *W*
Crichton, W H (Le Havre) 1906 *NZ*, *E*
Cristina, J (Montferrand) 1979 *R*
Cussac, P (Biarritz O) 1934 *G*
Cutzach, A (Quillan) 1929 *G*

Daguerre, F (Biarritz O) 1936 *G* 1
Daguerre, J (CASG) 1933 *G*
Dal Maso, M (Mont-de-Marsan) 1988 *R*(R), 1990 *NZ* 2
Danion, J (Toulon) 1924 *I*
Danos, P (Toulon, Béziers) 1954 *Arg* 1,2, 1957 *R* 2, 1958 *S*, *E*, *W*, *It*, *I*, *SA* 1,2, 1959 *S*, *E*, *It*, *W*, *I*, 1960 *S*, *E*
Darbos, P (Dax) 1969 *R*
Darracq, R (Dax) 1957 *It*
Darrieussecq, A (Biarritz O) 1973 *E*
Darrieussecq, J (Mont-de-Marsan) 1953 *It*
Darrouy, C (Mont-de-Marsan) 1957 *I*, *E*, *W*, *It*, *R* 1, 1959 *E*, 1961 *R*, 1963 *S*, *I*, *E*, *W*, *It*, 1964 *NZ*, *E*, *W*, *It*, *I*, *SA*, *Fj*, *R*, 1965 *S*, *I*, *E*, *It*, *R*, 1966 *S*, *I*, *E*, *W*, *It*, *R*, 1967 *S*, *A*, *E*, *It*, *W*, *I*, *SA* 1,2,4
Daudignon, G (SF) 1928 *S*
Dauga, B (Mont-de-Marsan) 1964 *S*, *NZ*, *E*, *W*, *It*, *I*, *SA*, *Fj*, *R*, 1965 *S*, *I*, *E*, *W*, *It*, *R*, 1966 *S*, *I*, *E*, *W*, *It*, *R*, 1967 *S*, *A*, *E*, *It*, *W*, *I*, *SA* 1,2,3,4, *NZ*, *R*, 1968 *S*, *I*, *NZ* 1,2,3, *A*, *SA* 1,2, *R*, 1969 *S*, *I*, *E*, *R*, 1970 *S*, *I*, *W*, *E*, *R*, 1971 *S*, *I*, *E*, *W*, *SA* 1,2, *A* 1,2, *R*, 1972 *S*, *I* 1, *W*
Dauger, J (Bayonne) 1945 *B* 1,2, 1953 *S*
Daulouede, P (Tyrosse) 1937 *G*, *It*, 1938 *G* 1, 1940 *B*
Decamps, P (RCF) 1911 *S*
Dedet, J (SF) 1910 *S*, *E*, *I*, 1911 *W*, *I*, 1912 *S*, 1913 *E*, *I*
Dedeyn, P (RCF) 1906 *NZ*
Dedieu, P (Béziers) 1963 *E*, *It*, 1964 *W*, *It*, *I*, *SA*, *Fj*, *R*, 1965 *S*, *I*, *E*, *W*
De Gregorio, J (Grenoble) 1960 *S*, *E*, *W*, *I*, *It*, *R*, *Arg* 1,2, 1961 *S*, *SA*, *E*, *W*, *I*, 1962 *S*, *E*, *W*, 1963 *S*, *W*, *It*, 1964 *NZ*, *E*
Dehez, J-L (Agen) 1967 *SA* 2, 1969 *R*
de Jouvencel, E (SF) 1909 *W*, *I*
de Laborderie, M (RCF) 1921 *I*, 1922 *I*, 1925 *W*, *E*
Delage, C (Agen) 1983 *S*, *I*
de Malherbe, H (CASG) 1932 *G*, 1933 *G*
de Malmann, R (RCF) 1908 *E*, *W*, 1909 *E*, *W*, *I*, 1910 *E*, *I*
de Muizon, J J (SF) 1910 *I*

Delaigue, G (Toulon) 1973 *J*, *R*
Delque, A (Toulouse) 1937 *It*, 1938 *G* 1, *R*, *G* 2
Descamps, P (SB) 1927 *G* 2
Desclaux, F (RCF) 1949 *Arg* 1,2, 1953 *It*
Desclaux, J (Perpignan) 1934 *G*, 1935 *G*, 1936 *G* 1,2, 1937 *G*, *It*, 1938 *G* 1, *R*, *G* 2, 1945 *B* 1
Deslandes, C (RCF) 1990 *A* 1, *NZ* 2, 1991 *W*1, 1992 *R*, *Arg* 1,2
Desnoyer, L (Brive) 1974 *R*
Destarac, L (Tarbes) 1926 *S*, *I*, *E*, *W*, *M*, 1927 *W*, *E*, *G* 1,2
Desvouges, R (SF) 1914 *W*
Detrez, P-E (Nimes) 1983 *A* 2 (R), 1986 *Arg* 1(R),2, *A* (R), *NZ* 1
Devergie, T (Nimes) 1988 *R*, 1989 *NZ* 1,2, *B*, *A* 2, 1990 *W*, *E*, *S*, *I*, *R*, *A* 1,2,3, 1991 *US*2, *W*2, 1992 *R* (R), *Arg* 2(R)
Deygas, M (Vienne) 1937 *It*
Deylaud, C (Toulouse) 1992 *R*, *Arg* 1,2, *SA* 1
Dintrans, P (Tarbes) 1979 *NZ* 1,2, *R*, 1980 *E*, *S*, *I*, *SA*, *R*, 1981 *S*, *I*, *W*, *E*, *A* 1,2, *R*, *NZ* 1,2, 1982 *W*, *E*, *S*, *I*, *R*, *Arg* 1,2, 1983 *E*, *W*, *A* 1,2, *R*, 1984 *I*, *W*, *E*, *S*, *NZ* 1,2, *R*, 1985 *E*, *S*, *I*, *W*, *Arg* 1,2, 1987 [R], 1988 *NZ* 1,2,3, 1989 *W*, *E*, *S*, 1990 *R*
Dizabo, P (Tyrosse) 1948 *A*, *S*, *E*, 1949 *S*, *I*, *E*, *W*, *Arg* 2, 1950 *S*, *I*, 1960 *Arg* 1,2,3
Domec, A (Carcassonne) 1929 *W*
Domec, H (Lourdes) 1953 *W*, *It*, 1954 *S*, *I*, *NZ*, *W*, *E*, *It*, 1955 *S*, *I*, *E*, *W*, 1956 *I*, *W*, *It*, 1958 *E*, *A*, *W*, *It*, *I*
Domenech, A (Vichy, Brive) 1954 *W*, *E*, *It*, 1955 *S*, *I*, *E*, *W*, 1956 *S*, *I*, *W*, *It*, *E*, *Cz*, 1957 *S*, *I*, *E*, *W*, *It*, *R* 1,2, 1958 *S*, *E*, *It*, 1959 *It*, 1960 *S*, *E*, *W*, *I*, *It*, *R*, *Arg* 1,2,3, 1961 *S*, *SA*, *E*, *W*, *It*, *I*, *NZ* 1,2,3, *A*, *R*, 1962 *S*, *E*, *W*, *I*, *It*, *R*, 1963 *W*, *It*
Domercq, J (Bayonne) 1912 *I*, *S*
Dorot, J (RCF) 1935 *G*
Dospital, P (Bayonne) 1977 *R*, 1980 *I*, 1981 *S*, *I*, *W*, *E*, 1982 *I*, *R*, *Arg* 1,2, 1983 *E*, *S*, *I*, *W*, 1984 *E*, *S*, *NZ* 1,2, *R*, 1985 *E*, *S*, *I*, *W*, *Arg* 1
Dourthe, C (Dax) 1966 *R*, 1967 *S*, *A*, *E*, *W*, *I*, *SA* 1,2, 3, *NZ*, 1968 *W*, *NZ* 3, *SA* 1,2, 1969 *W*, 1971 *SA* 2 (R), *R*, 1972 *I* 1,2, *A* 1,2, *R*, 1973 *S*, *NZ*, *E*, 1974 *I*, *Arg* 1,2, *SA* 1,2, 1975 *W*, *E*, *S*
Doussau, E (Angoulême) 1938 *R*
Droitecourt, M (Montferrand) 1972 *R*, 1973 *NZ* (R), *E*, 1974 *E*, *S*, *Arg* 1, *SA* 2, 1975 *SA* 1,2, *Arg* 1,2, *R*, 1976 *S*, *I*, *W*, *A* 1, 1977 *Arg* 2
Dubertrand, A (Montferrand) 1971 *A* 2, *R*, 1972 *I* 2, 1974 *I*, *W*, *E*, *SA* 2, 1975 *Arg* 1,2, *R*, 1976 *S*, *US*
Dubois, D (Begles) 1971 *S*
Dubroca, D (Agen) 1979 *NZ* 2, 1981 *NZ* 2 (R), 1982 *E*, *S*, 1984 *W*, *E*, *S*, 1985 *Arg* 2, 1986 *S*, *I*, *W*, *E*, *R* 1, *Arg* 2, *A*, *NZ* 1, *R* 2, *NZ* 2,3, 1987 *W*, *E*, *S*, *I*, [*S*, *Z*, *Fj*, *A*, *NZ*], *R*, 1988 *E*, *S*, *I*, *W*
Duché, A (Limoges) 1929 *G*
Duclos, A (Lourdes) 1931 *S*
Ducousso, J (Tarbes) 1925 *S*, *W*, *E*
Dufau, G (RCF) 1948 *I*, *A*, 1949 *I*, *W*, 1950 *S*, *E*, *W*, 1951 *S*, *I*, *E*, *W*, 1952 *SA*, *W*, 1953 *S*, *I*, *E*, *W*, 1954 *S*, *I*, *NZ*, *W*, *E*, *It*, 1955 *S*, *I*, *E*, *W*, *It*, 1956 *S*, *I*, *W*, *It*, 1957 *S*, *I*, *E*, *W*, *It*, *R* 1
Dufau, J (Biarritz) 1912 *I*, *S*, *W*, *E*
Duffaut, Y (Agen) 1954 *Arg* 1,2
Duffour, R (Tarbes) 1911 *W*
Dufourcq, J (SBUC) 1906 *NZ*, *E*, 1907 *E*, 1908 *W*
Duhard, Y (Bagnères) 1980 *E*
Duhau, J (SF) 1928 *I*, 1930 *I*, *G*, 1931 *I*, *S*, *W*, 1933 *G*
Dulaurens, C (Toulouse) 1926 *I*, 1928 *S*, 1929 *W*
Duluc, A (Béziers) 1934 *G*
Du Manoir, Y LeP (RCF) 1925 *I*, *NZ*, *S*, *W*, *E*, 1926 *S*, 1927 *I*, *S*
Dupont, C (Lourdes) 1923 *S*, *W*, *I*, 1924 *S*, *I*, *W*, *R*, *US*, 1925 *S*, 1927 *E*, *G* 1,2, 1928 *A*, *G*, *W*, 1929 *I*
Dupont, J-L (Agen) 1983 *S*
Dupont, L (RCF) 1934 *G*, 1935 *G*, 1936 *G* 1,2, 1938 *R*, *G* 2
Dupouy, A (SB) 1924 *W*, *R*
Duprat, B (Bayonne) 1966 *E*, *W*, *It*, *R*, 1967 *S*, *A*, *E*, *SA* 2,3, 1968 *S*, *I*, 1972 *E*, *W*, *I* 2, *A* 1
Dupré, P (RCF) 1909 *W*
Dupuy, J (Tarbes) 1956 *S*, *I*, *W*, *It*, *E*, *Cz*, 1957 *S*, *I*, *E*, *W*, *It*, *R* 2, 1958 *S*, *E*, *SA* 1,2, 1959 *S*, *E*, *It*, *W*, *I*, 1960 *W*, *I*, *It*, *Arg* 1,3, 1961 *S*, *SA*, *E*, *NZ* 2, *R*, 1962 *S*, *E*, *W*, *I*, *It*, 1963 *W*, *It*, *R*, 1964 *S*

Du Souich, C J (see Judas du Souich)
Dutin, B (Mont-de-Marsan) 1968 *NZ* 2, *A*, *SA* 2, *R*
Dutour, F X (Toulouse) 1911 *E*, *I*, 1912 *S*, *W*, *E*, 1913 *S*
Dutrain, H (Toulouse) 1945 *W*, 1946 *B*, *I*, 1947 *E*, 1949 *I*, *E*, *W*, *Arg* 1
Dutrey, J (Lourdes) 1940 *B*
Duval, R (SF) 1908 *E*, *W*, 1909 *E*, 1911 *E*, *W*, *I*

Echavé, L (Agen) 1961 *S*
Elissalde, E (Bayonne) 1936 *G* 2, 1940 *B*
Elissalde, J-P (La Rochelle) 1980 *SA*, *R*, 1981 *A* 1,2, *R*
Empereur-Buisson, H (Béziers) 1931 *E*, *G*
Erbani, D (Agen) 1981 *A* 1,2, *NZ* 1,2, 1982 *Arg* 1,2, 1983 *S* (R), *I*, *W*, *A* 1,2, *R*, 1984 *W*, *E*, *R*, 1985 *E*, *W*(R), *Arg* 2, 1986 *S*, *I*, *W*, *E*, *R* 1, *Arg* 2, *NZ* 1,2(R), 3, 1987 *W*, *E*, *S*, *I*, [*S*, *R*, *Fj*, *A*, *NZ*], 1988 *E*, *S*, 1989 *I*(R), *W*, *E*, *S*, *NZ* 1, *A* 2, 1990 *W*, *E*
Escaffre, P (Narbonne) 1933 *G*, 1934 *G*
Escommier, M (Montelimar) 1955 *It*
Esponda, J-M (RCF) 1967 *SA* 1,2, *R*, 1968 *NZ* 1,2, *SA* 2, *R*, 1969 *S*, *I*(R), *E*
Estève, A (Béziers) 1971 *SA* 1, 1972 *I* 1, *E*, *W*, *I* 2, *A* 2, *R*, 1973 *S*, *NZ*, *E*, *I*, 1974 *I*, *W*, *E*, *S*, *R*, *SA* 1,2, 1975 *W*, *E*
Estève, P (Narbonne, Lavelanet) 1982 *R*, *Arg* 1,2, 1983 *E*, *S*, *I*, *W*, *A* 1,2, *R*, 1984 *I*, *W*, *E*, *S*, *NZ* 1,2, *R*, 1985 *E*, *S*, *I*, *W*, 1986 *S*, *I*, 1987 [*S*, *Z*]
Etcheberry, J (Rochefort, Cognac) 1923 *W*, *I*, 1924 *S*, *I*, *E*, *W*, *R*, *US*, 1926 *S*, *I*, *E*, *M*, 1927 *I*, *S*, *W*, *G* 2
Etchenique, J-M (Biarritz O) 1974 *R*, *SA* 1, 1975 *E*, *Arg* 2
Etchepare, A (Bayonne) 1922 *I*
Etcheverry, M (Pau) 1971 *S*, *I*
Eutrope, A (SCUF) 1913 *I*

Fabre, E (Toulouse) 1937 *It*, 1938 *G* 1,2
Fabre, J (Toulouse) 1963 *S*, *I*, *E*, *W*, *It*, 1964 *S*, *NZ*, *E*
Fabre, L (Lezignan) 1930 *G*
Fabre, M (Béziers) 1981 *A* 1, *R*, *NZ* 1,2, 1982 *I*, *R*
Failliot, P (RCF) 1911 *S*, *W*, *I*, 1912 *I*, *S*, *E*, 1913 *E*, *W*
Fargues, G (Dax) 1923 *I*
Fauré, F (Tarbes) 1914 *I*, *W*, *E*
Fauvel, J-P (Tulle) 1980 *R*
Favre, M (Lyon) 1913 *E*, *W*
Ferrand, L (Chalon) 1940 *B*
Ferrien, R (Tarbes) 1950 *S*, *I*, *E*, *W*
Finat, R (CASG) 1932 *G*, 1933 *G*
Fite, R (Brive) 1963 *W*, *It*
Forestier, J (SCUF) 1912 *W*
Forgues, F (Bayonne) 1911 *S*, *E*, *W*, 1912 *I*, *W*, *E*, 1913 *S*, *SA*, *W*, 1914 *I*, *E*
Fort, J (Agen) 1967 *It*, *W*, *I*, *SA* 1,2,3,4
Fourcade, G (BEC) 1909 *E*, *W*
Foures, H (Toulouse) 1951 *S*, *I*, *E*, *W*
Fournet, F (Montferrand) 1950 *W*
Fouroux, J (La Voulte) 1972 *I* 2, *R*, 1974 *W*, *E*, *Arg* 1,2, *R*, *SA* 1,2, 1975 *W*, *Arg* 1, *R*, 1976 *S*, *I*, *W*, *E*, *US*, *A* 1, 1977 *W*, *E*, *S*, *I*, *Arg* 1,2, *NZ* 1,2, *R*
Francquenelle, A (Vaugirard) 1911 *S*, 1913 *W*, *I*
Furcade, R (Perpignan) 1952 *S*

Gabernet, S (Toulouse) 1980 *E*, *S*, 1981 *S*, *I*, *W*, *E*, *A* 1,2, *R*, *NZ* 1,2, 1982 *I*, 1983 *A* 2, *R*
Gachassin, J (Lourdes) 1961 *S*, *I*, 1963 *R*, 1964 *S*, *NZ*, *E*, *W*, *It*, *I*, *SA*, *Fj*, *R*, 1965 *S*, *I*, *E*, *W*, *It*, *R*, 1966 *S*, *I*, *E*, *W*, 1967 *S*, *A*, *It*, *W*, *I*, *NZ*, 1968 *I*, *S*, 1969 *S*, *I*
Galau, H (Toulouse) 1924 *S*, *I*, *E*, *W*, *US*
Galia, J (Quillan) 1927 *E*, *G* 1,2, 1928 *S*, *A*, *I*, *E*, *W*, 1929 *I*, *E*, *G*, 1930 *S*, *I*, *E*, *G*, *W*, 1931 *S*, *W*, *E*, *G*
Gallart, P (Béziers) 1990 *R*, *A* 1 (2(R),3, 1992 *S*, *I*, *R*, *Arg* 1,2, *SA* 1,2, *Arg*
Gallion, J (Toulon) 1978 *E*, *S*, *I*, *W*, 1979 *I*, *W*, *E*, *S*, *NZ* 2, *R*, 1980 *W*, *E*, *S*, *I*, 1983 *A* 1,2, *R*, 1984 *I*, *W*, *E*, *S*, *R*, 1985 *E*, *S*, *I*, *W*, 1986 *Arg* 2
Galthié, F (Colomiers) 1991 *R*, *US*1, [*R*, *Fj*, *C*, *E*], 1992 *W*, *E*, *S*, *R*, *Arg*
Galy, J (Perpignan) 1953 *W*
Garuet-Lempirou, J-P (Lourdes) 1983 *A* 1,2, *R*, 1984 *I*, *NZ* 1,2, *R*, 1985 *E*, *S*, *I*, *W*, *Arg* 1, 1986 *S*, *I*, *W*, *E*, *R* 1, *Arg* 1, *NZ* 1, *R* 2, *NZ* 2,3, 1987 *W*, *E*, *S*, *I*, [*S*, *R*, *Fj*, *A*, *NZ*], 1988 *E*, *S*, *Arg* 1,2, *R*, 1989 *E*(R), *S*, *NZ* 1,2, 1990 *W*
Gasc, J (Graulhet) 1977 *NZ* 2

Gasparotto, G (Montferrand) 1976 *A* 2, *R*
Gauby, G (Perpignan) 1956 *Cz*
Gaudermen, P (RCF) 1906 *E*
Gayraud, W (Toulouse) 1920 *I*
Geneste, R (BEC) 1945 *B* 1, 1949 *Arg* 2
Genet, J-P (RCF) 1992 *S, I, R*
Gensane, R (Béziers) 1962 *S, E, W, I, It, R*, 1963 *S*
Gerald, G (RCF) 1927 *E, G* 2, 1928 *S*, 1929 *I, S, W, E, G*, 1930 *S, I, E, G, W*, 1931 *I, S, E, G*
Gerintes, G (CASG) 1924 *R*, 1925 *I*, 1926 *W*
Geschwind, P (RCF) 1936 *G* 1,2
Giacardy, M (SBUC) 1907 *E*
Gimbert, P (Bègles) 1991 *R, US*1, 1992 *W, E*
Gommes, J (RCF) 1909 *I*
Gonnet, C-A (Albi) 1921 *E, I*, 1922 *E, W*, 1924 *S, E*, 1926 *S, I, E, W, M*, 1927 *I, S, W, E, G* 1
Gonzales, J-M (Bayonne) 1992 *Arg* 1,2, *SA* 1,2, *Arg*
Got, R (Perpignan) 1920 *I, US*, 1921 *S, W*, 1922 *S, E, W, I*, 1924 *I, E, W, R, US*
Gourdon, J-F (RCF, Bagnères) 1974 *S, Arg* 1,2, *R, SA* 1,2, 1975 *W, E, S, I, R*, 1976 *S, I, W, E*, 1978 *E, S*, 1979 *W, E, S, R*, 1980 *I*
Gourragne, J-F (Béziers) 1990 *NZ* 2, 1991 *W*1
Goyard, A (Lyon U) 1936 *G* 1,2, 1937 *G, It*, 1938 *G* 1, *R, G* 2
Graciet, A (SBUC) 1926 *I, W*, 1927 *S, G* 1, 1929 *E*, 1930 *W*
Graou, S (Auch) 1992 *Arg*(R)
Gratton, J (Agen) 1984 *NZ* 2, *R*, 1985 *E, S, I, W, Arg* 1,2, 1986 *S, NZ* 1
Graule, V (Arl Perpignan) 1926 *I, E, W*, 1927 *S, W*, 1931 *G*
Greffe, M (Grenoble) 1968 *W, Cz, NZ* 1,2, *SA* 1
Griffard, J (Lyon U) 1932 *G*, 1933 *G*, 1934 *G*
Gruarin, A (Toulon) 1964 *W, It, I, SA, Fj, R*, 1965 *S, I, E, W, It*, 1966 *S, I, E, W, It, R*, 1967 *S, A, E, It, W, I, NZ*, 1968 *S, I*
Guelorget, P (RCF) 1931 *E, G*
Guichemerre, J (Dax) 1920 *E*, 1921 *E, I*, 1923 *S*
Guilbert, A (Toulon) 1975 *E, S, I, SA* 1,2, 1976 *A* 1, 1977 *Arg* 1,2, *NZ* 1,2, *R*, 1979 *I, W, E*
Guillemin, P (RCF) 1908 *E, W*, 1909 *E, I*, 1910 *W, S, E, I*, 1911 *S, E, W*
Guilleux, P (Agen) 1952 *SA, It*
Guiral, M (Agen) 1931 *G*, 1932 *G*, 1933 *G*

Haget, A (PUC) 1953 *E*, 1954 *I, NZ, E, Arg* 2, 1955 *E, W, It*, 1957 *I, E, It, R* 1, 1958 *It, SA* 2
Haget, F (Agen, Biarritz O) 1974 *Arg* 1,2, 1975 *SA* 2, *Arg* 1,2, *R*, 1976 *S*, 1978 *S, I, W, R*, 1979 *I, W, E, S*, *NZ* 1,2, *R*, 1980 *W, S, I*, 1984 *S, NZ* 1,2, *R*, 1985 *E, S, I*, 1986 *S, I, W, E, R* 1, *Arg* 1, *A, NZ* 1, 1987 *S, I*, [*R, Fj*]
Haget, H (CASG) 1928 *S*, 1930 *G*
Halet, R (Strasbourg) 1925 *NZ, S, W*
Harislur-Arthapignet, P (Tarbes) 1988 *Arg* 4(R)
Harize, D (Cahors, Toulouse) 1975 *SA* 1,2, 1976 *A* 1, 2, *R*, 1977 *W, E, S, I*
Hauc, J (Toulon) 1928 *E, G*, 1929 *I, S, G*
Hauser, M (Lourdes) 1969 *E*
Hedembaigt, M (Bayonne) 1913 *S, SA*, 1914 *W*
Hericé, D (Begles) 1950 *I*
Herrero, A (Toulon) 1963 *R*, 1964 *NZ, E, W, It, I, SA, Fj, R*, 1965 *S, I, E, W*, 1966 *W, It, R*, 1967 *S, A, E, It, I, R*
Herrero, B (Nice) 1983 *I*, 1986 *Arg* 1
Heyer, F (Montferrand) 1990 *A* 2
Hiquet, J-C (Agen) 1964 *E*
Hoche, M (PUC) 1957 *I, E, W, It, R* 1
Hondagné-Monge, M (Tarbes) 1988 *Arg* 2 (R)
Hontas, P (Biarritz) 1990 *S, I, R*, 1991 *R*, 1992 *Arg*, 1993 *E, S, I, W*
Hortoland, J-P (Béziers) 1971 *A* 2
Houblain, H (SCUF) 1909 *E*, 1910 *W*
Houdet, R (SF) 1927 *S, W, G* 1, 1928 *G, W*, 1929 *I, S, E*, 1930 *S, E*
Hourdebaigt, A (SBUC) 1909 *I*, 1910 *W, S, E, I*
Hubert, A (ASF) 1906 *E*, 1907 *E*, 1908 *E, W*, 1909 *E, W, I*
Hueber, A (Lourdes, Toulon) 1990 *A* 3, *NZ* 1, 1991 *US*2, 1992 *I, Arg* 1,2, *SA* 1,2, 1993 *E, S, I, W*
Hutin, R (CASG) 1927 *I, S, W*

Icard, J (SF) 1909 *E, W*

Iguiniz, E (Bayonne) 1914 *E*
Ihingoué, D (BEC) 1912 *I, S*
Imbernon, J-F (Perpignan) 1976 *I, W, E, US, A* 1, 1977 *W, E, S, I, Arg* 1,2, *NZ* 1,2, 1978 *E, R*, 1979 *I*, 1981 *S, I, W, E*, 1982 *I*, 1983 *I, W*
Iraçabal, J (Bayonne) 1968 *NZ* 1,2, *SA* 1, 1969 *S, I, W, R*, 1970 *S, I, W, E, R*, 1971 *W, SA* 1,2, *A* 1, 1972 *E, W, I* 2, *A* 2, *R*, 1973 *S, NZ, E, W, I, J*, 1974 *I, W, E, S, Arg* 1,2, *SA* 2 (R)
Isaac, H (RCF) 1907 *E*, 1908 *E*
Ithurra, E (Biarritz O) 1936 *G* 1,2, 1937 *G*

Janeczek, T (Tarbes) 1982 *Arg* 1,2, 1990 *R*
Janik, K (Toulouse) 1987 *R*
Jarasse, A (Brive) 1945 *B* 1
Jardel, J (SB) 1928 *I, E*
Jaureguy, A (RCF, Toulouse, SF) 1920 *S, E, W, I, US*, 1922 *S, W*, 1923 *S, W, E, I*, 1924 *S, W, R, US*, 1925 *I, NZ*, 1926 *S, E, W, M*, 1927 *I, E*, 1928 *S, A, E, G, W*, 1929 *I, S, E*
Jaureguy, P (Toulouse) 1913 *S, SA, W, I*
Jeangrand, M-H (Tarbes) 1921 *I*
Jeanjean, P (Toulon) 1948 *I*
Jérôme, G (SF) 1906 *NZ, E*
Joinel, J-L (Brive) 1977 *NZ* 1, 1978 *R*, 1979 *I, W, E, S*, *NZ* 1,2, *R*, 1980 *W, E, S, I, SA*, 1981 *S, I, W, E, R*, *NZ* 1,2, 1982 *E, S, I, R*, 1983 *E, S, I, W, A* 1,2, *R*, 1984 *I, W, E, S, NZ* 1,2, 1985 *S, I, W, Arg* 1, 1986 *S, I, W, E, R* 1, *Arg* 1,2, *A*, 1987 [*Z*]
Jol, M (Biarritz O) 1947 *S, I, W, E*, 1949 *S, I, E, W, Arg* 1,2
Judas du Souich, C (SCUF) 1911 *W, I*
Junquas, L (Tyrosse) 1945 *B* 1,2, *W*, 1946 *B, I, K, W*, 1947 *S, I, W, E*, 1948 *S, W*

Kaczorowksi, D (Le Creusot) 1974 *I* (R)
Kaempf, A (St Jean-de-Luz) 1946 *B*

Labadie, P (Bayonne) 1952 *S, I, SA, W, E, It*, 1953 *S, I, It*, 1954 *S, I, NZ, W, E, Arg* 2, 1955 *S, I, E, W*, 1956 *I*, 1957 *I*
Labarthete, R (Pau) 1952 *S*
Labazuy, A (Lourdes) 1952 *I*, 1954 *S, W*, 1956 *E*, 1958 *A, W, I*, 1959 *S, E, It, W*
Laborde, C (RCF) 1962 *It, R*, 1963 *R*, 1964 *SA*, 1965 *E*
Lacans, P (Béziers) 1980 *SA*, 1981 *W, E, A* 2, *R*, 1982 *W*
Lacassagne, H (SBUC) 1906 *NZ*, 1907 *E*
Lacaussade, R (Begles) 1948 *A, S*
Lacaze, C (Lourdes, Angoulême) 1961 *NZ* 2,3, *A, R*, 1962 *E, W, I, It*, 1963 *W, R*, 1964 *S, NZ, E*, 1965 *It, R*, 1966 *S, I, E, W, It, R*, 1967 *S, E, SA* 1,3,4, *R*, 1968 *S, E, W, Cz, NZ* 1, 1969 *E*
Lacaze, H (Périgueux) 1928 *I, G, W*, 1929 *I, W*
Lacaze, P (Lourdes) 1958 *SA* 1,2, 1959 *S, E, It, W, I*
Lacazedieu, C (Dax) 1923 *W, I*, 1928 *A, I*, 1929 *S*
Lacombe, B (Agen) 1989 *B*, 1990 *A* 2
Lacome, M (Pau) 1960 *Arg* 2
Lacoste, R (Tarbes) 1914 *I, W, E*
Lacrampe, F (Béziers) 1949 *Arg* 2
Lacroix, P (Mont-de-Marsan, Agen) 1958 *A*, 1960 *W, I, It, R, Arg* 1,2,3, 1961 *S, SA, E, W, I, NZ* 1,2,3, *A, R*, 1962 *S, E, W, I, R*, 1963 *S, I, E, W*
Lacroix, T (Dax) 1989 *A* 1(R), 2, 1991 *W*1(R), 2(R), [*R, C*(R), *E*], 1992 *SA* 2, 1993 *E, S, I, W*
Lafarge, Y (Montferrand) 1978 *R*, 1979 *NZ* 1, 1981 *I* (R)
Laffitte, R (SCUF) 1910 *W, S*
Laffont, H (Narbonne) 1926 *W*
Lafond, A (Bayonne) 1922 *E*
Lafond, J-B (RCF) 1983 *A* 1, 1985 *Arg* 1,2, 1986 *S, I, W, E, R* 1, 1987 *I* (R), 1988 *W*, 1989 *I, W, E*, 1990 *W, A* 3(R), *NZ* 2, 1991 *S, I, W*1, *E, R, US*1, *W*2, [*R*(R), *Fj, C, E*], 1992 *W, E, S, I*(R), *SA* 2, 1993 *E, S, I, W*
Lagisquet, P (Bayonne) 1983 *A* 1,2, *R*, 1984 *I, W, NZ* 1,2, 1986 *R* 1 (R), *Arg* 1,2, *A, NZ* 1, 1987 [*S, R, Fj, A, NZ*], *R*, 1988 *S, I, W, Arg* 1,2,3,4, *R*, 1989 *I, W, E, S, NZ* 1,2, *B, A* 1,2, 1990 *W, E, S, I, A* 1,2,3, 1991 *S, I, W*, *US*2, [*R*]
Lagrange, J-C (RCF) 1966 *It*
Lalande, M (RCF) 1923 *S, W, I*
Lane, G (RCF) 1906 *NZ, E*, 1907 *E*, 1908 *E, W*, 1909 *E, W, I*, 1910 *W, E*, 1911 *S, W*, 1912 *I, W, E*, 1913 *S*
Langlade, J-C (Hyères) 1990 *R, A* 1, *NZ* 1

285

Laporte, G (Graulhet) 1981 *I*, *W*, *E*, *R*, *NZ* 1,2, 1986 *S*, *I*, *W*, *E*, *R* 1, *Arg* 1, *A* (R), 1987 [*R*, *Z*(R), *Fj*]
Larreguy, P (Bayonne) 1954 *It*
Larribau, J (Périgueux) 1912 *I*, *S*, *W*, *E*, 1913 *S*, 1914 *I*, *E*
Larrieu, J (Tarbes) 1920 *I*, *US*, 1921 *W*, *1923 S*, *W*, *E*, *I*
Larrieux, M (SBUC) 1927 *G* 2
Larrue, H (Carmaux) 1960 *W*, *I*, *It*, *R*, *Arg* 1,2,3
Lasaosa, P (Dax) 1950 *I*, 1952 *S*, *I*, *E*, *It*, 1955 *It*
Lascubé, G (Agen) 1991 *S*, *I*, *W1*, *E*, *US2*, *W2*, [*R*, *Fj*, *C*, *E*], 1992 *W*, *E*
Lassegue, J-B (Toulouse) 1946 *W*, 1947 *S*, *I*, *W*, 1948 *W*, 1949 *I*, *E*, *W*, *Arg* 1
Lasserre, F (René) (Bayonne, Cognac, Grenoble) 1914 *I*, 1920 *S*, 1921 *S*, *W*, *I*, 1922 *S*, *E*, *W*, *I*, 1923 *W*, *E*, 1924 *S*, *I*, *R*, *US*
Lasserre, J-C (Dax) 1963 *It*, 1964 *S*, *NZ*, *E*, *W*, *It*, *I*, *Fj*, 1965 *W*, *It*, *R*, 1966 *R*, 1967 *S*
Lasserre, M (Agen) 1967 *SA* 2,3, 1968 *E*, *W*, *Cz*, *NZ* 3, *A*, *SA* 1,2, 1969 *S*, *I*, *E*, 1970 *E*, 1971 *E*, *W*
Laterrade, G (Tarbes) 1910 *E*, *I*, 1911 *S*, *E*, *I*
Laudouar, J (Soustons, SBUC) 1961 *NZ* 1,2, *R*, 1962 *I*, *R*
Lauga, P (Vichy) 1950 *S*, *I*, *E*, *W*
Laurent, A (Biarritz O) 1925 *NZ*, *S*, *W*, *E*, 1926 *W*
Laurent, J (Bayonne) 1920 *S*, *E*, *W*
Laurent, M (Auch) 1932 *G*, 1933 *G*, 1934 *G*, 1935 *G*, 1936 *G* 1
Lavail, G (Perpignan) 1937 *G*, 1940 *B*
Lavaud, R (Carcassonne) 1914 *I*, *W*
Lavergne, P (Limoges) 1950 *S*
Lavigne, B (Agen) 1984 *R*, 1985 *E*
Lavigne, J (Dax) 1920 *E*, *W*
Lazies, H (Auch) 1954 *Arg* 2, 1955 *It*, 1956 *E*, 1957 *S*
Le Bourhis, R (La Rochelle) 1961 *R*
Lecointre, M (Nantes) 1952 *It*
Le Droff, J (Auch) 1963 *It*, *R*, 1964 *S*, *NZ*, *E*, 1970 *E*, *R*, 1971 *S*, *I*
Lefevre, R (Brive) 1961 *NZ* 2
Lefort, J-B (Biarritz O) 1938 *G* 1
Le Goff, R (Métro) 1938 *R*, *G* 2
Legrain, M (SF) 1909 *I*, 1910 *I*, 1911 *S*, *E*, *W*, *I*, 1913 *S*, *SA*, *E*, *I*, 1914 *I*, *W*
Lenient, J-J (Vichy) 1967 *R*
Lepatey, J (Mazamet) 1954 *It*, 1955 *S*, *I*, *E*, *W*
Lepatey, L (Mazamet) 1924 *S*, *I*, *E*
Lescarboura, J-P (Dax) 1982 *W*, *E*, *S*, *I*, 1983 *A* 1,2, *R*, 1984 *I*, *W*, *E*, *S*, *NZ* 1,2, *R*, 1985 *E*, *S*, *I*, *W*, *Arg* 1, 2, 1986 *Arg* 2, *A*, *NZ* 1, *R* 2, *NZ* 2, 1988 *S*, *W*, 1990 *R*
Lesieur, E (SF) 1906 *E*, 1908 *E*, *W*, 1909 *E*, *W*, *I*, 1910 *S*, *E*, *I*, 1911 *E*, *I*, 1912 *W*
Leuvielle, M (SBUC) 1908 *W*, 1913 *S*, *SA*, *E*, *W*, 1914 *W*, *E*
Levasseur, R (SF) 1925 *W*, *E*
Levée, H (RCF) 1906 *NZ*
Lewis, E W (Le Havre) 1906 *E*
Lhermet, J-M (Montferrand) 1990 *S*, *I*
Libaros, G (Tarbes) 1936 *G* 1, 1940 *B*
Lira, M (La Voulte) 1962 *R*, 1963 *I*, *E*, *W*, *It*, *R*, 1964 *W*, *It*, *I*, *SA*, 1965 *S*, *I*, *R*
Llari, (Carcassonne) 1926 *S*
Lobies, J (RCF) 1921 *S*, *W*, *E*
Lombard, F (Narbonne) 1934 *G*, 1937 *It*
Lombarteix, R (Montferrand) 1938 *R*, *G* 2
Londios, J (Montauban) 1967 *SA* 3
Lorieux, A (Grenoble, Aix) 1981 *A* 1, *R*, *NZ* 1,2, 1982 *W*, 1983 *A* 2, *R*, 1984 *I*, *W*, *E*, 1985 *Arg* 1,2(R), 1986 *R* 2, *NZ* 2,3, 1987 *W*, *E*, [*S*, *Z*, *Fj*, *A*, *NZ*], 1988 *S*, *I*, *W*, *Arg* 1,2,4, 1989 *W*, *A* 2
Loury, A (RCF) 1927 *E*, *G* 1,2, 1928 *S*, *A*, *I*
Loustau, M (Dax) 1923 *E*
Lubin-Lebrère, M-F (Toulouse) 1914 *I*, *W*, *E*, 1920 *S*, *E*, *W*, *I*, *US*, 1921 *S*, 1922 *S*, *E*, *W*, 1924 *W*, *US*, 1925 *I*
Lubrano, A (Béziers) 1972 *A* 2, 1973 *S*
Lux, J-P (Tyrosse, Dax) 1967 *E*, *It*, *W*, *I*, *SA* 1,2,4, *R*, 1968 *I*, *E*, *Cz*, *NZ* 3, *A*, *SA* 1,2, 1969 *S*, *I*, *E*, 1970 *S*, *I*, *W*, *E*, *R*, 1971 *S*, *I*, *E*, *W*, *A* 1,2, 1972 *S*, *I* 1, *E*, *W*, *I* 2, *A* 1,2, *R*, 1973 *S*, *NZ*, *E*, 1974 *I*, *W*, *E*, *S*, *Arg* 1,2, 1975 *W*

Maclos, P (SF) 1906 *E*, 1907 *E*
Magnanou, C (RCF) 1923 *E*, 1925 *W*, *E*, 1926 *S*, 1929 *S*, *W*, 1930 *S*, *I*, *E*, *W*
Magnol, L (Toulouse) 1928 *S*, 1929 *S*, *W*, *E*

Magois, H (La Rochelle) 1968 *SA* 1,2, *R*
Majerus, R (SF) 1928 *W*, 1929 *I*, *S*, 1930 *S*, *I*, *E*, *G*, *W*
Malbet, J-C (Agen) 1967 *SA* 2,4
Maleig, A (Oloron) 1979 *W*, *E*, *NZ* 2, 1980 *W*, *E*, *SA*, *R*
Malquier, Y (Narbonne) 1979 *S*
Manterola, T (Lourdes) 1955 *It*, 1957 *R* 1
Mantoulan, C (Pau) 1959 *I*
Marcet, J (Albi) 1925 *I*, *NZ*, *S*, *W*, *E*, 1926 *I*, *E*
Marchal, J-F (Lourdes) 1979 *S*, *R*, 1980 *W*, *S*, *I*
Marchand, R (Poitiers) 1920 *S*, *W*
Marfaing, M (Toulouse) 1992 *R*, *Arg* 1
Marocco, P (Montferrand) 1986 *S*, *I*, *W*, *E*, *R* 1, *Arg* 1,2, *A*, 1988 *Arg* 4, 1989 *I*, 1990 *E*(R), *NZ* 1(R), 1991 *S*, *I*, *W1*, *E*, *US2*, [*R*, *Fj*, *C*, *E*]
Marot, A (Brive) 1969 *R*, 1970 *S*, *I*, *W*, 1971 *SA* 1, 1972 *I* 2, 1976 *A* 1
Marquesuzaa, A (RCF) 1958 *It*, *SA* 1,2, 1959 *S*, *E*, *It*, *W*, 1960 *S*, *E*, *Arg* 1
Marracq, H (Pau) 1961 *R*
Martin, C (Lyon) 1909 *I*, 1910 *W*, *S*
Martin, H (SBUC) 1907 *E*, 1908 *W*
Martin, J-L (Béziers) 1971 *A* 2, *R*, 1972 *S*, *I* 1
Martin, L (Pau) 1948 *I*, *A*, *S*, *W*, *E*, 1950 *S*
Martine, R (Lourdes) 1952 *S*, *I*, *It*, 1953 *It*, 1954 *S*, *I*, *NZ*, *W*, *E*, *It*, *Arg* 2, 1955 *S*, *I*, *W*, 1958 *A*, *W*, *It*, *I*, *SA* 1,2, 1960 *S*, *E*, *Arg* 3, 1961 *S*, *It*
Martinez, G (Toulouse) 1982 *W*, *E*, *S*, *Arg* 1,2, 1983 *E*, *W*
Mas, F (Béziers) 1962 *R*, 1963 *S*, *I*, *E*, *W*
Maso, J (Perpignan, Narbonne) 1966 *It*, *R*, 1967 *S*, *R*, 1968 *S*, *W*, *Cz*, *NZ* 1,2,3, *A*, *R*, 1969 *S*, *I*, *W*, 1971 *SA* 1,2, *R*, 1972 *E*, *W*, *A* 2, 1973 *W*, *I*, *J*, *R*
Massare, J (PUC) 1945 *B* 1,2, *W*, 1946 *B*, *I*, *W*
Massé, A (SBUC) 1908 *W*, 1909 *E*, *W*, 1910 *W*, *S*, *E*, *I*
Masse, H (Grenoble) 1937 *G*
Matheu-Cambas, J (Agen) 1945 *W*, 1946 *B*, *I*, *K*, *W*, 1947 *S*, *I*, *W*, *E*, 1948 *I*, *A*, *S*, *W*, *E*, 1949 *S*, *I*, *E*, *W*, *Arg* 1,2, 1950 *E*, *W*, 1951 *S*, *I*
Mauduy, G (Périgueux) 1957 *It*, *R* 1,2, 1958 *S*, *E*, 1961 *W*, *It*
Mauran, J (Castres) 1952 *SA*, *W*, *E*, *It*, 1953 *I*, *E*
Mauriat, P (Lyon) 1907 *E*, 1908 *E*, *W*, 1909 *W*, *I*, 1910 *W*, *S*, *E*, *I*, 1911 *S*, *E*, *W*, *I*, 1912 *I*, *S*, 1913 *S*, *SA*, *W*, *I*
Maurin, G (ASF) 1906 *E*
Maury, A (Toulouse) 1925 *I*, *NZ*, *S*, *W*, *E*, 1926 *S*, *I*, *E*
Mayssonnié, A (Toulouse) 1908 *E*, *W*, 1910 *W*
Mazas, L (Colomiers) 1992 *Arg*
Melville, E (Toulon) 1990 *I*(R), *A* 1,2,3, *NZ* 1, 1991 *US2*
Menrath, R (SCUF) 1910 *W*
Menthiller, Y (Romans) 1964 *W*, *It*, *SA*, *R*, 1965 *E*
Meret, F (Tarbes) 1940 *B*
Mericq, S (Agen) 1959 *I*, 1960 *S*, *E*, *W*, 1961 *I*
Merquey, J (Toulon) 1950 *S*, *I*, *E*, *W*
Mesnel, F (RCF) 1986 *NZ* 2(R),3, 1987 *W*, *E*, *S*, *I*, [*S*, *Z*, *Fj*, *A*, *NZ*], *R*, 1988 *E*, *Arg* 1,2,3,4, *R*, 1989 *I*, *W*, *E*, *S*, *NZ* 1, *A* 1,2, 1990 *E*, *S*, *I*, *A* 2,3, *NZ* 1,2, 1991 *S*, *I*, *W1*, *E*, *R*, *US1*,2, *W2*, [*Fj*, *C*, *E*], 1992 *W*, *E*, *S*, *I*, *SA* 1,2, 1993 *E*(R), *W*
Mesny, P (RCF, Grenoble) 1979 *NZ* 1,2, 1980 *SA*, *R*, 1981 *I*, *W*(R), *A* 1,2, *R*, *NZ* 1,2, 1982 *I*, *Arg* 1,2
Meyer, G-S (Périgueux) 1960 *S*, *E*, *It*, *R*, *Arg* 2
Meynard, J (Cognac) 1954 *Arg* 1, 1956 *Cz*
Mias, L (Mazamet) 1951 *S*, *I*, *E*, *W*, 1952 *I*, *SA*, *W*, *E*, *It*, 1953 *S*, *I*, *W*, *It*, 1954 *S*, *I*, *NZ*, *W*, 1957 *R* 2, 1958 *S*, *E*, *A*, *W*, *I*, *SA* 1,2, 1959 *S*, *It*, *W*, *I*
Milliand, P (Grenoble) 1936 *G* 2, 1937 *G*, *It*
Minjat, R (Lyon) 1945 *B* 1
Mir, J-H (Lourdes) 1967 *R*, 1968 *I*
Mir, J-P (Lourdes) 1967 *A*
Modin, R (Brive) 1987 [*Z*]
Moga, A-M-A (Begles) 1945 *B* 1,2, *W*, 1946 *B*, *I*, *K*, *W*, 1947 *S*, *I*, *W*, *E*, 1948 *I*, *A*, *S*, *W*, *E*, 1949 *S*, *I*, *E*, *W*, *Arg* 1,2
Mommejat, B (Cahors, Albi) 1958 *It*, *I*, *SA* 1,2, 1959 *S*, *E*, *It*, *W*, *I*, 1960 *S*, *E*, *I*, *R*, 1962 *S*, *E*, *W*, *I*, *It*, *R*, 1963 *S*, *I*, *W*
Moncla, R (RCF, Pau) 1956 *Cz*, 1957 *I*, *E*, *W*, *It*, *R* 1, 1958 *SA* 1,2, 1959 *S*, *E*, *It*, *W*, *I*, 1960 *S*, *E*, *W*, *I*, *It*, *R*, *Arg* 1,2,3, 1961 *S*, *SA*, *E*, *W*, *It*, *I*, *NZ* 1,2,3
Monié, R (Perpignan) 1956 *Cz*, 1957 *E*
Monier, R (SBUC) 1911 *I*, 1912 *S*
Monniot, M (RCF) 1912 *W*, *E*

Montade, A (Perpignan) 1925 *I*, *NZ*, *S*, *W*, 1926 *W*
Montlaur, P (Agen) 1992 *E*(R)
Moraitis, B (Toulon) 1969 *E*, *W*
Morel, A (Grenoble) 1954 *Arg* 2
Morere, J (Toulouse) 1927 *E*, *G* 1, 1928 *S*, *A*
Moscato, V (Bègles) 1991 *R*, *US*1, 1992 *W*, *E*
Mougeot, C (Bègles) 1992 *W*, *E*, *Arg*
Mouniq, P (Toulouse) 1911 *S*, *E*, *W*, *I*, 1912 *I*, *E*, 1913 *S*, *SA*, *E*
Moure, H (SCUF) 1908 *E*
Moureu, P (Béziers) 1920 *I*, *US*, 1921 *W*, *E*, *I*, 1922 *S*, *W*, *I*, 1923 *S*, *W*, *E*, *I*, 1924 *S*, *I*, *E*, *W*, 1925 *E*
Mournet, A (Bagnères) 1981 *A* 1 (R)
Mouronval, F (SF) 1909 *I*
Muhr, A H (RCF) 1906 *NZ*, *E*, 1907 *E*
Murillo, G (Dijon) 1954 *It*, *Arg* 1

Namur, R (Toulon) 1931 *E*, *G*
Noble, J-C (La Voulte) 1968 *E*, *W*, *Cz*, *NZ* 3, *A*, *R*
Normand, A (Toulouse) 1957 *R* 1
Novès, G (Toulouse) 1977 *NZ* 1,2, *R*, 1978 *W*, *R*, 1979 *I*, *W*

Olive, D (Montferrand) 1951 *I*, 1952 *I*
Ondarts, P (Biarritz O) 1986 *NZ* 3, 1987 *W*, *E*, *S*, *I*, [*S*, *Z*, *Fj*, *A*, *NZ*], *R*, 1988 *E*, *I*, *W*, *Arg* 1,2,3,4, *R*, 1989 *I*, *W*, *E*, *NZ* 1,2, *A* 2, 1990 *W*, *E*, *S*, *I*, *R*(R), *NZ* 1,2, 1991 *S*, *I*, *W*1, *E*, *US*2, *W*2, [*R*, *Fj*, *C*, *E*]
Orso, J-C (Nice, Toulon) 1982 *Arg* 1,2, 1983 *E*, *S*, *A* 1, 1984 *E* (R), *S*, *NZ* 1, 1985 *I* (R), *W*, 1988 *I*
Othats, J (Dax) 1960 *Arg* 2,3
Ougier, S (Toulouse) 1992 *R*, *Arg* 1, 1993 *E*(R)

Paco, A (Béziers) 1974 *Arg* 1,2, *R*, *SA* 1,2, 1975 *W*, *E*, *Arg* 1,2, *R*, 1976 *S*, *I*, *W*, *E*, *US*, *A* 1,2, *R*, 1977 *W*, *E*, *S*, *I*, *NZ* 1,2, *R*, 1978 *E*, *S*, *I*, *W*, *R*, 1979 *I*, *W*, *E*, *S*, 1980 *W*
Palat, J (Perpignan) 1938 *G* 2
Palmié, M (Béziers) 1975 *SA* 1,2, *Arg* 1,2, *R*, 1976 *S*, *I*, *W*, *E*, *US*, 1977 *W*, *E*, *S*, *I*, *Arg* 1,2, *NZ* 1,2, *R*, 1978 *E*, *S*, *I*, *W*
Paoli, R (see Simonpaoli)
Paparemborde, R (Pau) 1975 *SA* 1,2, *Arg* 1,2, *R*, 1976 *S*, *I*, *W*, *E*, *US*, *A* 1,2, *R*, 1977 *W*, *E*, *S*, *I*, *Arg* 1, *NZ* 1,2, 1978 *E*, *S*, *I*, *W*, *R*, 1979 *I*, *W*, *E*, *S*, *NZ* 1,2, *R*, 1980 *W*, *E*, *S*, *SA*, 1981 *S*, *I*, *W*, *E*, *A* 1,2, *R*, *NZ* 1,2, 1982 *W*, *I*, *R*, *Arg* 1,2, 1983 *E*, *S*, *I*, *W*
Pardo, L (Hendaye) 1924 *I*, *E*
Pardo, L (Bayonne) 1980 *SA*, *R*, 1981 *S*, *I*, *W*, *E*, *A* 1, 1982 *W*, *E*, *S*, 1983 *A* 1 (R), 1985 *S*, *I*, *Arg* 2
Pargade, J-H (Lyon U) 1953 *It*
Paries, L (Biarritz O) 1968 *SA* 2, *R*, 1970 *S*, *I*, *W*, 1975 *E*, *S*, *I*
Pascalin, P (Mont-de-Marsan) 1950 *I*, *E*, *W*, 1951 *S*, *I*, *E*, *W*
Pascarel, J-R (TOEC) 1912 *W*, *E*, 1913 *S*, *SA*, *E*, *I*
Pascot, J (Perpignan) 1922 *S*, *E*, *I*, 1923 *S*, 1926 *I*, 1927 *G* 2
Paul, R (Montferrand) 1940 *B*
Pauthe, G (Graulhet) 1956 *E*
Pebeyre, E-J (Fumel, Brive) 1945 *W*, 1946 *I*, *K*, *W*, 1947 *S*, *I*, *W*, *E*
Pebeyre, M (Vichy, Montferrand) 1970 *E*, *R*, 1971 *I*, *SA* 1,2, 1973 *W*
Pecune, J (Tarbes) 1974 *W*, *E*, *S*, 1975 *Arg* 1,2, *R*, 1976 *I*, *W*, *E*, *US*
Pedeutour, P (Begles) 1980 *I*
Pellissier, L (RCF) 1928 *A*, *I*, *E*, *G*, *W*
Penaud, A (Brive) 1992 *W*, *E*, *S*, *I*, *R*, *Arg* 1,2, *SA* 1,2, *Arg*
Peron, P (RCF) 1975 *SA* 1,2
Perrier, A (Bayonne) 1982 *W*, *E*, *S*, *I* (R)
Pesteil, J-P (Béziers) 1975 *SA* 1, 1976 *A* 2, *R*
Petit, C (Lorrain) 1931 *W*
Peyrelade, H (Tarbes) 1940 *B*
Peyroutou, G (Périgueux) 1911 *S*, *E*
Phliponeau, J-F (Montferrand) 1973 *W*, *I*
Piazza, A (Montauban) 1968 *NZ* 1, *A*
Picard, T (Montferrand) 1985 *Arg* 2, 1986 *R* 1 (R), *Arg* 2
Pierrot, G (Pau) 1914 *I*, *W*, *E*
Pilon, J (Périgueux) 1949 *E*, 1950 *E*
Piqué, J (Pau) 1961 *NZ* 2,3, *A*, 1962 *S*, *It*, 1964 *NZ*, *E*, *W*, *It*, *I*, *SA*, *Fj*, *R*, 1965 *S*, *I*, *E*, *W*, *It*

Piquemal, M (Tarbes) 1927 *I*, *S*, 1929 *I*, *G*, 1930 *S*, *I*, *E*, *G*, *W*
Piquiral, E (RCF) 1924 *S*, *I*, *E*, *W*, *R*, *US*, 1925 *E*, 1926 *S*, *I*, *E*, *W*, *M*, 1927 *I*, *S*, *W*, *E*, *G* 1,2, 1928 *E*
Piteu, R (Pau) 1921 *S*, *W*, *E*, *I*, 1922 *S*, *E*, *W*, *I*, 1923 *E*, 1924 *E*, 1925 *I*, *NZ*, *W*, *E*, 1926 *E*
Plantefol, A (RCF) 1967 *SA* 2,3,4, *NZ*, *R*, 1968 *E*, *W*, *Cz*, *NZ* 2, 1969 *E*, *W*
Plantey, S (RCF) 1961 *A*, 1962 *It*
Podevin, G (SF) 1913 *W*, *I*
Poeydebasque, F (Bayonne) 1914 *I*, *W*
Poirier, A (SCUF) 1907 *E*
Pomathios, M (Agen, Lyon U, Bourg) 1948 *I*, *A*, *S*, *W*, *E*, 1949 *S*, *I*, *E*, *W*, *Arg* 1,2, 1950 *S*, *I*, *W*, 1951 *S*, *I*, *E*, *W*, 1952 *W*, *E*, 1953 *S*, *I*, *W*, 1954 *S*
Pons, P (Toulouse) 1920 *S*, *E*, *W*, 1921 *S*, *W*, 1922 *S*
Porra, M (Lyon) 1931 *I*
Porthault, A (RCF) 1951 *S*, *E*, *W*, 1952 *I*, 1953 *S*, *I*, *It*
Portolan, C (Toulouse) 1986 *A*, 1989 *I*, *E*
Potel, A (Begles) 1932 *G*
Prat, J (Lourdes) 1945 *B* 1,2, *W*, 1946 *B*, *I*, *K*, *W*, 1947 *S*, *I*, *W*, *E*, 1948 *I*, *A*, *S*, *W*, *E*, 1949 *S*, *I*, *E*, *W*, *Arg* 1, 2, 1950 *S*, *I*, *E*, *W*, 1951 *S*, *E*, *W*, 1952 *S*, *I*, *SA*, *W*, *E*, *It*, 1953 *S*, *I*, *E*, *W*, *It*, 1954 *S*, *I*, *NZ*, *W*, *E*, *It*, 1955 *S*, *I*, *E*, *W*, *It*
Prat, M (Lourdes) 1951 *I*, 1952 *S*, *I*, *SA*, *W*, *E*, 1953 *S*, *I*, *E*, 1954 *I*, *NZ*, *W*, *E*, *It*, 1955 *S*, *I*, *E*, *W*, *It*, 1956 *I*, *W*, *It*, *Cz*, 1957 *S*, *I*, *W*, *It*, *R* 1, 1958 *A*, *W*, *I*
Prevost, A (Albi) 1926 *M*, 1927 *I*, *S*, *W*
Prin-Clary, J (Cavaillon, Brive) 1945 *B* 1,2, *W*, 1946 *B*, *I*, *K*, *W*, 1947 *S*, *I*, *W*
Puech, L (Toulouse) 1920 *S*, *E*, *I*, 1921 *E*, *I*
Puget, M (Toulouse) 1961 *It*, 1966 *S*, *I*, *It*, 1967 *SA* 1,3,4, *NZ*, 1968 *Cz*, *NZ* 1,2, *SA* 1,2, *R*, 1969 *E*, *R*, 1970 *W*
Puig, A (Perpignan) 1926 *S*, *E*
Pujol, A (SOE Toulouse) 1906 *NZ*
Pujolle, M (Nice) 1989 *B*, *A* 1, 1990 *S*, *I*, *R*, *A* 1,2, *NZ* 2

Quaglio, A (Mazamet) 1957 *R* 2, 1958 *S*, *E*, *A*, *W*, *I*, *SA* 1,2, 1959 *S*, *E*, *It*, *W*, *I*
Quilis, A (Narbonne) 1967 *SA* 1,4, *NZ*, 1970 *R*, 1971 *I*

Ramis, R (Perpignan) 1922 *E*, *I*, 1923 *W*
Rancoule, H (Lourdes, Toulon, Tarbes) 1955 *E*, *W*, *It*, 1958 *A*, *W*, *It*, *I*, *SA* 1, 1959 *S*, *It*, *W*, 1960 *I*, *It*, *R*, *Arg* 1,2, 1961 *SA*, *E*, *W*, *It*, *NZ* 1,2, 1962 *S*, *E*, *W*, *I*, *It*
Rapin, A (SBUC) 1938 *R*
Raymond, F (Toulouse) 1925 *S*, 1927 *W*, 1928 *I*
Raynal, F (Perpignan) 1935 *G*, 1936 *G* 1,2, 1937 *G*, *It*
Raynaud, F (Carcassonne) 1933 *G*
Razat, J-P (Agen) 1962 *R*, 1963 *S*, *I*, *R*
Rebujent, R (RCF) 1963 *E*
Revailler, D (Graulhet) 1981 *S*, *I*, *W*, *E*, *A* 1,2, *R*, *NZ* 1,2, 1982 *W*, *S*, *I*, *R*, *Arg* 1
Revillon, J (RCF) 1926 *I*, *E*, 1927 *S*
Ribère, E (Perpignan, Quillan) 1924 *I*, 1925 *I*, *NZ*, *S*, 1926 *S*, *I*, *W*, *M*, 1927 *I*, *S*, *W*, *E*, *G* 1,2, 1928 *S*, *A*, *I*, *E*, *G*, *W*, 1929 *I*, *E*, *G*, 1930 *S*, *I*, *E*, *W*, 1931 *I*, *S*, *W*, *E*, *G*, 1932 *G*, 1933 *G*
Rives, J-P (Toulouse, RCF) 1975 *E*, *S*, *I*, *Arg* 1,2, *R*, 1976 *S*, *I*, *W*, *E*, *US*, *A* 1,2, *R*, 1977 *W*, *E*, *S*, *I*, *Arg* 1,2, *R*, 1978 *E*, *S*, *I*, *W*, *R*, 1979 *I*, *W*, *E*, *S*, *NZ* 1,2, *R*, 1980 *W*, *E*, *S*, *I*, *SA*, 1981 *S*, *I*, *W*, *E*, *A* 2, 1982 *W*, *E*, *S*, *I*, *R*, 1983 *E*, *S*, *I*, *W*, *A* 1,2, *R*, 1984 *I*, *W*, *E*, *S*
Rochon, A (Montferrand) 1936 *G* 1
Rodrigo, M (Mauléon) 1931 *I*, *W*
Rodriguez, L (Mont-de-Marsan, Montferrand, Dax) 1981 *A* 1,2, *R*, *NZ* 1,2, 1982 *W*, *E*, *S*, *I*, *R*, 1983 *E*, *S*, 1984 *I*, *NZ* 1,2, *R*, 1985 *E*, *S*, *I*, *W*, 1986 *Arg* 1, *A*, *R* 2, *NZ* 2,3 1987 *W*, *E*, *S*, *I*, [*S*, *Z*, *Fj*, *A*, *NZ*], *R*, 1988 *E*, *S*, *I*, *W*, *Arg* 1,2,3,4, *R*, 1989 *I*, *E*, *S*, *NZ* 1,2, *B*, *A* 1, 1990 *W*, *E*, *S*, *I*, *NZ* 1
Rogé, L (Béziers) 1952 *It*, 1953 *E*, *W*, *It*, 1954 *S*, *Arg* 1,2, 1955 *S*, *I*, 1956 *W*, *It*, *E*, 1957 *S*, 1960 *S*, *E*
Rollet, J (Bayonne) 1960 *Arg* 3, 1961 *NZ* 3, *A*, 1962 *It*, 1963 *I*
Romero, H (Montauban) 1962 *S*, *E*, *W*, *I*, *It*, *R*, 1963 *E*
Romeu, J-P (Montferrand) 1972 *R*, 1973 *S*, *NZ*, *E*, *W*, *I*, *R*, 1974 *W*, *E*, *S*, *Arg* 1,2, *R*, *SA* 1,2 (R), 1975 *W*, *SA* 2, *Arg* 1,2, *R*, 1976 *S*, *I*, *W*, *E*, *US*, 1977 *W*, *E*, *S*, *I*, *Arg* 1,2, *NZ* 1,2, *R*
Roques, A (Cahors) 1958 *A*, *W*, *It*, *I*, *SA* 1,2, 1959 *S*,

Villepreux, P (Toulouse) 1967 *It, I, SA* 2, *NZ*, 1968 *I*, *Cz, NZ* 1,2,3, *A*, 1969 *S, I, E, W, R*, 1970 *S, I, W, E, R*, 1971 *S, I, E, W, A* 1,2, *R*, 1972 *S, I* 1, *E, W, I* 2, *A* 1,2
Viviès, B (Agen) 1978 *E, S, I, W*, 1980 *SA, R*, 1981 *S, A* 1, 1983 *A* 1 (R)
Volot, M (SF) 1945 *W*, 1946 *B, I, K, W*

Weller, S (Grenoble) 1989 *A* 1,2, 1990 *A* 1, *NZ* 1
Wolf, J-P (Béziers) 1980 *SA, R*, 1981 *A* 2, 1982 *E*

Yachvili, M (Tulle, Brive) 1968 *E, W, Cz, NZ* 3, *A, R*, 1969 *S, I, R*, 1971 *E, SA* 1,2, *A* 1, 1972 *R*, 1975 *SA* 2

Zago, F (Montauban) 1963 *I, E*

FRENCH INTERNATIONAL RECORDS

Both team and individual records are for official French international matches, up to 31 March 1993.

TEAM RECORDS

Highest score
70 v Zimbabwe (70-12) 1987 Auckland
v individual countries
37 v Argentina (37-3) 1960 Buenos Aires
34 v Australia (34-6) 1976 Parc des Princes
19 v Canada (19-13) 1991 Agen
28 v Czechoslovakia (28-3) 1956 Toulouse
37 v England (37-12) 1972 Colombes
33 v Fiji (33-9) 1991 Grenoble
38 v Germany (38-17) 1933 Parc des Princes
44 v Ireland (44-12) 1992 Parc des Princes
60 v Italy (60-13) 1967 Toulon
30 v Japan (30-18) 1973 Bordeaux
24 v N Zealand (24-19) 1979 Auckland
59 v Romania (59-3) 1924 Colombes
28 v Scotland (28-22) 1987 Parc des Princes
29 v S Africa (29-16) 1992 Parc des Princes
41 v United States (41-9) 1991 Denver
36 v Wales (36-3) 1991 Parc des Princes
70 v Zimbabwe (70-12) 1987 Auckland

Biggest winning points margin
58 v Zimbabwe (70-12) 1987 Auckland
v individual countries
34 v Argentina (37-3) 1960 Buenos Aires
28 v Australia (34-6) 1976 Parc des Princes
6 v Canada (19-13) 1991 Agen
25 v Czechoslovakia (28-3) 1956 Toulouse
25 v England (37-12) 1972 Colombes
24 v Fiji (33-9) 1991 Grenoble
34 v Germany (34-0) 1931 Colombes
32 v Ireland (44-12) 1992 Parc des Princes
47 v Italy (60-13) 1967 Toulon
12 v Japan (30-18) 1973 Bordeaux
13 v N Zealand (16-3) 1986 Nantes

56 v Romania (59-3) 1924 Colombes
20 v Scotland (23-3) 1977 Parc des Princes
13 v S Africa (29-16) 1992 Parc des Princes
32 v United States (41-9) 1991 Denver
33 v Wales (36-3) 1991 Parc des Princes
58 v Zimbabwe (70-12) 1987 Auckland

Highest score by opposing team
49 Wales (14-49) 1910 Swansea
S Africa beat 'France' 55-6 at Parc des Princes on 3 January 1907, but it is not regarded as an official international match

by individual countries
27 Argentina (31-27) 1974 Buenos Aires
48 Australia (31-48) 1990 Brisbane
13 Canada (19-13) 1991 Agen
6 Czechoslovakia (19-6) 1968 Prague
41 England (13-41) 1907 Richmond
16 Fiji (31-16) 1987 Auckland
17 Germany { (16-17) 1927 Frankfurt / (38-17) 1933 Parc des Princes }
25 Ireland { (5-25) 1911 Cork / (6-25) 1975 Dublin }
13 Italy (60-13) 1967 Toulon
18 Japan (30-18) 1973 Bordeaux
38 N Zealand (8-38) 1906 Parc des Princes
21 Romania (33-21) 1991 Bucharest
31 Scotland (3-31) 1912 Inverleith
38 S Africa { (5-38) 1913 Bordeaux / (25-38) 1975 Bloemfontein }
17 United States (3-17) 1924 Colombes
49 Wales (14-49) 1910 Swansea
12 Zimbabwe (70-12) 1987 Auckland

Biggest losing points margin
42 v Wales (5-47) 1909 Colombes
The 6-55 defeat by S Africa in Paris in 1907 is regarded as unofficial

v individual countries
12 v Argentina (6-18) 1988 Buenos Aires
17 v Australia $\begin{cases} (15-32) \text{ 1989 Strasbourg} \\ (31-48) \text{ 1990 Brisbane} \end{cases}$
37 v England (0-37) 1911 Twickenham
3 v Germany (0-3) 1938 Frankfurt
24 v Ireland (0-24) 1913 Cork
30 v N Zealand (8-38) 1906 Parc des Princes
15 v Romania (0-15) 1980 Bucharest
28 v Scotland (3-31) 1912 Inverleith
33 v S Africa (5-38) 1913 Bordeaux
14 v United States (3-17) 1924 Colombes
42 v Wales (5-47) 1909 Colombes
No defeats v Canada, Czechoslovakia, Fiji, Italy, Japan or Zimbabwe

Most tries by France in an international
13 v Romania (59-3) 1924 Paris

INDIVIDUAL RECORDS

Most capped player
S Blanco 93 1980-91
in individual positions
Full-back
S Blanco 81(93)[1] 1980-91
Wing
P Lagisquet 46 1983-91
Centre
P Sella 81(88)[2] 1982-93
Fly-half
J-P Romeu 33(34)[3] 1972-77
Scrum-half
P Berbizier 56 1981-91
Prop
R Paparemborde 55 1975-83
Hooker
P Dintrans 50 1979-90
Lock
J Condom 61[4] 1982-90
Flanker
J-P Rives 59[4] 1975-84
No 8
G Basquet 33[4] 1945-52
[1] *S Blanco won 12 caps as a wing*
[2] *Sella has won 6 caps as a wing and one as a full-back*
[3] *Romeu was capped once as a replacement full-back. F Mesnel, 52 caps, won 29 as a centre and 23 at fly-half. D Camberabero, 36 caps, has won 30 at fly-half, 3 on the wing and 3 at full-back*

[4] *B Dauga and M Crauste, 63 caps each, are France's most-capped forwards. Dauga was capped as a lock and No 8; Crauste as a flanker and No 8*

Longest international career
F Haget 14 seasons 1974-87

Most consecutive Tests – 46
R Bertranne 1973-79

Most internationals as captain – 34
J-P Rives 1978-84

Most points in internationals – 354
D Camberabero (36 matches) 1982-93

Most points in International Championship in a season – 54
J-P Lescarboura (4 matches) 1983-84

Most points in an international – 30
D Camberabero v Zimbabwe 1987 Auckland

Most tries in internationals – 38
S Blanco (93 matches) 1980-91

Most tries in International Championship in a season – 5
P Estève (4 matches) 1982-83
E Bonneval (4 matches) 1986-87

Most tries in an international – 4
A Jauréguy v Romania 1924 Colombes
M Celhay v Italy 1937 Parc des Princes

Most conversions in internationals – 48
D Camberabero (36 matches) 1982-93

Most conversions in International Championship in a season – 7
P Villepreux (4 matches) 1971-72

Most conversions in an international – 9
G Camberabero v Italy 1967 Toulon
D Camberabero v Zimbabwe 1987
  Auckland
Father and son

Most dropped goals in internationals – 15
J-P Lescarboura (28 matches) 1982-90

Most penalty goals in internationals – 59
D Camberabero (36 matches) 1982-93

Most penalty goals in International Championship in a season – 10
J-P Lescarboura (4 matches) 1983-84

Most penalty goals in an international – 6
J M Aguirre v Argentina 1977 Buenos Aires

Most points on major tour – 112
S Viars (7 matches) 1992 Argentina

Most points in any match on tour – 28
P Lagisquet v Paraguayan XV 1988
  Ascunción
P Estève scored 32 points against East Japan in 1984, but this was not on a major tour

Most tries in a tour match – 7
P Lagisquet v Paraguayan XV 1988
  Ascunción
P Estève scored 8 tries v East Japan in 1984, but this was not on a major tour

MOMENTOUS YEAR OVERSHADOWED

THE 1992 SEASON IN SOUTH AFRICA
John Robbie *Radio 712*

It is tempting to equate the 1992 season in South Africa with the *annus horribilis* experienced by the British royal family. Both had rows, ructions and scandals behind the scenes and a rather poor set of public performances to add insult to injury. It's tempting to take that line, but it is not really accurate. Despite all the disappointments and dejection a lot was achieved in South Africa and, provided that lessons have been learned, one can argue that the rugby future looks bright. The best news, of course, was that international rugby came to South Africa and South Africa came back to the world. The tours are covered in detail elsewhere in the Yearbook.

Sadly, that future will be faced without the Doc. Dr Danie Craven passed away peacefully in January 1993 and was genuinely mourned by the rugby world. Perhaps he stayed at the helm of local rugby for too long; perhaps he had lost touch; perhaps he had failed to organise a successor; perhaps, through the Cavaliers, he had lost the trust of his international friends. Yet what is certain is that he was a rugby legend and, unlike Moses, he lived to experience the Promised Land of the return to legitimate international competition. That for the Doc would have been honey indeed.

Unfortunately, the results were not so sweet and the boasts about South Africa being surrogate world champions were cruelly exposed. The All Blacks, Australia, France and England were well ahead technically, and even a gutsy win over the French in one Test did little to soften the blow of this illumination. South Africa has much to learn and, in particular, the 26-3 defeat by Australia at Newlands left nobody in any doubt about the challenge ahead.

The season started off with unity between SARU and the SARB being finally achieved and the promise of tours whetting the appetites of all. Under the SARFU banner the Currie Cup campaign was an exciting one. Natal looked to be the best balanced side, and with imports Robert du Preez at scrum-half and Pieter Muller in the centre, most felt they would be there at the kill. They played a very controlled game, skipper Wahl Bartmann often leading the charge to commit opposition players. Full-back André Joubert suffered with injury and veteran Hugh Reece-Edwards again made the full-back position his own. He had a fine season and capped it, literally, with a place on the international tour.

Transvaal played expansive running rugby and broke all try-scoring records. Wings James Small and Pieter Hendriks revelled in the possession and both earned international caps along with full-back Theo van Rensburg. At 31 years of age coach Harry Viljoen was almost one of the players and his boldness was infectious. At one stage his side looked like completing the ten-match League section unbeaten, but in the end they once again seemed to lose momentum and had to settle for second place to Natal. So these two old rivals contested the September final, and what an occasion it was.

It was won 14-13 by Natal in front of 70,000 people at Ellis Park. Transvaal departed from their running game and even a late rally couldn't clinch things. Natal's try came early from young No 8 Garry Teichman, and it was when Transvaal centre Heinrich Fuls touched down after 58 minutes that the excitement really started. With minutes to go and Transvaal 13-14 down, Theo van Rensburg had a 45-metre kick to win. He narrowly missed and that was that. Transvaal had lost their fifth final since 1986 and retiring captain Jannie Breedt, a veteran of all five losses, won the respect of all with his dignity in defeat. Indeed, he was chaired off by the Natal players. Even a win in the Lion Cup final by 17-12 against Free State did not really save the season. The Lion Cup was played without the touring players and only 20,000 spectators came to watch. It is to be hoped that next season it will again become a major competition.

The 1991 holders, Northerns, were strangely inconsistent in 1992, although Naas Botha at times managed to compensate for team weaknesses. He returned late from Rovigo and kicked four penalties and a staggering five dropped goals in a 27-24 win over Natal. A number of fine young players emerged, including scrum-half Joost van der Westhuysen, and Northerns will challenge next season.

Western Province battled all year and indeed lost their three Currie Cup games. A strong pack was unable to compensate for deficiencies behind the scrum, although injuries certainly played a part. When he played Tiaan Strauss was inspirational and at times Lance Sherrel threatened to realise his huge potential. Dawie Snyman, who was at the helm during their marvellously successful run in the 1980s, returned as coach and will undoubtedly bring about improvements.

Eastern Province as usual promised much but achieved little. They were always hard to beat but never established a winning pattern. Alex Wyllie coached the B side, and with a number of top players moving to Port Elizabeth, including Garth Wright, confidence is high for next season. Captain Michael du Plessis was a disappointment and at times seemed to lack commitment.

Free State as so often played excellent rugby, but the loss of Muller and Joubert robbed them of the strikers of the year before. Young half-backs Hentie Martens and Jannie de Beer showed great maturity and are names to follow. Coach Gerrie Sonnekus was named as national coach after the axing of John Williams and, with Gysie Pienaar as his assistant, will no doubt encourage an expansive and running game.

Controversy surrounded a number of positive drug tests on provincial players. It appeared that unions supported their players rather than the interests of the game, and at one time legal actions were threatened. Thankfully, a policy in line with the rest of the world has now been introduced and regular random tests are the norm. The anthem row at Ellis Park before the All Black Test was a major issue in South Africa. Whether it was a mistake or a deliberate show of defiance is debatable, but at one time it threatened the very unity of the game. It is clear that until the country has settled down into a new democratic dispensation, symbols, flags and gestures will be important and around them compromise and sense must be shown.

Development in South African rugby means a programme to improve the opportunities for those who suffered under apartheid. It means training, facilities and encouragement plus a chance to develop potential. Development, or the lack of it, was also a controversial issue; indeed, the row caused the cancellation of a warm-up Test in Romania and Italy. Perhaps this contributed to the disasters on the international field. Happily, it would seem that programmes are now up and running, and a development side toured the South Pacific. They were unsuccessful on the field but important lessons were learned.

The great Naas Botha announced his retirement from the domestic game and so ended an era. He was a controversial figure and was criticised by many over his tour captaincy, particularly his leadership off the field. However, he was an inspirational player and captain for Northerns, and without isolation would certainly have established himself as one of the truly great match-winners of all time. He had weaknesses in defence and in individual running, but probably won more games with his kicking, tactical and goal, than any other player. He was enigmatic and that was part of his appeal. South Africa will never see his like again.

South African rugby has players of size and class, stadia unrivalled in the world and a burning desire to get back to the top. Many lessons must be learned, and private egos and provincial loyalties must be sacrificed for the good of the game. If that happens the World Cup in 1995 could be a victorious triumph. The world will look for improvement on and off the field in 1993.

Currie Cup winners: Natal
Lion Cup winners: Transvaal
Toyota Club champions: Rand Afrikaans U
Player of the Year: Tiaan Strauss (WP and South Africa)

Full details of the 1992 Currie Cup are given on page 112.

SOUTH AFRICAN INTERNATIONAL PLAYERS (*up to 31 March 1993*)

ABBREVIATIONS

A – Australia; *BI* – British Isles teams; *Cv* – New Zealand Cavaliers; *E* – England; *F* – France; *I* – Ireland; *NZ* – New Zealand; *S* – Scotland; *S Am* – South America; *US* – United States of America; *W* – Wales; *Wld* – World Invitation XV; (R) – Replacement

PROVINCIAL ABBREVIATIONS

Bor – Border; Bol – Boland; EP – Eastern Province; GW – Griqualand West; N – Natal; NT – Northern Transvaal; OFS – Orange Free State; R – Rhodesia; SET – South East Transvaal; SWA – South West Africa; SWD – South West Districts; Tvl – Transvaal; WP – Western Province; WT – Western Transvaal; Z-R – Zimbabwe-Rhodesia

Note: When a series has taken place, figures denote the particular matches in which players featured. Thus 1968 *BI* 1,2,4 indicates that a player appeared in the first, second and fourth Tests of the 1968 series against the British Isles.

Ackermann, D S P (WP) 1955 *BI* 2,3,4, 1956 *A* 1,2, *NZ* 1,3, 1958 *F* 2
Albertyn, P K (SWD) 1924 *BI* 1,2,3,4
Alexander, E (GW) 1891 *BI* 1,2
Allen, P B (EP) 1960 *S*
Allport, P (WP) 1910 *BI* 2,3
Anderson, J A (WP) 1903 *BI* 3
Anderson, J H (WP) 1896 *BI* 1,3,4
Andrew, J B (Tvl) 1896 *BI* 2
Andrews, K S (WP) 1992 *E*
Antelme, M J G (Tvl) 1960 *NZ* 1,2,3,4, 1960-61 *F*
Apsey, J T (WP) 1933 *A* 4,5, 1938 *BI* 2
Ashley, S (WP) 1903 *BI* 2
Aston, F T D (Tvl) 1896 *BI* 1,2,3,4
Aucamp, J (WT) 1924 *BI* 1,2

Baard, A P (WP) 1960-61 *I*
Babrow, L (WP) 1937 *A* 1,2, *NZ* 1,2,3
Barnard, A S (EP) 1984 *S Am* 1,2, 1986 *Cv* 1,2
Barnard, J H (Tvl) 1965 *S*, *A* 1,2, *NZ* 3,4
Barnard, R W (Tvl) 1970 *NZ* 2(R)
Barnard, W H M (NT) 1949 *NZ* 4, 1951-52 *W*
Barry, J (WP) 1903 *BI* 1,2,3
Bartmann, W J (Tvl, N) 1986 *Cv* 1,2,3,4, 1992 *NZ*, *A*, *F* 1,2
Bastard, W E (N) 1937 *A* 1, *NZ* 1,2,3, 1938 *BI* 1,3
Bates, A J (WT) 1969-70 *E*, 1970 *NZ* 1,2, 1972 *E*
Bayvel, P C R (Tvl) 1974 *BI* 2,4, *F* 1,2, 1975 *F* 1,2, 1976 *NZ* 1,2,3,4
Beck, J J (WP) 1981 *NZ* 2(R), 3 (R), *US*
Bedford, T P (N) 1963 *A* 1,2,3,4, 1964 *W*, *F*, 1965 *I*, *A* 1,2, 1968 *BI* 1,2,3,4, *F* 1,2, 1969 *A* 1,2,3,4, 1969-70 *S*, *E*, *I*, *W*, 1971 *F* 1,2
Bekker, H J (WP) 1981 *NZ* 1,3
Bekker, H P J (NT) 1951-52 *E*, *F*, 1953 *A* 1,2,3,4, 1955 *BI* 2,3,4, 1956 *A* 1,2, *NZ* 1,2,3,4
Bekker, M J (NT) 1960 *S*
Bekker, R P (NT) 1953 *A* 3,4
Bergh, W F (SWD) 1931-32 *W*, *I*, *E*, *S*, 1933 *A* 1,2,3,4,5, 1937 *A* 1,2, *NZ* 1,2,3, 1938 *BI* 1,2,3
Bestbier, A (OFS) 1974 *F* 2(R)
Bester, J J N (WP) 1924 *BI* 2,4
Bester, J L A (WP) 1938 *BI* 2,3
Beswick, A M (Bor) 1896 *BI* 2,3,4
Bezuidenhoudt, C E (NT) 1962 *BI* 2,3,4
Bezuidenhoudt, N S E (NT) 1972 *E*, 1974 *BI* 2,3,4, *F* 1,2, 1975 *F* 1,2, 1977 *Wld*
Bierman, J N (Tvl) 1931-32 *I*
Bisset, W M (WP) 1891 *BI* 1,3
Blair, R (WP) 1977 *Wld*
Bosch, G R (Tvl) 1974 *BI* 2, *F* 1,2, 1975 *F* 1,2, 1976 *NZ* 1,2,3,4
Bosman, N J S (Tvl) 1924 *BI* 2,3,4
Botha, D S (NT) 1981 *NZ* 1
Botha, H E (NT) 1980 *S Am* 1,2, *BI* 1,2,3,4, *S Am* 3,4, *F*, 1981 *I* 1,2, *NZ* 1,2,3, *US*, 1982 *S Am* 1,2, 1986 *Cv* 1,2,3,4, 1989 *Wld* 1,2, 1992 *NZ*, *A*, *F* 1,2, *E*
Botha, J (Tvl) 1903 *BI* 3
Botha, J P F (NT) 1962 *BI* 2,3,4
Botha, P H (Tvl) 1965 *A* 1,2
Boyes, H C (GW) 1891 *BI* 1,2

Brand, G H (WP) 1928 *NZ* 2,3, 1931-32 *W*,*I*, *E*, *S*, 1933 *A* 1,2,3,4,5, 1937 *A* 1,2, *NZ* 2,3, 1938 *BI* 1
Bredenkamp, M (GW) 1896 *BI* 1,3
Breedt, J C (Tvl) 1986 *Cv* 1,2,3,4, 1989 *Wld* 1,2, 1992 *NZ*, *A*
Brewis, J D (NT) 1949 *NZ* 1,2,3,4, 1951-52 *S*, *I*, *W*, *E*, *F*, 1953 *A* 1
Briers, T P D (WP) 1955 *BI* 1,2,3,4, 1956 *NZ* 2,3,4
Brink, D J (WP) 1906 *S*, *W*, *E*
Brooks, D (Bor) 1906 *S*
Brown, C (WP) 1903 *BI* 1,2,3
Brynard, G S (WP) 1965 *A* 1, *NZ* 1,2,3,4, 1968 *BI* 3,4
Buchler, J U (Tvl) 1951-52 *S*, *I*, *W*, *E*, *F*, 1953 *A* 1,2,3,4, 1956 *A* 2
Burdett, A F (WP) 1906 *S*, *I*
Burger, J M (WP) 1989 *Wld* 1,2
Burger, M B (NT) 1980 *BI* 2(R), *S Am* 3, 1981 *US* (R)
Burger, S W P (WP) 1984 *E* 1,2, 1986 *Cv* 1,2,3,4
Burger, W A G (Bor) 1906 *S*, *I*, *W*, 1910 *BI* 2

Carelse, G (EP) 1964 *W*, *F*, 1965 *I*, *S*, 1967 *F* 1,2,3, 1968 *F* 1,2, 1969 *A* 1,2,3,4, 1969-70 *S*
Carlson, R A (WP) 1972 *E*
Carolin, H W (WP) 1903 *BI* 3, 1906 *S*, *I*
Castens, H H (WP) 1891 *BI* 1
Chignell, T W (WP) 1891 *BI* 3
Cilliers, G D (OFS) 1963 *A* 1,3,4
Claassen, J T (WT) 1955 *BI* 1,2,3,4, 1956 *A* 1,2, *NZ* 1,2,3,4, 1958 *F* 1,2, 1960 *S*, *NZ* 1,2,3, 1960-61 *W*, *I*, *E*, *S*, *F*, 1961 *I*, *A* 1,2, 1962 *BI* 1,2,3,4
Claassen, W (N) 1981 *I* 1,2, *NZ* 2,3, *US*, 1982 *S Am* 1,2
Clarke, W H (Tvl) 1933 *A* 3
Clarkson, W A (N) 1921 *NZ* 1,2, 1924 *BI* 1
Cloete, H A (WP) 1896 *BI* 4
Cockrell, C H (WP) 1969-70 *S*, *I*, *W*
Cockrell, R J (WP) 1974 *F* 1,2, 1975 *F* 1,2, 1976 *NZ* 1,2, 1977 *Wld*, 1981 *NZ* 1,2(R),3, *US*
Coetzee, J H H (WP) 1974 *BI* 1, 1975 *F* 2(R), 1976 *NZ* 1,2,3,4
Cope, D (Tvl) 1896 *BI* 2
Cotty, W (GW) 1896 *BI* 3
Crampton, G (GW) 1903 *BI* 2
Craven, D H (WP) 1931-32 *W*, *I*, *S*, 1933 *A* 1,2,3,4,5, 1937 *A* 1,2, *NZ* 1,2,3, 1938 *BI* 1,2,3
Cronje, P A (Tvl) 1971 *F* 1,2, *A* 1,2,3, 1974 *BI* 3,4
Crosby, J H (Tvl) 1896 *BI* 2
Crosby, N J (Tvl) 1910 *BI* 1,3
Currie, C (GW) 1903 *BI* 2

D'Alton, G (WP) 1933 *A* 1
Daneel, G M (WP) 1928 *NZ* 1,2,3,4, 1931-32 *W*, *I*, *E*, *S*
Daneel, H J (WP) 1906 *S*, *I*, *W*, *E*
Davidson, M (EP) 1910 *BI* 1
De Bruyn, J (OFS) 1974 *BI* 3
De Jongh, H P K (WP) 1928 *NZ* 3
De Klerk, I J (Tvl) 1969-70 *E*, *I*, *W*
De Klerk, K B H (Tvl) 1974 *BI* 1,2,3(R), 1975 *F* 1,2, 1976 *NZ* 2(R),3,4, 1980 *S Am* 1,2, *BI* 2, 1981 *I* 1,2
De Kock, A (GW) 1891 *BI* 2

295

De Kock, J S (WP) 1921 *NZ* 3, 1924 *BI* 3
Delport, W H (EP) 1951-52 *S, I, W, E, F*, 1953 *A* 1,2,3,4
De Melker, S C (GW) 1903 *BI* 2, 1906 *E*
Devenish, C (GW) 1896 *BI* 2
Devenish, G St L (Tvl) 1896 *BI* 2
Devenish, M (Tvl) 1891 *BI* 1
De Villiers, D I (Tvl) 1910 *BI* 1,2,3
De Villiers, D J (WP, Bol) 1962 *BI* 2,3, 1965 *I, NZ* 1,3,4, 1967 *F* 1,2,3,4, 1968 *BI* 1,2,3,4, *F* 1,2, 1969 *A* 1,4, 1969-70 *E, I, W*, 1970 *NZ* 1,2,3,4
De Villiers, H A (WP) 1906 *S, W, E*
De Villiers, H O (WP) 1967 *F* 1,2,3,4, 1968 *F* 1,2, 1969 *A* 1,2,3,4, 1969-70 *S, E, I, W*
De Villiers, P du P (WP) 1928 *NZ* 1,3,4, 1931-32 *E*, 1933 *A* 4, 1937 *A* 1,2, *NZ* 1
Devine, D (Tvl) 1924 *BI* 3, 1928 *NZ* 2
De Vos, D J J (WP) 1965 *S*, 1969 *A* 3, 1969-70 *S*
De Waal, A N (WP) 1967 *F* 1,2,3,4
De Waal, P (WP) 1896 *BI* 4
De Wet, A E (WP) 1969 *A* 3,4, 1969-70 *E*
De Wet, P (WP) 1938 *BI* 1,2,3
Dinkelmann, E E (NT) 1951-52 *S, I, E, F*, 1953 *A* 1,2
Dirksen, C W (NT) 1963 *A* 4, 1964 *W*, 1965 *I,S*, 1967 *F* 1,2,3,4, 1968 *BI* 1,2
Dobbin, F J (GW) 1903 *BI* 1,2, 1906 *S, W, E*, 1910 *BI* 1, 1912-13 *S, I, W*
Dobie, J A R (Tvl) 1928 *NZ* 2
Dormehl, P J (WP) 1896 *BI* 3,4
Douglass, F W (EP) 1896 *BI* 1
Dryburgh, R G (WP) 1955 *BI* 2,3,4, 1956 *A* 2, *NZ* 1,4, 1960 *NZ* 1,2
Duff, B (WP) 1891 *BI* 1,2,3
Duffy, B A (Bor) 1928 *NZ* 1
Du Plessis, C J (WP) 1982 *S Am* 1,2, 1984 *E* 1,2, *S Am* 1,2, 1986 *Cv* 1,2,3,4, 1989 *Wld* 1,2
Du Plessis, D C (NT) 1977 *Wld*, 1980 *S Am* 2
Du Plessis, F (Tvl) 1949 *NZ* 1,2,3
Du Plessis, M (WP) 1971 *A* 1,2,3, 1974 *BI* 1,2, *F* 1,2, 1975 *F* 1,2, 1976 *NZ* 1,2,3,4, 1977 *Wld*, 1980 *S Am* 1,2, *BI* 1,2,3,4, *S Am* 4, *F*
Du Plessis, M J (WP) 1984 *S Am* 1,2, 1986 *Cv* 1,2,3,4, 1989 *Wld* 1,2
Du Plessis, N J (WT) 1921 *NZ* 2,3, 1924 *BI* 1,2,3
Du Plessis, P G (NT) 1972 *E*
Du Plessis, T D (NT) 1980 *S Am* 1,2
Du Plessis, W (WP) 1980 *S Am* 1,2, *BI* 1,2,3,4, *S Am* 3,4, *F*, 1981 *NZ* 1,2,3, 1982 *S Am* 1,2
Du Plooy, A J J (EP) 1955 *BI* 1
Du Preez, F C H (NT) 1960-61 *E, S*, 1961 *A* 1,2, 1962 *BI* 1,2,3,4, 1963 *A* 1, 1964 *W, F*, 1965 *A* 1,2, *NZ* 1,2,3,4, 1967 *F* 4, 1968 *BI* 1,2,3,4, *F* 1,2, 1969 *A* 1,2, 1969-70 *S, I, W*, 1970 *NZ* 1,2,3,4, 1971 *F* 1,2, *A* 1,2,3
Du Preez, J G H (WP) 1956 *NZ* 1
Du Preez, R J (N) 1992 *NZ, A*
Du Rand, J A (R, NT) 1949 *NZ* 2,3, 1951-52 *S, I, W, E, F*, 1953 *A* 1,2,3,4, 1955 *BI* 1,2,3,4, 1956 *A* 1,2, *NZ* 1,2,3,4
Du Toit, A F (WP) 1928 *NZ* 3,4
Du Toit, B A (Tvl) 1938 *BI* 1,2,3
Du Toit, P A (NT) 1949 *NZ* 2,3,4, 1951-52 *S, I, W, E, F*
Du Toit, P G (WP) 1981 *NZ* 1, 1982 *S Am* 1,2, 1984 *E* 1,2
Du Toit, P S (WP) 1958 *F* 1,2, 1960 *NZ* 1,2,3,4, 1960-61 *W, I, E, S, F*, 1961 *I, A* 1,2
Duvenhage, F P (GW) 1949 *NZ* 1,3

Edwards, P (NT) 1980 *S Am* 1,2
Ellis, J H (SWA) 1965 *NZ* 1,2,3,4, 1967 *F* 1,2,3,4, 1968 *BI* 1,2,3,4, *F* 1,2, 1969 *A* 1,2,3,4, 1969-70 *S, I, W*, 1970 *NZ* 1,2,3,4, 1971 *F* 1,2, *A* 1,2,3, 1972 *E*, 1974 *BI* 1,2,3,4, *F* 1,2, 1976 *NZ* 1
Ellis, M (Tvl) 1921 *NZ* 2,3, 1924 *BI* 1,2,3,4
Engelbrecht, J P (WP) 1960 *S*, 1960-61 *W, I, E, S, F*, 1961 *A* 1,2, 1962 *BI* 2,3,4, 1963 *A* 2,3, 1964 *W, F*, 1965 *I, S, A* 1,2, *NZ* 1,2,3,4, 1967 *F* 1,2,3,4, 1968 *BI* 1,2, *F* 1,2, 1969 *A* 1,2
Erasmus, F S (NT, EP) 1986 *Cv* 3,4, 1989 *Wld* 2
Etlinger, T E (WP) 1896 *BI* 4

Ferreira, C (OFS) 1986 *Cv* 1,2
Ferreira, P S (WP) 1984 *S Am* 1,2
Ferris, H H (Tvl) 1903 *BI* 3

Forbes, H H (Tvl) 1896 *BI* 2
Fourie, C (EP) 1974 *F* 1,2, 1975 *F* 1,2
Fourie, T T (SET) 1974 *BI* 3
Fourie, W L (SWA) 1958 *F* 1,2
Francis, J A J (Tvl) 1912-13 *S, I, W, E, F*
Frederickson, C A (Tvl) 1974 *BI* 2, 1980 *S Am* 1,2
Frew, A (Tvl) 1903 *BI* 1
Froneman, D C (OFS) 1977 *Wld*
Froneman, I L (Bor) 1933 *A* 1
Fuls, H T (Tvl) 1992 *NZ* (R)
Fry, S P (WP) 1951-52 *S, I, W, E, F*, 1953 *A* 1,2,3,4, 1955 *BI* 1,2,3,4

Gage, J H (OFS) 1933 *A* 1
Gainsford, J L (WP) 1960 *S, NZ* 1,2,3,4, 1960-61 *W, I, E, S, F*, 1961 *A* 1,2, 1962 *BI* 1,2,3,4, 1963 *A* 1,2,3,4, 1964 *W, F*, 1965 *I, S, A* 1,2, *NZ* 1,2,3,4, 1967 *F* 1,2,3
Geel, P J (OFS) 1949 *NZ* 3
Geere, V (Tvl) 1933 *A* 1,2,3,4,5
Geffin, A O (Tvl) 1949 *NZ* 1,2,3,4, 1951-52 *S, I, W*
Geldenhuys, A (EP) 1992 *NZ, A, F* 1,2
Geldenhuys, S B (NT) 1981 *NZ* 2,3, *US*, 1982 *S Am* 1,2, 1989 *Wld* 1,2
Gentles, T A (WP) 1955 *BI* 1,2,4, 1956 *NZ* 2,3, 1958 *F* 2
Geraghty, E M (Bor) 1949 *NZ* 4
Gerber, D M (EP, WP) 1980 *S Am* 3,4, *F*, 1981 *I* 1,2, *NZ* 1,2,3, *US*, 1982 *S Am* 1,2, 1984 *E* 1,2, *S Am* 1,2, 1986 *Cv* 1,2,3,4, 1992 *NZ, A, F* 1,2, *E*
Gerber, M C (EP) 1958 *F* 1,2, 1960 *S*
Gericke, F W (Tvl) 1960 *S*
Germishuys, J S (OFS, Tvl) 1974 *BI* 2, 1976 *NZ* 1,2,3,4, 1977 *Wld*, 1980 *S Am* 1,2, *BI* 1,2,3,4, *S Am* 3,4, *F*, 1981 *I* 1,2, *NZ* 2,3, *US*
Gibbs, B (GW) 1903 *BI* 2
Goosen, C P (OFS) 1965 *NZ* 2
Gorton, H C (Tvl) 1896 *BI* 1
Gould, R L (N) 1968 *BI* 1,2,3,4
Gray, B G (WP) 1931-32 *W, E, S*, 1933 *A* 5
Greenwood, C M (WP) 1961 *I*
Greyling, P J F (OFS) 1967 *F* 1,2,3,4, 1968 *BI* 1, *F* 1,2, 1969 *A* 1,2,3,4, 1969-70 *S, E, I, W*, 1970 *NZ* 1,2,3,4, 1971 *F* 1,2, *A* 1,2,3, 1972 *E*
Grobler, C J (OFS) 1974 *BI* 4, 1975 *F* 1,2
Guthrie, F H (WP) 1891 *BI* 1,3, 1896 *BI* 1

Hahn, C H L (Tvl) 1910 *BI* 1,2,3
Hamilton, F (EP) 1891 *BI* 1
Harris, T A (Tvl) 1937 *NZ* 2,3, 1938 *BI* 1,2,3
Hartley, A J (WP) 1891 *BI* 3
Hattingh, H (NT) 1992 *A* (R), *F* 2 (R), *E*
Hattingh, L B (OFS) 1933 *A* 2
Heatlie, B H (WP) 1891 *BI* 2,3, 1896 *BI* 1,4, 1903 *BI* 1,3
Hendriks, P (Tvl) 1992 *NZ, A*
Hepburn, T (WP) 1896 *BI* 4
Heunis, J W (NT) 1981 *NZ* 3(R), *US*, 1982 *S Am* 1,2, 1984 *E* 1,2, *S Am* 1,2, 1986 *Cv* 1,2,3,4, 1989 *Wld* 1,2
Hill, R A (R) 1960-61 *W, I*, 1961 *I, A* 1,2, 1962 *BI* 4, 1963 *A* 3
Hills, W G (NT) 1992 *F* 1,2, *E*
Hirsch, J G (EP) 1906 *I*, 1910 *BI* 1
Hobson, T E C (WP) 1903 *BI* 3
Hoffman, R S (Bol) 1953 *A* 3
Holton, D N (EP) 1960 *S*
Hopwood, D J (WP) 1960 *S, NZ* 3,4, 1960-61 *W, E, S, F*, 1961 *A* 1,2, 1962 *BI* 1,2,3,4, 1963 *A* 1,2,4, 1964 *W, F*, 1965 *S, NZ* 3,4
Howe, B F (Bor) 1956 *NZ* 1,4
Howe-Browne, N R F G (WP) 1910 *BI* 1,2,3
Hugo, D P (WP) 1989 *Wld* 1,2

Immelman, J H (WP) 1912-13 *F*

Jackson, D C (WP) 1906 *I, W, E*
Jackson, J S (WP) 1903 *BI* 2
Jansen, E (OFS) 1981 *NZ* 1
Jansen, J S (OFS) 1970 *NZ* 1,2,3,4, 1971 *F* 1,2, *A* 1,2,3, 1972 *E*
Jennings, C B (Bor) 1937 *NZ* 1
Johnstone, P G A (WP) 1951-52 *S, I, W, E, F*, 1956 *A* 1, *NZ* 1,2,4
Jones, C H (Tvl) 1903 *BI* 1,2
Jones, P S T (WP) 1896 *BI* 1,3,4

Jordaan, R P (NT) 1949 *NZ* 1,2,3,4
Joubert, A J (OFS) 1989 *Wld* 1 (R)
Joubert, S J (WP) 1906 *I*, *W*, *E*

Kahts, W J H (NT) 1980 *BI* 1,2,3, *S Am* 3,4, *F*, 1981 *I* 1,2, *NZ* 2, 1982 *S Am* 1,2
Kaminer, J (Tvl) 1958 *F* 2
Kelly, E W (GW) 1896 *BI* 3
Kenyon, B J (Bor) 1949 *NZ* 4
Kipling, H G (GW) 1931-32 *W*, *I*, *E*, *S*, 1933 *A* 1,2,3,4,5
Kirkpatrick, A I (GW) 1953 *A* 2, 1956 *NZ* 2, 1958 *F* 1, 1960 *S*, *NZ* 1,2,3,4, 1960-61 *W*, *I*, *E*, *S*, *F*
Knight, A S (Tvl) 1912-13 *S*, *I*, *W*, *E*, *F*
Knoetze, F (WP) 1989 *Wld* 1,2
Koch, A C (Bol) 1949 *NZ* 2,3,4, 1951-52 *S*, *I*, *W*, *E*, *F*, 1953 *A* 1,2,4, 1955 *BI* 1,2,3,4, 1956 *A* 1, *NZ* 2,3, 1958 *F* 1,2, 1960 *NZ* 1,2
Koch, H V (WP) 1949 *NZ* 1,2,3,4
Kotze, G J M (WP) 1967 *F* 1,2,3,4
Krantz, E F W (OFS) 1976 *NZ* 1, 1981 *I* 1
Krige, J D (WP) 1903 *BI* 1,3, 1906 *S*, *I*, *W*
Kritzinger, J L (Tvl) 1974 *BI* 3,4, *F* 1,2, 1975 *F* 1,2, 1976 *NZ* 4
Kroon, C M (EP) 1955 *BI* 1
Kruger, P E (Tvl) 1986 *Cv* 3,4
Kruger, T L (Tvl) 1921 *NZ* 1,2, 1924 *BI* 1,2,3,4, 1928 *NZ* 1,2
Kuhn, S P (Tvl) 1960 *NZ* 3,4 1960-61 *W*, *I*, *E*, *S*, *F*, 1961 *I*, *A* 1,2, 1962 *BI* 1,2,3,4, 1963 *A* 1,2,3, 1965 *I*, *S*

La Grange, J B (WP) 1924 *BI* 3,4
Larard, A (Tvl) 1896 *BI* 2,4
Lategan, M T (WP) 1949 *NZ* 1,2,3,4, 1951-52 *S*, *I*, *W*, *E*, *F*, 1953 *A* 1,2
Lawless, M J (WP) 1964 *F*, 1969-70 *E* (R), *I*, *W*
Ledger, S H (GW) 1912-13 *S*, *I*, *E*, *F*
Le Roux, M (OFS) 1980 *BI* 1,2,3,4, *S Am* 3,4, *F*, 1981 *I* 1
Le Roux, P A (WP) 1906 *I*, *W*, *E*
Little, E M M (GW) 1891 *BI* 1,3
Lochner, G P (WP) 1955 *BI* 3, 1956 *A* 1,2, *NZ* 1,2,3,4, 1958 *F* 1,2
Lochner, G P (EP) 1937 *NZ* 3, 1938 *BI* 1,2
Lockyear, R J (GW) 1960 *NZ* 1,2,3,4, 1960-61 *I*, *F*
Lombard, A C (EP) 1910 *BI* 2
Lotz, J W (Tvl) 1937 *A* 1,2, *NZ* 1,2,3, 1938 *BI* 1,2,3
Loubser, J A (WP) 1903 *BI* 3, 1906 *S*, *I*, *W*, *E*, 1910 *BI* 1,3
Lourens, M J (NT) 1968 *BI* 2,3,4
Louw, J S (Tvl) 1891 *BI* 1,2,3
Louw, M J (Tvl) 1971 *A* 2,3
Louw, M M (WP) 1928 *NZ* 3,4, 1931-32 *W*, *I*, *E*, *S*, 1933 *A* 1,2,3,4,5, 1937 *A* 1,2, *NZ* 2,3, 1938 *BI* 1,2,3
Louw, R J (WP) 1980 *S Am* 1,2, *BI* 1,2,3,4, *S Am* 3,4, *F*, 1981 *I* 1,2, *NZ* 1,3, 1982 *S Am* 1,2, 1984 *E* 1,2, *S Am* 1,2
Louw, S C (WP) 1933 *A* 1,2,3,4,5, 1937 *A* 1, *NZ* 1,2,3, 1938 *BI* 1,2,3
Luyt, F P (WP) 1910 *BI* 1,2,3, 1912-13 *S*, *I*, *W*, *E*
Luyt, J D (EP) 1912-13 *S*, *W*, *E*, *F*
Luyt, R R (WP) 1910 *BI* 2,3, 1912-13 *S*, *I*, *W*, *E*, *F*
Lyons, D (EP) 1896 *BI* 1
Lyster, P J (N) 1933 *A* 2,5, 1937 *NZ* 1

McCallum, I D (WP) 1970 *NZ* 1,2,3,4, 1971 *F* 1,2, *A* 1,2,3, 1974 *BI* 1,2
McCallum, R J (WP) 1974 *BI* 1
McCulloch, J D (GW) 1912-13 *E*, *F*
MacDonald, A W (R) 1965 *A* 1, *NZ* 1,2,3,4
Macdonald, D A (WP) 1974 *BI* 2
Macdonald, I (Tvl) 1992 *NZ*, *A*
McDonald, J A J (WP) 1931-32 *W*, *I*, *E*, *S*
McEwan, W M C (Tvl) 1903 *BI* 1,3
McHardy, E E (OFS) 1912-13 *S*, *I*, *W*, *E*, *F*
McKendrick, J A (WP) 1891 *BI* 3
Malan, A S (Tvl) 1960 *NZ* 1,2,3,4, 1960-61 *W*, *I*, *E*, *S*, *F*, 1962 *BI* 1, 1963 *A* 1,2,3, 1964 *W*, 1965 *I*, *S*
Malan, A W (NT) 1989 *Wld* 1,2, 1992 *NZ*, *A*, *F* 1,2, *E*
Malan, E (NT) 1980 *BI* 3(R),4
Malan, G F (WP) 1958 *F* 2, 1960 *NZ* 1,3,4, 1960-61 *E*, *S*, *F*, 1962 *BI* 1,2,3, 1963 *A* 1,2,4, 1964 *W*, 1965 *A* 1,2, *NZ* 1,2
Malan, P (Tvl) 1949 *NZ* 4
Mallett, N V H (WP) 1984 *S Am* 1,2

Mans, W J (WP) 1965 *I*, *S*
Marais, F P (Bol) 1949 *NZ* 1,2, 1951-52 *S*, 1953 *A* 1,2
Marais, J F K (WP) 1963 *A* 3, 1964 *W*, *F*, 1965 *I*, *S*, *A* 2, 1968 *BI* 1,2,3,4, *F* 1,2, 1969 *A* 1,2,3,4, 1969-70 *S*, *E*, *I*, *W*, 1970 *NZ* 1,2,3,4, 1971 *F* 1,2, *A* 1,2,3, 1974 *BI* 1,2,3,4, *F* 1,2
Maré, D S (Tvl) 1906 *S*
Marsberg, A F W (GW) 1906 *S*, *W*, *E*
Marsberg, P A (GW) 1910 *BI* 1
Martheze, W C (GW) 1903 *BI* 2, 1906 *I*, *W*
Martin, H J (Tvl) 1937 *A* 2
Mellett, T (GW) 1896 *BI* 2
Mellish, F W (WP) 1921 *NZ* 1,3, 1924 *BI* 1,2,3,4
Merry, J (EP) 1891 *BI* 1
Metcalf, H D (Bor) 1903 *BI* 2
Meyer, C du P (WP) 1921 *NZ* 1,2,3
Meyer, P J (GW) 1896 *BI* 1
Michau, J M (Tvl) 1921 *NZ* 1
Michau, J P (WP) 1921 *NZ* 1,2,3
Millar, W A (WP) 1906 *E*, 1910 *BI* 2,3, 1912-13 *I*, *W*, *F*
Mills, W J (WP) 1910 *BI* 2
Moll, T (Tvl) 1910 *BI* 2
Montini, P E (WP) 1956 *A* 1,2
Moolman, L C (NT) 1977 *Wld*, 1980 *S Am* 1,2, *BI* 1,2,3,4, *S Am* 3,4, *F*, 1981 *I* 1,2, *NZ* 1,2,3, *US*, 1982 *S Am* 1,2, 1984 *S Am* 1,2, 1986 *Cv* 1,2,3,4
Mordt, R H (Z-R, NT) 1980 *S Am* 1,2, *BI* 1,2,3,4, *S Am* 3,4, *F*, 1981 *I* 2, *NZ* 1,2,3, *US*, 1982 *S Am* 1,2, 1984 *S Am* 1,2
Morkel, A O (Tvl) 1903 *BI* 1
Morkel, D F T (Tvl) 1906 *I*, *E*, 1910 *BI* 1,3, 1912-13 *S*, *I*, *W*, *E*, *F*
Morkel, H J (WP) 1921 *NZ* 1
Morkel, H W (WP) 1921 *NZ* 1,2
Morkel, J A (WP) 1921 *NZ* 2,3
Morkel, J W H (WP) 1912-13 *S*, *I*, *W*, *E*, *F*
Morkel, P G (WP) 1912-13 *S*, *I*, *W*, *E*, *F*, 1921 *NZ* 1,2,3
Morkel, P K (WP) 1928 *NZ* 4
Morkel, W H (WP) 1910 *BI* 3, 1912-13 *S*, *I*, *W*, *E*, *F*, 1921 *NZ* 1,2,3
Morkel, W S (Tvl) 1906 *S*, *I*, *W*, *E*
Moss, C (N) 1949 *NZ* 1,2,3,4
Mostert, P J (WP) 1921 *NZ* 1,2,3, 1924 *BI* 1,2,4, 1928 *NZ* 1,2,3,4, 1931-32 *W*, *I*, *E*, *S*
Muller, G H (WP) 1969 *A* 3,4, 1969-70 *S*, *W*, 1970 *NZ* 1,2,3,4, 1971 *F* 1,2, 1972 *E*, 1974 *BI* 1,3,4
Muller, H L (OFS) 1986 *Cv* 4 (R), 1989 *Wld* 1(R)
Muller, H S V (Tvl) 1949 *NZ* 1,2,3,4, 1951-52 *S*, *I*, *W*, *E*, *F*, 1953 *A* 1,2,3,4
Muller, L J J (N) 1992 *NZ*, *A*
Muller, P G (N) 1992 *NZ*, *A*, *F* 1,2, *E*
Myburgh, F R (EP) 1896 *BI* 1
Myburgh, J L (NT) 1962 *BI* 1, 1963 *A* 4, 1964 *W*, *F*, 1968 *BI* 1,2,3, *F* 1,2, 1969 *A* 1,2,3,4, 1969-70 *E*, *I*, *W*, 1970 *NZ* 3,4
Myburgh, W H (WT) 1924 *BI* 1

Naude, J P (WP) 1963 *A* 4, 1965 *A* 1,2, *NZ* 1,3,4, 1967 *F* 1,2,3,4, 1968 *BI* 1,2,3,4
Neethling, J B (WP) 1967 *F* 1,2,3,4, 1968 *BI* 4, 1969-70 *S*, 1970 *NZ* 1,2
Nel, J A (Tvl) 1960 *NZ* 1,2, 1963 *A* 1,2, 1965 *A* 2, *NZ* 1,2,3,4, 1970 *NZ* 3,4
Nel, J J (WP) 1956 *A* 1,2, *NZ* 1,2,3,4, 1958 *F* 1,2
Nel, P A R O (Tvl) 1903 *BI* 1,2,3
Nel, P J (N) 1928 *NZ* 1,2,3,4, 1931-32 *W*, *I*, *E*, *S*, 1933 *A* 1,3,4,5, 1937 *A* 1,2, *NZ* 2,3
Nimb, C F (WP) 1961 *I*
Nomis, S H (Tvl) 1967 *F* 4, 1968 *BI* 1,2,3,4, *F* 1,2, 1969 *A* 1,2,3,4, 1969-70 *S*, *E*, *I*, *W*, 1970 *NZ* 1,2,3,4, 1971 *F* 1,2, *A* 1,2,3, 1972 *E*
Nykamp, J L (Tvl) 1933 *A* 2

Ochse, J K (WP) 1951-52 *I*, *W*, *E*, *F*, 1953 *A* 1,2,4
Oelofse, J S A (Tvl) 1953 *A* 1,2,3,4
Oliver, J F (Tvl) 1928 *NZ* 3,4
Olivier, E (WP) 1967 *F* 1,2,3,4, 1968 *BI* 1,2,3,4, *F* 1,2, 1969 *A* 1,2,3,4, 1969-70 *S*, *E*
Olivier, J (NT) 1992 *F* 1,2, *E*
Olver, E (EP) 1896 *BI* 1
Oosthuizen, J J (WP) 1974 *BI* 1, *F* 1,2, 1975 *F* 1,2, 1976 *NZ* 1,2,3,4
Oosthuizen, O W (NT, Tvl) 1981 *I* 1(R),2, *NZ* 2,3,

Van Heerden, J L (NT, Tvl) 1974 *BI* 3,4, *F* 1,2, 1975 *F* 1,2, 1976 *NZ* 1,2,3,4, 1977 *Wld*, 1980 *BI* 1,3,4, *S Am* 3,4, *F*
Van Jaarsveld, C J (Tvl) 1949 *NZ* 1
Van Jaarsveldt, D C (R) 1960 *S*
Van Niekerk, J A (WP) 1928 *NZ* 4
Van Reenen, G L (WP) 1937 *A* 2, *NZ* 1
Van Renen, C G (WP) 1891 *BI* 3, 1896 *BI* 1,4
Van Renen, W (WP) 1903 *BI* 1,3
Van Rensburg, J T J (Tvl) 1992 *NZ, A, E*
Van Rooyen, G W (Tvl) 1921 *NZ* 2,3
Van Ryneveld, R C B (WP) 1910 *BI* 2,3
Van Schoor, R A M (R) 1949 *NZ* 2,3,4, 1951-52 *S, I, W, E, F*, 1953 *A* 1,2,3,4
Van Vollenhoven, K T (NT) 1955 *BI* 1,2,3,4, 1956 *A* 1,2, *NZ* 3
Van Vuuren, T F (EP) 1912-13 *S, I, W, E, F*
Van Wyk, C J (Tvl) 1951-52 *S, I, W, E, F*, 1953 *A* 1,2,3,4, 1955 *BI* 1
Van Wyk, J F B (NT) 1970 *NZ* 1,2,3,4, 1971 *F* 1,2, *A* 1,2,3, 1972 *E*, 1974 *BI* 1,3,4, 1976 *NZ* 3,4
Van Wyk, S P (WP) 1928 *NZ* 1,2
Van Zyl, B P (WP) 1961 *I*
Van Zyl, C G P (OFS) 1965 *NZ* 1,2,3,4
Van Zyl, G H (WP) 1958 *F* 1, 1960 *S, NZ* 1,2,3,4, 1960-61 *W, I, E, S, F*, 1961 *I, A* 1,2, 1962 *BI* 1,3,4
Van Zyl, H J (Tvl) 1960 *NZ* 1,2,3,4, 1960-61 *I, E, S*, 1961 *I, A* 1,2
Van Zyl, P J (Bol) 1961 *I*
Veldsman, P E (WP) 1977 *Wld*
Venter, F D (Tvl) 1931-32 *W, S*, 1933 *A* 3
Versfeld, C (WP) 1891 *BI* 3
Versfeld, M (WP) 1891 *BI* 1,2,3
Vigne, J T (Tvl) 1891 *BI* 1,2,3
Viljoen, J F (GW) 1971 *F* 1,2, *A* 1,2,3, 1972 *E*
Viljoen, J T (N) 1971 *A* 1,2,3
Villet, J V (WP) 1984 *E* 1,2
Visagie, P J (GW) 1967 *F* 1,2,3,4, 1968 *BI* 1,2,3,4, *F*

1,2, 1969 *A* 1,2,3,4, 1969-70 *S, E*, 1970 *NZ* 1,2,3,4, 1971 *F* 1,2, *A* 1,2,3
Visagie, R G (OFS) 1984 *E* 1,2, *S Am* 1,2
Visser, J de V (WP) 1981 *NZ* 2, *US*
Visser, P J (Tvl) 1933 *A* 2
Viviers, S S (OFS) 1956 *A* 1,2, *NZ* 2,3,4
Vogel, M L (OFS) 1974 *BI* 2(R)

Wagenaar, C (NT) 1977 *Wld*
Wahl, J J (WP) 1949 *NZ* 1
Walker, A P (N) 1921 *NZ* 1,3, 1924 *BI* 1,2,3,4
Walker, H N (OFS) 1953 *A* 3, 1956 *A* 2, *NZ* 1,4
Walker, H W (Tvl) 1910 *BI* 1,2,3
Walton, D C (N) 1964 *F*, 1965 *I, S, NZ* 3,4, 1969 *A* 1,2, 1969-70 *E*
Waring, F W (WP) 1931-32 *I, E*, 1933 *A* 1,2,3,4,5
Wessels, J J (WP) 1896 *BI* 1,2,3
Whipp, P J M (WP) 1974 *BI* 1,2, 1975 *F* 1, 1976 *NZ* 1,3,4, 1980 *S Am* 1,2
White, J (Bor) 1931-32 *W*, 1933 *A* 1,2,3,4,5, 1937 *A* 1,2, *NZ* 1,2
Williams, A E (GW) 1910 *BI* 1
Williams, A P (WP) 1984 *E* 1,2
Williams, D O (WP) 1937 *A* 1,2 *NZ* 1,2,3, 1938 *BI* 1,2,3
Williams, J G (NT) 1971 *F* 1,2, *A* 1,2,3, 1972 *E*, 1974 *BI* 1,2,4, *F* 1,2, 1976 *NZ* 1,2
Wilson, L G (WP) 1960 *NZ* 3,4, 1960-61 *W, I, E, F*, 1961 *I, A* 1,2, 1962 *BI* 1,2,3,4, 1963 *A* 1,2,3,4, 1964 *W, F*, 1965 *I, S, A* 1,2, *NZ* 1,2,3,4
Wolmarans, B J (OFS) 1977 *Wld*
Wright, G D (EP, Tvl) 1986 *Cv* 3,4, 1989 *Wld* 1,2, 1992 *F* 1,2, *E*
Wyness, M R K (WP) 1962 *BI* 1,2,3,4, 1963 *A* 2

Zeller, W C (N) 1921 *NZ* 2,3
Zimerman, M (WP) 1931-32 *W, I, E, S*

SOUTH AFRICAN INTERNATIONAL RECORDS

Both team and individual records are for official South African international matches, up to 31 March 1993.

TEAM RECORDS

Highest score
50 v S America (50-18) 1982 Pretoria
v individual countries
30 v Australia (30-11) 1969 Johannesburg
34 v B Isles (34-14) 1962 Bloemfontein
35 v England (35-9) 1984 Johannesburg
38 v France $\begin{cases} \text{(38-5) 1913 Bordeaux} \\ \text{(38-25) 1975 Bloemfontein} \end{cases}$
38 v Ireland (38-0) 1912 Dublin
24 v N Zealand $\begin{cases} \text{(24-12) 1981 Wellington} \\ \text{(24-27) 1992 Johannesburg} \end{cases}$
33 v NZ Cavaliers (33-18) 1986 Pretoria
50 v S America (50-18) 1982 Pretoria
44 v Scotland (44-0) 1951 Murrayfield
38 v United States (38-7) 1981 New York
24 v Wales (24-3) 1964 Durban

Biggest winning points margin
44 v Scotland (44-0) 1951 Murrayfield
v individual countries
25 v Australia (28-3) 1961 Johannesburg
20 v B Isles (34-14) 1962 Bloemfontein
26 v England (35-9) 1984 Johannesburg
33 v France (38-5) 1913 Bordeaux
38 v Ireland (38-0) 1912 Dublin
17 v N Zealand (17-0) 1928 Durban
15 v NZ Cavaliers (33-18) 1986 Pretoria
32 v S America (50-18) 1982 Pretoria
44 v Scotland (44-0) 1951 Murrayfield
31 v United States (38-7) 1981 New York
21 v Wales (24-3) 1964 Durban

Highest score by opposing team
33 England (16-33) 1992 Twickenham
by individual countries
26 Australia (3-26) 1992 Cape Town
28 B Isles (9-28) 1974 Pretoria
33 England (16-33) 1992 Twickenham
29 France (16-29) 1992 Parc des Princes
15 Ireland (23-15) 1981 Cape Town
25 N Zealand (22-25) 1981 Auckland
19 NZ Cavaliers (18-19) 1986 Durban
21 S America (12-21) 1982 Bloemfontein
10 Scotland (18−10) 1960 Port Elizabeth
 7 United States (38-7) 1981 New York
 6 Wales (6-6) 1970 Cardiff

Biggest losing points margin
23 v Australia (3-26) 1992 Cape Town
v individual countries
23 v Australia (3-26) 1992 Cape Town
19 v B Isles (9-28) 1974 Pretoria
17 v England (16-33) 1992 Twickenham
13 v France (16-29) 1992 Parc des Princes
 3 v Ireland (6-9) 1965 Dublin
17 v N Zealand (3-20) 1965 Auckland
 1 v NZ Cavaliers (18-19) 1986 Durban
 9 v S America (12-21) 1982 Bloemfontein
 6 v Scotland (0-6) 1906 Glasgow
No defeats v United States or Wales

Most tries by South Africa in an international
10 v Ireland (38-0) 1912 Dublin

Most tries against South Africa in an international
5 { by B Isles (22-23) 1955 Johannesburg
{ by N Zealand (3-20) 1965 Auckland
{ by B Isles (9-28) 1974 Pretoria

Most points on overseas tour (all matches)
753 in Australia/N Zealand (26 matches) 1937

Most tries on overseas tour (all matches)
161 in Australia/N Zealand (26 matches) 1937

INDIVIDUAL RECORDS

Most capped player
F C H du Preez } 38 { 1960-71
J H Ellis   }   { 1965-76
in individual positions
Full-back
L G Wilson   27   1960-65
Wing
J P Engelbrecht   33   1960-69
Centre
J L Gainsford   33   1960-67
Fly-half
H E Botha   28   1980-92
Scrum-half
D J de Villiers   25   1962-70
Prop
J F K Marais   35   1963-74
Hooker
G F Malan   18   1958-65
Lock
F C H du Preez   31(38)[1]   1960-71
Flanker
J H Ellis   38   1965-76
No 8
D J Hopwood   22[2]   1960-65
[1]*du Preez won 7 caps as a flanker*
[2]*T P Bedford, 25 caps, won 19 at No 8 and 6 as a flanker*

Longest international career
J M Powell 13 seasons 1891-1903
B H Heatlie 13 seasons 1891-1903
D M Gerber 13 seasons 1980-1992-93
H E Botha 13 seasons 1980-1992-93
Gerber's and Botha's careers ended during a Northern Hemisphere season

Most consecutive internationals 25
S H Nomis 1967-72

Most internationals as captain
D J de Villiers 22 1965-70

Most points in internationals – 312
H E Botha (28 matches) 1980-92

Most points in an international – 22
G R Bosch v France 1975 Pretoria

Most tries in internationals – 19
D M Gerber (24 matches) 1980-92

Most tries in an international – 3
E E McHardy v Ireland 1912 Dublin
J A Stegmann v Ireland 1912 Dublin
K T van Vollenhoven v B Isles
  1955 Cape Town
H J van Zyl v Australia 1961 Johannesburg
R H Mordt v New Zealand 1981 Auckland
R H Mordt v United States
  1981 New York
D M Gerber v S America 1982 Pretoria
D M Gerber v England 1984 Johannesburg

Most conversions in internationals – 50
H E Botha (28 matches) 1980-92

Most conversions in an international – 7
A Geffin v Scotland 1951 Murrayfield

Most dropped goals in internationals – 18
H E Botha (28 matches) 1980-92

Most penalty goals in internationals – 50
H E Botha (28 matches) 1980-92

Most penalty goals in an international – 6
G R Bosch v France 1975 Pretoria

Most points in international series – 69
H E Botha (4 appearances) v
  NZ Cavaliers 1986

Most points in international series on tour – 35
H E Botha (3 appearances)
  1981 N Zealand

Most tries in international series on tour – 6
E E McHardy (5 appearances) 1912-13
  B Isles/France

Most points on overseas tour – 190
G H Brand (20 appearances) 1937
  Australia/N Zealand

Most tries on overseas tour – 22
J A Loubser (20 appearances) 1906-07
  B Isles/France

Most points in a tour match – 35
W J de Wet Ras v British Schools OB
  1980 Montevideo

Most tries in a tour match – 6
R G Dryburgh v Queensland 1956
  Brisbane

A JITTERY START ON A NEW COURSE

THE 1992 SEASON IN NEW ZEALAND
Donald Cameron *New Zealand Herald*

New Zealand rugby looked forward to the 1992 season mainly because it would mark the 100th year of the New Zealand Rugby Football Union – in prospect was an untroubled, even joyous, season of domestic bliss and fond regard for the deeds and men of the past. Instead, 1992 jerked New Zealand rugby into its second century with breakneck speed. Dramatic events were followed by sensations; the playing record started with disaster and ended in triumph. Instead of being a time of quiet and smug regard for the years past, 1992 gave notice that New Zealand rugby would be irretrievably altered in its second century.

First, a new All Black selection panel, led by the austere Laurie Mains of Otago, swept aside some old and favourite players as it sought a more positive style than the All Blacks had offered in the 1991 World Cup. New Zealand stumbled in the first of three 'tests' against a World XV and brushed Ireland aside in the second Test after a narrow escape in the first.

Then, as the South African rugby situation and therefore the fate of the New Zealand tour seemed to change with every passing week, the All Blacks pursued a jittery course through a difficult tour of Australia. The All Blacks lost injured players by the hatful; they also lost some friends with their ruthless style and, possibly deservedly, they lost the Bledisloe Cup 1-2. But all these memories faded away as the All Blacks brought South Africa back into Test rugby, and most satisfyingly, with a win that repaid any number of old debts incurred over the last century.

A month or so later New Zealand was immersed, for the first time in 100 years, in the thrills and spills of cup-tie rugby. Each of three divisional championships moved on to exciting semi-finals and then to finals, which brought bigger crowds than the home Tests of 1992 could manage, bigger even than Auckland could attract as they stretched their Ranfurly Shield tenure to 56 successful defences. The first-class rugby wagon had rumbled along for 84 years, and from 1976 the 27 teams competed for various championships. But only in 1992 did 'championship fever' strike, and there were full grounds and quite amazing scenes of provincial patriotism as Waikato, Taranaki and Nelson Bays respectively won the First, Second and Third Division titles. The face of inter-provincial rugby in New Zealand will never be the same again.

Had the 1992 season finished there it would have been acclaimed as a brilliant and very important time, offering a watershed for the second century. Alas, three days after the Championship finished there arose the allegation that Richard Loe, the All Black prop with a reputation for being difficult, had eye-gouged Greg Cooper, the Otago full-back, in the First Division final. Subsequently the NZRFU suspended Loe for nine months, but from 1 April 1993, so that he could attend, meanwhile, to his contractual duties in France. The French then refused to allow him in. The Loe affair will become a *cause célèbre*, and if it puts the fear of God into the mavericks and malcontents in the game, it will have set New Zealand on a course of fairer-minded rugby in its new century.

There will be many legacies from this amazing year. The Mains-method All Blacks have tried to take the best from the new and experimental laws, but they must also accept that their best side is more vulnerable than New Zealanders like to think. The cynics might say that Mains' men should have succeeded, for they rifled through close to 40 players before finding basically the right mix.

Old age and new laws brought Auckland back to the representative field. They held their beloved Ranfurly Shield, but lost the South Pacific title to Queensland, lost a Championship match to Wellington, and eventually conceded their First Division crown in a semi-final to Waikato.

What of the future? The All Blacks will not tour until late next year, and Mains will have to work hard on the autumn tour of England and Scotland. There may be another problem: the nationalistic ambitions of the South Pacific countries. Western Samoa has already exposed the dual-nationality difficulty, and now the Cook Islands want to press for World Cup recognition by using Maori players not required for the All Blacks. If the second century presents New Zealand rugby with one immediate difficulty, it is the classification of Pacific Island and New Zealand players. At the moment players can move between New Zealand and Western Samoan sides. The Cooks may be next, then Tonga and perhaps Fiji. The problem must be addressed, and solved, quickly – and certainly long before the 1995 World Cup.

NATIONAL CHAMPIONSHIP

First Division

	P	W	D	L	F	A	Pts
Auckland	8	7	0	1	253	127	28
Otago	8	6	0	2	203	147	25
North Harbour	8	6	0	2	222	157	24
Waikato	8	5	0	3	268	153	20
Wellington	8	4	0	4	183	182	18
King Country	8	3	0	5	144	245	12
Canterbury	8	2	0	6	197	198	10
Hawke's Bay	8	2	0	6	131	267	8
North Auckland	8	1	0	7	134	259	7

Semi-finals: Waikato 27, Auckland 21; Otago 26, North Harbour 23 (*aet*)
Final: Waikato 40, Otago 5

Second Division

	P	W	D	L	F	A	Pts
Taranaki	8	7	0	1	317	150	29
Counties	8	7	0	1	317	92	29
Bay of Plenty	8	5	0	3	171	128	21
Manawatu	8	5	0	3	263	202	21
Southland	8	5	0	3	283	161	21
Sth Canterbury	8	4	0	4	216	230	17
Wairarapa-Bush	8	2	0	6	143	326	8
Poverty Bay	8	1	0	7	101	382	4
Thames Valley	8	0	0	8	134	274	1

Semi-finals: Counties 31, Bay of Plenty 29; Taranaki 29, Manawatu 18
Final: Taranaki 12, Counties 0

Third Division

	P	W	D	L	F	A	Pts
Nelson Bays	8	8	0	0	328	94	32
Wanganui	8	7	0	1	306	102	28
Horowhenua	8	6	0	2	245	121	24
Mid-Canterbury	8	5	0	3	165	113	20
Buller	8	4	0	4	154	129	17
Marlborough	8	3	0	5	198	192	13
East Coast	8	2	0	6	160	243	8
North Otago	8	1	0	7	113	309	5
West Coast	8	0	0	8	47	413	0

Semi-finals: Nelson Bays 27, Mid-Canterbury 13; Horowhenua 30, Wanganui 22
Final: Nelson Bays 25, Horowhenua 23

RANFURLY SHIELD CHALLENGES

12 Aug, Lansdowne Road, Blenheim: Auckland 53 (4G 5T), Marlborough 3 (1PG); **22 Aug, Eden Park, Auckland:** Auckland 21 (2PG 3T), Otago 16 (1G 3PG); **29 Aug, McLean Park, Napier:** Auckland 40 (3G 2PG 1DG 2T), Hawke's Bay 9 (3PG); **2 Sept, Owen Delaney Park, Taupo:** Auckland 42 (4G 2PG 1DG 1T), King Country 15 (5PG); **5 Sept, Eden Park, Auckland:** Auckland 49 (5G 3PG 1T), North Auckland 3 (1PG); **12 Sept, Eden Park, Auckland:** Auckland 47 (5G 4PG), Canterbury 38 (3G 4PG 1T); **15 Sept, The Stadium, Pukekohe:** Auckland 24 (1G 4PG 1T), Counties 19 (1G 4PG); **19 Sept, Eden Park, Auckland:** Auckland 25 (1G 6PG), North Harbour 16 (1G 3PG)

NEW ZEALAND INTERNATIONAL PLAYERS *(up to 31 March 1993)*

ABBREVIATIONS

A – Australia; *Arg* – Argentina; *AW* – Anglo-Welsh; *BI* – British Isles teams; *C* – Canada; *E* – England; *F* – France; *Fj* – Fiji; *I* – Ireland; *It* – Italy; *R* – Romania; *S* – Scotland; *SA* – South Africa; *US* – United States; *W* – Wales; *Wld* – World Invitation XV; (R) – Replacement. Entries in square brackets [ ] indicate appearances in the Rugby World Cup.

Note: When a series has taken place, figures denote the particular matches in which players featured. Thus 1959 *BI* 2,4 indicates that a player appeared in the second and fourth Tests of the 1959 series against the British Isles.

Abbott, H L (Taranaki) 1906 *F*
Aitken, G G (Wellington) 1921 *SA* 1,2
Allen, F R (Auckland) 1946 *A* 1,2 1947 *A* 1,2, 1949 *SA* 1,2
Allen, N H (Counties) 1980 *A* 3, *W*
Alley, G T (Canterbury) 1928 *SA* 1,2,3
Anderson, A (Canterbury) 1983 *S*, *E*, 1984 *A* 1,2,3, 1987 [*Fj*]
Anderson, B L (Wairarapa-Bush) 1986 *A* 1
Archer, W R (Otago, Southland) 1955 *A* 1,2, 1956 *SA* 1,3
Argus, W G (Canterbury) 1946 *A* 1,2, 1947 *A* 1,2
Arnold, D A (Canterbury) 1963 *I*, *W*, 1964 *E*, *F*
Arnold, K D (Waikato) 1947 *A* 1,2
Ashby, D L (Southland) 1958 *A* 2
Asher, A A (Auckland) 1903 *A*
Ashworth, B G (Auckland) 1978 *A* 1,2
Ashworth, J C (Canterbury, Hawke's Bay) 1978 *A* 1,2,3, 1980 *A* 1,2,3, 1981 *SA* 1,2,3, 1982 *A* 1,2, 1983 *BI* 1,2,3,4, *A*, 1984 *F* 1,2 *A* 1,2,3, 1985 *E* 1,2, *A*
Atkinson, H (West Coast) 1913 *A* 1
Avery, H E (Wellington) 1910 *A* 1,2,3

Bachop, G T M (Canterbury) 1989 *W*, *I*, 1990 *S* 1,2, *A* 1,2,3, *F* 1,2, 1991 *Arg* 1,2, *A* 1,2, [*E*, *US*, *C*, *A*, *S*], 1992 *Wld* 1
Badeley, C E O (Auckland) 1921 *SA* 1,2
Baird, J A S (Otago) 1913 *A* 2
Ball, N (Wellington) 1931 *A*, 1932 *A* 2,3, 1935 *W*, 1936 *E*
Barrett, J (Auckland) 1913 *A* 2,3
Barry, E F (Wellington) 1934 *A* 2
Batty, G B (Wellington, Bay of Plenty) 1972 *W*, *S*, 1973 *E* 1, *I*, *F*, *E* 2, 1974 *A* 1,3, *I*, 1975 *S*, 1976 *SA* 1,2,3,4, 1977 *BI* 1
Batty, W (Auckland) 1930 *BI* 1,3,4, 1931 *A*
Beatty, G E (Taranaki) 1950 *BI* 1
Bell, R H (Otago) 1951 *A* 3, 1952 *A* 1,2
Bellis, E A (Wanganui) 1921 *SA* 1,2,3
Bennet, R (Otago) 1905 *A*
Berghan, T (Otago) 1938 *A* 1,2,3
Berry, M J (Wairarapa-Bush) 1986 *A* 3 (R)
Bevan, V D (Wellington) 1949 *A* 1,2, 1950 *BI* 1,2,3,4
Birtwistle, W M (Canterbury) 1965 *SA* 1,2,3,4, 1967 *E*, *W*, *S*
Black, J E (Canterbury) 1977 *F* 1, 1979 *A*, 1980 *A* 3
Black, N W (Auckland) 1949 *SA* 3
Black, R S (Otago) 1914 *A* 1
Blake, A W (Wairarapa) 1949 *A* 1
Boggs, E G (Auckland) 1946 *A* 2, 1949 *SA* 1
Bond, J G (Canterbury) 1949 *A* 2
Booth, E E (Otago) 1906 *F*, 1907 *A* 1,3
Boroevich, K G (Wellington) 1986 *F* 1, *A* 1, *F* 3 (R)
Botica, F M (North Harbour) 1986 *F* 1, *A* 1,2,3, *F* 2,3, 1989 *Arg* 1 (R)
Bowden, N J G (Taranaki) 1952 *A* 2
Bowers, R G (Wellington) 1954 *I*, *F*
Bowman, A W (Hawke's Bay) 1938 *A* 1,2,3
Braid, G J (Bay of Plenty) 1983 *S*, *E*
Bremner, S G (Auckland, Canterbury) 1952 *A* 2, 1956 *SA* 2
Brewer, M R (Otago) 1986 *F* 1, *A* 1,2,3, *F* 2,3, 1988 *A* 1, 1989 *A*, *W*, *I*, 1990 *S* 1,2, *A* 1,2,3, *F* 1,2, 1992 *I* 2, *A* 1
Briscoe, K C (Taranaki) 1959 *BI* 2, 1960 *SA* 1,2,3,4, 1963 *I*, *W*, 1964 *E*, *S*
Brooke, R M (Auckland) 1992 *I* 2, *A* 2,3, *SA*
Brooke, Z V (Auckland) 1987 [*Arg*], 1989 *Arg* 2 (R), 1990 *A* 1,2,3, *F* 1 (R), 1991 *Arg* 2, *A* 1,2, [*E*, *It*, *C*, *A*, *S*], 1992 *A* 2,3, *SA*

Brooke-Cowden, M (Auckland) 1986 *F* 1, *A* 1, 1987 [*W*]
Brown, C (Taranaki) 1913 *A* 2,3
Brown, O M (Auckland) 1992 *I* 2, *A* 1,2,3, *SA*
Brown, R H (Taranaki) 1955 *A* 3, 1956 *SA* 1,2,3,4, 1957 *A* 1,2 1958 *A* 1,2,3, 1959 *BI* 1,3, 1961 *F* 1,2,3, 1962 *A* 1
Brownlie, C J (Hawke's Bay) 1924 *W*, 1925 *E*, *F*
Brownlie, M J (Hawke's Bay) 1924 *I*, *W*, 1925 *E*, *F*, 1928 *SA* 1,2,3,4
Bruce, J A (Auckland) 1914 *A* 1,2
Bruce, O D (Canterbury) 1976 *SA* 1,2,4, 1977 *BI* 2,3,4, *F* 1,2, 1978 *A* 1,2, *I*, *W*, *E*, *S*
Bryers, R F (King Country) 1949 *A* 1
Budd, T A (Southland) 1946 *A* 2, 1949 *A* 2
Bullock-Douglas, G A H (Wanganui) 1932 *A* 1,2,3, 1934 *A* 1,2
Bunce, F E (North Harbour) 1992 *Wld* 1,2,3, *I* 1,2, *A* 1,2,3, *SA*
Burgess, G A J (Auckland) 1981 *SA* 2
Burgess, G F (Southland) 1905 *A*
Burgess, R E (Manawatu) 1971 *BI* 1,2,3, 1972 *A* 3, *W*, 1973 *I*, *F*
Burke, P S (Taranaki) 1955 *A* 1, 1957 *A* 1,2
Burns, P J (Canterbury) 1908 *AW* 2, 1910 *A* 1,2,3, 1913 *A* 3
Bush, R G (Otago) 1931 *A*
Bush, W K (Canterbury) 1974 *A* 1,2, 1975 *S*, 1976 *I*, *SA* 2,4, 1977 *BI* 2,3,4(R), 1978 *I*, *W*, 1979 *A*
Buxton, J B (Canterbury) 1955 *A* 3, 1956 *SA* 1

Cain, M J (Taranaki) 1913 *US*, 1914 *A* 1,2,3
Callesen, J A (Manawatu) 1974 *A* 1,2,3, 1975 *S*
Cameron, D (Taranaki) 1908 *AW* 1,2,3
Cameron, L M (Manawatu) 1980 *A* 3, 1981 *SA* 1(R),2,3, *R*
Carleton, S R (Canterbury) 1928 *SA* 1,2,3, 1929 *A* 1,2,3
Carrington, K R (Auckland) 1971 *BI* 1,3,4
Carter, M P (Auckland) 1991 *A* 2, [*It*, *A*]
Casey, S T (Otago) 1905 *S*, *I*, *E*, *W*, 1907 *A* 1,2,3, 1908 *AW* 1
Catley, E H (Waikato) 1946 *A* 1, 1947 *A* 1,2, 1949 *SA* 1,2,3,4
Caughey, T H C (Auckland) 1932 *A* 1,3, 1934 *A* 1,2, 1935 *S*, *I*, 1936 *E*, *A* 1, 1937 *SA* 3
Caulton, R W (Wellington) 1959 *BI* 2,3,4, 1960 *SA* 1,4 1961 *F* 2, 1963 *E* 1,2, *I*, *W*, 1964 *E*, *S*, *F*, *A* 1,2,3
Cherrington, N P (North Auckland) 1950 *BI* 1
Christian, D L (Auckland) 1949 *SA* 4
Clamp, M (Wellington) 1984 *A* 2,3
Clark, D W (Otago) 1964 *A* 1,2
Clark, W H (Wellington) 1953 *W*, 1954 *I*, *E*, *S*, 1955 *A* 1,2, 1956 *SA* 1,2,3,4
Clarke, A H (Auckland) 1958 *A* 3, 1959 *BI* 4, 1960 *SA* 1
Clarke, D B (Waikato) 1956 *SA* 3,4, 1957 *A* 1,2, 1958 *A* 1,3, 1959 *BI* 1,2,3,4, 1960 *SA* 1,2,3,4, 1961 *F* 1,2,3, 1962 *A* 1,2,3,4,5, 1963 *E* 1,2, *I*, *W*, 1964 *E*, *S*, *F*, *A* 2,3
Clarke, E (Auckland) 1992 *Wld* 2,3, *I* 1,2
Clarke, I J (Waikato) 1953 *W*, 1955 *A* 1,2,3, 1956 *SA* 1,2,3,4, 1957 *A* 1,2 1958 *A* 1,3, 1959 *BI* 1,2, 1960 *SA* 2,4, 1961 *F* 1,2,3, 1962 *A* 1,2,3, 1963 *E* 1,2
Clarke, R L (Taranaki) 1932 *A* 2,3
Cobden, D G (Canterbury) 1937 *SA* 1
Cockerill, M S (Taranaki) 1951 *A* 1,2,3
Cockroft, E A P (South Canterbury) 1913 *A* 3, 1914 *A* 2,3
Codlin, B W (Counties) 1980 *A* 1,2,3

Graham, W G (Otago) 1979 *F* 1(R)
Grant, L A (South Canterbury) 1947 *A* 1,2, 1949 *SA* 1,2
Gray, G D (Canterbury) 1908 *AW* 2, 1913 *A* 1, *US*
Gray, K F (Wellington) 1963 *I*, *W*, 1964 *E*, *S*, *F*, *A* 1,2,3, 1965 *SA* 1,2,3,4, 1966 *BI* 1,2,3,4, 1967 *W*, *F*, *S*, 1968 *A* 1, *F* 2,3, 1969 *W* 1,2
Gray, W N (Bay of Plenty) 1955 *A* 2,3, 1956 *SA* 1,2,3,4
Green, C I (Canterbury) 1983 *S*(R), *E*, 1984 *A* 1,2,3, 1985 *E* 1,2, *A*, *Arg* 1,2, 1986 *A* 2,3, *F* 2,3, 1987 [*It*, *Fj*, *S*, *W*, *F*], *A*
Grenside, B A (Hawke's Bay) 1928 *SA* 1,2,3,4, 1929 *A* 2,3
Griffiths, J L (Wellington) 1934 *A* 2, 1935 *S*, *I*, *W*, 1936 *A* 1,2, 1938 *A* 3
Guy, R A (North Auckland) 1971 *BI* 1,2,3,4

Haden, A M (Auckland) 1977 *BI* 1,2,3,4, *F* 1,2, 1978 *A* 1,2,3, *I*, *W*, *E*, *S*, 1979 *F* 1,2, *A*, *S*, *E*, 1980 *A* 1,2,3, *W*, 1981 *S* 2, *SA* 1,2,3, *R*, *F* 1,2, 1982 *A* 1,2,3, 1983 *BI* 1,2,3,4, *A*, 1984 *F* 1,2, 1985 *Arg* 1,2
Hadley, S (Auckland) 1928 *SA* 1,2,3,4
Hadley, W E (Auckland) 1934 *A* 1,2, 1935 *S*, *I*, *W*, 1936 *E*, *A* 1,2
Haig, J S (Otago) 1946 *A* 1,2
Haig, L S (Otago) 1950 *BI* 2,3,4, 1951 *A* 1,2,3, 1953 *W*, 1954 *E*, *S*
Hales, D A (Canterbury) 1972 *A* 1,2,3, *W*
Hamilton, D C (Southland) 1908 *AW* 2
Hammond, I A (Marlborough) 1952 *A* 2
Harper, E T (Canterbury) 1904 *BI*, 1906 *F*
Harris, P C (Manawatu) 1976 *SA* 3
Hart, A H (Taranaki) 1924 *I*
Hart, G F (Canterbury) 1930 *BI* 1,2,3,4, 1931 *A*, 1934 *A* 1, 1935 *S*, *I*, *W*, 1936 *A* 1,2
Harvey, B A (Wairarapa-Bush) 1986 *F* 1
Harvey, I H (Wairarapa) 1928 *SA* 4
Harvey, L R (Otago) 1949 *SA* 1,2,3,4, 1950 *BI* 1,2,3,4
Harvey, P (Canterbury) 1904 *BI*
Hasell, E W (Canterbury) 1913 *A* 2,3,
Hayward, H O (Auckland) 1908 *AW* 3
Hazlett, E J (Southland) 1966 *BI* 1,2,3,4, 1967 *A*, *E*
Hazlett, W E (Southland) 1928 *SA* 1,2,3,4, 1930 *BI* 1,2,3,4
Heeps, T R (Wellington) 1962 *A* 1,2,3,4,5
Heke, W R (North Auckland) 1929 *A* 1,2,3
Hemi, R C (Waikato) 1953 *W*, 1954 *I*, *E*, *S*, *F*, 1955 *A* 1,2,3, 1956 *SA* 1,3,4, 1957 *A* 1,2, 1959 *BI* 1,3,4
Henderson, P (Wanganui) 1949 *SA* 1,2,3,4, 1950 *BI* 2,3,4
Henderson, P W (Otago) 1991 *Arg* 1, [*C*], 1992 *Wld* 1,2,3, *I* 1
Herewini, M A (Auckland) 1962 *A* 5, 1963 *I*, 1964 *S*, *F*, 1965 *SA* 4, 1966 *BI* 1,2,3,4, 1967 *A*
Hewett, J A (Auckland) 1991 [*It*]
Hewson, A R (Wellington) 1981 *S* 1,2, *SA* 1,2,3, *R*, *F* 1,2, 1982 *A* 1,2,3, 1983 *BI* 1,2,3,4, *A*, 1984 *F* 1,2, *A* 1
Higginson, G (Canterbury, Hawke's Bay) 1980 *W*, 1981 *S* 1, *SA* 1, 1982 *A* 1,2, 1983 *A* 1
Hill, S F (Canterbury) 1955 *A* 3, 1956 *SA* 1,3,4, 1957 *A* 1,2, 1958 *A* 3, 1959 *BI* 1,2,3,4
Hines, G R (Waikato) 1980 *A* 3
Hobbs, M J B (Canterbury) 1983 *BI* 1,2,3,4, *A*, *S*, *E*, 1984 *F* 1,2, *A* 1,2,3, 1985 *E* 1,2, *A*, *Arg* 1,2, 1986 *A* 2,3, *F* 2,3
Holder, E C (Buller) 1934 *A* 2
Hook, L S (Auckland) 1929 *A* 1,2,3
Hooper, J A (Canterbury) 1937 *SA* 1,2,3
Hopkinson, A E (Canterbury) 1967 *S*, 1968 *A* 2, *F* 1,2,3, 1969 *W* 2, 1970 *SA* 1,2,3
Hore, J (Otago) 1930 *BI* 2,3,4, 1932 *A* 1,2,3, 1934 *A* 1,2, 1935 *S*, 1936 *E*
Horsley, R H (Wellington) 1960 *SA* 2,3,4
Hotop, J (Canterbury) 1952 *A* 1,2, 1955 *A* 3
Hughes, A M (Auckland) 1949 *A* 1,2, 1950 *BI* 1,2,3,4
Hughes, E (Southland, Wellington) 1907 *A* 1,2,3, 1908 *AW* 1, 1921 *SA* 1,2
Hunter, B A (Otago) 1971 *BI* 1,2,3
Hunter, J (Taranaki) 1905 *S*, *I*, *E*, *W*, 1906 *F*, 1907 *A* 1,2,3, 1908 *AW* 1,2,3
Hurst, I A (Canterbury) 1973 *I*, *F*, *E* 2, 1974 *A* 1,2

Ifwersen, K D (Auckland) 1921 *SA* 3
Innes, C R (Auckland) 1989 *W*, *I*, 1990 *A* 1,2,3, *F* 1,2, 1991 *Arg* 1,2, *A* 1,2, [*E*, *US*, *It*, *C*, *A*, *S*]
Innes, G D (Canterbury) 1932 *A* 2
Irvine, I B (North Auckland) 1952 *A* 1
Irvine, J G (Otago) 1914 *A* 1,2,3
Irvine, W R (Hawke's Bay, Wairarapa) 1924 *I*, *W*, 1925 *E*, *F*, 1930 *BI* 1
Irwin, M W (Otago) 1955 *A* 1,2, 1956 *SA* 1, 1958 *A* 2, 1959 *BI* 3,4, 1960 *SA* 1

Jackson, E S (Hawke's Bay) 1936 *A* 1,2, 1937 *SA* 1,2,3, 1938 *A* 3
Jaffray, J L (Otago, South Canterbury) 1972 *A* 2, 1975 *S*, 1976 *I*, *SA* 1, 1977 *BI* 2, 1979 *F* 1,2
Jarden, R A (Wellington) 1951 *A* 1,2, 1952 *A* 1,2, 1953 *W*, 1954 *I*, *E*, *S*, *F*, 1955 *A* 1,2,3, 1956 *SA* 1,2,3
Jefferd, A C R (East Coast) 1981 *S* 1,2, *SA* 1
Jessep, E M (Wellington) 1931 *A*, 1932 *A* 1
Johnson, L M (Wellington) 1928 *SA* 1,2,3,4
Johnston, W (Otago) 1907 *A* 1,2,3
Johnstone, B R (Auckland) 1976 *SA* 2, 1977 *BI* 1,2, *F* 1,2, 1978 *I*, *W*, *E*, *S*, 1979 *F* 1,2, *S*, *E*
Johnstone, P (Otago) 1949 *SA* 2,4, 1950 *BI* 1,2,3,4, 1951 *A* 1,2,3
Jones, I D (North Auckland) 1990 *S* 1,2, *A* 1,2,3, *F* 1,2, 1991 *Arg* 1,2, *A* 1,2, [*E*, *US*, *It*, *C*, *A*, *S*], 1992 *Wld* 1,2,3, *I* 1,2, *A* 1,2,3, *SA*
Jones, M G (North Auckland) 1973 *E* 2
Jones, M N (Auckland) 1987 [*It*, *Fj*, *S*, *F*], *A*, 1988 *W* 1,2, *A* 2,3, 1989 *F* 1,2, *Arg* 1,2, 1990 *F* 1,2, 1991 *Arg* 1,2, *A* 1,2, [*E*, *US*, *S*], 1992 *Wld* 1,3, *I* 2, *A* 1,3, *SA*
Jones, P F H (North Auckland) 1954 *E*, *S*, 1955 *A* 1,2, 1956 *SA* 3,4, 1958 *A* 1,2,3, 1959 *BI* 1, 1960 *SA* 1
Joseph, H T (Canterbury) 1971 *BI* 2,3
Joseph, J W (Otago) 1992 *Wld* 2,3(R), *I* 1, *A* 1(R),3, *SA*

Karam, J F (Wellington, Horowhenua) 1972 *W*, *S*, 1973 *E* 1, *I*, *F*, 1974 *A* 1,2,3, *I*, 1975 *S*
Katene, T (Wellington) 1955 *A* 2
Kearney, J C (Otago) 1947 *A* 2, 1949 *SA* 1,2,3
Kelly, J W (Auckland) 1949 *A* 1,2
Kember, G F (Wellington) 1970 *SA* 4
Ketels, R C (Counties) 1980 *W*, 1981 *S* 1,2, *R*, *F* 1
Kiernan, H A D (Auckland) 1903 *A*
Kilby, F D (Wellington) 1932 *A* 1,2,3, 1934 *A* 2
Killeen, B A (Auckland) 1936 *A* 1
King, R R (West Coast) 1934 *A* 2, 1935 *S*, *I*, *W*, 1936 *E*, *A* 1,2, 1937 *SA* 1,2,3, 1938 *A* 1,2,3
Kingstone, C N (Taranaki) 1921 *SA* 1,2,3
Kirk, D E (Auckland) 1985 *E* 1,2, *A*, *Arg* 1, 1986 *F* 1, *A* 1,2,3, *F* 2,3, 1987 [*It*, *Fj*, *Arg*, *S*, *W*, *F*], *A*
Kirkpatrick, I A (Canterbury, Poverty Bay) 1967 *F*, 1968 *A* 1(R), 2, *F* 1,2,3, 1969 *W* 1,2, 1970 *SA* 1,2,3,4, 1971 *BI* 1,2,3,4, 1972 *A* 1,2,3, *W*, *S*, 1973 *E* 1, *I*, *F*, *E* 2, 1974 *A* 1,2,3, *I* 1975 *S*, 1976 *I*, *SA* 1,2,3,4, 1977 *BI* 1,2,3,4
Kirton, E W (Otago) 1967 *E*, *W*, *F*, *S*, 1968 *A* 1,2, *F* 1,2,3, 1969 *W* 1,2, 1970 *SA* 2,3
Kirwan, J J (Auckland) 1984 *F* 1,2, 1985 *E* 1,2, *A*, *Arg* 1,2, 1986 *F* 1, *A* 1,2,3, *F* 2,3, 1987 [*It*, *Fj*, *Arg*, *S*, *W*, *F*], *A*, 1988 *W* 1,2, *A* 1,2,3, 1989 *F* 1,2, *Arg* 1,2, *A*, 1990 *S* 1,2, *A* 1,2,3, *F* 1,2, 1991 *Arg* 2, *A* 1,2, [*E*, *It*, *C*, *A*, *S*], 1992 *Wld* 1,2(R),3, *I* 1,2, *A* 1,2,3, *SA*
Kivell, A L (Taranaki) 1929 *A* 2,3
Knight, A (Auckland) 1934 *A* 1
Knight, G A (Manawatu) 1977 *F* 1,2, 1978 *A* 1,2,3, *E*, *S*, 1979 *F* 1,2, *A*, 1980 *A* 1,2,3, *W*, 1981 *S* 1,2, *SA* 1,3, 1982 *A* 1,2,3, 1983 *BI* 1,2,3,4, *A*, 1984 *F* 1,2, *A* 1,2,3, 1985 *E* 1,2, *A*, 1986 *A* 2,3
Knight, L G (Poverty Bay) 1977 *BI* 1,2,3,4, *F* 1,2
Koteka, T T (Waikato) 1981 *F* 2, 1982 *A* 3
Kreft, A J (Otago) 1968 *A* 2

Laidlaw, C R (Otago, Canterbury) 1964 *F*, *A* 1, 1965 *SA* 1,2,3,4, 1966 *BI* 1,2,3,4, 1967 *E*, *W*, *S*, 1968 *A* 1,2, *F* 1,2, 1970 *SA* 1,2,3
Laidlaw, K F (Southland) 1960 *SA* 2,3,4
Lambert, K K (Manawatu) 1972 *S*(R), 1973 *E* 1, *I*, *F*, *E* 2, 1974 *I*, 1976 *SA* 1,3,4, 1977 *BI* 1,4
Lambourn, A (Wellington) 1934 *A* 1,2, 1935 *S*, *I*, *W*, 1936 *E*, 1937 *SA* 1,2,3, 1938 *A* 3
Larsen, B P (North Harbour) 1992 *Wld* 2,3, *I* 1
Le Lievre, J M (Canterbury) 1962 *A* 4
Lendrum, R N (Counties) 1973 *E* 2
Leslie, A R (Wellington) 1974 *A* 1,2,3, *I*, 1975 *S*, 1976

307

Nicholls, M F (Wellington) 1921 *SA* 1,2,3, 1924 *I*, *W*, 1925 *E*, *F*, 1928 *SA* 4, 1930 *BI* 2,3
Nicholson, G W (Auckland) 1903 *A*, 1904 *BI*, 1907 *A* 2,3
Norton, R W (Canterbury) 1971 *BI* 1,2,3,4, 1972 *A* 1,2,3, *W*, *S*, 1973 *E* 1, *I*, *F*, *E* 2, 1974 *A* 1,2,3, *I*, 1975 *S*, 1976 *I*, *SA* 1,2,3,4, 1977 *BI* 1,2,3,4

O'Brien, J G (Auckland) 1914 *A* 1
O'Callaghan, M W (Manawatu) 1968 *F* 1,2,3
O'Callaghan, T R (Wellington) 1949 *A* 2
O'Donnell, D H (Wellington) 1949 *A* 2
Old, G H (Manawatu) 1981 *SA* 3, *R*(R), 1982 *A* 1(R)
O'Leary, M J (Auckland) 1910 *A* 1,3, 1913 *A* 2,3
Oliver, C J (Canterbury) 1929 *A* 1,2, 1934 *A* 1, 1935 *S*, *I*, *W*, 1936 *E*
Oliver, D J (Wellington) 1930 *BI* 1,2
Oliver, D O (Otago) 1954 *F*, *F*
Oliver, F J (Southland, Otago, Manawatu) 1976 *SA* 4, 1977 *BI* 1,2,3,4, *F* 1,2, 1978 *A* 1,2,3, *I*, *W*, *E*, *S*, 1979 *F* 1,2, 1981 *SA* 2
Orr, R W (Otago) 1949 *A* 1
Osborne, W M (Wanganui) 1975 *S*, 1976 *SA* 2(R), 4(R), 1977 *BI* 1,2,3,4, *F* 1(R),2, 1978 *I*, *W*, *E*, *S*, 1980 *W*, 1982 *A* 1,3
O'Sullivan, J M (Taranaki) 1905 *S*, *I*, *E*, *W*, 1907 *A* 3
O'Sullivan, T P A (Taranaki) 1960 *SA* 1, 1961 *F* 1, 1962 *A* 1,2

Page, J R (Wellington)1931 *A*, 1932 *A* 1,2,3, 1934 *A* 1,2
Palmer, B P (Auckland) 1929 *A* 2, 1932 *A* 2,3
Parker, J H (Canterbury) 1924 *I*, *W*, 1925 *E*
Parkhill, A A (Otago) 1937 *SA* 1,2,3, 1938 *A* 1,2,3
Parkinson, R M (Poverty Bay) 1972 *A* 1,2,3, *W*, *S*, 1973 *E* 1,2
Paterson, A M (Otago) 1908 *AW* 2,3, 1910 *A* 1,2,3
Paton, H (Otago) 1910 *A* 1,3
Pene, A R (Otago) 1992 *Wld* 1(R),2,3, *I* 1,2, *A* 1,2(R)
Phillips, W J (King Country) 1937 *SA* 2, 1938 *A* 1,2
Philpott, S (Canterbury) 1991 [*It*(R), *S*(R)]
Pickering, E A R (Waikato) 1958 *A* 2, 1959 *BI* 1,4
Pierce, M J (Wellington) 1985 *E* 1,2, *A*, *Arg* 1, 1986 *A* 2,3, *F* 2,3, 1987 [*It*, *Arg*, *S*, *W*, *F*], *A*, 1988 *W* 1,2, *A* 1,2,3, 1989 *F* 1,2, *Arg* 1,2, *A*, *W*, *I*
Pokere, S T (Southland, Auckland) 1981 *SA* 3, 1982 *A* 1,2,3, 1983 *BI* 1,2,3,4, *A*, *S*, *E*, 1984 *F* 1,2, *A* 2,3, 1985 *E* 1,2, *A*
Pollock, H R (Wellington) 1932 *A* 1,2,3, 1936 *A* 1,2
Porter, C G (Wellington) 1925 *F*, 1929 *A* 2,3, 1930 *BI* 1,2,3,4
Preston, J P (Canterbury) 1991 [*US*, *S*], 1992 *SA*(R)
Procter, A C (Otago) 1932 *A* 1
Purdue, C A (Southland) 1905 *A*
Purdue, E (Southland) 1905 *A*
Purdue, G B (Southland) 1931 *A*, 1932 *A* 1,2,3
Purvis, G H (Waikato) 1991 [*US*]
Purvis, N A (Otago) 1976 *I*

Quaid, C E (Otago) 1938 *A* 1,2

Rangi, R E (Auckland) 1964 *A* 2,3, 1965 *SA* 1,2,3,4, 1966 *BI* 1,2,3,4
Rankin, J G (Canterbury) 1936 *A* 1,2, 1937 *SA* 2
Reedy, W J (Wellington) 1908 *AW* 2,3
Reid, A R (Waikato) 1952 *A* 1, 1956 *SA* 3,4, 1957 *A* 1,2
Reid, H R (Bay of Plenty) 1980 *A* 1,2, *W*, 1983 *S*, *E*, 1985 *Arg* 1,2, 1986 *A* 2,3
Reid, K H (Wairarapa) 1929 *A* 1,3
Reid, S T (Hawke's Bay) 1935 *S*, *I*, *W*, 1936 *E*, *A* 1,2, 1937 *SA* 1,2,3
Reside, W B (Wairarapa) 1929 *A* 1
Rhind, P K (Canterbury) 1946 *A* 1,2
Richardson, J (Otago, Southland) 1921 *SA* 1,2,3, 1924 *I*, *W*, 1925 *E*, *F*
Rickit, H (Waikato) 1981 *S* 1,2
Ridland, A J (Southland) 1910 *A* 1,2,3
Roberts, E J (Wellington) 1914 *A* 1,2,3, 1921 *SA* 2,3
Roberts, F (Wellington) 1905 *S*, *I*, *E*, *W*, 1907 *A* 1,2,3, 1908 *AW* 1,3, 1910 *A* 1,2,3
Roberts, R W (Taranaki) 1913 *A* 1, *US*, 1914 *A* 1,2,3
Robertson, B J (Counties) 1972 *A* 1,3, *S*, 1973 *E* 1, *I*, *F*, 1974 *A* 1,2,3, *I*, 1976 *I*, *SA* 1,2,3,4, 1977 *BI* 1,3,4, *F* 1,2, 1978 *A* 1,2,3, *W*, *E*, *S*, 1979 *F* 1,2, *A*, 1980 *A* 2,3, *W*, 1981 *S* 1,2

Robertson, D J (Otago) 1974 *A* 1,2,3, *I*, 1975 *S*, 1976 *I*, *SA* 1,3,4, 1977 *BI* 1
Robilliard, A C C (Canterbury) 1928 *SA* 1,2,3,4
Robinson, C E (Southland) 1951 *A* 1,2,3, 1952 *A* 1,2
Rollerson, D L (Manawatu) 1980 *W*, 1981 *S* 2, *SA* 1,2,3, *R*, *F* 1(R), 2
Roper, R A (Taranaki) 1949 *A* 2, 1950 *BI* 1,2,3,4
Rowley, H C B (Wanganui) 1949 *A* 2
Rutledge, L M (Southland) 1978 *A* 1,2,3, *I*, *W*, *E*, *S*, 1979 *F* 1,2, *A*, 1980 *A* 1,2,3
Ryan, J (Wellington) 1910 *A* 2, 1914 *A* 1,2,3

Sadler, B S (Wellington) 1935 *S*, *I*, *W*, 1936 *A* 1,2, **Salmon, J L B** (Wellington) 1981 *R*, *F* 1,2(R)
Savage, L T (Canterbury) 1949 *SA* 1,2,4
Saxton, C K (South Canterbury) 1938 *A* 1,2,3
Schuler, K J (Manawatu, North Harbour) 1990 *A* 2(R), 1992 *A* 2
Schuster, N J (Wellington) 1988 *A* 1,2,3, 1989 *F* 1,2, *Arg* 1,2, *A*, *W*, *I*
Scott, R W H (Auckland) 1946 *A* 1,2, 1947 *A* 1,2, 1949 *SA* 1,2,3,4, 1950 *BI* 1,2,3,4, 1953 *W*, 1954 *I*, *E*, *S*, *F*
Scown, A I (Taranaki) 1972 *A* 1,2,3, *W*(R), *S*
Scrimshaw, G (Canterbury) 1928 *SA* 1
Seear, G A (Otago) 1977 *F* 1,2, 1978 *A* 1,2,3, *I*, *W*, *E*, *S*, 1979 *F* 1,2, *A*
Seeling, C E (Auckland) 1904 *BI*, 1905 *S*, *I*, *E*, *W*, 1906 *F*, 1907 *A* 1,2, 1908 *AW* 1,2,3
Sellars, G M V (Auckland) 1913 *A* 1, *US*
Shaw, M W (Manawatu, Hawke's Bay) 1980 *A* 1,2,3(R), *W*, 1981 *S* 1,2, *SA* 1,2, *R*, *F* 1,2, 1982 *A* 1,2,3, 1983 *BI* 1,2,3,4, *A*, *S*, *E*, 1984 *F* 1,2, *A* 1, 1985 *E* 1,2, *A*, *Arg* 1,2, 1986 *A* 3
Shelford, F N K (Bay of Plenty) 1981 *SA* 3, *R*, 1984 *A* 2,3
Shelford, W T (North Harbour) 1986 *F* 2,3, 1987 [*It*, *Fj*, *S*, *W*, *F*], *A*, 1988 *W* 1,2, *A* 1,2,3, 1989 *F* 1,2, *Arg* 1,2, *A*, *W*, *I*, 1990 *S* 1,2
Siddells, S K (Wellington) 1921 *SA* 3
Simon, H J (Otago) 1937 *SA* 1,2,3
Simpson, J G (Auckland) 1947 *A* 1,2, 1949 *SA* 1,2,3,4, 1950 *BI* 1,2,3
Simpson, V L J (Canterbury) 1985 *Arg* 1,2
Sims, G S (Otago) 1972 *A* 2
Skeen, J R (Auckland) 1952 *A* 2
Skinner, K L (Otago, Counties) 1949 *SA* 1,2,3,4, 1950 *BI* 1,2,3,4, 1951 *A* 1,2,3, 1952 *A* 1,2, 1953 *W*, 1954 *I*, *E*, *S*, *F*, 1956 *SA* 3,4
Skudder, G R (Waikato) 1969 *W* 2
Sloane, P H (North Auckland) 1979 *E*
Smith, A E (Taranaki) 1969 *W* 1,2, 1970 *SA* 1
Smith, B W (Waikato) 1984 *F* 1,2, *A* 1
Smith, G W (Auckland) 1905 *S*, *I*
Smith, I S T (Otago, North Otago) 1964 *A* 1,2,3, 1965 *SA* 1,2,4, 1966 *BI* 1,2,3
Smith, J B (North Auckland) 1946 *A* 1, 1947 *A* 2, 1949 *A* 1,2
Smith, R M (Canterbury) 1955 *A* 1
Smith, W E (Nelson) 1905 *A*
Smith, W R (Canterbury) 1980 *A* 1, 1982 *A* 1,2,3, 1983 *BI* 2,3, *S*, *E*, 1984 *F* 1,2, *A* 1,2,3, 1985 *E* 1,2, *A*, *Arg* 2
Snow, E M (Nelson) 1929 *A* 1,2,3
Solomon, F (Auckland) 1931 *A*, 1932 *A* 2,3
Sonntag, W T C (Otago) 1929 *A* 1,2,3
Speight, M W (Waikato) 1986 *A* 1
Spencer, J C (Wellington) 1905 *A*, 1907 *A* 1(R)
Spiers, J E (Counties) 1979 *S*, *E*, 1981 *R*, *F* 1,2
Spillane, A P (South Canterbury) 1913 *A* 2,3
Stanley, J T (Auckland) 1986 *F* 1, *A* 2,3, *F* 2,3, 1987 [*It*, *Fj*, *Arg*, *S*, *W*, *F*], *A*, 1988 *W* 1,2, *A* 1,2,3, 1989 *F* 1,2, *Arg* 1,2, *A*, *W*, *I*, 1990 *S* 1,2
Stead, J W (Southland) 1904 *BI*, 1905 *S*, *I*, *E*, 1906 *F*, 1908 *AW* 1,3
Steel, A G (Canterbury) 1966 *BI* 1,2,3,4, 1967 *A*, *F*, *S*, 1968 *A* 1,2
Steel, J (West Coast) 1921 *SA* 1,2,3, 1924 *W*, 1925 *E*, *F*
Steele, L B (Wellington) 1951 *A* 1,2,3
Steere, E R G (Hawke's Bay) 1930 *BI* 1,2,3,4, 1931 *A*, 1932 *A* 1
Stephens, O G (Wellington) 1968 *F* 3
Stevens, I N (Wellington) 1972 *S*, 1973 *E* 1, 1974 *A* 3
Stewart, A J (Canterbury, South Canterbury) 1963 *E* 1,2, *I*, *W*, 1964 *E*, *S*, *F*, *A* 3
Stewart, J D (Auckland) 1913 *A* 2,3

Stewart, K W (Southland) 1973 *E* 2, 1974 *A* 1,2,3, *I*, 1975 *S*, 1976 *I*, *SA* 1,3, 1979 *S*, *E*, 1981 *SA* 1,2
Stewart, R T (South Canterbury, Canterbury) 1928 *SA* 1,2,3,4, 1930 *BI* 2
Stohr, L B (Taranaki) 1910 *A* 1,2,3
Stone, A M (Waikato, Bay of Plenty) 1981 *F* 1,2, 1983 *BI* 3(R), 1984 *A* 3, 1986 *F* 1, *A* 1,3, *F* 2,3
Storey, P W (South Canterbury) 1921 *SA* 1,2
Strachan, A D (Auckland) 1992 *Wld* 2,3, *I* 1,2, *A* 1,2,3, *SA*
Strahan, S C (Manawatu) 1967 *A*, *E*, *W*, *F*, *S*, 1968 *A* 1,2, *F* 1,2,3, 1970 *SA* 1,2,3, 1972 *A* 1,2,3, 1973 *E* 2
Strang, W A (South Canterbury) 1928 *SA* 1,2, 1930 *BI* 3,4, 1931 *A*
Stringfellow, J C (Wairarapa) 1929 *A* 1(R),3
Stuart, K C (Canterbury) 1955 *A* 1
Stuart, R C (Canterbury) 1949 *A* 1,2, 1953 *W*, 1954 *I*, *E*, *S*, *F*
Stuart, R L (Hawke's Bay) 1977 *F* 1(R)
Sullivan, J L (Taranaki) 1937 *SA* 1,2,3, 1938 *A* 1,2,3
Sutherland, A R (Marlborough) 1970 *SA* 2,4, 1971 *BI* 1, 1972 *A* 1,2,3, *W*, 1973 *E* 1, *I*, *F*
Svenson, K S (Wellington) 1924 *I*, *W*, 1925 *E*, *F*
Swain, J P (Hawke's Bay) 1928 *SA* 1,2,3,4

Tanner, J M (Auckland) 1950 *BI* 4, 1951 *A* 1,2,3, 1953 *W*
Tanner, K J (Canterbury) 1974 *A* 1,2,3, *I*, 1975 *S*, 1976 *I*, *SA* 1
Taylor, H M (Canterbury) 1913 *A* 1, *US*, 1914 *A* 1,2,3
Taylor, J M (Otago) 1937 *SA* 1,2,3, 1938 *A* 1,2,3
Taylor, M B (Waikato) 1979 *F* 1,2, *A*, *S*, *E*, 1980 *A* 1,2
Taylor, N M (Bay of Plenty, Hawke's Bay) 1977 *BI* 2, 4(R), *F* 1,2, 1978 *A* 1,2,3, *I*, 1982 *A* 2
Taylor, R (Taranaki) 1913 *A* 2,3
Taylor, W T (Canterbury) 1983 *BI* 1,2,3,4, *A*, *S*, 1984 *F* 1,2, *A* 1,2, 1985 *E* 1,2, *A*, *Arg* 1,2, 1986 *A* 2, 1987 [*It*, *Fj*, *S*, *W*, *F*], *A*, 1988 *W* 1,2
Tetzlaff, P L (Auckland) 1947 *A* 1,2
Thimbleby, N W (Hawke's Bay) 1970 *SA* 3
Thomas, B T (Auckland, Wellington) 1962 *A* 5, 1964 *A* 1,2,3
Thomson, H D (Wellington) 1908 *AW* 1
Thorne, G S (Auckland) 1968 *A* 1,2, *F* 1,2,3, 1969 *W* 1, 1970 *SA* 1,2,3,4
Thornton, N H (Auckland) 1947 *A* 1,2, 1949 *SA* 1
Tilyard, J T (Wellington) 1913 *A* 3
Timu, J K R (Otago) 1991 *Arg* 1, *A* 1,2, [*E*, *US*, *C*, *A*], 1992 *Wld* 2, *I* 2, *A* 1,2,3, *SA*
Tindill, E W T (Wellington) 1936 *E*
Townsend, L J (Otago) 1955 *A* 1,3
Tremain, K R (Canterbury, Hawke's Bay) 1959 *BI* 2,3,4, 1960 *SA* 1,2,3,4, 1961 *F* 2,3, 1962 *A* 1,2,3, 1963 *E* 1,2, *I*, *W*, 1964 *E*, *S*, *F*, *A* 1,2,3, 1965 *SA* 1,2,3,4, 1966 *BI* 1,2,3,4, 1967 *A*, *E*, *W*, *S*, 1968 *A* 1, *F* 1,2,3,4
Trevathan, D (Otago) 1937 *SA* 1,2,3
Tuck, J M (Waikato) 1929 *A* 1,2,3
Tuigamala, V L (Auckland) 1991 [*US*, *It*, *C*, *S*], 1992 *Wld* 1,2,3, *I* 1, *A* 1,2,3, *SA*
Turner, R S (North Harbour) 1992 *Wld* 1,2(R)
Turtill, H S (Canterbury) 1905 *A*
Twigden, T M (Auckland) 1980 *A* 2,3
Tyler, G A (Auckland) 1903 *A*, 1904 *BI*, 1905 *S*, *I*, *E*, *W*, 1906 *F*

Udy, D K (Wairarapa) 1903 *A*
Urbahn, R J (Taranaki) 1959 *BI* 1,3,4
Urlich, R A (Auckland) 1970 *SA* 3,4
Uttley, I N (Wellington) 1963 *E* 1,2

Vincent, P B (Canterbury) 1956 *SA* 1,2
Vodanovich, I M H (Wellington) 1955 *A* 1,2,3

Wallace, W J (Wellington) 1903 *A*, 1904 *BI*, 1905 *S*, *I*, *E*, *W*, 1906 *F*, 1907 *A* 1,2,3, 1908 *AW* 2

Walsh, P T (Counties) 1955 *A* 1,2,3, 1956 *SA* 1,2,4, 1957 *A* 1,2, 1958 *A* 1,2,3, 1959 *BI* 1, 1963 *E* 2
Ward, R H (Southland) 1936 *A* 2, 1937 *SA* 1,3
Waterman, A C (North Auckland) 1929 *A* 1,2
Watkins, E L (Wellington) 1905 *A*
Watt, B A (Canterbury) 1962 *A* 1,4, 1963 *E* 1,2, *W*, 1964 *E*, *S*, *A* 1
Watt, J M (Otago) 1936 *A* 1,2
Watt, J R (Wellington) 1958 *A* 2, 1960 *SA* 1,2,3,4, 1961 *F* 1,3, 1962 *A* 1,2
Watts, M G (Taranaki) 1979 *F* 1,2, 1980 *A* 1,2,3(R)
Webb, D S (North Auckland) 1959 *BI* 2
Wells, J (Wellington) 1936 *A* 1,2
West, A H (Taranaki) 1921 *SA* 2,3
Whetton, A J (Auckland) 1984 *A* 1(R),3(R), 1985 *A*(R), *Arg* 1(R), 1986 *A* 2, 1987 [*It*, *Fj*, *Arg*, *S*, *W*, *F*], *A*, 1988 *W* 1,2, *A* 1,2,3, 1989 *F* 1,2, *Arg* 1,2, *A*, 1990 *S* 1,2, *A* 1,2,3, *F* 1,2, 1991 *Arg* 1, [*E*, *US*, *It*, *C*, *A*]
Whetton, G W (Auckland) 1981 *SA* 3, *R*, *F* 1,2, 1982 *A* 3, 1983 *BI* 1,2,3,4, 1984 *F* 1,2, *A* 1,2,3, 1985 *E* 1,2, *A*, *Arg* 2, 1986 *A* 2,3, *F* 2,3, 1987 [*It*, *Fj*, *Arg*, *S*, *W*, *F*], *A*, 1988 *W* 1,2, *A* 1,2,3, 1989 *F* 1,2, *Arg* 1,2, *A*, *W*, *I*, 1990 *S* 1,2, *A* 1,2,3, *F* 1,2, 1991 *Arg* 1,2, *A* 1,2, [*E*, *US*, *It*, *C*, *A*, *S*]
Whineray, W J (Canterbury, Waikato, Auckland) 1957 *A* 1,2, 1958 *A* 1,2,3, 1959 *BI* 1,2,3,4, 1960 *SA* 1,2,3,4, 1961 *F* 1,2,3, 1962 *A* 1,2,3,4,5, 1963 *E* 1,2, *I*, *W*, 1964 *E*, *S*, *F*, 1965 *SA* 1,2,3,4
White, A (Southland) 1921 *SA* 1, 1924 *I*, 1925 *E*, *F*
White, H L (Auckland) 1954 *I*, *E*, *F*, 1955 *A* 3
White, R A (Poverty Bay) 1949 *A* 1,2, 1950 *BI* 1,2,3,4, 1951 *A* 1,2,3, 1952 *A* 1,2, 1953 *W*, 1954 *I*, *E*, *S*, *F*, 1955 *A* 1,2,3, 1956 *SA* 1,2,3,4
White, R M (Wellington) 1946 *A* 1,2, 1947 *A* 1,2
Whiting, G J (King Country) 1972 *A* 1,2, *S*, 1973 *E* 1, *I*, *F*
Whiting, P J (Auckland) 1971 *BI* 1,2,4, 1972 *A* 1,2,3, *W*, *S*, 1973 *E* 1, *I*, *F*, 1974 *A* 1,2,3, *I*, 1976 *I*, *SA* 1,2,3,4
Williams, B G (Auckland) 1970 *SA* 1,2,3,4, 1971 *BI* 1,2,4, 1972 *A* 1,2,3, *W*, *S*, 1973 *E* 1, *I*, *F*, *E* 2, 1974 *A* 1,2,3, *I*, 1975 *S*, 1976 *I*, *SA* 1,2,3,4, 1977 *BI* 1,2,3,4, *F* 1, 1978 *A* 1,2,3, *I* (R), *W*, *E*, *S*
Williams, G C (Wellington) 1967 *E*, *W*, *F*, *S*, 1968 *A* 2
Williams, P (Otago) 1913 *A* 1
Williment, M (Wellington) 1964 *A* 1, 1965 *SA* 1,2,3, 1966 *BI* 1,2,3,4, 1967 *A*
Willocks, C (Otago) 1946 *A* 1,2, 1949 *SA* 1,3,4
Wilson, B W (Otago) 1977 *BI* 3,4, 1978 *A* 1,2,3, 1979 *F* 1,2, *A*
Wilson, D D (Canterbury) 1954 *E*, *S*
Wilson, H W (Otago) 1949 *A* 1, 1950 *BI* 4, 1951 *A* 1,2,3
Wilson, N A (Wellington) 1908 *AW* 1,2, 1910 *A* 1,2,3, 1913 *A* 2,3, 1914 *A* 1,2,3
Wilson, N L (Otago) 1951 *A* 1,2,3
Wilson, R G (Canterbury) 1979 *S*, *E*
Wilson, S S (Wellington) 1977 *F* 1,2, 1978 *A* 1,2,3, *I*, *W*, *E*, *S*, 1979 *F* 1,2, *A*, *S*, *E*, 1980 *A* 1, *W*, 1981 *S* 1,2, *SA* 1,2,3, *R*, *F* 1,2, 1982 *A* 1,2,3, 1983 *BI* 1,2,3,4, *A*, *S*, *E*
Wolfe, T N (Wellington, Taranaki) 1961 *F* 1,2,3, 1962 *A* 2,3, 1963 *E* 1
Wood, M E (Canterbury, Auckland) 1903 *A*, 1904 *BI*
Woodman, F A (North Auckland) 1981 *SA* 1,2, *F* 2
Wrigley, E (Wairarapa) 1905 *A*
Wright, T J (Auckland) 1986 *F* 1, *A* 1, 1987 [*Arg*], 1988 *W* 1,2, *A* 1,2,3, 1989 *F* 1,2, *Arg* 1,2, *A*, *W*, *I*, 1990 *S* 1,2, *A* 1,2,3, *F* 1,2, 1991 *Arg* 1,2, *A* 1,2, [*E*, *US*, *It*, *S*]
Wylie, J T (Auckland) 1913 *A* 1, *US*
Wyllie, A J (Canterbury) 1970 *SA* 2,3, 1971 *BI* 2,3,4, 1972 *W*, *S*, 1973 *E* 1, *I*, *F*, *E* 2

Yates, V M (North Auckland) 1961 *F* 1,2,3
Young, D (Canterbury) 1956 *SA* 2, 1958 *A* 1,2,3, 1960 *SA* 1,2,3,4, 1961 *F* 1,2,3, 1962 *A* 1,2,3,5, 1963 *E* 1,2, *I*, *W*, 1964 *E*, *S*, *F*

NEW ZEALAND INTERNATIONAL RECORDS

Both team and individual records are for official New Zealand international matches, up to 31 March 1993.

TEAM RECORDS

Highest score
74 v Fiji (74-13) 1987 Christchurch

v individual countries
60 v Argentina (60-9) 1989 Dunedin
38 v Australia { (38-13) 1936 Dunedin
                { (38-3) 1972 Auckland
38 v B Isles (38-6) 1983 Auckland
29 v Canada (29-13) 1991 Lille
42 v England (42-15) 1985 Wellington
74 v Fiji (74-13) 1987 Christchurch
38 v France (38-8) 1906 Paris
59 v Ireland (59-6) 1992 Wellington
70 v Italy (70-6) 1987 Auckland
14 v Romania (14-6) 1981 Bucharest
27 v S Africa (27-24) 1992 Johannesburg .
40 v Scotland (40-15) 1981 Auckland
51 v United States (51-3) 1913 Berkeley
54 v Wales (54-9) 1988 Auckland

Biggest winning points margin
64 v Italy (70-6) 1987 Auckland

v individual countries
51 v Argentina (60-9) 1989 Dublin
35 v Australia (38-3) 1972 Auckland
32 v B Isles (38-6) 1983 Auckland
16 v Canada (29-13) 1991 Lille
27 v England (42-15) 1985 Wellington
61 v Fiji (74-13) 1987 Christchurch
30 v France (38-8) 1906 Paris
53 v Ireland (59-6) 1992 Wellington
64 v Italy (70-6) 1987 Auckland
8 v Romania (14-6) 1981 Bucharest
17 v S Africa (20-3) 1965 Auckland
27 v Scotland (30-3) 1987 Christchurch
48 v United States (51-3) 1913 Berkeley
49 v Wales (52-3) 1988 Christchurch

Highest score by opposing team
30 Australia (16-30) 1978 Auckland

by individual countries
21 Argentina (21-21) 1985 Buenos Aires
30 Australia (16-30) 1978 Auckland
17 B Isles (18-17) 1959 Dunedin
13 Canada (29-13) 1991 Lille
16 England (10-16) 1973 Auckland

13 Fiji (74-13) 1987 Christchurch
24 France (19-24) 1979 Auckland
21 Ireland (24-21) 1992 Dunedin
21 Italy (31-21) 1991 Leicester
6 Romania (14-6) 1981 Bucharest
24 S Africa { (12-24) 1981 Wellington
            { (27-24) 1992 Johannesburg
25 Scotland (25-25) 1983 Edinburgh
6 United States (46-6) 1991 Gloucester
16 Wales (19-16) 1972 Cardiff

Biggest losing points margin
17 v S Africa (0-17) 1928 Durban

v individual countries
16 v Australia (10-26) 1980 Sydney
10 v B Isles (3-13) 1971 Wellington
13 v England (0-13) 1936 Twickenham
13 v France (3-16) 1986 Nantes
17 v S Africa (0-17) 1928 Durban
5 v Wales (8-13) 1953 Cardiff
No defeats v Argentina, Canada, Fiji, Ireland, Italy, Romania, Scotland or United States

---

Most tries by New Zealand in an international
13 v United States (51-3) Berkeley

Most tries against New Zealand in an international
5 by { S Africa (6-17) 1937 Auckland
     { Australia (16-30) 1978 Auckland
     { World XV (54-26) 1992 Wellington

Most points on overseas tour (all matches)
868 in B Isles/France (33 matches) 1905-06

Most tries on overseas tour
215 in B Isles/France (33 matches) 1905-06

INDIVIDUAL RECORDS

Most capped player
G W Whetton   58   1981-91
in individual positions
Full-back
D B Clarke   31   1956-64
Wing
J J Kirwan   54   1984-92
Centre (includes 2nd five-eighth)
B J Robertson   34   1972-81
1st five-eighth
G J Fox   41   1985-92
Scrum-half
S M Going   29   1967-77
Prop
S C McDowell   46   1985-92
Hooker
S B T Fitzpatrick   49   1986-92
Lock
G W Whetton   58   1981-91
Flanker
K R Tremain   36(38)[1]   1959-68
I A Kirkpatrick   36(39)[2]   1967-77
No 8
M G Mexted   34   1979-85
[1]*Tremain won 2 caps as a No 8*
[2]*Kirkpatrick won 3 caps as a No 8*

Longest international career
E Hughes   15 seasons   1907-21
C E Meads   15 seasons   1957-71

Most consecutive internationals – 47
S B T Fitzpatrick 1986-92

Most internationals as captain
W J Whineray   30   1958-65

Most points in internationals – 573
G J Fox (41 matches) 1985-92

Most points in an international – 26
A R Hewson v Australia 1982 Auckland
G J Fox v Fiji 1987 Christchurch

Most tries in internationals – 34
J J Kirwan (54 matches) 1984-92

Most tries in an international – 4
D McGregor v England 1905 Crystal Palace
C I Green v Fiji 1987 Christchurch

J A Gallagher v Fiji 1987 Christchurch
J J Kirwan v Wales 1988 Christchurch

Most conversions in internationals – 112
G J Fox (41 matches) 1985-92

Most conversions in an international – 10
G J Fox v Fiji 1987 Christchurch

Most dropped goals in internationals – 7
G J Fox (41 matches) 1985-92

Most penalty goals in internationals – 108
G J Fox (41 matches) 1985-92

Most penalty goals in an international – 6
D B Clarke v B Isles 1959 Dunedin
K J Crowley v England 1985 Christchurch
G J Fox v Argentina 1987 Wellington
G J Fox v Scotland 1987 Christchurch
G J Fox v France 1990 Parc des Princes

Most points in international series – 46
A R Hewson (4 appearances) v B Isles 1983

Most points in international series on tour – 38
G J Fox (2 appearances) 1990 France

Most tries in international series on tour – 5
K Svenson (4 appearances) 1924-25
 B Isles/France
Svenson scored in each match of the international series

Most points on tour – 230
W J Wallace (25 appearances) 1905-06
 B Isles/France

Most tries on tour – 42
J Hunter (23 appearances) 1905-06
 B Isles/France

Most points in a tour match – 43
R M Deans v South Australia 1984
 Adelaide

Most tries in a tour match – 8
T R Heeps v Northern NSW 1962
 Quirindi

WALLABIES – BATTERED AND BRUISED BUT STILL THE BEST

THE 1992 SEASON IN AUSTRALIA
Greg Campbell

Months after successfully securing rugby's most important trophy, the Webb Ellis Cup, the Wallabies faced an historic and challenging year. By the time the final whistle was blown, a weary and battle-scarred Australian team had completed their year of duty with a 7-1 winning record, the Bledisloe Cup in their trophy case and record victories against South Africa and Ireland.

Not only did the Australians face four different Test-playing nations, embark on two overseas tours and play under three different Test captains, but they also had to adjust mid-season from the old to the new laws. The team encountered a heavy injury toll which saw World Cup-winning team members Marty Roebuck, Jason Little, Michael Lynagh, Willie Ofahengaue, John Eales and Tony Daly all miss one or more Test matches while Tim Gavin again faced a period on the sideline. Both Simon Poidevin and Rob Egerton were unavailable for Test duties while Nick Farr-Jones announced his international retirement prior to the tour of Ireland and Wales after leading the Wallabies into a world record 36 Tests. These disruptions resulted in Paul Kahl, Peter Jorgensen, Garrick Morgan, Tim Kelaher, Richard Tombs and David Wilson all making their Test debuts.

It is only when one sits back and examines the Wallabies' difficulties that full appreciation of their outstanding results can be digested. Three tour matches were lost in Ireland and Wales as non-Test regulars were given their international wings. But Australia displayed their champion quality by bouncing back from these setbacks to rise triumphantly to the occasion, particularly when beating Wales 23-6 in Cardiff.

From the opening Test of the season, the Wallabies' class was evident. After a slow opening 40 minutes in the first Test against Scotland, the Wallabies took control to post a comfortable 27-12 win before convincingly disposing of the Scots 37-13 in the second Test. This final victory marked the last international played under the old laws. While the All Blacks had four tour matches to adjust to the new laws, Australia were forced to make an instant transition during the first Test for the Bledisloe Cup. The Wallabies remained calm and composed in a gripping see-sawing match before winning 16-15 in Sydney. They displayed the same qualities again in the second Test at Ballymore to secure the Bledisloe Cup for the first time since 1986 with a memorable 19-17 victory. The All Blacks ended Australia's ten-Test match-winning streak with a 26-23 victory only three days after being caned 40-15 by Sydney.

The All Black tour was not particularly pleasant as instances of foul play regularly submerged the tour in controversy, particularly the incident at Ballymore which resulted in Wallaby winger Paul Carozza suffering a broken nose after an incident involving Richard Loe of New Zealand.

This was not to be the only controversial tour involving the Australians. The Wallabies travelled to South Africa for the first time since 1969 and became the unfortunate victims of the Springbok-All Black Ellis Park anthem incident which plunged the Test against South Africa into jeopardy. It was during the week leading up to the Test that Australian Rugby Football Union president Mr Joe French played a key part in the continuation of the tour and the playing of the Test. French took a leading role in negotiations with the African National Congress. Before a packed Newlands Stadium, the Wallabies laid to rest any thought that their world title was perhaps unjustified by beating the Springboks by a record 26-3 margin. The mercurial David Campese celebrated the match by crossing for his 50th Test try.

Any idea of an easy post-season tour of Ireland and Wales was quickly erased when the Australians were beaten by Munster in the second of the 13 scheduled matches. The Wallabies, led by Michael Lynagh, recovered to trounce Ireland 42-17 and provide coach Bob Dwyer with an ideal victory in which to celebrate his 50th Test as coach. The Wallabies suffered further losses, criticism and injuries in Wales, but these setbacks only strengthened their resolve for the Test there. And the final result, a 23-6 victory, was a fitting finale to the year. Phil Kearns led the side from hooker.

Australia's fortunes at sevens did not duplicate the success of the 15-a-side team. Without key play-makers Campese and Lynagh, they reached the Cathay Pacific-Hong Kong Bank Invitation Sevens semi-finals, but were beaten in atrocious conditions by the eventual champions, Fiji.

On the domestic front, rugby continued to grow. An ARFU census revealed that youth rugby participation levels had soared by 21.9 per cent during the year. Added to the 17.5 increase in 1991, this shows a growth at this developmental level of almost 40 per cent in two years.

Queensland became the first non-New Zealand provincial team to capture the Super Six Championship. This Championship is to expand in 1993 to include three South African provinces plus an extra New Zealand province. Another radical step taken during the year was the decision that the Wallabies will play their first domestic night Test, in 1993 against the Springboks.

The club scene was again dominated by Randwick in Sydney and Southern Districts in Brisbane.

MAJOR PROVINCIAL MATCHES
Sydney Origin 30, NSW Country Origin 10; Queensland 23, NSW 16;
Queensland 18, NSW 15; NSW 30, ACT 17; Queensland 33, ACT 0
SYDNEY GRAND FINAL
Randwick 28, Gordon 14
BRISBANE GRAND FINAL
Southern Districts 44, Queensland 10

John Eales, the mighty Australian lock, whose tour of Wales, and indeed, his career, was disrupted by injury.

AUSTRALIAN INTERNATIONAL PLAYERS (*up to 31 March 1993*)

ABBREVIATIONS

Arg – Argentina; *BI* – British Isles teams; *C* – Canada; *E* – England; *F* – France; *Fj* – Fiji; *I* – Ireland; *It* – Italy; *J* – Japan; *M* – Maoris; *NZ* – New Zealand; *S* – Scotland; *SA* – South Africa; *SK* – South Korea; *Tg* – Tonga; *US* – United States of America; *W* – Wales; *WS* – Western Samoa; (R) – Replacement. Entries in square brackets [ ] indicate appearances in the Rugby World Cup

STATE ABBREVIATIONS

ACT – Australian Capital Territory; NSW – New South Wales; Q – Queensland; V – Victoria; WA – Western Australia

N.B. In the summer of 1986, the ARU retrospectively granted full Australian Test status to the five international matches played by the 1927-28 touring team to Europe. In 1988 Test status was extended to all those who played overseas in the 1920s.

Note: When a series has taken place, figures denote the particular matches in which players featured. Thus 1963 *SA* 2,4 indicates that a player appeared in the second and fourth Tests of the 1963 series against South Africa.

Abrahams, A M F (NSW) 1967 *NZ*, 1968 *NZ* 1, 1969 *W*
Adams, N J (NSW) 1955 *NZ* 1
Adamson, R W (NSW) 1912 *US*
Allan, T (NSW) 1946 *NZ* 1, *M*, *NZ* 2, 1947 *NZ* 2, *S*, *I*, *W*, 1948 *E*, *F*, 1949 *M* 1,2,3, *NZ* 1,2
Anlezark, E A (NSW) 1905 *NZ*
Armstrong, A R (NSW) 1923 *NZ* 1,2
Austin, L R (NSW) 1963 *E*

Baker, R L (NSW) 1904 *BI* 1,2
Baker, W H (NSW) 1914 *NZ* 1,2,3
Ballesty, J P (NSW) 1968 *NZ* 1,2, *F*, *I*, *S*, 1969 *W*, *SA* 2,3,4
Bannon, D P (NSW) 1946 *M*
Bardsley, E J (NSW) 1928 *NZ* 1,3, *M* (R)
Barker, H S (NSW) 1952 *Fj* 1,2, *NZ* 1,2, 1953 *SA* 4, 1954 *Fj* 1,2
Barnett, J T (NSW) 1907 *NZ* 1,2,3, 1908 *W*, 1909 *E*
Barry, M J (Q) 1971 *SA* 3
Barton, R F D (NSW) 1899 *BI* 3
Batch, P G (Q) 1975 *S*, *W*, 1976 *E*, *Fj* 1,2,3, *F* 1,2, 1978 *W* 1,2, *NZ* 1,2,3, 1979 *Arg* 2
Batterham, R P (NSW) 1967 *NZ*, 1970 *S*
Battishall, B R (NSW) 1973 *E*
Baxter, A J (NSW) 1949 *M* 1,2,3, *NZ* 1,2, 1951 *NZ* 1,2, 1952 *NZ* 1,2
Baxter, T J (Q) 1958 *NZ* 3
Beith, B McN (NSW) 1914 *NZ* 3
Bell, K R (Q) 1968 *S*
Bennett, W G (Q) 1931 *M*, 1933 *SA* 1,2,3
Bermingham, J V (Q) 1934 *NZ* 1,2, 1937 *SA* 1
Berne, J E (NSW) 1975 *S*
Besomo, K S (NSW) 1979 *I* 2
Betts, T N (Q) 1951 *NZ* 2,3, 1954 *Fj* 2
Biilmann, R R (NSW) 1933 *SA* 1,2,3,4
Birt, R (Q) 1914 *NZ* 2
Black, J W (NSW) 1985 *C* 1,2, *NZ*, *Fj* 1
Blackwood, J G (NSW) 1923 *NZ* 1,2,3, 1925 *NZ*, 1927 *I*, *W*, *S*, 1928 *E*, *F*
Blair, M R (NSW) 1928 *F*, 1931 *M*, *NZ*
Bland, G V (NSW) 1928 *NZ* 3, *M*, 1932 *NZ* 1,2,3, 1933 *SA* 1,2,4,5
Blomley, J (NSW) 1949 *M* 1,2,3, *NZ* 1,2, 1950 *BI* 1,2
Boland, S B (Q) 1899 *BI* 3,4, 1903 *NZ*
Bond, J H (NSW) 1921 *NZ*
Bonis, E T (Q) 1929 *NZ* 1,2,3, 1930 *BI*, 1931 *M*, *NZ*, 1932 *NZ* 1,2,3, 1933 *SA* 1,2,3,4,5, 1934 *NZ* 1,2, 1936 *NZ* 1,2, *M*, 1937 *SA* 1, 1938 *NZ* 1
Bosler, J M (NSW) 1953 *SA* 1
Bouffler, R G (NSW) 1899 *BI* 3
Bourke, T K (Q) 1947 *NZ* 2
Bowers, A J A (NSW) 1923 *NZ* 3, 1925 *NZ*, 1927 *I*
Boyce, E S (NSW) 1962 *NZ* 1,2, 1964 *NZ* 1,2,3, 1965 *SA* 1,2, 1966 *W*, *S*, 1967 *E*, *I* 1, *F*, *I* 2
Boyce, J S (NSW) 1962 *NZ* 3,4,5, 1963 *E*, *SA* 1,2,3,4, 1964 *NZ* 1,3, 1965 *SA* 1,2
Boyd, A (NSW) 1899 *BI* 3

Boyd, A F McC (Q) 1958 *M* 1
Brass, J E (NSW) 1966 *BI* 2, *W*, *S*, 1967 *E*, *I* 1, *F*, *I* 2, *NZ*, 1968 *NZ* 1, *F*, *I*, *S*
Breckenridge, J W (NSW) 1927 *I*, *W*, *S*, 1928 *E*, *F*, 1929 *NZ* 1,2,3, 1930 *BI*
Bridle, O L (V) 1931 *M*, 1932 *NZ* 1,2,3, 1933 *SA* 3,4,5, 1934 *NZ* 1,2, 1936 *NZ* 1,2, *M*
Broad, E G (Q) 1949 *M* 1
Brockhoff, J D (NSW) 1949 *M* 2,3, *NZ* 1,2, 1950 *BI* 1,2, 1951 *NZ* 2,3
Brown, B R (Q) 1972 *NZ* 1,3
Brown, J V (NSW) 1956 *SA* 1,2, 1957 *NZ* 1,2, 1958 *W*, *I*, *E*, *S*, *F*
Brown, R C (NSW) 1975 *E* 1,2
Brown, S W (NSW) 1953 *SA* 2,3,4
Bryant, H (NSW) 1925 *NZ*
Buchan, A J (NSW) 1946 *NZ* 1,2, 1947 *NZ* 1,2, *S*, *I*, *W*, 1948 *E*, *F*, 1949 *M* 3
Bull, D (NSW) 1928 *M*
Buntine, H (NSW) 1923 *NZ* 1(R)
Burdon, A (NSW) 1903 *NZ*, 1904 *BI* 1,2, 1905 *NZ*
Burge, A B (NSW) 1907 *NZ* 3, 1908 *W*
Burge, P H (NSW) 1907 *NZ* 1,2,3
Burge, R (NSW) 1928 *NZ* 1,2,3(R), *M* (R)
Burke, B T (NSW) 1988 *S* (R)
Burke, C T (NSW) 1946 *NZ* 2, 1947 *NZ* 1,2, *S*, *I*, *W*, 1948 *E*, *F*, 1949 *M* 2,3, *NZ* 1,2, 1950 *BI* 1,2, 1951 *NZ* 1,2,3, 1953 *SA* 2,3,4, 1954 *Fj* 1, 1955 *NZ* 1,2,3, 1956 *SA* 1,2
Burke, M P (NSW) 1984 *E* (R), *I*, 1985 *C* 1,2, *NZ*, *Fj* 1,2, 1986 *It* (R), *F*, *Arg* 1,2, *NZ* 1,2,3, 1987 *SK*, [*US*, *J*, *I*, *F*, *W*], *NZ*, *Arg* 1,2
Burnet, D R (NSW) 1972 *F* 1,2, *NZ* 1,2,3, *Fj*
Butler, O F (NSW) 1969 *SA* 1,2, 1970 *S*, 1971 *SA* 2,3, *F* 1,2

Calcraft, W J (NSW) 1985 *C* 1, 1986 *It*, *Arg* 2
Caldwell, B C (NSW) 1928 *NZ* 3
Cameron, A S (NSW) 1951 *NZ* 1,2,3, 1952 *Fj* 1,2, *NZ* 1,2, 1953 *SA* 1,2,3,4, 1954 *Fj* 1,2, 1955 *NZ* 1,2,3, 1956 *SA* 1,2, 1957 *NZ* 1, 1958 *I*
Campbell, J D (NSW) 1910 *NZ* 1,2,3
Campbell, W A (Q) 1984 *Fj*, 1986 *It*, *F*, *Arg* 1,2, *NZ* 1,2,3, 1987 *SK*, [*E*, *US*, *J*(R), *I*, *F*], *NZ*, 1988 *E*, 1989 *BI* 1,2,3, *NZ*, 1990 *NZ* 2,3
Campese, D I (ACT, NSW) 1982 *NZ* 1,2,3, 1983 *US*, *Arg* 1,2, *NZ*, *It*, *F* 1,2, 1984 *Fj*, *NZ* 1,2,3, *E*, *I*, *W*, *S*, 1985 *Fj* 1,2, 1986 *It*, *F*, *Arg* 1,2, *NZ* 1,2,3, 1987 [*E*, *US*, *J*, *I*, *F*, *W*], *NZ*, 1988 *E* 1,2, *NZ* 1,2,3, *E*, *S*, *It*, 1989 *BI* 1,2,3, *NZ*, *F* 1,2, 1990 *F* 2,3, *US*, *NZ* 1,2,3, 1991 *W*, *E*, *NZ* 1,2, [*Arg*, *WS*, *W*, *I*, *NZ*, *E*], 1992 *S* 1,2, *NZ* 1,2,3, *SA*, *I*, *W*
Canniffe, W D (Q) 1907 *NZ* 2
Carberry, C M (NSW, Q) 1973 *Tg* 2, *E*, 1976 *I*, *US*, *Fj* 1,2,3, 1981 *F* 1,2, *I*, *W*, *S*, 1982 *E*
Cardy, A M (NSW) 1966 *BI* 1,2, *W*, *S*, 1967 *E*, *I* 1, *F*, 1968 *NZ* 1,2
Carew, P J (Q) 1899 *BI* 1,2,3,4

Carmichael, P (Q) 1904 *BI* 2, 1907 *NZ* 1, 1908 *W*, 1909 *E*

Carozza, P V (Q) 1990 *F* 1,2,3, *NZ* 2,3, 1992 *S* 1,2, *NZ* 1,2,3, *SA*, *I*, *W*

Carpenter, M G (V) 1938 *NZ* 1,2

Carr, E T A (NSW) 1913 *NZ* 1,2,3, 1914 *NZ* 1,2,3

Carr, E W (NSW) 1921 *NZ* 1 (R)

Carroll, D B (NSW) 1908 *W*, 1912 *US*

Carroll, J C (NSW) 1953 *SA* 1

Carroll, J H (NSW) 1958 *M* 2,3, *NZ* 1,2,3, 1959 *BI* 1,2

Carson, J (NSW) 1899 *BI* 1

Carson, P J (NSW) 1979 *NZ*, 1980 *NZ* 3

Carter, D G (NSW) 1988 *E* 1,2, *NZ* 1, 1989 *F* 1,2

Casey, T V (NSW) 1963 *SA* 2,3,4, 1964 *NZ* 1,2,3

Catchpole, K W (NSW) 1961 *Fj* 1,2,3, *SA* 1,2, *F*, 1962 *NZ* 1,2,4, 1963 *SA* 2,3,4, 1964 *NZ* 1,2,3, 1965 *SA* 1,2, 1966 *BI* 1,2, *W*, *S*, 1967 *E*, *I* 1, *F*, *I* 2, *NZ*, 1968 *NZ* 1

Cawsey, R M (NSW) 1949 *M* 1, *NZ* 1,2

Cerutti, W H (NSW) 1928 *NZ* 1,2,3, *M*, 1929 *NZ* 1,2,3, 1930 *BI*, 1931 *M*, *NZ*, 1932 *NZ* 1,2,3, 1933 *SA* 1,2,3,4,5, 1936 *M*, 1937 *SA* 1,2

Challoner, R L (NSW) 1899 *BI* 2

Chapman, G A (NSW) 1962 *NZ* 3,4,5

Clark, J G (Q) 1931 *M*, *NZ*, 1932 *NZ* 1,2, 1933 *SA* 1

Clarken, J C (NSW) 1905 *NZ*, 1910 *NZ* 1,2,3

Cleary, M A (NSW) 1961 *Fj* 1,2,3, *SA* 1,2, *F*

Clements, P (NSW) 1982 *NZ* 3

Clifford, M (NSW) 1938 *NZ* 3

Cobb, W G (NSW) 1899 *BI* 3,4

Cocks, M R (NSW, Q) 1972 *F* 1,2, *NZ* 2,3, *Fj*, 1973 *Tg* 1,2, *W*, *E*, 1975 *J* 1

Codey, D (NSW Country, Q) 1983 *Arg* 1, 1984 *E*, *W*, *S*, 1985 *C* 2, *NZ*, 1986 *F*, *Arg* 1, 1987 *[US*, *J*, *F*(R)*]*, *W]*, *NZ*

Cody, E W (NSW) 1913 *NZ* 1,2,3

Coker, T (Q) 1987 *[E*, *US*, *F*, *W]*, 1991 *NZ* 2, *[Arg*, *WS*, *NZ*, *E]*, 1992 *NZ* 1,2,3, *W*(R)

Colbert, R (NSW) 1952 *Fj* 2, *NZ* 1,2, 1953 *SA* 2,3,4

Cole, J W (NSW) 1968 *NZ* 1,2, *F*, *I*, *S*, 1969 *W*, *SA* 1,2,3,4, 1970 *S*, 1971 *SA* 1,2,3, *F* 1,2, 1972 *NZ* 1,2,3, 1973 *Tg* 1,2, 1974 *NZ* 1,2,3

Collins, P K (NSW) 1937 *SA* 2, 1938 *NZ* 2,3

Colton, A J (Q) 1899 *BI* 1,3

Colton, T (Q) 1904 *BI* 1,2

Comrie-Thomson, I R (NSW) 1928 *NZ* 1,2,3, *M*

Connor, D M (Q) 1958 *W*, *I*, *E*, *S*, *F*, *M* 2,3, *NZ* 1,2,3, 1959 *BI* 1,2

Cook, M T (Q) 1986 *F*, 1987 *SK*, *[J]*, 1988 *E* 1,2, *NZ* 1,2,3, *E*, *S*, *It*

Cooke, B P (Q) 1979 *I* 1

Cooke, G M (Q) 1932 *NZ* 1,2,3, 1933 *SA* 1,2,3, 1946 *NZ* 2, 1947 *NZ* 2, *S*, *I*, *W*, 1948 *E*, *F*

Coolican, J E (NSW) 1982 *NZ* 1, 1983 *It*, *F* 1,2

Corfe, A C (Q) 1899 *BI* 2

Cornelsen, G (NSW) 1974 *NZ* 2,3, 1975 *J* 2, *S*, *W*, 1976 *E*, *F* 1,2, 1978 *W* 1,2, *NZ* 1,2,3, 1979 *I* 1,2, *NZ*, *Arg* 1,2, 1980 *NZ* 1,2,3, 1981 *I*, *W*, *S*, 1982 *E*

Cornes, J R (Q) 1972 *Fj*

Cornforth, R G W (NSW) 1947 *NZ* 1, 1950 *BI* 2

Cornish, P (ACT) 1990 *F* 2,3, *NZ* 1

Costello, P P S (Q) 1950 *BI* 2

Cottrell, N V (Q) 1949 *M* 1,2,3, *NZ* 1,2, 1950 *BI* 1,2, 1951 *NZ* 1,2,3, 1952 *Fj* 1,2, *NZ* 1,2

Cowper, D L (V) 1931 *NZ*, 1932 *NZ* 1,2,3, 1933 *SA* 1,2,3,4,5

Cox, B P (NSW) 1952 *Fj* 1,2, *NZ* 1,2, 1954 *Fj* 2, 1955 *NZ* 1, 1956 *SA* 2, 1957 *NZ* 1,2

Cox, M H (NSW) 1981 *W*, *S*

Cox, P A (NSW) 1979 *Arg* 1,2, 1980 *Fj*, *NZ* 1,2, 1981 *W*(R), *S*, 1982 *S* 1,2, *NZ* 1,2,3, 1984 *Fj*, *NZ* 1,2,3

Craig, R R (NSW) 1908 *W*

Crakanthorp, J S (NSW) 1923 *NZ* 3

Cremin, J F (NSW) 1946 *NZ* 1,2, 1947 *NZ* 1

Crittle, C P (NSW) 1962 *NZ* 4,5, 1963 *SA* 2,3,4, 1964 *NZ* 1,2,3, 1965 *SA* 1,2, 1966 *BI* 1,2, *S*, 1967 *E*, *I*

Croft, B H D (NSW) 1928 *M*

Cross, J R (NSW) 1955 *NZ* 1,2,3

Cross, K A (NSW) 1949 *M* 1, *NZ* 1,2, 1950 *BI* 1,2, 1951 *NZ* 2,3, 1952 *NZ* 1, 1953 *SA* 1,2,3,4, 1954 *Fj* 1,2, 1955 *NZ* 3, 1956 *SA* 1,2, 1957 *NZ* 1,2

Crossman, O C (NSW) 1925 *NZ*, 1929 *NZ* 2, 1930 *BI*

Crowe, P J (NSW) 1976 *F* 2, 1978 *W* 1,2, 1979 *I* 2, *NZ*, *Arg* 1

Crowley, D J (Q) 1989 *BI* 1,2,3, 1991 *[WS]*, 1992 *I*, *W*

Curley, T J P (NSW) 1957 *NZ* 1,2, 1958 *W*, *I*, *E*, *S*, *F*, *M* 1, *NZ* 1,2,3

Curran, D J (NSW) 1980 *NZ* 3, 1981 *F* 1,2, *W*, 1983 *Arg* 1

Currie, E W (Q) 1899 *BI* 2

Cutler, S A G (NSW) 1982 *NZ* 2(R), 1984 *NZ* 1,2,3, *E*, *I*, *W*, *S*, 1985 *C* 1,2, *NZ*, *Fj* 1,2, 1986 *It*, *F*, *NZ* 1,2,3, 1987 *SK*, *[E*, *J*, *I*, *F*, *W]*, *NZ*, *Arg* 1,2, 1988 *E* 1,2, *NZ* 1,2,3, *E*, *S*, *It*, 1989 *BI* 1,2,3, *NZ*, 1991 *[WS]*

Daly, A J (NSW) 1989 *NZ*, *F* 1,2, 1990 *F* 1,2,3, *US*, *NZ* 1,2,3, 1991 *W*, *E*, *NZ* 1,2, *[Arg*, *W*, *I*, *NZ*, *E]*, 1992 *S* 1,2, *NZ* 1,2,3, *SA*

D'Arcy, A M (Q) 1980 *Fj*, *NZ* 3, 1981 *F* 1,2, *I*, *W*, *S*, 1982 *E*, *S* 1,2

Darveniza, P (NSW) 1969 *W*, *SA* 2,3,4

Davidson, R A L (NSW) 1952 *Fj* 1,2, *NZ* 1,2, 1953 *SA* 1, 1957 *NZ* 1,2, 1958 *W*, *I*, *E*, *S*, *F*, *M* 1

Davis, C C (NSW) 1949 *NZ* 1, 1951 *NZ* 1,2,3

Davis, E H (V) 1947 *S*, *W*, 1949 *M* 1,2

Davis, G V (NSW) 1963 *E*, *SA* 1,2,3,4, 1964 *NZ* 1,2,3, 1965 *SA* 1, 1966 *BI* 1,2, *W*, *S*, 1967 *E*, *I* 1, *F*, *I* 2, *NZ*, 1968 *NZ* 1,2, *F*, *I*, *S*, 1969 *W*, *SA* 1,2,3,4, 1970 *S*, 1971 *SA* 1,2,3, *F* 1,2, 1972 *F* 1,2, *NZ* 1,2,3

Davis, G W G (NSW) 1955 *NZ* 2,3

Davis, R A (NSW) 1974 *NZ* 1,2,3

Davis, T S R (NSW) 1921 *NZ*, 1923 *NZ* 1,2,3

Davis, W (NSW) 1899 *BI* 1,3,4

Dawson, W L (NSW) 1946 *NZ* 1,2

Diett, L J (NSW) 1959 *BI* 1,2

Dix, W (NSW) 1907 *NZ* 1,2,3, 1909 *E*

Dixon, E J (Q) 1904 *BI* 3

Donald, K J (Q) 1957 *NZ* 1, 1958 *W*, *I*, *E*, *S*, *M* 2,3, 1959 *BI* 1,2

Dore, E (Q) 1904 *BI* 1

Dore, M J (Q) 1905 *NZ*

Dorr, R W (V) 1936 *M*, 1937 *SA* 1

Douglas, J A (V) 1962 *NZ* 3,4,5

Dowse, J H (NSW) 1961 *Fj* 1,2, *SA* 1,2

Dunbar, A R (NSW) 1910 *NZ* 1,2,3, 1912 *US*

Dunlop, E E (V) 1932 *NZ* 3, 1934 *NZ* 1

Dunn, P K (NSW) 1958 *NZ* 1,2,3, 1959 *BI* 1,2

Dunn, V A (NSW) 1921 *NZ*

Dunworth, D A (Q) 1971 *F* 1,2, 1972 *F* 1,2, 1976 *Fj* 2

Dwyer, L J (NSW) 1910 *NZ* 1,2,3, 1912 *US*, 1913 *NZ* 3, 1914 *NZ* 1,2,3

Eales, J A (Queensland) 1991 *W*, *E*, *NZ* 1,2, *[Arg*, *WS*, *W*, *I*, *NZ*, *E]*, 1992 *S* 1,2, *NZ* 1,2,3, *SA*, *I*

Eastes, C C (NSW) 1946 *NZ* 1,2, 1947 *NZ* 1,2, 1949 *M* 1,2

Egerton, R H (NSW) 1991 *W*, *E*, *NZ* 1,2, *[Arg*, *W*, *I*, *NZ*, *E]*

Ella, G A (NSW) 1982 *NZ* 1,2, 1983 *F* 1,2, 1988 *E* 2, *NZ* 1

Ella, G J (NSW) 1982 *S* 1, 1983 *It*, 1985 *C* 2 (R), *Fj* 2

Ella, M G (NSW) 1980 *NZ* 1,2,3, 1981 *F* 2, *S*, 1982 *E*, *S* 1, *NZ* 1,2,3, 1983 *US*, *Arg* 1,2, *NZ*, *It*, *F* 1,2, 1984 *Fj*, *NZ* 1,2,3, *E*, *I*, *W*, *S*

Ellem, M A (NSW) 1976 *Fj* 3(R)

Elliott, F M (NSW) 1957 *NZ* 1

Elliott, R E (NSW) 1921 *NZ*, 1923 *NZ* 1,2,3

Ellis, C S (NSW) 1899 *BI* 1,2,3,4

Ellis, K J (NSW) 1958 *NZ* 1,2,3, 1959 *BI* 1,2

Ellwood, B J (NSW) 1958 *NZ* 1,2,3, 1961 *Fj* 2,3, *SA* 1, *F*, 1962 *NZ* 1,2,3,4,5, 1963 *SA* 1,2,3,4, 1964 *NZ* 3, 1965 *SA* 1,2, 1966 *BI* 1

Emanuel, D M (NSW) 1957 *NZ* 2, 1958 *W*, *I*, *E*, *S*, *F*, *M* 1,2,3

Emery, N A (NSW) 1947 *NZ* 2, *S*, *I*, *W*, 1948 *E*, *F*, 1949 *M* 2,3, *NZ* 1,2

Erasmus, D J (NSW) 1923 *NZ* 1,2

Erby, A B (NSW) 1923 *NZ* 2,3

Evans, L J (Q) 1903 *NZ*, 1904 *BI* 1,3

Evans, W T (Q) 1899 *BI* 1,2

Fahey, E J (NSW) 1912 *US*, 1913 *NZ* 1,2, 1914 *NZ* 3

Fairfax, R L (NSW) 1971 *F* 1,2, 1972 *F* 1,2, *NZ* 1, *Fj*, 1973 *W*, *E*

Farmer, E H (Q) 1910 *NZ* 1

Farr-Jones, N C (NSW) 1984 *E*, *I*, *W*, *S*, 1985 *C* 1,2, *NZ*, *Fj* 1,2, 1986 *It*, *F*, *Arg* 1,2, *NZ* 1,2,3, 1987 *SK*, *[E*, *I*, *F*, *W*(R)]*, *NZ*, *Arg* 2, 1988 *E* 1,2, *NZ* 1,2,3, *E*, *S*, *It*, 1989 *BI* 1,2,3, *NZ*, *F* 1,2, 1990 *F* 1,2,3, *US*, *NZ* 1,2,3,

317

Massey-Westropp, M (NSW) 1914 *NZ* 3
Mathers, M J (NSW) 1980 *Fj, NZ* 2 (R)
Maund, J W (NSW) 1903 *NZ*
Meadows, J E C (V, Q) 1974 *NZ* 1, 1975 *S, W*, 1976 *I, US, Fj* 1,3, *F* 1,2, 1978 *NZ* 1,2,3, 1979 *I* 1,2, 1981 *I, S*, 1982 *E, NZ* 2,3, 1983 *US, Arg* 2, *NZ*
Meadows, R W (NSW) 1958 *M* 1,2,3, *NZ* 1,2,3
Meagher, F W (NSW) 1923 *NZ* 3, 1925 *NZ*, 1927 *I, W*
Meibusch, J H (Q) 1904 *BI* 3
Meibusch, L S (Q) 1912 *US*
Melrose, T C (NSW) 1978 *NZ* 3, 1979 *I* 1,2, *NZ, Arg* 1,2
Messenger, H H (NSW) 1907 *NZ* 2,3
Middleton, S A (NSW) 1909 *E*, 1910 *NZ* 1,2,3
Miller, A R (NSW) 1952 *Fj* 1,2, *NZ* 1,2, 1953 *SA* 1,2,3,4, 1954 *Fj* 1,2, 1955 *NZ* 1,2,3, 1956 *SA* 1,2, 1957 *NZ* 1,2, 1958 *W, E, S, F, M* 1,2,3, 1959 *BI* 1,2, 1961 *Fj* 1,2,3, *SA* 2, *F*, 1962 *NZ* 1,2, 1966 *BI* 1,2, *W, S*, 1967 *I* 1, *F, I* 2, *NZ*
Miller, J M (NSW) 1962 *NZ* 1, 1963 *E, SA* 1, 1966 *W, S*, 1967 *E*
Miller, J S (Q) 1986 *NZ* 2,3, 1987 *SK, [US, I, F], NZ, Arg* 1,2, 1988 *E* 1,2, *NZ* 2,3, *E, S, It*, 1989 *BI* 1,2,3, *NZ*, 1990 *F* 1,3, 1991 *W, [WS, W, I]*
Miller, S W J (NSW) 1899 *BI* 3
Mingey, N (NSW) 1923 *NZ* 1,2
Monaghan, L E (NSW) 1973 *E*, 1974 *NZ* 1,2,3, 1975 *E* 1,2, *S, W*, 1976 *E, I, US, F* 1, 1978 *W* 1,2, *NZ* 1, 1979 *I* 1,2
Monti, C I A (Q) 1938 *NZ* 2
Moon, B J (Q) 1978 *NZ* 2,3, 1979 *I* 1,2, *NZ, Arg* 1,2, 1980 *Fj, NZ* 1,2,3, 1981 *F* 1,2, *I, W, S*, 1982 *E, S* 1,2, 1983 *US, Arg* 1,2, *NZ, It, F* 1,2, 1984 *Fj, NZ* 1,2,3, *E*, 1986 *It, F, Arg* 1,2
Mooney, T P (Q) 1954 *Fj* 1,2
Moran, H M (NSW) 1908 *W*
Morgan, G (Q) 1992 *NZ* 1(R), 3(R), *W*
Morrissey, C V (NSW) 1925 *NZ*
Morrissey, W (Q) 1914 *NZ* 2
Morton, A R (NSW) 1957 *NZ* 1,2, 1958 *F, M* 1,2,3, 1959 *BI* 1,2
Mossop, R P (NSW) 1949 *NZ* 1,2, 1950 *BI* 1,2, 1951 *NZ* 1
Moutray, I E (NSW) 1963 *SA* 2
Munsie, A (NSW) 1928 *NZ* 2
Murphy, P J (Q) 1910 *NZ* 1,2,3, 1913 *NZ* 1,2,3, 1914 *NZ* 1,2,3
Murphy, W (Q) 1912 *US*

Nasser, B P (Q) 1989 *F* 1,2, 1990 *F* 1,2,3, *US, NZ* 2, 1991 *[WS]*
Nicholson, F C (Q) 1904 *BI* 3
Nicholson, F V (Q) 1903 *NZ*, 1904 *BI* 1
Niuqila, A S (NSW) 1988 *S, It*, 1989 *BI* 1
Nothling, O E (NSW) 1921 *NZ*, 1923 *NZ* 1,2,3
Nucifora, D V (Queensland) 1991 *[Arg(R)]*

O'Brien, F W H (NSW) 1937 *SA* 2, 1938 *NZ* 3
O'Connor, J A (NSW) 1928 *NZ* 1,2,3, *M*
O'Connor, M D (ACT, Q) 1979 *Arg* 1,2, 1980 *Fj, NZ* 1,2,3, 1981 *F* 1,2, *I*, 1982 *E, S* 1,2
O'Donnell, C (NSW) 1913 *NZ* 1,2
O'Donnell, I C (NSW) 1899 *BI* 3,4
O'Donnell, J B (NSW) 1928 *NZ* 1,3, *M*
O'Donnell, J M (NSW) 1899 *BI* 4
O'Gorman, J F (NSW) 1961 *Fj* 1, *SA* 1,2, *F*, 1962 *NZ* 2, 1963 *E, SA* 1,2,3,4, 1965 *SA* 1,2, 1966 *W, S*, 1967 *E, I* 1, *F, I* 2
O'Neill, D J (Q) 1964 *NZ* 1,2
O'Neill, J M (Q) 1952 *NZ* 1,2, 1956 *SA* 1,2
Ofahengaue, V (NSW) 1990 *NZ* 1,2,3, 1991 *W, E, NZ* 1,2, *[Arg, W, I, NZ, E]*, 1992 *S* 1,2, *SA, I, W*
Osborne, D H (V) 1975 *E* 1,2, *J* 1
Outterside, R (NSW) 1959 *BI* 1,2
Oxenham, A McE (Q) 1904 *BI* 2, 1907 *NZ* 2
Oxlade, A M (Q) 1904 *BI* 2,3, 1905 *NZ*, 1907 *NZ* 2
Oxlade, B D (Q) 1938 *NZ* 1,2,3

Palfreyman, J R L (NSW) 1929 *NZ* 1, 1930 *BI*, 1931 *NZ*, 1932 *NZ* 3
Papworth, B (NSW) 1985 *Fj* 1,2, 1986 *It, Arg* 1,2, *NZ* 1,2,3, 1987 *[E, US, J* (R), *I, F], NZ, Arg* 1,2
Parker, A J (Q) 1983 *Arg* 1 (R), 2, *NZ*
Parkinson, C E (Q) 1907 *NZ* 2

Pashley, J J (NSW) 1954 *Fj* 1,2, 1958 *M* 1,2,3
Pauling, T P (NSW) 1936 *NZ* 1, 1937 *SA* 1
Pearse, G K (NSW) 1975 *W* (R), 1976 *I, US, Fj* 1,2,3, 1978 *NZ* 1,2,3
Penman, A P (NSW) 1905 *NZ*
Perrin, P D (Q) 1962 *NZ* 1
Perrin, T D (NSW) 1931 *M, NZ*
Phelps, R (NSW) 1955 *NZ* 2,3, 1956 *SA* 1,2, 1957 *NZ* 1,2, 1958 *W, I, E, S, F, M* 1, *NZ* 1,2,3, 1961 *Fj* 1,2,3, *SA* 1,2, *F*, 1962 *NZ* 1,2
Phipps, J A (NSW) 1953 *SA* 1,2,3,4, 1954 *Fj* 1,2, 1955 *NZ* 1,2,3, 1956 *SA* 1,2
Phipps, W J (NSW) 1928 *NZ* 2
Pilecki, S J (Q) 1978 *W* 1,2, *NZ* 1,2, 1979 *I* 1,2, *NZ, Arg* 1,2, 1980 *Fj, NZ* 1,2, 1982 *S* 1,2, 1983 *US, Arg* 1,2, *NZ*
Piper, B J C (NSW) 1946 *NZ* 1, *M* 2, 1947 *NZ* 1, *S, I, W*, 1948 *E, F*, 1949 *M* 1,2,3
Poidevin, S P (NSW) 1980 *Fj, NZ* 1,2,3, 1981 *F* 1,2, *I, W, S*, 1982 *E, NZ* 1,2,3, 1983 *US, Arg* 1,2, *NZ, It, F* 1,2, 1984 *Fj, NZ* 1,2,3, *E, I, W, S*, 1985 *C* 1,2, *NZ, Fj* 1,2, 1986 *It, F, Arg* 1,2, *NZ* 1,2,3, 1987 *SK, [E, J, I, F, W], Arg* 1, 1988 *NZ* 1,2,3, 1989 *NZ*, 1991 *E, NZ* 1,2, *[Arg, W, I, NZ, E]*
Pope, A M (Q) 1968 *NZ* 2 (R)
Potter, R T (Q) 1961 *Fj* 2
Potts, J M (NSW) 1957 *NZ* 1,2, 1958 *W, I*, 1959 *BI* 1
Prentice, C W (NSW) 1914 *NZ* 3
Prentice, W S (NSW) 1908 *W*, 1909 *E*, 1910 *NZ* 1,2,3, 1912 *US*
Price, R A (NSW) 1974 *NZ* 1,2,3, 1975 *E* 1,2, *J* 1,2, 1976 *US*
Primmer, C J (Q) 1951 *NZ* 1,3
Proctor, I J (NSW) 1967 *NZ*
Prosser, R B (NSW) 1967 *E, I* 1,2, *NZ*, 1968 *NZ* 1,2, *F, I, S*, 1969 *W, SA* 1,2,3,4, 1971 *SA* 1,2,3, *F* 1,2, 1972 *F* 1,2, *NZ* 1,2,3, *Fj*
Pugh, G H (NSW) 1912 *US*
Purcell, M P (Q) 1966 *W, S*, 1967 *I* 2
Purkis, E M (NSW) 1958 *S, M* 1

Ramalli, C (NSW) 1938 *NZ* 2,3
Ramsay, K M (NSW) 1936 *M*, 1937 *SA* 1, 1938 *NZ* 1,3
Rankin, R (NSW) 1936 *NZ* 1,2, *M*, 1937 *SA* 1,2, 1938 *NZ* 1,2
Rathie, D S (Q) 1972 *F* 1,2
Raymond, R L (NSW) 1921 *NZ*
Redwood, C (Q) 1903 *NZ*, 1904 *BI* 1,2,3
Reid, E J (NSW) 1925 *NZ*
Reid, T W (NSW) 1961 *Fj* 1,2,3, *SA* 1, 1962 *NZ* 1
Reilly, N P (Q) 1968 *NZ* 1,2, *F, I, S*, 1969 *W, SA* 1,2,3,4
Reynolds, L J (NSW) 1910 *NZ* 2 (R), 3
Reynolds, R J (NSW) 1984 *Fj, NZ* 1,2,3, 1985 *Fj* 1,2, 1986 *Arg* 1,2, *NZ* 1, 1987 *[J]*
Richards, E W (Q) 1904 *BI* 1,3, 1905 *NZ*, 1907 *NZ* 1 (R), 2
Richards, G (NSW) 1978 *NZ* 2 (R), 3, 1981 *F* 1
Richards, T J (Q) 1908 *W*, 1909 *E*, 1912 *US*
Richards, V S (NSW) 1936 *NZ* 1,2 (R), *M*, 1937 *SA* 1, 1938 *NZ* 1
Richardson, G C (Q) 1971 *SA* 1,2,3, 1972 *NZ* 2,3, *Fj*, 1973 *Tg* 1,2, *W*
Rigney, W A (NSW) 1925 *NZ*
Riley, S A (NSW) 1903 *NZ*
Roberts, B T (NSW) 1956 *SA* 2
Roberts, H F (Q) 1961 *Fj* 1,3, *SA* 2, *F*
Robertson, I J (NSW) 1975 *J* 1,2
Roche, C (Q) 1982 *S* 1,2, *NZ* 1,2,3, 1983 *US, Arg* 1,2, *NZ, It, F* 1,2, 1984 *Fj, NZ* 1,2,3, *I*
Rodriguez, E E (NSW) 1984 *Fj, NZ* 1,2,3, *E, I, W, S*, 1985 *C* 1,2, *NZ, Fj* 1, 1986 *It, F, Arg* 1,2, *NZ* 1,2,3, 1987 *SK, [E, J, W* (R)*], NZ, Arg* 1,2
Roebuck, M C (NSW) 1991 *W, E, NZ* 1,2, *[Arg, WS, W, I, NZ, E]*, 1992 *S* 1,2, *NZ* 2,3, *SA, I, W*
Rose, H A (NSW) 1967 *I* 2, *NZ*, 1968 *NZ* 1,2, *F, I, S*, 1969 *W, SA* 1,2,3,4, 1970 *S*
Rosenblum, M E (NSW) 1928 *NZ* 1,2,3, *M*
Rosenblum, R G (NSW) 1969 *SA* 1,3, 1970 *S*
Rosewell, J S H (NSW) 1907 *NZ* 1,3
Ross, A W (NSW) 1927 *I, W, S*, 1928 *E, F*, 1929 *NZ* 1, 1930 *BI*, 1931 *M, NZ*, 1932 *NZ* 2,3, 1933 *SA* 5, 1934 *NZ* 1,2
Ross, W S (Q) 1979 *I* 1,2, *Arg* 2, 1980 *Fj, NZ* 1,2,3,

1982 *S* 1,2, 1983 *US, Arg* 1,2, *NZ*
Rothwell, P R (NSW) 1951 *NZ* 1,2,3, 1952 *Fj* 1
Row, F L (NSW) 1899 *BI* 1,3,4
Row, N E (NSW) 1907 *NZ* 1,3, 1909 *E*, 1910 *NZ* 1,2,3
Rowles, P G (NSW) 1972 *Fj*, 1973 *E*
Roxburgh, J R (NSW) 1968 *NZ* 1,2, *F*, 1969 *W, SA* 1,2,3,4, 1970 *S*
Ruebner, G (NSW) 1966 *BI* 1,2
Russell, C J (NSW) 1907 *NZ* 1,2,3, 1908 *W*, 1909 *E*
Ryan, J R (NSW) 1975 *J* 2, 1976 *I, US, Fj* 1,2,3
Ryan, K J (Q) 1958 *E, M* 1, *NZ* 1,2,3
Ryan, P F (NSW) 1963 *E, SA* 1, 1966 *BI* 1,2

Sampson, J H (NSW) 1899 *BI* 4
Sayle, J L (NSW) 1967 *NZ*
Schulte, B G (Q) 1946 *NZ* 1, *M*
Scott, P R I (NSW) 1962 *NZ* 1,2
Scott-Young, S J (Q) 1990 *F* 2,3 (R), *US, NZ* 3, 1992 *NZ* 1,2,3
Shambrook, G G (Q) 1976 *Fj* 2,3
Shaw, A A (Q) 1973 *W, E*, 1975 *E* 1,2, *J* 2, *S, W*, 1976 *E, I, US, Fj* 1,2,3, *F* 1,2, 1978 *W* 1,2, *NZ* 1,2,3, 1979 *I* 1,2, *NZ, Arg* 1,2, 1980 *Fj, NZ* 1,2,3, 1981 *F* 1,2, *I, W, S*, 1982 *S* 1,2
Shaw, G (NSW) 1925 *NZ* (R)
Shaw, G A (NSW) 1969 *W, SA* 1 (R), 1970 *S*, 1971 *SA* 1,2,3, *F* 1,2, 1973 *W, E*, 1974 *NZ* 1,2,3, 1975 *E* 1,2, *J* 1,2, *W*, 1976 *E, I, US, Fj* 1,2,3, *F* 1,2, 1979 *NZ*
Sheehan, W B J (NSW) 1923 *NZ* 1,2,3, 1927 *W, S*
Shehadie, N M (NSW) 1947 *NZ* 2, 1948 *E, F*, 1949 *M* 1,2,3, *NZ* 1,2, 1950 *BI* 1,2, 1951 *NZ* 1,2,3, 1952 *Fj* 1,2, *NZ* 2, 1953 *SA* 1,2,3,4, 1954 *Fj* 1,2, 1955 *NZ* 1,2,3, 1956 *SA* 1,2, 1957 *NZ* 2, 1958 *W, I*
Sheil, A G R (Q) 1956 *SA* 1
Shepherd, D J (V) 1964 *NZ* 3, 1965 *SA* 1,2, 1966 *BI* 1,2
Simpson, R J (NSW) 1913 *NZ* 2
Skinner, A J (NSW) 1969 *W, SA* 4, 1970 *S*
Slack, A G (Q) 1978 *W* 1,2, *NZ* 1,2, 1979 *NZ, Arg* 1,2, 1980 *Fj*, 1981 *I, W, S*, 1982 *E, S* 1, *NZ* 3, 1983 *US, Arg* 1,2, *NZ, It*, 1984 *Fj, NZ* 1,2,3, *E, I, W, S*, 1986 *It, F, NZ* 1,2,3, 1987 *SK, [E, US, J, I, F, W]*
Slater, S H (NSW) 1910 *NZ* 3
Slattery, P J (Q) 1990 *US* (R), 1991 *W*(R), *E*(R), *[WS*(R), *W, I*(R)], 1992 *I, W*
Smairl, A M (NSW) 1928 *NZ* 1,2,3
Smith, B A (Q) 1987 *SK, [US, J, I* (R), *W]*, *Arg* 1
Smith, F B (NSW) 1905 *NZ*, 1907 *NZ* 1,2,3
Smith, L M (NSW) 1905 *NZ*
Smith, N C (NSW) 1923 *NZ* 1
Smith, P V (NSW) 1967 *NZ*, 1968 *NZ* 1,2, *F, I, S*, 1969 *W, SA* 1
Smith, R A (NSW) 1971 *SA* 1,2, 1972 *F* 1,2, *NZ* 1,2 (R), 3, *Fj*, 1975 *E* 1,2, *J* 1,2, *S, W*, 1976 *E, I, US, Fj* 1,2,3, *F* 1,2
Smith, T S (NSW) 1921 *NZ*, 1925 *NZ*
Snell, H W (NSW) 1928 *NZ* 3
Solomon, H J (NSW) 1949 *M* 3, *NZ* 2, 1950 *BI* 1,2, 1951 *NZ* 1,2, 1952 *Fj* 1,2, *NZ* 1,2, 1953 *SA* 1,2,3, 1955 *NZ* 1
Spragg, S A (NSW) 1899 *BI* 1,2,3,4,
Stanley, R G (NSW) 1921 *NZ*, 1923 *NZ* 1,2,3
Stapleton, E T (NSW) 1951 *NZ* 1,2,3, 1952 *Fj* 1,2, *NZ* 1,2, 1953 *SA* 1,2,3,4, 1954 *Fj* 1, 1955 *NZ* 1,2,3, 1958 *NZ* 1
Steggall, J C (Q) 1931 *M, NZ*, 1932 *NZ* 1,2,3, 1933 *SA* 1,2,3,4,5
Stegman, T R (NSW) 1973 *Tg* 1,2
Stephens, O G (NSW) 1973 *Tg* 1,2, *W*, 1974 *NZ* 2,3
Stewart, A A (NSW) 1979 *NZ, Arg* 1,2
Stone, A H (NSW) 1937 *SA* 2, 1938 *NZ* 2,3
Stone, C G (NSW) 1938 *NZ* 1
Stone, J M (NSW) 1946 *M, NZ* 2
Storey, G P (NSW) 1927 *I, W, S*, 1928 *E, F*, 1929 *NZ* 3 (R), 1930 *BI*
Storey, K P (NSW) 1936 *NZ* 2
Storey, N J D (NSW) 1962 *NZ* 1
Strachan, D J (NSW) 1955 *NZ* 2,3
Street, N O (NSW) 1899 *BI* 2
Streeter, S F (NSW) 1978 *NZ* 1
Stuart, R (NSW) 1910 *NZ* 2,3
Stumbles, B D (NSW) 1972 *NZ* 1 (R), 2,3, *Fj*
Sturtridge, G S (V) 1929 *NZ* 2, 1932 *NZ* 1,2,3, 1933 *SA* 1,2,3,4,5
Sullivan, P D (NSW) 1971 *SA* 1,2,3, *F* 1,2, 1972 *F* 1,2,

NZ 1,2, *Fj*, 1973 *Tg* 1,2, *W*
Summons, A J (NSW) 1958 *W, I, E, S, M* 2, *NZ* 1,2,3, 1959 *BI* 1,2
Suttor, D C (NSW) 1913 *NZ* 1,2,3
Swannell, B I (NSW) 1905 *NZ*
Sweeney, T L (Q) 1953 *SA* 1

Taafe, B S (NSW) 1969 *SA* 1, 1972 *F* 1,2
Tancred, A J (NSW) 1927 *I, W, S*
Tancred, J L (NSW) 1928 *F*
Tanner, W H (Q) 1899 *BI* 1,2
Tasker, W G (NSW) 1913 *NZ* 1,2,3, 1914 *NZ* 1,2,3
Tate, M J (NSW) 1951 *NZ* 3, 1952 *Fj* 1,2, *NZ* 1,2, 1953 *SA* 1, 1954 *Fj* 1,2
Taylor, D A (Q) 1968 *NZ* 1,2, *F, I, S*
Taylor, H C (NSW) 1923 *NZ* 1,2,3
Taylor, J I (NSW) 1971 *SA* 1, 1972 *F* 1,2, *Fj*
Teitzel, R G (Q) 1966 *W, S*, 1967 *E, I* 1, *F, I* 2, *NZ*
Thompson, C E (NSW) 1923 *NZ* 1
Thompson, E G (Q) 1929 *NZ* 1,2,3, 1930 *BI*
Thompson, F (NSW) 1913 *NZ* 1,2,3, 1914 *NZ* 1,2,3
Thompson, J (Q) 1914 *NZ* 1
Thompson, P D (Q) 1950 *BI* 1
Thompson, R J (WA) 1971 *SA* 3, *F* 2 (R), 1972 *Fj*
Thorn, A M (NSW) 1921 *NZ*
Thorn, E J (NSW) 1923 *NZ* 1,2,3
Thornett, J E (NSW) 1955 *NZ* 1,2,3, 1956 *SA* 1,2, 1958 *W, I, S, F, M* 2,3, *NZ* 2,3, 1959 *BI* 1,2, 1961 *Fj* 2,3, *SA* 1,2, *F*, 1962 *NZ* 2,3,4,5, 1963 *E, SA* 1,2,3,4, 1964 *NZ* 1,2,3, 1965 *SA* 1,2, 1966 *BI* 1,2, 1967 *F*
Thornett, R N (NSW) 1961 *Fj* 1,2,3, *SA* 1,2, *F*, 1962 *NZ* 1,2,3,4,5
Thorpe, A C (NSW) 1929 *NZ* 1 (R)
Timbury, F R V (Q) 1910 *NZ* 1,2
Tindall, E N (NSW) 1973 *Tg* 2
Toby, A E (NSW) 1925 *NZ*
Tolhurst, H A (NSW) 1931 *M, NZ*
Tombs, R C (NSW) 1992 *S* 1,2
Tonkin, A E J (NSW) 1947 *S, I, W*, 1948 *E, F*, 1950 *E, F, NZ* 1,2,3, 1954 *Fj* 1,2, 1955 *NZ* 1,2,3, 1957 *NZ* 1,2
Towers, C H T (NSW) 1927 *I*, 1928 *E, F, NZ* 1,2,3, *M*, 1929 *NZ* 1,3, 1930 *BI*, 1931 *M, NZ*, 1934 *NZ* 1,2, 1937 *SA* 1,2
Trivett, R K (Q) 1966 *BI* 1,2
Turnbull, A (V) 1961 *Fj* 3
Turnbull, R V (NSW) 1968 *I*
Tuynman, S N (NSW) 1983 *F* 1,2, 1984 *E, I, W, S*, 1985 *C* 1,2, *NZ, Fj* 1,2, 1986 *It, F, Arg* 1,2, *NZ* 1,2,3, 1987 *SK, [E, US, J, I, W], NZ, Arg* 1 (R), 2, 1988 *E, It*, 1989 *BI* 1,2,3, *NZ*, 1990 *NZ* 1
Tweedale, E (NSW) 1946 *NZ* 1,2, 1947 *NZ* 2, *S, I*, 1948 *E, F*, 1949 *M* 1,2,3

Vaughan, D (NSW) 1983 *US, Arg* 1, *It, F* 1,2
Vaughan, G N (V) 1958 *E, S, F, M* 1,2,3
Verge, A (NSW) 1904 *BI* 1,2

Walden, R J (NSW) 1934 *NZ* 2, 1936 *NZ* 1,2, *M*
Walker, A K (NSW) 1947 *NZ* 1, 1948 *E, F*, 1950 *BI* 1,2
Walker, A S B (NSW) 1912 *US*, 1921 *NZ*
Walker, L F (NSW) 1988 *NZ* 2,3, *S, It*, 1989 *BI* 1,2,3, *NZ*
Walker, L R (NSW) 1982 *NZ* 2,3
Wallace, A C (NSW) 1921 *NZ*, 1927 *I, W, S*, 1928 *E, F*
Wallach, C (NSW) 1913 *NZ* 1,3, 1914 *NZ* 1,2,3
Walsh, J J (NSW) 1953 *SA* 1,2,3,4
Walsh, P B (NSW) 1904 *BI* 1,2,3
Walsham, K P (NSW) 1962 *NZ* 3, 1963 *E*
Ward, P G (NSW) 1899 *BI* 1,2,3,4
Ward, T (Q) 1899 *BI* 2
Watson, G W (Q) 1907 *NZ* 1
Watson, W T (NSW) 1912 *US*, 1913 *NZ* 1,2,3, 1914 *NZ* 1
Weatherstone, L J (ACT) 1975 *E* 1,2, *J* 1,2, *S* (R), 1976 *E, I*
Webb, W (NSW) 1899 *BI* 3,4
Wells, B G (NSW) 1958 *M* 1
Westfield, R E (NSW) 1928 *NZ* 1,2,3, *M*, 1929 *NZ* 2,3
White, C J B (NSW) 1899 *BI* 1, 1903 *NZ*, 1904 *BI* 1
White, J M (NSW) 1904 *BI* 3
White, J P L (NSW) 1958 *NZ* 1,2,3, 1961 *Fj* 1,2,3, *SA* 1,2, *F*, 1962 *NZ* 1,2,3,4,5, 1963 *E, SA* 1,2,3,4, 1964

NZ 1,2,3, 1965 *SA* 1,2
White, M C (Q) 1931 *M, NZ,* 1932 *NZ* 1,2, 1933 *SA* 1,2,3,4,5
White, S W (NSW) 1956 *SA* 1,2, 1958 *I, E, S, M* 2,3
White, W G S (Q) 1933 *SA* 1,2,3,4,5, 1934 *NZ* 1,2, 1936 *NZ* 1,2, *M*
White, W J (NSW) 1928 *NZ* 1, *M,* 1932 *NZ* 1
Wickham, S M (NSW) 1903 *NZ,*1904 *BI* 1,2,3, 1905 *NZ*
Williams, D (Q) 1913 *NZ* 3, 1914 *NZ* 1,2,3
Williams, I M (NSW) 1987 *Arg* 1,2, 1988 *E* 1,2, *NZ* 1,2,3, 1989 *BI* 2,3, *NZ, F* 1,2, 1990 *F* 1,2,3, *US, NZ* 1
Williams, J L (NSW) 1963 *SA* 1,3,4
Williams, S A (NSW) 1980 *Fj, NZ* 1,2, 1981 *F* 1,2, 1982 *E, NZ* 1,2,3, 1983 *US, Arg* 1 (R), 2, *NZ, It, F* 1,2, 1984 *NZ* 1,2,3, *E, I, W, S,* 1985 *C* 1,2, *NZ, Fj* 1,2
Wilson, B J (NSW) 1949 *NZ* 1,2
Wilson, C R (Q) 1957 *NZ* 1, 1958 *NZ* 1,2,3

Wilson, D (Q) 1992 *S* 1,2, *NZ* 1,2,3, *SA, I, W*
Wilson, V W (Q) 1937 *SA* 1,2, 1938 *NZ* 1,2,3
Windon, C J (NSW) 1946 *NZ* 1,2, 1947 *NZ* 1, *S, I, W,* 1948 *E, F,* 1949 *M* 1,2,3, *NZ* 1,2, 1951 *NZ* 1,2,3, 1952 *Fj* 1,2, *NZ* 1,2
Windon, K S (NSW) 1937 *SA* 1,2, 1946 *M*
Windsor, J C (Q) 1947 *NZ* 2
Winning, K C (Q) 1951 *NZ* 1
Wogan, L W (NSW) 1913 *NZ* 1,2,3, 1914 *NZ* 1,2,3, 1921 *NZ*
Wood, F (NSW) 1907 *NZ* 1,2,3, 1910 *NZ* 1,2, 1913 *NZ* 1,2,3, 1914 *NZ* 1,2,3
Wood, R N (Q) 1972 *Fj*
Woods, H F (NSW) 1925 *NZ,* 1927 *I, W, S,* 1928 *E*
Wright, K J (NSW) 1975 *E* 1,2, *J* 1, 1976 *US, F* 1,2, 1978 *NZ* 1,2,3

Yanz, K (NSW) 1958 *F*

AUSTRALIAN INTERNATIONAL RECORDS

Both team and individual records are for official Australian international matches, up to 31 March 1993.

TEAM RECORDS

Highest score
67 v United States (67-9) 1990 Brisbane
v individual countries
39 v Argentina (39-19) 1986 Brisbane
30 v British Isles (30-12) 1989 Sydney
59 v Canada (59-3) 1985 Sydney
40 v England (40-15) 1991 Sydney
52 v Fiji (52-28) 1985 Brisbane
48 v France (48-31) 1990 Brisbane
42 v Ireland (42-17) 1992 Dublin
55 v Italy (55-6) 1988 Rome
50 v Japan (50-25) 1975 Brisbane
30 v N Zealand (30-16) 1978 Auckland
37 v Scotland $\begin{cases} \text{(37-12) 1984 Murrayfield} \\ \text{(37-13) 1992 Brisbane} \end{cases}$
26 v South Africa (26-3) 1992 Cape Town
65 v South Korea (65-18) 1987 Brisbane
30 v Tonga (30-12) 1973 Sydney
67 v United States (67-9) 1990 Brisbane
63 v Wales (63-6) 1991 Brisbane
9 v Western Samoa (9-3) 1991 Pontypool

Biggest winning points margin
58 v United States (67-9) 1990 Brisbane
v individual countries
26 v Argentina (26-0) 1986 Sydney
18 v British Isles (30-12) 1989 Sydney
56 v Canada (59-3) 1985 Sydney
25 v England (40-15) 1991 Sydney
24 v Fiji (52-28) 1985 Brisbane
17 v France $\begin{cases} \text{(32-15) 1989 Strasbourg} \\ \text{(48-31) 1990 Brisbane} \end{cases}$

25 v Ireland (42-17) 1992 Dublin
49 v Italy (55-6) 1988 Rome
30 v Japan (37-7) 1975 Sydney
16 v N Zealand (26-10) 1980 Sydney
25 v Scotland (37-12) 1984 Murrayfield
23 v South Africa (26-3) 1992 Cape Town
47 v South Korea (65-18) 1987 Brisbane
18 v Tonga (30-12) 1973 Sydney
58 v United States (67-9) 1990 Brisbane
57 v Wales (63-6) 1991 Brisbane
6 v Western Samoa (9-3) 1991 Pontypool

Highest score by opposing team
38 $\begin{cases} \text{N Zealand (13-38) 1936 Dunedin} \\ \text{N Zealand (3-38) 1972 Auckland} \end{cases}$
by individual countries
27 Argentina (19-27) 1987 Buenos Aires
31 British Isles (0-31) 1966 Sydney
15 Canada (43-15) 1985 Brisbane
28 England (19-28) 1988 Twickenham
28 Fiji (52-28) 1985 Brisbane
34 France (6-34) 1976 Paris
27 Ireland (12-27) 1979 Brisbane
18 Italy (39-18) 1986 Brisbane
25 Japan (50-25) 1975 Brisbane
38 $\begin{cases} \text{N Zealand (13-38) 1936 Dunedin} \\ \text{N Zealand (3-38) 1972 Auckland} \end{cases}$
24 Scotland (15-24) 1981 Murrayfield
30 South Africa (11-30) 1969 Johannesburg
18 South Korea (65-18) 1987 Brisbane
16 Tonga (11-16) 1973 Brisbane

12 United States (47-12) 1987 Brisbane
28 Wales (3-28) 1975 Cardiff
 3 Western Samoa (9-3) 1991 Pontypool

Biggest losing points margin
35 v N Zealand (3-38) 1972 Auckland
v individual countries
15 v Argentina (3-18) 1983 Brisbane
31 v British Isles (0-31) 1966 Brisbane
17 v England $\left\{\begin{array}{l}\text{(3-20) 1973 Twickenham}\\\text{(6-23) 1976 Twickenham}\end{array}\right.$
 2 v Fiji $\left\{\begin{array}{l}\text{(15-17) 1952 Sydney}\\\text{(16-18) 1954 Sydney}\end{array}\right.$
28 v France (6-34) 1976 Paris
15 v Ireland (12-27) 1979 Brisbane
35 v New Zealand (3-38) 1972 Auckland
 9 v Scotland (15-24) 1981 Murrayfield
25 v South Africa (3-28) 1961 Johannesburg
 5 v Tonga (11-16) 1973 Brisbane
25 v Wales (3-28) 1975 Cardiff
No defeats v Canada, Italy, Japan, South Korea, United States or Western Samoa.

Most tries by Australia in an international
13 v South Korea (65-18) 1987 Brisbane

Most tries against Australia in an international
9 by N Zealand (13-38) 1936 Dunedin

Most points on overseas tour (all matches)
500 in B Isles/France (35 matches)
 1947-48

Most tries on overseas tour (all matches)
115 in B Isles/France (35 matches)
 1947-48

INDIVIDUAL RECORDS

Most capped player
D I Campese   72   1982-92
in individual positions
Full-back
R G Gould   25   1980-87

Wing
D I Campese   56(72)[1]   1982-92
Centre
A G Slack   39   1978-87
Fly-half
M P Lynagh   52(60)[2]   1984-92
Scrum-half
N C Farr-Jones   58(59)[3]   1984-92
Prop
A J McIntyre   38   1982-89
Hooker
P G Johnson   42   1959-71
Lock
S A G Cutler   40   1982-91
Flanker
S P Poidevin   59   1980-91
No 8
S N Tuynman   28(34)[4]   1983-90
[1]*Campese has played 16 times as a full-back*
[2]*Lynagh has played 7 times as a centre and once as a replacement full-back*
[3]*Farr-Jones was capped once as a replacement wing*
[4]*Tuynman played 6 times as a flanker*

Longest international career
G M Cooke 16 seasons 1932-1947/8
A R Miller 16 seasons 1952-1967
Cooke's career ended during a Northern hemisphere season

Most consecutive internationals – 37
P G Johnson 1959-68

Most internationals as captain
N C Farr-Jones   36   1988-92
Includes wins against the British Isles and all senior IB nations – a unique feat

---

Most points in internationals – 760
M P Lynagh (60 matches) 1984-92

Most points in an international – 24
M P Lynagh v France 1990 Brisbane
M P Lynagh v United States 1990 Brisbane

Most tries in internationals – 52
D I Campese (72 matches) 1982-92

Most tries in an international – 4
G Cornelsen v N Zealand 1978 Auckland
D I Campese v United States 1983 Sydney

Most conversions in internationals – 125
M P Lynagh (60 matches) 1984-92

Most conversions in an international – 8
M P Lynagh v Italy 1988 Rome
M P Lynagh v United States 1990 Brisbane

Most dropped goals in internationals – 9
P F Hawthorne (21 matches) 1962-67
M P Lynagh (60 matches) 1984-92

Most penalty goals in internationals – 145
M P Lynagh (60 matches) 1984-92

Most penalty goals in an international – 6
M P Lynagh v France 1986 Sydney
M P Lynagh v England 1988 Brisbane

Most points in international series on tour – 42
M P Lynagh (4 appearances) 1984
  B Isles

Most tries in international series on tour – 4
G Cornelsen (3 appearances) 1978
  N Zealand
M G Ella (4 appearances) 1984
  B Isles
Ella scored in each match of the international series

Most points on overseas tour – 154
P E McLean (18 appearances) B Isles
  1975-76

Most tries on overseas tour – 23
C J Russell B Isles 1908-09

Most points in a tour match – 26
A J Leeds v Buller (NZ) 1986 Westport

Most tries in a tour match – 6
J S Boyce v Wairarapa (NZ) 1962
  Masterton

INTERNATIONAL MATCH APPEARANCES FOR BRITISH ISLES TEAMS (*up to 31 March 1993*)

From 1910 onwards, when British Isles teams first became officially representative of the four Home Unions. (*Uncapped when first selected to play in a Test match for the British Isles.)

ABBREVIATIONS

A – Australia; *NZ* – New Zealand; *SA* –South Africa; (R) – Replacement.

CLUB ABBREVIATIONS

NIFC – North of Ireland Football Club; CIYMS – Church of Ireland Young Men's Society

Note: When a series has taken place, figures have been used to denote the particular matches in which players have featured. Thus 1962 *SA* 1,4 indicates that a player appeared in the first and fourth Tests of a series.

Aarvold, C D (Cambridge U, Blackheath and England) 1930 *NZ* 1,2,3,4, *A*
Ackerman, R A (London Welsh and Wales) 1983 *NZ* 1,4(R)
Ackford, P J (Harlequins and England) 1989 *A* 1,2,3
Alexander, R (NIFC and Ireland) 1938 *SA* 1,2,3
Andrew, C R (Wasps and England) 1989 *A* 2,3
Arneil, R J (Edinburgh Acads and Scotland) 1968 *SA* 1,2,3,4
Ashcroft, A (Waterloo and England) 1959 *A* 1, *NZ* 2

Bainbridge, S J (Gosforth and England) 1983 *NZ* 3,4
Baird, G R T (Kelso and Scotland) 1983 *NZ* 1,2,3,4
Baker, A M (Newport and Wales) 1910 *SA* 3
Baker, D G S (Old Merchant Taylors' and England) 1955 *SA* 3,4
Bassett, J (Penarth and Wales) 1930 *NZ* 1,2,3,4, *A*
Beamish, G R (Leicester, RAF and Ireland) 1930 *NZ* 1,2,3,4, *A*
Beattie, J R (Glasgow Acads and Scotland) 1983 *NZ* 2(R)
Beaumont, W B (Fylde and England) 1977 *NZ* 2,3,4, 1980 *SA* 1,2,3,4
Bebb, D I E (Swansea and Wales) 1962 *SA* 2,3, 1966 *A* 1,2, *NZ* 1,2,3,4
Bennett, P (Llanelli and Wales) 1974 *SA* 1,2,3,4, 1977 *NZ* 1,2,3,4
Bevan, J C (Cardiff Coll of Ed, Cardiff and Wales) 1971 *NZ* 1
Black, A W (Edinburgh U and Scotland) 1950 *NZ* 1,2
Black, B H (Oxford U, Blackheath and England) 1930 *NZ* 1,2,3,4, *A*
Blakiston, A F (Northampton and England) 1924 *SA* 1,2,3,4
Bowcott, H M (Cambridge U, Cardiff and Wales) 1930 *NZ* 1,2,3,4, *A*
Boyle, C V (Dublin U and Ireland) 1938 *SA* 2,3
Brand, T N (NIFC and *Ireland) 1924 *SA* 1,2
Bresnihan, F P K (UC Dublin and Ireland) 1968 *SA* 1,2,4
Brophy, N H (UC Dublin and Ireland) 1962 *SA* 1,4
Brown, G L (W of Scotland and Scotland) 1971 *NZ* 3,4, 1974 *SA* 1,2,3, 1977 *NZ* 2,3,4
Budge, G M (Edinburgh Wands and Scotland) 1950 *NZ* 4
Burcher, D H (Newport and Wales) 1977 *NZ* 3
Butterfield, J (Northampton and England) 1955 *SA* 1,2,3,4

Calder, F (Stewart's-Melville FP and Scotland) 1989 *A* 1,2,3
Calder, J H (Stewart's-Melville FP and Scotland) 1983 *NZ* 3
Cameron, A (Glasgow HSFP and Scotland) 1955 *SA* 1,2
Campbell, S O (Old Belvedere and Ireland) 1980 *SA* 2(R), 3,4, 1983 *NZ* 1,2,3,4
Campbell-Lamerton, M J (Halifax, Army and Scotland) 1962 *SA* 1,2,3,4, 1966 *A* 1,2, *NZ* 1,3

Carleton, J (Orrell and England) 1980 *SA* 1,2,4, 1983 *NZ* 2,3,4
Chalmers, C M (Melrose and Scotland) 1989 *A* 1
Cleaver, W B (Cardiff and Wales) 1950 *NZ* 1,2,3
Clifford, T (Young Munster and Ireland) 1950 *NZ* 1,2,3, *A* 1,2
Cobner, T J (Pontypool and Wales) 1977 *NZ* 1,2,3
Colclough, M J (Angoulême and England) 1980 *SA* 1,2,3,4, 1983 *NZ* 1,2,3,4
Connell, G C (Trinity Acads and Scotland) 1968 *SA* 4
Cotton, F E (Loughborough Colls, Coventry and England) 1974 *SA* 1,2,3,4, 1977 *NZ* 2,3,4
Coulman, M J (Moseley and England) 1968 *SA* 3
Cove-Smith, R (Old Merchant Taylors' and England) 1924 *SA* 1,2,3,4
Cowan, R C (Selkirk and Scotland) 1962 *SA* 4
Cromey, G E (Queen's U, Belfast and Ireland) 1938 *SA* 3
Cunningham, W A (Lansdowne and Ireland) 1924 *SA* 3

Dancer, G T (Bedford) 1938 *SA* 1,2,3
Davies, C (Cardiff and Wales) 1950 *NZ* 4
Davies, D M (Somerset Police and Wales) 1950 *NZ* 3,4, *A* 1
Davies, D S (Hawick and Scotland) 1924 *SA* 1,2,3,4
Davies, H J (Newport and Wales) 1924 *SA* 2
Davies, T G R (Cardiff, London Welsh and Wales) 1968 *SA* 3, 1971 *NZ* 1,2,3,4
Davies, T J (Llanelli and Wales) 1959 *NZ* 2,4
Davies, T M (London Welsh, Swansea and Wales) 1971 *NZ* 1,2,3,4, 1974 *SA* 1,2,3,4
Davies, W G (Cardiff and Wales) 1980 *SA* 2
Davies, W P C (Harlequins and England) 1955 *SA* 1,2,3
Dawes, S J (London Welsh and Wales) 1971 *NZ* 1,2,3,4
Dawson, A R (Wanderers and Ireland) 1959 *A* 1,2, *NZ* 1,2,3,4
Dixon, P J (Harlequins and England) 1971 *NZ* 1,2,4
Dodge, P W (Leicester and England) 1980 *SA* 3,4
Dooley, W A (Preston Grasshoppers and England) 1989 *A* 2,3
Doyle, M G (Blackrock Coll and Ireland) 1968 *SA* 1
Drysdale, D (Heriot's FP and Scotland) 1924 *SA* 1,2,3,4
Duckham, D J (Coventry and England) 1971 *NZ* 2,3,4
Duggan, W P (Blackrock Coll and Ireland) 1977 *NZ* 1,2,3,4
Duff, P L (Glasgow Acads and Scotland) 1938 *SA* 2,3

Edwards, G O (Cardiff and Wales) 1968 *SA* 1,2, 1971 *NZ* 1,2,3,4, 1974 *SA* 1,2,3,4
Evans, G (Maesteg and Wales) 1983 *NZ* 3,4
Evans, G L (Newport and Wales) 1977 *NZ* 2,3,4
Evans, I C (Llanelli and Wales) 1989 *A* 1,2,3
Evans, R T (Newport and Wales) 1950 *NZ* 1,2,3,4, *A* 1,2
Evans, T P (Swansea and Wales) 1977 *NZ* 1
Evans, W R (Cardiff and Wales) 1959 *A* 2, *NZ* 1,2,3

Farrell, J L (Bective Rangers and Ireland) 1930 *NZ* 1,2,3,4, *A*
Faull, J (Swansea and Wales) 1959 *A* 1, *NZ* 1,3,4
Fenwick, S P (Bridgend and Wales) 1977 *NZ* 1,2,3,4
Fitzgerald, C F (St Mary's Coll and Ireland) 1983 *NZ* 1,2,3,4
Foster, A R (Queen's U, Belfast and Ireland) 1910 *SA* 1,2

Gibson, C M H (Cambridge U, NIFC and Ireland) 1966 *NZ* 1,2,3,4, 1968 *SA* 1(R),2,3,4, 1971 *NZ* 1,2,3,4
Giles, J L (Coventry and England) 1938 *SA* 1,3
Gravell, R W R (Llanelli and Wales) 1980 *SA* 1 (R),2,3,4
Graves, C R A (Wanderers and Ireland) 1938 *SA* 1,3
Greenwood, J T (Dunfermline and Scotland) 1955 *SA* 1,2,3,4
Grieve, C F (Oxford U and Scotland) 1938 *SA* 2,3
Griffiths, G M (Cardiff and Wales) 1955 *SA* 2,3,4
Griffiths, V M (Newport and Wales) 1924 *SA* 3,4
Guscott, J C (Bath and England) 1989 *A* 2,3

Hall, M R (Bridgend and Wales) 1989 *A* 1
Handford, F G (Manchester and England) 1910 *SA* 1,2,3
Harding, W R (Cambridge U, Swansea and Wales) 1924 *SA* 2,3,4
Harris, S W (Blackheath and England) 1924 *SA* 3,4
Hastings, A G (London Scottish and Scotland) 1989 *A* 1,2,3
Hastings, S (Watsonians and Scotland) 1989 *A* 2,3
Hay, B H (Boroughmuir and Scotland) 1980 *SA* 2,3,4
Hayward, D J (Newbridge and Wales) 1950 *NZ* 1,2,3
Henderson, N J (Queen's U, Belfast, NIFC and Ireland) 1950 *NZ* 3
Henderson, R G (Northern and Scotland) 1924 *SA* 3,4
Hendrie, K G P (Heriot's FP and Scotland) 1924 *SA* 2
Hewitt, D (Queen's U, Belfast, Instonians and Ireland) 1959 *A* 1,2, *NZ* 1,3,4, 1962 *SA* 4
Higgins, R (Liverpool and England) 1955 *SA* 1
Hinshelwood, A J W (London Scottish and Scotland) 1966 *NZ* 2,4, 1968 *SA* 2
Hodgson, J McD (Northern and *England) 1930 *NZ* 1,3
Holmes, T D (Cardiff and Wales) 1983 *NZ* 1
Hopkins, R (Maesteg and Wales) 1971 *NZ* 1(R)
Horrocks-Taylor, J P (Leicester and England) 1959 *NZ* 3
Horton, A L (Blackheath and England) 1968 *SA* 2,3,4
Howard, W G (Old Birkonians) 1938 *SA* 1
Howie, R A (Kirkcaldy and Scotland) 1924 *SA* 1,2,3,4

Irvine, A R (Heriot's FP and Scotland) 1974 *SA* 3,4, 1977 *NZ* 1,2,3,4, 1980 *SA* 2,3,4
Irwin, D G (Instonians and Ireland) 1983 *NZ* 1,2,4
Isherwood, G A M (Old Alleynians, Sale) 1910 *SA* 1,2,3

Jackson, P B (Coventry and England) 1959 *A* 1,2, *NZ* 1,3,4
Jarman, H (Newport and Wales) 1910 *SA* 1,2,3
Jeeps, R E G (Northampton and *England) 1955 *SA* 1,2,3,4, 1959 *A* 1,2, *NZ* 1,2,3, 1962 *SA* 1,2,3,4
Jenkins, V G J (Oxford U, London Welsh and Wales) 1938 *SA* 1
John, B (Cardiff and Wales) 1968 *SA* 1, 1971 *NZ* 1,2,3,4
John, E R (Neath and Wales) 1950 *NZ* 1,2,3,4, *A* 1,2
Jones, B L (Devonport Services, Llanelli and Wales) 1950 *NZ* 4, *A* 1,2
Jones, D K (Llanelli, Cardiff and Wales) 1962 *SA* 1,2,3, 1966 *A* 1,2, *NZ* 1
Jones, E L (Llanelli and *Wales) 1938 *SA* 1,3
Jones, Ivor (Llanelli and Wales) 1930 *NZ* 1,2,3,4, *A*
Jones, J P (Newport and Wales) 1910 *SA* 1,2,3
Jones, K D (Cardiff and Wales) 1962 *SA* 1,2,3,4
Jones, K J (Newport and Wales) 1950 *NZ* 1,2,4
Jones, R N (Swansea and Wales) 1989 *A* 1,2,3
Jones, S T (Pontypool and Wales) 1983 *NZ* 2,3,4

Keane, M I (Lansdowne and Ireland) 1977 *NZ* 1
Kennedy, K W (CIYMS, London Irish and Ireland) 1966 *A* 1,2, *NZ* 1,2
Kiernan, M J (Dolphin and Ireland) 1983 *NZ* 2,3,4

Kiernan, T J (Cork Const and Ireland) 1962 *SA* 3, 1968 *SA* 1,2,3,4
Kininmonth, P W (Oxford U, Richmond and Scotland) 1950 *NZ* 1,2,4
Kinnear, R M (Heriot's FP and *Scotland) 1924 *SA* 1,2,3,4
Kyle, J W (Queen's U, Belfast, NIFC and Ireland) 1950 *NZ* 1,2,3,4, *A* 1,2

Laidlaw, F A L (Melrose and Scotland) 1966 *NZ* 2,3
Laidlaw, R J (Jedforest and Scotland) 1983 *NZ* 1(R),2,3,4
Lamont, R A (Instonians and Ireland) 1966 *NZ* 1,2,3,4
Lane, M F (UC Cork and Ireland) 1950 *NZ* 4, *A* 2
Larter, P J (Northampton, RAF and England) 1968 *SA* 2
Lewis, A R (Abertillery and Wales) 1966 *NZ* 2,3,4
Lynch, J F (St Mary's Coll and Ireland) 1971 *NZ* 1,2,3,4

McBride, W J (Ballymena and Ireland) 1962 *SA* 3,4, 1966 *NZ* 2,3,4, 1968 *SA* 1,2,3,4, 1971 *NZ* 1,2,3,4, 1974 *SA* 1,2,3,4
Macdonald, R (Edinburgh U and Scotland) 1950 *NZ* 1, *A* 2
McFadyean, C W (Moseley and England) 1966 *NZ* 1,2,3,4
McGeechan, I R (Headingley and Scotland) 1974 *SA* 1,2,3,4, 1977 *NZ* 1,2,3(R),4
McKay, J W (Queen's U, Belfast and Ireland) 1950 *NZ* 1,2,3,4, *A* 1,2
McKibbin, H R (Queen's U, Belfast and Ireland) 1938 *SA* 1,2,3
McLauchlan, J (Jordanhill and Scotland) 1971 *NZ* 1,2,3,4, 1974 *SA* 1,2,3,4
McLeod, H F (Hawick and Scotland) 1959 *A* 1,2, *NZ* 1,2,3,4
McLoughlin, R J (Gosforth, Blackrock Coll and Ireland) 1966 *A* 1,2, *NZ* 4
MacNeill, H P (Oxford U and Ireland) 1983 *NZ* 1,2,4(R))
Macpherson, N C (Newport and Scotland) 1924 *SA* 1,2,3,4
Macrae, D J (St Andrew's U and Scotland) 1938 *SA* 1
McVicker, J (Collegians and Ireland) 1924 *SA* 1,3,4
Marques, R W D (Harlequins and England) 1959 *A* 2, *NZ* 2
Marsden-Jones, D (London Welsh and Wales) 1924 *SA* 1,2
Martin, A J (Aberavon and Wales) 1977 *NZ* 1
Martindale, S A (Kendal and England) 1930 *A*
Matthews, J (Cardiff and Wales) 1950 *NZ* 1,2,3,4, *A* 1,2
Maxwell, R B (Birkenhead Park) 1924 *SA* 1
Mayne, R B (Queen's U, Belfast and Ireland) 1938 *SA* 1,2,3
Meredith, B V (Newport and Wales) 1955 *SA* 1,2,3,4, 1962 *SA* 1,2,3,4
Meredith, C C (Neath and Wales) 1955 *SA* 1,2,3,4
Millar, S (Ballymena and Ireland) 1959 *A* 1,2, *NZ* 2, 1962 *SA* 1,2,3,4, 1968 *SA* 2
Milliken, R A (Bangor and Ireland) 1974 *SA* 1,2,3,4
Moore, B C (Nottingham and England) 1989 *A* 1,2,3
Morgan, C I (Cardiff and Wales) 1955 *SA* 1,2,3,4
Morgan, D W (Stewart's-Melville FP and Scotland) 1977 *NZ* 3(R),4
Morgan, G J (Clontarf and Ireland) 1938 *SA* 3
Morgan, H J (Abertillery and Wales) 1959 *NZ* 3,4, 1962 *SA* 2,3
Morgan, M E (Swansea and Wales) 1938 *SA* 1,2
Morley, J C (Newport and Wales) 1930 *NZ* 1,2,3
Mulcahy, W A (UC Dublin and Ireland) 1959 *A* 1, *NZ* 4, 1962 *SA* 1,2,3,4
Mullen, K D (Old Belvedere and Ireland) 1950 *NZ* 1,2, *A* 2
Mulligan, A A (Wanderers, London Irish and Ireland) 1959 *NZ* 4
Mullin, B J (London Irish and Ireland) 1989 *A* 1
Murphy, N A A (Cork Const and Ireland) 1959 *A* 2, *NZ* 1,2,4, 1966 *A* 1,2, *NZ* 2,3
Murray, P F (Wanderers and Ireland) 1930 *NZ* 1,2,4, *A*

Neale, M E (Bristol, Blackheath and *England) 1910 SA 1,2,3
Neary, A (Broughton Park and England) 1977 NZ 4
Nelson, J E (Malone and Ireland) 1950 NZ 3,4, A 1,2
Nicholson, B E (Harlequins and England) 1938 SA 2
Norris, C H (Cardiff and Wales) 1966 NZ 1,2,3
Norster, R L (Cardiff and Wales) 1983 NZ 1,2, 1989 A 1
Novis, A L (Blackheath and England) 1930 NZ 2,4, A

O'Donnell, R C (St Mary's Coll and Ireland) 1980 SA 1
O'Driscoll, J B (London Irish and Ireland) 1980 SA 1,2,3,4, 1983 NZ 2,4
O'Neill, H O'H (Queen's U, Belfast and Ireland) 1930 NZ 1,2,3,4, A
O'Reilly, A J F (Old Belvedere and Ireland) 1955 SA 1,2,3,4, 1959 A 1,2, NZ 1,2,3,4
Orr, P A (Old Wesley and Ireland) 1977 NZ 1
O'Shea, J P (Cardiff and Wales) 1968 SA 1

Parker, D (Swansea and Wales) 1930 NZ 1,2,3,4, A
Pask, A E I (Abertillery and Wales) 1962 SA 1,2,3, 1966 A 1,2, NZ 1,3,4
Patterson, C S (Instonians and Ireland) 1980 SA 1,2,3
Patterson, W M (Sale and *England) 1980 SA 1
Paxton, I A M (Selkirk and Scotland) 1983 NZ 1,2,3,4
Pedlow, A C (CIYMS and Ireland) 1955 SA 1,4
Pillman, C H (Blackheath and England) 1910 SA 2,3
Piper, O J S (Cork Const and Ireland) 1910 SA 1
Poole, H (Cardiff) 1930 NZ 3
Preece, I (Coventry and England) 1950 NZ 1
Prentice, F D (Leicester and England) 1930 NZ 2, A
Price, B (Newport and Wales) 1966 A 1,2, NZ 1,4
Price, G (Pontypool and Wales) 1977 NZ 1,2,3,4, 1980 SA 1,2,3,4, 1983 NZ 1,2,3,4
Price, M J (Pontypool and Wales) 1959 A 1,2, NZ 1,2,3
Prosser, T R (Pontypool and Wales) 1959 NZ 4
Pullin, J V (Bristol and England) 1968 SA 2,3,4, 1971 NZ 1,2,3,4

Quinnell, D L (Llanelli and *Wales) 1971 NZ 3, 1977 NZ 2,3, 1980 SA 1,2

Ralston, C W (Richmond and England) 1974 SA 4
Rees, H E (Neath and *Wales) 1977 NZ 4
Reeve, J S R (Harlequins and England) 1930 NZ 1,3,4, A
Reid, T E (Garryowen and Ireland) 1955 SA 2,3
Renwick, J M (Hawick and Scotland) 1980 SA 1
Rew, H (Blackheath, Army and England) 1930 NZ 1,2,3,4
Reynolds, F J (Old Cranleighans and England) 1938 SA 1,2
Richards, D (Leicester and England) 1989 A 1,2,3
Richards, D S (Swansea and Wales) 1980 SA 1
Richards, M C R (Cardiff and Wales) 1968 SA 1,3,4
Richards, T J (Bristol and Australia) 1910 SA 1,2
Rimmer, G (Waterloo and England) 1950 NZ 3
Ringland, T M (Ballymena and Ireland) 1983 NZ 1
Risman, A B W (Loughborough Colls and England) 1959 A 1,2, NZ 1,4
Robbie, J C (Greystones and Ireland) 1980 SA 4
Robins, J D (Birkenhead Park and Wales) 1950 NZ 1,2,3, A 1,2
Robins, R J (Pontypridd and Wales) 1955 SA 1,2,3,4
Rogers, D P (Bedford and England) 1962 SA 1,4
Rowlands, K A (Cardiff and Wales) 1962 SA 1,2,4
Rutherford, D (Gloucester and England) 1966 A 1
Rutherford, J Y (Selkirk and Scotland) 1983 NZ 3

Savage, K F (Northampton and England) 1968 SA 1,2,3,4
Scotland, K J F (Cambridge U, Heriot's FP and Scotland) 1959 A 1,2, NZ 1,3,4
Sharp, R A W (Oxford U, Redruth and England) 1962 SA 3,4
Slattery, J F (Blackrock Coll and Ireland) 1974 SA 1,2,3,4
Slemen, M A C (Liverpool and England) 1980 SA 1
Smith, A R (Edinburgh Wands, London Scottish and Scotland) 1962 SA 1,2,3
Smith, D F (Richmond and England) 1910 SA 1,2,3

Smith, D W C (London Scottish and Scotland) 1950 A 1
Smith, G K (Kelso and Scotland) 1959 A 1,2, NZ 1,3
Smith, I S (Oxford U, London Scottish and Scotland) 1924 SA 1,2
Smyth, T (Malone, Newport and Ireland) 1910 SA 2,3
Sole, D M B (Edinburgh Acads and Scotland) 1989 A 1,2,3
Spong, R S (Old Millhillians and England) 1930 NZ 1,2,3,4, A
Spoors, J A (Bristol) 1910 SA 1,2,3
Squire, J (Newport, Pontypool and Wales) 1977 NZ 4, 1980 SA 1,2,3,4, 1983 NZ 1
Squires, P J (Harrogate and England) 1977 NZ 1
Stagg, P K (Oxford U, Sale and Scotland) 1968 SA 1,3,4
Steele, W C C (Bedford, RAF and Scotland) 1974 SA 1,2
Stephens, I (Bridgend and Wales) 1983 NZ 1
Stephens, J R G (Neath and Wales) 1950 A 1,2
Stevenson, R C (St Andrew's U and Scotland) 1910 SA 1,2,3

Tanner, H (Swansea and Wales) 1938 SA 2
Taylor, A R (Cross Keys and Wales) 1938 SA 1,2
Taylor, J (London Welsh and Wales) 1971 NZ 1,2,3,4
Taylor, R B (Northampton and England) 1968 SA 1,2,3,4
Teague, M C (Gloucester and England) 1989 A 2,3
Telfer, J W (Melrose and Scotland) 1966 A 1,2, NZ 1,2,4, 1968 SA 2,3,4
Thomas, M C (Devonport Services, Newport and Wales) 1950 NZ 2,3, A 1, 1959 NZ 2
Thomas, R C C (Swansea and Wales) 1955 SA 3,4
Thomas, W D (Llanelli and *Wales) 1966 NZ 2,3, 1968 SA 3(R),4, 1971 NZ 1,2,4(R)
Thompson, R H (Instonians, London Irish and Ireland) 1955 SA 1,2,4
Travers, W H (Newport and Wales) 1938 SA 2,3
Tucker, C C (Shannon and Ireland) 1980 SA 3,4
Turner, J W C (Gala and Scotland) 1968 SA 1,2,3,4

Underwood, R (RAF, Leicester and England) 1989 A 1,2,3
Unwin, E J (Rosslyn Park, Army and England) 1938 SA 1,2
Uttley, R M (Gosforth and England) 1974 SA 1,2,3,4

Voyce, A T (Gloucester and England) 1924 SA 3,4

Waddell, G H (Cambridge U, London Scottish and Scotland) 1962 SA 1,2
Waddell, H (Glasgow Acads and Scotland) 1924 SA 1,2,4
Walker, S (Instonians and Ireland) 1938 SA 1,2,3
Wallace, W (Percy Park) 1924 SA 1
Waller, P D (Newport and Wales) 1910 SA 1,2,3
Ward, A J P (Garryowen and Ireland) 1980 SA 1
Waters, J A (Selkirk and Scotland) 1938 SA 3
Watkins, D (Newport and Wales) 1966 A 1,2, NZ 1,2,3,4
Watkins, S J (Newport and Wales) 1966 A 1,2, NZ 3
Webb, J (Abertillery and Wales) 1910 SA 1,2,3
Welsh, W B (Hawick and Scotland) 1930 NZ 4
Weston, M P (Richmond, Durham City and England) 1962 SA 1,2,3,4, 1966 A 1,2
Wheeler, P J (Leicester and England) 1977 NZ 2,3,4, 1980 SA 1,2,3,4
White, D B (London Scottish and Scotland) 1989 A 1
Whitley, H (Northern and *England) 1924 SA 1,3,4
Willcox, J G (Oxford U, Harlequins and England) 1962 SA 1,2,4
Williams, B L (Cardiff and Wales) 1950 NZ 2,3,4, A 1,2
Williams, C (Swansea and Wales) 1980 SA 1,2,3,4
Williams, D (Ebbw Vale and Wales) 1966 A 1,2, NZ 1,2,4
Williams, D B (Cardiff and *Wales) 1977 NZ 1,2,3
Williams, J J (Llanelli and Wales) 1974 SA 1,2,3,4, 1977 NZ 1,2,3
Williams, J P R (London Welsh and Wales) 1971 NZ 1,2,3,4, 1974 SA 1,2,3,4
Williams, R H (Llanelli and Wales) 1955 SA 1,2,3,4, 1959 A 1,2, NZ 1,2,3,4
Williams, S H (Newport and *England) 1910 SA 1,2,3

Williams, W O G (Swansea and Wales) 1955 *SA* 1,2,3,4
Willis, W R (Cardiff and Wales) 1950 *NZ* 4, *A* 1,2
Wilson, S (London Scottish and Scotland) 1966 *A* 2, *NZ* 1,2,3,4
Windsor, R W (Pontypool and Wales) 1974 *SA* 1,2,3,4, 1977 *NZ* 1
Winterbottom, P J (Headingley and England) 1983 *NZ* 1,2,3,4
Wood, B G M (Garryowen and Ireland) 1959 *NZ* 1,3
Wood, K B (Leicester) 1910 *SA* 1,3

Woodward, C R (Leicester and England) 1980 *SA* 2,3

Young, A T (Cambridge U, Blackheath and England) 1924 *SA* 2
Young, D (Cardiff and Wales) 1989 *A* 1,2,3
Young, J (Harrogate, RAF and Wales) 1968 *SA* 1
Young, J R C (Oxford U, Harlequins and England) 1959 *NZ* 2
Young, R M (Queen's U, Belfast, Collegians and Ireland) 1966 *A* 1,2, *NZ* 1, 1968 *SA* 3

RESULTS OF BRITISH ISLES MATCHES
(*up to 31 March 1993*)

From 1910 onwards – the tour to South Africa in that year was the first fully representative one in which the four Home Unions co-operated.

v SOUTH AFRICA

Played 30   British Isles won 8, South Africa won 18, Drawn 4

1910 *1* Johannesburg
South Africa 1G 3T (14) to 1DG 2T (10)

2 Port Elizabeth
British Isles 1G 1T (8) to 1T (3)

3 Cape Town
South Africa 3G 1PG 1T (21) to 1G (5)
South Africa won series 2-1

1924 *1* Durban
South Africa 1DG 1T (7) to 1T(3)

2 Johannesburg
South Africa 1G 1PG 3T (17) to 0

3 Port Elizabeth
Drawn 1T (3) each

4 Cape Town
South Africa 1DG 4T (16) to 1PG 2T (9)
South Africa won series 3-0, with 1 draw

1938 *1* Johannesburg
South Africa 4G 2PG (26) to 4PG (12)

2 Port Elizabeth
South Africa 2G 2PG 1T (19) to 1T (3)

3 Cape Town
British Isles 1G 1PG 1DG 3T (21)
to 2G 1PG 1T (16)
South Africa won series 2-1

1955 *1* Johannesburg
British Isles 4G 1T (23) to 2G 2PG 2T (22)

2 Cape Town
South Africa 2G 5T (25) to 1PG 2T (9)

3 Pretoria
British Isles 1PG 1DG 1T (9)
to 2PG (6)

4 Port Elizabeth
South Africa 2G 1DG 3T (22)
to 1G 1T (8)
Series drawn 2-2

1962 *1* Johannesburg
Drawn 1T (3) each

2 Durban
South Africa 1PG (3) to 0

3 Cape Town
South Africa 1G 1PG (8) to 1DG (3)

4 Bloemfontein
South Africa 5G 2PG 1T (34)
to 1G 1PG 2T (14)
South Africa won series 3-0, with 1 draw

1968 *1* Pretoria
South Africa 2G 4PG 1T (25)
to 1G 5PG (20)

2 Port Elizabeth
Drawn 2PG (6) each

3 Cape Town
South Africa 1G 2PG (11) to 2PG (6)

4 Johannesburg
South Africa 2G 1DG 2T (19) to 2PG (6)
South Africa won series 3-0, with 1 draw

1974 *1* Cape Town
British Isles 3PG 1DG (12) to 1DG (3)

2 Pretoria
British Isles 1G 1PG 1DG 4T (28)
to 2PG 1DG (9)

3 Port Elizabeth
British Isles 1G 2PG 2DG 2T (26)
to 3PG (9)

4 Johannesburg
Drawn British Isles 1G 1PG 1T (13)
South Africa 3PG 1T (13)
British Isles won series 3-0, with 1 draw

1980 *1* Cape Town
South Africa 3G 2T (26)
to 5PG 1DG 1T (22)

2 Bloemfontein
South Africa 2G 2PG 2T (26)
to 1G 3PG 1T (19)

3 Port Elizabeth
South Africa 1G 1PG 1DG (12)
to 2PG 1T (10)

4 Pretoria
British Isles 1G 1PG 2T (17)
to 3PG 1T (13)
South Africa won series 3-1

v NEW ZEALAND

Played 28   British Isles won 5, New Zealand won 21, Drawn 2

1930 *1* Dunedin
British Isles 2T (6) to 1T (3)

2 Christchurch
New Zealand 2G 1GM (13) to 2G (10)

3 Auckland
New Zealand 1G 1DG 2T (15)
to 2G (10)

4 Wellington
New Zealand 2G 4T (22) to 1G 1PG (8)
New Zealand won series 3-1

1950 *1* Dunedin
Drawn 1PG 2T (9) each

2 Christchurch
New Zealand 1G 1T (8) to 0

3 Wellington
New Zealand 1PG 1T (6) to 1PG (3)

4 Auckland
New Zealand 1G 1DG 1T (11)
to 1G 1PG (8)
New Zealand won series 3-0, with 1 draw

1959 *1* Dunedin
New Zealand 6PG (18)
to 1G 1PG 3T (17)

2 Wellington
New Zealand 1G 2T (11) to 1G 1PG (8)

3 Christchurch
New Zealand 2G 1PG 1DG 2T (22)
to 1G 1PG (8)

4 Auckland
British Isles 3T (9) to 2PG (6)
New Zealand won series 3-1

1966 *1* Dunedin
New Zealand 1G 2PG 1DG 2T (20)
to 1PG (3)

2 Wellington
New Zealand 2G 1PG 1T (16)
to 3PG 1DG (12)

3 Christchurch
New Zealand 2G 2PG 1T (19) to 2T (6)

4 Auckland
New Zealand 3G 1PG 1DG 1T (24)
to 1G 1PG 1T (11)
New Zealand won series 4-0

1971 *1* Dunedin
British Isles 2PG 1T (9) to 1PG (3)

2 Christchurch
New Zealand 2G 1PG 3T (22)
to 1PG 1DG 2T (12)

3 Wellington
British Isles 2G 1DG (13) to 1T (3)

4 Auckland
Drawn British Isles 1G 2PG 1DG (14)
New Zealand 1G 2PG 1T (14)
British Isles won series 2-1, with 1 draw

1977 *1* Wellington
New Zealand 2G 1T (16) to 4PG (12)

2 Christchurch
British Isles 3PG 1T (13) to 3PG (9)

3 Dunedin
New Zealand 1G 2PG 1DG 1T (19)
to 1PG 1T (7)

4 Auckland
New Zealand 2PG 1T (10) to 1G 1PG (9)
New Zealand won series 3-1

1983 *1* Christchurch
New Zealand 3PG 1DG 1T (16)
to 3PG 1DG (12)

2 Wellington
New Zealand 1G 1PG (9) to 0

3 Dunedin
New Zealand 1G 3PG (15) to 2T (8)

4 Auckland
New Zealand 4G 2PG 2T (38) to 2PG (6)
New Zealand won series 4-0

v AUSTRALIA

Played 10   British Isles won 8, Australia won 2, Drawn 0

1930 *1* Sydney
Australia 2T (6) to 1G (5)

1950 *1* Brisbane
British Isles 2G 2PG 1DG (19)
to 2PG (6)

2 Sydney
British Isles 3G 1PG 2T (24) to 1T (3)
British Isles won series 2-0

1959 *1* Brisbane
British Isles 1G 2PG 1DG 1T (17)
to 2PG (6)

2 Sydney
British Isles 3G 1PG 2T (24) to 1PG (3)
British Isles won series 2-0

1966 *1* Sydney
British Isles 1G 1PG 1T (11)
to 1G 1PG (8)

2 Brisbane
British Isles 5G 1PG 1DG (31) to 0
British Isles won series 2-0

1989 *1* Sydney
Australia 4G 1PG 1DG (30)
to 3PG 1DG (12)

2 Brisbane
British Isles 1G 2PG 1DG 1T (19)
to 1G 2PG (12)

3 Sydney
British Isles 5PG 1T (19) to 1G 4PG (18)
British Isles won series 2-1

BRITISH ISLES RECORDS
(*up to 31 March 1993*)

From 1910 onwards – the tour to South Africa in that year was the first fully representative one in which the four Home Unions co-operated.

TEAM RECORDS

Highest score
31 v Australia (31-0) 1966 Brisbane
v individual countries
28 v S Africa (28-9) 1974 Pretoria
17 v New Zealand (17-18) 1959 Dunedin
31 v Australia (31-0) 1966 Brisbane

Biggest winning points margin
31 v Australia (31-0) 1966 Brisbane
v individual countries
19 v S Africa (28-9) 1974 Pretoria
10 v New Zealand (13-3) 1971 Wellington
31 v Australia (31-0) 1966 Brisbane

Highest score by opposing team
38 New Zealand (6-38) 1983 Auckland
by individual countries
34 S Africa (14-34) 1962 Bloemfontein
38 New Zealand (6-38) 1983 Auckland
30 Australia (12-30) 1989 Sydney

Biggest losing points margin
32 v New Zealand (6-38) 1983 Auckland
v individual countries
20 v S Africa (14-34) 1962 Bloemfontein
32 v New Zealand (6-38) 1983 Auckland
18 v Australia (12-30) 1989 Sydney

Most tries by B Isles in an international
5 {
v Australia (24-3) 1950 Sydney
v S Africa (23-22) 1955 Johannesburg
v Australia (24-3) 1959 Sydney
v Australia (31-0) 1966 Brisbane
v S Africa (28-9) 1974 Pretoria
}

Most tries against B Isles in an international
7 by South Africa (9-25) 1955 Cape Town

Most points on overseas tour (all matches)
842 in Australia, New Zealand and Canada (33 matches) 1959
(includes 582 points in 25 matches in New Zealand)

Most tries on overseas tour (all matches)
165 in Australia, New Zealand and Canada (33 matches) 1959
(includes 113 tries in 25 matches in New Zealand)

INDIVIDUAL RECORDS

Most capped player
W J McBride 17 1962-74
in individual positions
Full-back
J P R Williams   8[1]   1971-74
Wing
A J F O'Reilly   9(10)[2]   1955-59
Centre
C M H Gibson   8(12)[3]   1966-71
Fly-half
P Bennett   8   1974-77
Scrum-half
R E G Jeeps   13   1955-62
Prop
G Price   12   1977-83
Hooker
B V Meredith   8   1955-62
Lock
W J McBride   17   1962-74
Flanker
N A A Murphy   8   1959-66
No 8
T M Davies   8[4]   1971-74

[1]*A R Irvine, 9 Tests, played 7 times at full-back and twice as a wing*
[2]*O'Reilly played once as a centre*
[3]*Gibson played 4 times as a fly-half. I R McGeechan, 8 Tests, played 7 times as a centre and once, as a replacement, on the wing*
[4]*Both A E I Pask and J W Telfer (8 Tests each), played 4 Tests at No 8 and 4 Tests at flanker*

Longest international career
W J McBride   13 seasons   1962-74

Most consecutive Tests – 15
W J McBride 1966-74

Most internationals as captain – 6
A R Dawson 1959

Most points in internationals – 44
P Bennett (8 appearances) 1974-77

Most points in an international – 18
A J P Ward v S Africa 1980 Cape Town

Most tries in internationals – 6
A J F O'Reilly (10 appearances) 1955-59

Most tries in an international – 2
C D Aarvold v New Zealand 1930
   Christchurch
J E Nelson v Australia 1950 Sydney
M J Price v Australia 1959 Sydney
M J Price v New Zealand 1959 Dunedin
D K Jones v Australia 1966 Brisbane
T G R Davies v New Zealand 1971
   Christchurch
J J Williams v S Africa 1974 Pretoria
J J Williams v S Africa 1974 Port Elizabeth

Most conversions in internationals – 6
S Wilson (5 matches) 1966

Most conversions in an international – 5
S Wilson v Australia 1966 Brisbane

Most dropped goals in internationals – 2
D Watkins (6 matches) 1966
B John (5 matches) 1968-71
P Bennett (8 matches) 1974-77
*(P F Bush also dropped 2 goals in Tests played by British
teams prior to 1910)*

Most penalty goals in internationals – 11
T J Kiernan (5 matches) 1962-68

Most penalty goals in an international – 5
T J Kiernan v South Africa 1968 Pretoria
A J P Ward v South Africa 1980 Capetown
A G Hastings v Australia 1989 Sydney

**Most points for B Isles on overseas tour
– 188**
B John (17 appearances) 1971 Australia/
   N Zealand
(including 180 points in 16 appearances in
   N Zealand)

**Most tries for B Isles on overseas tour
– 22***
A J F O'Reilly (23 appearances) 1959
   Australia/N Zealand/Canada
(includes 17* tries in 17 appearances in
   N Zealand)
*Includes one penalty try

**Most points for B Isles in international
series – 35**
T J Kiernan (4 appearances) 1968 S Africa

**Most tries for B Isles in international
series – 4**
J J Williams (4 appearances) 1974 S Africa

**Most points for B Isles in any match on
tour – 37**
A G B Old v South Western Districts
   1974 Mossel Bay, S Africa

**Most tries for B Isles in any match on
tour – 6**
D J Duckham v West Coast-Buller 1971
   Greymouth, N Zealand
J J Williams v South Western Districts
   1974 Mossel Bay, S Africa
(A R Irvine scored 5 tries from full-back
   v King Country-Wanganui 1977
   Taumarunui, N Zealand)

LEADING CAP-WINNERS
(up to 31 March 1993)

ENGLAND

R Underwood	60
P J Winterbottom	58
W A Dooley	55
C R Andrew	52
B C Moore	45
A Neary	43
J V Pullin	42
W D C Carling	42
P J Wheeler	41
J A Probyn	37
D J Duckham	36
G S Pearce	36
D P Rogers	34
W B Beaumont	34
J P Scott	34
D Richards	34
J M Webb	33
P W Dodge	32
W W Wakefield	31
F E Cotton	31
M A C Slemen	31
E Evans	30
R Cove-Smith	29
C R Jacobs	29
M P Weston	29
P J Squires	29
R J Hill	29
J Butterfield	28
S J Smith	28
P A G Rendall	28
J C Guscott	28
A T Voyce	27
J S Tucker	27
M C Teague	27
J Carleton	26
C N Lowe	25
J D Currie	25
M S Phillips	25
C B Stevens	25
W H Hare	25
M J Colclough	25
J Leonard	25

SCOTLAND

J M Renwick	52
C T Deans	52
A R Irvine	51
A B Carmichael	50
A J Tomes	48
R J Laidlaw	47
S Hastings	46
A G Hastings	45
A F McHarg	44
K W Robertson	44
I G Milne	44
D M B Sole	44
J McLauchlan	43

J Y Rutherford	42
D B White	41
J Jeffrey	40
H F McLeod	40
D M D Rollo	40
J MacD Bannerman	37
I Tukalo	37
I A M Paxton	36
F Calder	34
A R Smith	33
C M Chalmers	33
I S Smith	32
F A L Laidlaw	32
I R McGeechan	32
D G Leslie	32
N S Bruce	31
I H P Laughland	31
G L Brown	30
A G Stanger	30
W I D Elliot	29
S R P Lineen	29
A P Burnell	29
W M Simmers	28
P K Stagg	28
G Armstrong	28
D F Cronin	28
J W Y Kemp	27
K J F Scotland	27
P C Brown	27
J H Calder	27
D I Johnston	27
G R T Baird	27
W E Maclagan	26
D Drysdale	26
J C McCallum	26
G P S Macpherson	26
J B Nelson	25
J P Fisher	25
J R Beattie	25
J W Telfer	25
K S Milne	25

IRELAND

C M H Gibson	69
W J McBride	63
J F Slattery	61
P A Orr	58
T J Kiernan	54
D G Lenihan	52
M I Keane	51
J W Kyle	46
K W Kennedy	45
B J Mullin	45
M J Kiernan	43
G V Stephenson	42
N A A Murphy	41
W P Duggan	41
K D Crossan	41

N J Henderson	40
R J McLoughlin	40
P M Matthews	38
S Millar	37
H P MacNeill	37
J R Kavanagh	35
W A Mulcahy	35
E O'D Davy	34
T M Ringland	34
D C Fitzgerald	34
P M Dean	32
A C Pedlow	30
G T Hamlet	30
W E Crawford	30
J D Clinch	30
J L Farrell	29
B G M Wood	29
A J F O'Reilly	29
M T Bradley	29
M Sugden	28
J S McCarthy	28
A M Magee	27
A R Dawson	27
M G Molloy	27
J J Moloney	27
W A Anderson	27
J C Walsh	26
R M Young	26
J B O'Driscoll	26
G R Beamish	25
K D Mullen	25
F P K Bresnihan	25
A T A Duggan	25
B J McGann	25
T O Grace	25
S A McKinney	25
C F Fitzgerald	25
D G Irwin	25
S J Smith	25

WALES

J P R Williams	55
G O Edwards	53
T G R Davies	46
R N Jones	46
K J Jones	44
G Price	41
T M Davies	38
P H Thorburn	37
D Williams	36
I C Evans	36
R M Owen	35
B V Meredith	34
D I E Bebb	34
W D Morris	34
A J Martin	34
R L Norster	34
W J Bancroft	33
P T Davies	33

B Price	32
J R G Stephens	32
G A D Wheel	32
M G Ring	32
J J Williams	30
S P Fenwick	30
W J Trew	29
C I Morgan	29
P Bennett	29
J Squire	29
R W Windsor	28
A J Gould	27
W C Powell	27
M C Thomas	27
H J Morgan	27
A M Hadley	27
J Davies	27
R C C Thomas	26
A E I Pask	26
S J Watkins	26
J Taylor	26
G Travers	25
H Tanner	25
B John	25
N R Gale	25
W D Thomas	25
T D Holmes	25
M R Hall	25

FRANCE

S Blanco	93
P Sella	88
R Bertranne	69
M Crauste	63
B Dauga	63
J Condom	61
J-P Rives	59
P Berbizier	56
L Rodriguez	56
R Paparemborde	55
A Domenech	52
F Mesnel	52
J Prat	51
W Spanghero	51
J-L Joinel	51
M Celaya	50
P Dintrans	50
A Boniface	48
J-P Lux	47
J-C Skréla	46
D Erbani	46
P Lagisquet	46
M Vannier	43
J-P Garuet	42
E Champ	42
P Ondarts	42
J Dupuy	40
C Darrouy	40
F Haget	40
J-M Aguirre	39
G Dufau	38
D Camberabero	36
J-B Lafond	36
G Boniface	35

E Cester	35
A Paco	35
E Ribère	34
J Bouquet	34
P Villepreux	34
J Iraçabal	34
J-P Romeu	34
O Roumat	34
G Basquet	33
C Lacaze	33
C Dourthe	33
D Dubroca	33
L Armary	33
J Gachassin	32
J-P Bastiat	32
A Cassayet	31
A Jauréguy	31
M Prat	31
F Moncla	31
G Cholley	31
D Codorniou	31
M Cecillon	31
P Albaladéjo	30
A Roques	30
R Bénésis	30
A Lorieux	30
R Biénès	29
L Mias	29
J Trillo	28
J-P Lescarboura	28
H Rancoule	27
P Lacroix	27
J-C Berejnoi	27
C Carrère	27
J Fouroux	27
J Gallion	27
P Saint-André	27
B Chevallier	26
J Barthe	26
J-M Cabanier	26
A Gruarin	26
J-L Azarète	26
A Vaquerin	26
M Andrieu	26
R Martine	25
J Maso	25
J-L Averous	25
P Estève	25

SOUTH AFRICA

F C H Du Preez	38
J H Ellis	38
J F K Marais	35
J P Engelbrecht	33
J L Gainsford	33
J T Claassen	28
H E Botha	28
F du T Roux	27
L G Wilson	27
T P Bedford	25
D J de Villiers	25
P J F Greyling	25
S H Nomis	25
P J Visagie	25

L C Moolman	24
D M Gerber	24
D J Hopwood	22
A C Koch	22
M Du Plessis	22
J A du Rand	21
M T S Stofberg	21
J S Germishuys	20

NEW ZEALAND

G W Whetton	58
C E Meads	55
J J Kirwan	54
S B T Fitzpatrick	49
S C McDowell	46
A M Haden	41
G J Fox	41
I A Kirkpatrick	39
K R Tremain	38
B G Williams	38
R W Loe	38
G A Knight	36
A G Dalton	35
A J Whetton	35
B J Robertson	34
S S Wilson	34
M G Mexted	34
W J Whineray	32
D B Clarke	31
M W Shaw	30
T J Wright	30
S M Going	29
M N Jones	28
R W Norton	27
J T Stanley	27
M J Pierce	26
I D Jones	26
B J Lochore	25
B E McLeod	24
K F Gray	24
I J Clarke	24
J C Ashworth	24
D S Loveridge	24
W T Taylor	24
R A White	23
B G Fraser	23
D J Graham	22
D Young	22
W T Shelford	22
G N K Mourie	21
M J B Hobbs	21
W K Little	21
K L Skinner	20
C R Laidlaw	20
I N MacEwan	20
P J Whiting	20
C I Green	20

AUSTRALIA

D I Campese	72
M P Lynagh	60
S P Poidevin	59
N C Farr-Jones	59

Olivier Roumat: 34 caps for France.

P G Johnson	42	S N Tuynman	34	R J McCall	26
A R Miller	41	N M Shehadie	30	R B Prosser	25
T A Lawton	41	P E McLean	30	G Cornelsen	25
S A G Cutler	40	M E Loane	28	M G Ella	25
G V Davis	39	S A Williams	28	R G Gould	25
A G Slack	39	P N Kearns	28	P C Grigg	25
A J McIntyre	38	K W Catchpole	27	M J Hawker	25
J E Thornett	37	G A Shaw	27	A J Daly	25
J N B Hipwell	36	C T Burke	26	T J Horan	25
A A Shaw	36	E E Rodriguez	26	J K Lenehan	24
B J Moon	35	J S Miller	26	J P L White	24

J W Cole	24	J E C Meadows	22	A N McGill	21
G Fay	24	W A Campbell	22	W H Cerutti	21
E J A McKenzie	24	B T Gavin	22	J S Little	21
R Phelps	23	E T Bonis	21	A S Cameron	20
M P Burke	23	P F Hawthorne	21	B J Ellwood	20
R A Smith	22	R J Heming	21	C J Windon	20

WORLD'S LEADING CAP-WINNERS
(up to 31 March 1993)

For purposes of comparison, the following list includes appearances for individual countries in major international matches.

S Blanco	France	93	C E Meads	New Zealand	55
P Sella	France	88	J P R Williams	Wales	55
D I Campese	Australia	72	R Paparemborde	France	55
C M H Gibson	Ireland	69	W A Dooley	England	55
R Bertranne	France	69	T J Kiernan	Ireland	54
M Crauste	France	63	J J Kirwan	New Zealand	54
W J McBride	Ireland	63	G O Edwards	Wales	53
B Dauga	France	63	A Domenech	France	52
J Condom	France	61	J M Renwick	Scotland	52
J F Slattery	Ireland	61	C T Deans	Scotland	52
M P Lynagh	Australia	60	F Mesnel	France	52
R Underwood	England	60	C R Andrew	England	52
J-P Rives	France	59	J Prat	France	51
S P Poidevin	Australia	59	W Spanghero	France	51
N C Farr-Jones	Australia	59	A R Irvine	Scotland	51
P A Orr	Ireland	58	M I Keane	Ireland	51
G W Whetton	New Zealand	58	J-L Joinel	France	51
P J Winterbottom	England	58	M Celaya	France	50
L Rodriguez	France	56	A B Carmichael	Scotland	50
P Berbizier	France	56	P Dintrans	France	50

The following list incorporates appearances by home countries' players for British Isles teams (the Lions) in international matches against New Zealand, Australia and South Africa (up to 31 March 1993). The number of Lions' appearances is shown in brackets.

S Blanco	France	93		L Rodriguez	France	56	
P Sella	France	88		P Berbizier	France	56	
C M H Gibson	Ireland	81	(12)	C E Meads	New Zealand	55	
W J McBride	Ireland	80	(17)	R Paparemborde	France	55	
D I Campese	Australia	72		J J Kirwan	New Zealand	54	
R Bertranne	France	69		C R Andrew	England	54	(2)
J F Slattery	Ireland	65	(4)	J M Renwick	Scotland	53	(1)
G O Edwards	Wales	63	(10)	G Price	Wales	53	(12)
J P R Williams	Wales	63	(8)	A Domenech	France	52	
M Crauste	France	63		C T Deans	Scotland	52	
B Dauga	France	63		J W Kyle	Ireland	52	(6)
R Underwood	England	63	(3)	M I Keane	Ireland	52	(1)
P J Winterbottom	England	62	(4)	F Mesnel	France	52	
J Condom	France	61		J Prat	France	51	
A R Irvine	Scotland	60	(9)	W Spanghero	France	51	
M P Lynagh	Australia	60		T G R Davies	Wales	51	(5)
T J Kiernan	Ireland	59	(5)	J McLauchlan	Scotland	51	(8)
J-P Rives	France	59		J-L Joinel	France	51	
P A Orr	Ireland	59	(1)	R J Laidlaw	Scotland	51	(4)
S P Poidevin	Australia	59		M Celaya	France	50	
N C Farr-Jones	Australia	59		A B Carmichael	Scotland	50	
G W Whetton	New Zealand	58		P Dintrans	France	50	
W A Dooley	England	57	(2)				

Most appearances for the Lions are by W J McBride 17, R E G Jeeps (England) 13, C M H Gibson 12, G Price 12, and A J F O'Reilly (Ireland), R H Williams (Wales), and G O Edwards 10 each, up to 31 March 1993.

INTERNATIONAL REFEREES 1992-93

Leading Referees

Up to 31 March 1993, in major international matches. These include all matches for which senior members of the International Board have awarded caps, and also all matches played in the World Cup final stages.

12 or more internationals

C Norling	Wales	25	B S Cumberlege	England	16
K D Kelleher	Ireland	23	J M Fleming	Scotland	16
D G Walters	Wales	23	D I H Burnett	Ireland	15
M Joseph	Wales	22	C H Gadney	England	15
R C Williams	Ireland	21	I David	Wales	14
K V J Fitzgerald	Australia	21	Dr I R Vanderfield	Australia	14
F A Howard	England	20	O E Doyle	Ireland	14
A M Hosie	Scotland	19	R G Byres	Australia	13
Capt M J Dowling	Ireland	18	J P Murphy	New Zealand	13
A E Freethy	Wales	18	N R Sanson	Scotland	13
R C Quittenton	England	18	K H Lawrence	New Zealand	13
J R West	Ireland	18	S R Hilditch	Ireland	13
J B Anderson	Scotland	18	R F Johnson	England	12
R Hourquet	France	18	T D Schofield	Wales	12
W D Bevan	Wales	18	T H Vile	Wales	12
D P D'Arcy	Ireland	17	W Williams	England	12
F Palmade	France	17	A R MacNeill	Australia	12
D J Bishop	New Zealand	17			

Major international match appearances 1992-93

Matches controlled between 1 April 1992 and 31 March 1993.

1992

NZ v Wld(2)	W D Bevan (Wales)	F v Arg	R J Megson (Scotland)
NZ v Wld	D J Bishop (New Zealand)	W v A	A Spreadbury (England)
F v R	K W McCartney (Scotland)		
NZ v I(2)	A R MacNeill (Australia)	**1993**	
A v S	*L L McLachlan (New Zealand)	S v I	E Morrison (England)
A v S	C J Hawke (New Zealand)	E v F	J M Fleming (Scotland)
A v NZ	J M Fleming (Scotland)	F v S	W D Bevan (Wales)
Arg v F(2)	F Burger (South Africa)	W v E	*J Dumé (France)
A v NZ(2)	P Robin (France)	S v W	J Dumé (France)
SA v NZ	A R MacNeill (Australia)	I v F	D Leslie (Scotland)
SA v A	D J Bishop (New Zealand)	W v I	A R MacNeill (Australia)
E v C	*G Simmonds (Wales)	E v S	B W Stirling (Ireland)
F v SA(2)	B Kinsey (Australia)	F v W	O E Doyle (Ireland)
I v A	E Morrison (England)	I v E	A R MacNeill (Australia)
E v SA	S R Hilditch (Ireland)		

*Denotes debut in a major international

Referees dismissing players in a major international

A E Freethy	E v NZ	1925	D I H Burnett	E v W	1980
K D Kelleher	S v NZ	1967	C Norling	F v I	1984
R T Burnett	A v E	1975	K V J Fitzgerald	NZ v W	1987*
W M Cooney	A v Fj	1976	F A Howard	A v W	1987*
N R Sanson (two)	W v I	1977	K V J Fitzgerald	Fj v E	1988

O E Doyle	Arg v F	1988	**C Norling**	A v F	1990
B W Stirling (two)	E v Fj	1989	**C J Hawke**	E v Arg	1990
F A Howard	W v F	1990	**E Morrison**	R v F	1991
F A Howard	S v F	1990	**J M Fleming** (two)	Arg v WS	1991*
F A Howard	Nm v W	1990	**S R Hilditch** (two)	F v E	1992
A Spreadbury	A v F	1990	**D J Bishop**	NZ v Wld	1992

World Cup matches

INTERNATIONAL REFEREES

The list which follows shows referees who have controlled major internationals (i.e. games for which a senior member country of the IB has awarded caps, or the final stages of the official World Cup) since 1876, when referees were first appointed, up to 31 March 1993.

ABBREVIATIONS

A – Australia; *Arg* – Argentina; *AW* – Anglo-Welsh; *B* – British Forces' and Home Union Teams; *Bb* – Barbarians; *BI* – British Isles; *C* – Canada; *Cv* – New Zealand Cavaliers; *Cz* – Czechoslovakia; *E* – England; *F* – France; *Fj* – Fiji; *GB* – Great Britain; *G* – Germany; *I* – Ireland; *It* – Italy; *J* – Japan; *K* – New Zealand Kiwis; *M* – New Zealand Maoris; *Nm* – Namibia; *NZ* – New Zealand; *NZA* – New Zealand Army; *P* – President's XV; *R* – Romania; *S* – Scotland; *SA* – South Africa; *SAm* – South America; *SK* – South Korea; *Tg* – Tonga; *US* – United States of America; *W* – Wales; *Wld* – World XV; *WS* – Western Samoa; *Z* – Zimbabwe; (C) – Special Centenary Match; (R) – Replacement. Entries in square brackets [ ] indicate matches in the World Cup final stages.

N.B. The Australian Rugby Union now recognises the internationals played by the New South Wales touring teams of the 1920s as cap matches.

Ackermann, C J (South Africa) 1953 *SA v A* (2), 1955 *SA v BI*, 1958 *SA v F*
Acton, W H (Ireland) 1926 *W v E*, *E v S*
Adams, A (South Africa) 1991 *US v F* (2)
Alderson, F H R (England) 1903 *S v I*
Allan, M A (Scotland) 1931 *I v W*, *I v SA*, 1933 *E v I*, *I v W*, 1934 *I v E*, 1935 *E v I*, *I v W*, 1936 *I v E*, 1937 *I v W*, 1947 *I v E*, 1948 *I v W*
Allen, J W (Ireland) 1906 *W v S*, *S v E*
Anderson, C (Scotland) 1928 *I v F*
Anderson, J B (Scotland) 1981 *W v E*, *I v A*, 1982 *R v F*, 1983 *I v E*, *A v NZ*, 1984 *E v W*, 1986 *W v F*, *NZ v A*, 1987 [*A v US*, *A v I*, *F v A*], 1988 *A v NZ*(2), 1989 *I v F*, *R v E*, *F v B*, 1991 [*E v It*, *Arg v WS*]
Anderson, J H (South Africa) 1903 *SA v GB*
Angus, A W (Scotland) 1924 *W v E*, 1927 *I v A*
Ashmore, H L (England) 1890 *S v I*, 1891 *S v W*, 1892 *S v I*, 1894 *I v S*, 1895 *S v I*
Austin, A W C (Scotland) 1952 *W v F*, 1953 *I v E*, 1954 *I v W*
Austry, R (France) 1972 *E v I*

Badger, Dr (England) 1900 *I v S*
Baise, M (South Africa) 1967 *SA v F* (2), 1968 *SA v BI* (2), 1969 *SA v A*, 1974 *SA v BI* (2)
Baise, S (South Africa) 1969 *SA v A*
Barnes, P (Australia) 1938 *A v NZ*
Baxter, J (England) 1913 *F v S*, *S v I*, 1914 *I v S*, 1920 *S v I*, 1921 *W v S*, *I v S*, 1923 *W v S*, 1925 *W v S*, *I v W*
Bean, A S (England) 1939 *W v S*, 1945 *W v F*, 1946 *F v W*, 1947 *F v W*, *W v A*, 1948 *S v F*, *W v F*, 1949 *S v I*
Beattie, R A (Scotland) 1937 *E v W*, 1938 *W v E*, 1945 *B v F*, 1947 *W v E*, *I v A*, 1948 *E v W*, 1949 *I v E*, 1950 *E v I*, *I v W*
Beattie, W H (Australia) 1899 *A v GB*, 1904 *A v GB*
Bell, T (Ireland) 1932 *S v W*, 1933 *E v W*
Bevan, W D (Wales) 1985 *E v R*, 1986 *F v E*, *NZ v A* (2), 1987 [*NZ v Fj*, *F v Z*], *A v NZ*, 1988 *I v WS*, 1990 *NZ v S*, 1991 *I v F*, [*F v Fj*, *S v WS*, *E v A*], 1992 *S v E*, *E v I*, *NZ v Wld* (2), 1993 *F v S*
Beves, G (South Africa) 1896 *SA v GB*
Bezuidenhout, G P (South Africa) 1976 *SA v NZ* (3)

Bishop, D J (New Zealand) 1986 *Fj v W*, *R v F*, *I v R*, 1987 [*W v Tg*, *W v C*], 1988 *A v E* (2), *E v A*, *S v A*, 1990 *S v E*, *I v W*, 1991 *S v W*, *W v I*, [*A v Arg*, *F v E*], 1992 *NZ v Wld*, *SA v A*
Bissett, W M (South Africa) 1896 *SA v GB*
Bonnet, J-P (France) 1979 *W v E*, 1980 *S v E*, *SA v BI* (2), 1981 *I v E*, *Arg v E* (2), 1982 *W v S*
Bott, J G (Scotland) 1931 *W v S*, 1933 *W v S*
Boundy, L M (England) 1955 *S v I*, 1956 *W v S*, 1957 *F v S*, *I v F*, *S v I*, *R v F*, 1958 *S v F*, 1959 *S v I*, 1961 *S v SA*
Bowden, G (Scotland) 1910 *F v E*
Bowen, D H (Wales) 1905 *E v S*
Bradburn, T J (England) 1928 *F v A*, 1929 *F v G*
Bressy, J (France) 1988 *W v S*
Brook, P G (England) 1963 *F v W*, 1964 *W v S*, 1965 *W v I*, *I v SA*, 1966 *F v I*, *It v F*, *R v F*
Brown, A (Australia) 1907 *A v NZ*
Brown, D A (England) 1960 *I v W*, *It v F*
Brunton, J (England) 1924 *W v NZ*
Buchanan, A (Scotland) 1877 *I v S*, 1880 *S v I*
Bullerwell, I M (England) 1988 *W v R*, 1990 *F v R*
Burger F (South Africa) 1989 *F v A* (2), 1990 *S v Arg*, 1992 *S v F*, *F v I*, *Arg v F* (2)
Burmeister, R D (South Africa) 1949 *SA v NZ* (2), 1953 *SA v A*, 1955 *SA v BI* (2), 1960 *SA v NZ* (2), 1961 *SA v A*
Burnand, F W (England) 1890 *I v W*
Burnet, W (Scotland) 1932 *I v E*, 1934 *W v I*
Burnett, D I H (Ireland) 1977 *W v E*, 1979 *F v W*, 1980 *E v W*, 1981 *S v W*, *E v S*, 1982 *W v F*, *F v Arg*, 1983 *E v F*, 1984 *S v E*, *A v NZ*, 1985 *E v F*, *NZ v A*, 1986 *S v F*, 1987 [*S v Z*, *NZ v S*]
Burnett, R T (Australia) 1973 *A v Tg*, 1974 *A v NZ*, 1975 *A v E*, *A v J*, 1978 *A v W*
Burrell, G (Scotland) 1958 *E v I*, 1959 *W v I*
Burrell, R P (Scotland) 1966 *I v W*, 1967 *I v F*, *F v NZ*, 1969 *I v E*, *F v W*
Butt, C C (Australia) 1914 *A v NZ*
Byrnes, R G (Australia) 1976 *A v Fj*, 1978 *A v W*, 1979 *A v I* (2), *A v NZ*, 1980 *A v NZ*, 1981 *NZ v S*, 1982 *A v S* (2), 1983 *NZ v BI* (2), 1984 *I v W*, *W v F*

338

Calitz, M (South Africa) 1961 *SA v I*
Calmet, R (France) 1970 *E v W*
Calver, E W (England) 1914 *F v I*
Camardon, A (Argentina) 1960 *Arg v F*
Campbell, A (New Zealand) 1908 *NZ v AW* (2)
Carlson, K R V (South Africa) 1962 *SA v BI*
Cartwright, V H (England) 1906 *I v S*, 1909 *S v I*, 1910 *I v S*, *F v I*, 1911 *S v I*
Castens, H H(South Africa) 1891 *SA v GB*
Ceccon, A (France) 1991 *I v E, R v S*
Chambers, J (Ireland) 1888 *W v S, I v M*, 1890 *S v E*, 1891 *E v S*
Chapman, W S (Australia) 1938 *A v NZ* (2)
Charman, R (England) 1919 *W v NZA*
Chevrier, G (France) 1980 *I v S*
Chiene, Dr J (Scotland) 1879 *I v S*
Clark, K H (Ireland) 1973 *E v F*, 1974 *S v F*, 1976 *F v E*
Cochrane, C B (Australia) 1907 *A v NZ*
Coffey, J J (Ireland) 1912 *S v E*
Colati, L (Fiji) 1991 *[I v J]*
Coles, P (England) 1903 *W v I*, 1905 *S v I*
Collett C K (Australia) 1981 *NZ v S*
Combe, A (Ireland) 1876 *I v E*
Cook, H G (Ireland) 1886 *S v E*
Cooney, R C (Australia) 1929 *A v NZ*, 1930 *A v BI*, 1932 *A v NZ*, 1934 *A v NZ*
Cooney, W M (Australia) 1972 *A v F*, 1975 *A v E, A v J*, 1976 *A v Fj*
Cooper, Dr P F (England) 1952 *I v W*, 1953 *S v W*, *W v I*, *F v It*, *W v NZ*, 1954 *I v NZ*, *W v S*, *It v F*, 1956 *F v I*, *W v F*, *It v F*, 1957 *F v W*
Corley, H H (Ireland) 1906 *S v SA*, 1908 *S v E*
Corr, W S (Australia) 1899 *A v GB* (2)
Costello, J (Fiji) 1972 *Fj v A*
Craven, W S D (England) 1920 *F v W*
Crawford, S H (Ireland) 1913 *W v E, S v W*, 1920 *S v W*, 1921 *S v E*
Cross, W (Scotland) 1877 *S v E*
Crowe, K J (Australia) 1965 *A v SA*, 1966 *A v BI*, 1968 *A v NZ*, 1976 *A v Fj*
Cumberlege, B S (England) 1926 *S v I, W v I*, 1927 *S v F, I v S, I v W*, 1928 *S v I*, 1929 *F v I, S v F, I v S*, 1930 *I v F, S v I*, 1931 *I v S*, 1932 *S v SA, S v I*, 1933 *I v S*, 1934 *S v I*
Cunningham, J G (Scotland) 1913 *W v I*, 1921 *F v I*
Cuny, Dr A (France) 1976 *W v S*
Curnow, J (Canada) 1976 *US v F*
Currey, F I (England) 1887 *S v W*

Dallas, J D (Scotland) 1905 *W v NZ*, 1908 *I v W*, 1909 *W v E, I v E*, 1910 *E v W, I v W*, 1911 *I v E*, 1912 *I v W*
D'Arcy, D P (Ireland) 1967 *F v E, E v S, F v W, F v R*, 1968 *E v W, S v E, F v SA*, 1969 *E v F, W v E*, 1970 *W v S*, 1971 *W v E*, 1973 *F v NZ, F v W, F v R*, 1975 *E v S, F v Arg, W v A*
David, I (Wales) 1938 *E v S*, 1939 *S v E*, 1947 *E v S*, 1952 *S v F, I v S, E v I*, 1953 *S v I*, 1954 *S v F, E v NZ, S v NZ, F v NZ, F v E*, 1955 *I v F*, 1956 *F v E*
Davidson, I G (Ireland) 1911 *S v W*
Day, H L V (England) 1934 *S v W*
Day, P W (South Africa) 1903 *SA v GB*
Dedet, L (France) 1906 *F v NZ, F v E*
De Bruyn, C J (South Africa) 1969 *SA v A*, 1974 *SA v BI* (2)
Delany, M G (Ireland) 1899 *S v W*, 1900 *S v E*
Desclaux, M (France) 1992 *W v S*
Dickie, A I (Scotland) 1954 *F v I, E v I, W v F*, 1955 *I v E, W v I*, 1956 *E v I, I v W*, 1957 *W v E, I v E*, 1958 *W v A, W v F*
Dodds, I (Ireland) 1898 *S v E*
Domercq, G (France) 1972 *S v NZ*, 1973 *W v E*, 1976 *E v W*, 1977 *S v W*, 1978 *I v W*
Donaldson, S (Ireland) 1937 *S v E*
Donaldson, W P (Scotland) 1903 *SA v GB*
Don Wauchope, A R (Scotland) 1889 *W v I*, 1890 *E v I*, 1893 *I v E*
Doocey, T F (New Zealand) 1976 *NZ v I*, 1983 *E v S*, *F v W*
Douglas, W M (Wales) 1891 *I v E*, 1894 *E v I*, 1896 *S v E*, 1903 *E v S*
Doulcet, J-C (France) 1989 *S v W*
Dowling, M J (Ireland) 1947 *S v W*, 1950 *W v S, S v E, W v F*, 1951 *W v E, S v W, F v W, E v S, S v SA*, 1952 *W v S, F v SA, S v E*, 1953 *W v E, E v S*, 1954 *E v W*,

1955 *S v W*, 1956 *S v F, S v E*
Downes, A D (New Zealand) 1913 *NZ v A*
Doyle, O E (Ireland) 1984 *W v S, R v S, W v A*, 1987 *E v S*, 1988 *F v E, Arg v F* (2), *W v WS*, 1989 *F v S*, 1990 *F v E*, 1991 *[It v US, Fj v R]*, 1992 *W v F*, 1993 *F v W*
Drennan, V (Ireland) 1914 *W v S*
Duffy, B (New Zealand) 1977 *NZ v BI*
Dumé, J (France) 1993 *W v E, S v W*
Duncan, J (New Zealand) 1908 *NZ v AW*
Durand, C (France) 1969 *E v S*, 1970 *I v S*, 1971 *E v S*

Eckhold, A E (New Zealand) 1923 *NZ v A*
Elliott, H B (England) 1955 *F v S, F v It*, 1956 *I v S*
Engelbrecht, Dr G K (South Africa) 1964 *SA v W*
Evans, F T (New Zealand) 1904 *NZ v GB*
Evans, G (England) 1905 *E v NZ*, 1908 *W v A*
Evans, W J (Wales) 1958 *I v A, F v E*

Farquhar, A B (New Zealand) 1961 *NZ v F* (3), 1962 *NZ v A* (2), 1964 *NZ v A*
Faull, J W (Wales) 1936 *E v NZ, S v I*, 1937 *E v I*
Ferguson, C F (Australia) 1963 *A v E*, 1965 *A v SA*, 1968 *A v F*, 1969 *A v W*, 1971 *A v SA* (2)
Ferguson, P (Australia) 1914 *A v NZ*
Findlay, D G (Scotland) 1895 *I v E*, 1896 *E v W, E v I*, 1897 *I v E*, 1898 *E v I*, 1899 *I v E*, 1900 *E v I*
Findlay, J C (Scotland) 1902 *I v W*, 1903 *I v E*, 1904 *E v W, I v W*, 1905 *I v NZ*, 1911 *I v F*
Finlay, A K (Australia) 1961 *A v Fj*, 1962 *A v NZ*
Fitzgerald, K V J (Australia) 1985 *I v F, W v I, NZ v E* (2), *Arg v NZ* (2), 1987 *[I v W, E v US, NZ v W, NZ v F]*, 1988 *Fj v E*, 1989 *S v I, W v E, SA v Wld* (2), 1990 *A v US*, 1991 *F v W, S v I, [Fj v C, NZ v It, S v E]*
Fleming, G R (Scotland) 1879 *S v E*
Fleming, J M (Scotland) 1985 *I v E*, 1986 *A v Arg* (2), 1987 *E v F*, [*A v J, Fj v Arg*], *F v R*, 1989 *F v W*, 1990 *NZ v A*, 1991 *W v F*, [*E v NZ, Arg v WS* (R)], *I v A, NZ v A*], 1992 *A v NZ*, 1993 *E v F*
Fleury, A L (New Zealand) 1959 *NZ v BI*
Fong, A S (New Zealand) 1946 *NZ v A*, 1950 *NZ v BI*
Fordham, R J (Australia) 1986 *E v W, F v I, Arg v F* (2), 1987 [*NZ v It, F v R*]
Fornès, E (Argentina) 1954 *Arg v F* (2)
Forsyth, R A (New Zealand) 1958 *NZ v A*
Frames, P R (South Africa) 1891 *SA v GB*
Francis, R C (New Zealand) 1984 *E v A, I v A*, 1985 *Arg v F* (2), 1986 *W v S, S v E, WS v W*
Freeman, W L (Ireland) 1932 *E v SA*
Freethy, A E (Wales) 1923 *F v E*, 1924 *E v F, I v NZ, F v US*, 1925 *E v NZ, I v S, S v E, F v E*, 1926 *E v F*, 1927 *F v E*, 1928 *I v E, E v F*, 1929 *E v I, F v E*, 1930 *I v E, E v F*, 1931 *E v I, F v E*
Fright, W H (New Zealand) 1956 *NZ v SA* (2)
Frood, J (New Zealand) 1952 *NZ v A*
Fry, H A (England) 1945 *F v B*
Furness, D C (Australia) 1952 *A v Fj* (2), 1954 *A v Fj*

Gadney, C H (England) 1935 *S v NZ, W v NZ*, 1936 *S v W, W v I*, 1937 *W v S, I v S*, 1938 *S v W, S v I*, 1939 *I v S*, 1940 *F v B*, 1946 *F v B*, 1947 *F v S, S v I*, 1948 *F v A, I v S*
Games, J (Wales) 1909 *E v A*, 1913 *E v F*, 1914 *F v E*
Gardiner, F (Ireland) 1912 *S v E*
Gardner, J A (Scotland) 1884 *E v W*, 1887 *W v I*
Garling, A F (Australia) 1981 *A v NZ* (2)
Garrard, W G (Australia) 1899 *A v GB*
Gilchrist, N R (New Zealand) 1936 *M v A*
Gillespie, J I (Scotland) 1907 *W v E*, 1911 *W v E*
Gilliard, P (England) 1902 *W v S*
Gillies, C R (New Zealand) 1958 *NZ v A* (2), 1959 *NZ v BI* (2)
Gilliland, R W (Ireland) 1964 *It v F*, 1965 *S v W, E v F, F v W, F v R*, 1966 *E v W*, 1967 *F v A*
Gillmore, W N (England) 1956 *F v Cz*, 1958 *I v S, It v F*
Glasgow, O B (Ireland) 1953 *F v S, F v W*, 1954 *S v E*, 1955 *W v E, F v W*
Goulding, W J (Ireland) 1882 *I v W*
Gourlay, I W (South Africa) 1976 *SA v NZ*
Gouws, Dr J (South Africa) 1977 *SA v Wld*
Greenlees, Dr J R C (Scotland) 1913 *I v E*, 1914 *E v W*
Grierson, T F E (Scotland) 1970 *I v SA*, 1971 *F v R*, 1972 *F v E*, 1973 *W v I*, 1975 *E v F*
Griffin, Dr (South Africa) 1891 *SA v GB*

McMahon, D C J (Scotland) 1961 *W v I*, 1963 *E v F*, 1964 *E v NZ*, 1967 *E v NZ*, *W v E*, 1969 *W v I*
McMullen, R F (New Zealand) 1973 *NZ v E*
MacNeill, A R (Australia) 1988 *F v Arg* (2), 1989 *W v NZ*, *I v NZ*, 1990 *F v NZ* (2), 1991 [*C v R*], 1992 *NZ v I* (2), *SA v NZ*, 1993 *W v I*, *I v E*
Magee, J T (Ireland) 1897 *W v S*, *E v S*, 1898 *E v W*, 1899 *E v S*
Magrath, R M (Ireland) 1928 *F v S*
Mailhan, L (France) 1933 *F v G*, 1935 *F v G*, 1937 *F v G*
Malan, Dr W C (South Africa) 1970 *SA v NZ*, 1971 *SA v F* (2)
Marie, B (France) 1960 *Arg v F* (2), 1965 *F v W* (R), 1966 *E v I*
Marsh, F W (England) 1907 *W v I*
Martelli, E (Ireland) 1903 *S v W*
Martin, N B (Australia) 1910 *A v NZ* (2)
Matheson, A M (New Zealand) 1946 *NZ v A*
Maurette, G (France) 1987 *W v I*, [*J v US*, *I v Tg*], 1988 *NZ v W* (2), 1989 *E v S*
Mayne, A V (Australia) 1929 *A v NZ* (2), 1932 *A v NZ*
Megson, R J (Scotland) 1987 *W v E*, 1988 *I v W*, *I v It*, 1991 *W v E*, *A v NZ*, 1992 *E v W*, *F v Arg*
Miles, J H (England) 1913 *F v W*, *I v F*, 1914 *W v F*
Millar, D H (New Zealand) 1965 *NZ v SA*, 1968 *NZ v F*, 1977 *NZ v BI* (2), 1978 *NZ v A* (3)
Millar, W A (South Africa) 1924 *SA v BI* (2)
Mitchell, R (Ireland) 1955 *E v F*, 1956 *E v W*, 1957 *E v S*
Moffat, F J C (Scotland) 1932 *W v E*
Moffitt, J (New Zealand) 1936 *NZ v A*
Moolman, Dr J (South Africa) 1972 *SA v E*
Moore, D F (Ireland) 1886 *E v W*, *W v S*
Moore, T W (Australia) 1947 *A v NZ*, 1950 *A v BI*, 1951 *A v NZ*, 1954 *A v Fj*, 1956 *A v NZ*
Morgan, C E (Australia) 1907 *A v NZ*, 1910 *A v NZ*
Morgan, K (Wales) 1967 *F v It*
Morrison, D (USA) 1981 *US v SA*
Morrison, E (England) 1991 *F v S*, *R v F*, [*S v J*, *A v WS*], 1992 *I v A*, 1993 *S v I*
Mortimer, S (England) 1888 *W v M*
Morton, D S (Scotland) 1893 *W v E*
Muller, F (South Africa) 1982 *SA v SAm*, 1988 *S v F*, *F v I*
Mullock, R (Wales) 1886 *I v E*
Muntz, J (France) 1924 *F v R*
Murdoch, W C W (Scotland) 1951 *W v I*, *I v SA*, 1952 *E v SA*, *F v E*
Murphy, J P (New Zealand) 1959 *NZ v BI*, 1963 *NZ v E*, 1964 *NZ v A* (2), 1965 *NZ v SA* (3), 1966 *NZ v BI* (3), 1968 *NZ v F*, 1969 *NZ v W* (2)
Myburgh, P A (South Africa) 1962 *SA v BI*, 1963 *SA v A* (3)

Neilson, A E (New Zealand) 1921 *NZ v SA* (2)
Neser, V H (South Africa) 1924 *SA v BI*, 1928 *SA v NZ* (4), 1933 *SA v A* (4)
Neville, Dr W C (Ireland) 1882 *I v E*
Nicholls, E G (Wales) 1909 *E v S*
Nicholls, F (England) 1904 *W v S*
Nicholson, G W (New Zealand) 1913 *NZ v A*
Noon, O (Argentina) 1949 *Arg v F*
Norling, C (Wales) 1978 *I v NZ*, 1979 *E v S*, 1980 *F v E*, 1981 *I v F*, *NZ v SA* (2), *F v NZ*, 1982 *I v S*, 1983 *A v Arg* (2), 1984 *F v I*, 1985 *E v S*, 1986 *E v I*, 1987 *I v F*, [*C v Tg*, *F v Fj*], 1988 *E v I*, *R v F*, 1989 *NZ v Arg* (2), 1990 *I v S*, *A v F* (2), 1991 *Nm v I* (2)
Nugent, G P (Ireland) 1880 *I v E*

Oakley, L D (South Africa) 1924 *SA v BI*
O'Callaghan, B J (Australia) 1959 *A v BI*
O'Leary, J (Australia) 1958 *A v M*

Palmade, F (France) 1973 *F v S* (R), *S v W*, 1974 *I v S*, 1975 *I v E*, 1977 *I v E*, 1978 *E v I*, 1979 *S v W*, 1980 *SA v BI* (2), 1981 *W v I*, *SA v I* (2), 1982 *E v W*, 1983 *NZ v BI* (2), 1985 *W v E*, 1986 *I v S*
Parfitt, V J (Wales) 1953 *E v F*, 1954 *I v S*
Parkes, Dr N M (England) 1958 *W v S*, *F v A*, *I v W*, *F v I*, 1959 *F v It*, *F v W*, 1960 *W v E*, *F v W*, 1961 *F v W*, 1962 *W v S*, *I v S*
Parkinson, F G M (New Zealand) 1955 *NZ v A*, 1956 *NZ v SA* (2)

Paton, R J (New Zealand) 1931 *M v A*
Pattinson, K A (England) 1973 *F v S*, *W v A*, 1974 *I v W*, *R v F*, 1975 *F v W*, 1976 *S v F*
Pattisson, A S (Scotland) 1883 *E v I*
Pauling, T G (Australia) 1904 *A v GB* (2), 1914 *A v NZ*
Peake, J F (New Zealand) 1923 *NZ v A*
Pearce, T N (England) 1948 *F v I*, *W v S*, 1949 *F v S*, *I v F*, *W v I*, 1950 *F v I*, *I v S*, 1951 *F v S*, *I v F*, *S v I*, 1952 *F v I*
Peard, L J (Wales) 1989 *I v E*, 1991 *E v F*, [*F v R*, *E v US*]
Petrie, A G (Scotland) 1882 *S v I*
Phillips, T H (Wales) 1936 *E v S*
Phillips, W D (Wales) 1887 *I v E*, 1889 *I v S*
Pontin, A C (USA) 1976 *US v A*
Potter-Irwin, F C (England) 1909 *W v I*, 1911 *W v I*, 1912 *W v S*, *I v S*, *S v SA*, *I v SA*, *W v SA*, 1920 *F v S*, *W v I*
Pozzi, S (Italy) 1957 *F v R*, 1960 *R v F*
Pretorius, N F (South Africa) 1938 *SA v BI*
Price, F G (Wales) 1963 *I v F*
Prideaux, L (England) 1980 *W v S*, *I v W*, *SAm v SA* (2), 1981 *S v I*, *NZ v SA*, 1985 *F v S*
Priest, T E (England) 1952 *It v F*, 1953 *I v F*
Pring, J P G (New Zealand) 1966 *NZ v BI*, 1967 *NZ v A*, 1968 *NZ v F*, 1971 *NZ v BI* (4), 1972 *NZ v A*
Purcell, N M (Ireland) 1927 *S v E*

Quittenton, R C (England) 1977 *Arg v F* (2), 1978 *W v NZ*, 1979 *I v F*, *F v S*, *S v NZ*, 1981 *S v A*, 1982 *NZ v A*, 1983 *S v W*, *F v R*, 1984 *A v NZ* (2), 1986 *R v S*, 1987 *S v I*, [*Arg v It*, *NZ v Arg*], 1988 *I v S*, 1989 *W v I*

Rainie, R D (Scotland) 1890 *E v W*, 1891 *W v E*, 1894 *I v W*
Rea, M D M (Ireland) 1978 *R v F*, 1981 *S v R*, 1982 *F v E*
Reading, L S (England) 1912 *US v A*
Reilly, J R (Australia) 1972 *A v F*
Reordan, D (United States) 1991 [*S v Z*]
Richards, A (Wales) 1980 *R v F*, 1981 *A v F*, 1982 *E v A*, 1983 *F v S*
Richards, A R (South Africa) 1896 *SA v GB*
Robbertse, P (South Africa) 1967 *SA v F*, 1969 *SA v A*, 1970 *SA v NZ* (2)
Roberts, E (Wales) 1924 *F v S*
Roberts, R A (England) 1924 *F v W*
Robertson, W A (Scotland) 1920 *E v F*, *I v E*
Robin, P (France) 1988 *It v A*, 1989 *S v Fj*, 1990 *E v I*, 1991 [*W v WS*], 1992 *A v NZ* (2)
Robinson, H L (Ireland) 1882 *E v S*
Robson, C F (New Zealand) 1963 *NZ v E*
Roca, J (France) 1937 *F v It*
Rowlands, K (Wales) 1980 *SA v SAm* (2), 1981 *F v S*, 1982 *S v E*, 1986 *SA v Cv* (4)
Rowsell, A (England) 1891 *W v I*
Royds, P M R (England) 1921 *W v F*, 1923 *F v I*
Rutherford, C F (Scotland) 1908 *F v E*
Rutter, A (England) 1876 *E v S*

St Guilhem, J (France) 1974 *S v E*, 1975 *W v I*
Sanson, N R (Scotland) 1974 *W v F*, *F v SA*, 1975 *I v P* (C), *SA v F* (2), *F v R*, 1976 *I v A*, *I v W*, 1977 *W v I*, 1978 *F v E*, *E v W*, *E v NZ*, 1979 *E v NZ*
Schoeman, J P J (South Africa) 1968 *SA v BI*
Schofield, T D (Wales) 1907 *E v S*, 1908 *E v I*, 1910 *E v I*, 1911 *E v S*, 1912 *E v I*, *F v E*, 1913 *E v S*, 1914 *E v I*, *S v E*, 1920 *E v S*, 1921 *E v I*, 1922 *S v I*
Schwoenberg, M (Germany) 1938 *R v F*
Scott, J M B (Scotland) 1923 *E v W*
Scott, R L (Scotland) 1927 *F v I*, *E v W*
Scriven, G (Ireland) 1884 *E v S*
Short, J A (Scotland) 1979 *F v R*, 1982 *I v W*
Simmonds, G (Wales) 1992 *E v C*
Simpson, J W (Scotland) 1906 *I v W*
Simpson, R L (New Zealand) 1913 *NZ v A*, 1921 *NZ v A*, 1923 *NZ v A*
Sklar, E (Argentina) 1991 [*NZ v US*]
Slabber, M J (South Africa) 1955 *SA v BI*, 1960 *SA v NZ*
Smith, J A (Scotland) 1892 *E v I*, 1894 *E v W*, 1895 *W v E*
Spreadbury, A (England) 1990 *A v F*, 1992 *I v S*, *W v A*
Stanton, R W (South Africa) 1910 *SA v GB* (3)

341

WORLD INTERNATIONAL RECORDS

Both team and individual records are for official cap matches played by senior members of the International Board, up to 31 March 1993.

TEAM RECORDS

Highest score – 74
New Zealand (74-13) v Fiji 1987
  Christchurch

Biggest winning margin – 64
New Zealand (70-6) v Italy 1987 Auckland

Most tries in an international – 13
England v Wales 1881 Blackheath
New Zealand v United States 1913 Berkeley
France v Romania 1924 Paris
France v Zimbabwe 1987 Auckland

Most conversions in an international – 10
New Zealand v Fiji 1987 Christchurch

Most penalty goals in an international – 7
South Africa v France 1975 Pretoria
England v Wales 1991 Cardiff

Most consecutive international
  victories – 17
New Zealand between 1965 and 1969

Most consecutive internationals
  undefeated – 23
New Zealand between 1987 and 1990

Most points in an international
  series – 109
New Zealand v Argentina (2 matches)
  1989 in New Zealand

Most tries in an international series – 18
New Zealand v Wales (2 matches) 1988
  in New Zealand

Most points in Five Nations
Championship in a season – 118
England 1991-92

Most tries in Five Nations
Championship in a season – 21
Wales 1909-10

Most points on an overseas tour
(all matches) – 868
New Zealand to B Isles/France
  (33 matches) 1905-06

Most tries on an overseas tour
(all matches) – 215
New Zealand to B Isles/France
  (33 matches) 1905-06

Biggest win on a major tour
(all matches)
117-6 New Zealand v S Australia 1974
  Adelaide

INDIVIDUAL RECORDS

*including appearances for British Isles,
shown in brackets*

Most capped player
S Blanco (France) 93 1980-91
in individual positions
Full-back
S Blanco (France) 81[1] 1980-91
Wing
R Underwood (England) 63(3)[2] 1984-93
Centre (includes 2nd five-eighth)
P Sella (France) 81[3] 1982-93
Fly-half (includes 1st five-eighth)
C R Andrew (England) 53(2)[4] 1986-93

Scrum-half
G O Edwards (Wales) 63(10) 1967-78
Prop
P A Orr (Ireland) 59(1) 1976-87
Hooker
C T Deans (Scotland) 52 1978-87
Lock
W J McBride (Ireland) 80(17) 1962-75
Flanker
J F Slattery (Ireland) 65(4) 1970-84
No 8
T M Davies (Wales) 46(8)[5] 1969-76

[1] *Blanco also played 12 times as a wing*
[2] *D I Campese (Australia), 72 caps, has won 56 as a wing*
[3] *Sella has also played 6 times on the wing and once at full-back*
[4] *Andrew has also played once for England as a full-back. M P Lynagh (Australia), 60 caps in all, has played 52 times at fly-half, 7 at centre and once at full-back*
[5] *Several French utility forwards won more caps than Davies, but none has played as frequently at No 8*

Most consecutive internationals for a country – 53
G O Edwards (Wales) 1967-78

Most internationals as captain – 36
N C Farr-Jones (Australia) 1988-92

Most points in internationals – 760
M P Lynagh (Australia) (60 matches) 1984-92

Most points in an international – 30
D Camberabero (France) v Zimbabwe 1987 Auckland

Most tries in internationals – 52
D I Campese (Australia) (72 matches) 1982-92

Most tries in an international – 5
G C Lindsay (Scotland) v Wales 1887 Edinburgh
D Lambert (England) v France 1907 Richmond
R Underwood (England) v Fiji 1989 Twickenham

Most conversions in internationals – 125
M P Lynagh (Australia) (60 matches) 1984-92

Most conversions in an international – 10
G J Fox (New Zealand) v Fiji 1987 Christchurch

Most dropped goals in internationals – 18
H E Botha (South Africa) (28 matches) 1980-92

Most dropped goals in an international – 3
P Albaladejo (France) v Ireland 1960 Paris
P F Hawthorne (Australia) v England 1967 Twickenham
H E Botha (South Africa) v S America 1980 Durban
H E Botha (South Africa) v Ireland 1981 Durban
J-P Lescarboura (France) v England 1985 Twickenham
J-P Lescarboura (France) v New Zealand 1986 Christchurch
D Camberabero (France) v Australia 1990 Sydney

Most penalty goals in internationals – 145
M P Lynagh (Australia) (60 matches) 1984-92

Most penalty goals in an international – 7
S D Hodgkinson (England) v Wales 1991 Cardiff

Fastest player to 100 points in internationals
G J Fox (New Zealand) in his 6th match

Fastest player to 200 points in internationals
G J Fox (New Zealand) in his 13th match

Fastest player to 300 points in internationals
G J Fox (New Zealand) in his 18th match

Fastest player to 400 points in internationals
G J Fox (New Zealand) in his 26th match

Most points in a Five Nations match – 24
S Viars (France) v Ireland 1992

Most points in Five Nations Championship in a season – 67
J M Webb (England) (4 matches) 1991-92

Most tries in Five Nations Championship in a season – 8
C N Lowe (England) (4 appearances) 1913-14
I S Smith (Scotland) (4 appearances) 1924-25

Tries in each match of a Five Nations Championship
H C Catcheside (England) 1923-24
A C Wallace (Scotland) 1924-25
P Estève (France) 1982-83
P Sella (France) 1985-86

Most penalty goals in Five Nations Championship in a season – 18
S D Hodgkinson (England) (4 matches) 1990-91

Most conversions in Five Nations Championship in a season – 11
J Bancroft (Wales) (4 appearances) 1908-09
J M Webb (England) (4 matches) 1991-92

Most dropped goals in Five Nations Championship in a season – 5
G Camberabero (France) (3 appearances) 1966-67
J-P Lescarboura (France) dropped a goal in each Championship match 1983-84, a unique feat

---

Most points on an overseas tour – 230
W J Wallace (NZ) (25 appearances) in B Isles/France 1905-06

Most tries on an overseas tour – 42
J Hunter (NZ) (23 appearances) in B Isles/France 1905-06

Most points in any match on tour – 43
R M Deans (NZ) v South Australia 1984 Adelaide

Most tries in any match on tour – 8
T R Heeps (NZ) v Northern NSW 1962
P Estève scored 8 for France v East Japan in 1984, but this was not on a major tour

---

PARTNERSHIP RECORDS

Centre threequarters.
S Hastings and S R P Lineen (Scotland) 28
Half-backs
M P Lynagh and N C Farr-Jones (Australia) 47
Front row
S C McDowell, S B T Fitzpatrick and R W Loe (New Zealand) 33
Second row
A J Martin and G A D Wheel (Wales) 27
Back row
J Matheu, G Basquet and J Prat (France) 22

OTHER INTERNATIONAL MATCH RECORDS

Up to 31 March 1993. These are included for comparison and cover performances since 1971 by teams and players in Test matches for nations which are not senior members of the International Board.

Most points in a match
By a team
111 Zimbabwe v Nigeria 1987 Nairobi
By a player
31 M Grobler Zimbabwe v Nigeria 1987
29 S Bettarello Italy v Canada 1983

Most tries in a match
By a team
20 Zimbabwe v Nigeria 1987 Nairobi
By a player
5 R Tsimba Zimbabwe v Nigeria 1987
5 M Neill Zimbabwe v Nigeria 1987

Most conversions in a match
By a team
14 Zimbabwe v Nigeria Nairobi 1987
By a player
14 M Grobler Zimbabwe v Nigeria 1987

Most penalty goals in a match
By a team
8 Canada v Scotland 1991 St John
By a player
8 M A Wyatt Canada v Scotland 1991
St John

Most dropped goals in a match
By a team
3 Argentina v SA Gazelles 1971 Pretoria
3 Argentina v Australia 1979
Buenos Aires

3 Argentina v New Zealand 1985
Buenos Aires
By a player
3 T A Harris-Smith
Argentina v SA Gazelles 1971
3 H Porta Argentina v Australia 1979
3 H Porta Argentina v New Zealand 1985

Most points in matches
530 H Porta Argentina/South America
483 S Bettarello Italy

Most tries in matches
21 M Marchetto Italy

Most conversions in matches
54 H Porta Argentina/South America
46 S Bettarello Italy

Most penalties in matches
109 H Porta Argentina/South America
104 S Bettarello Italy

Most dropped goals in matches
25 H Porta Argentina/South America
17 S Bettarello Italy

Most matches as captain
43 H Porta Argentina/South America

THE WORLD CUP 1991

SECOND TOURNAMENT IN BRITAIN, IRELAND AND FRANCE

POOL 1	P	W	D	L	F	A	Pts
New Zealand	3	3	0	0	95	39	9
England	3	2	0	1	85	33	7
Italy	3	1	0	2	57	76	5
USA	3	0	0	3	24	113	3

3 October, Twickenham
NEW ZEALAND 18 (1G 4PG)   **ENGLAND 12** (3PG 1DG)

NEW ZEALAND: Wright; Kirwan, Innes, McCahill, Timu; Fox, Bachop; McDowell, Fitzpatrick, Loe, I D Jones, G W Whetton (*capt*), A J Whetton, Brooke, M N Jones
Replacement Earl for Brooke (70 mins)
Scorers *Try:* M N Jones   *Conversion:* Fox   *Penalty Goals:* Fox (4)
ENGLAND: Webb; Underwood, Carling (*capt*), Guscott, Oti; Andrew, Hill; Leonard, Moore, Probyn, Ackford, Dooley, Teague, Richards, Winterbottom
Scorers *Penalty Goals:* Webb (3)   *Dropped Goal:* Andrew
Referee J M Fleming (Scotland)

5 October, Otley
ITALY 30 (4G 2PG)   **USA 9** (1G 1PG)

ITALY: Troiani; Vaccari, Gaetaniello, Barba, Marcello Cuttitta; Dominguez, Francescato; Massimo Cuttitta, Pivetta, Properzi-Curti, Favaro, Croci, Saetti, Checchinato, Zanon (*capt*)
Scorers *Tries:* Barba, Francescato, Vaccari, Gaetaniello   *Conversions:* Dominguez (4)
Penalty Goals: Dominguez (2)
USA: Nelson; Hein, Williams, Higgins, Whitaker; De Jong, Daily; Lippert, Flay, Paoli, Swords, Leversee, Vizard (*capt*), Ridnell, Farley *Replacement* Lipman for Vizard (57 mins)
Scorers *Try:* Swords   *Conversion:* Williams   *Penalty Goal:* Williams
Referee O E Doyle (Ireland)

8 October, Gloucester
NEW ZEALAND 46 (4G 2PG 4T)   **USA 6** (2PG)

NEW ZEALAND: Wright; Timu, Innes, McCahill, Tuigamala; Preston, Bachop; McDowell, Fitzpatrick, Purvis, I D Jones, G W Whetton (*capt*), A J Whetton, Earl, M N Jones
Scorers *Tries:* Wright (3), Earl, Purvis, Timu, Innes, Tuigamala
Conversions: Preston (4)   *Penalty Goals:* Preston (2)
USA: Sheehy; Hein, Williams, Burke, Whitaker; O'Brien, Pidcock; Lippert, Johnson, Mottram, Swords (*capt*), Tunnacliffe, Sawicki, Ridnell, Lipman *Replacement* Manga for Lippert (51 mins)
Scorers *Penalty Goals:* Williams (2)
Referee E Sklar (Argentina)

8 October, Twickenham
ENGLAND 36 (4G 4PG)   **ITALY 6** (1G)

ENGLAND: Webb; Oti, Carling (*capt*), Guscott, Underwood; Andrew, Hill; Leonard, Moore, Probyn, Ackford, Redman, Teague, Richards, Winterbottom
Replacement Rendall for Probyn (53 mins)
Scorers *Tries:* Underwood, Guscott (2), Webb   *Conversions:* Webb (4)

Penalty Goals: Webb (4)
ITALY: Troiani; Vaccari, Gaetaniello, Barba, Marcello Cuttitta; Dominguez, Francescato; Massimo Cuttitta, Pivetta, Properzi-Curti, Favaro, Croci, Saetti, Zanon (*capt*), Giovanelli *Replacement* Bonomi for Troiani (48 mins)
Scorers *Try:* Marcello Cuttitta   *Conversion:* Dominguez
Referee J B Anderson (Scotland)

11 October, Twickenham
ENGLAND 37 (4G 3PG 1T)   **USA 9** (1G 1PG)

ENGLAND: Hodgkinson; Heslop, Carling (*capt*), Halliday, Underwood; Andrew, Hill; Leonard, Olver, Pearce, Dooley, Redman, Skinner, Richards, Rees
Scorers *Tries:* Underwood (2), Carling, Skinner, Heslop   *Conversions:* Hodgkinson (4)
Penalty Goals: Hodgkinson (3)
USA: Nelson; Hein, Williams, Higgins, Sheehy; O'Brien, Pidcock; Manga, Flay, Mottram, Tunnacliffe, Swords (*capt*), Lipman, Ridnell, Farley *Replacements* de Jong for Higgins (40 mins); Wilkerson for Farley (70 mins)
Scorers *Try:* Nelson   *Conversion:* Williams   *Penalty Goal:* Williams
Referee L J Peard (Wales)

13 October, Leicester
NEW ZEALAND 31 (3G 3PG 1T)   **ITALY 21** (2G 3PG)

NEW ZEALAND: Wright; Kirwan, Innes, Little, Tuigamala; Fox, Hewett; McDowell, Fitzpatrick, Loe, I D Jones, G W Whetton (*capt*), A J Whetton, Brooke, Carter *Replacement* Philpott for Wright (73 mins)
Scorers *Tries:* Innes, Brooke, Tuigamala, Hewett   *Conversions:* Fox (3)
Penalty Goals: Fox (3)
ITALY: Vaccari; Venturi, Gaetaniello, Dominguez, Marcello Cuttitta; Bonomi, Francescato; Massimo Cuttitta, Pivetta (*capt*), Properzi-Curti, Favaro, Croci, Bottacchiari, Checchinato, Giovanelli *Replacement* Grespan for Properzi-Curti (44 mins)
Scorers *Tries:* Marcello Cuttitta, Bonomi   *Conversions:* Dominguez (2)
Penalty Goals: Dominguez (3)
Referee K V J Fitzgerald (Australia)

POOL 2	P	W	D	L	F	A	Pts
Scotland	3	3	0	0	122	36	9
Ireland	3	2	0	1	102	51	7
Japan	3	1	0	2	77	87	5
Zimbabwe	3	0	0	3	31	158	3

5 October, Murrayfield
SCOTLAND 47 (5G 3PG 2T)   **JAPAN 9** (1G 1DG)

SCOTLAND: A G Hastings; Stanger, S Hastings, Lineen, Tukalo; Chalmers, Armstrong; Sole (*capt*), Allan, Burnell, Gray, Weir, Jeffrey, White, Calder *Replacements* Wyllie for Chalmers (70 mins); D Milne for Sole (75 mins)
Scorers *Tries:* penalty try, White, Tukalo, G Hastings, S Hastings, Stanger, Chalmers
Conversions: G Hastings (5)   *Penalty Goals:* G Hastings (2), Chalmers
JAPAN: Hosokawa; Masuho, Kutsuki, Hirao (*capt*), Yoshida; Matsuo, Murata; Ota, Kunda, Takura, Hayashi, Tifaga, Kajihara, Latu, Nakashima
Scorer *Try:* Hosokawa   *Conversion:* Hosokawa   *Dropped Goal:* Hosokawa
Referee E Morrison (England)

6 October, Lansdowne Road
IRELAND 55 (4G 5PG 4T)   **ZIMBABWE 11** (1PG 2T)

IRELAND: Staples; Geoghegan, Cunningham, Curtis, Crossan; Keyes, Saunders; Popplewell, Smith, D C Fitzgerald, Lenihan, Francis, Matthews (*capt*), Robinson,

Hamilton
Scorers *Tries:* Robinson (4), Popplewell (2), Curtis, Geoghegan   *Conversions:* Keyes (4)
Penalty Goals: Keyes (5)
ZIMBABWE: Currin (*capt*); Brown, Letcher, Tsimba, Walters; Kuhn, Ferreira;
Hunter, Beattie, Garvey, Martin, Demblon, Botha, Catterall, Dawson
Replacement Schultz for Kuhn (29 mins)
Scorers *Tries:* Dawson, Schultz   *Penalty Goal:* Ferreira
Referee K H Lawrence (New Zealand)

9 October, Lansdowne Road
IRELAND 32 (2G 4PG 2T)   JAPAN 16 (2G 1T)

IRELAND: Staples; Clarke, Mullin, Curtis, Crossan; Keyes, Saunders; J J Fitzgerald,
Kingston (*capt*), Halpin, Galwey, Francis, O'Hara, Mannion, Hamilton
Replacement Cunningham for Crossan (60 mins)
Scorers *Tries:* Staples, O'Hara, Mannion (2)   *Conversions:* Keyes (2)
Penalty Goals: Keyes (4)
JAPAN: Hosokawa; Masuho, Kutsuki, Hirao (*capt*), Yoshida; Matsuo, Horikoshi; Ota,
Fujita, Takura, Hayashi, Oyagi, Tifaga, Latu, Kajihara *Replacements* Kunda for Fujita
(52 mins); Miyamato for Tifaga (73 mins)
Scorers *Tries:* Yoshida, Hayashi, Kajihara   *Conversions:* Hosokawa (2)
Referee L Colati (Fiji)

9 October, Murrayfield
SCOTLAND 51 (5G 2PG 1DG 3T)   ZIMBABWE 12 (2G)

SCOTLAND: Dods (*capt*); Stanger, S Hastings, Lineen, Tukalo; Wyllie, Oliver;
Burnell, K S Milne, Watt, Cronin, Weir, Turnbull, White, Marshall
Replacement Chalmers for Stanger (78 mins)
Scorers *Tries:* Tukalo (3), Stanger, Turnbull, Hastings, Weir, White
Conversions: Dods (5)   *Penalty Goals:* Dods (2)   *Dropped Goal:* Wyllie
ZIMBABWE: Currin (*capt*); Schultz, Tsimba, Letcher, Walters; Brown, MacMillan;
Nicholls, Beattie, Garvey, Martin, Nguruve, Muirhead, Catterall, Dawson
Replacements Hunter for Garvey (46 mins); Chimbima for Walters (56 mins); Roberts for
Hunter (78 mins)
Scorers *Tries:* Garvey (2)   *Conversions:* Currin (2)
Referee D Reordan (USA)

12 October, Murrayfield
SCOTLAND 24 (2G 3PG 1DG)   IRELAND 15 (4PG 1DG)

SCOTLAND: A G Hastings; Stanger, S Hastings, Lineen, Tukalo; Chalmers,
Armstrong; Sole (*capt*), Allan, Burnell, Gray, Weir, Jeffrey, White, Calder
Replacement Shiel for Chalmers (43 mins)
Scorers *Tries:* Shiel, Armstrong   *Conversions:* G Hastings (2)
Penalty Goals: G Hastings (3)   *Dropped Goal:* Chalmers
IRELAND: Staples; Geoghegan, Curtis, Mullin, Crossan; Keyes, Saunders; Popplewell,
Smith, D C Fitzgerald, Lenihan, Francis, Matthews (*capt*), Robinson, Hamilton
Scorer *Penalty Goals:* Keyes (4)   *Dropped Goal:* Keyes
Referee F A Howard (England)

14 October, Belfast
JAPAN 52 (5G 2PG 4T)   ZIMBABWE 8 (2T)

JAPAN: Hosokawa; Masuho, Kutsuki, Hirao (*capt*), Yoshida; Matsuo, Horikoshi; Ota,
Kunda, Takura, Hayashi, Oyagi, Tifaga, Latu, Kajihara
Scorers *Tries:* Yoshida (2), Masuho (2), Kutsuki (2), Horikoshi, Tifaga, Matsuo
Conversions: Hosokawa (5)   *Penalty Goals:* Hosokawa (2)

ZIMBABWE: Currin (*capt*); Schultz, Tsimba, Letcher, Walters; Brown, MacMillan; Nicholls, Beattie, Garvey, Martin, Botha, Nguruve, Catterall, Dawson
Replacement Snyder for Garvey (70 mins)
Scorers *Tries:* Tsimba, Nguruve
Referee R Hourquet (France)

POOL 3	P	W	D	L	F	A	Pts
Australia	3	3	0	0	79	25	9
Western Samoa	3	2	0	1	54	34	7
Wales	3	1	0	2	32	61	5
Argentina	3	0	0	3	38	83	3

4 October, Llanelli
AUSTRALIA 32 (3G 2PG 2T)   **ARGENTINA 19** (1G 1PG 2DG 1T)

AUSTRALIA: Roebuck; Campese, Little, Horan, Egerton; Lynagh, Farr-Jones (*capt*); Daly, Kearns, McKenzie, Coker, McCall, Poidevin, Eales, Ofahengaue
Replacement Nucifora for Kearns (50 mins)
Scorers *Tries:* Campese (2), Horan (2), Kearns   *Conversions:* Lynagh (3)
Penalty Goals: Lynagh (2)
ARGENTINA: del Castillo; Teran, Laborde, Garcia Simon, Cuesta Silva; Arbizu, Camardon; Mendez, Le Fort, Cash, Sporleder, Llanes, Garreton (*capt*), Carreras, Santamarina *Replacement* Bosch for Le Fort (40 mins)
Scorers *Tries:* Teran (2)   *Conversion:* del Castillo   *Penalty Goal:* del Castillo
Dropped Goals: Arbizu (2)
Referee D J Bishop (New Zealand)

6 October, Cardiff Arms Park
WESTERN SAMOA 16 (1G 2PG 1T)   **WALES 13** (1G 1PG 1T)

WESTERN SAMOA: Aiolupo; Lima, Vaega, Bunce, Tagaloa; Bachop, Vaea; Fatialofa (*capt*), Toomalaiti, Alalatoa, Birtwistle, Keenan, Vaifale, Lam, Perelini
Scorers *Tries:* Vaega, Vaifale   *Conversion:* Vaea   *Penalty Goals:* Vaea (2)
WALES: Clement; I C Evans (*capt*), Gibbs, Hall, Emyr; Ring, Jones; Griffiths, Waters, Delaney, May, Moseley, Lewis, Davies, Collins *Replacements* Morris for May (29 mins); Rayer for Clement (48 mins); Jenkins for Collins (52 mins)
Scorers *Tries:* Emyr, Evans   *Conversion:* Ring   *Penalty Goal:* Ring
Referee P Robin (France)

9 October, Pontypool
AUSTRALIA 9 (3PG)   **WESTERN SAMOA 3** (1PG)

AUSTRALIA: Roebuck; Campese, Herbert, Horan, Flett; Lynagh, Farr-Jones (*capt*); Lillicrap, Kearns, Crowley, Coker, Cutler, Miller, Eales, Nasser *Replacement* Slattery for Farr-Jones (10 mins)
Scorer *Penalty Goals:* Lynagh (3)
WESTERN SAMOA: Aiolupo; Lima, Vaega, Bunce, Faamasino; Bachop, Vaea; Fatialofa (*capt*), Toomalatai, Alalatoa, Birtwistle, Keenan, Paramore, Perelini, Kaleopa
Replacement Tagaloa for Lima (52 mins)
Scorer *Penalty Goal:* Vaea
Referee E Morrison (England)

9 October, Cardiff Arms Park
WALES 16 (4PG 1T)   **ARGENTINA 7** (1PG 1T)
WALES: Rayer; I C Evans (*capt*), Hall, Gibbs, Emyr; Ring, Jones; Griffiths, Jenkins, Delaney, Arnold, Moseley, Lewis, P T Davies, Webster
Scorers *Try:* Arnold   *Penalty Goals:* Ring (3), Rayer

ARGENTINA: del Castillo; Teran, Laborde, Garcia Simon, Cuesta Silva; Arbizu, Camardon; Mendez, Le Fort, Molina, Sporleder, Llanes, Garreton (*capt*), Carreras, Santamarina
Scorers *Try:* Garcia Simon   *Penalty Goal:* del Castillo
Referee R Hourquet (France)

12 October, Cardiff Arms Park
AUSTRALIA 38 (4G 2PG 2T)   WALES 3 (1PG)

AUSTRALIA: Roebuck; Campese, Horan, Little, Egerton; Lynagh, Slattery; Daly, Kearns, McKenzie, McCall, Eales, Poidevin, Ofahengaue, Miller
Scorers *Tries:* Roebuck (2), Slattery, Campese, Lynagh, Horan   *Conversions:* Lynagh (4)
Penalty Goals: Lynagh (2)
WALES: Clement; I C Evans (*capt*), Hall, Gibbs, Emyr; Ring, Jones; Griffiths, Jenkins, Delaney, Arnold, Moseley, Lewis, P T Davies, Webster *Replacements* D W Evans for Emyr (75 mins); Rayer for Gibbs (79 mins)
Scorer *Penalty Goal:* Ring
Referee K H Lawrence (New Zealand)

13 October, Pontypridd
WESTERN SAMOA 35 (4G 1PG 2T)   ARGENTINA 12 (1G 2PG)

WESTERN SAMOA: Aiolupo; Lima, Vaega, Bunce, Tagaloa; Bachop, Vaea; Fatialofa (*capt*), Toomalatai, Alalatoa, Birtwistle, Keenan, Vaifale, Lam, Perelini
Scorers *Tries:* Tagaloa (2), Lima (2), Bunce, Bachop   *Conversions:* Vaea (4)
Penalty Goal: Vaea
ARGENTINA: Angaut; Teran, Laborde, Garcia Simon, Cuesta Silva; Arbizu, Camardon; Aguirre, Bosch, Cash, Buabse, Sporleder, Irarrazabal, Santamarina, Garreton (*capt*) *Replacements* Meson for Angaut (53 mins); Carreras for Irarrazabal (60 mins)
Scorers *Try:* Teran   *Conversion:* Arbizu   *Penalty Goals:* Laborde, Arbizu
Referee B Anderson (Scotland) *Replacement* J M Fleming (40 mins)

POOL 4	P	W	D	L	F	A	Pts
France	3	3	0	0	82	25	9
Canada	3	2	0	1	45	33	7
Romania	3	1	0	2	31	64	5
Fiji	3	0	0	3	27	63	3

4 October, Béziers
FRANCE 30 (1G 4PG 3T)   ROMANIA 3 (1PG)

FRANCE: Blanco (*capt*); Saint-André, Lacroix, Mesnel, Lagisquet; Camberabero, Galthié; Lascubé, Marocco, Ondarts, Cadieu, Roumat, Champ, Benazzi, Cabannes
Replacement Lafond for Lagisquet (70 mins)
Scorers *Tries:* penalty try, Saint-André, Roumat, Lafond   *Conversion:* Camberabero
Penalty Goals: Camberabero (4)
ROMANIA: Dumitru; Sasu, Lungu, Sava, Racean; Nichitean, Neaga; Leonte, Ion, Stan, Ciorascu, Cojocariu, Dinu, Dumitras (*capt*), Guranescu
Scorer *Penalty Goal:* Nichitean
Referee L J Peard (Wales)

5 October, Bayonne
CANADA 13 (3PG 1T)   FIJI 3 (1DG)

CANADA: D S Stewart; Palmer, C Stewart, Lecky, Gray; Rees, Tynan; Evans, Speirs, Jackart, Robertsen, Hadley, Charron, Ennis (*capt*), MacKinnon
Scorers *Try:* D S Stewart   *Penalty Goals:* Rees (3)

FIJI: Koroduadua; Seru, Aria, Nadruku, Lovo; Serevi, Tabulutu; Taga (*capt*), Naivilawasa, Naituivau, Savai, Domoni, Kato, Tawake, Dere *Replacement* Baleiwai for Naivilawasa (76 mins)
Scorer *Dropped Goal:* Serevi
Referee K V J Fitzgerald (Australia)

8 October, Grenoble
FRANCE 33 (3G 1PG 3T) FIJI 9 (1G 1PG)

FRANCE: Blanco (*capt*); Lafond, Sella, Mesnel, Saint-André; Camberabero, Galthié; Lascubé, Marocco, Ondarts, Cadieu, Roumat, Champ, Benazzi, Cabannes
Scorers *Tries:* Lafond (3), Sella (2), Camberabero *Conversions:* Camberabero (3)
Penalty Goal: Camberabero
FIJI: Koroduadua; Seru, Aria, Naisoro, Lovo; Serevi, Vosanibole; Taga (*capt*), Baleiwai, Vuli, Savai, Domoni, Naruma, Tawake, Dere *Replacements* Tabulutu for Vosanibole; Volavola for Taga; Kato for Domoni
Scorers *Try:* Naruma *Conversion:* Koroduadua *Penalty Goal:* Koroduadua
Referee W D Bevan (Wales)

9 October, Toulouse
CANADA 19 (1G 2PG 1DG 1T) ROMANIA 11 (1PG 2T)

CANADA: Wyatt (*capt*); Palmer, C Stewart, Lecky, D S Stewart; Rees, Graf; Evans, Svoboda, Jackart, van den Brink, Hadley, Breen, Ennis, MacKinnon
Scorers *Tries:* MacKinnon, Ennis *Conversion:* Wyatt *Penalty Goals:* Wyatt (2)
Dropped Goal: Rees
ROMANIA: Dumitru; Sasu, Lungu, Fulina, Racean; Nichitean, Neaga; Leonte, Ion, Stan, Ciorascu, Cojacariu, Dinu, Dumitras (*capt*), Doja *Replacements* Brinza for Doja (15 mins); Sava for Dumitru (33 mins); Vlad for Leonte (70 mins)
Scorers *Tries:* Lungu, Sasu *Penalty Goal:* Nichitean
Referee A R MacNeill (Australia)

12 October, Brive
ROMANIA 17 (1G 1PG 2T) FIJI 15 (2PG 3DG)

ROMANIA: Racean; Sasu, Lungu, Fulina, Colceriu; Nichitean, Neaga; Stan, Ion, Vlad, Ciorascu, Cojocariu, Dinu, Dumitras (*capt*), Marin *Replacement* Ivanciuc for Nichitean
Scorers *Tries:* Ion, Dumitras, Sasu *Penalty Goal:* Nichitean *Conversion:* Racean
FIJI: Turuva; Seru, Nadruku, Naisoro, Vonolagi; Rabaka, Tabulutu; Volavola, Baleiwai, Vuli, Savai, Nadolo, Tawake, Olsson, Dere (*capt*) *Replacements* Naituivau for Volavola; Naruma for Olsson
Scorers *Penalty Goals:* Turuva (2) *Dropped Goals:* Rabaka (2), Turuva
Referee O E Doyle (Ireland)

13 October, Agen
FRANCE 19 (1G 3PG 1T) CANADA 13 (2PG 1DG 1T)

FRANCE: Blanco (*capt*); Lafond, Sella, Mesnel, Saint-André; Camberabero, Galthié; Lascubé, Marocco, Ondarts, Cadieu, Roumat, Champ, Benazzi, Cabannes
Replacements Lacroix for Camberabero (40 mins); Sadourny for Sella (50 mins)
Scorers *Tries:* Lafond, Saint-André *Conversion:* Camberabero
Penalty Goals: Lacroix (2), Camberabero
CANADA: Wyatt (*capt*); Palmer, C Stewart, Woods, Gray; Rees, Tynan; Evans, Svoboda, Jackart, Robertsen, Hadley, Charron, Ennis, MacKinnon
Replacements van den Brink for Robertsen (25 mins); D S Stewart for Wyatt (45 mins)
Scorers *Try:* Wyatt *Dropped Goal:* Rees *Penalty Goals:* Wyatt, Rees
Referee S R Hilditch (Ireland)

KNOCKOUT STAGES

QUARTER-FINAL 19 October, Murrayfield
SCOTLAND 28 (2G 4PG 1T)   WESTERN SAMOA 6 (1PG 1DG)

SCOTLAND: A G Hastings; Stanger, S Hastings, Shiel, Tukalo; Chalmers, Armstrong; Sole (*capt*), Allan, Burnell, Gray, Weir, Jeffrey, White, Calder
Scorers *Tries:* Jeffrey (2), Stanger   *Conversions:* A G Hastings (2)
Penalty Goals: A G Hastings (4)
WESTERN SAMOA: Aiolupo; Lima, Vaega, Bunce, Tagaloa; Bachop, Vaea; Fatialofa (*capt*), Toomalatai, Alalatoa, Birtwistle, Ioane, Vaifale, Lam, Perelini
Scorers *Penalty Goal:* Vaea   *Dropped Goal:* Bachop
Referee W D Bevan (Wales)

QUARTER-FINAL 19 October, Parc des Princes
ENGLAND 19 (1G 3PG 1T)   FRANCE 10 (2PG 1T)

ENGLAND: Webb; Heslop, Carling (*capt*), Guscott, Underwood; Andrew, Hill; Leonard, Moore, Probyn, Ackford, Dooley, Skinner, Teague, Winterbottom
Scorers *Tries:* Underwood, Carling   *Conversion:* Webb   *Penalty Goals:* Webb (3)
FRANCE: Blanco (*capt*); Saint-André, Sella, Mesnel, Lafond; Lacroix, Galthié; Lascubé, Marocco, Ondarts, Cadieu, Roumat, Champ, Cecillon, Cabannes
Scorers *Try:* Lafond   *Penalty Goals:* Lacroix (2)
Referee D J Bishop (New Zealand)

QUARTER-FINAL 20 October, Lansdowne Road
AUSTRALIA 19 (2G 1PG 1T)   IRELAND 18 (1G 3PG 1DG)

AUSTRALIA: Roebuck; Campese, Little, Horan, Egerton; Lynagh, Farr-Jones (*capt*); Daly, Kearns, McKenzie, McCall, Eales, Poidevin, Ofahengaue, Miller
Replacement Slattery for Farr-Jones (18 mins)
Scorers *Tries:* Campese (2), Lynagh   *Conversions:* Lynagh (2)   *Penalty Goal:* Lynagh
IRELAND: Staples; Geoghegan, Mullin, Curtis, Clarke; Keyes, Saunders; Popplewell, Smith, D C Fitzgerald, Lenihan, Francis, Matthews (*capt*), Robinson, Hamilton
Scorers *Try:* Hamilton   *Conversion:* Keyes   *Penalty Goals:* Keyes (3)
Dropped Goal: Keyes
Referee J M Fleming (Scotland)

QUARTER-FINAL 20 October, Lille
NEW ZEALAND 29 (3G 1PG 2T)   CANADA 13 (1G 1PG 1T)

NEW ZEALAND: Timu; Kirwan, Innes, McCahill, Tuigamala; Fox, Bachop; McDowell, Fitzpatrick, Loe, I D Jones, G W Whetton (*capt*), A J Whetton, Brooke, Henderson
Scorers *Tries:* Timu (2), Kirwan, Brooke, McCahill   *Conversions:* Fox (3)
Penalty Goal: Fox
CANADA: Wyatt (*capt*); D S Stewart, C Stewart, Woods, Gray; Rees, Tynan; Evans, Speirs, Szabo, van den Brink, Hadley, Charron, Ennis, MacKinnon
Scorers *Tries:* Tynan, Charron   *Conversion:* Rees   *Penalty Goal:* Wyatt
Referee F A Howard (England)

SEMI-FINAL 26 October, Murrayfield
ENGLAND 9 (2PG 1DG)   SCOTLAND 6 (2PG)

ENGLAND: Webb; Halliday, Carling (*capt*), Guscott, Underwood; Andrew, Hill; Leonard, Moore, Probyn, Ackford, Dooley, Skinner, Teague, Winterbottom
Scorers *Penalty Goals:* Webb (2)   *Dropped Goal:* Andrew
SCOTLAND: A G Hastings; Stanger, S Hastings, Lineen, Tukalo; Chalmers, Armstrong; Sole (*capt*), Allan, Burnell, Gray, Weir, Jeffrey, White, Calder

Scorer *Penalty Goals:* A G Hastings (2)
Referee K V J Fitzgerald (Australia)

SEMI-FINAL 27 October, Lansdowne Road
AUSTRALIA 16 (1G 2PG 1T)   NEW ZEALAND 6 (2PG)

AUSTRALIA: Roebuck; Campese, Little, Horan, Egerton; Lynagh, Farr-Jones (*capt*);
Daly, Kearns, McKenzie, McCall, Eales, Poidevin, Coker, Ofahengaue
Scorers *Tries:* Campese, Horan   *Conversion:* Lynagh   *Penalty Goals:* Lynagh (2)
NEW ZEALAND: Crowley; Kirwan, Innes, McCahill, Timu; Fox, Bachop;
McDowell, Fitzpatrick, Loe, I D Jones, G W Whetton (*capt*), A J Whetton, Brooke,
Carter
Scorer *Penalty Goals:* Fox (2)
Referee J M Fleming (Scotland)

THIRD-FOURTH PLAY-OFF 30 October, Cardiff Arms Park
NEW ZEALAND 13 (3PG 1T)   SCOTLAND 6 (2PG)

NEW ZEALAND: Wright; Kirwan, Innes, Little, Tuigamala; Preston, Bachop;
McDowell, Fitzpatrick, Loe, I D Jones, G W Whetton (*capt*), Earl, Brooke, M N Jones
Replacement Philpott for Tuigamala (40 mins)
Scorers *Try:* Little   *Penalty Goals:* Preston (3)
SCOTLAND: A G Hastings; Stanger, S Hastings, Lineen, Tukalo; Chalmers,
Armstrong; Sole (*capt*), Allan, Burnell, Gray, Weir, Jeffrey, White, Calder
Replacement Dods for Stanger (47 mins)
Scorer *Penalty Goals:* A G Hastings (2)
Referee S R Hilditch (Ireland)

FINAL 2 November, Twickenham
AUSTRALIA 12 (1G 2PG)   ENGLAND 6 (2PG)

AUSTRALIA: Roebuck; Campese, Little, Horan, Egerton; Lynagh, Farr-Jones (*capt*);
Daly, Kearns, McKenzie, McCall, Eales, Poidevin, Coker, Ofahengaue
Scorers *Try:* Daly   *Conversion:* Lynagh   *Penalty Goals:* Lynagh (2)
ENGLAND: Webb; Halliday, Carling (*capt*), Guscott, Underwood; Andrew, Hill;
Leonard, Moore, Probyn, Ackford, Dooley, Skinner, Teague, Winterbottom
Scorer *Penalty Goals:* Webb (2)
Referee W D Bevan (Wales)

TOP SCORERS 1992-93

Peter Jackson *Daily Mail*

David Johnson played his first match for Gosforth as a 15-year-old schoolboy. He was still there 23 seasons later, potting the goals which took his home-town club into the First Division. Now that they are up there among the élite, complete with the Newcastle prefix, it remains to be seen whether Tyneside can afford to give their prodigious fly-half the luxury of retirement for no better reason than that he will be 38 some time in November.

One of few contemporary players to start in senior rugby the season before the 1971 Lions had been heard of, Johnson has now topped 5,000 points. The figure would have been even larger but for the odd knee injury. The worst blow coincided with England picking him for the only time, for the uncapped tour of the United States in 1982. The damage, 'à la Gazza', put paid to his chances of a cap – not that Johnson expected one. 'Playing for England B and the Northern Division was about my limit,' he says. 'I could do the business and not look out of place. You have to be a ten-out-of-ten player for international rugby. Maybe I was a nine-out-of-ten . . .'

Last season he was out on his own, the only senior player in Britain or Ireland to score 400 points for the season. The rest, among them the Liley brothers, were some way behind.

Ieuan Evans' flair for the big occasion ensured he finished the domestic season as the nation's joint leading try-scorer before resuming in New Zealand with the Lions. Two more Welsh Cup final tries, in the SWALEC Trophy thriller against Neath, brought Llanelli's distinguished wing level with one from the nether regions of the Courage Leagues. Steve Titcombe's highly consistent finishing helped Sudbury climb into the Third Division.

If it hadn't been for a troublesome finale to the season, Nigel Walker might not have been seen for dust. Instead the fastest wing in the game had to be content with 25 at a rate of more than one a game, not bad for his first season as an ex-sprint hurdler.

POINTS

404 – David Johnson (Newcastle Gosforth); **365** – Andy Green (Exeter); **355** – John Liley (Leicester); **339** – Colin Stephens (Llanelli); **335** – Keith McGarry (Dungannon); **324** – Dave Barrett (West of Scotland); **321** – Rob Liley (Wakefield); **316** – Adrian Davies (Cardiff); **310** – Steve Dyble (Sudbury); **308** – Neil Jenkins (Pontypridd); **307** – Mike Hamlin (London Welsh); **305** – Simon Hogg (Clifton); **304** – Martin Livesey (Richmond); **297** – Mark Rodgers (Sheffield); **294** – George O'Sullivan (Highfield); **287** – Alastair Donaldson (Currie); **286** – Michael Corcoran (London Irish); **279** – John Stabler (West Hartlepool); **277** – Murray Thompson (Stewart's-Melville FP); **276** – Peter Rutledge (Otley); **275** – Simon Pinnington (Stourbridge), Richard Mills (Walsall); **274** – Peter Smith (High Wycombe); **270** – Mark Tainton (Bristol); **264** – Aled Williams

David Johnson of Newcastle Gosforth, leading points-scorer in 1992-93 with 404. He is one of few players to have topped 5,000 points in his career.

(Swansea); **260** – Andy Halford (Lydney); **259** – Kenny Smith (Garryowen); **256** – Aidan O'Halloran (Young Munster); **254** – David Richards (Lichfield); **251** – John Bland (Durham City); **249** – Paul Thatcher (Weston-super-Mare); **242** – Paul Grayson (Waterloo); **231** – Jimmy Morris (Llanharan); **221** – Jonathan Webb (Bath); **216** – Luc Evans (Bridgend); **214** – Paul Thorburn (Neath), Andy Higgin (Liverpool St Helens); **207** – Jonathan Callard (Bath); **203** – Jonathan Newton (Dundee HSFP); **201** – Rowen Shepherd (Edinburgh Academicals); **200** – Murry Walker (Boroughmuir); **197** – Kevin Thomas (Redruth); **196** – Guy Gregory (Nottingham), Darren Chapman (Camborne); **194** – Paul Challinor (Harlequins); **193** – Mark Thomas (Dunvant); **190** – Stewart Laing (Ballymena), Adam Carr (Pontypool); **188** – Andy Finnie (Bedford); **187** – Andrew Hay (Ayr); **186** – Graeme Aitchison (Kelso), Kenny Halliday (Grangemouth); **181** – John Mitchell (Kirkcaldy); **176** – Gregor McKechnie (Jedforest); **175** – John Graves (Rosslyn Park), Cliff Livingstone (Musselburgh); **174** – Jonathan Westwood (Newport); **172** – Erin Corsey (Clarkston); **170** – Ben Childs (Tenby Utd); **166** – Richard Angell (Coventry), Phil Jee (Sale); **162** – David Love (Aberavon).

TRIES

32 – Ieuan Evans (Llanelli), Steve Titcombe (Sudbury); **28** – Mark Sephton (Liverpool St Helens); **26** – Dave Catchpole (Southend); **25** – Nigel Walker (Cardiff); **24** – Garry Parker (Melrose); **23** – Wayne Proctor (Llanelli), John Hewes (High Wycombe); **22** – Doug Woodman (Clifton), Dale Lyon (Grangemouth); **21** – Steve Ford (Cardiff), Shaun White (Pontypool), James Reynolds (Neath), Andrew Lewis (Newport); **20** – Mark Moncrieff (Gala); **19** – Jonathan Callard (Bath), Keith Suddon (Hawick), Robbie Smith (Boroughmuir); **18** – Tony Clark (Morley), Richard Porter (Edinburgh Academicals), John McKenzie (Stewart's-Melville FP), Alan Drysdale (Wigtownshire); **17** – Jon Eagle (Leeds), Gary Quilligan (Garryowen), David Drysdale (Wigtownshire), Billy O'Shea (Shannon); **16** – Steve Hackney (Leicester), Peter Smith (High Wycombe), Mark Rodgers (Sheffield), Steve Bowling (Neath); **15** – Tony Swift (Bath), Cameron Little (Glasgow High/Kelvinside), Eddie Saunders (Rugby), Michael O'Riordan (Sunday's Well), Harvey Thorneycroft (Northampton), Kelvin Smithman (Camborne), Mickey Bell (London Welsh), Andy Maunder (Exeter), John Price (Clarkston); **14** – Neil Boobyer (Llanelli), John Pawson (Glasgow Academicals), Simon Geoghegan (London Irish), Simon Davies (Swansea), Mark Chatterton (Exeter), Chris Johns (Askeans), Matt Hoskins (Leeds), Jimmy Turnbull (Gala), Henry Murray (Heriot's FP), James Adams (Kilmarnock), Simon Burns (Edinburgh Academicals), Steve Baker (Harrogate), David Osborne (Askeans), Barry Evans (Coventry), Brian Hay-Smith (Edinburgh Academicals); **13** – Andrew Harriman (Harlequins), Derek Stark (Boroughmuir), Frank Packman (Northampton), Graham Mackay (Glasgow Academicals), Jonathan Sleightholme (Wakefield), Alan Linton (Selkirk), Kerry Morley (Wakefield), John Mitchell (Kirkcaldy).

SCOTLAND AND IRELAND GATHER STRENGTH: PROBLEMS OF SCALE HOLD BACK THE GAME

WOMEN'S RUGBY 1992-93
Alice Cooper

Ten years after the establishment of the WRFU, the union can now proudly boast over 170 clubs and is ever-growing. The West Country has been a particular expansion area. It was certainly an evolutionary season – probably more changed than in any previous season in the women's game. This has happened for several reasons. First the standard of play at the top of the game has made a huge leap forward. Certainly, the English national team are working towards creating a viable challenge to the Americans in the 1994 World Cup. More players are being brought in (sometimes without qualifying through the proper channels), and there are now four coaches/selectors. The new-look team left out such established players as Debbie Francis and Maxine Edwards, who both recently had babies. No thought was given to long-term squad-building using the experience of such players, and Francis has taken her experience away to Scotland.

However, the pressures of playing at the top – time out for fixtures, training and so on – are making unbelievable demands on many players who are still trying to hold down careers. A change of attitude from employers would be welcomed – surely, an international athlete on the staff may benefit them.

For the first time, Scotland and Ireland emerged as international playing nations. They are still some way behind the English, but this was undoubtedly a major step. They met at Edinburgh Academicals on 14 February, a match which Scotland won 10-0. Next season will see the creation of Exiles sides for both countries to create comprehensive national trials.

Wales maintained their standard despite having to wrangle with domestic problems which involved administrative difficulties. They also had yet another change in coach (with the promotion of Darryl Edwards), which must cause continuity problems for the players. Their annual meeting with England at Northampton resulted in another defeat, by 23-5.

An important feature of the season was the further development of youth sides, at Maidstone, Richmond and Wimbledon, amongst others. Also, schools nationwide are starting to allow girls to play rugby. This is an excellent step forward with so many girls coming up through the minis sections. At club level, players are starting to move between clubs at the top. England captain Karen Almond left Wasps for Saracens, internationals Paula George and Giselle Prangnell joined

Wasps from Richmond and Nicky Ponsford moved to Clifton from Waterloo. In addition, an increasing number of guest players from other international teams gained experience in England.

One less positive development is the nepotism currently raising its ugly head. Right up to international level, there is a worrying trend for wives or girlfriends to be selected by coaches irrespective of their ability or fitness. This is surely not healthy, and if nothing else, it lowers standards by keeping worthier players out of teams.

INTERNATIONAL RESULTS

9 October: England Select 27, American Grizzlies 0 **14 February:** England 23, Wales 5; Scotland 10 Ireland 0 **22 March:** Wales A 3, England A 10 **3 April:** Scotland 12, North 10 **18 April:** England Select 27, Nomads 0

Divisionals: *The divisional matches had a new system as national trials. Regional matches were played and the best of the regional players then joined established national players in the divisionals. The aim is to give less experienced players, who would normally be kept out by an established player, the chance of playing above club level.*
Winners: Midlands

Regional Results: North-West 17, South-East 17; London 72, East Midlands 0; Scottish 36, North-West 0; Scottish 24, North-East 0
UAU Cup final: Loughborough University 26, Cardiff IHE 0
National Cup: Saracens 70, Waterloo 0
Scottish Cup: Edinburgh Academicals 5, Edinburgh University 0
BSSA Cup winners: Cheltenham & Gloucester College
Plate Winners: Portsmouth University
London Sunday Rugby Festival final: Richmond 19, Saracens 0
National Sevens: Saracens

WRFU NATIONAL LEAGUES

Saracens emerged as the super club winning the First Division and the National Cup. Wasps narrowly lost the League, while Richmond came a poor third when compared to previous years.

In Division Two, Cardiff had an outstanding year and deserve their promotion, while Eton Manor have raised their standard from scratch in just three seasons to come second.

Division 1

	P	W	D	L	F	A	Pts
Saracens	14	13	0	1	569	59	26
Wasps	14	12	1	1	292	75	25
Richmond	14	10	1	3	268	75	21
Clifton	14	5	1	8	106	203	11
Lampeter	14	5	0	*9	128	173	10
Blackheath	14	4	0	10	131	303	8
Waterloo	14	4	0	10	91	366	8
Leeds	14	1	1	12	26	357	3

* Lampeter defaulted 2 fixtures
Relegated: Leeds, Waterloo.

Division 2

	P	W	D	L	F	A	Pts
Cardiff	12	11	0	1	339	58	22
Eton Manor	12	10	0	2	238	81	20
Richmond II	12	6	1	5	205	159	13
Medway	11	4	1	*6	127	85	9
Bury	11	4	0	*7	50	218	8
Sale	10	3	0	7	49	147	6
Northampton	10	0	0	10	36	296	0

* Medway defaulted fixture
Promoted: Cardiff, Eton Manor. Relegated: Northampton.

Division 3 North

	P	W	D	L	F	A	Pts
York	4	4	0	0	91	0	12
Novocastrians	4	3	0	1	106	15	10
Congleton	4	2	0	2	97	103	8
Waterloo II	4*	1	0	1	0	34	4
Manchester	4*	0	0	3	5	147	3

* Waterloo II defaulted 2 games, Manchester 1

Division 3 London

	P	W	D	L	F	A	Pts
Wasps II	9	7	1	1	163	25	24
St Albans	9	7	1	1	145	39	24
Teddington	9	7	0	2	0	138	24
Southend	9*	6	0	2	86	39	20
Saracens II	9	4	1	4	237	52	18
Wimbledon	9	3	3	3	106	109	18
Swindon SM	9*	4	1	3	246	173	17
Littlemore	9*	1	1	6	60	223	11
O Abbotsonians	9*	2	0	4	5	182	10
Northolt	9*	0	0	5	0	373	5

* Defaulted matches
Division 3 winners: Wasps II.
Promoted in play-offs: Wasps II.

Division 3 Midlands East

	P	W	D	L	F	A	Pts
Witham	6	5	1	0	83	20	17
Sudbury	6	5	0	1	246	17	16
Norwich	6	4	1	1	150	41	15
Bury St Ed	6*	3	0	2	23	64	11
Shelford	6	2	0	4	107	107	10
Crusaders	6*	1	0	4	10	191	7
Colchester	6*	0	0	4	0	179	4

* Defaulted matches

Division 3 South-East

	P	W	D	L	F	A	Pts
Crawley	9	9	0	0	362	15	27
Staines	9	8	0	1	201	61	25
Richmond III	9	6	0	3	164	119	21
London Welsh	9	6	0	3	96	150	21
Alton	9	4	1	4	102	67	18
Camberley	9	3	0	6	91	284	15
Nomads	9	3	1	4	87	108	15
Hove	9	3	0	5	42	235	14
Sevenoaks	9*	1	0	3	7	214	6
Blackheath II	9*	1	0	2	10	31	5

* Defaulted matches

Division 3 Midlands West

	P	W	D	L	F	A	Pts
Selly Oak	7	6	0	1	184	12	19
N'pton OS	7	6	0	1	132	25	19
O Leamingtons	7	6	0	1	125	24	19
Sutton Coldfd	7	4	0	3	118	44	15
Nottingham	7	3	0	4	56	110	13
Shipston	7	2	0	5	61	201	11
Newbold on A	7	1	0	6	30	196	9
King's Norton	7*	0	0	5	7	186	5

* Defaulted matches
Promoted in play-offs: Northampton Old Scouts.

CLUBS SECTION

Records of most-capped players are complete up to 30 April 1993

ENGLAND
Bath

Year of formation 1865
Ground Recreation Ground, London Road, Bath   Tel: Bath (0225) 425192
Colours Blue, white and black
Most capped player D M B Sole (Scotland) 44 caps
Captain 1992-93 R A Robinson
Courage Leagues Div 1 *Winners* **Pilkington Cup** Lost 8-9 to Waterloo (3rd round)

League Record 1992-93

Date	Venue	Opponents	Result	Scorers
19 Sept	H	Harlequins	22-6	*T:* Guscott *C:* Webb *PG:* Webb (5)
26 Sept	H	London Irish	42-19	*T:* Ubogu (2), de Glanville, Clarke, Barnes *C:* Webb (4) *PG:* Webb (3)
10 Oct	A	Northampton	8-11	*T:* Clarke *PG:* Barnes
24 Oct	H	Orrell	39-3	*T:* Hall (2), Hill, Webb, Redman *C:* Webb (4) *PG:* Webb (2)
31 Oct	A	Bristol	31-8	*T:* Swift (2), Clarke, Webb *C:* Webb (4) *PG:* Webb
21 Nov	A	Leicester	13-3	*T:* Adebayo, Redman *PG:* Webb
9 Jan	H	Rugby	61-7	*T:* Barnes (2), Adebayo (2), O'Leary, Robinson, Redman, Webb, Guscott *C:* Webb (5) *PG:* Webb (2)
13 Feb	A	Gloucester	20-0	*T:* Swift *PG:* Webb (5)

Action from a bitter and crucial match as Andy Robinson of Bath, the eventual champions, falls to the challenges of Rob Andrew and Kevin Dunn of Wasps, the eventual runners-up, in Courage League Division 1.

13 Mar	H	Wasps	22-11	*T:* Guscott *C:* Webb *PG:* Webb (4) *DG:* Barnes
27 Mar	A	West Hartlepool	38-10	*T:* Barnes (3), Callard (2) *C:* Callard, Barnes *PG:* Barnes (3)
3 Apr	H	London Scottish	40-6	*T:* Swift, Barnes, Ubogu, Clarke, Callard, de Glanville *C:* Barnes, Callard *PG:* Barnes (2)
24 Apr	A	Saracens	19-13	*T:* Callard (2) *PG:* Barnes (3)

Bedford

Year of formation 1886
Ground Goldington Road, Bedford   Tel: Bedford (0234) 354619 or 359160
Colours Hoops in Oxford and Cambridge blue
Most capped player D P Rogers (England) 34 caps
Captain 1992-93 P Alston
Courage Leagues Div 2 7th *relegated* **Pilkington Cup** Lost 14-27 to Rugby (3rd round)

League Record 1992-93

Date	Venue	Opponents	Result	Scorers
19 Sept	A	Moseley	9-9	*PG:* Finnie (3)
26 Sept	A	Wakefield	3-27	*PG:* Finnie
3 Oct	H	Richmond	22-16	*T:* Rennell *C:* Marment *PG:* Marment (5)
10 Oct	A	Rosslyn Park	16-13	*T:* Taylor *C:* Marment *PG:* Marment (2) *DG:* Jones
24 Oct	H	Fylde	24-12	*T:* Chandler, Taylor *C:* Marment *PG:* Marment (4)
21 Nov	H	Sale	9-9	*PG:* Marment (3)
9 Jan	A	Waterloo	8-28	*T:* Whetstone *PG:* Finnie
13 Feb	H	Nottingham	15-9	*PG:* Finnie (5)
13 Mar	A	Blackheath	12-16	*T:* Garrett, Rennell *C:* Finnie
27 Mar	H	Coventry	30-15	*T:* Finnie, Howe *C:* Finnie *PG:* Finnie (4) *DG:* Finnie (2)
3 Apr	A	Newcastle Gos	13-19	*T:* Allen *C:* Finnie *PG:* Finnie (2)
24 Apr	H	Morley	25-10	*T:* Whetstone, Rennell, Garratt *C:* Finnie (2) *PG:* Finnie (2)

Blackheath

Year of formation 1858
Ground Rectory Field, Blackheath, London SE3   Tel: 081-858 1578 and 858 3677
Colours Red and black hoops
Most capped player C N Lowe (England) 25 caps
Captain 1992-93 R Howe
Courage Leagues Div 2 10th *relegated* **Pilkington Cup** Lost 3-72 to Harlequins (3rd round)

League Record 1992-93

Date	Venue	Opponents	Result	Scorers
19 Sept	H	Wakefield	9-9	*PG:* Eagle (2) *DG:* Eagle
26 Sept	H	Nottingham	5-46	*T:* Griffiths
10 Oct	A	Coventry	15-38	*T:* McIntyre, Mercer *C:* Mercer *PG:* Mercer
24 Oct	H	Newcastle Gos	9-12	*PG:* Eagle (3)
31 Oct	A	Morley	23-8	*T:* McIntyre (2) *C:* Eagle (2) *PG:* Eagle (3)
21 Nov	A	Richmond	23-13	*T:* Eagle, Griffiths *C:* Eagle (2) *PG:* Eagle (3)
9 Jan	H	Rosslyn Park	18-14	*PG:* Eagle (6)
13 Feb	A	Fylde	9-9	*PG:* Eagle (3)
13 Mar	H	Bedford	16-12	*T:* McIntyre (2) *PG:* Eagle (2)

27 Mar	A	Moseley	6-23	*PG:* Eagle *DG:* Eagle
3 Apr	H	Sale	3-20	*PG:* Eagle
24 Apr	A	Waterloo	6-27	*PG:* Eagle (2)

Bristol

Year of formation 1888
Ground Memorial Ground, Filton Ave, Horfield, Bristol   Tel: Bristol (0272) 514448
Colours Navy blue and white
Most capped player J V Pullin (England) 42 caps
Captain 1992-93 D J Eves
Courage Leagues Div 1 6th **Pilkington Cup** Lost 15-20 to Saracens (3rd round)

League Record 1992-93

Date	Venue	Opponents	Result	Scorers
19 Sept	A	Northampton	6-16	*PG:* May (2)
26 Sept	H	West Hartlepool	19-11	*T:* Knibbs, Hull *PG:* May (3)
3 Oct	A	London Scottish	11-8	*T:* Lloyd *PG:* Tainton (2)
10 Oct	H	Saracens	12-7	*PG:* Tainton (4)
24 Oct	A	London Irish	7-9	*T:* Morgan *C:* Tainton
31 Oct	H	Bath	8-31	*T:* Johnston *PG:* Tainton
21 Nov	H	Orrell	23-11	*T:* Wring, pen try *C:* Tainton (2) *PG:* Tainton (3)
13 Feb	A	Harlequins	0-16	
13 Mar	H	Leicester	15-10	*T:* Barrow, Bracken *C:* Tainton *PG:* Tainton
27 Mar	A	Rugby	32-21	*T:* Eves (3), Waghorn *C:* Tainton (3) *PG:* Tainton (2)
3 Apr	H	Gloucester	9-22	*PG:* Tainton (3)
24 Apr	A	Wasps	6-7	*PG:* Tainton (2)

Coventry

Year of formation 1874
Ground Coundon Road, Coventry   Tel: Coventry (0203) 591274 and 593399
Colours Navy and white
Most capped player D J Duckham (England) 36 caps
Captain 1992-93 B Evans
Courage Leagues Div 2 11th *relegated* **Pilkington Cup** Lost 14-28 to Nottingham (3rd round)

League Record 1992-93

Date	Venue	Opponents	Result	Scorers
19 Sept	H	Morley	41-3	*T:* Gee (3), Hickey, M Thomas *C:* M Thomas (5) *PG:* M Thomas (2)
26 Sept	H	Waterloo	6-32	*PG:* M Thomas (2)
3 Oct	A	Nottingham	10-16	*T:* Evans (2)
10 Oct	H	Blackheath	38-15	*T:* Jones, P Thomas, Hickey, Mackie *C:* Angell (3) *PG:* Angell (4)
31 Oct	A	Newcastle Gos	3-26	*PG:* Angell
21 Nov	A	Wakefield	0-8	
9 Jan	H	Richmond	13-18	*T:* Hickey *C:* Harwood *PG:* Angell (2)
13 Feb	A	Rosslyn Park	10-32	*T:* Evans *C:* Harwood *PG:* Angell
13 Mar	H	Fylde	37-10	*T:* P Thomas (2), Barden, Turner, Curtis *C:* Angell (3) *PG:* Angell (2)
27 Mar	A	Bedford	15-30	*T:* Evans, Harwood *C:* M Thomas *DG:* Angell
3 Apr	H	Moseley	19-22	*T:* Hickey *C:* Angell *PG:* Angell (2) *DG:* Lakie (2)
24 Apr	A	Sale	0-24	

Fylde

Year of formation 1919
Ground Woodlands Memorial Ground, Blackpool Road, Lytham St Annes
Tel: Lytham (0253) 734733
Colours Claret, gold and white
Most capped player W A Dooley (England) 55 caps
Captain 1992-93 M Jackson
Courage Leagues Div 2 12th *relegated* **Pilkington Cup** Lost 6-19 to Moseley (3rd round)

League Record 1992-93

Date	Venue	Opponents	Result	Scorers
19 Sept	A	Sale	3-51	*PG:* Jackson
26 Sept	A	Richmond	6-29	*PG:* Jackson (2)
3 Oct	H	Rosslyn Park	9-22	*PG:* Jackson (3)
24 Oct	A	Bedford	12-24	*PG:* Jackson (3) *DG:* Gough
31 Oct	H	Moseley	15-15	*T:* Gough, Nicholson *C:* Jackson *PG:* Jackson
21 Nov	H	Waterloo	14-15	*T:* Jackson *PG:* I Barclay (3)
9 Jan	A	Nottingham	8-19	*T:* Gough *PG:* I Barclay
13 Feb	H	Blackheath	9-9	*PG:* I Barclay (3)
13 Mar	A	Coventry	10-37	*T:* Nicholson *C:* I Barclay *PG:* I Barclay
27 Mar	H	Newcastle Gos	5-32	*T:* Hanavan
3 Apr	A	Morley	10-10	*T:* Moffatt, I Barclay
24 Apr	H	Wakefield	7-27	*T:* Russell *C:* Taylor

Gloucester

Year of formation 1873
Ground Kingsholm, Kingsholm Road, Gloucester   Tel: Gloucester (0452) 520901
Colours Cherry and white
Most capped player A T Voyce (England)/M C Teague (England) 27 caps
Captain 1992-93 I R Smith
Courage Leagues Div 1 5th **Pilkington Cup** Lost 10-13 to Newcastle Gosforth (3rd round)

League Record 1992-93

Date	Venue	Opponents	Result	Scorers
19 Sept	A	London Scottish	3-8	*PG:* T Smith
26 Sept	A	Leicester	21-22	*T:* Perrins, Hannaford *C:* T Smith *PG:* T Smith (3)
3 Oct	H	Rugby	21-12	*T:* Morgan, pen try *C:* T Smith *PG:* T Smith (3)
24 Oct	A	Wasps	9-14	*PG:* T Smith (3)
31 Oct	H	West Hartlepool	6-21	*PG:* T Smith, Matthews
21 Nov	H	Saracens	19-5	*T:* West, Morgan *PG:* Roberts (3)
9 Jan	A	London Irish	18-6	*T:* Roberts, pen try *C:* Roberts *PG:* Roberts (2)
13 Feb	H	Bath	0-20	
13 Mar	A	Northampton	21-16	*T:* Holford, Morris *C:* Beech *PG:* T Smith (2), Beech
27 Mar	H	Orrell	8-13	*T:* T Smith *PG:* T Smith
3 Apr	A	Bristol	22-9	*T:* Caskie, T Smith, Phillips *C:* Beech (2) *PG:* Beech
24 Apr	H	Harlequins	25-5	*T:* Morris, Fowke, T Smith *C:* T Smith (2) *PG:* T Smith (2)

Harlequins

Year of formation 1866
Ground Stoop Memorial Ground, Craneford Way, Twickenham, Middlesex
Tel: 081-892 0822
Colours Light blue, magenta, chocolate, French grey, black and light green
Most capped player P J Winterbottom (England) 58 caps
Captain 1992-93 P J Winterbottom
Courage Leagues Div 1 8th **Pilkington Cup** Lost 16-23 to Leicester (final)

League Record 1992-93

Date	Venue	Opponents	Result	Scorers
19 Sept	A	Bath	6-22	*PG:* Pears, Challinor
26 Sept	H	Wasps	13-15	*T:* Evans *C:* Thresher *PG:* Thresher (2)
3 Oct	A	West Hartlepool	12-9	*PG:* Challinor (4)
10 Oct	H	London Scottish	22-22	*T:* Carling, Sheasby, Wedderburn *C:* Thresher (2) *PG:* Thresher
24 Oct	A	Saracens	18-3	*T:* Glenister, Thresher *C:* Thresher *PG:* Thresher (2)
31 Oct	H	London Irish	47-24	*T:* Glenister (2), Challinor, Carling, Harriman, Thresher *C:* Thresher (4) *PG:* Thresher (3)
21 Nov	H	Northampton	7-12	*T:* Challinor *C:* Thresher
9 Jan	A	Orrell	16-18	*T:* Thresher, Wedderburn *PG:* Challinor (2)
13 Feb	H	Bristol	16-0	*T:* Carling, Sheasby *PG:* Challinor *DG:* Challinor
27 Mar	A	Leicester	0-23	
3 Apr	H	Rugby	35-14	*T:* Alexander (2), Winterbottom (2), Challinor *C:* Challinor (2) *PG:* Challinor (2)
24 Apr	A	Gloucester	5-25	*T:* Wedderburn

Leicester

Year of formation 1880
Ground Welford Road, Leicester Tel: Leicester (0533) 540276 and 541607
Colours Scarlet, green and white
Most capped player R Underwood (England) 60 caps
Captain 1992-93 J Wells
Courage Leagues Div 1 3rd **Pilkington Cup** *Winners* Beat Harlequins 23-16 (final)

League Record 1992-93

Date	Venue	Opponents	Result	Scorers
19 Sept	A	London Irish	30-14	*T:* Liley, T Underwood, Richardson *C:* Liley (3) *PG:* Liley (3)
26 Sept	H	Gloucester	22-21	*T:* Hackney, Kardooni, Richardson *C:* Liley (2) *PG:* Liley
3 Oct	A	Wasps	13-14	*T:* Potter *C:* Liley *PG:* Liley (2)
10 Oct	H	West Hartlepool	21-8	*T:* Potter, Liley *C:* Liley *PG:* Liley (3)
24 Oct	A	London Scottish	18-11	*T:* Poole, T Underwood *C:* Liley *PG:* Liley (2)
31 Oct	H	Saracens	30-3	*T:* Cockerill, R Underwood, pen try *C:* Liley (3) *PG:* Liley (2) *DG:* Harris
21 Nov	H	Bath	3-13	*PG:* Liley
9 Jan	A	Northampton	13-12	*T:* Back *C:* Liley *PG:* Liley (2)
13 Feb	H	Orrell	9-0	*PG:* Liley (3)
13 Mar	A	Bristol	10-15	*T:* Kardooni *C:* Liley *PG:* Liley
27 Mar	H	Harlequins	23-0	*T:* Richardson, Povoas *C:* Liley (2) *PG:* Liley (2) *DG:* Harris
24 Apr	A	Rugby	28-5	*T:* T Underwood, R Underwood, Grewcock *C:* Harris (2) *PG:* Kilford *DG:* Harris (2)

London Irish

Year of formation 1898
Ground The Avenue, Sunbury-on-Thames, Middlesex   Tel: Sunbury (0932) 783034
Colours Emerald green
Most capped player K W Kennedy (Ireland) 45 caps
Captain 1992-93 J E Staples
Courage Leagues Div 1 7th **Pilkington Cup** Lost 8-13 to West Hartlepool (3rd round)

League Record 1992-93

Date	Venue	Opponents	Result	Scorers
19 Sept	H	Leicester	14-30	*T:* Corcoran *PG:* Corcoran (3)
26 Sept	A	Bath	19-42	*T:* Geoghegan *C:* Corcoran *PG:* Corcoran (2) *DG:* Hennessey, Burke
3 Oct	H	Northampton	12-3	*PG:* Corcoran (4)
10 Oct	A	Orrell	12-8	*PG:* Corcoran (4)
24 Oct	H	Bristol	9-7	*PG:* Corcoran *DG:* Burke (2)
31 Oct	A	Harlequins	24-47	*T:* Young, Curtis *C:* Corcoran *PG:* Corcoran (4)
21 Nov	A	Rugby	14-0	*T:* Geoghegan *PG:* Corcoran (2) *DG:* Burke
9 Jan	H	Gloucester	6-18	*PG:* Corcoran *DG:* Burke
13 Feb	A	Wasps	9-18	*PG:* Corcoran (3)
13 Mar	H	West Hartlepool	25-13	*T:* Collins, Corcoran, Geoghegan *C:* Corcoran (2) *PG:* Corcoran *DG:* Burke
27 Mar	A	London Scottish	21-28	*PG:* Corcoran (6), Burke
3 Apr	H	Saracens	10-9	*T:* Halpin *C:* Burke *PG:* Burke

London Scottish

Year of formation 1878
Ground Richmond Athletic Ground, Richmond, Surrey   Tel: 081-332 2473
Colours Blue jersey with red lion crest
Most capped player A G Hastings (Scotland) 46 caps
Captain 1992-93 R I Cramb
Courage Leagues Div 1 10th *relegated* **Pilkington Cup** Lost 11-20 to Leicester (3rd round)

League Record 1992-93

Date	Venue	Opponents	Result	Scorers
19 Sept	H	Gloucester	8-3	*T:* Eriksson *PG:* Appleson
26 Sept	A	Orrell	10-13	*T:* Mair *C:* Appleson *PG:* Appleson
3 Oct	H	Bristol	8-11	*T:* Morrison *PG:* Appleson
10 Oct	A	Harlequins	22-22	*T:* Cronin, White *PG:* Grecian (3), Appleson
24 Oct	H	Leicester	11-18	*T:* Burnell *PG:* Appleson *DG:* Cramb
31 Oct	A	Rugby	45-20	*T:* Appleson (2), Harrold, Troup, Renwick, Scott, White *C:* Appleson (2) *PG:* Appleson (2)
21 Nov	A	Wasps	6-10	*PG:* Grecian (2)
9 Jan	H	West Hartlepool	10-15	*T:* Wichary *C:* Wichary *PG:* Wichary
13 Mar	A	Saracens	17-41	*T:* Millard (2) *C:* Wichary (2) *PG:* Grecian
27 Mar	H	London Irish	28-21	*T:* Renwick (2), Leckie *C:* Grecian (2) *PG:* Grecian (2) *DG:* Cramb
3 Apr	A	Bath	6-40	*PG:* Grecian (2)
24 Apr	H	Northampton	21-34	*T:* Renwick, Scott, Appleson *PG:* Grecian (2)

Morley

Year of formation 1878
Ground Scatcherd Lane, Morley, Leeds   Tel: Leeds (0532) 533487

Colours Maroon
Most capped player G H Marsden (England) 3 caps
Captain 1992-93 J Georgiou
Courage Leagues Div 2 13th *relegated* **Pilkington Cup** Lost 3-21 to West Hartlepool
(4th round)

League Record 1992-93

Date	Venue	Opponents	Result	Scorers
19 Sept	A	Coventry	3-41	*PG:* Grayshon
26 Sept	H	Moseley	6-13	*PG:* Booth (2)
3 Oct	A	Sale	0-34	
10 Oct	H	Waterloo	12-27	*PG:* Grayshon (4)
24 Oct	A	Nottingham	0-78	
31 Oct	H	Blackheath	8-23	*T:* Clark *PG:* Grayshon
21 Nov	H	Newcastle Gos	13-36	*T:* Clark *C:* Grayshon *PG:* Grayshon (2)
13 Feb	A	Wakefield	15-16	*PG:* Grayshon (3) *DG:* Grayshon (2)
13 Mar	H	Richmond	6-28	*PG:* Grayshon (2)
27 Mar	A	Rosslyn Park	24-43	*T:* Sales, Yule *C:* Grayshon *PG:* Grayshon (3) *DG:* Grayshon
3 Apr	H	Fylde	10-10	*T:* Collins *C:* Grayshon *PG:* Grayshon
24 Apr	A	Bedford	10-25	*T:* Rowland, Faulkner

Moseley

Year of formation 1873
Ground The Reddings, Reddings Road, Moseley, Birmingham   Tel: 021-499 2149
Colours Red and black
Most capped player M C Teague (England) 27 caps
Captain 1992-93 P Shillingford
Courage League Div 2 6th **Pilkington Cup** Lost 15-37 to Northampton (quarter-final)

League Record 1992-93

Date	Venue	Opponents	Result	Scorers
19 Sept	H	Bedford	9-9	*PG:* Houston (3)
26 Sept	A	Morley	13-6	*T:* Massey, Shillingford *PG:* Houston
3 Oct	H	Wakefield	3-14	*PG:* Houston
10 Oct	A	Richmond	21-28	*T:* Parry, Spiller *C:* Massey *PG:* Massey (3)
24 Oct	H	Rosslyn Park	32-10	*T:* Shillingford, Massey, Purdy, James *C:* Kerr (3) *PG:* Kerr *DG:* Hardcastle
31 Oct	A	Fylde	15-15	*T:* Linnett, Fenley *C:* Kerr *PG:* Kerr
9 Jan	A	Sale	13-6	*T:* Parry *C:* Reed-Daunter *PG:* Reed-Daunter (2)
13 Feb	H	Waterloo	9-12	*PG:* Reed-Daunter (3)
13 Mar	A	Nottingham	5-9	*T:* Purdy
27 Mar	H	Blackheath	23-6	*T:* Massey, Burley, Parry, Sherriffe *DG:* Drane
3 Apr	A	Coventry	22-19	*T:* Fenley *C:* Massey *PG:* Massey (4) *DG:* Hardcastle
24 Apr	H	Newcastle Gos	19-16	*T:* Linnett, Spiller *PG:* Reed-Daunter (3)

Newcastle Gosforth

Year of formation 1877
Ground Kingston Park, Brunton Road, Kenton Bank Foot, Newcastle-upon-Tyne
Tel: Tyneside (091) 214 0422
Colours Green and white
Most capped player R J McLoughlin (Ireland) 40 caps

Captain 1992-93 N Frankland
Courage Leagues Div 2 *Winners* **Pilkington Cup** Lost 3-33 to Northampton (4th round)

League Record 1992-93

Date	Venue	Opponents	Result	Scorers
26 Sept	H	Sale	7-3	*T:* Murray *C:* Johnson
3 Oct	A	Waterloo	13-3	*T:* Wilkinson *C:* Johnson *PG:* Johnson (2)
10 Oct	H	Nottingham	28-6	*T:* Wilkinson *C:* Johnson *PG:* Johnson (6) *DG:* Johnson
24 Oct	A	Blackheath	12-9	*PG:* Johnson (3) *DG:* Johnson
31 Oct	H	Coventry	26-3	*T:* Wilkinson, Clark *C:* Johnson (2) *PG:* Johnson (4)
21 Nov	A	Morley	36-13	*T:* Roberts (2), Curry, Johnson, Douglas *C:* Johnson (4) *PG:* Johnson
9 Jan	H	Wakefield	17-20	*T:* Chandler, Douglas, Meadows *C:* Johnson
13 Feb	A	Richmond	21-9	*T:* Chandler, Robinson *C:* Johnson *PG:* Johnson (3)
13 Mar	H	Rosslyn Park	14-3	*T:* Chandler *PG:* Johnson (3)
27 Mar	A	Fylde	32-5	*T:* Wilkinson, Penn, Fuller, Curry *C:* Johnson (3) *PG:* Johnson (2)
3 Apr	H	Bedford	19-13	*T:* Wilkinson *C:* Johnson *PG:* Johnson (3) *DG:* Johnson
24 Apr	A	Moseley	16-19	*T:* Wilkinson *C:* Johnson *PG:* Johnson (3)

Northampton

Year of formation 1888
Ground Franklins Gardens, Weedon Road, Northampton
Tel: Northampton (0604) 751543
Colours Black, green and gold

Wayne Shelford on the burst in Northampton's 11-8 Courage League victory against Bath. The influential Shelford was in the last season of an inspiring stint at Northampton.

Most capped player G S Pearce (England) 36 caps
Captain 1992-93 C J Olver
Courage Leagues Div 1 4th **Pilkington Cup** Lost 6-28 to Leicester (semi-final)

League Record 1992-93

Date	Venue	Opponents	Result	Scorers
19 Sept	H	Bristol	16-6	*T:* Rodber *C:* Steele *PG:* Steele (3)
26 Sept	H	Saracens	21-17	*T:* Thorneycroft, Packman *C:* Steele *PG:* Steele (3)
3 Oct	A	London Irish	3-12	*PG:* Steele
10 Oct	H	Bath	11-8	*T:* Beal *PG:* Steele (2)
31 Oct	A	Orrell	10-9	*T:* Hunter *C:* Tubb *PG:* Tubb
21 Nov	A	Harlequins	12-7	*PG:* Steele (3) *DG:* Dawson
9 Jan	H	Leicester	12-13	*T:* Packman, Thorneycroft *C:* Steele
13 Feb	A	Rugby	13-7	*T:* Thorneycroft *C:* Steele *PG:* Tubb, Steele
13 Mar	H	Gloucester	16-21	*T:* Packman *C:* Steele *PG:* Tubb (2), Steele
27 Mar	A	Wasps	12-20	*T:* MacNaughton, Ward *C:* Beal
3 Apr	H	West Hartlepool	55-9	*T:* Rodber (2), Baldwin, Dawson, Shelford, Thorneycroft, Packman, Ward *C:* Beal (6) *PG:* Beal
24 Apr	A	London Scottish	34-21	*T:* Thorneycroft (2), Ward, Pask, Rees *C:* Tubb (3) *PG:* Tubb

Nottingham

Year of formation 1877
Ground Ireland Avenue, Beeston, Nottingham   Tel: Nottingham (0602) 254238
Colours White and green
Most capped player C R Andrew (England) 52 caps
Captain 1992-93 C A Gray
Courage Leagues Div 2 4th **Pilkington Cup** Lost 3-28 to Leicester (4th round)

League Record 1992-93

Date	Venue	Opponents	Result	Scorers
19 Sept	H	Richmond	17-12	*T:* Gabriel *PG:* Hodgkinson (3) *DG:* Gregory
26 Sept	A	Blackheath	46-5	*T:* Byrom, Cook, Gabriel, pen try *C:* Hodgkinson (4) *PG:* Hodgkinson (5) *DG:* Gregory
3 Oct	H	Coventry	16-10	*T:* Jackson, Byrom *PG:* Hodgkinson, Gregory
10 Oct	A	Newcastle Gos	6-28	*PG:* Hodgkinson *DG:* Gregory
24 Oct	H	Morley	78-0	*T:* Walker (3), Gabriel, Gregory, Hindmarch, Furley, Jones, Bradley, Byrom, Freer, Carbutt *C:* Gregory (9)
31 Oct	A	Wakefield	9-22	*PG:* Gregory (3)
21 Nov	A	Rosslyn Park	18-6	*PG:* Gregory (4) *DG:* Gregory (2)
9 Jan	H	Fylde	19-8	*T:* Pepper *C:* Gregory *PG:* Gregory (2) *DG:* Gregory (2)
13 Feb	A	Bedford	9-15	*PG:* Gregory (3)
13 Mar	H	Moseley	9-5	*PG:* Gregory *DG:* Gregory (2)
27 Mar	A	Sale	8-25	*T:* Freer *PG:* Gregory
3 Apr	H	Waterloo	14-9	*T:* Gray *PG:* Gregory (3)

Orrell

Year of formation 1927
Ground Edge Hall Road, Orrell, Lancashire   Tel: Upholland (0695) 623193
Colours Black and amber

Most capped player J Carleton (England) 26 caps
Captain 1992-93 S Taberner
Courage Leagues Div 1 9th **Pilkington Cup** Lost 3-8 to Waterloo (4th round)

League Record 1992-93

Date	Venue	Opponents	Result	Scorers
26 Sept	H	London Scottish	13-10	*T:* Ashurst, Halsall *PG:* Ainscough
3 Oct	A	Saracens	9-6	*PG:* Ainscough (3)
10 Oct	H	London Irish	8-12	*T:* Morris *PG:* Ainscough
24 Oct	A	Bath	3-39	*PG:* Ainscough
31 Oct	H	Northampton	9-10	*PG:* Ainscough (3)
21 Nov	A	Bristol	11-23	*T:* Morris *PG:* Ainscough (2)
9 Jan	H	Harlequins	18-16	*T:* Taberner, Cleary, Hamer *PG:* Ainscough
13 Feb	A	Leicester	0-9	
13 Mar	H	Rugby	66-0	*T:* Hamer (4), Ashurst (2), Kimmins, Halsall, Horrocks, Taberner, Manley *C:* Ainscough (4) *PG:* Ainscough
27 Mar	A	Gloucester	13-8	*T:* Morris *C:* Ainscough *PG:* Ainscough (2)
3 Apr	H	Wasps	10-11	*T:* Hamer *C:* Ainscough *PG:* Ainscough
24 Apr	A	West Hartlepool	15-39	*PG:* Langford (4), Ainscough

Richmond

Year of formation 1861
Ground Athletic Ground, Richmond, Surrey   Tel: 081-940 0397
Colours Old gold, red and black
Most capped player C W Ralston (England) 22 caps
Captain 1992-93 K G Boroevich
Courage Leagues Div 2 9th *relegated* **Pilkington Cup** Lost 22-25 to Wakefield (3rd round)

League Record 1992-93

Date	Venue	Opponents	Result	Scorers
19 Sept	A	Nottingham	12-17	*PG:* Livesey (3) *DG:* Livesey
26 Sept	H	Fylde	29-6	*T:* Sole (2), Lloyd, Hancock *C:* Livesey (3) *PG:* Livesey
3 Oct	A	Bedford	16-22	*T:* McAllister *C:* Livesey *PG:* Livesey (3)
10 Oct	H	Moseley	28-21	*T:* Lloyd, Clarke, Livesey, Elliott *C:* Livesey (4)
24 Oct	A	Sale	10-21	*T:* Elliott *C:* Livesey *PG:* Livesey
31 Oct	H	Waterloo	12-16	*PG:* Livesey (3) *DG:* Livesey
21 Nov	H	Blackheath	13-23	*T:* Saunders *C:* Hoad *PG:* Livesey (2)
9 Jan	A	Coventry	18-13	*T:* Hornung, Greenwood *C:* Clark *PG:* Clark (2)
13 Feb	H	Newcastle Gos	9-21	*PG:* Hoad (2), Clark
13 Mar	A	Morley	28-6	*T:* Boroevich, Hoad, Sole *C:* Livesey (2) *PG:* Livesey (3)
27 Mar	H	Wakefield	11-6	*T:* Greenwood *PG:* Livesey *DG:* Livesey
24 Apr	A	Rosslyn Park	18-24	*T:* Greenwood, Della-Savina *C:* Livesey *PG:* Livesey (2)

Rosslyn Park

Year of formation 1879
Ground Priory Lane, Roehampton, London SW15   Tel: 081-876 1879
Colours Red and white
Most capped player A G Ripley (England) 24 caps
Captain 1992-93 A Brooks
Courage Leagues Div 2 8th *relegated* **Pilkington Cup** Lost 10-37 to Wasps (3rd round)

League Record 1992-93

Date	Venue	Opponents	Result	Scorers
19 Sept	A	Waterloo	9-12	*PG:* Graves (3)
3 Oct	A	Fylde	22-9	*T:* Abraham, Stratford *PG:* Abraham (4)
10 Oct	H	Bedford	13-16	*T:* Thomas *C:* Abraham *PG:* Abraham (2)
24 Oct	A	Moseley	10-32	*T:* Thomas *C:* Abraham *PG:* Abraham
31 Oct	H	Sale	18-8	*PG:* Graves (5) *DG:* Holder
21 Nov	H	Nottingham	6-18	*PG:* Graves (2)
9 Jan	A	Blackheath	14-18	*T:* Barnett *PG:* Graves (3)
13 Feb	H	Coventry	32-10	*T:* Graves, Stratford, Moon *C:* Graves *PG:* Graves (5)
13 Mar	A	Newcastle Gos	3-14	*PG:* Abraham
27 Mar	H	Morley	43-24	*T:* Essenhigh (2), Allison, Pickup, Abraham *PG:* Abraham (6)
3 Apr	A	Wakefield	15-20	*T:* Allison, Blake *C:* Abraham *DG:* Abraham
24 Apr	H	Richmond	24-18	*T:* Roiser, Essenhigh *C:* Roblin *PG:* Roblin (3) *DG:* Roblin

Rugby

Year of formation 1873
Ground Webb Ellis Road (off Bilton Road), Rugby   Tel: Rugby (0788) 542252
Colours Orange, black and white
Most capped player G S Conway (England) 18 caps
Captain 1992-93 D Bishop
Courage Leagues Div 1 13th *relegated* **Pilkington Cup** Lost 5-11 to Moseley (4th round)

League Record 1992-93

Date	Venue	Opponents	Result	Scorers
19 Sept	A	Saracens	9-14	*PG:* Mapletoft (3)
3 Oct	A	Gloucester	12-21	*PG:* Mapletoft (3) *DG:* Pell
10 Oct	H	Wasps	3-34	*PG:* Mapletoft
24 Oct	A	West Hartlepool	6-5	*PG:* Mapletoft *DG:* Pell
31 Oct	H	London Scottish	20-45	*T:* Bromley, Pell, Saunders *C:* Pell *PG:* Pell
21 Nov	H	London Irish	0-14	
9 Jan	A	Bath	7-61	*T:* Riley *C:* Pell
13 Feb	H	Northampton	7-13	*T:* Bromley *C:* Mapletoft
13 Mar	A	Orrell	0-66	
27 Mar	H	Bristol	21-32	*T:* Saunders, Cockerill *C:* MacLeod *PG:* MacLeod (2) *DG:* MacLeod
3 Apr	A	Harlequins	14-35	*T:* Saunders, Cockerill *C:* MacLeod (2)
24 Apr	H	Leicester	5-28	*T:* Bishop

Sale

Year of formation 1861
Ground Heywood Road, Brooklands, Sale, Cheshire   Tel: Manchester (061) 973 6348
Colours Blue and white
Most capped player F E Cotton (England) 31 caps
Captain 1992-93 M Whitcombe
Courage Leagues Div 2 5th **Pilkington Cup** Lost 3-20 to Orrell (3rd round)

League Record 1992-93

Date	Venue	Opponents	Result	Scorers
19 Sept	H	Fylde	51-3	*T:* Warr (2), Young, Powell, Jee, Dobson *C:* Turner (3) *PG:* Turner (4) *DG:* Turner

26 Sept	A	Newcastle Gos	3-7	*PG:* Turner
3 Oct	H	Morley	34-0	*T:* Stocks, Young, Erskine *C:* Jee, Turner *PG:* Jee(2), Turner *DG:* Turner(2)
10 Oct	A	Wakefield	12-6	*T:* Young, Davies *C:* Jee
24 Oct	H	Richmond	21-10	*T:* Macfarlane, Warr *C:* Jee *PG:* Jee(3)
31 Oct	A	Rosslyn Park	8-18	*T:* Warr *PG:* Turner
21 Nov	A	Bedford	9-9	*PG:* Jee(2) *DG:* Jee
9 Jan	H	Moseley	6-13	*PG:* Jee(2)
13 Mar	A	Waterloo	24-25	*T:* Erskine, Birch *C:* Jee *PG:* Jee(3) *DG:* Jee
27 Mar	H	Nottingham	25-8	*T:* Mallinder, Kenrick, Young, Diamond *C:* Turner *PG:* Turner
3 Apr	A	Blackheath	20-3	*T:* Turner, Whitcombe *C:* Jee, Turner *PG:* Jee(2)
24 Apr	H	Coventry	24-0	*T:* Rowlands(2), Mallinder, Harper *C:* Turner(2)

Saracens

Year of formation 1876
Ground Bramley Sports Ground, Green Road, Southgate, London N14
Tel: 081-449 3770
Colours Black with red star and crescent
Most capped player J Leonard (England) 25 caps
Captain 1992-93 B Davies
Courage Leagues Div 1 11th *relegated* **Pilkington Cup** Lost 17-18 to Wasps (4th round)

League Record 1992-93

Date	*Venue*	*Opponents*	*Result*	*Scorers*
19 Sept	H	Rugby	14-9	*T:* Crawley *PG:* Rudling(3)
26 Sept	A	Northampton	17-21	*T:* Reed *PG:* Rudling(3) *DG:* Rudling
3 Oct	H	Orrell	6-9	*PG:* Rudling(2)
10 Oct	A	Bristol	7-12	*T:* Cassell *C:* Rudling
24 Oct	H	Harlequins	3-18	*PG:* Rudling
31 Oct	A	Leicester	3-30	*PG:* Rudling
21 Nov	A	Gloucester	5-19	*T:* O'Leary
9 Jan	H	Wasps	9-13	*PG:* Rudling(3)
13 Feb	A	West Hartlepool	10-3	*T:* O'Leary, Crawley
13 Mar	H	London Scottish	41-17	*T:* Wilson, Adamson, Dooley, Crawley, O'Leary, Buckton *C:* Tunningley(4) *PG:* Tunningley
3 Apr	A	London Irish	9-10	*PG:* Tunningley(2) *DG:* Hughes
24 Apr	H	Bath	13-19	*T:* Davies *C:* Tunningley *DG:* Hughes(2)

Wakefield

Year of formation 1901
Ground Pinderfields Road, College Grove, Wakefield   Tel: Wakefield (0924) 372038
Colours Black and gold hoops
Most capped player M E Harrison (England) 15 caps
Captain 1992-93 D Scully
Courage Leagues Div 2 3rd **Pilkington Cup** Lost 18-47 to Harlequins (4th round)

League Record 1992-93

Date	*Venue*	*Opponents*	*Result*	*Scorers*
19 Sept	A	Blackheath	9-9	*PG:* Liley(3)
26 Sept	H	Bedford	27-3	*T:* Sleightholme(2), Atkinson *C:* Liley(3) *PG:* Liley *DG:* Liley

3 Oct	A	Moseley	14-3	T: Thompson PG: Liley (3)
10 Oct	H	Sale	6-12	PG: Liley (2)
24 Oct	A	Waterloo	11-22	T: Liley PG: Liley (2)
31 Oct	H	Nottingham	22-9	T: Bramley, Atkinson, Sleightholme C: Liley (2) DG: Barley
21 Nov	H	Coventry	8-0	T: Thompson PG: Liley
9 Jan	A	Newcastle Gos	20-17	T: Sleightholme, pen try C: Liley (2) PG: Liley (2)
13 Feb	H	Morley	16-15	T: Morley C: Liley PG: Liley (3)
27 Mar	A	Richmond	6-11	PG: Liley (2)
3 Apr	H	Rosslyn Park	20-15	T: Sleightholme PG: Liley (4) DG: Liley
24 Apr	A	Fylde	27-7	T: Sleightholme (2), Thompson, Sowerby C: Liley, Barley PG: Liley

Wasps

Year of formation 1867
Ground Repton Avenue (off Rugby Road), Sudbury, Middlesex   Tel: 081-902 4220
Colours Black with gold wasp on left breast
Most capped player C R Andrew (England) 52 caps
Captain 1992-93 D Ryan
Courage Leagues Div 1 2nd **Pilkington Cup** Lost 13-14 to Harlequins (semi-final)

League Record 1992-93

Date	Venue	Opponents	Result	Scorers
19 Sept	A	West Hartlepool	19-6	T: White C: Buzza PG: Buzza (4)
26 Sept	A	Harlequins	15-13	T: Childs, Emeruwa C: Buzza PG: Buzza
3 Oct	H	Leicester	14-13	T: Dunn PG: Buzza (3)
10 Oct	A	Rugby	34-3	T: Buzza (2), Oti, Ryan, White C: Buzza (2), Pilgrim PG: Buzza
24 Oct	H	Gloucester	14-9	T: Oti PG: Pilgrim (3)
21 Nov	H	London Scottish	10-6	T: Davies C: Pilgrim PG: Pilgrim
9 Jan	A	Saracens	13-9	T: Oti C: Buzza PG: Buzza (2)
13 Feb	H	London Irish	18-9	T: Hopley (2), Bates PG: Hopley
13 Mar	A	Bath	11-22	T: Hopley PG: Andrew (2)
27 Mar	H	Northampton	20-12	T: Davies PG: Andrew (4) DG: Andrew
3 Apr	A	Orrell	11-10	T: Oti PG: Andrew (2)
24 Apr	H	Bristol	7-6	T: Hopley C: Andrew

Waterloo

Year of formation 1882
Ground St Anthony's Road, Blundellsands, Liverpool   Tel: Liverpool (051) 924 4552
Colours Green, red and white
Most capped player H G Periton (England) 21 caps
Captain 1992-93 N Allott
Courage Leagues Div 2 2nd **Pilkington Cup** Lost 14-21 to Harlequins (quarter-final)

League Record 1992-93

Date	Venue	Opponents	Result	Scorers
19 Sept	H	Rosslyn Park	12-9	PG: Aitchison (3), Swindells
26 Sept	A	Coventry	32-6	T: Swindells, Grayson, Buckton, Saverimutto C: Grayson (3) PG: Grayson DG: Grayson
3 Oct	H	Newcastle Gos	3-13	PG: Grayson
10 Oct	A	Morley	27-12	T: Buckton, Allott C: Grayson PG: Grayson (4) DG: Grayson
24 Oct	H	Wakefield	22-11	T: Buckton C: Grayson PG: Grayson (3) DG: Grayson, Saverimutto

31 Oct	A	Richmond	16-12	*T:* Healey (2) *PG:* Grayson (2)
21 Nov	A	Fylde	15-14	*PG:* Grayson (5)
9 Jan	H	Bedford	28-8	*T:* Handley, Fraser, Saverimutto
				C: Grayson (2) *PG:* Grayson (2) *DG:* Grayson
13 Feb	A	Moseley	12-9	*PG:* Grayson (4)
13 Mar	H	Sale	25-24	*T:* Healey *C:* Grayson *PG:* Grayson (4)
				DG: Grayson (2)
3 Apr	A	Nottingham	9-14	*PG:* Grayson (3)
24 Apr	H	Blackheath	27-6	*T:* Fraser (2), Buckton, Bracegirdle
				C: Swindells (2) *DG:* Healey

West Hartlepool

Year of formation 1881
Ground Brierton Lane, Hartlepool   Tel: Hartlepool (0429) 272640
Colours Red, green and white hoops
Most capped player C D Aarvold (England) 16 caps
Captain 1992-93 J Stabler
Courage Leagues Div 1 12th *relegated* **Pilkington Cup** Lost 9-15 to Wasps (quarter-final)

League Record 1992-93

Date	*Venue*	*Opponents*	*Result*	*Scorers*
19 Sept	H	Wasps	6-19	*PG:* Stabler (2)
26 Sept	A	Bristol	11-19	*T:* Brown *PG:* Stabler (2)
3 Oct	H	Harlequins	9-12	*PG:* Stabler (3)
10 Oct	A	Leicester	8-21	*T:* Evans *PG:* Stabler
24 Oct	H	Rugby	5-6	*T:* Stabler
31 Oct	A	Gloucester	21-6	*T:* Brown, Lee *C:* Stabler *PG:* Stabler (3)
9 Jan	A	London Scottish	15-10	*T:* Cook, Whitelock *C:* Stabler
				PG: Stabler
13 Feb	H	Saracens	3-10	*PG:* Stabler
13 Mar	A	London Irish	13-25	*T:* Mitchell *C:* Stabler *PG:* Stabler (2)
27 Mar	H	Bath	10-38	*T:* Havery *C:* Stabler *PG:* Stabler
3 Apr	A	Northampton	9-55	*PG:* Stabler (3)
24 Apr	H	Orrell	39-15	*T:* Evans, Cooke, Stabler, Brown, pen try
				C: Stabler (4) *PG:* Stabler (2)

SCOTLAND
Ayr

Year of formation 1897
Ground Millbrae, Alloway, Ayr KA7 4PJ   Tel: Alloway (0292) 441944
Colours Pink and black
Most capped player S Munro (Scotland) 10 caps
Captain 1992-93 George McMillan
1st XV 1992-93 P29 W11 D1 L17 F415 A590
McEwan's/SRU Div 2 6th

League Record 1992-93

Date	*Venue*	*Opponents*	*Result*	*Scorers*
26 Sept	A	Musselburgh	3-20	*PG:* Hay
3 Oct	H	Stewart's-Melville FP	24-35	*T:* Fairgrieve, George McMillan *C:* Hay
				PG: Hay (4)
10 Oct	A	Kirkcaldy	6-13	*PG:* Hay (2)
17 Oct	A	Peebles	15-10	*PG:* Hay (5)
24 Oct	H	West of Scotland	8-29	*T:* Kemp *PG:* Kemp
31 Oct	A	Wigtownshire	17-11	*T:* George McMillan *PG:* Hay (3) *DG:* Hay

374

7 Nov	H	Preston Lodge FP	19-12	*T:* Fairgrieve *C:* Hay *PG:* Hay (4)
14 Nov	A	Dunfermline	3-0	*PG:* Hay
9 Jan	H	Edinburgh Wands	22-16	*T:* Buchanan, Horne, George McMillan *C:* Hay (2) *PG:* Hay
30 Jan	A	Kilmarnock	9-7	*PG:* Hay (3)
13 Feb	H	Grangemouth	22-12	*T:* Buchanan *C:* Hay *PG:* Hay (5)
27 Feb	A	Glasgow Acads	12-20	*T:* Potter (2) *C:* Hay
13 Mar	H	Clarkston	5-25	*T:* Horne

Boroughmuir

Year of formation 1919 (Boroughmuir FP until 1974)
Ground Meggetland, Colinton Road, Edinburgh EH14 1AS   Tel: 031-443 7571
Colours Blue and green quarters
Most capped player S R P Lineen (Scotland) 29 caps
Captain 1992-93 G J Drummond
1st XV 1992-93 P32 W17 D0 L15 F700 A688
McEwan's/SRU Div 1 6th

League Record 1992-93

Date	Venue	Opponents	Result	Scorers
26 Sept	A	Gala	9-11	*PG:* Walker (3)
3 Oct	A	Heriot's FP	12-3	*PG:* Walker (4)
10 Oct	H	Glasgow High/K'side	34-18	*T:* Drummond, Lineen, Reid, Stark *C:* Walker (4) *PG:* Walker (2)
17 Oct	A	Selkirk	39-17	*T:* Stark (2), Walker (3) *C:* Walker (4) *PG:* Walker (2)
24 Oct	H	Jedforest	27-10	*T:* Drummond, Finnie, Stark, Walker *C:* Walker (2) *PG:* Walker
31 Oct	A	Currie	25-11	*T:* Burns, Hall, Reid, Stark *C:* Walker *PG:* Walker
7 Nov	H	Melrose	0-16	
14 Nov	A	Watsonians	37-15	*T:* Lineen, Robertson, Stark (2), Walker *C:* Reekie, Walker (2) *PG:* Reekie, Walker
9 Jan	H	Edinburgh Acads	7-10	*T:* Smith *C:* Walker
27 Feb	A	Kelso	12-18	*T:* Smith, Stark *C:* Seagar
27 Mar	A	Stirling County	6-33	*PG:* Reekie (2)

Clarkston

Year of formation 1937
Ground Braidholm, Braidholm Road, Giffnock, Glasgow G46 6EB Tel: 041-637 5850
Colours Red, white and green hoops
Captain 1992-93 K Fairbairn
1st XV 1992-93 P30 W12 D1 L16 Ab1 F507 A603
McEwan's/SRU Div 2 5th

League Record 1992-93

Date	Venue	Opponents	Result	Scorers
26 Sept	H	Peebles	10-16	*T:* Aitken *C:* Cossey *PG:* Cossey
3 Oct	A	West of Scotland	12-26	*T:* Aitken, G McIlwham *C:* Cossey
10 Oct	H	Wigtownshire	38-6	*T:* Aitken, McGrane (2), Speight *C:* Cossey (3) *PG:* Cossey (4)
17 Oct	A	Preston Lodge FP	22-16	*T:* Biggin, Price (2) *C:* Cossey (2) *PG:* Cossey
24 Oct	H	Dunfermline	39-15	*T:* Aitken, Keith, Price, Raath *C:* Cossey (2) *PG:* Cossey (5)
31 Oct	A	Edinburgh Wands	8-11	*T:* Raath *PG:* Cossey
7 Nov	H	Kilmarnock	47-7	*T:* Cossey, Keith, Menzies, Price (2), Speight (2) *C:* Cossey (6)

14 Nov	A	Grangemouth	24-20	*T:* Price (2) *C:* Cossey *PG:* Cossey (4)
9 Jan	H	Glasgow Acads	6-6	*PG:* Cossey (2)
30 Jan	H	Kirkcaldy	25-0	*T:* Orsi (2), Price *C:* Cossey (2)
				PG: Cossey (2)
13 Feb	A	Musselburgh	8-21	*T:* B Middler *PG:* Cossey
27 Feb	H	Stewart's-Melville FP	3-24	*PG:* Cossey
13 Mar	A	Ayr	25-5	*T:* Cossey, Jackson, Speight *C:* Cossey (2)
				PG: Cossey (2)

Currie

Year of formation 1970
Ground Malleny Park, Balerno, Edinburgh EH14 5HA   Tel: 031-449 2432
Colours Amber and black
Captain 1992-93 A Donaldson
1st XV 1992-93 P27 W16 D0 L11 F584 A497
McEwan's/SRU Div 1 4th

League Record 1992-93

Date	*Venue*	*Opponents*	*Result*	*Scorers*
26 Sept	A	Edinburgh Acads	14-18	*T:* Kay *PG:* Donaldson (3)
10 Oct	A	Hawick	11-31	*T:* C Robertson *PG:* Donaldson
				DG: Donaldson
17 Oct	H	Kelso	33-23	*T:* Forrester, Ward, Wilson *C:* Donaldson (3)
				PG: Donaldson (2) *DG:* Donaldson (2)
24 Oct	A	Dundee HSFP	13-11	*T:* Forrester, Manclark *DG:* Donaldson
31 Oct	H	Boroughmuir	11-25	*T:* Dickson *PG:* Donaldson (2)
7 Nov	A	Heriot's FP	23-18	*T:* Dickson, Donaldson *C:* Donaldson (2)
				PG: Donaldson (3)
9 Jan	A	Selkirk	12-9	*PG:* Donaldson (3) *DG:* Donaldson
23 Jan	H	Jedforest	20-6	*T:* Mack, A Robertson *C:* Donaldson (2)
				PG: Donaldson (2)
30 Jan	H	Stirling County	22-14	*T:* Russell, Te Whaiti *PG:* Donaldson (4)
13 Feb	A	Gala	13-47	*T:* Mack *C:* Donaldson *PG:* Donaldson (2)
27 Feb	A	Melrose	7-16	*T:* Tonkin *C:* Donaldson
13 Mar	H	Watsonians	19-6	*T:* Donaldson (2), Laugerson *C:* Donaldson (2)
27 Mar	H	Glasgow High/K'side	20-18	*T:* Dickson, Manclark *C:* Donaldson (2)
				PG: Donaldson (2)

Dundee High School FP

Year of formation 1880
Ground Mayfield, Arbroath Road, Dundee   Tel: Dundee (0382) 453517 (ground)
and 451045 (clubhouse)
Colours Blue and red
Most capped player D G Leslie (Scotland) 32 caps
Captain 1992-93 W A Keys
1st XV 1992-93 P29 W16 D0 L13 F608 A430
McEwan's/SRU Div 1 14th *relegated*

League Record 1992-93

Date	*Venue*	*Opponents*	*Result*	*Scorers*
26 Sept	H	Heriot's FP	27-9	*T:* Nicol, Rouse *C:* J R Newton
				PG: J R Newton (4) *DG:* J R Newton
3 Oct	A	Glasgow High/K'side	0-41	
10 Oct	H	Selkirk	12-18	*PG:* J R Newton (4)
17 Oct	A	Jedforest	9-20	*PG:* B R Easson (2), Rouse
24 Oct	H	Currie	11-13	*T:* Cousin *PG:* Easson, Rouse
31 Oct	A	Melrose	6-46	*PG:* Easson, Rouse

7 Nov	H	Watsonians	15-29	*PG:* J R Newton (5)
14 Nov	A	Edinburgh Acads	12-43	*PG:* J R Newton (2) *DG:* J R Newton (2)
9 Jan	H	Stirling County	8-9	*T:* J R Newton *PG:* J R Newton
23 Jan	A	Hawick	3-12	*PG:* J R Newton
13 Feb	H	Kelso	23-16	*T:* Cousin (2), Nicol *C:* J R Newton
				PG: J R Newton (2)
27 Feb	H	Gala	16-13	*T:* Douglas *C:* J R Newton
				PG: J R Newton (3)

Dunfermline

Year of formation 1904
Ground McKane Park, Dunfermline, Fife   Tel: Dunfermline (0383) 721279
Colours Royal blue with white band
Most capped player J T Greenwood (Scotland) 20 caps
Captain 1992-93 D H Mitchell
1st XV 1992-93   P28   W10   D3   L15   F417   A639
McEwan's/SRU Div 2 13th *relegated*

League Record 1992-93

Date	Venue	Opponents	Result	Scorers
26 Sept	A	Edinburgh Wands	9-25	*PG:* Pulfrey (3)
10 Oct	A	Grangemouth	0-25	
17 Oct	H	Glasgow Acads	18-26	*T:* Keir, Shirtliff *C:* Pulfrey *PG:* Pulfrey (2)
24 Oct	A	Clarkston	15-39	*T:* Cruickshank, Smith *C:* Pulfrey
				PG: Pulfrey
31 Oct	H	Musselburgh	17-10	*T:* Burdon, Drummond *C:* Pulfrey (2)
				PG: Pulfrey
7 Nov	A	Stewart's-Melville FP	0-42	
14 Nov	H	Ayr	0-3	
19 Dec	H	Kilmarnock	27-10	*T:* Cruickshank, Dalton, Pulfrey *PG:* Dalton (3)
				DG: Dalton
9 Jan	A	Peebles	8-29	*T:* Keir *PG:* Cross
30 Jan	H	West of Scotland	16-38	*T:* Charleston *C:* Dalton *PG:* Dalton (2)
				DG: Dalton
13 Feb	A	Wigtownshire	13-13	*T:* Keir, Shirtliff *PG:* Dalton
27 Feb	H	Preston Lodge FP	18-18	*T:* McKenzie, Mitchell *C:* Dalton
				PG: Dalton (2)
13 Mar	A	Kirkcaldy	0-44	

Edinburgh Academicals

Year of formation 1857
Ground Raeburn Place, Stockbridge, Edinburgh EH4 1HQ   Tel: 031-332 1070
Colours Blue and white hoops
Most capped player D M B Sole (Scotland) 44 caps
Captain 1992-93 S A D Burns
1st XV 1992-93   P31   W20   D2   L9   F784   A489
McEwan's/SRU Div 1 joint 2nd

League Record 1992-93

Date	Venue	Opponents	Result	Scorers
26 Sept	H	Currie	18-14	*T:* Burns, Porter, Shepherd *PG:* Shepherd
3 Oct	A	Melrose	0-14	
10 Oct	H	Watsonians	16-12	*T:* Porter, Swanson *PG:* Shepherd (2)
17 Oct	H	Gala	33-20	*T:* Hay-Smith (2), Patterson, Porter
				C: Shepherd (2) *PG:* Hay-Smith, Shepherd
				DG: Hay-Smith

24 Oct	A	Stirling County	16-3	*T:* McLean, Scott *PG:* Shepherd (2)
31 Oct	H	Hawick	46-12	*T:* Hay-Smith, Porter (3), Simmers, Wilson
				C: Hay-Smith (2) *PG:* Shepherd (4)
7 Nov	A	Kelso	16-26	*T:* Porter, Swanson *PG:* Hay-Smith (2)
14 Nov	H	Dundee HSFP	43-12	*T:* McIvor, Simmers (2), Wainwright, Wilson
				C: Hay-Smith (3) *PG:* Hay-Smith (3)
				DG: Hay-Smith
9 Jan	A	Boroughmuir	10-7	*T:* Porter *C:* Shepherd *DG:* Shepherd
13 Feb	A	Glasgow High/K'side	22-13	*T:* Burns, McIvor, Swanson *C:* Shepherd (2)
				PG: Shepherd
27 Feb	H	Selkirk	6-6	*PG:* Shepherd *DG:* Hay-Smith
13 Mar	H	Jedforest	10-11	*T:* McIvor *C:* Shepherd *PG:* Shepherd
27 Mar	H	Heriot's FP	29-5	*T:* Bowe (2), Burns, pen try, Hay-Smith
				C: Shepherd (2)

Edinburgh Wanderers

Year of formation 1868
Ground Murrayfield, Edinburgh EH12 5QG   Tel: 031-337 2196
Colours Red and black
Most capped player A R Smith (Scotland) 33 caps
Captain 1992-93 S Dennis
1st XV 1992-93 P27 W10 D1 L16 F489 A632
McEwan's/SRU Div 2 joint 10th

League Record 1992-93

Date	Venue	Opponents	Result	Scorers
26 Sept	H	Dunfermline	25-9	*T:* Godfrey, Graham, Horne *C:* Little (2)
				PG: Little *DG:* C Docherty
3 Oct	H	Kirkcaldy	11-19	*T:* E S Gillies *PG:* Little (2)
10 Oct	A	Kilmarnock	13-25	*T:* E S Gillies (2) *PG:* Little
17 Oct	H	Grangemouth	20-12	*T:* Boswell, Dunlop, E S Gillies *C:* Little
				PG: Little
24 Oct	A	Glasgow Acads	12-28	*T:* G W M Hamilton, Rowley *C:* MacPhail
31 Oct	H	Clarkston	11-8	*T:* Godfrey *PG:* Little (2)
7 Nov	A	Musselburgh	5-24	*T:* Chirat
14 Nov	H	Stewart's-Melville FP	13-24	*T:* Boswell, Little *PG:* Little
9 Jan	A	Ayr	16-22	*T:* C C Docherty, E S Gillies *PG:* MacPhail (2)
30 Jan	H	Peebles	18-17	*T:* Boswell, Hepburn, Throssell *PG:* Little
13 Feb	A	West of Scotland	12-35	*PG:* Little (2), MacPhail (2)
27 Feb	H	Wigtownshire	9-15	*PG:* Little (3)
13 Mar	A	Preston Lodge FP	11-15	*T:* Boswell *PG:* Little (2)

Gala

Year of formation 1875
Ground Netherdale, Nether Road, Galashiels TD1 3HE   Tel: Galashiels (0896) 55145
Colours Maroon
Most capped player D G Leslie (Scotland) 32 caps
Captain 1992-93 I Corcoran
1st XV 1992-93 P28 W20 D1 L7 F735 A430
McEwan's/SRU Div 1 joint 2nd

League Record 1992-93

Date	Venue	Opponents	Result	Scorers
26 Sept	H	Boroughmuir	11-9	*T:* Little *PG:* Dods, Townsend
3 Oct	A	Watsonians	13-5	*T:* Maitland *C:* Townsend *PG:* Dods
				DG: Dods

10 Oct	H	Heriot's FP	35-28	*T:* Farquharson, Laing, Tod, Turnbull *C:* Dods (3) *PG:* Dods (3)
17 Oct	A	Edinburgh Acads	20-33	*T:* Maitland, Moncrieff (2) *C:* Dods *PG:* Dods
24 Oct	H	Glasgow High/K'side	28-3	*T:* Amos, Bryson, Isaac *C:* Dods (2) *PG:* Dods (3)
31 Oct	A	Stirling County	14-9	*T:* Amos *PG:* Dods (2) *DG:* Townsend
7 Nov	H	Selkirk	43-10	*T:* Bryson, Crooks, Dods, Townsend, Turnbull *C:* Dods (3) *PG:* Dods (4)
9 Jan	H	Jedforest	8-6	*T:* B A J Swan *PG:* Learmonth
23 Jan	A	Kelso	22-0	*T:* Turnbull, Farquharson, Dalgleish *C:* Dods (2) *PG:* Dods
30 Jan	A	Hawick	9-9	*PG:* Dods (3)
13 Feb	H	Currie	47-13	*T:* Dalgleish, Learmonth, Moncrieff, B A J Swan, Townsend (2) *C:* Townsend (4) *PG:* Townsend (3)
27 Feb	A	Dundee HSFP	13-16	*T:* Dalgleish *C:* Townsend *PG:* Townsend (2)
13 Mar	H	Melrose	14-30	*T:* Moncrieff, Walker *C:* Maitland (2)

Glasgow Academicals

Year of formation 1867
Ground New Anniesland, Helensburgh Drive, Glasgow   Tel: 041-959 1101
Colours Navy blue and white hoops
Most capped player W M Simmers (Scotland) 28 caps
Captain 1992-93 S M Simmers
1st XV 1992-93 P27 W14 D1 L12 F629 A566
McEwan's/SRU Div 2 4th

League Record 1992-93

Date	Venue	Opponents	Result	Scorers
26 Sept	H	West of Scotland	13-21	*T:* Pawson *C:* C G MacGregor *PG:* C G MacGregor *DG:* C G MacGregor
3 Oct	A	Wigtownshire	55-7	*T:* Afuakwah, Mackay (2), Maclean, J F Mason (3), Peoples, Sturges *C:* C G MacGregor (5)
10 Oct	H	Preston Lodge FP	34-10	*T:* Mackay, J F Mason, Ogle, Pawson (2) *C:* C G MacGregor (3) *PG:* C G MacGregor
17 Oct	A	Dunfermline	26-18	*T:* Mackay (2), Ogle, S M Simmers *PG:* C G MacGregor (2)
24 Oct	H	Edinburgh Wands	28-12	*T:* C G MacGregor (2), J F Mason, Sturgess *C:* S M Simmers *PG:* C G MacGregor (2)
31 Oct	A	Kilmarnock	41-5	*T:* Mackay (4), Maclean, Mason, Ogle *C:* C G MacGregor (3)
7 Nov	H	Grangemouth	25-10	*T:* Mackay, Pawson, Pirrie, S M Simmers *C:* C G MacGregor *PG:* S M Simmers
14 Nov	H	Kirkcaldy	27-13	*T:* Mackay, Maclean, J F Mason, pen try *C:* Milne (2) *PG:* Milne
9 Jan	A	Clarkston	6-6	*PG:* C G MacGregor (2)
30 Jan	H	Musselburgh	18-35	*T:* Ker, G T MacGregor *C:* C G MacGregor *PG:* C G MacGregor (2)
13 Feb	A	Stewart's-Melville FP	18-32	*T:* Mackay, S M Simmers *C:* C G MacGregor *PG:* C G MacGregor *DG:* C G MacGregor
27 Feb	H	Ayr	20-12	*T:* G T MacGregor (3) *C:* C G MacGregor *PG:* C G MacGregor
13 Mar	A	Peebles	20-27	*T:* Pawson (2) *C:* C G MacGregor (2) *PG:* C G MacGregor (2)

Glasgow High/Kelvinside

Year of formation 1982 (on amalgamation of Glasgow High RFC and Kelvinside Academicals)

Ground Old Anniesland, 637 Crow Road, Glasgow   Tel: 041-959 1154
Colours Navy blue, green and white
Most capped player A G J Watt (Scotland) 2 caps (before amalgamation J M Bannerman (Glasgow HSFP) was capped 37 times and D M White (Kelvinside Academicals) 4 times, both for Scotland)
Captain 1992-93 C E Little
1st XV 1992-93   P26   W15   D0   L11   F743   A411
McEwan's/SRU Div 1 13th *relegated*

League Record 1992-93

Date	Venue	Opponents	Result	Scorers
26 Sept	A	Kelso	14-24	*T:* Halley, Hawkes *C:* Breckenridge (2)
3 Oct	H	Dundee HSFP	41-0	*T:* Breckenridge, Little, Munro, Umaga, F D Wallace *C:* Breckenridge (5) *PG:* Breckenridge (2)
10 Oct	A	Boroughmuir	18-34	*T:* Ness, Watt *C:* Breckenridge *PG:* Breckenridge (2)
17 Oct	H	Heriot's FP	56-13	*T:* Hawkes, Kernohan, McDiarmid, McInnes, Manning (2), Umaga, F D Wallace *C:* Breckenridge (5) *PG:* Breckenridge (2)
24 Oct	A	Gala	3-28	*PG:* Breckenridge
31 Oct	A	Selkirk	22-24	*T:* Malcolm, Umaga *PG:* Breckenridge (4)
7 Nov	H	Jedforest	23-13	*T:* Murphy, Umaga (2) *C:* Breckenridge *PG:* Breckenridge *DG:* Breckenridge
9 Jan	H	Melrose	18-33	*T:* Hawkes (2) *C:* Breckenridge *PG:* Breckenridge (2)
30 Jan	A	Watsonians	15-21	*T:* Kernohan, McKee, Malcolm
13 Feb	H	Edinburgh Acads	13-22	*T:* Devlin *C:* Little *PG:* Breckenridge (2)
27 Feb	A	Stirling County	11-23	*T:* Devlin *PG:* Breckenridge *DG:* Breckenridge
13 Mar	H	Hawick	39-0	*T:* Dow, Little, Manning, Waddell (2), M I Wallace *C:* Little (3) *PG:* Little
27 Mar	A	Currie	18-20	*T:* Devlin, Little, Waddell *PG:* Little

Grangemouth

Year of formation 1929
Ground Glensburgh, Glensburgh Road, Grangemouth
Tel: Grangemouth (0324) 486142
Colours Red and black hoops
Captain 1992-93 Alan Mackenzie
1st XV 1992-93   P26   W12   D0   L14   F589   A581
McEwan's/SRU Div 2 joint 10th

League Record 1992-93

Date	Venue	Opponents	Result	Scorers
26 Sept	H	Wigtownshire	25-10	*T:* Halliday, Rutherford, Stewart *C:* Halliday (2) *PG:* Halliday (2)
3 Oct	A	Preston Lodge FP	9-34	*PG:* Halliday (3)
10 Oct	H	Dunfermline	25-0	*T:* Innes, McGregor (2) *C:* Halliday (2) *PG:* Halliday (2)
17 Oct	A	Edinburgh Wands	12-20	*T:* Lyon (2) *C:* Halliday
24 Oct	H	Kilmarnock	14-20	*T:* Rutherford *PG:* Halliday (3)
31 Oct	H	Kirkcaldy	13-8	*T:* Carter *C:* Halliday *PG:* Halliday (2)
7 Nov	A	Glasgow Acads	10-25	*T:* Lyon, Stewart
14 Nov	H	Clarkston	20-24	*T:* Rutherford *PG:* Halliday (5)
9 Jan	A	Musselburgh	0-23	
30 Jan	H	Stewart's-Melville FP	18-23	*T:* McMillan, McWatt *C:* Halliday *PG:* Halliday (2)

13 Feb	A	Ayr	12-22	*T:* Forsyth, Innes *C:* Halliday
27 Feb	H	Peebles	25-0	*T:* Lyon (3) *C:* Halliday (2) *PG:* Halliday (2)
13 Mar	A	West of Scotland	6-52	*PG:* Halliday (2)

Hawick

Year of formation 1873
Ground Mansfield Park, Mansfield Road, Hawick, Roxburghshire
Tel: Hawick (0450) 74291
Colours Dark green
Most capped player J M Renwick/C T Deans (Scotland) 52 caps
Captain 1992-93 J A Hay
1st XV 1992-93 P31   W16   D2   L13   F606   A608
McEwan's/SRU Div 1 7th

League Record 1992-93

Date	Venue	Opponents	Result	Scorers
26 Sept	H	Selkirk	39-8	*T:* Oliver, B L Renwick, Stokes, Turnbull *C:* D Gray (2) *PG:* D Gray (3) *DG:* Welsh (2)
3 Oct	A	Jedforest	12-15	*PG:* D Gray (3) *DG:* Welsh
10 Oct.	H	Currie	31-11	*T:* Bannerman, Suddon, Turnbull, Welsh *C:* Welsh *PG:* Welsh (3)
17 Oct	A	Melrose	14-20	*T:* Stanger *PG:* D Gray (2) *DG:* Welsh
24 Oct	H	Watsonians	11-14	*T:* Suddon *PG:* D Gray (2)
31 Oct	A	Edinburgh Acads	12-46	*PG:* Welsh (4)
7 Nov	H	Stirling County	22-8	*T:* Suddon *C:* Welsh *PG:* Welsh (5)
9 Jan	A	Kelso	20-6	*T:* Grant, Stanger (2) *C:* Oliver *PG:* Oliver
23 Jan	H	Dundee HSFP	12-3	*PG:* Bannerman (4)
30 Jan	H	Gala	9-9	*PG:* Bannerman (3)
27 Feb	H	Heriot's FP	15-20	*T:* Grant, Reid *C:* Gordon *PG:* Gordon
13 Mar	A	Glasgow High/K'side	0-39	

Heriot's FP

Year of formation 1890
Ground Goldenacre, Bangholm Terrace, Edinburgh EH3 5QN   Tel: 031-552 5925
Colours Blue and white horizontal stripes
Most capped player A R Irvine (Scotland) 51 caps
Captain 1992-93 K S Milne
1st XV 1992-93 P29   W11   D0   L18   F630   A756
McEwan's/SRU Div 1 joint 8th

League Record 1992-93

Date	Venue	Opponents	Result	Scorers
26 Sept	A	Dundee HSFP	9-27	*PG:* Glasgow (3)
3 Oct	H	Boroughmuir	3-12	*DG:* Whitaker
10 Oct	A	Gala	28-35	*T:* Murray, Robertson, Watt *C:* Glasgow (2) *PG:* Glasgow (3)
17 Oct	A	Glasgow High/K'side	13-56	*T:* Lessels *C:* Glasgow *PG:* Glasgow (2)
24 Oct	H	Selkirk	33-20	*T:* Rafferty (3) *PG:* Glasgow (4) *DG:* Glasgow (2)
31 Oct	A	Jedforest	11-14	*T:* Watt *PG:* Glasgow *DG:* Glasgow
7 Nov	H	Currie	18-23	*T:* Allingham, Whitaker *C:* Glasgow *PG:* Glasgow (2)
14 Nov	A	Melrose	15-24	*T:* Lister, Whitaker *C:* Glasgow *PG:* Glasgow
9 Jan	H	Watsonians	30-15	*T:* H R Gilmour, Lawrie (3), Murray *C:* Lawrie *PG:* Lawrie

13 Feb	H	Stirling County	24-7	*T:* Adam, K S Milne, Murray, Stoddart *C:* Lawrie (2)
27 Feb	A	Hawick	20-15	*T:* Stoddart (2) *C:* Lawrie (2) *PG:* Lawrie (2)
13 Mar	H	Kelso	86-8	*T:* Allingham, Buchanan-Smith, H R Gilmour, S Gilmour, Glasgow (2), Lawrie, Macdonald, McRobbie, Murray (4), Stoddart *C:* Glasgow (6), Lawrie (2)
27 Mar	A	Edinburgh Acads	5-29	*T:* Allingham

Jedforest

Year of formation 1885
Ground Riverside Park, Jedburgh   Tel: Jedburgh (0835) 62855
Colours Royal blue
Most capped player R J Laidlaw (Scotland) 47 caps
Captain 1992-93 H G Hogg
1st XV 1992-93 P24 W14 D0 L10 F529 A401
McEwan's/SRU Div 1 5th

League Record 1992-93

Date		*Venue Opponents*	*Result*	*Scorers*
26 Sept	A	Stirling County	9-8	*PG:* McKechnie (2) *DG:* Shiel
3 Oct	H	Hawick	15-12	*PG:* McKechnie (5)
10 Oct	A	Kelso	18-13	*T:* Amos, Kirkpatrick *C:* McKechnie *PG:* McKechnie (2)
17 Oct	H	Dundee HSFP	20-9	*T:* Kirkpatrick *PG:* McKechnie (2) *DG:* Hogg (2), McKechnie
24 Oct	A	Boroughmuir	10-27	*T:* K Armstrong *C:* McKechnie *PG:* McKechnie
31 Oct	H	Heriot's FP	14-11	*T:* Amos *PG:* Shiel (2) *DG:* Shiel
7 Nov	H	Glasgow High/K'side	13-23	*T:* Amos, G Armstrong PG: McKechnie
9 Jan	A	Gala	6-8	*PG:* McKechnie (2)
23 Jan	A	Currie	6-20	*PG:* McKechnie (2)
30 Jan	H	Selkirk	18-20	*T:* C J Brown, McKechnie *C:* McKechnie *PG:* McKechnie (2)
13 Feb	H	Melrose	16-19	*T:* A J Douglas, Liddle *PG:* McKechnie *DG:* McKechnie
27 Feb	A	Watsonians	50-5	*T:* Amos, K Armstrong (2), A J Douglas, Hogg, Yule (2) *C:* Amos (3) *PG:* McKechnie (3)
13 Mar	H	Edinburgh Acads	11-10	*T:* Amos *PG:* McKechnie (2)

Kelso

Year of formation 1876
Ground Poynder Park, Bowmont Street, Kelso, Roxburghshire
Tel: Kelso (0573) 224300 and 223773
Colours Black and white
Most capped player J Jeffrey (Scotland) 40 caps
Captain 1992-93 J Jeffrey
1st XV 1992-93 P28 W11 D0 L17 F518 A702
McEwan's/SRU Winners Div 1 joint 8th

League Record 1992-93

Date		*Venue Opponents*	*Result*	*Scorers*
26 Sept	H	Glasgow High/K'side	24-14	*T:* J Jeffrey, G Laing, Oliver *C:* Aitchison (3) *PG:* Aitchison
3 Oct	A	Selkirk	28-8	*T:* Forbes, Bennet, J Jeffrey, Oliver *C:* Aitchison *PG:* Aitchison (2)

10 Nov	H	Jedforest	13-18	*T:* J Jeffrey, Roxburgh *PG:* S Lang
17 Oct	A	Currie	23-33	*T:* Fairley (2), J Jeffrey *C:* Aitchison
				PG: Aitchison (2)
24 Oct	H	Melrose	13-50	*T:* C Millar *C:* Aitchison *PG:* Aitchison (2)
31 Oct	A	Watsonians	17-27	*T:* Bennet, Roxburgh, Tait *C:* Aitchison
7 Nov	H	Edinburgh Acads	26-16	*T:* Aitchison, Heseltine *C:* Aitchison (2)
				PG: Aitchison (4)
14 Nov	A	Stirling County	19-18	*T:* Fairley, Heseltine, MacArthur
				C: Aitchison (2)
9 Jan	H	Hawick	6-20	*PG:* Aitchison (2)
23 Jan	H	Gala	0-22	
13 Feb	A	Dundee HSFP	16-23	*T:* J Jeffrey *C:* Aitchison *PG:* Aitchison (3)
27 Feb	H	Boroughmuir	18-12	*T:* Roxburgh, Walker *C:* Aitchison
				PG: Aitchison (2)
13 Mar	A	Heriot's FP	8-86	*T:* Baird *PG:* Aitchison

Kilmarnock

Year of formation 1868
Ground Bellsland, Queens Drive, Kilmarnock, Ayrshire   Tel: Kilmarnock (0563) 22314
Colours White with red hoop and white Maltese cross
Most capped player W Cuthbertson (Scotland) 22 caps
Captain 1992-93 R S Carswell
1st XV 1992-93 P27   W9   D1   L17   F395   A673
McEwan's/SRU Div 2 14th *relegated*

League Record 1992-93

Date	*Venue*	*Opponents*	*Result*	*Scorers*
26 Sept	H	Preston Lodge FP	0-14	
10 Oct	H	Edinburgh Wands	25-13	*T:* Carswell (2), Pattie *C:* A W McCall (2)
				PG: A W McCall *DG:* A W McCall
17 Oct	H	Kirkcaldy	17-29	*T:* J W R Adams, McIntyre *C:* A W McCall (2)
				PG: A W McCall
24 Oct	A	Grangemouth	20-14	*T:* Muirhead (2) *C:* A W McCall (2)
				PG: A W McCall *DG:* A W McCall
21 Oct	H	Glasgow Acads	5-41	*T:* Crawford
7 Nov	A	Clarkston	7-47	*T:* Kerr *C:* Barrie
14 Nov	H	Musselburgh	20-27	*T:* J W R Adams, Carswell, McIntyre
				C: Stewart *PG:* Stewart
19 Dec	A	Dunfermline	10-27	*T:* Shanks, Wallace
9 Jan	A	Stewart's-Melville FP	0-53	
30 Jan	H	Ayr	7-9	*T:* Muirhead *C:* Stewart
13 Feb	A	Peebles	0-9	
27 Feb	H	West of Scotland	3-55	*PG:* A W McCall
13 Mar	A	Wigtownshire	6-38	*PG:* A W McCall (2)

Kirkcaldy

Year of formation 1873
Ground Beveridge Park, Balwearie Road, Kirkcaldy   Tel: Kirkcaldy (0592) 263470
Colours Royal blue
Most capped player D D Howie/R Howie (Scotland) 9 caps
Captain 1992-93 A D Henderson
1st XV 1992-93 P31   W17   D1   L13   F660   A516
McEwan's/SRU Div 2 9th

League Record 1992-93

Date	*Venue*	*Opponents*	*Result*	*Scorers*
26 Sept	H	Stewart's-Melville FP	12-19	*PG:* J R Mitchell (4)

3 Oct	A	Edinburgh Wands	19-11	*T:* Ferguson *C:* J R Mitchell *PG:* J R Mitchell (4)
10 Oct	H	Ayr	13-6	*T:* Smith *C:* J R Mitchell *PG:* J R Mitchell (2)
17 Oct	A	Kilmarnock	29-17	*T:* Bonner (3) *C:* J R Mitchell *PG:* J R Mitchell (4)
24 Oct	H	Peebles	3-3	*PG:* J R Mitchell
31 Oct	A	Grangemouth	8-13	*T:* J R Mitchell *PG:* J R Mitchell
7 Nov	H	West of Scotland	24-40	*T:* J R Mitchell (2), Porter *C:* J R Mitchell (3) *PG:* J R Mitchell
14 Nov	A	Glasgow Acads	13-27	*T:* Carruthers, Bonner *PG:* J W Thomson
9 Jan	H	Wigtownshire	55-17	*T:* Bonner, R R Dewar, Macdonald, Mitchell (4), Sullivan, J W Thomson *C:* Mitchell (5)
30 Jan	A	Clarkston	0-25	
13 Feb	H	Preston Lodge FP	17-31	*T:* Brett, Cuthbert, R R Dewar *C:* J W Thomson
27 Feb	A	Musselburgh	0-25	
13 Mar	H	Dunfermline	44-0	*T:* R R Dewar (3), Ferguson, Hannah, Macdonald, Merritt *C:* Carruthers (3) *PG:* Carruthers

Melrose

Year of formation 1877
Ground The Greenyards, Melrose, Roxburghshire TD6 9SA
Tel: Melrose (089 682) 2993 (office) and 2559 (clubrooms)
Colours Yellow and black hoops
Most capped player K W Robertson (Scotland) 44 caps
Captain 1992-93 Robbie Brown
1st XV 1992-93 P28 W25 D1 L2 F776 A323
McEwan's/SRU Div 1 *Winners*

League Record 1992-93

Date	*Venue*	*Opponents*	*Result*	*Scorers*
26 Sept	A	Watsonians	14-13	*T:* Bell *PG:* Parker (3)
3 Oct	H	Edinburgh Acads	14-0	*T:* B W Redpath *PG:* Chalmers (3)
10 Oct	A	Stirling County	9-13	*PG:* Parker (3)
17 Oct	H	Hawick	20-14	*T:* A Redpath *PG:* Parker (4) *DG:* Bain
24 Oct	A	Kelso	50-13	*T:* Hogg (3), C Redpath (2), Shiel (2), Weir *C:* Parker (5)
31 Oct	H	Dundee HSFP	46-6	*T:* Ross Brown, Millan Browne, Hogg, Joiner, Parker, Weir (2) *C:* Parker (4) *PG:* Parker
7 Nov	A	Boroughmuir	16-0	*T:* Joiner, Shiel *PG:* Parker *DG:* Parker
14 Nov	H	Heriot's FP	24-15	*T:* Robbie Brown, Chalmers, Parker, B W Redpath *C:* Parker (2)
9 Jan	A	Glasgow High/K'side	33-18	*T:* Robbie Brown, Parker, C Redpath, Turnbull *C:* Parker (2) *PG:* Parker (3)
23 Jan	H	Selkirk	35-5	*T:* Robbie Brown (2), Chalmers, White *C:* Parker (3) *PG:* Parker (3)
13 Feb	A	Jedforest	19-16	*T:* Brotherstone, Parker *PG:* Parker *DG:* Chalmers (2)
27 Feb	H	Currie	16-7	*T:* Weir *C:* Parker *PG:* Parker (3)
13 Mar	A	Gala	30-14	*T:* Brotherstone, A Redpath B W Redpath (2), C Redpath (2)

Musselburgh

Year of formation 1921
Ground Stoneyhill, Stoneyhill Farm Road, Musselburgh   Tel: 031-665 3435
Colours Navy blue with narrow white hoops
Captain 1992-93 A D McColl
1st XV 1992-93 P29 W20 D1 L8 F675 A416
McEwan's/SRU Div 2 joint 1st (3rd on points difference)

League Record 1992-93

Date	Venue	Opponents	Result	Scorers
26 Sept	H	Ayr	20-3	T: Lockhart PG: Lockhart (5)
3 Oct	A	Peebles	17-3	T: Weatherhead PG: Lockhart (2) DG: C Livingstone (2)
10 Oct	H	West of Scotland	24-13	T: Campbell, Stewart (2) PG: C Livingstone (3)
17 Oct	A	Wigtownshire	20-6	T: McLeod, Ramsay C: C Livingstone, Lockhart PG: C Livingstone (2)
24 Oct	H	Preston Lodge FP	23-14	T: Campbell, McLeod C: Lockhart (2) PG: Lockhart (2) DG: C Livingstone
31 Oct	A	Dunfermline	10-17	T: C Livingstone, Maxwell
7 Nov	H	Edinburgh Wands	24-5	T: C Livingstone, MacMillan, Pow, Weatherhead C: C Livingstone (2)
14 Nov	A	Kilmarnock	27-20	T: Ramsay (2), Weatherhead PG: Lockhart (4)
9 Jan	H	Grangemouth	23-0	T: C Livingstone, McLeod, Ramsay C: C Livingstone PG: C Livingstone (2)
30 Jan	A	Glasgow Acads	35-18	T: Campbell, Horsburgh, MacMillan, Ramsay C: C Livingstone (3) PG: C Livingstone (3)
13 Feb	H	Clarkston	21-8	T: C Livingstone, McLeod C: C Livingstone PG: C Livingstone (2) DG: C Livingstone
27 Feb	H	Kirkcaldy	25-0	T: Campbell, Laird, McLeod C: C Livingstone (2) PG: C Livingstone (2)
13 Mar	A	Stewart's-Melville FP	14-17	T: Ramsay, Weatherhead C: C Livingstone (2)

Peebles

Year of formation 1923
Ground Hay Lodge Park, Neidpath Road, Peebles EH45 8NN
Tel: Peebles (0721) 21600
Colours Red with white hoops
Captain 1992-93 S W Ferguson
1st XV 1992-93 P27 W13 D1 L13 F431 A495
McEwan's/SRU Div 2 7th

League Record 1992-93

Date	Venue	Opponents	Result	Scorers
26 Sept	A	Clarkston	16-10	T: Greenshields, Nisbet PG: Mutch (2)
3 Oct	H	Musselburgh	3-17	PG: Mutch
10 Oct	A	Stewart's-Melville FP	0-37	
17 Oct	H	Ayr	10-15	T: G Wilson C: McBride PG: McBride
24 Oct	A	Kirkcaldy	3-3	PG: Nisbet
31 Oct	A	West of Scotland	3-16	PG: Mutch
7 Nov	H	Wigtownshire	23-3	T: Collins (2), Mutch, Nisbet PG: Mutch
14 Nov	A	Preston Lodge FP	10-6	T: pen try C: Mutch PG: Mutch
9 Jan	H	Dunfermline	29-8	T: Ferguson, Knox, McBride, Nisbet, Ross C: Nisbet (2)
30 Jan	A	Edinburgh Wands	17-18	T: Knox, Nisbet C: Mutch (2) PG: Mutch
13 Feb	H	Kilmarnock	9-0	PG: Mutch (3)
27 Feb	A	Grangemouth	0-25	
13 Mar	H	Glasgow Acads	27-20	T: Knox, Nisbet, Ross (2) C: Mutch (2) PG: Mutch

Preston Lodge FP

Year of formation 1929
Ground Pennypit Park, Rope Walk, Prestonpans, East Lothian EH32 9BN
Tel: 0875 810309
Colours Black with maroon band edged in white

Most capped player R F Cunningham (Scotland) 3 caps
Captain 1992-93 R Allan
1st XV 1992-93 P30 W11 D2 L17 F438 A655
McEwan's/SRU Div 2 8th

League Record 1992-93

Date	Venue	Opponents	Result	Scorers
26 Sept	A	Kilmarnock	14-0	*T:* Payne *PG:* Gordon (3)
3 Oct	H	Grangemouth	34-9	*T:* S Gilliland, McMillan, McSorley, Payne, Watt *C:* S Gilliland, Gordon (2) *PG:* S Gilliland
10 Oct	A	Glasgow Acads	10-34	*T:* Henderson *C:* S Gilliland *PG:* S Gilliland
17 Oct	H	Clarkston	16-22	*T:* S Gilliland *C:* S Gilliland *PG:* S Gilliland (3)
24 Oct	A	Musselburgh	14-23	*T:* Donaldson *PG:* S Gilliland, Ramage (2)
31 Oct	H	Stewart's-Melville FP	12-6	*PG:* S Gilliland (3), Ramage
7 Nov	A	Ayr	12-19	*PG:* S Gilliland (3), Ramage
14 Nov	H	Peebles	6-10	*PG:* Ramage (2)
9 Jan	A	West of Scotland	12-26	*T:* Redpath (2) *C:* Gordon
23 Jan	H	Wigtownshire	10-10	*T:* O'Brien *C:* Watters *PG:* Watters
13 Feb	A	Kirkcaldy	31-17	*T:* R Allan, S Gilliland, McLeod, Smith *C:* Watters (4) *PG:* Watters
27 Feb	A	Dunfermline	18-18	*PG:* Watters (6)
13 Mar	H	Edinburgh Wands	15-11	*T:* Newton, Watt *C:* Watters *PG:* Watters

Selkirk

Year of formation 1907
Ground Philiphaugh, Selkirk Tel: Selkirk (0750) 20403
Colours Navy blue
Most capped player J Y Rutherford (Scotland) 42 caps
Captain 1992-93 I Tukalo
1st XV 1992-93 P26 W10 D1 L15 F500 A524
McEwan's/SRU Div 1 12th

League Record 1992-93

Date	Venue	Opponents	Result	Scorers
26 Sept	A	Hawick	8-39	*T:* McGauchie *PG:* Brett
3 Oct	H	Kelso	8-28	*T:* Buckley *PG:* Brett
10 Oct	A	Dundee HSFP	18-12	*T:* Brett, Tukalo *C:* Brett *PG:* Brett (2)
17 Oct	H	Boroughmuir	17-39	*T:* Tukalo *PG:* Brett (4)
24 Oct	A	Heriot's FP	20-33	*T:* Johnston, Linton *C:* Brett (2) *PG:* Brett (2)
31 Oct	H	Glasgow High/K'side	24-22	*T:* Linton (2) *C:* S A Nichol *PG:* S A Nichol (3) *DG:* S A Nichol
7 Nov	A	Gala	10-43	*T:* Johnston *C:* S A Nichol *PG:* S A Nichol
9 Jan	H	Currie	9-12	*PG:* Brett (3)
23 Jan	A	Melrose	5-35	*T:* Linton
30 Jan	A	Jedforest	20-18	*T:* Guntley *PG:* Brett (5)
13 Feb	H	Watsonians	16-19	*T:* Marshall *C:* Brett *PG:* Brett (3)
27 Feb	A	Edinburgh Acads	6-6	*PG:* Brett (2)
13 Mar	H	Stirling County	33-10	*T:* Jaffray (2), Nichol, Tukalo *C:* Pow (2) *PG:* Pow (3)

Stewart's-Melville FP

Year of formation 1973 (on amalgamation of Daniel Stewart's College FP and Melville College FP)
Ground Inverleith, Ferry Road, Edinburgh EH5 2DW Tel: 031-552 1515

Colours Scarlet with broad black and narrow gold bands
Most capped player F Calder (Scotland) 38 caps
Captain 1992-93 D S Wyllie
1st XV 1992-93 P28 W17 D0 L11 F724 A417
McEwan's/SRU Div 2 joint 1st (2nd points difference) *promoted*

League Record 1992-93

Date	Venue	Opponents	Result	Scorers
26 Sept	A	Kirkcaldy	19-12	*T:* MacKenzie *C:* M M Thomson *PG:* M M Thomson (4)
3 Oct	A	Ayr	35-24	*T:* MacKenzie, M M Thomson, Wyllie (2) *C:* M M Thomson (3) *PG:* M M Thomson (3)
10 Oct	H	Peebles	37-0	*T:* Milligan, Penny, Roxburgh, Wilson, Wyllie *C:* M M Thomson (3) *PG:* M M Thomson (2)
17 Oct	A	West of Scotland	23-18	*T:* MacKenzie, J M Scott (2) *C:* Stirling *PG:* Stirling (2)
24 Oct	H	Wigtownshire	19-24	*T:* MacKenzie, Wilson *PG:* M M Thomson (3)
31 Oct	A	Preston Lodge FP	6-12	*PG:* M M Thomson (2)
7 Nov	H	Dunfermline	42-0	*T:* Dobson, Kittle, MacKenzie, J M Scott (2), pen try *C:* Stirling, Wyllie (2) *PG:* Stirling, Wyllie
14 Nov	A	Edinburgh Wands	24-13	*T:* MacKenzie, Wyllie *C:* M M Thomson *PG:* M M Thomson (3) *DG:* Wyllie
9 Jan	H	Kilmarnock	53-0	*T:* Burns (3), Flockhart, MacKenzie, McNulty, Stirling (3) *C:* M M Thomson (4)
30 Jan	A	Grangemouth	23-18	*T:* Burns, MacKenzie, Stirling *C:* M M Thomson *PG:* M M Thomson (2)
13 Feb	H	Glasgow Acads	32-18	*T:* Burnside, MacKenzie, Milligan (3) *C:* M M Thomson, Wyllie *DG:* Wyllie
27 Feb	A	Clarkston	24-3	*T:* F Calder, Stirling, M M Thomson *PG:* M M Thomson (2) *DG:* Wyllie
13 Mar	H	Musselburgh	17-14	*T:* Stirling, Wyllie *C:* M M Thomson (2) *PG:* M M Thomson

Stirling County

Year of formation 1904
Ground Bridgehaugh Park, Causewayhead Road, Stirling Tel: Stirling (0786) 74827
Colours Red, white and black
Most capped player K M Logan (Scotland) 2 caps
Captain 1992-93 K G M Harper
1st XV 1992-93 P28 W15 D1 L12 F490 A303
McEwan's/SRU Div 1 joint 8th

League Record 1992-93

Date	Venue	Opponents	Result	Scorers
26 Sept	H	Jedforest	8-9	*T:* Turner *PG:* M McKenzie
10 Oct	H	Melrose	13-9	*T:* Crawford *C:* M McKenzie *PG:* M McKenzie (2)
17 Oct	A	Watsonians	24-15	*T:* Ireland, K D McKenzie, Turner (2) *C:* MacDonald (2)
24 Oct	H	Edinburgh Acads	3-16	*PG:* MacDonald
31 Oct	H	Gala	9-14	*PG:* MacDonald (3)
7 Nov	A	Hawick	8-22	*T:* K D McKenzie *PG:* MacDonald
14 Nov	H	Kelso	18-19	*T:* Brough, Turner *C:* MacDonald *PG:* MacDonald (2)
9 Jan	A	Dundee HSFP	9-8	*PG:* J P Stewart (3)
30 Jan	A	Currie	14-22	*T:* McVey, Mailer *C:* J P Stewart (2)
13 Feb	A	Heriot's FP	7-24	*T:* K M Logan *C:* J P Stewart

27 Feb	H	Glasgow High/K'side	23-11	*T:* Elliott, K M Logan, McVey *C:* M McKenzie
				PG: K M Logan, M McKenzie
13 Mar	A	Selkirk	10-33	*T:* Elliot *C:* M McKenzie *PG:* M McKenzie
27 Mar	H	Boroughmuir	33-6	*T:* Blues, K M Logan, M D McKenzie
				M McKenzie *C:* M McKenzie (2)
				PG: K M Logan, M McKenzie
				DG: M McKenzie

Watsonians

Year of formation 1875
Ground Myreside, Myreside Road, Edinburgh EH10 5DB   Tel: 031-447 5200
Colours Maroon and white hoops
Most capped player S Hastings (Scotland) 46 caps
Captain 1992-93 D S Henderson
1st XV 1992-93 P25 W9 D0 L16 F369 A514
McEwan's/SRU Div 1 joint 8th

League Record 1992-93

Date	Venue	Opponents	Result	Scorers
26 Sept	H	Melrose	13-14	*T:* A G Hastings, F M Henderson
				PG: A G Hastings
3 Oct	H	Gala	5-13	*T:* Lee
10 Oct	A	Edinburgh Acads	12-16	*PG:* A G Hastings (4)
17 Oct	H	Stirling County	15-24	*T:* F M Henderson, Johnston *C:* A G Hastings
				PG: A G Hastings
24 Oct	A	Hawick	14-11	*T:* Kelly, MacDonald *C:* Kelly (2)
31 Oct	H	Kelso	27-17	*T:* S Hastings, D S Henderson, Kelly, Rudkin
				C: F M Henderson, Lee *PG:* Lee
7 Nov	A	Dundee HSFP	29-15	*T:* Couser, A G Hastings, F M Henderson, Lee
				C: A G Hastings (3) *PG:* A G Hastings
14 Nov	H`	Boroughmuir	15-37	*T:* A G Hastings, Laws *C:* Lee
				PG: A G Hastings
9 Jan	A	Heriot's FP	15-30	*PG:* A G Hastings (5)
30 Jan	H	Glasgow High/K'side	21-15	*T:* Garry, A G Hastings *C:* A G Hastings
				PG: A G Hastings (2) *DG:* Lee
13 Feb	A	Selkirk	19-16	*T:* Lee *C:* A G Hastings *PG:* A G Hastings (4)
27 Feb	H	Jedforest	5-50	*T:* Garry
13 Mar	A	Currie	6-19	*PG:* Ker (2)

West of Scotland

Year of formation 1865
Ground Burnbrae, Glasgow Road, Milngavie, Glasgow G62 6HX
Tel: 041-956 3116 and 041-956 1960
Colours Red and yellow hoops
Most capped player A B Carmichael (Scotland) 50 caps
Captain 1992-93 D N Barrett
1st XV 1992-93 P26 W19 D0 L7 F675 A447
McEwan's/SRU Div 2 joint 1st (winners on points difference) *promoted*

League Record 1992-93

Date	Venue	Opponents	Result	Scorers
26 Sept	A	Glasgow Acads	21-13	*T:* Barrett, A Williamson *C:* Barrett
				PG: Barrett (3)
3 Oct	H	Clarkston	26-12	*T:* McIntosh, McKee *C:* Barrett (2)
				PG: Barrett (3) *DG:* Barrett

10 Oct	A	Musselburgh	13-24	*T:* A Williamson *C:* Barrett *PG:* Barrett *DG:* Barrett
17 Oct	H	Stewart's-Melville FP	18-23	*PG:* Barrett (6)
24 Oct	A	Ayr	29-8	*T:* Carmichael, Robertson *C:* Barrett (2) *PG:* Barrett (5)
31 Oct	H	Peebles	16-3	*T:* Lonergan (2) *PG:* Barrett (2)
7 Nov	A	Kirkcaldy	40-24	*T:* Barrett, Carmichael, Clark (2), Lonergan, Stott *C:* Barrett (5)
14 Nov	A	Wigtownshire	8-0	*T:* Carmichael *PG:* Barrett
9 Jan	H	Preston Lodge FP	26-12	*T:* McKee, Macpherson *C:* Barrett (2) *PG:* Barrett (4)
30 Jan	A	Dunfermline	38-16	*T:* Cochrane, Fletcher, McKee (2), Robertson, Stott *C:* Barrett (4)
13 Feb	H	Edinburgh Wands	35-12	*T:* Barrett (2), Robertson, Williamson *C:* Barrett (3) *PG:* Barrett (3)
27 Feb	A	Kilmarnock	55-3	*T:* Barrett, Carmichael, Munro, Robertson, Tasker, A Williamson (2) *C:* Barrett (4) *PG:* Barrett (4)
13 Mar	H	Grangemouth	52-6	*T:* Barrett, Carmichael, Fletcher (2), McKee, Munro *C:* Barrett (5) *PG:* Barrett (4)

Wigtownshire

Year of formation 1922
Ground London Road Playing Fields, Ladies Walk, Stranraer   Tel: Stranraer (0776) 4133
Colours Royal blue
Captain 1992-93 Douglas Drysdale
1st XV 1992-93 P25   W11   D2   L12   F474   A469
McEwan's/SRU Div 2 joint 10th

League Record 1992-93

Date	Venue	Opponents	Result	Scorers
26 Sept	A	Grangemouth	10-25	*T:* A Drysdale *C:* Scott Kelly *PG:* Scott Kelly
3 Oct	H	Glasgow Acads	7-55	*T:* Tennant *C:* Scott Kelly
10 Oct	A	Clarkston	6-38	*PG:* Scott Kelly (2)
17 Oct	H	Musselburgh	6-20	*PG:* Scott Kelly (2)
24 Oct	A	Stewart's-Melville FP	24-19	*T:* David Drysdale, Gemmell, Kilker, M I Hose *C:* Scott Kelly (2)
31 Oct	H	Ayr	11-17	*T:* David Drysdale *PG:* Scott Kelly (2)
7 Nov	A	Peebles	3-23	*PG:* David Drysdale
14 Nov	H	West of Scotland	0-8	
9 Jan	A	Kirkcaldy	17-55	*T:* David Drysdale (2) *C:* McHenry (2) *PG:* McHenry
23 Jan	A	Preston Lodge FP	10-10	*T:* Andrew Hose, Kerr
13 Feb	H	Dunfermline	13-13	*T:* A Drysdale, David Drysdale *PG:* David Drysdale
27 Feb	A	Edinburgh Wands	15-9	*T:* Hannah, Kilker *C:* Stewart Kelly *PG:* Stewart Kelly
13 Mar	H	Kilmarnock	38-6	*T:* A Drysdale (2), David Drysdale, Gemmell, Hannah, Andrew Hose *C:* Stewart Kelly (4)

IRELAND
Ballymena

Year of formation 1922
Ground Eaton Park, Raceview Road, Ballymena   Tel: Ballymena 656746
Colours Black
Most capped player W J McBride (Ireland) 63 caps
Captain 1992-93 K Andrew

1st XV 1992-93   P27   W13   D2   L12   F581   A471
Insurance Corporation League Div 1 9th *relegated* **First Trust Bank Ulster Senior Cup**
Lost 18-20 to Dungannon (final)

League Record 1992-93

Date	Venue	Opponents	Result	Scorers
10 Oct	A	Young Munster	6-11	*PG:* McAleese (2)
7 Nov	H	Garryowen	15-12	*PG:* Laing (2), McAleese *DG:* Laing (2)
14 Nov	A	St Mary's Coll	6-26	*PG:* Laing (2)
9 Jan	H	Old Wesley	17-19	*T:* Chambers *PG:* McAleese (3) *DG:* McAleese
23 Jan	A	Dungannon	15-26	*PG:* McAleese (5)
30 Jan	H	Shannon	9-6	*PG:* McAleese (2), Laing
6 Feb	A	Greystones	6-13	*PG:* Laing (2)
13 Feb	H	Cork Const	23-38	*T:* Pollock, Simpson *C:* Laing, McAleese *PG:* McAleese (2) *DG:* Laing

Bangor

Year of formation 1885
Ground Upritchard Park, Bloomfield Road South, Bangor   Tel: Bangor 462670
Colours Old gold, royal blue and black
Most capped player J J McCoy (Ireland) 16 caps
Captain 1992-93 D Whittle
1st XV 1992-93   P24   W9   D1   L14   F448   A442
Insurance Corporation League Div 2 9th **First Trust Bank Ulster Senior Cup** Lost 8-10
to Malone (quarter-final)

League Record 1992-93

Date	Venue	Opponents	Result	Scorers
10 Oct	H	Wanderers	6-25	*PG:* McCall (2)
7 Nov	A	Galwegians	10-10	*T:* Hooks *C:* McCall *PG:* McCall
14 Nov	H	Blackrock Coll	6-23	*PG:* Millar (2)
21 Nov	A	Dolphin	11-15	*T:* Long *PG:* Millar (2)
9 Jan	H	Instonians	16-22	*T:* Rogers *C:* McCall *PG:* McCall (2) *DG:* McMaster
23 Jan	H	Terenure Coll	7-16	*T:* McCoy *C:* McCall
30 Jan	A	Old Crescent	15-18	*PG:* McCall (3) *DG:* McMaster (2)
6 Feb	H	Lansdowne	25-32	*T:* Maxwell (3) *C:* McCall (2) *PG:* McCall (2)
13 Feb	A	Clontarf	16-13	*T:* pen try *C:* McCall *PG:* McCall *DG:* McMaster (2)

Blackrock College

Year of formation 1882
Ground Stradbrook Road, Blackrock, Dublin   Tel: Dublin 2805967
Colours Royal blue and white hoops
Most capped player J F Slattery (Ireland) 61 caps
Captain 1992-93 B J Mullin
1st XV 1992-93   P25   W12   D1   L12   F474   A413
Insurance Corporation League Div 2 3rd *promoted* **Smithwicks Leinster Senior Cup**
Lost 10-23 to St Mary's College (1st round)

League Record 1992-93

Date	Venue	Opponents	Result	Scorers
10 Oct	A	Dolphin	8-14	*T:* Rolland *PG:* McGowan
7 Nov	H	Clontarf	19-8	*T:* Rolland, Ridge *PG:* McGowan (2) *DG:* McGowan

14 Nov	A	Bangor	23-6	*T:* Ridge *PG:* McGowan (6)
21 Nov	H	Old Crescent	27-12	*T:* Rolland, Ridge *C:* McGowan
				PG: McGowan (5)
9 Jan	A	Lansdowne	6-16	*PG:* Woods, Mullin
23 Jan	A	Galwegians	6-6	*PG:* McGowan (2)
30 Jan	H	Instonians	20-12	*T:* Beggy, Woods *C:* McGowan, Mullin
				PG: McGowan *DG:* McGowan
6 Feb	A	Wanderers	32-18	*T:* Woods (2), Costello *C:* McGowan
				PG: McGowan (5)
13 Feb	H	Terenure Coll	8-3	*T:* Woods *PG:* McGowan

Clontarf

Year of formation 1876
Ground Castle Avenue, Clontarf, Dublin   Tel: Dublin 332621
Colours Red and blue hoops
Most capped player G J Morgan (Ireland) 19 caps
Captain 1992-93 R Foley
1st XV 1992-93 P30 W10 D1 L19 F547 A624
Insurance Corporation League Div 2 10th *relegated* **Smithwicks Leinster Senior Cup**
Lost 11-26 to Greystones (quarter-final)

League Record 1992-93

Date	*Venue*	*Opponents*	*Result*	*Scorers*
10 Oct	A	Lansdowne	8-15	*T:* Matthews *PG:* Matthews
7 Nov	A	Blackrock Coll	8-19	*T:* Foley *PG:* Reilly
14 Nov	H	Galwegians	19-11	*T:* Carroll, O'Brien, Quinn *C:* Reilly (2)
21 Nov	A	Instonians	3-13	*PG:* Reilly
9 Jan	H	Wanderers	3-25	*PG:* Moore
23 Jan	A	Dolphin	10-15	*T:* Lawless *C:* Moore *PG:* Moore
30 Jan	A	Terenure Coll	10-11	*T:* Fitzsimmons *C:* Smith *PG:* Smith
6 Feb	H	Old Crescent	12-18	*T:* Fitzsimmons, Carroll *C:* Smith
13 Feb	H	Bangor	13-16	*T:* Carroll (2) *PG:* Smith

Cork Constitution

Year of formation 1892
Ground Temple Hill, Ballintemple, Cork   Tel: Cork 292563
Colours White
Most capped player T J Kiernan (Ireland) 54 caps
Captain 1992-93 L Dineen
1st XV 1992-93 P32 W25 D1 L6 F757 A462
Insurance Corporation League Div 1 2nd **Carling Munster Senior Cup** Lost 13-15 to
Garryowen (semi-final)

League Record 1992-93

Date	*Venue*	*Opponents*	*Result*	*Scorers*
10 Oct	H	Old Wesley	17-6	*T:* Corkery *PG:* K Murphy (2), Haly, Byrne
7 Nov	A	Dungannon	29-25	*T:* Walsh, Bradley, Haly *C:* Keyes
				PG: Keyes (4)
14 Nov	H	Shannon	15-8	*T:* K Murphy, Murray, Crotty
21 Nov	A	Greystones	23-20	*T:* Haly (2), Murray *C:* Keyes *PG:* Keyes (2)
23 Jan	H	Young Munster	13-16	*T:* Murray *C:* K Murphy *PG:* K Murphy (2)
30 Jan	A	Garryowen	20-18	*T:* Walsh *PG:* K Murphy (5)
6 Feb	H	St Mary's Coll	11-12	*T:* Howell *PG:* K Murphy *DG:* Crotty
13 Feb	A	Ballymena	38-23	*T:* Murray (2), Walsh (2), Corkery
				C: K Murphy (2) *PG:* K Murphy
				DG: Bradley (2)

Dolphin

Year of formation 1902
Ground Musgrave Park, Cork   Tel: Cork 962435
Colours Navy blue, yellow and white
Most capped player M J Kiernan (Ireland) 43 caps
Captain 1992-93 T Keogh
1st XV 1992-93   P30   W15   D0   L15   F512   A487
Insurance Corporation League Div 2 4th **Carling Munster Senior Cup** Lost 0-15 to
Young Munster (semi-final)

League Record 1992-93

Date	Venue	Opponents	Result	Scorers
10 Oct	H	Blackrock Coll	14-8	*T:* O'Mahony *PG:* O'Mahony (2) *DG:* Kidney
7 Nov	A	Terenure Coll	12-16	*PG:* O'Mahony (3) *DG:* O'Mahony
14 Nov	A	Instonians	10-22	*T:* Kidney *C:* Kiernan *PG:* O'Mahony
21 Nov	H	Bangor	15-11	*T:* J Clarke, Holden *C:* O'Mahony *PG:* O'Mahony
9 Jan	A	Old Crescent	12-9	*PG:* O'Mahony (4)
23 Jan	H	Clontarf	15-10	*T:* J Clarke, O'Donoghue, O'Shea
30 Jan	A	Lansdowne	24-28	*T:* O'Shea, Kelleher, Keogh *C:* Kidney (2), O'Mahony *DG:* Kidney
6 Feb	H	Galwegians	21-8	*T:* Kidney, O'Shea, O'Neill *PG:* Kiernan (2)
13 Feb	A	Wanderers	10-12	*T:* Keogh *C:* Kidney *PG:* Kiernan

Dungannon

Year of formation 1873
Ground Stevenson Park, Dungannon   Tel: Dungannon 22387
Colours Blue and white hoops
Most capped player W A Anderson (Ireland) 27 caps
Captain 1992-93 W A Anderson
1st XV 1992-93   P33   W21   D1   L11   F978   A557
Insurance Corporation League Div 1 6th **First Trust Bank Ulster Senior Cup** *Winners*
Beat Ballymena 20-18 (final)

League Record 1992-93

Date	Venue	Opponents	Result	Scorers
10 Oct	A	Greystones	15-29	*T:* Carey, Boyd *C:* McGarry *PG:* McGarry
7 Nov	H	Cork Const	25-29	*T:* Jy Hastings *C:* McGarry *PG:* Blair (3), Archer (2) *DG:* Archer
14 Nov	A	Young Munster	15-22	*PG:* McGarry (5)
21 Nov	H	Garryowen	16-11	*T:* Jy Hastings (2) *PG:* McGarry (2)
9 Jan	A	St Mary's Coll	12-30	*PG:* Blair (3), McGarry
23 Jan	H	Ballymena	26-15	*T:* Boyd (2), Anderson *C:* Blair *PG:* Blair, McGarry *DG:* Blair
30 Jan	A	Old Wesley	24-20	*T:* McDowell, Carey *C:* Blair *PG:* Blair *DG:* Archer (2), McGarry
13 Feb	H	Shannon	11-16	*T:* Howe *PG:* McGarry (2)

Galwegians

Year of formation 1922
Ground Crowley Park, Glenina, Galway   Tel: Galway 53435
Colours Sky blue
Most capped player P J A O'Sullivan (Ireland) 15 caps

Captain 1992-93 S Guerin
1st XV 1992-93 P31 W10 D3 L18 F465 A597
Insurance Corporation League Div 2 8th **Smithwicks Connacht Senior Cup** Lost 3-17
to Athlone (1st round)

League Record 1992-93

Date	Venue	Opponents	Result	Scorers
10 Oct	H	Instonians	3-13	*PG:* O'Donnell
7 Nov	H	Bangor	10-10	*T:* Leahy *C:* Lee *PG:* O'Donnell
14 Nov	A	Clontarf	11-19	*T:* O'Donnell *PG:* Lee (2)
21 Nov	H	Lansdowne	8-13	*T:* Clarke *PG:* Beatty
9 Jan	A	Terenure Coll	15-31	*T:* Clarke, Molloy *C:* O'Donnell
				PG: O'Donnell
23 Jan	H	Blackrock Coll	6-6	*PG:* McGowan (2)
30 Jan	H	Wanderers	5-12	*T:* O'Donnell
6 Feb	A	Dolphin	8-21	*T:* Dooley *PG:* McGowan
13 Feb	A	Old Crescent	31-18	*T:* Rogers, Carty, Beatty, Murphy
				C: McGowan (4) *PG:* McGowan

Garryowen

Year of formation 1884
Ground Dooradoyle, Limerick   Tel: Limerick 27672
Colours Light blue with white five-pointed star
Most capped player B G M Wood (Ireland) 29 caps
Captain 1992-93 D Larkin
1st XV 1992-93 P32 W20 D0 L12 F618 A454
Insurance Corporation League Div 1 8th **Carling Munster Senior Cup** *Winners* Beat
Young Munster 12-5 (final)

League Record 1992-93

Date	Venue	Opponents	Result	Scorers
10 Oct	H	St Mary's Coll	30-16	*T:* Quilligan (2), Wood, Murphy *C:* Smith (2)
				PG: Smith *DG:* Larkin
7 Nov	A	Ballymena	12-15	*PG:* Smith (4)
14 Nov	H	Old Wesley	29-13	*T:* Quilligan, Larkin *C:* Smith (2)
				PG: Smith (4) *DG:* Larkin
21 Nov	A	Dungannon	11-16	*T:* Cronin *PG:* Smith (2)
23 Jan	A	Greystones	15-24	*PG:* Smith (3) *DG:* Larkin (2)
30 Jan	H	Cork Const	18-20	*PG:* Smith (6)
6 Feb	A	Young Munster	6-13	*PG:* Smith (2)
27 Feb	H	Shannon	11-27	*T:* Quilligan *PG:* Smith, Larkin

Greystones

Year of formation 1937
Ground Dr J J Hickey Park, Delgany Road, Greystones, Co Wicklow
Tel: Dublin 2874640
Colours Green and white narrow hoops
Most capped player A J P Ward (Ireland) 19 caps
Captain 1992-93 J N Murphy
1st XV 1992-93 P30 W21 D1 L8 F797 A566
Insurance Corporation League Div 1 4th **Smithwicks Leinster Senior Cup** Lost 8-28 to
Old Wesley (semi-final)

League Record 1992-93

Date	Venue	Opponents	Result	Scorers
10 Oct	H	Dungannon	29-15	T: Heaney, Power, McVitty, Dignam C: O'Farrell (3) PG: O'Farrell
7 Nov	A	Shannon	15-13	PG: Dunne (4) DG: Dunne
21 Nov	H	Cork Const	20-23	T: Vance, Murphy C: Dunne (2) PG: Dunne (2)
9 Jan	A	Young Munster	3-3	PG: Dunne
23 Jan	H	Garryowen	24-15	T: Keyes, Quinn, Magennety C: Dunne (3) PG: Dunne
30 Jan	A	St Mary's Coll	15-41	PG: Dunne (5)
6 Feb	H	Ballymena	13-6	T: Carney C: Keyes PG: Keyes DG: McVitty
13 Feb	A	Old Wesley	13-6	T: Carney C: Keyes PG: Keyes DG: Vance

Instonians

Year of formation 1919
Ground Shane Park, Stockman's Lane, Belfast   Tel: Belfast 660629
Colours Purple, yellow and black
Most capped player K D Crossan (Ireland) 41 caps
Captain 1992-93 B McKibbin
1st XV 1992-93 P25 W14 D2 L9 F501 A374
Insurance Corporation League Div 2 6th **First Trust Bank Ulster Senior Cup** Lost 11-31 to Ballymena (1st round)

League Record 1992-93

Date	Venue	Opponents	Result	Scorers
10 Oct	A	Galwegians	13-3	T: Crossan C: Russell PG: Russell (2)
7 Nov	A	Wanderers	6-15	PG: Strutt (2)
14 Nov	H	Dolphin	22-10	T: Wylie C: Russell PG: Russell (5)
21 Nov	H	Clontarf	13-3	T: Bell, Strutt PG: Russell
9 Jan	A	Bangor	22-16	T: Lamont, Strutt, Crossan C: Russell (2) PG: Russell
23 Jan	H	Old Crescent	8-13	T: Russell PG: Russell
30 Jan	A	Blackrock Coll	12-20	PG: Strutt, Russell DG: Strutt, Wylie
6 Feb	H	Terenure Coll	13-11	T: Wylie C: Strutt PG: Strutt (2)
13 Feb	H	Lansdowne	15-35	T: Russell, Lamont C: Russell DG: Russell

Lansdowne

Year of formation 1872
Ground Lansdowne Road, Dublin   Tel: Dublin 689300
Colours Red, yellow and black
Most capped player M I Keane (Ireland) 51 caps
Captain 1992-93 L F P Aherne   •
1st XV 1992-93 P30 W25 D1 L4 F701 A404
Insurance Corporation League Div 2 *Winners* **Smithwicks Leinster Senior Cup** Lost to St Mary's College 6-17 (semi-final)

League Record 1992-93

Date	Venue	Opponents	Result	Scorers
10 Oct	H	Clontarf	15-8	T: Ahern, Aherne C: O'Shea DG: Elwood
7 Nov	A	Old Crescent	16-15	T: Whelan C: Elwood PG: Elwood (2) DG: Elwood

14 Nov	H	Terenure Coll	32-3	*T:* Sexton, Shalloe, Aherne, Elwood
				C: O'Shea (2), Elwood *PG:* O'Shea (2)
21 Nov	A	Galwegians	13-8	*T:* Mannion *C:* Elwood *PG:* O'Shea
				DG: Elwood
9 Jan	H	Blackrock Coll	16-6	*T:* Dwyer, Aherne *PG:* Elwood (2)
23 Jan	A	Wanderers	22-14	*T:* Sexton *C:* Elwood *PG:* Elwood (3)
				DG: Elwood, Aherne
30 Jan	H	Dolphin	28-24	*T:* Sexton, Doyle, Elwood *C:* Elwood (2)
				PG: Elwood (3)
6 Feb	A	Bangor	32-25	*T:* Glennon (3), Brady *C:* Elwood (3)
				PG: Elwood *DG:* Elwood
13 Feb	A	Instonians	35-15	*T:* Whelan (2), Mannion, Shalloe
				C: Elwood (3) *PG:* Elwood (3)

Old Crescent

Year of formation 1947
Ground Rosbrien, Limerick   Tel: Limerick 228083
Colours Navy, blue and white hoops
Most capped player P Lane (Ireland) 1 cap
Captain 1992-93 P Boland
1st XV 1992-93 P32   W14   D0   L18   F538   A487
Insurance Corporation League Div 2 7th **Carling Munster Senior Cup** Lost 17-20 to Cork Constitution (1st round)

League Record 1992-93

Date	Venue	Opponents	Result	Scorers
10 Oct	A	Terenure Coll	3-19	*PG:* Tuohy
7 Nov	H	Lansdowne	15-16	*PG:* Begley (5)
14 Nov	H	Wanderers	24-26	*T:* T Browne (2) *C:* Begley *PG:* Begley (3)
				DG: Tuohy
21 Nov	A	Blackrock Coll	12-27	*PG:* Begley (4)
9 Jan	H	Dolphin	9-12	*PG:* Begley (3)
23 Jan	A	Instonians	13-8	*T:* O'Sullivan *C:* Begley *PG:* Begley (2)
30 Jan	H	Bangor	18-15	*PG:* Begley (6)
6 Feb	A	Clontarf	18-12	*T:* Begley, Tolland *C:* Begley *PG:* Begley
				DG: Barrett
13 Feb	H	Galwegians	18-31	*T:* O'Sullivan, Boland *C:* Begley
				PG: Begley, Barrett

Old Wesley

Year of formation 1891
Ground Donnybrook, Dublin   Tel: Dublin 609893
Colours White with blue and red band
Most capped player P A Orr (Ireland) 58 caps
Captain 1992-93 D Strong
1st XV 1992-93 P36   W26   D1   L9   F708   A500
Insurance Corporation League Div 1 5th **Smithwicks Leinster Senior Cup** Lost 6-12 to St Mary's College (final)

League Record 1992-93

Date	Venue	Opponents	Result	Scorers
10 Oct	A	Cork Const	6-17	*PG:* Strong *DG:* Farren
7 Nov	H	Young Munster	26-17	*T:* Cody *PG:* Farren (6) *DG:* Farren
14 Nov	A	Garryowen	13-29	*T:* Porter *C:* Farren *PG:* Farren, Strong
21 Nov	H	St Mary's Coll	0-28	
9 Jan	A	Ballymena	19-17	*T:* Bursey *C:* Farren *PG:* Farren (3)
				DG: Strong

30 Jan	H	Dungannon	20-24	*T:* Strong, Pim *C:* Farren (2) *PG:* Farren (2)
6 Feb	A	Shannon	7-6	*T:* Jackson *C:* Farren
13 Feb	H	Greystones	16-13	*T:* Pim *C:* Farren *PG:* Farren (3)

Shannon

Year of formation 1884
Ground Thomond Park, Limerick   Tel: Limerick 452350
Colours Black and blue hoops
Most capped player G A J McLoughlin (Ireland) 18 caps
Captain 1992-93 M J Galwey
1st XV 1992-93 P28 W14 D1 L13 F581 A471
Insurance Corporation League Div 1 7th **Carling Munster Senior Cup** Lost 6-15 to Young Munster (quarter-final)

League Record 1992-93

Date	Venue	Opponents	Result	Scorers
7 Nov	H	Greystones	13-15	*T:* Kenny, Roche *PG:* Pearse
14 Nov	A	Cork Const	8-15	*T:* Gallagher *PG:* W O'Shea
21 Nov	H	Young Munster	6-15	*PG:* Pearse (2)
23 Jan	H	St Mary's Coll	3-3	*PG:* W O'Shea
30 Jan	A	Ballymena	6-9	*PG:* W O'Shea (2)
6 Feb	H	Old Wesley	6-7	*PG:* W O'Shea (2)
13 Feb	A	Dungannon	16-11	*T:* Gallagher *C:* W O'Shea *PG:* W O'Shea (2) *DG:* Galvin
27 Feb	A	Garryowen	27-11	*T:* W O'Shea, Fitzgerald *C:* W O'Shea *PG:* W O'Shea (4) *DG:* Galvin

St Mary's College

Year of formation 1900
Ground Templeville Road, Templeogue, Dublin   Tel: Dublin 900440
Colours Royal blue with five-pointed white star
Most capped player P M Dean (Ireland) 32 caps
Captain 1992-93 S Jameson
1st XV 1992-93 P32 W23 D3 L6 F796 A410
Insurance Corporation League Div 1 3rd **Smithwicks Leinster Senior Cup** *Winners* Beat Old Wesley 12-6 (final)

League Record 1992-93

Date	Venue	Opponents	Result	Scorers
10 Oct	A	Garryowen	16-30	*T:* D Hernan *C:* White *PG:* White (3)
14 Nov	H	Ballymena	26-6	*T:* Wall, White *C:* White (2) *PG:* White (3) *DG:* Barry
21 Nov	A	Old Wesley	28-0	*T:* Wall (2), Cunningham *C:* White (2) *PG:* White (3)
9 Jan	H	Dungannon	30-12	*T:* Wall (2), Jameson *C:* White (3) *PG:* White (3)
23 Jan	A	Shannon	3-3	*PG:* White
30 Jan	H	Greystones	41-15	*T:* Gillen (2), Dowling, Wall, Devlin *C:* White (2) *PG:* White (4)
6 Feb	A	Cork Const	12-11	*PG:* White (4)
13 Feb	H	Young Munster	14-17	*T:* Wall *PG:* White (2) *DG:* Barry

Terenure College

Year of formation 1941
Ground Lakelands Park, Greenlea Grove, Terenure, Dublin   Tel: Dublin 907572

Colours Purple, black and white hoops
Most capped player M L Hipwell (Ireland) 12 caps
Captain 1992-93 P Hennebry
1st XV 1992-93 P26 W20 D1 L5 F695 A255
Insurance Corporation League Div 2 5th **Smithwicks Leinster Senior Cup** Lost 7-10 to
Old Wesley (quarter-final)

League Record 1992-93

Date	Venue	Opponents	Result	Scorers
10 Oct	H	Old Crescent	19-3	*T:* Costello (2) *PG:* Hennebry (3)
7 Nov	H	Dolphin	16-12	*T:* Costello, Walsh *PG:* Cullen (2)
14 Nov	A	Lansdowne	3-32	*PG:* Cullen
21 Nov	A	Wanderers	13-21	*T:* Tynan *C:* Walsh *PG:* Walsh (2)
9 Jan	H	Galwegians	31-15	*T:* Hennebry, Costello, C Clarke, pen try
				C: Hennebry (4) *PG:* Hennebry
23 Jan	A	Bangor	16-7	*T:* Costello, White *PG:* Hennebry (2)
30 Jan	H	Clontarf	11-10	*T:* Hennebry *PG:* Hennebry *DG:* Hennebry
6 Feb	A	Instonians	11-13	*T:* Daly *PG:* Hennebry, Daly
13 Feb	A	Blackrock Coll	3-8	*PG:* Walsh

Wanderers

Year of formation 1870
Grounds Lansdowne Road, Dublin   Tel: Dublin 689277; Merrion Road, Dublin
Tel: Dublin 695272
Colours Blue, black and white
Most capped player J R Kavanagh (Ireland) 35 caps
Captain 1992-93 M Murphy
1st XV 1992-93 P28 W20 D1 L7 F716 A423
Insurance Corporation League Div 2 2nd *promoted* **Smithwicks Leinster Senior Cup**
Lost 6-34 to St Mary's College (quarter-final)

League Record 1992-93

Date	Venue	Opponents	Result	Scorers
10 Oct	A	Bangor	25-6	*T:* Leahy (2), Finnegan *C:* Wyse (2)
				DG: Wyse (2)
7 Nov	H	Instonians	15-6	*T:* Leahy, McGoey *C:* Wyse *PG:* Wyse
14 Nov	A	Old Crescent	26-24	*T:* Leahy (2), Wyse *C:* Wyse *PG:* Wyse (3)
21 Nov	H	Terenure Coll	21-13	*T:* Leahy (2) *C:* Wyse *PG:* Wyse (3)
9 Jan	A	Clontarf	25-3	*T:* Kenny, Wyse *PG:* Wyse (5)
23 Jan	H	Lansdowne	14-22	*T:* Walker *PG:* Wyse (3)
30 Jan	A	Galwegians	12-5	*T:* Culliton, Garth *C:* Wyse
6 Feb	H	Blackrock Coll	18-32	*T:* Walker, Culliton *C:* Wyse *PG:* Wyse (2)
13 Feb	H	Dolphin	12-10	*PG:* Wyse (3) *DG:* Wyse

Young Munster

Year of formation 1895
Ground Tom Clifford Park, Greenfields, Limerick   Tel: Limerick 228433
Colours Black and amber hoops
Most capped player T Clifford (Ireland) 14 caps
Captain 1992-93 G Clohessy
1st XV 1992-93 P28 W19 D3 L6 F534 A301
Insurance Corporation League Div 1 *Winners* **Carling Munster Senior Cup** Lost 5-12 to
Garryowen (final)

League Record 1992-93

Date	Venue	Opponents	Result	Scorers
10 Oct	H	Ballymena	11-6	*T:* N McNamara *PG:* Benson *DG:* O'Halloran
7 Nov	A	Old Wesley	17-26	*T:* Ryan *PG:* O'Halloran (2), Benson *DG:* O'Halloran
14 Nov	H	Dungannon	22-15	*T:* Clohessy *C:* O'Halloran *PG:* O'Halloran (4) *DG:* O'Halloran
21 Nov	A	Shannon	15-6	*PG:* O'Halloran (4) *DG:* O'Halloran
9 Jan	H	Greystones	3-3	*PG:* O'Halloran
23 Jan	A	Cork Const	16-13	*T:* N McNamara *C:* O'Halloran *PG:* O'Halloran (3)
6 Feb	H	Garryowen	13-6	*T:* pen try *C:* O'Halloran *PG:* O'Halloran (2)
13 Feb	A	St Mary's Coll	17-14	*T:* Earls *PG:* O'Halloran (2) *DG:* O'Halloran (2)

WALES
Aberavon

Year of formation 1876
Ground Talbot Athletic Ground, Manor Street, Port Talbot, West Glamorgan
Tel: Port Talbot (0639) 882427
Colours Red and black hoops
Most capped player A J Martin (Wales) 34 caps
Captain 1992-93 L Lewis
1st XV 1992-93 P40 W20 D0 L20 F743 A695
Heineken League Div 1 9th **SWALEC Cup** Lost 5-9 to Fleur-de-Lys (4th round)

League Record 1992-93

Date	Venue	Opponents	Result	Scorers
5 Sept	H	Cardiff	6-15	*PG:* Love (2)
12 Sept	A	Newbridge	21-19	*T:* M Evans, J Griffiths, D Griffiths *PG:* Love (2)
19 Sept	H	Maesteg	15-23	*T:* N Griffiths, M Evans *C:* N Griffiths *PG:* N Griffiths
26 Sept	A	S Wales Police	24-0	*T:* G Evans (2) *C:* Love *PG:* Love (4)
3 Oct	H	Llanelli	3-19	*PG:* N Griffiths
10 Oct	A	Neath	16-38	*T:* Shenton, W Morris *PG:* Love *DG:* Love
17 Oct	H	Pontypool	11-26	*T:* Dragone *PG:* Vauden (2)
24 Oct	A	Bridgend	10-18	*T:* D Griffiths *C:* N Griffiths *PG:* N Griffiths
31 Oct	H	Newport	20-42	*T:* Diplock, Hamley, G Evans *C:* Love *DG:* Love
14 Nov	A	Maesteg	17-7	*T:* D Davies, Bucknell *C:* Love (2) *PG:* Love
28 Nov	A	Swansea	13-25	*T:* Spender *C:* Love *PG:* Love (2)
5 Dec	H	Pontypridd	19-14	*T:* D Davies *C:* Love *PG:* Love (4)
12 Dec	A	Cardiff	12-46	*T:* G Thomas, Love *C:* Love
9 Jan	H	Newbridge	6-12	*PG:* Love (2)
16 Jan	H	S Wales Police	9-0	*PG:* Love (2) *DG:* Love
30 Jan	A	Llanelli	12-46	*T:* D Davies, N Griffiths *C:* N Griffiths
13 Feb	H	Neath	13-12	*T:* Jardine *C:* Love *PG:* Love (2)
13 Mar	A	Pontypool	7-28	*T:* D Griffiths *C:* Love
27 Mar	H	Bridgend	15-19	*PG:* Love (4) *DG:* Love
10 Apr	A	Newport	0-50	
17 Apr	H	Swansea	12-6	*PG:* Love (2), G Thomas *DG:* Love
1 May	A	Pontypridd	10-36	*T:* Diplock *C:* N Griffiths *PG:* N Griffiths

Abertillery

Year of formation 1884
Ground The Park, Abertillery, Gwent Tel: Abertillery (0495) 212555

Colours Green and white hoops
Most capped player H J Morgan (Wales) 27 caps
Captain 1992-93 M Picton
1st XV 1992-93 P41 W18 D3 L20 F626 A679
Heineken League Div 2 7th **SWALEC Cup** Lost 8-23 to Bonymaen (4th round)

League Record 1992-93

Date	Venue	Opponents	Result	Scorers
5 Sept	H	Tredegar	45-0	*T:* Picton (2), M Williams, Ford, L Davies, J Williams *C:* J Williams (6) *PG:* J Williams
12 Sept	A	Blaina	22-15	*T:* M Williams, Atkins *PG:* J Williams (2) *DG:* J Williams (2)
19 Sept	H	Dunvant	3-28	*PG:* M Williams
26 Sept	A	Tenby Utd	11-21	*T:* Ford *PG:* J Williams (2)
3 Oct	H	Cross Keys	3-23	*PG:* J Williams
10 Oct	A	Ebbw Vale	9-12	*PG:* J Williams (3)
17 Oct	H	Glamorgan W	23-14	*T:* Graham, A Richards *C:* J Williams (2) *PG:* J Williams (3)
24 Oct	H	Llandovery	31-14	*T:* McCluney (2), Cross *C:* M Williams (2) *PG:* M Williams (4)
31 Oct	A	Narberth	5-34	*T:* Ford
14 Nov	A	Dunvant	3-16	*PG:* M Williams
28 Nov	H	Llanharan	8-15	*T:* Hillman *PG:* M Williams
12 Dec	A	Tredegar	20-12	*T:* L Phillips, McCluney, Worgan *C:* M Williams *PG:* M Williams
16 Jan	H	Tenby Utd	13-22	*T:* Atkins *C:* M Williams *PG:* M Williams (2)
30 Jan	A	Cross Keys	13-18	*T:* Picton *C:* M Williams *PG:* M Williams (2)
13 Feb	H	Ebbw Vale	21-6	*T:* Worgan, Hillman *C:* M Williams *PG:* M Williams (3)
27 Feb	A	Penarth	25-18	*T:* R Roberts, Picton, McCluney *C:* M Williams (2) *PG:* M Williams (2)
13 Mar	A	Glamorgan W	17-28	*T:* Corlett (2) *C:* M Williams (2) *PG:* M Williams
27 Mar	A	Llandovery	10-3	*T:* Worgan *C:* M Williams *PG:* M Williams
30 Mar	H	Blaina	27-6	*T:* R Roberts, Wilkins, Corlett *C:* M Williams (3) *PG:* M Williams (2)
10 Apr	H	Narberth	27-13	*T:* Corlett (2), McCluney, Atkins, Hillman *C:* M Williams
17 Apr	A	Llanharan	10-21	*T:* McCluney *C:* G Thomas *PG:* G Thomas
1 May	H	Penarth	20-16	*T:* Gladwin *PG:* Rossiter (3) *DG:* Rossiter (2)

Blaina

Year of formation 1875
Ground Central Park, Blaina, Gwent   Tel: Blaina (0495) 290363
Colours Scarlet
Most capped player J Williams (Wales) 7 caps
Captain 1992-93 N Davies
1st XV 1992-93 P40 W14 D2 L24 F539 A829
Heineken League Div 2 12th *relegated* **SWALEC Cup** Lost 9-17 to Pontypool (4th round)

League Record 1992-93

Date	Venue	Opponents	Result	Scorers
5 Sept	A	Ebbw Vale	10-17	*T:* Dobbs *C:* Walbyoff *PG:* D Evans
12 Sept	H	Abertillery	15-22	*PG:* D Evans (4), Walbyoff
19 Sept	A	Llandovery	10-21	*T:* Archer *C:* D Evans *PG:* D Evans
26 Sept	A	Narberth	3-18	*PG:* D Evans
3 Oct	A	Llanharan	8-15	*T:* G Powell *PG:* D Evans

10 Oct	H	Penarth	42-5	T: Hales, Beynon, N Davies, B Powell, Mattravers
				C: D Evans (4) PG: D Evans (3)
17 Oct	H	Tredegar	13-9	T: Hales, B Powell PG: D Evans
24 Oct	A	Glamorgan W	14-22	T: Beynon PG: Walbyoff (3)
31 Oct	H	Dunvant	6-36	PG: D Evans (2)
14 Nov	H	Llandovery	14-22	T: D Evans PG: D Evans (3)
28 Nov	A	Tenby Utd	0-27	
5 Dec	H	Cross Keys	3-52	PG: Walbyoff
12 Dec	H	Ebbw Vale	10-15	T: Beynon C: D Evans PG: D Evans
16 Jan	A	Narberth	9-17	PG: D Evans (3)
30 Jan	H	Llanharan	3-29	PG: D Evans
13 Feb	A	Penarth	0-39	
12 Mar	A	Tredegar*	6-3	PG: D Evans (2)
27 Mar	H	Glamorgan W	14-32	T: Beynon PG: D Evans (3)
30 Mar	A	Abertillery	6-27	PG: D Evans (2)
10 Apr	A	Dunvant	3-48	PG: D Evans
17 Apr	H	Tenby Utd	3-28	PG: M Powell
1 May	A	Cross Keys	7-45	T: Dobbs C: D Evans

*Abandoned after 39 minutes

Bridgend

Year of formation 1878
Ground Brewery Field, Tondu Road, Bridgend, Mid-Glamorgan
Tel: Bridgend (0656) 659032
Colours Blue and white hoops
Most capped player J P R Williams (Wales) 55 caps
Captain 1992-93 D J Bryant
1st XV 1992-93 P42   W22   D3   L17   F783   A775
Heineken League Div 1 6th **SWALEC Cup** Lost 15-33 to Neath (semi-final)

League Record 1992-93

Date	Venue	Opponents	Result	Scorers
5 Sept	H	S Wales Police	41-10	T: M Lewis (2), Bradshaw, Webbe, Spender,
				Apsee, D Jones C: Howley (2), M Jones
12 Sept	A	Llanelli	15-53	T: Howley, O Lloyd C: Howley PG: Howley
19 Sept	H	Neath	20-24	T: Webbe, Bradshaw C: Howley (2)
				PG: Howley (2)
26 Sept	A	Pontypool	13-24	T: Webbe C: L Evans PG: L Evans (2)
3 Oct	H	Pontypridd	12-12	PG: L Evans (4)
10 Oct	H	Newport	5-24	T: P Wintle
17 Oct	A	Swansea	6-29	PG: L Evans (2)
24 Oct	H	Aberavon	18-10	T: S Jones, P Wintle C: L Evans
				PG: L Evans (2)
31 Oct	A	Cardiff	7-39	T: P Wintle C: Howley
20 Nov	A	Neath	6-12	PG: L Evans (2)
28 Nov	H	Newbridge	25-0	T: M Lewis, M Jones, Apsee C: L Evans (2)
				PG: L Evans (2)
5 Dec	A	Maesteg	25-14	T: P Jones, Apsee, Howley C: L Evans (2)
				PG: L Evans (2)
12 Dec	A	S Wales Police	35-5	T: L Evans (2), P Wintle (2), Spender
				C: L Evans (2) PG: L Evans (2)
2 Jan	H	Llanelli	18-8	T: Howley, Bradshaw, P Jones PG: L Evans
16 Jan	H	Pontypool	15-6	T: P Jones (2) C: L Evans PG: L Evans
13 Feb	A	Newport	17-13	T: D Davies, P Jones C: Howley (2)
				PG: Howley
13 Mar	H	Swansea	16-25	T: Spender, D Rees PG: L Evans (2)
23 Mar	A	Pontypridd	6-17	PG: L Evans (2)
27 Mar	A	Aberavon	19-15	T: G Davies, Wilkins PG: Wilkins (2), D Davies
7 Apr	H	Cardiff	29-17	T: P Wintle, Howley C: L Evans (2)
				PG: L Evans (5)

17 Apr	A	Newbridge	17-19	*T:* D Davies, G Davies *C:* M Jones (2)
				DG: M Jones
1 May	H	Maesteg	37-24	*T:* N Jones, D Jones, L Evans, Bradshaw
				C: L Evans (4) *PG:* L Evans (3)

Cardiff

Year of formation 1876
Ground Cardiff Arms Park, Westgate Street, Cardiff   Tel: Cardiff (0222) 383546
Colours Cambridge blue and black
Most capped player G O Edwards (Wales) 53 caps
Captain 1992-93 M R Hall
1st XV 1992-93 P37   W29   D0   L8   F1334   A493
Heineken League Div 1 2nd   **SWALEC Cup** Lost 14-16 to St Peter's (5th round)

League Record 1992-93

Date	*Venue*	*Opponents*	*Result*	*Scorers*
5 Sept	A	Aberavon	15-6	*PG:* A Davies (4) *DG:* A Davies
12 Sept	H	Pontypridd	37-3	*T:* A Davies (3), Rayer (2), Hill *C:* A Davies (2)
				PG: A Davies
19 Sept	H	Newbridge	39-14	*T:* Walker (3), Rayer, A Davies *C:* A Davies (4)
				PG: A Davies (2)
26 Sept	A	Maesteg	21-11	*T:* Moore, C Thomas *C:* A Davies
				PG: A Davies (3)
3 Oct	H	S Wales Police	65-8	*T:* Walker (2), Ford (2), Greenslade (2), Kawulok,
				Palfrey, A Davies *C:* A Davies (7)
				PG: A Davies *DG:* A Davies
10 Oct	A	Llanelli	16-20	*T:* A Davies *C:* A Davies *PG:* A Davies (2)
				DG: A Davies
17 Oct	H	Neath	31-20	*T:* Budd (2), Kawulok *C:* A Davies (2)
				PG: A Davies *DG:* A Davies (2), Ring
24 Oct	A	Pontypool	31-24	*T:* Walker (2), Sedgemore *C:* A Davies (2)
				PG: A Davies (4)
31 Oct	H	Bridgend	39-7	*T:* Rayer, Budd, A Davies, Hill, M Edwards
				C: A Davies (4) *PG:* A Davies (2)
14 Nov	A	Newbridge	24-12	*T:* Hall (2) *C:* Rayer *PG:* Rayer (4)
28 Nov	A	Newport	39-3	*T:* Armstrong (2), Budd, Ford, Walker, Booth
				C: A Davies (3) *PG:* A Davies
5 Dec	H	Swansea	8-6	*T:* Ford *PG:* A Davies
12 Dec	H	Aberavon	46-12	*T:* Walker (4), Hill (3), A Davies *C:* A Davies (3)
16 Jan	H	Maesteg	54-0	*T:* Laity (2), Roy (2), Hill, Rayer, Moore,
				C Thomas *C:* A Davies (4) *PG:* A Davies (2)
26 Jan	A	Pontypridd	6-3	*PG:* A Davies (2)
30 Jan	A	S Wales Police	36-7	*T:* Walker (2), Roy, Taylor, Budd, Hall
				C: A Davies (3)
13 Feb	H	Llanelli	13-18	*T:* C Thomas, Budd *PG:* A Davies
13 Mar	A	Neath	6-11	*PG:* A Davies (2)
27 Mar	H	Pontypool	41-16	*T:* A Davies (2), Roy (2), Laity, Sedgemore
				C: A Davies (4) *PG:* A Davies
7 Apr	A	Bridgend	17-29	*T:* Hill *PG:* A Davies (3) *DG:* A Davies
17 Apr	H	Newport	36-20	*T:* Laity, Budd, G Lewis, Palfrey *C:* A Davies (2)
				PG: A Davies (4)
1 May	A	Swansea	16-10	*T:* Hill *C:* Rayer *PG:* Rayer (2)
				DG: A Davies

Cross Keys

Year of formation 1885
Ground Pandy Park, Cross Keys, Gwent   Tel: Cross Keys (0495) 270289
Colours Black and white
Most capped player S Morris (Wales) 19 caps
Captain 1992-93 N Rossiter/I Reynolds

1st XV 1992-93 P43 W28 D4 L11 F1036 A647
Heineken League Div 2 2nd *promoted* **SWALEC Cup** Lost 15-24 to Neath (quarter-final)

League Record 1992-93

Date	Venue	Opponents	Result	Scorers
19 Sept	H	Glamorgan W	23-12	*T:* Rossiter, N Griffiths *C:* Fleet (2) *PG:* Fleet (3)
26 Sept	H	Ebbw Vale	12-6	*PG:* Fleet (4)
3 Oct	A	Abertillery	23-3	*T:* Parry, Withers *C:* Fleet, Parry *PG:* Fleet, Parry (2)
10 Oct	H	Llandovery	50-19	*T:* T Williams, Powell, N Griffiths, Withers, Nicholls, Marshall *C:* Fleet (4) *PG:* Fleet (3) *DG:* Withers
17 Oct	A	Narberth	10-13	*T:* Powell *C:* Parry *PG:* Parry
24 Oct	H	Llanharan	18-10	*T:* Withers, Parkes *C:* Fleet *PG:* Fleet (2)
31 Oct	A	Penarth	32-0	*T:* N Griffiths, Nicholls, Marshall, J Rees, A Thomas *C:* Fleet (2) *PG:* Fleet
7 Nov	H	Dunvant	11-17	*T:* Parry *PG:* Fleet (2)
14 Nov	A	Glamorgan W	12-10	*T:* N Griffiths (2) *C:* Parry
22 Nov	A	Tenby Utd	12-16	*T:* Nicholls, Marshall *C:* Fleet
5 Dec	A	Blaina	52-3	*T:* Withers (2), Glastonbury (2), Foster, N Griffiths, Marshall, pen try *C:* Fleet (6)
12 Dec	A	Dunvant	6-21	*PG:* Fleet (2)
2 Jan	H	Tenby Utd	6-3	*PG:* Fleet (2)
16 Jan	A	Ebbw Vale	22-14	*T:* Withers, A Thomas *PG:* Fleet (4)
30 Jan	H	Abertillery	18-13	*T:* A Thomas, Marshall *C:* Fleet *PG:* Fleet (2)
13 Feb	A	Llandovery	20-16	*T:* Marshall (2) *C:* Fleet (2) *PG:* Fleet (2)
23 Feb	H	Tredegar	36-12	*T:* Marshall, Gladwin, Parry, Forster, Withers *C:* Parry *PG:* Parry (3)
13 Mar	H	Narberth	20-15	*T:* Glastonbury *PG:* Fleet (5)
27 Mar	A	Llanharan	13-13	*T:* Foster *C:* Fleet *PG:* Fleet (2)
10 Apr	H	Penarth	8-29	*T:* Reid *PG:* Fleet
17 Apr	A	Tredegar	25-16	*T:* A Thomas, Parry, Marshall *C:* Fleet (2) *PG:* Fleet (2)
1 May	H	Blaina	45-7	*T:* A Thomas (2), Forster (2), Marshall, K Jones, N Griffiths *C:* Fleet (5)

Dunvant

Year of formation 1888
Ground Broadacre, Killay, Swansea   Tel: Swansea (0792) 207291
Colours Red and green hoops
Captain 1992-93 R Greenwood
1st XV 1992-93 P25 W23 D1 L1 F514 A153
Heineken League Div 2 *Winners promoted* **SWALEC Cup** Drew 10-10 with Cross Keys (6th round). Lost 2-1 on try-count

League Record 1992-93

Date	Venue	Opponents	Result	Scorers
12 Sept	H	Ebbw Vale	25-9	*T:* D Evans, Hutchings, W Lloyd *C:* M Thomas, D Evans *PG:* M Thomas (2)
19 Sept	A	Abertillery	28-3	*T:* P Morris, Crane, Hutchings *C:* M Thomas (2) *PG:* M Thomas (2) *DG:* M Thomas
26 Sept	H	Llandovery	21-3	*PG:* M Thomas (6), D Evans
3 Oct	A	Narberth	6-5	*PG:* M Thomas (2)
10 Oct	H	Llanharan	19-3	*T:* Farnworth (3) *C:* M Thomas (2)
17 Oct	A	Penarth	60-3	*T:* W Lloyd (2), Farnworth (2), Llewellyn (2), N Lloyd, D Evans, Bolton, P John *C:* M Thomas (5)
24 Oct	H	Tredegar	28-0	*T:* M Thomas, Farnworth, Bolton, P John *C:* M Thomas *PG:* M Thomas (2)

31 Oct	A	Blaina	36-6	*T:* Bolton (2), N Lloyd, D Morris
				C: M Thomas (2) *PG:* M Thomas (4)
7 Nov	A	Cross Keys	17-11	*T:* P John *PG:* M Thomas (4)
14 Nov	H	Abertillery	16-3	*T:* W Lloyd, Farnworth *PG:* M Thomas (2)
5 Dec	H	Tenby Utd	21-9	*T:* Callaghan, M Thomas *C:* M Thomas
				PG: M Thomas (2), D Evans
12 Dec	H	Cross Keys	21-6	*T:* P Morris, pen try *C:* M Thomas
				PG: M Thomas (3)
9 Jan	A	Glamorgan W	17-3	*T:* Niblo, Callaghan, Bolton *C:* M Thomas
16 Jan	A	Llandovery	15-0	*T:* Hutchings, Llewellyn *C:* M Thomas
				PG: M Thomas
30 Jan	H	Narberth	16-15	*T:* Butler *C:* M Thomas *PG:* M Thomas (2)
				DG: M Thomas
13 Feb	A	Llanharan	3-12	*PG:* M Thomas
13 Mar	H	Penarth	23-18	*T:* Bolton, Farnworth, Jeffries *C:* M Thomas
				PG: M Thomas *DG:* M Thomas
27 Mar	A	Tredegar	14-6	*T:* Jeffries *PG:* D Evans, M Thomas (2)
10 Apr	H	Blaina	48-3	*T:* Callaghan (2), D Evans (2), Farnworth,
				Greenwood, P Morris, M Thomas
				C: M Thomas (3), D Evans
17 Apr	H	Glamorgan W	25-10	*T:* M Thomas, Waygood, N Lloyd
				C: M Thomas (2) *PG:* M Thomas (2)
26 Apr	A	Ebbw Vale	12-0	*T:* Hutchings, pen try *C:* M Thomas
1 May	A	Tenby Utd	7-6	*T:* Farnworth *C:* M Thomas

Ebbw Vale

Year of formation 1880
Ground Eugene Cross Park, Ebbw Vale, Gwent   Tel: Ebbw Vale (0495) 302955
Colours Red, white and green
Most capped player D Williams (Wales) 36 caps
Captain 1992-93 P Booth
1st XV 1992-93   P31   W9   D0   L22   F334   A624
Heineken League Div 2 10th   **SWALEC Cup** Lost 15-16 to Talywain (4th round)

League Record 1992-93

Date	Venue	Opponents	Result	Scorers
5 Sept	H	Blaina	17-10	*T:* Parfitt *PG:* Strange (4)
12 Sept	A	Dunvant	9-25	*PG:* Strange (3)
19 Sept	H	Tenby Utd	23-14	*T:* Bowden, C Price *C:* Strange (2)
				PG: Strange (2) *DG:* Strange
26 Sept	A	Cross Keys	6-12	*PG:* Strange (2)
3 Oct	H	Glamorgan W	13-21	*T:* C Price *C:* Strange *PG:* Strange (2)
10 Oct	H	Abertillery	12-9	*PG:* Strange (4)
17 Oct	A	Llandovery	6-3	*PG:* Strange *DG:* Strange
24 Oct	H	Narberth	9-22	*PG:* McKie (3)
31 Oct	A	Llanharan	10-18	*T:* Boycott *C:* McKie *PG:* McKie
14 Nov	A	Tenby Utd	8-30	*T:* I Davies *PG:* Strange
28 Nov	H	Penarth	3-21	*PG:* Strange
5 Dec	A	Tredegar	3-0	*PG:* Strange
12 Dec	A	Blaina	15-10	*PG:* Hardacre (3), Strange *DG:* Strange
16 Jan	H	Cross Keys	14-22	*T:* Strange *PG:* Strange (3)
30 Jan	A	Glamorgan W	0-6	
13 Feb	A	Abertillery	6-21	*PG:* Strange (2)
13 Mar	H	Llandovery	21-13	*T:* C Price (3) *PG:* Strange (2)
27 Mar	A	Narberth	0-18	
10 Apr	H	Llanharan	8-32	*T:* Bowden *PG:* Strange
17 Apr	A	Penarth	0-20	
26 Apr	H	Dunvant	0-12	
30 Apr	H	Tredegar	0-16	

Glamorgan Wanderers

Year of formation 1893
Ground The Memorial Ground, Stirling Road, Ely, Cardiff   Tel: Cardiff (0222) 591039
Colours Cambridge blue, black and white
Captain 1992-93 D St John
1st XV 1992-93   P37   W18   D0   L19   F677   A741
Heineken League Div 2 6th   **SWALEC Cup** Lost 3-13 to Trimsaran (4th round)

League Record 1992-93

Date	Venue	Opponents	Result	Scorers
5 Sept	H	Tenby Utd	14-6	*T:* De Lloyd *PG:* Bolderson (3)
12 Sept	A	Llanharan	14-13	*T:* De Lloyd *PG:* Bolderson (3)
19 Sept	A	Cross Keys	12-23	*PG:* Bebb (3) *DG:* Bebb
26 Sept	H	Penarth	55-5	*T:* Edmunds (2), Rogers, Blackmore, St John, Bebb, Norman, Clarke *C:* Bebb (6) *PG:* Bebb
3 Oct	A	Ebbw Vale	21-13	*T:* Miller, Norman *C:* Bebb *PG:* Bebb (3)
10 Oct	H	Tredegar	44-9	*T:* Norman (3), Thompson, Roke, Bebb *C:* Bebb (4) *PG:* Bebb *DG:* Bebb
17 Oct	A	Abertillery	14-23	*T:* Clarke *PG:* Bolderson (3)
24 Oct	H	Blaina	22-14	*T:* Prickett *C:* Bebb *PG:* Bebb (5)
31 Oct	A	Llandovery	7-17	*T:* Norman *C:* Bebb
14 Nov	H	Cross Keys	10-12	*T:* Lintern *C:* Bebb *PG:* Bebb
5 Dec	A	Narberth	8-20	*T:* Lintern *PG:* S Williams
12 Dec	A	Tenby Utd	10-64	*T:* Norman *C:* Bebb *PG:* Bebb
2 Jan	H	Llanharan	0-41	
9 Jan	H	Dunvant	3-17	*PG:* Norman
16 Jan	A	Penarth	0-13	
30 Jan	H	Ebbw Vale	6-0	*PG:* Norman (2)
13 Feb	A	Tredegar	16-10	*T:* Gibbon, Harrington *PG:* Harrington, Norman
13 Mar	H	Abertillery	28-17	*T:* Norman (2), Prickett, Gibbon *C:* Holland *PG:* Holland (2)
27 Mar	A	Blaina	32-14	*T:* Clarke (2), Collins, Jacas, St John *C:* M Jones, Patterson *PG:* M Jones
10 Apr	H	Llandovery	19-16	*T:* Duly, Gibbon *PG:* M Jones (2) *DG:* M Jones
17 Apr	A	Dunvant	10-25	*T:* Duly, Blackmore
1 May	H	Narberth	12-37	*T:* Norman (2) *C:* M Jones

Llandovery

Year of formation 1878
Ground Church Bank, Llandovery, Dyfed   Tel: Llandovery (0550) 2389
Colours Red and white hoops
Most capped player C P Lewis (Wales) 5 caps
Captain 1992-93 C Davies
1st XV 1992-93   P29   W9   D1   L19   F352   A482
Heineken League Div 2 8th   **SWALEC Cup** Lost 0-41 to Bridgend (6th round)

League Record 1992-93

Date	Venue	Opponents	Result	Scorers
5 Sept	H	Penarth	39-0	*T:* Rowlands, Chris Davies, H Jones, A Thomas, Giles *C:* H Jones (4) *PG:* H Jones (2)
12 Sept	A	Tredegar	13-23	*T:* H Jones *C:* H Jones *PG:* H Jones (2)
19 Sept	H	Blaina	21-10	*T:* Chris Davies (2) *C:* H Jones *PG:* H Jones (3)
26 Sept	A	Dunvant	3-21	*PG:* H Jones
3 Oct	H	Tenby Utd	7-8	*T:* Chris Davies *C:* H Jones

10 Oct	A	Cross Keys	19-50	*T:* H Thomas, A Thomas, Olsen *C:* H Jones (2)
17 Oct	H	Ebbw Vale	3-6	*PG:* H Jones
24 Oct	A	Abertillery	14-31	*T:* Allnutt, A Williams *C:* Roe (2)
31 Oct	H	Glamorgan W	17-7	*T:* Olsen, pen try *C:* H Jones (2) *PG:* H Jones
14 Nov	A	Blaina	22-14	*T:* Giles *C:* H Jones *PG:* H Jones (4) *DG:* H Jones
28 Nov	H	Narberth	6-12	*PG:* H Jones (2)
5 Dec	A	Llanharan	8-30	*T:* Chris Davies *PG:* Doran
12 Dec	A	Penarth	16-8	*T:* D Morgan, D Thomas *PG:* H Jones (2)
2 Jan	H	Tredegar	28-7	*T:* M Rees, Rowlands, Giles *C:* H Jones (2) *PG:* H Jones (3)
16 Jan	H	Dunvant	0-15	
30 Jan	A	Tenby Utd	7-0	*T:* Rowlands *C:* H Jones
13 Feb	H	Cross Keys	16-20	*T:* Giles *C:* C Williams *PG:* C Williams (3)
13 Mar	A	Ebbw Vale	13-21	*T:* Roe *C:* H Jones *PG:* H Jones (2)
27 Mar	H	Abertillery	3-10	*PG:* H Jones
3 Apr	A	Narberth	8-14	*T:* Olsen *PG:* H Jones
10 Apr	A	Glamorgan W	16-19	*T:* H Jones, I Jones *PG:* H Jones (2)
1 May	H	Llanharan	6-19	*PG:* H Jones (2)

Llanelli

Year of formation 1872
Ground Stradey Park, Llanelli, Dyfed   Tel: Llanelli (0554) 774060
Colours Scarlet
Most capped player I C Evans (Wales) 36 caps
Captain 1992-93 R H StJ B Moon
1st XV 1992-93   P36   W32   D1   L3   F1328   A432
Heineken League Div 1 *Winners* **SWALEC Cup** *Winners* Beat Neath 21-18 (final)

League Record 1992-93

Date	Venue	Opponents	Result	Scorers
5 Sept	A	Pontypool	44-20	*T:* Proctor (2), N Davies, Quinnell, G Jones, Boobyer, I Evans *C:* Stephens (3) *PG:* Stephens
12 Sept	H	Bridgend	53-15	*T:* Ian Jones (3), Stephens, I Evans, Iwan Jones, Moon, Boobyer *C:* Stephens (5) *DG:* Stephens
19 Sept	A	Newport	79-10	*T:* I Evans (3), Stephens (3), Moon, L Jones, Joseph, Proctor, pen try *C:* Stephens (9) *PG:* Stephens (2)
26 Sept	H	Swansea	7-14	*T:* L Jones *C:* Stephens
3 Oct	A	Aberavon	19-3	*T:* Proctor, Boobyer *PG:* H Williams (2) *DG:* H Williams
10 Oct	H	Cardiff	20-16	*T:* S Davies, Perego, I Evans *C:* Stephens *PG:* Stephens
17 Oct	A	Newbridge	52-7	*T:* Iwan Jones (2), Joseph, Proctor, May, N Davies, Wake *C:* Stephens (4) *PG:* Stephens (3)
24 Oct	H	Maesteg	82-13	*T:* I Evans (6), P Davies (2), Proctor (2), Ian Jones, Boobyer, N Davies, Moon *C:* H Williams (6)
31 Oct	A	S Wales Police	33-11	*T:* Boobyer (2), I Evans, Gary Jones, H Williams *C:* Stephens (3), A Richards
28 Nov	A	Pontypridd	11-11	*T:* I Evans *PG:* Stephens (2)
5 Dec	H	Neath	24-16	*T:* Proctor (2), P Davies *C:* Stephens (2), H Williams *PG:* Stephens
12 Dec	H	Pontypool	36-13	*T:* H Williams, Stephens, Gary Jones, S Davies, Proctor *C:* Stephens (4) *PG:* Stephens
2 Jan	A	Bridgend	8-18	*T:* Lamerton *PG:* Stephens
15 Jan	A	Swansea	15-10	*T:* N Davies, Proctor *C:* H Williams *PG:* H Williams
30 Jan	H	Aberavon	46-12	*T:* Quinnell (2), Stephens, P Davies, N Davies, Ian Jones, L Davies *C:* L Davies *PG:* Stephens (2) *DG:* Stephens

13 Feb	A	Cardiff	18-13	T: Stephens (2), Moon PG: Stephens
9 Mar	H	Newport	72-10	T: Proctor (2), L Davies (2), Quinnell (2), P Jones, L Jones, Wintle, Perego, Lewis, Moon C: Stephens (6)
13 Mar	H	Newbridge	53-13	T: Ian Jones (2), Proctor (2), Quinnell, Boobyer, L Davies, Wintle, G Jones C: Stephens (4)
27 Mar	A	Maesteg	58-12	T: Quinnell (2), Lamerton (2), I Evans, Boobyer, Stephens, pen try C: Stephens (6) PG: Stephens (9)
10 Apr	H	S Wales Police	93-0	T: Proctor (3), I Evans (3), Boobyer (3), Wintle (2), Quinnell, L Jones, Stephens, H Williams C: Stephens (9)
28 Apr	H	Pontypridd	47-3	T: Proctor (2), I Evans (2), I Jones, Copsey, Lewis C: Stephens (3) PG: Stephens (2)
1 May	A	Neath	31-14	T: Richards, Quinnell, H Williams, L Davies, P Jones C: H Williams (3)

Llanharan

Year of formation 1891
Ground Bridgend Road, Llanharan, Mid-Glamorgan   Tel: Llanharan (0443) 222209
Colours White with black and blue hoops
Captain 1992-93 M Reynolds
1st XV 1992-93 P34 W23 D1 L10 F707 A384
Heineken League Div 2 3rd **SWALEC Cup** Lost 9-17 to Tondu (4th round)

League Record 1992-93

Date	Venue	Opponents	Result	Scorers
5 Sept	A	Narberth	6-9	PG: J Morris (2)
12 Sept	H	Glamorgan W	13-14	T: Poucha C: J Morris PG: J Morris (2)
19 Sept	H	Penarth	46-9	T: P Hughes J Morris, Collins, Brain, Wyllie C: J Morris (3) PG: J Morris (5)
26 Sept	A	Tredegar	18-3	T: J Griffiths (2) C: J Morris PG: J Morris (2)
3 Oct	H	Blaina	15-8	T: A Evans, Dodd C: J Morris PG: J Morris
10 Oct	A	Dunvant	3-19	PG: J Morris
17 Oct	H	Tenby Utd	9-8	PG: J Morris (3)
24 Oct	A	Cross Keys	10-18	T: A Price C: J Morris PG: J Morris
31 Oct	H	Ebbw Vale	18-10	T: A Price, Poucha C: J Morris PG: J Morris (2)
14 Nov	A	Penarth	28-6	T: Hiscocks, P Hughes, S Pryce C: J Morris (2) PG: J Morris (3)
28 Nov	A	Abertillery	15-8	PG: J Morris (5)
5 Dec	H	Llandovery	30-8	T: Hiscocks, J Morris, Dodd, Poucha C: J Morris (2) PG: J Morris (2)
12 Dec	H	Narberth	12-0	T: Reynolds, J Morris C: J Morris
2 Jan	A	Glamorgan W	41-0	T: D Emyr, Langdon, Martin, H James, A Price, B Lewis C: J Morris (4) PG: J Morris
16 Jan	H	Tredegar	31-21	T: Dodd, B Lewis, Hiscocks, A Evans, Reynolds PG: J Morris (2)
30 Jan	A	Blaina	29-3	T: Langdon, Pritchard, J Morris C: J Morris PG: J Morris (3) DG: J Morris
13 Feb	H	Dunvant	12-3	PG: J Morris DG: J Morris (3)
13 Mar	A	Tenby Utd	14-18	T: Merry, Dodd C: J Morris (2)
27 Mar	H	Cross Keys	13-13	T: P John C: J Morris PG: J Morris (2)
10 Apr	A	Ebbw Vale	32-8	T: Reynolds, Hiscocks, Pritchard, Pick, Thompson C: A Price, J Morris PG: J Morris
17 Apr	H	Abertillery	21-10	T: J Morris, Cornelius, A Price C: J Morris (3)
1 May	A	Llandovery	19-6	T: Reynolds, Hiscocks, Langdon C: Dodd (2)

Maesteg

Year of formation 1882
Ground Old Parish Ground, Llynvi Road, Maesteg, Mid-Glamorgan
Tel: Maesteg (0656) 732283
Colours Black and amber hoops
Most capped player G Evans (Wales) 10 caps
Captain 1992-93 H Woodland/G Davies
1st XV 1992-93 P40 W12 D2 L26 F720 A938
Heineken League Div 1 11th *relegated* **SWALEC Cup** Lost 3-55 to Cardiff (4th round)

League Record 1992-93

Date	Venue	Opponents	Result	Scorers
5 Sept	A	Newport	13-37	*T:* D Williams *C:* D Williams *PG:* D Williams (2)
12 Sept	H	Swansea	6-35	*PG:* D Williams (2)
19 Sept	A	Aberavon	23-15	*T:* Buckle, Woodland, A Williams *C:* D Williams *PG:* D Williams (2)
26 Sept	H	Cardiff	11-21	*T:* N Lewis *PG:* D Williams, D Edwards
3 Oct	A	Newbridge	13-20	*T:* D Williams *C:* D Williams *PG:* D Williams (2)
10 Oct	A	Pontypridd	20-29	*T:* N Lewis, Woodland *C:* D Edwards (2) *PG:* D Edwards (2)
17 Oct	H	S Wales Police	0-0	
24 Oct	A	Llanelli	13-82	*T:* A Williams *C:* D Williams *PG:* D Williams (2)
31 Oct	H	Neath	21-31	*T:* P Thomas, D Edwards *C:* D Williams *PG:* D Edwards (3)
14 Nov	H	Aberavon	7-17	*T:* N Lewis *C:* D Williams
28 Nov	A	Pontypool	8-14	*T:* J Hopkins *PG:* D Williams
5 Dec	H	Bridgend	14-25	*T:* S Lewis *PG:* D Edwards (3)
12 Dec	H	Newport	18-7	*T:* H Lewis, Wilcox *C:* D Edwards *PG:* D Edwards (2)
9 Jan	A	Swansea	11-15	*T:* P Thomas *PG:* D Edwards (2)
16 Jan	A	Cardiff	0-54	
30 Jan	H	Newbridge	12-6	*PG:* D Edwards (4)
13 Feb	H	Pontypridd	8-21	*T:* A Williams *PG:* D Edwards
13 Mar	A	S Wales Police	14-29	*T:* Yardley *PG:* D Edwards (2) *DG:* D Williams
27 Mar	H	Llanelli	12-58	*T:* D Williams, Yardley *C:* D Edwards
10 Apr	A	Neath	3-49	*PG:* D Edwards
24 Apr	H	Pontypool	27-30	*T:* Davey, Harvey, A Williams *C:* D Edwards (3) *PG:* D Edwards (2)
1 May	A	Bridgend	24-37	*T:* Gilbey, P Thomas, pen try *C:* Davey (2), D Williams *PG:* Davey

Narberth

Year of formation 1882
Ground Lewis Lloyd Ground, Spring Gardens, Narberth, Dyfed
Tel: Narberth (0834) 860462
Colours Sky blue and navy hoops
Captain 1992-93 D Setaro
1st XV 1992-93 P34 W23 D2 L9 F679 A361
Heineken League Div 2 4th **SWALEC Cup** Lost 8-22 to St Peter's (4th round)

League Record 1992-93

Date	Venue	Opponents	Result	Scorers
5 Sept	H	Llanharan	9-6	*PG:* Pearce (2), A Phillips

12 Sept	A	Penarth	46-6	*T:* A Phillips (2), Pearce, D Setaro, D Griffiths, Andrew Young, pen try *C:* Pearce (4) *PG:* Pearce
19 Sept	H	Tredegar	11-6	*T:* Andrew Young *PG:* Pearce (2)
26 Sept	A	Blaina	18-3	*PG:* Pearce (4) *DG:* Pearce (2)
3 Oct	H	Dunvant	5-6	*T:* Roderick
10 Oct	A	Tenby Utd	13-6	*T:* C Phillips *C:* A Phillips *PG:* A Phillips (2)
17 Oct	H	Cross Keys	13-10	*T:* McDonald *C:* A Phillips *PG:* A Phillips *DG:* D Setaro
24 Oct	A	Ebbw Vale	22-9	*T:* D Thomas, D Setaro *PG:* A Phillips (2) *DG:* Pearce (2)
31 Oct	H	Abertillery	34-5	*T:* Roderick (2), D Thomas, C Phillips, D Setaro, Pearce *C:* A Phillips, D Setaro
14 Nov	A	Tredegar	3-3	*PG:* Pearce
28 Nov	A	Llandovery	12-6	*PG:* Pearce (4)
5 Dec	H	Glamorgan W	20-8	*T:* McDonald, D Griffiths *C:* Pearce (2) *PG:* Pearce (2)
12 Dec	A	Llanharan	0-12	
2 Jan	H	Penarth	13-8	*T:* Roderick, McDonald *PG:* Pearce
16 Jan	H	Blaina	17-9	*T:* D Setaro *PG:* A Phillips (3) *DG:* Vobe
30 Jan	A	Dunvant	15-16	*T:* Roderick, C Phillips *C:* Pearce *PG:* Pearce
13 Feb	H	Tenby Utd	10-23	*T:* C Phillips *C:* A Phillips *PG:* A Phillips
13 Mar	A	Cross Keys	15-20	*T:* C Phillips, pen try *C:* Pearce *PG:* Pearce
27 Mar	H	Ebbw Vale	18-0	*T:* McDonald, pen try *C:* Pearce *PG:* Pearce, A Phillips
3 Apr	H	Llandovery	14-8	*T:* Pearce *PG:* Pearce (3)
10 Apr	A	Abertillery	13-27	*T:* Roderick *C:* Pearce *PG:* Pearce (2)
1 May	A	Glamorgan W	37-12	*T:* McDonald (2), Roderick, D Setaro, E Jones *C:* Pearce (3) *PG:* Pearce (2)

Neath

Year of formation 1871
Ground The Gnoll, Gnoll Park Road, Neath, West Glamorgan   Tel: Neath (0639) 636547
Colours Black with white Maltese cross
Most capped player P H Thorburn (Wales) 37 caps
Captain 1992-93 G O Llewellyn
1st XV 1992-93 P39 W28 D0 L11 F1101 A504
Heineken League Div 1 4th **SWALEC Cup** Lost 18-21 to Llanelli (final)

League Record 1992-93

Date	Venue	Opponents	Result	Scorers
5 Sept	A	Pontypridd	11-9	*T:* Bowling *PG:* Bird (2)
12 Sept	H	Pontypool	37-16	*T:* Reynolds (2), S Williams (2), J Davies, R Jones *C:* Ball, Bird *PG:* Ball
19 Sept	A	Bridgend	24-20	*T:* Varney (2), Bowling, Reynolds *C:* Ball (2)
26 Sept	H	Newport	32-10	*T:* Ball (2), McCarthy, Boobyer *C:* Ball (2), Bird *PG:* Ball (2)
3 Oct	A	Swansea	12-29	*T:* Varney, Bowling *C:* Ball
10 Oct	H	Aberavon	38-16	*T:* R Jones (2), Bowling, P Jones, Phillips *C:* Thorburn (5) *PG:* Thorburn
17 Oct	A	Cardiff	20-31	*T:* Thorburn, McCarthy, G D Llewellyn *C:* Thorburn *PG:* Thorburn
24 Oct	H	Newbridge	21-14	*T:* J Davies, Phillips *C:* Thorburn *PG:* Thorburn (3)
31 Oct	A	Maesteg	31-21	*T:* R Jones, McCarthy, Reynolds, A Hughes *C:* Bird *PG:* McCarthy (2), Bird
20 Nov	H	Bridgend	12-6	*PG:* Thorburn (4)
28 Nov	H	S Wales Police	27-15	*T:* S Williams, Bowling, Reynolds, G D Llewellyn *C:* Thorburn (2) *PG:* Thorburn
5 Dec	A	Llanelli	16-24	*T:* R Jones *C:* Thorburn *PG:* Thorburn (3)
12 Dec	H	Pontypridd	28-15	*T:* S Williams, Varney *PG:* Thorburn (6)

16 Jan	A	Newport	0-17	
30 Jan	H	Swansea	8-18	*T:* Bowling *PG:* Thorburn
13 Feb	A	Aberavon	12-13	*T:* Thorburn, R Jones *C:* Thorburn
13 Mar	H	Cardiff	11-6	*T:* Varney *PG:* Thorburn (2)
27 Mar	A	Newbridge	13-17	*T:* Thorburn *C:* Thorburn *PG:* Thorburn (2)
10 Apr	H	Maesteg	49-3	*T:* Reynolds (3), N Lewis (2), Morris, R Jones *C:* Thorburn (4) *PG:* Thorburn (2)
12 Apr	A	Pontypool	7-9	*T:* Isaac *C:* Thorburn
17 Apr	A	S Wales Police	25-19	*T:* Reynolds (3), G O Llewellyn *C:* Bird *PG:* Bird
1 May	H	Llanelli	14-31	*T:* D Jones, Gerrard *C:* Bird (2)

Newbridge

Year of formation 1888
Ground Welfare Ground, Bridge Street, Newbridge, Gwent
Tel: Newbridge (0495) 243247
Colours Blue and black hoops
Most capped player D Hayward (Wales) 15 caps
Captain 1992-93 D Rees/S Fealey
1st XV 1992-93 P40 W19 D0 L21 F641 A849
Heineken League Div 1 10th **SWALEC Cup** Lost 3-67 to Llanelli (6th round)

League Record 1992-93

Date	Venue	Opponents	Result	Scorers
5 Sept	A	Swansea	13-17	*T:* Hayward *C:* Hayward *PG:* Hayward (2)
12 Sept	H	Aberavon	19-21	*T:* Egan *C:* Hayward *PG:* Hayward (4)
19 Sept	A	Cardiff	14-39	*T:* Fealey (2) *C:* Hayward (2)
26 Sept	A	Pontypridd	3-22	*PG:* A Harries
3 Oct	H	Maesteg	20-13	*T:* Manley, D Roberts *C:* P Williams (2) *PG:* P Williams *DG:* P Williams
10 Oct	A	S Wales Police	11-6	*T:* G Taylor *PG:* Hayward (2)
17 Oct	H	Llanelli	7-52	*T:* Fealey *C:* Hayward
24 Oct	A	Neath	14-21	*T:* Hibbs, Manley *C:* Hayward (2)
31 Oct	H	Pontypool	27-14	*T:* D Rees (2), Hayward, Pook *C:* Hayward, P Williams *PG:* Hayward
14 Nov	H	Cardiff	12-24	*T:* Manley, Hibbs *C:* Hayward
28 Nov	H	Bridgend	0-25	
12 Dec	H	Swansea	0-28	
9 Jan	A	Aberavon	12-6	*T:* Waters, Fealey *C:* Hayward
16 Jan	H	Pontypridd	8-13	*T:* Glasson *PG:* Hayward
30 Jan	H	Maesteg	6-12	*PG:* A Harries (2)
8 Feb	H	Newport	3-20	*PG:* A Harries
13 Feb	H	S Wales Police	14-27	*T:* Manley *PG:* Hayward (3)
13 Mar	A	Llanelli	13-53	*T:* Brown, Morelli *PG:* Brown
27 Mar	H	Neath	17-13	*T:* Harding *PG:* P Williams (3) *DG:* P Williams
10 Apr	A	Pontypool	8-36	*T:* Waters *PG:* P Williams
17 Apr	H	Bridgend	19-17	*T:* Fisher, P Williams *PG:* P Williams (2) *DG:* P Williams
1 May	A	Newport	18-57	*T:* Hayward, Glasson *C:* Hayward *PG:* Hayward (2)

Newport

Year of formation 1874
Ground Rodney Parade, Rodney Road, Newport, Gwent
Tel: Newport (0633) 258193 and 267410
Colours Black and amber hoops
Most capped player K J Jones (Wales) 44 caps
Captain 1992-93 G M George

1st XV 1992-93   P39   W21   D0   L18   F898   A787
Heineken League Div 1 7th   **SWALEC Cup** Lost 16-18 to Bridgend (quarter-final)

League Record 1992-93

Date	Venue	Opponents	Result	Scorers
5 Sept	H	Maesteg	37-13	*T:* McCracken (2), George, A Lewis, Carter, Bidgood, Withey *C:* Westwood
12 Sept	A	S Wales Police	42-0	*T:* McCracken (2), Bidgood (2), Withey, A Lewis *C:* Westwood (3) *PG:* Westwood (2)
19 Sept	H	Llanelli	10-79	*T:* A Lewis, Bidgood
26 Sept	A	Neath	10-32	*T:* B Watkins *C:* Westwood *PG:* Westwood
3 Oct	H	Pontypool	20-9	*T:* Orrell, Westwood, A Lewis *C:* Westwood *PG:* Westwood
10 Oct	A	Bridgend	24-5	*T:* A Lewis, R Jones *C:* Westwood *PG:* Westwood (4)
17 Oct	H	Pontypridd	10-17	*T:* A Lewis *C:* Westwood *PG:* Westwood
24 Oct	H	Swansea	20-44	*T:* George, R Jones *C:* Westwood (2) *PG:* Westwood (2)
31 Oct	A	Aberavon	42-20	*T:* A Lewis (3), Duggan, R Jones *C:* Westwood (4) *PG:* Westwood (2) *DG:* Yendle
28 Nov	H	Cardiff	3-39	*PG:* Westwood
12 Dec	A	Maesteg	7-18	*T:* Westwood *C:* Westwood
16 Jan	H	Neath	17-0	*T:* Roderick, A Lewis *C:* Westwood (2) *PG:* Westwood
30 Jan	A	Pontypool	33-14	*T:* Bidgood, A Lewis, Jeffreys *C:* J Williams (3) *PG:* J Williams (4)
8 Feb	A	Newbridge	20-3	*T:* Carter, Jeffreys, George, Withey
13 Feb	H	Bridgend	13-17	*T:* D Rees *C:* J Williams *PG:* J Williams (2)
9 Mar	A	Llanelli	10-72	*T:* Roderick *C:* J Williams *DG:* J Williams
13 Mar	A	Pontypridd	3-30	*DG:* D Rees
23 Mar	H	S Wales Police	49-14	*T:* Yendle (2), Scott (2), Westwood, D Rees *C:* Westwood (5) *PG:* Westwood (2) *DG:* D Rees
6 Apr	A	Swansea	16-32	*T:* Jeffreys, A Lewis *PG:* Westwood (2)
10 Apr	H	Aberavon	50-0	*T:* Yendle (2), A Lewis (2), Watkins, McCracken, Waters, Llewellyn *C:* D Rees (4), Westwood
17 Apr	A	Cardiff	20-36	*T:* Waters, Jeffreys *C:* J Williams (2) *PG:* J Williams (2)
1 May	H	Newbridge	57-18	*T:* Orrell (2), A Lewis (2), George, Westwood, Voyle, I Jones *C:* J Williams (6), Westwood *PG:* Westwood

Penarth

Year of formation 1880
Ground Athletic Field, Lavernock Road, Penarth, South Glamorgan
Tel: Penarth (0222) 708402
Colours Royal blue with white chevron
Most capped player J A Bassett (Wales) 15 caps
Captain 1992-93 C Clark
1st XV 1992-93   P39   W13   D0   L26   F653   A1035
Heineken League Div 2 9th   **SWALEC Cup** Lost 16-19 to Tenby Utd (4th round)

League Record 1992-93

Date	Venue	Opponents	Result	Scorers
5 Sept	A	Llandovery	0-39	
12 Sept	H	Narberth	6-46	*PG:* Goult (2)
19 Sept	A	Llanharan	9-46	*PG:* Goult (3)
26 Sept	A	Glamorgan W	5-55	*T:* Graham Lewis

3 Oct	H	Tredegar	5-3	T: D Williams
10 Oct	A	Blaina	5-42	T: Crozier
17 Oct	H	Dunvant	3-60	PG: A Williams
24 Oct	A	Tenby Utd	7-76	T: Clark C: A Williams
31 Oct	H	Cross Keys	0-32	
14 Nov	H	Llanharan	6-28	PG: Goult (2)
28 Nov	A	Ebbw Vale	21-3	T: Goult, M Evans C: M Thomas
				PG: M Thomas (3)
12 Dec	H	Llandovery	8-16	T: Fifield PG: M Thomas
2 Jan	A	Narberth	8-13	T: Bernard PG: M Thomas
16 Jan	H	Glamorgan W	13-0	T: S Thomas C: M Thomas PG: M Thomas (2)
30 Jan	A	Tredegar	3-8	PG: M Thomas
13 Feb	H	Blaina	39-0	T: M Evans (2), M Thomas, Jackson, Hardman, Crothers C: M Thomas (3) PG: M Thomas
27 Feb	H	Abertillery	18-25	T: D Williams (2) C: M Thomas PG: M Thomas, Hardman
13 Mar	A	Dunvant	18-23	T: Hardman, D Williams C: Hardman PG: M Thomas DG: Howells
27 Mar	H	Tenby Utd	6-3	PG: Howells (2)
10 Apr	A	Cross Keys	29-8	T: Graham Lewis (2), Crothers, M Thomas C: Hardman (3) PG: Hardman
17 Apr	H	Ebbw Vale	20-0	T: Jackson (2), Graham Lewis C: Hardman PG: Hardman
1 May	A	Abertillery	16-20	T: Nicholas, Fifield PG: Hardman (2)

Pontypool

Year of formation 1901
Ground The Park, Pontypool, Gwent   Tel: Pontypool (0495) 763492 or 762524
Colours Black, white and red hoops
Most capped player G Price (Wales) 41 caps
Captain 1992-93 R Goodey
1st XV 1992-93 P43 W24 D1 L18 F1062 A769
Heineken League Div 1 8th **SWALEC Cup** Lost 18-21 to Pontypridd (6th round)

League Record 1992-93

Date	Venue	Opponents	Result	Scorers
5 Sept	H	Llanelli	20-44	T: White (2), Hanson C: Carr PG: Carr
12 Sept	A	Neath	16-37	T: Spiller C: Carr PG: Carr (3)
19 Sept	H	Pontypridd	29-24	T: M Taylor (2), White C: Carr PG: Carr (2) DG: Hanson (2)
26 Sept	H	Bridgend	24-13	T: Jackson (2) C: Carr PG: Carr (4)
3 Oct	A	Newport	9-20	PG: Hanson (3)
10 Oct	H	Swansea	27-37	T: Jackson, Hanson C: Carr PG: Carr (4) DG: Hanson
17 Oct	A	Aberavon	26-11	T: White (2), Jacas, M Jones PG: Carr (2)
24 Oct	H	Cardiff	24-31	T: Hanson, P Taylor C: Carr PG: Carr (4)
31 Oct	A	Newbridge	14-27	T: S Smith PG: Carr (2) DG: Hanson
14 Nov	A	Pontypridd	24-20	T: Young, Meek C: M Jones PG: M Jones (4)
28 Nov	H	Maesteg	14-8	T: Pickering PG: Carr (3)
5 Dec	A	S Wales Police	9-16	PG: M Jones (3)
12 Dec	A	Llanelli	13-36	T: White C: M Jones PG: M Jones (2)
16 Jan	A	Bridgend	6-15	PG: M Jones (2)
30 Jan	H	Newport	14-33	T: White PG: Carr (3)
13 Feb	A	Swansea	30-38	T: Hanson, B Taylor, Bridges C: Ring (3) PG: Ring (2) DG: Ring
13 Mar	H	Aberavon	28-7	T: White (2), Lintern C: Ring (2) PG: Ring (2) DG: Ring
27 Mar	A	Cardiff	16-41	T: White C: Ring PG: Ring DG: Ring (2)
10 Apr	H	Newbridge	36-8	T: White (2), W Taylor, Ring C: Ring (2) PG: Ring (4)
12 Apr	H	Neath	9-7	PG: Ring (3)

24 Apr	A	Maesteg	30-27	*T:* Bridges (2), L Jones, V Davies *C:* Ring (2)
				DG: Ring (2)
1 May	H	S Wales Police	71-8	*T:* B Taylor (3), L Jones (2), W Taylor, Spiller, Rogers, Carr, White, Goodey *C:* Carr (8)

Pontypridd

Year of formation 1876
Ground Sardis Road Ground, Pwllgwaun, Pontypridd   Tel: Pontypridd (0433) 405006
Colours Black and white hoops
Most capped player R J Robins (Wales) 13 caps
Captain 1992-93 N Bezani
1st XV 1992-93   P40   W24   D3   L13   F1011   A661
Heineken League Div 1 5th **SWALEC Cup** Lost 6-24 to Llanelli (quarter-final)

League Record 1992-93

Date	Venue	Opponents	Result	Scorers
5 Sept	H	Neath	9-11	*PG:* G Jones (3)
12 Sept	A	Cardiff	3-37	*PG:* G Jones
19 Sept	A	Pontypool	24-29	*T:* Back (2), G Owen, A Roberts *C:* G Jones (2)
26 Sept	H	Newbridge	22-3	*T:* Earland, A Roberts *PG:* K Davies (3)
				DG: K Davies
3 Oct	A	Bridgend	12-12	*PG:* N Jenkins (4)
10 Oct	H	Maesteg	29-20	*T:* McIntosh, N Jenkins, D Hughes, G Jones
				PG: N Jenkins (3)
17 Oct	A	Newport	17-10	*T:* N Jenkins, G Jones *C:* N Jenkins (2)
				PG: N Jenkins
24 Oct	H	S Wales Police	25-13	*T:* G Jones (2), N Jenkins *C:* N Jenkins (2)
				PG: N Jenkins (2)
31 Oct	A	Swansea	15-21	*T:* N Jenkins (2) *C:* N Jenkins *PG:* N Jenkins
14 Nov	H	Pontypool	20-24	*T:* Rowley, M Lloyd, Paul John *C:* G Jones
				PG: K Davies
28 Nov	H	Llanelli	11-11	*T:* S Lewis *PG:* N Jenkins (2)
5 Dec	A	Aberavon	14-19	*T:* D Hughes, S Lewis *C:* G Jones (2)
12 Dec	A	Neath	15-28	*T:* Back, G Jones *C:* G Jones *PG:* G Jones
16 Jan	A	Newbridge	13-8	*T:* G Jones *C:* N Jenkins *PG:* N Jenkins (2)
26 Jan	H	Cardiff	3-6	*PG:* N Jenkins
13 Feb	A	Maesteg	21-8	*T:* G Jones, N Jenkins *C:* N Jenkins
				PG: N Jenkins (3)
13 Mar	H	Newport	30-3	*T:* N Jenkins (2), McIntosh, D Hughes
				C: N Jenkins (2) *PG:* N Jenkins
				DG: N Jenkins
23 Mar	H	Bridgend	17-6	*T:* N Jenkins *PG:* N Jenkins (4)
27 Mar	A	S Wales Police	26-15	*T:* Prosser *PG:* N Jenkins (7)
10 Apr	H	Swansea	35-12	*T:* J Lewis, S Lewis, Earland, D Hughes
				C: N Jenkins (3) *PG:* N Jenkins (3)
28 Apr	A	Llanelli	3-47	*PG:* N Jenkins
1 May	H	Aberavon	36-10	*T:* N Jenkins (2), Back, N Jones *C:* N Jenkins (2)
				PG: N Jenkins (3) *DG:* N Jenkins

South Wales Police

Year of formation 1969
Ground Waterton Cross, Bridgend, Mid-Glamorgan   Tel: Bridgend (0656) 655555 x 218
Colours Red, white and blue
Most capped player B Bowen (Wales) 22 caps
Captain 1992-93 M Pugh
1st XV 1992-93   P36   W13   D1   L22   F589   A982
Heineken League Div 1 12th *relegated* **SWALEC Cup** Lost 11-27 to Swansea (6th round)

League Record 1992-93

Date	Venue	Opponents	Result	Scorers
5 Sept	A	Bridgend	10-41	T: A Price C: J Price PG: A Hughes
12 Sept	H	Newport	0-42	
19 Sept	A	Swansea	24-73	T: Williams-Jones, Cox, Parfitt C: Marshall (3) PG: Marshall
26 Sept	H	Aberavon	0-24	
3 Oct	A	Cardiff	8-65	T: Matthews DG: J Price
10 Oct	H	Newbridge	6-11	PG: Marshall (2)
17 Oct	A	Maesteg	0-0	
24 Oct	A	Pontypridd	13-25	T: Matthews C: Marshall PG: Marshall (2)
31 Oct	H	Llanelli	11-33	T: R Williams PG: Marshall (2)
14 Nov	H	Swansea	16-24	T: P Phillips, Higgs PG: Marshall (2)
28 Nov	A	Neath	15-27	PG: Marshall (5)
5 Dec	H	Pontypool	16-9	T: Parfitt C: Marshall PG: Marshall (3)
12 Dec	H	Bridgend	5-35	T: Hillman
16 Jan	A	Aberavon	0-9	
30 Jan	H	Cardiff	7-36	T: J Williams C: Marshall
13 Feb	A	Newbridge	27-14	T: P Phillips (2), Higgs C: Marshall (3) PG: Marshall (2)
13 Mar	H	Maesteg	29-14	T: Poole, Higgs, Donovan, Payne C: Marshall (3) PG: Marshall
23 Mar	A	Newport	14-49	T: Legge, Hemburrow C: A Hughes (2)
27 Mar	H	Pontypridd	15-26	T: P Phillips, Parfitt C: A Hughes PG: A Hughes
10 Apr	A	Llanelli	0-93	
17 Apr	H	Neath	19-25	T: Collins, Marshall, Apsee C: Marshall (2)
1 May	A	Pontypool	8-71	T: Matthews PG: Cox

Swansea

Year of formation 1873
Ground St Helen's, Swansea, West Glamorgan   Tel: Swansea (0792) 464918
Colours White
Most capped player R N Jones (Wales) 46 caps
Captain 1992-93 Stuart Davies
1st XV 1992-93   P36   W25   D3   L8   F887   A559
Heineken League Div 1 3rd **SWALEC Cup** Lost 18-29 to Llanelli (semi-final)

League Record 1992-93

Date	Venue	Opponents	Result	Scorers
5 Sept	H	Newbridge	17-13	T: B Taylor, Simon Davies, Ian Davies C: A Williams
12 Sept	A	Maesteg	35-6	T: Simon Davies (2), Reynolds, Titley, R Jones C: R Jones (2) PG: R Jones (2)
19 Sept	H	S Wales Police	73-24	T: Simon Davies (3), Colclough (2), Kehoe, Stuart Davies, Weatherley, M Morgan, Titley, Clement C: Titley (9)
26 Sept	A	Llanelli	14-7	T: Titley PG: A Williams (3)
3 Oct	H	Neath	29-12	T: Stuart Davies, Simon Davies, Gibbs, A Williams PG: A Williams (2), Titley
10 Oct	A	Pontypool	37-27	T: Titley, A Williams, G Jenkins C: A Williams (2) PG: A Williams (4) DG: A Williams (2)
17 Oct	H	Bridgend	29-6	T: Titley (2), Michael, R Jones, Webster C: A Williams (2)
24 Oct	A	Newport	44-20	T: R Jones, Clement, Ian Davies, Simon Davies, Gibbs C: A Williams (2) PG: A Williams (3) DG: A Williams (2)
31 Oct	H	Pontypridd	21-15	T: A Williams, G Jenkins C: A Williams PG: A Williams (3)

14 Nov	A	S Wales Police	24-16	*T:* Stuart Davies, R Jones *C:* S Jones
				PG: Ball (4)
28 Nov	H	Aberavon	25-13	*T:* Arnold, Titley, Hopkins *C:* A Williams (2)
				PG: A Williams (2)
5 Dec	A	Cardiff	6-8	*PG:* A Williams (2)
12 Dec	A	Newbridge	28-0	*T:* A Williams (2), Simon Davies
				C: A Williams (2) *PG:* A Williams (3)
9 Jan	H	Maesteg	15-11	*T:* Weatherley, A Williams *C:* A Williams
				PG: A Williams
15 Jan	H	Llanelli	10-15	*T:* A Williams *C:* A Williams *PG:* A Williams
30 Jan	A	Neath	18-8	*T:* Clement, Simon Davies *C:* A Williams
				PG: A Williams (2)
13 Feb	H	Pontypool	38-30	*T:* A Williams, Ian Davies, Hopkins, R Jones
				C: A Williams (3) *PG:* A Williams (4)
13 Mar	A	Bridgend	25-16	*T:* Webster (2), Arnold, Barclay, Clement
6 Apr	H	Newport	32-16	*T:* Ian Davies, Greenslade, Gibbs, Webster
				C: S Jones (3) *PG:* S Jones *DG:* Titley
10 Apr	A	Pontypridd	12-35	*PG:* A Williams (3) *DG:* A Williams
17 Apr	A	Aberavon	6-12	*PG:* Ball *DG:* Ball
1 May	H	Cardiff	10-16	*T:* Robbie Jones *C:* A Williams
				DG: A Williams

Tenby United

Year of formation 1901
Ground Heywood Lane, Tenby   Tel: Tenby (0834) 842909
Colours Black and scarlet hoops
Captain 1992-93 C Harts
Ist XV 1992-93 P34 W22 D1 L11 F845 A397
Heineken League Div 2 5th **SWALEC Cup** Lost 6-22 to Swansea (5th round)

League Record 1992-93

Date	*Venue*	*Opponents*	*Result*	*Scorers*
5 Sept	A	Glamorgan W	6-14	*PG:* Scotcher (2)
19 Sept	A	Ebbw Vale	14-23	*T:* Sutton *PG:* Scotcher (3)
26 Sept	H	Abertillery	21-11	*T:* M Griffiths, Hartland *C:* Scotcher
				PG: Scotcher (3)
3 Oct	A	Llandovery	8-7	*T:* Truman *PG:* Scotcher
10 Oct	H	Narberth	6-13	*PG:* Scotcher (2)
17 Oct	A	Llanharan	8-9	*T:* J Richards *PG:* Scotcher
24 Oct	H	Penarth	76-7	*T:* Sutton (2), P Hopkins (2), P Morris (2),
				A Morgan (2), Truman, F Setaro, Gale, Childs
				C: Childs (8)
31 Oct	A	Tredegar	13-13	*T:* P Hopkins *C:* Childs *PG:* Childs
				DG: Childs
14 Nov	H	Ebbw Vale	30-8	*T:* Hartland, F Setaro, Goodwin, M Evans
				C: Childs (2) *PG:* Childs (2)
22 Nov	H	Cross Keys	16-12	*T:* C Evans *C:* Childs *PG:* Childs (3)
28 Nov	H	Blaina	27-0	*T:* F Setaro, Sutton, M Griffiths *C:* Childs (3)
				PG: Childs (2)
5 Dec	A	Dunvant	9-21	*PG:* Childs (3)
12 Dec	H	Glamorgan W	64-10	*T:* Sutton (2), P Hopkins (2), Goodwin (2), Childs,
				Hartland, G Thomas *C:* Childs (8) *PG:* Childs
2 Jan	A	Cross Keys	3-6	*DG:* Childs
16 Jan	A	Abertillery	22-13	*T:* A Morgan, Truman *PG:* Childs (3)
				DG: Childs
30 Jan	H	Llandovery	0-7	
13 Feb	A	Narberth	23-10	*T:* Goodwin *PG:* Childs (6)
13 Mar	H	Llanharan	18-14	*T:* Goodwin, C Evans *C:* Childs
				PG: Childs (2)
27 Mar	A	Penarth	3-6	*PG:* Scotcher

10 Apr	H	Tredegar	31-20	T: M Evans, P Hopkins, M Griffiths
				C: Childs (2) PG: Childs (3) DG: Childs
17 Apr	A	Blaina	28-3	T: Hartland, Childs, Lawrence C: Childs (2)
				PG: Childs (2) DG: Childs
1 May	H	Dunvant	6-7	PG: A Morgan (2)

Tredegar

Year of formation 1893
Ground Recreation Ground, Parc Hill, Tredegar, Gwent   Tel: Tredegar (0495) 252879
Colours Red, black and white
Captain 1992-93 J Richards
1st XV 1992-93   P39   W12   D3   L24   F589   A657
Heineken League Div 2 11th *relegated* **SWALEC Cup** Lost 0-21 to S Wales Police (5th round)

League Record 1992-93

Date	Venue	Opponents	Result	Scorers
5 Sept	A	Abertillery	0-45	
12 Sept	H	Llandovery	23-13	T: Daley, K Smith, Moyle C: Green
				PG: Green (2)
19 Sept	A	Narberth	6-11	PG: K Smith (2)
26 Sept	H	Llanharan	3-18	PG: K Smith
3 Oct	A	Penarth	3-5	PG: K Smith
10 Oct	A	Glamorgan W	9-44	PG: K Smith (3)
17 Oct	A	Blaina	9-13	PG: K Smith (3)
24 Oct	A	Dunvant	0-28	
31 Oct	H	Tenby Utd	13-13	T: J Williams, Marsh PG: Green
14 Nov	H	Narberth	3-3	PG: Green
5 Dec	H	Ebbw Vale	0-3	
12 Dec	H	Abertillery	12-20	PG: Green (4)
2 Jan	A	Llandovery	7-28	T: J Williams C: Green
16 Jan	A	Llanharan	21-31	T: Daley, Medlicott C: Bolderson
				PG: Bolderson (3)
30 Jan	H	Penarth	8-3	T: Moyle PG: Bolderson
13 Feb	H	Glamorgan W	10-16	T: Phillips C: Bolderson PG: Bolderson
23 Feb	A	Cross Keys	12-36	PG: Bolderson (3) DG: Green
12 Mar	H	Blaina*	3-6	PG: Bolderson
27 Mar	H	Dunvant	6-14	PG: Bolderson (2)
10 Apr	A	Tenby Utd	20-31	T: Daley, J Williams C: Bolderson (2)
				PG: Bolderson DG: Green
17 Apr	H	Cross Keys	16-25	T: Green C: Bolderson PG: Bolderson (2)
				DG: Hunt
30 Apr	A	Ebbw Vale	16-0	T: Moore C: Bolderson PG: Bolderson (3)

*Abandoned after 39 minutes

OBITUARY 1992-93 (*up to 1 May 1993*)

Dr James Gilbert ABERCROMBIE (Edinburgh University, Scotland) won seven caps as a hooker in 1949 and 1950 when he was a medical student at Edinburgh University. In his last international, against England in 1950, he scored a vital try in a match destined to be Scotland's last Calcutta Cup win for 14 years. 'Gibby', who later settled in New Zealand, died at his home in Auckland on 23 August 1992, aged 64.

Rev. Peter Watts Pitt BROOK (Cambridge University, Harlequins, England) died in Bristol on 6 August 1992, aged 85. After winning four Cambridge Blues between 1928 and 1931, he played three times for England in the 1930s, making an impact as a useful jumper at the tail of the line-out. For many years he was chaplain of Clifton College, where he made a big contribution as coach of the First XV.

Sir Giles Lionel BULLARD KCVO, CMG (Oxford University), the noted diplomat, died on 11 November 1992, aged 66. A lock forward, he scored a try and kicked two conversions when leading the Dark Blues to a resounding 13-0 victory in the 1951 Varsity match.

Raoul BONAMY (Stade Bordelais, France), a loose forward capped twice in 1928, died on 21 April 1993, aged 87. In the 1930s he also won caps for France as a Rugby League player.

James Christopher CASEY (Young Munster, Ireland) was the first player to represent Ireland out of the Young Munster club, winning caps against Scotland in 1930 and England in 1932. 'Ter' Casey died in Limerick on 4 August 1992, aged 89.

Stanley Randall COUCHMAN (Old Cranleighans), who died in November 1992, aged 79, was the president of the RFU in 1978-79 and a hard-working administrator for both Surrey and the RFU. An uncompromising forward in the 1930s, he appeared in several England trials and toured South Africa with the 1938 Lions.

Dr Daniel Hartman CRAVEN (W Province, E Province, N Transvaal, South Africa) was rugby football's most senior administrator. During a distinguished lifetime in the game, he first made his mark as a gifted player. In the 1930s he was chiefly recognised as the scrum-half who perfected the dive-pass. However, in an extraordinary Test career which brought him 16 caps, he also appeared as centre, fly-half and No 8. He became an innovative coach and later enjoyed a high profile as chairman of the International Board. From 1956 he was president of the former South African Rugby Board and when, in 1992, the SARFU became the sport's new governing body in the Republic, Dr Craven was

Danie Craven, the late lamented Mr Rugby of South Africa.

immediately installed as its joint president to oversee South Africa's return to the international rugby fold. He died in Stellenbosch on 4 January 1993, aged 82.

Dr Morgan Patrick CROWE (Lansdowne, Leicester, Ireland), a centre who won 13 caps between 1929 and 1934, died at his Dublin home on 8 April 1993, aged 86. Three times in 1931 he played alongside Ned Lightfoot, Jack Arigho and Eugene Davy when his Lansdowne club supplied Ireland with its entire threequarter line. Dr Crowe's brother Phil and son Jim also played for Ireland.

Jean DARRIEUSECQ (Mont-de-Marsan, France), who died on 27 December 1992, aged 72, won one cap as a scrum-half against Italy in 1953. A schoolmaster, he twice led his club to the French championship final.

Eiryn Gwyn DAVIES (Cardiff, Wales) made his cap debut as a teenager in 1928 and won the last of his three caps in 1930, when he was on the wing of an all-Cardiff threequarter line which represented Wales against Scotland. A distinguished Rugby League career with Wigan followed, bringing him further international honours, including a tour with the 1936 Great Britain team in Australia. He died in Wigan on 14 July 1992, aged 84.

Jack Gale Wilmot DAVIES OBE (Blackheath), the accomplished all-round sportsman who became the secretary to the Cambridge University Appointments Board, died on 5 November 1992, aged 81. At rugby football Jack Davies was a noted centre, good enough to play in the first England trial in 1938.

Colin EVANS (Pontypool, Wales), the scrum-half whose long pass gave his fly-half partners so much time and room in which to manoeuvre, died in Leeds on 23 November 1992, aged 56. He won his sole Rugby Union cap against England in 1960 before joining Leeds Rugby League club.

Albert Charles FALWASSER (Hawke's Bay, Taranaki, Auckland) was one of the best wings never to play for New Zealand. He did, however, tour Europe with the Maori side of 1926-27, scoring 23 tries and appearing in 30 of the 31 matches, including the only Test match of the visit, against France. Alby died in Surfers' Paradise on 31 August 1992, aged 89.

Allan Leslie FLEURY (Otago), the New Zealand referee in the first Test between the All Blacks and the Lions in 1959, died in Dunedin on 3 August 1992, aged 70. In his only Test appointment Mr Fleury courted controversy for persistently penalising the Lions. As a result, Don Clarke became the first player to kick six penalty goals in an international and the Lions were pipped 18-17.

Rev. Peter Maurice Sydney GEDGE (Edinburgh Wanderers, Scotland) played on the wing for Scotland in 1933 when they beat Ireland to win the Triple Crown. Educated at Loretto and Cambridge University, where he missed his Blue, Peter Gedge became a schoolmaster and was the head of St George's, Harpenden between 1950 and 1970, before taking holy orders. Rev. Gedge, whose father played for Scotland in the 1890s, died in Scarborough on 27 February 1993, aged 82.

Malcolm Leith GRANT (Harlequins, Scotland), a red-haired Cambridge graduate who won four caps between 1955 and 1957 as a fly-half-cum-centre, died in Edinburgh on 29 October 1992, aged 64. Described as a Harlequin club man to the core, 'Micky' Grant's international qualification was through his Scottish father.

Kenneth Francis GRAY MBE (Wellington, New Zealand) was the automatic choice as prop in 24 New Zealand Tests between 1963 and 1969. The All Blacks created a world record of 17 successive Test wins during that period, their success deriving from a magnificent pack in which Ken Gray was a key figure. At the time of his death on 18 November 1992, he was a Labour Party candidate for the 1993 New Zealand election. He was 54.

William Ngataiawhio GRAY (Bay of Plenty, New Zealand), a Maori second five-eighth renowned for his strength and courage in defence, died suddenly in Rotorua on 10 January 1993, aged 60. Bill played in six Tests for the All Blacks in the mid-1950s, including the home series against South Africa in 1956, in which the All Blacks took a rubber off the Springboks for the first time.

Stewart Cathie GRIFFITH (Dulwich College), better known as Billy Griffith, former England cricketer and late secretary of MCC, was a talented rugby footballer as a schoolboy at Dulwich College. After the war he was also a respected rugby critic for a number of newspapers and journals. He died on 7 April 1993, aged 78.

William Edward HADLEY (Bay of Plenty, Auckland, New Zealand), who died in Auckland on 30 September 1992, aged 82, was New Zealand's hooker in eight consecutive Tests between 1934 and 1936. On the 1935-36 All Blacks visit to Britain his jaw was broken in the opening tour match. He recovered, however, to play in 16 of the matches, including the four internationals.

Laurence Stokes HAIG (Otago, New Zealand), vice-captain of the fourth All Blacks to Britain, Ireland and France in 1953-54, died in Dunedin on 10 July 1992, aged 69. A Scot by birth, Laurie Haig was first capped against the 1950 Lions and went on to play in nine Tests for the All Blacks as a five-eighth who had a sharp eye for an opening.

Terence Anthony HARRIS (Transvaal, South Africa), who died on 7 March 1993, aged 76, was Danie Craven's half-back partner against the All Blacks in 1937 when, for the only time to date, South Africa won a Test series in New Zealand. He was one of the best all-round sportsmen ever produced by South Africa. Besides winning five rugby caps in 1937 and 1938, he returned from war service with the SAAF to play Test cricket for his country between 1947 and 1949.

Robert HOWIE (Kirkcaldy, Scotland), a 1924 Lion in South Africa and one of the last two survivors of the 1925 Scottish Grand Slam team, died on 14 May 1992, aged 93. He was plucked from the obscurity of junior club rugby to play in the Scottish trials of November 1923 and went straight into the Scottish pack for the four internationals of 1924. On tour with the Lions he was a forceful scrummager and skilful dribbler in the loose, becoming an integral part of the Test pack.

Eric David HILL (Auckland), who died aged 84 on 14 June 1992, was one of New Zealand's leading referees before and after the last war. He controlled the First Test between New Zealand and Australia in 1949 and refereed two of the tour matches played by the 1950 Lions.

Gordon Donald INNES (Canterbury, New Zealand) was an All Black in Australia in 1932, when he played in his only Test for New Zealand, as a second five-eighth. A year later he joined Wigan Rugby League team and in 1935 he became the first All Black to represent England in a Rugby League international, turning out against France. He died on 6 November 1992, aged 82.

John Meadows JEFFS, who died in Wellington on 21 August 1992, aged 76, was the secretary-treasurer of the NZRFU from 1973 to 1978.

Thomas KATENE (King Country, Wellington, New Zealand) appeared in one Test for New Zealand, in 1955 against Australia. A powerful wing and a useful place-kicker, he regularly represented the Maoris in the 1950s. He died on 6 June 1992 in Auckland. He was 62.

Brian Alexander KILLEEN (Wellington, Auckland, New Zealand) was capped once as a second five-eighth for New Zealand against the 1936 Wallabies. The same year he captained both Auckland and the North Island. He died on 9 March 1993, aged 81.

Richard Martin Alford KINGSWELL (Headingley), the 1972-73 president of the RFU, died in London on 5 June 1992, aged 80. As a player in the 1930s, he was an uncomplicated scrum-half who came close to winning caps for England.

Seamus LAVELLE (Hendon) died tragically on 15 March 1993 after losing consciousness during a Courage League match two days earlier. He suffered head injuries after a punch was allegedly thrown. He was 30.

Hugh Campbell McLAREN (Waikato, Auckland, New Zealand), a mobile forward who was able to play in all three rows of the scrum, died at Tauranga on 9 May 1992, aged 65. After a brilliant Test debut against Australia in 1952, he had to withdraw from the second Test through injury. Although he never again played for the All Blacks, he successfully led Waikato during their Ranfurly Shield run of victories between 1951 and 1953.

Harold Maurice MILLIKEN (Canterbury, New Zealand), who died on 10 January 1993, aged 78, played for the All Blacks as a lock on the 1938 tour of Australia, winning three caps. The following year he was a member of the New Zealand Rugby League team whose tour of England was interrupted by the outbreak of war. He returned to Rugby Union in 1950, playing senior club rugby in Auckland and Waikato.

André MOGA (Bègles), a vice-president of the FFR between 1966 and 1991, died on 22 December 1992, aged 71. He was capped twice for France B in the 1940s and, at 6 feet 3 inches and 15 stones, was the biggest French forward of his generation. His brother 'Bambi' Moga won 22 caps for France.

Jack Deryk Erle MONTEITH (Queen's University, Belfast, Ireland), who captained Ireland twice while winning three caps in 1947, died on 26 June 1992, aged 72. He represented Ulster on numerous occasions, performing with equal facility as full-back or centre. A dentist by profession, he was a respected sports administrator in Northern Ireland.

Jean-Luc PELAEZ (Bayonne), a member of the victorious French squad at the 1992 Students World Cup, died in a car accident on 23 February 1993, aged 23.

Terence Graham PRICE (Llanelli, Hendy, London Welsh, Wales) died in a road accident at Bicester on 7 April 1993, aged 47. After a brilliant career in schoolboy rugby at Llanelli GS, he made his Welsh debut as a teenager in 1965 and was the wizard of a team which carried off the Triple Crown and Championship. His accurate kicking brought him 22 points for the season, which included a prodigious dropped goal from 40 metres at a crucial moment in the Triple Crown decider against Ireland. Capped eight times, he toured New Zealand with the 1966 Lions before turning professional with Bradford Northern a year later. After a successful career in Rugby League he went to America, making a name for himself as a place-kicker with the Buffalo Bills.

Jean-Claude ROUAN (Narbonne, France), France's full-back in their opening Five Nations matches in 1953, had been honorary secretary of Narbonne club for the past 20 years at the time of his death on 23 January 1993. He was 59.

Edward Harding SADLER (Army, England), who died on 26 December 1992, aged 82, uniquely played Rugby Union and Rugby League for England before returning to the 15-a-side game to represent England again in services internationals during the war. He scored a try on his debut against Ireland in 1933 and won two caps before Oldham Rugby League club bought him out of the Army the same year.

Col Frank William SIMPSON DSO (Cambridge University, Army), the distinguished soldier who died in August 1992, aged 83, was a talented scrum-half between the wars. A gifted all-round sportsman, he won rugby Blues at Cambridge in 1930 and 1931, played club rugby for Waterloo and Blackheath, and was twice chosen as an England reserve.

Mark Sprot STEWART (Stewart's FP, Scotland), Scotland's captain in 1934 and the president of the SRU in 1966-67, died at his home near Melrose on 2 March 1993, aged 88. A mobile lock forward during his playing days, he won nine caps between 1932 and 1934, and was a mainstay of the pack which paved the way for the Scottish Triple Crown win of 1933.

Josias Johannes Nicolaas SWART (South-West Africa, South Africa), the first player from the former South-West Africa team to be capped by South Africa, died in Windhoek, Namibia, on 18 January 1993, aged 58. Sias Swart won his only cap for the Springboks in the pulsating First Test of the series against the Lions in 1955, scoring a try in a 22-23 defeat for South Africa.

Kelvin Robert TREMAIN (Canterbury, Hawke's Bay, New Zealand) died of cancer at Napier on 2 May 1992, aged 54. During the 1960s Kel was regarded as the world's outstanding flanker. In his 38 Tests between 1959 and 1968, when the All Blacks enjoyed a great run of success at international level, he scored nine tries, establishing a record for a New Zealand forward.

Group Captain Carlton Lang TROOP CBE (Army, England), the back-row forward who was twice capped in 1933, died at a residential home near Rye on 2 June 1992. He was 81.

John William Cleet TURNER (Gala, Scotland), a natural footballer who won 20 caps between 1966 and 1971 as a centre, fly-half and full-back, died suddenly on 19 May 1992, aged 48. A stout defender and a penetrative attacker, Jock Turner toured South Africa with the 1968 Lions, appearing at centre in all four of the Tests. He was one of the most talented products of his club and captained Gala in 1968-69.

Jeremiah Charles WALSH (UC Cork, Sunday's Well, Ireland), who died on 28 September 1992, aged 53, won 26 caps as a centre between 1960 and 1967. An outstanding crash-tackler, Jerry went as a Lion to Australia in 1966 but had to return prematurely owing to the death of his father. He scored his only try for Ireland in his last international, against Australia in 1967.

Arthur WHEATLEY (Coventry, England), who was England's lock in the 1937 Triple Crown side and packed down behind his brother Harold in 1938, died in March 1993, aged 84. The Wheatleys were the last pair of brothers to play together for England before Tony and Rory Underwood lined up against South Africa in 1992.

Rhys Haydn WILLIAMS (Llanelli, Wales), the Welshman who was a legend in his own line-out during 23 games for Wales and ten Tests for the Lions, died at his home in Whitchurch on 27 January 1993, aged 62. 'RH' was the first British forward to win worldwide acclaim. His line-out work and mauling in South Africa with the 1955 Lions provided crucial possession for a lively back division, and his outstanding service for the 1959 Lions in New Zealand greatly impressed the All Blacks, who elected him one of their five players of the season. For 15 years he served the WRU, resigning in 1989 in the wake of the South African centenary celebrations affair.

Air Vice-Marshal Brian YOUNG CB, CBE (Wasps), the former commandant-general of the RAF Regiment who died on 26 July 1992, aged 74, was in the winning Wasps team at the 1948 Middlesex Sevens and captained his club in 1950-51.

FIXTURES 1993-94

Venues and fixtures are understood to be correct at the time of going to press, but are subject to alteration. We should like to thank all those who have assisted in the compilation of this list, especially those at the various headquarters of the Home Unions.

Saturday, 28 August

Selkirk Sevens

Wednesday, 1 September

Lancashire v Munster (Manchester)
Hertfordshire v Eastern Counties
  (Hertford)
Amman Utd v S Wales Police
Ayr v West of Scotland
Bridgend v Llanharan
Broughton Park v Wigan
Burton v Nuneaton
Coventry v Rugby
Ebbw Vale v Tredegar
Fylde v Lancs Police
Harlequins v Richmond
Jedforest v Langholm
Kelso v Hawick
Lydney v Gloucester
Maesteg v Birchgrove
Melrose v Selkirk
Morley v Wakefield
Newbury v Havant
Newcastle Gosforth v Tynedale
Northampton v Met Police
Peebles v Gala
Penarth v Newport
Plymouth Albion v Cork Const
Pontypool v Gwent Police
Redruth v Camborne
Watsonians v Stirling County
West Hartlepool v Middlesbrough

Thursday, 2 September

Exeter v Devon
Liverpool St Helens v De La Salle
  Palmerston

Saturday, 4 September

WRU Heineken Leagues
Division 1
Cardiff v Aberavon
Cross Keys v Bridgend
Dunvant v Newport
Llanelli v Pontypool
Neath v Pontypridd
Newbridge v Swansea

Division 2
Llanharan v Narberth
Maesteg v Mountain Ash
Penarth v Llandovery
S Wales Police v Abertillery
Tenby Utd v Glam Wands
Treorchy v Ebbw Vale

Cornwall v Cork Const (Redruth)
Askeans v London Welsh
Bath v Toulouse
Bedford v Moseley
Boroughmuir v Newcastle Gosforth
Brixham v Clifton
Coventry v Northampton
Fylde v Kendal
Gala v Saracens
Havant v Harlequins
Hawick v Ballymena
Heriot's FP v Lansdowne
Jedforest v Selkirk
Kelso v Melrose
London Irish v Richmond
London Scottish v Rosslyn Park
Lydney v Taunton
Northern v Liverpool St Helens
Nuneaton v Middlesbrough
Otley v Halifax
Rugby v Morley
Stewart's-Melville FP v Glasgow Acads
Stourbridge v Exeter
Tynedale v Watsonians
Wakefield v Harrogate
Wanderers v Nottingham
Wasps v West Hartlepool
Waterloo v Broughton Park
West of Scotland v Vale of Lune
Wharfedale v Sheffield

Sunday, 5 September

Kelso Sevens
Northern Sevens
Newton Abbot v Clifton

Tuesday, 7 September

WRU Heineken Leagues
Division 1
Bridgend v Llanelli
Pontypridd v Cardiff

Wednesday, 8 September

WRU Heineken Leagues
Division 1
Pontypool v Neath
Swansea v Dunvant

Devon v Somerset (Tiverton)
Morley v Hull Ionians
Newport v Cross Keys

Saturday, 11 September

RFU Courage Leagues
Division 1
Bristol v Bath
Gloucester v Wasps
Harlequins v London Irish
Northampton v Leicester
· Orrell v Newcastle Gosforth
Division 2
London Scottish v Sale
Nottingham v Otley
Saracens v Moseley
Wakefield v Rugby
West Hartlepool v Waterloo

SRU McEwan's Leagues
Division 1
Edinburgh Acads v Jedforest
Hawick v West of Scotland
Kelso v Heriot's FP
Melrose v Gala
Stewart's-Melville FP v Boroughmuir
Stirling County v Selkirk
Watsonians v Currie
Division 2
Biggar v Wigtownshire
Clarkston v Ayr
Dundee HSFP v Kirkcaldy
Edinburgh Wands v Preston Lodge
Glasgow Acads v Peebles
Grangemouth v Glasgow High/Kelvinside
Musselburgh v Haddington

WRU Heineken Leagues
Division 1
Cross Keys v Swansea
Dunvant v Aberavon
Llanelli v Newport
Neath v Bridgend
Newbridge v Cardiff
Pontypridd v Pontypool
Division 2
Abertillery v Treorchy
Ebbw Vale v Maesteg
Glam Wands v Llanharan

Llandovery v S Wales Police
Mountain Ash v Tenby Utd
Narberth v Penarth

RFU Pilkington Cup *1st round*
RFU Junior Clubs Cup *1st round*
Aspatria v Fylde
Bedford v Richmond
Birkenhead Park v Liverpool St Helens
Broughton Park v Manchester
Harrogate v Blackheath
Havant v Sutton-Epsom
Middlesbrough v Sheffield
Morley v Leeds
Plymouth Albion v Exeter
Rosslyn Park v Clifton
Taunton v Redruth
Vale of Lune v Macclesfield
Wanderers v Coventry

Tuesday, 14 September

Eastern Counties v Holland (Shelford)
Northampton v London Welsh
Wasps v Blackheath

Wednesday, 15 September

Cardiff v Penarth
Morley v Durham City
Preston Grasshoppers v Vale of Lune

Saturday, 18 September

RFU Courage Leagues
Division 1
Bath v Northampton
Leicester v Orrell
London Irish v Bristol
Newcastle Gosforth v Gloucester
Wasps v Harlequins
Division 2
Moseley v Wakefield
Otley v West Hartlepool
Rugby v Nottingham
Sale v Saracens
Waterloo v London Scottish

RFU County Championship
Division 1 (South)
Cornwall v Gloucestershire (Redruth)
Hampshire v Middlesex (US Portsmouth)
Division 1 (North)
Durham v Northumberland (Hartlepool Rovers)
Lancashire v Yorkshire (Preston Grasshoppers)

Division 2 (South)
Dorset & Wilts v Surrey
Devon v Kent (Teignmouth)
Division 2 (North)
Cheshire v Leicestershire (New Brighton)
Warwickshire v Cumbria
Division 3 (South)
Hertfordshire v Somerset
Sussex v Buckinghamshire
Division 3 (North)
North Midlands v Staffordshire
Notts, Lincs & Derbys v East Midlands
Division 4
Berkshire v Eastern Counties (Reading)

SRU McEwan's Leagues
Division 1
Boroughmuir v Gala
Currie v Edinburgh Acads
Heriot's FP v Stewart's-Melville FP
Jedforest v Stirling County
Melrose v Watsonians
Selkirk v Hawick
West of Scotland v Kelso
Division 2
Ayr v Musselburgh
Dundee HSFP v Edinburgh Wands
Glasgow High/Kelvinside v Glasgow Acads
Haddington v Kirkcaldy
Peebles v Clarkston
Preston Lodge v Biggar
Wigtownshire v Grangemouth

IRFU Insurance Corporation Leagues
Division 1
Blackrock Coll v St Mary's Coll
Cork Const v Garryowen
Greystones v Old Wesley
Shannon v Dungannon
Young Munster v Lansdowne
Division 2
Dolphin v Old Belvedere
Galwegians v Instonians
Malone v Ballymena
Terenure Coll v Sunday's Well
Division 3
Athlone v Clontarf
Bective Rangers v Highfield
NIFC v City of Derry
Portadown v De La Salle Palmerston

WRU Heineken Leagues
Division 1
Aberavon v Cross Keys
Bridgend v Pontypool
Cardiff v Dunvant

Newbridge v Pontypridd
Newport v Neath
Swansea v Llanelli
Division 2
Glam Wands v Mountain Ash
Maesteg v Abertillery
Penarth v Llanharan
S Wales Police v Narberth
Tenby Utd v Ebbw Vale
Treorchy v Llandovery

WRU SWALEC Cup *1st round*
Askeans v Southend
Blackheath v London Welsh
Broughton Park v Morley
Clifton v Basingstoke
Exeter v Launceston
Harrogate v Coventry
Havant v Torquay Ath
Kendal v Vale of Lune
Liverpool St Helens v Fylde
Penryn v Redruth
Plymouth Albion v Lydney
Sheffield v Bedford
Walsall v Rosslyn Park

Sunday, 19 September

IRFU Insurance Corporation Leagues
Division 2
Old Crescent v Ballina
Division 3
Corinthians v Sligo

Tuesday, 21 September

Rosslyn Park v Wasps

Wednesday, 22 September

Bedford v Beds Police
Cambridge U v Cambridge City

Saturday, 25 September

RFU Courage Leagues
Division 1
Gloucester v Leicester
Harlequins v Bristol
Northampton v London Irish
Orrell v Bath
Wasps v Newcastle Gosforth
Division 2
London Scottish v Otley
Nottingham v Moseley
Sale v Waterloo
Saracens v Wakefield
West Hartlepool v Rugby

RFU County Championship
Division 1 (South)
Cornwall v Hampshire (Camborne)
Middlesex v Gloucestershire (Imber
  Court)
Division 1 (North)
Durham v Lancashire (Gateshead Fell)
Yorkshire v Northumberland
Division 2 (South)
Dorset & Wilts v Devon
Kent v Surrey (Blackheath)
Division 2 (North)
Leicestershire v Cumbria
Warwickshire v Cheshire
Division 3 (South)
Somerset v Buckinghamshire
  (Bridgwater)
Sussex v Hertfordshire
Division 3 (North)
Notts, Lincs & Derbys v North Midlands
Staffordshire v East Midlands
Division 4
Oxfordshire v Berkshire

SRU McEwan's Leagues
Division 1
Boroughmuir v Heriot's FP
Edinburgh Acads v Melrose
Gala v Watsonians
Hawick v Jedforest
Kelso v Selkirk
Stewart's-Melville FP v West of Scotland
Stirling County v Currie
Division 2
Biggar v Dundee HSFP
Clarkston v Glasgow High/Kelvinside
Glasgow Acads v Wigtownshire
Grangemouth v Preston Lodge
Haddington v Ayr
Kirkcaldy v Edinburgh Wands
Musselburgh v Peebles

IRFU Insurance Corporation Leagues
Division 1
Dungannon v Blackrock Coll
Garryowen v Young Munster
Old Wesley v Shannon
St Mary's Coll v Cork Const
Wanderers v Greystones
Division 2
Ballina v Malone
Bangor v Galwegians
Instonians v Terenure Coll
Old Belvedere v Old Crescent
Sunday's Well v Dolphin

Division 3
City of Derry v Bective Rangers
Collegians v NIFC
De La Salle Palmerston v Athlone
Highfield v Corinthians
Sligo v UC Cork

WRU Heineken Leagues
Division 1
Cross Keys v Cardiff
Dunvant v Newbridge
Llanelli v Aberavon
Neath v Swansea
Pontypool v Newport
Pontypridd v Bridgend
Division 2
Abertillery v Tenby Utd
Ebbw Vale v Mountain Ash
Llandovery v Maesteg
Llanharan v S Wales Police
Narberth v Treorchy
Penarth v Glam Wands

Bedford v Liverpool St Helens
Cambridge U v Sheffield
Clifton v Havant
Coventry v Lydney
Fylde v Vale of Lune
Kendal v Broughton Park
Maidstone v Blackheath
Morley v Rotherham
Rosslyn Park v Southend
Sidcup v Askeans

Sunday, 26 September

Redruth v Launceston
Torquay Ath v Plymouth Albion

Tuesday, 28 September

Exeter v Barbarians
Pontypridd v Maesteg
Wasps v Richmond

Wednesday, 29 September

Wales A v Japanese (Llanelli)
Cambridge U v St Mary's Hosp
Lydney v Penarth
Nuneaton v Loughborough Students
Oxford U v CLOB

Saturday, 2 October

BC Development XV v Australians
  (Vancouver) (provisional)

RFU Courage Leagues
Division 1
Bath v Gloucester
Bristol v Northampton
Leicester v Wasps
London Irish v Orrell
Newcastle Gosforth v Harlequins
Division 2
Moseley v West Hartlepool
Otley v Sale
Rugby v London Scottish
Wakefield v Nottingham
Waterloo v Saracens

RFU County Championship
Division 1 (South)
Gloucestershire v Hampshire (Lydney)
Middlesex v Cornwall
Division 1 (North)
Northumberland v Lancashire
  (Tynedale)
Yorkshire v Durham
Division 2 (South)
Kent v Dorset & Wilts (Maidstone)
Surrey v Devon
Division 2 (North)
Cumbria v Cheshire
Leicestershire v Warwickshire
Division 3 (South)
Buckinghamshire v Hertfordshire
  (Marlow)
Somerset v Sussex
Division 3 (North)
East Midlands v North Midlands
Staffordshire v Notts, Lincs & Derbys
Division 4
Eastern Counties v Oxfordshire
  (Thurrock)

SRU McEwan's Leagues
Division 1
Currie v Hawick
Heriot's FP v Gala
Jedforest v Kelso
Melrose v Stirling County
Selkirk v Stewart's-Melville FP
Watsonians v Edinburgh Acads
West of Scotland v Boroughmuir
Division 2
Ayr v Kirkcaldy
Dundee HSFP v Grangemouth
Edinburgh Wands v Biggar
Glasgow High/Kelvinside v Musselburgh
Peebles v Haddington
Preston Lodge v Glasgow Acads
Wigtownshire v Clarkston

IRFU Insurance Corporation Leagues
Division 1
Blackrock Coll v Old Wesley
Cork Const v Dungannon
Lansdowne v Garryowen
Shannon v Wanderers
Young Munster v St Mary's Coll
Division 2
Ballymena v Ballina
Dolphin v Instonians
Malone v Old Belvedere
Terenure Coll v Bangor
Division 3
Athlone v UC Dublin
Bective Rangers v Collegians
Clontarf v De La Salle Palmerston
Corinthians v City of Derry
Portadown v Sligo

WRU Heineken Leagues
Division 1
Aberavon v Neath
Cardiff v Llanelli
Dunvant v Pontypridd
Newbridge v Cross Keys
Newport v Bridgend
Swansea v Pontypool
Division 2
Glam Wands v Ebbw Vale
Maesteg v Narberth
Mountain Ash v Abertillery
S Wales Police v Penarth
Tenby Utd v Llandovery
Treorchy v Llanharan

Askeans v Maidstone
Blackburn v Vale of Lune
Blackheath v Clifton
Coventry v Broughton Park
Exeter v Nuneaton
Harrogate v Fylde
High Wycombe v Havant
Liverpool St Helens v Morley
Plymouth Albion v Cheltenham
Redruth v Truro
Rosslyn Park v Cambridge U
Rotherham v Sheffield

Sunday, 3 October

IRFU Insurance Corporation Leagues
Division 2
Old Crescent v Sunday's Well
Division 3
UC Cork v Highfield

Tuesday, 5 October

Newport v Barbarians
Maesteg v Swansea
Wasps v Loughborough Students

Wednesday, 6 October

Canada A v Australians (Calgary)
East Wales v Japanese (Abertillery)
Bedford v West London Inst
Clifton v Exeter
Henley v Oxford U
Royal Navy v Havant

Saturday, 9 October

CANADA v AUSTRALIA (Calgary)
West Wales v Japanese (Narberth)

RFU Courage Leagues
Division 1
Gloucester v London Irish
Harlequins v Northampton
Newcastle Gosforth v Leicester
Orrell v Bristol
Wasps v Bath
Division 2
London Scottish v Moseley
Sale v Rugby
Saracens v Nottingham
Waterloo v Otley
West Hartlepool v Wakefield

SRU McEwan's Leagues
Division 1
Boroughmuir v Selkirk
Gala v Edinburgh Acads
Hawick v Melrose
Heriot's FP v West of Scotland
Kelso v Currie
Stewart's-Melville FP v Jedforest
Stirling County v Watsonians
Division 2
Ayr v Peebles
Clarkston v Preston Lodge
Glasgow Acads v Dundee HSFP
Grangemouth v Edinburgh Wands
Haddington v Glasgow High/Kelvinside
Kirkcaldy v Biggar
Musselburgh v Wigtownshire

IRFU Insurance Corporation Leagues
Division 1
Dungannon v Young Munster
Greystones v Shannon
Old Wesley v Cork Const
St Mary's Coll v Lansdowne

Wanderers v Blackrock Coll
Division 2
Bangor v Dolphin
Galwegians v Terenure Coll
Instonians v Old Crescent
Old Belvedere v Ballymena
Sunday's Well v Malone
Division 3
City of Derry v UC Cork
Collegians v Corinthians
Highfield v Portadown
NIFC v Bective Rangers
UC Dublin v Clontarf

WRU Heineken Leagues
Division 1
Aberavon v Newbridge
Division 2
Abertillery v Ebbw Vale
Llandovery v Mountain Ash
Llanharan v Maesteg
Penarth v Treorchy
S Wales Police v Glam Wands

Bridgend v Rosslyn Park
Exeter v Basingstoke
Fylde v Broughton Park
Liverpool St Helens v Preston
    Grasshoppers
London Welsh v Havant
Lydney v Birmingham
Morley v Harrogate
Newport v Richmond
Nuneaton v Plymouth Albion
Oxford U v Loughborough Students
Pontypool v Weston-super-Mare
Streatham-Croydon v Askeans
Sheffield v Kendal
Stourbridge v Clifton
Swansea v Coventry
Vale of Lune v Stoke

Sunday, 10 October

IRFU Insurance Corporation Leagues
Division 3
Sligo v Athlone

Tuesday, 12 October

Welsh Selection v Japanese (Pontypridd)
Cambridge U v Crawshay's Welsh
Aberavon v Penarth
Maesteg v Newport
Neath v Llanharan

Wednesday, 13 October

Wales A v North of England (Pontypool)
Newcastle Gosforth v Morpeth

Friday, 15th October

Ebbw Vale v Blaina
Maesteg v Pontypool
Newport v Glam Wands
Penarth v Cross Keys
S Wales Police v Bridgend

Saturday, 16 October

WALES v JAPAN (Cardiff)
French Selection v Australians (Dax)

RFU Divisional Championship
Northern Division v London Division
 (Newcastle Gosforth)
South & South-West Division v
 Midlands Division (Bath)

IRFU Provincial Championship
Connacht v Leinster
Ulster v Exiles

SRU McEwan's Leagues
Division 1
Currie v Stewart's-Melville FP
Edinburgh Acads v Stirling County
Jedforest v Boroughmuir
Melrose v Kelso
Selkirk v Heriot's FP
Watsonians v Hawick
West of Scotland v Gala
Division 2
Biggar v Grangemouth
Dundee HSFP v Clarkston
Edinburgh Wands v Glasgow Acads
Glasgow High/Kelvinside v Ayr
Peebles v Kirkcaldy
Preston Lodge v Musselburgh
Wigtownshire v Haddington

RFU Pilkington Cup *2nd round*
RFU Junior Clubs Cup *2nd round*
Bristol v Sale
Dublin U v Cambridge U
Llanelli v Bath
London Irish v Oxford U
Northampton v Aberavon
Nottingham v Loughborough Students
Orrell v Wakefield
Rugby v Greystones
Saracens v Harlequins
Vale of Lune v Durham City

Wasps v London Scottish
West Hartlepool v Northern

Sunday, 17 October

WRU Heineken Leagues
Division 2
Narberth v Tenby Utd

Tuesday, 19 October

Gloucester v SA Barbarians
Bath v Oxford U

Wednesday, 20 October

French Selection v Australians (Agen)

Thursday, 21 October

Leicester v SA Barbarians

Saturday, 23 October

London Division v New Zealanders
 (Twickenham)
French Selection v Australians
 (Narbonne)

RFU Divisional Championship
South & South-West Division v
 Northern Division (Gloucester)

SRU District Championship *Semi-finals*
Glasgow Dist v Edinburgh Dist
South of Scotland v Scottish North &
 Midlands

IRFU Provincial Championship
Connacht v Ulster
Exiles v Leinster

RFU Courage Leagues
Division 3
Coventry v Exeter
Fylde v Richmond
Havant v Morley
Redruth v Blackheath
Rosslyn Park v Bedford
Division 4
Askeans v Sheffield
Broughton Park v Liverpool St Helens
Harrogate v Clifton
Leeds v Aspatria
Plymouth Albion v Sudbury
Division 5 (South)
Basingstoke v Camborne
Met Police v Maidstone
North Walsham v Lydney
Reading v Berry Hill

Tabard v London Welsh
Weston-super-Mare v High Wycombe
Division 5 (North)
Bradford & Bingley v Preston
  Grasshoppers
Hereford v Durham City
Kendal v Nuneaton
Stoke-on-Trent v Birmingham Solihull
Stourbridge v Lichfield
Winnington Park v Rotherham

WRU Heineken Leagues
Division 1
Bridgend v Swansea
Cross Keys v Dunvant
Llanelli v Newbridge
Neath v Cardiff
Pontypool v Aberavon
Pontypridd v Newport
Division 2
Ebbw Vale v Llandovery
Glam Wands v Abertillery
Maesteg v Penarth
Mountain Ash v Narberth
Tenby Utd v Llanharan
Treorchy v S Wales Police

WRU Cup *2nd round*
Bath v Nottingham
Boroughmuir v Ayr
Cambridge U v Northampton
Edinburgh Acads v Heriot's FP
Gala v Wakefield
Grangemouth v West of Scotland
Harlequins v London Scottish
Langholm v Kelso
Newcastle Gosforth v Waterloo
Orrell v West Hartlepool
Oxford U v UC Cork
Sale v Loughborough Students
Saracens v London Irish
Stewart's-Melville FP v Watsonians
Wasps v Moseley
Wharfedale v Otley

Monday, 25 October

Newport v SA Barbarians

Tuesday, 26 October

Midlands Division v New Zealanders
  (Leicester)
French Selection v Australians
  (Grenoble)
Bedford v Cambridge U
Neath v Oxford U

Wednesday, 27 October

Llanelli v SA Barbarians

Saturday, 30 October

FRANCE v AUSTRALIA
**South & South-West Division v New
  Zealanders** (Redruth)

**RFU Divisional Championship
Midlands Division v London Division**
  (Leicester)

SRU District Championship *Final &
  play-off*

**IRFU Provincial Championship
Exiles v Connacht
Munster v Leinster**

RFU Courage Leagues
Division 3
Bedford v Fylde
Blackheath v Coventry
Exeter v Rosslyn Park
Morley v Redruth
Richmond v Havant
Division 4
Aspatria v Broughton Park
Clifton v Leeds
Liverpool St Helens v Askeans
Sheffield v Plymouth Albion
Sudbury v Harrogate
Division 5 (South)
Berry Hill v North Walsham
High Wycombe v Basingstoke
London Welsh v Reading
Lydney v Weston-super-Mare
Maidstone v Tabard
Southend v Met Police
Division 5 (North)
Birmingham Solihull v Kendal
Durham City v Stoke-on-Trent
Lichfield v Hereford
Preston Grasshoppers v Winnington Park
Rotherham v Stourbridge
Walsall v Bradford & Bingley

WRU Heineken Leagues
Division 1
Aberavon v Bridgend
Cardiff v Pontypool
Cross Keys v Pontypridd
Dunvant v Llanelli
Newbridge v Neath
Swansea v Newport

Division 2
Llandovery v Abertillery
Llanharan v Mountain Ash
Narberth v Ebbw Vale
Penarth v Tenby Utd
S Wales Police v Maesteg
Treorchy v Glam Wands

Bath v Loughborough Students
Boroughmuir v West of Scotland
Cambridge U v Wasps
Gala v Jedforest
Heriot's FP v Royal HSFP
Kelso v Ballymena
Langholm v Melrose
Northampton v Moseley
Nottingham v Bristol
Orrell v Waterloo
Rugby v Harlequins
Sale v Hawick
Stewart's-Melville FP v Selkirk
Watsonians v Glasgow Acads
West Hartlepool v Newcastle Gosforth

Sunday, 31 October

London Irish v Nuneaton

Monday, 1 November

Bridgend v SA Barbarians

Tuesday, 2 November

Northern Division v New Zealanders
(Liverpool FC)
French Selection v Australians (Toulon)
Abertillery v Lydney
Leicester v Cambridge U
Northampton v Oxford U

Wednesday, 3 November

Bristol v Combined Services

Saturday, 6 November

FRANCE v AUSTRALIA (Paris)

RFU Divisional Championship
**London Division v South & South-
West Division**
Midlands Division v Northern Division
(Northampton)

Bath v SA Barbarians
Scottish Exiles v Auckland

428

RFU Courage Leagues
Division 3
Blackheath v Morley
Coventry v Rosslyn Park
Fylde v Exeter
Havant v Bedford
Richmond v Redruth
Division 4
Aspatria v Clifton
Broughton Park v Askeans
Harrogate v Sheffield
Leeds v Sudbury
Plymouth Albion v Liverpool St Helens

SRU McEwan's Leagues
Division 1
Boroughmuir v Currie
Gala v Stirling County
Hawick v Edinburgh Acads
Heriot's FP v Jedforest
Kelso v Watsonians
Stewart's-Melville FP v Melrose
West of Scotland v Selkirk
Division 2
Ayr v Wigtownshire
Clarkston v Edinburgh Wands
Glasgow Acads v Biggar
Haddington v Preston Lodge
Kirkcaldy v Grangemouth
Musselburgh v Dundee HSFP
Peebles v Glasgow High/Kelvinside

WRU Heineken Leagues
Division 1
Bridgend v Cardiff
Llanelli v Cross Keys
Neath v Dunvant
Newport v Aberavon
Pontypool v Newbridge
Pontypridd v Swansea
Division 2
Abertillery v Narberth
Ebbw Vale v Llanharan
Glam Wands v Llandovery
Mountain Ash v Penarth
Tenby Utd v S Wales Police

RFU Junior Clubs Cup *3rd round*
Cambridge U v Harlequins
Kendal v Sale
London Irish v London Scottish
Lydney v Hereford
Moseley v Bristol
Nottingham v Gloucester
Orrell v Otley
Oxford U v Wasps

Rugby v London Welsh
Saracens v Northampton
Vale of Lune v Birkenhead Park
Wakefield v Newcastle Gosforth
West Hartlepool v Durham City

Sunday, 7 November

England A v New Zealanders (Gateshead)

Tuesday, 9 November

Edinburgh Dist v Auckland
Bath v Combined Services

Wednesday, 10 November

South of Scotland v New Zealanders
(Gala)
Oxford U v Penguins

Thursday, 11 November

French Barbarians v Australians
(Clermont-Ferrand)
Toulouse U v Cambridge U

Friday, 12 November

Boroughmuir v Hawick
Kelso v Gala

Saturday, 13 November

IRELAND v ROMANIA (Dublin)
Scotland A v New Zealanders (Hawick)

RFU Courage Leagues
Division 1
Bath v Newcastle Gosforth
Bristol v Gloucester
Leicester v Harlequins
London Irish v Wasps
Northampton v Orrell
Division 2
Moseley v Sale
Nottingham v West Hartlepool
Otley v Saracens
Rugby v Waterloo
Wakefield v London Scottish
Division 3
Bedford v Redruth
Exeter v Havant
Morley v Coventry
Richmond v Blackheath
Rosslyn Park v Fylde
Division 4
Askeans v Plymouth Albion
Clifton v Broughton Park

Liverpool St Helens v Harrogate
Sheffield v Leeds
Sudbury v Aspatria
Division 5 (South)
Basingstoke v Lydney
Camborne v High Wycombe
North Walsham v London Welsh
Reading v Maidstone
Tabard v Southend
Weston-super-Mare v Berry Hill
Division 5 (North)
Hereford v Rotherham
Kendal v Durham City
Nuneaton v Birmingham Solihull
Stoke-on-Trent v Lichfield
Stourbridge v Preston Grasshoppers
Winnington Park v Walsall

WRU Heineken Leagues
Division 1
Aberavon v Swansea
Cardiff v Newport
Cross Keys v Neath
Dunvant v Pontypool
Llanelli v Pontypridd
Newbridge v Bridgend
Division 2
Llanharan v Abertillery
Maesteg v Glam Wands
Narberth v Llandovery
Penarth v Ebbw Vale
S Wales Police v Mountain Ash
Treorchy v Tenby Utd

Jedforest v Melrose
Preston Lodge v Heriot's FP
Stewart's-Melville FP v Kirkcaldy
Watsonians v Clarkston

Sunday, 14 November

Scottish Districts XV v Auckland

Tuesday, 16 November

Scottish Development XV v New
Zealanders (Myreside)
Llanharan v Pontypridd

Wednesday, 17 November

Oxford U v Major R V Stanley's XV

Friday, 19 November

Ayr v Melrose
Boroughmuir v Heriot's FP
Clarkston v Gala

Edinburgh Wands v Stewart's-Melville FP
Hawick v Langholm
Kelso v Jedforest
Musselburgh v Watsonians

Saturday, 20 November

SCOTLAND v NEW ZEALAND
(Murrayfield)

RFU Courage Leagues
Division 1
Gloucester v Northampton
Leicester v Bath
Newcastle Gosforth v London Irish
Orrell v Harlequins
Wasps v Bristol
Division 2
London Scottish v Nottingham
Otley v Rugby
Sale v Wakefield
Saracens v West Hartlepool
Waterloo v Moseley
Division 3
Blackheath v Bedford
Coventry v Fylde
Havant v Rosslyn Park
Morley v Richmond
Redruth v Exeter
Division 4
Aspatria v Sheffield
Broughton Park v Plymouth Albion
Clifton v Sudbury
Harrogate v Askeans
Leeds v Liverpool St Helens
Division 5 (South)
Berry Hill v Basingstoke
London Welsh v Weston-super-Mare
Lydney v Camborne
Maidstone v North Walsham
Met Police v Tabard
Southend v Reading
Division 5 (North)
Bradford & Bingley v Winnington Park
Durham City v Nuneaton
Lichfield v Kendal
Preston Grasshoppers v Hereford
Rotherham v Stoke-on-Trent
Walsall v Stourbridge

IRFU Insurance Corporation Leagues
Division 1
Cork Const v Greystones
Garryowen v Dungannon
Old Wesley v Lansdowne
Shannon v Blackrock Coll

Wanderers v Young Munster
Division 2
Ballina v Old Belvedere
Ballymena v Sunday's Well
Dolphin v Galwegians
Malone v Instonians
Old Crescent v Bangor
Division 3
Athlone v Collegians
Clontarf v City of Derry
De La Salle Palmerston v Highfield
Portadown v NIFC
UC Cork v Bective Rangers
UC Dublin v Sligo

WRU Heineken Leagues
Division 1
Bridgend v Dunvant
Neath v Llanelli
Newport v Newbridge
Pontypool v Cross Keys
Pontypridd v Aberavon
Swansea v Cardiff
Division 2
Abertillery v Penarth
Ebbw Vale v S Wales Police
Glam Wands v Narberth
Llandovery v Llanharan
Mountain Ash v Treorchy
Tenby Utd v Maesteg

WRU SWALEC Cup *3rd round*
Loughborough Students v Cambridge U

Monday, 22 November

Oxford U v Scottish Students

Tuesday, 23 November

**England Emerging Players v New
Zealanders** (Gloucester)
Bedford v Oxford U
Exeter v Exeter U

Wednesday, 24 November

Cambridge U v M R Steele-Bodger's XV
Gloucester v Combined Services

Friday, 26 November

Bristol v Havant
Northampton v West London Inst
Nottingham v Cambridge U

Saturday, 27 November

ENGLAND v NEW ZEALAND
(Twickenham)

IRFU Provincial Championship
Leinster v Ulster
Munster v Exiles

SRU McEwan's Leagues
Division 1
Currie v Heriot's FP
Edinburgh Acads v Kelso
Jedforest v West of Scotland
Melrose v Boroughmuir
Selkirk v Gala
Stirling County v Hawick
Watsonians v Stewart's-Melville FP
Division 2
Biggar v Clarkston
Dundee HSFP v Haddington
Edinburgh Wands v Musselburgh
Glasgow High/Kelvinside v Kirkcaldy
Grangemouth v Glasgow Acads
Preston Lodge v Ayr
Wigtownshire v Peebles

WRU Heineken Leagues
Division 1
Aberavon v Cardiff
Bridgend v Cross Keys
Newport v Dunvant
Pontypool v Llanelli
Pontypridd v Neath
Swansea v Newbridge
Division 2
Abertillery v S Wales Police
Ebbw Vale v Treorchy
Glam Wands v Tenby Utd
Llandovery v Penarth
Mountain Ash v Maesteg
Narberth v Llanharan

RFU Pilkington Cup *3rd round*
RFU Junior Clubs Cup *4th round*
Bath v London Scottish
Bradford & Bingley v Otley
Durham U v Oxford U
Gloucester v Sale
Harlequins v Moseley
Huddersfield v Broughton Park
Leeds v Wharfedale
New Brighton v Liverpool St Helens
Newcastle Gosforth v Harrogate
Penzance-Newlyn v Redruth
Rugby v Orrell
Vale of Lune v Sheffield

Monday, 29 November

Cornwall v Devon (Launceston)

Tuesday, 30 November

Combined Services v New Zealanders
(Devonport)

WRU Heineken Leagues
Division 1
Cardiff v Pontypridd
Cross Keys v Newport
Dunvant v Swansea
Llanelli v Bridgend
Neath v Pontypool

Boroughmuir v Edinburgh Wands

Thursday, 2 December

**Oxford U Greyhounds v Cambridge U
LX Club**

Saturday, 4 December

Barbarians v New Zealanders (Cardiff)
Glasgow Dist v Munster
Leinster v Edinburgh Dist
Scottish North & Midlands v Connacht
Ulster v South of Scotland

RFU Courage Leagues
Division 1
Bristol v Newcastle Gosforth
Harlequins v Bath
London Irish v Leicester
Northampton v Wasps
Orrell v Gloucester
Division 2
Moseley v Otley
Nottingham v Sale
Saracens v Rugby
Wakefield v Waterloo
West Hartlepool v London Scottish
Division 3
Bedford v Morley
Exeter v Blackheath
Fylde v Havant
Richmond v Coventry
Rosslyn Park v Redruth
Division 4
Askeans v Leeds
Liverpool St Helens v Aspatria
Plymouth Albion v Harrogate
Sheffield v Clifton
Sudbury v Broughton Park
Division 5 (South)
Basingstoke v London Welsh

Camborne v Berry Hill
High Wycombe v Lydney
North Walsham v Southend
Reading v Met Police
Weston-super-Mare v Maidstone
Division 5 (North)
Birmingham Solihull v Durham City
Hereford v Walsall
Kendal v Rotherham
Nuneaton v Lichfield
Stoke-on-Trent v Preston Grasshoppers
Stourbridge v Bradford & Bingley

WRU Heineken Leagues
Division 1
Aberavon v Dunvant
Bridgend v Neath
Cardiff v Newbridge
Newport v Llanelli
Pontypool v Pontypridd
Swansea v Cross Keys
Division 2
Llanharan v Glam Wands
Maesteg v Ebbw Vale
Penarth v Narberth
S Wales Police v Llandovery
Tenby Utd v Mountain Ash
Treorchy v Abertillery

Ayr v Heriot's FP
Boroughmuir v Glasgow High/Kelvinside
Edinburgh Acads v Watsonians
Gala v Dundee HSFP
Hawick v Edinburgh Wands
Langholm v Jedforest
Melrose v Glasgow Acads
Stewart's-Melville FP v Musselburgh
West of Scotland v Wigtownshire

Tuesday, 7 December

Oxford U v Cambridge U (Twickenham)
**Oxford U Under-21s v Cambridge U
   Under-21s**

Saturday, 11 December

Connacht v Glasgow Dist
Edinburgh Dist v Ulster
Munster v Scottish North & Midlands
South of Scotland v Leinster

RFU Courage Leagues
Division 1
Bath v London Irish
Gloucester v Harlequins
Leicester v Bristol

Newcastle Gosforth v Northampton
Wasps v Orrell
Division 2
London Scottish v Saracens
Otley v Wakefield
Rugby v Moseley
Sale v West Hartlepool
Waterloo v Nottingham
Division 3
Bedford v Richmond
Blackheath v Rosslyn Park
Havant v Coventry
Morley v Exeter
Redruth v Fylde
Division 4
Aspatria v Askeans
Clifton v Liverpool St Helens
Harrogate v Broughton Park
Leeds v Plymouth Albion
Sudbury v Sheffield
Division 5 (South)
Berry Hill v High Wycombe
London Welsh v Camborne
Maidstone v Basingstoke
Met Police v North Walsham
Southend v Weston-super-Mare
Tabard v Reading
Division 5 (North)
Bradford & Bingley v Hereford
Lichfield v Birmingham Solihull
Preston Grasshoppers v Kendal
Rotherham v Nuneaton
Walsall v Stoke-on-Trent
Winnington Park v Stourbridge

WRU Heineken Leagues
Division 1
Cross Keys v Aberavon
Dunvant v Cardiff
Llanelli v Swansea
Neath v Newport
Pontypool v Bridgend
Pontypridd v Newbridge
Division 2
Abertillery v Maesteg
Ebbw Vale v Tenby Utd
Llandovery v Treorchy
Llanharan v Penarth
Mountain Ash v Glam Wands
Narberth v S Wales Police

Colts County Championship *Final*
   (Twickenham)
Glasgow High/Kelvinside v Gala
Heriot's FP v Kilmarnock

Jedforest v Dundee HSFP
Kelso v Boroughmuir
Langholm v Hawick
Peebles v Melrose
Stewart's-Melville FP v Ballymena
Watsonians v Kirkcaldy
West of Scotland v Haddington

Wednesday, 15 December

Territorial Army v Army

Saturday, 18 December

Italy v Scotland A

IRFU Provincial Championship
Leinster v Connacht
Ulster v Munster

RFU Courage Leagues
Division 3
Coventry v Bedford
Fylde v Blackheath
Havant v Redruth
Richmond v Exeter
Rosslyn Park v Morley
Division 4
Askeans v Clifton
Broughton Park v Sheffield
Harrogate v Leeds
Liverpool St Helens v Sudbury
Plymouth Albion v Aspatria
Division 5 (South)
Basingstoke v Southend
Camborne v Maidstone
High Wycombe v London Welsh
Lydney v Berry Hill
North Walsham v Tabard
Weston-super-Mare v Met Police
Division 5 (North)
Birmingham Solihull v Rotherham
Durham City v Lichfield
Hereford v Winnington Park
Kendal v Walsall
Nuneaton v Preston Grasshoppers
Stoke-on-Trent v Bradford & Bingley

RFU Pilkington Cup *4th round*
RFU Junior Clubs Cup *5th round*
WRU SWALEC Cup *4th round*
Boroughmuir v Dundee HSFP
Heriot's FP v Kelso
Langholm v Gala
Melrose v Hawick
Preston Lodge v Stewart's-Melville FP
Stirling County v West of Scotland
Watsonians v Ayr

Monday, 20 December

Scotland Schools v France Schools

Tuesday, 21 December

Newbridge v Ebbw Vale
S Wales Police v Pontypool

Wednesday, 22 December

Aberavon v Maesteg
Newport v Gloucester

Thursday, 23 December

Hillhead Jordanhill v West of Scotland
Kelso v Langholm

Sunday, 26 December

Abertillery v Ebbw Vale
London Irish v Old Millhillians
Northampton v Stirling County

Monday, 27 December

Bath v Clifton
Bedford v Old Paulines
Camborne v Redruth
Coventry v Moseley
Currie v Boroughmuir
Exeter v President's XV
Gala v Melrose
Gloucester v Lydney
Havant v Bournemouth
Heriot's FP v Watsonians
Jedforest v Hawick
Llanelli v London Welsh
Maesteg v Bridgend
Met Police v London Irish
Morley v Bradford & Bingley
Newport v Bristol
Northern v Newcastle Gosforth
Nuneaton v Rugby
Orrell v Liverpool St Helens
Otley v Leeds
Pontypool v Tredegar
Preston Grasshoppers v Fylde
Richmond v Harlequins
Sale v Broughton Park
Selkirk v Kelso
West Hartlepool v Hartlepool Rovers

Tuesday, 28 December

Scotland A v Ireland A
Leicester v Barbarians
Swansea v S Wales Police

433

Wednesday, 29 December

Stroud v Lydney

Thursday, 30 December

Alnwick v Kelso

Saturday, 1 January 1994

Ireland Trial (Dublin)
Bath v Cardiff
Bristol v Clifton
Fylde v Blackburn
Harlequins v Blackheath
Hawick v Heriot's FP
London Irish v Rosslyn Park
London Welsh v Bedford
Northampton v Nottingham
Novocastrians v Newcastle Gosforth
Sheffield v Hull Ionians
Wakefield v Leeds

Sunday, 2 January

Exeter v Barnstaple

Monday, 3 January

WRU Heineken Leagues
Division 1
Aberavon v Llanelli
Bridgend v Pontypridd
Cardiff v Cross Keys
Newbridge v Dunvant
Swansea v Neath
Division 2
Glam Wands v Penarth
Mountain Ash v Ebbw Vale
S Wales Police v Llanharan
Tenby Utd v Abertillery
Treorchy v Narberth

Askeans v Sutton
Broughton Park v Rotherham
Dundee HSFP v Stewart's-Melville FP
Edinburgh Wands v West of Scotland
Gala v Selkirk
Glasgow High/Kelvinside v Melrose
Liverpool St Helens v Wakefield
Lydney v Nuneaton
Musselburgh v Boroughmuir
Newcastle Gosforth v Middlesbrough
Newport v Watsonians
Orrell v Coventry
Otley v Morley
Peebles v Jedforest
Pontypool v Maesteg
Redruth v St Ives

Stockton v West Hartlepool
Vale of Lune v Preston Grasshoppers
Wasps v Saracens

Tuesday, 4 January

Scotland A v Spain

Wednesday, 5 January

Wales Schools v Scotland Schools

Saturday, 8 January

RFU Courage Leagues
Division 1
Bath v Bristol
London Irish v Harlequins
Leicester v Northampton
Newcastle Gosforth v Orrell
Wasps v Gloucester
Division 2
Moseley v Saracens
Otley v Nottingham
Rugby v Wakefield
Sale v London Scottish
Waterloo v West Hartlepool
Division 3
Bedford v Exeter
Blackheath v Havant
Morley v Fylde
Redruth v Coventry
Richmond v Rosslyn Park
Division 4
Aspatria v Harrogate
Clifton v Plymouth Albion
Leeds v Broughton Park
Sheffield v Liverpool St Helens
Sudbury v Askeans
Division 5 (South)
London Welsh v Lydney
Maidstone v High Wycombe
Met Police v Basingstoke
Reading v North Walsham
Southend v Camborne
Tabard v Weston-super-Mare
Division 5 (North)
Bradford & Bingley v Kendal
Preston Grasshoppers v Birmingham
  Solihull
Rotherham v Durham City
Stourbridge v Hereford
Walsall v Nuneaton
Winnington Park v Stoke-on-Trent

SRU McEwan's Leagues
Division 1
Boroughmuir v Watsonians

Gala v Hawick
Heriot's FP v Melrose
Kelso v Stirling County
Selkirk v Jedforest
Stewart's-Melville FP v Edinburgh Acads
West of Scotland v Currie
Division 2
Ayr v Dundee HSFP
Clarkston v Grangemouth
Glasgow High/Kelvinside v Wigtownshire
Haddington v Edinburgh Wands
Kirkcaldy v Glasgow Acads
Musselburgh v Biggar
Peebles v Preston Lodge

IRFU Insurance Corporation Leagues
Division 1
Blackrock Coll v Greystones
Cork Const v Wanderers
Garryowen v St Mary's Coll
Lansdowne v Dungannon
Young Munster v Old Wesley
Division 2
Bangor v Malone
Galwegians v Old Crescent
Instonians v Ballymena
Terenure Coll v Dolphin
Division 3
Athlone v Highfield
Clontarf v Sligo
Corinthians v NIFC
De La Salle Palmerston v UC Dublin
Portadown v City of Derry
UC Cork v Collegians

WRU Heineken Leagues
Division 1
Newbridge v Aberavon
Newport v Pontypool

Bridgend v S Wales Police
Ebbw Vale v Pontypridd
Penarth v Berry Hill
Swansea v Maesteg

Sunday, 9 January

IRFU Insurance Corporation Leagues
Division 2
Sunday's Well v Ballina

Tuesday, 11 January

Llanharan v Aberavon
Pontypool v Cheltenham

Wednesday, 12 January

RAF v Civil Service
Exeter v Royal Navy
Lydney v Bridgwater Albion

Thursday, 13 January

West of Scotland v Glasgow Acads

Friday, 14 January

Wales Under-21s v Scotland Under-21s
  (Cardiff)
Welsh Us v Scottish Us
Abertillery v Pontypool
Alnwick v Melrose
Boroughmuir v Llanelli
Coventry v Loughborough Students
Hawick v Tynedale
Kelso v Stewart's-Melville FP
Llanelli v Boroughmuir
Maesteg v Newbridge
Newport v Glasgow High/Kelvinside
Pontypridd v S Wales Police
Tredegar v Ebbw Vale

Saturday, 15 January

WALES v SCOTLAND (Cardiff)
FRANCE v IRELAND (Paris)

RFU Courage Leagues
Division 1
Bristol v London Irish
Gloucester v Newcastle Gosforth
Harlequins v Wasps
Northampton v Bath
Orrell v Leicester
Division 2
London Scottish v Waterloo
Nottingham v Rugby
Saracens v Sale
Wakefield v Moseley
West Hartlepool v Otley

RFU County Championship *Semi-finals*
Askeans v Westcombe Park
Broughton Park v Middlesbrough
Cambridge U v Durham U
Gala v Kilmarnock
Leeds v Fylde
Liverpool St Helens v Vale of Lune
Maidstone v Clifton
Morley v Sheffield
Redruth v Bridgwater Albion
Rosslyn Park v London Welsh
Salisbury v Lydney
Weston-super-Mare v Exeter

Wednesday, 19 January

Army v Civil Service (Aldershot)
Cambridge U v RAF
Royal Navy v Oxford U

Saturday, 22 January

RFU Pilkington Cup *5th round*
WRU SWALEC Cup *5th round*

RFU Courage Leagues
Division 3
Bedford v Rosslyn Park
Blackheath v Redruth
Exeter v Coventry
Morley v Havant
Richmond v Fylde
Division 4
Aspatria v Leeds
Clifton v Harrogate
Liverpool St Helens v Broughton Park
Sheffield v Askeans
Sudbury v Plymouth Albion

SRU McEwan's Leagues
Division 1
Currie v Selkirk
Edinburgh Acads v Boroughmuir
Jedforest v Gala
Hawick v Kelso
Melrose v West of Scotland
Stirling County v Stewart's-Melville FP
Watsonians v Heriot's FP
Division 2
Biggar v Haddington
Dundee HSFP v Peebles
Edinburgh Wands v Ayr
Glasgow Acads v Clarkston
Grangemouth v Musselburgh
Preston Lodge v Glasgow High/Kelvinside
Wigtownshire v Kirkcaldy

IRFU Insurance Corporation Leagues
Division 1
Dungannon v St Mary's Coll
Greystones v Young Munster
Lansdowne v Wanderers
Old Wesley v Garryowen
Shannon v Cork Const
Division 2
Ballina v Instonians
Ballymena v Bangor
Malone v Galwegians
Old Belvedere v Sunday's Well
Old Crescent v Terenure Coll

Division 3
Athlone v Bective Rangers
Clontarf v NIFC
De La Salle Palmerston v Collegians
Portadown v Corinthians
Sligo v Highfield
UC Dublin v City of Derry

RFU Junior Clubs Cup *6th round*
Barker's Butts v Vale of Lune
Bradford & Bingley v Wakefield
Bristol v Bedford
Halifax v Nuneaton
Hull Ionians v Otley
London Irish v London Welsh
Oxford U v Bristol U
Rugby v Gloucester
Sale v Bath
Wasps v Nottingham
West London Inst v Cambridge U

Wednesday, 26 January

Army v Hampshire (Aldershot)
Cambridge U v Royal Navy
Oxford U v RAF

Saturday, 29 January

RFU Courage Leagues
Division 1
Bath v Orrell
Bristol v Harlequins
Leicester v Gloucester
London Irish v Northampton
Newcastle Gosforth v Wasps
Division 2
Moseley v Nottingham
Otley v London Scottish
Rugby v West Hartlepool
Wakefield v Saracens
Waterloo v Sale
Division 3
Coventry v Blackheath
Fylde v Bedford
Havant v Richmond
Redruth v Morley
Rosslyn Park v Exeter
Division 4
Askeans v Liverpool St Helens
Broughton Park v Aspatria
Harrogate v Sudbury
Leeds v Clifton
Plymouth Albion v Sheffield
Division 5 (South)
Basingstoke v Tabard

Berry Hill v London Welsh
Camborne v Met Police
High Wycombe v Southend
Lydney v Maidstone
Weston-super-Mare v Reading
Division 5 (North)
Birmingham Solihull v Walsall
Durham City v Preston Grasshoppers
Kendal v Winnington Park
Lichfield v Rotherham
Nuneaton v Bradford & Bingley
Stoke-on-Trent v Stourbridge

IRFU Insurance Corporation Leagues
Division 3
Bective Rangers v Portadown
City of Derry v De La Salle Palmerston
Collegians v Clontarf
Corinthians v UC Cork
Highfield v UC Dublin
NIFC v Athlone

WRU Heineken Leagues
Division 1
Bridgend v Newport
Cross Keys v Newbridge
Llanelli v Cardiff
Neath v Aberavon
Pontypool v Swansea
Pontypridd v Dunvant
Division 2
Abertillery v Mountain Ash
Ebbw Vale v Glam Wands
Llandovery v Tenby Utd
Llanharan v Treorchy
Narberth v Maesteg
Penarth v S Wales Police

Edinburgh Wands v Watsonians
Gala v Langholm
Glasgow Acads v Jedforest
Kelso v Musselburgh
Oxford U v Dublin U
Stewart's-Melville FP v Heriot's FP
Vale of Lune v Hereford
West of Scotland v Trinity Acads

Tuesday, 1 February

Clifton v Bristol U
Edinburgh Wands v Heriot's FP
Lydney v Cheltenham
Northampton v Loughborough Students
Penarth v Neath
S Wales Police v Tredegar

Wednesday, 2 February

IRFU Insurance Corporation Leagues
Division 3
UC Cork v UC Dublin

Bedford v RAF
Cambridge U v Army
Oxford v Oxford U
Royal Navy v Redruth

Friday, 4 February

Ireland A v Wales A (Dublin)
Scottish Us v English Us
Scottish Students v English Students
   (Edinburgh)
Askeans v Cambridge U
Bath v Newbridge
Boroughmuir v West Hartlepool
Bridgend v Bristol
Clifton v Stroud
Cross Keys v S Wales Police
Dunfermline v Stewart's-Melville FP
Gala v Northampton
Gloucester v Pontypool
Hawick v Currie
Jedforest v Rugby
Kelso v Northern
Leicester v Coventry
Maesteg v Cardiff
Melrose v Wasps
Plymouth Albion v Weston-super-Mare
Tiverton v Exeter

Saturday, 5 February

SCOTLAND v ENGLAND
   (Murrayfield)
IRELAND v WALES (Dublin)
Blackheath v London Irish
Bedford v Saracens
Brixham v Redruth
Exeter v Devonport Services
Furness v Vale of Lune
Fylde v Sheffield
Lydney v Torquay Ath
Met Police v Havant
Moseley v Rosslyn Park
Newcastle Gosforth v Durham U
Nottingham v Harlequins
Orrell v Sale
Nuneaton v Maidstone
Waterloo v Liverpool St Helens

Sunday, 6 February

Ireland Under-21s v Wales Under-21s
(Dublin)

Tuesday, 8 February

Newbridge v S Wales Police
Penarth v Pontypool
Wasps v London Welsh

Wednesday, 9 February

Bridgend v Maesteg
Civil Service v Royal Navy
Oxford U v Army
Swansea v Ebbw Vale

Saturday, 12 February

RFU Courage Leagues
Division 1
Gloucester v Bath
Harlequins v Newcastle Gosforth
Northampton v Bristol
Orrell v London Irish
Wasps v Leicester
Division 2
London Scottish v Rugby
Nottingham v Wakefield
Sale v Otley
Saracens v Waterloo
West Hartlepool v Moseley
Division 3
Bedford v Havant
Exeter v Fylde
Morley v Blackheath
Redruth v Richmond
Rosslyn Park v Coventry
Division 4
Askeans v Broughton Park
Clifton v Aspatria
Liverpool St Helens v Plymouth Albion
Sheffield v Harrogate
Sudbury v Leeds
Division 5 (South)
Maidstone v Berry Hill
Met Police v High Wycombe
North Walsham v Weston-super-Mare
Reading v Basingstoke
Southend v Lydney
Tabard v Camborne
Division 5 (North)
Bradford & Bingley v Birmingham Solihull
Hereford v Stoke-on-Trent
Preston Grasshoppers v Lichfield
Stourbridge v Kendal
Walsall v Durham City
Winnington Park v Nuneaton

SRU McEwan's Leagues
Division 1
Boroughmuir v Stirling County
Gala v Kelso
Heriot's FP v Edinburgh Acads
Jedforest v Currie
Selkirk v Melrose
Stewart's-Melville FP v Hawick
West of Scotland v Watsonians
Division 2
Ayr v Biggar
Glasgow High/Kelvinside v Dundee HSFP
Haddington v Grangemouth
Kirkcaldy v Clarkston
Musselburgh v Glasgow Acads
Peebles v Edinburgh Wands
Wigtownshire v Preston Lodge

IRFU Insurance Corporation Leagues
Division 3
Bective Rangers v Corinthians
City of Derry v Athlone
Collegians v Portadown
Highfield v Clontarf
NIFC v UC Cork
Sligo v De La Salle Palmerston

Ebbw Vale v Newbridge
Llanharan v Bridgend
Newport v Maesteg
Pontypool v Glam Wands

Tuesday, 15 February

Clifton v RAF
S Wales Police v Swansea

Wednesday, 16 February

Army v Surrey (Aldershot)
Cambridge U v Luddites
London Irish v Royal Navy
Newcastle Gosforth v Newcastle U
Oxfordshire v Oxford U

Friday, 18 February

England Students v Ireland Students
(Bournemouth)
Aberavon v S Wales Police
Askeans v Blackheath
Bath v Pontypool
Bective Rangers v Northampton
Bristol v Cardiff
Brixham v Exeter
Clifton v Lydney
Coventry v Nottingham

Gloucester v Newport
Leicester v Bedford
London Irish v Garryowen
Newbridge v Maesteg
Penarth v Pontypridd
Wasps v Wanderers

Saturday, 19 February

ENGLAND v IRELAND (Twickenham)
WALES v FRANCE (Cardiff)
Broughton Park v Wakefield
Camborne v Plymouth Albion
Durham City v Newcastle Gosforth
Fylde v Orrell
Glasgow Acads v Stewart's-Melville FP
Glasgow High/Kelvinside v Heriot's FP
Harlequins v West London Inst
Hawick v Gala
Jedforest v Ayr
Kelso v Aspatria
Liverpool St Helens v Winnington Park
Llanharan v London Welsh
Melrose v Harrogate
Middlesbrough v Boroughmuir
Redruth v Torquay Ath
Rosslyn Park v Old Wesley
Rugby v Nuneaton
Sheffield v Otley
Vale of Lune v Cambridge U
Waterloo v Morley
Watsonians v Dundee HSFP
West of Scotland v Biggar
West Hartlepool v Rotherham

Sunday, 20 February

France A v Scotland A

Tuesday, 22 February

Newport v Ebbw Vale

Wednesday, 23 February

Surrey v Royal Navy
Army v CLOB (Aldershot)
Cambridge U v Penguins
Lydney v RAF
Oxford U v Anti-Assassins

Saturday, 26 February

RFU Pilkington Cup *Quarter-finals*
WRU SWALEC Cup *6th round*

RFU Courage Leagues
Division 3
Blackheath v Richmond

Coventry v Morley
Fylde v Rosslyn Park
Havant v Exeter
Redruth v Bedford
Division 4
Aspatria v Sudbury
Broughton Park v Clifton
Harrogate v Liverpool St Helens
Leeds v Sheffield
Plymouth Albion v Askeans

SRU McEwan's Leagues
Division 1
Currie v Gala
Edinburgh Acads v West of Scotland
Hawick v Boroughmuir
Kelso v Stewart's-Melville FP
Melrose v Jedforest
Stirling County v Heriot's FP
Watsonians v Selkirk
Division 2
Biggar v Peebles
Clarkston v Musselburgh
Dundee HSFP v Wigtownshire
Edinburgh Wands v Glasgow High/
   Kelvinside
Glasgow Acads v Haddington
Grangemouth v Ayr
Preston Lodge v Kirkcaldy

IRFU Insurance Corporation Leagues
Division 1
Blackrock Coll v Cork Const
Greystones v Lansdowne
St Mary's Coll v Old Wesley
Wanderers v Garryowen
Young Munster v Shannon
Division 2
Bangor v Ballina
Dolphin v Old Crescent
Galwegians v Ballymena
Instonians v Old Belvedere
Terenure Coll v Malone
Division 3
Bective Rangers v Clontarf
City of Derry v Sligo
Collegians v UC Dublin
NIFC v De La Salle Palmerston
UC Cork v Portadown

WRU Heineken Leagues
Division 2
Maesteg v Llandovery

RFU Junior Clubs Cup *Quarter-finals*
Bath v Moseley

Bristol v Aberavon
Harlequins v Newport
Lydney v Bournemouth
Newcastle Gosforth v West Hartlepool
Nottingham v Orrell
Nuneaton v Cheltenham
Otley v Huddersfield
Rugby v London Irish
Wakefield v Northampton
Wasps v Swansea
Wilmslow v Vale of Lune

Sunday, 27 February

IRFU Insurance Corporation Leagues
Division 3
Corinthians v Athlone

Tuesday, 1 March

Clifton v Bristol

Wednesday, 2 March

CLOB v RAF (Esher)
Royal Navy v Cornwall (Devonport)
Cambridge U v Anti-Assassins
Met Police v Army
Pontypridd v Llanharan
Swansea U v Oxford U

Friday, 4 March

Irish Students v Scottish Students
French Students v English Students
Ireland Under-21s v Scotland Under-21s
Askeans v West London Inst
Bective Rangers v Gala
Boroughmuir v Stewart's-Melville FP
Dungannon v Hawick
Exeter v Bristol
Northampton v Coventry
Old Belvedere v Watsonians
Old Wesley v Kelso
West of Scotland v Howe of Fife

Saturday, 5 March

FRANCE v ENGLAND (Paris)
IRELAND v SCOTLAND (Dublin)

WRU Heineken Leagues
Division 1
Aberavon v Pontypool
Cardiff v Neath
Dunvant v Cross Keys
Newbridge v Llanelli
Newport v Pontypridd

Swansea v Bridgend
Division 2
Ebbw Vale v Abertillery
Glam Wands v S Wales Police
Maesteg v Llanharan
Mountain Ash v Llandovery
Tenby Utd v Narberth
Treorchy v Penarth

Bradford & Bingley v Cambridge U
Broughton Park v Stourbridge
Clifton v Walsall
Durham U v Vale of Lune
Havant v Salisbury
Kendal v Liverpool St Helens
London Irish v Lydney
London Welsh v Rosslyn Park
Morley v West Hartlepool
Nottingham v Bedford
Rugby v Bath
St Ives v Redruth
Sale v Newcastle Gosforth
Saracens v Blackheath
Sheffield v Preston Grasshoppers
Stroud v Nuneaton
Wakefield v Harlequins
Waterloo v Fylde

Sunday, 6 March

Racing Club de France v Wasps

Tuesday, 8 March

Maesteg v Neath
S Wales Police v Pontypridd

Wednesday, 9 March

East Midlands v Barbarians
   (Northampton)
Cardiff U v Oxford U
Pontypool v Ebbw Vale

Saturday, 12 March

RFU Courage Leagues
Division 1
Bath v Wasps
Bristol v Orrell
Leicester v Newcastle Gosforth
London Irish v Gloucester
Northampton v Harlequins
Division 2
Moseley v London Scottish
Nottingham v Saracens
Otley v Waterloo
Rugby v Sale
Wakefield v West Hartlepool

Division 3
Bedford v Blackheath
Exeter v Redruth
Fylde v Coventry
Richmond v Morley
Rosslyn Park v Havant
Division 4
Askeans v Harrogate
Liverpool St Helens v Leeds
Plymouth Albion v Broughton Park
Sheffield v Aspatria
Sudbury v Clifton
Division 5 (South)
Basingstoke v North Walsham
Berry Hill v Southend
Camborne v Reading
High Wycombe v Tabard
London Welsh v Maidstone
Lydney v Met Police
Division 5 (North)
Birmingham Solihull v Winnington Park
Durham City v Bradford & Bingley
Kendal v Hereford
Lichfield v Walsall
Nuneaton v Stourbridge
Rotherham v Preston Grasshoppers

SRU McEwan's Leagues
Division 1
Boroughmuir v Kelso
Currie v Melrose
Gala v Stewart's-Melville FP
Heriot's FP v Hawick
Jedforest v Watsonians
Selkirk v Edinburgh Acads
West of Scotland v Stirling County
Division 2
Ayr v Glasgow Acads
Glasgow High/Kelvinside v Biggar
Haddington v Clarkston
Kirkcaldy v Musselburgh
Peebles v Grangemouth
Preston Lodge v Dundee HSFP
Wigtownshire v Edinburgh Wands

IRFU Insurance Corporation Leagues
Division 1
Dungannon v Old Wesley
Garryowen v Greystones
Lansdowne v Shannon
St Mary's Coll v Wanderers
Young Munster v Blackrock Coll
Division 2
Ballina v Galwegians
Ballymena v Terenure Coll
Malone v Dolphin

Old Belvedere v Bangor
Sunday's Well v Instonians
Division 3
Athlone v UC Cork
Clontarf v Corinthians
De La Salle Palmerston v Bective Rangers
Highfield v City of Derry
Sligo v Collegians
UC Dublin v NIFC

Cardiff v Maesteg
Cross Keys v Penarth
Glam Wands v Newport
Llanharan v Swansea
Pontypool v S Wales Police

Tuesday, 15 March

Bristol v Royal Navy
Glam Wands v Pontypool
Maesteg v Pontypridd
Newport v Abertillery
Northampton v RAF
Penarth v Aberavon

Wednesday, 16 March

Nuneaton v Coventry

Friday, 18 March

Wales A v France A
English Students v Welsh Students
  (Oxford)
Scottish Students v French Students
Scotland Under-21s v France Under-21s
Bedford v Rugby
Blackheath v Crawshay's Welsh XV
Blaina v Ebbw Vale
Boroughmuir v Jedforest
Brixham v Plymouth Albion
Cheltenham v Penarth
Clifton v Berry Hill
Coventry v Harlequins
Hawick v Selkirk
Howe of Fife v Stewart's-Melville FP
Kelso v Middlesbrough
Leicester v Nottingham
London Irish v S Wales Police
Moseley v Northampton
Pontypridd v Bristol
Swansea v Bath
Tredegar v Pontypool
Wasps v Llanelli
West of Scotland v Clarkston

Saturday, 19 March

ENGLAND v WALES (Twickenham)
SCOTLAND v FRANCE (Murrayfield)

IRFU Insurance Corporation Leagues
Division 1
Blackrock Coll v Lansdowne
Cork Const v Young Munster
Greystones v St Mary's Coll
Shannon v Garryowen
Wanderers v Dungannon
Division 2
Bangor v Sunday's Well
Dolphin v Ballymena
Galwegians v Old Belvedere
Old Crescent v Malone
Terenure Coll v Ballina
Division 3
Bective Rangers v UC Dublin
Collegians v Highfield
Corinthians v De La Salle Palmerston
NIFC v Sligo
Portadown v Athlone
UC Cork v Clontarf

Boroughmuir v Jedforest
Broughton Park v Bradford & Bingley
Camborne v Exeter
Fylde v Sale
Gala v Alnwick
Liverpool St Helens v Tynedale
Melrose v Langholm
Newcastle Gosforth v Morley
Orrell v Saracens
Redruth v Penryn
Rosslyn Park v Harrogate
Rotherham v Otley
Sheffield v Waterloo
Vale of Lune v Nuneaton
Watsonians v Glasgow High/Kelvinside
West Hartlepool v Leeds

Wednesday, 23 March

England Schools v Wales Schools
 (Bournemouth)
London Irish v RAF
Penarth v Cardiff

Saturday, 26 March

**CATHAY PACIFIC-HONG KONG
 BANK SEVENS**
Royal Navy v Army (Twickenham)

RFU Courage Leagues
Division 1
Gloucester v Bristol
Harlequins v Leicester
Newcastle Gosforth v Bath
Orrell v Northampton
Wasps v London Irish
Division 2
London Scottish v Wakefield
Sale v Moseley
Saracens v Otley
Waterloo v Rugby
West Hartlepool v Nottingham
Division 3
Blackheath v Exeter
Coventry v Richmond
Havant v Fylde
Morley v Bedford
Redruth v Rosslyn Park
Division 4
Aspatria v Liverpool St Helens
Broughton Park v Sudbury
Clifton v Sheffield
Harrogate v Plymouth Albion
Leeds v Askeans
Division 5 (South)
Met Police v Berry Hill
North Walsham v Camborne
Reading v High Wycombe
Southend v London Welsh
Tabard v Lydney
Weston-super-Mare v Basingstoke
Division 5 (North)
Bradford & Bingley v Lichfield
Hereford v Nuneaton
Stoke-on-Trent v Kendal
Stourbridge v Birmingham Solihull
Walsall v Rotherham
Winnington Park v Durham City

WRU Heineken Leagues
Division 1
Bridgend v Aberavon
Llanelli v Dunvant
Neath v Newbridge
Newport v Swansea
Pontypool v Cardiff
Pontypridd v Cross Keys
Division 2
Abertillery v Glam Wands
Llandovery v Ebbw Vale
Llanharan v Tenby Utd
Narberth v Mountain Ash
Penarth v Maesteg
S Wales Police v Treorchy

Scottish Youth v Scotland Schools
(Murrayfield)
Dunfermline v West of Scotland
Gala v Glasgow Acads
Glasgow High/Kelvinside v Jedforest
Hawick v Kirkcaldy
Kilmarnock v Melrose
Watsonians v Boroughmuir

Sunday, 27 March

**CATHAY PACIFIC-HONG KONG
BANK SEVENS**
Wales Youth v England Colts (Cardiff)

Tuesday, 29 March

Ebbw Vale v Pontypool
Lydney v Tredegar
Moseley v Coventry
Nuneaton v Nottingham

Wednesday, 30 March

Blackheath v RAF

Friday, 1 April

Redruth v St Mary's Hosp

Saturday, 2 April

Cardiff v Barbarians
RFU Pilkington Cup *Semi-finals*
WRU SWALEC Cup *Quarter-finals*

WRU Heineken Leagues
Division 2
Maesteg v Treorchy

RFU Junior Clubs Cup *Semi-finals*
Italy Under-21s v Scotland Under-21s
Scotland Under-21s v Spain Under-21s
Bath v Saracens
Bristol v Bridgend
Dundee HSFP v West of Scotland
Fylde v Preston Grasshoppers
Hereford v Lydney
Liverpool St Helens v Sale
Newcastle Gosforth v Alnwick
Newport v Coventry
Northampton v Bedford
Nottingham v Rosslyn Park
Otley v Harrogate
Rugby v Plymouth Albion
Sheffield v West Hartlepool
Southend v Havant
S Wales Police v Newbridge
Torquay Ath v Exeter

Wakefield v Morley
Waterloo v Orrell
Weston-super-Mare v Clifton
Widnes v Broughton Park

Monday, 4 April

Swansea v Barbarians
Ireland Schools v Scotland Schools
Broughton Park v Davenport
Maesteg v Aberavon
Newport v London Welsh
Plymouth Albion v Torquay Ath
Pontypool v Penarth
Rugby v Nuneaton
Stroud v Lydney
Vale of Lune v Kendal

Wednesday, 6 April

CLOB v Royal Navy

Saturday, 9 April

RFU Courage Leagues
Division 1
Bath v Leicester
Bristol v Wasps
Harlequins v Orrell
London Irish v Newcastle Gosforth
Northampton v Gloucester
Division 2
Moseley v Waterloo
Nottingham v London Scottish
Rugby v Otley
Wakefield v Sale
West Hartlepool v Saracens
Division 3
Coventry v Havant
Exeter v Morley
Fylde v Redruth
Richmond v Bedford
Rosslyn Park v Blackheath
Division 4
Askeans v Aspatria
Broughton Park v Harrogate
Liverpool St Helens v Clifton
Plymouth Albion v Leeds
Sheffield v Sudbury
Division 5 (South)
Berry Hill v Tabard
Camborne v Weston-super-Mare
High Wycombe v North Walsham
London Welsh v Met Police
Lydney v Reading
Maidstone v Southend
Division 5 (North)
Birmingham Solihull v Hereford

Durham City v Stourbridge
Lichfield v Winnington Park
Nuneaton v Stoke-on-Trent
Preston Grasshoppers v Walsall
Rotherham v Bradford & Bingley

IRFU Insurance Corporation Leagues
Division 1
Dungannon v Greystones
Garryowen v Blackrock Coll
Lansdowne v Cork Const
Old Wesley v Wanderers
St Mary's Coll v Shannon
Division 2
Ballina v Dolphin
Ballymena v Old Crescent
Instonians v Bangor
Old Belvedere v Terenure Coll
Sunday's Well v Galwegians
Division 3
City of Derry v Collegians
Clontarf v Portadown
De La Salle Palmerston v UC Cork
Highfield v NIFC
Sligo v Bective Rangers
UC Dublin v Corinthians

WRU Heineken Leagues
Division 1
Aberavon v Newport
Cardiff v Bridgend
Cross Keys v Llanelli
Dunvant v Neath
Newbridge v Pontypool
Swansea v Pontypridd
Division 2
Abertillery v Llandovery
Ebbw Vale v Narberth
Glam Wands v Treorchy
Maesteg v S Wales Police
Mountain Ash v Llanharan
Tenby Utd v Penarth

Melrose Sevens
England Under-19s v Scotland Under-19s (Waterloo)
Ireland Under-18s v Scotland Under-18s
RFSU Schools Cup *Final* (Twickenham)
England Under-16s v Wales Under-16s (Twickenham)

Wednesday, 13 April
RAF v Royal Navy (Twickenham)
England Under-18s v Ireland Under-18s (Durham)

London Irish v Army

Saturday, 16 April
RFU County Championship *Final* (Twickenham)
WRU SWALEC Cup *Semi-finals*

WRU Heineken Leagues
Division 2
Llandovery v Glam Wands
Llanharan v Ebbw Vale
Narberth v Abertillery
Penarth v Mountain Ash
S Wales Police v Tenby Utd
Treorchy v Maesteg

Scotland Under-19s v Wales Under-19s
Askeans v Met Police
Bedford v Bath
Bridgwater Albion v Nuneaton
Broughton Park v Preston Grasshoppers
Exeter v Plymouth Albion
Harlequins v Rosslyn Park
Harrogate v West Hartlepool
Havant v Maidstone
Lydney v Brixham
Moseley v Orrell
Newcastle Gosforth v Leeds
Newport v Nottingham
Northampton v Richmond
Otley v Broughton Park
Redruth v Barnstaple
Rugby v Fylde
Sale v Leicester
Sheffield v Wakefield
Stourbridge v Liverpool St Helens
Vale of Lune v Aspatria
Wasps v Waterloo

Wednesday, 20 April
RAF v Army (Twickenham)

Saturday, 23 April
RFU Courage Leagues
Division 1
Bath v Harlequins
Gloucester v Orrell
Leicester v London Irish
Newcastle Gosforth v Bristol
Wasps v Northampton
Division 2
London Scottish v West Hartlepool
Otley v Moseley
Rugby v Saracens
Sale v Nottingham

Waterloo v Wakefield
Division 3
Bedford v Coventry
Blackheath v Fylde
Exeter v Richmond
Morley v Rosslyn Park
Redruth v Havant
Division 4
Aspatria v Plymouth Albion
Clifton v Askeans
Leeds v Harrogate
Sheffield v Broughton Park
Sudbury v Liverpool St Helens

WRU Heineken Leagues
Division 1
Bridgend v Newbridge
Neath v Cross Keys
Newport v Cardiff
Pontypool v Dunvant
Pontypridd v Llanelli
Swansea v Aberavon
Division 2
Abertillery v Llanharan
Ebbw Vale v Penarth
Glam Wands v Maesteg
Llandovery v Narberth
Mountain Ash v S Wales Police
Tenby Utd v Treorchy

Ulster Senior Cup *Final*
Bridgwater Albion v Lydney
New Brighton v Vale of Lune
Nuneaton v London Welsh

Wednesday, 27 April

Redruth v Penzance Newlyn

Saturday, 30 April

RFU Courage Leagues
Division 1
Bristol v Leicester
Harlequins v Gloucester
London Irish v Bath
Northampton v Newcastle Gosforth
Orrell v Wasps
Division 2
Moseley v Rugby

Nottingham v Waterloo
Saracens v London Scottish
Wakefield v Otley
West Hartlepool v Sale
Division 3
Coventry v Redruth
Exeter v Bedford
Fylde v Morley
Havant v Blackheath
Rosslyn Park v Richmond
Division 4
Askeans v Sudbury
Broughton Park v Leeds
Harrogate v Aspatria
Liverpool St Helens v Sheffield
Plymouth Albion v Clifton

WRU Heineken Leagues
Division 1
Aberavon v Pontypridd
Cardiff v Swansea
Cross Keys v Pontypool
Dunvant v Bridgend
Llanelli v Neath
Newbridge v Newport
Division 2
Llanharan v Llandovery
Maesteg v Tenby Utd
Narberth v Glam Wands
Penarth v Abertillery
S Wales Police v Ebbw Vale
Treorchy v Mountain Ash

Connacht Senior Cup *Final*
Leinster Senior Cup *Final*
Munster Senior Cup *Final*
Lydney v Walsall
Nuneaton v Met Police
Vale of Lune v Bradford & Bingley

Saturday, 7 May

RFU Pilkington Cup *Final* (Twickenham)
WRU SWALEC Cup *Final* (Cardiff)

Saturday, 14 May

Middlesex Sevens (Twickenham)

MAJOR TOURS

NEW ZEALANDERS TO SCOTLAND, ENGLAND AND WALES

October

23 **London & South-East Division**
    (Twickenham)
26 **Midlands Division** (Leicester)
30 **South-West Division** (Redruth)

November

 2 **Northern Division** (Liverpool FC)
 7 **England A** (Gateshead)
10 **South of Scotland** (Gala)
13 **Scotland A** (Hawick)
16 **Scottish Development XV**
    (Myreside)
20 **SCOTLAND** (Murrayfield)
23 **English Emerging Players**
    (Gloucester)
27 **ENGLAND** (Twickenham)
30 **Combined Services** (Devonport)

December

 4 **Barbarians** (Cardiff)

AUSTRALIANS TO CANADA AND FRANCE

October

 2 **British Columbia Development XV**
    (Vancouver)
 6 **Canada A** (Calgary)
 9 **CANADA** (Calgary)

16 **French Selection** (Dax)
20 **French Selection** (Agen)
23 **French Selection** (Narbonne)
26 **French Selection** (Grenoble)
30 **FRANCE**

November

 2 **French Selection** (Toulon)
 6 **FRANCE** (Paris)
11 **French Barbarians** (Clermont-
    Ferrand)

SOUTH AFRICAN BARBARIANS TO ENGLAND AND WALES

October

19 **Gloucester**
21 **Leicester**
25 **Newport**
27 **Llanelli**

November

 1 **Bridgend**
 6 **Bath**

JAPANESE TO WALES

September

29 **Wales A** (Llanelli)

October

 2 **Dunvant**
 6 **East Wales** (Abertillery)
 9 **West Wales** (Narberth)
12 **Welsh Selection** (Pontypridd)
16 **WALES** (Cardiff)

MAJOR FIXTURES 1993-94

September

29   Wales A v Japanese (Llanelli)

October

9   **CANADA v AUSTRALIA** (Calgary)
13   **Wales A v North of England**
     (Pontypool)
16   **WALES v JAPAN** (Cardiff)
     RFU Divisional Championship
23   **RFU Divisional Championship**
30   **FRANCE v AUSTRALIA**
     RFU Divisional Championship

November

6   **FRANCE v AUSTRALIA** (Paris)
     RFU Divisional Championship
7   **England A v New Zealanders**
     (Gateshead)
13   **IRELAND v ROMANIA** (Dublin)
     Scotland A v New Zealanders
     (Hawick)
20   **SCOTLAND v NEW ZEALAND**
     (Murrayfield)
27   **ENGLAND v NEW ZEALAND**
     (Twickenham)

December

4   **Barbarians v New Zealanders**
     (Cardiff)
7   **Oxford U v Cambridge U**
     (Twickenham)
18   **Italy v Scotland A**
28   **Scotland A v Ireland A**

January 1994

1   **Ireland Trial** (Dublin)

4   **Scotland A v Spain**
15   **WALES v SCOTLAND** (Cardiff)
     FRANCE v IRELAND (Paris)

February

4   **Ireland A v Wales A** (Dublin)
5   **SCOTLAND v ENGLAND**
     (Murrayfield)
     IRELAND v WALES (Dublin)
19   **ENGLAND v IRELAND**
     (Twickenham)
     WALES v FRANCE (Cardiff)
20   **France A v Scotland A**

March

5   **IRELAND v SCOTLAND** (Dublin)
     FRANCE v ENGLAND (Paris)
18   **Wales A v France A**
19   **ENGLAND v WALES**
     (Twickenham)
     SCOTLAND v FRANCE
     (Murrayfield)
26   **CATHAY PACIFIC-HONG**
     KONG BANK SEVENS
     Royal Navy v Army (Twickenham)
27   **CATHAY PACIFIC-HONG**
     KONG BANK SEVENS

April

13   **Royal Navy v RAF** (Twickenham)
16   **RFU County Championship Final**
     (Twickenham)
20   **Army v RAF** (Twickenham)

May

7   **RFU Pilkington Cup Final**
     (Twickenham)
     WRU SWALEC Cup Final (Cardiff)
14   **Middlesex Sevens** (Twickenham)

More bestselling non-fiction from Headline

ROTHMANS FOOTBALL YEARBOOK 1993-94	Jack Rollin	£16.99
ROTHMANS RUGBY LEAGUE YEARBOOK 1993-94	Howes/Fletcher	£14.99
PLAYFAIR FOOTBALL ANNUAL 1993-94	Jack Rollin	£3.99
PLAYFAIR EUROPEAN FOOTBALL ANNUAL 1993-94	Bruce Smith	£3.99
PLAYFAIR CRICKET ANNUAL 1993	Bill Frindall	£3.99
BOBBY MOORE: A TRIBUTE	David Emery	£9.99
MARTIN PIPE: THE CHAMPION TRAINER'S STORY	Martin Pipe	£5.99
HEART AND SOLE	David Sole	£5.99
DALGLISH	Stephen F Kelly	£5.99

All Headline books are available at your local bookshop or newsagent, or can be ordered direct from the publisher. Just tick the titles you want and fill in the form below. Prices and availability subject to change without notice.

Headline Book Publishing Ltd, Cash Sales Department, Bookpoint, 39 Milton Park, Abingdon, OXON OX14 4TD, UK. If you have a credit card you may order by telephone – 0235 831700.

Please enclose a cheque or postal order made payable to Bookpoint Ltd to the value of the cover price and allow the following for postage and packing:
UK & BFPO: £1.00 for the first book, 50p for the second book and 30p for each additional book ordered up to a maximum charge of £3.00.
OVERSEAS & EIRE: £2.00 for for the first book, £1.00 for the second book, and 50p for each additional book.

NAME (Block Letters) ....

ADDRESS ....

....

....

If you would prefer to pay by credit card, please complete:
Please debit my Visa/Access/Diner's Card/American Express (delete as applicable) card no:

Signature..Expiry Date....................